International Directory of
COMPANY HISTORIES

International Directory of

COMPANY HISTORIES

VOLUME 7

Editor
Paula Kepos

St J

St James Press

Detroit   London   Washington D.C.

Copyright © 1993 by St. James Press
835 Penobscot Building
Detroit, MI 48226

Library of Congress Catalog Number: 89-190943

British Library Cataloguing in Publication Data

International directory of company histories. Vol. 7
I. Paula Kepos
338.7409

ISBN 1-55862-322-1

Printed in the United States of America
Published simultaneously in the United Kingdom

I(T)P™

The trademark **ITP** is used under license.

Cover photograph courtesy of the Toronto Stock Exchange.

CONTENTS _____

Company Histories

PREFACE

International Directory of Company Histories provides detailed information on the development of the world's largest and most influential companies. To date, *Company Histories* has covered more than 1500 companies in seven volumes.

Inclusion Criteria

Most companies chosen for inclusion in *Company Histories* have achieved a minimum of US$500 million in annual sales. Some smaller companies are included if they are leading influences in their respective industries or geographical locations. State-owned companies that are important in their industries and that may operate much like public or private companies also are included. Wholly owned subsidiaries of other companies are presented if they meet the requirements for inclusion.

St. James Press does not endorse any of the companies or products mentioned in this book. Companies that appear in *Company Histories* were selected without reference to their wishes and have in no way endorsed their entries. The companies were given the opportunity to read their entries for factual inaccuracies, and we are indebted to many of them for their comments and corrections. We also thank them for allowing the use of their logos for identification purposes.

Entry Format

Each entry in this volume begins with a company's legal name, the address of its headquarters, its telephone number and fax number, and a statement of public, private, or state ownership. A company with a legal name in both English and the language of its headquarters country is listed by the English name, with the native-language name in parentheses.

Also provided are the company's earliest incorporation date, the number of employees, and the most recent sales figures available, which are for fiscal year 1992 unless otherwise noted. Sales figures are given in local currencies with equivalents in U.S. dollars. For some private companies, sales figures are estimates. The entry lists the exchanges on which a company's stock is traded, as well as the company's principal Standard Industrial Classification codes. American spelling is used, and the word ''billion'' is used in its American sense of a thousand million.

Sources

The histories were compiled from publicly accessible sources such as general and academic periodicals, books, annual reports, and material supplied by the companies themselves. *Company Histories* is intended for reference use by students, business people, librarians, historians, economists, investors, job candidates, and others who want to learn more about the historical development of the world's most important companies.

Indexes

A cumulative Index to Companies and Persons provides access to companies and individuals discussed in the text. Beginning with Volume 7, a cumulative Index to Industries allows researchers to locate companies by their principal industry.

A.B.	Aktiebolaget (Sweden)
A.G.	Aktiengesellschaft (Germany, Switzerland)
A.S.	Atieselskab (Denmark)
A.S.	Aksjeselskap (Denmark, Norway)
A.Ş.	Anomin Şirket (Turkey)
B.V.	Besloten Vennootschap met beperkte, Aansprakelijkheid (The Netherlands)
Co.	Company (United Kingdom, United States)
Corp.	Corporation (United States)
G.I.E.	Groupement d'Intérêt Economique (France)
GmbH	Gesellschaft mit beschränkter Haftung (Germany)
H.B.	Handelsbolaget (Sweden)
Inc.	Incorporated (United States)
KGaA	Kommanditgesellschaft auf Aktien (Germany)
K.K.	Kabushiki Kaisha (Japan)
LLC	Limited Liability Company (Middle East)
Ltd.	Limited (Canada, Japan, United Kingdom, United States)
N.V.	Naamloze Vennootschap (The Netherlands)
OY	Osakeyhtiöt (Finland)
PLC	Public Limited Company (United Kingdom)
PTY.	Proprietary (Australia, Hong Kong, South Africa)
S.A.	Société Anonyme (Belgium, France, Switzerland)
SpA	Società per Azioni (Italy)

ABBREVIATIONS FOR CURRENCY _____

DA	Algerian dinar	Dfl	Netherlands florin
A$	Australian dollar	NZ$	New Zealand dollar
Sch	Austrian schilling	N	Nigerian naira
BFr	Belgian franc	NKr	Norwegian krone
Cr	Brazilian cruzado	RO	Omani rial
C$	Canadian dollar	P	Philippine peso
DKr	Danish krone	Esc	Portuguese escudo
E£	Egyptian pound	SRls	Saudi Arabian riyal
Fmk	Finnish markka	S$	Singapore dollar
FFr	French franc	R	South African rand
DM	German mark	W	South Korean won
HK$	Hong Kong dollar	Pta	Spanish peseta
Rs	Indian rupee	SKr	Swedish krona
Rp	Indonesian rupiah	SFr	Swiss franc
IR£	Irish pound	NT$	Taiwanese dollar
L	Italian lira	B	Thai baht
¥	Japanese yen	£	United Kingdom pound
W	Korean won	$	United States dollar
KD	Kuwaiti dinar	B	Venezuelan bolivar
LuxFr	Luxembourgian franc	K	Zambian kwacha
M$	Malaysian ringgit		

International Directory of
COMPANY HISTORIES

ACCO WORLD CORPORATION

500 Lake Cook Road
Suite 150
Deerfield, Illinois 60615-0818
U.S.A.
(708) 405-9000
Fax: (800) 962-0576

Wholly Owned Subsidiary of American Brands Corporation
Incorporated: October 26, 1970
Employees: 9,300
Sales: $1 billion (approximately)
Stock Exchanges: New York, Amsterdam, Brussels, Düsseldorf, Frankfürt, Geneva, Paris, London, Tokyo, Zürich
SICs: 3496 Miscellaneous Fabricated Wire Products; 2782 Blankbooks & Looseleaf Binders; 2621 Paper Mills; 6719 Holding Companies, Nec

ACCO World Corporation is one of the largest suppliers of office products. Built largely on the growth of paperwork over the last century, ACCO World has tied its recent growth to the proliferation of office product superstores, which have emerged as the most efficient high-volume channel for retail sales.

Thoroughly diversified within its market, ACCO World provides a wide variety of office products, from paper clips and bindery products to integrated computer accessories, workstations, and peripherals. As a result, it is likely that virtually every office contains at least one, and probably several, of the company's products.

ACCO World has several predecessor companies, but the core organization that gave it its name was the Clipper Manufacturing Company. Clipper was founded in 1903 by Fred J. Kline. Originally located in Long Island City, New York, Clipper had one product: paper clips. Seemingly insignificant at only a fraction of a cent per piece, Clipper eventually turned out billions of the little wire contraptions.

In 1910 Kline changed the name of his firm to the grander sounding American Clip Company. Two years later, he invented a new paper fastener that he dubbed the "ACCO Fastener" after his company's acronym. This two-pronged, locking paper compressor proved highly successful and cleared the way for several new products, including folders, binders, punches,

and clamps. Also marketed under the ACCO brand name, these items became more well known than the company that made them. This prompted Kline to change the name of the company again in 1922, this time to ACCO Products, Inc.

Operating under the claim, "ACCO originates and develops," the company prospered from the proliferation of paperwork in consumers' business and personal affairs. ACCO Products grew tremendously on this expanding market. In 1924 Kline established an English subsidiary and, three years later, added another in Canada. The company also established a new product line, pressboard binders, in 1928. Available in five colors, these binders became common office supplies and represented the company's continuing effort to broaden its product line.

In 1933 ACCO Products changed its distribution channels. Rather than serving as the exclusive distributor of its own products, the company enlisted a network of commercial vendors and later began printing mail order catalogs. Within one year, as the distribution network grew dramatically, a much greater demand for the company's products was created. This led to another company tagline, "We're easy and profitable to do business with."

During this time, another ACCO World company got its start. Swingline, Inc., a manufacturer of staplers, was established in 1925 by Jack Linsky. From its factory on the Lower East Side of New York City, Swingline made a name for itself by developing more efficient stapler designs.

Swingline was one of the first companies to package staples in glued rows. Prior to this, staples had to be loaded individually or came attached to overly sturdy sheets of metal that did not break away cleanly. The glued staples, called frozen wire staples, allowed Swingline to introduce another innovation during the 1930s, the open channel stapler, in which rows of 50 or more staples could be dropped in at once. Swingline also developed a stroke control that almost eliminated the common problem of staples jamming.

ACCO and Swingline were deeply affected by the outbreak of World War II. With government controls on production, rationing, and the diversion of metal stocks to the defense industry, both companies had to find a new way to do business. Far from being pressed into action as war materials suppliers, the companies' products proved to be essential because of the increased need for government record keeping.

ACCO Products fared better, having developed a paper clip made of pressed paper fiber as an alternative to metal clips and staples. In addition, the company reduced the metal content of its product line, manufacturing paper punches out of wood, but with metal hole punchers. It also introduced laced binders and lace ties for envelope binders. On the strength of wartime demand, ACCO Products had become a large company; in fact, after the war it was forced to relocate to a larger facility in Ogdensburg, New York, in 1947. This plant had been requisitioned during World War II to handle production for the government.

ACCO Products continued to prosper after the war as a steady business expansion occurred in all industries. As the nation's commerce grew, so did the need for record keeping. By the mid

1950s, however, ACCO Products had become an attractive takeover target.

Gary Industries, a private holding company based in Chicago, acquired ACCO Products in 1956. Meanwhile, ACCO Products continued its growth by expansion and by this time was a major office supply manufacturer offering a complete line of products. Gary Industries did not become actively involved in ACCO Product's affairs until 1966, when the parent moved the operation from Ogdensburg to Chicago. At that time, Gary brought in Douglas K. Chapman, formerly head of ACCO Products' Canadian operations, to run the company, which was now known as the ACCO Division of Gary Industries.

Swingline, Inc., achieved its own recovery from World War II on the strength of the same postwar business boom that had catapulted ACCO Products to a leading position in the industry. Still limited to the manufacture of staplers, however, the company sought to diversify, and in 1960 took over the operations of the Wilson Jones Company.

Wilson Jones was founded in 1893 as the Chicago Shipping and Receipt Book Company. The company's original proprietor was a Chicago jeweler who invented and began manufacturing a simple aluminum paper clasp. Six years later, the small company was taken over by Ralph B. Wilson. In 1904 the company developed the first three-ring binder, an invention that greatly contributed to its growth. Also that year, Wilson merged his company with the Jones Improved Loose Leaf Specialty Company, run by W. Gifford Jones and his two brothers. As the Wilson Jones Company, the enterprise benefited from a wider product line and a more efficient combined sales force.

ACCO Products redoubled international sales efforts in the 1960s and 1970s. In 1964 the company established a subsidiary in Holland and entered into a joint venture in Mexico. These were followed in 1970 by a joint venture in Jamaica and, in 1972, in Venezuela. To standardize the company's identity, a new corporate design was introduced in 1968 that featured distinctive red and black bars. Two years later ACCO Products was reorganized under a new parent company, ACCO World Corporation. This holding company assumed centralized ownership of the American and European operations.

In 1971, however, Chapman and a group of senior executives launched a leveraged buyout of ACCO World. They succeeded and, having won their autonomy from Gary Industries, began several efforts to boost sales. The increase in product demand caused a need to move to larger, more modern quarters. At the time, however, the nation was in the grips of a serious recession, exacerbated by an oil embargo perpetrated by Middle Eastern countries. In spite of the adverse conditions, Chapman pressed on with plans to build a new headquarters facility in Wheeling, Illinois. After the move was completed in 1976, Chapman remarked that the decision to erect the new building was "one of the most positive things we could tell our employees, customers and suppliers about our optimism for the future."

Meanwhile, ACCO World continued its international expansion with the establishment of a French subsidiary in 1975, another in West Germany in 1977, and joint ventures in New Zealand, Nigeria, Brazil, and Australia. At this time, ACCO Products, which was renamed ACCO International, started a new company, the Polyblend Corporation, based in St. Charles, Illinois. Polyblend was established specifically to extrude polyethylene, a plastic used in the manufacture of ACCO binders.

In 1982 the company's Toronto-based ACCO Canada Ltd. subsidiary acquired Plymouth Tool and Stamping, Ltd. Plymouth, which had been an important supplier to ACCO International, was one of the most sophisticated tool and dye manufacturers in Canada.

In February of 1983 senior management took ACCO International—the American side of the business—public and gained a listing on the New York Stock Exchange. In May of that year the company purchased the Systems Furniture Company and in 1984 acquired Twinlock PLC, a British office products manufacturer, through its European subsidiary. In 1986 ACCO International also took over Kensington Microware, which produced computer workstation products. These acquisitions were intended to shore up ACCO's position in the broader office market by adding furniture and other products to the line.

The Twinlock acquisition resulted in European wholesalers offering two competing product lines from the same company to their customers. In 1986, however, the ACCO International logo was incorporated into individual brand names to further solidify the company's identity.

In 1987 American Brands, a tobacco, food, consumer products and financial services conglomerate, announced a bid to acquire ACCO World for $603 million. American Brands had acquired Swingline in 1970 and Wilson Jones in 1972. This caused the U.S. Justice Department to oppose the transaction on the grounds that American would enjoy excessive control over the fastener market.

In August of 1987 American Brands allowed the transaction to proceed by agreeing to divest itself of a substantial portion of its fastener business. The company sold its Swingline punch and two-hole fastener operations to Bates Manufacturing, and ACCO International sold its stapler business to Hunt Manufacturing.

The following year, ACCO International and Swingline coordinated their manufacturing and marketing operations, resulting in the expansion of ACCO's Wheeling plant. American Brands, meanwhile, acquired Vogel Peterson Furniture Company, another office products and furniture manufacturer, and Day-Timers, Inc., which made diaries and time planners. Vogel Peterson was consolidated with Systems Furniture in 1990, and its headquarters were relocated to Garden Grove, California.

In 1990 ACCO World introduced a new "Worldmark" logo for its American companies, which now included ACCO, Swingline, Wilson Jones, Vogel Peterson, Kensington and, through an earlier acquisition, Perma Products. The following year, ACCO International, Swingline and Wilson Jones were merged into one company—ACCO USA. The individual brand names, however, were retained.

ACCO brand products include fastening, computer, and bindery items. Swingline, the industry's leading stapling products brand, offers a line that includes the tiny Swingline Tot 50, of which more than 100 million have been sold. Other models include conventional manual and electric devices. Swingline also makes desk accessories, task lighting, and clips for holding paper beside a computer terminal. The Wilson Jones line consists of accounting supplies, business forms, and DublLock binding kits. And, to dispose of it all, the company manufactures paper shredders.

ACCO World European operations belong to a separate parent company, ACCO-Rexel Group Holdings, PLC, whose revenues comprise roughly half of ACCO World's total. ACCO-Rexel maintains an extensive distributor network throughout Europe, the Middle East, Latin America, Africa, and the Pacific Basin. The company is primarily involved in the manufacture of binding machines, manila and plastic folders, staples, pencils, filing products, computer supplies, and office furniture.

ACCO-Rexel has more than 100 subsidiaries, including 65 in the United Kingdom alone. The largest of these subsidiaries are Eastlight Limited in Britain, ACCO-Benelux in Holland, Hetzel & Company in Germany, King-Mec in Italy, Val-Rex in France, ACCO-Rexel in Ireland, and Marbig-Rexel and OPI in Australia.

ACCO World Corporation may best be described as an international network of companies focused on one market: office products. Perhaps due to the noncyclical nature of the office supply business, the company has avoided forays into fields outside its expertise, such as electronics, real estate, and transportation. As a result, ACCO World has avoided poor and nonstrategic investments that could have derailed its core businesses or burdened it with debt.

Principal Subsidiaries: ACCO USA; ACCO-Rexel Group Holdings, PLC; Perma Products; Vogel Peterson Furniture Company; Day-Timers, Inc.; Kensington Microware, Ltd.; ACCO Canada Ltd.

Further Reading: "Justice Department Approves Plan to Acquire Acco World," *Wall Street Journal,* August 10, 1987; "ACCO World Timeline," Deerfield, IL, ACCO World Corporation, 1992; "History of ACCO World," ACCO World Corporation, 1993.

—John Simley

ADAM OPEL AG

Postfach 17
10, Bahnhofsplatz 1
D-6090 Rüsselsheim
Germany
(61 42) 66-2822
Fax: (61 42) 66-4859

Wholly Owned Subsidiary of General Motors Corp.
Incorporated: 1862
Employees: 56,782
Sales: DM 27.1 billion (US$16.59 billion)
SICs: 3711 Motor Vehicles & Car Bodies; 3714 Motor
   Vehicle Parts & Accessories; 5012 Automobiles & Other
   Motor Vehicles—Wholesale; 5013 Motor Vehicle Supplies
   & New Parts—Wholesale

Adam Opel AG is a large German car manufacturer, wholly owned and operated by the American automotive giant General Motors Corp. Founded in the mid-19th century, Opel, which started out making sewing machines, turned to the manufacture of automobiles in the earliest days of the industry, producing popular cars that were available to the common man. Opel survived the devastation of two world wars to enjoy the auto boom from the 1950s through 1970s, only to experience difficulties later as the market moved toward smaller, more economical cars.

Opel was founded in 1862 by Adam Opel in Rüsselsheim-am-Main, Germany. Against the wishes of his father, a locksmith, Opel formulated a plan to manufacture sewing machines. After working in Paris to learn his trade as a journeyman, he returned home to open a workshop in the cow stables belonging to his uncle. The first machines produced were crafted by hand, and sold quickly. Opel's fledgling business flourished, and by 1868 it had grown prosperous enough for him to rent space in a factory building.

With the success of his business, Opel was able to turn his attention to starting a family, and he and his wife Sophie had five boys. As they grew, Opel's sons developed an avid interest in bicycling, and Opel purchased five of the machines for his family, over the objections of his wife. Observing his son's bicycles, Opel realized that the high, three-wheeled mechanisms could provide a new mode of transportation, as well as a new source of revenue for his factory. In 1886, the first bicycle left the Opel works. Before long the Opel factory was turning out 16,000 bicycles a year. The popularity of the Opel bike was enhanced by the fame of the five Opel sons, who won hundreds of bike races across Europe.

Adam Opel died in 1895, bringing to an end the first era of the Opel firm. Inheriting the business, his five sons looked to modernize, turning to new products in order to maintain the company's competitive edge. The men set their sights on the automobile, one of the latest products to be developed.

To obtain the expertise needed to convert their production line from bicycles to cars, the brothers hired Friedrich Lutzmann, a famous inventor and master metalworker previously employed by the court of Dessau, in 1894. Five years later, Lutzmann produced the first Opel automobile, a coach-like vehicle with a one cylinder rear engine and a maximum speed of 20 kilometers per hour.

By the turn of the century, the Opel factory was producing six different auto bodies, all of which were labeled with "Opel-Patented Lutzmann Motor Wagon System." Lutzmann left the Opel firm in 1901, joining forces with the pioneering French automobile firm, Darracq, and Opel and Darracq entered into cooperation. The French firm supplied engines, which were shipped to the Opel works in Rüsselsheim, while Opel manufactured auto bodies, combining them with the French parts for sale under the name Opel-Darracq.

The first car built entirely by the Opel brothers went on the market in 1902. The compact Tonneau had a two cylinder engine that was upgraded to four cylinders within a year. During this time, Opel cars were winning races in Germany, France, Belgium, and the United States, bringing fame to the company name.

Since each car produced by the Opel factory at this time was extremely expensive, it was available to only a small segment of the population: in 1906 the company's top-of-the-line luxury touring vehicle was priced at DM 22,000. In an effort to broaden their market, the brother's decided to build a less expensive form of transportation, and soon, motorized two-wheel bicycles were rolling out of the Opel factory. A line of more affordable cars was also introduced in 1908. Half the size of a larger four-seater, the 10/18 PS cost just DM 8,500. The following year, the company introduced what would become its famous "Doctor Car." With a four-cylinder, eight horsepower engine, the car cost just DM 3,950. In addition to an autobody crafted by hand, the car featured standardized tire rims, which, for the first time, made it possible to change a punctured tire easily. Purchased by many lawyers and country doctors, the car was rugged enough to withstand poor rural roads, and the Opel factory received many letters of appreciation from satisfied new automobile owners.

The company continued to upgrade its product, introducing new, more aerodynamic torpedo-shaped autobodies. At the factory, division of labor was introduced, as engines and autobodies were mixed and matched according to size, and parts were standardized and made interchangeable. In 1911 the Opel brothers broadened the company's offerings further when they began to manufacture four-cylinder engines for airplanes, and a four-cylinder motor plow, for use in agriculture.

In August of 1911, the Opel factory was consumed by flames. In the wake of the fire, which struck in particular the portion of the plant where sewing machines were still being assembled from individual parts, the Opel company when out of the sewing machine business, having produced more than a million of these devices. A newly rebuilt factory was completed in time for the company's 50th anniversary in 1912.

To commemorate the half-century mark, Opel introduced a new flagship automobile, to succeed the Doctor Car. With a four-cylinder engine, this car garnered even wider popularity, and was followed two years later by a new model that was given the nickname "*Puppchen*," meaning Dolly. With more than 3,000 cars manufactured in one year, Opel became the largest auto-maker in Germany.

Germany entered World War I in August of 1914, and Opel's production was converted to provide material for the armed forces. The company manufactured trucks for the war effort, producing in particular a three-ton truck. For the first time, many parts were standardized, allowing them to be taken from one truck and used to fix another. Since 2,500 Opel men—a large part of the factory's workforce—were conscripted into the army and sent off to war, women and prisoners-of-war were used to operate the plant. As the war progressed, Opel experienced extreme shortages of resources, including rubber, and by 1915 the factory was turning out trucks with iron wheels.

The war affected the Opel family in ways that extended beyond the business. The youngest of Adam Opel's five sons died in battle. In 1917 his surviving sons were made knights, and the following year, the family was given the right to add the noble prefix "von" to their names.

In the wake of Germany's defeat, the Opel factory was occupied by French troops in December of 1918, who surveilled production closely, controlling the plant's output. The country's strained economic circumstances increased demand for cheap transportation, and Opel began to build and sell more bikes and motorcycles. In 1919 the company began to market a bike with an accessory motor, which attached to its side. Production of automobiles was resumed that year, though at a slowed pace given the low demand.

In the early 1920s Germany suffered hyper-inflation, which quickly consumed the capital of the middle class. Under these conditions, Opel's cheapest car in 1922 sold for DM 225,000, an astronomical sum out of the reach of almost all consumers. In 1923 Opel was compelled to print its own emergency money with which to pay its worker's salaries, and finally, in August, the plant was forced to close.

Facing this crisis, two of the Opel sons travelled to America to learn about modernized car manufacturing methods, particularly the assembly line technique perfected by Henry Ford. They returned convinced that this was the key to rapid car manufacturing in the future, instead of the piece work method currently practiced in Germany. A 45-meter-long assembly line was installed in the Opel factory, and in the spring of 1924, the first car rolled off this line. Called the "Country Frog" because of its standard green color, this sturdy two-seater featured a directly-operated transmission.

Opel sold more than 100,000 of the Country Frogs throughout the 1920s. From 1924 to 1928, the company steadily reduced the prices of its products until the cost to buy the company's cheapest car had sunk below DM 2,000 at the end of the decade. In addition to possessing 37 percent of the German market, Opel was the country's largest exporter.

In March of 1929 Opel formalized its contacts with the American automobile industry when General Motors (GM) purchased 80 percent of the company's stock. Two years later GM acquired the remaining 20 percent of Opel. In 1932 Opel increased its geographic reach when it opened manufacturing facilities in China, Japan, South America, and India.

The company also continued to expand its model lines. In 1931, Opel rolled out a new line of trucks, called Blitz, after a contest was conducted to find a name. Four years later, the company introduced its Olympia model at the Berlin car show. Using techniques developed for airplanes, this car had a detachable autobody, which could be separated from its engine block. Two other models added in the next few years, the Kadett and the Kapitän, which was designed for use on the newly constructed Autobahn, contained this feature.

In 1935 Opel opened a second factory, in Brandenburg, in eastern Germany. Four years later, Germany entered the Second World War, and Opel's main plant, in Rüsselsheim, which had produced over one million cars, was converted to wartime use, making cockpit covers and fuselages for fighter planes. During the war, Opel, as many German factories did, made use of slave labor to keep its production lines running. In August of 1944, Allied bombers destroyed Opel's Brandenburg factory entirely. A year later the facility on the Main was targeted and more than half of it was destroyed. At war's end, Opel, along with the rest of the country, was in ruins.

By May of 1945, Opel workers had begun to clear rubble from the factory, and within a brief period the first machines were running. The company soon learned, however, that its facility at Brandenburg would be demolished, not returned to use. In addition, Opel was compelled to sacrifice its entire Kadett production line to the Soviet Union as part of Germany's war reparations. Consequently, the Soviet model Moskwitsch 400 is a renamed 1947 Opel Kadett.

Since Germany needed trucks for reconstruction, Opel resurrected its old Blitz model, turning it out with the six cylinder engine previously used for the pre-war Kapitän luxury car. In December of 1947, the company began automobile production once again. Opel's old partner, General Motors, resumed management of the firm the next year, as German currency reform stabilized the economy and enabled citizens to once again consider the purchase of a car. To take advantage of this new situation, Opel marketed the Kapitän, at a price of DM 10,000.

In the 1950s, Germany's new federal republic prospered, and Opel marketed cars which reflected this new affluence in their design. Opel cars were loaded with chrome, their style heavily influenced by American automobiles. The 1952 Olympia Rekord featured a famous "shark mouth" grille, and the 1957 Rekord had "panorama" windows. Opel also adopted the practice of updating its models every year, as American car makers did, and the company began to export its models to the United

States. In 1956, the two millionth car rolled off Opel's assembly lines.

In 1962, Opel's one-hundredth anniversary, the company opened a second large factory complex, in Bochum, and also expanded its facilities at its flagship site in Rüsselsheim. In 1966 a testing center in Dudenhofer and a third factory in Kaiserslautern were also opened.

Throughout the 1960s Opel continued to expand its model line, adding the Kadett A to compete with compact cars, and revamping older models. In 1970 the company introduced the Ascona and the Manta, both designed with a more sporty look. The Manta quickly gained a place in German popular culture as the working-man's dream car. By the end of 1972 Opel held the largest portion of the German car market with 20.4 percent.

In 1975 West Germany's automobile market entered a boom period, and Opel expanded its production capacity to keep pace with demand, adding 10,000 workers at its Rüsselsheim plant in just four years. The resultant crowding and pressure to produce created tensions between the plant's workers and its GM management.

In 1977 Opel added to its model line with the Senator, designed to appeal to Germany's ever-more-affluent middle class. Two years later the company added its first car with an engine over the front wheels, rather than behind the car. By this time, however, the German auto boom was over, as rising fuel costs made larger models unattractive. Opel's overly optimistic sales estimates caused it to suspend production at its main plant for ten days at the end of the year, in order to ease an over-supply of its larger cars.

In 1979 GM managers announced an ambitious $2.5 billion investment plan to revamp Opel facilities, build new factories in Spain and Austria, and introduce new models in the important compact and sub-compact ranges. The company planned to produce a subcompact car called the Corsa at a plant in Zaragosa, Spain, and to start the production of a newly-redesigned, aerodynamically sleek Kadett at Opel's Bochum works. These steps were part of an attempt to change Opel's image from that of a traditional, conservatively dependable car to a technologically sophisticated car.

As Opel's slump continued into the 1980s, the company's financial problems began to foster dissent among its workers, and the company developed a reputation for the worst labor relations in Germany as it laid off 5,000 workers at its Rüsselsheim plant. Employees complained that they had no say in decisions being made about the company in GM's headquarters in Detroit, Michigan, and objected in particular to plans for producing cars in Spain. In the fall of 1980 GM replaced Opel's American head, and took steps to streamline the administration of its German subsidiary.

Opel's sales continued to lag in the early 1980s. Far from the days when it was known as GM's "money machine," Opel—and its British affiliate—lost $426.7 million in 1981. By the start of the following year, however, the company's sales had started to pick up, spurred in part by its introduction of new, smaller, fuel-efficient models, such as a revamped Ascona. Opel's market share in Germany rose to 18.8 percent in 1982, led by sales of the Kadett and the Ascona, which trailed only Volkswagen's Golf.

This progress was stymied in part the next year, however, due to the company's continuing labor difficulties. A 50-day metalworker's strike in mid-1983 cost Opel 13 percent of its annual production. Despite this setback, the company managed to retain 18.5 percent of the German market, turning a profit of $100 million.

By 1984, however, Opel was back in the red, with production down and losses totalling $227 million. In 1986 the company lost $372.1 million, as lowered prices and rising costs for advertising offset increases in sales. Facing a flat market for automobile sales, Opel managers looked to reduce its labor force further, increase automation, and overhaul inefficient systems. To this end, in 1988, the company announced a plan to cut 5,200 jobs. To further economize, the company began to purchase parts from other automakers, entering into an agreement with Isuzu Motors of Japan, in particular.

In 1989 Opel announced that it would begin to market a line of mid-sized family cars called Vectra. In a nod to environmental sensitivity, the company began to install catalytic converters on all of its cars, and also adopted a water-based painting process in its plant at Bochum, in order to cut down on solvent emissions. With these moves, the company once again began to report a profit.

During 1989 West Germany was reunited with the formerly Communist East Germany, and Opel moved quickly to take advantage of the changed situation, negotiating the purchase of an automobile plant in eastern Germany, in the town of Eisenach. The computerized plant opened in September of 1992 and was slated to produce the Vectra line of cars. As it looked forward to the mid-1990s, with its long history of automobile manufacturing behind it, Opel appeared well situated to conduct business in the challenging environment of the future Germany, as it had been in the Germany of the past.

Principal Subsidiaries: GM Service, GmbH; Gemeinnuetzige Opel-Wohnbau GmbH; Saginaw Deutschland GmbH; Adam Opel Unterstuetzungskasse; General Motors Espana S.A. (26.5%); General Motors France, S.A. (49.6%); General Motors Turkiye Ltd.; General Motors Coordination Center N.V. (78.1%); Saab Automobile AB.

Further Reading: Geddes, John M., "Ford and G.M. Cut Back At German Subsidiaries," *New York Times,* November 23, 1979; Gooding, Kenneth, "A German Gear Change for General Motors," *Financial Times,* November 18, 1980; Tagliabue, John, "European Push by G.M., Ford," *New York Times,* October 19, 1982; Tagliabue, John, "G.M.'s Sputtering Opel Unit," *New York Times,* June 24, 1986; *Stationen: 125 Jahre Opel,* Rüsselsheim, Germany, Adam Opel AG, 1987; Widman, Miriam, "GM Thrives in Eastern Germany," *Journal of Commerce,* May 28, 1991.

—Elizabeth Rourke

AEROSPATIALE 9

AEROSPATIALE

37, boulevard de Montmorency
75781 Paris Cedex 16
France
(1) 42 24 24 24
Fax: (1) 42 24 20 93

State-Owned Company
Incorporated: 1970 as Société Nationale Industrielle
  Aerospatiale
Employees: 45,200
Sales: FFr 52.3 billion (US$9.46 billion)
SICs: 3721 Aircraft; 3761 Guided Missiles & Space Vehicles

Aerospatiale, a French state-owned company, is one of the world's leaders in the development and manufacturing of aerospace equipment. The most diversified aerospace company in Europe, its expertise covers civil and military airplanes and helicopters; strategic and tactical weapon systems, including antitank and strategic ballistic missiles; and space systems, launch vehicles, and satellites. Its development of the Concorde in partnership with Great Britain is one of the best known example of Aerospatiale's commitment to cooperation with other countries. A significant portion of the company's business is done in such international consortiums as Airbus Industrie, ATR, Euromissile, and Eurocopter SA.

Aerospatiale's many products and research projects can be divided into four basic categories: aircraft, helicopters, missile systems, and space equipment. The company's aircraft division, with approximately 14,000 employees, has sales of about FFr 21 billion. As part of Airbus Industrie, a consortium that also includes Deutsche Aerospace Airbus, British Aerospace plc, and CASA, Aerospatiale produces a successful line of commercial jets, the Airbus A300-600, the Airbus A310, A320, A330, and A340. ATR, the company's cooperative venture with Alenia, supplies such regional transport aircraft as the ATR 42, a 50-seater, and ATR 72, with 70 seats, used by feeder airlines. The aircraft division is also working with companies in Europe and the United States on a successor to the Concorde.

Aerospatiale conducts its commercial helicopter business through Eurocopter SA, a subsidiary owned 70 percent by Aerospatiale and 30 percent by Deutsche Aerospace Airbus (DASA). The world's leading exporter of helicopters, Eurocopter supplies 120 countries with vehicles for civil and military

purposes. Aerospatiale's space and defense division produces France's nuclear weapons, both land-based and sea-launched strategic missiles, including the SSBS (Surface-to-Surface Ballistic Strategic) and the MSBS (Sea-to-Surface Ballistic Strategic) systems. In the field of tactical missiles, Aerospatiale is involved in several international projects: Euromissile, a cooperative venture with DASA; EMDG, a partnership with DASA and British Aerospace; and Eurosam, a Franco-Italian grouping with Aerospatiale, Thomson S.A., and Alenia.

Aerospatiale's space ventures are all done in cooperation with other companies. As a member of Arianespace, Aerospatiale is the "industrial architect" for the Ariane 4 launch vehicles and plays an important role in the development of Ariane 5. The company is also the lead contractor in a number of international satellite programs, including direct television transmission and communications for meteorology and scientific applications. Aerospatiale, Alenia, Alcatel, DASA, and Loral Corp. work together in the world's leading satellite company.

Incorporated in 1970, Aerospatiale can actually trace its history back to the early days of aviation. Aerospatiale is the product of a long series of mergers in the French aerospace industry that began when eight major companies were nationalized in 1936 and 1937. These companies had been built by pioneers in aviation, including Louis Bleriot, Gabriel Voisin, and Henri Farman. As far back as 1901 Bleriot sketched airplanes, although the machines they depicted would not be manufactured until 1906. Voisin, who initially collaborated with Bleriot, became his major competitor in aircraft manufacturing. Farman, who bought his first plane from Voisin, set several records, including, in 1908, the first one-kilometer closed loop flight. He then founded what was to become a leading manufacturer of aircraft in France.

Competition in the limited market for aircraft was fierce. For example, Bleriot was almost bankrupt in 1909 and saved his company by being the first to cross the English channel in an airplane. Not only did the prize money from the *Daily Mail* newspaper come in handy, but his instant fame brought in many orders for the Bleriot XI.

Aerospatiale's founding companies benefited in the succeeding years from the Army's interest in airplanes. The military observed planes in such large-scale maneuvers as the Reims Competition in 1911, in which manufacturers competed to make the aircraft best suited to the military's operational requirements. Aircraft orders boomed in World War I. For instance, 13 Bleriot SPAD VII and SPAD XIII were made a day, for a total of 13,000 by the end of the war—Bleriot representing just one manufacturer.

After the war, companies began concentrating on the development of commercial air transportation, and the French manufacturers were at the forefront of the industry. In 1918 Farman designed the Goliath, which in the next six years set several world records, including its 1919 two-stage flight from Paris to Casablanca to Dakar, totaling 2200 kilometers. Bleriot supplied Europe's first airlines with "Berlines," and in the 1920s and early 1930s, Potez's plant was reputed to be the world's most modern aeronautical facility. Manufacturing flourished in this period, with French aircraft setting records and fulfilling much of Europe's need for air transportation.

In 1936 the Popular Front Government assumed power and France's major aviation companies were nationalized. Farman, Hanriot, Potez, Marcel Bloch, Louis Bleriot, Dyle et Bacalan, Loire Nieuport, Liore Olivie, and Dewoitine were combined into six companies according to geographical criteria: the Sociétés Nationales de Constructions Aeronautiques du Centre (SNCAC), du Sud-Ouest (SNCASO), du Sud-Est (SNCASE), du Midi (SNCAM), du Nord (SNCAN), and de l'Ouest (SNCAO). These were reduced to two companies, SNCASO and SNCASE, in 1941.

In 1940, with the signing of the Armistice, France submitted to German occupation. According to the Armistice agreement, aircraft plants were required to manufacture material for the German forces, thus subjecting the manufacturers to Allied bombing. During the war, bombing destroyed aircraft facilities and work tools, holding up development. The U.S. and British aeronautical industries advanced far ahead of the French in the next five years.

When France was liberated in 1945, the aeronautical industry struggled to catch up. Many studies that had been secretly pursued during the Occupation bore fruit and sped France's return to the level of the U.S. and British industries. For example, the country's first jet, the Triton, had been secretly developed during the war and was tested only one year after France was liberated. However, their attempts to develop a helicopter were frustrated by mechanical problems and the closing of SNCAC in 1949. With the development of the Djinn by SNCASO in the mid-1950s, the French helicopter industry got its real start, producing 150 units between 1956 and 1960. The French-owned companies also produced several enduring aircraft in this period, including the Noratlas and the Fouga Magister, which were both flown for several decades.

The mid-1950s began a critical period for the companies that were to become Aerospatiale. Their helicopter designs moved to the forefront of the industry when they replaced piston-driven engines with high-capacity turbo engines. The helicopter utilizing these engines, the Alouette I introduced in 1955, and the subsequent Alouette II, sold well both nationally and as an export. The companies also gained ground with their studies in supersonic aircraft, developing the Durandal in 1956. Their experimentation with combined turbo/ram-jet propulsion systems on the Griffon II eventually led to the application of this technology on modern tactical missiles.

This period also saw the beginning of Aerospatiale's subsequent dedication to cooperative agreements with other countries. After the reconciliation between France and West Germany, the two countries worked together in the tactical missile field, developing the Milan and Hot antitank missiles in the early 1960s. They extended their cooperative endeavors to include the development of the Airbus program. France and Great Britain together pursued the creation of a supersonic transport plane, resulting in the 1969 maiden flight of the Concorde.

Aerospatiale's immediate predecessors—Sud-Aviation; Nord-Aviation; and SEREB, the Société pour l'Étude et la Realisation d'Engins Balistiques—had all been formed by the late 1950s from those companies initially nationalized by the French government. SEREB's initial job was to develop the Strategic Ballistic Surface-to-Surface Missile and the Strategic Ballistic Sea-to-Surface Missile for National Defense. These developments provided a solid base for the implementation of France's later nuclear policy. In addition, these ballistic studies led to a space launcher program in 1962. The resulting Diamant, successfully fired in 1965, established France as the third leading space developer, behind the United States and the USSR.

In order to eliminate duplication in marketing, customer service, and research and development, the French government decided to merge its three aerospace companies in 1970. It was hoped that the new company, Société Nationale Industrielle Aerospatiale, would increase efficiency and France's competitiveness in the aerospace industry. Initially, management was reorganized but production remained unchanged. A lack of aircraft orders led to losses three years in a row—$100 million in 1973 alone. These continued losses prompted the government to demand reorganization along departmental lines, creating aircraft, helicopter, missile, and space divisions. Layoffs were also threatened for several years in a row, but major unemployment in France caused the government to hold off. Instead, the government held the company together with a $100 million advance in capital.

Aerospatiale's performance in the 1970s was held back by a continuing lack of orders for the aircraft division. The Concorde, scheduled to begin service in 1975, had only nine orders in 1973, and those were from the countries sponsoring the aircraft's development, France and England. Aerospatiale was finding it difficult to market to other countries because cost overruns and environmental problems had raised the price of a Concorde from $15 million to $65 million. In addition, operating costs for the Concorde, already quite high, rose dramatically with skyrocketing oil prices. Interest in the United States was particularly low because the aircraft would not be allowed to fly supersonically over land. Airbus Industrie's Airbus A 300 B, a twin-engine wide body aircraft, was also in financial trouble because of a low number of orders.

Aerospatiale's first years were successful ones for its other divisions. The helicopter line was improved with the introductions of Ecureuil, the Super-Puma, and the Dauphin. This division remained profitable during Aerospatiale's tough times in the 1970s, becoming, in fact, the world's leading exporter. Aerospatiale also developed plans inherited from SEREB for France's first strategic nuclear missiles. The company installed 18 land-based S1 missiles in 1971. The same year, it introduced its M1 missiles for submarines. Throughout the 1970s, Aerospatiale was improving its missile designs, replacing the S2 with S3 missiles in 1980 and continuing to upgrade its M series submarine missiles. The decade also saw work on the Exocets, a series of antiship missiles to be launched from surface ships, combat aircraft, coastline battery, or submarines.

France's space programs had suffered from cuts and delays because of a lack of funds in the late 1960s, a situation the country hoped to solve with the creation of Aerospatiale. Indeed, Aerospatiale played a major role in the European space cooperation that began in 1972. The company became the industrial architect of the Ariane space launchers, first successfully fired in 1979, and the prime contractor for several satellite programs.

In 1973 the French government gave Aerospatiale emergency financial support in the form of government guarantees for a $26 million public bond issue. Despite this aid and the strong performances of the helicopter, tactical missile, and ballistic systems divisions, the company still registered losses in 1974 and 1975.

"We are dying a slow death," Andre Gintrand, financial vice president of Aerospatiale, lamented in *Business Week* in 1974. "With the American competition in the market, we can't breathe." President Charles Cristofini felt more transnational aircraft would help fight the U.S. aircraft leaders by encouraging more national airlines to buy European products. Aerospatiale was also competing with Avions Marcel Dassault-Breguet Aviation for military contracts and felt that the government was favoring Dassault.

Aerospatiale's aircraft division continued their policy of forming international cooperative ventures. They joined forces with Alenia in 1982 to form ATR. The company created the ATR 42, a small regional transport aircraft and, later, the ATR 72.

The company also continued to work with British Aerospace, forming plans in the mid-1980s for a second generation Concorde, although evaluating its feasibility was expected to take years. Airbus Industrie expanded its line and soon offered a large series of commercial aircraft. Orders gradually improved during the 1980s; in 1989 aircraft orders totalled over 39 million francs, and in 1990 Airbus Industrie had 1250 firm orders for A300s, A310s, and A320s.

Aerospatiale's other divisions continued to expand throughout the 1980s. The helicopter division maintained its position as the world's leading exporter and, in 1988, had the biggest market share in the civil sector in the United States, where the company has a subsidiary. Its space division was at the forefront of European space technology, suggesting and studying the feasibility of such projects as an unmanned space station and a small winged space shuttle-type vehicle called Hermes. Aerospatiale remained a prime contractor for the European Space Agency's Ariane family of launch vehicles and became the head of the ESA team charged with building Hermes, production of which was delayed by a ministerial conference at the end of 1992.

In 1990 France and Britain began a three-year study into the commercial and technical feasibility of a second generation supersonic transport. The study was to examine the ATSF (Future Supersonic Transport Aircraft), and a hypersonic aircraft, the AGV (High-Speed Aircraft), which would fly 12,000 to 15,000 km at Mach 5, but would not require passengers to have astronaut training. In theory, the ATSF could be in service by 2005, and the AGV by 2030 to 2040, but both would need broad-based international cooperation to make development feasible. There were many problems to overcome, including the assurance of a market for 400-500 aircraft.

In 1991 Aerospatiale and Italy's state-owned Alenia made a bid for De Havilland, an ailing Canadian subsidiary of Boeing Co. The European Commission, a decision-making body of the European Community (EC), did not allow the deal to go

through, however, arguing the venture would have a "dominant position," giving the two companies together a 50 percent share of the world market and 65 percent of the EC market for commuter planes with 20 to 70 seats.

The next year Aerospatiale, DASA, and Alenia were planning a new consortium called Regioliner, which would produce a 120-seat jet by 1996. Many companies saw the market for a new generation of small jet aircraft that could be used for short routes, but lacked the money to develop them. The companies were hoping for government funds to help start them on this proposed $2.5 billion project.

Aerospatiale's creation of new subsidiaries and cooperative ventures accelerated in the early 1990s, as it attempted to distribute the burden of research and development and receive the benefits of governmental subsidies from several nations. In 1990 Aerospatiale, DASA, Alenia, and Dassault, formed a single company, Euro-Hermespace to oversee the development and production of the Hermes spaceplane. France provided funding for a 43.5 percent share of the company; the country's interests were then to be administered by a new company, Hermespace France, owned jointly by Aerospatiale, with 51 percent, and Dassault, with the remainder. However, Hermes and the Columbus space station encountered financial, political, and management problems in the early 1990s. While the ESA evaluated the cost of the station and waited to see what NASA did with their plans for a space station, a ministerial conference decision delayed the production of Hermes in 1992. Eventually, the Hermes program was postponed indefinitely, and Euro-Hermespace was dissolved.

In 1991 Aerospatiale and DASA merged the commercial operations of their helicopter divisions. The new company, Eurocopter Holding, is owned 60 percent by Aerospatiale and 40 percent by DASA. However, Eurocopter SA, which directs the activity of the French and German helicopter divisions, is owned 75 percent by Eurocopter Holding and 25 percent Aerospatiale directly. Before the merger, Aerospatiale held 33 percent of the world helicopter market, based on sales from 1985 to 1989, whereas MBB held only 8 percent. Revenue from the two helicopter divisions equaled about $1.6 billion in 1990. The new company will combine sales, service, and support operations.

With the end of the cold war, many military contractors were threatened with budget cutbacks and program cancellations. Most of Aerospatiale's international projects, including the Aster surface-to-air system and their third generation of anti-tank weapons, were going forward in the early 1990s. However, the backlog of missile orders dropped and that area of business activity was hurt by the cancellation of the S-45 strategic missile program and the Hades short-range nuclear missile. Aerospatiale was forced to cut 1,145 jobs in 1992.

The downturn in the global market in the early 1990s increased the complaints by the United States and others that subsidies and non-tariff barriers gave Aerospatiale an unfair advantage in the world market. Jacques Balazard, vice president of research and development, claimed in *Design News,* "Such phenomena . . . are less marked in Europe than in many other regions. . . . If you consider the very large proportion of U.S.-made aircraft in

European airlines, you will undoubtedly acknowledge that the U.S. industry does not suffer from these alleged barriers.''

In 1992 Crédit Lyonnais, a state-owned French bank, acquired 20 percent of Aerospatiale from the French government. Thus, Aerospatiale increased its capital, enabling the company to reduce its debt and finance new investments.

Principal Subsidiaries: Seca; Socata; Sogerma-Socea; Eurocopter Holding (60%); Eurocopter SA (25% held directly, Eurocopter Holding holds an additional 75%); Euromissile (50%); ATR (50%); Airbus Industrie Group (37.9%); Sextant Avionique (50%); Unilaser; Aerospatiale, Inc. (U.S.A.); Aerospatiale Canada Inc.; Aerospatiale UK Ltd.

Further Reading: Fink, Donald E. ''France Reorganizing Aerospace Industry,'' *Aviation Week and Space Technology,* March 3, 1969; ''France: Aircraft Makers Take a Nose Dive,'' *Business Week,* September 15, 1973; ''France: Emergency Refueling for Aerospatiale,'' *Business Week,* November 2, 1974; ''France Searching for Solutions To Continued Aerospatiale Losses,'' *Aviation Week and Space Technology,* April 19, 1976; Lenorovitz, Jeffrey M., ''French Plan Unmanned Space Station,'' *Aviation Week and Space Technology,* August 3, 1981; Lenorovitz, Jeffrey M., ''Aerospatiale Defines Con-

corde Follow-On for 21st Century,'' *Aviation Week and Space Technology,* January 20, 1986; ''Cooperative Ventures Aid Expansion,'' ''Civil Transports: From the ATR to Hypersonic Aircraft,'' ''Helicopters: The World's Top Exporter,'' ''A Pillar of French Defense, Backed by Strong R&D'' and ''The Foundation of European Space Leadership'' Market Supplements, *Aviation Week and Space Technology,* January 20, 1990; Shifrin, Carole A., ''Britain and France Begin Concorde Follow–On Study,'' *Aviation Week and Space Technology,* May 14, 1990; Lenorovitz, Jeffrey M., ''Company Formed to Manage Next Phase of Europe's Hermes Spaceplane Program,'' *Aviation Week and Space Technology,* November 12, 1990; Lenorovitz, Jeffrey M., ''Aerospatiale, MBB Merge Helicopter Commercial Sectors,'' *Aviation Week and Space Technology,* May 20, 1991; ''War by Competition Policy,'' *The Economist,* October 12, 1991; ''Europe's Growing Impact on High Technology,'' *Design News,* March 23, 1992; ''Consortiamania,'' *The Economist,* May 23, 1992; ''Credit Lyonnais to Buy 20% Stake in Aerospatiale from French Government,'' *Aviation Week and Space Technology,* August 3, 1992; ''Aerospatiale,'' *Aviation Week and Space Technology,* October 19, 1992; ''Aerospatiale, Dassault Aviation Agree to Develop Stronger Bonds,'' *Aviation Week and Space Technology,* January 4, 1993.

—Susan Windisch Brown

AFFILIATED PUBLICATIONS, INC.

135 Morrisey Boulevard
P.O. Box 2378
Boston, Massachusetts 02107-2378
U.S.A.
(617) 929-3300
Fax: (617) 929-3490

Public Company
Incorporated: 1978 as Globe Newspaper Company
Employees: 2406
Sales: $413.9 million
Stock Exchanges: New York
SICs: 2711 Newspapers

Affiliated Publications, Inc., is the owner and operator of The Boston Globe, the principal newspaper of the Boston metropolitan area and the surrounding states of New England. Run by one family for over a century, this journal has served as a civic institution, rising slowly to prominence over its many competitors, almost all of which are now defunct. In the 1970s, the owners of the Globe sold stock to the public for the first time and expanded into a number of new fields, seeking to build the Globe into a full-fledged media and communications conglomerate. After 20 years of this activity, however, the company came more or less full circle, concentrating again most fully on the Globe as the center of its activities.

The Boston Globe was founded in 1872 by a group of six prominent Boston businessmen who put up a total of $100,000 to start a new journal in a city that already had ten of them. The new paper's first issue came out on March 4, 1872. Published only on weekday mornings, it sold for four cents and featured news of local cultural events, as well as a summary of recent sermons from Boston churches entitled "The Sunday Pulpit."

In the paper's early months, advertising revenue was scarce and the enterprise's initial capitalization was quickly depleted. In November 1872 Boston was struck by a devastating fire, which wiped out much of the city. Although The Globe's building was spared, its financial situation was not improved, and by June of the following year, the failing paper's backers had begun to pull out. In an effort to resurrect the Globe, its remaining owners convinced veteran newspaperman Charles H. Taylor to join the

paper. Taylor was a printer, reporter, and Civil War veteran whose own monthly journal, the American Homes Magazine, had suffered a major setback in the fire. Taylor had previously worked as a correspondent for the New York Tribune, covering news all across New England, and in politics, as the secretary to the governor of Massachusetts, as a state representative, and as the clerk of the state House of Representatives. In August 1873 Taylor began his association with the Globe. By December of that year, he had signed a two-year contract as general manager. At the same time, the Globe appointed a new editor, Edwin Munroe Bacon, who, though only 29 years old, had worked as a correspondent for a New York paper for ten years. Under the leadership of these two men, the Globe began its climb to preeminence in the Boston newspaper world.

The early stages of this process were not easy, as the Globe combatted the effects of a financial crash and panic in 1873 that lasted throughout the rest of the decade. The paper reduced its price per copy to three cents, increased advertising incrementally, and tried to raise its circulation. Issues were produced on a single printing press and featured woodcuts and cartoons as illustrations. In 1877 the Globe printed its first story transmitted by Alexander Graham Bell's new invention, the telephone, after a reporter relayed an account of a promotional speech by Bell to an assistant in Boston over the wires set up for Bell's demonstration.

Despite these technological advances, the paper continued to lose money. In 1878 the Globe was reorganized when Eben Jordan, owner of the Jordan Marsh department store and one of the paper's original founders, paid off the Globe's debts and put it on a sound financial footing. Eventually, Taylor and Jordan would split ownership of the paper evenly, although Taylor alone managed the business. The newspaper's newfound financial security enabled Taylor to introduce a Sunday edition and an evening paper. In addition, he changed the Globe's content, switching its political loyalties from the Republican to Democratic party, introducing a higher standard of impartiality and objectivity in reporting, and adding sections to appeal to women and children. These innovations, combined with a drop in price to two cents, resulted in a dramatic increase in circulation for the Globe. Between 1878 and 1881 the number of copies sold increased from 8,000 to 30,000. In 1879 the paper broke even for the first time, and by the end of the 1880s, the Globe had become the dominant paper of the New England region.

Taking note of the demographics of Boston, the paper cultivated the city's burgeoning population of Irish immigrants and supported the crusades of organized labor. Not unrelated to this, the paper instituted "Help Wanted" and "Situations Wanted" advertisements, which would grow into a major source of revenue. In 1884 another key member of the Globe's staff was hired when James Morgan, a 22-year-old Kentucky telegraph operator who had previously worked as the Boston correspondent for the fledgling United Press syndicate, was hired as an editor. Morgan soon became a reporter and covered the political beat for more than 60 years. Throughout his long tenure on the Globe, Morgan enjoyed the complete confidence of Taylor and his descendents, and his sensibility shaped the Globe throughout that time.

In the mid-1880s the Globe added columns devoted to the concerns of women to its Sunday edition, in line with the suffragist sentiment of the day. This helped to push the paper's circulation above 100,000 in 1886. The following year, the paper moved into a new building, with space for new presses, to produce a much larger number of newspapers. At seven stories, the Globe building was the tallest on the Boston street that would come to be known as "Newspaper Row."

Within five years the Globe claimed a circulation of 200,000. The purchase of a second building enabled the Globe to add an array of new equipment and services, including ten telegraph operators and a linotype machine, which could be used to set type more quickly and efficiently. Reporters began to use typewriters to turn out their copy, and papers were delivered by horse-drawn wagon and by train to outlying areas. In 1894 the paper introduced color printing. Three years later, this innovation enabled the Globe to introduce color comics to its product. With this and other new features attracting readers, the level of advertising in the Globe continued to grow throughout the 1890s, despite the general economic recession.

Continuity in running the Globe was assured in the 1890s when all three of Taylor's sons joined the family business. By the end of the century, the paper's days of innovation were over. The Globe had taken on a staid, institutional quality, as it established itself as the foremost journal of the New England region. With the exception of the period covering the Spanish-American War, when the sales of all newspapers went up dramatically, the Globe's circulation stabilized, rising incrementally as it kept pace with the size of the community it covered. In the early years of the twentieth century, two brash upstart papers arose to challenge the Globe in Boston, and the sensationalism of these new competitors paradoxically contributed to the Globe's emphasis on conventional news coverage. The paper relied on its large staff and heavy use of lighter features to cover the news thoroughly and keep readers interested in reading it during the quiet years before the First World War.

When World War I broke out on August 14, 1914, the Globe quickly published dispatches from war correspondents in Europe. The paper also became embroiled in the controversy over whether or not the United States should maintain its isolationist stance or become more involved in the war. By 1916, the paper, which had moved from its early Democratic boosterism to a solid middle-of-the-road position, had allied itself firmly with the progressive policies of Woodrow Wilson. When the U.S. did enter the European conflict, the Globe sent its top war reporter to travel with the Yankee Division, made up of men from New England.

With the death in June 1921 of Charles Taylor, regarded as the Globe's founder, an era at the paper came to an end. Taylor turned leadership over to his second son, William O. Taylor, who ran the paper in conjunction with his older brother, Charles H. Taylor, Jr. Under their stewardship, the Globe prospered during the general economic boom of the 1920s. The stock market crash of 1929, however, coupled with the ensuing Depression, dramatically changed the country's financial landscape.

The economic downturn proved a trying time for the Globe. With the failure of many businesses, advertising revenue dropped off sharply. With no less than five morning papers and four evening papers competing for a shrinking number of dollars, the Globe dropped to third place in circulation in its market. The new leader was the Boston Herald, which had purchased new printing equipment that allowed it to put out a larger, better organized paper. By 1935 the Herald's daily circulation topped the Globe's by 30,000 copies. In the following year, the Globe's profit had dwindled to a mere $50,000, and salaries at the paper were cut.

In 1937 Charles H. Taylor, Jr., son of the paper's founder, retired. The Globe resorted to contests, previously considered beneath the paper's dignity, to shore up its circulation and enable it to retain its national advertising accounts. The basic problem, however, was not solely financial. The Globe had become a cautious paper with a dulled instinct for the news. Critics charged that the newspaper's coverage of controversial issues was severely lacking and reflected an abdication of civic responsibility. In a sign of the paper's archaic nature, the Globe continued the old-fashioned practice of running advertisements instead of headlines across the tops of its inside pages up until 1936. (Advertisements stayed on the paper's front page well into the 1960s.)

By the mid-1930s, however, it was time for a renewal of the Globe's energy. This was accomplished through the retirement in 1937 of many of the Globe's old hands, and the promotion of younger men into their jobs. Chief among them was Laurence Winship, who became the paper's managing editor.

Under Winship the Globe began its slow climb back to preeminence in the Boston market. The newspaper appointed its first picture editor in recognition of the growing importance of photography for a newspaper. The Globe also began to commission and use market research to shape its offerings to readers. It undertook various promotional activities to increase advertising and readership, as well as to bring in young readers. In addition, the Globe began to shift its distribution emphasis from sales at commuter rail stations and other key points to home delivery in the rapidly growing suburbs and the city.

These efforts had begun to pay off when the United States entered World War II in late 1941. For the Globe, as for other papers, covering the events in Europe proved a major challenge. The paper strived to present the most accurate account of distant events possible, marking questionable information "unconfirmed" in bold letters over the story.

The conflict brought a severe shortage of newsprint. With this came a restriction on the number of advertisements possible and the number of copies available to be sold. Although the Globe's fair handling of these restrictions limited its revenues severely during the war, the paper rebounded during the post-war boom.

During the 1950s, the Globe's tradition of sensitivity to the Irish Catholic members of its reading population led it to shrink from any criticism of the demagogic tactics of Senator Joseph McCarthy, just as twenty years earlier it had failed to object to the book bannings and other actions of Boston's corrupt Irish mayor, James Curley. The paper's quiescence began to diminish in the mid-1950s, after the death of publisher William O.

Taylor and the ascension of his son, William Davis Taylor, in 1955. The following year, the rival Boston Post went out of business, and the Globe, accustomed to the middle spot in a three-way contest (which tended to solidify its middle-of-the-road tendencies), found itself in a one-on-one battle with the Boston Herald. Armed with a modern printing plant that produced a clean, sophisticated-looking paper, the Herald's circulation had been increasing for decades while the Globe's remained static, hampered by its outmoded equipment and less attractive product. Both papers sought to increase their advertising and readership in a media market that now included television.

Seeking to set itself apart from its competitor, the Globe began to lobby in its pages for civic change and reform. By the end of the 1950s these efforts paid off as the paper picked up a modest number of new readers. In 1958 the Globe abandoned its historic but cramped home on newspaper row and moved south to a modern new plant in the neighborhood of Dorchester, near highways and rail lines. The facility cost $14 million and was partly funded by a loan from the John Hancock Life Insurance Company. It was the first time that the paper had sought outside financing since its early years. The new plant allowed the Globe to produce larger editions than its competitor, and the daily morning paper's circulation increased by 100,000 in the next seven years as the Globe took a commanding lead in its war with the Herald.

In the 1960s the Globe fully came into its own as an activist journal, taking strong editorial positions on controversial issues and lobbying for civic improvements under the editorial leadership of Laurence Winship's son Thomas, who succeeded his father as editor of the paper in 1965. These efforts were rewarded in 1965 when the paper won the first Pulitzer Prize to be awarded to a Boston journal in 45 years. Under the stewardship of the younger Winship, the Globe moved firmly from a staff of reporters with general assignments to the development of a pool of specialized writers who brought a higher level of expertise and background to the topics they covered. The Globe added critics of the arts, and also sought to recruit younger and more ethnically diverse reporters.

Throughout the 1960s, the Boston Globe continued to expand the printing capacity at its Dorchester plant, and in 1968 the paper introduced multiple sections to its large Sunday edition paper. The following year, the paper redid its typeface and design in search of a more modern look. With these changes, the paper continued to show steady gains in Sunday and morning readership, while circulation for the evening edition fell as the Boston area's population shifted to the suburbs.

In the 1970s the Globe continued its trend toward activist reporting as it covered such stories as the U.S. involvement in Vietnam and the burgeoning counterculture. In August 1973 the Globe's financial structure underwent a major change when the trustees of Eben Jordan's trust and various members of the Taylor family sold stock in the company to the public for the first time. The stock sale was structured so that the Jordan trust and Taylor family effectively remained in control of the new company, named Affiliated Publications, Inc.

With the capital raised by the sale, Affiliated began to expand its scope of operations beyond its core urban newspaper tradition into new forms of media and communications. In late 1975 the company acquired Research Analysis Corporation to conduct and market demographic surveys. The following year the company purchased radio stations in New York and Ohio, and bought a small Massachusetts newspaper.

Affiliated's media purchases continued in the late 1970s, as the company added six radio stations around the country to its holdings. In 1981 the company entered a new field when it purchased a 45-percent share in McCaw Cellular Communications, a Washington-state-based cable television operator, for $12 million. The following year, Affiliated and McCaw augmented their holdings by buying two West Coast cable television properties, the Southern Oregon Broadcasting Company and Pacific Teletronics, Inc.

In 1983 Affiliated made a major investment in what remained the centerpiece of its holdings, the Boston Globe, when it opened a satellite printing press for the newspaper in Billerica, Massachusetts, outside Boston. Newspaper pages were made up at the main Globe facility in town and then sent over wires to the plant to be printed. Two years later, this move allowed the Globe to produce its largest daily issue ever—216 pages—and the largest Sunday paper, totalling 1,050 pages, one month later on December 1, 1985.

Following these successes, Affiliated began to streamline its operations. First, the company sold off its radio properties, divesting itself of its first two purchases separately, and then handing off an additional nine radio stations to EZ Communications for $65.5 million in 1986. At the end of that year, Affiliated and McCaw sold their cable television operations for $755 million. Affiliated then announced plans to enter the fledgling cellular phone industry through McCaw, with expectations that profits in the largely untried field would be high.

In a move more in line with its traditional strength in print media, Affiliated purchased Billboard Publications, Inc. (BPI), a trade magazine publisher, for $100 million in 1987. The following year, this subsidiary, now called BPI Communications, Inc., bought two publications—Plants, Sites & Parks and The Hollywood Reporter. Affiliated also increased its holdings in McCaw slightly. The acquisitions expanded the company's profits to more than $200 million for the fiscal year ending in December 1987.

By the end of 1988, however, the economy of New England fell into a recession, sharply limiting the profitability of the Globe. In an effort to bring order to its somewhat disparate activities, Affiliated reorganized itself in early 1989, spinning off its core publishing businesses, the Globe Newspaper Company and BPI Communications, Inc., and merging its remaining businesses into McCaw. These transactions, all accomplished on a tax-free basis, left Affiliated's stockholders holding both Affiliated stock and McCaw stock. In total, Affiliated had invested $80 million into McCaw. On May 31, 1989, the day these transactions were finalized, the public market valuation of Affiliated's stock interest in McCaw was approximately $2.6 billion.

As part of the process of returning to its roots, Affiliated purchased a majority interest in Adweek magazine in 1990 through

BPI Communications, continuing the company's focus on print media. Affiliated turned a profit in 1989 and 1990. In the throes of regional recession, however, Affiliated's operating income in 1991 was only one third of what it had been in 1988. Affiliated decided to streamline its operations further, selling off two-thirds of its BPI Communications, Inc., subsidiary to a partnership formed by the subsidiary's management and a venture capital house. In an effort to adapt to the changing advertising climate for the Globe, the company created Community Direct, Inc., to provide specialized marketing services to Globe advertisers.

As Affiliated moved into the mid-1990s, it looked to the Boston Globe, its first and principal holding, as the focus of its activities. Keeping this institution, founded in the nineteenth century, relevant and profitable in the twenty-first century will comprise the company's main challenge in the years to come.

Principal Subsidiaries: Globe Newspaper Company; Community Newsdealers Inc.; Wilson Tisdale Company.

Further Reading: Lyons, Louis M., *Newspaper Story: One Hundred Years of the Boston Globe*, Cambridge, MA, Belknap Press, 1971.

—Elizabeth Rourke

AGWAY, INC.

333 Butternut Drive
Dewitt, New York 13214
U.S.A.
(315) 449-6431
Fax: (315) 449-6078

Private Company
Incorporated: 1964 as GLF-Eastern States Association
Employees: 6,200
Sales: $3.26 billion
Stock Exchanges: American (Curtice Burns Foods)
SICs: 5159 Farm-Product Raw Materials Nec; 2911
  Petroleum Refining

Agway, Inc. ranks behind Farmland Industries as one of the largest agricultural cooperatives in the United States. As recently as 1990, however, it held the number one position in both assets and revenue. Its 91,000 members populate 12 northeastern states but, through its diversified food businesses, Agway markets many of its products nationwide. Like most major cooperatives, Agway is divided into several different operations. Its Agriculture Group manufactures and sells farm production supplies, including fertilizer and bulk feed; this group also carries out dairy research and testing. The Agway Energy Group supplies home heating fuels to both farmers and nonfarmers in the Northeast. Agway also furnishes a broad line of insurance products as well as capital financing for farmers and other agricultural businesses. Agway's Consumer Group (which sells yard and garden equipment, pet food and supplies, farm-related equipment, and a small number of processed foods) and food subsidiaries Curtice Burns Foods and H. P. Hood together comprise the cooperative's largest branch of operations. The Consumer Group operates some 230 stores and employs 364 franchised representatives to market its Big Red and other product lines.

Agway was created in 1964 from the merger of three regional cooperatives serving the northeastern United States. The oldest of the three, Eastern States Farmers Exchange, was founded in 1920 and headquartered in West Springfield, Massachusetts. The second, the Cooperative Grange League Federation Exchange (GLF), was founded in 1920 and headquartered in Ithaca, New York. The third, Pennsylvania Farm Bureau Cooperative Association (PFB), was founded in 1934 and headquar-

tered in Harrisburg, Pennsylvania. Cumulative sales for the three totaled $375 million. The idea to merge first arose in January 1960 at the annual meeting of the National Council of Farmer Cooperatives in Atlanta. There the general manager of GLF, Edmund H. Fallon, invited the assistant general manager of Eastern States, William H. Prigmore, to his room for a private discussion on the future of agriculture, particularly as it affected cooperative activity in the Northeast. Both men agreed that one large cooperative might better serve the area than the three already in place. In later informal meetings, at Fallon's request, PFB was included in the plans for consolidation. In June 1960 the presidents and the general managers of all three co-ops met at GLF headquarters and launched the "PEG" study (named after the initial letters of the three businesses).

The PEG study offered a cautious approach to merging. Its guiding principle was to discover whether profitability could be enhanced by joint operation of some or all of the facilities of the parent corporations. Although the answer might well have been obvious, another reason for proceeding cautiously was the difficulty of merging three different governing boards, with varying goals, into some new organizational system. However, within three years, an executive study committee had reported that the best and most workable solution was a complete consolidation. GLF and Eastern were committed to proceed rapidly, but PFB had, during the interim, contracted with Cooperative Mills of Baltimore to run one of its mills. Furthermore, PFB's committee member, L. A. Thomas, Jr., had neglected to participate in feed deliberations, the primary focus of the PEG study.

GLF and Eastern decided to hammer out an initial merger and then include PFB at a later date; a merger of all three at once, had it been possible at the time, would only have multiplied the many logistical problems that were due to arise. As explained in Nathaniel E. White's "The Birth of Agway," GLF and Eastern "were structured quite differently. GLF was a stock cooperative with the farmer's membership validated by the ownership of common stock. Eastern States was a membership cooperative with no securities outstanding—the farmer's membership was activated solely by patronage." Negotiators for the two co-ops proposed that the new requirements for membership be that a person not only farmed but held common stock in the company and was a user of the company's products and services. The board was to be large at first (27 members) and then reduced over time to the recommended number of 18. Following unanimous adoption of these and other settlements by the directors of both co-ops in November 1963, the first merger was incorporated in January 1964 under the temporary name of GLF-Eastern States Association. A month later Agway, Inc. was approved by the new board of directors as a concise name signifying the general enterprise while not indicating any geographical restriction. A final mandate for the merger was awarded in a landslide vote by members of the two co-ops. By July a makeshift headquarters had been established in Syracuse and Fallon became Agway's first general manager.

Now only PFB remained to be merged. "In many respects," writes White, "the PFB merger was more difficult than the initial merger of GLF and Eastern States. The federated PFB system was made up of 35 separately chartered agricultural cooperative corporations consisting of a regional cooperative, a marketing cooperative, and 33 county cooperatives." However, by June 1965, all obstacles had been overcome—including the 32 mergers within PFB—and PFB's assets were transferred to Agway. A year later all securities transactions were complete and Agway was beginning to operate as a single entity.

During this initial period another co-op, centered in upstate New York, was launched under the auspices of Agway. Named Pro-Fac (from produce facilities), this cooperative of fruit and vegetable farmers was also the result of a merger. In this case, Curtice Brothers Co. and Burns-Alton joined to form the public company of Curtice Burns, Inc. (now named Curtice Burns Foods, Inc.), while the New York farmers, many of them Agway members, joined to form the Pro-Fac Cooperative. A perfect symbiotic business relationship resulted. James Cook, in a 1981 article, explained it this way: "Curtice-Burns, Inc. of Rochester, N.Y., is in a class by itself. Not because it ranks as the fastest-growing branded foods company in the country these days . . . What makes Curtice-Burns so special is that it is the public half of Pro-Fac Cooperative, Inc., an 880-member, tax-exempt agricultural cooperative that sells its output exclusively to Curtice-Burns."

Because of this special arrangement, Curtice Burns quickly became the most visible barometer of growth for Agway as a major foods company. Between 1971 and 1981 the food-processor and marketer acquired no less than eight other companies, including Nalley's Fine Foods, Comstock Foods, National Brands Beverage, and National Oats Co. Annual sales, which in 1962 totaled just $13 million, now approached $400 million. Aside from unusual and highly beneficial funding arrangements available through Pro-Fac, Curtice Burns attained its elite status by focusing on successful regional brands. "Here's a company," according to Barron's, "that seeks out markets that aren't ever going to be big. But the secret is that sauerkraut, say, is only a $60 million market—too small to interest the big players and too tiny to carry national advertising budgets that the company isn't large enough to match." Agway continues to govern the still swelling company, which in fiscal 1992 posted sales of $896.9 million, through its 34 percent ownership and 70 percent voting power. The subsidiary operates 56 facilities in 17 states and western Canada.

The success of Curtice Burns has led Agway to explore similar public company/co-op partnerships. In July 1980 Agway purchased H.P. Hood Inc., a Boston-based processor and distributor of dairy and other food products. Hood is a major food concern, with $575 million in 1992 revenues. In management's discussion of the company's financial condition in 1992, declines in overall revenue (3.1 percent in 1991, 6.1 percent in 1990) were largely attributed to Hood, "which has experienced pricing pressures to maintain private label sales, along with volume decreased in fluid milk, ice cream and cultured products." Still valued by the company "as an innovative marketer in a highly competitive industry," Hood operates ten manufacturing plants in the northeastern United States.

Under new chief executive officer Charlie Saul, Agway has pledged itself to an internal reorganization project titled "Customer Driven: 1995—Focusing on the 21st Century." Agway incurred a $75 million restructuring charge impacting fiscal 1992 earnings; the result was a reported loss of $58.8 million on total sales of $3.3 billion. A program of voluntary early retirement, chosen by some 439 employees, was one of several factors contributing to the large cost.

Principal Subsidiaries: Agway Insurance Companies; Curtice Burns Foods, Inc. (34%); H.P. Hood Inc. (99%); Telmark Inc.

Further Reading: Cook, James, "Tea for Two," *Forbes,* March 2, 1981; "Companies Involved in Largest Insider Purchases: Curtice-Burns, Inc.," *The Insiders' Chronicle,* June 23, 1986; Cochran, Thomas N., and Pauline Uyelys, "Curtice Burns Foods Inc.: Its Secret Is in Finding the Sauerkraut Markets," *Barron's,* September 26, 1988; White, Nathaniel E., "The Birth of Agway: Northeast Agriculture in Transition," Dewitt, New York, Agway, Inc., 1989; "The Forbes Nonprofit 500: Agricultural Cooperatives," *Forbes,* November 26, 1990; *The Agway Extra* (Special 1992 Annual Meeting Edition), October 1992; *Agway Cooperator,* December 1992.

—Jay P. Pederson

ALBERTSON'S INC.

250 Parkcenter Boulevard
Boise, Idaho 83726
U.S.A.
(208) 385-6200
Fax: (208) 385-6110

Public Company
Incorporated: 1945
Employees: 60,000
Sales: $8.68 billion
Stock Exchanges: New York Boston Pacific Midwest
SICs: 5411 Grocery Stores; 5912 Drug Stores & Proprietary
　Stores

In 1939, Joe Albertson left his position as a district manager for Safeway Stores and, with partners L. S. Skaggs, whose family helped build Safeway, and Tom Cuthbert, Skaggs's accountant, opened his first one-stop shopping market on a Boise, Idaho corner. Albertson thought big from the start—his first newspaper ad promised customers "Idaho's largest and finest food store." And indeed, the store was huge by contemporary standards; at 10,000 square feet it was approximately eight times as large as the average grocery store of that era. The store included specialties such as an in-store bakery, one of the country's first magazine racks, and homemade "Big Joe" ice cream cones. Customers liked what they saw, and the store pulled in healthy first-year profits of $9,000.

Today, Albertson's Inc. is the sixth-largest grocery chain in the United States, operating more than 550 stores in 17 western and southern states. Yet Albertson's has not forgotten the lessons of its small-town beginnings during its expansion. "Albertson's is, in effect, a big store with a specialty store approach," claims its corporate philosophy, adopted in 1973. "We must be 'big' in terms of low prices, convenience and wide selection of brands. We must be a 'specialty' store in terms of quality, personal service and specialized selection."

Albertson's fosters this small-town style both through management and consumer services. The corporation implements a strong employee incentive program which returns 15 percent of each store's profits directly to its store director and department heads, and store management teams are kept informed of the accounting figures that make or break their unit's profitability.

Among their specialty consumer services, Albertson's stores provide personal service at in-store "scratch" bakeries, delicatessens, and meat departments. Larger stores carry ethnic foods geared toward the neighborhoods in which they are located, and, according to *Forbes,* Albertson's is cleaned "with a Disney-like fanaticism."

While Albertson's may owe its style to small-town roots, its history turns on the expansion of the one-stop shopping concept, which led to the growth of larger stores carrying more diverse products and eventually to the jumbo food-and-drug stores that were the key to Albertson's tremendous success.

Albertson's grew slowly at first. Sales remained constant during the war years, and in 1945, Joe Albertson dissolved the partnership and Albertson's was incorporated. By 1947, the chain had six stores operating in Idaho, and had established a complete poultry-processing operation. In 1949, the Dutch Girl ice cream plant opened in Boise, and Albertson's adopted the Dutch Girl as its early trademark.

Albertson's expanded during the 1950s into Washington, Utah, Oregon, and Montana. In 1957 the company built its first frozen foods distribution house, which served its southern Idaho and eastern Oregon stores. Albertson's also operated a few department stores during the 1950s but these were phased out rapidly as the company decided to focus on the sale of food and drugstore items. In 1959, Albertson's introduced its private label, Janet Lee, named after the executive vice president's daughter. The company also went public in 1959, and with that capital began to expand its markets aggressively.

Albertson's moved into its sixth state, Wyoming, in 1961, and opened its 100th store in 1962. In 1964 the company broke into the California market by acquiring Greater All American Markets, based in Los Angeles. The same year, Albertson turned the position of chief executive over to J. L. Berlin, although he continued to chair the executive board.

Under Berlin's leadership, the company strengthened its Californian position by merging with Semrau and Sons, an Oakland-based grocery store chain, in 1965. This added eight markets in northern California, which Albertson's continued to operate under the name of Pay Less. In 1967 the company purchased eight Colorado supermarkets from Fury's Inc., a Lubbock, Texas concern. Between these purchases and construction of new units, Albertson's operated more than 200 stores by the end of the decade and annual sales were well over $400 million.

In the late 1960s, Albertson's set several company policies that would secure its snowballing success. One of these was the company's ongoing renovation program. In 1980, vice chairman Bolinder pointed out that "almost every failure of previously profitable supermarket companies can be attributed to stores becoming outdated." Albertson's has avoided this pitfall by constantly upgrading its facilities, remodeling and enlarging older stores, and closing those that have become obsolete.

Anticipating the ever-increasing competition for profitable operating sites, Albertson's also took care during the 1960s to build a sophisticated property-development task force of lawyers, economic analysts, negotiators, engineers, architects, and construction supervisors that has allowed the company to stay on top of industry trends. In addition, it expanded its employee training and incentive programs to encourage employees to make a lifetime career with the company.

During its first three decades Albertson's primarily sold groceries, although it did introduce drugstore departments into units where possible. In 1970, however, the company pioneered a unique and exceptionally profitable concept in supermarket design. J. L. Scott, who had become chief executive officer in 1966, announced in 1969 that Albertson's would enter into partnership with Skaggs Drugs Centers, based in Salt Lake City, Utah, and headed by Albertson's former partner, to jointly finance and manage six jumbo combination food and drug stores in Texas. While the average contemporary supermarket was 30,000 square feet or smaller, the combination stores covered as many as 55,000 square feet. And while conventional stores carried strictly grocery items, which have a slim profit margin of 1 percent to 2 percent, the Skaggs-Albertson's combination stores stocked not only groceries but also nonfood items such as cosmetics, perfumes, pharmacy products, camera supplies, and electrical equipment. Banking on the higher profit margin of nonfood items as well as on an aggressive five-year plan, Scott also predicted in 1969 that Albertson's sales would double within five years. His optimism was not unfounded. By 1974, sales reached $852.3 million, with net earnings of $8.9 million.

The first Skaggs-Albertson's combination stores were opened in Texas in 1970, the year after the New York Stock Exchange began to trade Albertson's shares. In the early 1970s, Albertson's and Skaggs considered merging, but ultimately decided against the move. Albertson's continued its beneficial partnership with Skaggs until 1977, opening combination drug and grocery stores throughout Texas, Florida, and Louisiana.

Along with rapid growth, Albertson's faced some minor setbacks during the early 1970s. In 1972 Albertson's had acquired Mountain States Wholesale of Idaho, a subsidiary of DiGiorgio Corporation. In 1974, the Justice Department filed a civil antitrust suit against Albertson's, asserting that at the time of the purchase, Albertson's was the largest retail grocer in the southern Idaho and eastern Oregon market, while Mountain States carried 43 percent of the wholesale grocery market, and that Albertson's purchase created an illegal monopoly.

Robert D. Bolinder, chief executive officer from 1974 through 1976, claimed that the suit was without basis and that Albertson's had in fact preserved competition in the area by acquiring Mountain States. Although Bolinder still claimed that the Justice Department had misunderstood Albertson's reasons for buying the wholesaler, noting that the subsidiary was not financially integral to the company but accounted for only 3.4 percent of its total sales in 1973, the settlement, in 1977, required Albertson's to divest Mountain States and barred the company from acquiring any retail or wholesale grocery businesses in southern Idaho or eastern Oregon for five years.

Also in 1974, in the Portland, Seattle, and Denver areas, the Federal Trade Commission found fault with Albertson's advertising practices. The company complied with an FTC order requiring that advertised sale items be available to customers and that rain checks be issued when sale items were out of stock, although Bolinder maintained that Albertson's had not violated any laws and emphasized that compliance would not require any change in the company's previously established advertising policies.

In 1976, after chairing the board for 37 years, Joe Albertson became chairman of the executive committee. Warren McCain, who began his career with Albertson's as a merchandising supervisor in 1951, became chairman of the board and chief executive officer. In the same year, Albertson's began to build superstores, which would carry an even higher ratio of nonfood items. A slightly smaller version of the combination store, the superstores range in size from 35,000 to 48,000 square feet and feature more fresh foods and perishables. It was during 1976 that the corporation slowly began to phase out its conventional markets. Although a few profitable ones are still in existence today, most were closed or converted into larger stores during the late 1970s and early 1980s. Albertson's also installed its first electric price scanner in 1976. By the late 1980s, 85 percent of Albertson's stores used scanners.

Relying principally on outside distributors, Albertson's successfully penetrated markets located throughout a broad geographic area, but the rapid expansion of its markets during the 1970s called for expansion of company-owned distribution facilities. Two of the company's four full-line distribution facilities were built during this period. The first of these went up in 1973 in Brea, California, and the other was completed in 1976 in Salt Lake City. All Albertson's distribution facilities are built, and operate, as profit centers, contributing a return on investment that equals or exceeds that of the company's retail stores.

In 1977 Albertson's and Skaggs dissolved their partnership amicably, splitting their assets equally. For Albertson's, the breakup resulted in the formation of Southco, the company's southern division. Southco assumed operation of 30 of the 58 combination stores formerly run by the partnership. Albertson's continued opening combination stores, concentrating them principally in southern states, but also opening a few in South Dakota and Nebraska. In 1978 Albertson's strengthened its stronghold in southern California by acquiring 46 supermarkets located in the Los Angeles area from Fisher Foods, Inc.

In 1979 Albertson's took the "bigger is better" concept to the drawing boards again and introduced its first warehouse stores. As inflation drove prices up, Albertson's needed to cut overhead to preserve its profit margin. To this end, it converted, between 1979 and 1981, seven stores into full-line, mass-merchandise warehouse stores run under the name Grocery Warehouse. These no-frills stores carried nonfood items but emphasized groceries, with substantial savings on meat and liquor. While these stores continue to be successful, they did not eclipse the profitability of the more broadly appealing superstores.

The introduction of the combination store and the continuing readaptation of older stores—87 percent of the company's stores were newly built or completely remodeled during the 1970s—allowed Albertson's to prosper despite the economically hostile environment of the late-1970s and early-1980s. In 1983, just after the country's most severe recession since the

Depression, Albertson's boasted 13 years of record sales. The combination stores, both jumbo and smaller, were largely responsible for this success. In 1983, these units accounted for only one-third of the chain's 423 stores but were the source of 65 percent of its profits.

Since Albertson's had grown by expanding over a wide geographic area rather than increasing its dominance in a smaller area, it did not hold superior market share in many of the areas where it operated. But it was this diversification, in part, that had allowed Albertson's to weather the economic storms of the 1970s and 1980s so successfully. As it happened, the areas of Albertson's concentration were the areas of relative economic prosperity. In 1981 Albertson's was operating in 17 of the fastest growing standard metropolitan areas, as identified by the U.S. Department of Commerce. Stores in relatively stable areas helped balance losses in more depressed markets.

Although Albertson's did break into the Nebraska and North and South Dakota markets in 1981, during the 1980s it concentrated principally on increasing its presence in established markets. For example, in an effort to expand its market in Texas, Albertson's modified its advertising strategy. In 1984, Albertson's reentered the Dallas-Fort Worth area, a very competitive market that no new firm had entered since Skaggs opened its first store there in 1972. The standard advertising strategy was to offer gimmicks like double-value coupons and promotional games to attract customers. Albertson's had used such techniques, but chose to approach the Dallas-Fort Worth market with an "every day low-cost" image instead. Store circulars explained "we won't be advertising weekly specials . . . we'll pass the savings on advertising costs on to you. Tell your friends and neighbors to help us keep prices down." The campaign sparked fierce competition, but the Albertson's units continued to prosper. Although the company traditionally held an upscale profile, it began to extend the new image to other suitable markets, and today about half of its stores operate on this basis.

As Albertson's continues to build larger concentrations of stores, its behind-the-scenes operations continue to grow. In 1982, retail management was reorganized into four regions: California, northwest, intermountain, and Southco. This subdivision allows each regional director and his management team to more effectively focus marketing and retail sales strategies, and more closely guide employee and real estate development. Albertson's built another distribution center in the Denver area in 1984, and completed its first fully mechanized distribution center in Portland, Oregon, in 1988. In addition, the Salt Lake City facility was substantially expanded in late 1988, and the Brea, California, center was expanded and mechanized in 1989.

The expansion of Albertson's distribution network, combined with new computerized inventory and checkout scanners, enabled the chain to begin to handle its own distribution in 1990. By 1993, almost two-thirds of the items purchased by Albertson's stores were distributed by its own system.

In December of 1991 Albertson's announced a five-year expansion plan that called for $2.4 billion investments in: the construction of 250 new stores, the renovation of 175 older stores, and the acceleration of computerization chain-wide. By the end of fiscal year 1991 (January 1992), more than half of Albertson's stores had computerized time and attendance systems, all of the pharmacies had automated prescription systems, and 96 percent of the stores were equipped with checkout scanners.

The company's plans are ambitious, especially considering that it took Albertson's all of the 1980s to build or acquire 283 stores. But Albertson's is well-positioned for growth. In an industry that has been shaken by huge mergers and leveraged buyouts, Albertson's is conservatively financed, with long-term debt at about ten percent of total assets. In southern California, Albertson's competition consists of three chains hamstrung by debt: American Stores, Von's, and Ralph's. The company acquired 74 Jewel Osco food and drug stores in Texas, Oklahoma, Arkansas, and Florida from American Stores in 1992.

Albertson's is targeting its growth for California, Texas, Florida, and Arizona, some of the United States' fastest-growing markets. Chief Executive Officer Warren McCain targeted growth for smaller cities and suburbs where plentiful, inexpensive land allows Albertson's to maximize profits.

Gary Michael became chairman of the board and chief executive officer of Albertson's on February 1, 1991, and initiated the "Service First" employee award program. The plan recognizes and rewards excellence in customer service. Michael also implemented a quarterly video news program that promotes employee understanding of Albertson's goals and objectives. The employee relations efforts resulted in a 16 percent decrease in the worker turnover rate.

Public relations in the 1990s has focused on "Service First" and a new advertising theme, "It's Your Store." The slogan hopes to instill customers with a sense of partnership through convenience, quality, competitive pricing, and service. The HOPE (Helping Our Planet's Ecology) line of environmentally safer paper products reinforces Albertson's commitment to the ecosystem.

By January of 1992, Albertson's ran 562 grocery stores in 17 Western and Southern states, employing 60,000 workers. The company's 1991 sales and earnings hit record highs for the 22nd year: net income rose 10.3 percent to $258 million and sales grew 5.6 percent to $8.68 billion. Even though same-store sales growth dropped from 5.5 percent in 1990 to 1.1 percent in 1991, industry analysts forecast continuing growth in sales and profits through the mid-1990s for the United States' sixth-largest retail food-drug chain. Distribution facilities are also headed for major expansion, as Albertson's seeks to supply all its markets except North Dakota and Florida by 1993.

The key to Albertson's success has been a steady sensitivity to the changing desires of consumers. It continues to groom its top executives the old-fashioned way, promoting from within the corporation. Most of the current top officers began in typical entry-level positions and have seen their careers grow with the company. Years of familiarity with Albertson's strengths and style allow top executives to adapt the company to changing consumer desires effectively. And while this modern business sensibility has cultivated Albertson's billion-dollar success, the solid, small-town philosophy of founder Joe Albertson—giving customers quality merchandise at a reasonable price—is at its root.

Further Reading: Beauchamp, Marc, ''Food for Thought,'' *Forbes,* April 17, 1989, p. 73; Hughes, Terri, editor, ''Yesterday and Tomorrow 1939–1989,'' *Albertson's Today,* July, 1989; Alster, Norm, ''One Man's Poison . . .'' *Forbes,* October 16, 1989, pp. 38–39; Johnston, Melanie, ''Supermarkets Feed Phoenix Glut,'' *Advertising Age,* November 13, 1989, p. 66; Baldo, Anthony, ''Fleming: Food Fight,'' *Financial World,* January 8, 1991, pp. 40–41; ''Albertson's Massive Deployment,'' *Discount Merchandiser,* March, 1991, pp. 26–27; Byrne, Harlan S., ''Albertson's: Food and Drug Retailer Boasts Top Earnings Growth, High Rate of Return,'' *Barron's,* April 13, 1992, pp. 55–56.

—updated by April Dougal

AMERICAN GREETINGS CORPORATION

10500 American Road
Cleveland, Ohio 44144
U.S.A.
(216) 252-7300
Fax: (216) 252-6777

Public Company
Incorporated: 1944 as American Greetings
Employees: 21,400
Sales: $1.57 billion
Stock Exchanges: NASDAQ
SICs: 2771 Greeting Cards; 2671 Paper Coated &
    Laminated—Packaging; 2656 Sanitary Food Containers;
    3999 Manufacturing Industries Nec

American Greetings Corporation, which advertises itself as "the world's largest publicly owned manufacturer of greeting cards and related personal communications products," is second only to Hallmark (a privately held corporation) in what has become an increasingly crowded, competitive, and tight-margin industry. Since its founding in 1906 as a small Cleveland jobber's shop, American Greetings has enjoyed 86 consecutive years of increased revenue. Within recent decades growth has been driven especially by the company's creation, marketing, and licensing of such characters as Ziggy, the Care Bears, Holly Hobbie, and Strawberry Shortcake, as well as by a pronounced emphasis on "anytime" cards, a fast-growing niche area of the historically holiday- and occasional-oriented market. One strategy by which American plans to expand this niche area as well as appeal to a new card-buying public is through its CreataCard vending machines, which allow shoppers to personally design and print their own cards, via touchscreen, both quickly and economically. The company operates 31 plants in the United States, Canada, the United Kingdom, and Mexico, and distributes its products through a network of 97,000 retail outlets in over 50 countries.

The birth of American Greetings roughly coincides with the birth of the U.S. greeting card industry, which was marked by the advent of occasional cards to complement the seasonal Christmas card trade. A Polish emigré named Jacob Sapirstein entered the fledgling industry in 1906 as an independent salesman. Sapirstein (known as "J. S.") had had some experience

working with relatives in a hotel card shop. When the shop closed he established his own business, which consisted of buying picture postcards and reselling them to such local outlets as novelty shops, candy stores, and drug stores. Conducting his wholesaling enterprise from a horse-drawn wagon, J. S. enjoyed modest success and by 1918 welcomed his eldest son, nine-year-old Irving, as the first partner. In 1926 the Sapirstein Greeting Card Company solidified itself as a family business with the additional employment of Irving's brother Morris. Two years later, through the sales efforts of Morris and Irving, the company received its largest order since inception, a postcard contract worth $24,000. During 1929, a year after the Hall Brothers Company (Hallmark) had begun to advertise nationally, the Sapirsteins greatly furthered their eventual position as a mainstay of the market by becoming the first distributor to utilize display cabinets for its greeting cards. Three years later, the company began phasing out its dependency on suppliers, whose products were often inferior, by manufacturing its own line of greeting cards. Although Hallmark would retain until the 1980s a formidable industry lead due to its well-established name and high-quality image, the Sapirstein business was at least preparing itself to compete with the market leader.

The Great Depression had minimal negative impact on the company, as evinced by a continuing string of "firsts" during the 1930s. These included the hiring of the first sales representative in 1934; youngest son Harry's first year with the company in 1935; the opening of the first branch office and the first major manufacturing facility in 1936; and the introduction of the first line of Forget Me Not cards in 1939. With the advent of the next decade the company, which had now renamed itself American Greetings Publishers, catapulted to national prominence with annual sales exceeding $1 million. In 1944 the family-owned and family-run business incorporated under its present name and in 1952, due to rapid population growth and subsequent plans for both acquisitions and expansion, the company went public.

A new era dawned in 1960 when J. S. became chairman of the board and Irving (who, like his brothers, had changed his last name to Stone) became president. This same year the company launched a cabinet manufacturing plant in Forest City, North Carolina, the first of many large capital expenditures necessary to keep pace with growth and fortify the company's large position in the industry. In 1967 the company introduced the Holly Hobbie character to wide public approval; this important creative move, which had huge potential for licensing spinoffs, eventually led to the formation of Those Characters From Cleveland, a subsidiary operation active since 1980 that has become a valuable contributor to the company's financial health. The year following Holly Hobbie's debut, overall sales surpassed $100 million.

The 1970s were marked by a number of major events. The decade opened with the introduction of Soft Touch cards, so labeled for their combination of soft focus photography and touching sentiment. This new line became the most successful of any introduced in American Greetings' history. In 1972 the world was introduced to Ziggy, "the world's most lovable loser." Even more so than Holly Hobbie (who by 1977 was the most popular female licensed character in the world), Ziggy became a perennial money-maker for the company, due especially to the royalty profits and publicity generated by his syndicated newspaper cartoon series, the creative rights for which were sold to Universal Press. In 1978 Irving Stone became chairman and CEO and Morry Weiss, Irving's son-in-law, was named president. During this changeover year, two new subsidiaries were established: Plus Mark, Inc., a manufacturer of Christmas gift wrap, boxed cards, and accessories, and A.G. Industries, Inc., the largest display fixture company in the country. By this time American Greetings possessed a view of itself as a leading mass-marketer to pharmacies, variety stores, discount stores, and supermarkets of lower-cost cards. Hallmark, which had ignored such venues until 1959, was now beginning to represent a serious threat to American's market share through its Ambassador card line. The most comforting news for American was that it, indisputably, dominated in terms of licensing revenue; the company reinforced this fact in 1980 with the unveiling of Strawberry Shortcake, whose array of products grossed $100 million in the first marketing year alone.

American celebrated its 75th anniversary in 1981 by recreating its 21-year-old emblem of the rose. This symbolic affirmation of quality and beauty dovetailed nicely with other key components of the new corporate identity program, including American's first foray into national television advertising as the Fresh Idea Company. Investors sensed a new surge in growth as they nearly doubled the stock price of American shares from October 1981 to May 1982. It was around this time that Weiss fueled investor fever by proclaiming, "We want to be the dominant force in the industry." *Forbes* writer Jeff Blyskal noted that the company was "actively upgrading its products and prices" and opined: "American Greetings is making a bold move. Weiss is pouring his licensing profits into an aggressive and well-timed campaign to challenge Hallmark." From 1981 to 1985 American grew from a half-billion to a billion-dollar company and thus attained one of the key corporate objectives it had set for itself. However, more important than this increase in total revenue was American's astonishing net income increase of 613 percent in a ten-year period. What the company had failed to do, unfortunately, was enhance its market share with respect to Hallmark.

Gibson Greetings, the No. 3 card-seller, shook the industry in 1986 with a vicious price war, which it commenced in an effort to increase its own 10-percent share. The price war ended the following year, but all three companies suffered profit losses from it, with virtually no change in their respective market positions (Hallmark still led with 45 percent and American followed with 35 percent; the bottom tier was still comprised of Gibson and several hundred much smaller manufacturers). American's recovery from this siege, as well as from downswings in non-card sales, was difficult. A 1988 *Forbes* article labeled the company "Flounder," finding support for its dismal forecast in new earnings estimates ($1.05 per share versus $2.35 in 1985) and a 60 percent drop in stock price from its mid-1986 high of 42. However, after hitting bottom this year with a devastating drop in profits from $63 million to $33 million, American rebounded in 1989 to $44 million.

Since then, American has more than doubled its net income and once again become a feisty contender for the No. 1 position. Although Hallmark's revenues are roughly double those of American, American showed 10 percent growth in sales for cards and related goods in 1991 while Hallmark reported only 1 percent. At least some of this renewed vigor is due to the appointment of long-time employee Ed Fruchtenbaum as the fourth and first non-family president and the elevation of Weiss to CEO status. Under Weiss, American cut costs, streamlined its operations, and improved its idea-to-market development time (Desert Storm cards were shipped to retailers within a mere three-week period from initiation). With Fruchtenbaum, American is expected to further hone its day-to-day operations by placing special emphasis on its information systems (IS) technology. Through its IS department, the company creates software to aid management, the sales force, and their retail customers in tracking inventories and reacting to buying trends. With the ability to supply sales managers and retailers with block-by-block demographic data, IS will be an indispensable component of Fruchtenbaum's future plans, for pinpoint marketing represents the cutting edge of the industry. As Laurel Touby has observed, "To keep his sales growing, Fruchtenbaum is [already] targeting narrow consumer segments, such as college students, while continuing to beef up service to retailers." Touby also speculates that "the company, whose assets include a picture-frame maker, a hair-accessory manufacturer, and a licensing arm, may also make more acquisitions in and out of cards."

The most important and promising acquisition by American during 1992 was the purchase of Custom Expressions, Inc., maker of the CreataCard units. Although Hallmark, which owns Touch Screen Greetings and the Personalize It! method, has filed suit against American for patent infringement, American is confident that its video touchscreen system is not only unique but also superior. According to its own promotional copy, Creatacard is the only system that offers the customer complete control over the selection, design, and printing of individualized cards. The current format being test-marketed around the country features approximately 1,000 card options and is capable of producing cards for consumers, priced at $3.50 each, in less than 4 minutes. The company optimistically estimates that annual sales from CreataCard will approach $500 million within its first ten years of business.

American, as might be expected, will continue to fight for its market share not only through CreataCard but also through its Anytime Card lines, which include Kid Zone, 78TH STREET, and the Forget Me Not line. Guiding the company's strategy will be an ongoing analysis of population figures, which according to its own appraisal will tend to favor new surges in growth. The Annual Report for 1992 asserts that, "throughout the '90s and into the year 2000, the Baby Boom generation will be irreversibly advancing into the age group categories that buy the greatest number of greeting cards per capita." Furthermore, "this developing surge in demand is headed directly towards value priced retailers. That's our primary market. And we are determined to ensure that we, and the retail accounts we serve, realize the optimum benefits." Ironically, Gibson, the very company that helped precipitate American's fall during the 1980s, may pounce again during the 1990s and possibly leave Weiss and Fruchtenbaum with only a modest and short-lived celebration of their swift corporate turnaround. Termed a "rapid climber" by Susan Caminiti, Gibson posted sales growth at twice the rate of American from 1987 to 1991. Although American reported impressive increases in total revenue and net income for the first half of 1992—an indication that neither Hallmark nor Gibson can dictate its financial performance—the company's future is no less secure than it was a decade ago. To remain the Fresh Idea Company, let alone the clear successor to the card industry throne, American needs to repeatedly create "the future of greeting cards," in advance of the competition, as it has claimed to have done with CreataCard.

Principal Subsidiaries: Acme Frame Products, Inc.; A.G. Industries, Inc.; Carlton Cards, France; Carlton Cards, Ltd. (Canada); Carlton Cards, Ltd. (UK); Felicitaciones Nacionales S. A. de C.V.; Plus Mark; Rust Craft Canada; The Summit Corporation; Summit-Canada; Those Characters From Cleveland; Wilhold.

Further Reading: Blyskal, Jeff, "Greetings from the Competition," *Forbes*, March 29, 1982, pp. 36–7; Chiu, Tony, and Joyce Wansley, "Who's Red and Sweet and Filthy Rich? Strawberry Shortcake, Toyland's Newest Tyke-Coon," *People Weekly*, May 10, 1982, pp. 91–3; Sanger, Elizabeth, "Salutes for American Greetings," *Barron's*, October 27, 1986, p. 83; "Jacob Sapirstein, 102; Founded Card Concern," *New York Times Biographical Service*, Vol. 18, p. 624; Jaffe, Thomas, "Flounder," *Forbes*, April 25, 1988, p. 352; Rifkin, Glenn, "A Sentimental Journey to Success," *Computerworld*, August 28, 1989, pp. 55, 59; Schwartz, Ela, "The Next Cycle in Greeting Cards," *Discount Merchandiser*, July 1990, pp. 68–69; Oliver, Suzanne, "Christmas Card Blues," *Forbes*, December 24, 1990, p. 100; Caminiti, Susan, "The Fortune 500: America's Fastest-Growing Companies," *Fortune*, April 22, 1991, pp. 67–76; McCune, Jenny C., "Street Smart Selling," *Success*, May 1991, p. 22; "Chronological History: American Greetings," November 1991; Laurel, Touby, "Congratulations on Your Big Earnings Increase!" *Business Week*, August 17, 1992, p. 58; Maturi, Richard J., "High Tech Makes for High Touch: Managerial Know-how Keeps American Greetings Close to Customers," *Industry Week*, August 17, 1992, pp. 50–1; "American Greetings Launches Custom Card System," *Greetings Magazine*, September 1992, p. 14; "Hallmark, American at Odds Over Custom Card Patents," *Greetings Magazine*, November 1992, p. 13.

—Jay P. Pederson

AMERICA'S FAVORITE CHICKEN COMPANY, INC.

Two Concourse Parkway
Suite 600
Atlanta, Georgia 30328
U.S.A.
(404) 901-6200
Fax: (404) 901-6202

Private Company
Incorporated: 1972 as Popeyes Famous Fried Chicken and
    Biscuits, Inc.
Employees: 13,057
Sales: $415 million
SICs: 5812 Eating Places; 6794 Patent Owners & Lessors

America's Favorite Chicken Company, Inc. (AFC), is the parent company to two fast-food chicken restaurant chains, Popeyes Famous Fried Chicken and Biscuits, Inc. and Church's Fried Chicken, Inc. AFC as a whole ranks second in size among fast-food chicken operations, trailing Pepsico's Kentucky Fried Chicken (KFC) chain by a large margin. The Popeyes chain, specializing in a Cajun-style fried chicken that is spicier than most conventional recipes, consists of 917 units, 694 of which are franchised. Popeyes restaurants are located in 38 states, and include 30 units around the world, with locations in Germany, France, Japan, Dubai, Guam, Korea, Saudi Arabia, Honduras, and the Philippines. Total sales for the Popeyes system were $550 million in 1991. Church's, which features a Southern-style menu, numbers 1,087 units, 621 of which are company-owned. Church's has domestic sites in 30 states, as well as 127 international restaurants in Canada, Mexico, Puerto Rico, Taiwan, Malaysia, and Singapore. The Church's system recorded sales of over $513 million in 1991.

AFC is held in majority by Canadian Imperial Bank of Commerce (CIBC), which owns 82 percent of the company's common stock and 89.3 percent of its preferred stock. CIBC obtained control of AFC as a result of two years of bankruptcy proceedings in Austin, Texas. Acting as an agent for a syndicate of lending institutions, CIBC submitted a plan that was ultimately accepted by the Federal Bankruptcy Court for the reorganization of Al Copeland Enterprises, Inc., previous owner of Popeyes and Church's. Under the plan, Copeland Enterprises lost ownership of the two chicken chains and was replaced as

parent company by the newly created AFC in October 1992. AFC also assumed control of Copeland Enterprises subsidiary Far West Products, a manufacturer of food service equipment such as refrigerators, freezers, and fryers.

The first Popeyes was opened by company founder, Al Copeland, in June 1972. Copeland's success with Popeyes is a classic rags-to-riches tale. A native of New Orleans, Copeland dropped out of tenth grade at age 16 to help support his ailing mother and, after working for some time as a soda jerk, was hired by his older brother who ran a chain of donut shops. At 18, Copeland sold his car for capital to open his own one-man donut operation, thereby becoming his brother's first franchisee. He quickly turned the shop into the chain's biggest money-maker, and went on to spend ten modestly successful years in the donut business. The opening of a Kentucky Fried Chicken store in New Orleans in 1966, however, caught Copeland's eye when he saw that KFC—with a shorter workday—was making about four times as much money per week as his donut shop. Inspired by KFC's success, Copeland used his donut profits to open a restaurant in 1971 named Chicken on the Run.

After six months of operation, Chicken on the Run was grossing only $1,100 a week—$900 short of the break-even point—which prompted Copeland to close the store and begin planning for another donut shop. In a last-ditch effort at success in the chicken business, however, he chose a spicier Louisiana Cajun-style recipe and reopened the restaurant under the name Popeyes Mighty Good Fried Chicken, after Popeye Doyle, Gene Hackman's character in the film *The French Connection.* In its third week of operation, Copeland's revived chicken restaurant brought in $2,100 of receipts, breaking the profit barrier for the first time.

Copeland opened his second Popeyes in New Orleans about a year later, by which time the original location was selling over $5,000 worth of chicken a week. By the end of 1974, there were fifteen Popeyes in operation, and within only two years of the second Popeyes the number had grown to 24. Unable to find a bank willing to finance the chain's early expansion, Copeland relied upon the company's own cash flow. In 1975, what would become the company's most popular advertising campaign was launched, featuring the "Love That Chicken" jingle performed by local musician Dr. John. The jingle became wildly popular in New Orleans, so much so that it was once spontaneously sung in unison by the Superdome crowd at a New Orleans Saints football game.

Copeland began franchising Popeyes in 1977 and brought in his brother Bill to handle the expansion program. At the time, there were already about 50 company-owned stores in the chain. Although the Popeyes system increased its sales in 1977 to $21.5 million—about $5 million more than the previous year—the company recorded a $391,381 net loss. In 1978, the company nearly folded when the chain's rapid expansion led to overextended credit. Rather than scale back the pace of growth, however, Copeland continued his aggressive marketing tactics and proceeded with developing a strong territorial franchising system. By mid-1978, Popeyes restaurants were located in 28 cities, for a total of 125 units ranging geographically from El Paso to Miami to Detroit. That same year, company-owned stores averaged over $12,000 in sales per week, while franchised units brought in roughly $9,000. Popeyes advertising continued to emphasize the company's New Orleans roots, featuring local landmarks and the jazz music of Louisiana-based artists. Popeyes menu included, along with its trademark spicy chicken, homemade onion rings, corn on the cob, deep-fried clams, and Louisiana Dirty Rice dressing.

By the early 1980s, Popeyes was the third largest fast-food chicken chain, behind KFC and Church's. Under Popeyes corporate structure, company-owned stores—which numbered 76 in November 1982—were held by Al Copeland Enterprises, Inc., while the 239 outside-owned franchises were overseen by a subsidiary of Al Copeland Enterprises named Popeyes Famous Fried Chicken and Biscuits. In the Popeyes system, stores were franchised five at a time; buyers paid $25,000 for the first unit, and $10,000 each for options on the other four. Franchisees typically operated 15 to 20 restaurants in an area for which they were licensed. By late 1982, Popeyes restaurants were located in five countries, with a roughly half-and-half mix between urban and suburban sites. Copeland Enterprises's sales for 1982 were about $185 million, about $20 million higher than in 1981. New menu items included chicken tacos, barbecued beans, red beans and rice, and, most importantly, a new biscuit. The biscuit alone was responsible for an over 20 percent unit-sales increase. To ensure consistent product quality, all mid-level managers were required to participate in a two- to three-day training course in biscuit preparation at company headquarters.

In 1983, Popeyes began test-marketing breakfast items, including grits, eggs, and fried potatoes, and sandwiches made with Popeyes popular biscuit. Beer and wine were also tested in some stores. In 1984, Copeland Enterprises launched a chain of more upscale full-service Cajun-American restaurants, appropriately named Copeland's. Debuting in New Orleans, Copeland's featured a 100-item menu overseen personally by its owner. The same year, the Popeyes chain consisted of about 400 outlets in 35 states and 5 foreign countries, generating sales of $250 million and earnings of $6 million. Sales slumped somewhat, however, partly as a result of McDonald's newly introduced Chicken McNuggets, which brought in about $1 billion. Popeyes was slow to counter with its own version, due to Al Copeland's dissatisfaction with the quality control of his company's entry into that market.

By the mid-1980s, with a personal fortune of close to $100 million, Copeland had become a noted celebrity around New Orleans. His hobbies included racing 50-foot powerboats, touring New Orleans in Rolls-Royces and Lamborghinis, and decorating his Lake Pontchartrain with lavish Christmas decorations, including half a million lights and a three-story-tall snowman. Copeland's wealth was derived primarily from his 100 percent ownership of Copeland Enterprises and his 95 percent interest in the Popeyes franchising arm. By 1985, Copeland Enterprises operated about 100 company-owned Popeyes outlets, approximately half of them in the New Orleans area. The chain's total of over 500 stores included locations in Puerto Rico, Panama, and Kuwait. Popeyes most visible advertising campaign in 1985, produced by its new agency, Doyle Dane Bernbach of New York, depicted eating spicy Cajun-style chicken as a "hair-raising experience." Customers eating the chicken were shown with their hair literally standing on end

after tasting the product. The spots continued to use the ten-year-old "Love That Chicken" slogan. In 1985, the Popeyes system spent 3 percent of gross sales for advertising expenditures, a relatively low figure for the industry. The following year, Popeyes separated from its agency and began producing its commercials in-house.

In 1986, sales for the entire Popeyes system reached $420 million. That same year, Popeyes began to test-market Cajun popcorn shrimp in nearly 100 Chicago and New Orleans stores, as well as home delivery in New Orleans and Houston. In New Orleans, where 4 of 50 company units were involved in the experimental home delivery program, a central computer relayed orders to the appropriate Popeyes outlet. The program was discontinued in 1987, however, as its high costs resulted in a $4.7 million loss for Copeland Enterprises—leaving the company in the red for the year. Also in 1987, Popeyes introduced 39-cent miniature chicken sandwiches called Little Chickadees, consisting of a Cajun-spiced one-ounce square chicken patty, pickles, and a mayonnaise-based sauce all on a toasted bun. The sandwiches were a response to plans by KFC to launch a similar product. Popeyes advertising budget for 1987—between $12 million to $17 million—was largely spent on a new campaign showing Popeyes as the clear winner in side-by-side taste tests with KFC and Church's.

Popeyes grew to 700 units by 1988. For the first time, Copeland realized that Copeland Enterprises had outgrown its management structure, and that he needed to delegate some of his responsibilities. As a result, he created the positions of president, chief financial officer, and executive vice-president of operations. Copeland then recruited a pair of executives from Church's in a move that brought about accusations of company secrets being given away by defectors. Later in the year, Copeland made a play for control of Church's with an unsolicited $296 million bid. The day after Copeland's $8-a-share offer, active trading elevated Church's stock to an $8.25 price. The move came on the heels of a 1987 takeover attempt by Church's former president, Richard Sherman, whose $12.25-a-share buyout offer was declined by company management.

In February 1989, Church's agreed to be acquired by Al Copeland Enterprises, Inc., for $392 million. Under the terms of the agreement, $11 per share was paid for the first 86.5 percent of Church's stock, and the remaining shares were swapped for .44 shares of newly created preferred stock in the merged company. The new company, named Al Copeland Enterprises, Inc., controlled about 17 percent of the $10 billion fried chicken market, but together the two chains were still only about one-third the size of KFC. Within a couple months of the takeover, Copeland fired 12 percent of Church's staff, including Ernest Renaud, the company's president and chief executive. Copeland himself replaced Renaud as CEO and also became chairman of Church's board, while James Flynn, president of Copeland Enterprises, became Church's president.

The acquisition of Church's soon proved to be lethal to Copeland Enterprises. To finance the acquisition, Copeland Enterprises borrowed about $450 million from a group of lending institutions led by the Canadian Imperial Bank of Commerce and Merrill Lynch and Company. This move, however, created interest costs of at least $100,000 a day and could not be covered by Church's revenues, which had been declining since 1985 to the point of a $14.5 million loss in 1988. Since a far higher percentage of Church's outlets were company-owned than Popeyes, Copeland Enterprises began selling Church's franchises to their managers in an effort to raise money. The drive brought in only $21 million, however, and in 1989 Copeland Enterprises reported a net loss of $35.9 million on revenue of $415 million—a loss largely due to interest payments of $55.6 million to CIBC and Merrill Lynch.

In November 1990, Copeland Enterprises announced itself in default on $391 million in debts and that it was in danger of bankruptcy if payment was demanded by one of its lenders. The company, operating at a net loss of over $11 million for the first three quarters of the year, failed to make payments due in September of $3.3 million in bridge-loan interest and $4.2 million on principal. By that time, Popeyes had overtaken the struggling Church's chain for the number-two spot in market share, garnering 11.4 percent on sales of $547 million at 783 stores, to Church's 10.7 percent on sales of $514 million at 1,163 outlets.

Copeland Enterprises filed for bankruptcy law protection in April 1991 when attempts to restructure its debts failed. During the summer, a settlement plan appeared imminent which would result in Merrill Lynch owning about 85 percent of the company. The tentative agreement also called for Al Copeland to relinquish ownership of the company and his secret recipe, and to receive $31 million in cash, five Popeyes stores, and a company jet. In return, Copeland would have a $3 million personal debt to the company forgiven and would retain a contract to supply the chain with spices. When Merrill Lynch began to withdraw its support for this plan, however, the court invited CIBC, Copeland Enterprises, and Copeland himself to submit individual reorganization plans. The plan submitted by CIBC called for full ownership of the company to be given to CIBC, for Merrill Lynch to come up empty-handed, and for Copeland to continue receiving royalties for his ownership of the Popeyes recipe. Under the plan entered by Copeland, Copeland would retain ownership of the company while creditors would receive reduced debt payments after the company emerged from bankruptcy.

In October 1992, Judge Frank Monroe chose the CIBC reorganization plan, and shortly thereafter America's Favorite Chicken Company, Inc., was created as the new parent company to Popeyes and Church's. Named AFC chairman and chief executive was Frank J. Belatti, former president of Arby's Inc.,

the fast-food roast-beef sandwich chain. AFC established headquarters in Atlanta, and in November 1990 announced a 100-day action plan for Popeyes and Church's. The plan, set to go into action in 1993, included programs to enhance the system's image, to improve employee and franchise relations, and to upgrade operational efficiency and quality. Today, as the second-largest fast-food chicken corporation, AFC appears to have a secure niche in the industry. Whether the company's new management is able to return AFC to a position of profitability and more reasonable growth, however, as well as to chip away at KFC's market dominance, remains to be seen.

Principal Subsidiaries: Popeyes Famous Fried Chicken and Biscuits, Inc.; Church's Fried Chicken, Inc.

Further Reading: Marshall, Christy, "Popeyes Fights Off KFC with Fast, Spicy Chicken," *Advertising Age,* July 10, 1978; Liesse, Julie, "Popeyes Muscles In," *Restaurants and Institutions,* January 1, 1983; Fadiman, Mark T., "The Popeye Challenge," *Forbes,* February 13, 1984; Schoifet, Mark, "Copeland Beefs Up Popeyes," *Nation's Restaurant News,* July 8, 1985; Donovan, Sharon, "Popeyes Strums Cajun Theme in Chicken," *Advertising Age,* July 15, 1985; Schoifet, Mark, "Popeyes Tests Delivery at 17 Southern Outlets," *Nation's Restaurant News,* May 26, 1986; Romeo, Peter, "Popeyes Abandons Home-Delivery Test," *Nation's Restaurant News,* March 30, 1987; Alva, Marylin, "Popeyes Rolls Little Chickadees as KFC Readies Sandwich Blitz," *Nation's Restaurant News,* June 22, 1987; Alva, Marylin, "Popeyes Pops Hard-Sell Ads," *Nation's Restaurant News,* July 20, 1987; Bruno, Karen, "Copeland Makes Church's Bid," *Nation's Restaurant News,* November 7, 1988; Blumenthal, Karen, "Church's Agrees to Be Acquired By Copeland Unit," *Wall Street Journal,* February 16, 1989; Andrews, Nina, "Fried-Chicken Merger Creates No. 2 Concern," *New York Times,* February 17, 1989; Charlier, Marj, "Spicy Cajun," *Wall Street Journal,* March 22, 1989; Romeo, Peter, "Copeland Ousts Renaud, Lays Off 12% at Church's," *Nation's Restaurant News,* April 10, 1989; Barrier, Michael, "Chicken That Packs a Punch," *Nation's Business,* July 1989; Blumenthal, Karen, "Copeland Says It's in Default on $391 Million," *Wall Street Journal,* November 7, 1990; Fisher, Christy, "Popeyes Touts New Orleans," *Advertising Age,* March 4, 1991; Ortega, Bob, "Copeland Emerges from Bankruptcy Minus Its Founder," *Wall Street Journal,* October 21, 1992.

—Robert R. Jacobson

AMSTED INDUSTRIES INCORPORATED

Boulevard Towers South
44th Floor
205 North Michigan Avenue
Chicago, Illinois 60601
U.S.A.
(312) 645-1700
Fax: (312) 819-8425

Private Company
Incorporated: 1902 as American Steel Foundries
Employees: 7,900
Sales: $827.1 million
SICs: 3321 Gray & Ductile Iron Foundries

Amsted Industries Incorporated is comprised of seven companies divided into railroad, construction and building, and general industrial divisions. The company maintains 35 plants—including three in Canada and five overseas—and is principally engaged in the manufacture of cast steel freight components, road wheels, ductile iron pipe, automotive parts, cooling towers, roller chain, and wire rope.

Amsted Industries was created as the American Steel Foundries (ASF) on June 26, 1902, upon the merger of several steel companies operating eight plants between New Jersey and Illinois. Unable to compete as effectively as independent concerns, these companies were organized along the lines of United States Steel, which was formed only a few years earlier.

ASF, in fact, was established by many of the same men who helped to put together U.S. Steel. Among them were Judge Elbert H. Gary, who chaired U.S. Steel's executive committee, Edward Shearson, comptroller of U.S. Steel and later founder of the Shearson-Hammill brokerage house, and Charles M. Schwab, who later established Bethlehem Steel. Also involved in the partnership were Dan Eagan, president of the American Steel Casting Company, W. D. Sargent, head of the Sargent Steel Company, and Edward F. Goltra and George B. Leighton, who controlled steel interests in St. Louis, Missouri.

Headquartered in New York City, American Steel Foundries expanded its capitalization from $9 million to $40 million during its first year through the issue of new shares. The company's first products ranged from 16-ounce cams to 38-ton

ocean liner shaft bearings. ASF was not a steel producer, but rather a finisher of steel products. Steel entered the company's factories as raw ingots but left as finished products, which eventually included locomotive and boxcar frames, couplers, and axle assemblies.

Having outgrown the small Sargent plant at Englewood, near Chicago, ASF built a huge new casting facility at Indiana Harbor. Early workers commuted to the Greenfield site by train and often had to dump sand out of their shoes after a shift.

ASF issued annual reports its first two years but skipped the third year because of mounting reverses. In fact, the company came perilously close to failure, prompting Schwab to leave the concern to establish Bethlehem Steel.

With a fair volume of business, ASF took the unusual step of acquiring another company, not for its business, but to raid its management for more capable leaders. This enterprise, the Simplex Railway Appliance Company of Hammond, Indiana, also manufactured parts for railroad freight cars. In the fall of 1905 Simplex agreed to a merger, and its president, William V. Kelley, assumed responsibility for the entire operation, moving the company from New York to Chicago, center of the nation's railroad commerce.

Kelley took control at a most opportune time. He helped restore profitability in 1906 and 1907, before United States industry was racked by a financial crisis that dried up factory orders. Had the company still been financially weak, ASF would surely have gone broke. Kelley was later succeeded in 1912 by Robert P. Lamont, after the company had begun a special effort to help design and test railroad couplers. Previously, foundries such as ASF were asked simply to manufacture to a customer's specifications. But by helping clients to improve their designs, the company developed a superior product.

In 1910 ASF established a full-fledged product engineering facility in Granite City, Illinois, where testing was expanded to other car parts, including springs.

During World War I, ASF was pressed into service manufacturing shell casings. By the end of the war, the company had produced more than a million of these casings.

In 1919, with advent of the automobile, ASF began manufacturing smaller springs for automobiles. This business dried up quickly, however, after auto manufacturers established their own parts operations. That year, Lamont moved on an opportunity to purchase the Griffin Wheel Company, which was founded on October 5, 1877. A leader in hard chilled iron technology, Griffin operated nine plants across the United States and did a steady business with the railroads.

While tied to the uncertain fortunes of the maturing railroad industry, Lamont reasoned that, even with no orders for new railroad cars, the market for repair and replacement was sure to be ongoing—freight car wheels would need to be replaced continually. Indeed, in 1923 alone, the company turned out more than 1.5 million wheels.

American Steel Foundries purchased the Galesburg Malleable Castings Company in 1921 and the Damascus Brake Beam

Company in 1923 but later closed these operations when new brake shoe technologies made their products obsolete. In 1926 the company took over the Verona Steel Castings Company near Pittsburgh. In the first year of the Great Depression, however, the foundry was forced to close.

Lamont, meanwhile, left American Steel Foundries in 1929 to serve as commerce secretary in President Herbert Hoover's administration. He was succeeded by George E. Scott, a veteran of Simplex. Scott, noting that the company's Pittsburgh plant had outgrown its boxed-in facilities, decided to move its operations to the shuttered Verona facility in 1936. This was the first of several site consolidations that left the company with only four of its original eight foundries, plus the rest of those it had acquired.

In 1939, however, a remaining facility at Newark was converted into an alloy metals plant specializing in corrosion-resistant products. ASF's timing was highly advantageous as hostilities had erupted in Europe, causing the government to undertake a rearmament program. The plant was soon turning out parts for 50-caliber antiaircraft guns, bomb parts, valves, and fittings.

Also in 1939, Scott died suddenly and was replaced as president by Thomas Drever, a Scottish accountant and comptroller of American Steel Foundries. By 1940 ASF operated 21 plants and was recording sales of $26.3 million.

In 1942 Drever oversaw American Steel Foundries' construction of a war materiel plant in East Chicago that turned out, among other things, tank parts and vessels for the atomic bomb program. Also that year, ASF acquired the Charles F. Elmes Engineering Works, a company specializing in steel engineering.

By 1945 ASF had poured 200,000 tons of cast armor—26 percent of the country's total output during World War II. At the end of the war, however, the company was almost exclusively a producer of castings for railroad freight cars. Drever appointed R. D. Brizzolara to study opportunities for ASF to diversify.

The first step in the process of diversification came shortly before the end of the war, when the company began manufacturing semi trailer turrets. Then, in 1948, American Steel Foundries acquired the King Machine Tool Company in Cincinnati. A year later, the Elmes factory was consolidated with the King Company.

Drever retired in 1949 and was succeeded by another financial type, Charles C. Jarchow. Continuing the effort to diversify, ASF acquired the Diamond Chain Company of Indianapolis in December of 1950. Diamond, a manufacturer of bicycle and industrial roller chains since 1890, helped divert the company's focus on the railroad industry.

After briefly returning to the cast armor business during the Korean War, ASF secured new business supplying Canadian railroads. In January of 1955 ASF acquired the Pipe Line Service Company (later called Plexco), which applied anticorrosive coatings to petroleum transmission pipes.

As steam locomotives gave way to diesels, and as freight capacities increased, a demand arose for more durable railroad wheels. Griffin responded with a patented controlled pressure pouring method that was capable of producing superhardened wheels. Unable to keep up with demand for the wheels, Griffin constructed six wheel plants between 1952 and 1963.

In 1959 Joseph B. Lanterman became president and chief executive officer of ASF, and sales hit $94 million. Under Lanterman, ASF converted an idle factory in Council Bluffs, Iowa, into a water pipe manufacturing plant. Specially engineered water pipes were in significant demand in the 12 states of the Midwest, as the population increased and farming became more mechanized.

Feeling that the company was sufficiently diversified to warrant a new, less specific name, Lanterman hired New York marketing consultants Lippincott and Margulies to develop a name that abandoned the words "steel" and "foundries." Settling on AMS, for American Steel, and TED, for Transportation Equipment Division—the company's largest operation—they recommended Amsted. The change became official on January 23, 1962, but the name American Steel Foundries was retained for a division.

Later in 1962 Amsted purchased the R. D. Wood Company, a Florence, New Jersey-based cast iron pressure pipe manufacturer that was later folded into a new subsidiary, Griffin Pipe Products Company. Continuing to grow by acquisition, Amsted bought the Macwhyte Company in July of 1967 and ten months later, the Burgess-Norton Mfg. Co. Macwhyte made wire rope, a basic tool in numerous heavy industries, while Burgess-Norton produced piston pins and powdered metal parts. Amsted then acquired Standard Automotive Parts—later merged with Burgess-Norton—in 1969. A year later, the company purchased the Extron Corporation, a manufacturer of plastic pipe and fittings. Extron became part of the company's Plexco division. Griffin, meanwhile, took over the Glamorgan Pipe & Foundry Company in 1971.

In 1973 Amsted bought J&B Plastics, which was added to Plexco. Two years later, Amsted entered the filtration business by acquiring the Hydromation Company. Though suspending its acquisition binge in 1976 and 1977 to concentrate on internal expansion, Amsted made its biggest acquisition to date in 1978 when it bought the Henry Pratt Company for $58 million.

In 1980 Lanterman retired as chairman. He chose Goff Smith to succeed him and Robert H. Wellington as president. That year, Amsted's sales reached $915 million. By 1981, however, record railcar orders dropped by 40 percent. While buoyed somewhat by diversification, Amsted still reported a 29 percent drop in earnings. This performance was repeated in the recession year of 1982, when earnings dropped a further 65 percent, led by persistent weakness in the railcar sector. That year, Smith retired.

After a third bad year, things finally rebounded for Amsted in 1984. With sales up, Amsted purchased the Broderick and Bascom Rope Company, a wire rope manufacturer, and combined the company with its Macwhyte division. The following year, Amsted acquired the Baltimore Aircoil Company—a manufacturer of evaporative coding and heat transfer equipment—from Merck & Company for $91 million. Later in 1985, the company collected Nipak Pipe and merged it with Plexco.

In April of 1985 the United States Securities and Exchange Commission received a form 13D, disclosing that a corporate raider, Charles Hurwitz, held more than eight percent of Amsted's shares. Rather than be taken over and carved up for quick profits by a disinterested raider, the company decided—on the advice of Goldman Sachs—to arrange a leveraged buyout through an employee stock ownership plan. A number of shareholders objected to the scheme and the buyout price; some even sued. In the end, on March 5, 1986, Amsted was taken private by its own employees for a price of $529 million. Even with this distraction, Amsted finished 1985 and 1986 in the black.

Litho-Strip, a metal precoating operation, was sold off in February of 1987, because it was no longer considered a core business. A year later, the company got rid of its PACO pumps operation, and in 1989 sold both Plexco and Henry Pratt. The $183 million in proceeds was devoted to debt reduction resulting from the leveraged buyout.

Hurt slightly by a five-week strike at the American Steel Foundries division in 1990, Amsted suffered more significant reverses in 1991, reporting declining sales in all three of its operating divisions. There was, however, a small recovery in 1992, when Amsted acquired the Ceramic Cooling Tower Company, a manufacturer of low-maintenance cooling tower units, and folded it into Baltimore Aircoil.

Protected from possible future takeovers by virtue of its unique employee ownership plan, Amsted was free to concentrate in the early 1990s on its business. As the number of employees was declining—from nearly 9,000 in 1988 to slightly more than 7,000 in 1993—the company's cost structures had fallen in line. In addition, the sale of certain noncore assets helped to ensure that the company was sufficiently focused to compete in the markets it knows best.

Principal Subsidiaries: American Steel Foundries; Baltimore Aircoil Company; Burgess-Norton Mfg. Co.; Diamond Chain Company; Griffin Pipe Products Company; Griffin Wheel Company Griffin Canada, Inc.; Macwhyte Company; Amsted Industries International.

Further Reading: Reck, Franklin M., *Sand in Their Shoes,* American Steel Foundries Company, 1952; ''The History of Amsted: 1902 to the Present,'' Chicago, Amsted Industries Incorporated; ''How Amsted Got Its Name,'' *Chicago Daily News,* January 31, 1962; ''Did the Amsted LBO Shortchange Shareholders?'' *Barron's,* February 16, 1987; Amsted Industries Incorporated annual reports, 1988–92.

—John Simley

ARCH MINERAL CORPORATION

City Place 1
St. Louis, Missouri 63141
U.S.A.
(314) 994-2700
Fax: (314) 444-0159

Private Company
Incorporated: 1969
Employees: 3,206
Sales: $600 million
SICs: 1221 Bituminous Coal & Lignite—Surface; 1222
   Bituminous Coal—Underground

Arch Mineral Corporation is a private coal company owned in equal parts by Ashland Oil Company and the Hunt family. From its headquarters in the St. Louis, Missouri, suburb of Creve Coeur, it oversees a nearly completely decentralized system of mines in Wyoming, Illinois, Alabama, Virginia, West Virginia, and Kentucky.

Arch was founded in 1969 by Merl Kelce, with backing from Ashland Oil. In 1955 Kelce and his brothers had merged their family-owned Sinclair Coal Company into the larger Peabody Coal Company. They gained operating control of Peabody and in succeeding years built it into the industry's leader. Eventually becoming tired of running a huge organization, the brothers decided in the mid-1960s to sell out.

Merl Kelce tried to sell the company to Ashland Oil but then, in 1968, came to terms with Kennecott Copper. The Kelce family received $58 million of the $585 million purchase price, and Merl Kelce himself received approximately $33 million.

Following his involvement with Peabody, Merl Kelce remained interested in coal. Early in 1969 he and longtime associate William "Guy" Heckman formed Sinclair Associates to make selected coal investments. They set up offices in St. Louis and brought in Hubert Hagen, another former employee, to seek possible acquisitions in the West.

Around the same time, Ashland Oil's chief executive officer, Orin Atkins, and his special assistant, Buck Weaver, visited Kelce and asked him to help Ashland evaluate a possible acquisition, Ayshire Collieries. Kelce was not interested in that type of business but told Atkins and Weaver about his ambition to build a new coal company. The three men discussed a possible partnership and after negotiations, agreed to form a new company with a capital layout of $10 million. Ashland and Kelce each would receive 50 percent of the stock, though Ashland would put up $7.5 million, or 75 percent of the money.

Even before Arch Mineral was officially incorporated on June 20, 1969, Kelce began looking in the West for low-sulfur coal. He believed that low-sulfur western coal—previously untouched because of transportation costs—would become profitable as environmental concerns were felt in the marketplace. With this in view, he decided to try to obtain western coal rights held by the Union Pacific Railroad.

Kelce had several projects in mind, but Arch's $10 million in capital was not nearly enough to finance them. Arch had no assets, and banks were reluctant to loan Kelce money. He eventually obtained a form of collateral through the Tennessee Valley Authority (TVA), which like other power producers, was worried about the availability of coal in coming years. Agreeing to buy coal from Arch, TVA head Jim Watson produced a letter of intent that Kelce in turn used to get a $10 million loan from Citibank of New York.

With the loaned money Kelce bought a mine in Fabius, Alabama, and initiated purchases of a coal preparation plant, reserves in southern Illinois, and draglines from the Marion Power Shovel Company. These moves required further capital from Ashland, which might have balked had it not been for the strong support of Atkins and Weaver.

By May of 1970 Merl Kelce had gotten Arch firmly under way. The fledgling company's success, however, was by no means assured, and perhaps nothing could have been more threatening to it than the sudden death of Arch's founder. On May 9, 1970, Kelce learned he had colon cancer; he died three days later.

The management of Arch was left to Heckman, who had the support of Ashland's Atkins. Heckman was a financial man who did not fit the typical up-from-the-mine chief executive officer profile that was common in the coal industry. Nevertheless, he was able to close several complex deals, many of which were already in the works when Kelce died.

With some difficulty, Heckman purchased a Corona, Alabama, coal reserve, signed a contract to supply Georgia Power, and, in exchange for an Arch commitment to supply coal to the government-owned utility, persuaded the TVA to guarantee the $24.5 million in bonds Arch used to purchase the Fabius facility.

Heckman also pursued Kelce's western strategy. In partnership with Kansas Power & Light, he bid on and won mineral rights in the Hanna Basin of Wyoming. Unfortunately, these rights formed a kind of checkerboard with rights held by the Rocky Mountain Energy Company, a Union Pacific Railroad subsidiary. Arch and Kansas tried to lease Rocky Mountain's land, but after complex negotiations in which Rocky Mountain Energy essentially attempted to muscle its way into mining the area, Kansas Power dropped out of the venture.

Into this breach stepped the Hunt brothers, who were looking to broaden their holdings from a base in oil. As a condition of their involvement, the Hunts demanded a 50 percent share of the company. Both Heckman and Atkins agreed. The Hunts acquired the Kelce shares, and Arch issued enough new shares to equalize the Hunt holdings with those of Ashland. Key employees such as Heckman and David Kelce also retained small but significant holdings.

With the Hunts behind them and a commitment from Commonwealth Edison to buy the western coal, Heckman obtained financing from Citibank and the First National Bank of St. Louis and began work on the Seminoe I and Seminoe II mines in Wyoming. In June of 1971 Heckman wrote a memo to Herbert Hunt and Ashland's Buck Weaver suggesting the possible availability of Southwestern Illinois Coal Company. Southwestern's high-sulfur reserves were huge and it had long-term, low-priced contracts with Commonwealth Edison. A consulting report estimated Southwestern's worth at $54 million—several times that of Arch, but not too much for Ashland and the Hunts. The question was whether or not Arch could operate Southwestern's Captain mine efficiently enough to profit off such an acquisition.

Heckman, Atkins, and the Hunts decided Southwestern could be profitable, and on April 11, 1972, they bid more than $58 million to narrowly win Southwestern. "With this purchase," Atkins wrote to Ashland's directors, as cited in *Buried Treasure,* "Arch will be producing in excess of 12 million tons of coal a year, with the potential of moving into the range of 14-15 million tons. This will place it among the top ten coal companies in the country." In fact, the Captain mine served for many years as the company's flagship operation.

At this point—though work was underway on Seminoe I and II—Arch's Hanna Basin holdings were not all in use. Construction of a third mine was being held up by Rocky Mountain Energy, which was demanding terms in exchange for involvement. Rocky Mountain had a great deal of leverage, since Arch would have to drill in a less profitable checkerboard pattern without its land. Rocky Mountain also needed Arch, since it too would be stuck with checkerboard holdings without a deal.

Heckman decided to drill and see if Rocky Mountain would come around. And, just as Heckman ordered equipment onto the land early in November of 1972, Rocky Mountain's John Kelly agreed to terms. Arch and Rocky Mountain would create a joint venture called Medicine Bow Coal Company located 15 miles from the Seminoe II mine.

While these plans were proceeding in the West, however, Arch faced difficulties in the East. The Fabius mine was losing money and having trouble meeting its commitment to the TVA. Early in 1973, the mine defaulted on its notes reverted to the TVA, which had guaranteed them three years earlier. Saddled with Arch's debt, the TVA could have taken control of the mines. Instead, it decided to let Arch continue under its management.

During the early 1970s, Arch's financial fortunes were erratic. The company lost $1.049 million in 1970 on sales of $1.3 million, $540,000 on 1971 sales of $6.1 million, and made $617,000 in 1972 on sales of $13.3 million. In 1973 problems at the Fabius mine caused $3.2 million worth of red ink—despite the opening of Seminoe II—and it was only after the Arab oil boycott caused coal prices to rise that Arch's balance sheet moved firmly into the black with $4.3 million worth of profits in 1974.

Heckman had much to be proud of, but a heart attack prevented him from enjoying his accomplishments. During his convalescence, Arch's ace coal marketer, Jerry Patrick, had ascended to the helm as acting chief executive officer. Patrick was brilliant but impatient. When Heckman returned, Patrick was made president and, despite having no formal technical background, was put in charge of operations.

In 1975 the Medicine Bow mine opened and profits soared to $27 million on sales of $116 million. The balance sheet, though, masked problems, especially at the Captain mine in Illinois where Patrick was not attending to efficiency. Patrick allegedly had alienated much of the original staff and caused many of Kelce's original circle to leave.

Despite problems and miscalculations, Arch remained profitable through the late 1970s and early 1980s. In December of 1977 Jerry Patrick pushed through a special $28 million bucket and wheel system for the Captain Mine. The system was supposed to improve efficiency, but since it failed in the rain and was stopped by boulders, it ultimately proved counterproductive.

In mid-December of 1977 the coal industry was hit with a four-month strike, which threatened Arch's commitments. Nonunion operations in Wyoming worked overtime, though, and in June of 1978, Arch reported profits of $14.1 million on sales of $156.8 million.

By 1979 problems were increasing at the operating level. Morale was down, absenteeism was up, and Jerry Patrick's name was mentioned all too often as a cause. Finally, Heckman moved Patrick out of operations.

In the early 1980s, profits hovered between $6 and $8 million—not very impressive considering that the company was selling assets and that Heckman had the foresight in 1977 to arrange for a fixed rate 8.5 percent line of credit, which, in a time of high interest rates, was saving the company $4 to $8 million a year. After Heckman fired Patrick in June of 1982, he began conversations with R. E. Samples, chief executive officer of Consolidated Coal (Consol). Samples, one of the bright, younger executives of the industry, who felt constrained by Consol's parent, Dupont, approached Heckman about moving to Arch. Hoping Samples could provide the technical leadership the company needed, Heckman hired him as president in September of 1982.

Samples acted quickly, reducing overhead especially at headquarters, where he eliminated the entire public relations department. He probed the staff, sent desk men into the field, appointed a vice-president for human resources, and placed human resources people and controllers at mine sites. At the Captain mine, he removed the bucket wheel excavator and substituted more efficient equipment.

From an operations point of view, things at Arch began to improve. Samples placed new management at several mines. Unafraid to make unconventional choices, he put controller Terry Sullivan, a man skilled at spotting troubles but lacking operational experience, in charge of the troubled Corona mine.

Sullivan knew enough to listen to the people who worked for him and increased production and productivity. He did so well, in fact, that management eventually moved him to the troubled Captain Mine.

With operations strengthened, Heckman and Samples focused on acquisitions. In 1984 they paid $145 million for troubled U.S. Steel's coal business. This was Arch's first Appalachian operation and it included three fully staffed "drift mines" (tunneled horizontally into the mountainside) in Lynch, Kentucky, and more than 400 million tons of low-sulfur reserves in Kentucky and Virginia. By June of that year, Arch's coal production reached 10.3 million tons, and net earnings hit a record $28.3 million.

In 1985 Arch began winding down operations at Seminoe I and Medicine Bow. But while old operations were closing, new ones were opening. At the Captain Mine in Illinois, management unveiled the underground Kathleen mine to help meet obligations. At the end of 1985 Arch of Illinois acquired the Leahy mine from Amax and the following year opened the Horse Creek mine three miles northeast of the Captain mine.

Still on the acquisition trail, in the fall of 1985, Heckman and Samples began negotiating to buy troubled Diamond Shamrock's coal operation. With reserves of six or seven hundred million tons, including the Falcon Coal Company in eastern Kentucky, the Amherst Coal Company in West Virginia, and the Trail Mountain Coal Company in Utah, Diamond Shamrock would lift Arch into the ranks of major coal companies. After problem-filled, on-again-off-again negotiations, Arch paid $135 million for Diamond Shamrock Coal in 1987.

To make the Diamond Shamrock properties profitable, Arch followed the pattern it established with previous acquisitions. According to Coal, Arch took "once underutilized operations typically running at high costs with low productivity," trimmed Diamond Shamrock's costs "by as much as two-thirds," and increased productivity by "three-fold or more." In practice this meant introducing young management teams, initiating safety and employee communications programs, commencing management development programs, revamping labor relations, and working to instill pride in employees.

An example of Arch's efforts could be observed at the North Fork, which, under Diamond Shamrock, was hamstrung with labor and contractor agreements, diminishing reserves, and high costs. Arch ended an expensive cost-plus contract with truckers and offered a purchase agreement on which truckers bid. For miners, it imposed a new agreement despite a two-and-a-half week strike. "At no time," Arch on the North Fork President Ron Gaudiano told Coal, "were there surprises. Everything we did was up-front and was told to our employees verbally and in writing. We communicated with them and built a trust. They may not have liked what we were saying, but they appreciated being told. That continues today."

The U.S. Steel and Diamond Shamrock acquisitions dramatically increased Arch's presence in Appalachia. In 1988 Arch created Catenary Coal "primarily," Catenary president Gerald Peacock explained in Coal, "to develop contractor operations on isolated small pockets of [Appalachian] reserves that do not lend themselves to large operations, and whose coals can be shipped primarily raw."

By June of 1989 Arch Mineral was producing 23 million tons of coal annually. It had acquired more reserves from Lawson Hamilton properties and in July of 1989, Arch of Wyoming acquired the Stansbury mine in Wyoming from Bitter Creek Resources. Growth continued with the acquisition of Blue Diamond Coal, and in April of 1991, Arch and the University of Kentucky resolved a long-running dispute that previously prevented Arch from mining lands adjacent to a University forest research project.

By 1992 Arch was one of the country's leading and fastest-growing coal producers. Perhaps the only cloud on its horizon was the Clean Air Act, which might cause some clients to reassess their use of Arch of Illinois's high sulfur coal. Company officials however did not seem to be worried. Steve Carter, head of marketing for the expanding company, told Coal, "The feeling here at Arch is that the effect of the act will be less than some other producers believe. Much of our high-sulfur coal, which comes primarily from the Illinois operations, is already going to utilities equipped with scrubbers. We think too, that many Midwestern utilities that are potential customers for our Illinois coal will opt for the use of scrubbers."

Principal Subsidiaries: Arch of West Virginia, Inc.; Arch of Kentucky, Inc.; Arch on the North Fork; Catenary Coal Co.; Arch of Illinois, Inc.; Arch of Wyoming, Inc.; Arch Transportation Co., Inc.; Arch Coal Sales Inc.

Further Reading: Scott, Otto, *Buried Treasure: The Story of Arch Mineral Corporation,* Washington, DC, Braddock Communications, Inc., 1989; Sanda, Arthur, Russell Carter, Peter Darling, and Paul C. Merritt, "Arch Mineral Shows the Way to Grow," *Coal,* October 1990.

—Jordan Wankoff

AUTOMOBILES CITROEN

62, boulevard Victor-Hugo
92200 Neuilly-sur-Seine (Hauts-de-Seine)
France
(1) 47 48 32 52
Fax: (1) 47 48 40 68

Subsidiary of PSA Peugeot-Citroen Group (90%)
Incorporated: 1924 as Societe Anonyme Automobiles
    Citroen
Employees: 58,700
Sales: FF 68,800 million
SICs: 3711 Motor Vehicles & Car Bodies

One of the world's first automobile manufacturers, Automobiles Citroen is today one of two car manufacturing divisions of France's PSA Peugeot-Citroen Group, the largest private car manufacturer in France. With manufacturing or assembly plants in 12 countries, Citroen has worldwide sales in 85 countries.

Andre Citroen established the company's precursor, the Citroen Gear Company, in 1913. In order to work smoothly, the teeth on the gears had the form of chevrons, the shape that became the emblem of the Citroen name. Andre Citroen soon began importing modern industrial working methods to France, allowing him to produce economical cars in large quantities. In 1916 M. Citroen began preparations to convert his Paris munitions factory on the Quai de Javel into a car factory. By the end of 1919, the factory was producing thirty cars a day.

The factory produced the Type A, appearing in June 1919, the first European car to be mass-produced and the first low-cost car to be sold fully equipped (with, among other things, electric starter and lighting, hood, spare wheel, and tire). It was also the first car designed with the intention of reaching the popular market.

In 1920 Citroen's fame took off at rapid speed after the company won the fuel economy grand prix at Le Mans. As a result, the company greatly increased its rate of production; from a total of 2,810 cars built in 1919, the company had a production total of 12,244 in 1920.

Citroen first became known in foreign markets in 1921, when it exported a total of approximately 3,000 cars. This move sent the company on a long trek of expansion through numerous international territories throughout the century. Andre Citroen established the basis of a network of subsidiaries in Brussels, Amsterdam, Cologne, Milan, Geneva, and Copenhagen in 1924; the company exported a total of 17,000 vehicles during that year.

Also in 1921, the company took another turn that was to establish its direction for decades to come. It produced three types of "half-trucks," the B2 engine-powered-model which was to accomplish the first vehicle crossing of the Sahara. This mission, led by Haardt and Audouin Dubreuil, left Algiers in December 1922 and arrived successfully in Timbuktu in February 1923. In the ensuing decades, Citroen gained world renown by participating in motor expeditions, rallies, and mass treks across desert landscapes in both Asia and Africa.

In 1922 the company began offering credit sales, with repayments spread over 12 or 18 months. These arrangements helped to jumpstart the popularization of the automobile throughout France. Also in 1922, the company presented the 5CV Type C, a model that contributed to the "democratization" of the automobile because it was economical and easy to drive—so easy, in fact, that it was dubbed the first "ladies' car." The model was mostly painted yellow; hence, its popular nickname was "petite citron," or little lemon.

The year 1924 marked the official beginning of Automobiles Citroen. Andre Citroen founded the Societe Anonyme Automobiles Citroen with a capital of FF 100 million. In the same year, the company presented the B10, the first automobile to have an all-steel body instead of the conventional mixed wood-and-steel construction. Made of cold-pressed panels welded together, the new body offered much better resistance to impact. Production increased in 1924 to 300 vehicles per day, for a total output that year of 55,387 automobiles.

In 1925 the company also shaped and welded its dealer network in France; the number of dealers increased from 200 in 1919 to 5,000 in 1925. The fame of Citroen continued to spread as Haardt and Audouin Dubreuil led their second mission, the Croisiere Noire, between October 1924 and July 1925. The Citroen Central African Expedition consisted of sixteen men and eight half-trucks traveling a total of 20,000 kilometers from Colomb-Bechar (Algeria) to Antananarivo (Madagascar).

From 1925 until 1934, the name "Citroen" was in lights, in letters 30 meters high, on the Eiffel Tower; Charles Lindbergh said he used the illuminated tower as a beacon for his solo flight across the Atlantic in 1927. Andre Citroen organized a reception for Lindbergh at the Javel factory, where 6,000 workers were present to greet him.

By 1928 Citroen's factories employed 30,000 workers and maintained a total production capacity of 1,000 vehicles per day; the company had 14 distributors in France and North Africa, ten subsidiary companies, and four factories in foreign countries. Overseas sales represented 45 percent of all French motor industry exports.

After the crash of the New York Stock Exchange in 1929, Citroen, along with the rest of the world, entered an era of economic crisis. The company's yearly production fell in 1932 to 41,348 vehicles. Milestones in the 1930s, nevertheless, included Citroen's first bus, a 22-passenger vehicle with all-steel bodywork and a six-cylinder engine, built at the Levallois factory in 1931. In 1932 the company announced the C4G and C6G, containing the first engines carried on soft mountings to eliminate vibration; a swan in flight between the double chevrons of the Citroen badge symbolized the advance. Also in the 1930s, Haardt and Audouin Dubreuil completed their third expedition: the Croisiere Jaune. Forty men and 14 half-trucks traveled 12,000 kilometers from Beirut to Peking via the Himalayas, the Gobi desert, and China from April 1931 to February 1932.

Even as the Depression continued to dampen the high spirits of the French motor industry, Andre Citroen clung to his original thinking: the greater the number of products, the cheaper production becomes. In 1933 he set two goals: production of 1,000 vehicles per day, and the introduction of the new front-driven model developed by Citroen designer Andre Lefebvre. The company announced the 7A in April of 1934, the first of a line of Traction Avant models that were produced until 1957. The model had bold specifications: aerodynamic bodywork, unitary steel body with no chassis or running-boards, all-independent suspension, and hydraulic brakes.

M. Citroen's plans came to a standstill, however, when the company's financial difficulties led to an inability to pay its debts. In 1934 the French government asked the Michelin company, Citroen's principal creditor, to take financial control and re-float the company. Under the direction of Michelin, 8,000 layoffs took place. The company's production plummeted from 51,546 in 1934 to 29,101 in 1935.

In 1935 Andre Citroen died after a serious illness. The following year the company conceived one of its all-time classics, the legendary 2CV (or "deux chevaux"). The idea was for a low-priced car with a very small engine, described by the design department as "four wheels under an umbrella." In 1939 the declaration of war prevented the company from announcing the 2CV. In May of that year, the company destroyed all of its 250 prototypes except one to maintain secrecy. In 1940 the Quai de Javel factory was bombed and Citroen's Belgian factory was partly destroyed. The company's production gradually fell to zero in 1943, partly due to management's refusal to comply with the demands of the Vichy government.

Production built up slowly from 1,600 in 1945 to 12,600 in 1946. In 1948 the 2CV appeared at the Paris Motor Show. From October 1949 to the end of 1984, the company built over 3 million examples of the immensely popular vehicle. With an outer appearance that Steven Greenhouse of the *New York Times* called a cross between a camel and a frog, the 2CV was long the least expensive French car on the market. A cult developed around what became something of a national symbol for the car of the proletariat. Manifestations of popular enthusiasm for the 2CV included odes, sculptures, and water races (contestants removed the car's tires and floated it on oil drums). As the company entered the fifties, the demand for the 2CV stretched the delivery delay to six years.

In 1953 Citroen began decentralizing its production organization with the opening of the Rennes-la Barre Thomas factory in Brittany. It was not until the end of the 1970s, however, that the company achieved a balance between the Paris region and the provinces.

Citroen's design and development department pioneered a technical breakthrough in 1954: constant-height hydropneumatic rear suspension. The system combined the actions of a gas and a liquid to achieve greatly improved road handling. In 1955 the company announced the DS19, with no front grille and a completely smooth nose. This model was revolutionary not only because of its aerodynamic shape, but also because of its technical features, including the newly developed hydropneumatic suspension. All major systems (gearchange, clutch, steering, and brakes) were power operated. The model was an instant success: Citroen received 12,000 orders by the end of the first day.

In 1958 the factory of the Societe Citroen Hispania at Vigo (Spain) began to produce 2CV vans for the Spanish market and for export. This gave the company representation in a market where imports were strictly limited by quotas. Also in 1958, the company announced the four-wheel-drive 2CV Sahara, especially useful for oil exploration and mining teams in desert areas; the vehicle was capable of climbing a sandy, 40 percent slope fully laden. In 1959 a Citroen ID19 driven by Coltelloni, Alexandre, and Desrosiers won the Monte Carlo Rally; this led the company to its decision to participate in motor sports events in the years to come.

As Citroen entered the 1960s, the company expanded by establishing subsidiaries and signing joint ventures in foreign locations. In 1960, it reached an agreement with the Yugoslav Tomos concern for the assembly of the 2CV in Yugoslavia. In 1962 Citroen established sales companies in Montreal and Vienna. In 1963 the company set up a subsidiary in Chile for assembly and sales; it also reached an agreement with the Sedica company for the assembly of the 2CV and 3CV in Madagascar. In 1964 the Mangualde factory in Portugal came into operation to manufacture the 2CV; this move again allowed Citroen access to a market with severe restrictions on the import of fully assembled cars.

New models in the 1960s included the Ami 6, a model categorized as top-of-the-range, and the Dyane, a model categorized between the 2CV and Ami 6.

In 1965 Citroen acquired the Panhard factory at Reims (France), a facility specializing in the manufacture of mechanical components for commercial vehicles. In 1967 after signing an industrial collaboration agreement for the production of common designs, Citroen took a majority shareholding in the company Berliet, the European Economic Community's largest producer of commercial vehicles.

Citroen underwent major reorganization the following year. A holding company was created (Citroen SA) to oversee the activities of Citroen, Berliet, and Panhard. Citroen SA gathered within its structure more than 20 subsidiary companies, including the Societe Anonyme Automobiles Citroen (handling production) and the Societe Commerciale Citroen (handling sales).

Citroen signed a technical and commercial agreement in 1968 with the Italian sports car company Maserati. It also signed an agreement with Fiat to set up a holding company, Pardevi, which would hold the majority of Citroen shares, and in which Fiat would have a 49 percent shareholding, and Michelin 51 percent. Under the terms of the agreement, Autobianchi models were to be sold through Citroen dealerships in France, Belgium, Switzerland, and Portugal; Citroens were to be sold through the Autobianchi dealerships in Italy.

In 1970 the company organized the Paris-Kabul-Paris "raid" with 1,300 participants in 2CVs, Dyanes, and Meharis. In March of that year, the company launched the SM, a luxury coupe made possible by the 1968 agreement with Maserati.

In 1971 the company reached agreements with Inda SA of Paraguay, Quinatar SA of Uruguay, and Aviles Alfaro in Equador for the assembly of 2CV and 3CV models. In 1972 it signed an agreement with the Yugoslav concerns Tomos and Iskra for the creation of a joint Franco-Yugoslav company, Cimos, to manufacture the 2CV, Dyane, Ami 8, GS and mechanical components in Yugoslavia. The company also created an industrial and commercial subsidiary in Johannesburg, and reached agreement with a company in Tunisia for the assembly of 2CV and 3CV models.

In 1973 the decision of Middle East oil exporters to increase oil prices dramatically led to a severe international economic crisis. Production at the company fell in 1974. Citroen staged a recovery in 1975, largely due to an increase in exports, which represented 55 percent of the total sales volume.

In 1973 the company opened the Aulnay-sous-Bois factory in the Paris region, intended to gradually replace the original Quai de Javel factory. The new facility was one of the most modern of its day; it had body assembly transfer lines, an automated paint system, and computer-controlled buffer stores and production systems. In the same year, Fiat withdrew from Pardevi and returned its 49 percent shareholding to Michelin.

In 1974 Michelin and the Peugeot group decided to merge Automobiles Citroen and Automobiles Peugeot in order to create a truly internationally competitive company. The two groups retained their own sales networks and product ranges; they agreed upon joint research policies as well as joint purchasing and investment in order to achieve economies of scale. In the same year, Berliet left the Citroen group, and the famous factory at Quai de Javel closed its doors.

In the mid-seventies, Citroen opened a completely computer-controlled factory, the Charleville-Meziere foundry in Ardennes (France). Affected adversely by the energy crisis, the company ended production of its luxury SM model. It announced a new model, the CX2200, which in 1975 won the awards of "Car of the Year," "Prix de la Securite," and "Award Style Auto." In 1976 as part of the merging process, the Peugeot group took an 89.95 percent shareholding in Citroen and created the PSA holding company.

In 1978 a sister company of Citroen and Peugeot, the SMAE or Societe Mecanique Automobile de l'Est, was founded at Metz (Lorraine); the company's two factories supplied mechanical assemblies to both PSA companies. Also in 1978, the company announced the FAF, or Facile a Fabriquer ("easy to manufacture") at the Dakar fair in Senegal. Developed with the needs of the "Third World" in mind, the model had a body built up from a folded steel sheet which could be made without heavy machinery. Citroen signed assembly agreements with several African countries, including Senegal, the Ivory Coast, Guinea-Bissau, and the Central African Republic.

Modern management theories had their impact on Citroen as the company's first Quality Circles appeared in 1980. Five to ten volunteers in each circle worked to apply quality control techniques to solve problems as they arose. Another sister company, the SMAN (Societe Mecanique Automobile du Nord) began operations at Valenciennes in northern France in 1980; it supplied the three companies of the group with gearboxes for mid-range vehicles. Citroen felt the effects of the second energy crisis as production fell in 1980; losses in 1982 and 1983 were the equivalent of $142 million.

The early 1980s threw yet another roadblock in the company's way when workers went on strike in several factories in the Paris area; the strikes prevented production for several weeks. On the foreign front, however, the company covered yet more new territory by signing its first contract with China. With the sale of 150 CXs to the Dong Fang Hotel in Canton, Citroen made its entry in the Chinese market.

In 1983 the company began operations in the Meudon factory that were completely controlled by computer, worked 24 hours a day, and needed no manual intervention to check prototype and small- and medium-series components. In the same year, Citroen entered the European market for top-class long-distance cruisers with the announcement of the CX 25 RD Turbo and CX 25 TRD Turbo saloon and estate.

The company shifted its image in the mid-1980s by inaugurating a new corporate identity campaign featuring a herd of thoroughbred horses running wild. It also replaced the old dealer network colors of blue and yellow with red and white. In July 1985 Citroen participated in the first Chinese motor show in Shanghai and signed a contract for the delivery of 250 CXs. In 1986 the company again became profitable after six years of financial losses.

The company continued on the quality control route by introducing the Plan Mercure program in its production facilities in 1986. The plan introduced product diversification, cost-cutting schemes, shorter delivery schedules, shorter chains of command, and value-added job profiles. The company also prepared to launch its new AX by adopting a single publicity strategy—identification of the model with China and the Great Wall.

Citroen's strategies began to pay off handsomely in the last half of the decade. End-of-the-year 1987 figures showed a tripling of 1986 profits; in 1988, profits were 78.24% higher than in 1987, and the PSA Group's profits reached FF 8.8 billion. Citroen exports increased by 12 percent, with the most significant gains in Portugal, Spain, and Britain.

Citroen began major preparations in 1988 to introduce its new luxury model XM. Investments reached FF 7.5 billion, including FF 1.2 billion in research and development. The company completely refurbished the final assembly plant for the model at Rennes-La Janais. Citroen displayed the XM at the Frankfurt Motor Show, using an avant-garde stand with a centerpiece representing movement into the future.

As Citroen entered the 1990s, it set up a joint Citroen-Mazda distribution network in Japan, known as Eunos. It also established a network of 80 Citroen dealers in eastern Germany, and associated with Peugeot in a coordinated logistics program for spare parts over the whole of Europe. The company signed a joint-venture contract with the Chinese manufacturer S.A.W. (Second Automobile Works), creating a company to manufacture and market the Citroen ZX.

The company officially returned to international motor competition with the announcement of the Citroen ZX Rallye-Raid. Winning drivers for Citroen included Ari Vatanen and Bruno Berglund in the eighth Baja Aragon Multi-Terrain race, and Christine Driano in the 1990 French Rally Championships. The company came out ahead not only in sports: the Citroen XM won 14 national and international awards and was voted "Car of the Year 1990." Also in 1990, Citroen launched a "customized" series with models designed to fit customer lifestyles, such as "image," "relaxation," "sport." One lifestyle philosophy, however, disappeared altogether: The last 2CV rolled off the production line and rode into history on July 27, 1990.

In 1991 European markets important to Citroen contracted as the European car industry entered a recession. Citroen officially introduced the ZX to the general public at the Geneva motor show, targeted for the mid-range market as a collection of four models. The company also signed an agreement with trade unions that addressed job classification, training, easier access to supervisory grades, and the creation of clear promotional paths to executive status. Finally, an international jury of 100 journalists in association with the *Auto-Moto* magazine voted Citroen car-maker of the century. While the manufacturer may face economic obstacles in the last leg of the road to the twenty-first century, its innovative character should keep it driving forward well beyond.

Principal Subsidiaries: Societe Mecanique Automobile de l'Est (75%); Societe de Construction d'Equipements, de Mecanisation et de Machines (SCEMM); Societe Commerciale Citroen; Citroen Deutschland AG (Germany); Citroen Commerce AG (Germany); Citroen Hispania S.A. (Spain; 93%); Citroen Italia SpA (Italy; 96%); Comercial Citroen S.A. (Spain); Citroen (U.K.) Ltd. (United Kingdom).

Further Reading: Ducorroy, Regis, *Dates,* Neuilly-sur-Seine, France, Automobiles Citroen, 1991; Greenhouse, Steven, "Valiant Little Companion of the Road, Au Revior!" *New York Times,* March 9, 1988; Smith, Timothy K., "Why a Little Car Won a Big Place in Europe's Heart," *Wall Street Journal,* July 11, 1984.

—Dorothy Walton

AVONDALE INDUSTRIES, INC.

5100 River Road
Avondale, Louisiana 70094
U.S.A.
(504) 436-2121
Fax: (504) 436-5304

Public Company
Incorporated: 1938 as Avondale Marine Ways, Inc.
Employees: 6–8,000
Sales: $592 million
Stock Exchanges: NASDAQ
SICs: 3731 Ship Building & Repairing; 3441 Fabricated
   Structural Metal

Avondale Industries, Inc., is a diversified company whose primary business is the construction, repair, conversion, and "jumboization" of ships, barges, tugboats, and other vessels. The company is a major supplier of non-combat vessels to the United States Navy, constructing a full range of destroyer escorts, frigates, cutters, fleet oilers, landing ship docks, and landing craft aircushion (LCAC) at shipyards and repair and manufacturing facilities in Louisiana and Mississippi. It is also involved in non-marine, industrial construction projects as well as other ventures in Louisiana, Mississippi, and Texas.

Avondale grew out of a small barge repair business, Avondale Marine Ways, Inc., which was founded in 1938 by James G. Viavant, Harry Koch, and Perry N. Ellis about 12 miles upriver from New Orleans on the Mississippi River. Almost immediately it began building river boats and barges, at first as a way of keeping employees busy between repair jobs, which were much more profitable. By 1941 the company employed about 200 workers.

With the United States gearing up for World War II, the government took control of the flow of metals and other raw materials. In 1941 James Viavant flew to Washington to find out from the Maritime Commission whether there were any small vessels that Avondale could bid on. The result was a contract to manufacture four tugboats, the company's first major building contract. This was followed by a contract to construct 14 M3 coastal cargo ships, 300-foot shallow draft vessels. Avondale continued to build ships including tankers, tugs, and other coastal vessels for the government for the duration of the war, which required expansion of the original shipyard facilities.

After the war, the company continued to grow as the oil industry in southern Louisiana expanded during the 1940s and 1950s. Avondale began building drilling barges and work boats, and built its first submersible drilling barge in 1951. As river and intercoastal traffic grew, there was increasing need for repair facilities. Avondale purchased a major new site in 1946 at Harvey Canal and continued to expand its repair facilities throughout the period. The company's name was changed to Avondale Shipyards, Inc., in 1960.

In 1959 Avondale was sold to the Ogden Corporation of New York for $14 million. The company remained a subsidiary of Ogden until 1985, building guided missile destroyers, destroyer escorts, auxiliary oilers, and other vessels for the Navy; various types of commercial vessels, including cargo vessels, offshore drilling rigs, tugs, oil tankers, LASH cargo vessels, dredges, tug/supply vessels, product tankers, container vessels, and miscellaneous barges; and Coast Guard cutters. In 1985 Ogden sold seven companies including Avondale Shipyards to the employees, and these became Avondale Corporation under an Employee Stock Ownership Plan (ESOP). The ESOP, one of the largest ever formed, was 70 percent employee-owned, with Ogden retaining a 30 percent share. Ogden continued to have a minor interest in the company, but concentrated on its food service, building maintenance, waste recovery and management, and allied businesses. In 1987 Avondale Industries divested itself of six of those companies. The shipyard, with its various divisions centered around New Orleans, continued as Avondale Industries, Inc. In 1988 the company was taken public; the employees owned approximately 44 percent of the common stock in 1989. In 1991 that figure was about 54 percent.

After World War II Japan became the leader in innovative methods of building high quality ships utilizing modular construction, also known as "zone outfitting." In this mode of construction, large projects are broken up into manageable modules, which are worked on simultaneously in different workshops or facilities, sometimes many miles apart. The modules are then transported to the ship site. This method results in tremendous cost savings, although it requires complex planning, logistics, and engineering in order to maintain tight tolerances between the modules.

In the late 1970s Avondale made the decision to study and adapt the Japanese system. To this end, Avondale management, under Chief Executive Albert L. Bossier, entered into a unique technology transfer agreement with Ishikawajima-Harima Heavy Industries (IHI) of Japan in 1980–81. It took the company approximately five years to retrain and retool, but modular construction eventually gave Avondale a decisive competitive advantage in the shipbuilding industry. While Avondale thrived, other shipbuilders such as General Dynamics and Lockheed closed shipyards, and Todd Shipyards and Morrison Knudsen experienced severe losses. The relationship with IHI has continued, but on a case-by-case consulting basis.

In addition to its changeover to modular construction, Avondale also invested heavily in facility improvements and expansion. Between 1970 and 1992, the company plowed more than $258 million into new manufacturing shops, modular assembly buildings, and state-of-the-art equipment. In 1992 its lifting equipment included a 600-ton floating crane, seven cranes with capacity above 130 tons, and 29 cranes with capacity greater than 50 tons. Avondale also had an 81,000-ton drydock measuring 900' x 220' and a 20,000-ton panamax drydock measuring 705' x 118'. Equipment of this size has enabled Avondale to specialize in "jumboization," a process whereby a ship is cut in half and a matching section is inserted in order to lengthen the vessel.

The company has used modular construction in some industrial non-marine projects as well. These have included a 192-mega-watt hydroelectric plant in Vidalia, Louisiana, four hazardous waste treatment plants for Ogden, compressor and pump modules for the oil industry, sulphur recovery units, cryogenic gas separation systems, sub-sea oil treatment units for oil companies, and a floating detention center for New York City capable of housing 800 inmates delivered in 1992.

By 1989 defense-related contracts, mainly with the Navy, accounted for as much as 85 percent of Avondale's business. In 1991 the Secretary of the Navy advised Congress that by 1995 the Navy's fleet would be pared from about 550–600 ships to 450, and the actual number might drop even lower. In terms of expenditures, this meant that the Navy's annual budget for shipbuilding would be reduced from $12–14 billion in the 1980s to $6–8 billion in the 1990s. In addition, because the Navy planned to concentrate on combat ships and submarines, vessels that Avondale had not previously produced, the effect of the cutbacks on Avondale would be that much greater.

In 1990 Avondale reported a net loss of $25.8 million and then a loss of $140.9 million in 1991. These losses were, however, not attributable to military downsizing, but rather to cost overruns on seven T-AO (auxiliary oil tanker) and three LSD-CV (landing ship dock-cargo variant) contracts due to be completed in 1994 and 1995. In early 1992 the company applied for requests for equitable adjustments (REAs) of $300–340 million from the Navy. As Albert L. Bossier, Jr., Avondale's chairman, president, and CEO stated at the time, "The REAs we are pursuing with the Navy are intended to seek reimbursement for the portion of our cost overruns resulting from disruption of work caused by contract delays and changes initiated by the Navy." While the REAs had not been settled as of January 1993, the Navy released $15 million of earned retentions from previous contracts, which helped alleviate a cash shortfall for 1992.

In 1992 Avondale learned that a competitor had been awarded a contract to build as many as seven MHC-51 minehunters despite the fact that Avondale was already building four such vessels. On the other hand, the Navy changed its contract on three of the T-AOs already being built by Avondale to make them double-hulled. The company was also awarded a $1.2 million contract to design ships for "Sealift," the ocean transport of weapons and supplies for ground troops. The company also launched the T-AGS 45 oceanographic survey ship for the Navy as well as several other ships in that year. In spite of the dropoff in Navy contracts, Avondale did show a small second-quarter profit and a third-quarter profit of about $280,000, although revenues declined for the sixth straight quarter from $205 million in the first quarter of 1991 to $139 million in the third quarter of 1992.

The combination of the Navy's cutbacks, the economic recession, and factors peculiar to the industry and/or Avondale hit the company particularly hard in its efforts to diversify. Congress passed the Oil Pollution Act of 1990 in the aftermath of the *Exxon Valdez* disaster. The Act mandated that all oil tankers entering U.S. ports after January 1, 2000, be double-hulled. While this created some immediate opportunities for Avondale, the company found that the physical capacity of its main shipyard, the draft of the river, and the height of bridges spanning the Mississippi precluded it from making bids to retrofit or build ultra-large oil tankers. As of January 1993, Avondale had not received orders for commercial double-hulled tankers.

In addition, while international demand for the replacement of large commercial ships was projected to be above average in the 1990s, most of Avondale's foreign competitors were subsidized by their governments, placing Avondale at a competitive disadvantage. In response to this, Avondale entered into a unique joint venture with Peter Gast Shipping GmbH, of Hamburg, Germany, and Wilhelm Wilhelmsen Ltd., of Oslo, Norway, in January 1991. Avgain Marine A/S, based in Oslo, was created to be an international broker of ship components, allowing Avondale to cut materials expenses by pooling purchasing power, and to boost Gast's efforts to market Avondale-built ships in Europe and elsewhere. It was thought that the lower value of the dollar would partially offset the disadvantage posed by European government subsidization. As Gast put it, "Avondale's ship prices are now more competitive."

Avondale's attempts to transfer its shipbuilding and managerial skills to non-marine projects met with only limited success during this period. One bright spot during 1991, however, was a five-year contract worth approximately $63 million obtained by Avondale Technical Services, a subsidiary, to operate and maintain specialized commuter services for the handicapped and elderly in Dallas, Texas. The company was also looking into the possibility of getting back into the offshore construction business, principally offshore oil platforms for the international market.

In spite of the global recession, cost overruns, and Navy cutbacks that so adversely affected Avondale in the early 1990s, the company can draw on its more than 50 years of technical and managerial innovation and expertise. Its experience with modular construction would seem to position it ideally to take on industrial, non-marine contracts during a period of economic recovery. The company also appears well suited to profit from the Oil Pollution Act of 1990. In addition, the strategy institutionalized in Avgain Marine A/S shows promise of expanding Avondale's business base beyond the United States when the world economy expands.

Principal Subsidiaries: Avondale Technical Services, Inc.; Crawford Technical Services, Inc.; Avondale Gulfport Marine, Inc.; Avondale Enterprises, Inc.; Genco Industries, Inc.

Further Reading: Bonney, Joseph, "Ogden Sells Avondale To Workers," *Journal of Commerce,* July 19, 1985; "Big Easy Survivor," *Forbes,* January 9, 1989; Toll, Erich E., "US Shipbuilder to Join Norwegians, Germans in Unusual Partnership," *Journal of Commerce,* January 10, 1991; "1991 Annual Report,'' Avondale Industries, Inc., Avondale, Louisiana; ''Avondale Industries Posts Net Loss, Cites Cost Overruns on Navy Pacts,'' *Journal of Commerce,* April 20, 1992; *Avondale Industries, Inc.—A Diversified Company,* Avondale, Avondale, Louisiana; ''Avondale Industries, Inc. Shipyards Division,'' Avondale, Avondale, Louisiana; ''Avondale—1938–1974,'' Avondale, Avondale, Louisiana.

—Kenneth F. Kronenberg

BAUER PUBLISHING GROUP

Burchardstrasse 11
2000 Hamburg 1
Germany
(40) 30 19 33 70
Fax: (40) 33 56 52

Private Company
Incorporated: 1875
Employees: 6,400
Sales: DM 2.8 billion; US$1.714 billion
SICs: 2721 Periodicals: Publishing, or Publishing & Printing

Bauer Publishing Group is the largest magazine publisher in Germany and one of the largest in Europe, offering a wide variety of light-information periodicals for a mainstream readership. Five of Germany's best-selling magazines are Bauer creations: *TV Hören und Sehen, Fernsehwoche* and *Auf Einen Blick,* all of which combine television guides with elements of women's and family magazines; *Neue Post,* which is targeted at older women, and *Tina,* which its publisher describes as a "classic women's magazine." In addition, Bauer publishes the German editions of *Esquire* and *Playboy.* As recently as 1988, the publisher was able to claim 42 percent of all magazines sold in West Germany. Bauer also publishes three magazines in the United States—*Woman's World, First for Women* and *Soap Opera Update*—and numerous magazines in other European countries, many of them foreign editions of its domestic staples. Bauer owns an extensive printing and distribution operation, making it a fully integrated publishing concern.

Bauer Publishing traces its origins back to 1875 when a young resident of Hamburg named Louis Bauer went into business as a printer, setting up shop in his home in Billhorner Roehrendamm and using a borrowed press. Bauer was a lithographer by training but, when he found himself out of work in the midst of an economic downturn, he decided to go into business for himself. This home-grown operation proved so successful that at the turn of the century, the payroll of Louis Bauer's print shop had grown from one to 20.

When Bauer's son Heinrich Bauer became a partner in the company in 1903, the family business began to branch out, acquiring a typesetting machine and a high-speed press and setting up a stationer's in the building next door. Soon after, the Bauers published their first periodical, a free advertising news-

paper called *Rothenburgsorter Zeitung.* They added a second newspaper, *Hammerbrooker Zeitung,* shortly thereafter. The success of these two publishing ventures enabled the company to buy a new duotone printing press in 1913.

Heinrich Bauer's son Alfred joined the company in 1918, and it continued to grow and diversify in the interwar years. In 1920 the company began publishing *Extrablatt am Montag,* a weekly newspaper that eventually converted to a sports-only format. Three years later, now operating under the name Heinrich Bauer Buch-und-Verlagsdruckerei, the company moved to its current address on Burchardstrasse in Hamburg. In 1927 another weekly, *Rundfunkkritik* (later renamed *Funk-Wacht*) made its debut and became the Bauer family's greatest success yet, achieving a circulation of more than 500,000.

The outbreak of World War II put a stop to the company's plans for further expansion. Patriarch Louis Bauer died in Hamburg in 1941 at the age of 90. After the war, Bauer Publishing, like the rest of the nation, found itself having to rebuild and remake itself. It proved quite adept at this task and quickly became one of the most prominent publishers of periodicals in West Germany. In 1948 Bauer began publishing the illustrated weekly *Quick.* In 1953 the company acquired a number of regional publications that served as guides to television programming and consolidated them into a national periodical named *Hören und Sehen.* In 1958 Bauer Publishing acquired Wiesbaden-based magazine publisher Schwabe-Verlag and its popular fashion magazine *Neue Mode.* Also during the 1950s, Bauer began publishing *Fix und Foxi,* a children's comic that would become a longtime German favorite. And in 1961 the company acquired Kurt Möller Verlag, publisher of *Neue Post.*

Also in 1961, 22-year-old Heinz Bauer, great-grandson of Louis Bauer, became the chief executive officer of the nascent Bauer publishing empire. This latest member of the Bauer clan to run the family business presented a combination of old ways and new: He studied business administration at a university, but like his predecessors, also apprenticed as a printer before joining the company.

Under Heinz Bauer, the company continued to expand during the 1960s. Bauer Publishing created its popular illustrated weekly, *Neue Revue,* by merging two magazines, *Neue Illustrierte* and *Revue.* Because circulation kept expanding, production capacity at the company's Hamburg printing facilities was exhausted by the end of the decade. As a consequence, the company expanded southward from its base in the Hanseatic north. It acquired Du Mont Press in Köln, which it renamed Bauer Druck Köln. By 1990 this facility was turning out 28 million copies per week on state-of-the-art equipment. Also, Bauer Publishing expanded its editorial facilities in Munich and demolished its old printing facilities in Hamburg to make way for a larger, more modern plant.

In the following decades, the company continued to grow. Two of its best-selling titles made their debut in the 1970s; *Fernsehwoche* appeared in 1970, followed by *Tina* in 1975. The 1980s saw Bauer Publishing expanding its horizons and looking to foreign markets for revenue growth. In 1981 it created an American subsidiary, Heinrich Bauer North America, based in Englewood Cliffs, New Jersey. Bauer North America's first offering was a supermarket weekly called *Woman's World*. In 1987 Bauer Publishing created subsidiaries in Great Britain (Heinrich Bauer Publishing) and Spain (Bauer Ediciones); Heinrich Bauer Publishing launched *Bella*, a women's magazine along the lines of *Tina*, while Bauer Ediciones came out with *TV Plus*, which attempted to duplicate Bauer's successful combination of television program information and homemaker/family-oriented light information. Also in 1987, Bauer Publishing began producing the West German edition of *Esquire*. The next year, the company chalked up two titles in France through its subsidiary there (Editions Bauer France), launching yet another TV guide/women's magazine, *Aujord'hui Madame*, and acquiring the popular fashion magazine *Marie France*.

Bauer North America achieved great success with the introduction of *Woman's World*. Within ten years, the magazine drew a circulation of 1.5 million readers and was generating estimated annual revenues of $15 million for the parent company. The success of *Woman's World* encouraged Bauer to take another plunge into the American market. In 1989 the company launched *First for Women*, which targeted homemakers with light information in a magazine format.

Unfortunately for Bauer, however, *First for Women* had more difficulty turning a profit than its predecessor. Some analysts claim that Bauer, in its rush to conquer unexplored territory, had neglected to learn how the American periodical business works. German mass circulation periodicals rely heavily on sales to readers to generate revenues, whereas in the United States circulation figures are simply held out as a lure for advertisers. (Advertising sales are what will turn a magazine profitable.) Bauer ran *Woman's World* and *First for Women* based on the German model. While this did not hurt *Woman's World*, it nearly crippled *First for Women*, which competed directly with two popular U.S. magazines, *Woman's Day* and *Family Circle*.

Despite impressive circulation figures, *First for Women* lost money initially—some observers estimated the deficit at as much as $60 million over its first two years—because of scanty advertisement sold at low rates.

Far from souring Bauer on the American market, however, this experience with *First for Women* simply provided a learning experience for solidifying its presence in the United States. In 1992 it entered the lucrative and growing field of covering daytime television serials when it acquired *Soap Opera Update* from the magazine's founders, Jerome and Angela Shapiro.

Bauer Publishing's expansion since the end of World War II has been impressive, and significant opportunities for future growth remain. The reunification of Germany in 1990 opened up a lucrative market for the entire West German publishing industry. Bauer and rivals Axel Springer, Gruner, Jahr and Burda jumped at the possibilities, each wasting little time in creating their own distribution networks and forming joint ventures with their eastern counterparts. The long-term winner of the circulation battles that were joined in eastern Germany in the early 1990s has yet to be determined. But, if its experience in West Germany, the rest of Western Europe and the United States is a good indication, Bauer Publishing Group would be a dangerous player to bet against.

Principal Subsidiaries: Heinrich Bauer Vertreibs KG; Editions Bauer France; Heinrich Bauer North America, Inc.; Heinrich Bauer Publishing; Bauer Ediciones S.C.

Further Reading: *Verlagsgruppe Bauer in Formation,* Bauer Publishing Group, Hamburg, 1989; Ynostroza, Roger, "Golden Age for German Magazines," *Graphic Arts Monthly,* April 1990; Fabrikant, Geraldine, "Many Readers, Few Ads for Bauer," *New York Times,* May 22, 1991.

—Douglas Sun

BAUSCH & LOMB INC.

One Lincoln First Square
Rochester, NY 14601
U.S.A.
(716) 338-6000
Fax: (716) 338-6007

Public company
Incorporated: 1853 as Bausch & Lomb Optical Co.
Sales: $1.52 billion
Employees: 13,700
Stock Exchanges: New York
SICs: 3851 Ophthalmic Goods; 3843 Dental Equipment &
    Supplies; 2834 Pharmaceutical Preparations; 3842 Surgical
    Appliances & Supplies

Bausch & Lomb Inc. is the United States' leading ophthalmic goods firm and stand as one of the premiere contact lens manufacturers in the world. The company also produces the flagship brand Ray-Ban sunglasses, as well as a variety of pharmaceuticals and health care products for the eyes, mouth, and ears.

Bausch & Lomb Optical Co., an eyeglass store and manufacturer of eyeglass frames, was founded in 1853 by two German immigrants, John Jacob Bausch and Henry Lomb, in Rochester, New York. Bausch's son Edward learned to make microscopes, and the company prospered after it began to manufacture them. In 1890 Edward Bausch contacted Carl Zeiss, a German optics firm, and soon arranged for Bausch & Lomb to license Zeisses' patents, with the exclusive rights to the U.S. market. The most important patents were to Zeisses' new photographic lens and its first prism binoculars. Bausch & Lomb expanded, opening offices in Chicago, Boston, New York City, and Frankfurt, Germany. Bausch & Lomb gradually became a leading name in optics in the United States, supplying microscopes to schools and laboratories and manufacturing the U.S. Navy's first telescopic gun sights.

In the early 1900s, Zeiss perfected the military range finder. Impressed by U.S. manufacturing expertise, Zeiss eventually decided that, rather than build its own factory, it would allow Bausch & Lomb to manufacture range finders in the United States. In 1907 Zeiss bought 20 percent of Bausch & Lomb, granting the company free use of Zeiss patents in the United States. Zeiss, on the other hand, sold to the rest of the world and was paid in dividends rather than royalty payments. Bausch &

Lomb also sent technicians to Germany for training at Zeiss laboratories. Military products accounted for only a small amount of Bausch & Lomb's production, but as the only U.S. manufacturer of many optical products, production was nevertheless vital to the U.S. military. As a result, the U.S. Navy stationed technical experts in the company's plant in 1912.

Bausch & Lomb's arrangement with Zeiss unraveled after the outbreak of World War I. The company had sold the Allies equipment without Zeisses' approval in Europe, which was not one of their markets. In 1915 Zeiss sold its 20-percent share back to Bausch & Lomb, and until 1921, the two companies had no dealings with one another (although Bausch & Lomb continued to use Zeiss patents). Because of the war, Bausch & Lomb became the major U.S. supplier of scientific precision glass, from which the lenses used by the military were ground. After the war, the other U.S. companies which had learned to make the glass stopped production, making Bausch & Lomb the only producer of scientific precision glass in the Western Hemisphere. In 1921 Zeiss made all of its military patents exclusively available to Bausch & Lomb for use in the United States.

In 1926 John Jacob Bausch died, and Edward Bausch became chairman of the board. In the 1937 Bausch & Lomb went public, selling $3.6 million worth of stock to raise working capital. At the time the company made 17,000 products, from eyeglasses to spectroscopes. Bausch & Lomb made 28 percent of U.S. eyeglass lenses and a large percentage of the country's microscopes and binoculars. Even after the offering, the company was still closely held, with family members owning significant percentages of Bausch & Lomb stock and holding most top management positions.

During the late 1930s, as Europe once again headed toward war, Bausch & Lomb focused on becoming self-sufficient by searching for U.S. sources of most materials to make optical glass and stockpiling two year's worth of foreign supplies. During this time, the firm emerged as a leading provider of professional photographic lenses, particularly for the film industry. Bausch & Lomb's Cinephor coated projection lenses were used by almost all U.S. movie houses, while its high-speed lenses were used for projecting background scenes. Bausch & Lomb was awarded an honorary Oscar for these contributions. With help from these new products, company sales increased from $16.2 million in 1938 to about $21 million in 1940.

Despite these accomplishments, Bausch & Lomb's image was tarnished somewhat by a 1940 federal suit regarding its relationship with Zeiss. The U.S. Justice department charged both companies with anti-trust violations because of their agreed-upon division of world markets. The government alleged that this resulted in inflated prices and also questioned the propriety of a German company dictating the sales of optical products by a U.S. company. While denying any wrongdoing, Bausch & Lomb paid a fine and again severed its relationship with Zeiss. The company was expanding for a new rearmament program and bidding on navy contracts, and industry analysts assumed that Bausch & Lomb wanted to incident put behind them as quickly as possible.

During World War II Bausch & Lomb produced optical instruments including range finders and field scopes. As one of the earliest manufacturers of high-quality sunglasses, the company also benefited from the use of Ray-Ban sunglasses by U.S. Army Air Corps pilots and General Douglas MacArthur.

During the war, the percentage of company output relating to the military soared, but by the early-1950s, military sales had fallen to 15 percent of the total. Sales had increased to about $48.5 million, and the firm had more than 150 prescription labs for grinding and polishing glass lenses throughout the United States. Bausch & Lomb spent less than 2 percent of sales on research and development. Meanwhile, as Japanese firms recovered from the war, they became competitive. In 1951 Bausch & Lomb realized it was slowly losing its competitive edge and began allocating more money—some of it borrowed—into research and development. As a result, the company moved into the growing electronic optics field in 1954. By the early 1960s the firm was spending approximately 6.5 percent of sales on research and development. Bausch & Lomb also upgraded its marketing department to determine customer demand prior to developing new product lines.

In 1959 William McQuilkin became the first president not related to the families of Bausch & Lomb's founders. The firm dropped Optical from its title in 1961, reflecting its move into other technologies and measurements. Sales reached $70 million in 1962. The company moved into the school market, which was growing quickly and required inexpensive, rugged instruments. In 1963 the firm released a $12 microscope targeted at the elementary and secondary school market. The instrument, with features usually reserved for expensive models, was made of tough plastics. Bausch & Lomb released two additional school microscopes priced under $50. Company earnings were static for much of the 1960s, however, because low-margin ophthalmic products such as eyeglass lenses and frames still accounted for a sizable portion of its sales.

In 1966 Bausch & Lomb made its most important decision since World War II when it negotiated a license to make and sell contact lenses made from a fluid-absorbing hydrophilic plastic. The material had been invented in Czechoslovakia and Western Hemisphere rights were purchased by National Patent Development Corp., from whom Bausch & Lomb licensed them. Bausch & Lomb spent $3.3 million on research and development, learning how to make viable soft contact lenses from the material. Many people experienced so much discomfort with hard contact lenses that they refused to wear them. The company hoped soft contact lenses would garner a huge share of the contact lens market. Because the soft-contact lenses conformed to the shape of the cornea, people with irregularly shaped corneas initially could not wear them. Other problems cropped up, including eye infections. Further, the U.S. Food and Drug Administration (FDA) classified soft contact lenses as a drug, which meant that Bausch & Lomb's product encountered numerous regulatory hurdles. Nonetheless, many doctors greeted the new lenses with enthusiasm. The firm's Softlens contacts were released in 1971 and sold about 100,000 pairs that year.

Because of the excitement generated by soft contact lenses, Bausch & Lomb's stock tripled in value in less than a year and, at one point, sold for 75 times annual earnings. At that time, approximately 44 percent of Bausch & Lomb's sales came from scientific instruments, mostly optical instruments sold to medi-

cal, industrial, military, film, and educational customers. The company served as the major supplier of lenses for Xerox Corp.'s copy machines. Bausch & Lomb also sold consumer goods such as microscopes, binoculars, and rifle scopes.

By 1973 Softlens contact lenses accounted for 14 percent of company earnings and 51 percent of revenues. Bausch & Lomb had little competition and made roughly $14 per pair of contact lenses sold. The market for lenses was enormous; surveys found that more than 50 percent of Americans wore prescription glasses or contact lenses, and industry analysts predicted that large numbers of them might eventually get soft contact lenses. Yet the price of soft contacts—more than $300 including prescription and doctor's visit—held down sales. There was also slow acceptance of lenses among some doctors who had been offended by Bausch & Lomb's initial, high-pressure marketing. Additionally, certain doctors and lens wearers were disappointed with the slim selection of lenses offered. Bausch & Lomb worked hard to correct this, spending $3.5 million a year on Softlens research and development and hoping to offer at least five lenses. Despite these problems, trade sources estimated that 350,000 patients throughout the world bought Bausch & Lomb's soft contacts in 1973, and an additional 500,000 customers were added in 1974.

Competitors, however, were eager to enter such a large, untapped market. In 1974 Soft Lenses Inc. won FDA permission to produced soft lenses for vision correction. Warner-Lambert Co. received approval to produce lenses for therapeutic reasons and also applied to furnish vision-corrective lenses. Bausch & Lomb managed to maintain a large portion of its market share because of a three-year lead, name identification, and marketing strategies that reduced retailers inventory costs. The company also cut wholesale prices by 25 percent, reducing retail of lenses to between $25 and $30 a pair. Despite price cuts, soft lenses accounted for 27 percent of company sales in 1979 and 63 percent of profits. By 1979 Bausch & Lomb still had a 55 to 65 percent share of the soft contact lens market, which had grown to $400 million a year. The firm was also selling gallons of lens cleaning and soaking solutions. Its saline solution had a 56 percent market share, its lens lubricant had 50 percent, and its daily cleaner 32 percent. In 1979 Bausch & Lomb began a lens fitting system that allowed 90 percent of new lens wearers to be fit with the firm's new Ultra Thin lenses with a single visit. The company also introduced a prescription version of its AmberMatic sunglasses, that darkened as light levels increased.

In 1980 Daniel Gill, a former marketing specialist with Abbott Labs, became Bausch & Lomb's company chairman. He felt that the company was too dependent on contact lenses and too bloated by low-performance products. Gill restructured the company by selling off low-profit businesses. One of the first to go was prescription eyeglasses. Gill justified this change because the firm had missed a trend to plastic lenses and was also being pinched by cheaper imported lenses. Yet with its traditional business gone, the company went into an upheaval, and many top managers left.

The market for soft contact lenses continued to grow more competitive as it grew larger. By 1982 competitors included large companies such as Johnson & Johnson, Revlon, and Ciba-

Geigy. Although Bausch & Lomb continued to hold nearly half of the market, new competitors were introducing products Bausch & Lomb either did not have or had no lead on, such as gas-permeable hard lenses, extended-wear soft lenses, bifocal contacts and color-tinted contacts. The competitors pushed these products with expensive television advertising campaigns. While Bausch & Lomb's cost for producing soft-contacts had dropped to $1.50 to $2 each, American Hydron reported that it was nearly finished with a system that would produce contacts for $1.

Bausch & Lomb moved quickly into the extended-wear lens market, an area in which it had been losing new lens wearers. While waiting for FDA approval of its own lens, Bausch & Lomb leased an extended-wear system from American Medical Optics. The lenses were lathe cut, not spin cast like the Softlens, and cost $7 to $8 a pair to manufacture. When FDA approval came in 1984, Bausch & Lomb displayed its marketing power by supplying new lenses to 90 percent of the U.S. outlets selling contact lenses within a month. Within four months the company's extended-wear lenses had 37 percent of the market and stood as the leading brand. Part of that success came through aggressive pricing. The lenses wholesaled for $20 a pair, while the industry average was $30. As a result, Bausch & Lomb was soon embroiled in a price war with rival CooperVision.

Sunglasses sales were also improving. The firm had signed a $50,000-a-year agreement with Unique Product Placement in 1982 to feature Ray-Bans in films. The Ray-Ban Wayfarer line did particularly well. The company sold 16,000 pairs in 1982, but after Tom Cruise wore them in the 1983 film *Risky Business,* sales jumped to 360,000. Wayfarers were also worn by actors on the *Miami Vice* and *Moonlighting* television series. By 1986 sales reached 1.5 million, and Ray-Ban's 40 lines accounted for one-third of the $500 million U.S. market for premium sunglasses.

Meanwhile restructuring within Bausch & Lomb continued. In 1983 the company entered a new business when it bought the Charles River Laboratory, the world's largest supplier of laboratory mice and rats, for $108 million in stock. Though the business was not related to optics, it offered a steady supply of cash and operating profit margins of more than 20 percent. In 1984 most of the $217 million instrument business was sold to its management, except for microscopes and telescopes. The unit had lost $16 million over the two preceding years.

Bausch & Lomb earned $74.7 million on sales of $698.9 million in 1986, despite a leveling off of soft contact lens sales. The market was damaged by reports of people wearing extended-wear lenses and subsequently developing eye infections. The biggest market for contacts, women between the ages of 18 and 25, began shrinking. The firm fought to maintain sales and market share by introducing new contact lens technologies. In 1987 it won FDA approval to sell lenses with a Teflon-like surface that protected against protein buildup and made the lenses more comfortable. Bausch & Lomb also tried new marketing strategies such as introducing disposable contact lenses meant to be worn for a week or two and then thrown out. The primary difference between the disposable and regular soft lenses was the packaging, which was less expensive and durable for the disposables. Bausch & Lomb faced tough competition for this niche, however. Johnson & Johnson beat them to market by introducing its Acuvue lenses before Bausch & Lomb's SeeQuence.

Despite the leveling off of the contact lens market, Bausch & Lomb continued to expand by moving into businesses using similar distribution methods, especially ear, mouth, and skin care products. The company's strategy was to offer technologically advanced products that had few competitors and therefore high margins. Bausch & Lomb also began focusing on sales outside of the United States, an area which accounted for only 17 percent of sales in 1984. In 1986 the firm agreed to a joint venture with Beijing Contact Lens. Ltd. to produce contact lenses and solutions in China. Bausch & Lomb then bought Dr. Gerhard Mann Pharma, a ophthalmic drugs company based in West Germany, for $97 million. The firm also began designing and marketing products specifically for countries in Europe, Asia, and Latin America. For example, Bausch & Lomb had mainly sold adjustable metal-frame sunglasses in Japan because the firm's more popular plastic models did not offer comparable fit. In 1987 Bausch & Lomb redesigned its plastic sunglasses and sales took off.

In 1988 Bausch & Lomb bought Dental Research for $133 million. Included in this sale was Interplak, a patented, sophisticated electric toothbrush used to remove plaque. The device had been sold on the retail market, but Bausch & Lomb used dentists to let consumers know about it, and its sales climbed to approximately $110 million by 1989. In 1989 the firm acquired 80 percent of Voroba Hearing Systems, a maker of hearing aids. Bausch & Lomb also announced plans to introduce a line of sunglasses containing a synthetic version of melanin, the pigment that protects the skin from ultraviolet rays.

By 1990, sales outside of the United States accounted for 40 percent of the firm's total sales. When Bausch & Lomb began concentrating on international sales, it gave local managers more flexibility. One result was that European sales managers pushed for flashier styles of Ray-Ban sunglasses. These styles proved popular and fetched higher prices than in the United States. Partly due to this, operating income doubled in Europe between 1987 and 1990. In 1991 half of Ray-Ban's new styles were developed for international markets, and by 1992 Ray-Bans accounted for 40 percent of premium international sunglasses sales. Managers in China advised making contact lenses there inexpensive to make money from volume rather than sales margin. As a result, lens sales in China were third in the world in 1992, after the United States and Japan.

By the early 1990s, Gill's restructuring seemed a clear success. Sales were growing more than 10 percent a year, the company was expanding internationally and had moved away from its dependence on contact lens sales. The company's pharmaceuticals were beginning to pay off their start-up costs, and the firm's debt was relatively low. These factors, combined with the company's contact lens and sunglasses stronghold, have helped Bausch & Lomb Inc. hold its position as the number one ophthalmic goods firm in the United States.

Principal Subsidiaries: Charles River Laboratories, Inc.; Polymer Technology Corp.; Latin America Export Association.

Further Reading: "Long Grind," *Time,* January 24, 1938; "Optical Restraint of Trade?" *Time,* April 8, 1940; "Bausch & Lomb," *Fortune,* October 1940; "Getting One-Up on the Japanese," *Business Week,* October 19, 1963; Du Bois, Peter C., "The Old Fish Eye," *Barron's,* November 25, 1974; "Back in Focus," *Financial World,* November 1, 1979; Reynes, Roberta, "New Contact Lens Competition Focuses on Bausch & Lomb," *Barron's,* August 1, 1983; Troxell, Thomas N., Jr., "Broader Focus," *Barron's,* August 18, 1986; Benoit, Ellen, "Through a Glass, Slowly," *Financial World,* November 28, 1989; "Bausch & Lomb: Hardball Pricing Helps it to Regain its Grip on Contact Lenses," *Business Week,* July 16, 1984; Leinster, Colin, "A Tale of Mice and Lens," *Fortune,* September 28, 1987; Hirsch, James S., "Bausch & Lomb Applies an Above-the Neck Strategy," *Wall Street Journal,* February 27, 1990; Jacob, Rahul, "Trust the Locals, Win Worldwide," *Fortune,* May 4, 1992.

—Scott Lewis

BETHLEHEM STEEL CORPORATION

Bethlehem, Pennsylvania 18016
U.S.A.
(215) 694-2424
Fax: (215) 694-5743

Public Company
Incorporated: 1904
Employees: 22,000
Sales: $4.0 billion
Stock Exchanges: New York Midwest
SICs: 3312 Blast Furnaces & Steel Mills; 3731 Ship
   Building & Repairing; 3443 Fabricated Plate Work—
   Boiler Shops; 3317 Steel Pipe & Tubes

Bethlehem Steel Corporation is the second-largest integrated steel producer in the United States, with control of supply sources, production, and distribution, from raw materials to products. The company manufactures and sells a wide variety of steel-mill products. Bethlehem also is involved in the repair of ships and offshore-drilling-platform businesses and in the manufacture of forgings and castings. The company is the nation's number one supplier of steel to the domestic construction industry.

The company began operations in 1857 as the Saucona Iron Company in South Bethlehem, Pennsylvania. Its primary business was the rolling of iron railroad rails. In 1899, after broadening the product line to include heavy forging for electric generators, tool steels for metal cutting, and armor plate for U.S. Navy ships, the company's name was changed to the Bethlehem Steel Company.

Bethlehem Steel Corporation was incorporated in December of 1904 by Charles M. Schwab, a former Andrew Carnegie disciple and first president of United States Steel Corporation (U.S. Steel). Schwab left U.S. Steel over difficulties that he felt inhibited his freedom to run the company properly. At its incorporation the company included Bethlehem Steel, a Cuban iron ore mine, and several shipbuilding concerns in California and Delaware. Schwab became president and chairman of the board.

Soon after the formation of the company, Schwab hired an electrical engineer, Eugene G. Grace, whose management skills allowed the more entrepreneurial Schwab the freedom he needed to plan the growth of the company. Together, the two men became the team that built Bethlehem from a small producer with an ingot capacity of less that one percent of the national total in 1905 to the world's second-largest producer in fewer than 35 years.

In 1908 the two men staked the company's future on a new type of mill invented by Henry Grey. It was capable of rolling a wide flange structural steel section that was stronger, lighter, and less expensive than the fabricated steel sections that were being used at the time. The gamble paid off for Bethlehem. The wide-flange section made it possible to build skyscrapers and modern cities.

In the years preceding World War I, the company acquired an interest in a Chilean iron ore mine with ore of a higher quality than available from the U.S. upper-Great Lakes region. As a result of the acquisition, the company built a fleet of ore carriers and entered the ocean transportation business. With the outbreak of the war, Bethlehem became a business of international scope, building warships for Great Britain at the company's shipyards. Bethlehem also filled orders for guns and munitions, armor, and ordnance placed by the British, French, and Russians. In the process of contributing to the Allied cause in Europe, Bethlehem created a financial base that would help in expanding the company's steelmaking facilities.

Grace was named president of the company in 1916, with Schwab staying on as chairman of the board. In that same year, bolstered by wartime profits, Bethlehem acquired American Iron and Steel Manufacturing Company, Pennsylvania Steel Company, and Maryland Steel Company. In the years following World War I, the company continued its growth with the acquisition of Lackawanna Steel & Ordnance Company, Midvale Steel and Ordnance Company, and Cambria Steel Company. In the years preceding the Great Depression, the company boosted its steelmaking capacity to 8.5 million tons and employed more than 60,000 people.

Bethlehem's growth was tied to an incentive program from which its upper management profited handsomely. In 1929 Grace received a bonus in excess of $1.6 million, or about 3.3 percent of earnings. The policy of paying out such large awards to its executives eventually caused problems. In early 1931 a group of stockholders filed suit against Schwab and 12 other officers of the company, charging that the bonus program constituted a misuse of company funds. The suit asked that a total of $36 million in bonuses distributed since 1911 be returned to the company's coffers. The action resulted in the formation of the Protective Committee for Stockholders of Bethlehem Steel Corporation, a watchdog group that sought the elimination of the bonus program in its existing form. Though no funds were returned to the company, the suit was settled in July of 1931, about six months after it was filed. The settlement resulted in a new policy that included the publication of executive bonuses in the company's annual reports and a revised executive salary and bonus package. In subsequent years labor unions used the bonus issue in their demands for higher compensation and benefits for the rank-and-file steelworkers.

The 1920s were years of growth for Bethlehem. In the early years of the Great Depression, the company weathered the economic storm and continued to improve its production plants and introduce new products. The Depression caught up with Bethlehem in September of 1931 when the company posted a quarterly loss for the first time since 1909. In the face of a stagnant economy and an eroding demand for steel products, the company had overexpanded and was forced to shut down many of its facilities, including a newly constructed, jumbo-sized open hearth at the Sparrows Point, Maryland, plant. Bethlehem, along with other major steel producers, struggled through the Depression. Help arrived with President Franklin D. Roosevelt's New Deal and the National Industrial Recovery Act of 1933. The government suspended antitrust laws, and the steel industry established codes approved by the National Recovery Administration providing for labor reform, workers rights to organize, minimum wages, and maximum work hours. In December of 1933 Bethlehem reported a modest net profit in excess of $600,000 after nine quarters totaling more than $30 million in losses.

During the 1930s Bethlehem acquired steelmaking plants in Los Angeles and San Francisco, California, and Seattle, Washington. McClintic-Marshall, a large fabricator and builder of bridges, was also purchased, enabling Bethlehem to participate in the construction of San Francisco's Golden Gate Bridge. Through this subsidiary, Bethlehem was also involved in the construction of other large bridges and notable buildings, including Rockefeller Plaza and the Waldorf Astoria Hotel in New York City; the Chicago Merchandise Mart; and the U.S. Supreme Court Building in Washington, D.C.

During the mid-1930s Bethlehem went through an expensive retooling. With the largest capital expenditure since before the Depression, the company spent approximately $20 million on the construction of a continuous strip and tin-plate mill at Sparrows Point. A primary reason for the new project was beer. After six years of research and development, the American Can Company had produced a coated tin can suitable for packaging beer, and the tin-plate market exploded.

Schwab died in September of 1939, leaving Bethlehem under the tight controls of Grace. With U.S. involvement in World War II imminent, Grace geared the company's entire capacity toward war production. Furnaces, shops, and mills worked around the clock producing armor plate for ships and structural steel for defense plants, munitions, and aircraft engines. Between 1941 and 1944 Grace pushed production at Bethlehem to 101 percent of usual capacity. During the war, the company's 15 shipyards produced more than 1,100 ships, including aircraft carriers, destroyers, heavy cruisers, and cargo ships. In 1943 alone the company built 380 vessels.

During World War II, from 1940 to 1945, Bethlehem produced more than 73 million tons of steel. This total represented almost one-third of the armor plate and gun forgings used by the United States in the war. Prior to the U.S. entrance into the war, the company's gross sales were $135 million. In 1945 sales topped $1.33 billion, with more than 300,000 employees. Bethlehem became a global giant in the steel industry. In December of 1945, six years after the death of Schwab, Grace was elected the company's chairman. Arthur B. Homer, director of the Bethlehem's wartime shipbuilding program, became president.

With the war's end, the global demand for steel was even greater than during the conflict. Consumer demands for new cars and household goods, along with the massive amounts of structural steel needed to rebuild war-torn economies, resulted in further expansion. Bethlehem built new furnaces and mills at many of its plants and by the late 1950s was capable of producing 23 million tons annually. The nature of the company's shipbuilding business began to change as Bethlehem produced larger, longer cargo ships. Forerunners to supertankers, the new ships produced by Bethlehem cost less per unit, carried more tonnage, and were able to cruise at speeds 30 percent faster than their prewar predecessors. More iron ore was delivered in less time. In 1957, Bethlehem's peak postwar production year, the company made more than 19 million tons of steel and earned $190 million on sales of $2.6 billion. At the close of the decade, Bethlehem's full-time postwar employee roster stood at 165,000.

In 1960 the United States imported more steel than it exported for the first time in the American steel industry's history. This situation was a harbinger. The deterioration of Bethlehem's enterprises, as well as those of other U.S. steel manufacturers, can be traced to several major factors. High wages, foreign competition, and the enormous costs of environmental clean-up of the lands and waters around the company's many production plants cut deeply into the company's profits and cash reserves. In addition, decades of unlimited growth, expansion, and profits had made Bethlehem's leadership complacent. Antitrust and price fixing suits against several U.S. steel giants including Bethlehem followed. Throughout the 1960s and 1970s, company leaders believed that procedures could continue as they had been for over a half century without change in processes or structure.

Bethlehem's leaders did not engage in product research, innovation, or reorganization. The company, like its competitors, relied on continual price increases to protect profits. These policies allowed opportunities for entrance into the U.S. market by Japanese and other foreign steelmakers, who rebuilt their steel industries after World War II and captured the competitive edge worldwide. This new competition, a shrinking domestic market, and the expansion of steel substitutes such as aluminum and plastics, created a still-existent threat to Bethlehem's future. Following Grace's death in 1960, Homer, the company's new chairman, committed the company to a $3 billion modernization and expansion program. The old mentality still prevailed as the company pushed to produce more tonnage. Bigger still seemed to be better.

Two important factors permitted Bethlehem to sustain its business and expansion through the early 1970s. First, pressure was put on the U.S. government to limit the amount of foreign steel allowed into the country. Early in 1969 the State Department persuaded Japanese and European steel producers voluntarily to cut their imports to the United States by 25 percent. The second factor that helped sustain Bethlehem during the 1970s was the Vietnam War, which stimulated production in all sectors of the U.S. economy. Bethlehem again pushed for more production and higher steel prices. After the price of steel rose steeply in 1969, the administration of President Richard Nixon instituted price controls on steel in August of 1971.

The company faced growing competition from mini-mills. These small operations challenged the premise that the steel business had to be huge and integrated to survive. Using scrap metal melted down in electric furnaces, the small operations were capable of producing simple iron and steel products at a much lower cost than the large steelmakers. In light of increased competition, the company chose to grow with the construction of a huge blast furnace at Sparrows Point. Named Big L, it was built at a cost of $275 million. The furnace began operations three years after the end of the early-1970s boom years and one year after the company had shown a net operating loss of over $448 million. Bethlehem Steel was in trouble.

Drastic action was needed to save the company. In 1980 Donald Trautlein, Bethlehem's controller, was named chairman. Trautlein began to cut away at the company's cost of doing business. The company possessed outmoded production plants, steep labor costs, rising foreign and domestic competition, and eroding profits at a time when the steel industry was experiencing the worst downturn in more than 50 years. Trautlein had other problems as well. He knew little about the business of steelmaking; he felt that most of Bethlehem's problems were due to external forces beyond the company's control. Trautlein chose first to diversify, then to remain exclusively in the steel business, and then began a diversification that was not completed.

The company's new chairman began cutting costs at the top. Salaries were cut by 20 percent over a four-year period. Lump-sum retirement packages were offered to employees over the age of 55; vacations were cut back; and by the fall of 1982, 13 upper echelon executives had taken early retirement. These measures were accompanied by mass firings and layoffs. Further cutbacks eliminated such perquisites as company limousines and drivers, security forces for executives' homes, and a fleet of jet airplanes. By 1984, the number of Bethlehem employees had shrunk by almost 50 percent. Trautlein replaced some of the executive-level positions made vacant with professional managers who had little or no experience in the steel business; many positions were left unfilled.

The company also began the liquidation of some subsidiaries. During the 1980s, 11 of the company's operations were sold. In that same period, Bethlehem began to consolidate many of its steelmaking operations by closing marginal facilities and modernizing aging plants. The company closed its West Coast steel plants and scaled back shipbuilding operations, and in 1983 steelmaking was discontinued at the Lackawanna plant.

Between 1982 and 1985 the company posted losses of $1.9 billion. Under pressure and criticism, Trautlein resigned in 1986. He was replaced by the company's president, Walter F. Williams, who had more than 30 years of experience in the business. Williams was faced with a downward momentum that would be difficult to reverse. The company's stock hovered around an all-time low of $4 per share.

Williams instituted a campaign to improve and revitalize Bethlehem's basic steel business. He began by selling off the assets that were not related to steel. He smoothed relations with both customers and suppliers and persuaded bankers to stay with the company. Slowly, Williams's program began to make a difference. For the year ending December 31, 1987, the company reported more than $174 million in profits compared to a net loss of over $150 million the previous year. In 1988 the company increased its sales volume another 18 percent over 1987 sales figures and reported record earnings of more than $400 million. Two important problems were solved in 1989. First, a 50-month labor contract that included cost-of-living increases and profit sharing was signed with the United Steelworkers. Second, the U.S. government's steel-trade-liberalization program with other countries extended voluntary restraint arrangements previously negotiated with other countries by President Ronald Reagan's administration. In 1990 and 1991 Bethlehem worked at increasing its market share in products that produced higher profit margins. Further, the company focused on modernization and the development of high-technology production methods, and increased research and development into new products and processes.

The severe recession of the early 1990s, though, affected Bethlehem earlier than most American industries, dampening the effects of management's determined modernization and streamlining efforts. Steel prices and domestic demand sank to all-time lows. With the capacity to produce 16 million tons of steel annually, Bethlehem produced only eight million tons in 1991. Unfortunately, the economic recession also exacerbated longstanding problems of the company, such as high employment costs and, in particular, skyrocketing health insurance costs (two to three times higher than that of foreign steel competitors). By the end of 1991 Bethlehem posted a $191 million loss.

Under the leadership of Chairman and CEO Williams, Bethlehem forged ahead with $564 million worth of capital expenses for the modernization of Sparrows Point, improvement of flat rolled operations at the Burns Harbor plant, and completion of a new galvanizing line for the production of coated sheet products. In 1991, the worst year of the recession, such leading automotive companies as Ford, Mazda, and Nissan presented the Burns Harbor plant with outstanding quality awards.

Restructuring continued: Bethlehem sold its Freight Car Division and most of its coal properties. The company discontinued the manufacture of trackwork at its Steelton, Pennsylvania, plant as well as its coke production operations at its Sparrows Point, Maryland, plant. These capital outlays and structural changes were all part of management's comprehensive plan (which was approved by the board of directors in January of 1992) to revitalize Bethlehem during the recession. The plan also called for the elimination of the quarterly stock dividend and a reduction in the work force by 6,500 employees. The leaner, more streamlined company weathered the storm, just as it had in previous and even more severe economic downturns. By 1993, Bethlehem had recovered its 12 percent domestic market share and had become a world producer of coated sheet products for both the construction industry and domestic and U.S.-based foreign automobile companies.

Demand for steel has increased steadily and is likely to spiral, especially in view of the federal government's plan to invest billions of dollars in upgrading the nation's infrastructure of bridges (40 percent of 576,000 bridges are in need of serious repairs), highways (60 percent of 1.1 million miles of highway in need of repair), and public transportation systems. With serious attention being paid by the federal government to rising health care costs, this financial drain on the company eventually will be significantly reduced before the end of the decade.

With a return to profitability, Bethlehem is the biggest low-cost steel producer in the United States. The company also boasts thoroughly modern, world-class facilities for producing steel—especially high quality flat rolled sheets, a product that holds great future promise and that already accounts for 80 percent of the company's sales. Getting Bethlehem back on track has been the major accomplishment of recently retired Chairman Williams. The challenge for the incoming CEO and Chairman Curtis H. Barnette, former top counsel in Bethlehem's legal department, will be not only to maintain this record but to make Bethlehem the number one steelmaker on the domestic scene.

Principal Subsidiaries: Bethlehem Hibbing Corp.; Bethlehem Mines Corp.; Bethlehem Steel International Corp.

Further Reading: Fisher, Douglas Alan, *The Epic of Steel,* New York, Harper & Row, 1963; Strohmeyer, John, *Crisis in Bethlehem: Big Steel's Struggle to Survive,* Bethesda, Maryland, Adler & Adler, 1986; Reutter, Mark, *Sparrows Point: Making Steel—the Rise and Ruin of American Industrial Might,* New York, Summit Books, 1988; Hessen, Robert, *Steel Titan: The Life of Charles M. Schwab,* Pittsburgh, University of Pittsburgh Press, 1990; *A Brief History of Bethlehem Steel,* Bethlehem, Pennsylvania, Bethlehem Steel Corporation, 1990; Annual Report: Bethlehem Steel, 1991; Woutat, Donald, "Restructured Steel Firms Face New Problems," *Los Angeles Times,* February 9, 1992; McQueen, Rod, "U.S. Charges Likely Against Canada's Steel," *Financial Post,* June 30, 1992; Cotter, Wes, "Still Suffering U.S. Steel Producers Seek Relief from Product Dumping," *Pittsburgh Business Times & Journal,* July 6, 1992; Kleiner, Kurt, "Steel Companies Crying Foul," *Baltimore Business Journal,* July 10, 1992; Prizinsky, David, "Steel Firms Benefit as Bethlehem Drops Lines," *Crain's Cleveland Business,* July 20, 1992; Ritz, Joseph P, "Bethlehem Workers Eye Bleak Future as Bar Mill Closes in Lackawanna," *Buffalo News,* September 26, 1992; "Steel Makers Unite to Seek Higher Flat-Rolled Prices," *Cincinnati Enquirer,* October 9, 1992; Scolieri, Peter, "Walter F. Williams Takes Union Regret into his Retirement," *American Metal Market,* October 27, 1992.

—William R. Grossman
updated by Sina Dubovoj

BRITISH BROADCASTING CORPORATION

Broadcasting House
London, W1A 1AA
England
(071) 580-4468
Fax: (071) 637-1630

State-Owned Company
Incorporated: 1922 as British Broadcasting Company
    Limited
Employees: 27,000
Sales: £1.55 billion (US$2.25 billion)
SICs: 4832 Radio Broadcasting Stations; 4833 Television
    Broadcasting Stations

The British Broadcasting Corporation (BBC) is a public service broadcasting corporation that broadcasts within and from the United Kingdom. The corporation's domestic services consist of two national color television channels, five national radio networks, regional television and radio services, and 38 local radio stations throughout England, Scotland, Wales, and Northern Ireland. Domestic operations are financed largely through the sale of television licenses to households with at least one television set. In February of 1993, the price of a color license was £80 ($116), among the lowest in Europe. Additional funding for U.K. programming comes from the BBC Enterprises Group, the commercial arm of the Corporation which includes such profitable and renowned subsidiaries as BBC Video and BBC Books. The BBC World Service, on the other hand, is financed directly through grants-in-aid provided by the British Government on the understanding that editorial control over all broadcasts remains firmly within the BBC.

The BBC derives its authority from a royal charter granting it the right to operate throughout the United Kingdom. Because the charter is issued by the British monarch and not by a political party, the BBC's independence and impartiality are constitutionally guaranteed. The terms and conditions under which the BBC operates its transmitters and technical apparatus are embodied in a second document, the BBC License, issued by the home secretary (the government minister responsible for broadcasting). The license prohibits the corporation from carrying advertising or allowing sponsorship of any kind. In theory the license also allows the home secretary to veto broadcasts which are deemed inappropriate, but this right has never been exercised. The BBC is governed by a 12-person board of governors appointed by the monarch in consultation with a council of senior politicians from the main political parties in the United Kingdom and the British Commonwealth. It is the responsibility of the board to safeguard the public interest by ensuring that the BBC's output reflect the uncompromising standards enshrined in its constitution. The governors in turn appoint a director-general and other experienced industry executives to oversee the day-to-day operations of the BBC. Governors and management are jointly responsible for policy and general strategy decisions.

Throughout its history, the BBC has been characterized by an emphasis on enhancing the public good through quality programming and impartial news coverage. By 1992, domestic BBC programs were being purchased by broadcasters in more than 100 countries, while the BBC World Service was offering radio news service in 38 languages. With its reputation for high quality and reliability, the BBC has come to be regarded as the standard for public broadcasting worldwide.

The history of this august institution parallels the history of broadcasting itself. The British Broadcasting Company Limited, as it was originally known, came into being on October 18, 1922. It represented a collaboration between leading radio manufacturers—such as the Marconi Company and the General Post Office (GPO)—that wanted to introduce a national service in Britain while preventing any individual manufacturer from gaining monopoly power. The new company had a share capital of £100,000, shares being allotted only to "genuine British manufacturers employing genuine British labor," and generated income in two ways. It was entitled to half of the Post Office license fee of ten shillings (75 cents) and would receive royalties on the sale of radio transceivers made by member companies. The license was introduced on November 1, 1922. By December 31 of the same year, 35,744 licenses had been issued.

On the evening of November 14, 1922, Arthur Burrows the company's first director of programs, read two news bulletins from Marconi House in London. These were the first daily transmissions at the BBC. The following day, radio stations opened in Manchester and Birmingham, and by the end of the month, British radio enthusiasts could tune into five hours of broadcasting daily. Despite the fact that the original broadcasters had little experience in the field—or perhaps because of it—the standards they established in both news service and children's programming set the tone for decades to come. Their success partially due to the influence of John C. Reith who, at the age of 33, became the company's first general manager. Reith was a Scottish war veteran with a background in engineering and a clear vision of what public broadcasting could achieve if run by an idealistic team. He determined company policy and dictated the program mix. In Reith's first year at the helm, programming expanded to include outside broadcasts of opera and theater, daily weather forecasts and live commentaries of sporting events. To keep track of this range of programs, the BBC published a guide called the *Radio Times,* that included scheduling information, commentaries, and articles on the development of the new medium. By the end of 1923, an experimental broadcast had reached America, and a Radiola Paris transmission had been relayed to listeners in the south of England. Meanwhile, the number of U.K. stations operated by the BBC had increased to ten while the number of employees had risen from four in December of 1922 to 177 in December of the following year.

The number of stations grew over the next few years, as did the power of broadcasting. During the general strike of May 1926, publication of most newspapers was suspended for a week. During this time, the BBC increased its daily news broadcasts to five, becoming the sole medium of mass communication in many parts of the country. Although government pressure prevented the BBC from interviewing striking miners on the air, Reith campaigned successfully to maintain the company's editorial independence with respect to reporting on strike developments. The BBC's position was strengthened on January 1, 1927, when the British Broadcasting Company became the British Broadcasting Corporation, established under a new royal charter guaranteeing that it was not "a creature of Parliament and connected with political activity." The motto of the new company was "And nation shall speak peace unto nation." Sir John Reith was appointed director-general, a post he maintained until 1938. The postmaster general (the chief executive of the Post Office) continued to collect license fees from the public and place restrictions on permitted broadcasting hours, but policy making responsibility was transferred to a five-person board of governors, a tradition which continues to the present day. During the depression years of 1930–31, 1000 licenses per day were issued, and by 1935 an estimated 95 percent of the population were able to receive at least one BBC program in their homes. Complete reception coverage was a guiding principle of the BBC, and indeed it was perhaps among the poorest classes and in the most remote regions of the country that the service was most appreciated. It was also during this period that the first foreign-language broadcasts were made from Bush House in London. An Arabic service was inaugurated in January of 1938, to be followed two months later by service in Portuguese and Spanish.

Television service had a more difficult birth. The BBC had been experimenting with television broadcasts since 1932 and, in November of 1936, was able to launch the world's first high-definition black-and-white service under the leadership of director of television Gerald Cock. During the first three years, the prohibitive cost of television sets limited the number of viewers to 20,000, but the range of programming was impressive and foreshadowed the tremendous influence which television would exert in the postwar years. Among the events covered by fledgling BBC Television was the coronation of King George VI and Queen Elizabeth and a performance of *Macbeth* with Laurence Olivier in the title role. On September 1, 1939, however, television broadcasts ceased. The television transmitter at Alexandra Palace in London was a perfect aircraft direction finder, and, for national security reasons, the service remained off the air for the duration of World War II. The BBC reopened in June of 1946, when 100,000 viewers in the greater London area watched a broadcast of the victory parade celebrating the end of the war, and reached a high point on June 2, 1953 with the historic televising of Elizabeth II's coronation inside Westminster Abbey.

BBC radio had a tremendous impact with its informative broadcasts during the war years. Its influence was felt far beyond the borders of the United Kingdom; it was in foreign-language broadcasts to the occupied territories that the Overseas Service came into its own. The BBC approach to news reporting was captured succinctly by R. T. Clark, director of foreign news, who told his augmented news staff: "It's war now ... tell the truth ... that's our job ... thanks very much and good luck." Meanwhile, on the domestic front, home broadcasting stations were restricted to a single wavelength named the Home Service, which introduced innovative if still rather high-brow programming in a supreme effort to boost the country's morale through the early war years. In January of 1940, a second program was introduced with the aim of lifting the morale of British troops stationed overseas. Attractions such as popular American variety stars quickly helped the Forces Program secure a huge civilian audience in Britain. At the end of the war the Forces Program was renamed the Light Program, becoming the BBC's first formal admission that frivolity had a permanent place in the radio schedule.

By 1946 a combined radio and television license was being offered for £2 ($2.90), and the Home and Light Programs had been supplemented with the addition of a third program, designed to meet what was controversially perceived as "the virtually insatiable demand for serious literature and drama, for good music and intelligent discussion." Classical music fans in particular benefited from the change. In 1947 the BBC was granted a third royal charter and, in spite of fuel shortages which led to the temporary suspension of all television service and some radio service, continued to expand the geographical scope and variety of its operations.

In 1950 the number of permanent employees at the BBC topped 12,000, and new television studios were opened at Lime Grove in London. In the same year, the Beveridge Committee on Broadcasting published a lengthy report which upheld the BBC's right to exercise a broadcasting monopoly. In 1951, however, the Labour government of the austere postwar period was replaced by a Conservative government which deplored nationalization and stressed the importance of the free market in raising Britain's depressed standard of living. As unemployment rates continued to fall and demand for consumer goods soared, and public debate focused on television as a legitimate medium for advertising the exciting new products. The Television Act of 1954, sponsored by the Conservative government, broke the BBC's television monopoly. As a direct consequence of the Television Act, an Independent Television Authority (ITA) was formed, and on September 22, 1955, the first commercial broadcast went on the air. Although advertising was now permitted on independent stations, it remained strictly regulated, and most analyses of the first decade of independent television focus on the many similarities between the ITA and the BBC, rather than on their differences.

Meanwhile, television technology was also developing apace. In October of 1955 the first experimental color television transmissions began from Alexandra Palace in London. By this point, approximately 95 percent of the population could receive television at home. Program hours were increased accordingly, from 38 hours per week in 1954 to 50 hours a week in 1955. A new emphasis was placed on regional broadcasts and regional offices were given greater programming autonomy. Outside broadcasts, too, became more adventurous. In October of 1959, for example, the popular astronomy program *Sky at Night* included photographs taken by a Russian spacecraft on the far side of the moon. These innovations were achieved at a price, and, as concern about the financing of the BBC mounted, the government took the unusual step in 1963 of abolishing the excise duty on the television license and allowing the BBC to keep the full £4 fee. One result of this improvement in finances was the introduction in April of 1964 of the second television channel BBC2, which was described by Director-General Hugh Greene as a "complement rather than a competitor" to BBC1. Greene was a controversial figure, much criticized by more conservative elements in the press for encouraging irreverent satire and populist drama at a time when the BBC was supposed to provide an alternative to the commercialism of the independent channel. However, BBC2 quickly established itself as a forum for minority and specialized programming in much the same way as the Third Program had done for radio listeners eighteen years previously. Initially available in the London region only, transmission capability spread in a few years to all corners of the United Kingdom.

In July of 1967, BBC2 followed the American lead, and became the first European television station to offer regular color television service using the PAL system. The success of the color venture led to the introduction of a supplementary £5 license fee in 1968, with color service being extended to BBC1 and the independent channel in November of 1969. A parallel development was the spread of stereo VHF radio stations throughout the United Kingdom. In keeping with the enhanced broadcast capabilities of the VHF system, the BBC introduced a fourth radio network in 1967 that was devoted to popular music and named it Radio 1. The existing networks became Radios 2, 3, and 4 respectively. A fifth radio network would open in August 1990.

By the 1970s many critics felt that in its determination to maintain audience viewing figures, the venerable "Beeb," as it was affectionately known, was producing lowbrow, rather than substantial, programs. Representatives of the corporation pointed to a long list of award-winning shows in rebuttal of this argument. Of graver concern to BBC executives was the company's long-term financial health. In 1975 expenditure exceeded income for the first time. A series of highly publicized budget cuts at the BBC in the early 1980s highlighted the relative financial strength of the big commercial networks, that were now producing lavish period pieces like *Brideshead Revisited,* once the BBC's exclusive preserve. Commercial television was also beginning to take the initiative in new kinds of programming. The introduction of breakfast time television on the BBC in January of 1983, for example, was a response to a similar venture on the commercial network.

In the summer of 1985, an incident occurred which focused attention on the BBC's accountability to the British government. At the center of the controversy was a BBC documentary about Northern Ireland titled *At the Edge of the Union* that featured an interview with the alleged chief of staff of the Provisional IRA. Several days before the program was due to be screened, the board of governors of the BBC bowed to pressure from Leon Brittan, the home secretary, to withdraw the documentary on the grounds that it offered a legitimate platform to terrorism. This decision led to a disagreement with the corporation's director-general, Alasdair Milne, who objected to what he viewed as unacceptable levels of censorship both within and external to the BBC. Journalists at the Home Services and the World Service staged a one-day strike in protest, and, when colleagues at the rival commercial network walked out in sympathy, news coverage in the United Kingdom was effectively suspended for the day. The strike ended when the director-general announced that *At the Edge of the Union* would be broadcast at a future date with some minor explanatory additions. The offending interview would not be cut.

The effect of this incident on morale within the BBC and on the corporation's reputation worldwide was considerable. The timing of the controversy was also unfortunate, since Leon Brittan had recently appointed a committee under the chairmanship of professor Alan Peacock to look into financing options for the BBC. The Peacock report was published in July of 1986. It firmly rejected the idea of introducing advertising, a stance strongly supported in the press. On the other hand, the criticisms in the report did inspire a new set of guidelines for producers, giving them much greater flexibility in financing their productions. The following year, the company's commercial activities were expanded with the creation of BBC Subscription Television Limited as a fully owned subsidiary of BBC Enterprises. BBCSTV, a provider of late-night niche subscription services, was a timely response to fundamental changes in the structure of the broadcasting industry. A second BBC initiative was realized in April of 1991 with the launch of BBC World Service Television Limited in Europe. Designed as a self-funding cable subscription service, World Service Television offered 18 ten-minute international news bulletins a day, in addition to highlights from the domestic services produced by BBC1 and BBC2. In November of 1991 World Service Television was extended to Asia, a market with an estimated 170 million English speakers. This new venture was especially popular in India, where early reports indicated that it was watched by seven times as many people as CNN.

With the sixth royal charter up for renewal in 1996, the BBC entered the 1990s engaged in much soul-searching. Sixteen task forces were appointed and spent a year looking at the entire scope of BBC operations from the inside. The result was an 88-page document titled "Extending Choice—The BBC's Role in the New Broadcasting Age," that highlighted the BBC's arguments for charter renewal. In summarizing the document, the chairman identified three factors that he believed were crucial to the corporation's future success: efficiency, accountability, and, above all, a "robust spirit of independence from political pressures and commercial interests." Only if all three areas were addressed, he continued, could one of the most highly regarded broadcasting companies in the world continue to fulfill its historic commitment to public service.

Principal Subsidiaries: BBC Enterprises Limited; BBC World Service Television Limited; BBC Subscription Television Limited; BBC Investments Limited; Opinion and Broadcasting Research (OBR) Limited; Lionheart Television International Incorporated (USA); BBC Telecordiale (SARL) (France); Redwood Publishing Limited (77.5%); World Publications Limited (76%); Hartog Hutton Publishing Limited; Video

World Publishing Limited; Ealing Studios Limited; BBC Enterprises (Investments) Limited.

Further Reading: Black, Peter, *The Biggest Aspidistra in the World,* '' London, British Broadcasting Corporation, 1972; Trethowen, Ian, ''Turning Point at the BBC,'' *World Press Review,* August 1980; Antcliffe, John, ''Politics of the Airwaves,'' *History Today,* March 1984; Briggs, Asa, *The BBC: The First Fifty Years,* Oxford, Oxford University Press, 1985; Leapman, Michael, *The Last Days of the Beeb,* London, Allen & Unwin, 1986; McDonnell, J., *Public Service Broadcasting: A Reader,* London, Routledge, 1991; *Guide to the BBC 1992,* London, British Broadcasting Corporation, 1992; *This Is the BBC,* London, British Broadcasting Corporation, April 1992.

—Moya Verzhbinsky

BRITISH PETROLEUM COMPANY PLC

1 Finsbury Circus
London EC2M 7BA
United Kingdom
(071) 496-4000
Fax: (071) 496-5656

Public Company
Incorporated: 1909 as Anglo-Persian Oil Company
Employees: 115,250
Sales: £37.65 billion (US$54.59 billion)
Stock Exchanges: London New York Toronto Tokyo Paris
    Zürich Amsterdam Frankfurt
SICs: 1311 Crude Petroleum & Natural Gas; 1221
    Bituminous Coal and Lignite Surface Mining; 2911
    Petroleum Refining; 2048 Prepared Feed and Feed
    Ingredients for Animals and Fowls, Except Dogs and Cats;
    6719 Offices of Holding Companies, Nec

British Petroleum (BP) is one of the world's leading oil companies, and the United Kingdom's largest corporation. The company, which was the pioneer of the Middle Eastern oil industry, discovered oil in Iran before World War I and eventually became involved in all aspects of oil exploration, production, refining, transportation, and marketing. It has significant interests in chemicals and plastics, including a range of specialty products—mostly detergents, advanced composite materials, and advanced ceramic engineered materials.

BP has its origins in the activities of William Knox D'Arcy, who had made a fortune in Australian mining, and who in 1901 secured a concession from the reigning shah to explore for petroleum throughout almost all of the Persian empire. The search for oil proved extremely costly and difficult, since Persia was devoid of infrastructure and politically unstable. Within a few years D'Arcy was in need of capital. Eventually, after intercession by members of the British Admiralty, the Burmah Oil Company joined D'Arcy in a Concessionary Oil Syndicate in 1905 and supplied further funds in return for operational control. In May of 1908 oil was discovered in the southwest of Persia at Masjid-i-Suleiman. This was the first oil discovery in the Middle East. The following April the Anglo-Persian Oil Company was formed, with the Burmah Oil Company holding most of the shares.

The dominant figure in the early years of the Anglo-Persian Oil Company was Charles Greenway. Greenway's career had begun in the firm of managing agents who handled the marketing of Burmah Oil's products in India. He was invited by Burmah Oil to help in the formation of Anglo-Persian Oil. He became a founding director, was appointed managing director in 1910, and took the position of chairman in 1914. The first few years of the company's existence were extremely difficult, and it was largely through Greenway's skill that it survived as an independent entity. Although Anglo-Persian Oil had located a prolific oil field, there were major problems in refining the crude oil. The company also lacked a tanker fleet and a distribution network to sell its products.

For a time it seemed that Anglo-Persian Oil would be absorbed by one of the larger oil companies, such as the Royal Dutch/Shell group, with whom it signed a ten-year marketing agreement in 1912. But in 1914 Greenway preserved the independence of Anglo-Persian Oil by a unique agreement with the British government. Under the terms of this agreement negotiated with Winston Churchill, then first lord of the Admiralty, Greenway signed a long-term contract with the British Admiralty for the supply of fuel oil, which the Royal Navy wished to use as a replacement for coal.

At the same time, in an unusual departure from the United Kingdom's laissez-faire traditions, the British government invested £2 million in Anglo-Persian Oil, receiving in return a majority shareholding that it would retain for many years. The transaction provided the company with funds for further investment in refining equipment and an initial investment in transport and marketing in fulfillment of Greenway's ambition to create an independent, integrated oil business. In return for its investment, the British government was allowed to appoint two directors to the company's board with powers of veto, which could not, however, be exercised over commercial affairs. In fact, the government directors never used their veto throughout the period of state shareholding in the company. Despite the fact that Anglo-Persian Oil was nominally state controlled until the 1980s, in practice it functioned as a purely commercial company.

World War I created considerable opportunities for the fledgling enterprise. Although within Persia the authority of the shah had almost disintegrated, and in 1915 Anglo-Persian Oil's pipeline to the coast was cut by dissident tribesmen and German troops, demand for oil products was soaring. Between 1912 and 1918 there was a tenfold increase in oil production in Iran. The war also created opportunities for Greenway to further his ambition of establishing an integrated oil business. In 1915 Greenway founded a wholly owned oil tanker subsidiary, and within five years Anglo-Persian Oil had more than 30 oil tankers. In 1917, in his biggest coup, Greenway acquired British Petroleum Company, the British marketing subsidiary of the European Petroleum Union. The European Petroleum Union, a Continental alliance with significant Deutsche Bank participation, had been expropriated by the British government as an enemy property. In 1917 Greenway also decided to establish a refinery at Swansea, Wales, with improved refining technology that could produce petroleum products for British and European markets.

World War I, coupled with Greenway's skill, led to Anglo-Persian Oil's emergence by the late 1920s as one of the world's largest oil companies, matching Royal Dutch/Shell and Standard Oil of New Jersey in stature. During the 1920s the company made a major expansion in marketing, establishing subsidiaries in many European countries and, after the expiration of the agreement with Shell in 1922, in Africa and Asia. New refineries were established in Scotland and France, and a research laboratory erected in Sunbury, Great Britain, in 1917 greatly expanded the company's activities. In the early 1920s there were some criticisms of the management of Anglo-Persian Oil within the British government and some suggestions that the state shareholding should be privatized, but in November of 1924 a decision was made to retain the government's equity stake.

Greenway's successor was John Cadman, a former mining engineer who had been a professor of mining at Birmingham University before World War I, and who had become a major figure in official British oil policy during the war. In 1923 he became a managing director of Anglo-Persian Oil, and in 1927, chairman. He introduced major administrative reforms and, in the words of business historian Alfred Chandler, as quoted in *Scale and Scope: The Dynamics of Industrial Capitalism,* "was one of the few effective British organizational builders." Cadman was successful in overcoming the excessive departmentalism and lack of coordination that had formerly characterized the company. He was also a leading figure alongside Henri Deterding of the Shell group and Standard Oil of New Jersey in the late 1920s attempts to regulate and cartelize the world oil industry.

In the 1930s one of Cadman's greatest challenges came from the growth of Persian nationalism. Previously, in 1921, the old dynasty of shahs had been overthrown by an army colonel, Reza Khan, who made himself shah in 1925. Reza Khan was determined to reverse the foreign political and economic domination of his country. Anglo-Persian Oil had a symbolic role as a bastion of British imperialism and, following growing resentment of declining royalty payments from the company due to its falling profits during the Great Depression, the government of Persia cancelled its concession in November of 1932. The dispute eventually went to the League of Nations, and in 1933 a new 60-year concession agreement was signed with Anglo-Persian Oil, the main effects of which were to reduce the area of the concession to about a quarter of the original and to introduce a new tonnage basis of assessment for royalty payments. Anglo-Persian Oil had the formidable backing of the British government, and Persia gained little out of the dispute.

The oil company, which was renamed Anglo-Iranian Oil in 1935—the year Persia became Iran—became a renewed target of nationalist discontent after World War II. The Iranians complained that their dividends were too small, and the signing of 50-50 profit-sharing agreements between governments and oil companies elsewhere—in Venezuela in 1948 and Saudi Arabia in 1950—fueled criticism of Anglo-Iranian Oil within Iran. There were extensive negotiations between the company and the Iranian government. Anglo-Iranian Oil eventually offered substantial concessions, but they came too late and were repudiated by the nationalist government of Muhammad Mussadegh.

On May 1, 1951, the Iranian oil industry was formally nationalized. Several years of complex negotiations followed, and eventually, a 1953 coup—in which the British government and the United States Central Intelligence Agency (CIA) were implicated—resulted in the overthrow of Mussadegh. After his removal from power, an agreement was reached that allowed the return to Iran of Anglo-Iranian Oil—renamed the British Petroleum Company in 1954—but not on such favorable terms as the company had secured after the early 1930s dispute. Under the accord, which was reached in August of 1954, British Petroleum held a 40 percent interest in a newly created consortium of Western oil companies, formed to undertake oil exploration, production, and refining in Iran.

The events of 1951–54 had encouraged BP to diversify away from its overdependence on a single source of crude oil. The Iranian nationalization deprived the company of two-thirds of its production. The company responded by increasing output in Iraq and Kuwait and by building new refineries in Europe, Australia, and Aden. Oil exploration activities were launched in the Arabian Gulf, Canada, Europe, North Africa, East Africa, and Australia. Meanwhile, BP, which had first moved into petrochemicals in the late 1940s, became the second-largest chemicals business in the United Kingdom in 1967.

The company's future was secured at the end of the 1960s by major oil discoveries in Alaska and the North Sea. In 1965 BP found gas in British waters of the North Sea. In October of 1970 it discovered the Forties field, the first major commercial oil find in British waters. Throughout the 1960s BP had also been looking for oil in Alaska, and in 1969 this effort was rewarded by a major discovery at Prudhoe Bay on the North Slope. In the previous year BP had acquired the U.S. East Coast refining and marketing operations from Atlantic Richfield Company, and the stage was now set for a surge of expansion in the United States. Through its large share in Prudhoe Bay, BP owned more than 50 percent of the biggest oil field in the United States, and it needed outlets for this oil.

The solution was found in an agreement with the Standard Oil Company of Ohio, signed in August of 1969. The Standard Oil Company of Ohio was the market leader in Ohio and several neighboring states. Under the agreement, Standard took over BP's Prudhoe Bay leases as well as the downstream facilities acquired from Atlantic Richfield. In return, BP acquired 25 percent of Standard's equity. BP and Standard engaged in a seven-year struggle—lasting from 1970 to 1977—to develop the Prudhoe Bay oil field and construct the 800-mile Trans Alaska Pipeline system, which was finally completed in 1977. By the following year BP had taken a majority holding in Standard. Later, in 1987, it would be acquired outright and merged with BP's other interests in the United States to form a new company: BP America.

The oil price shocks and the transformation of the balance of power between oil companies and host governments that occurred in the 1970s caused many problems for BP, as for other western oil companies. BP lost most of its direct access to crude oil supplies produced in countries that belonged to OPEC (Organization of Petroleum Exporting Countries). The company's oil assets were nationalized in Libya in 1971 and Nigeria in 1979. BP and Shell clashed with the British government in 1973 over the allocation of scarce oil supplies. BP's chairman, Sir Eric Drake, refused to give priority to supplying the United Kingdom, despite forceful reminders from Prime Minister Edward Heath that the government owned half of the company.

Problems in the oil industry prompted BP to diversify away from its traditional role as an integrated oil company heavily dependent on Middle Eastern oil production. Retrospectively, it can be seen that this strategy was not always a wise one, and by the late 1980s BP was actively divesting its noncore businesses. BP's chemical interests grew, especially after 1978 when it acquired major European assets from Union Carbide and Monsanto. The major world recession after 1979 led to considerable overcapacity, though, and BP was forced to close down or sell off parts of its chemicals business in the early 1980s.

From the mid-1970s BP further diversified, building up a large coal business, especially in the United States, Australia, and South Africa. In 1989 and 1990, however, many of these coal interests were sold. Also in the mid-1970s BP became active in mineral mining. The company eventually acquired Selection Trust, a Great Britain-based mining finance house, in what was at the time the London stock market's largest-ever takeover bid. In 1981 Standard Oil acquired Keiecott, the largest U.S. copper producer. In 1989, however, most of BP's minerals assets were sold to the British mining company Rio Tinto Zinc for £2.38 billion. As a result of its divestments, BP came to be focused on its four core businesses: oil exploration and production, oil refining and marketing, chemicals, and nutrition.

The years since the late 1980s saw considerable changes at BP. In October of 1987 the government under Prime Minister Margaret Thatcher sold its remaining shareholding in the company as part of a privatization program. The timing of the share issue was particularly unfortunate, as the world's stock markets collapsed between the opening and closing of the offer. One result of the sale was that by March of 1988 the Kuwait Investment Office had built up a 21.6 percent stake in the company; government regulatory authorities subsequently reported that this share was reduced to less than 10 percent.

A second major development for BP in 1987 was the launch of a successful bid to acquire Britoil, a company established by the British government in the 1970s to participate in North Sea oil exploration. Britoil had become one of the largest independent oil exploration and production companies, and in acquiring it, BP almost doubled its exploration acreage in the North Sea.

In 1990 BP announced a fundamental change of its corporate structure, known as Project 1990. The primary aims were to reduce organizational complexity, reshape the central organization and reduce its cost, and reposition BP for the 1990s. Project 1990 was the brainchild of BP's chairman, Robert Horton. Horton earned a reputation for saving money and rose to prominence at BP by cutting costs first at the company's tanker division, then progressing to BP's chemicals subsidiary. Eventually becoming chairman and chief executive officer of BP Oil in 1990, he set out to cut costs throughout the conglomerate and revamp the corporate culture. At the heart of the scheme was a conviction that BP had become over-bureaucratic, and that strategic flexibility was handicapped as a result.

Under Project 1990, nearly 90 percent of corporate center committees—a total of 70—were abolished, with individuals taking responsibility instead. Hierarchically structured departments were to be replaced by small flexible teams with more open and less formal lines of communication.

Unfortunately, Project 1990 quickly came to represent wholesale job cuts and low morale. Between 1990 and mid-1992, 8,000 positions were cut, and up to 11,000 more workers faced unemployment if BP was to meet its goal of saving $750 million annually. The intended result of the job cuts was to shorten the lines of command and promote individual responsibility, but workloads were not redistributed in the process.

Project 1990 earned a poor reputation among employees, since some of the most basic measures to promote good communication and efficiency were eschewed for job elimination. For example, British Petroleum's Houston, London, Glasgow, and Alaska operations each had separate computer systems for geological appraisal and analysis of prospective oil fields, a configuration that could not have promoted good communication between those departments. Horton also insisted on maintaining BP's dividend—despite cuts in other vital areas.

As a result of Project 1990's inefficiencies, many employees lost faith in it, according to a 1991 internal survey. Horton's personal abrasiveness and tendency to dictate, rather than cultivate, change led to his forced resignation on June 25, 1992.

Horton's role was split between Lord Ashburton, the nonexecutive director who had led the mutiny, and David Simon, chief operating officer-turned chief executive officer. BP's problems did not depart with Horton, however. From 1987 to 1992 British Petroleum had a negative cash flow of approximately £6 billion, and by March 1990 the company's debt-to-equity ratio had skyrocketed to 81 percent.

Many of the conglomerate's problems stemmed from the poor performance of its American subsidiary, BP Oil. In 1991 BP Oil's profits dropped by two-thirds, and the subsidiary lost $27 million in the first nine months of 1992. Cost-cutting measures at BP Oil have run the gamut from selling 300 California and Florida gas stations, to employee buyouts eliminating 600 to 700 jobs, to the close scrutinization of travel vouchers. Ashburton and Simon also planned to cut BP's dividend, a measure Horton had been reluctant to take.

In the early 1990s British Petroleum sought to consolidate its activities to focus on its traditional areas of strength in ''upstream'' areas—oil and gas exploration, field development, production, pipeline transportation and gas marketing—and ''downstream'' areas—oil supply trading, refining and marketing—as well as in chemicals manufacturing.

After a five-year acquisitions binge costing approximately £10 billion, BP had started to consolidate its upstream business through divestment in the late 1980s. The company sold its coal businesses in the United States, Canada, Indonesia, Australia, and South Africa, netting £428 million. Another sale of selected worldwide oil and gas interests and assets brought in US$1.3

billion. In 1990 and 1991 sales of exploration interests and assets in New Zealand, France, the Netherlands, and from the BP Exploration division in particular totaled £830 million.

BP, alongside Imperial Chemical Industries PLC, represents one of the success stories of twentieth-century British business. Its achievement in penetrating the international oil oligopoly of the early 1900s was impressive, as was the survival of the loss of the Iranian oil fields in the early 1950s.

Principal Subsidiaries: BP International; BP Oil International; BP Exploration; BP Chemicals (International); Exploration Operating Co.; BP Shipping; BP Capital; BP Chemicals; BP Oil UK; Britoil (85%); BP Austria; BP Belgium (85%); BP France (86%); Deutsche BP; BP Greece; BP Nederland; BP Portuguesa; BP España; Svenska BP; BP Switzerland; BP Petrolleri; BP Middle East; BP Africa; BP Southern Africa; BP Singapore; BP Australia; BP Finance Australia; BP Developments Australia; BP Oil New Zealand; BP Canada (57%); BP America/Standard Oil.

Further Reading: Ferrier, R. W., *The History of the British Petroleum Company,* vol. 1, Cambridge, Cambridge University Press, 1982; Ferrier, R. W., ''Sir Maurice Richard Bridgeman,'' ''John Cadman,'' ''William Knox D'Arcy,'' ''Sir Arthur Eric Courtney Drake,'' ''William Milligan Fraser,'' ''Charles Greenway,'' *Dictionary of Business Biography: A Biographical Dictionary of Business Leaders Active in Britain in the Period, 1860–1980,* 5 vols., edited by David Jeremy, London, Butterworth, 1984–86; Jones, Geoffrey, *The State and the Emergence of the British Oil Industry,* London, Macmillan, 1981; ''The Road From Persia: A Brief History of BP,'' London, BP Briefing Paper, April 1989; Beck, Robert J. ''State Companies Lead OGJ100 World Reserves, Production List,'' *Oil & Gas Journal,* September 28, 1992; ''Big Problems: British Petroleum,'' *The Economist,* February 8, 1992; ''BP After Horton,'' *The Economist,* July 4, 1992; Yerak, Rebecca, ''Plugging the Drain at BP Oil,'' *Plain Dealer* (Cleveland), January 26, 1993.

—Geoffrey Jones
updated by April Dougal

Bruno's, Inc.

BRUNO'S INC.

800 Lakeshore Parkway
P.O. Box 2486
Birmingham, Alabama 35201-2486
U.S.A.
(205) 940-9400
Fax: (205) 940-9568

Public Company
Incorporated: 1959
Employees: 23,454
Sales: $2.66 billion
Stock exchanges: NASDAQ
SICs: 5411 Grocery Stores; 5912 Drug Stores & Proprietary
    Stores

One of the biggest, most productive, and most profitable super-market chains in the United States, Bruno's, Inc., boasts the highest sales volume of 129 companies in Alabama and is one of America's top 20 supermarket chains. The corporation operates more than 250 stores, including a variety of retail food stores, pharmacies, and combination food and drug stores in Alabama, Georgia, Florida, Mississippi, Tennessee, and South Carolina. Located in urban and rural settings, these stores consist of: Food World, Bruno's Food and Pharmacy, FoodMax, Vincent's, Food Fair, Bruno's Finer Foods, Consumer Warehouse Foods, and Piggly Wiggly.

In 1932 during the Great Depression, Joe Bruno, the son of Sicilian immigrants, opened his first grocery, a 20 by 40 foot corner store in Birmingham, Alabama. Using his family's savings for an initial investment of $600, Joe would achieve the kind of success that young immigrants still dream of. Joe's cash-only policy enabled him to keep prices low, and customers came from all over Birmingham to the first Bruno's store. As they became old enough to work, Joe's three brothers, Anthony, Angelo, and Lee, joined the business. By April 1, 1959, when the company was incorporated in Alabama as Bruno's, Inc., all four Bruno sons were well established in the business.

Alabama remains at the center of Bruno's operating area and is home to more than 120 of the chain's 250 stores. In some parts of the state, Bruno's has market shares of up to 30 percent. There are close to 100 Bruno's stores in Georgia; the balance are in Florida, Mississippi, Tennessee, and South Carolina.

The success of Bruno's is due in part to its variety of stores. Bruno's strategy is to divide each market and open stores directed at each segment. This way, the corporation gains market share and comes to dominate each market segment. The stores have different sizes, designs, and products, and each is geared to a particular demographic or economic community.

Bruno's Food and Pharmacy stores are higher-end stores that stock gourmet items from the United States and overseas while featuring the everyday low prices of the lower-end stores. With about 50,000 square feet per store, Bruno's Food and Pharmacy features one-stop shopping, in-store banks, and specialty items. The combination food and drug stores are committed to customer service, with such amenities as bag boys carrying groceries to customers' cars. At a 1987 opening in Huntsville, Alabama, Cajun Chef Paul Prudhomme gave a cooking demonstration, and samples from store departments included fresh strawberry shortcake, chocolate and champagne ice cream balls, and fresh Beluga caviar. The opening, called "The Art of Food," was billed as a benefit for the local art museum, and invitations were sent to museum patrons, who were regarded as the cosmopolitan, affluent consumers that Bruno's wanted to attract to the store.

Vincent's, which also carries gourmet foods in an upscale setting, offers catering services for small gatherings and large parties. There is only one Vincent's store, located in Homewood, a suburb of Birmingham. It carries fine, expensive wines, and probably stocks more gourmet items than any other store in the south.

FoodMax stores, many of which are open 24 hours a day, emphasize an everyday low-price image while attracting upscale customers. They are super-warehouse size, with between 48,000 and 60,000 square feet. A FoodMax in Mableton, Georgia, features wide aisles, 20 kinds of fresh fish, and a bakery that can produce 450 loaves of bread per hour.

Food World stores are more than 40,000 square feet in area and display shelves of food in manufacturers' cartons. More than 80 Food World stores are in operation—far more than any other Bruno's chain. Theirs is a no frills, economical image that encourages high sales volume and low overhead. Food World was the first chain in the region to forgo periodic sales on selected merchandise in favor of everyday low prices. The strategy has been so successful that it has been widely imitated.

Food Fair stores are similar to Food World, but smaller, at only approximately 30,000 square feet. The 58 Piggly Wiggly stores now owned by Bruno's are conventional supermarkets that are typically 28,000 square feet in size. They offer store specials, double manufacturers' coupons, and weekly selected merchandise specials. All of Bruno's stores emphasize high volume and competitive prices.

Bruno's has a reputation in the industry for aggressive, effective management and practices. For instance, it buys most of its food directly from manufacturers, rather than from wholesalers. When manufacturers want their products sold at Bruno's stores, they make presentations directly to a committee of Bruno's managers, many of whom are part of the Bruno family. If the committee decides to buy the products, they usually buy large quantities and qualify for the largest volume discounts. That way, Bruno's can save money and pass the savings on to their customers.

Bruno's store managers are compensated according to how much money their stores make. This puts pressure on them to keep inventories moving, but most Bruno's managers are happy to hustle, especially knowing they may earn as much as $80,000 in a good year. Many of these managers started at Bruno's while they were still in high school and have stayed, and this loyalty has served the company well.

In September 1987 Angelo Bruno, co-founder and then chairperson, signed a joint venture agreement with K Mart. Considered a bold move for Bruno's, the idea was to build hypermarkets of approximately 200,000 square feet all over the country. Hypermarkets combine groceries and general merchandise, selling everything from vegetables to clothing, and featuring up to 50 checkout stands. Such shopping centers already existed in Europe, and this was not the first time hypermarkets would open in the United States. However, this venture represented the first partnership between a grocery chain with the food expertise of Bruno's, and a general retailer with expertise in merchandise sales. The management of Bruno's felt that the new sales could boost growth, even in the traditionally slow grocery trade. Three American Fare hypermarkets owned jointly by Kmart and Bruno's opened between 1989 and 1991 in Atlanta, Georgia; Charlotte, North Carolina; and Jackson, Mississippi.

On April 20, 1988, Bruno's acquired PWS Holding Corp., which held Piggly Wiggly Southern, Inc. This helped Bruno's achieve a substantial expansion in northern Georgia and Florida. The acquisition of 58 Piggly Wiggly stores was Bruno's first major competitive purchase. The price was 2,498,251 shares of Bruno's common stock. Bruno's retained some of Piggly Wiggly's management, naming the former Piggly Wiggly Southern president, William White, executive vice president of Bruno's for merchandising and operations.

Always on the lookout for new technology to improve operations in its stores, in the early 1990s Bruno's installed minicomputers connected to the Birmingham mainframe computer in its stores. These computers are used primarily to improve direct store buying and delivery. The system also enables stores to monitor customer traffic in order to adjust labor needs. They also use the computers to keep track of store employees' attendance and working hours. The warehouse is also highly computerized. Food arrives from manufacturers and is priced, inventoried, and loaded onto Bruno's trucks for delivery to stores. The shipments, arrivals, pricing, and deliveries are also tracked on computer.

A tremendous test to Bruno's organization came in a tragic accident on December 11, 1991, when six Bruno's executives and three others were killed in the crash of the corporate jet shortly after takeoff in Rome, Georgia. The executives, including co-founders Angelo Bruno and his brother Lee Bruno, were on their annual Christmas visit to all of their stores when the crash occurred. Also killed were Sam Vacarella, the senior vice president for merchandising; Edward Hyde, vice president for store operations; Randolph Page, a vice president for personnel; Karl Mollica, produce director; Mary Faust, an advertising ac-

count executive working with Bruno's; and the co-pilots Joe Tesney and Rob Stamps. The accident took an emotional toll on the family business and required much shifting of personnel. Angelo's son Ronald Bruno, who had been groomed to run the company and who had already been designated president and chief executive officer, was elected to the chair. In August 1992 Bruno's, Inc., bought 3.6 million shares of common stock from the estates of Angelo and Lee Bruno.

Bruno's entered the 1990s in the top 40 of some 270 food stores ranked by sales volume. National competition consisted of such chains as American Stores, Kroger, Safeway, Winn-Dixie, and Jewel, while Food Lion, Albertson's, and Giant Food competed with Bruno's mainly in the southeast region. Many of Bruno's competitors in Georgia suffered after Bruno's 1988 acquisition of Piggly Wiggly. But Bruno's continues to keep watch over its competition as Warehouse clubs and Wal-Mart supercenters begin to pose a challenge to Bruno's in several of its larger markets.

In June 1992 Bruno's announced an end to its joint venture with K Mart. K Mart assumed full ownership of the hypermarkets, taking over Bruno's 49 percent interest in Atlanta and Charlotte, and its 51 percent interest in the Jackson store. Bruno's management noted "We felt it was time to eliminate our loss from the American Fare stores and focus our full attention on our primary store concerns." The company took a charge of $.13 a share, or $10.8 million for the fiscal year ending in June 1992.

Also during fiscal 1992, Bruno's finalized plans to consolidate the Piggly Wiggly division offices from Vidalia, Georgia to a unit in the Birmingham corporate office. According to Ronald Bruno, savings from the closed Vidalia division offices would be in the vicinity of $5 million. The offices were officially closed in 1992, but the distribution center in Vidalia remained. Bruno's planned to use the facility as a jumping-off point for new operations in that geographic area.

Bruno's, like many food retailers and supermarket operators, suffered during the recession of the late 1980s and early 1990s. Some store sales were slow while consumer spending plummeted. Food prices went down, and consumers were spending less money on food. The outlook brightened slightly as the economy began to improve, and Brunos' management team seems to have successfully ridden out the worst of the storm. Forecasts for food retailing growth remain modest, but some analysts have expected Bruno's to be able to resume its annual growth rate of 15 to 20 percent. Bruno's planned to open 33 new stores in fiscal 1993. Half of these were to be FoodMax stores, and the others were to be combination grocery and drug stores.

Principal Subsidiaries: PWS Holding Corporation

Further Reading: Donegan, Priscilla, "Merchandising the Store," *Progressive Grocer,* August, 1987; "Getting Hyper," *Forbes,* January 11, 1988; Kindel, Stephen, "Rebel Sell," *Financial World,* January 9, 1990; Grossman, Laurie M. and Martha Brannigan, "Six Bruno's Officials and Three Others Die in Jet Crash During Goodwill Tour," *The Wall Street Journal,* December 12, 1991; Smothers, Ronald, "Crash of Private Plane in Georgia Kills 9," *The New York Times,*

December 12, 1991; ''Bruno's Executives Die in Plane Crash,'' *Progressive Grocer,* January, 1992; Merrefield, David, ''Bruno's: Pulling Together,'' *Supermarket News*, March 30, 1992; ''Bruno's Leaves American Fare Venture With KMart,'' *The New York Times,* June 11, 1992; ''Bruno's After the Crash,'' *Forbes*, July 6, 1992.

—Fran Shonfeld Sherman

▌▐▌CABLEVISION

CABLEVISION SYSTEMS CORPORATION

One Media Crossways
Woodbury, NY 11797
U.S.A.
(516) 364-8450
Fax: (516) 364-5314

Public Company
Incorporated: 1985
Sales: $603 million
Employees: 5,400
Stock Exchanges: American
SICs: 4841 Cable & Other Pay Television Services

Cablevision Systems Corporation is the fourth largest cable systems operator in the United States, providing service to about 2.08 million subscribers in 19 states. Through its subsidiary, Rainbow Programming Holdings, Cablevision has also been an innovator in cable television programming, offering movie, news, and sports channels.

Charles F. Dolan, the founder and chair of the board of directors of Cablevision, entered the cable television business in its infancy. A maker of industrial films, he became a pioneer of cable television in 1960 when he began wiring hotels in New York City for reception of his cable news service. In 1965 Dolan's company, Sterling Manhattan, won a franchise to operate a cable television system in the southern half of Manhattan. Sterling had wealthy partners—Time, Inc. in particular—and was able to raise money for the cable system through a stock offering, but he was unable to amass enough funds to complete the system. Sterling's debts multiplied until 1973 when Time, having become the owner of 80 percent of the company, decided to liquidate. Time bought the Home Box Office (HBO) channel—the first nationwide pay-TV channel in the United States, which Dolan had founded in 1970—from Sterling, and HBO went on to become the leading pay-TV channel in the United States.

Although Time had lost faith in the marketability of cable service on Long Island, where many free television channels were already offered, Dolan firmly believed that people wanted the commercial-free television with programming alternatives that cable offered. Using part of the $675,000 he received from Time for his Sterling stock, he bought back the Long Island cable franchises from Time and quickly created another cable company, Long Island Cable Communication Development Company. The company offered a free month of HBO to its 1,500 Long Island customers, and was rewarded when over 90 percent of them opted to continue the service for six dollars a month.

Early successes like this enabled Cablevision to begin raising venture capital and attracting more customers. The densely populated Long Island proved an especially auspicious market. Its proximity to Manhattan made it easy to pick up the microwave signals HBO and other transmitters were still using. Dolan won still more customers by gaining the rights to New York Mets, Islanders, Nets, and Yankees games that were blacked-out locally. Cablevision received the highest revenue per subscriber in the United States, partly because Long Island provided an affluent customer base, and partly because of its strategy of selling pay-TV channels in blocks for a lower sum than they would bring individually.

While Cablevision produced significant cash flow, there was little profit due to the capital intensive nature of the cable business. To keep the company afloat and expanding, Dolan turned to limited partnerships, attracting business magnates such as Hugh Hefner and Milton Friedman as investors. Cablevision slowly expanded, adding systems in Yonkers, New York, New Jersey, and suburban Chicago. By 1980, at about the time the cable industry began receiving significant nationwide attention, Cablevision had 155,000 customers and $14 million of cash flow. It was worth $250 million and had a debt of $45 million. The 50 miles of cable it had owned in 1973 grew to 4,000 miles.

In 1980 Cablevision formed a subsidiary, Rainbow Programming Services, to create cable programming. This programming soon included the American Movie Classics channel, which showed vintage Hollywood films, and Bravo, which showed classic American and foreign films, exclusive Broadway plays, music and dance performances, and educational presentations. In 1983 Cablevision began offering the Newsday Channel, a 24-hour news and information channel produced in conjunction with the New York newspaper *Newsday*. The station did not attract enough viewer support to survive long, however. Cablevision also started SportsChannel, which broadcast New York Nets basketball games, and Islander and Devils hockey games, in addition to Yankees and Mets games. The channel received revenue from advertisers and subscribers, and became one of the cable industry's most successful sports services.

In 1984 Cablevision moved aggressively to win a cable franchise in Boston. It won the bidding with a basic cable fee of two dollars a month, considered low for the cable industry. The firm planned to make up for the lost revenue by tiering pay services like HBO. It ran into construction problems in laying the cable, however, delaying completion of the system—and its capacity for bringing in much-needed revenue—for years. Cablevision was also expanding into New York City, where it won franchises for The Bronx and two-thirds of Brooklyn. Although there were more setbacks—in 1985 Cablevision lost its 47.5 percent stake in a Sacramento cable system when it was unable to pay off a $34 million obligation to partner Scripps Howard

Inc.—Cablevision became the fifteenth-largest cable systems operator in the United States in 1986, with 595,000 subscribers.

In 1986, with the price of cable televisions systems at an all-time high, Dolan decided to create a publicly held company with 390,000 of Cablevision's subscribers. The systems going public were in Long Island, Westchester County, New York City, and New Jersey. Systems in Boston and Chicago that had not yet become profitable were not included in the new company until they went into the black. The initial stock price worked out to about $1,700 per subscriber. The stock offering was structured in such a way that it left Dolan with a large percentage of the company's voting rights and control of 75 percent of the board of directors. Dolan received some criticism because the systems he was taking public were believed to have grown about as large as they were going to. Cablevision's debt stood at about $290 million from acquisitions and the buying out of limited partners. Dolan reportedly wanted to use the $80 million he raised through the offering to pay off part of this debt. Dolan also wanted to spend $25 million on further cable construction in New York City.

In July 1986 Cablevision agreed to acquire two cable systems from Scripps Howard Inc. for $175 million. The systems were also partly held by Dolan, though how much each party owned was not revealed. The systems were located in Fairfield County, Connecticut and added 120,000 subscribers to the Cablevision system. Later in the year Cablevision acquired the portions of Rainbow Programming Services it did not already own for about $57 million. In 1987 Cablevision bought Adams-Russell Co., a cable TV company based in Waltham, Massachusetts.

Cablevision also expanded its programming services. In December, 1986, Cablevision tried again to offer a 24-hour local news channel. News 12, offered on all Long Island cable systems, not just Cablevision's, won numerous awards for its news coverage, and has become Long Island's premier news service.

In early 1987, Cablevision joined a group of cable operators and investor Kirk Kerkorian in investing $550 million in Turner Broadcasting System Inc. (TBS). The investment in TBS allowed chair of the board Ted Turner to keep control of his company. Cablevision and the other investors desired this because Turner Broadcasting was an important source of programming, and they wanted it to maintain its independence. The group of investors were allowed to name five of TBS's 11 board members.

Increasing its involvement with cable programming, Cablevision bought the Washington Post Company's interests in four of California's SportsChannels in June 1987 for six million dollars. At this point, Cablevision had sports channels in Chicago, New York, New England, Philadelphia, and Florida. The firm also increased its expansion out of the Eastern seaboard when it bought First Carolina Communication cable systems in Cleveland and Toledo, Ohio.

In 1988 Gulf & Western outbid Cablevision for the rights to Yankees games. To protest, Cablevision dropped Gulf & Western's Madison Square Garden Network, which broadcast the games as part of its regular service. The move angered many of the 400,000 Cablevision subscribers in New York, New Jersey, and Connecticut, who were unable to watch the games. It also

upset many cable systems operators, who worried that the controversy would attract unwanted attention from the U.S. federal government. Congress had just deregulated cable in 1987, and as consumers complained about cable service, some lawmakers considered reregulation. Cablevision settled with Gulf & Western in 1989, agreeing to offer the Madison Square Garden Network as an option in its service package, priced and promoted equally to its own SportsChannel.

In 1989 Cablevision and the National Broadcasting Co. (NBC) formed a joint venture to market a national cable network as well as regional news and sports networks. They also agreed to offer the first pay-per-view Olympics coverage of the 1992 Summer Games in Barcelona. It was the first time that a broadcast network and a cable system had cooperated in a programming venture, and many industry analysts had doubts that it would work. NBC and Cablevision had competing interests: cable television was a threat to the audiences of NBC's affiliate stations, and cable operators were suspicious of NBC's forays into cable programming. NBC received a 50 percent stake in most of Rainbow's programming services, while Cablevision took 50 percent of NBC's cable venture, Consumer News and Business Channel, and $137.5 million to develop programming for it. The two companies also intended to create a series of regional cable news stations and 10 sports channels in addition to the five already operated by Cablevision.

Cablevision had borne a high debt load since its inception, having borrowed heavily to lay cable and buy other companies. In the late 1980s the firm's debt increased significantly as it made a number of large purchases. Cablevision bought a regional sports channel in Los Angeles for $18 million. It also bought two cable systems in suburban Cleveland and Long Island from Viacom Inc. for $549 million. Cablevision also received 20 percent of another system under construction in Cleveland and a five percent stake in The Movie Channel and Showtime, two Viacom pay channels. The sale added 120,000 subscribers to the 310,000 Cablevision already had in Long Island and added 75,000 subscribers to the 85,000 it had in Cleveland. Cablevision became the eighth largest cable systems operator in the United States, with over 1.3 million customers in 11 states. But with rising interest payments on its significant debt, Cablevision lost $22.6 million in 1988 on sales of $493 million.

In February 1990 Cablevision announced it would invest one billion dollars with three other media companies in Sky Cable, a direct-broadcast satellite service that was to offer up to 108 channels. The plan fell apart in little more than a year, however, due to conflicting interests among the partners.

In the meantime, Cablevision continued to create new programming. It announced plans for a channel that would cover important or sensational court trials. The In Court channel was hampered by a lack of unused channels on most cable systems, as well as a rival channel to be started by American Lawyer Media. Tentative plans to merge the channels were announced before either went on the air. In 1991 the Cablevision and NBC partnership agreed to start a sports-news cable channel. The channel was to be distributed through the SportsChannel America network. Critics pointed out that sports fans wanted to see the games themselves, and that sports news was already covered by a variety of media outlets.

Cablevision and NBC spent $40 million on marketing their pay-per-view Olympics service, and $60 million producing it, but the actual sales were disappointing. The cost of the service to the consumer was high, starting at $95 for weekend coverage, and 160 hours of Olympic coverage was already available on free television. Far fewer subscribers signed up than expected and Cablevision lost $50 million on the venture. Partly as a result of this, Cablevision lost $82.7 million in the second quarter of 1992.

In 1992 Cablevision's debt was more than one billion dollars, and the price of its Class A stock declined to the extent that the company canceled a public offering that had been scheduled. But business analysts observed that Dolan continued to think big, and despite its heavy debt, Cablevision continued to grow. In 1991, for instance, Cablevision bought Gateway Cable, a

42,000-subscriber system serving Newark and South Orange, New Jersey. By 1992 Cablevision owned 23 cable systems and had a total of about 2 million basic subscribers.

Further Reading: Sloan, Allan, "The Man Who Hated Commercials," *Forbes,* October 27, 1980; Bloch, Jeff, "How High Is Up?," *Forbes,* January 27, 1986; Fabrikant, Geraldine, "Cablevision, Runner of Risks," *New York Times,* November 13, 1986; Kneale, Dennis, "Cablevision to Buy 2 Cable-TV Systems of Viacom," *Wall Street Journal,* August 17, 1988; Landro, Laura, "NBC Cable Venture Unites Natural Foes," *Wall Street Journal,* February 8, 1989; Lieberman, David, "A Cable Mogul's Darning Dance on the High Wire," *Business Week,* June 5, 1989; Robichaux, Mark, "Cable Channel for Sports News Is Coming to Bat," *Wall Street Journal,* August 28, 1991; Goldman, Kevin, "Olympics '92: Some Games Have Begun," *Wall Street Journal,* July 20, 1992.

—Scott M. Lewis

Campbell Soup Company

CAMPBELL SOUP COMPANY

Campbell Place
Camden, New Jersey 08103-1799
U.S.A.
(609) 342-4800
Fax: (609) 342-3878

Public Company
Incorporated: 1922
Employees: 43,256
Sales: $6.26 billion
Stock Exchanges: New York Philadelphia London Swiss
SICs: 2032 Canned Specialties; 2038 Frozen Specialties Nec;
2051 Bread, Cake & Related Products; 2052 Cookies &
Crackers; 2034 Dehydrated Fruits, Vegetables & Soups;
0812 Food Crops Grown Under Cover; 5148 Fresh Fruits
& Vegetables; 0161 Vegetables & Melons; 2015 Poultry
Slaughtering & Processing; 5149 Groceries & Related
Products Nec.

Campbell Soup Company is the number-one maker of soups in
the United States and is also a leading manufacturer of other
products, including frozen entrees, baked goods, fruit juices,
pickles, spaghetti sauces, and ready-to-eat salads.

The roots of the Campbell Soup Company can be traced back to
1860, when Abraham Anderson opened a small canning factory
in Camden, New Jersey. In 1869 Philadelphia produce merchant Joseph Campbell became Anderson's partner, forming
Anderson and Campbell. The company canned vegetables,
mince meat, jams and jellies, and a variety of soups. In 1876
Anderson and Campbell dissolved their partnership and Campbell bought Anderson's share of the business, changing its name
to Joseph Campbell Preserve Company. In 1882 a partnership
was formed between Campbell's son-in-law, Walter S. Spackman; Campbell's nephew, Joseph S. Campbell; and Arthur Dorrance, Spackman's personal friend who brought a cash infusion
to the partnership. At this time the company was renamed
Joseph Campbell Preserving Company. The senior Campbell
maintained daily involvement in the company until his death in
1900.

In 1896 the company built a large factory in Camden and
expanded its product line to include prepared meats, sauces,
canned fruits, ketchup, and plum pudding. The next year Arthur
Dorrance hired his nephew John Thompson Dorrance, a chemi-

cal engineer and organic chemist. By 1899 John Dorrance had
successfully developed a method of canning condensed soup.
This innovation helped Campbell outstrip its two soup-canning
competitors. While others were still shipping heavy, uncon-
densed soup, Campbell was able to ship and sell its product at
one-third cost. As the company began increasing the variety of
soups it offered, it began canning less produce. John Dorrance
became director of the company in 1900 and soon after the
company was renamed the Joseph Campbell Company.

Campbell's soup began finding its way into American kitchens
at a time when the prepared-food industry was growing rapidly
yet was still small. By 1904 the company sold 16 million cans of
soup a year. Boasting 21 varieties of soup by 1905, Campbell
began to eye a bigger market; in 1911 Campbell began doing
business in California market, thus becoming one of the first
companies to serve the entire nation.

In 1910 Dorrance was made general manager of the company,
and in 1914 he became president. Dorrance focused on soup and
discontinued the marginal line of ketchups, preserves, and jams.
In 1915 Dorrance became sole owner of Campbell when he
bought out his uncle, Arthur Dorrance.

In 1912 Campbell began growing its own produce in an effort to
standardize quality. This program was the first of an ongoing
series of efforts Campbell has made to grow what it processes.
At that time, during the eight summer weeks in which tomatoes
were harvested, the Campbell plant devoted its entire effort to
the production of tomato soup and tomato juice. During World
War I almost half of Campbell's sales were from these two
products.

In 1921 Campbell acquired the Franco-American Food Company, and the next year the company was renamed the Campbell
Soup Company. In 1923 Arthur C. Dorrance, John Dorrance's
brother, became Campbell's general manager. In 1929 Arthur
C. Dorrance was made a director and vice-president of the board
of directors. When John Dorrance died in 1930, Arthur C.
Dorrance was elected president.

Throughout this period Campbell continued to grow. In 1929
the company opened a second major facility in Chicago. In the
early-1930s Campbell opened subsidiaries in Canada—
Campbell Soup Company Ltd.—and Great Britain—
Campbell's Soups Ltd. In 1936 Campbell began making its own
cans and in 1939 its agricultural research department was
formed. In 1942 sales topped $100 million for the first time. In
1946 Arthur C. Dorrance died and James McGowen, Jr. became
president. The following year Campbell began growing its own
mushrooms in Prince Crossing, Illinois.

Despite this growth, Campbell was slow to diversify. In 1948
the company acquired V-8 juice, but its first major purchase was
not made until 1955, when it bought the Omaha, Nebraska-
based C.A. Swanson & Sons, producers of the first complete
meal frozen entrees called TV dinners.

In the midst of this growth, W. B. Murphy was elected president, following McGowan's retirement in 1953. In 1954 Campbell took its stock public and, in 1957, the company formed an
international division to oversee its foreign concerns. In 1958
sales exceeded $500 million for the first time and Campbell

established Campbell's Soups, S.p.A. in Italy. This venture was followed, in 1959, by the opening of subsidiaries in Mexico and Australia.

Throughout the 1960s Campbell was conservatively managed and quite successful. In that decade the company opened two mushroom-growing facilities and 11 new plants on three continents. In the 1960s Campbell's growth—which underwent a slight shift in emphasis—began to include regular acquisitions in addition to internal expansion. In 1961 Campbell acquired Pepperidge Farm, a maker of quality baked goods, and a similar Belgian company, Biscuits Delacre. In 1965 Campbell created a food-service division and, in 1966, began marketing EfficienC, its own brand of food-service products through that division. Also in 1966 Campbell formed Godiva Chocolatier to distribute the Belgian-made chocolates in the United States. In 1974 the company completed a purchase of the European Godiva company and became its sole owner. Campbell created Champion Valley Farms, a pet food concern, in 1969.

During the 1970s the company's slow but steady growth continued. Campbell, which had built its fortune on Dorrance's invention of condensed soup, introduced the first Chunky brand of ready-to-serve soups. This became a highly successful enterprise. In 1971, for the first time, Campbell's sales topped $1 billion. In 1972 Murphy retired and was replaced by President Harold A. Shaub. Also that year, Swanson introduced Hungry Man meals, a line of frozen dinners with larger-than-average portions. In 1973 Campbell acquired Pietro's Pizza Parlors, a chain based in the Pacific Northwest. This led, in 1974, to the formation of a restaurant division, and heralded Campbell's intention to add more restaurants to its growing list of subsidiaries.

In 1978 Campbell purchased Vlasic Foods, a Michigan-based producer of pickles and similar condiments, for approximately $35 million in capital stock. This acquisition gave Campbell the lead over archrival H. J. Heinz in the pickle-packing business. Campbell added seven small European food-producing companies and three domestic operations in 1979. That same year sales topped $2 billion for the first time. In 1978 Campbell made a brief and unsuccessful foray into the Brazilian soup market.

The diversification movement started by Shaub in the early 1970s prepared the company for long-term growth. Campbell's debt remained low and the company's new products and acquisitions have provided it with popular brand names in a variety of food-industry sectors. Campbell realized that the key to growth in this mature market is diversification. Shaub changed a long-standing policy on new-product development requiring a profit within the first year. His most notable innovation, however, was his decentralization of marketing for major product lines.

To sustain these growth-oriented policies, Campbell broke its tradition of relying on internally generated funds to finance its efforts. In June of 1980 the company entered the debt market with a $100 million ten-year offering. As a cautious food producer, Campbell's earning have always been healthy, but Shaub hoped to increase both sales and profits margins. A key reason for Shaub's determination to allow Campbell to diversify was the recognition that the market for many of these products had matured and growth had slowed.

In 1980 R. Gorden McGovern succeeded Shaub as president and Campbell made two acquisitions—Swift-Armour S.A. Argentina and a small American poultry-processing plant used by Swanson for its frozen chicken dinners. Campbell's efforts in Argentina were not entirely fruitful; much of the difficulty has been related to currency-transaction adjustments. Also in 1980 Campbell acquired additional bakery, pasta, and pickle operations.

In 1981 McGovern reorganized management structure, dividing the company into two new divisions—Campbell U.S.A. and Campbell International—and about 50 business groups. This new structure was meant to foster entrepreneurship and heighten management's sensitivity to consumer opinion, long a weakness at Campbell. The company acquired Snow King Frozen Foods, a large producer of uncooked frozen specialty meats, and introduced the wildly successful Prego spaghetti sauce nationally in 1981. In 1982 Campbell acquired Mrs. Paul's Kitchens, a processor of frozen prepared seafood and vegetables. Several of the company's subsidiaries also made major purchases. Vlasic Foods acquired Win Schuler Foods, a specialty-foods producer, and Pepperidge Farm completed the purchase of an apple juice processor, Costa Apple Products, with markets primarily on the East Coast. Also in 1982, Juice Bowl Products, a fruit juice processor, was acquired.

A variety of other acquisitions in the early 1980s added Annabelle's, a restaurant chain; Triangle, a manufacturer of physical-fitness and sports-medicine products; a fresh-produce distributor; a Puerto Rican canning company; and an Italian manufacturer of premium biscuits.

McGovern further increased emphasis on marketing and new-product development in an effort to shift the company away from its production-oriented focus. McGovern also introduced Total Systems, a worker-oriented system designed to increase quality and efficiency that is similar to the successful worker management strategies employed by many Japanese companies.

One of McGovern's primary concerns was turning Campbell into a "market-sensitive food company." After McGovern publicly referred to some of the company's Swanson TV dinner line as "junk food" in 1982, Campbell initiated Project Fix in an effort to upgrade food quality and improve packaging of its older products. As McGovern told *Business Week* in 1983, one of the most important facets his make over was making the company "somebody who is looking after [consumers'] well-being." The 1983 Triangle Manufacturing purchase and 1982 formation of a health-and-fitness unit were both designed to meet that goal. Campbell's involvement in frozen fish, juices, and produce were also part of the new market sensitivity urged by McGovern.

In addition, Campbell has attempted to market products regionally and according to age group. The central marketing was broken into 20 regions to allow tailoring of advertising and marketing to fit each region's peculiar demographics. For instance, the company sells spicier nacho cheese soup in Texas than the rest of the country. The company also aimed its national brands at regional audience, with spots featuring local celebrities and locally arranged promotions. Campbell, which reached half the nation's homes just by sponsoring the television show *Lassie* in the 1950s, spent 15 percent of its advertising budget in regional efforts in 1983. That figure was expected to eventually reach 50 percent.

McGovern increased Campbell's sales and earnings significantly in his first few years. His encouragement of new-product development and line extensions may have been overzealous. The company introduced frozen entrees to compete with Stouffer's, dried soups to challenge Lipton, and name-brand produce such as Farm Fresh mushrooms and tomatoes, complemented by exotic varieties of mushrooms, refrigerated salads and pasta sauces, and juices. In all, Campbell introduced 334 new products in the first half of the 1980s. This included several costly mistakes, such as the 1984 failure of Pepperidge Farm's Star Wars cookies, which did not fit the brand's high-quality image. Yet spurred on by successes such as Le Menu frozen dinners, McGovern concentrated on marketing and new-product development. In 1985, however, the company decided to cut back on new-product gambles and McGovern reevaluated his goals and returned the company's focus to product quality and efficiency.

Throughout this period, during which it became increasingly clear that McGovern's plan was destined to fail, acquisitions and group formations continued, but at a pace reminiscent of the old Campbell. The company purchased a Belgian food producer and 20 percent of Arnotts Ltd., an Australian biscuit manufacturer, in 1985. In 1986 the company bought two more American food companies and established Campbell Enterprises to oversee non-grocery products. Meanwhile new products were gradually but steadily introduced.

In 1984 John T. Dorrance Jr., the son of condensed soup's inventor, retired as chairman of the board and became director of the board's executive committee. He was posthumously inducted into Junior Achievement's National Business Hall of Fame in 1991. He was succeeded by William S. Cashel, Jr. Dorrance and other members of his family, however, still controlled 58 percent of Campbell's stock and showed no interest in selling, keeping the company safe from takeover.

By 1987 McGovern began selling off some of Campbell's less-successful ventures. In 1987 the company sold its disappointing pet food, Triangle physical fitness, and Juice Works beverage businesses. In 1988 the Pietro's pizza and Annabelle's restaurants were also sold, taking Campbell out of the restaurant business entirely.

However, Campbell also bought several smaller companies in 1987 and 1988 that were more compatible with its traditional lines of business. These included a French cookie maker, the Open Pit barbecue sauce line, an American olive producer, and Campbell's largest acquisition to date, Freshbake Foods Group PLC, a British producer of frozen foods. Also in 1988, Robert J. Vlasic, whose Vlasic Foods Campbell had purchased in 1978, became chairman of Campbell.

Campbell's management crisis was exacerbated by the death, in April of 1989, of John Dorrance. Dorrance's 31 percent of the company's stock was split between his three children, who have demonstrated an interest in preserving family control of the company. The remaining 27 percent of the family-owned stock is split among other members of the clan, some of whom (representing about 17.4 percent of the company's stock) have

expressed a desire to sell Campbell. But Chairman Vlasic had loaded the board with family members loyal to the company (six of the 15 board members are family members, including John Dorrance's three children), so a proxy battle seems unlikely.

McGovern left Campbell in late 1989. His final attempt to recoup Campbell's losses, a $343 million restructuring program, earned him little praise. Although sales had doubled during his term, profits had dropped 90 percent as a result of his aggressive capital commitments. From 1988 to 1990 alone, earnings fell from $274.1 million to $4.4 million.

In January of 1990 David W. Johnson was elected president and CEO. Johnson came to Campbell from Gerber Products Company, where he had been successful in streamlining that company's operations. Johnson employed a "back-to-basics" strategy that called for drastic restructuring. The new CEO oversaw the divestment of whole businesses, including mushroom farms, a salmon processing plant, the refrigerated salads line, and cookie maker Lazzaroni. By June of 1991, Johnson had closed or sold 20 plants worldwide, reduced the company's 51,700 person work force by 15.5 percent, and pulled unprofitable lines from store shelves. And while Johnson purported to support marketing, he also cut Campbell's advertising budget.

The product Johnson was most interested in promoting was soup, the company's core. Even into the early 1990s, Campbell soups had 66 percent, or $1.6 billion, of the $2.6 billion U.S. soup market, which contributed almost half of the conglomerate's $570 million operating profits.

In anticipation of the North American Free Trade Agreement, Johnson also supervised the combination of Campbell's Canadian operations, some Mexican companies, and the U.S. businesses into one division called Campbell North America. Late in 1991, Campbell also focused on the impending European Community's single market, which promised 344 million consumers (50 percent more than the United States) and had potential for future growth. The cookie subsidiary of Campbell Soup, Campbell Biscuits Europe, got a head start on the market in February of 1990, when it reorganized its European corporate structure, consolidated marketing, and standardized packaging.

By the end of 1991, some indicators showed that Johnson's efforts had paid off: Campbell's earnings through the first three quarters of 1991 had risen 33 percent, making the company's profits the second-fastest growing in the food industry. But some analysts warned that the profits came at the expense of core brand promotion, which was cut in 1991. The earnings were not based on sales, which only rose 1.9 percent during the same period.

Johnson has been given an overall good rating in the quick turnaround at Campbell. In 1992 the company made bolder goals, with a vision expressed as "Campbell Brands Preferred Around the World." The plan made further preparations for the European Community's single market and expanded those efforts around the world. The company was reorganized into three multi-national divisions. Campbell North and South America grouped Campbell's Swift-Armour subsidiary in Argentina with the previously-organized North American group. Campbell Biscuit and Bakery united Pepperidge Farm in North

America with Delacre in Europe and Australia's market-leading biscuit company, Arnotts Limited (of which Campbell owns 58 percent). Campbell Europe/Asia is a growth-oriented division that comprises the company's "greatest opportunity and challenge," according to the 1992 annual report.

Campbell's good performance, maintenance of high stock prices ($80 in mid-1991), and 58 percent Dorrance family ownership has staved off any threat of takeover by such giants as Philip Morris and Unilever. Campbell hopes to maintain those qualities by building brand strength, concentrating on global marketing, and continuing strategic asset divestment.

Principal Subsidiaries: Campbell Finance Corp.; Campbell Investment Co.; Campbell Sales Co.; Casera Foods, Inc.; Godiva Chocolatier, Inc.; Herider Farms, Inc.; Joseph Campbell Co.; Mrs. Paul's Kitchens, Inc.; Pepperidge Farm, Inc.; Vlasic Foods, Inc.; Swift-Armour Sociedad Anonima Argentina; N.V. Biscuits Delacre S.A. (Belgium); Campbell Foods P.L.C. (England); Societe Francaise des Biscuits Delacre S.A. (France); Campbell's de Mexico, S.A. de C.V.; Compania Envasadora Loreto, S.A. (Spain); Campbell Soup Co. Ltd. Les Soupes Campbell Ltee (France); Campbell S. Australasia Pty. Ltd. (Australia); Campbell S. Fresh, Inc.; Campbell S. U.K. Ltd. (United Kingdom); NV Campbell Food & Confectionar Coordination Center Continental Europe; ESA; NV Godiva Belgium, SA; Royal American Foods Corp.; Sanwa Foods Inc. (Japan).

Further Reading: Sim, Mary B., *History of Commercial Canning in New Jersey,* Trenton, New Jersey, New Jersey Agricultural Society, 1951; *A History,* Camden, New Jersey, Campbell Soup Company, 1988; "From Soup to Nuts and Back to Soup," *Business Week,* November 5, 1990, pp. 114, 116; Nulty, Peter, "The National Business Hall of Fame," *Fortune,* March 11, 1991, pp. 98–103; Barrett, Amy, "Campbell Soup: Hail to the Chef," *Financial World,* June 11, 1991, pp. 52–54; Weber, Joseph, "Campbell is Bubbling, But for How Long?" *Business Week,* June 17, 1991, pp. 56–57; Dagnoli, Judann, "Campbell Ups Ad $," *Advertising Age,* July 1, 1991, pp. 1, 25; "Recession Stalks Food Aisles," *Advertising Age,* July 15, 1991, pp. 1, 39; Saporito, Bill, "Campbell Soup Gets Piping Hot," *Fortune,* September 9, 1991, pp. 142–48; "New Product Search," *Advertising Age,* December 2, 1991; Wentz, Laurel, "Europe: How Smart Marketers Cash In," *Advertising Age,* December 2, 1991, pp. S-1, S-9; Abernathy, Chris A., "Company Study: Building Networks of Small Brands," *Journal of Services Marketing,* winter 1991, pp. 29–34; "Seizing the Dark Day," *Business Week,* January 13, 1992, pp. 26–28; Glosserman, Brad, "Campbell Soup Works for Spill Over Effect," *Japan Times Weekly International Edition,* May 11–May 17, 1992, p. 17; Woods, Wilton, "The Global 500: The World's Largest Industrial Corporations," *Fortune,* July 27, 1992, pp. 176–232; "Campbell: Now It's M-M-Global," *Business Week,* March 15, 1993, pp. 52–54.

—updated by April Dougal

CARRIER CORPORATION

One Carrier Place
Farmington, Connecticut 06032
U.S.A.
(203) 674-3000
Fax: (203) 674-3139

Subsidiary of United Technologies Corporation
Public Company
Incorporated: 1930
Employees: 28,000
Sales: $4 billion
Stock Exchanges: New York London Paris Frankfurt
    Amsterdam Brussels Geneva Zürich Basel Lausanne
SICs: 3585 Refrigeration & Heating Equipment

Carrier Corporation leads the world in the manufacture of residential and commercial heating, ventilating, and air conditioning (HVAC) systems and equipment. Its businesses also include commercial, industrial, and transport refrigeration and cryogenic cooling. Carrier manufactures and sells more than 350 product lines, among them heat pumps, furnaces, window room air conditioners, portable air conditioners, package thermal air conditioners, chillers, ducted and ductless systems, and packaged systems. These products are available in more than 10,000 model configurations.

On July 6, 1979, Carrier Corporation became a wholly owned subsidiary of United Technologies Corporation (UTC), the Hartford-based aerospace giant best known for its Pratt & Whitney jet engine division, in a contentious takeover that drew the attention of the federal government. Today, Carrier is one of UTC's global enterprises: together with the Otis Elevator Company, it forms the parent company's Building Systems division, which in 1991 accounted for 38 percent of UTC's revenues. Carrier leads the HVAC industry in many of the world's fastest growing markets and maintains distribution channels in 118 countries. It conducts about half of its manufacturing activities outside of the United States.

Though incorporated under its present name in 1930, the organization's roots extend back to the beginning of the century when a newly graduated Cornell engineer, Willis Haviland Carrier, started work at the Buffalo Forge Company, Buffalo, New York, on July 1, 1901. The story of Carrier Corporation begins with its founder, who, by being the first researcher to

combine air cooling with humidity control, became known as the inventor of modern air conditioning. Born November 26, 1876, on a farm in Angola, New York, a community in rural Erie County, Willis Haviland Carrier was the only child of Duane Carrier—who taught music to native Americans, tried running a general store, served a brief stint as postmaster, then took up farming—and his wife, Elizabeth Haviland, a descendent of a family of New England Quakers. Willis Carrier believed that he inherited his mechanical ability from his mother; she passed away when he was 11 years old.

Carrier graduated from Angola Academy, the local high school, in 1894 in the midst of a financial depression. Despite the problematic economics of his situation, he aspired to attend Cornell University, in Ithaca, New York. Carrier moved in with relatives in Buffalo and spent a year (1896–97) at Central High School in that city. In 1897, Carrier enrolled at Cornell on scholarships he had won through competitive examinations, graduating four years later with a degree in electrical engineering. He worked at odd jobs while in college to earn money for his living expenses.

Upon joining the Buffalo Forge Company shortly after graduation, Carrier was put to work on designs for a heating plant, boilers, and various types of systems for drying materials. He also began early on to pursue valuable research for his employer on the heat absorption of air when it circulated over steam-heating coils. Not surprisingly, the young engineer's first concentration, both practical and theoretical, was on heat, the core of Buffalo Forge's business.

The importance of Carrier's research activities was not lost on his managers and colleagues at Buffalo Forge. The company inaugurated a research program in 1902, with Willis Carrier as its unofficial director. That spring, Carrier's experiments drew the attention of a man who would become perhaps the most important figure in Carrier's career: J. Irvine Lyle, who was involved in sales and management for Buffalo Forge and in 1902 headed up the New York office. Like Carrier, Irvine Lyle was a farm boy; he grew up in Woodford County, Kentucky, and earned a degree in mechanical engineering in 1896. What prompted Lyle to seek out Carrier was a problem brought to Lyle by a consulting engineer working on behalf of the Sackett-Wilhelms Lithographing and Publishing Company of Brooklyn. High humidity levels in Sackett-Wilhelms's plant were causing production problems and the company was looking for a way to control airborne moisture.

Carrier threw himself into research on air dehumidification and by July 17, 1902, had completed drawings for what came to be recognized as the world's first scientific air conditioning system. Designed for Sackett-Wilhelms, the system was installed beginning in the summer of 1902 and continuing into 1903. By October 1903, Lyle was able to report back to Buffalo Forge's home office on the success of the first modern air conditioner. In the words of Carrier's biographer, "Out of Willis Carrier's research and ingenuity and Irvine Lyle's faith and salesmanship, a new industry was conceived and given birth."

Carrier continued to develop his ideas for conditioning air by controlling moisture. On September 16, 1904, he applied for a patent on an invention he called an "Apparatus for Treating

Air''; patent number 808897 was issued for the device on January 2, 1906. The ''Apparatus for Treating Air'' was the first spray-type air conditioning equipment, designed to humidify or dehumidify air by heating or cooling water. It ''was to open thousands of industrial doors.'' The LaCrosse National Bank of LaCrosse, Wisconsin, became the first purchaser of the system in 1904. By 1907, the spray-type air conditioning equipment had been installed for a number of significant customers, principally manufacturers in such businesses as textiles, shoes, and pharmaceuticals. The Wayland silk mill in Wayland, New York, acquired the first automatically operated modern air conditioning system, which took into account the added heat of the sun. Air conditioning had also found its way overseas to a silk mill in Yokohama, Japan.

At the end of 1907, Carrier came up with another ''invention''—a new company. He proposed the idea of creating a spinoff of Buffalo Forge to engineer and market air conditioning systems. In early 1908, Carrier Air Conditioning Company of America, a wholly owned subsidiary of Buffalo Forge Company, was in actual operation. The suggestion that the fledgling venture bear Carrier's name came from Lyle, perhaps with the intention of shielding the parent company if the air conditioning business failed. In any event, Carrier became vice-president of the subsidiary, although he remained in the employ of Buffalo Forge as its chief engineer and director of research, positions he had held since 1905. The sales manager of Carrier Air Conditioning Company of America, with headquarters in New York, was Irvine Lyle; the construction superintendent was Edmund P. Heckel; and the members of Lyle's staff included Boston-based Ernest T. Lyle, Irvine's younger brother and an experienced Buffalo Forge salesman, and Philadelphia-based Edward T. Murphy. In New York, Alfred E. Stacey, Jr., was chief engineer. When Stacey was transferred to Chicago in 1909, L. Logan Lewis joined the company as chief engineer. Murphy had worked with Carrier and Lyle in 1902 on the first air conditioner installation at Sackett-Wilhelms; Stacey and Heckel had worked with them on the Wayland silk mill system. Together, these men—the ''original seven''—who had been together on the very first air conditioning projects would later found the organization that was the immediate precursor of Carrier Corporation.

By the end of Carrier Air Conditioning Company of America's first year in existence, the foundation of the air conditioning industry was firmly in place. Between 1908 and 1914, the firm took on one industry after another: tobacco, steel, and hospitality, among others. It sold air conditioning systems to paper mills, breweries, department stores, hotels, soap and rubber factories, candy and processed food plants, film studios, bakeries, and meat packers—more than doubling its sales in the two-year period from 1912 to 1914. Despite this success, however, the Buffalo Forge Company decided in 1914, on the cusp of world war, to confine its activity to manufacturing. This alteration would require major changes at the air conditioning subsidiary. All the employees of Carrier Air Conditioning Company of America were to be discharged except Irvine Lyle, who was to be offered his old job as manager of Buffalo Forge's sales office in New York, and Willis Carrier, who was actually an employee of the parent company.

Although secure in their positions at Buffalo Forge Company, Carrier and Lyle decided that they could not simply let go of the new industry they had built. Moving forward with their air conditioning venture necessitated moving away from Buffalo Forge. On June 26, 1915, Carrier Engineering Corporation was officially formed under the laws of New York State, and the ''original seven'' were in business for themselves. The founders were Willis Carrier, Irvine Lyle, Edward Murphy, L. Logan Lewis, Ernest Lyle, A.E. Stacey, Jr., and Edmund Heckel; Carrier was president and Irvine Lyle assumed the positions of treasurer and general manager. Carrier Engineering Corporation opened its headquarters in Buffalo and its offices in New York, Chicago, Philadelphia, and Boston on July 1, 1915. The original capital was stock subscriptions totaling $2,500.

The new corporation's first decade saw not only a continuation of the previous success achieved in the air conditioning business (Carrier Engineering closed 40 contracts by the end of 1915), but also a breakthrough in refrigeration technology, another result of Willis Carrier's research creativity. By the early 1920s, Carrier Engineering Corporation had begun manufacturing and selling the centrifugal refrigeration machines that its president and engineers had developed, equipment that represented the first major advance in mechanical refrigeration since David Boyle introduced the original ammonia compressor in 1872. The first sale of the centrifugal refrigeration system was to Stephen F. Whitman & Sons of Philadelphia, a candy maker.

While 1921 was a productive year for the highly promising refrigeration product line, it was a key year in other areas as well. Seeking space for expansion into manufacturing to produce the centrifugal refrigerators as well as for offices to house the company's headquarters, Carrier Engineering bought a building on Frelinghuysen Avenue in Newark, New Jersey. Willis Carrier went to Europe in search of low-cost suppliers of components for the refrigeration system and to help complete the organization of Carrier Engineering Company, Ltd., of England. Much was riding on the success of the Carrier centrifugal refrigerating machine, which at that time was barely off the drawing boards.

Once that success was assured, Carrier Engineering set a new goal for the mid-1920s and beyond: to pioneer into a new market—comfort air conditioning. This market began to open in 1924 when Irvine Lyle sold the company's first ''comfort job,'' a centrifugal refrigeration system to cool the J.L. Hudson Department Store in Detroit. However, it was the introduction of the new centrifugal systems to movie houses that truly launched comfort cooling. Carrier Engineering's first such installation was at the Palace Theater in Dallas in the summer of 1924. Perhaps the firm's crowning contract in the new comfort market was its installation, completed in 1929, of the first air conditioning systems in the U.S. Senate and House of Representatives.

The history of the company that operates today under the UTC umbrella dates to the following year—October 31, 1930—when Carrier Corporation was incorporated in Delaware. The new entity was a consolidation of the Carrier Engineering Corporation and its subsidiaries, Carrier Construction Company, Inc., and W.J. Gamble Corporation, as well as several refrigeration and heating companies. Carrier Corporation's growth through the next three decades can be traced in the continuation of its merger and acquisition activities, which brought in, among other additions: Affiliated Gas Equipment, Inc., of Cleveland in 1955; the Elliott Company, a major subsidiary, in 1957; and a significant number of overseas organizations throughout the 1960s and 1970s. By the fourth quarter of 1977, shortly before UTC's unsolicited overtures, Carrier Corporation had more than 38 subsidiaries in locations as far flung as Japan, Singapore, and Australia; it operated, from its Syracuse, New York, headquarters, more than ten million square feet of manufacturing, warehouse, and office facilities in 23 states and 12 foreign countries; and it had diversified into a range of businesses that included energy process equipment (e.g., centrifugal air, gas compressors, and turbines), solid waste handling equipment, potentiometers (i.e., instruments for measuring electromotive forces), large electric motors, chemical specialty products for industry (e.g., inks and paints), and finance.

A "snapshot" view of Carrier Corporation in 1965 shows it riding the crest of the construction wave that swept households and businesses from the cities to the suburbs in the period of rapid economic expansion following World War II. During that year one in every four new houses in the United States was air conditioned, up from one in nine just five years earlier, boosting total domestic home air conditioner sales to a record $1.2 billion. Commercial air conditioning represented a $1.15 billion market in 1965, with one new industrial plant in three being HVAC equipped. Even schools had become potential customers for systems that were now capable of cooling, heating, controlling humidity, eliminating dust, and reducing noise. Carrier Corporation, number one in this burgeoning U.S. air conditioning market in the mid-1960s, reported a jump in sales in fiscal year 1964 to $325 million, up nine percent, as well as a 22 percent increase in new orders and a 58 percent increase in profits during the first quarter of 1965. Exports, particularly to reverse-season continents such as Australia and South America, had helped make air conditioning a year-round enterprise by the 1960s, fueling the growth of all the firms offering HVAC products. Moreover, Carrier Corporation had landed several large, high-profile air conditioning projects, including the Houston Astrodome, the 19-building complex to house New York State's governmental offices in Albany, and the new London headquarters of Scotland Yard.

In the following decade, however, the U.S. growth curve began heading downward, bringing slower activity in the industrial and construction sectors that were so vital to Carrier Corporation's health. In the aftermath of UTC's hostile takeover of the company—a protracted and bitter struggle that finally ended with Carrier's becoming a wholly owned subsidiary of UTC on July 6, 1979—the decade of the 1980s saw Carrier Corporation in a deteriorating competitive position: it lagged well behind the other companies in the industry in new product development, its costs were as much as ten percent higher than the competition's, and it had developed a reputation among dealers for poor quality and service. These problems were compounded by a shrinking U.S. market for air conditioning and heating equipment as new home sales dropped 10.1 percent between 1989 and 1990 alone and the overbuilt office and commercial real estate markets depressed demand for Carrier's products by as much as 30 percent.

After assuming the chairmanship of UTC in 1986, Robert F. Daniell went to work on the Carrier subsidiary as part of his efforts to give the parent company an overhaul. This involved $600 million worth of cost cuts at UTC and the sale of more than $1.5 billion of its assets. By 1990, Daniell had disposed of unrelated Carrier Corporation businesses such as trout farming and dumpsters and eliminated $100 million in overhead. Carrier president William A. Wilson reduced the number of white-collar employees by 30 percent during his six-year tenure which ended in 1990. He also initiated an updating of Carrier's product line, with the result that in 1990 new or redesigned products represented 75 percent of North American sales. Among the new offerings were a residential furnace designed to cut home energy costs by 45 percent and a home air conditioner featuring a 25 percent reduction in noise. Research and development initiatives included office air conditioning systems to cool the air without releasing the chlorofluorocarbons that deplete the atmosphere's ozone layer, as well as a $100 million investment in a new compressor to be manufactured in a state-of-the-art plant in the United States rather than in Japan, where such components had traditionally been purchased by air conditioner makers.

In 1992, after a four-year slide and despite downsizings and reorganizations, Carrier Corporation remained a troubled subsidiary and a drag on the parent's performance. Nevertheless, UTC cited the end of a lengthy recession and indications of a turnaround in UTC's overall operations as signs that its decision to hold on to its units, including Carrier, was going to pay off. In early 1992 it unveiled an ambitious restructuring plan in which more than 100 plants were to be closed or merged and 11,000 jobs cut. At the Carrier division, the push to add new products and to reduce both inventories and delivery time to customers meant consolidating and reengineering production processes and installing new technology at its manufacturing sites. In line with the plans of many U.S. corporations in the early 1990s, the goal at Carrier was to maintain current output with fewer workers and less space at lower costs. At a Carrier facility in Indianapolis, where assembly lines were reconfigured and component manufacturing was moved nearby, annual inventory was reduced by $12 million and productivity improved by as much as 20 percent.

Looking ahead, UTC expects the world market for HVAC equipment to grow by more than 65 percent, to approximately $40 billion, by the year 2000, with more than half that total market centered in the Asia-Pacific region. The blueprint for Carrier Corporation calls for expansion outside current slow-growth markets to secure a presence in developing areas globally. Quality and customer-satisfaction initiatives also continue to be emphasized, with the result that quality problems, and the accompanying warranty-claims costs, connected with new installations of the company's main line of home air conditioning compressors have declined by half since 1986. To meet its goal of greater responsiveness to changing customer requirements, Carrier is building the add-on and replacement segments of the heating and air conditioning business (both residential and commercial). Research and development is another area in which Carrier is concentrating, spending $100 million on research in 1991 and committing itself to an additional $550 million research and development investment during the five subsequent years. The strategic focus is to be on such core technologies as compression, electronics and controls, refrigerants (particularly non-ozone-depleting alternatives), air management, heat transfer, and indoor air quality.

While UTC's plans envision a more internationally competitive Carrier, they also mandate a still-leaner company. Employment at the subsidiary is targeted for a 1,525-job reduction by 1994, manufacturing capacity is to shrink by 1.7 million square feet, and plant closings will take place in California, Tennessee, Georgia, and at overseas locations. What observers will be looking for in the immediate future are indications that Carrier is finally carrying its own weight within the UTC fold.

Further Reading: Ingels, Margaret, *Willis Haviland Carrier: Father of Air Conditioning,* New York, Country Life Press, 1952; "Warm News at Carrier," *Time,* March 5, 1965; Vogel, Todd, "Can Carrier Corp. Turn Up the Juice?" *Business Week,* September 3, 1990; Naj, Amal Kumar, "United Technologies Navigates a Turnaround Course," *Wall Street Journal,* April 7, 1992.

—Nancy Hitchner

CBI INDUSTRIES, INC.

800 Jorie Boulevard
Oak Brook, Illinois 60522-7001
U.S.A.
(708) 572-7000
Fax: (708) 572-7405

Public Company
Incorporated: 1889 as Chicago Bridge & Iron Company
Employees: 12,950
Sales: $1.67 billion
Stock Exchanges: New York
SICs: 3443 Fabricated Plate Work—Boiler Shops; 2813
  Industrial Gases; 1629 Heavy Construction Nec; 6719
  Holding Companies Nec

CBI Industries, Inc. is the world's leading manufacturer of vessels for oil, gas, and water storage and, through its Liquid Carbonic subsidiary, the largest producer of industrial gases. Principally involved in the energy supply and municipal projects businesses, CBI operates in hundreds of countries throughout the world.

The Chicago Bridge & Iron Company, forerunner to CBI Industries, was established in 1889 through the merger of two companies. One of these companies was a Minneapolis-based engineering concern run by Horace Ebenezer Horton, who had distinguished himself by building some the country's first metallic span bridges over the Mississippi River. The other was the Kansas City Bridge and Iron Company, operated by George Wheelock and A.M. Blodgett. In the three years before the merger, this company built more than 500 structures across the United States.

The new company relocated to Washington Heights, Illinois, a suburb of Chicago, which provided easy rail transportation to the foundries and steel mills in the area. Though it took several months to relocate machinery from Kansas City, Chicago Bridge & Iron immediately began accepting jobs to build bridges.

In 1890 Chicago Bridge & Iron absorbed the operations of the Des Moines-based George E. King Bridge Company. King was an established bridge builder in Iowa, a market that Horton and his new partners had been unable to crack. Meanwhile, King was attracted to an interest in his new partners' reliable metal fabricating facility.

The demand for bridges at this time was extraordinary. In the decades after the Civil War, railroads helped to establish burgeoning rural communities. As commerce grew, demands on transportation followed. Between so many points, there were rivers, streams and gulleys, and each route required its own span.

Until that time, wooden bridges were the order of the day. But while these were sturdy, they were susceptible to rot and structural failure. The answer was in iron bridges, which few foundries were equipped to design or manufacture. With demand high, Chicago Bridge & Iron won contracts to build several hundred bridges by 1893. Other structures they were contracted to build included the first metallic water towers and standpipes and a Horse Exchange Amphitheatre for the Chicago stockyards.

That year, however, irregularities in railroad financing, shoddy banking practices, and the failure of agricultural crops caused a severe four-year economic depression that nearly closed Chicago Bridge & Iron. Then, in 1897, a devastating fire destroyed nearly the entire operation. Faced with the tremendous task of rebuilding, King opted to leave the corporation to concentrate on his more profitable banking and agricultural interests. While it took Horton nearly six years to pay King off, he did emerge as the company's sole shareholder.

As the Washington Heights plant was rebuilt, work under contract was gradually brought back from other factories working under subcontract. Also, the company's water towers became extremely popular after Horton's son George Horton perfected a hemispherical tank bottom that eliminated the need for a complex tank deck. This business helped the company weather an extremely difficult period in which all sales offices outside of Chicago were closed.

By the turn of the century the company was once again on its feet and taking on its first ventures in Canada. But a covert trade dispute waged by Canadian firms and the government convinced Horton to abandon Canada and never again do business there. His son George, however, succeeded in winning several important contacts on his own, purchasing the materials from his father's company.

The company entered 1907 on strong growth, with contracts for several hundred water tanks, hundreds of bridges, and miscellaneous structures. Later that year a second financial panic sent the American economy into a tailspin. Public funds, which municipalities used to purchase water tanks and bridges, evaporated almost over night. Contracts were canceled and, once again, Chicago Bridge & Iron was forced into retrenchment.

These conditions were made more difficult by the fact that all steel products at this time were subject to artificial shipping costs from Pittsburgh, regardless of where they were made. This prevented Chicago Bridge & Iron from competing effectively in the East. In an effort to open this new market, the company established a second facility in 1911 at Greenville, Pennsylvania, outside Pittsburgh.

Horton died on July 28, 1912, leaving the business to his wife and five children. The eldest son George later emerged as leader of the company. Unencumbered by his father's anti-Canadian prejudice, George Horton quickly merged his own Canadian operations with Chicago Bridge & Iron, establishing a new factory at Bridgeburg, Ontario, near Niagara Falls. Other business arose in Cuba, where the demand was for molasses, water, and, later, oil tanks. Soon afterward the company was asked to build water tanks in the shapes of a milk bottle, a pineapple, and a ''peachoid.'' Diversifying further, Chicago Bridge & Iron was asked to build water pumping facilities for the City of Chicago.

By 1914, as the war in Europe began to heat up, the belligerents began to purchase more and more war material from American manufacturers. This energized the American economy and drastically assisted Chicago Bridge & Iron's growth. Only three years later, after the United States entered the war and many of the company's employees left for the army, Chicago Bridge & Iron received hundreds of war-related orders, including one to build 150 5,000-ton barges.

At the close of the war in 1919, George Horton decided not to involve his company in the reconstruction of Europe. Governments there, he was told, were not as credit worthy as Central and South American governments. This decision paid off when Chicago Bridge & Iron began taking large orders for huge oil storage tanks, first in the United States and then in Cuba, Venezuela, Aruba, and Mexico. Additional orders later came from the Dutch East Indies, Malaya, India, and China. The tremendous tank business also prompted Horton to phase out the company's bridge building business in favor of plate steel structures.

Horton made an important discovery during this time. Noting how his engineers spent so much time boring rivet holes with templates, Horton conceived of a 12-hole rivet punch, capable of boring a dozen perfectly placed rivet holes at once. This ''Chibridge Spacer'' shortened production schedules, enabling the company to secure more business. Later, Horton abandoned rivets altogether, favoring leak-proof welded seams.

Meanwhile, the company experienced a brief labor strike in October 1919 when, soon after organizing, workers walked out. Queried as to why they went on strike, workers replied that their union was seeking a closed shop and better benefits. The strike was resolved after 18 days.

In 1922 Chicago Bridge & Iron purchased the rights to a ''floating roof'' storage system patented by a Bureau of Mines engineer named John H. Wiggins. The design allowed the tank's roof to float on the stored product, trapping the contents within and preventing losses to leakage or evaporation. Another major product for the oil industry, intended for natural gas storage, was the Hortonsphere, a spherical steel vessel capable of holding gas under great pressure.

In December of 1923 the Horton Steel Works in Bridgeburg suffered a debilitating fire. During reconstruction of this plant, Chicago Bridge & Iron merged the Horton plant with another Canadian firm, Des Moines Steel. In 1929, on the strength of its tank business, Chicago Bridge & Iron absorbed the large Reeves Brothers plant in Birmingham, Alabama. Later that year, however, a stock market crash plunged the world into the Great Depression. Once again, Chicago Bridge & Iron's orders were either deferred or canceled, profits took a nosedive, and employees were laid off.

But, surviving on a trickle of work from the oil industry—namely, in the Middle East, the Dutch East Indies, and Italy—Chicago Bridge & Iron forged ahead with plans to incorporate new electric arc welding technology into its products. This new process allowed entire structures, rather than just tank bottoms and roofs, to be welded. This greatly reduced the weight of the structures, resulting in more efficient designs.

The company once again faced labor trouble in 1930 when new labor laws lifted certain restrictions on union organization of workers. But when the matter came up before unrepresented workers at Chicago Bridge & Iron, the employees rejected outside labor representatives and established their own independent union. Still, the company's nomadic tank builders were left unrepresented. Local Boilermakers unions incited battles with the company's ''tankees,'' and killed many during gun fights. The Boilermakers later agreed to negotiations which led to the establishment of an associated union for transient tank builders.

Chicago Bridge & Iron entered several new fields during the 1930s. While the Canadian plant began building heat exchangers and welded ships, the repeal in 1933 of Prohibition led to massive brewery contracts for the American plants. Once again public works projects, including work on the San Francisco Bay Bridge and the Tennessee Valley Authority, provided much needed income. Layoffs were reversed in 1934 and in the following year the company began taking on new hires. Later work included barge building and work on chemical and infant nuclear plants.

The outbreak of war in December of 1941 put Chicago Bridge & Iron on a war footing. By agreement with the government the company was assigned to build drydocks and ships, for which it purchased land in Morgan City, Louisiana. In January of 1942 Chicago Bridge & Iron took control of a Pacific yard at Eureka, California, and later established facilities in Newburgh, New York, and Seneca, Illinois. As construction commenced at these sights, entire families were relocated from the company's other locations. Employment ballooned from 4,000 employees in 1941 to 20,000 the following year.

The company's first contract was for 40 Landing Ship Tanks, or LSTs, which were designed to deliver heavy mobile machinery from ships to beachheads. Construction began on LSTs immediately. In fact, ships were built as the yard was built, and few of the employees were trained shipbuilders. Many learned their jobs as they went. The company also built drydocks, capable of lifting 100,000-ton ships out of the water for repairs, and underground fuel storage facilities at Pearl Harbor and, near the end of the war, in Subic Bay in the Philippines.

As the war drew to a close, Chicago Bridge & Iron was highly regarded for its excellent production schedule and cost control. After building 157 LSTs, George Horton reminded employees in February of 1945 that war production was ending and that, ''a contractor without contracts does not amount to much.'' A month later, Horton was killed in a car accident. The company's directors, eager to prevent ruinous disorganization, elected George Horton's younger brother Horace president of the company, and career engineer Merle Trees chairman of the board.

Later that year, John Wiggins announced that he was terminating his design and consulting agreements with Chicago Bridge & Iron and going to work for a rival, the General American Transportation Corporation. This threatened to knock the company out of its most profitable peacetime line at precisely the wrong moment. Trees issued a challenge to his engineers to develop an improved floating roof technology free of Wiggins' patent. Operating under a short deadline, the engineers succeeded in designing an original Horton model.

The company entered the postwar period in very solid financial condition, holding no bank loans. Market conditions were favorable for strong growth, owing to pent-up demand for public works and industrial projects. Chicago Bridge & Iron received orders for a variety of its standard products—water and oil tanks—but also was asked to construct pressure and containment vessels for the emerging nuclear testing and power industries.

But the company faced two serious impediments to postwar business. First, few companies could find enough skilled draftsmen to design these products. While some talent could be hired away from competitors, the company's design offices still couldn't keep up. There also was a shortage of experienced construction engineers. And, secondly, CB&I, as it had become known, was faced with recurrent shortages of steel, which was still being rationed in monthly allocations. During the war, however, the Geneva steel mill that had been established at Salt Lake City lacked a large local customer base. Seeing it as the perfect supplier, the company immediately began construction of a full scale fabricating plant at that sight.

By March 1946, the company encountered a boat glut. The company's shipbuilding unit, which employed 12,000 workers during the war, was now down to 12 employees. But growth in overseas markets more than made up for this loss. With tax incentives to invest in Latin America, as part of the Roosevelt Administration's "Good Neighbor Policy," CB&I established subsidiaries in Venezuela and Brazil. Later, the company decided to aggressively pursue foreign licensing to boost sales and protect patent rights. Licensees were established throughout the world, including France, Germany, Japan, and Australia.

In 1948, the first year of postwar profitability, CB&I won a contract to modernize U.S. Steel's massive South Chicago Works. A few years later the company was invited to build an enormous tank farm in Aden for British Petroleum, which later led to the establishment of a British subsidiary.

Employees ran on nine-hour days and six-day work weeks. As the job backlog lightened up, this was scaled back to eight hours and five days, avoiding layoffs. By 1953, however, the backlog had disappeared, forcing the company to institute layoffs and a "necessary absence" plan.

By 1954 CB&I had become involved in cryogenics, hydroelectric and nuclear power, liquified natural gas, and, later, built wind tunnels and vessels for the space program. Returning to bridgework after nearly 40 years, the company built caissons for the Mackinac Straights Bridge in Michigan.

Also in 1954, Merle Trees died. He was replaced as chairman by Horace B. Horton, who was himself replaced as president by E. E. Michaels. Michaels was well suited to lead the company at that time. He was an experienced corporate diplomat, capable of maintaining a balance between two opposing ownership forces within the company. He was also, however, a good manager, unafraid to assert his own views.

With the discovery of oil in Western Canada, CB&I established a facility in North Lethbridge, Alberta, where it manufactured vessels for the oil, gas, pulp, and fertilizer industries. In 1957 the company became involved in sewage projects. In 1958, as international expansion continued, the company established an Argentine subsidiary, Cometarsa, which failed to perform well and was sold nine years later. Still, massive water desalinization projects, particularly one in Kuwait, were undertaken in partnership with G. & J. Weir Ltd. of Glasgow. Building on its aeronautical business, CB&I acquired an interest in the Minneapolis-based FluiDyne Engineering Corporation.

In September 1959 Horace B. Horton died and was succeeded as chairman by his son Arthur. Later, in 1962, E. E. Michaels resigned to run, unsuccessfully, as a Republican for the U.S. House of Representatives. He was replaced by Josh Clarke.

In 1960 the company established subsidiaries in Germany and Holland and, later, in Mexico. The company also restructured its Australian interests, forming Chicago Bridge Lennox with its Australian licensee, but later dissolved it in favor of a wholly owned company called CBI Constructors. Additional operations were later established in the Philippines, Italy, and Japan. Back home, in 1961, CB&I broke ground on a new headquarters building in Oak Brook, Illinois. Two years later, recognizing the tremendous growth the company had experienced, the Board of Directors decided to take the company public.

In 1963 CB&I won a contract to build major sections of the large Mangla Dam in Pakistan. This successful project led to work on a second, the Tarbela Dam, in 1971. In 1964 CB&I acquired three engineering companies, Rebikoff Oceanics, Copeland Process, a specialist in industrial waste disposal, and Walker Process, which built equipment for water and sewage plants. And, to keep up with the growing volume of nuclear plant projects, CB&I opened a new facility specifically for supplying nuclear reactors in Memphis. The company continued to bolster its engineering ranks in 1967, when it set up a new research lab at Plainfield, Illinois and staffed it with some of the best engineers in the world.

During the 1960s, the liquified natural gas (LNG) business began to take off. As a pioneer in engineering these projects, CB&I became the industry leader in vessel manufacturing, both for land storage and on ships. In 1969 the company formed a gas transportation subsidiary called American LNG. That year CB&I also built an enormous oil storage and loading device designed to sit on the seafloor. This project, Khazzan Dubai, was built for the Gulf Sheikdom of Dubai, and was nominated for honors by the National Society of Professional Engineers. Unfortunately the project's competitors were the Apollo space program and the Boeing 747.

John Horton, son of Horace B. Horton, who succeeded Josh Clarke as president in 1968, stepped down after only 11 months in office to pursue personal interests. He was replaced as president by Marvin Mitchell, a career CB&I engineer. Early in 1973 Arthur Horton, who had been inflicted with polio as a boy, died after a long illness. Mitchell succeeded him as chairman of the company.

The Arab oil embargo of 1973–1974 was a tremendous boon to the company. Oil consumers, used to frequent oil deliveries, had little storage capacity for oil, which now was available only when you could get it. With sales up 80 percent in 1973, CB&I was again awash in a backlog of orders. The energy crisis caused by the embargo set into motion plans to exploit huge oil reserves in Alaska. Here, too, CB&I was asked to supply equipment and storage tanks for the Alyeska Pipeline Company between Barrow and Valdez. The company also opened a new facility at Prairieville, Louisiana, to service projects in the Gulf of Mexico and train underwater welders.

But, after the embargo ended, Mitchell grew weary of the cyclical and unpredictable nature of the energy business. He moved to diversify the company and in 1975 purchased Virginia-based Fairmac Corporation, a real estate developer. In 1977, however, CB&I unveiled a more economical process of extracting carbon dioxide from LNG, called Cryex. This patented process only helped to push CB&I further into the energy business. In 1979 CB&I took control of Circle Bar, an oil drilling company based in New Orleans.

Management affected a corporate reorganization in 1979, creating a holding company called CBI Industries, which took ownership of Chicago Bridge & Iron. The name change was deemed necessary because the company was no longer based in Chicago, did not build bridges, and hadn't used iron for decades.

CBI won new contracts for large petroleum projects in the North Sea and in Abu Dhabi and, in 1983, once again tried to diversify. Its search ended in 1984 when the company purchased Liquid Carbonic, the world's leading supplier of carbon dioxide. Liquid Carbonic was founded in 1888 to supply carbon dioxide gas to soda fountains and soft drink bottlers. In 1926 the company began commercial sales of solid carbon dioxide, or "dry ice." After World War II, Liquid Carbonic branched into frozen food technologies and commercial sales of oxygen, nitrogen, and argon which, unlike carbon dioxide, are extracted from the atmosphere.

Marvin Mitchell resigned as chairman of the company upon turning 65 in 1981 and was replaced by Bill Pogue. Pogue served as chairman until 1989 when he, too, turned 65. Pogue was succeeded by John Jones, a former vice-chairman and chief operating officer.

After a difficult period of adjustment during the mid-1980s, caused primarily by cyclical retrenchment in the energy construction business, CBI entered the 1990s with a stronger, revitalized organization built on more than 100 years of successful projects. While Liquid Carbonic has helped to insulate CBI from the ups and downs of energy development, it remains to be seen whether the company will continue to pursue additional businesses that are equally stable.

Principal Subsidiaries: Chicago Bridge & Iron Company; Liquid Carbonic Industries Corporation; Statia Terminals, N.V.; Integrated Drilling and Exploration, Inc.

Further Reading: The Bridge Works: A History of Chicago Bridge & Iron, CBI Industries, Inc., Mobium Press, Chicago, 1987; "Companies to Watch," *Fortune,* November 5, 1990; *CBI Industries, Inc. Annual Report,* 1990 and 1991; *Total Capability in Carbon Dioxide,* Liquid Carbonic Publication; *Capabilities,* Chicago Bridge & Iron Company Publication.

—John Simley

CENTRAL INDEPENDENT TELEVISION PLC

Central House
Broad Street
Birmingham B1 2I9
Great Britain
071-486 6688
Fax: 071-468 9898

Public Company
Incorporated: 1982
Sales: $211,000,000
Employees: 830
Stock Exchange: London International Stock Exchange
SICs: 4833 Television Broadcasting Stations

Central Independent Television plc is Britain's largest Independent Television (ITV) broadcaster, producing, broadcasting, and distributing news and drama programs in its British home market and abroad. Central's audience is comprised of nine million homes in the British Midlands region. Because of its expertise in distributing material abroad, Central also sells programs on behalf of 20 international broadcasters, including Zenith, Royal Geographic Society, WGBH Boston (part of the U.S. Public Broadcasting Service) and Television New Zealand.

Central, which ranked as Britain's 193rd largest public company on the London Stock Exchange at the end of 1992, has three major divisions: Central Broadcasting, Central Productions, and Central Television Enterprises. The Birmingham-based Central Broadcasting division operates the company's broadcasting license and is responsible for commissioning, marketing, scheduling, and broadcasting all the company's programs. It also controls the production of all regional programming, including regional news and current affairs output. The Nottingham-based Central Productions division produces programs in studios and regionally for the ITV network and for other British and international broadcasters. Finally, the London-based Central Television Enterprises (CTE) division is the company's program distributor, selling Central's programs to fellow broadcasters, cable operators, and video distributors internationally.

Central's roots as a broadcaster date back to 1954 when independent commercial television was introduced in England to break the monopoly of the BBC, the country's state-run television network. In February of 1956, Independent Television (ITV) arrived in the Midlands with weekend broadcasts, which were replaced by daily programming by the end of the year. Programming was handled by Associated Television (ATV), a subsidiary of Associated Communications Corporation (ACC), during the weekdays, and by ABC on the weekends.

ATV was granted the franchise for the Midlands broadcasting operation in 1968 and held it until January of 1982, when the Independent Broadcasting Authority (IBA), Britain's television regulatory body at the time, announced the franchise would not be automatically re-awarded. What was more, the IBA stipulated that ACC could hold no more than a 51 percent interest in Central, and had to build and operate studios in regions served by the broadcaster with the latest in equipment.

A new company named Central Independent Television was formed to take control of the new Midlands franchise in January of 1982. Major stockholders included ACC (51 percent), leisure group Ladbrokes (10 percent), publishing group DC Thomson (15 percent) and Pergamon (9 percent), led by the late Robert Maxwell. Central's boundaries at the time ranged from the borders of Wales in the west to Lincolnshire in the east, and from Cheshire in the north to the Home Counties in the south. Covering an estimated 14,000 square miles and serving more than 9 million people, Central had the largest audience of Britain's 12 independent ITV broadcasters.

In May 1982, ACC was taken over by TVW Enterprises, led by Australian media magnate, Robert Holmes a Court. The IBA ruled that ACC's 51 percent stake in Central be put in trust, thus freezing its voting right until ACC had reduced its shareholding in the broadcaster. Therefore, in May 1983, ACC sold off its stake in Central. Sears Holdings purchased a 20 percent shareholding, Ladbrokes and DC Thomson increased their stakes to 20 percent each and Pergamon took its ownership to 12.5 percent.

In line with IBA requirements, renovation of Central's four Birmingham studios at Broad Street was completed in 1982. A new broadcast center was opened a year later. In addition, Nottingham saw the opening of the $42.5 million, four-studio East Midlands Television Center in late 1983. The formal ribbon-cutting ceremony in March of 1984 was attended by the Duke of Edinburgh.

In October 1986, Central issued public shares to be listed on the London International Stock Exchange. Institutional investors in London were among the broadcaster's leading stockholders.

From its beginnings, Central had a mandate to operate a local news service broadcast to each of the company's three main markets: Central West, East, and South. The broadcaster eventually had the most morning and evening local news viewers of any ITV news program. For its news broadcasts, Central was supplied with national and international programs by Independent Television News (ITN), the national news bureau owned and operated by all ITV regional broadcasters.

Central also continued to produce strong drama and entertainment programs for broadcast in its own market and throughout Britain and internationally. The broadcaster's most popular programs include the satirical weekly *Spitting Image,* the investigative current affairs program *The Cook Report,* and drama series like *Inspector Morse* and *Soldier Soldier.*

Much, though certainly not all, of Central's drama output, tended towards high-brow content for sale abroad. The popular *Legacy of Civilization* series, a six-part documentary exploring the effects of ancient history on modern life, was an early example. British television has always emphasized cultural programming. Central and other ITV franchises still broadcast a large amount of ballet and opera to complement their lighter drama and entertainment content. Broadcasts of the established arts, though top sellers in foreign markets for Central, are in part defensive. Because quality of programming is a key factor in the granting of franchises to broadcasting companies, a tendency for high culture is often observed in ITV programming when franchises are up for renewal.

In 1986, Central established Television Sales and Marketing Services Ltd. (TSMS), a joint venture between itself and Anglia Television, another ITV broadcaster. The role of TSMS was to secure airtime sales and program sponsorships, in part to recover production costs. In addition, TSMS acts as consultant to international broadcasters like BBC Select, Nederland 1 in The Netherlands, and Westcountry.

In 1989, Central spent $10 million to build a high-tech regional news center at Abingdon, near Oxford. That gave the broadcasters three main regional centers: Abingdon, Nottingham, and Birmingham. In addition, Central operated offices in London, New York, Sydney, and Hamburg. Besides functioning as news-gathering centers, these international bureaus also facilitated international sales and sponsorship of Central's programs.

International cooperation between program makers had become the buzzword in the increasingly global television market during the late 1980s. Broadcasters found they could spread out the cost—and the risk—of producing programs if they could bring in overseas partners. The key was recognizing, and taking advantage of, the demands of the television industry beyond their own home markets. British English-language programming—Central's included—had long secured wide audiences around the world, a legacy of the British Empire. Central looked to tap into this growing international system of coproduction, cofinancing, sales, pre-sales, and sponsor-packaging to reduce the cost of its own program production by pooling resources with others, and securing yet more markets for its output.
Central also had to keep pace with rapid changes in the technology of the television industry. In the mid to late 1980s, the number of terrestrial, cable, and satellite television channels worldwide was mushrooming. In addition, a revolution was taking place in high-definition television. Program production and distribution was entering the world of digital compression, which would multiply the available frequency spectrum and transform home television viewing.

The regional broadcaster was also looking to counter the growing influence of American programs being sold to Europe and worldwide. As Leslie Hill, Central's managing director, said in 1990: "American culture seems to be in danger of overwhelming that of some other countries, including Britain. I believe we should guard against that." Hill felt that cooperation between foreign broadcasters, especially between those in Canada, Europe, and Australia, could not only reduce production costs but counter an American programming offensive. "This international activity may appear to boost the ego and self-importance of an industry notoriously aware of its image, but it is this international cooperation that lies behind some of our more ambitious program projects."

International coproductions Central completed included the 1988 *Legacy of Civilization* documentary series, made in conjunction with Maryland Public Television. Another series, *Nuclear Age,* was produced along with WGBH, a Boston-based public television station, and NHK, a Japanese broadcaster.

Deregulation of the British television industry, first introduced by the then Prime Minister Margaret Thatcher in 1988, had a profound effect on Central Television's future. The British government sought to shake up the country's television market by ending the monopoly that existing ITV franchise broadcasters, including Central, seemingly enjoyed. The 1989 Broadcasting Bill, introduced by the government and leading to the 1990 Broadcasting Act, called for 16 ITV contractors to bid in May 1991 to retain their franchises against rival tenders.

With no anticipated rival bidders for its franchise, Central was expected to emerge strongly from the 1991 auction, since it could bid low and win. Prior to the bid, the broadcasting company had focused on its core strengths: program production and distribution, and aiming to maintain quality output so potential competitors would be deterred. The strategy worked. Central's application was unchallenged in May 1991, and it was granted the seven-day-a-week broadcast license in October 1991, extending from January 1, 1993 through the year 2002. For the East, West, and South Midlands television regions, Central bid a mere $4000 annual bid. That figure paled in comparison to other ITV franchise bidders, who offered many millions as part of annual bids to the British treasury, and yet often did not emerge as victors against rivals.

Under the license auction, Central agreed to pay the British Treasury a percentage, set by the Independent Television Commission (TIC), of annual qualifying revenue, or a part of advertising, subscription, and sponsorship income. In addition, it was to pay the cash bid, or $4000, each year.

At the same time, Central profited yet again from the ITV auction after Meridian, a consortium in which Central held a 20 percent stake, was successful in securing the license to broadcast in South and South East England. Meridian was led by MAI, a financial services group whose businesses included moneybroking and market research, and had a 65 percent stake in the bidding consortium.

In September 1991, just prior to the announcement of license awards, David Justham, chair of Central, died. He was immediately replaced by Leslie Hill as chair of the board of directors and chief executive officer of Central.

In November 1991, after having its license award confirmed, Central purchased its rented headquarters in Birmingham. The building was renamed the West Midlands Television Center. Also that year, Television Sales and Marketing Services acquired the airtime sales operation of Ulster Television in Northern Ireland. Continued cost-cutting measures at this time included the sale in 1991 of Film Fair, the film animation company owned by Central. The broadcaster also disposed of its 25 percent stake in Starstream, the British children's channel, and Central Communications Network, once Central's in-house public relations department before becoming a consultancy. Central also refocused its business by severing ties with Chris Bearde Entertainment, a small production house, and Wordstar, a company providing newspapers and magazines with entertainment news worldwide.

Central's fortune after the ITV auction was reflected in its bottom line. Although advertising revenue had fallen throughout the British broadcast market owing to the harsh recession of the early 1990s, Central still posted pre-tax profits up nearly 25 percent at 24.4 million pounds sterling for fiscal 1991, compared with a figure of 19.2 million sterling a year earlier. This profit rise came as company sales continued falling. Revenue of 306.6 million sterling in 1991 was down 2.7 percent from a year earlier, or 315.1 million sterling in 1990. This performance was accomplished on pre-tax profits of 27 million sterling posted in fiscal 1989, prior to the recession.

In 1992, Zodiac, Central's USA program production subsidiary, unveiled its second animated program, *Mr. Bogus.* Its first series, *Widget,* began re-runs in the all-important U.S. television market. Also that year, Central Music was formed as a separate company within Central Productions to produce music-based programs largely funded by music companies and video distribution. Among its first programs was *Bedrock II,* a late night music series, and *Lafter Hours,* featuring popular British comedians. *Lafter Hours* triggered a video distribution deal with Virgin Music, a leading British record producer and retailer.

Looking to the future, Central appeared in an enviable position among ITV broadcasters in holding the largest franchise, and yet paying the lowest Exchequer levy of a mere $4000 annually. At the same time, a strong balance sheet has made Central a favorable takeover target after January 1, 1994, when acquisitions of ITV franchises will become possible. Indeed, takeover bids may well come from continental broadcasters as Britain continues opening up its frontiers to the European Community.

Principal Subsidiaries: World International Network; Zodiac; Television Sales and Marketing Services; Central Television Enterprises.

Further Reading: Root, Jane Open the Box: About Television, Comedia Publishing Group, London, 1986; "Programming Free-For-All," *Financial Weekly,* March 23–29, 1990; "Big Two Face Toughest TV Franchise Fight," *Guardian,* May 16, 1991; "The Darling Bids of May," *Observer,* May 19, 1991; "Bidders Facing Becher's Brook of Quality TV," *Observer,* May 19, 1991.

—Etan Vlessing

CENTRAL SOYA

CENTRAL SOYA COMPANY, INC.

P.O. Box 1400
Fort Wayne, Indiana 46801-1400
U.S.A.
(219) 425-5100
Fax: (219) 425-5153

Wholly owned subsidiary of CSY Agri-Processing, Inc.
Incorporated: 1934
Employees: 4,000
Sales: $2.06 billion
SICs: 2075 Soybean Oil Mills; 2048 Prepared Feeds Nec

Central Soya Company, Inc. is a leading international agribusiness company that processes, refines, and manufactures oilseed and animal feed products. Principal operations include soybean processing, feed manufacturing, vegetable oil refining, and grain merchandising, as well as the manufacture of soy protein and lecithin. Beginning in the mid-1980s, the company underwent several changes that affected its structure as it entered the 1990s. In July 1985 it was acquired by Shamrock Capital L.P. in a leveraged buy-out. By September of 1987 it was sold to Ferruzzi Agricola Finanziario, representing the largest U.S. acquisition ever made by an Italian company. The Ferruzzi deal opened up extensive new international markets, especially in Europe. Major strategic alliances were made in 1990, resulting in the establishment of CSY Agri-Processing, a holding company controlling Central Soya Company, Inc., Oilseed Products Group, Central Soya Feed Company, Inc., Privimi Holding B.V., Innovative Pork Concepts, and CanAmera Foods. Thus, in order to most flexibly respond to market demands of the 1990s, Central Soya became a member of a group designed to collectively coordinate soybean processing, feed manufacturing, grain merchandising, vegetable oil refining, the manufacture of soy proteins and lecithin, and pork processing.

When Central Soya was founded in 1934, in Decatur, Indiana, its primary objectives were to process soybeans, market soybean meal and oil, and manufacture and market livestock and poultry feeds. At that time, the soybean was a relatively new crop in the United States, even though it had been widely used in the Far East since 200 B.C., and possibly earlier. Although the U.S. Department of Agriculture began significant importation of varieties from Asian countries in 1898, the bean did not

take off commercially until after World War II. The industry quickly grew, however, becoming the world leader by the 1970s and accounting for approximately 65 percent of the global crop by 1990.

Due to a powerful concentration of amino acids, soybeans contain twice as much protein as beef and are high in nutrition. They are inexpensive and are characterized by extremely high yield under optimal weather conditions. A single seed can create a bushy plant averaging three feet in height; a single plant can produce up to 100 pods; and a bushel of soybeans (59 pounds) can be processed into more than 11 pounds of oil and 47 pounds of meal translating into protein-rich food supplements, among other things. Dale W. McMillen Sr., the founder of Central Soya, pioneered this relatively new crop by exploiting its naturally high protein content for livestock and poultry feeds (and eventually for human consumption as well). In 1953, his sons—Chairperson Harold and President Dale Jr.—assumed control and furthered their father's innovations.

The first years of Central Soya's business focused primarily on the expansion of its original business, processing beans and producing soybean meal, crude soybean oil, and animal feed. In 1940, the company built its Gibson City, Illinois, soybean processing plant, which proved consistently successful, employing 150 workers and yielding $141 million in sales by 1991. After World War II, the industry developed highly sophisticated processing methods for extracting meal and oil, resulting in production boosts, often to the overcapacity level.

Such overproduction, paired with the characteristically unsteady crop output (due to fluctuations in climate and in planting strategies), resulted in a period of low profits. In response, Central Soya and others entered a period of diversification into grain merchandising and, in the soybean product line, the development of soy protein and lecithin products. In 1956, the company moved into grain merchandising because it had excess space to store grain in the summer, when soybean stocks were down. By 1966, grain merchandising accounted for approximately 15 percent of sales and profits. As the company had already diversified into the feed industry, consuming much of its own meal, it next went one step further, into the poultry and egg business. In November of 1962, Central Soya acquired Tennessee Egg Co., and in 1964 it acquired Selby Food Co., a turkey grower from Iowa. Furthermore, in 1961, the company began refining industrial soybean oil, and by 1970 it had opened its first edible vegetable oils refinery in Decatur, Indiana. In 1964, it expanded its feeds market by opening the first of many feed manufacturing plants outside the United States, in this case Guatemala. Thus the overall trend, from the 1950s onward, was one of diversification and of growing interdependence between its own processing and its own end products.

By the late 1960s and early 1970s, diversification and growth had paid off. The soybean had reached its heyday. In 1966, the harvest soared to about 880 million bushels, up from a record 844 the previous year; soybeans toppled wheat on the Chicago Board of Trade, ranking in dollar trading as the country's leading commodity. Central Soya became a market leader, handling 84 million bushels a year and seeing its earnings rise to $4.75 a share, up from $3.13 in 1965. The company expanded rapidly, acquiring McKee Feed & Grain Co., Clinton Milling

Co., Austin Farms, Inc., and A.B.C. Grain Corp. all in a matter of months.

An era of American affluence created a booming market for meats and poultry, which in turn positively affected the soy and feed industries. At the same time, a trend toward more healthful foods accelerated growth in the market for high protein soy products, which were low in fat and cholesterol. A process developed in the 1950s, by a chemist named Robert Boyer, enabled food manufacturers to transform the soybean into a wide variety of high protein, textured foods resembling hamburger, chicken, beef, bacon, dried fruit, potato chips, or other foods requiring inexpensive, healthy substitutes. Soy margarine, "soyburgers," and tofu became not only viable but fashionable alternatives. Central Soya developed a 97 percent pure protein called "Promine," marketed as a binder for sausages, bologna, and other process meats. In addition, the company developed a dairy substitute that could be frozen into an ice-cream-like dessert or exported as a flexible dietary supplement. In conjunction with these endeavors, Central Soya entered the processed food industry, acquiring Fred's Frozen Foods, Inc. in 1970, which it sold to International Multifoods Corp. 16 years later. Soy extracts became increasingly important in other industrial products ranging from paints to printing inks, insect sprays, adhesives, and nail polish. A 1966 article in *Barron's*, entitled "Jack and the Soy Bean," epitomized the crop's tremendous potential by referring to the folktale in which a bean stalk grows uncontrollably, carrying its cultivator up to a different world.

Soybeans carried Central Soya to different continents, as the international market took off in the 1960s, turning soybeans into the number one export crop in the United States. West Germany represented the largest European market, followed closely by other countries of the common market, where grain production could not keep pace with demand for meat, milk, and eggs. Japanese markets also increased dramatically, reflecting rapidly rising consumption of animal protein. In 1972, Central Soya acquired Industriele B Bonda-Rotterdam N.V.(Bonda Industrial Corp.), a holding company controlling a group of companies manufacturing and marketing livestock and poultry feed concentrates principally in Holland, Belgium, Portugal, and Canada. Central Soya had become a major player in international agribusiness.

Despite such growth, the market was volatile, and Central Soya's profits oscillated dramatically. Pretax earnings swung from $30 million in 1971 up to $64 million in 1974 and then down to $34 million in 1975; in 1976, earnings were back up to $71 million and then down to $22 million in 1977; in 1980, $57.3 million marked a fall from $59 million in 1979. In order to stabilize the profit base, chairperson, president, and CEO Douglas Fleming drafted a plan that would trim grain merchandising, develop new feed products with higher margins, and expand in processed foods and chemurgy.

To secure itself against changes in the soy market, the company also depended on its vital practice of hedging soybean purchases in order to fix its processing margins. Roughly, hedging works as follows: when a firm contracts to buy beans, it sells a futures contract for an identical amount. If prices drop, inventory values fall. Gains on the future sales, however, offset the inventory losses. If prices rise, the inventory appreciation is offset by losses on the futures sales. Creative hedging is necessary for survival in the soybean industry.

In April 1985, Shamrock Capital L.P., a limited partnership wholly owned by the Roy E. Disney family, acquired Central Soya in a leveraged buy-out. Shamrock bought all outstanding shares of common stock at $24.25 cash per share, amounting to an aggregate of $275 million. In August, Fleming retired, ceding the post of chair and chief executive to Donald P. Eckrich. With Central Soya's debt at 89.5 percent of capitalization, Standard & Poor lowered the company's senior debt ratings to "B" from "BBB" and removed them from Credit-Watch, where they had been listed in March. In a July letter to employees, Eckrich welcomed the Shamrock executive, Stanley P. Gold, to his new post as chairperson of Central Soya, and expressed plans for "a stronger, larger company with emphasis on increasing our market share, margins and profitability."

Two years later, in September of 1987, Shamrock announced the sale of Central Soya, which had been refocused to its core businesses, to Ferruzzi Agricola Finanziario, a holding company of the Ferruzzi Group based in Ravenna, Italy. In a news briefing, Central Soya's president and chief executive expressed appreciation for the restructuring input and growth associated with Shamrock as well as optimism at "expanded product lines in Europe as an integral part of the Ferruzzi organization." Ferruzzi, one of the largest agribusiness organizations in the world, comprised three major operations: soy, corn, and sugar processing; commodity trading; and chemical engineering. The Ferruzzi/Central Soya merger promised accelerated growth and stronger competition.

In some ways, growth was too strong, resulting in a July 1989 lawsuit in which the Chicago Board of Trade (CBOT) sued Ferruzzi/Central Soya for trying to corner the soybean market. In January 1992, Ferruzzi settled—without admitting or denying charges—by paying CBOT $2 million in fines, $1 million in court expenses, and resigning its exchange seat. The case and its outcome were controversial, with some farmers arguing that CBOT employed an inefficient regulating system that weakened market prices.

The 1990s marked a change in growth strategy. Under the direction of David H. Swanson, Central Soya established the CSY Agri-Processing holding company in 1990. This holding company linked various businesses, all related to the production of food for human consumption, with an emphasis on added value through technology. The five primary holdings were: 1) Central Soya Company, Inc., for soybean processing, refined oil, and chemurgy; 2) Central Soya Feed Co., divided into the Domestic Feed Division, Animal Health and Nutrition, and International Feed; 3) Provimi Holding B.V., a significant exporter and developer/manager of technical service agreements with other feed manufacturers in Europe; 4) Innovative Pork Concepts, a joint venture with Mitsubishi Corp., running a fully automated pork processing facility, Indiana Packers Co., and providing genetic research and breeding stock facilities for hog producers; and 5) CanAmera Foods, a Canadian oilseed processing and vegetable oil refining venture. CSY was organized in order to decentralize the company and to best respond to complex market demands. Initial figures were promising: net sales increased in 1991 to $2.06 billion, from $1.95 billion the year before, and gross earnings increased 20.8 percent, to $64.4 million from $53.3 million, according to the 1991 annual report.

The company also renewed emphasis on research. Feed research, operating from Decatur and Kerkdriel, in the Netherlands, developed better feeding programs and production systems for feeds and feed concentrates. Oilseeds Research, based in Fort Wayne, Indiana, explored value-added products like proteins and lecithin.

Rapid growth, paired with the Ferruzzi affiliation, helped expand an already growing international market. Changes in the former Soviet Union and Eastern Europe opened new markets. In January 1990, for example, Agrokomplex-Central Soya was established. With 30.2 percent of its stock held by Central Soya, and 45 percent by Provimi Holding Co. (also owned by Central Soya), it produced around 18 percent of Hungary's animal feed. Central Soya entered India in November of 1991, agreeing on a joint venture with Birla Group, the largest industrial group in that country. In February of 1992, Central Soya and Germany's Stern Lecithin & Soja GmbH merged to form a venture that would yield an estimated annual revenue of $25 million, according to a European Information Service report. These and many other international ventures marked an increasingly global agenda.

While these represented promising signs for agribusiness, some analysts identified dangers. In the *Des Moines Register*, Douglas Constance and William Heffernan, two University of Missouri sociologists, warned that the world's large food corporations were replacing governments as shapers of agricultural policy. "The implications are devastating for nation-states trying to establish food security," they claimed. Even so, the soybean industry will continue to grow, along with Central Soya. In a 1966 *Barron's* article, John Haymaker, of Cargill, Inc., compared the beans to "those little animals in the Li'l Abner comic strip called Schmoos. . . . When it comes to versa-tility, the Schmoos' only competitor is the soybean." With such a crop as its keystone, Central Soya is bound to excel.

Principal Subsidiaries: Central Soya Far East, Inc.; B.G. Management Co., Inc.; Central Soya Del Norte, Inc.; Central Soya Export Co., Inc. (V.I.); Music City Supplement, Inc.; McMillen Feed Mills, Inc.; Central Soya Feed Company, Inc.; Tindle Mills, Inc; C.S. Services, Inc.; C.S. Trading, Inc.; CSY Holdings, Inc.; Feed Specialities Co., Inc.; Mac-Page, Inc.; Nutra-Tech, Inc.; Midwest Pork, Inc.; Precision Microblenders, Inc.; Jip Hong International (HK) Ltd. (100%); Weifang Zhongji Animal Feed Co., Ltd. (50%); Central Soya Bretagne, S.A. (France); Total Nutrition Technologies Co., Ltd. (50%); Central Soya Overseas, B.V. (Netherlands); Provimi Portuguesa-Concentrados para Alimentacao de Animais, Ltda. (Portugal); Belegging B.V.

Further Reading: "The Golden Beans," *Forbes,* April 15, 1966; "Jack and the Soybean," *Barron's,* September 5, 1966; "Shorter Swings? Central Soya Heads for Strong Year," *Barron's,* January 19, 1981; "Shamrock Capital Agrees to Acquire Central Soya," *Business Wire,* April 1, 1985; "S&P Rates Central Soya Senior Debt," *PR Newswire,* August 27, 1985; "Shamrock to Sell Central Soya to Ferruzzi Agricola Finanziario," *Business Wire,* September 14, 1987; Parikh, Kirit S., et al, *Towards Free Trade in Agriculture,* Boston, Marinus Nijhoff Publishers, 1988; "Central Soya and Birla Announce Joint Venture," *Food Engineering,* January, 1991; "Mega-Food Corporations Shape Government Food Policy," *Des Moines Register,* May 10, 1991; Forrestal, Jan J., *The Kernel and the Bean,* New York, Simon and Schuster, 1992; CSY Agri-Processing, Inc., *1991 Annual Report,* 1992; "Indiana Packers; American Pork Goes Global," *Food Engineering,* November, 1992; "Illinois Farm Bureau Lashes out at CBOT," *Chicago Tribune,* January 25, 1992; "Ferruzzi, Stern-Wymiol to Merge Units," *Reuter's Dateline,* February 10, 1992.

—Kerstan Cohen

CHIQUITA BRANDS INTERNATIONAL, INC.

250 East 5th Street
Cincinnati, Ohio 45202-5190
U.S.A.
(513) 784-8011
Fax: (513) 784-8030

Public Company
Incorporated: 1885 as the Boston Fruit Company
Employees: 50,000
Sales: $4.62 billion
Stock Exchanges: New York Boston Pacific
SICs: 0179 Fruits & Tree Nuts Nec; 5148 Fresh Fruits &
    Vegetables; 2037 Frozen Fruits & Vegetables

One of the world's foremost marketers of fresh fruits and vegetables, Chiquita Brands International, Inc. is a food conglomerate whose name will forever be linked with the Chiquita Banana, a perennial market leader with a long and colorful history. Sales for the Chiquita Banana are the driving force of the company's $2.4 billion Fresh Foods Group. The company has also capitalized on the Chiquita name in its Prepared Foods Group, which accounts for the remainder of sales and features John Morrell and other name-brand meats, as well as a line of blended fruit juices, processed vegetables, salads, and other value-added products.

Management under Carl H. Lindner has richly rewarded shareholders: Chiquita shares purchased in 1984 and held through 1991 increased in value by 1,000 percent. Lindner's American Financial Corporation, a large Ohio-based holding company founded in 1955, retains 48 percent of the voting stock of Chiquita Brands.

During the pre-Lindner era, Chiquita was known first as the United Fruit Company and was reviled in some corners as the creator and perpetuator of "banana republics." Beginning in the 1950s the company began diversifying widely, while repairing its image, and eventually became the United Brands Company in 1970 under Eli Black. After suffering a $70 million dollar loss in 1974, which was followed by the suicide of Black and revelations of corporate scandal in early 1975, the future of Chiquita was in jeopardy. Now, nearly two decades later, the Chiquita name is not only intact but has become the company's

leading image, governing its product line and propelling it onward as "a global leader in premium branded foods."

The idea for a dominant international banana company was first launched in 1870 when Captain Lorenzo Dow Baker speculatively sold 160 bunches of Jamaican bananas in Jersey City at an enormous profit. The delicate fruit—coupled with the vagaries of transportation, weather, and prices—made for a particularly risky business. In addition, the American public was, until the Philadelphia Centennial Exposition of 1876, largely unfamiliar with the many merits of bananas. However, Baker soon found an ally in Boston produce agent Andrew Preston, who agreed to handle marketing. The two men, aided by Preston's other partners, eventually joined to form the Boston Fruit Company in 1885. When three other banana companies, including railroad pioneer Minor Keith's concern, agreed to merge in 1899 with Boston Fruit, the United Fruit Company was born.

The strategy behind the merger was to create a broad base of operations in an effort to continue trade when droughts, floods, or political upheavals were disrupting one or another of the harvesting lands. From then until well into the twentieth century, the company operated principally in Ecuador, Nicaragua, and Panama, though shipments also came from Colombia, Guatemala, and Honduras. The governments of these Central and South American countries were eager to develop, but were unable to finance the construction of railroads and ports themselves. For North American companies who were willing to buy land, which was cheaply priced, and do the building themselves, the situation offered unimaginable potential. Although United faced some competition, namely from the Standard Fruit and Steamship Company of New Orleans, for all practical purposes, it became *the* U.S. banana company and guided not only the economic but the political developments in the countries it had invested in.

Technologically, too, United led the fruit-producing and importation industry. In 1903 it became the first company to transport refrigerated cargo; in 1904 it established commercial radio on its ships; and in 1910 it successfully introduced uninterrupted radio service between headquarters in Boston and New York and its various crop-producing outposts. Aside from continuing to acquire more plantation land with its profits, the company expanded into the Cuban sugar trade with acquisitions in 1907 and 1912. A much later acquisition of Samuel Zemurray's Cuyamel Fruit Company in 1930 led to new management three years later under Cuyamel's largest shareholder, Zemurray himself.

From this period through the mid-1950s the company prospered and wielded considerable influence, both at home and abroad. Several of the Central American governments felt powerless when negotiating land rights and new development with "The Fruit Company;" Hondurans commonly referred to the corporation as "the Octopus," for its control seemed to reach virtually everywhere. In the United States the company enjoyed a far better image, particularly with the federal government, which found United indispensable during World War II and in later years for maintaining security (in 1961 United supplied the government with ships for the failed Bay of Pigs invasion) and the free flow of both durable and nondurable goods throughout the Caribbean. In 1944 the company unleashed its single greatest public relations campaign with the creation of the "Chiquita Banana Song" for radio. Soon such notables as Xavier Cugat, the King Sisters, and Carmen Miranda transformed the Calypso jingle into a long-running, nationwide hit. More importantly, the name Chiquita (meaning "little one") became imprinted in the American consciousness and domestic banana consumption rose rapidly. In 1947 the company solved the problem of distinguishing their bananas from the competition's with the colorful Chiquita sticker. In so doing, United made advertising history by creating a branded premium product out of what was essentially a common commodity.

From the early 1950s through the early 1960s the company experienced radical and disturbing changes. Although United's share of the banana market had been declining since 1910, the company still had a near monopoly of the market. Earnings of $45 million during the early 1950s translated into profit margins of around 15 percent. A decade later the company was posting losses of half a million. As John M. Fox, the executive charged with reorganizing operations in the 1960s, recounted: "No longer was United Fruit the major source of quality bananas. No longer was the 'Great White Fleet,' as United Fruit's ocean ships were called, the only dependable furnisher of refrigerated transport of fruit from the tropics." With rising production costs and dropping prices, the company was in serious trouble. Contributing to the dire situation was the gradual evolution of the banana republics into the role of self-sustaining exporters as well as the outbreak of Panama disease, a fusarium wilt virus that was proving to be a huge capital drain on the company. In addition, antitrust action by the U.S. Justice Department would ultimately require United to help establish a domestic competitor through the sale of a portion of its operations.

United's response was to hire new management to better integrate its three often autonomously run branches of production, shipping, and sales. Greater competition in the commodity market also suggested that the company begin diversifying; United proceeded to acquire a miscellany of companies, including the A & W Root Beer Company, Baskin-Robbins, and Foster Grant. The result was a relatively unfocused stream of purchases that ended when United Fruit merged with AMK Corporation in 1970. In 1966 AMK, originally a producer of milk-bottle caps, had acquired a third of the common shares of John Morrell and Company (a meat packer once involved with orange-trading during the early nineteenth century) and in December of the following year acquired the rest. Eli Black, the president and chairman of AMK, gained a reputation for financial wizardry with this acquisition because Morrell, the fourth-largest meat packer in the country, was twenty times larger than AMK.

Unfortunately, Black's triumph as chief executive officer of the expanded United was short-lived, punctuated only by a few years of solid earnings and the company's considerable strides forward in eradicating injustices against workers. During the mid-1970s United Brands experienced some of the worst losses in its history. In April 1974 Central American governments began levying a large export tax on their bananas. Then, in September 1974, hurricane Fifi hit Central America, wiping out 70 percent of the company's Honduran plantations and causing losses of more than $20 million. Black sent relief teams to the victims of the hurricane, but he could do nothing to help the

company. Losses continued to mount; because of high cattle feed costs, the John Morrell division contributed another $6 million in losses to United Brands' $70 million operating loss in 1974, compared to a $16 million profit the previous year. Black's final attempt to alleviate the company's troubles was to sell United's interest in Foster Grant—once touted as the company's "crown jewel"—for almost $70 million at the very end of the year. The sale was considered a tremendous success, but apparently it was not enough for Black, who committed suicide on February 3, 1975.

Investigations into Black's death uncovered a bribery scandal that was to plague United Brands for more than three years. In April 1975 the Securities and Exchange Commission (SEC) charged United Brands with having paid a bribe of $1.25 million and having agreed to pay another $1.25 million to a Honduran official in exchange for a reduction in export taxes. The SEC also accused United of bribing European officials for $750,000. Trade in United Brands stock was halted for almost a week. Black's culpability, however, offered only a partial explanation for his leap to death from his Manhattan offices. Jefferson Grigsby surmised that the scandal was simply "the last straw." Through his so-called wizardry Black "had created a giant company . . . but he had also made a classic mistake. By merging a cash-rich company with a capital-hungry company, he had hoped to create one strong company but instead created a weak one. In this case, one plus one had equaled zero."

In May 1975 Wallace Booth, a former executive at Rockwell International, succeeded the string of chairmen who had headed the company by committee-rule in the wake of Eli Black's death. Booth is credited with leveling the rocky operation by methodically tightening management control, streamlining banana delivery systems, and updating meat-packing technology at John Morrell. Yet United was far from recovery. In 1972 it had been forced by the government to sell its Guatemalan operations to Del Monte. Perhaps the sale came as a relief—Guatemala had for a long time been the company's most politically volatile producer region. Yet the transaction also signalled a weakening of the once monolithic food company that, unlike fruit-producers Del Monte or Dole, was still largely dependent on a single, highly perishable cash crop. Booth lasted only until 1977.

Until 1984 a series of chairmen and presidents, including Paul and Seymour Milstein, managed to keep United Brands afloat, but profits slipped and net losses increased steadily. John Morrell came close to closing a plant in the early 1980s and in 1983 tropical storms in Panama and Costa Rica inflicted further damage. *Fortune* writer Eleanor Tracy, in 1984, summarized United's downward spiral: "For more than a decade United Brands has looked about as appealing to investors as a black banana. The debt-ridden successor to the old United Fruit Co. had cumulative profits of only $97 million from 1974 through 1982. In fiscal 1983 . . . it lost $167 million on revenues of $2.4 billion." Another *Fortune* writer called the ailing company "a case study in corporate calamity."

Carefully watching these developments was board member and American Financial founder Carl Lindner. Since 1973 Lindner had been amassing stock in United. Beginning in 1982 he accelerated his purchases and prepared to overtake the company two years later by buying out the company's principal share-holders: Max Fisher and the Milsteins. With 87 percent control of the company, Lindner named himself the new chief executive officer. He quickly moved the company away from large diversified operations and toward a narrower focus on stable profits. He and the four new directors he elected doubled United's cash flow between 1985 and 1988. Lindner streamlined the company's operations by selling some of its extraneous operations (i.e., soft drinks, animal feeds, domestic lettuce, and telecommunications) and lowered its overhead by moving the headquarters from New York to Cincinnati. Most importantly, under Lindner the company succeeded in recapturing from Dole its position as the number one marketer of bananas worldwide.

In 1988 Lindner, after beginning to reduce his stake in the company, quieted rumors that he was planning to either take the company private or sell it. A health-conscious American public, new ad campaigns, and Lindner's financial savvy had all served to revive Chiquita and there was little reason to be suspicious of the company's future. In 1990 the company changed its name to Chiquita Brands International and ushered in a new age of aggressive, food-related business acquisitions. The Chiquita label began to appear on a wide variety of fruits, including kiwis, melons, and pineapples; fresh produce, though limited to 45 percent of the company's sales, was contributing some 90 percent to operating profits.

With the new age, however, came new problems. A 1990 rebellion by Honduran growers pointed out the fact that Chiquita was offering a full 30 percent less for its banana shipments than British competitor Fyffes. Although an agreement between Chiquita and its growers, securing such prices, remained in effect until 1992, it did little to assuage flaring tempers or halt strikes by underpaid workers. Given Chiquita's reliance on independent suppliers for 50 percent of its banana production, maintaining good trade relations had become and would continue to be a primary concern for the company.

Most of Chiquita's profits during the period, from earnings and from public offerings, were funneled into enormous capital expenditures on land and equipment. In 1990 such investment totaled $282 million; in 1991, $400 million. A commitment to buy more refrigerated freighters promises investments of similar scale in the coming years. Chiquita also remains acquisition-hungry and has made overtures to buy both Castle and Cooke's Dole and Polly Peck International's Del Monte Tropical Fruit.

After eight years of solid performance, however, the company faltered in 1992. For the nine months ended on September 30th, it reported a $90.6 million net loss. This compared to record earnings during the previous year of $119.2 million. Poor banana quality (due to El Niño and outbreaks of banana disease), a sluggish European market, and increased domestic competition among meat packers were all cited as contributing factors. A *New York Times* article dated July 8, 1992, declared that Chiquita was involved in "the great banana war of 1992." Reporter Eben Shapiro explained that, "as the world's biggest banana marketer and the only one of the Big Three that relies on bananas for its fortunes, Chiquita Brands International has been kicked hardest" through plummeting stock prices.

For all of its difficulties, Chiquita still spends alot of its income on advertising. Shapiro remarked, "Chiquita's hard knocks show the difficulty of dressing up what is essentially a commodity food as a premium brand. The Cincinnati-based company spends about $20 million a year on television and magazine advertising to convince shoppers, grocers, and its stockholders that bananas blessed with the Chiquita seal are somehow worth more than the others."

As president, Carl Lindner's son Keith is now faced with turning the company around yet again. The possibility of large acquisitions remains a realistic solution to some of the company's problems, as does a management buyout of its nonfruit properties. Still, the investment community remains wary. In February of 1993 Chiquita's stock price hovered near its 52-week low of $15.75, far distant from its 1991 high of $50.75. For the foreseeable future a return to the heyday of early Lindner management seems unlikely—and yet, the Chiquita banana endures. Perpetual risk versus potentially high profit margins mean nothing to the average consumer. The look, flavor, and nutritional benefits of bananas (the most popular fruit in the country), however, will always be important. For many shoppers, if the name says "Chiquita," so much the better.

Principal Subsidiaries: Chiquita Brands, Inc.; Chiquita Ventures, Inc.; Compania Mundimar; Compania Palma Tica; John Morrell & Co.; Polymer United G.C. Inc.; UB-N26LB, Inc.; United Brands Food Ventures Ltd.; United Brands Japan Co., Ltd. (89%).

Further Reading: Lavine, Harold, "Bright New Image for the 'Octopus'," *Saturday Review World,* April 20, 1974; "United Brands Trades More Assets for Cash," *Business Week,* January 13, 1975; "Who Calls the Shots at United Brands," *Business Week,* May 26, 1975; "Sorting Out the Wreckage," *Fortune,* June 1975; Grigsby, Jefferson, "The Wonder Is That It Works at All," *Forbes,* February 18, 1980; Fox, John M., "How 'Chiquita' Helped United Fruit, *Agribusiness Worldwide,* February/March 1980; Tracy, Eleanor Johnson, "United Brands' Hidden Charms for Carl Lindner," *Fortune,* March 19, 1984; Jaffe, Thomas, "Don't Slip," *Forbes,* July 1, 1985; "Lindner's Buildup at United Brands," *Business Week,* August 26, 1985; Hannon, Kerry, "Ripe Banana," *Forbes,* June 13, 1988; "The Banana Rebellion," *Time,* June 11, 1990; Shapiro, Eben, "Revitalized Chiquita Seeks Growth," *New York Times,* September 11, 1990; Mejia, John, "Chiquita, Polly Peck Deny Reports of Del Monte Sale," *Supermarket News,* March 4, 1991; Shapiro, Eben, "Yes, They Have Too Many Bananas," *New York Times,* July 8, 1992; "Chiquita Cites Lower Meat Margins in Results," *Feedstuffs,* December 21, 1992; De Cordoba, Jose, "Fruit Fight: Two Banana Empires, Latin and Caribbean, Battle Over Europe," *Wall Street Journal,* January 15, 1993.

—Jay P. Pederson

CITIZENS UTILITIES

UTILITIES

CITIZENS UTILITIES COMPANY

High Ridge Park
Stamford, Connecticut 06905-1390
U.S.A.
(203) 329-8800
Fax: (203) 329-4602

Public Company
Incorporated: 1935
Employees: 2,335
Sales: $589.3 million
Stock Exchanges: New York
SICs: 4813 Telephone Communications Except
   Radiotelephone; 4911 Electric Services; 4923 Gas
   Transmission & Distribution; 4941 Water Supply

Citizens Utilities Company is likely the most fully diversified utility company in the United States. The company provides telecommunications, electric power, gas, water, and wastewater treatment services to more than 800,000 customers in 13 states. Through such operational and geographic diversity, Citizens has managed to de-emphasize the effects of crisis and regulation in any one area of jurisdiction. For example, disastrous weather or heavy regulation impacting one region is largely offset by the performance of another operation.

Citizens Utilities was created in 1935 during a government reorganization of the utilities industries. The company was formed from several smaller utilities companies previously controlled by the Public Utilities Consolidated Corporation which, like Citizens Utilities, was a highly diversified company. Public Utilities was assembled by W. B. Foshay. During the 1920s, Foshay had a relatively easy time acquiring utility assets and other properties with unsecured debt. The company owned telephone, electric power, and gas operations in several states and controlled additional businesses in Alaska and Nicaragua. Unable to sustain his business, however, Foshay's company was forced to reorganize in 1928 in order to avoid bankruptcy.

The financial crisis in 1929 that began the Great Depression was caused by thousands of investors whose holdings were financed with up to 90 percent debt. When confidence in this huge debt collapsed, capital markets dried up, forcing companies like Public Utilities to fail almost immediately; the company went into reorganization. Still based in Minneapolis, the reconstituted company was incorporated in 1935 in Delaware as the Citizens

Utilities Company. The company—under essentially the same management, including president Joseph Chapman—continued operation for several years during the Depression, maintaining stable performance but unimpressive growth through most of the war years.

In 1945, however, Citizens was discovered by a group of New York financiers. With a reasonable rate of return on investment and with a mandate that precluded competition, Citizens presented this group of investors with a high potential for improvement and financial growth. After securing interest from the existing board members, the financiers hired Richard Rosenthal to ever see their investment. Rosenthal, at that time a 29-year old financial consultant who was born in Canada and raised in Brooklyn, had studied finance at New York University and, after stints as an analyst with several Wall Street firms, set up his own consulting firm specializing in utility acquisitions.

During his first year in Minneapolis, as a director for Citizens Utilities, Rosenthal doubled shareholders' dividends and proposed so many changes in the company that he and his backers successfully waged a proxy fight to have him installed as president of the company. In 1946 Rosenthal, at age 30, became the youngest company president in the industry at the time.

During his first ten years as president, Rosenthal doubled revenues and net income and reduced long-term debt from 85 percent of capitalization to 60 percent. Rosenthal's financial approach to the industry was unusual at the time for an industry dominated by engineers. But running a regulated company did present Rosenthal with new problems. At every turn, his management decisions were second-guessed by state public utility commissions. He responded in a way that was to become his trademark: when commissions tried to stop him, he fought until he prevailed; this bulldog approach quite often succeeded, making him the nemesis of regulators.

Rosenthal felt Citizens Utilities should be in the business of serving the public, not battling the government. He worked diligently to reduce unit costs and raise shareholder equity. But Rosenthal, a self-described "financial type," recognized the limited benefits from these efforts and set out to do more for shareholders.

Regulatory commissions rejected the idea of raising rates to increase shareholder dividends, so Rosenthal investigated other ways to maximize shareholder value. He found a method in the federal tax code. After having moved the company to Connecticut, first to Greenwich and then to Stamford, Rosenthal in 1955 asked the Treasury Department to rule on a proposal to reclassify Citizens' common stock into two classes: one paying cash and the other paying dividends in the form of tax-deferred issues of additional stock. These stock dividends, earned as interest, would only be subject to taxation when they were sold, and then only as a capital gain. Despite this highly unconventional approach, the Treasury Department allowed Rosenthal's plan.

The following year the company queried its shareholders as to how they would prefer to receive their dividends, all in cash, all in stock, or a bit of both. Seventy-five percent of Citizens Utilities shareholders opted to receive stock-based dividends, for which they were issued new Series A shares. The remainder held the cash-paying stock, which under the reclassification was renamed Series B. Under the reclassification arrangement, the stock dividend paid on Series A was equal in fair market value to the cash dividend paid on Series B.

Thereafter, every year when Citizens Utilities distributed a stock dividend, it created additional shares of Series A stock. This enabled the company to plow cash back into the business for maintenance, improvements and acquisitions, while avoiding the paperwork and costs of floating additional shares.

While the idea was quite unusual, Citizens received a favorable ruling on its tow-series structure from the Internal Revenue Service, which was subsequently barraged with similar requests from other companies. At this point the Internal Revenue Service decided that a Pandora's box had been opened, and that unless the process was amended, the government would suffer huge losses in tax revenue. The Congress held a series of hearings from 1956 to 1959, at which Rosenthal personally defended the plan. Congress later amended the earlier Treasury Department ruling to prevent other companies from issuing stock as a tax-deferred dividend while also paying a cash dividend. However, Citizens Utilities was allowed to continue its unique arrangement under a grandfather clause, which expired in 1990 and was not renewed. In 1990 Citizens initiated stock dividends on its Series B, because by paying stock dividends on both its Series A and Series B stock, those stock dividends could remain tax deferred, taxed only when sold. In addition, the company in 1992 introduced an optional plan for Series B shareholders that enables them to receive cash by having their quarterly stock dividends sold in the market and the cash sent to them each quarter. As of 19092, three quarters of the outstanding common stock was in Series A and the remainder in Series B.

During the 1950s, 1960s, and well into the 1970s, Citizens Utilities went on an acquisition binge, snapping up numerous rural utilities in Arizona, California, Hawaii, Illinois, Indiana, Ohio, and Pennsylvania. While the majority of these were small water utilities, the company expanded in every area of its business, including its electric, gas, and telephone operations as well as its cold storage business in Alaska, which it eventually sold in 1976 because it was neither a core business nor strategically related to its other businesses.

In the early and mid-1960s, when nuclear power generation was growing in popularity, Citizens elected to stay out of the business. Rosenthal refused to believe that the projected costs of nuclear plants would not rise. The cost of nuclear plants did in fact rise, and exploded into impracticality fifteen years later when a partial meltdown at Three Mile Island led to a virtual moratorium on new plants. Nevertheless, instead of "going nuclear," Citizens Utilities continued to develop fossil fuel and hydro plants in partnership with other electric power companies.

The most notable growth in the company's electric power business came in 1969, when Citizens Utilities acquired the Kauai Electric Company for $10 million. This company, which serves the entire island of Kauai, northernmost in the Hawaiian chain, marked Citizens' largest acquisition to date, and its move into yet another state. The company also won the unofficial title

of "super utility," operating 27 subsidiaries in five different industries in nearly a dozen states, from Vermont to Hawaii. From 1945 to 1970 Citizens experienced impressive growth, with its number of customers increasing from 28,000 to 177,000. Revenues grew from $2 million to $31 million, and profits rose from $179,000 to $7 million. By 1970, Citizens was operating in ten states.

In 1970 Rosenthal was elected chairman (also continuing as CEO), and Ishier Jacobson, who had joined Citizens in 1954 in an administrative management position, became president and chief operating officer. Later, in 1981, Jacobson assumed the CEO position.

By the mid 1970s, Citizens Utilities' electric power business grew to 40 percent of total earnings. The lucrative three-state telephone operation contributed 31 percent, while water constituted 15 percent, and gas and sewage each registered seven percent.

Although heavily diversified, both operationally and geographically, Citizens was not immune to inflation, and particularly to the skyrocketing costs of construction. Unable to win timely rate increases to meet these conditions, many utility companies were hit hard. Virtually all suffered reduced earnings credit downgrades.

Citizens' unique stock dividend policy was critical to the company's strong performance. Other companies, unable to secure loans, were forced to issue new shares of stock. These substantial issues, however, diluted the value of existing stock, depressing the value of all shares. However, because it created shares gradually, on the basis of earnings, Citizens Utilities suffered no depression in share value, even on a short-term basis. In addition, as funding became especially difficult, the two-series capital structure enabled the company to devote much of its cash profit to servicing existing debt or financing new construction. As a result, Citizens was the only one of 33 utility companies to avoid a credit downgrade. In fact, its credit rating was promoted, further lowering the company's cost of borrowing.

By 1984, the company had received Standard & Poor's and Moody's highest credit ratings as well as Standard & Poor's highest common stock ranking. As of 1992, these ratings remained intact, with the exception of Citizens' Debentures, which received Moody's second-highest rating.

After the divestiture of AT&T in 1984 and the rise of new competitive ventures in telecommunications, the profitability of telephone operations began to rise. Those run by Citizens Utilities constituted the fastest growing segment in the company, overtaking even Citizens' traditionally large electric sector.

In 1989, after 44 years at the helm of Citizens, Rosenthal retired as chairman of the company. One year later, Jacobson retired as president and chief executive. As a result of the two-series capital structure he put in place in 1956, Rosenthal's holdings in Citizens had grown to about two percent ownership, making him the company's largest shareholder. Concurrent with his retirement, Rosenthal sold the substantial portion of his holdings to Century Communications Corp. (ASE), a cable television and cellular telephone company. Century also acquired two other blocks of Citizens' stock, bringing its total purchase to more than 900,000 Series A shares.

In 1989 Century Communications' founder and chairman, Leonard Tow, was elected to Citizens' board of directors. In 1990, recognizing Tow's ability to aggressively expand businesses into growing markets and his management philosophy of emphasizing the highest quality of service to customers, the board named him chairman and chief executive officer. When he took over as chairman, Tow's intention was to focus on Citizens being customer-driven, to continue the company's uninterrupted record of increased earnings and dividends (48 straight years as of 1992), and to generate more growth through acquisitions. Also in 1990 Daryl Ferguson, who had joined Citizens in 1989 after having served as a vice-president of Centel Corporation, was elected president and CEO of Citizens.

Quick to seize on growth opportunities under Tow's direction, in 1990 Citizens acquired, by merger, Louisiana General Services, Inc. (LGS), the largest natural gas distribution company in Louisiana. This expanded Citizens' geographic spread into a 13th state and significantly increased its presence in the natural gas business. To date, the LGS purchase, a stock swap valued at about $94 million, represents Citizens' largest acquisition. The company continued growth through acquisitions when it took over Southern Union Company's northern Arizona gas operations in 1991 for $46 million in cash and assumed liabilities and acquired two water/wastewater utilities in the suburban Chicago area.

In the mid-1980s Citizens had acquired several licenses to provide, through partnerships, cellular telephone service in areas of Arizona, California, and Nevada. Cellular operations, however, quickly became overvalued and most, including Citizens', were too small to deliver high returns on a larger scale. In order to affect higher rates of growth and take advantage of more favorable economies of scale, in 1991 Citizens merged its Citizens Cellular subsidiary into Century Cellular, a subsidiary of Century Communications Corp. Citizens Utilities retained a 32 percent residual equity position in the new company, called Centennial Cellular Corp. (NASDAQ), marking yet another of many consolidations in the cellular field.

In an acquisition closely related to the cellular field, Citizens acquired AAlert Paging Company in 1986, a company providing mobile pager services in several western cities, including Sacramento, San Francisco, San Diego, Tucson, Phoenix, and Salt Lake City. Citizens, however, sold its paging business in 1993 because it had not met its growth expectations.

In telecommunications, Citizens Utilities has invested in bypass operations, those secondary telephone networks that may be used instead of the local telephone company. In the early 1990s, the company's bypass operations remained limited to the Pacific Northwest, in Seattle and Portland. The company has plans, though, to construct a fiber-optic route from Nevada to Arizona that will give its Arizona telephone customers centralized equal access service and make it possible for the company to enter the long-distance market as a competitor.

In 1992 telecommunications represented 33 percent of the company's revenues, followed by gas with 32 percent, electric with 25 percent, and water/wastewater with 10 percent. While it operates in 13 states (Arizona, California, Colorado, Hawaii, Idaho, Illinois, Indiana, Louisiana, Ohio, Oregon, Pennsylvania, Vermont, and Washington), it is most heavily concentrated in Arizona, where it provides all five utility services, and in California, where it has telecommunications and water operations. Citizens provides no services in Connecticut, the state in which it is headquartered.

Principal Subsidiaries: Citizens Communications Services, Inc.; Citizens Resources Company; Citizens Utilities Company of California; Citizens Utilities Company of Illinois; Citizens Utilities Company of Pennsylvania; Citizens Utilities Home Water Company; Citizens Utilities Rural Company, Inc.; Citizens Utilities Water Company of Pennsylvania; Blue Mountain Consolidated Water Company; DuPage Utility Company; Derby Meadows Utility Company; CU CapitalCorp; LGS Natural Gas Company; Citizens Utilities Company of Ohio; Southwestern Capital Corporation; Southwestern Investments, Inc.; Sun City Sewer Company; Sun City Water Company; Sun City West Utilities Company; Citizens Mohave Cellular Company.

Further Reading: ''Along the Highways and Byways of Finance,'' *New York Times*, June 11, 1950; ''Mighty Midget,'' *Forbes*, May 15, 1955; ''Citizens Utilities Company,'' Harvard Business School Case Study, 1959; ''Richard Rosenthal Runs His Utility Like a Business,'' *Fortune*, September 25, 1978; ''Light and Heat,'' *Barron's*, August 18, 1980; ''Profile,'' *Fairfield County*, September, 1981; ''Richard Rosenthal— Utility Dynamo,'' *NYU Business,* Fall 1982; interview with Leonard Tow, *Wall Street Transcript*, September 14, 1992; Citizens Utilities Company Annual Reports, 1936, 1988, 1990, and 1991.

—John Simley

COMCAST CORPORATION

1234 Market Street
Philadelphia, Pennsylvania
U.S.A.
(215) 665-1700
Fax: (215) 981-7790

Public Company
Incorporated: 1969
Employees: 6,000
Sales: $721 million
Stock Exchanges: NASDAQ
SICs: 4841 Cable & Other Pay Television Services; 4812
   Radiotelephone Communications

Comcast Corporation is the fifth largest cable television company in the United States. Although a leader in the cable industry, Comcast has also made bold moves to enter the telephone industry as a high-tech competitor. Most of Comast's operations are centered in greater Philadelphia, but the company operates systems in 15 states and the United Kingdom.

Comcast has its origin in American Cable Systems, Inc., a small cable operation serving Tupelo, Mississippi. At the time, in the early 1960s, American was one of only a few community antenna television (CATV) services in the nation. The CATV business was predicated on the fact that rural areas were underserved by commercial television stations that catered to large metropolitan areas. Without CATV services—and its huge antennas that pulled in distant signals—consumers in these areas had little use for television. Although required to pay for CATV, customers considered the benefits worth the cost.

In 1963 Ralph J. Roberts and his brother Joe sold their interest in Pioneer Industries, a men's accessories business in Philadelphia and were looking to invest the proceeds in a new industry. After some research, they learned that the Jerrold Electronics Company, the owner of American Cable Systems, wished to sell the CATV concern. The Roberts brothers enlisted a young CPA named Julian Brodsky, who had helped them liquidate Pioneer Industries, and Daniel Aaron, a former system director at Jerrold Electronics, to help them evaluate the opportunity. The four agreed that while the system carried only five channels and served only 1500 customers, the investment had great potential. Ralph Roberts bought American Cable Systems and

later asked Brodsky and Aaron to join him in managing the company.

Growth within Tupelo was difficult, however. At times, the three were forced to serve as door-to-door salesmen. By 1964 they decided to buy additional franchises in Meridian, Laurel and West Point, in eastern Mississippi. The following year, American acquired more franchises in Okolona and Baldwyn, Mississippi. While these acquisitions succeeded in increasing subscribership, they failed to have much effect on penetration; for the cost of setting up a local system, there remained an insufficient number of subscribers to deliver a high return.

Roberts turned his attention to the bigger potential market of Philadelphia. In 1966 he bid successfully for cable franchises in Abington, Cheltenham, and Upper Darby, all northern suburbs of Philadelphia. He then purchased the Westmoreland cable system that served four other communities in western Pennsylvania. To achieve better economies of scale, Roberts dovetailed Westmoreland's operations with those of his other franchises. After establishing a strong foothold in suburban Philadelphia, Roberts extended his company's presence into six additional local communities.

Highly leveraged from this acquisition binge, but eager for more opportunities, Roberts enlisted the *Philadelphia Bulletin* newspaper for a joint venture to build additional cable systems serving Sarasota and Venice, Florida. As part of a limited diversification in 1968, Ralph Roberts joined his brother Joe—by then a minor partner in American but also an executive vice-president of Muzak Corporation—in purchasing a large franchise to provide the subscription "elevator music" service in Orlando, Florida.

Having decided that the name American Cable Systems sounded too generic for his growing company, Roberts decided in 1969 to change its name. In an effort to build a more technological identity, he took portions of the words "communication" and "broadcast," creating Comcast Corporation and re-incorporating the company in Pennsylvania.

Comcast reorganized its operations somewhat in 1970, selling off its Florida operations to Storer Communications and forming a limited partnership to purchase Multiview Cable, a local franchise serving Hartford County in Maryland. Limited partnerships enabled Comcast to finance growth with a minimal use of operating funds and were used to finance subsequent acquisitions. Predicting growth in the Muzak business, Comcast also acquired a franchise in 1970 for the service in Denver. The company later purchased Muzak franchises in Dallas, San Diego, Detroit, and Hartford, Connecticut.

Boasting 40,000 customers, but hampered by a continued stagnation in subscriber penetration rates, Comcast still needed funds to finance further expansion. In 1972 Roberts decided to take the company public, offering shares on the OTC market. In 1974 Comcast purchased a cable franchise for Paducah, Kentucky, and in 1976 acquired systems in Flint, Hillsdale, and Jonesville, Michigan. The following year, Comcast bought out its partners' interest in Multiview.

Cable by this time had become much more than an antenna service. For several years, cable operators included local access and special programming channels, as well as programming from large independent stations such as WGN in Chicago and WTBS in Atlanta. The government restricted what programming a cable operator could offer, often blocking access to programs that customers clearly wanted. Dan Aaron, a manager with Comcast, was active in the National Cable Television Association (NCTA), lobbying effectively for the relaxation of programming and other restrictions. In 1977, as chairman of the NCTA, Aaron brought many of the industry's efforts to fruition. As the cable industry was allowed to mature, additional cable-only stations were added, making the service viable within metropolitan areas that were well served by broadcasters.

With this added strength in the product, Comcast was able to win franchises to serve parts of northern New Jersey in 1978, as well as Lower Merion, Pennsylvania, and Warren and Clinton, Michigan in 1979. Through limited partnerships, the company later won franchises for Sterling Heights and St. Clair Shores, Michigan and Corinth, Mississippi. By 1983, Comcast had purchased Muzak franchises in Indianapolis, Buffalo, Scranton, Pennsylvania, and Peoria, Illinois.

The company made an important move in 1983 when, in partnership with a British gambling and entertainment enterprise, Ladbrokes, it won a license to establish a cable television system in the residential suburbs of London. Most cable licenses in the United States had been taken, and those that remained were expensive or only marginally profitable. But the industry was still in its infancy in the United Kingdom. In addition, British viewers would appreciate cable's selection; Britain had only about five stations, offering mostly government-supported programming.

In 1984, as Comcast added a cable partnership in Baltimore County and a Muzak franchise for Tyler, Texas, an important change took place in another industry. After a half century of antitrust litigation, the United States government broke up the Bell System. As a result, AT&T and its long distance operations were separated from 22 local Bell companies. Each of these Bell companies was organized into one of seven companies that saw cable television as the next logical course of progression for their telephone networks. The United States Congress, however, had already enacted legislation that would prevent telephone companies from taking over the still fragile cable industry. The Cable Act, which was written primarily to guarantee fair pole attachment rates to cable companies, had the effect of locking telephone companies out of the cable business.

Free for the moment from the ominous threat of competition from any of these multi-billion-dollar companies, Comcast proceeded with growth through acquisition. In 1985, after purchasing cable operations in Pontiac/Waterford, Michigan, Fort Wayne, Indiana and Jones County, Mississippi, Comcast won a plum: the right to serve the densely populated northeast Philadelphia area. In 1986 Comcast took over a cable system serving Indianapolis and purchased a 26-percent interest in Group W, one of the country's largest cable companies. This brought the company's cable subscribership to more than one million customers. The following year, Comcast acquired a cable system in northwest Philadelphia from Heritage Communications and cemented its position in suburban Philadelphia.

Turning more toward investments in other cable companies than in actual franchises, Comcast purchased a 20-percent share of Heritage Communications and a 50-percent share of Storer Communications in 1988. The Storer acquisition brought subscribership to more than two million customers and elevated Comcast to the fifth-largest cable company in the United States. Consolidating its partnerships, the company took full control of its Maryland Limited Partnership, Comcast Cablevision of Indiana, and Comcast Cable Investors, a venture capital subsidiary.

Also in 1988, Comcast turned an important strategic corner regarding telephone companies when it purchased American Cellular Network, or Amcell, a cellular telephone business serving New Jersey. For the first time, cable and telephone companies, prevented from competition in landline services, were facing each other in the cellular telephone business. And for the first time, a cable company was able to offer telephone customers an alternative to the telephone company.

In 1990, a year after relocating the corporate offices from Bala Cynwyd, Pennsylvania, to Philadelphia, Ralph Roberts shocked the company and the industry by naming his 30-year-old son Brian to succeed him as president of the company, while the he remained as chairman. Brian Roberts, who had impeccable academic credentials, silenced critics by proving to be a highly effective manager. Also, having begun work in the company at the age of seven, he had 23 years seniority, more than virtually anyone but his father.

Also in 1990, after having purchased an interest in an additional franchise serving suburban London, the company's newly-formed International unit won more British franchises, allowing the company to serve Cambridge and Birmingham. Comcast now counted more than one million customers in Britain alone. Increasingly, however, Comcast's smaller companies—such as Amcell—were beginning to experience slower growth. Rather than allow Amcell to be swallowed up later by a larger suitor, Comcast struck a deal in 1991 with the Metromedia Company, in which it purchased that company's Metrophone cellular unit for $1.1 billion. The new joint company, established in 1992, quadrupled Comcast's potential market to more than 7.3 million customers.

Later that year, however, the company's offices at One Meridian Plaza in Philadelphia were destroyed by a fire that took 19 hours to control. Only eight days later, the company set up shop four blocks away at 1234 Market Street. While officially a "temporary" location, the entire Meridian operation and 250 employees were once again in business.

In 1991 Comcast won one of only a few licenses granted by the Federal Communications Commission to test a Personal Communications Network system (PCN), more or less a cross between cordless and cellular telephones. PCNs are predicted to grow in popularity, decline in price and—to the dismay of telephone companies—render conventional telephones obsolete.

In September of 1992, Comcast staged a five-way international telephone call using the Comcast network and a long distance carrier. The purpose was to demonstrate that the company could handle telephone calls and completely bypass the local telephone network. While the demonstration was intended to raise investor hype over such bypass operations, it also succeeded in scaring telephone companies sufficiently to argue for permission to offer cable television services. The company continued to bolster its position in the bypass business in November of 1992, when it purchased a 51-percent interest in Eastern Tele-logic, a fiber optic-based bypass company based in King of Prussia, Pennsylvania.

In other areas of technological advance, Comcast is working to bring high-definition television and interactive television technologies to market, primarily through a research agreement with the industry-funded Cable Labs. Late in 1992, Comcast took over 50 percent of Storer Communications, dividing the assets of that company with Denver-based Tele-Communications, another leading cable firm. Storer was forced into dissolution by heavy debt carried at high interest. The proceeds for the sale enabled Storer's parent company, SCI Holdings, to retire much of that debt.

Comcast, built mainly on growth through acquisition, remains financially sound enough to avoid crises such as those suffered by Storer. But the era of this type of growth is coming to an end. It is likely that Comcast will attempt to maintain its impressive growth by making important, but expensive, strategic investments in telecommunications. Understanding that telephony is graduating to the airwaves, while television is graduating to wires, Comcast is in the right place.

Principal Subsidiaries: Comcast Cable Communications, Inc.; Comcast Cellular Communications, Inc.; Comcast Sound Communications, Inc.; Comcast International Holdings, Inc.

Further Reading: ''Comcast Names Brian Roberts President, Extending Family's Hold on Cable Firm,'' *Wall Street Journal,* February 1, 1990; Comcast Annual Report, 1991; ''Comcast Agrees to Buy Metromedia's Cellular Operations in $1.1 Billion Deal,'' *Wall Street Journal,* May 8, 1991; ''Comcast Corporation, a Historical Perspective,'' *Metrophonelines,* Company Publication, March 1992; ''Making a Point Long Distance,'' *Philadelphia Inquirer,* September 11, 1992; ''Cable/Cellular/CAP Combo Demos Competition for LECs,'' *Telephony,* September 14, 1992; ''Please Hold, Mr. Roberts Will Connect You,'' *Business Week,* October 26, 1992.

—John Simley

COMMERCE CLEARING HOUSE, INC.

2700 Lake Cook Road
Riverwoods, Illinois 60015-3888
U.S.A.
(708) 940-4600
Fax: (708) 940-0113

Public Company
Incorporated: 1927
Employees: 6,600
Sales: $659.4 million
Stock Exchanges: NASDAQ
SICs: 2741 Miscellaneous Publishing; 7389 Business
   Services Nec; 7374 Data Processing and Preparation; 8111
   Legal Services

The world's largest publisher of tax and business law news reports and books, Commerce Clearing House, Inc. (CCH) is a family-dominated service company composed of 18 subsidiaries, chief of which are CCH Computax (part of the company's Computer Processing Services division) and CCH Legal Information Services (representing the entire Corporate Services division). However, more than half of consolidated revenues for the company are derived from its extensive publishing division, with subsidiaries in Canada, England, Germany, Mexico, Australia, New Zealand, Singapore, and Japan. CCH also owns New York-based Facts on File, which controls U.S. rights for the *Guiness Book of World Records* and produces a number of general reference texts. Since going public in 1961, CCH has gained a reputation as a top-performing *Fortune* 500 company—return on shareholder equity from 1979 to 1984 averaged 47 percent.

Commerce Clearing House was founded in Chicago in 1892 to provide various services for lawyers, principally paper filing and document handling—important but bothersome tasks for large law offices. At that time, the legal publishing industry was attaining maturity under Minnesota-based West Publishing, a leader in the reporting of federal and state case law. CCH carved out its own niche in the legal publishing industry some fifteen years later. The catalyst was Oakleigh Thorne, a wealthy local banker who, in 1907, purchased an interest in the business. Thorne saw the publication of legislative reports and other legal and business reference works as an opportunity for future growth. His entry proved fortuitous to the still fledgling firm; six years later federal income tax laws were introduced and CCH was prepared to capitalize on the new demands for information. Like West, CCH had found its place in the lucrative government and legal field.

By 1935 CCH had ousted all major competitors and was blossoming into a major corporation. Thorne died in 1948 and his half ownership in the concern was transferred to a family holding company. Thorne's son Oakleigh L. Thorne ultimately became sole stockholder of the estate. The company went public in 1961 yet has, due to the ongoing ownership and management of the Thorne family, retained a low profile typical of most private companies. Oakleigh B. Thorne, a member of the third generation, has served as chairman since 1975. Oakleigh Thorne, a member of the fourth generation, was elected executive vice-president and group president in 1988 and a member of the executive committee in 1992. Edward L. Massie serves as president and chief executive officer.

CCH's biggest waves have been on the stock market and in its annual reports. The company's greatest growth occurred during the 1980s, but its livelihood is ensured indefinitely due to the seemingly paper-addicted federal government. As *Fortune* writer Stratford P. Sherman explained in 1984: "Thanks to tax laws so voluminous and arcane that even professionals cannot untangle them unaided, CCH has come to derive over half its $379 million annual sales from its tax products alone and now cheerfully counts the IRS as its largest customer." Sherman estimated the company's market share at 50 percent, with enviable pretax profit margins of 17 percent and 25 percent in its publishing and legal services divisions, respectively.

Chief Executive Officer Richard T. Merrill was responsible for CCH's cautious move into database research services, first pioneered by Mead Data's LEXIS system during the early 1970s. Although CCH had led the field of computerized tax-return processing with Computax, the move to high-tech had brought with it a host of competitors. Computax alone was responsible for a $12-million loss in 1983 due to a saturated software market and an increase in the number of accounting firms now beginning to offer full in-house services. CCH's quandary was how to remain competitive in the new information age without suffering further losses. While it remained a publishing powerhouse—with nearly double the subscriber base of its closest competitor, Research Institute of America—it struggled on the electronic front behind Mead, Research, and others. Andy Zipser, writing in *Barron's* in February of 1991, reflected on CCH's impending fall: "Once an earnings powerhouse that in 1980 churned out a 63 percent return on equity, CCH went into a decade-long slide that saw 1989 ROE slip to 16 percent and net income fall to $34.3 million from a 1987 high of $52.8 million." Although "decade-long" overstates the severity of the situation (during the first half of the 1980s corporate profits rose 56 percent on revenue increases of 45 percent), CCH and its stockholders certainly suffered. Zipser noted that an analyst who regularly follows CCH stock, Alan Bird, remains optimistic. Referring to a new on-line research service called ACCESS, Bird remarked, " 'This is their first innovation in decades, and if it cost a couple of years' earnings to do it, I don't think that's too high a price to pay.' " Bird's optimism remains warranted in light of CCH's introduction of

12 CD-ROM editions and a series of practice systems in 1992. Sales of these products have exceeded expectations and CCH Online was successfully upgraded and relaunched late in 1992.

With Computax, ACCESS Online and CCH ACCESS CD-ROM have become integral parts of the conservative but forward-looking CCH of the 1990s. Publishing, still CCH's largest segment, posted $411 million in sales for 1992. However, computer processing services, at $151 million in sales, now dwarfs the company's original business of legal services. For many years, CCH enjoyed a profitable business in mainframe-based service bureau tax return processing. By 1991, however, customers were beginning to use microcomputer tax software. CCH was well positioned for this change; the company had acquired 1040 Solutions in 1985 and PFX in 1989. Notable management announcements in 1992 included a reduction of 150 positions at CCH Computax and the sale of Fiduciary Tax Systems (FTS), a small segment of the computer division, to Computer Language Research Inc.

In February of 1993, CCH announced its agreement to acquire the federal and state tax service of Matthew Bender & Company, Inc. "This important acquisition not only strengthens CCH's leadership position on tax publishing but also demonstrates CCH's commitment to be the best in both analytical and topical reporting," according to CCH president Edward L. Massie.

In 1992 CCH completed the first phase of a planning process begun in 1991 and launched a new corporate mission. That ten-year mission involves becoming the leading global provider of knowledge. CCH plans to renew the core tax and business law product lines to restore earnings growth and then move into new areas to broaden its business base.

The company recorded a loss in the 1992 fiscal years, but expects a turnaround. The company completed a shift from mainframe to microcomputer-based tax return processing and software licensing, incurring a $50 million restructuring charge. The company also changed its methods of accounting for retiree health benefits. Yet, according to company officials, CCH stands in a strong financial position.

Its long-term course still a puzzle, CCH may nonetheless be expected in the next few years to redouble its publishing efforts overseas, a market that constitutes 25 percent of all publication revenue. The acquisition of Bender's tax service line also sig-nals a new CCH that is committed to developing new products, establishing strategic partnerships, and exploring other market opportunities. Also possible are more joint ventures modeled on CCH's 1992 agreement with West to furnish its long-standing money-maker, the *Standard Federal Tax Reporter,* to WEST-LAW database subscribers. A testimonial to CCH's golden years and the wisdom of the first Thorne manager, the 19-volume *Reporter* (at an annual cost over $1,000) is also one of the company's recurrent bright spots. Its renewal rate among subscribers—businesses, libraries, law and accounting firms, and the federal government—is 90 percent. Perhaps this is palliative enough for a company that continues to streamline, retrench, and rethink as it faces the twenty-first century.

Principal Subsidiaries: CCH Asia Limited; CCH Australia Limited; CCH Canadian Limited; CCH Computax, Inc.; CCH Editions Limited; CCH Europe Inc.; CCH Japan Limited; CCH Legal Information Services, Inc.; CCH New Zealand Limited; C T Corporation System; Facts on File, Inc.; Les Publications CCH/FM Ltée; LYF, S.A. de C.V. (49%); McCord Company; National Quotation Bureau, Inc.; State Capital Information Service, Inc.; Trademark Research Corporation; Washington Service Bureau, Inc.

Further Reading: "Commerce Clearing House, Inc.," *Datamation,* June 1981; Sherman, Stratford P., "The Company That Loves the U.S. Tax Code," *Fortune,* November 26, 1984; Oneal, Michael, "Commerce Clearing House Gets Rich on Tax Reform," *Business Week,* September 1, 1986; Allen, Michael Patrick, "Oakleigh Thorne," *The Founding Fathers: A New Anatomy of the Super-Rich Families in America,* New York, Truman Talley Books, 1987; Goodman, Jordan E., and Andrea Rock, "Commerce Clearing: Cashing in on Tax Confusion," *Money,* January 1987; Stovall, Robert H., "In the Rubble," *Financial World,* January 10, 1989; Tirbutt, Edmund, "The Business Book Business: CCH Editions," *Accountancy,* April 1989; Loomis, Carol J., "Secrets of the Superstars," *Fortune,* April 24, 1989; "Facts On File No Longer For Sale," *New York Times,* June 21, 1990; Byrne, Harlan S., Pauline Yuelys, and James P. Meagher, "Commerce Clearing House Inc.," *Barron's,* July 30, 1990; Zipser, Andy, "Clearly Commerce," *Barron's,* February 25, 1991; "West Publishing to Offer Tax Reports," *Star Tribune,* August 19, 1992.

—Jay P. Pederson

COMMODORE INTERNATIONAL LTD.

1200 Wilson Drive
West Chester, Pennsylvania 19380-4231
U.S.A.
(215) 431-9100
Fax: (215) 431-9465

Public Company
Incorporated: 1958 as Commodore Portable Typewriter Co.,
  Ltd.
Employees: 4,500
Sales: $887 million
Stock Exchanges: New York
SICs: 3571 Electronic Computers

Commodore International Ltd. produces the Amiga multimedia
line of computers, a range of PC-compatible computers, and the
entry-level Commodore 64 system. It is incorporated in the
Bahamas but has its main office in West Chester, Pennsylvania.
Commodore's primary market is Europe, where, especially in
Germany, it is a leading brand.

Commodore was founded by Jack Tramiel, an autocratic Polish-
born Canadian who had survived the German Nazi concentration camps of World War II. Tramiel incorporated Commodore
on October 10, 1958, as the Commodore Portable Typewriter
Co., Ltd., a Canadian corporation that *Forbes* referred to as "a
typewriter repair shop in the Bronx."

In the succeeding four years Tramiel successfully moved Commodore first into the assembly and marketing of typewriters and
mechanical adding machines and then into the manufacture of
electromechanical typewriters and adding machines. In February 1962 he changed the company's name to Commodore Business Machines Ltd.

Tramiel's initial success was soon overshadowed by controversy about his business methods. In 1965 it was revealed that
he and C. Powell Morgan, Commodore's chairman and president of the bankrupt Atlantic Acceptance Corporation, had,
according to *Forbes,* issued misleading financial statements,
used inside information to bolster share prices, and profited
from dummy companies that borrowed money from Atlantic
and re-lent it to Commodore. Tramiel was never indicted and, in
response to these charges, which were made in the report of the
Canadian Royal Commission investigating the collapse of the

Atlantic Acceptance Corporation, he claimed he was merely
following orders. Convinced otherwise, however, was Ontario
Supreme Court Justice Samuel H. S. Hughes, who wrote, according to *Forbes,* that Tramiel "was not, and probably never
had been the man who appeared, on his own showing, to be the
dutiful and helpless instrument of Morgan's schemes."

The financial fallout from the Atlantic bankruptcy plunged
Commodore itself near bankruptcy. In need of new capital,
Tramiel turned to Canadian investor Irving Gould, who in 1966
paid less than $500,000 for control of 17.9 percent of Commo-
dore's stock.

Once in control, Gould reduced Commodore's debt and sold
company assets, including manufacturing facilities. He brought
Commodore's designs to low-cost producers in Japan, where he
and Tramiel also saw early electronic calculators. Impressed by
these devices, he and Tramiel became convinced that the future
lay in electronics and subsequently contracted Casio and others
to manufacture calculators for sale in North America.

Sales and profits increased rapidly in 1968 when Commodore
introduced the first of these calculators. Between that year and
1970 sales rose from $4.1 million to $9.4 million while profits
expanded from $130,000 to $700,000. In 1973 Commodore
made $1.3 million on sales of $32.8 million.

Taking advantage of the economic climate, Tramiel and Gould
moved to take control of manufacturing and introduce new
products. In 1969 they arranged to begin manufacturing calculators using semiconductor chips made by Texas Instruments. In
1971 they introduced the C106, the first mass-market compact
electronic calculator for consumers. In 1973, in response to
exploding demand, they opened manufacturing plants in Palo
Alto, California; Bristol, Virginia; and Eaglescliff, England.

By 1974, although sales increased to $49.8 million, earnings
began to fall due to a surplus of calculators on the market. Prices
spiralled downward and the glut of products led to massive
returns by retailers. The situation worsened in 1975 when the
swiftly-evolving electronics industry left Commodore with $6.5
million in obsolete inventory. As a result, the company reported
losses of $4.4 million on sales of $55.9 million.

To avoid similar future disasters, Tramiel cut costs. He phased
out the Bristol plant, moved Japanese headquarters closer to its
assemblers' facilities, sold only to volume buyers who paid
promptly, and reincorporated as Commodore International Ltd.,
in the tax-free Bahamas. Most importantly, he decided to tackle
the actual manufacturing of chips so that Commodore could
govern its own supply.

In pursuit of this "vertical integration" he and Gould acquired
several small companies, the most important of which proved to
be MOS Technology. Unbeknownst to Tramiel or Gould, MOS
had developed the 6502 microprocessor—the chip that Commodore used to build its first computer and which Apple and
Atari used to build their early home computers.

By 1976 management realized that the calculator market had
reached maturity and Commodore needed new products. They
put together a prototype of a small computer and exhibited it at a
trade show. The prototype generated so much excitement that
Tramiel decided to manufacture a stand-alone home computer.

To develop the product, though, Commodore needed a bank loan and banks, mindful of the Atlantic Acceptance episode, refused to loan Commodore the money. In the end, Gould was forced to personally guarantee the $3 million note.

While the computer was being developed, Tramiel struggled to keep Commodore in the black. He divided the company into four divisions, each of which he hoped would devise new products and sell them through international distributors: the consumer products division would handle electronic calculators and watches; the components division would market semiconductor components and watch modules; the metal products group would deal in steel office furniture; and the systems division would sell personal computers and small microprocessor systems.

In 1977 Commodore's systems division unveiled the Pet, Commodore's first home computer and one of the very first home computers on the market. By the standards of the mid-1990s, the Pet was primitive, with little practical use. In 1977, however, it had tremendous novelty value and, at $795, was the first stand-alone home computer priced under $1,000. The Pet did well, but in the United States its low price made financing its promotion difficult. Due in part to the lack of promotion, its share of the market fell to just 10 percent in 1981, compared to 23 percent for Apple and 16 percent for Tandy. In Europe, where Commodore's distribution facilities were intact and the Pet's price was significantly higher ($1,295), the computer did much better. This disparity between European and American sales would become a trend for Commodore, which would ultimately garner more than 90 percent of its sales earnings outside North America.

Commodore grew quickly, especially in its systems and metal products divisions, the latter of which had been bolstered by the acquisition of Nortex Products and Gildon Metal Enterprises. Sales for 1978 reached $50.1 million, and profits hit $3.4 million. In 1979, a year when Commodore made $6.5 million on sales of $71.1 million, stock prices bolted from 5½ to 48⅞ before a 3-for-2 split.

Throughout the late 1970s and early 1980s Commodore continued to issue new products, including the CBM, which was aimed at the small business market and priced just under $5,000. Its next real success came in late 1980 when it introduced the Vic 20, the first home computer priced under $300. More advanced than a video game machine and less powerful than the personal computers that would soon appear, the Vic 20 was extremely successful and established Commodore as the leading microcomputer manufacturer in Europe and a top manufacturer in North America.

Fueled by the success of the Vic 20 as well as the giddy atmosphere surrounding the personal computer industry, Commodore's share price rose to 138¼ before a 3-for-1 split in 1981. By 1982 Commodore was selling 800,000 Vic 20s a year as well as a large number of semiconductor components to other manufacturers. That year the company reported profits of $40.6 million on sales of $304 million.

With the introduction of the Commodore 64 in August 1982, Commodore again placed itself at the leading edge of the personal computer market. Intended as an alternative to the Apple II, its base price of $600 was $400 less. According to *Forbes,* the price differential was made possible by "having chip and equipment designers working hand in hand." The 64, like the Vic 20, proved extremely popular. Profits were so high that management declared a 50 percent stock dividend. Even so, Commodore continued to have problems on the domestic market. Only 30 percent of the company's 1982 sales came from the United States.

In the 1984 fiscal year Commodore made $143 million and reported sales of $1.27 billion. Both Tramiel and Gould, however, could see that the company's future fortunes were uncertain. While Apple was trying new products and IBM had entered the race for home computer dollars, Commodore had nothing to replace the 64. Given the situation, Gould's forced out a whole cadre of top management, including Tramiel, who departed that January.

As his new president, Gould chose Marshall F. Smith, a professional manager who had previously headed the diversified industrial company Thyseen-Bornemisza, Inc. Smith repopulated Commodore's management ranks with professionals from Apple, Nabisco, and other firms. He and Gould also focused on finding a next generation computer to compete with the Macintosh and IBM's rapidly improving offerings. Smith and Gould found their new computer in the Amiga Corporation, a small Silicon Valley start-up that they bought for $25 million in December 1984. Amiga would provide Commodore with 27 new engineers and a computer chip essential to the development of a line of computers touting greatly advanced graphics capabilities.

Commodore was then sued by Jack Tramiel, who, after his ouster from Commodore, had bought the computer game maker Atari Corporation from Warner Communications. Atari filed suit against Commodore alleging that Amiga had pledged to sell its chips only to Atari.

Despite the lawsuit, Commodore went ahead with the deal and in July 1985 introduced the Amiga. Priced at $1,295 and based on the Motorola 68000 microprocessor as well as three custom chips, the Amiga was superior to the Macintosh in several respects. It displayed in color, worked faster, and could perform several computing jobs at once. The Amiga was oriented toward video, audio, and graphics. Douglas Cayne of the Garttner Group said in *Fortune* that "The Amiga is absolutely the most spectacular, most wonderful, most powerful machine for the home market today." The reviews of the machine, however, were not universally positive. An anonymous reviewer in *Byte* described it as "so poorly documented that many features were as confusing as bugs." The operating system, AmigaDOS, was incapable of running DOS-based software, and software writers were frustratingly slow in writing programs specifically for it.

Commodore also failed to define the Amiga's niche in the video and sound portion of the marketplace and didn't actually deliver it to stores until mid-November of 1985, missing much of that winter's holiday shopping season. Because of Amiga's slow start, Commodore's cash flow, according to *Forbes,* "dried to a trickle." The company lost $113 million in 1985 and $127 million in 1986.

The losses brought Commodore close to bankruptcy. Smith cut costs by closing a semiconductor plant in Costa Mesa, California, and a computer assembly plant in Corby, England. In mid-

1985 the company went into technical default and its banks set a deadline of January 31, 1986, for the renegotiation of loans. The deadline was successfully negotiated but a month later Smith resigned. It was speculated that the resignation was part of Commodore's agreement with its banks.

Thomas Rattigan, a former PepsiCo vice-president who had become Commodore's president in 1985, succeeded Smith as chief executive officer. In the summer of 1986 Rattigan returned Commodore to profitability. He introduced a line of IBM-compatible PCs and presided over continued successes in Europe, where the Amiga became a leading computer for business. Rattigan and Gould, however, clashed over the poor United States sales, which continued to account for just 30 percent of revenues. The conflict became a question of board loyalty and in April 1987 Rattigan resigned amidst suits and countersuits.

With Rattigan gone, Gould left the presidency vacant and took over as chief executive. In April 1988 he presided over the introduction of the Amiga 2000. The 2000 improved the Amiga's performance in areas the computer already dominated, such as desk-top video. It was more rugged and expandable than the 1000, and Commodore gave it an optional bridgeboard that would allow it to run DOS-based programs. The 2000 and its lower priced cousin, the Amiga 500, were lauded by the computer press and found a niche among sound and video enthusiasts. But they did not really enter the mainstream and did not threaten Apple or IBM.

Nevertheless, the combination of the Amiga, DOS-based PCs, and the surprisingly large sales of the veteran Commodore 64 system led to reasonable profits. In 1988 Commodore made $48.2 million on sales of $871.1 million. In 1989 it cleared $50.1 million on sales of $939 million. Commodore did run into trouble with the IRS, however, which disagreed with Commodore's tax tactics and claimed it owed $74.1 million for the years 1981, 1982, and 1983.

While profits continued, Amiga technology advanced. The company introduced the Amiga 2500, which *Forbes* lauded for its ability to capture video and overlay it with text, graphics, and four channel sound. The 2500 model, which was well supplied with software and conformed to both the United States and European television standards, was better with video than most computers and ideal for computing's burgeoning role in training and business presentations.

Despite this technological advance, Commodore reported losses in the first two quarters of fiscal 1990—losses *Forbes* magazine placed at the feet of Irving Gould. *Forbes* criticized Gould's penchant for hiring and firing executives and described him as an absentee landlord who, as a Canadian citizen, could spend no more than three days a week in the United States without paying American taxes. One analyst told *Forbes,* "Irving tries to minimize taxes, hates the day-to-day stuff and doesn't like to push the product."

In April 1990 Commodore introduced the Amiga 3000. Released in the midst of an industry buzz about the possibilities of multi-media systems—a concept Commodore had been pushing since its beginning—the 3000 retained Amiga's edge. It cost thousands less than competing systems and *Byte* called it

"the most capable multimedia platform you can get in a single box." It also came with an authoring system that, according to the *Wall Street Journal,* made "it rather easy to pull together a multi-media presentation." Moreover, according to *Byte,* Commodore had "finally defined a focus for the Amiga line and staked its claim to the emerging multimedia market." Perhaps because of this, Commodore convinced many retailers—some still smarting from the company's mid-1980s decision to sell to discount chains—to carry the system.

In fiscal 1992 Commodore sold more than one million Amigas, pushing that computer's installed base to well over 3.7 million. Nevertheless, overall sales fell from $1.04 billion to $911 million, primarily because of lower peripheral sales, a discontinuation of lower end MS-DOS based PCs, price reductions on the ever-surprising Commodore 64 (650,000 units sold), and disappointing sales of CDTV, a new system that combined compact disc sound and video with interactive Amiga technology. As a result, Commodore reported a loss for its fourth quarter and yearly profits that fell to $27.6 million from 1991's $48.2 million.

Commodore continues to enjoy great success in Europe, where it accounts for the great majority of its sales. Its historic position as a major player in that market remains unchanged. The company continues to struggle for market share in the United States, however, and its sales in Asia and Australia have not been as substantial as the company hoped. The remainder of the decade will no doubt prove interesting for Commodore as it continues its many-fronted battle in the computer industry.

Principal Subsidiaries: Commodore B.V. (Netherlands); Commodore Electronics Ltd. (Bahamas); Commodore Business Machines Ltd. (Canada); Commodore Business Machines Inc. (U.S.A.); Commodore Business Machines Inc. Ltd. (New Zealand); Commodore France S.A.R.L.; Commodore Business Machines, U.K. Ltd.; Commodore Business Machines Pty. Ltd. (Australia); Commodore Buromaschinen GmbH (Germany); Commodore Japan Ltd.; Commodore AB (Sweden); Commodore AG (Switzerland); Commodore Amiga, Inc.; Commodore Data A/S (Denmark); Commodore Computers Norge A/S (Norway); Commodore Italiana S.p.A. (Italy); Commodore Computer N.V./S.A. (Belgium); Commodore Business Machines Ltd. (Hong Kong); Commodore Semiconductor Group; Commodore European Support and Coordination Company (Netherlands); Commodore S.A. (Spain); Commodore Computer GmbH (Austria); Commodore Protuguesa Electronica, S.A. (Portugal).

Further Reading: Chakravarty, Subrata N., "Albatross," *Forbes,* January 17, 1983; Monci Jo Williams, "How Commodore Hopes To Survive," *Fortune,* January 6, 1986; Heath, Charlie, "Commodore Opens the Amiga," *Byte,* April 1988; McGlinn, Evan, "Lost Opportunity," *Forbes,* November 13, 1989; "Four Multimedia Gospels," *Byte,* February 1990; Ryan, Bob, "Commodore Sets Course for Multimedia," *Byte,* May 1990; "The Datamation 100," *Datamation,* June 15, 1991; "The Datamation 100," *Datamation,* June 15, 1992; "Users Column," *Byte,* September 1992.

—Jordan Wankoff

In May of 1963, inspired by the growth of television advertising, the popularity of television programs, and the introduction of color broadcasts, Hostetter and Grousbeck pooled $3,000 and devised a narrowly-focused plan to serve areas that were underserved by conventional broadcast television. They settled upon two rural communities in northwestern Ohio, Fostoria and Tiffin, which, they reasoned, would be unable to pull in a decent signal from major cities without the help of a cable system.

The two men negotiated franchises to serve the area but needed an additional $650,000 to finance construction of the system. It took them both nearly a year to raise the funds, and after they secured backing from Boston Capital, they returned to Ohio to discover that local authorities had grown impatient with them and awarded a competing franchise to a local radio station that had already begun construction.

Faced with a situation in which the market was ''overbuilt'' and realizing that competition in the fragile market would destroy both companies, Hostetter and Grousbeck began negotiations to purchase their competitor's system and eventually reached an agreement to buy out the competitor for $80,000—a steep sum at that time. Although Hostetter and Grousbeck were successful, the fiasco proved an expensive lesson in good government and community relations. With only a few thousand customers, the two men went into business, operating the systems, carrying out marketing initiatives, and answering the phones.

In 1965, Hostetter and Grousbeck took their Continental Cablevision venture to the Mississippi River community of Quincy in west central Illinois. The lessons they learned with their Ohio operations helped them establish a franchise in Quincy without a hitch. From that time, Grousbeck handled the Illinois operations while Hostetter managed the Ohio properties. This arrangement soon demonstrated to both men that local operating decisions were best made by the managers who worked and lived in the community. This philosophy of decentralization and empowerment would later be cited as the defining quality of Continental's success.

In 1969 Hostetter and Grousbeck appointed new managers for their Ohio and Illinois businesses and returned to Boston, establishing a headquarters for Continental in a warehouse in Boston's Lewis Wharf. From there, they planned the acquisition of additional franchises and began to assemble a crack management team.

By the early 1970s, Continental served 65,000 subscribers. While many franchise opportunities arose, Continental restricted its bids to only the most promising. Interestingly, despite its location in Boston, Continental never bid on a contract to serve the city.

Hostetter, a banker and corporate financier by training, also learned the importance of marketing. In order to fund the construction of a cable system, Continental first had to have enough subscriber cash flow to cover loan payments, maintenance, salaries, and other expenses. Subscriber cash flow could only be maximized through good marketing and customer service. This simple point drove the company though a period of explosive growth through the 1970s and remains the company mantra.

CONTINENTAL CABLEVISION, INC.

The Pilot House
Lewis Wharf
Boston, Massachusetts 02110
U.S.A.
(617) 742-9500
Fax: (617) 742-0530

Private Company
Incorporated: 1963
Employees: 8,000
Sales: $1.1 billion
SICs: 4841 Cable & Other Pay Television Services

Continental Cablevision is a leader in the cable television industry and is renowned for its enlightened community relations practices and its commitment to customer service. Consequently, Continental Cablevision has enjoyed greater success than most cable providers when negotiating for new franchises.

The notion of paying to receive television signals over coaxial cable predates cable-exclusive programming by more than 25 years. When it was first proposed as a business in the early 1950s, cable television was intended to provide clear reception of distant signals to subscribers in remote areas. At the time, only large cities had a full range of television programming from the three major networks, while some cities also had an independent or educational broadcast system. Using large antennae mounted on tall towers, fledgling cable companies could pick up signals from these cities and bring television to vast unserved rural areas. With much of suburban and rural America without adequate television service, the industry was built for growth.

This fact was not lost upon Amos ''Bud'' Hostetter, a graduate of the Harvard Business School class of 1961. In 1962, Hostetter, then an employee of Boston-based Cambridge Capital, became involved in a proposition to finance a cable television system for industry pioneer Bill Daniels in Keene, New Jersey. Hostetter recommended that Cambridge help finance the deal and found himself responsible for keeping an eye on its activity. Soon Hostetter developed a personal interest in cable television and invited a Harvard classmate, Irving Grousbeck, to join him in bidding on other franchises.

In 1972, for his efforts as a director of the National Cable Television Association, Hostetter was elected to the organization's chair, and he became an outspoken opponent of federal regulation that threatened to retard the growth of the industry. Hostetter joined the board of the Corporation for Public Broadcasting in 1975 and the board of the Children's Television Workshop in 1980. In 1979 he helped to establish C-SPAN, a network devoted to televising congressional proceedings.

In the mid-1970s, Continental continued to operate a group of small franchises scattered across Ohio and Illinois and around Richmond, Virginia. During this time, the industry experienced an investor shock. Faced with possible competition from telephone companies, the apparent exhaustion of undeveloped franchises, and the threat of overbuilding, banks and venture capitalists began to abandon the industry. Growth came to a standstill, forcing many cable companies to renegotiate their agreements with local governments. Continental, however, was not as broadly exposed to any of the dangers that caused investors to balk. Through conservative financial management and a measured construction schedule, Continental was able to weather the storm with no ill effect. In fact, because some companies were forced to sell off portions of their systems, it became a buyer's market for the stronger, smaller companies in the industry, such as Continental.

During this time antitrust litigation against the Bell System was entering its final stages and the federal government was beginning to address the major public policy questions related to cable television and telecommunications. Hostetter was instrumental in numerous FCC regulatory decisions, including one that guaranteed cable operators a fair rate for attachment rights on telephone and power utility poles. The new regulations ensured that utilities would not conspire to extract excessive funds from cable subscribers through high pole attachment rates.

Another regulation prevented telephone companies from competing with cable companies, thus preserving exclusive cable franchises. This allowed cable companies to build out their systems, free from potentially ruinous competition from multibillion dollar monopolies. Both industrial guidelines later were incorporated into the 1984 congressional Cable Act.

In 1978, Continental claimed more than 200,000 subscribers. The company continued to purchase smaller 3000- to 5000-subscriber systems, favoring a gradual expansion incorporating proven technologies. This approach won the interest of Dow Jones & Company, Inc. which was looking for strategic investments in information industries outside the print medium, and in 1981, Dow Jones negotiated the purchase of a 25 percent share in Continental for $80 million. The deal also marked an important alliance against telephone companies who, it was feared, were committed to building cable systems to compete with publishers for the attention of readers—and advertising dollars.

The Dow Jones investment provided Continental with enough capital to bid on or buy out franchises in lucrative suburban markets around Boston, Cleveland, Detroit, Chicago, and St. Louis. The company scored its first major buyout in 1984, when it acquired a mismanaged, 82,000-subscriber system in Jacksonville, Florida. By redoubling service efforts in that market—and applying its marketing charm—Continental succeeded in doubling subscribership in Jacksonville within three years.

Continental's local management in the city later negotiated exclusive rights to carry the United States Football League's Jacksonville Bulls home games. This move brought in 5,000 new subscribers overnight. In another notable marketing effort in 1987, Continental sponsored a three-hour special promoting cable television—on a Jacksonville broadcast station. At the time, the Jacksonville deal was the largest in the industry. Continental paid nearly $1,600 per subscriber but, as penetration increased, that figure fell to about $600 per subscriber—representing a bargain.

Continental also began a foray into the cellular telephone industry by purchasing an operating license to serve some communities in the northeastern United States. This experiment, however, was unsuccessful, as the cellular phone and cable businesses proved too dissimilar. The company had not purchased enough cellular licenses to realize profitable economies of scale, and the investment languished for some time as an alternative to land-line telephone service. In 1986, Continental negotiated the sale of its troublesome cellular telephone operation to Colony Communications. In exchange, Continental received cash and several of Colony's cable systems in eastern Massachusetts.

In 1984, Continental purchased a poorly run cable system from McClatchy Newspapers serving Fresno, California. The following year marked its one millionth customer with the opening of a 1000-mile cable system in St. Paul, Minnesota.

In 1985, however, Continental made its largest acquisition to date, taking over American Cablesystems, a company modeled after Continental by its founder, Steven Dodge. Five days after the deal was announced, however, Wall Street experienced the worst one-day stock crash in history; investors were dazed by the 500-point drop in the Dow Jones Industrial Average. Undeterred, and buoyed by an excellent record of financial management, Continental pressed forward. The sale was completed in 1988, giving Continental access to 900,000 customers in greater Los Angeles.

The newly acquired system presented Continental with several new challenges, particularly that of attempting to increase sales in areas where previous franchise owners proved unable to bring market penetration above 25 percent. Nevertheless, Continental eventually saw penetration rates nearly double that.

Also in 1985, Hostetter negotiated the repurchase of Dow Jones' 25 percent interest in the business, ensuring that Continental's management would retain full control over the company. Irving Grousbeck, a partner in the business for more than 20 years, left Continental two years later to pursue other business ventures and to take up a teaching position at Stanford University. Hostetter remained to chair the enterprise.

In 1989, Continental Cablevision began making large investments in programming from Turner Broadcasting System, Inc. and the Viewers Choice pay-per-view network. Continental is bullish on pay-per-view, one of the few high-margin premium services in the cable market. The company also began to profit from locally programmed advertising on its systems.

In 1992, isolated abuses in the cable industry led the United States Congress to enact legislation that would allow reregulation of the cable television industry. While all cable companies argued that this would load regulatory costs into customers' bills, Continental was particularly chagrined that, after doing its job correctly for nearly 30 years, it was subject to a punishment intended for other companies.

Continental attributes its success to three factors. First, after trying, and ultimately failing, to make a success of its cellular properties, Continental focuses only on those things it can do well. Second, the company maintains a decentralized organizational structure that will not support a large bureaucracy. In 1989, Hostetter told *Multichannel News,* "We at headquarters are not smart enough to know what the right answers are. We're not there day in and day out. Our decision makers have to go home and read the town paper and see the mayor the next day. That's a different approach from two guys in dark suits who fly out of New York to renegotiate a franchise and leave the next day." In fact, the company's senior marketing managers are in the field. They are given responsibility for drawing up their own budgets and are expected to make major decisions on their own authority in the belief that decisions must be made as close to the customer as possible. Finally, Continental concentrates on hiring creative, energetic managers under the assumption that they will, in turn, hire staffers with similar values. Company vice chairperson Tim Neher told *Cable Marketing,* "We don't lose a lot of people, because they like what they're doing and where they're doing it. It's fun to be in a job where you have all the authority to do the job well."

These precepts helped Continental to become the third largest Multiple System Operator in the United States, serving 2.9 million subscribers in 600 communities in 16 states. In addition to being highly profitable, Continental is renowned for its exceptional customer service and is consistently chosen by its peers in the industry as one of the best-managed companies in the business.

Principal Subsidiaries: Insight Communications, Inc.; Teleport Communications, Inc. (20%); Turner Broadcasting (Minority Stake); E! Entertainment Broadcasting Company (Minority Stake).

Further Reading: "Continental Cable: Top of the Line," *Channels,* October 1986; "Amos Hostetter, Jr.: A Profile," *Cable Television Business,* January 1, 1988; "Readers' Choice Awards," *CableVision,* May 9, 1988; "Excelling at the Basics," *Channels,* July/August 1988; "Continental at 25," *Cable Marketing,* April, 1989; "Continental: Sterling After 25 Years," *Multichannel News,*" April 17, 1989; "The 'Elegant Package' that is Amos Hostetter," *CableVision,* April 24, 1989; Annual Report, 1992.

—John Simley

CROWN CENTRAL PETROLEUM CORPORATION

The Blaustein Building
One North Charles Street
P.O. Box 1168
Baltimore, Maryland 21203
U.S.A.
(410) 539-7400
Fax: (410) 659-4730

Public Company
Incorporated: 1923 as United Central Oil Corporation
Employees: 3,894
Sales: $1.76 billion
Stock Exchanges: American
SICs: 2911 Petroleum Refining; 5541 Gasoline Service
   Stations

Crown Central Petroleum Corporation is an independent refiner and marketer of petroleum products, including petrochemical feedstocks. It operates two refineries, one located near Houston, Texas, and another in Tyler, Texas, with rated capacities of 100,000 and 50,000 barrels per day (b/d), respectively. Crown's principle business is the wholesale and retail sale of its products in the Mid-Atlantic, Southeastern, and Midwestern United States, with approximately 435 gasoline stations and convenience stores in operation. The company relies heavily on the high volume, multi-pump concept in gasoline retail that it pioneered in the early 1970s.

The 1990s have brought several challenges to Crown's fiscal well-being. Stringent environmental regulations, stronger competition, and tighter profit margins, exacerbated by conflict in the Middle East that sent shock waves through every branch of the oil industry, have all combined to rock Crown's foundations. Like other independent firms, Crown has been forced to react expeditiously to increased competition in the industry.

Crown Central's history began in 1917 on a nondescript plot of land in Harris County, Texas. A drilling crew of the recently founded Crown Oil and Refining Company struck oil at Well Number 3, Goose Creek Field. With the revenue generated by that well, the fledgling company was first able to compensate its crew—whose paychecks had run out before their momentous find—and then, in 1918, to construct its own 65-acre refinery,

one of the first on the Houston Ship Channel. In 1920 it began production of one product: 500 viscosity red oil, commonly called lube oil. At that time, the majority of Crown Oil and Refining Company's stock was held by White Oil Corporation.

In 1923 Delaware-based United Central Oil Corporation acquired White Oil and, by extension, the business of Crown. In 1925 United Central Oil began production of gasoline at the Houston refinery and changed its name to Crown Central Petroleum Corporation, acquiring the "Crown" trademark in September of that year. In 1930 the American Trading and Production Corporation, operated by the Maryland-based Blaustein family, purchased a controlling interest in Crown—an interest that remained at 48 percent of Crown stock well into the 1990s.

The convoluted nature of Crown's early history was attributable in part to the general disorder prevalent in the early oil industry, as well as to its history with the Blaustein family, which involved itself in a maze of oil investments from the 1920s onward. Through various privately held companies, the family has owned more than $100 million in apartment houses and office buildings; manufacturing companies; considerable bank stock; and tankers. In addition, the family reigns as the largest stockholder in Indiana Standard Oil Company since the late 1950s.

In 1910 the patriarch of the family, Louis Blaustein, founded American Oil Company, which marketed gasoline under the Amoco brand name. In the late 1920s the Blausteins started a private firm, the American Trading and Production Corporation. By the 1980s the firm had concentrated its operations on exploration and production of crude oil and natural gas in the United States and western Canada, utilizing its own fleet of tankers to transport crude and finished products. In the 1920s the Blausteins and Crown had, as yet, an impersonal relationship; Crown supplied gasoline to Amoco. But the Blausteins had founded American Trading in order "to consolidate, expand, and diversify the Blaustein family business activities," according to Henry A. Rosenberg, Blaustein's grandson. In 1930 American Trading acquired a controlling share of Crown as an extension of that plan. In 1937 the Blaustein imprint became an indelible one as Crown moved its state of incorporation from Delaware to Maryland, the home state of its controlling family. The plan worked, inasmuch as Crown grew rapidly until the 1980s and set national standards for gasoline retail sales facilities.

The Second World War further boosted Crown's operations. The United States Bureau of Standards and the Department of the Navy both recognized Crown for its quality products. In addition, the company pioneered the manufacturing of high efficiency, 100-octane aviation gasoline for warplanes. An early "wing and star" logo was modeled after the Army Air Corps pilots' wing emblem, a reference to Crown's effective military service.

The post-war era marked Crown's entry into the retail gas business. By this time the company had already established itself as a growing force as a wholesaler of gasoline and distillates. In 1943 the company opened its first service station in Baltimore, beginning a gas-station colonization of the Mid-Atlantic and Southeastern states. As this business grew, so did the product transport system. Initially, the company used the Plantation Pipeline to move its product—60–65 percent gasoline and 35–40 percent distillate—to the Atlantic Coast. It eventually expanded to the Colonial Pipeline as well, while also relying on some of its own trucks to distribute their product to service stations and/or its 11 terminals in Houston; Atlanta; Baltimore; Birmingham, Alabama; Norfolk, Richmond, and Newington, Virginia; Columbus, Georgia; Spartanburg, South Carolina; Elizabeth, New Jersey; and Charlotte, North Carolina.

Crown's relatively steady growth was interrupted in the 1970s by increases in crude costs, initiated by the 1973 Arab oil embargo. Crown, now led by Henry A. Rosenberg, Jr., who succeeded his father as the company's top executive in 1976, attempted a change in strategy, away from traditional refining and retail sales and toward diversification. The company attempted to expand its exploration and production operations to increase its self-sufficiency in crude oil.

Like other independent refiners, Crown dealt primarily with foreign producers, such as Nigerian National Corp. and Algeria's Sonatrach, through short-term contracts that were subject to quarterly renegotiation and summary cancellation where negotiations fell through. After having lost on a bid for Burmah Oil Co., Ltd., Crown set its sights on Kewanee Industries. In a combined bid with the National Cooperative Refinery Association (NCRA) and Hamilton Brothers, an independent producer, Crown offered $430.5 million for the firm. NCRA pulled out of the deal, leaving Crown and Hamilton in no position to outbid Gulf, which won the deal.

In other attempts at diversification to bolster its place in the stagnant market in the 1970s, Crown ventured into coal and gold mining, launched an oil exploration partnership with the Nigerian government, and started an East Coast refinery construction project. All of these endeavors eventually lost money. It also acquired Continental American Life Insurance Company in 1980. The merger's life span was cut short, however, when Crown sold American Life to Provident Mutual Life Insurance Co. for $44 million.

In the 1980s Crown refocused its efforts in retailing, trying to maximize efficiency in order to gain greater control over prices and increase profit margins. Fierce competition made this more difficult to execute than to plan. Although Crown had been a pioneer in developing the modern service station—a clean, well-lit, open 24-hours unit, equipped with multi-product pumps and convenience stores—by the 1980s similar models operated by its competitors were commonplace. Keeping continuous vigil along the country's superhighways and high-traffic intersections were similar, if not identical, service stations affiliated with BP America, Coastal Marketing, Getty Petroleum, and Atlantic Refining & Marketing, as well as such convenience store giants as Cumberland Farms and Circle K. The figures were daunting: Atlantic Richfield Co., for example, expanded its 750 "am/pm mini marts" in many of the territories where Crown operated; and Southland Corp. of Dallas bought its own refinery and added gasoline service to many of the company's 7,300 7-Eleven stores.

In order to build what CEO Rosenberg called "better mousetraps" to lure gasoline and grocery customers, Crown cut un-

profitable outlets and opened more promising ones. In 1983 the company acquired two highly profitable chains, Zippy Mart and Fast Fare, comprising 642 new units, although most were furnished with obsolete pumps and needed overall refurbishing. Along similar lines, Crown acquired 68 BP service stations in Maryland in 1986, doubling the number of outlets it owned in the state. In 1987, concentrating on its core businesses of refining and marketing, the company sold its small but profitable crude oil and natural gas business for $166 million. Crown used the money to balance its books and get rid of all outstanding debt, according to Rosenberg.

In 1989 the company increased its refining capacities by 50,000 barrels a day with the purchase of La Gloria Oil and Gas Company in Tyler, Texas. Increased production was intended to more efficiently stock the company's expanding retail chains, which grew again in 1991 as Crown acquired 48 existing retail properties in Virginia for $21 million. Marketing strategies to draw consumers to these service stations included payment plans offered with either Crown fleet credit cards or WEX cards, available through Wright Express Corporation. Crown also cosponsored Oldsmobile in 1988 on the NASCAR Winston Cup circuit, a series of racing events that drew 14 million fans and 165 million television spectators. In 1991 Crown expanded its wholesale capabilities with the completion of a pipeline directly linking the Houston refinery to the Texas Eastern pipeline system.

A combination of political and economic barriers in the 1980s and 1990s hindered further growth. A lingering recession affected all aspects of the business, from deliveries of petroleum products in the U.S. to a sizable decline in oil's share of domestic energy consumption (it fell to 41 percent in 1991, the lowest in 40 years, according to company sources). While the repercussions of the Persian Gulf War triggered temporary industry turmoil and a tremendous price surge in early 1991, *Standard & Poor's Industry Surveys* also identified a stabilizing effect on the market, as the "price hawks" in OPEC had had their wings clipped as a result of the conflict.

Crown's independent status and relatively small size also complicated matters, as industry trends favored the larger conglomerates who were better protected against market fluctuations. In addition, major oil companies such as Exxon, Mobil, and Texaco could typically afford substantial oil reserves that immediately appreciated in value when the price of oil surged, providing instant profit when sold. Without such cushions, independent refiners such as Crown were at a significant disadvantage.

One tactical recourse was in the realm of pricing: adjusting retail prices to reflect wholesale prices and thereby maximize margins. In March 1979 the Department of Energy (DOE) had implemented its "tilt" regulation permitting refiners to pass along increased costs in higher gasoline prices. This legislation gave independents additional leverage against major corporations. Nevertheless, Crown found itself embroiled in numerous suits for alleged pricing violations. In June 1982 the DOE proposed that Crown pay more than $33 million to gasoline and heating oil customers in compensation for overcharges and other violations of federal oil price and allocation regulations. Over the years, Crown had sustained a long chain of similar allegations. In 1964 the Federal Trade Commission ordered the company to halt price-fixing practices. In 1977 Crown and five other firms were convicted of conspiring to fix prices from 1967 to 1974. In 1980 Crown faced charges from the Federal Council on Wage and Price Stability. Finally, the DOE charged Crown with overcharging gasoline and heating oil customers by more than $709,000 in 1978. The DOE pricing mechanisms, then, while helpful to Crown in certain respects, had historically also proven somewhat troublesome.

The late 1980s and 1990s were marked by heightened environmental considerations that reverberated throughout the oil industry. Whether enforced by government legislation or mandated by environmentally conscious consumers, oil companies took costly measures to produce cleaner-burning fuels and to minimize ecological damage in oil prospecting and transportation. Crown thus placed environmental issues at the top of its priority list for the 1990s. According to the Clean Air Act (CAA) of 1990, the EPA mandated new gasoline specifications to be developed in two main phases. Phase I required the substitution of oxygenates for a percentage of the aromatics by 1995. Oxygenates are octane enhancers that burn more completely, while Aromatics are octane enhancers that are less efficient. The most commonly produced oxygenate is methyl tertiary butyl ether (MTBE). For refiners, Phase I costs had been estimated at $3 billion to $5 billion to retrofit facilities by 1996, according to Standard and Poor's. Crown estimated that from 1991 to 1995, 80 percent of total capital allocation at its refineries would be for environmentally directed projects.

Other regulations were being designed to determine liability in oil spill incidents. In June 1990 an explosion aboard the supertanker Mega Borg caused fire damage and spillage of approximately 2,000 gallons of oil into the Gulf of Mexico. The tanker was owned primarily by a Norwegian firm, carrying Angolan crude owned by the French company Société Nationale Elf Aquitaine, and bound for delivery to Crown Central Corp. Legal arguments in the incident's aftermath hinged on determining legal culpability for the accident. Subsequent legislation resulted in foreign reluctance to ship crude and other raw materials to the United States. Crown adapted by purchasing a portion of its waterborne crude at the point of origin, requiring the company to assume greater responsibility for the material's safe transport.

Crown expended considerable effort and funds to comply with the varied environmental concerns being raised. In November 1982 it became the first licensee of a process to recover liquids from refinery fuel gas, an application that would help contain refinery flares. In 1989 Crown began producing MTBE at a rate of 1,500 barrels a day at its Houston refinery. Both Crown refineries began work on facilities for the production of low-sulfur diesel fuel and the efficient processing of higher sulfur, and therefore much cheaper, feedstocks. The company complied with new training and documentation guidelines published by the Occupational Safety and Health Administration. New regulations monitored gasoline evaporation at gas pumps and gas leakage from underground storage tanks (USTs). Crown projects the cost of modifications to refinery and other operations in order to meet environmental guidelines to reach $200 million through 1997.

Crown's fiscal outlook in the early 1990s was a bleak one. In 1991 the company had a net loss of $6 million ($.61 per share), compared to net income of $26 million ($2.65 per share) for 1990. Sales and operating revenues were $1.8 billion in 1991, compared to $2.1 billion in 1990. In 1992 William D. Hyler of Oppenheimer & Co. noted that the refining business was a "mess," with the "spread"—the difference between what it costs for a barrel of oil and what a refiner can get for the refined gasoline—at its lowest in 10 years. Yet Standard & Poor's forecasted that refining would be the first sector of the battered petroleum industry to rebound from the 1991 fall. Crown Central Petroleum Corporation hopes to take a leading role in that recovery.

Principal Subsidiaries: Continental American Corp. (Delaware); Coronet Security Systems, Inc. (Delaware); Coronet Software, Inc. (Delaware); Crown Central Pipe Line Co. (Texas); Crown Gold, Inc. (Maryland); Crown Central International, Ltd. (U.K); Crown Nigeria, Inc. (Maryland); Crown Oil & Gas Co. (Maryland); Crown-Rancho Pipe Line Corp. (Texas); Crown Stations, Inc. (Maryland); La Gloria Oil & Gas Co. (Delaware); Crowncen International N.V. (Netherlands Antilles); FZ Corp. (Maryland); Fast Fare, Inc. (Delaware); Crown Central Holdings Corp.(Maryland); Locot, Inc. (Maryland); McMurrey Pipe Line Co. (Texas); Tiara Insurance Co. (Vermont); Tongue Brooks (Bermuda, Ltd.) (Bermuda); Tongue, Brooks & Company, Inc. (Maryland); Health Plan Administrators, Inc. (Maryland)

Further Reading: "Can't Lose for Winning," *Forbes*, July 15, 1977; Santry, David G. "Refinery Values that Look Tempting," *Business Week*, March 26, 1979; Hamilton, Martha, "Crown is Asked to Pay Refunds for Overcharges," *Washington Post*, June 26, 1982; "Recovering Liquids from Refinery Fuel Gas," *Chemical Week*, November 17, 1982; Wachter, Jerry, "Crown Central Petroleum: Taking on the Big Guys," *Business Week*, September 12, 1983; Dorfman, John R. "On the Prowl?" *Forbes*, February 28, 1983; "Amoco to Buy Crown Central Unit," *Chicago Tribune*, November 17, 1987; Hattie, Wicks, "Why Crown Central is Worth Watching," *National Petroleum News*, 1988; Reier, Sharon, "Life on the Knife's Edge," *Financial World*, October 31, 1989; Krauss, Alan, "Oil-Spill Legislation Hits Snag in Congress," *Investor's Daily*, June 13, 1990; Potts, Mark, "Crown Central: Caught in Oil's Vise," *Washington Post*, August 16, 1990; *1991 Annual Report*, Crown Central Petroleum Corporation, Baltimore, MD, 1992; Hinden, Stan, "The Tarnish on Crown Central Petroleum's Stock," *Washington Post*, July 27, 1992.

—Kerstan Cohen

Curtice Burns Foods

CURTICE-BURNS FOODS, INC.

90 Linden Place
P.O. Box 681
Rochester, New York 14603-0681
U.S.A.
(716) 383-1850
Fax: (716) 383-1281

Public Company
Incorporated: 1961
Employees: 7,400
Sales: $896.9 million
Stock Exchanges: American Midwest
SICs: 2033 Canned Fruits & Vegetables; 2099 Food
  Preparations Nec; 2011 Meat Packing Plants; 2037 Frozen
  Fruits & Vegetables; 2096 Snack Foods

Curtice-Burns Foods Inc. is a fruit, vegetable, and food processor, that grows, packages, ships, and markets a range of food products internationally. The company's range of products include canned and frozen fruits and vegetables, desserts, oat-based cereals, condiments, snack foods, microwaveable main dish meals, and breaded specialty vegetables.

The fruit and vegetable processor got started through the work of the Curtice brothers and the Burns-Alton Corp. late in the nineteenth century. First, in 1868, brothers Simeon and Edgar Curtice founded a small grocery store in Rochester, New York. Soon thereafter, they formed a canning business called Curtice Brothers to save surplus vegetables and fruits they could not sell in the store. Working first from a Water Street plant, the business expanded to Curtice Street, and before long additional plants were built in Vernon, New York, and Woodstown, New Jersey.

At this time, the commercial tinning and canning industry was still developing. Technology for mass market preserving was rudimentary, and the use of chemical preservatives brought occasional digestive side effects. Nevertheless the Curtice Brothers business grew; the company, along with other food processors, discovered that products tastefully packaged could find strategic markets.

In 1920, both Curtice brothers having died, control of the company was handed over to the Security Trust Company, which shortly thereafter sold its stake to Douglas C. Townson.

The Burns half of Curtice Burns began as the Burns-Alton Corp. in Alton, New York. In 1900, founder C. F. Burns began packing dried and fresh apples and dried beans. His son Ed joined the family business in 1925, and the company's name was changed to C. F. Burns and Son, Inc.

Much of the company's food products at this time were shipped to Europe, a market that slowly shrank during the 1920s. In 1927, the Burns's plant was re-equipped to process applesauce. One year later, 50,500 cases, mostly applesauce, had been processed at the plant.

The merger of the Curtice Brothers and C. F. Burns & Son operations occurred in the early 1960s. Both companies were active in the fruit and vegetable growing regions in central and western New York state. They and other food processors were adjusting to the end of lucrative government contracts for canned food during the World War II years. With sales down, companies found fixed and overhead costs rising.

A shakeout of the regional industry was inevitable, with resulting mergers among rivals. One consolidation involved talks beginning in 1958 between Curtice Brothers, Burns-Alton Corp., and Haxton Foods Inc. of Oakfield, New York. All the owners of these companies were getting along in years and wanted out of the business, so their main incentive was to find a buyer for their companies. An additional incentive was locating capital to fund the purchase of new labor-saving equipment and obtaining an increased market share in the expanding frozen food business. The drawback was continuing pricecutting in the marketplace, which further dented already slender profit lines achieved by each company.

The merger talks did not progress well. A large agricultural cooperative, Cooperative Grange League Federation Inc. (GLF) of Ithaca, New York, was recruited in early 1959 to seek ways to establish a joint venture of farmers and processors involving the three companies. That year, the death of George W. Haxton led to the withdrawal of Haxton Foods from the joint venture talks. This left GLF consultants to establish the processing venture with Curtice Brothers and Burns-Alton.

Further study concluded that the best solution would be to merge Curtice Brothers and Burns-Alton into a new operating company with a contractual arrangement for marketing cooperation, owned and operated by farmers. So, in October of 1960, Pro-Fac Cooperative Inc. opened for business. By March 31, 1961, more than 500 central and western New York state fruit and vegetable farmers had bought common stock in Pro-Fac. They pledged to deliver a predetermined tonnage of raw produce to the cooperative over the next three years.

This meant that Curtice Burns Inc. would be incorporated to process and sell products grown and delivered by Pro-Fac Cooperative to supermarket chains. Achieving this vertical integration called for Pro-Fac to acquire the plants and equipment of the former Curtice Brothers and Burns-Alton operations for approximately $3 million. The new, merged company achieved sales of $13 million in 1962, its first fiscal year.

In June of 1962, Haxton Foods was ultimately bought by Pro-Fac and Curtice Burns for $1.5 million. Haxton Foods brought to the deal such branded products as its Blue Boy food line as well as operating plants in Oakfield, Waterville, LeRoy, Barker, and Wyoming.

Beginning in 1962, Curtice Burns, under the leadership of President Stanley Macklem, set about becoming a regionally focused company. The idea was to operate a series of small, locally based businesses on a cost-effective basis, enabling Curtice Burns to become a national force serving regional markets in ways that large, national competitors could not.

The company came by this grand strategy the hard way. Beginning as a processor and marketer of Pro-Fac products, Curtice Burns served the private label business, marketing canned string beans, beets, corn, and applesauce to such supermarket chains as Shop Rite Foods Inc. or Grand Union stores. Serving private label chains was profitable when national brands were in short supply. But in periods of oversupply, Curtice Burns suffered. In 1962, for example, the company's second year of business, prices for private label food products plummeted, and the company lost money. Worse, Pro-Fac growers received 15 percent below the average market price for their raw product.

Curtice Burns sought to establish a regional edge to stabilize its earnings. A mere ten percent fluctuation in the national supply of a product group could greatly alter a company's profit and loss statement. The unpredictability of supplies is often driven by crop yields, themselves subject to weather and annual planting patterns. A plan to diversify regionally allowed Curtice Burns to give Pro-Fac members more than full market value for their raw product in all but two years between 1962 and 1980.

Curtice Burns began offering frozen vegetable products with regional appeal, marketing, for example, southern style frozen vegetables in the southern United States. The company could also provide quick delivery of products.

In 1963 Morton Adams, who had been executive vice-president of Burns-Alton when it merged with Curtice Brothers in 1961, became president of Curtice Burns. Two years later in September of 1965, Curtice Burns purchased the canned sauerkraut maker Empire State Pickling Company, based in Phelps, New York, adding the well-known Silver Floss label. The company also added Finger Lakes Packaging to its operations portfolio. Pro-Fac built two can-making plants in Alton and LeRoy, New York that year and leased them to Continental Can Co.

In February of 1967 Curtice Burns expanded outside New York state when it purchased the P. J. Ritter Company, headquartered in Bridgeton, New Jersey. Along with Indiana-based subsidiary Brooks Foods, P. J. Ritter made branded tomato ketchup and specialty bean products under the Brooks label. P. J. Ritter/ Brooks products were sold in one-third of the U.S. market. Acquiring them allowed Curtice-Burns to further diversify regionally in the United States and decrease its weather and national oversupply risks by adding branded commodity products and growing areas to its portfolio.

Curtice Burns's next big acquisition came in June of 1972 with the purchase of Pennsylvania based Snyder's Potato Chips. Snyder's packaged its chip products in foil bags aimed at the convenience food market. The company also sold other potato chip, corn chip, and snack products.

A year later, Curtice Burns issued 220,000 shares of common stock with a value of $10.50 each. The shares were to be listed on NASDAQ, a stock exchange for emerging publicly listed companies. The proceeds of the 1973 issue helped in that year's purchase of Michigan Fruit Canners, headquartered in Benton Harbor, Michigan. The acquired company's products, marketed mainly under the Thank You brand label, brought Curtice Burns into markets ranging from Denver to Pittsburgh and Atlanta.

In July of 1975, Curtice Burns moved out west by purchasing Nalley's Fine Foods, based in Tacoma, Washington. Bought from the W.R. Grace & Co., Nalley's had four main product groups: canned meats, pickles, salad dressings, and snack foods. Nalley's brand products were sold mostly in the western United States market.

In December of 1975 Curtice Burns made a second public offering of 413,294 shares, valued at $11.50 each. Early in the following year, the company's stock gained a listing on the American Stock Exchange.

More companies were brought under the Curtice Burns umbrella in the ensuing years. In 1976 the company acquired Nalley's Canada Ltd., based in Vancouver, British Columbia. In May of 1977 Curtice Burns acquired Comstock Foods, headquartered in Newark, New Jersey, from Borden. A year later, the Canadian arm of Curtice Burns purchased Bonus Foods for $428,000.

Curtice Burns had by now installed Hugh Cummings as president of the company. He oversaw the June 1979 acquisition of National Brands Beverage Division, which was bought from Canada Dry Bottling Co. of Syracuse, New York, for approximately $1.7 million. For the first time, Curtice Burns had entered into the branded soft drinks market, initially in New York state.

Earnings at Curtice Burns were dented by the early 1980s slowdown in the U.S. market, causing squeezed profit margins. Company sales in 1980 totalled $357.6 million, compared to $303.7 million posted a year earlier. Net income fell in that period from $5.13 million in 1979 to $4.6 million in 1980.

At the same time, Curtice Burns recognized that a slumping market is a good time to buy struggling rivals. In January of 1980, the National Oats Co. Inc., headquartered in Cedar Rapids, Iowa, was picked up from the Liggett Group. National Oats produced milled oat food products and corn for popping.

Curtice Burns's U.S. expansion was furthered a year later when Lucca Packing Company, a California-based canned and frozen Italian and Mexican food maker, was purchased. Soon thereafter, it bought the southern division of Seabrook Foods Company. Henceforth to be named the Southern Frozen Foods division of Curtice Burns, the newly acquired company sold primarily McKenzie's brand southern style frozen vegetables in 11 southeastern states.

In February of 1984 Curtice Burns purchased the 7-Up Bottling Company of Binghamton Inc. from a private concern for $1.15 million. Two years later, the company added fruit fillings, frozen fruits, and maraschino cherries to its line when it bought for $41 million the assets of Wilderness Foods, Naturally Good

Foods, and Cerise Foods Divisions of Cherry Central Cooperative Inc. The acquired company served markets in the western United States from its Sodus, Michigan, headquarters.

The acquisitions were meant to serve the company's long-term growth. As company president David McDonald expressed in 1988, "Our principal focus in any year is not on short term earnings, but on the structuring of Curtice Burns in a manner that will, over the long term, maintain a rate of growth that is at the top of the industry."

Curtice Burns's marketing strategy included achieving dominant positions in niche food categories; for example, two meat snack companies were purchased, the Smoke Craft Division of International Multifoods, in December, 1986, and, in December, 1988, Lowrey's Meat Specialties, Inc., based in Denver. Lowrey's was the leading maker of meat snack products, including beef jerky, for which Curtice Burns became the largest supplier in the U.S. market. The two companies later merged to form the Curtice Burns Meat Snacks division. Other important acquisitions in this period were Adams, a producer of natural branded peanut butter, and Farman Brothers Pickle Co.

Another niche market was Mexican frozen food products, part of the larger frozen dinner market then becoming popular in the United States. In January of 1989 the company acquired from Pillsbury the Van de Kamp Mexican Frozen Dinner line. Sales of frozen Mexican food were then increasing 16 percent annually in the U.S. market. Eighty percent of sales were made in the growing San Francisco and Los Angeles markets.

The company was also making cuts wherever possible to remain a low-cost producer. Due to a variety of factors, mainly competitive, Curtice Burns got out of the branded soft drinks market in 1988 when it sold its National Brands Beverage business to eleven separate bottlers. Only private labels were retained in a series of deals that netted the company $6.6 million in profit.

Perhaps more importantly, the company was focusing on growing low per capita food categories in its regional brand marketing. For example, in 1988, sales of canned vegetables nationwide reached around $63 million, and canned desserts attained $105 million in sales. Although small in size, Curtice Burns believed no food processing giant could make inroads in such markets by advertising on television at great cost. This meant the battleground for products like sauerkraut and fruit toppings shifted from the living room to the grocery store shelf, where Curtice Burns's cost effective operations could successfully outplay bigger companies in the market.

The company's two-year acquisitions spree that began in 1986 led to a sales increase that in 1989 reached $807.2 million. Reflecting this growth, stock in Curtice Burns soared 34 percent in value to $32. By now, the Pro-Fac Cooperative numbered 774 members; Curtice Burns itself had more than 7000 full and seasonal employees on its payroll.

Adverse weather conditions and high raw product costs contributed to earnings falling 22 percent to $11.6 million in 1990. The early effects of the recession in North American markets was being felt. That year, the company was decentralized into ten major operating divisions: Southern Frozen Foods, headquartered in Montezuma, Georgia; Comstock Michigan Fruit, based in Rochester, New York; Finger Lakes Packaging, operating out of Lyons, New York; Snack Foods Group, headquartered in Rochester; Curtice Burns Meat Snacks of Denver; Nalley's Fine Foods, based in Tacoma, Washington; Nalley's Canada Ltd. in Vancouver, British Columbia; Brooks Foods, headquartered in Mount Summit, Indiana; Lucca Packing of San Francisco, California; and National Oats Company, based in Cedar Rapids, Iowa.

Curtice Burns's acquisitions continued apace at this time. David McDonald, the company's president and chief executive officer during that period, announced in July of 1992, according to *Refrigerated & Frozen Foods:* "If we could find an acquisition that would get us into another part of the country on an economic basis, we would make that acquisition. We'd buy any size company. We've bought them as small as a couple of million or as big as $100 million. It depends on the company."

McDonald's boldness came at a time when the recession was further affecting the company's balance sheet. 1991 sales remained stagnant at $933 million, compared to $926.8 million a year earlier. Profits were down from $7.4 million in 1990 to $3.6 million in 1991. The earnings decline was most marked in oat cereal sales. Following an oat bran craze that required increased plant capacity, demand nationally for oat products decreased, and the company had to adjust its National Oats division to market erosion and reduced profit margins. Two other major factors in the earnings decline were oversupply in vegetables and high material costs for meat snacks.

The early 1990s recession also meant widespread price cutting in the snack food industry and record low earnings by North American food retailers that the company served with private label products. Still, through 1992, Curtice Burns achieved a 68 percent jump in earnings to $6.14 million. Cost efficiencies were made possible that year with the opening of the company's first national sales office in Memphis, Tennessee, to aid in customer sales and servicing.

Curtice Burns's earnings recovery continued into fiscal year 1993. First-quarter income jumped from $1.1 million a year earlier to $1.33 million. Looking to the future, Curtice Burns hoped to profit from its continuing focus on core businesses in regional markets, where a cost effective dominance of that product category could be maintained. When the product commodity cycles—worsened by the recession of the early 1990s—return to stability with the recovery, the company's earnings would likely show similar improvement.

Principal Subsidiaries: Southern Frozen Foods; Comstock Michigan Fruit; Finger Lakes Packaging; Snack Foods Group; Curtice Burns Meat Snacks; Nalley's Fine Foods; Nalley's Canada Ltd; Brooks Foods; National Oats Company.

Further Reading: "Curtice Burns Foods Inc.: A History," Curtice-Burns Public Relations, November 1991; "Regional Edge," *Refrigerated & Frozen Foods,* July 1992.

—Etan Vlessing

CYPRUS MINERALS COMPANY

9100 East Mineral Circle
P.O. Box 3299
Englewood, Colorado 80155-3299
U.S.A.
(303) 643-5000
Fax: (303) 643-5642

Public Company
Incorporated: 1969 as Amoco Minerals Co.
Employees: 7,000
Sales: $1.64 billion
Stock Exchanges: New York
SICs: 1021 Copper Ore Mining; 1222 Bituminous Coal
Underground Mining; 1221 Bituminous Coal and Lignite
Surface Mining

Cyprus Minerals Company is the second largest U.S. copper producer, a world leader in molybdenum production, a top 20 U.S. coal producer, and the world's leading producer of lithium. Cyprus also produces iron ore and gold. It operates in 24 states and seven countries and conducts base and precious metals exploration worldwide.

The Cyprus Minerals Company first appeared in July of 1985 as a spinoff from the Amoco Corporation. The company's history, however, dates back to 1969 when Amoco created Amoco Minerals Company to handle mineral rights. In 1979, that subsidiary's president, Kenneth J. Barr, acquired Cyprus Mines Corporation, which then mined copper, talc, calcium carbonate, and kaolin and explored for uranium, gold, and molybdenum. Amoco kept the Cyprus name and in the early 1980s built it into a large concern that produced coal, copper, and industrial minerals.

In 1980 Amoco created Cyprus Coal, a subsidiary that, in turn, acquired coal mines in Colorado, Pennsylvania, and Kentucky. The coal operation was immediately profitable, and Donald P. Bellum installed efficient longwalls, draglines, shovels, and haul trucks to reduce costs. At some mines, these efforts cut costs by as much as 40 percent. By 1985, coal accounted for 56 percent of Cyprus's $706 million in sales.

Cyprus Industrial Minerals handled talc, limestone, calcium carbonate, clay, and barite—products in production before the Amoco takeover.

Cyprus's third subsidiary was Cyprus Metals which mined copper for construction and molybdenum for steel and lubricants. Under Amoco, Cyprus Metals expanded Cyprus Mines' Baghdad copper mine in Arizona and built the Thompson Creek molybdenum mine—which was later shut down—in Challice, Idaho. Each facility was an efficient producer but each suffered when prices dipped in 1983 and 1984. In the last half of 1984 metals lost $70.8 million due to slackening molybdenum demand and copper prices, which had fallen from one dollar to 60 cents a pound.

Cyprus experienced extensive losses in 1984 and 1985. Ironically the cost cutting these losses induced put Cyprus in a position to grow once it became independent from Amoco, which decided to spin it off in July of 1985. "As a spin-off," then-Chairman John C. Duncan wrote in Cyprus's 1985 report, "we emerged with low debt, well equipped and in a very strong position relative to our competitors."

Once independent Barr began expanding the company. Almost immediately, Cyprus bought coal mines in Utah, Colorado, and Virginia, increasing coal capacity to over 18 million tons. "The companies wanted to get out of this business," Barr told *Barron's,* "and we were able to help them out with a good deal for ourselves."

In succeeding years, Barr would acquire and make profitable many unwanted operations, so many that *Forbes* called him a "junk pitcher" and lauded him for "acquiring . . . almost dead or dying U.S. mining properties for pennies on the dollar and [bringing] them back to life."

At this point, most of Cyprus's operations were producing a profit—Cyprus reported operating revenues of $32 million in its first six months. Three businesses, however, looked unlikely to ever return their investment. Rather than carry these investments, the company decided to sell a barge operation, close and upgrade the Baghdad copper mine, and write down the company's entire $398 million investment in the Thompson Creek molybdenum mine. In all, 1985 asset write-downs totaled $675.7 million. Nevertheless, Barr told *Barron's,* "I see a good, steady earnings picture." The sacrifice was ultimately profitable. With lower depreciation and amortization costs and more efficient operations at Baghdad, Cyprus reported 1986 profits of $21.1 million on sales of $811 million.

In 1986 Cyprus Metals recorded its first profits in more than three years, and in March Barr added to its strength by acquiring the Sierrita copper and molybdenum mine near Tucson, Arizona. Sierrita made Cyprus the third-largest copper producer in the United States and the third-largest producer of molybdenum in the world.

Cyprus Coal also finished in the black, though not quite as profitably as officials had hoped. The coal operation had been on its way to a very good year, but the LTV Corporation filed in U.S. Bankruptcy Court for Chapter 11 protection and canceled long-term contracts with the Emerald and Knox Creek mines. This caused second half losses, and led Cyprus to sell Knox Creek early in 1987. On the positive side, Cyprus's Plateau mine in Utah, its Empire mine in Colorado, and several recently acquired mines in Kentucky achieved higher profits.

Though Cyprus was becoming quite successful in its core businesses, Barr felt that new products, especially gold, would enhance shareholder value. "It's one of those areas that adds value in the minds of investors," he told *Barron's*. "A gold company carries a greater price to earnings multiple than a copper company."

Barr established Cyprus Gold late in 1985, and, in 1986, that subsidiary began identifying prospects. Concentrating on proper ties with the potential to produce gold at cash costs of less than $200 per ounce, the company located four gold ore bodies in Australia and one in the United States. In 1987 Cyprus's board advanced Cyprus Gold $25 million to pursue these investments through joint ventures.

Although they did begin gold production at Gidgee in Australia and Copperstone in Arizona, gold was far from the only forum Barr and Duncan used to expand Cyprus in 1987. Among other subsidiaries, Cyprus Coal acquired the Shoshone coal mine in Wyoming, while Cyprus Metals acquired the Casa Grande copper mine in Arizona, the Piños Altos copper mine in New Mexico, and Metec, a New Jersey producer of specialty molybdenum products.

For 1987, profits reached $26.2 million, though sales fell to $795.3 million. Much of the improved profits picture came from Cyprus Metals, which, through acquisitions, had increased capacity by more than 50 percent and was benefiting from copper prices, which soared above $1.40 a pound that December. But while metals operating profits doubled, coal profits suffered from a soft market and industrial mineral profits fell to $2.9 million, despite further reorganization.

In 1988 Cyprus's growth campaign swung into high gear. The company bought a Colorado coal mine and acquired ARCO's inactive Tonopah, Nevada molybdenum mine—which was later shut down—making Cyprus the largest molybdenum producer in the United States. The following year Cyprus acquired an 82 percent interest in Foote Mineral Company, the world's largest producer of lithium, a material used in pharmaceuticals, greases, ceramics, aluminum alloys, and high-performance batteries.

Financing for all this expansion came from soaring copper prices, and Barr did not neglect to expand this most profitable area. In 1988 Cyprus acquired the Arizona assets of the Inspiration Consolidated Copper Company and signed a long-term lease at the Twin Buttes mine, which was adjacent to Sierrita in Arizona. The Inspiration copper company was renamed Cyprus Miami. New assets included a smelter, a refinery, and a rod plant, and Cyprus, which had become the second-largest copper producer in the United States, would now begin the process of vertical integration. The company was nearly self-sufficient in smelting, a big cost cutter.

High copper and molybdenum prices led to 1988 earnings of $170 million ($6.31 a share) on sales of $1.3 billion. There were, however, two setbacks. Cyprus Gold was hurt by start-up problems and coal profits fell to $8.2 million due to reduced contract prices and a $6.1 million charge for closing three Kentucky mines.

In 1989, copper prices remained high and copper production grew 28 percent to 594 million pounds. In total, copper accounted for nearly 90 percent of that year's record $250.1 million in profits. However, while the copper was bringing in substantial income, management was becoming aware of problems with costs and price fluctuations. Cyprus's copper costs were high for the industry, and costs rose even further in the final quarter of 1989 when the company unsuccessfully tried to mix ore from four different pits at Sierrita and Twin Buttes. If copper prices fell, Cyprus would find itself in trouble.

Furthermore, Cyprus's other products were barely contributing. Operating earnings from lithium and talc fell almost 50 percent to $26.7 million. Cyprus Gold lost $1.7 million because of low prices, and the coal company, which battled inefficiency and low prices, was only marginally profitable.

Cyprus officials worked to squeeze more profits from these other businesses. They exchanged shares in three small Australian mines for a larger interest in a more efficient Queensland, Australia operation. They also consolidated some Kentucky operations and closed some costly Kentucky coal mines.

But while attention was beginning to focus on efficiency, acquisitions were by no means finished. In 1989 Cyprus entered two new businesses when Barr leased the inactive Groundhog zinc mill in Deming, New Mexico and paid $52 million for the Reserve Mining Company's Babbit iron mine and processing plant in Silver Bay, Minnesota. Since Reserve's mine had been idle since LTV's 1986 bankruptcy, Cyprus had to spend an additional $30 million on capital improvements to bring it up to speed. By March of 1993 the mine was up for sale.

In 1990 Cyprus zeroed in on costs, budgeting $200 million to increase efficiency. Copper had earned most of the company's $111 million in 1990 profits and remained very profitable. To keep it so, the company installed larger haul trucks and a power shovel at Sierrita and took steps to correct problems with metal recovery, stripping, conveyors, and ore grade at Twin Buttes. At Miami, it began a $100 million smelter expansion and modernization project, which would make the company self-sufficient in smelting and reduce overall copper production costs.

Cyprus Coal suffered from cost increases despite state-of-the-art long wall equipment at Twentymile and Emerald and good longwall equipment at Plateau and Empire. At Shoshone, failed longwall machinery led to $25 million worth of repairs, and at Kanawha lower reserves and higher reclamation costs led to $31 million in writedowns.

Most of Cyprus's other products seemed to be in a down cycle. A Molybdenum glut caused $50 million in losses at the Tonopah mine, which Cyprus put on a care and maintenance basis. Lithium production shifted to a low-cost Chilean operation where the company completed a $9 million expansion. Talc suffered from the maturing product life cycle of Airways Vapor and needed to return to what the company called "acceptable levels of profitability."

In February of 1991 Barr retired. Board member Calvin A. Campbell, Jr., became chairperson and Chester B. Stone, Jr., who had previously been chief financial officer and senior vice-president for coal and iron ore, became president and chief executive officer.

That year a worldwide economic slowdown dragged earnings down to $42.7 million on sales of $1.9 billion. Copper prices fell one-third from their 1988 high, molybdenum prices remained depressed, and spot coal prices continued to decline. Despite lower prices, copper continued to lead the way, combining with molybdenum to report operating earnings of $132 million on revenues of $905.7 million. Coal finished $4 million in the black despite falling prices and a strike at the Empire mine in Colorado. What dragged profits down were $37.6 million in combined losses from lithium, gold, iron ore, zinc, and talc, including a $35 million pretax writedown for the sale of the company's talc business.

In early February 1992, Stone announced his retirement as president and CEO, and Campbell assumed both of those posts. Campbell was an interim choice but by no means a caretaker. "There's so much to be done at Cyprus and the things that have to be done have to be done now," he told the New York Times. Indeed copper, coal, and other minerals were all losing money by mid-1992 and needed immediate attention.

Campbell outlined his strategy for the company in Cyprus's 1991 annual report. He planned to narrow the company's focus to copper and coal and possibly one other material. Moreover, he aimed to develop low cost international sources of copper, increase marketing expertise, and reduce costs by a variety of means, including reducing staff. By mid-March Campbell announced plans to review the cost of goods and services and lay off 25 percent of the company's headquarters staff.

In April of 1992, Cyprus named Milton H. Ward chair and chief executive. Ward almost immediately wrote down $315 million in assets and told security analysts, according to the New York Times, that he would update the company's mining equipment and narrow Cyprus from eight commodities to three or four, including copper, coal, and lithium.

As Cyprus Minerals headed into 1993, it hoped to grow through carefully selected acquisitions. The company also planned such internal improvements as an increase in its coal-producing capacity and a heightened dedication to environmental responsibility.

Principal Subsidiaries: Cyprus Coal Co.; Cyprus Western Coal Co.; Cyprus Yampa Valley Coal Corp.; Colorado Yampa Coal Co.; Twenty-Mile Coal Co.; Cyprus Mountain Coals Corp.; Buckhorn Processing Co.; MCI Mining Corp.; Cyprus Metals Co.; Sociedad Chilena de Litio Limitada; Minera Bismark S.A. de C.V.

Further Reading: Rosenberg, Hilary, "Richer Vein," *Barron's,* April 21, 1986; Norman, James R., "Will the Bargain Still Be a Bargain?," *Forbes,* June 11, 1990; Cyprus Minerals Company annual reports, 1991-92.

—Jordan Wankoff

DAIHATSU MOTOR COMPANY, LTD.

1-1, Daihatsu-cho, Ikeda-shi
Osaka 563
Japan
(0727) 51-8811

Public Company
Incorporated: 1951
Sales: 787,502 yen (1991)
Employees: 11,328
Stock Exchanges: Tokyo
SICs: 3711 Motor Vehicles & Car Bodies; 3713 Truck &
　Bus Bodies; 3714 Motor Vehicle Parts & Accessories

A world leader in the manufacture and sale of high-quality minivehicles, small passenger cars, trucks, and utility vehicles, Daihatsu Motor Company, Ltd. is also a pioneer in the development of the electric car. Daihatsu was the first automobile company in the world to produce a one liter diesel engine, and the first to realize in the postwar era the need for three- and four-wheel small delivery vehicles; as a result, in the 1950s the company introduced its extremely successful "Midget" minivehicle (marketed in the United States as the "Trimobile"). Despite recent recessionary times, which have forced Daihatsu to close down its American operations, the company is still a highly successful competitor internationally in the small vehicle and electric car markets. In 1992, J.D. Power & Associates, the leading market researcher of the automotive industry, rated Daihatsu first in terms of customer satisfaction after two to three years of ownership.

Daihatsu Motor Company began as the Hatsudoki Seizo Company, Ltd., established in Osaka in 1907 by a team of professors from Osaka University whose project it was to advance Japan's domestic motor vehicle industry. That year there was little demand for the six horse power automobile built by the Hatsudoki Seizo Company. After the First World War, when the importance of automotive vehicles in modern warfare was established, domestic vehicle production was encouraged. During this time Hatsudoki Seizo focused its production on trucks for the military, motorcycles, and small three-wheeled vehicles that could easily negotiate Japan's narrow streets and alleyways.

Despite encouragement from the military, resulting in large purchase orders for domestic motor vehicles, passenger cars were considered too risky an investment for Japan's big manufacturers. Lacking a sophisticated machine tool infrastructure, Japan produced only 1,000 passenger cars in 1929, while it imported nearly 15,000, primarily from the United States. This foreign monopoly of the Japanese automobile market ended with the military takeover of the Japanese government in the mid-1930s. The Automotive Manufacturing Industries Law was enacted in 1935, providing tax incentives and other benefits to producers of domestic motor vehicles. Still, neither the Hatsudoki Seizo Company nor other automotive businesses in Japan were willing to risk investing in passenger cars, but continued instead to focus on wartime needs, especially medium-sized military trucks and weaponry.

In 1930 Hatsudoki Seizo became the first Japanese automotive business to produce a three-wheeled vehicle with a domestically manufactured engine. Seven years later they introduced the first "mini four wheeler." As a result of its reputation as a machinery and small vehicle manufacturer, Hatsudoki Seizo was increasingly relied upon by the military, and the company began to expand; the first major plant opened in Ikeda in 1939.

After World War II, with Japanese industrial facilities destroyed and the country occupied by the allied military powers, Japanese manufacturers were encouraged to rebuild and resume production of motor vehicles, especially trucks and urban transportation vehicles. However, as in prewar days, the import of foreign automobiles resumed. The first real stimulus to the domestic automobile industry as well as to Hatsudoki Seizo—which adopted the name Daihatsu Motor Company, Ltd. in 1951—was the outbreak of the Korean War. Japanese industry recovered as huge purchase orders were received from the allied occupation government.

In the 1950s Japanese automakers entered into technical agreements with European manufacturers in order to improve passenger car technology. The Japanese government, no longer pressured by military demands as in prewar days, stepped in to support and protect the domestic auto industry, especially by imposing restrictions on imported vehicles.

Benefiting most from these incentives were companies well experienced in the manufacture of motor vehicles and machinery, particularly Daihatsu and its chief competitor, Suzuki. In the mid 1950s, a thoroughly modern market research study of consumer needs, undertaken by Daihatsu, indicated a widespread desire for a high-quality, lightweight, three-wheel truck; in 1957, Daihatsu marketed the Midget minivehicle. In that year alone, over 80,000 Midgets were sold in Japan. The golden years of the minivehicle and small passenger car had arrived.

The Midget was marketed as the "Trimobile" in the United States in 1959, and its phenomenal success at home and abroad enabled Daihatsu to expand and market new products, such as the lightweight four-wheel truck "Hijet" in 1961, followed two years later by the four-wheel "Compagno Van." In February 1964, Daihatsu introduced a small, four-wheel passenger car, the "Compagno Berlina."

In the mid-1960s, the Japanese auto industry underwent a major transformation. Mergers took place among the major motor vehicle manufacturers, and Toyota embarked on a joint venture with Daihatsu and Hino, while Nissan merged with other Japanese auto firms. Together, these two main auto-producing groups controlled over 60 percent of the Japanese car market. Pooling resources in this way enabled Daihatsu to expand further into the small vehicle market, increasingly gearing itself to exports. Over 50 percent of Japanese car production after 1968 would be for the international market.

The 1960s and 1970s marked the heyday of the minivehicle and small passenger cars, which were affordable and therefore popular among the middle and working class. Daihatsu produced several small passenger car models, including the ''Fellow'' in 1966, the ''Charmant'' in 1974, and the highly popular and acclaimed ''Charade'' in 1977, which won the Car of the Year Award in 1978 and other prizes in following years. In 1980, the highly successful minivehicle ''Mira'' was introduced. Daihatsu's small car and minivehicle production passed the ten million mark in 1985.

European and Asian exports remain Daihatsu's lifeline. In 1979, a European branch office was established in Belgium, and in 1984, production and sales of Daihatsu vehicles began in Taiwan as well as limited production on mainland China. There are Daihatsu sales offices in Australia, Indonesia, Malaysia and Hong Kong. For the sake of greater efficiency, Indonesia became the main parts supplier for Daihatsu in the all-important southeast Asian market. With the production of the locally built Mira mini pickup in Thailand, sales picked up in that country 50 percent in 1990, and with the fall of communism in eastern Europe and the unification of Germany, Daihatsu established offices in Poland and a branch in Germany, Daihatsu Deutschland G.m.b.H. Also, a joint venture was concluded with Piaggio of Italy to produce and market vehicles like the ''Hijet'' pickups and vans. In all, Daihatsu vehicles are driven in over 160 countries, and its profits continue to grow, as in 1991, when they rose 69 percent over the previous year.

In the United States, by the 1980s, the ''big three'' auto manufacturers in the United States had become as vulnerable to Japanese competition as Japanese automakers had been to American competitors fifty years earlier, and in July 1986 Daihatsu opened a new branch, Daihatsu America, Inc., headquartered in California. Nevertheless, Daihatsu struggled in the highly competitive American car market for several reasons. In the early 1990s, in response to U.S. economic concerns, Japan's government restricted its automotive exports to the United States. Furthermore, unlike other Japanese auto companies, Daihatsu had unfortunately delayed establishing assembly plants in the United States. With its exports restricted and without production facilities in the country, Daihatsu was forced to withdraw its offices from the United States. Furthermore, while competition in the small vehicle market was intense, the demand appeared to be declining. The company had not achieved renown in the United States as had other Japanese car brands, and it deemed the cost and effort required to launch a massive advertising campaign prohibitive under the circumstances.

Despite its problems in the American market, Daihatsu's ongoing concern with environmental standards bodes well for the company's future. Striving to meet the stringent environmental controls of most developed countries, Daihatsu has discontinued using harmful chlorofluorocarbons in its air conditioning systems and in the cleaning of its parts, and it continues its intensive research and development efforts on the automobile of the future, the electric car.

As early as 1965, the company's research and development team began designing a silent, high-quality electric car. The prototype electric car was unveiled in 1966. Four years later, Japan's Ministry of International Trade and Industry commissioned Daihatsu to produce nearly 300 electric buses to drive visitors about Japan's first International Exposition in Osaka, where the vehicles ran without any problems, over a period of six months. Since then, the number of electric vehicles in Japan has grown steadily. Daihatsu supplies electric golf carts, newspaper and milk delivery vehicles, and security patrol cars, while the Ministry of Construction successfully employs Daihatsu Rugger electric vehicles that can run on an eight-hour charge.

Daihatsu remains concerned with developing a low-cost electric vehicle for the twenty first century. While some analysts are skeptical of Daihatsu's, or any automobile firm's, ability to bring down the prohibitive cost of electric cars, most acknowledge Daihatsu's leadership role in the development of the electric vehicle and point to the fact that unlike most automotive companies, Daihatsu has gone well beyond the planning and design stage: it already has working models. In 1977, at Chicago's International Electric Vehicle Expo, Daihatsu unveiled its electric ''Hijet'' model as well as its electric three wheeler. While sales of electric vehicles remain low, in 1988 Japan's Environment Agency developed a long range plan to encourage their research and development.

Under the management of president Jiro Osuga and chairperson Tomonaru Eguchi, Daihatsu is extremely well poised to enter the twenty-first century. While some analysts point to a permanent decline in the demand for small passenger cars and to Daihatsu's poor performance in the United States, Daihatsu is flourishing in the international market, particularly the market it knows and understands best, Asia, and remains far ahead of most manufacturers in the development of the electric vehicle.

Principal Subsidiaries: Daihatsu Auto Body Co., Ltd.; Daihatsu Metal Industry Co., Ltd.; Daihatsu Transportation Co., Ltd.; Daihatsu Credit Co., Ltd.; Daihatsu Estate Co., Ltd.; Daihatsu America, Inc.; Daihatsu Deutschland G.m.b.H.

Further Reading: Snyder, Jesse, ''Daihatsu Seeks North American Tie,'' *Automotive News,* August 17, 1987; Stark, Harry A., ''No Riddle Here: Charade Aims at Specific U.S. Market Niche,'' *Ward's Auto World,* November 1987; Knee, Richard, ''Daihatsu Gets Piece of the Pie, (Car Shipment via Ships and Trucks),'' *American Shipper,* January 1988; Hiromoto, Toshiro, ''Another Hidden Edge—Japanese Management Accounting,'' *Harvard Business Review,* July/August 1988; Chappell, Lindsay, ''Catch-22: Japan's Export Restrictions Hinder Daihatsu's Growth in U.S.,'' *Automotive News,* March 19, 1990; *Annual Report: Daihatsu Motor Company, Ltd.,* 1991, 1987; *Daihatsu Motor Company, Ltd.,* Daihatsu Motor Co., Ltd., 1991; ''High Octane Relationships,'' *Business Korea,*

November 1991; Donaldson, K.C., "Daihatsu Motor Co., Ltd.—Company Report," *Salomon Bros., Inc.,* November 14, 1991; O'Dell, John, "Daihatsu's Little Struggle to Succeed," *Los Angeles Times,* February 10, 1991; O'Dell, John, "Daihatsu Quits U.S. Market; Although Offering Quality, the Company Failed to Woo Many American Customers," *Los Angeles Times,* February 14, 1992; Elliot, Stuart, "Daihatsu Move," *The New York Times,* February 18, 1992.

—Sina Dubovoj

DAIRY MART CONVENIENCE STORES, INC.

One Vision Dr.
Enfield, Connecticut 06082
U.S.A.
(203) 741-6808
Fax: (203) 741-2704

Public Company
Incorporated: 1972 as Snow White Dairies Inc.
Employees: 5,100
Sales: $795 million
Stock Exchanges: NASDAQ Over-The-Counter
SICs: 5411 Grocery Stores; 2026 Fluid Milk

Dairy Mart Convenience Stores, Inc. is the third-largest convenience store chain in the United States with approximately 1,100 stores in 11 states.

Dairy Mart's origins date back to 1949, when Charles Nirenberg began selling ice cream from the back of his truck in the backlot of a Springfield, Massachusetts, gas station. Four years later Nirenberg had more than 60 ice cream trucks in various locations and a winter business that also sold coffee and doughnuts.

The success of these businesses showed Nirenberg there was money to be made by offering consumers convenience. In order to cash in on this opportunity, he opened his first store in 1957 with $1,500. Nirenberg first named the shop Dairy Land, but soon changed it after receiving complaints from another retailer using the same name. To save money, Nirenberg settled on the name Dairy Mart so he would only have to change three of the letters on his sign. Despite saving money on new signage, the store went bankrupt a year later. Nirenberg blamed the failure on the store's location next to a high-rise apartment building. Initially he reasoned the location would guarantee him plenty of customers, but many of the residents were elderly with smaller budgets for food and impulse items.

Instead of giving up, Nirenberg opened two more stores soon after, and by 1972 he was running a chain of 37 outlets with sales of $6 million. The stores were incorporated under the name Snow White Dairies Inc.

Nirenberg decided the success of the company warranted a public offering, but before any stock could be issued, the company attracted the interest of Giant Stores, Inc., a retail chain based in Chelmsford, Massachusetts, which sought to acquire the company. Nirenberg decided he couldn't turn the offer down and sold his company for Giant stock. "They made . . . a deal to give me 86,000 shares of Giant stock, which at the time was selling for $18.60 a share and within a matter of weeks it hit $26 a share," Nirenberg told *New England Business* correspondent Gregory Sandler. "[Giant] quickly made me a paper millionaire. Except the problem was the following year, they went bankrupt and I became a paper pauper." Undaunted, Nirenberg borrowed $250,000, bought back the 37 Dairy Mart outlets from Giant in 1974 and started again.

In 1975 Dairy Mart Convenience Stores, Inc. relocated to Enfield, Connecticut. In addition, a $2.6 million milk processing plant was built in order to expand the business. The plant produced ice cream, frozen desserts and other dairy items for Dairy Mart outlets. Milk, orange juice, and fruit drinks were also processed in the facility.

By 1980 Dairy Mart was poised for bigger and better things, and a goal was set to build the company into a 1,000-store chain. In an effort to meet this objective Dairy Mart began an aggressive plan of acquisition. In 1981 the company purchased Sunnybrook Farms and its 66 stores, followed in 1983 by the acquisition of Dutchland Farms's 32 stores, and IPO with 143 stores. Still far from the goal, Dairy Mart found itself in need of more capital. Spearheading the aggressive growth period was then-Vice President of Real Estate/Corporate Development Frank Colaccino. To help fund its growth, the company went public in 1983. Sales were $60.3 million and net income was $439,000. The stock offering raised $3 million.

Two years later Dairy Mart was ready to expand beyond its stronghold in the Northeast. The company made this bold move with the acquisition of The Lawson Co. from Sara Lee Corp. The 779-outlet chain, based in Ohio, was three times the size of Dairy Mart, and the $45 million deal included a dairy plant and a distribution center. While such competitors as Circle K were buying stores for as much as $350,000, Dairy Mart estimated its cost per Lawson store somewhere between $40,000 and $50,000.

Dairy Mart soon began to feel the effects of its rapid growth. Three months after Dairy Mart bought the company, workers at the Lawson dairy plant went on strike when their demands for higher wages were turned down. Replacement workers were hired to fill the jobs, sparking more controversy. A boycott was organized, some stores were damaged, one security guard was shot, and rumors were spread about poisoned milk. Dairy Mart suffered yet another boycott in 1986, this time by the American Family Association, an anti-pornography group upset with Dairy Mart's decision to continue selling adult magazines.

The Lawson acquisition still wasn't enough to put Dairy Mart over the 1,000 store mark, and in 1986 the company bought CONNA Corp., the Louisville, Kentucky, franchisor of the Convenient Food Mart chain with 369 stores. The $25 million purchase gave Dairy Mart a total of 1,207 stores in 11 states. Negotiating the purchase was not an easy task, however.

Convenient Food Mart Inc. (CFMI), a group of Chicago-based franchisors and owners of Convenient Food Marts, also wanted to buy CONNA, though Dairy Mart would be required to pay franchisor's fees to CFMI if the acquisition went through. After extensive negotiations, the two parties agreed to divide the outlets. CFMI retained the stores in its region, as well as 72 stores in New England, while Dairy Mart received the balance. Now Dairy Mart had three divisions—one in Connecticut, another in Kentucky, representing the former CONNA stores, and the third in Ohio, overseeing the Lawson interest.

Under the terms of the CONNA acquisition, Dairy Mart was paying CFMI a substantial annual fee for its franchise of Convenient Food Marts. However, with the 1987 court ruling that stated "convenient" is a generic name, Dairy Mart took the opportunity to buy its way out of the franchise agreement with CFMI and give the former CONNA stores the Dairy Mart name. Those stores, however, proved to be well worth the trouble it took to get and keep them. That division is considered the most profitable part of the company, due in large part to the stores' high gasoline sales.

Dairy Mart's aggressive acquisition and expansion strategy since going public began to take its toll in the late 1980s. Financial performance was shaky, and the company's stock fluctuated from 15 points to 6 and 1/8. Dairy Mart's 1,207 stores garnered $482 million in sales in 1987, but the company still posted a $3.5 million loss because of a $3.3 million pension settlement and a slide in store margins. The company also carried a high debt to equity ratio. In fiscal year 1987, the rate was 2.86 to 1 compared to 1.4 to 1 the year before. Dairy Mart began to move forward again in 1988, however, with a leap in sales to $723 million and a net income of $4 million. Though some stores identified as weak performers were closed, and sales dropped to $717 million, this was offset with $3 million from the sale of Dairy Mart's Midwest distribution center. In all, the company ended the year with a net income of $4.1 million.

In 1989 a team led by Nirenberg, which included four senior managers and the Salomon Brothers Holding Co., formed DCMS Holdings Inc. to attempt a leveraged buyout of Dairy Mart and take it private. The move would put Nirenberg and his managers in control of the firm and give Salomon Bros. a hefty 37.5 percent share. Charlie and Jan Nirenberg, who owned 35 percent of Dairy Mart's outstanding shares along with 60 percent of the voting power, stood to make a profit of $22 million. They would also have the opportunity to pay just $5 per share of the newly private Dairy Mart. Armed with an $80 million loan commitment from the Bank of Boston, Salomon's promise to sell $35 million in junk bonds, and another $35 million in bonds that were already in place, DCMS Holdings offered shareholders $14.50 for each of their Dairy Mart shares, which were then trading at $8. The value of the buyout would have been about $150 million.

The deal, however, was challenged by United Acquisitions—a New York company that owns Red Apple supermarkets—when they countered with an offer of $15 a share. DCMS quickly raised its offer to match it. When United tried again with a $16 a share offer, DCMS had already signed a definitive merger agreement, and the offer was ignored.

DCMS still wasn't in the clear as it turned out. The deal collapsed when the Bank of Boston pulled back its financing support. The bank blamed Dairy Mart's weak first-quarter earnings, but Nirenberg surmised that the bank was abandoning the risky leveraged buyout business, particularly in light of the federal regulatory pressures on the struggling New England banking system at the time. Rather than increase its reliance on junk bonds or eat into its low buyout price, DCMS Holdings dropped its goal of once again making Dairy Mart a private company.

The failed deal turned out to be a blessing in disguise and helped the firm avoid the heavy debt burdens of its competitors, including Circle K, the Southland Corp., operators of the 7-Eleven chain, and Convenient Food Mart Inc., which filed for bankruptcy in 1989. Without the debt burden, in 1990 Dairy Mart went on to purchase 137 Stop-N-Go stores from the Sun Company, Inc. for $16.2 million. The stores are located in Ohio, Kentucky, and Michigan, rounding out the company's presence in the Midwest.

Even after buying Stop-N-Go, Dairy Mart retained its strong position. Fiscal year 1991 was the company's best ever with sales reaching $809 million, up from $742 million the previous year. Net income was $3.8 million versus $682,000 the year before. The 1991 figures were especially healthy in light of the fact that the country was suffering from a recession, and gasoline sales had been hurt by the high prices caused by the Persian Gulf War.

With its acquisition fervor over for the time being, Dairy Mart turned its attention to modernizing its stores. In 1991, the company began testing a point-of-sale system in ten stores, hoping to reduce the paperwork burdens of store managers and increase store margins by half of a percent. The system, scheduled for a company-wide roll-out in 1993, provided an electronic link between each site's personal computer, cash register, gas consoles and money-order dispenser. The computer tallied all of the day's transactions, including sales and deposits, deliveries and accounts payable, bundled the information and sent it to Dairy Mart's headquarters for processing. With little or no paperwork, store managers could then focus more closely on their customers and other needs. The second phase of the project involved installing the technology to give stores price scanning capability.

Dairy Mart also began to focus more on customer relations. In 1991 the company started a new program called MAGIC, or Make A Good Impression on the Customer. Store employees were trained in customer service skills and rewarded for providing good service through a recognition system.

In 1992, Charlie and Jan Nirenberg decided to sell their controlling interest to a limited partnership headed by Frank Colaccino, Dairy Mart's president. Nirenberg abdicated his position as chief executive officer, but remains chairman of the board. Colaccino, who had long been groomed by Nirenberg for the job, took the title of CEO. In addition to Nirenberg, the limited partnership also included several other members of Dairy Mart's senior management team. News of the transition came as Dairy Mart entered its fifth consecutive year of profitability. Sales were $795 million, a decline from the year before due to the closing of another 62 low-volume stores and a drop in the price of gasoline. Pre-tax earnings were $7 million and net income was $4 million.

The changing of the guard at Dairy Mart coincided with a major step in ensuring the company's future growth. Dairy Mart entered into a joint venture agreement with two international firms to establish a network of convenience stores in Mexico. The venture, called Dairy Mart de Mexico, is the company's new strategy for growth in the 1990s. While the company had consulted with and licensed its name to convenience store operators in Japan, England, France, Australia, Germany, and Korea, it had done so for a one-time fee, payable at the outset of the arrangements. The Mexican deal represented the first time that Dairy Mart, with a one-third stake of the business, would hold equity in a foreign operation. Dairy Mart's partners in the deal were Grupo Corvi S.A. de C.V., a Mexican food distributor, and Filles S.A. de C.V., a distribution, canning and real estate company. Unlike their U.S. counterparts, Mexican Dairy Marts will not be designed around its driving customers and will be geared, instead, to walk-in traffic.

In 1992 the company unveiled the prototype of a new outlet combining gasoline service and a convenience store. The prototype emphasized the gasoline islands, which are sometimes ignored by consumers more comfortable filling their tanks at a regular gas station where they might also be able to pick up a carton of milk or some snacks. Earmarked for 432 stores, the design called for T-shaped canopies to be placed over extended gas dispensers, more closely linking the area to the convenience store. By placing emphasis on the gas pumps, the company hoped to increase its already significant gasoline volume. In 1990, for example, the 420 Dairy Marts that sold gas contributed 35 percent of the company's total revenues. The prototype building also served to highlight the company's food service and beverage programs. In addition to popcorn, pizza, and fried chicken, the site also included a counter for store-made, shrink-wrapped sandwiches.

By 1992, Dairy Mart's dairy operations also saw some new developments. In addition to the 400,000 gallons of milk the company's two processing plants produced every week, the Cuyahoga Falls, Ohio, facility began production of a low fat line of frozen yogurt and ice milk. The increased product line, combined with expanded distribution of Dairy Mart brand ice cream to its Southeast stores, helped increase the plant's distribution by 25 percent.

Dairy Mart is poised for the rest of the decade with an eye toward rolling out its new prototype, modernizing existing facilities with new technologies and more attractive interior designs, the production of new products, and improved training for its more than 5,000 employees. Under Colaccino, who spearheaded Dairy Mart's overseas franchise agreements, Dairy Mart will also continue to expand its foreign operations. Having recovered from significant financial hardships during its history, the early 1990s have proven to be very healthy years for Dairy Mart Convenience Stores, Inc., placing the company in a strong position for the future.

Principal Subsidiaries: Dairy Mart Midwest; Dairy Mart Southeast.

Further Reading: Sandler, Gregory, "Ahead of the Herd," *New England Business,* October 1990; "Charlie Nirenberg, Running With the Bulls," *Convenience Store People,* June 1991; "Retailing's Entrepreneurs of the Year," *Chain Store Age Executive,* December 1991; "Transition at Dairy Mart," *Convenience Store People,* March 1992; Geehern, Christopher, "New Dairy Mart CEO Describes Chain's Foreign Plans," *Union-News,* June 10, 1992; Anderer, Charles, "Dual Purpose Prototype," *Convenience Store News,* August 31, 1992; *Dairy Mart: On the Way to the Top* (annual report), Enfield, Connecticut, Dairy Mart Convenience Stores, Inc., 1992.

—Julie Monahan

IC

DANAHER CORPORATION

DANAHER CORPORATION

1250 24th St. N.W.
Suite 800
Washington, DC 20037
U.S.A.
(202) 828-0850
Fax: (202) 828-0860

Public Company
Incorporated: 1984
Sales: $955.5 million
Employees: 7,000
Stock Exchanges: New York Pacific
SICs: 3714 Motor Vehicle Parts & Accessories; 3011 Tires
& Inner Tubes; 3824 Fluid Meters & Counting Devices

Danaher Corporation, a holding company established in 1984, currently consists of thirteen wholly owned subsidiaries that manufacture such diverse product lines as automotive and industrial tools, transportation products, and precision instruments and machines. The company achieved the status of a Fortune 500 company barely two years after being established, and in less than a decade saw its sales revenues climb from $300 million to $1 billion dollars. It is the world's largest producer of drill chucks, the country's largest producer and marketer of Swiss screw machine components, and the leading automotive tools supplier to both the National Automotive Parts Association (NAPA) and Sears.

Danaher had its origins in 1969 when its predecessor, DMG, Inc., was organized as a Massachusetts real estate investment trust. DMG restructured in 1978, becoming a Florida corporation under the name of Diversified Mortgage Investors, Inc. (DMI). In 1980 a new holding company was formed under the name DMG, of which DMI became a subsidiary. Until 1984 all operations of DMG had been in real estate, but that year the holding company underwent a major transformation when it acquired two new subsidiaries. Continuing its real estate operations in the DMI subsidiary, DMG entered the business of tire manufacturing with its acquisition of Mohawk Rubber Company and entered into the manufacture and distribution of vinyl building products with its purchase of Master Shield Inc. Steven and Mitchell Rales, the majority stockholders of DMG, Inc., named the reorganized holding company Danaher Corporation—after a favorite mountain stream in western Montana.

Steven M. Rales, 33 years old at the time, became the chief executive officer and chair of the board of the new company.

Danaher's founders developed a carefully considered strategy of acquisition that was centered around the purchase of companies that had "high performance potential" but were not, for a variety of reasons, performing their best at the time of purchase. They also sought to acquire companies with well-known trademarked brands, high market shares, a reputation for innovative technology, and extensive distribution channels on which to build. Once acquired, Danaher's subsidiaries were grouped according to product lines and potential markets. If a company did not perform well after acquisition, Danaher's directors divested it and used the resulting capital to invest in new technologies or industries.

Utilizing this strategy, Danaher acquired another twelve companies within two years of its founding. By then, Danaher was listed as a Fortune 500 company, and revenues had climbed from $300 million in 1984 to $456 million by 1986. The fourteen subsidiaries were grouped into four business units: automotive/transportation, instrumentation, precision components, and extruded products. At least twelve of Danaher's products were market leaders.

The automotive/transportation unit produced and marketed tools for the professional auto mechanic as well as transportation parts. This unit consisted of well-known companies and leading market brands including Coats, a highly regarded trademark of wheel service products (such as tire changers and wheel balancers), Matco Tools, Jacobs Engine Brake, and Fayette Tubular Products, which was a leader in car air-conditioning parts.

The instrumentation unit of Danaher manufactured counting and sensing instruments, including devices that kept track of motion (magnetic encoders, electronic counters, and electronic voting machines), and instruments measuring and recording temperature. This unit boasted such prestigious companies as Veeder-Root—which supplies instruments for four out of five gas pumps worldwide—Dynapar, Partlow, and QualiTROL.

The precision components unit manufactured such diverse products as Swiss screw machine parts, the famous Allen wrench, and drill chucks. Finally, the extruded products unit, manufacturing vinyl siding and plastics, included Mohawk Rubber, Master Shield, and A. L. Hyde Company, a leading American plastics manufacturer. With the exception of A. L. Hyde, most of these companies no longer remain as Danaher subsidiaries. Among Danaher's biggest customers were petroleum, aerospace, telecommunications, electronics, and automotive firms, including Toyota and Honda.

Chairman and Chief Executive Officer Steven Rales and Executive Committee Chairman Mitchell Rales maintained that they were seeking the best—not just good, but superior products and service; not just to be a leading company, but a world leader. According to analysts, they had become skilled in aggressive competition, divestment of unprofitable businesses, consolidation of facilities, and debt and cost reduction. Each year the company grew by more than eight percent and boasted record sales. In 1987 net sales increased 141 percent over 1986.

During 1989 Danaher reassessed and restructured. George M. Sherman, an executive officer from Black & Decker, became president and chief executive officer, bringing to Danaher his own corporate vision, which included increasing the company's hitherto negligible international sales. Danaher's fourteen subsidiaries were reduced to twelve (and shortly thereafter grew to thirteen), while its four business segments were reduced from four to three: tools, process/environmental controls, and transportation.

The tool unit was greatly expanded by Danaher's 1989 merger with Easco Hand Tools, Inc., and by 1991 tools made up 49 percent of Danaher's sales.

The entirely new process/environment unit reflected a new emphasis on environmental instruments and machines, which included Veeder-Root's underground fuel storage sensors, Dynapar's motion control devices, and QualiTROL's instruments for measuring pressure and temperature, used widely by the electrical transformer industry. The A. L. Hyde Company belonged to the "process/environment" category by virtue of its extruded plastics production. This business segment is by far Danaher's fastest growing.

Transportation, accounting for 29 percent of Danaher's sales in 1991, included such leading brand names as Hennessy/Ammco (producing wheel balancers, tire changers, brake repair lathes), Jacobs Brake (producing engine retarders for heavy diesel trucks), and Fayette Tubular Products for car air-conditioning components.

Danaher's reorganization and streamlining contributed to its continued record sales, growth, and development of new products. In 1991 Sears, Roebuck & Co. selected Danaher as its only source for the manufacture of Sears mechanics' hand tools. Danaher was already marketing the Jacob Engine Brake diesel engine retarders in Japan, and, in 1991, Danaher acquired Normond/CMS, the leading manufacturer and marketer in Great Britain of environmental products. Danaher was already the leading supplier of hand tools to the National Automotive Parts Association.

The recession of the late 1980s and early 1990s affected Danaher, though not severely. Facilities were consolidated and some restructuring occurred (the firms Dynapar and Veeder-Root were combined into Danaher Controls, for instance, to eliminate duplicate services), but net sales of $832 million in 1991 were only one percent below the previous year, and in 1992, sales increased significantly to $897 million, the best year in the company's history for per share earnings. Chief Executive Officer George Sherman attributed the relatively mild effects of the recession to the company's investment in capital spending and in research and development at a time when most other firms practiced a timid "wait and see" policy.

With the worst of the recession over by 1993, Danaher's fortunes seemed secure. In part this was because of increasingly stringent environmental regulations and the growing demand for such environmental products as underground storage tank monitoring devices and fuel pump computers. This was already Danaher's fastest growing segment of business. Medical technology will probably be another increasingly important area in the company's future. International markets also continued to grow in importance. Under the presidency of George Sherman, Danaher's international sales were rising significantly, to just over 10 percent of total sales, and market analysts predict that the percentage will double by the year 2000.

Principal Subsidiaries: Danaher Controls; Danaher Tool Group; Fayette Tubular Products; Hennessy Industries, Inc.; Holo-Krome Co.; A. L. Hyde Co.; Iseli Co.; Jacobs Brake Manufacturing Co.; Jacobs Chuck Manufacturing Co.; Matco Tools; Partlow Corp.; QualiTROL Corp.; Veeder-Root Co.

Further Reading: Gubernick, Lisa, "Raiders in Short Pants (S. and M. Rales of Danaher Corp.)," *Forbes,* November 18, 1985; Ichniowski, Tom, "A Portrait of the Takeover Artist as a Young Man," *Business Week,* August 22, 1988; "Danaher Takeover of Easco Likely: Shareholders to Vote Today on Proposal," *Washington Post,* June 7, 1990, p. E1; "Danaher: Riding the Rales: The Rales Brothers Build Their Dream Conglomerate," *Financial World,* September 18, 1990; Potts, Mark, "Danaher Corp. (Executive Changes)," *New York Times,* September 20, 1990; pp. C4(N) and D4(L); "The Washington Area's Largest Public Companies (The District of Columbia)," *Washington Post,* April 8, 1991, p. WB11; *Annual Reports: Danaher Corp.,* Washington, DC, 1985–1991; "Danaher Forms Industrial Groups (Will Form Danaher Tool Group, Industrial Prods. Div.)," *Industrial Distribution,* August, 1991, pp. 11–12; Woo, Junda, "Shareholder Can Bring Derivative Suit after Merger (Case Involving Danaher Corp. and Easco Hand Tools Inc. Merger and Arthur Blasband's Derivative Action Case)," *Wall Street Journal,* August 7, 1992, pp. B3(W) and B2(E); "Danaher Corp. (Third Quarter Earnings)," *Washington Post,* October 22, 1992, p. D13.

—Sina Dubovoj

DDI CORPORATION

Ichibancho FS Bldg 8
Ichibancho Chiyoda-ku
Tokyo 102
Japan
(03) 3221-9536
Fax: (03) 3221-9527

Private Company
Incorporated: 1984 as Daini Denden Planning, Inc.
Employees: 1620
Sales: ¥155.0 billion (US$1.21 billion)
Stock Exchanges: Tokyo
SICs: 4813 Telephone Communications, Except Radio

DDI Corporation is a Japanese long distance telephone company established to challenge the monopoly of Nippon Telegraph and Telephone Corporation. From its conception in the early 1980s, DDI has grown much faster than any of the other monopoly challengers and has achieved a large portion of long distance market share in Japan.

The idea for DDI was conceived in 1983 by Kazuo Inamori, founder and chairperson of Kyocera, a Japanese ceramics company that had begun diversification into electronic components, such as computers, digital switches, and other high-technology products. During this time, in the United States, a federal court battle was taking place that would end the monopoly of communications leader AT&T, dividing that concern into eight new companies. Inamori followed the developments of the case as did legislators in Japan's parliament who proposed a plan to introduce competition to Japan's telecommunications market, then dominated by NTT.

Inamori reasoned that Kyocera stood a good chance of competing successfully in the telecommunications market, specifically against NTT, then an inefficient long distance monopoly with high-priced services. With no experience in the communications industry, Inamori first had to find capable managers to run the enterprise, and he soon struck up a friendship with Sachio Semmotobc, an NTT engineer involved in setting up NTT's Integrated Services Digital Network prototype, called INS. Semmoto was well connected with MCI and Ameritech, American companies created out of the AT&T divestiture. Inamori and Semmoto then convinced ten other key NTT managers to join the new concern. Subsequent hires were carefully chosen;

Inamori wanted only the most dedicated people, with proven records of success, as his employees.

The venture was initially backed by personal investments by Inamori, Semmoto, and Akio Morita, chair of the Sony Corporation. Inamori later won additional financial support from Ushio, Secom, Mitsubishi, and Sony. The company was incorporated in June 1984 as Daini Denden Planning, Inc.

Shortly thereafter, two other contenders announced plans to compete with NTT. One, Japan Telecom, was launched by the Japan Railways Group, which had access to thousands of miles of railroad right of way in which to lay cable. The other company, Teleway Japan, was backed by Toyota Motor Corporation and by the Japan Highway Public Corporation, which also offered thousands of miles of right of way. Unlike Inamori's concern, these companies chose to work closely with the NTT and later received managerial and technological assistance from the local carrier.

Because it opted not to work within the established structure and use traditional methods of industry cooperation, Daini Denden was generally expected to fail. In April 1985, however, the Japanese government permitted Daini Denden to develop a new network under the new Telecommunications Business Law. That month, the company was reincorporated as DDI Corporation.

The company's first task was to construct the network, and the first option open to the company was to use combinations of NTT lines, purchasing traffic rights at a lower tariffed "bulk rate," and passing, in effect, the "wholesale" price on to consumers in the form of lower prices. The company decided to construct an entirely separate network using microwave dishes to relay traffic from one area of Japan to another. This was an extremely expensive proposition and, if unsuccessful, would incur costs of about ¥100 billion.

In establishing its microwave network, DDI faced several difficulties. First, the company had to purchase or win easements for small plots of land where relay stations could be established. Furthermore, due to the nature of microwave radiation, the company faced unanticipated opposition from environmental groups as well as from residents opposed to the location of the company's Tokyo Network Center. But, after negotiating with the community for more than a year, the company prevailed.

In September 1987, with its Tokyo-Nagoya-Osaka network in place, DDI was at last ready for business. It established more than a dozen interconnections with the NTT network. As NTT's local switches were not yet equipped to allow individual subscribers to have their long distance calls automatically routed to DDI, customers were required to precede every call with a special carrier access code. This code, 0077, instructed the local telephone switch to route the call to DDI, rather than NTT, where it would otherwise have been routed automatically.

Fearing that this added inconvenience constituted an anticompetitive barrier, DDI fought NTT for the necessary upgrade in switching software. But this was an expensive and time-consuming process, and, unwilling to wait for NTT to comply, the company turned to Kyocera engineers to develop a solution.

Only months later, DDI introduced a small box that attached to customer's telephone lines. The box determined the lowest cost routing for the call, and automatically dialed the 0077 prefix whenever DDI service was less expensive. Because DDI prices were generally lower, the boxes ensured that the bulk of long distance traffic would be handled by DDI. The boxes were distributed to many of the company's usage-heavy business customers at no charge.

Inamori understood early on that pricing was extremely important. Pricing largely determined the company's operating costs. If higher prices allowed higher operating costs to become the norm, the company would have a much harder time keeping up with cost competition when a price war began. Still, Inamori had seen that low prices alone couldn't guarantee success. For example, in the United States, when MCI advertised lower prices than AT&T, the competitor responded by claiming that it offered vastly superior service. Rather than allow NTT to respond as AT&T had, Inamori decided that DDI should make customer service its number one priority. He dispatched several work groups to the United States to observe customer service operations at several American telecommunications companies. These lessons were modified slightly for the Japanese market and were then instituted under a comprehensive training scheme. The company established a network of 67 customer service offices, each heavily staffed. Having started out with less than 100 employees in 1984, DDI soon grew to employ more than 1,500.

When the company's president, Shingo Moriyama, died, Inamori chose a successor carefully. Feeling a need for a stronger administrative system within the growing company, Inamori sought someone with a great deal of experience in setting up and administering large organizations. He soon asked Nobusuke Kanda, a former vice chair of the giant Sanwa Bank, to succeed Moriyama.

Upon accepting the job, Kanda was given simple instructions: build a highly efficient managerial structure, superior even to NTT. Kanda succeeded in this task, populating the company with energetic, youthful managers, and he is credited with establishing the company's current lean, low-cost managerial structure.

Kanda also established a system of cost accounting in which transfers between work groups, numbering five to 100 people, had to be negotiated. This kept each group highly cost conscious and ensured that lowest cost providers were used.

As DDI began to steadily take away market share from NTT, Inamori grew concerned that competition would one day become so efficient that virtually all of the profit margins from land-based telephony businesses would be severely squeezed. In order to avoid that possibility, he began studying other lines in the communications business. Inamori was among the first in Japan to recognize the potential of cellular telephones. At the time, cellular phones were bulky and expensive, and the fees for airtime were prohibitive. Inamori reasoned that if more people were able to use the phones, the rates would become cheaper, and that if cellular phone manufacturers could compete on the basis of size as well as price of their phones, the devices would grow in popularity.

An internal feasibility study of the industry confirmed Inamori's conclusions, but suggested that personal paging systems would provide higher growth than cellular telephony. In addition, the company's directors cautioned against such a risky adventure when DDI had not yet consolidated its position in the long distance market.

Overruling the study and his directors, Inamori pressed on, fighting for as many cellular phone licenses as possible. In 1987 the government awarded DDI a license to operate in nonurban markets throughout Japan, from Hokkaido to Okinawa, while reserving the most lucrative cellular licenses, serving Tokyo and Nagoya, for a group led by Teleway Japan, called Nippon Idou Tsushin (IDO).

While IDO moved slowly in setting up its operation, choosing to serve only the 23 wards of greater Tokyo, DDI quickly established large cellular operations in Japan's other industrial centers, beginning with Kansai, Kyushu, and Chugoku in 1987. Unable to secure the huge amounts of start-up capital that were necessary—even from its deep-pocketed backers—DDI turned instead to local electric power utilities. Through a series of cooperative agreements with these and other local companies, DDI received manpower and marketing support. By 1989 the company succeeded in setting up four more regional cellular companies, serving Tohoku, Hokuriku, Hokkaido, and Shikolu, and established an eighth cellular company in Okinawa in 1991.

In a further break with the establishment, DDI elected to build its cellular network using the total access communication system (TACS), rather than a rival system developed by NTT and adopted by IDO. Inamori reasoned that relying on the same system would place DDI at a competitive disadvantage to NTT.

Also controversial was DDI's 1986 decision to use American suppliers for its cellular operation. In an interview, Inamori proclaimed the superiority of American cellular technology to that of the Japanese, a statement that did not sit well with Japanese manufacturers. However, in choosing a system built by Motorola, DDI faced both lower infrastructure and terminal equipment costs.

IDO's market strategy, largely at the insistence of its benefactor Toyota, was to promote the use of cellular phones in automobiles, particularly in urban areas. However, the large volumes of pedestrian and automobile traffic typically found in Japan's cities made driving difficult, commanding the motorist's undivided attention, and cellular phones in cars therefore proved unpopular. DDI, on the other hand, envisioned millions of commuters and pedestrians using pocket phones, and it fought to import Motorola's calculator-sized MicroTac phones, the smallest in the industry.

In 1989 Japanese cellular operators encountered a new kind of problem: it was excluded from the large urban markets where Motorola's tiny phone would be most marketable. In addition, Motorola products were subject to stiff import restrictions. Determined to resolve the problem, Motorola brought its trade dispute to the U.S. trade representative, who publicly censured Japanese trade practices as discriminatory and anticompetitive. Consequently, the Japanese parliament summarily amended the import restriction law and opened the Tokyo and Nagoya cellular markets to Motorola.

DDI customers were thus able to use their MicroTac in Tokyo and Nagoya, as well as in rural areas.

DDI was unable to immediately set up operations in Tokyo. Rather than permit IDO to benefit from a slow construction schedule, DDI formed a partnership with Nissan called TUKA Cellular Tokyo and, with a substantial investment from Nissan, began construction immediately.

The company targeted its cellular sales at residential and small business customers, hoping to appeal to a larger customer base than that of the corporate business world. By 1991 the company controlled 20 percent of the Japanese cellular market.

DDI attempted to repeat this success in the battle for long distance market share. However, it was impractical to offer the bulky autorouting boxes to millions of residential customers, whose urban living spaces are notoriously small. Instead, Inamori ordered a team of engineers to reduce the works in the box to a more compact size, a technologically feasible but expensive proposition.

At the end of 1990 the engineering team reduced the autorouting box onto a single microchip. DDI promoted the "Alpha" chip with equipment manufacturers, including Kyocera, Sony, Sharp, Sanyo, and Toshiba, and won a deal to jointly market telephone sets and fax machines with DDI long distance service. Customers who purchased the equipment could register for DDI long distance service and activate it by dialing a telephone number. All the customer information was registered and verified by the equipment's Alpha chip.

In terms of growth, 1990 was a banner year for DDI. The customer base increased by 50 percent that year, from 3.6 million subscribers to 5.4 million. The following year, the customer base increased again by two million customers.

In 1991, DDI finalized a strategy that would move the company into the equipment manufacturing business and further de-emphasize its exposure to the increasingly less profitable long distance market. With substantial records on all its customers, DDI possessed a huge marketing database useful in selling equipment. Furthermore, DDI regards this database as a potentially effective tool for marketing information services—an industry still in the developmental stages in Japan.

Now in control of more than ten percent of Japan's long distance business and 20 percent of its cellular market, DDI has accomplished more than any other upstart telecommunications competitor in the world. This has caused considerable concern at NTT, which was forced to begin lowering its rates in 1991 in order to stem losses to DDI. Welcoming the competitive response from NTT, Semmoto assured *Telephony* in 1991 that "a king without an enemy cannot be strong."

Principal Subsidiaries: Kansai Cellular Telephone Company (64.3%); Kyushu Cellular Telephone Company (63.5%); Chugoku Cellular Telephone Company (63.2%); Tohoku Cellular Telephone Company (64.1%); Hokuriku Cellular Telephone Company (63.3%); Hokkaido Cellular Telephone Company (63.2%): Shikoku Cellular Telephone Company (62.7%); Okinawa Cellular Telephone Company (60%).

Further Reading: "No One Is Laughing at Japan's DDI Now," *Telephony*, September 2, 1991; *Telecommunications in the Far East,* McGraw-Hill, 1992; "DDI Corporation," *Harvard Business School Case Study,* September 18, 1992; Business Report, 1992.

—John Simley

DE BEERS CONSOLIDATED MINES LIMITED / DE BEERS CENTENARY AG

36 Stockdale Street
Kimberley 8301
Republic of South Africa
(531) 22171
Fax: (531) 24611

Langensandstrasse 27
6000 Luzern 14
Switzerland
(41) 403 540
Fax: (41) 444 468

Public Company
Incorporated: 1888 and 1990
Employees: 27,000
Sales: US$3.4 billion
Stock Exchanges: Johannesburg London Paris Brussels
    Frankfurt Zürich Geneva Basel
SICs: 1499 Miscellaneous Nonmetallic Minerals; 3961
    Costume Jewelry

The De Beers Group dominates the world market in rough diamonds. In 1990 it was split into two basic parts, De Beers Consolidated Mines Limited (De Beers Consolidated) and De Beers Centenary AG (Centenary). The first is a South African holding company controlling the group's South African assets. The second is a Swiss-registered holding company created to direct all the De Beers interests outside South Africa, accounting for 79 percent of attributable earnings and 56 percent of equity-accounted earnings of combined results in 1992. The two share identical boards of directors and their stock is traded as a linked unit. De Beers Consolidated has a 9.5 percent interest in Centenary.

The combined group's main activities include: prospecting for and mining diamonds; the tightly controlled global marketing of its own rough—that is, uncut and unpolished—diamond production and that of cooperating producers via the Central Selling Organisation (CSO), the De Beers marketing arm; and, exceptionally (given that it does not retail the finished product), the worldwide advertising and promotion of diamond jewelry. It also manufactures synthetic diamond and abrasive products. In

1991 De Beers produced nearly 50 percent of the world's rough gem diamonds, and through the CSO, based in London, was marketing approximately 80 percent of the world diamond production. The group has a considerable investment portfolio, affording it the financial strength to keep stocks of rough diamonds, particularly important at times when the market cannot absorb them. Stocks in 1992 were valued at $3.765 billion.

Formed by Cecil Rhodes and others, De Beers is a close associate of the Anglo American Corporation of South Africa (Anglo), founded by Ernest Oppenheimer in 1917. Together they are often referred to as the Oppenheimer empire or ''greater group,'' forged by Ernest Oppenheimer. Since 1929 they have almost always shared the same chairman. De Beers Consolidated holds 39 percent in Anglo, and Anglo has a 33 percent holding in De Beers Consolidated and 29 percent in Centenary. The greater group wields significant influence within the South African economy. The vision and dogged determination of three chairmen, Cecil Rhodes, Ernest Oppenheimer, and the latter's son, Harry Oppenheimer, have dictated the path taken by De Beers and the modern diamond trade over most of its existence.

The first authenticated diamond discovery in South Africa occurred in 1866, setting the modern diamond industry in motion. Prospectors came by the thousands to stake claims along the Orange and Vaal rivers. Between 1869 and 1871 six major diamond pipes or veins were discovered: Bultfontein, Koffiefontein, Jagersfontein, Dutoitspan, De Beers, and Kimberley, or the ''Big Hole,'' as it became known. Rhodes arrived at the New Rush settlement, renamed Kimberley in 1873. He began by supplying drinking water and ice to the community and contracting to pump water from the De Beers and Dutoitspan mines with a friend, Charles Rudd; the two bought a claim apiece, and from here Rhodes was to build his business empire.

De Beers Mining Company Ltd. was founded on April 28, 1880, by Rhodes and Rudd, with other partners. The company arose once the restrictions on the number of claims individuals could hold were lifted. Barney Barnato, Rhodes's main rival in acquiring dominant control of South African diamond production, meanwhile purchased claims in the center of the Kimberley mine and in 1885 merged with the Kimberley Central Mining Company. Rhodes, however, raised a £1 million loan from the London merchant bank N. M. Rothschild & Sons to outbid Barnato in 1887 to acquire the important Compagnie Française des Mines de Diamants du Cap claims adjacent to those of Kimberley Central. Rhodes and Barnato drained each other's profits by their rivalry through the mid-1880s. Barnato, however, eventually gave way to Rhodes's vision of a single controlling company and agreed to exchange his shares in the Kimberley Central mine for shares in De Beers.

De Beers Consolidated Mines was established on March 12, 1888, controlling around 90 percent of contemporary world diamond production. It owned the De Beers mine, three quarters of the Kimberley mine, and held controlling interests in the Dutoitspan and Bultfontein mines. The merger of the De Beers and Kimberley Central mines was contested in court by unhappy Kimberley Central shareholders. Rhodes and Barnato overcame this obstacle by liquidating Kimberley Central. De Beers paid the liquidators £5.34 million for Kimberley Central.

The move toward the consolidation of South African production was followed by a centralization in the control of sales of South African diamonds. Prior to De Beers Consolidated's creation, individual mines sold their production through different London dealers. In February of 1890 De Beers concluded a sales contract with a new dealers' and brokers' syndicate, the London Diamond Syndicate. Ties between production and sales control were thus strengthened, several of the dealing firms having significant shareholdings in De Beers.

Fluctuation in demand, however, led to great ups and downs in these early days. In 1890, for instance, the company closed down operations at Dutoitspan, which was proving uneconomical. A new pipe, Wesselton in Kimberley, was discovered the same year. De Beers purchased it in 1891, determinedly continuing its policy of acquisition. De Beers, though, was deprived of the excitement of the discovery in 1893 of the Excelsior diamond at Jagersfontein, the second-largest rough diamond ever found. The Jagersfontein mine would finally be acquired by De Beers in 1930.

The end of the century was marked in South Africa by political upheaval and the Boer War. Kimberley lay under siege by the Afrikaners between October of 1899 and February of 1900. Once the war was over, the great threat at the start of the new century came from the Premier (Transvaal) Diamond Mining Company, founded in 1902 following the discovery of diamonds near Pretoria. Its chairman was Thomas Cullinan, after whom the world's largest rough diamond, 3,106 carats, found at Premier in 1905, was named. The rich finds at the Premier mine opened a new period of bruising competition.

The American financial crisis of 1907 to 1908 severely affected the demand for diamonds, and coupled with Premier's bid for independence of sales when it abandoned selling via the syndicate in 1906, had a crippling effect on trade. Premier soon recommended selling via the syndicate after the price it was receiving per carat had almost halved in a year, and the two companies agreed to limit sales. But De Beers had already had to reduce its mining activities considerably.

Still more significantly, diamonds were discovered in 1908 along the coast of the then German South West Africa. Exclusive prospecting and mining rights were given to German companies. The Germans set up the Diamond Regie to regulate their production and marketing. For a brief period De Beers, with the London Diamond Syndicate, had an agreement to purchase diamonds from the Regie. But the latter moved to selling first to an Antwerp syndicate, then onto the open market by tender.

The discovery of diamonds in South West Africa heralded a great expansion in the areas of diamond production, further threatening De Beers's control. Alluvial diamond gravels were discovered in the Belgian Congo (now Zaire) in 1912. The Belgian Société Internationale Forestière et Minière (La Forminière) began production in 1913. The year 1912 also saw the discovery of diamonds in Angola. The Companhia de Pesquisas Mineras de Angola (Pema) was created to exploit these finds.

The outbreak of World War I brought De Beers to a standstill. Mining was suspended in 1914, and the Diamond Syndicate stopped its contract. Only an essential core of workers remained, many others leaving to join the forces. In 1915 South Africa invaded South West Africa, defeating the German forces there and paving the way for the takeover of German diamond interests in the region.

Ernest Oppenheimer, who had arrived in South Africa in 1902—the year of Rhodes's death—to work as an agent for the diamond brokers A. Dunkelsbuhler & Co., founded Anglo in 1917. One of this company's primary aims was to mine gold on the eastern Witswatersrand. In 1919 it set about acquiring diamond interests in South West Africa previously belonging to the members of the German Diamond Regie, beating De Beers in securing them. These interests were transferred to the specially incorporated Consolidated Diamond Mines of South West Africa Ltd. (CDM) in 1920—the year in which the League of Nations mandated South West Africa to South African administration.

De Beers had secured a controlling share of its previous rival, the Premier mine, in 1917. At the time the purchase seemed important for maintaining its control of diamond production. Under Francis Oats, chairman of De Beers from 1908 to 1918, it was slow to respond to its encirclement by Ernest Oppenheimer, who continued busily acquiring diamond interests outside South Africa. Added to this, in 1918 the world's largest contemporary diamond deposits were found by a Belgian rail company in the Bakwanga region of the Belgian Congo.

While De Beers faced another depression in world markets at the beginning of the 1920s, exacerbated by the sale by the new government of the Soviet Union of diamonds and jewelry confiscated during the Russian Revolution, Anglo continued buying into various areas of the southern African diamond industry. In 1923 it purchased a 16 percent share in Diamang, the new name given to Pema in 1917. Then in 1924 it was granted membership of the London Diamond Syndicate, only to rock the boat. Anglo and Dunkelsbuhler were asked to retire from the syndicate, having attempted to bid for the entire South African output.

The new Diamond Syndicate created in 1925 by Sir Ernest (Oppenheimer was knighted in 1921) quickly caused the London Diamond Syndicate's dissolution by offering better terms, and bought out its assets. Oppenheimer had been steadily building up his shareholding in De Beers and cementing a friendship with De Beers's largest shareholder, Solly Joel and his firm, Barnato Brothers. In 1926 Oppenheimer was elected to the De Beers board.

Spectacular new diamond discoveries were made in South Africa in 1926 and 1927, first in Lichtenburg, where hundreds of prospectors were allowed to rush off from a starting line to stake their claims, and then in Alexander Bay. By January of 1927 Oppenheimer had secured a controlling interest in the Lichtenburg region and by 1929 he had bought out the remaining interests belonging to Dr. Merensky, the discoverer of the Alexander Bay deposits, for just over £1 million. The markets were flooded, however, by these massive discoveries, and De Beers suffered considerably. Through Oppenheimer's dynamic policies, his ever-expanding acquisitions of diamondiferous areas, and his control of the syndicate, he was elected chairman of De Beers in December of 1929. He took the helm as the Great

Depression began. Sales throughout the 1930s were poor to nonexistent, and in 1932, mining came to a complete halt.

However, important structural changes for De Beers and the diamond sales pipeline were put in place during the decade. Oppenheimer felt the original purpose of a diamond syndicate to sell South African production was becoming too restricted. He envisioned a single organization for the producers and sellers of rough diamonds that would become, as far as possible, the exclusive marketing channel for world rough diamond production. The Diamond Corporation Ltd. was founded in 1930. De Beers, CDM, Premier, and other leading producers took a 50 percent holding, the Diamond Syndicate the other 50 percent. Sir Ernest became chairman. Anglo gave up its CDM holding for De Beers shares in the same year. This arrangement radically diminished the divergence of interests between the diamond producers and the sellers of rough diamonds, and effectively saw the start of a single central selling organization. The Diamond Corporation also established important financial resources to enable it to acquire further outside production. The Diamond Trading Company (DTC) was further formed as a subsidiary of the Diamond Corporation in 1934 to sell at "sights," the process by which boxes of rough gems prepared by the DTC (which painstakingly grades the individual diamonds and selects a percentage of the graded categories) are offered to the individual clients or "sightholders," diamond manufacturers and dealers it has carefully chosen from the world's cutting centers. The combined structures have become known as the CSO.

The concept behind the Diamond Corporation was expanded with the creation in 1934 of the Diamond Producers' Association (DPA), encompassing the members of the Diamond Corporation and representatives of the South African government and the administration of South West Africa. The DPA arose to create a pooling arrangement to enable the large producers to protect the market together. On the industrial diamond side, the Diamond Development Company Ltd. was created in 1934 to explore new uses for industrial diamonds. By 1936, a British company, Sierra Leone Selection Trust, entered into an initial marketing agreement with the Diamond Corporation.

World War II brought production to a halt. But just prior to the outbreak of the war, De Beers embarked on a significant new venture advocated by Harry Oppenheimer: its first advertising campaign, which was launched in the United States. Thus De Beers, selling the rough product, built a bridge of promotional support and solidarity with the jewelers, retailers of the final product. The De Beers campaigns, and in particular such catchphrases as "A Diamond Is Forever" and "Diamonds Are a Girl's Best Friend," have become something of a legend, promoting the romantic image of gem diamonds.

During World War II the company's production of industrial diamonds acquired greater importance. Sales of these rose to £4.3 million in 1942, representing nearly 40 percent of the total trade in diamonds. Surprisingly, the diamond market recorded record sales in 1943 (£20.5 million) and 1945 (£24.5 million). Conflict, however, arose with the U.S. government, which accused De Beers of being unwilling to loosen control of its diamond stockpile to help the war effort; it was further concerned about the shortage of industrial diamonds, and about

Britain falling under enemy control. Sir Ernest denied the accusation and the shortage, and proposed the compromise of stockpiling in Canada. Industrial diamond sales were in fact supervised by the British government and prices were frozen. But Sir Ernest had angered the U.S. government, which pursued De Beers as an anti-competitive cartel. The U.S. Justice Department filed antitrust actions against De Beers in 1945, 1957, and 1974. De Beers did not take up the challenge of the U.S. courts and does not operate in the United States.

A further important discovery of diamonds had been made in Tanganyika (now Tanzania) at the beginning of the 1940s by a Canadian, Dr. John Williamson. Williamson first agreed to join the Producers' Association in 1947, but then changed his mind. He stockpiled his production and threatened to damage the CSO's position. Harry Oppenheimer eventually managed to negotiate a settlement. On Williamson's death, he negotiated with the heirs and secured a 50 percent share in the Williamson mine in 1958, the government taking the other 50 percent.

In 1952 De Beers was to benefit from a windfall profit of £40 million thanks to the sale of a stockpile of diamonds held since the Depression, helping to strengthen substantially its financial base. The unknown quantity for De Beers in the 1950s came from the production of synthetic diamonds by foreign companies. The Swedish Allmanna Svenska Elektriska Aktiebolaget was the first to successfully create synthetic diamonds. But it failed to secure the patent rights, taken up exclusively by the U.S. General Electric Company (SEC) in 1955. In response, De Beers set up its Adamant Research Laboratory in Johannesburg. By 1960 De Beers founded Ultra High Pressure Units Limited for the commercial manufacturing of synthetic diamonds. Only in 1966 would a lengthy and costly dispute with SEC over the patent rights be resolved. De Beers Industrial Diamond Division continues, with SEC, to be one of the main market leaders in synthetic industrial diamond production.

In 1955 De Beers began prospecting in the Bechuanaland Protectorate (now Botswana), and 1956 saw its founding of the Diamond Corporation Sierra Leone Limited (Dicosil). The Sierra Leone government granted it sole exclusive exporting rights. Outside De Beers control, Russia had been finding diamonds in the Urals and Siberia. In 1959 the first short-lived marketing deal was signed between the Diamond Corporation and the Soviet government for sales via the CSO. Diamond buying offices were established by the CSO across West Africa with the incorporation in 1961 of the Diamond Corporation West Africa Ltd. (Dicorwaf). The offices purchased diamonds from the independent individual alluvial diggers, helping to maintain market price stability.

That year independent prospectors discovered rich diamond deposits: Sammy Collins made a discovery on the coast off CDM's concessions, and Allister Fincham and William Schwabel (forming the Finsch mine) made a discovery in South Africa, northwest of Kimberley. By 1962, De Beers had secured a contract to prospect the latter; in 1963 it bought the rights to the Finsch pipe for £2.3 million, leasing the 70 percent state share. By 1965, it had taken a controlling stake in Sammy Collins's Marine Diamond Corporation by buying 53 percent of his Sea Diamonds Limited. De Beers's pursuit of rights may have been relentless, but certain smaller interests remained outside its control, for example in Ghana, the Central African Republic, Guinea, and South America.

A dramatic discovery, the Orapa pipe on the edge of the Kalahari desert in Botswana, was made in 1967 by De Beers geologists. De Beers Botswana Mining Company Limited (Debswana) was incorporated in 1969 as a joint venture between De Beers and the Botswana government. Diamonds are now responsible for about 45 percent of Botswana's Gross Domestic Product and more than half of government revenue. Further discoveries ensued at Letlhakane and Jwaneng, the latter—buried some 150 feet in the sand—hailed as a particular technological triumph. Debswana became a 5.27 percent shareholder in De Beers in 1987 in exchange for De Beers's acquisition of the diamond stocks built up by Debswana from 1982 to 1985.

Business cooperation did not always go so smoothly with the other African diamond-producing countries through the 1960s, 1970s, and 1980s. Newfound independence, political upheaval, vacillating policies, and illegal mining led to certain unstable relationships for De Beers. Sierra Leone declared an open market in 1974. Dicorwaf, which had superseded Dicosil, lost its sole exclusive exporting rights. Its supposed monopoly had been undermined by theft from and illegal mining on Selection Trust's concessions.

For some 50 years, until the early 1970s, sales of Angolan diamonds by Diamang via the CSO went smoothly. The Portuguese withdrawal before the country's independence in 1975 and the civil war that raged afterwards saw this position collapse. Diamang's operations disintegrated, leaving a great deal of production to be smuggled out to Lisbon in Portuguese luggage and to Antwerp. The volume of this trade was so important that the CSO was forced to buy quantities of these diamonds, when they came onto the open market in Belgium, to maintain price stability. In 1977 the government took a majority interest in Diamang, later to become Endiama, and De Beers was left with a nominal shareholding. The government could not be seen to be dealing with a South African company, being officially at war with her neighbor. Thirty Cornish tin miners were recruited in London by Mining and Technical Services, a Liberian-registered company with several members of De Beers as directors, to go to Angola to advise and assist the state company. Endiama sold what diamond production there was by tender to Antwerp dealers. Following growth in production, however, Endiama signed an agreement with the CSO in 1991 for the marketing of all the diamonds from the important Cuango River region and for help in extending production.

After independence, the Tanzanian government fully nationalized the Mwadui (formerly Williamson) mine and set up its own sorting and valuing office. Production has been run down and investment lacking, but the diamonds continue to be sold via the CSO. And in Zaire, the CSO had set up a buying company, British Zaire Diamond Distributors Limited (Zaïrebrit, later Britmond) on the former La Forminière site, and from 1972 embarked on exploration. De Beers's involvement in Zaire underwent a serious crisis when the Zaire government broke off its contract (in operation since 1967) for the exclusive marketing of the Société Minière de Bakwanga (MIBA) diamonds by the CSO. Unhappy at being offered equal sales rights as one of four, the CSO withdrew from the country. The situa-

tion was resolved in 1983, first when the government allowed the CSO amongst others to buy the open-market production, and then when a new agreement was signed for the exclusive marketing of MIBA's production via the CSO. Elicit mining and black market buying have been even more rife here than in Sierra Leone.

In Namibia, De Beers's CDM has enjoyed a remarkably stable position since the 1920s, only briefly troubled by Sammy Collins. To exploit the foreshore alluvial reserves of very high-quality gems, it has developed sophisticated techniques, basically shifting sand dunes seaward, pushing the sea back by up to a quarter of a mile along ten miles. The area is said to have the most concentrated fleet of earth-moving equipment in the world. Security is high, although diamond theft is a problem. In the late 1960s and early 1970s, CDM production accounted for up to 40 percent of De Beers's total taxed profits. Since 1974, no separate accounts have been published. South Africa ignored the United Nations' lifting in 1966 of its Namibia mandate and the International Court of Justice's 1971 ruling that the territory be surrendered. Namibia finally achieved independence in 1989. De Beers was accused in the early 1980s by an ex-employee of deliberately overmining its Namibian territory before it might lose out with independence, and of transfer pricing. The Thirion commission supported allegations of overmining and tax evasion, but a government white paper later exonerated CDM on both counts. At present CDM remains 100 percent De Beers-owned and holds the lease on the area until 2010.

The largest diamond discoveries in the 1970s and 1980s have been in Australia, now the world's largest diamond producer in carats. The mainly Australian Katalumburu Joint Venture began prospecting in Kimberley, Northwest Australia, in 1972. Conzinc Riotinto of Australia Ltd. (CRA) joined the consortium in 1976, building up a 35 percent stake, which increased to almost 70 percent some years later. In 1977 it took over the management of the joint venture, now named Ashton Joint Venture (AJV). Ironically, De Beers had surveyed and dismissed the region in the 1960s. In 1982 CRA and Ashton Mining Ltd., holding 95 percent of the Australian production sales rights, approved a sales contract with the CSO until the end of the decade, the CSO guaranteeing its purchase of the entire production regardless of the state of the markets. This important contract was renewed in 1991.

In the late 1970s speculation by diamond traders, who had purchased and stockpiled large quantities of rough diamonds as a hedge against inflation, resulted in large numbers of diamonds in excess to jewelry demand later being released on the markets. Consequently, the early 1980s were adversely marked for De Beers. It had to limit its sales substantially so that the stocks that had built up in the cutting centers could be absorbed into the retail markets. Owing to De Beers's strict control over supply and thanks to the strength of its investments outside diamonds, it managed to ride out the severe recession.

The Soviet Union, which became one of the world's largest diamond producers, had abandoned official dealings with the CSO in 1963 because of De Beers's South African status, although it was revealed in the media that the Soviets were involved in covert dealings via a third party. Having developed their own cutting industry, though, the Soviets were able to sell certain stocks onto the open market independently. Occasionally they dumped large amounts onto the international market, for example in 1984. Once again, the CSO weathered the storm. In 1990 dealing between the two parties came back into the open, and Centenary concluded an extraordinary US$5 billion sales agreement with Glavalmazzoloto, the main precious metals and diamonds administrative body in the USSR, under which the CSO will market the USSR's rough diamond production for five years.

The acrimonious takeover bid by Minorco—an international mining investment house of the greater Anglo-De Beers empire in which Centenary now holds 21 percent—for Consolidated Gold Fields (Consgold) brought De Beers unwanted publicity. Rudolph Agnew, chairman of Consgold, argued the undesirability of a South African group wielding such power over the gold industry, and attempted to discredit De Beers by asking the British Office of Fair Trading (OFT) to investigate the CSO as a "negative monopoly." In May of 1989 Minorco's bid fell through due to legal obstacles, but in August of 1989 the OFT announced that it would not mount an investigation into the CSO.

It is not without controversy that De Beers exercises its formidable power over the diamond industry. It has frequently been attacked as an anti-competitive, secretive cartel. De Beers likes to refer to the system as a "producers' cooperative." De Beers is also attacked for profiting initially from exploitation through colonialism and then from the system of apartheid. Within South Africa, De Beers and Anglo are considered liberal. The greater group has consistently opposed the government on its racial policy. Harry Oppenheimer served for many years as a member of parliament for the anti-apartheid opposition, but progress in conditions for black workers has been slow.

A fully integrated wage scale was established for all employees, regardless of race, in 1978. In 1981, for the first time in South African mining history, a recognition agreement with an established black trade union was signed, allowing for the representation of black employees in wage and other negotiations. At the end of the 1980s most of the black workers still migrated to the mines from neighboring states or South Africa's so-called homelands and lived in single-sex hostels away from their families. In 1988 the law was changed, giving blacks the right to acquire blasting certificates, opening the way for them to fill more skilled posts. Black workers' pay at the end of the 1980s was, on average, one-sixth of that of white workers, who were generally skilled workers. De Beers, with Anglo, makes major investments in social programs, calculated on a percentage of Anglo-De Beers dividend payments, via the joint Chairman's Fund. It embarked in 1987 on an employee share-ownership scheme to which 9,000 have subscribed, and on a small-scale home-ownership scheme. It is encouraging small black business enterprises by contracting out work to them and is a major contributor to the Urban Foundation for black housing. The greater group is recognized to have led the way in South Africa in such initiatives, and for its business in the future, as well as for social reasons, sees its interest in encouraging the creation of a prosperous, capitalist black middle class. However, partly due to the cyclical nature of such a luxury-goods market, its shares trade at a discount to the asset worth of the company.

New exploration and operations are continuing all the time, with particularly important new developments for the 1990s at the Venetia mine in South Africa, at Elizabeth Bay, Auchas in Namibia, and in North Saskatchewan in Canada. Harry Oppenheimer stepped down as chairman in 1984 to be replaced by Julian Ogilvie Thompson, now also chairman of Anglo and of Minorco, and Harry Oppenheimer's son Nicky became deputy chairman of De Beers and chairman of the CSO.

At the end of the 1980s sales soared to new heights, reaching a record $4.17 billion in 1988, almost four times what they stood at in the early 1980s. The massive De Beers advertising budget of around $172 million was spent on major campaigns in 29 countries. Twenty-five years ago, the tradition of the diamond engagement ring hardly existed in Japan; now 77 percent of Japanese brides receive one. In 1992 De Beers Marine recovered some 360,000 carats from CDM's off-shore areas, and is developing the technology for sea-floor mining.

Political, ethical, and economic problems have plagued De Beers in the early 1990s. International calls for an end to apartheid in South Africa have had repercussions for the country's largest conglomerates. The African National Congress (ANC) has rallied for the unbundling of South Africa's largest conglomerates, including Anglo and De Beers. ANC leaders feel that the eventual dissolution of these companies will open big business to more blacks. More than 80 percent of the Johannesburg Stock Exchange is comprised of South Africa's six largest companies. Leaders of the ANC insist that the country's economy is constricted by the conglomerates, and that the lack of competition inherent in the South African economy discourages foreign investors. But De Beers and Anglo spokesmen see their company's strengths as a necessary attribute for world competition once South Africa becomes a fully accepted member of the community of trading nations. The differences between these two groups will have to be resolved in the near future.

In April of 1992 De Beers ethical standards came under the scrutiny of the U.S. Justice Department, which accused the diamond giant of price-fixing in cooperation with General Electric Company. Although industrial diamonds fall outside the CSO's purview (and in any case bring only 1 percent of the price of gems), the Justice Department's lawsuit claimed that GE and De Beers conspired to control over 90 percent of the worldwide market for high-grade industrial diamonds.

De Beers's control of the gem market has been threatened in the early 1990s by the twin demons of recession and rogue diamond producers. The worldwide economic downturn depressed diamond sales in the United States and Japan, which together account for 66 percent of diamond jewelry sales. In response, De Beers cut back its purchases from diamond producers 25 percent in 1992 to adjust supplies according to demand.

Unfortunately, as De Beers limited its supplies, political upheaval in Angola resulted in over 50,000 unauthorized diamond diggers in that country's rich diamond fields. De Beers was forced to spend an estimated $6 million per week on these illegal diamonds to guarantee a stable market. Add that to De Beers's contracts for $4.5 billion in diamonds and total rough sales at $3.5 billion, and a deficit situation was clearly at hand by September of 1992. The company was forced again to reduce all its contracts by another 25 percent that month.

To make matters worse, Russian suppliers in the Sakha region began to demand more control over the sale of diamonds produced in that region. They base their demands on the fact that, by value, Russia has the world's largest diamond production as well as a stockpile of diamonds rivaling De Beers's own $3.3 billion reserves. The Russian central government, which sells 75 percent of the country's production through De Beers, has entered into negotiations with the Sakha regional government and De Beers officials to effect an agreement. Sakha produces 98 percent of Russia's diamonds and allocates 80 percent of that production to the country's central government. It receives income generated by the sale of the remaining twenty percent directly from De Beers.

A contract between De Beers and Russia expires in 1995, adding a sense of urgency to the situation. Some sources estimate that $5 million to $7 million in Russian rough diamonds were released to world markets from unauthorized sources in 1992. The Russian threat constitutes the most serious threat to De Beers's predominance in the diamond industry, and may bring an end to the company's century-long dominance over the market. But De Beers executives, confident that the Angolan situation will subside and the Russians will work with them to ensure market stability, see the crisis as more of a short-term public relations problem than a collapse of their company's control.

The great aim of De Beers through its history has been to maintain the long-term stability of diamond prices for the prosperity of the diamond industry. De Beers prides itself on the fact that the price of diamonds has shown a steady growth more consistent than any other commodity since World War II and that market fluctuations and volatility have been avoided. *Fortune* magazine ranked De Beers second in the world in 1989 among the companies with the highest returns on sales and tenth among those with the highest returns on assets.

All the major diamond producers now sell through De Beers. Only some small producers do not. De Beers keeps a very tight grip on the diamond industry. Despite the uncertainty of South Africa's political future, De Beers, with its expertise in technol-ogy and marketing and its sound financial footing, seems set to maintain the industry's stability and its preeminent position.

Principal Subsidiaries: CDM Properties (Pty) Ltd.; CDM Prospecting (Pty) Ltd.; De Beers Consolidated Investments (Pty) Ltd.; De Beers Diamantes Industriais do Brasil Ltda; De Beers Holdings (Pty) Ltd.; De Beers Industrial Diamond Division (Ireland) Ltd.; De Beers Industrial Diamonds (Ireland) Ltd.; De Beers Industrial Diamond Division (Pty) Ltd.; De Beers Industrial Diamonds (South Africa) (Pty) Ltd.; De Beers Marine (Pty) Ltd.; De Beers Prospecting Botswana (Pty) Ltd.; Diamond Corp. (Pty) Ltd.; Eronia Investments Ltd.; Exclusive Properties (Pty) Ltd.; Manne Diamond Corp. (Pty) Ltd.; Marine Group Investments (Pty) Ltd.; Olivia Properties (Pty) Ltd.; Orama Holdings (Pty) Ltd.; Premier (Transvaal) Diamond Mining Co. (Pty) Ltd.; Sea Diamond Corp. (Pty) Ltd.; Finsch Diamonds (Pty) Ltd.; (80.78%); Griqualand West Diamond Mihing Co. Dutoitspan Mine Ltd. (72.87%); Consolidated Co Bultfontein Mine Ltd. (67.47%); International Diamond Products Ltd. (50%); Ultra High Pressure Units (Pty) Ltd.; Ultra High Pressure Units (Ireland) Ltd. (50%).

Further Reading: Chilvers, Hedley A., *The Story of De Beers,* London, Cassell and Company, Ltd., 1939; Gregory, Sir Theodore, *Ernest Oppenheimer and the Economic Development of Southern Africa,* Cape Town, Oxford University Press, 1962; Hocking, Anthony, *Oppenheimer and Son,* Johannesburg, McGraw-Hill, 1973; Jessup, Edward, *Ernest Oppenheimer: A Study in Power,* London, Rex Collins, 1979; Green, Timothy, *The World of Diamonds,* London, Weidenfeld & Nicolson, 1981; Newbury, Colin, *The Diamond Ring Business, Politics and Precious Stones in South Africa, 1867–1947,* Oxford, Clarendon Press, 1989; Jamieson, Bill, *Goldstrike: The Oppenheimer Empire in Crisis,* London, Hutchinson Business Books, 1990; Hilzenrath, David S., and Steven Pearlstein, "U.S. Probing Possible Price-Fixing by GE," *Washington Post,* April 23, 1992; Frank, David, "Unbundling into Power," *Euromoney,* September 1992; "Is It a Crack or a Scratch?," *Economist,* September 12, 1992; Shor, Russell, "Russia to De Beers: 'We Want More Control,'" *Jewelers' Circular-Keystone,* January 1993.

—Philippe A. Barbour
updated by April Dougal

DEAN FOODS COMPANY

3600 North River Road
Franklin Park, Illinois 60131
U.S.A.
(312) 625-6200
(708) 678-1680
Fax: (708) 671-8744

Public Company
Incorporated: 1925 as Dean Evaporated Milk Company
Sales: $2.29 billion
Employees: 10,100
Stock Exchanges: New York
SICs: 2026 Fluid Milk; 2024 Ice Cream & Frozen Desserts;
2033 Canned Fruits & Vegetables; 2035 Pickles, Sauces,
& Salad Dressings

Through thoughtful acquisitions and balanced diversification, Dean Foods Company has grown from a small regional dairy into a food company with sales of more than $2 billion. Dean's trademark has been acquiring private companies, then boosting their profits by modernizing operations and increasing productivity. Absorbing regional dairy operations and providing those private labels as well as Dean's own to grocery chains, retail stores, and food service outlets has positioned Dean just behind dairy industry leader Borden, Inc. Dean is also the second-largest pickle business in the United States, and the third-largest vegetable processor. Success in these areas has helped Dean to counteract the fluctuations in the fluid milk market.

Sam Dean, Sr., was working with a brokerage firm in Chicago when he decided to start his own company. As he had been brokering evaporated milk, it seemed logical to enter that business. When he founded the Dean Evaporated Milk Company in 1925, it consisted of one plant in Pecatonica, Illinois. Soon, two more plants were added. Dean entered the fresh milk industry in the mid-1930s, and until 1947 Dean's market was mostly fluid milk in Northern Illinois. In 1947 Dean also entered the ice cream business.

The company's strategy of growth through careful acquisition began with its founder. In order to expand geographically, Dean began acquiring solid performers in other regions. Until World War II, Dean had been strictly a Midwestern dairy. After the war, it spread further, going as far as Kentucky. A research and development lab was established as early as 1943. One of the

lab's first innovations was a powdered non-dairy coffee creamer. This marked the origin of another company strength: more than half of Dean's later growth came from expanded markets and new products.

A major milestone for the company came in 1961, with the purchase of Green Bay Food Company. This acquisition marked Dean's entry into the pickle business, and Green Bay continues to lead this profitable Dean division. Four years later, Howard M. Dean, grandson of the founder and at the time a supply officer for the navy, was tapped by his uncle, who was then chairman, to join the company. Howard Dean became company president in 1970, along with some other changes in management that signalled a new era for Dean Foods. Included in that new era was an acquisition strategy—perfected by Kenneth J. Douglas—that set the stage for the company's next decade. Most often, Dean absorbed well-known regional brands and companies that were small and healthy. Dean provided them with infusions of capital—especially to upgrade facilities—as well as access to marketing and managing expertise.

Dean was remarkable for its decentralized management structure, allowing acquired companies relative autonomy. In nearly all cases, acquired companies saw increased earnings within a year or two of joining the Dean family. All but one acquisition through 1992 were privately held companies, often family-owned. Where other industry giants relied on brand-name, premium-priced products, Dean made its reputation through low-margin markets, providing regionally labeled goods to leading grocery chains and restaurants. For this reason, the Dean name was often not as recognized as some of its regional product lines. The company built itself on the success of well-known local favorites.

Dean acquired a few more Midwestern dairy concerns in the 1960s, including Wisconsin's Fieldcrest Sales, purchased in 1966. Changes in the dairy industry, where competition necessitated economies of scale, caused many smaller companies to look to Dean for survival. Seven out of the 12 companies Dean acquired up to 1991 had approached Dean. Gandy's Dairies, Inc. of Texas was acquired in 1976, followed by Bell Dairy Products and Price's Creameries in 1978. Creamland Dairy of Albuquerque, New Mexico, also joined the family that year. In 1980, Florida companies McArthur Dairy Inc. and T.G. Lee Foods, Inc. were purchased, granting Dean a solid entry into that region. Later, Hart's Dairy of Florida was added to that state's holdings. Moving out of the largely Midwestern markets proved profitable for Dean as early as 1985, when its Southern and Southwestern regions became the company's strongest performers.

Dean began serving the Pennsylvania and eastern Ohio regions with its 1984 purchase of a Sharpsville, Pennsylvania, dairy. A Kentucky-based dairy specialty company brought Dean into that area through a 1985 acquisition. Dean's sales hit the $1 billion mark, after 13 consecutive years of record earnings, in 1985. In spring of that year, Jewel Food Stores was forced to close its own dairy operations after an outbreak of salmonella. The Chicago-area Jewel stores at that time accounted for nearly one-third of retail grocery business there. Dean stepped in to assist Jewel, providing the stores' fluid milk supply within 48 hours of the onset of the crisis. While this one market accounted for nearly 90 percent of Dean's sales growth that year, the growth wasn't immediately reflected in profits because of the costs of expansion and start-up services.

Meanwhile, Dean's dairy division was also benefiting from the explosion of public awareness of the health benefits of calcium. Fluid milk consumption, after 20 years of stagnation, increased in 1984 and 1985. Research linking osteoporosis, or bone deterioration, to calcium-deficient diets not only gave a boost to milk sales, but generated a new product line: Dean Foods quickly introduced Nature's Calcium Plus and other calcium-added items.

Dairy products accounted for nearly 70 percent of Dean's total sales in 1984. Fluid milk was the largest dairy category at that time, but Dean's ice cream business was also thriving. Dean was area franchiser and exclusive supplier to more than 400 Baskin-Robbins stores in the West and Midwest. Ice cream sales nearly doubled when Dean began supplying Jewel in 1986. Several more healthy dairy companies were added to the fold about this time, including Reiter Dairy, Inc. of Akron, Ohio, in 1986. Representing $100 million in annual sales in that state, with excellent brand identity and growth records, Reiter's product line included fluid milk, cottage cheese, and ice cream. Ryan Milk Company of Kentucky, also acquired in 1986, brought with it a line of aseptic products and a distribution network that reached 40 states. Ryan brought Dean solidly into the ultra-high temperature (UHT) processed products market. UHT products have longer shelf lives and include such things as flavored milks, half-and-half, whipping creams, and non-dairy coffee creamers, of which Dean is the nation's largest producer. With the purchase of Elgin Blenders, Inc. in 1986, Dean began supplying stabilizers and other products to McDonald's Corporation.

While best known for its dairy products, Dean's fastest growing area was its specialty segment. Specialty foods included such things as pickles, dips, sauces, and relishes. Another watershed event for Dean in 1986 was when it merged with Larsen Company and entered the vegetable business. Considered the creator of canned mixed vegetables, Larsen was a cornerstone in the canned and frozen vegetables industry as the processor of successful retail brands such as Veg-All and Freshlike. Larsen's annuals sales were $170 million. This acquisition was one of Dean's largest and represented a notable diversification. It also reflected a revised corporate strategy regarding acquisitions—one that targeted companies with larger sales and different markets. At the time, more than three-quarters of Dean's volume was in dairy operations. The expense of this merger, combined with a bountiful crop at that time which lowered selling prices, hurt Dean initially, but the company recovered. With increased public attention to diet and health concerns, sales of frozen vegetables especially soared in the 1980s. By 1987, Dean ranked third in frozen and canned vegetables sales, after Pillsbury's Green Giant and Nabisco's Del Monte. Dean also began to service international vegetable markets. However, the vegetable glut combined with higher raw-milk prices in 1987 to slow Dean's net income that year. Profits for the company were flat. Whereas the government stabilized prices in the milk industry by buying surpluses, a surplus of vegetables meant only waste and depressed margins.

Dean purchased Verifine Dairy Products Corp. at the end of 1987. The $25 million Wisconsin dairy was quickly computerized and its automated systems updated. Fairmont Products, Inc. of Belleville, Pennsylvania, came on board that year as well. In large part because of these two purchases, Dean's fluid milk sales grew 14 percent in 1988. In this same year, Dean spent $9 million to settle a price-fixing case brought by school boards based in Florida. The charge was that two of Dean's subsidiaries—acquired in 1980—were among ten dairies and distributors who allegedly conspired to rig bids for school milk-supply contracts in Florida, between 1965 and 1987.

Dean greatly strengthened its position in the frozen vegetable market by purchasing Richard A. Shaw, Inc. in 1988. Shaw's annual sales in 1989 were $55 million. The California-based company supplied major grocery chains and food service accounts and was Dean's entry into the West Coast vegetable market. Shaw also helped round out Dean's Midwestern produce line with crops grown mostly in the West. Dean then expanded its canned vegetable business in 1989 with the acquisition of Big Stone Inc. This Minnesota-based vegetable processor had sales of $24 million and two processing plants located near thriving sources of corn, peas, and green beans. Still more prime growing areas were accessed with the 1990 purchase of Bellingham Frozen Foods, Inc., whose plants in Washington and Michigan garnered annual sales of $30 million. A 1988 drought brought prices back up after they had been depressed by the earlier crop surplus, though this same drought depressed milk production.

Dean also made some internal changes in 1989: Howard Dean became chairman; William Fischer became president; and Kenneth Douglas became vice-chairman. The cost of acquisitions and the anti-trust settlement combined with the drought-related fall-off in milk production caused a dip in earnings leading into 1989. Another drain was the company's unprofitable transportation unit, which operated in a highly competitive market, providing a wide range of transportation and distribution services. Only 20 percent of the division's business was transporting Dean's products.

Dean sold its retail Baskin-Robbins ice cream business in 1989, though it continued to be the stores' sole supplier for two of their major distribution areas. Shortly after that sale, Dean acquired Charles F. Cates & Sons, Inc., a pickle processor based in North Carolina with annual sales of $84 million. This boosted Dean's presence in the East and Southeast, regions in which it was not strong. Meanwhile, the company was the target of takeover talk and updated its poison-pill measure late in 1989. Dean also continued its product innovations, introducing a very successful non-fat yogurt with artificial sweetener and Extra Light sour creams and dips. A frozen yogurt, which Dean had introduced 14 years earlier with no success, suddenly began performing well in the climate of nutritional and health awareness.

Dean launched 1990 with the purchase of Mayfield Dairy Farms, Inc. As one of the largest remaining family-owned dairy farms, Mayfield was a force in the Southeast—primarily Tennessee and Georgia—with annual sales near $110 million. Another new product was introduced in 1990: a low-fat milk with reduced lactose, a sugar that caused digestion problems for some milk drinkers. Dean also acquired Ready Food Products, Inc. of Philadelphia, a specialty dairy processor representing sales of $28 million. Expanding its specialty food segment helped Dean to balance the shortfall in dairy profits caused by further increases in raw-milk prices in 1989 and 1990. The operating earnings in specialty foods exceeded Dean's dairy products segment for the first time in fiscal 1990.

Three more dairies acquired in early 1991 brought with them $150 million of annual revenues. At the same time, Dean sold its McCadam Cheese Company unit, a private-label, New York supplier of natural cheeses. As raw-milk prices returned to pre-drought levels by summer 1991, the company refocused upon its acquisition program. Dean purchased Cream o'Weber Dairy, Inc. of Utah in April 1991. It also acquired Frio Foods, Inc., a Texas-based vegetable processor, and Meadow Brook Dairy Company of Pennsylvania. The Cream o'Weber purchase typified Dean's strategy: even before the acquisition was completed, Cream o'Weber's plants were being consolidated and updated. Another advantage of being part of the Dean team was the sharing between divisions. An example of this came during the frozen yogurt boom in 1990, when Dean's T.G. Lee and McArthur affiliates wanted to enter this market. Starting a new product from scratch might have taken more than six months. Instead, these dairies were able to take advantage of the expertise of a fellow Dean division, Mayfield Dairy Farms, which produced one of Dean's best frozen yogurts. In just about five weeks, these companies had a new product on the market under their own names. Sharing between companies and a decentralized management style are part of what makes Dean so successful.

Dean passed the $2 billion mark for the first time in 1991. However, an excess of crops in fiscal 1992 put a squeeze on Dean's profits in the vegetable segment. At this time, the vegetable line was 55 percent frozen and 45 percent canned, with roughly two-thirds of its output for private label. Dairy remained Dean's primary business, with more than 21 milk-processing plants and nearly 6 percent of the total market, making Dean a very close second to Borden, the industry leader. Dean was well positioned to continue its dairy operation acquisitions, and diversified enough to balance out market fluctuations. These factors should contribute to its continued success in the future.

Principal Subsidiaries: McArthur Dairy, Inc.; T. G. Lee Foods, Inc.; Hart's Dairy Inc.; Dean Milk Company, Inc.; Ryan Milk Company, Inc.; Liberty Dairy; Creamland Dairies, Inc.; Reiter Dairy Inc.; Gilt Edge Farms, Inc.; Dean Dairy Products Co.; Fairmont Products Inc.; Meadow Brook Dairy Company; Ready Food Products Inc.; Mayfield Dairy Farms, Inc.; Price's Creameries; Bell Dairy Products, Inc.; Gandy's Dairies, Inc.; Cream o'Weber Dairy Inc.; St. Thomas Dairies; Fieldcrest Sales; Verifine Dairy Products; Atkins Pickle Co.; Western Food Products; Pilgrim Farms, Inc.; Green Bay Food Company; Aunt Jane Foods; Charles F. Cates & Sons, Inc.; Amboy Specialty Foods; Elgin Blenders, Inc.; E.B.I. Foods Ltd.; Richard A. Shaw, Inc.; Big Stone; Bellingham Frozen Foods, Inc.; The Larsen Company; DFC Transportation Company.

Further Reading: "Lucky 13th," *Barron's,* July 5, 1985; Horwich, Andrea, "Boosting Sales by Boning Up on Calcium," *Dairy Foods,* October 1986; Otto, Alison, "The Year-End Juggling Act," *Dairy Foods,* December 1986; Otto, Alison, "A Prognosis of Progress," *Dairy Foods,* April 1986; Cahill, William R., "Galloping Gourmet," *Barron's,* December 8, 1986; Leibowitz, David, "Of Gum, Tools and Milk," *Financial World,* February 24, 1987; "Dean's List," *Forbes,* June 15, 1987; "Dean Foods," *Dairy Foods,* April 1987; Andrews, Nina, "Financial Officer Named President of Dean Foods," *New York Times,* January 2, 1989; Therrien, Lois, "Dean Goes Looking for a Diet Supplement," *Business Week,* March 14, 1988; "Dean Foods," *Dairy Foods,* April 1989; Siler, Charles, "Ripe for the Picking," *Forbes,* April 3, 1989; "Dean Foods Co.: A Big Processor Survives a Dry Spell," *Barron's,* April 10, 1989; "Dean Foods Co.," *Wall Street Journal,* August 22, 1989; Crown, Judith, "Dean Foods Catches a Chill," *Crain's Chicago Business,* September 18, 1989; "Dean Foods' Poison Pill," *Wall Street Journal,* December 11, 1989; "Dean Foods," *Dairy Foods,* February 1990; "Dean Foods Co.," *Dairy Foods,* April 1990; Byrne, Harlan S., "Dean Foods Co.: Diversification Paying Off for Big Seller of Dairy Products," *Barron's,* May 7, 1990; Therrien, Lois, "Making the Undrinkable Thinkable," *Business Week,* May 14, 1990; "Dean Foods to Post an Earnings Record for Its Latest Year," *Wall Street Journal,* July 17, 1990; "Firm Completes Unit's Sale to Finnish Dairy Collective," *Wall Street Journal,* January 4, 1991; Schexnayder, Karla, " 'Whey' Ahead of the Game," *Dairy Foods,* March 1991; "Dean Foods Completes Purchase," *Wall Street Journal,* May 1, 1991; Reiter, Jeff, "Small Niche, Big Potential," *Dairy Foods,* May 1991; Byrne, Harlan S., "Dean Foods Co.: See-Saw Markets Don't Slow Its Trek to Another Record Year," *Barron's,* June 3, 1991; "Dean Foods Expects to Split Stock, Boost Payout, as Profit Rises," *Wall Street Journal,* July 17, 1991; Oloroso, Arsenio, "Dean Foods' Dry Spell Ends," *Crain's Chicago Business,* July 29, 1991; Lingle, Rick, "A Tale of Two Lines," *Dairy Foods,* August 1991; Dexheimer, Ellen, "Dean Dynasty," *Dairy Foods,* November 1991; Reiter, Jeff, "All Together Now," *Dairy Foods,* November 1991; Mans, Jack, "Hey, Big Spender!" *Dairy Foods,* November 1991; "Dean Foods Completes Purchase," *Wall Street Journal,* November 21, 1991; Palmer, Jay, "Growing Again," *Barron's,* July 6, 1992; *Dean Foods Company: Company Profile,* Franklin Park, Illinois, Dean Foods Company; *Dean Foods Company: 1992 Annual Report,* Franklin Park, Illinois, Dean Foods Company.

—Carol I. Keeley

DEL MONTE CORPORATION

One Market Plaza
P.O. Box 193575
San Francisco, California 94119-3575
U.S.A.
(415) 442-4000
Fax: (415) 442-4894

Private Company
Incorporated: 1916 as California Packing Corporation
Employees: 14,500
Sales: $1.43 billion
SICs: 2033 Canned Fruits & Vegetables; 2086 Bottled and
  Canned Soft Drinks

The Del Monte Corporation, doing business as Del Monte Foods, is the largest canner of fruits and vegetables in the United States. Yet its size now is little more than half what it was at the beginning of the 1980s, when it was under the ownership of R. J. Reynolds Industries. R. J. Reynolds became RJR Nabisco, which in 1988 was consumed by Kohlberg Kravis Roberts & Co. (KKR). KKR quickly divested itself of a number of RJR Nabisco properties, including Del Monte's fresh fruits operations (purchased by British-based Polly Peck International) and its processed foods and Japanese rights (purchased by Kikkoman). Although Del Monte management and an investor group led by Merrill Lynch & Co. bought the company's remaining businesses in early 1990, they were also forced to divest various branches of the company, including the Hawaiian Punch and European canned food divisions. In mid- to late 1992 plans surfaced for more Del Monte sales, both of the original and the ancillary businesses. Nevertheless, as the decade progressed, San Francisco-based Del Monte Foods remained intact and tied to its heritage: that of a quality marketer of fruit under an internationally recognized, albeit increasingly confused, brand name.

Del Monte traces its origins to the pioneering nineteenth-century figures in West Coast canning Daniel Provost and Francis Cutting. Along with the influx of settlers from the California gold rush came a need for new regional food manufacturers, and these men led the way. While Provost holds the distinction of forming the first foodpacking operation there, Cutting became the first of a long line of entrepreneurs to manufacture metal and glass containers—rather than having them shipped from the East—and the first to export California-processed fruit back to the East Coast as well as Europe. As the California orchard industry grew, so did the canning industry; a virtual boom in agriculture came to the region during the 1800s, following construction of the first railroad networks, and dozens of canneries were established.

One such business, the Oakland Preserving Company, was launched in 1891. At this time, uniformity in labeling and product quality, under the auspices of the recently established California Canned Goods Association, was becoming a foremost marketing concern. The intent of this service organization was to ensure that the label "California grown" stood for an uncommonly high standard; its efforts ultimately led to effective legislation governing the canning industry. Oakland's own efforts in this area generated the Del Monte brand, a name that would soon become synonymous with exceptional value.

During this time the need arose for sustaining high consumer demand within an industry that now seemed to be rapidly outgrowing its economic limits. Talks of consolidation among canners eventually produced the California Fruit Canners Association (CFCA) in 1899. CFCA represented a historical merger of 18 separate canneries, including the Oakland Preserving Company. Upon consolidation, CFCA was so vast that it comprised approximately half of the entire California canning industry and ranked, in effect, as the largest canner of fruits and vegetables in the world. There were several key promoters of the CFCA consolidation, including Frederick Tillman, Jr., of Oakland Preserving; Sydney Smith of Cutting Fruit Packing Company; Robert and Charles Bentley of Sacramento Packing; and Mark Fontana and William Fries of Fontana & Co. By popular assent, Fries became the company's president.

Given CFCA's wide area of operations and the strong wills of its various principals, true integration of the canneries never materialized. Furthermore, the retention of a large number of name brands prevented CFCA from developing a strong, cohesive marketing presence during its early years. Nonetheless, the multidimensional cannery prospered, spreading beyond the borders of California with the acquisitions of the Oregon Packing Company and the Hawaii Preserving Company. Like the other canneries already within the fold, these continued to operate fairly autonomously. However, as William Braznell pointed out in his *History of the Del Monte Corporation*, "One notable concession made to corporate solidarity was the adoption of the *Del Monte* label as the association's premier brand." The brand name, courtesy of Tillman and the Oakland Preserving Company, derived from a coffee blend prepared by Tillman and a partner for the Hotel Del Monte in Monterey as early as 1886. Now the Del Monte label graced over 50 products, including squash, sweet potatoes, peppers, berries, jams, jellies, cranberry sauce, and olives.

CFCA's reliance upon commission agents to sell most of its produce led to a curious chain of events and, ultimately, the formation of the California Packing Corporation (Calpak), the immediate ancestor of the Del Monte Corporation. For some time, CFCA employed San Francisco-based J. K. Armsby Co., the West Coast's largest wholesaler, as its exclusive agent. After CFCA terminated the arrangement, Armsby sought out the region's second-largest manufacturer, Central California

Canneries (CCC). This new arrangement soured when the Armsby brothers, J. K. and George, began rapidly accumulating stock in CCC. George, the more aggressive and visionary-minded of the two, had begun to conceive of a single, dominant food concern that would, at the very least, include the Armsby Co., CCC, and CFCA. Although CCC president William Hotchkiss managed to repel the takeover attempt, he eventually proved amenable to the idea of such a merger.

On November 19, 1916, after numerous meetings, disagreements, and compromises, George Armsby's dream was realized and the monolithic Calpak was formed. Joining the three major companies in the merger were Alaska Packers Association and Griffin & Skelley. Save for Alaska Packers, all of the consolidated companies were headquartered in San Francisco within a short distance of each other. By 1917, a new headquarters had been established and a committee system of management adopted. J. K. Armsby and Fries were elected to serve as president and chairperson, respectively. Like the CFCA merger, the Calpak merger presented a host of organizational problems for the new management, not the least of which was establishing production consistency within the 71 plants in California, Washington, Oregon, and Idaho, as well as the territories of Alaska and Hawaii. According to Braznell, what held everything together was the understanding by the owners that "California Packing Corporation would present a solid front in the market place. There would be only one premium Calpak label—Del Monte. It would stand for products of uniformly high quality, and it would be promoted for all it was worth."

A year after the merger, Calpak made promotional history by placing its first Del Monte advertisement in the *Saturday Evening Post*. Mass advertising was a new medium, and Calpak's intent was to use it to create a national market for its Del Monte label. What the company hoped to overcome was the prevailing image among consumers that canned goods were "rainy day" items, adequate though not preferable replacements for fresh produce. The concept of brand loyalty was another potential stumbling block for the company, for most grocers at the time were "full service," filling customers orders themselves and paying little attention to manufacturers or labels. Piggly Wiggly was among the first grocery chains to alter this practice. By the 1920s the evolution toward self-service supermarkets in the grocery industry was well underway, and the success of the Del Monte marketing plan was ensured.

However, Calpak entered the 1920s in a precarious situation. Although earnings were some $7 million on revenues of $85 million following record-high commodity prices, an agricultural depression loomed, made worse by the plight of many farmers who had heavily mortgaged their land to sink new capital into their operations. The company weathered the crisis better than many of its growers, strengthening itself through the establishment of a national sales network and the initiation of mass production, quality assurance, and other internal systems that both improved efficiency and enhanced the Del Monte brand. A major development came in 1925, when Calpak acquired Rochelle Canneries of Rochelle, Illinois. The purchase of this Midwest company signified Calpak's expansion into corn and pea packing, then the two most lucrative segments of the vegetable canning industry. Related acquisitions included plants in Wisconsin and Minnesota. Several overseas ventures,

in such countries as the Philippines and Haiti, also highlighted the decade.

With the onset of the Great Depression, Calpak's earnings crumbled. From 1930 to 1931 they fell from $6.16 per share to just 9¢ per share. In 1932, the company posted the worst losses in its history. Yet, within two years, earnings began to rebound and, after one more unfavorable year, the company was firmly back in the black. In addition to the poor economy and fierce competition from other major canners, Calpak also faced pressure at the time from a flurry of new canneries. Enormous changes within the industry also came about as a result of the agricultural labor movement. The International Longshoremen and Warehousemen's Union (ILWU), after demonstrating its clout through well-planned strikes, eventually won the right to represent cannery workers in wage, plant safety, and benefit negotiations.

Having aided the allied effort during World War II, while sustaining profit losses and the temporary closing of operations in the Philippines, Calpak emerged a much stronger company during the late 1940s due to the postwar expansion and rising per capita consumption of canned products. In 1948 the company acquired East Coast producer Edgar H. Hurff Co. Two years later Calpak moved into new headquarters, and in 1951 the company named its seventh president, Roy Lucks. Braznell characterized him as: "coolly logical, an avid student of management sciences . . . a leader who recognized no jurisdictional boundaries and no allegiances other than those owed to the corporation and its shareholders." Under Lucks, wrote Braznell, "Calpak/Del Monte moved into the modern era."

By 1951, Calpak had an estimated worth of $158 million and annual revenues of $223 million. Yet it remained an unwieldy business whose potential for growth had barely been tapped. Until the end of his presidency in 1963, Lucks drove the company forward not so much by acquisition as by a devotion to marketing research, field sales, new promotions, new product introductions (including fruit drinks), and a consolidation of its operating units. Of course one merger did prove singularly beneficial to Calpak. This was the purchase of a two-thirds interest in Canadian Canners Limited in 1956. The $14-million-dollar deal attracted considerable attention from industry analysts, for it not only gave Calpak a controlling voice in the operations of the world's second-largest fruit and vegetable canner, but it also ensured a dominant position for the company in the prized British trade bloc.

When Jack Countryman succeeded Lucks, he fortified Del Monte's competitive advantages by establishing a highly efficient warehouse distribution system. In 1967, in an attempt to heighten the company's profile and attract new management talent, he gave Calpak the name it had come to prize above all others, Del Monte. After streamlining its now famous shield logo, the Del Monte Corporation launched boldly into the new territory of soft drinks (which was abandoned after four years) as well as an entire line of canned fruit drinks (which survived until 1974). Other forays included potato chips, frozen french fries, fruit turnovers, frozen prepared entrees, and real estate. Only the last two held any real promise for the company. Strong earnings growth typified the period not because of these attempts at diversification but because of Countryman's parallel commitment to international expansion. The president also proved astute in thwarting a potential takeover from United Fruit (now Chiquita Brands) by acquiring a Miami-based banana importer which, under a U.S. District Court antitrust ruling, nullified any such attempt. United would later sell its Guatemalan operations to Del Monte for $20 million, thus conferring status on the canner as a potentially major player in the fresh fruit market. Alfred W. Eames, Jr. assumed the reins from Countryman in 1968, just prior to a "canner's recession." Accordingly, profits during 1969 and 1970 dropped substantially.

Profit Improvement Project, or PIP, teams dominated Del Monte corporate culture during the 1970s. U.S. Grocery Products, U.S. Subsidiaries, International Grocery Products, and Seafood were named as the company's major divisions and decentralization became the guiding management philosophy. By 1978, Del Monte had weathered several economic crises—the devaluation of the dollar, rising manufacturing costs, and price freezes—to emerge with record sales of $1.56 billion. Through conservative management of its assets, it was positioning itself for a pivotal acquisition of large proportions that might render it less vulnerable to downswings in its core industry. However, the company's balance sheets were beginning to look so attractive that its privately issued stock, which was once closely held but now freely traded among a widening circle of private investors, began unexpectedly ratcheting upward. In August 1978, J. Paul Sticht and Joseph Abely, Jr. of R. J. Reynolds Industries arranged a meeting with the new Del Monte president, Dick Landis. In a little over a month an agreement to merge, worth $618 million, was reached and then officially ratified in early 1979, with Del Monte becoming the acquired rather than the acquirer.

For the next ten years, Del Monte benefited from the added RJR Foods labels (Hawaiian Punch, Chun King, Patio, etc.) but also suffered from RJR managerial impulses. The company underwent at least four reorganizations, as well as a succession of managers, and saw its longtime San Francisco headquarters moved to Miami. All of this came to an abrupt end in 1988, when KKR effected the biggest leveraged buyout in U.S. history, purchasing RJR for more than $24 billion. In order to reduce debt incurred by the transaction, substantial portions of Del Monte were auctioned off to overseas buyers. A new Del Monte management led by Ewan Macdonald, who had served as marketing vice-president since 1985, salvaged the remainder of the business via another leveraged buyout in 1990. The cost of this acquisition was $1.48 billion, 80 percent of which was financed with outside capital. According to Fara Warner in

Adweek's Marketing Week: "Del Monte is one of the success stories to come out of the RJR leveraged buyout, despite the heavy debt load the current owners incurred in buying Del Monte from RJR; sales have grown annually by 9 percent during Macdonald's tenure." Most attribute the success to Macdonald's strategy of advertising only in magazines. Yet, a $50 million dollar campaign to introduce the failed Del Monte Vegetable Classics, a considerable portion of which was earmarked for television ads, belied this strategy. Although Del Monte still ranks number one in brand preference in several categories and controls 16 percent of the $3.5 billion canned vegetable market, its future is far from clear. In May 1992, a number of newspapers reported that Italian financier Sergio Cragnotti, owner of Cragnotti & Partners Capital Investment, was preparing to offer a cash and debt-assumption package worth $800 million for the U.S. food concern. George Anders, writing in the *Wall Street Journal,* surmised that "If Del Monte's owners aren't able to fetch more money for the food company, they may choose to forgo a sale at present and hold on to the business for another year or two, in hopes of brighter sales prospects later on."

Further Reading: Braznell, William, *California's Finest: The History of the Del Monte Corporation,* San Francisco: Del Monte Corporation, 1982; Paris, Ellen, "Swimming Through Syrup," *Forbes,* November 21, 1983; Elliott, Dorinda, "Dole and Del Monte Are Staying Put—No Matter What," *Business Week,* November 18, 1985; Maremont, Mark, "Meet Asil Nadir, the Billion-Dollar Fruit King," *Business Week,* September 18, 1989; Waldman, Peter, "RJR Completes Del Monte Sale for $1.48 Billion," *Wall Street Journal,* January 11, 1990; Loeffelholz, Suzanne, "Thrice Shy: Del Monte and Sansui Are the Jewels in Polly Peck's Crown," *Financial World,* May 29, 1990; "Del Monte Names Macdonald CEO," *Advertising Age,* October 22, 1990; Johnson, Bradley, "Vexed over Vegetables: Churlish Children Hawk Del Monte's New Line," *Advertising Age,* January 14, 1991; "A Century of Growing," San Francisco: Del Monte Corporation, 1991; "A Time to Grow," *Brand News: A Quarterly Publication for the Employees of Del Monte Foods,* March 1991; "Refinancing of Debt Related to Buy-Out Is Completed," *Wall Street Journal,* September 13, 1991; Warner, Fara, "What's Happening at Del Monte Foods?," *Adweek's Marketing Week,* November 18, 1991; Anders, George, "Italian Financier Begins Talks Aimed at Buying Del Monte for $300 Million," *Wall Street Journal,* May 28, 1992; Warner, Fara, "Del Monte Has a Rendezvous with an Italian Suitor," *Adweek's Marketing Week,* June 1, 1992.

—Jay P. Pederson

Delaware North Companies
Incorporated

DELAWARE NORTH COMPANIES INCORPORATED

438 Main Street
Buffalo, New York 14202
U.S.A.
(716) 858-5000
Fax: (716) 858-5266

Private Company
Incorporated: 1915 as Jacobs Brothers
Employees: 40,000
Sales: $1.5 billion
SICs: 5812 Eating Places; 3339 Primary Nonferrous Metals
Nec; 2731 Book Publishing; 6719 Holding Companies Nec

Delaware North Companies Incorporated is a privately owned holding company that operates over 200 subsidiaries. The two largest companies in the Delaware North family are Sportsystems Corporation and Sportservice Corporation. Sportsystems, which owns and operates nine horse- and dog-racing tracks, runs the most extensive chain of pari-mutuel wagering facilities in the United States. The pari-mutuel business accounts for about half of Delaware North's yearly revenue. Sportservice specializes in large venue food service, most notably at sports arenas. Sportservice provides the concessions for six major league baseball teams, three National Hockey League teams, and one member each of the National Basketball Association and the National Football League. It also operates concessions at convention centers and parks. Food service and concessions account for about 31 percent of Delaware North's revenue. Delaware North also owns the Boston Garden, home to the NBA's Boston Celtics and the NHL's Boston Bruins, while the Bruins team is owned by Delaware North owner Jeremy Jacobs. Through its Concession Air Corporation subsidiary, Delaware North provides airport and in-flight food service to over 250 million travelers each year. Further areas in which Delaware North businesses operate include publishing, metals, and typography.

The three Jacobs brothers, Marvin, Charles, and Louis, began the concession business that would grow to become Delaware North in 1915. Their parents, Polish immigrants, had moved the family to Buffalo from Manhattan's Lower East Side around the turn of the century. From a very early age, the brothers were hawking food and services at public gathering places. Louis sold peanuts at Buffalo's ball park and popcorn at a local burlesque house. His older brothers worked the Delaware Park Lake, renting canoes, shining shoes, and selling newspapers. From these humble roots, they learned the trade and saved the money to open more concession booths.

Furthermore, the brothers opened stands in theaters in other cities and their first baseball park concession operation at the old field in Jersey City. Their baseball business grew quickly after World War I, expanding in 1919 into the ballpark occupied by the Baltimore team of the International League. They began operating the concessions at Buffalo Bisons baseball games back home as well. The Jacobs brothers would eventually become shareholders, and later, outright owners of that team. The company's first major break came in 1927, when it was awarded its first major league concession contract by Frank Navin, owner of the Detroit Tigers. Overseen by Louis, the first year operations at Navin Field were so successful that the company brought in twice as much money as the previous operator had. At the end of the season, Louis gave Navin a check for $12,500, explaining that the contract had been unfair and the owner deserved a bigger cut. Needless to say, this gesture played well around the league, and the Jacobses began receiving calls from team owners throughout the country. Sportservice was still handling concessions for the Tigers 65 years later.

As Sportservice Co., the company made further inroads into major league baseball concessions in the 1930s, with Louis Jacobs in charge. An important tactic for Jacobs was to loan money to struggling sports franchises in return for guaranteed concessions contracts. During this time, Jacobs dealt with several well-known figures in baseball, including Bill Veeck, who worked with Jacobs on franchise deals in Milwaukee, Cleveland, St. Louis, and Chicago. Although decreased baseball attendance due to the Depression pushed Sportservice to the brink of bankruptcy in 1932, the company was bailed out by a group of baseball owners led by Navin and the Pittsburgh Pirates' Barney Dreyfuss. Thus the relationship between the Jacobses and baseball owners was cemented. Another example of this special tie occurred in 1951, when the legendary Connie Mack borrowed $250,000 interest-free from Jacobs to assist his financially struggling Philadelphia Athletics. Jacobs later helped Mack sell the team, which was then moved to Kansas City.

The company began to diversify in the 1930s and 1940s, especially into professional hockey and pari-mutuel racing, first as foodservice providers, and later owning some facilities. In the mid-1930s, Sportservice invented the ice show. The earliest ice shows were merely exhibitions put on by skating clubs, bearing little resemblance to such lavish modern descendants as the Ice Capades. Sportservice was active in the formation of the Arena Managers Association, which underwrote attractions that single arenas could not afford to produce. The Ice Follies first appeared in Minneapolis, then moved to a Chicago hotel, where they were initially a major flop. In 1937, Jacobs joined with a group of investors to help support the floundering Syracuse team of the International Hockey League. When all of the other members of the group dropped out one by one, Jacobs became the team's owner by default. The team was moved to Buffalo, but it never really recovered financially. It was eventually sold to the Chicago Blackhawks system. In 1939, Sportservice made an agreement with the American Hockey League franchise in

Providence that covered not only concession rights, but also granted Sportservice final authority on any sale or transfer of the club until 1999. This incredible contract was not publicly known until the late 1960s, when a Boston financial consultant tried to buy the Providence team and the Rhode Island Auditorium. The deal was nearly complete before he uncovered the remarkable 60-year agreement. It turned out later that Sportservice owned even the land on which the auditorium was built.

Sportservice received a long-term contract in 1939 for the concession operations at Washington National Airport. The company's income from this new pursuit was held back at first by a struggle for jurisdiction over the airport between the District of Columbia and the Commonwealth of Virginia. Virginia won, which meant that no alcohol could be served in airport restaurants, a prohibition Jacobs had not figured into his bid. The company began serving food at drive-in movie theaters in the early 1940s, beginning in western New York and quickly spreading throughout the United States. Among the racing facilities at which Sportservice began handling concessions in the 1940s was Hazel Park Raceway, located just outside of Detroit. The company later acquired a 12 percent interest in that facility, a holding which would later draw much negative attention, since the track was largely controlled by reputed organized crime members, and this control was largely financed by Jacobs.

In 1948, Jacobs moved the headquarters of the Sportservice operation into a cramped second floor office at 703 Main Street in Buffalo, where it remained for decades. Sportservice's move to become a corporate giant began in the early 1950s, when Charles and Marvin Jacobs retired. They sold their shares in the company to Louis, leaving him in complete control of the business. In 1952, the company began in-flight foodservice on planes bound out of Buffalo, an operation formerly handled by an outfit called Sky Chefs. The race track business also expanded briskly in the 1950s. Among Sportservice's acquisitions in the area was Magnolia Park in Louisiana, later called Jefferson Downs. Sportservice began running concessions there in 1954, and ended up controlling the facility when it came close to bankruptcy several years later, another episode that yielded bad press and corruption allegations for the company.

The 1960s were a decade of remarkable growth for Sportservice. The company entered the decade by operating the concessions for the 1960 Olympic Games in Rome. In 1961, Jacobs formed the Emprise Corporation, a holding company whose function was to keep separate the company's proprietorship of racetracks and sports arenas from the operations of Sportservice, its principal subsidiary. Emprise began to dabble in real estate and distributorships as well, including among its acquisitions the Joseph Strauss Co., western New York's Zenith distributorship. In 1963, the Jacobs family obtained controlling interest in the Cincinnati Royals professional basketball team and the Cincinnati Gardens, the site of the Royals' home court. Louis had invested in the Gardens when it was first constructed, and as the arena's finances required, had increased his stake to 40 percent. In the 1963 acquisition, the family paid just over $400,000 for an additional 40 percent of the Gardens and 56 percent of the team. Max Jacobs, one of Louis's sons, was later elected chair of the Royals' board.

Emprise's expansion in the 1960s was international as well. Sportservice became concessionaire to royalty in the early 1960s, when it began serving food at England's Royal Ascot Race Track. The company also won concession rights for the New York World's Fair and for Expo '67 in Montreal. In 1968, a year after the deaths of brothers Charles and Marvin, Louis Jacobs died—at his desk as he had long predicted. Shortly after Louis's death, an editorial appeared in *The Sporting News* recommending that Louis and his brothers be enshrined in the Baseball Hall of Fame at Cooperstown, New York for their unique contribution to the game. By this time, the company had grown to over 30 times its 1953 size. Sportservice had over 500 operating units, and sold concessions in more race tracks and sports stadiums than anyone else. The company was feeding fans in such diverse settings as Puerto Rican racetracks, posh Florida jai alai frontons, and middle American bowling alleys. Sportservice's estimated gross revenues for 1968 were around $50 million.

Leadership of Emprise was assumed by Louis Jacobs's two sons, Jeremy and Max. Jeremy had learned the business at his father's side over the previous fourteen years, and he became president of Emprise at age 28. Max, three years older than Jeremy, had joined the company only two years earlier, after a moderately successful stretch as a Broadway actor. He became executive vice-president and secretary. The company did not lose a step through the generational leadership transition. The company continued to loan millions of dollars to strapped baseball teams. The Jacobs brothers loaned $2 million to the Montreal Expos and received a multi-year exclusive concession contract. A similar deal was cut with the Seattle Pilots, who, after their move to Milwaukee in 1970, awarded Sportservice concession rights for 25 years. $12 million in financing for Busch Stadium in St. Louis resulted in another multi-decade concession arrangement for Sportservice.

However, Emprise was rocked by a series of scandals, accusations, and convictions in the early 1970s. In 1972, the U.S. Justice Department began investigating Emprise in regard to possible antitrust violations. Papers filed in Buffalo suggested that Emprise's lending power gave it an unfair edge over other companies in competition for sports concession business. A similar antitrust action was undertaken in Atlanta to investigate Emprise's racetrack operations in the southeastern part of the country. The Justice Department also began to look into several of the company's labor union contracts. Later that year, the House Select Committee on Crime began to hold hearings concerning Emprise's connections with organized crime figures. Much of this attention focused on Emprises well-documented associations with Anthony Zerilli and Michael Polizzi, two of Emprise's co-investors in Detroit's Hazel Park Racing Association. Investigations revealed that Louis Jacobs had made interest-free loans in the 1950s to Zerilli and to Jack Tocco, a reputed member of the Detroit Mafia. In a related case, Emprise and six individuals, including Zerilli and Polizzi, were convicted of concealing ownership of the Frontier Hotel and Casino in Las Vegas. The defendants were also found guilty of related racketeering charges. In the aftermath of these convictions, Emprise was forced to give up control of a number of its betting facilities. The company's dog racing operations in Arizona were placed under the legal authority of a trustee appointed by the Arizona State Racing Commission. The liquor control authorities in Missouri also put the Emprise units operating concessions at Busch Stadium, the St. Louis Arena, and Kiel Auditorium into trusteeship.

In the fall of 1975, Sportservice, and Jeremy, Max, and Lawrence Jacobs individually, purchased the Boston Bruins of the NHL, plus their home stadium, the Boston Garden, from Storer Broadcasting Company. However, the investigations of Emprise continued into this period, and by the end of 1976, the company's fitness to retain its contracts had been challenged in eight of the 28 states in which it held liquor licenses, and six of the nine states in which it had pari-mutuel operations. Although several states restored Emprise's operating licenses on appeal, the company's plea for a presidential pardon in 1977 was rejected, leading a number of states to deny Emprise licenses according to those states' laws prohibiting convicted felons from holding liquor licenses. In 1977, a new parent holding company, Sportsystems Corporation, was developed. The company's revenues were estimated that year at $275 million. Of that total, $125 million came from arena food service, $80 million from subsidiaries in steel, smelting, and appliance distribution, and $70 million from the eight horse tracks, eight dog tracks, and two jai alai fronton the company owned, either wholly or in part.

Emprise was dissolved in 1978, and as Sportsystems, the company diversified further into the metals industry during the late 1970s. In 1977, Sportsystems acquired Fitzsimons Steel Co., a manufacturer of cold-finished bars based in Youngstown, Ohio. Sportsystems already owned Ramco Steel Inc. of Buffalo by that time. Two years later, Pennsylvania Steel Foundry and Machine Co. was purchased, and one additional metal concern, Aluminum Smelting and Refining Co. of Maple Heights, Ohio, was also acquired during this period.

In 1980, the name of the parent company was changed from Sportsystems to Delaware North Companies Incorporated. Sportsystems continued to exist as the subsidiary that owned and managed pari-mutuel facilities. In the early 1980s, Sportservice tapped into the southern Florida leisure market by acquiring the concession rights for the elaborate new Miami Metrozoo. The company's revenue from foodservice alone in 1981 reached $174 million. Sportservice embarked on a campaign around that time to modernize its stadium concession facilities. $12 million was spent refurbishing the concession areas and restaurants, and an ambitious training program for employees was added as well. These efforts produced a 200 percent jump in sales at the company's five major league ball parks.

Through the 1980s, Delaware North seemed to recover completely from the controversy surrounding it during the 1970s. The company's public image was enhanced by such programs as Sportservice's temperance campaign of 1985, in which concession stand workers were trained to recognize intoxicated patrons and limit sales of alcohol to such patrons. In the next few years, Sportservice expanded its convention center concession business. Two such venues were added in 1987, the San Jose Convention and Cultural Center and the Bakersfield Civic Auditorium. With these facilities added, the company's convention center operations contributed over $50 million to annual revenues. Sportservice also expanded its minor league concession business, which included food service for Nashville Sounds and Louisville Redbirds games. Sportservice used the minor league operations much as the teams themselves did: to prepare managers for future promotion to a big league ballpark.

In the late 1980s, Delaware North began to focus even more on its bread-and-butter businesses, dog- and horse-racing, airport concessions, and sports concessions. The company's airport concession operations were given a major boost by the purchase of the restaurant and concession division of Sky Chefs from Onyx Capital Corp., and its merger with Delaware North's Air Terminal Services subsidiary. This lifted the company's Concession Air Corp. subsidiary into the number two spot nationally among airport food service companies. During this period, Delaware North built a new dog track in Phoenix, converted a Florida jai alai facility into a dog track, and purchased three existing dog-racing sites. In 1989 and 1990, the company made somewhat of an exit from the parking facilities business, both in the United States and in Europe. By 1991, parking accounted for only about 8 percent of company revenue, down from 23 percent in 1985.

Delaware North expanded its international operations substantially in the early 1990s. The company maintained its parking operations in Australia and Hungary when most of its domestic parking business was sold off. Concession operations in Australia and New Zealand were beefed up by the purchase of three Australian companies. Additionally, concession contracts were obtained for two Budapest horse-racing tracks. In late 1991, Delaware North, in a joint venture with a company based in the United Arab Emirates, won the food service contract for the fire-fighting and engineering efforts in Kuwait's oil fields following the war there. In 1992, the company's Australian subsidiary was awarded a ten-year contract worth $70 million for food service at Melbourne's Tullamarine Airport. Later that year, Delaware North signed with the Moscow Circus to provide food and souvenir concessions for 40 years. Domestically, the Sportservice subsidiary gained concession rights for a number of sports teams in 1992. These included the San Francisco Giants of major league baseball, the NFL's Buffalo Bills, the Charlotte Hornets of the NBA, and the NHL's Tampa Bay Lightning. With long-term concession contracts in every major sport, racetrack holdings throughout America, and airport concession contracts throughout the world, Delaware North seems to have a secure future as long as people continue to enjoy airline travel, gambling, and sporting events.

Principal Subsidiaries: Sportservice Corporation; Sportsystems Corporation; Concession Air Corporation; New Boston Garden Corporation; Boston Professional Hockey Association, Inc.; Delaware North (Australia) Pty. Ltd.; Halsey Publishing Company; Arrow Typographers, Inc.

Further Reading: "An Empire Built on Peanuts, pts 1–7," *Buffalo News,* October 1968; Gapay, Les, "Fair or Foul?" *Wall Street Journal,* March 7, 1972; Underwood, John, "Look What Louie Wrought," *Sports Illustrated,* May 29, 1972; "Emprise Corp., 6 Men Draw Stiff Penalties in Frontier Hotel Case," *Wall Street Journal,* July 11, 1972; Cady, Steve, "Albany is Beginning Inquiry into Emprise, a Racing Operator," *New York Times,* December 28, 1976; Marro, Anthony, "Emprise Corp. Loses Plea for U.S. Pardon," *New York Times,* September 29,

1977; Timmins, Mary, "Sportservice Stalks Leisure Market in Miame," *Restaurant Business,* June 1, 1982; "Sportservice— There've Been Some Changes Made," *Restaurants and Institutions,* September 1, 1982; "Sportservice Launches Temperance Campaign," *Nation's Restaurant News,* May 20, 1985; Newman, Melinda, "Convention Center Biz Focus of Sportservice Expansion," *Amusement Business,* August 29, 1987; Hackett, Vernell, "Sportservice, Tiger Stadium Working Relationship Still Strong After 60 Years," *Amusement Business,* July 23, 1990; Robinson, David, "Delaware North Realigns Global Operations," *Buffalo News,* May 24, 1992; O'Brien, Tim, "Sportservice's Six New Contracts Could Mean $4 Million Annually," *Amusement Business,* June 1, 1992; Delaware North Companies, Company Brochure, Buffalo, New York: Delaware North Companies Incorporated, 1992.

—Robert R. Jacobson

 **DELUXE** CORPORATION

DELUXE CORPORATION

1080 West Company Road F
P.O. Box 64399
St. Paul, Minnesota 55164-0399
U.S.A.
(612) 483-7111
Fax: (612) 481-4163

Public Company
Incorporated: 1920 as DeLuxe Check Printers, Inc.
Employees: 17,400
Sales: $1.53 billion
Stock Exchanges: New York
SICs: 2759 Commercial Printing Nec; 2782 Blankbooks &
    Looseleaf Binders; 3953 Marking Devices; 2761 Manifold
    Business Forms

A shining example of a company built upon the right idea at the right time, Deluxe Corporation is the largest supplier of checks, deposit slips, and other financial documents in the United States, holding over 50 percent market share in a $1.9 billion industry. Since its 1987 purchase of Current, Inc., it has also become the nation's foremost direct-mail marketer of greeting cards and related products. The company's long and enviable track record has in large part mirrored the evolution of American banking and financial services technology, from the relatively simple boom-and-bust 1920s through the complex decades of the 1950s and 1960s, when electronic automation revolutionized the industry, to the current rise of electronic funds transfer (EFT). As recently as 1985, check printing accounted for 96 percent of Deluxe's sales. However, under the leadership of CEO Harold Haverty, this figure was lowered to 69 percent by 1989 through an expanded focus on such product-services as processing software, account verification, ATM cards, sales development, business and health care forms, and the specialty products offered through Current. For many analysts, the diversification was long overdue, particularly given repeated predictions that checks would soon be obsolete; yet, 54 consecutive years of sales increases, regular returns on equity of 25–30 percent, and the continuing viability of the personal check, have proved the company right in its slow and judicious move away from its original market.

The foundation for Deluxe was laid in 1905 when William Roy Hotchkiss purchased a small Wisconsin newspaper named *The*

Barron County Shield. Well acquainted with the printing business since boyhood, Hotchkiss thought he had found his niche, particularly after he became publisher and co-owner of the more prestigious *Dunn County News* of Menomonie in 1908. For the next five years Hotchkiss oversaw the development of this paper into the largest and most respected weekly in the state. A protracted illness, however, forced his early retirement from the newspaper business and his relocation to the more congenial climate of southern California. His entrepreneurial drive still intact, Hotchkiss decided to raise chickens but failed, despite conceiving the idea of selling pre-cut chickens to grocery stores.

In 1915 Hotchkiss returned to the Midwest and settled in St. Paul, vowing, according to company annals, "to do one thing and one thing only, but do it better, faster and more economically than anyone else." Recalling his printing days and a special assignment of printing bank checks for a friend, Hotchkiss decided to claim the creation and marketing of personalized checks as his business. The distinctive feature of his checks would be quality imprinting of information unique to each customer. Hotchkiss borrowed $300 to secure the necessary equipment and a small office in the People's Bank Building in downtown St. Paul. In the two months of operations for 1915 the eager salesman attracted $23 in orders against $293 in expenses. Despite such unpromising numbers, the company would soon find success. As Terry Blake wrote in *A History of the Deluxe Corporation, 1915–1990*, several factors favored Hotchkiss's enterprise, particularly the printer's choice of location. The Minneapolis/St. Paul area, already densely populated with financial institutions, was destined to become a major national banking center—and therefore a major check clearinghouse—through Minneapolis's selection as the site of the Federal Reserve Bank of the Ninth District. Equally important was Hotchkiss's timing. In 1915 approximately five billion checks were being written by American businesses each year. This immense market was being served by various printing houses, none of which was more than regionally dominant, particularly noteworthy for its service, or even remotely prepared to foster new business in a virtually untapped domain: individual consumers.

Hotchkiss's early marketing of his company's services consisted of mail-order brochures sent to all regions of Minnesota. His first customers were healthy outstate banks, with less deposits than the Twin Cities banks but also far fewer check-printing competitors. In 1916 Hotchkiss succeeded in tapping the metropolitan market with contracts from both the People's Bank and the Western State Bank of St. Paul. Sales for his first full year of business reached $4,173. This same year Hotchkiss welcomed printer Einer Swanson as a business partner. Swanson replaced Hotchkiss as chief salesman and may also have been responsible for determining the company's name. The new arrangement allowed Hotchkiss, an instinctive inventor, the freedom to design and develop new machinery to enhance printing quality, speed delivery time, and save money. By 1918 the company's sales had soared to $18,961 and Hotchkiss issued his first catalog. The following year, as sales more than doubled, the company relocated to its first, full-sized plant. In 1920 Swanson and Hotchkiss incorporated as DeLuxe Check Printers, Inc. and became equal partners.

Growth during the 1920s was phenomenal because of both timing and the special imprint of Hotchkiss's vision. From the beginning he had decided that his business would emphasize quality and service. Service, for him, became synonymous with speed; he instituted the still standing company goal of 48-hour turnaround on any order, or "in one day, out the next." As the Federal Reserve established new banking districts, Deluxe, as soon as it was able, moved in to claim its share of the check business. First came Chicago, then Kansas City, then Cleveland, then New York. By the end of the decade, sales and net income had risen to $579,000 and $42,000, respectively.

Perhaps more indicative of the company's long-term prospects were Hotchkiss's unique advancements in check products and printing technology during the 1920s. In 1922 he developed one of the first small pocket checks—nicknamed the LH, or "Little Handy"—to complement the larger, end-register-style business check. The initial market for this new check was to be the wise and discerning consumer. As catalog copy from this era declared, "The Individualized Check today is considered almost as necessary in leading social and business circles as the calling or business card. It marks the user as a man of distinction and discrimination." Yet, as Blake pointed out, "Hotchkiss had no definite strategy for marketing the personalized Handy checks. Bankers, too, were skeptical of the horizontal register and deemed Hotchkiss's invention a fad. As a result, the LH, destined to become the most successful product in Deluxe's history, remained an obscure novelty for a number of years." Hotchkiss realized more immediate profits from a series of important, speed-enhancing inventions, which included the Hotchkiss Imprinting Press (HIP), patented in 1925; a two-way perforator, perfected the same year; and the Hotchkiss Lithograph Press (HLP), patented in 1928.

With the stock market crash in 1929 came an end to a free-spending era. From 1920 to 1929, Deluxe saw sales increase by an average of 32.3 percent annually. By comparison, from 1930 to 1939, sales increased only 55 percent for the entire ten-year span. After suffering its only full-year loss in 1932, the company began to rebound as newly elected President Franklin D. Roosevelt's sweeping reforms for the banking industry took hold. A potentially devastating period was transformed and, like F.D.R., Deluxe hastened the transformation with a revolutionary new sales program. The program was guided not by Hotchkiss but by George McSweeney, a former Deluxe paper supplier hired by the company in 1932 expressly for the task of building a sales force and boosting revenue. McSweeney emphasized personalized attention over catalog promotions and worked closely with bankers in developing personalized check programs. Viewing Deluxe as a service—rather than product-oriented—business, he sought ways to aid financial institutions in boosting their own incomes. Promoting small checking accounts for individual customers, all of whom represented potential loan clients, became a mutual goal and the LH the mutually agreed upon tool to attract these customers. McSweeney also directed his sales force to refocus attention on serving rural banks; by 1939, this segment had grown to represent 58 percent of Deluxe's annual revenue. Finally, McSweeney instilled in his sales force a "guidance and counsel" approach. With the passing of the Social Security Act in 1935 came an opportunity for McSweeney and his representatives to thoroughly research the law and then educate their banking customers. "To Mc-

Sweeney," writes Blake, "it was important for Deluxe to establish itself as a leader, and Deluxe's impressive anticipation of an industry-altering event like Social Security set a precedent the company has always followed."

In 1940 Deluxe saw sales surpass $1 million. A year later, McSweeney became company president at his own request. LH orders had multiplied from 1,000 in 1938 to 100,000 and would continue to grow exponentially. With World War II and the ration banking program which necessitated new ration checks, sales also jumped dramatically. A new service-monitoring system was instituted by production superintendent Joe Rose in 1948. Within a year, two-day delivery fulfillment advanced from 75 percent to nearly 90 percent. The advent of the teletypesetter and new plant construction in Chicago, Kansas City, and St. Paul capped the decade.

During the 1950s, overall sales rose by 275 percent. Much of the company's growth could be attributed to the widespread popularity of the LH. Equally important was Deluxe's national coverage of the commercial banking industry. By 1960 it had contracted for a portion of sales with 99 percent of the country's commercial banks. Meanwhile, Deluxe's largest competitor, New York-based Todd Company, was struggling to hold market share after a corporate takeover. With ten plants strategically spread across the United States to better serve its customers, Deluxe could boast sales of $24 million and anticipate a bright future, with steadily rising numbers for total domestic checks written, which now numbered nearly 13 billion. Furthermore, many bankers now accorded Deluxe special status as an industry leader. This was particularly true after Deluxe's fundamental involvement with the development of magnetic ink character recognition (MICR), which after years of back-and-forth negotiations between the American Bankers Association, leading high-tech companies, and check printers, was now becoming the industry norm.

With McSweeney's death in 1962 and the continuing maturation of MICR technology came numerous changes for the company. McSweeney's successor, Joe Rose, was faced with dire predictions that a checkless society would be a reality by 1970. Deluxe's recourse was to embrace MICR for all types of document processing and to launch a New Products Research Division. By 1967, sales for the three-year-old division from loan coupon books, process control documents, and deposit/withdrawal slips topped $1 million. Deluxe underwent another difficult, though ultimately beneficial, change in 1965 when it went public after pressure from various estates who complained of the artificially low trading prices for their stock. This same year, Rose satisfactorily settled another potential setback when the U.S. Post Office announced new coding and presorting regulations. A major user of the public mails, Deluxe could ill afford increased expenses or undue delays caused by the new regulations. Consequently, Rose met directly with the deputy postmaster general and obtained permission to establish his own in-plant post offices where mail could be easily sorted and sent to save the company and the local post offices both time and money. Rose closed the 1960s with more than $85 million in sales.

Despite serious inflation during the 1970s which caused production costs to rise, Deluxe performed well. By 1979 sales had risen to $366 million and net income to $39 million. This was especially impressive after considering the large capital expenditures involved in new plant openings, which arose at the pace of three per year. A considerable amount of new equipment, including minicomputers and the Deluxe Encoder Printer (DEP), also made their debut during this decade. Under Gene Olson, who became president in 1976 and CEO in 1978, Deluxe acceded to critics on Wall Street—long wary of the company's dependency on essentially one product—and cautiously diversified into pre-inked endorsement stamps.

Growth continued unabated during the 1980s; by 1988 sales had surpassed $1 billion. Among the new products that kept Deluxe firmly in place as a financial products market leader were three-on-a-page, computer-form business checks, pegboard checks, and money market related documents. Although the financial industry suffered repeatedly by failures of large-sized banks, such developments actually increased Deluxe's competitiveness, for as the institutions failed, numerous small check printers ceased business as well. By 1989, less than ten full-service printers remained. In one sense, however, such events were singularly frightening, for few could anticipate the future of banking. Harold Haverty, elected president in 1983 and CEO in 1986, wrestled anew with the problem of diversification (analysts for *Forbes* had twice predicted the company's downfall, due to its traditionally cautious acquisition policy). In part to satisfy the analysts, but also to increase its presence as a provider of wide business services, Deluxe purchased Chex Systems, John A. Pratt and Associates, and Colwell Systems, consequently entering such new fields as account verification, marketing services, and direct-mail supply to the dental and medical industry. In 1986 Deluxe purchased A. O. Smith Data Systems and instantly became a leader in the burgeoning EFT industry. In 1987 the company purchased Current, which it now touts as "the nation's largest direct mail marketer of greeting cards and consumer specialty products."

Doubts about the company and its future have largely ceased. As reported by Ignatius Chithelen for *Forbes,* "Deluxe's new businesses have grown to the point where they now account for 35 percent of Deluxe's revenues and an estimated 25 percent of its operating income." In fiscal 1991, the Data Systems Division (responsible now not only for EFT, but also electronic benefit transfer, point-of-sale retail, and automated clearing house processing) reported 12 percent sales growth. The Business Systems Division (responsible for short-run business forms for small businesses) experienced 11 percent growth. Deluxe Check Printers, as evidenced by the company's recent name change, has now become a contributing unit to, rather than the centerpiece of, the corporation. "What happens if checkbooks eventually go the way of the buggy whip and the vacuum tube?" asked Reed Abelson, a *Forbes* forecaster. "Deluxe," he decided, "seems to be well prepared." Nonetheless, checks continue to be cashed and Deluxe reigns as the market leader in service (99.56 percent error-free delivery, 97.2 percent on-time delivery).

Principal Subsidiaries: ChexSystems, Inc.; Current, Inc.; Deluxe Data Systems, Inc.; Electronic Transaction Corp.; Nelco, Inc.

Further Reading: Zemke, Ron, and Dick Schaaf, "Deluxe Corporation," *The Service Edge: 101 Companies That Profit from Customer Care,* New York: New American Library, 1989; Blake, Terry, *A History of Deluxe Corporation, 1915–1990,* St. Paul: Deluxe Corporation, 1990; Barthel, Matt, "To Bolster Checks, Deluxe Buys Authorization Service," *American Banker,* January 4, 1991, p. 3; Chithelen, Ignatius, "Printing Money," *Forbes,* March 18, 1991, p. 116; Sawaya, Zina, "The Underpaid: Relative Pain (Harold Haverty)," *Forbes,* May 27, 1991, p. 222; Abelson, Reed, "The Check Is in the (Electronic) Mail," *Forbes,* January 6, 1992, p. 99; Kutler, Jeffrey, "3 ACH Operators Band Together," *American Banker,* April 20, 1992, p. 3; "Company Profile," July 1992, St. Paul: Deluxe Corporation.

—Jay P. Pederson

DEUTSCHE BP

DEUTSCHE BP AKTIENGESELLSCHAFT

Überseering 2
2000 Hamburg 60
Germany
(040) 6395-2162
Fax: (040) 6395-2314

*Wholly Owned Subsidiary of the British Petroleum Company
  PLC*
Incorporated: 1904 as Aktiengesellschaft für österreichische
  und ungarische Mineralölprodukte (OLEX)
Employees: 4,199 including affiliates
Sales: DM 9.55 billion (US$6.30 billion; DM 14.06 billion
  before mineral oil tax)
SICs: 1311 Crude Petroleum and Natural Gas; 1382 Oil and
  Gas Exploration Services; 2911 Petroleum Refining; 5172
  Petroleum Products

Deutsche BP Aktiengesellschaft is one of the top suppliers of
petroleum products in the competitively fragmented German
market. The company is actively engaged in all facets of the
petroleum industry: exploration, crude oil supplies, refining,
and petroleum products. Through its affiliates and subsidiaries,
Deutsche BP is also involved in petroleum transport and pipelines, a network of filling stations, and the chemical industry.
The only companies in Germany with a similar range of activities that are larger than Deutsche BP are Deutsche Shell and
Esso.

Although it is a subsidiary of the British Petroleum Company
(BP), Deutsche BP has a long history of its own going back to
the first decade of this century, and its predecessor was founded
a few years before that of BP. Despite two world wars, German
and British oil companies had long been doing business with
each other. In fact, British Petroleum—originally the Anglo-
Persian Oil Company—took its current name from a *German*
oil marketing company, British Petroleum Ltd., which it acquired in 1926.

Deutsche BP's history began in neighboring Austria, but it was
founded with the aim of serving the German market as well.
At the turn of the century the Austro-Hungarian Empire's oil
fields in Hungary, Rumania, and Galicia (now divided between
Poland and Ukraine) were among the few developed oil fields in
the world.

On July 1, 1904, a group of Viennese industrialists founded the
"Aktiengesellschaft für österreichische und ungarische Mineralölprodukte" (corporation for Austrian and Hungarian mineral oil products) with the initial capital of one million Kronen.
This essentially was a corporation to replace a cartel of Austrian
refineries, the Exportbüro der österreichischen Petroleum Raffinerien of 1902. The board of directors included the leading
figures of the Austrian oil and banking businesses. The first
president was Robert Freiherr Biedermann von Turnoy, and
vice presidents were Oskar Szirmai and Ludwig von Neurath.
Its business functions were, as entered in the Vienna commercial register: "Trade in petroleum and its by-products for itself
and third parties, especially export; the storage of petroleum and
its by-products as well as the rental, acquisition and establishment of reservoirs, storage areas and other facilities for storage
and shipment; and the investment in enterprises which operate
similar businesses."

Management of the young corporation was in the hands of a 30-
year-old bank clerk, Carl Adler, who had become familiar with
the financial interests of the oil industry through his administrative position in a Prague bank. He had also managed the predecessor business, the Exportbüro der österreichischen Petroleum
Raffinerien. Adler employed the next 12 partners. The firm soon
became known in Germany, Belgium, Holland, and Switzerland
by its telegram address of OLEX, derived from Petrolexport.

Europe at that time represented the largest and most profitable
market and the seat of the most intense competition. To compete with the excellence of American petroleum, OLEX's first
task was to standardize the quality of Austrian petroleum.
OLEX also sought to follow the American example of becoming a regional business, and thus acquired a series of subsidiaries for marketing its lighting oil in the major German cities:
Mainz, Breslau, Düsseldorf, Dresden, Munich, Hamburg, and
Berlin. In its first year, OLEX received important assistance
from the German regime, which had granted it favorable rail
cargo fares within Germany. To take full advantage of the
German market, in 1910 OLEX centralized its management at
its Berlin subsidiary, OLEX-Petroleum-Gesellschaft mbH, and
thus became a German-based company. The following year
OLEX became a subsidiary and sales organization for the
Deutsche Erdol Aktiengesellschaft (German crude oil corporation).

The primary consumer product derived from petroleum at the
time was still kerosene, for which the company also marketed
its own brand of lamps. However, it was not long before
gasoline and other fuel oils became the major business. In 1922
OLEX opened in Berlin the first modern "fuel station" in
Germany. By 1926 OLEX had 1226 gas pumps in service at
1086 filling stations and was planning the construction of another 1000 pumps.

In 1926 OLEX merged with the Deutsche Petroleum-Verkaufsgesellschaft mbH (German petroleum sales company) to become the OLEX Deutsche Petroleum-Verkaufsgesellschaft
mbH. It was here that the British became involved. The Anglo-
Persian Oil Company (APOC) of London, predecessor of Brit-

ish Petroleum, participated 40% in the new OLEX merger and thus obtained a German marketing organization for its products derived from its own crude oil deposits.

In that same year APOC also purchased another German oil company, a subsidiary of the Bremen-based Europäische Petroleum Union named the British Petroleum Company Ltd. This name, in which the word "British" originally reflected the fact that it marketed the Union's petroleum products in the United Kingdom, was ultimately assumed by APOC to become the BP of today. Three years later APOC increased its shares in OLEX to 75%. In 1930 the latter changed its name to OLEX Deutsche Benzin und Petroleum GmbH and took over the trademark BP, which by then was being used by APOC. The following year APOC became the sole stockholder of OLEX. This was also a time of great growth for OLEX, which quadrupled its sales between 1926 and 1932.

With the Soviet blockade of Berlin in 1948, OLEX permanently moved its headquarters from Berlin to Hamburg. Two years later its parent, the Anglo-Iranian Oil Company (previously APOC) brought into OLEX shares of two other German petroleum companies, the Europaischen Tanklager- und Transport AG (EUROTANK) and Runo-Everth Treibstoff und Ol AG. The resulting enterprise was renamed BP Benzin und Petroleum GmbH. In 1957 the firm legally changed from a private company to a joint-stock corporation, and accordingly changed its name to BP Benzin und Petroleum Aktiengesellschaft. It kept that name until 1974, when it assumed its current name, Deutsche BP Aktiengesellschaft.

Through the takeover of the Hamburg EUROTANK Refinery (renamed BP Refinery Hamburg-Finkenwerder) Deutsche BP also became a manufacturing company. In 1953 a platforming facility (for petroleum refining using a platinum catalyst) was erected at this refinery, the first such facility in the Federal Republic of Germany. In subsequent decades the addition of other refineries reflected BP's growth. In 1960 it put into operation the BP Ruhr Refinery in Hünxe bei Dinslaken, and in 1968 the BP Bavaria Refinery in Vohburg. With a capacity of 4 million tons, the Dinslaken refinery was the second-largest in the country at the time. However, in 1985, as a consequence of the radical changes in the energy market, the processing facilities of the refineries of Ruhr and Hamburg-Finkenwerder had to be closed. These sites continued to function as trade centers, though. Growth again in the late 1980s led to the founding in 1988 of a new refinery enterprise, Raffineriegesellschaft Vohburg/Ingolstadt mbH, as a technical association between BP Raffinerie Bayern in Vohburg and the Erdölraffinerie Ingolstadt AG. In 1991 output was 6.7 million tons annually, over half of which was automotive fuels. The following year work began on expanding the refinery's capabilities in order to satisfy the growing demand for automotive fuels and to improve their quality, by adding a second catalytic cracking unit and a deisohexanizer (to remove isohexane), a project in which DM 180 ($118.8) million would be invested over the next few years.

Deutsche BP also expanded by investing in the petrochemical industry. In 1957 it participated in the founding of EC Erdolchemie GmbH in Cologne-Worringen, a joint venture with Bayer AG, with each party owning 50%. EC Erdölchemie has since become one of the largest petrochemical companies in Europe. This was merely the first of a number of enterprises going beyond fuel oil production and distribution in which Deutsche BP would get involved. In 1967 BP Benzin und Petroleum acquired a majority share of the Oelwerken Julius Schindler GmbH (later to be renamed BP Oiltech GmbH) of Hamburg from the British Petroleum Company Limited. Subsequently its ownership was increased to 100%. Specializing in motor oils, BP Oiltech has grown to produce one-fifth of all lubricants sold on the German market. BP Oiltech also produces bitumen (a tar for asphalt) used in road building. In 1979 Deutsche BP purchased BP Chemie GmbH (today BP Chemicals) as a wholly owned subsidiary, with activities based in Düsseldorf in the marketing and sales of chemicals, solvents, and plastics. In 1986 Deutsche BP acquired a majority share in Globol GmbH and Globol International Vertriebs- und Entwicklungs-GmbH in Neuburg an der Donau, which is one of the leading manufacturers of household insecticides and hygiene products in Europe.

In the 1970s BP also began to make acquisitions in the plastics industry. In 1973 BP Benzin und Petroleum acquired its first shares of the synthetics manufacturer Alkor-Oerlikon Plastic GmbH in Wasserburg, which later became known as AOE Plastic GmbH. Two years later BP acquired a 50% share of the Polydress Plastic GmbH in Michelstadt/Odenwald, which it subsequently increased to 100% ownership. In 1977 BP acquired the synthetics manufacturer Etimex Kunstoffwerke GmbH in Stuttgart. However, towards the end of 1991 the group of four plastics manufacturers that had made up Deutsche BP's plastics arm were merged into a single company, BP Chemicals PlasTec GmbH, and ownership was transferred within the international BP Group to BP Chemicals Investments Ltd., London.

Although Deutsche BP has made forays into the petrochemicals industry, it has continued to develop its interests in its core petroleum business. In 1979 the BP-Veba agreement was approved under which Deutsche BP acquired the restructured Gelsenberg AG from Veba, thus breaking up the union of the Gelsenberg and Veba, whose merger in 1974 formed the largest single share in the domestic petroleum market in Germany. The most important holdings of Gelsenberg AG included a 25% share in Ruhrgas AG, Essen; the network of filling stations of Fanal GmbH, Mülheim/Ruhr; the fuel trading firm Stromeyer GmbH, through which Deutsche BP also gained access to the coal industry; and 50% of the shares in the refinery Erdölraffinerie Ingolstadt AG. Its stake in Ruhrgas AG remains Deutsche BP's principle participation in the natural gas business. In 1989 a trademark agreement was made with the company Merk & Cie KG of Landshut whereby 90 filling stations of the name "Deltin" were transferred to Deutsche BP.

Deutsche BP has also been involved in the supply of fuel oils for commercial transport. In 1982 Helmuth Hardekopf Bunker GmbH (renamed BP Bunker GmbH in 1984) was founded with the responsibility of supplying fuel and lubricants to inland and coastal navigating vessels. International shipping in German seaports, on the other hand, is supplied bunker oils (heavy residual petroleum fuel oils) and lubricants by BP Marine. A supplier of aviation fuel, Air BP was by 1991 providing one-sixth of such fuel sold in Germany at both international and domestic airports.

By the end of the 1980s most of Deutsche BP's operational business had been delegated to its subsidiaries, which act on behalf of Deutsche BP. The head office of Deutsche BP both acts as a holding company and is responsible for fixing corporate objectives and strategies and monitoring their implementation. Thus, in 1989 the trade activities of Deutsche BP became centralized under a new subsidiary, BP Handel GmbH.

Deutsche BP has been a leader in consumer services at its filling stations in Germany, which are now operated by its subsidiary BP Tankstellen GmbH. In 1959 Deutsche BP came out with SUPERMIX, the first homogeneous blend of super and regular gasoline. In 1964 Deutsche BP was the first company to introduce the coin operated gasoline pump in West Germany. In 1970 it was the first oil company whose filling stations offered self-service. In 1988 Deutsche BP filling stations were the first in Germany to accept a credit card, and by 1991 about 90% of Deutsche BP's 1518 retail outlets accepted credit card and electronic cash payments. In 1990 Deutsche BP opened its first truck stop near Hannover, and by 1992 it had three in operation. Attention continues to be devoted to improving customer services with multi-product dispensing pumps (choice of grades from a single pump), more service stations open around the clock, and over 100 mini supermarkets.

At the same time, Deutsche BP, in its capacity as a holding company, decided to cut back in other investment activities, such as real estate, in order to concentrate on its core business of petroleum. In December 1990 Deutsche BP sold off its parking garage business. It completely turned over 27 parking garages to an English-Belgian consortium. According to the *Süddeutsche Zeitung* the proceeds of the garage sales were primarily used for the buildup of Deutsche BP's petroleum activities in the new states of eastern Germany.

Deutsche BP has endeavored to stay at the forefront of modern technology, especially in the 1980s in the area of environmental protection. In 1981 the company earned an energy research award for its project "Fuel from Sludge." The German Federal Environmental Office and Deutsche BP in 1985 put forth a prototype of a quiet tanker, "Flüstertanker". Also in that year Deutsche BP organized its conference "Environment '85" in Bonn. In 1987 Deutsche BP introduced the product "Rigidoil" for the removal of oil pollutants from inland waters, installed a dust removing facility for the catalytic cracker at the refinery in Bavaria, and also introduced a gas recovery system to reduce the hydrocarbon emissions during the transfer of oil products within refineries and oil depots. A vapor recovery system for gasoline dispensing was installed at filling stations in 1991.

In the summer of that year Deutsche BP founded the Technology Center Hamburg (TCH) on the site of the BP Oiltech GmbH in Hamburg/Neuhof. The center combines the research and development sectors together with the applied technology facilities. The TCH is primarily engaged in the further development of petroleum products and related technical services, such as quality assurance, technical advisory services, and environmental protection analysis. The TCH also conducts development projects in the fuels and lubricants sector for BP Oil Europe toward the improvement of motor oils and the expansion of environmentally friendly biolubricants.

Deutsche BP was quick to take advantage of the changes in the East. In 1990 Deutsche BP opened its first filling station in the former German Democratic Republic in Dresden, which within a year after reunification had become one the company's highest through-put stations. In December of 1990 a cooperation agreement was signed with two companies of former East Germany, Leuna-Werke AG of Leuna and Intrac Handelsgesellschaft mbH of Berlin, for the marketing of Leuna's petroleum products. Under this agreement three joint-venture companies were established, of which each partner owns a third: a wholesale company to sell finished petroleum products according to BP specifications; an operating company in which Deutsche BP has invested DM 60 ($40) million to build a road tanker loading facility with an annual capacity of 3 million tons; and a marketing company to distribute the products from Leuna under the BP name to intermediate dealers and customers. The 5 million ton annual output of the Leuna refinery will also supply Deutsche BP's own filling stations in the eastern states.

Deutsche BP's objective is to achieve by the mid-1990s the same market share in the East, 10%, as it has in western Germany. To do so, it began establishing extremely modern, high-volume retail outlets at prime locations within the urban centers of the states of Thuringia, Saxony, Saxony-Anhalt, and East Berlin. During the year 1991 Deutsche BP put 16 high-volume retail outlets into operation in eastern Germany and planned to build another 25 in 1992. In 1991 Deutsche BP invested more than half of the DM 175 ($116) million it had allocated to the retail oil sector toward developing its retail network in the eastern states; this move began to pay off immediately with a greater increase in gasoline sales in the East than in the West for that year. By 1995 BP hopes to undertake the construction of more than 100 stations in the eastern states with a further DM 500 ($330) million investment planned. Sixty-five percent of the orders to erect the filling stations will be allocated to local enterprises. Looking for additional means of supply, in April 1991 Deutsche BP became part of a consortium of Hamburg-based oil companies constructing a 450-kilometer product pipeline from Hamburg to the Saxony regions and Dresden, which was expected to become operational in 1994–95.

In 1991 sales in virtually all of its petroleum products increased overall by 7% in volume over the previous year. While gasoline sales stagnated in western Germany, largely due to an increase in the Mineral Oil Tax that became effective July 1, increased motorization in the East led to an increase there. The subsidiaries belonging to the group's chemicals sector contributed less towards earnings, reflecting the weaker trend in chemicals and depressed prices. However, this decline was more than compensated for by the favorable earnings in the oil business.

Deutsche BP saw increasing sales from a low in 1988 through 1991, but in the early 1990s, profits were checked by new taxes and investment expenditures, and prospects for the near future did not look very good. The world oil supply, despite the Gulf War and the collapse of the Soviet Union, remained abundant and prices relatively low, meaning competition would remain keen. Furthermore, the continued economic recession meant that the oil industry would not see an expansion in the near future. Deutsche BP nevertheless was expected to maintain its present market share.

Principal Subsidiaries: BP Oiltech GmbH; BP Handel GmbH; BP Tankstellen GmbH; BP Bunker GmbH; BP Flüssiggas GmbH; BP Transport und Logistik GmbH; Raffineriegesellschaft Vohburg/Ingolstadt mbH (62.5%); BP Chemicals GmbH; Carborundum Deutschland GmbH; Gelsenberg AG; Globol GmbH (75%); EC Erdölchemie GmbH (50%).

Further Reading: Geschichte einer Ölgesellschaft, Hamburg, BP Benzin und Petroleum GmbH, 1954; Pruskil, Werner, *Geographie und staatsmonopolistischer Kapitalismus,* Leipzig, VEB Hermann Haack, 1971; Förster, Fren, *Geschichte der Deutschen BP 1904–1979,* Hamburg, Deutsche BP Aktiengesellschaft, 1980; Ferrier, R. W., *The History of the British Petroleum Company,* New York, Cambridge University Press, 1982; Polster, Bernd, *Tankstellen: Die Benzingeschichte,* Berlin, TRANSIT, 1982; ''BP trennt sich von ihren Parkhäusern,'' *Süddeutsche Zeitung,* December 9, 1990; ''BP kooperiert mit ostdeutschen Partnern,'' *Süddeutsche Zeitung,* January 7, 1991; ''Deutsche BP verdient im Ölgeschäft gläzend,'' *Süddeutsche Zeitung,* February 28, 1992; *Report of the Financial Year 1991,* Hamburg, Deutsche BP Aktiengesellschaft, 1992.

—Heather Behn Hedden

DIEBOLD®

INCORPORATED

DIEBOLD, INC.

P.O. Box 8230
Canton, Ohio 44711-8230
U.S.A.
(216) 489-4000
Fax: (216) 588 3794

Public Company
Incorporated: 1876 as Diebold Safe & Lock Co.
Employees: 3,975
Sales: $543 million
Stock Exchange: New York
SICs: 3499 Fabricated Metal Products, Except Machinery
and Transportation Equipment; 3669 Electronic and Other
Electrical Equipment and Components, Except Computer
Equipment; 3578 Calculating & Accounting Equipment

In the wake of the 1871 Great Chicago Fire, natural disaster proved a boon for Diebold Bahmann & Co. when word spread that all 878 Diebold safes in the area, along with their contents, survived the flames. The safes' reputation as a haven from the elements came full circle more than a century later when Hurricane Andrew devastated much of South Florida in August of 1992. A bank executive in Homestead, Florida, the city that bore the worst of the storm, reported weathering 160-mile-per-hour winds in a Diebold safe. Over the years, the company has diversified considerably, becoming the international leader in the production and servicing of Automated Teller Machines (ATMs), while continuing to make safes, office equipment, and a variety of security and surveillance systems.

Charles Diebold first organized Diebold Bahmann in 1859, as a manufacturer of safes and vaults in Cincinnati, Ohio. In 1872, Diebold had outgrown its space in Cincinnati and transferred plant and headquarters to Canton, Ohio, where most of the post-fire orders were filled. In 1874, Wells Fargo of San Francisco chose Diebold to make what would be the world's largest vault. In 1875, a special 47-car train transported the 32-foot-long, 27-foot-wide, 12-foot-high vault to San Francisco. In 1876, the company was incorporated under Ohio law as Diebold Safe & Lock Co. Following the Wells Fargo feat, Diebold continued to traffic in the colossal, selling the largest-ever commercial bank vault to Detroit National Bank in 1921. In 1968, the First National Bank of Chicago purchased the largest-ever double vault doors, with a combined weight of 87 1/2 tons. Size aside,

the company's abiding interest lay in developing equipment to stay one step ahead of bank robbers. In 1890, the company introduced manganese steel doors that were billed as TNT-proof. Through time, combination locks replaced keys, which could be copied. Safety hinges were introduced along with locks that jammed automatically after banking hours.

The company made a splash in 1954 by putting visually pleasing vault doors on the market. In the process of mechanically redesigning its bank vault equipment, the company canvassed bankers for suggested improvements to the standard. The overwhelming answer was that a plain slab of steel, particularly on the inside of the door—the side customers see—was an unworthy complement to a bank's carefully decorated public spaces. The company then hired Charles Deaton, a St. Louis industrial designer, to retool both the interior and exterior of the vaults. Despite the fact that the newly designed vaults cost around twice as much as the simpler models, they dominated new orders from customers.

While better and more secure vaults and safes continued to be key features in Diebold's product line, the market for safes and vaults has not always been dependable, relying as it does on the health of the banking industry. In the 1930s, Diebold began to diversify. In slightly over a decade, the company made seven major moves toward expansion. In 1936, the company acquired United Metal Products Co., also of Canton, a manufacturer of hollow metal doors and door frames. In 1938 Diebold made its first entrance into the office equipment business by introducing the Cardineer Rotary File System. This was followed in 1944 with the acquisition of the Visible Records Equipment Company of Chicago, a former subsidiary and a manufacturer of vertical filing systems and other record-keeping equipment. The same year, Diebold bought the patents and manufacturing rights for Flofilm, a process that allowed companies to microfilm records in-house with a one-hour automatic developer. In 1945, buying rights to the Safe-T-Stak Steel Storage File further augmented Diebold's growing office equipment business. In 1946, Diebold bought the safe and vault business of the York Safe & Lock Company. Finally, in January of 1947, the bank equipment division of O. B. McClintock Co. of Minneapolis went over to Diebold. The products acquired from McClintock included burglar alarms, a bank vault ventilator (in case of lock-ins), and after-hour depositories.

Several factors motivated Diebold's first expansion. World War II brought the safe and vault business as a whole out of rough years with a flurry of government armament contracts. Following the dismal economy of the 1930s, the war created a demand for manufacturers accustomed to high-precision work with hardened steels. For Diebold, as well as its main competitors York Safe and Mosler Safe Co., the war effort spelled a windfall. In 1942 Diebold, Inc., which had previously grossed around $3 million per year, brought in $40 million.

When the dust settled and the contracts disappeared with the end of the war, the company was fiscally sound but its executives were having trouble agreeing on Diebold's path of postwar reconversion. Amid the confusion, Eliot Ness joined the company's board in 1944. A former prohibition agent and Cleveland director of safety, he represented the Rex family, who owned the largest single block of Diebold shares (38%). Ness, who became chairman of the board, engineered a spectacular take-over of York Safe. Located in York, Pennsylvania, York was the largest prewar producer of safes and vaults, with a strong sales base on the East Coast. However, the company had let its sales division deteriorate during the war, while Diebold's was intact. Seeing York's weakness, Diebold moved in. The deal came together with the help of Clint Murchison, Sr., a Texas oilman and a friend of future chair and board member Daniel Maggin. Murchison arranged for several insurance companies to make loans to Diebold for the purchase and personally guaranteed them. Diebold acquired all of York's patents, tools, service contracts, and orders as well as its sales branches. However, the York company had diversified to include plastics production and microfilm equipment and Diebold left the remaining business free-standing under the name York Industries, Inc.

In the 1950s, Diebold cashed in on America's postwar migration to suburban areas, which created a demand for new bank branches and orders for safes as well as the full complement of office and security equipment. Thanks to its expansion during the 1940s, the company was able to meet the new demand for its products. The automobile-oriented suburban life brought buyers for the company's drive-in teller windows, which Diebold had started selling after the purchase of McClintock, along with the Diebold-McClintock burglar alarm and several models of after-hour depositories. In 1955, Diebold acquired K. F. Kline Co., a maker of steel lockers, shelving parts, storage bins, and storage and wardrobe cabinets. The Kline acquisition, combined with Diebold's previous business in record-handling and storage equipment, brought business equipment to account for approximately 50 percent of total volume in 1957.

In August of 1958, Diebold acquired the entire stock of Herring-Hall-Marvin Safe Co. of Canada, Ltd., which became Diebold of Canada, Ltd. In September of 1959, Diebold acquired Herring-Hall-Marvin Safe Co. of Hamilton, Ohio. In addition to safes, Herring-Hall made teller counter equipment and the acquisition expanded Diebold's range of service to banks even further. The U.S. government subsequently took the merger to court on anti-trust grounds, saying that Diebold and Herring-Hall were two of only three companies in the United States producing bank vault equipment. Southern District Court of Ohio dismissed the case on the so-called "failing company doctrine," under which an acquisition in danger of anti-trust challenges could be justified if it can be shown that the object of a takeover is in such poor shape that its continued existence would not substantially alter the competitive environment. In 1961, the Justice Department asked the Supreme Court to review the case, saying that the defense should be less broadly defined. The high court recommended that the district court that dismissed the case should try it. In April of 1963, before a trial could take place, Diebold and the Justice Department reached an agreement. Diebold would sell the safe and vault part of the Herring-Hall-Marvin operation within the year and agree not to buy any other vault or safe companies for another five years. That limitation would be stretched to ten years if Herring-Hall was not sold within that time frame.

In the meantime, Diebold continued to expand. Along with the postwar growth in the number of banks in the country, the late 1950s and early 1960s saw an explosion in the per-person use of checks. This prompted Diebold to buy into the check-imprinting business. In 1963, the company acquired Consolidated Business Systems, Inc. and its subsidiary Young & Selden. That company was a maker of business forms and magnetic ink imprinting for checks. Diebold then sold off the business forms part of the business at a loss, but profitably ventured further into the check business with the purchase of the ThriftiCheck Service Corporation later the same year. Diebold sold some assets of Young & Selden in 1970 and all of ThriftiCheck in 1974. Diebold was first listed on the New York Stock Exchange in April, 1964, under the symbol DBD.

In 1965 the company added the products of the Lamson Corporation of Syracuse, New York, to its line of office equipment. A maker of materials-handling systems, Lamson became a division of Diebold. Among its products was a message-carrying system that used pneumatic tubes. When Diebold took over, it expanded the operations of the Syracuse plant and invested in research and development, resulting in the computer-regulated tube transport systems that were used to carry material between floors in large office buildings and continue to be used in drive-up remote teller stations. In 1970, Diebold acquired Florida Development Services, a Clearwater, Florida company that made "modular" bank buildings. Those structures, used for small branch offices, could be transported to a site and assembled within 90 days. The following year the name was changed to Diebold Contracting Services, Inc. The concern was sold in 1979.

In the early 1970s, Diebold was faced with a slowdown in sales of security equipment. The company, led by long-time President and Chief Executive Officer Raymond Koontz, decided to respond by looking ahead and taking a chance on ATMs. Diebold invested heavily in electronic research, applied computer technology, ergonomic design, and software development and, in 1973, introduced the first ATM model. The ATM trade turned out to be a natural for the company that had been doing business with banks for over a century. While Diebold was a relative newcomer to this type of computer technology, its experience with cash-handling systems and security concerns made Diebold ATMs an attractive choice for banks. Within five years, up against competing products from IBM, NCR, Burroughs, TRW, and Honeywell, Diebold had captured 45 percent of the domestic market. In 1979 banks using Diebold ATMs included Bank of America, Citibank, Marine Midland, and the Shawmut Corp.

Through the early 1980s, the business press portrayed Diebold's ATM dominance over IBM and NCR as the pin-striped battle between David and a two-headed Goliath. "Those three letters I-B-M are the first thing we think of when we awake," *Forbes* quoted Earl Wearstler, then Diebold executive vice president, as saying in 1980. But Diebold held its ground, working out a reciprocal sales agreement with Bunker Ramo, a maker of microcomputer-driven teller terminals with strong sales in Europe and the U.S. To gain access to the Canadian ATM market, the company signed a sales and service agreement with Phillips, the international electronics company.

In 1985 and 1986, ATM orders from banks sagged in pace with a general slowdown in bank equipment sales. Diebold had to cut back on costs, but kept the research and development funds flowing toward finding additional applications for ATM technology and aggressively sought out non-bank ATM buyers. In 1985, National Transactions Systems ordered 1,000 cash-dispensing machines to be placed in West Coast 7-Eleven and Safeway stores. In 1986, Diebold announced 26 new products. These included self-serve video rental machines, credit card-activated gas station pumps, and interactive video systems to be used for dispensing tickets and information. For banks that wanted lower-cost cash networks, they also came out with automatic teller machines that were smaller and performed fewer operations, such as dispensing cash but not taking deposits.

In July of 1990, Diebold, the company that professed to having nightmares about IBM a decade earlier, announced a joint venture with its erstwhile competitor, which was dubbed Inter-Bold. At the time, Diebold held a larger proportion of the domestic and world ATM markets than IBM, but the venture was designed to make the most of each parent company's expertise. Diebold owns the majority share of the partnership, at 70 percent. Through InterBold, Diebold benefitted from IBM's strengths in software development and systems integration as well as from the company's strong position in Europe, Asia, and Latin America. Within a year of the venture, InterBold introduced the *i* Series TM ATM, the only model ATM that uses "image-lift" technology. Image-lift allows ATM users to see a picture of deposited checks on the ATM screen, and addresses customers' fears about trusting deposits to the machines. As of 1992, InterBold had the only networked ATMs in Poland and held the leading position in Mexico, where the banking industry is in the process of privatization. As the former Eastern Bloc countries develop free-market economies and Western Europe moves toward increased economic integration, the demand for ATMs can be expected to expand rapidly through the 1990s.

At the same time, retail applications for card-activated transaction equipment continue to multiply. InterBold has developed a "multi-media dispenser" capable of self-service distribution of postage stamps, airline tickets, travelers' checks, food stamps, and public transportation passes, among other items. In 1992, Diebold formed a joint venture with Nelson Vending Technology Limited of Toronto to distribute automated videocassette vending systems to convenience stores, drug stores, apartment complexes, business centers, hotels, hospitals, and other commercial centers.

AT&T, which owns NCR, remained Diebold's major competitor in global ATM sales and service in 1992. In security products, Mosler of Hamilton, Ohio, Diebold's century-old rival, was a major competitor, along with LeFebure Corp., Honeywell, and ATD Ltd. Diebold has maintained manufacturing facilities in Canton and Newark, Ohio, Lynchburg, Virginia, and Sumter, South Carolina.

Principal Subsidiaries: Diebold of Nevada, Inc.; The Diebold Co. of Canada, Ltd.; Diebold Investment Co.; DBD Investment Management Co.; Diebold Foreign Sales Corp.; Diebold Finance Co., Inc.; Diebold International, Inc.; Diebold Pacific, Ltd.; Diebold Holding Company, Inc.; InterBold; InterBold Pacific Limited.

Further Reading: "Diebold Annexes York's Line," *Business Week,* January 12, 1946; "Selling Banks a High-Style Door for Vaults," *Business Week,* September 11, 1954; "Earnings of Diebold Vault to Higher Level on Rapid U.S. Bank Expansion," *Barron's,* November 26, 1956; "Diebold Cashes In on Bank Growth, Office Automation," *Barron's,* December 2, 1957; "High Court to Review Anti-Merger Suit Defense: Firm Was Failing," *Wall Street Journal,* November 7, 1961; "Diebold Agrees to Sell Concern It Bought in 1959," *Wall Street Journal,* April 11, 1963; "Waiting for New Deals to Click," *Business Week,* June 6, 1964; "The Safe Makers," *Financial World,* October 14, 1964; "To Catch a Thief," *Forbes,* December 15, 1973; "Diebold: A Future to Bank On—At Last," *Financial World,* July 15, 1979; "The Early Risers," *Forbes,* October 27, 1980; "Diebold Inc.: Banking on an Industry's Needs for Security, Automation," *Barron's,* February 8, 1988; "Diebold Inc.: Belt-tightening Reshapes Automated-teller Leader," *Barron's,* December 4, 1989; "IBM, Diebold Form Venture to Develop, Sell Bank Machines," *Wall Street Journal,* July 13, 1990.

—Martha Schoolman

DIRECTORATE GENERAL OF TELECOMMUNICATIONS

31 E. Aikuo Road
Taipei, Taiwan
Republic of China
(02) 334-3691
Fax: (02) 394-7324

State-Owned Company
Incorporated: 1943
Employees: 36,384
Sales: NT$100.43 billion (US$3.92 billion)
SICs: 4813 Telephone Communications; 4822 Telegraph & Other Message Communications; 4899 Communications Services Nec

Initially developed as a telegraph service for the military over 100 years ago, Taiwan's Directorate General of Telecommunications (DGT) is a state-owned and operated enterprise that is the major supplier of phone and other telecommunication service throughout Taiwan. The DGT is also branching out into international telecommunications including satellite communications.

The history of the DGT begins with the introduction of telegraph service to China during the 1880s. Telegraph service was first proposed in 1874 to improve military communications in the face of increasing Japanese military harassment. In July 1877 the government began laying a submarine cable between the Chinese mainland and its island province Taiwan, which the Japanese had claimed as their own.

Although this connection was not completed until nine years later, additional lines were started in 1881 for military communications between other Chinese marine bases. These links helped the military to respond to attacks from other foreign armies and domestic warlords. Until these telegraph lines were installed, crucial battlefield communications were delivered on foot and subject to long delays.

Local officials later won grants from the imperial government to establish a public telegraph service, initially linking Shanghai and Tianjin. This line, which included seven switching stations along its route, took eight months to complete.

But, because the Chinese language is based on pictographic characters rather than on an alphabet, it was impossible to transmit Chinese words using standard Morse code dots and dashes. Instead engineers developed an ingenious method of dots and dashes that indicated the position and number of strokes of each radical in a given Chinese character. In this way a character could be described with Morse code. And, in time, this method grew into such a highly efficient shorthand that telegraph operators could transmit messages almost as fast as their English-language counterparts. This same method remains in use in China today.

To help establish this new electronic language, and to assist in the growth of telecommunications in China, the government established a school at Tianjin which it staffed with foreign engineers and teachers.

The network was plagued by frequent outages. Where weather or poor workmanship was not to blame, peasant farmers were usually responsible. Many did not trust those who operated the system, seeing it as an aid to bureaucrats and tax collectors. Others simply didn't want the poles on their farmland and yet others found better uses for the wood and wire. As a result, farmers became a major hazard to the system, taking down what workers spent months putting into place.

In 1890, as officials continued to struggle with telegraphy, the telephone was introduced to China. The first service was set up by a telegraph office in Nanjing connecting 14 customers—all of them government offices. This system and others like it expanded rapidly as businesses and then wealthy residents requested their own lines. Often growth outstripped the capacity of switching offices, forcing Chinese operators to handle hundreds of connections at a single station.

In 1896 China lost a war with Japan and was forced to cede Taiwan to the Japanese government. As a result, the excellent communications established for the defense of Taiwan was now in Japanese hands.

The Japanese military began construction of large telephone networks during 1897 in the areas of China that it occupied, but these were primarily for administrative use. By 1900, however, the Japanese began offering telephone service commercially, including local and long distance services. At this time there were only about 30,000 telephone customers in all of China, and 80 percent of them were Japanese.

After the establishment of the Chinese Republic in 1911, demand for telephone lines exploded. As more customers requested telephones, the average costs of providing services were reduced, making the telephone affordable to even more customers.

By 1927 every large city in China had Strowger-type switches, which allowed calls to be placed automatically by dialing a customer's number. At this time, telecommunications authorities had completed a major long distance network connecting more than 7,000 customers in seven provinces. In addition, the government took over international services, which had previously been offered only by foreign companies operating in China. New connections were established from the Northeastern city of Shenyang to Germany and France. By 1930 backbone construction of the national telephone network was completed.

Telegraphy, however, was not dead. In 1905 the first wireless telegraph system was installed. While restricted mainly to military applications, the wireless gained widespread commercial application in the late 1920s. A decade later, after the Japanese invasion of Manchuria, the wireless became essential to military operations, as wireline networks were easily and frequently destroyed by enemy action. A wireless telephone service between China and the United States was inaugurated shortly before the outbreak of full-scale war between China and Japan.

The Chinese government evacuated Guangzhou (Canton) to Japanese forces and later moved a thousand miles inland to Chongqing, capital of Sichuan province. It was here that the ruling Nationalist government reorganized administrative organs, creating a Ministry of Transportation and Telecommunications. Within this ministry, on May 19, 1943, the government established a Directorate General of Telecommunications, whose mission was to develop telephone and telegraph communications in China.

During World War II China suffered tremendous damage at the hand of the Japanese. So complete was Japan's scorched earth policy that occupation authorities ordered all telephones impounded and destroyed. In the waning days of the war, as Japan's defeat became inevitable, Japanese authorities on Taiwan ordered the total destruction of the telecommunications network, much of which it had developed over the previous 50 years.

After Japan's surrender in 1945 the DGT inherited a system that was in complete ruin. Even lines that could be salvaged were nearly unusable because they were built with inferior war-grade Japanese wire. Rehabilitation of the network was extremely difficult and costly.

Shortly after the war the communists under Mao Zedong and the ruling Nationalist faction under Chiang Kai-shek ended their anti-Japanese cooperation. Subsequent hostilities between the parties later escalated into a destructive civil war.

In 1948, amid the battles raging throughout the country, the government's DGT introduced telex service, and telephone subscribership in China peaked at 167,000 customers. The Guomindang, however, began losing to the Communists and in 1949 was forced off the mainland to take refuge on Taiwan. At that time the government had to abandon the entire telecommunications network on the mainland to the Communists.

Repairs on Taiwan's telephone system began as soon as Chinese control was re-established on the island in 1945. But after 1949, with the newly arrived government in exile, thousands of refugees and hundreds of businesses from the mainland, public demands on the network continued to outrun what the service could provide. In 1949 Taiwan had only five international circuits.

The government on Taiwan struggled to arm itself against a "final" offensive from the mainland. This required highly taxing investments in local industry and infrastructure, which drained commercial financing. With investment prioritized for

shipbuilding, steel, and heavy machinery, little was left for modernization of the telephone network.

One major accomplishment, however, was the establishment of rural telephone service along the Taiwanese seacoast. These new rural lines, constructed for military use in 1949, brought telephone service to thousands of farmers. But it wasn't until 1952 that reconstruction of the basic network was declared complete.

During the remainder of the 1950s the state-run telecommunications agency struggled to keep its network operating with the most modern technology it could afford. Emphasis was shifted from merely getting lines strung to improving signal quality. In 1957 the company introduced FM-band telegraphy and in the following year it perfected a Chinese-language telegram typewriter. These breakthroughs extended the life of telegraphy in Taiwan and greatly increased telegram traffic.

Gradually, by the mid-1960s, after basic industries had been firmly established in Taiwan, funding for improvements in the telephone network became available. Under government direction, the Taiwanese economy was designed to generate wealth from export earnings. Export-led growth began in certain sectors of the economy during the 1960s and exploded in the early 1970s.

Led by small manufacturers of toys, machinery, and handicrafts, Taiwan's strong growth provided tremendous personal income. This income created further demand for telecommunications services, fueling a period of extremely strong growth for the DGT.

In 1969 DGT began widespread automated switching, eliminating all operator-connecting calling. That year the company also completed construction of a modern satellite communications facility that greatly expanded the capacity for international calls. Microwave communications systems were also established between Taiwan, the Philippines, and Hong Kong. This had a great effect on Taiwanese commerce, as exporters now found it much easier to remain in contact with their customers.

By 1971 DGT had nearly 400,000 telephone customers with 600,000 telephones—about twice the number on the entire Chinese mainland. Again, strong demand lowered average costs, making the telephone affordable to even more people.

The DGT placed several thousand public telephones throughout Taiwan during the 1970s. First introduced shortly after World War II, DGT's first public phones collected charges only after a call was completed. In 1955 credit accounts were introduced. By 1976, however, the company had installed nearly 27,000 standard coin-operated phones and had introduced paging services.

In 1980 the DGT completed an eight-year campaign to bring telephone coverage to all rural areas in the Republic of China, including many offshore islands. This campaign also helped the company to achieve extremely high rates of growth, averaging 20 percent per year. During the 1970s, as investment in the network averaged a staggering 0.7 percent of the entire nation's gross national product, Taiwan's telecommunications industry moved from developing country levels to those of modern industrial nations. By 1981 the DGT served more than 2.7 million customers with more than 3.7 million telephones.

In 1981 the DGT introduced digital switching, which, in addition to allowing calls to be placed more quickly and accurately, enabled the company to introduce touch-tone service and, later, new "vertical" services such as call waiting and speed dialing. The company also began direct international dialing, high-speed telex, and data and computer services.

In 1989 the company introduced cellular service and began setting up large networks in each of its major urban markets. By 1992 cellular coverage was extended to the Chungshan Freeway and other trunk highways as well as to remote industrial parks and resorts, such as Sun Moon Lake, Kenting National Park, and Snow Dan International Park. Cellular subscription in 1992 exceeded 220,000 customers.

The DGT began installing fiber optic cable on major long distance and trunk routes during the late 1980s. These upgrades have allowed increases in switching capacity and improvements in signal quality. The fiber optic backbone has even been extended offshore to Kinmen, Penghu, and Matsu, an island immediately adjacent to the mainland which the Nationalists continue to control.

As a partner in several tran-Asian submarine cable projects, the DGT offers a variety of international services, including satellite communications. The company also maintains a radio-based maritime coastal communications system for the shipping industry and a computer-based videotex service that provides an array of information services.

The DGT is divided into three operating regions, encompassing northern, central, and southern Taiwan. Each of these regions contains a major metropolis (Taipei, Taichung, and Kaoshiung, respectively). Due to the high density of these cities, they are routinely targeted to receive advanced services before other areas. The company also operates an advanced telecommunications laboratory for network planning and product development.

While governments around the world are privatizing their state-owned telephone utilities, government proposals to privatize DGT have only recently surfaced. This is because privatizations are usually carried out to introduce competitive practices and increase the efficiency of an operation and the DGT is already viewed as an efficient operation. Perhaps in anticipation of "corporatization," the company is already run like an enterprise rather than a bureau. The company has begun a public identity campaign and even publishes annual reports.

DGT's logo is based on the Chinese character for electricity, which is used in the words for telephone and telegraph. But the logo symbol also resembles another word which means "to work hard." Such dual symbolism is extremely important and profound in Chinese society.

In addition the DGT contributes about half of its annual revenue directly to government coffers—an important source of revenue that the government will not easily give away. Privatization of DGT would most likely require a restructuring of the industry and the appearance of competitors modeled after Japan's DDI or Britain's Mercury.

After nearly 50 years in Taiwan, the DGT has helped to elevate the island's economy to one of the most powerful in Asia. While currently limited to serving Taiwan, it is plausible that the company may be allowed to participate in the development of telecommunications on the Chinese mainland. But, because the DGT is an agency of a government which is a rival to that in China, such participation would be contingent upon a wider political rapprochement.

Principal Subsidiaries: Data Communication Institute; Telecommunications Training Institute; Telecommunications Laboratories; Long Distance Telecommunications Administrations; Northern Taiwan Telecommunications Administrations; Central Taiwan Telecommunications Administrations; Southern Taiwan Telecommunications Administrations

Further Reading: "The Origin of Telecommunications in China" (in Chinese), Directorate General of Telecommunications, Taipei, 1981; "A Brief History of Telecommunication Development in Taiwan" (in Chinese), Directorate General of Telecommunications, Taipei, 1981; "Chairman's Speech on the 100th Telecommunications Day, December 28, 1981" (in Chinese), Directorate General of Telecommunications, Taipei, 1981; "Taiwan's Telecommunication: A Profile of Progress," *Telephony,* March 24, 1986.

—John Simley

DOMINO'S PIZZA, INC.

30 Frank Lloyd Wright Drive
P.O. Box 997
Ann Arbor, Michigan 48106-0997
U.S.A.
(313) 930-3030
Fax: (313) 668-1946

Private Company
Incorporated: 1965
Sales: $2.45 billion
Employees: 145,000
SICs: 5250 Eating Places; 6794 Patent Owners & Lessors

Privately held Domino's Pizza, Inc., is the largest pizza-delivery company in the world, operating more than 5,000 units internationally. One-fifth of those units are company-run, with the majority franchised. Domino's pioneered a pizza delivery guarantee of thirty minutes or less, and has maintained that standard in all its franchises throughout its company history. Notable as well is the company's basic menu, which includes two sizes of pizza, eleven topping choices, and—until 1990—only one beverage, cola; in 1992 the company added salads and breadsticks to its menu.

Tom Monaghan, founder of Domino's Pizza, was born in 1937 near Ann Arbor, Michigan. Following his father's death in 1941, Monaghan lived in a succession of foster homes, including a Catholic orphanage, for much of his childhood. His mother, after finishing nursing school and buying a house, made two attempts to have Tom and his brother live at home with her; but she and Tom failed to get along. During these years Monaghan worked a lot of jobs, many of them on farms, to stay busy. His father's aunt took him in his senior year of high school, but after that he was once again on his own. Significantly, a quote from Monaghan in his high school yearbook read: ''The harder I try to be good the worse I get; but I may do something sensational yet.''

For several years Monaghan worked to try and save money for college; he joined the marines and saved $2,000 but gave it in several installments to a fly-by-night ''oil man'' he met hitchhiking, who took the money and ran. Monaghan returned to Ann Arbor to live with his brother, who worked for the post office and did occasional carpentry work at a pizza shop called DomiNick's. Within a year Jim Monaghan overheard the pizza shop owner discussing a possible sale; he mentioned buying it as a possibility to Tom. With the aid of a $900 loan from the post office credit union, in December 1960 Jim and Tom Monaghan were in business in Ypsilanti, Michigan.

Within eight months, Jim Monaghan took a beat-up Volkswagen as a trade for his half of the partnership. Tom moved in across the street from his shop. The store Monaghan bought had little room for sit-down dining; from the start delivery was key. The first drivers, unemployed workers from a factory, agreed to work on commission. After only $99 in sales the first week, profits climbed steadily to $750 a week. Early on, Monaghan made decisions which streamlined work and greatly enhanced profits: he cut six-inch pizzas and submarine sandwiches from his menu on two separate occasions, when he was shorthanded at his shop. He figured he and his staff could cope with the rush better without making special-sized pizzas or sandwiches in addition to regular pizzas. When he went over the numbers the day after, both times Monaghan found his volume and profits increased. Keeping it simple made financial sense.

Though his salary rose to $20,000 a year, Monaghan wasn't satisfied. On the advice of Jim Gilmore, a local chef with some restaurant experience, Monaghan opened a Pizza King store offering free delivery in Mt. Pleasant, near the Central Michigan University campus. Gilmore would run the original DomiNick's, as a full partner with Monaghan. By spring 1962, Gilmore had run the Ypsilanti store down, yet he persuaded Monaghan to open a Pizza King at a new Ann Arbor location, which Gilmore would oversee while Monaghan went and whipped the original DomiNick's back into shape. Gilmore convinced Monaghan to continue expanding in a financially dangerous way; since Gilmore had been bankrupt when the partnership began, all papers were in Monaghan's name. By 1964, when Gilmore became ill, he made his differences clear: he liked sit-down stores while Monaghan ran delivery. He asked for $35,000 for his share in the pizzerias. Though Monaghan considered the price preposterous, he did want to separate from Gilmore. He hired lawyer Larry Sperling, who worked out a deal where Monaghan would pay Gilmore $20,000. Gilmore would keep two restaurants in Ann Arbor; Monaghan, two pizzerias in Ypsilanti and one in Ann Arbor. Though their partnership was dissolved, Monaghan was still dependent on Gilmore's success in business. In February 1966 Monaghan bought one more shop from Gilmore, but later that year Gilmore filed for bankruptcy, with a total debt of $75,000, in Monaghan's name. Monaghan managed to sell Gilmore's Restaurant, leaving him immediately responsible for only $20,000, with the new owner of Gilmore's to pay off related debts on a month-by-month basis.

As Monaghan's operations grew, the original owner of DomiNick's decided to maintain rights to the name. Under deadline for a Yellow Pages ad, driver Jim Kennedy came up with the name Domino's Pizza. The new company incorporated in 1965. Free from the Gilmore-related debts, Monaghan was ready to begin franchising. The first board of directors included Tom, his wife and bookkeeper, Margie, and Larry Sperling. Sperling drafted a franchise agreement in which Domino's would keep 2.5 percent as royalties from sales, 2 percent to cover advertising, and 1 percent for bookkeeping. As Monaghan stated in his autobiography *Pizza Tiger:* ''By today's standards, the royalties were far too favorable to the franchisee. But it served our purpose then, and I was not concerned about covering all future contingencies.''

The first franchisee, Chuck Gray, was a man visible in local and state politics; he took over an original store on the east side of Ypsilanti. While Sperling and Monaghan hammered out financial matters—the former wanted to control costs, the latter to build sales—Domino's Pizza slowly gathered a base of corporate staff. The second franchisee, Dean Jenkins, was handpicked by Monaghan: he would take over the first store to be built from the ground up. By July 1967, when Jenkins' store was up and running, Domino's Pizza moved to East Lansing, home of Michigan State University. Its dormitory population, at approximately 20,000, was the largest in the nation. Dave Kilby, originally hired to do some radio copy-writing for Domino's, later bought into a franchise, then began working at company headquarters, located above the Cross Street shop in Ypsilanti. Kilby then worked on franchisee expansion with Monaghan.

In February 1968 a fire swept through Monaghan's original pizza store. Advertising manager Bob Cotman escaped the building just in time, climbing down a fireman's ladder. While the pizza shop reopened within two days, headquarters was wiped out and Domino's first commissary, with $40,000 of stored goods, was destroyed. The staff pulled together, with each existing store location responsible for producing one pizza item—cheese, dough, chopped toppings—which drivers then ferried from one store to the next to keep operations running.

The biggest challenge for Monaghan was not simply covering the total fire losses of $150,000 (only $13,000 paid for by insurance)—he also had to pay the leases on five new franchises and find store operators as soon as possible. While Tom worked on his task, Margie Monaghan brought in Mike Paul, her contact at the Ypsilanti bank, who soon joined Domino's to run the commissary. Paul fired half of the staff and cleaned up operations; he introduced caps, aprons, and periodic spot-checks for employee neatness.

Monaghan learned a lot in the early years of Domino's, due in part to road trips he took early on to research business and learn from competitors. When observing the competition didn't result in better methods, Monaghan innovated. Looking for equipment ideas at a Chicago convention, he found a meat-grinder which he used to chop cheese as well as mix consistent pizza dough in less than a minute. Standard mixers at the time took eight to ten minutes to mix dough. Dough, once mixed, was stored on oiled pans, with towels covering it; this method failed to keep the outside edges of the dough from hardening. Monaghan discovered an air-tight fiberglass container that stored dough very well; the practice later became a standard in the industry. Monaghan was also dissatisfied with standard pizza boxes: they were too flimsy to stack, and heat and steam from the pizza weakened them. Monaghan prodded his salesman to work with the supplier and devise a corrugated box with airholes, which also became an industry standard.

Plans began in earnest for Midwest expansion as Domino's jumped on the 1960s franchise bandwagon. While Monaghan had worked on his plan to expand on college campuses, opening a new store a week in late 1968 proved to be the beginning of a nightmare. Monaghan opened up 32 stores in 1969 and was hailed as Ypsilanti's boy wonder. Spurred by McDonald's great success going public in 1965, Monaghan planned to do the same. With the aid of loans, he bought a fleet of 85 new delivery cars, and spruced up his personal image; he also hired a CPA firm for accounting, and computerized bookkeeping. When moving information from paper to computer, Domino's lost all its records. Perhaps as a result, the company underpaid the Internal Revenue Service by $36,000. Monaghan was forced to sell his stock for the first time to raise the money to pay the IRS.

Monaghan tried to do too much, too fast. Ohio stores opened before Domino's regional reputation spread that far. Sales in these stores were poor. This was only the beginning of the downturn: Monaghan lost control of Domino's on May 1, 1970. Dan Quirk, who had bought Monaghan's stock, recommended he contact Ken Heavlin, a local man known for turning businesses around. Heavlin, in exchange for Monaghan's remaining stock, would run the company, get loans to cover IRS debts, and after two years keep a controlling 51 percent interest in the company, with Monaghan getting 49 percent. In the meantime, Domino's became the target of lawsuits from various franchisees, creditors, and the law firm Cross, Wrock.

In March of 1971 Heavlin ended his agreement with Monaghan, who shortly went to speak with each franchisee, persuading them that Domino's would survive the crisis and they would all fare better working with him rather than against him. Their lawsuit was dropped. Monaghan pushed on, and Domino's was back in business, however tight its financial strings. One man instrumental in the growth of the early 1970s was Richard Mueller. Originally from Ohio, Mueller bought a franchise in 1970, during Domino's lowest period. After Mueller ran this Ann Arbor store for a year, Monaghan sent him to Columbus to revive an ailing store; within three months, sales shot to $7,000 a week from a dismal $600. Mueller soon operated ten Domino's franchises and incorporated as Ohio Pizza Enterprises, Inc. Within six-and-a-half years Mueller opened fifty stores. As Domino's grew, Mueller went on to become vice-president of operations in 1978.

Quick to rebuild Domino's, Monaghan encouraged trusted employees and friends to expand. Steve Litwhiler opened five stores in Vermont, while Dave Kilby, who had relocated during the Domino's slump, managed to build a strong base in Florida. A significant hire by Kilby was Dave Black, a top-selling manager who later rose to become president and COO of Domino's Pizza.

The year 1973 was a turning point for Domino's. The company introduced its first delivery guarantee, ''a half hour or a half dollar off,'' as stated in the company newsletter *The Pepperoni Press.* The College of Pizzarology was founded to train potential franchisees. The company decentralized as well: accounting was moved from Ypsilanti headquarters to local accountants, while the commissary was reorganized as a separate company.

Domino's introduced its corporate logo—a red domino flush against two blue rectangles—in 1975. The company was sued the same year by Amstar Corporation, parent company of Domino Sugar, for the right to use the name. After a five-year battle, Domino's won; but not until after having opened more than thirty new stores under the interim name Pizza Dispatch.

Free to expand, Domino's planned to grow by 50 percent each year. By the late 1970s, several acquisitions contributed significantly to company growth. Domino's merged with PizzaCo Inc., in 1978, gaining 23 open stores plus a handful more under lease. The merger with this Boulder-based company allowed Domino's to move into Kansas, Arizona, and Nebraska. The following year, joining with Dick Mueller's Ohio Pizza Enterprises, Inc., Domino's added 50 stores in Ohio and Texas, for a total of 287 stores. The company ended 1979 by announcing plans to expand internationally.

The 1980s was a decade of phenomenal growth for Domino's Pizza, but this time the company was prepared. Monaghan learned from the financial dive Domino's took in 1970. While he always feared that formal budgeting systems promoted bureaucracy, with the advice of Doug Dawson, Monaghan decided to design company-wide budgeting procedures, which Domino's continued to use as training tools for potential franchisees. Dawson implemented the new accounting methods and moved on to become vice-president of marketing and corporate treasurer. Instrumental in Domino's surge was John McDevitt, a financial consultant Monaghan met in 1977. Among other accomplishments, he created and became president of TSM Leasing, Inc., a financial services company which loaned money to franchisees who could not find other start-up financing.

To Monaghan, operations was the backbone of the business. When Dick Mueller left the post of vice-president of operations in 1981 to work as a franchiser once again, Monaghan decided to regionalize Domino's operations. Mueller's previous job entailed far too much travel, and changes were necessary. Monaghan set up six geographic regions, with a director fully responsible for each territory. The regional system, as Monaghan stated in *Pizza Tiger,* "gave us the long communication lines with tight controls at the working ends that we needed for rapid but well-orchestrated growth."

At the executive level, Bob Cotman took over as senior vice-president of operations; his position included marketing. Dave Black advanced from field consultant and regional director to vice-president of operations. Both men (like Dick Mueller and Monaghan himself) had climbed every step of the Domino's ladder, after beginning as delivery driver and pizza maker. In 1981 Black carried Monaghan's favored "defensive management" strategy—where each store concentrated on keeping the customers it had—to a new level, by moving company focus away from the top-performing stores to the weakest ones. Bringing the lower performers up worked extremely well. As the company added an average of nearly 500 stores each year through the decade, newer, weaker stores were constantly given attention to improve sales.

One other element vital to Domino's 1980s growth spurt was choosing Don Vlcek, formerly in the meat business, to head the eight commissary operations. Vlcek went through the nuts-and-bolts problems, no matter how basic. One commissary saved on laundry bills by rinsing tray-drying towels, making them last a

week before cleaning was necessary. Vlcek made all commissaries do the same thing. Another commissary's manager was buying from a local, more expensive, cheese distributor instead of a national one. The manager reworked his purchasing policies. Vlcek moved sauce-mixing from the commissaries to the company's tomato-packing plant, which resulted in highly consistent, quality pizza sauce. Once Vlcek had taken care of the basics, in one eight-month period he opened a new commissary a month, all with state-of-the-art equipment.

All the support Monaghan received gave him time to fulfill boyhood dreams on a dramatic scale. In 1983 Monaghan bought the Detroit Tigers baseball team, which went on to win the World Series in 1984. He followed with the planning of Domino's Farms in Ann Arbor, a $120 million corporate headquarters modeled after architect Frank Lloyd Wright's Golden Beacon tower. Wright advocated the integration of a high-rise building in a rural setting, rather than an urban one. Monaghan planned to set up a working farm adjacent to the tower.

In 1985, *Advertising Age* placed Domino's "among the fastest-growing money makers in the restaurant industry." The company had to keep pace with not only its own growth but that of its competition—number one Pizza Hut had more than 4,000 units as compared to Domino's 2,300. Domino's stepped up advertising, increasing media spending 249 percent from the previous year. Pizza Hut entered the delivery business in 1986, the biggest threat yet to Monaghan's baby.

Domino's sales hit $1.44 billion by 1987. The company had grown to 3,605 units, spreading to Canada, Australia, the United Kingdom, West Germany, and Japan. While 33 percent of U.S. stores were company-run, international units were franchised, usually to one operator who could opt to subfranchise. The international marketing challenge was to convince buyers of the need for delivery. Back in the United States, Domino's imitated McDonald's by tailoring an ad campaign to attract the Hispanic market. Competition in the late 1980s got so tough, Monaghan was quoted in *Advertising Age* as saying, "I want people here in the company to think of it as a war." Unfortunately, with wars come casualties.

By 1989, more than twenty deaths had occurred involving Domino's drivers, calling the company's 30-minute delivery guarantee into question. A Pittsburgh-based attorney representing a couple whose car was broadsided by a driver subpoenaed Domino's for its records. Citizen's groups, major news networks, and the National Safe Work Place Institute joined in the heated criticism. Domino's responded with a national ad campaign, and with various tactics at the franchise level. One franchisee hired an off-duty police officer to track his drivers to ensure they obeyed the law.

Domino's opened its 5,000th store by January 1989, moving into Puerto Rico, Mexico, Guam, Honduras, Panama, Colombia, Costa Rica, and Spain. U.S. sales hit $2 billion. Monaghan named Dave Black as president and chief operating officer, with intentions to spend more time in community work. Domino's introduced pan pizza in May, its first new product in 28 years. This news was hardly as big, however, as Monaghan's October announcement to sell the company. After a buyout attempt in the form of an employee stock ownership plan failed, Monaghan went shopping for buyers. By April 1990 Domino's cut its public relations and international marketing departments and continued cutting executive and corporate support staff as part of a company-wide effort to improve profitability. Payroll that year decreased by $24 million. Kevin Williams, who made his name as a regional director, replaced Mike Orcutt as vice-president of operations. At the store level, Domino's opened fewer than 300 units in both 1989 and 1990.

Monaghan returned to Domino's in March 1991; by December he fired David Black, along with other top executives. Former franchisee Phil Bressler became vice-president of operations. Domino's closed 155 stores, cut regional offices from 16 to 9, and unloaded a number of pricey appendages such as corporate planes, a three-masted ship, a travel agency, a lavish Ann Arbor Christmas display, and various sports sponsorships. Monaghan made some personal sacrifices too, leaving his post on the boards of directors of sixteen Catholic colleges and organizations.

Adding three new senior executives, the company geared up to battle Pizza Hut, which had aired an ad showing unkempt Domino's drivers buying Pizza Hut products. Domino's moved its advertising accounts to New York's Grey Advertising, Inc., from the local ad agency Group 243. While Monaghan was away, Pepsico's Pizza Hut had converted half of its 7,000 units for home delivery.

Under fire, Monaghan insisted on maintaining Domino's original concept of a simple menu which speeds order preparation, allowing the company to uphold its thirty-minute guarantee. In the effort to be flexible—and to compete with Pizza Hut's pan pizza—Domino's offered a new pizza with more cheese and an increased amount of toppings. Taking another tip from its rival, Domino's worked on developing a single U.S. phone order number for Domino's customers. Also in the works was a new computer system to track sales, costs, and trends. The company closed the Columbus and Minneapolis offices, with corporate in Ann Arbor resuming those duties. The overall goal was to decrease debt. Monaghan considered making a public stock offering again in 1992. The company also worked to lessen the number of company-owned stores in the 1990s.

Domino's entered its fourth decade an international company competing in a global market. A key to meeting or exceeding competition was to maintain good internal service. Domino's franchisees, commissaries, regional offices, and corporate staff continually rated their peers on services they received from one another. As Patricia Sellers stated in *Fortune*, "A number of companies are discovering that employees who view one another as customers usually treat the actual buyers better." Domino's management hoped that this continued emphasis on customer service would contribute to their success in the future.

Principal Subsidiaries: Domino's Pizza International Inc.; Domino's Pizza Distribution Corporation.

Further Reading: Serafin, Raymond, "Domino's Pizza Delivers on the Basics," *Advertising Age,* July 8, 1985; Serafin, Raymond, "Domino's Pizza Finds Global Going Slow," *Advertising Age,* January 6, 1986; Monaghan, Tom, with Robert Anderson, *Pizza Tiger,* New York, Random House, 1986; Serafin, Raymond, "Domino's Plans Hispanic Push," *Advertising Age,* June 15, 1987; Zellner, Wendy, "Tom Monaghan: The Fun-Loving Prince of Pizza," *Business Week,* February 8, 1988; Chaudhry, Rajan, "Domino's Truck Kills 2 En Route to Delivery," *Nation's Restaurant News,* August 29, 1988; Serafin, Raymond, "Making Domino's Deliver," *Advertising Age,* November 28, 1988; Sellers, Patricia, "Getting Customers to Love You," *Fortune,* March 13, 1989; Carlino, Bill, "Domino's Launches Safety Ads," *Nation's Restaurant News,* August 14, 1989; Prewitt, Milford, "Domino's Franchisees Set Sights on #1," *Nation's Restaurant News,* August 21, 1989; Prewitt, Milford, "Domino's Cuts 19 Jobs; More May Follow," *Nation's Restaurant News,* April 30, 1990; *Domino's Thirtieth Anniversary,* Ann Arbor, Domino's Pizza, Inc., 1990; Hume, Scott, and Raymond Serafin, "Domino's Burned Up over Pizza Hut Spot," *Advertising Age,* January 7, 1991; Prewitt, Milford, "Domino's Restructures Executive Team," *Nation's Restaurant News,* March 18, 1991; "Domino's Pizza: Kevin A. Williams," *Fortune,* April 22, 1991; Driscoll, Lisa, and David Woodruff, "With Tom Monaghan Back, Can Domino's Deliver?" *Business Week,* October 28, 1991; Sympson, Ron, "Can Monaghan Deliver?" *Restaurant Business,* April 10, 1992.

—Frances E. Norton

E & J GALLO WINERY

P.O. Box 1130
Modesto, California 95353
U.S.A.
(209) 579-3111
Fax: (209) 579-3192

Private Company
Incorporated: 1933
Employees: 5,000
Sales: $1 billion (est.)
SICs: 2084 Wines, Brandy, and Spirits

E & J Gallo Winery is the largest winemaker in the world. In 1990, the wine industry newsletter *Impact* estimated Gallo's sales at over $1 billion on shipments of 67 million cases, and in 1991 Gallo produced one in every three bottles of wine made in the United States. Gallo grows approximately five percent of the wine grapes it uses, the remaining ninety-five percent coming from hundreds of independent growers. While best known for its inexpensive jug wines, in the last decade Gallo has aggressively followed consumer preference into more expensive categories, notably cork-finished varietals. By 1991, according to estimates by investment banking firm Hambrecht and Quist, Gallo was the largest producer of varietals in the United States, selling an estimated eight million cases that year. The winery's crowning achievement will undoubtedly be its introduction of a limited-production, estate-bottled $60 Cabernet Sauvignon and $30 Chardonnay from the Gallo property in California's Sonoma County. These wines will be released when the company feels that their quality equals or exceeds other offerings in the most expensive super-premium category. In pursuit of this goal, the Gallo brothers have almost 2,300 acres of prime Sonoma land in vine, making them the largest landowners in the region. The company is also a market leader in sherry, vermouth, and port, marketed under the Gallo trade name; their other leading brands include André sparkling wine and E & J brandy.

Gallo's phenomenal success rests on the shoulders of two publicity-shy octogenarians, brothers Ernest and Julio Gallo, who founded the winery in Modesto, California, in 1933 and who remain with their families its sole owners. Ernest is regarded as the marketing and distribution expert, while Julio oversees wine production. The Gallos' contribution to every aspect of their business is widely acknowledged throughout the industry. Ernest is credited with almost single-handedly increasing domestic demand in the 1960s and 1970s, while Julio's technical innovations include the widespread adoption of stainless-steel fermentation tanks to replace the traditional wood casks for all but the most expensive wines. In an era when most of the big winemakers are publicly listed conglomerates, Gallo remains resolutely family-oriented. The second generation of Gallo family members has been active in management of the winery for many years, and the third generation has recently begun to make its mark.

The growth of the Gallo winery parallels the emergence of California winemaking as a world-class industry. California had been successful in international competitions as far back as the early 1900s, but with the arrival of Prohibition in January 1920, the thriving industry was almost destroyed. Thousands of acres of carefully cultivated wine grapes were uprooted and replaced with cash crops such as apples and walnuts. When Prohibition was repealed on December 5, 1933, a mere 160 of California's original 700 wineries were intact, and federal and state taxation and legislation had decimated domestic wine consumption.

In 1933 Ernest and Julio Gallo, aged 24 and 23 years, respectively, entered the wine business. They had worked since childhood in the modest vineyards of their immigrant Italian father, and after the death of both their parents, they decided to start making their own wine. Their technical expertise was gleaned from two pre-Prohibition wine pamphlets in the Modesto Public Library. Ernest and Julio obtained the necessary Government license, purchased winemaking equipment on credit, and leased a small Modesto warehouse for $60 a month. They then visited local growers, offering them a share of the profits in return for the use of their grapes. By the time Repeal came in December 1933, Ernest had made his first sale of 6,000 gallons of wine to Pacific Wine Company, a Chicago distributor. Profit in the first year was $34,000, a sum which was immediately ploughed back into the business.

The first Gallo winery was built at Dry Creek in Modesto and until the late 1930s sold table wine to local bottlers, who sold it under a variety of labels. In 1940, however, the first wine was introduced under the Gallo label, and business increased substantially. Bottled in Los Angeles and New Orleans, the original selection consisted of the varietal wines Zinfandel and Dry Muscat, in addition to sherry and muscatel. It was during this early period that Ernest developed the strategic vision which would make him renowned throughout the industry. Realizing that consumption would never rise while wine was relegated to a secondary position behind hard liquor, he introduced the novel concept of salesmen who sold wine exclusively, a highly successful idea which was soon widely imitated. He recruited a team of zealous salesmen to push Gallo products and guarantee them high visibility on liquor store shelves. From the beginning, Gallo followed a strategy of expansion into new markets only when existing markets were conquered. Twenty-five years later, Gallo brands were available nationwide, and the company's distribution system was regarded as its greatest competitive strength.

The company was also admired for its enological accomplishments. The Prohibition era had wreaked havoc on crops of better varieties of wine grape, which had been largely supplanted by inferior table and raisin varieties. The Gallo brothers addressed this problem with the purchase in 1942 of 2,000 acres of land in Livingston, California. Starting in 1945, they pursued an ambitious research and experimentation program which covered all aspects of viticulture, from rootstocks to irrigation methods. Grapes grown on the Livingston land were transported to a special research winery in Modesto for further testing. When a particular variable was determined to be beneficial, it was introduced into day-to-day winery operations. Many of the experiments, such as an innovative pest control system, were well ahead of their time and had far-reaching beneficial effects on the entire industry. In 1958, a research laboratory went into operation. By 1993, the research staff of twenty included chemical engineers, microbiologists, and biochemists, and a total of fifty research papers had been submitted by the Winery to the American Society of Enology and Viticulture. The company also maintained a technical library designed to keep researchers and growers abreast of latest developments in their respective fields.

In 1957 the Gallo brothers built a customized glass plant in Modesto, a step in the process of vertical integration which would eventually encompass the Fairbanks Trucking Company, an intra-state transportation company established in 1961, and Midcal Aluminum, an aluminum bottle-cap and foil manufacturing plant founded the same year. In 1957, the company introduced Thunderbird, a citrus-flavored fortified wine which reflected consumer tastes of the period. Over the years, the brand began to sell particularly well in depressed neighborhoods because of its high alcohol content and low price. Although Thunderbird was undoubtedly one of Gallo's early marketing successes, it also contributed to the company's downmarket image. By 1989, in the face of public concern over alcoholism and internal family pressure, Gallo had asked distributors not to sell its flavored fortified wines to retailers in low-income neighborhoods.

Consumption of table wine in the United States increased more than sixfold between 1960 and 1980, corresponding to a period of great growth for the Gallo company. Production techniques were developed to provide high quality at lower cost than the competition. Wine industry experts unanimously praised Gallo's achievement in "bringing new wine drinkers to the fold" with their clean, consistent, and competitively priced product. As early as 1972 the wine critic of the *Los Angeles Times* identified Gallo Hearty Burgundy, priced at $1.25 a bottle, as "the best wine value in the country today." This wine was credited with influencing Americans to buy more California jug wines. In 1965 Julio Gallo established a Grower Relations staff of wine professionals who continue to work with growers, recommending new technologies and practices developed largely at Gallo's research facility. Among the most important developments of this period was a quality drive initiated by the company with California growers in 1967. In exchange for replacing existing grapes with grape varieties of Gallo's choice, growers were offered ten- to fifteen-year contracts guaranteeing them a fair price for their harvest. More than one hundred growers signed contracts, thus ensuring the re-emergence of such classic grapes as Chardonnay, Cabernet Sauvignon, and Sauvignon Blanc. As a result of the increasing supply

of true wine grapes, Gallo was able to discontinue use of the inferior Thompson seedless grape in 1972.

In 1976 the Federal Trade Commission charged Gallo with unfair competition, and the winery signed a consent agreement restricting its ability to control its wholesalers. The consent order was designed to prevent Gallo from vertically integrating to a point where competitors would be unable to distribute their products effectively. In September 1982, Gallo successfully filed a petition to have the order set aside, arguing that "dramatic changes in the wine industry," specifically the entry of conglomerates such as Coca-Cola and Seagrams, had rendered the terms of the original order obsolete.

During the 1980s Gallo made a strong move into the premeium wine market. In 1981 a premium Chardonnay was launched, to be followed one year later with a vintage-dated Cabernet from 1978. In late 1988, having dropped some of its original cork-finished varietals, Gallo introduced others, such as a successful new "blush" category of varietals. A vintage year was added across the Wine Cellars label, a trend the winery had resisted for many years. Given the company's production, marketing, and distribution expertise, no one in the industry was surprised when Gallo quickly took a leading role in the premium wine market. At the same time, Gallo was experiencing great success with the Bartles and Jaymes wine cooler, a beverage containing a mixture of wine, fruit juices, and carbonated water, and having less alcohol than table wine. The Bartles and Jaymes product was introduced in 1985 and within a year had become market leader in a highly competitive and burgeoning segment. Many analysts attributed its success to an inspired ad campaign by Hal Riney and Partners, featuring a pair of eccentric characters named Frank Bartles and Ed Jaymes. The wine cooler phenomenon was short-lived, however; by 1993 demand had plummeted and Gallo and Seagrams were the only wine cooler producers left in the market. Advertising expenditure dropped accordingly. New introductions in the 1990s included the Eden Roc champagne brand, priced somewhat higher than the company's market leader André champagne.

In April 1986, Ernest and Julio filed suit against their younger brother Joseph, charging him with trademark infringement. Joseph had begun to market cheese under the Gallo name. The case was important because it brought into question the right of an individual to use a personal name which had already been registered as a trademark by someone else. Several months later, Joseph filed a countersuit, claiming that he had been deprived of his rightful one-third share of their parents' winery, in effect a substantial share in the E & J Gallo Winery itself. Ernest and Julio's defense rested on the assertion that their winery was completely self-funded and had nothing to with their parents' estate. In September 1988, Joseph's counterclaim was dismissed. In June 1989, a U.S. District Court judge settled the trademark infringement case in favor of the plaintiffs, and Joseph Gallo was given 30 days to stop using the Gallo name on his cheese.

Ernest and Julio show no signs of retiring; indeed they still keep a demanding daily schedule. Such is their influence on every aspect of their business that analysts have speculated on the future of Gallo when they do finally leave. However, for many years they have been transferring responsibility for day-to-day running of the winery to the second generation. Ernest's son Joseph is in charge of sales and domestic and international marketing, while his son David holds an important position in marketing. Julio's son Robert and son-in-law James Coleman are active in the production side of the business. Ernest, the company chairman, is still responsible for overall marketing and sales strategies, while Julio oversees production. Although per capita consumption of wine in the United States has been shrinking since the health-conscious 1980s, the Gallo brothers have managed to maintain their formidable output. They have exploited their tremendous distribution strength to the full. They have invested large sums in distinctive advertising campaigns. They have an almost infallible sense for what their customers want. In the 1980s, wine coolers were extremely popular. In the 1990s, Gallo is poised to capitalize on the long-term trend toward drinking more expensive wines. Ultimately, however, the company's success can be summed up in the words of Ernest Gallo as ''a constant striving for perfection in every aspect of our business.'' Competitors would surely agree.

Principal Subsidiaries: E & J Gallo Winery Europe; Gallo Glass Company Inc.; Gallo Sales Company Inc.; Pio Bartolomeo Inc.; Fairbanks Trucking Company; Frei Brothers Winery Inc.; Midcal Aluminum Inc.

Further Reading: ''American Wine Comes of Age,'' *Time,* November 27, 1972; Fierman, Jaclyn, ''How Gallo Crushes the Competition,'' *Fortune,* September 1, 1986; Laube, James, ''Gallo Brothers' Growing Stake in Sonoma,'' *The Wine Spectator*, May 31, 1991; Shanken, Marvin R., ''Gallo's Dramatic Shift to Fine Varietals,'' *The Wine Spectator*, September 15, 1991; Prial, Frank J., ''Passing the Jug,'' *New York Times Magazine*, November 15, 1992; Fisher, Lawrence M., ''The Gallos Go for the Gold,'' *New York Times*, November 22, 1992.

—Moya Verzhbinsky

THE E.W. SCRIPPS COMPANY

312 Walnut Street, 28th Floor
Cincinnati, Ohio 45202
U.S.A.
(513) 977-3825
Fax: (513) 977-3721

Public Company
Incorporated: 1878 as Scripps and Sweeney Co.
Employees: 8,200
Sales: $1.3 billion
Stock Exchanges: New York
SICs: 2711 Newspapers; 4833 Television Broadcasting
    Stations; 4841 Cable & Other Pay Television Services;
    4832 Radio Broadcasting Stations

The E. W. Scripps Company is one of the largest media companies in the United States, with 21 daily newspapers, 10 television stations, 5 radio stations, and cable television systems in 10 states. It is also a worldwide syndicator of newspaper features and comics.

The E. W. Scripps Company began life in 1878 as Scripps and Sweeney Co. when 24-year-old Edward Willis Scripps, with his cousin John Sweeney and other family members, founded his first newspaper, the *Cleveland Penny Press.* Scripps had $10,000 in capital and owned 20 percent of the paper. The rest was owned by his half-brothers George Henry and James Edmund Scripps—each of whom received 30 percent stakes in the company—and other partners.

E. W. Scripps was a populist who thought that most newspapers were geared towards the rich. He wanted his newspaper to keep the poor informed through short, simple stories that could be understood by those without extensive education. He got many of these ideas from James Scripps, an English immigrant who started the *Detroit Evening News* in 1873. E. W. also added his interest in personal stories to the mix, later giving a raise to an editor who published the fact that he had been fined $10 for riding a horse while intoxicated.

At the time the *Cleveland Penny Press* was founded, most newspapers had a party affiliation. They also sold for more than a penny, and many contemporaries were skeptical that the *Press* would succeed. E. W. Scripps's formula proved successful, however, and within weeks the *Cleveland Penny Press* had a circulation of approximately 10,000. It was not a profitable operation, however, until James Scripps ordered E. W. to run the paper for $400 a week.

As soon as the *Penny Press* was making money, E. W. persuaded his brothers to buy the St. Louis *Chronicle.* He then spent a year in St. Louis managing the paper. E. W. bought a 55 percent in the *Penny Post* —part of which was already owned by James—went to Cincinnati to manage it, and changed the paper's name to the *Cincinnati Post.* He subsequently began taking on political corruption and winning circulation.

From 1887 to 1889 James Scripps was in Europe receiving medical treatment while E. W. managed the *Detroit News.* Although E. W. expanded advertising and circulation, James was angry with the changes his brother made; upon his return, James removed E. W. from every position he could. In 1890 E. W. started his own paper, the *Kentucky Post,* in Covington, across the Ohio River from Cincinnati.

Also in 1890 E. W. Scripps entered into a partnership with his business manager, Milton McRae; the two called their newspaper company the Scripps-McRae League. McRae handled day-to-day management of the papers and received one-third of the profits, while Scripps set editorial guidelines and long-term policy. In 1890, with his business running smoothly, Scripps began building a ranch outside of San Diego, California.

In 1894 George Scripps joined Scripps-McRae. This gave the group a controlling interest in the *Cleveland Press.* Later in the 1890s the group started the *Akron Press* and *Kansas City World.* As his chain expanded, E. W. Scripps chose young, growing towns to start new newspapers. He invested as little in machinery or plants as possible, usually buying old presses and renting run-down buildings. He would then hire young ambitious editors who were given a minority stake in their paper; many of them became rich if their newspapers succeeded. With E. W. Scripps spending most of his time in California, McRae often exceeded his authority and put editorial pressure on newspaper editors. Scripps would periodically venture out of California, discover what McRae was doing, and reverse it.

Scripps next began a series of West Coast newspapers unassociated with the Scripps-McRae League group. They included papers in Los Angeles, San Francisco, Fresno, Berkeley, and Oakland, California, as well as Seattle, Tacoma, and Spokane, Washington. In 1900 George Scripps died, leaving his stock to E. W. James Scripps contested the will, however, and James and E. W. settled out of court. E. W. was forced to give all of his stock in the Detroit newspapers to James, who in return gave E. W. all of his stock in newspapers outside Detroit.

In 1902 Scripps started the Newspaper Enterprise Association (NEA), a service for exchanging and distributing illustrations, cartoons, editorials, and articles on such specialized subjects as sports and fashion. Newspapers in the Scripps chain paid a monthly fee and received information and illustrations none of them could have afforded individually. Though the NEA was originally only for Scripps papers, demand for its services was so great that it soon became available to any newspaper.

In 1906 Scripps entered another period of expansion, buying or starting papers in Denver and Pueblo, Colorado; Evansville and

Terre Haute, Indiana; Memphis and Nashville, Tennessee; Dallas, Texas; and Oklahoma.

In 1907 Scripps combined the NEA, the Scripps McRae Press Association, and Publishers Press into the United Press Association wire service in order to provide 12,000 words of copy a day by telegraph to 369 subscribers in the United States. A similar service, the Associated Press (AP), already existed and was far larger and better financed. Scripps viewed AP as monopolistic and too close to the establishment and deliberately set out to oppose it. AP was also geared toward morning newspapers, while most of Scripps's were evening newspapers. Scripps therefore had each of his papers send out stories from their area during the day and combined them with information gathered at offices set up in important news-producing cities like Washington, D.C., and other world capitals.

In 1908 Scripps retired from active management, appointing his son James G. Scripps chairman of the board. During World War I, Scripps was a passionate advocate of United States intervention on the side of the allies and moved to Washington, D.C., to push his cause. Shortly thereafter, a family crisis erupted, during which Scripps's son James detached the five West Coast newspapers and the *Dallas Dispatch* from the chain. In 1918 United Press caused a storm of controversy when it reported the end of World War I four days before it actually ended. Scripps's health started declining during the war, and by its end he was largely living on his yacht. In 1920 he gave direct control of the chain to his son Robert and Roy W. Howard and in 1922 incorporated all of his stock, news services, and newspapers into the E.W. Scripps Company, based in Cincinnati. The profits went to the Scripps Trust, set up for his heirs.

Despite his semiretirement, Scripps had the energy to direct a last burst of expansion in the 1920s. He made Roy Howard chairman and business director in 1921. Howard had played an important role in building the United Press. By 1924, he was placed in full charge of both business and editorial by E. W.'s son Robert. The newspaper chain was renamed the Scripps Howard League. Beginning in 1921, newspapers were bought or started in Birmingham, Alabama; Indianapolis, Indiana; Baltimore, Maryland; and Pittsburgh. Sales for 1925 came to about $28 million. In 1926 the Denver-based *Rocky Mountain News* and *Times* were bought.

At the time of E. W. Scripps's death in 1926, the Scripps Howard League was the second-largest newspaper chain in the United States, after William Randolph Hearst's. E. W. Scripps was one the most successful newspaper owners of the era of the so-called Press Barons. Because of his reclusive personality, though, he was one of the least known. He stood up for the working class but in many ways despised them. And, he encouraged his newspapers to crusade for female suffrage but considered women inferior to men.

All in all, Scripps started 32 newspapers. Some of them did not stay in business long; some were unsophisticated but remained fiercely independent. Their emphasis on human interest stories was welcomed by new immigrants who had lost their former communities.

Roy Howard's stock holding in the company was small, but with his strong personality he influenced the Scripps heirs and took working control of the company, managing it as if it were his own and bringing his own family into the company hierarchy. In 1927 Scripps Howard bought the *New York Telegram.* Four years later, it purchased the *New York World* and merged the two newspapers into the *World-Telegram.* In 1936 Howard gave up his position as chairman of the chain and became president.

In the 1930s United Press built a network of bureaus in South and Central America and in the Far East, though its coverage was weaker in Europe, and it remained smaller than AP. Also that decade the newspaper chain began to shrink as less-profitable papers were sold or consolidated and six-day evening papers began to lose their appeal.

After World War II Scripps Howard's sales grew dramatically, from nearly $50 million in 1940 to more than $100 million in 1948 and $140 million in 1952. Profits, however, were not increasing. Due to the rising cost of labor, newsprint, and printing machinery, profits were hovering around $10 million, according to *Forbes* magazine. In 1953 E. W. Scripps's grandson Charles E. Scripps became company chairman at the age of 33, and Roy Howard's son Jack R. became company president at the age of 42. By this time Scripps Howard had 19 newspapers with a total circulation of 4 million. The company was also expanding into broadcasting and owned radio and television stations in Cleveland and Cincinnati as well as in Knoxville and Memphis, Tennessee. The Scripps family trust still owned nearly 75 percent of the company. Management was decentralized with general operations in New York, editorial policy centered in Washington, and finances handled in Cincinnati.

In 1958 United Press merged with the Hearst Corporation's troubled International News Service to become United Press International (UPI). Hearst gained five percent ownership of UPI, but most former International News Service employees were laid off. Also that year Scripps bought the *Cincinnati Times-Star* and merged it into the *Post,* giving the company control of all of Cincinnati's daily newspapers. The *Cincinnati Enquirer* —which had been acquired in 1956—was carefully kept separate from the other papers to diminish possible charges of a monopoly. In 1964, however, the U.S. Department of Justice accused Scripps Howard of owning a monopoly and ordered it to sell the *Enquirer.* The *Enquirer* was far stronger financially, but the trust's lawyers advised the firm that it would be better off selling it, rather than trying to sell the *Post.*

In the meantime, Scripps continued building its broadcast division, buying WPTV in West Palm Beach, Florida, for $2 million in 1961. In 1963 the broadcast properties were taken public under the name Scripps Howard Broadcasting Company. The initial offering quickly sold out, leaving the E.W. Scripps Company with two-thirds ownership.

Roy Howard died in 1964. One of the problems Jack Howard—who had succeed Roy Howard as president in 1953—faced was that the company was still run for the beneficiaries of the E.W. Scripps trust, and the trustees' lawyers sometimes had a large role in significant corporate decisions. More importantly, with the rise of television after World War II, evening newspapers across the United States found their circulations declining: people read the newspaper in the morning and watched the news on TV in the evening. In addition, management of Scripps had become so conservative that critics charged it had no long-range plans and did little beyond preserve its assets. More and more Scripps newspapers took advantage of a law that allowed newspapers in danger of failing to partially merge with stronger rivals, keeping only editorial departments separate. By 1980 eight of the 16 remaining Scripps dailies were in such arrangements, a higher percentage than any other major chain.

In 1976 Jack Howard retired as president of E.W. Scripps but remained a director of E.W. Scripps and chairman of Scripps Howard Broadcasting. Edward Estlow became E.W. Scripps's first chief executive officer who was not from the Scripps or Howard families; he had been the chain's general business manager.

Scripps slowly began to change in the 1970s. In 1977 the company bought for $29 million the 90 percent of Media Investment Co. that it did not already own. Media Investment had holdings in some of Scripps's newspapers and radio and TV stations. The purpose of acquiring the investment company was to permit employees to own shares in the diversified E.W. Scripps Company.

UPI losses were continuing to increase—$24 million between 1975 and 1980. In addition some of Scripps's newspapers were operating in the red, including the flagship *Cleveland Press*. In 1980 Scripps sold the *Press* for an undisclosed amount to Cleveland retailer Joseph E. Cole. The chain then had 16 daily newspapers, making it the seventh-largest in the United States. Scripps continued a policy of not reporting financial data, but the *Wall Street Journal* cited its sales at approximately $550 million.

In 1981 the E.W. Scripps Company began looking for a buyer for UPI. Estlow said that part of the reason was the possibility that the beneficiaries of the Scripps trust fund might bring legal action forcing the closing or selling of the wire service. In 1982 the firm found a buyer for UPI: Media News Corporation, a private firm started for the purpose of buying UPI, which had 224 bureaus and 2,000 employees. The purchase price was not disclosed, but industry analysts felt it could not have been much more than the value of UPI's assets, which the *New York Times* estimated were worth about $20 million.

In the early 1980s Scripps began funneling money into its chain of weekly business journals. The publications were losing readership and advertising revenue, and some criticized them as lacking hard news. In 1985 Lawrence A. Leser became president of Scripps and quickly began making changes. He sold many of the weeklies, as well as a videotape-publishing business, and concentrated on building the cable, broadcast, and daily newspaper operations, particularly in the rapidly growing South and West.

In 1986 the company bought two television stations from Capital Cities Communications and the American Broadcasting Co. Scripps paid an estimated $246 million for WXYZ in Detroit and WFTS in Tampa. The company was also building a string of cable TV systems. And in 1986 Scripps merged with the John P. Scripps newspaper chain, which was comprised of six California newspapers and one Washington newspaper.

These purchases, along with a cable system being built in Sacramento, left the company with millions of dollars in debt. Partly in an effort to pay off this debt, the Scripps family members who controlled the Scripps trust fund decided to take the company public. In 1987, as a prelude to its stock offering, the firm officially released financial data for the first time, reporting an operating income of $150 million on sales of $1.15 billion. It owned 20 daily newspapers and 9 TV stations and cable systems in 10 states. The 1988 stock offering left the Scripps Trust with approximately 75 percent ownership of the company.

In December of 1988 The E.W. Scripps Company formed Scripps Howard Productions to produce and market TV programs. In February of 1989 it sold the six-day *Florida Sun-Tattler* for an undisclosed amount and bought Cable USA's system in Carroll County, Georgia. Profits for 1989 were $89.3 million on sales of $1.27 billion.

In 1990 Scripps began the Sportsouth Network to provide regional sports programming on cable-TV in six southern states. Most of the firm's revenue continued to come from newspapers, but it believed that future growth would come from cable-TV. As of the early 1990s, the firm had 672,000 cable subscribers, making it one of the 20 largest cable system operators in the United States.

The E.W. Scripps Company also negotiated to buy WMAR-TV in Baltimore from Gillett Holdings for $154.7 million. Scripps backed out of the deal at the last minute and was sued by Gillett. The firms settled out of court, and Scripps bought the station for $125 million in cash. In late 1991 the company announced a modernization of the *Pittsburgh Press* delivery systems. The modernization, which would cause hundreds of layoffs, resulted in a crippling strike that lasted well into 1992; the newspaper was sold on December 31, 1992.

In February of 1993 The E.W. Scripps Company sold its Pharos Books and World Almanac Education to K-III Communications. In March of that year, the company offered for sale its four radio stations in a continuing effort to focus its attention on television.

Principal Subsidiaries: Scripps Howard Broadcasting Company.

Further Reading: Cochran, Negley D., *E. W. Scripps,* New York, Harcourt, Brace and Company, 1933; "Scripps and Howard," *Forbes,* October 1953; "Roy W. Howard, Publisher, Dead," *New York Times,* November 21, 1964; King, Michael J., "Weakened Chain," *Wall Street Journal,* November 28, 1980; Pace, Eric, "U.P.I. Sold to New Company," *New York Times,* June 3, 1982; Brendon, Piers, *The Life and Death of the Press Barons,* New York, Atheneum, 1983; Abrams, Bill, "Capital Cities, ABC to Sell 2 TV Outlets To Scripps Howard," *Wall Street Journal,* July 29, 1985; Phillips, Stephen, and David Lieberman, "Extra! Extra! Get Yer Share of Scripps," *Business Week,* July 11, 1988; The E.W. Scripps Company Annual Report, 1991; Scripps Howard Broadcasting Company Annual Report, 1991.; The E.W. Scripps Company news releases, December 31, 1992, February 16, 1993, and March 10, 1993.

—Scott M. Lewis

EASTMAN KODAK COMPANY

343 State Street
Rochester, New York 14650
U.S.A.
(716) 724-4000
Fax: (716) 724-0663

Public Company
Incorporated: 1901
Employees: 132,600
Sales: $20.18 billion
Stock Exchange: New York
SICs: 3861 Photographic Equipment and Supplies; 5043
   Photographic Equipment & Supplies; 2869 Industrial
   Organic Chemicals; 2899 Chemical Preparations; 2865
   Cyclic Crudes & Intermediates; 3572 Computer Storage
   Devices; 3577 Computer Peripheral Equipment; 7372
   Prepackaged Software; 7373 Computer Integrated Systems
   Design; 2796 Platemaking Services; 2833 Medicinals &
   Botanicals; 2821 Plastics Materials & Resins; 2823
   Cellulosic Man-Made Fibers

A multinational corporation whose name and film products are familiar to photographers around the world, Eastman Kodak Company is a diversified manufacturer of photographic imaging equipment and supplies, chemicals, health-care products, and information systems. Kodak is recognized widely as a tightly managed company with superior international marketing.

The company bears the name of its founder, George Eastman, who became interested in photography during the late 1870s while planning a vacation from his job as a bank clerk in Rochester, New York. Taking a coworker's suggestion to make a photographic record of his intended trip to Santo Domingo, the 24-year-old Eastman soon discovered that the camera, film, and wet-plate-developing chemicals and equipment he had purchased were far too bulky. Instead of following through with his original vacation plans, Eastman spent the time studying how to make photography more convenient. He discovered a description of a dry-plate process that was being used by British photographers. He tried to replicate this process in his mother's kitchen at night after work.

After three years Eastman produced a dry glass plate with which he was satisfied. He obtained a U.S. patent for the dry plate and for a machine for preparing many plates at one time, and started

manufacturing dry plates for sale to photographers. Henry A. Strong, a local businessman impressed by Eastman's work, joined him on January 1, 1881, to form the Eastman Dry Plate Company. Eastman left his position at the bank later that year to give his complete attention to the new company.

The new venture almost collapsed several times during its early years because the quality of the dry plates was inconsistent and Eastman insisted that the defective plates be replaced at no charge to the customer. Despite these setbacks, he was determined to make the camera ''as convenient as the pencil.''

As his business grew, Eastman experimented to find a lighter and more flexible substitute for the glass plate. In 1884 he introduced a new film system using gelatin-coated paper packed in a roll holder that could be used in almost every plate camera available at that time. The company was recognized as Eastman Dry Plate and Film Company. Strong was president and Eastman treasurer and general manager of the 14-shareholder corporation. The company also opened a sales office in London in 1885 to take advantage of the growing European photography market.

In 1888 Eastman's company introduced its first portable camera. Priced at $25, it included enough film for 100 pictures. After shooting the roll of film, the owner sent both the film and the camera to Rochester for processing. For $10, the company sent back the developed prints and the camera loaded with a new roll of film. This breakthrough is considered to be the birth of snapshot photography. It was also at this time that Eastman trademarked ''Kodak,'' which he invented by experimenting with words that began and ended with his favorite letter, ''K.'' The company advertised its new camera extensively using the slogan, ''You push the button, we do the rest.''

The following year, the Eastman Photographic Materials Company was incorporated in the United Kingdom to distribute Kodak products outside the United States from its headquarters in London. The company built a manufacturing plant in 1891 outside London to accommodate the growing product demand overseas, and set up additional distribution sites in France, Germany, and Italy by 1900.

In 1889 the firm's name was changed to Eastman Company and in 1892 to Eastman Kodak Company. Eastman became president of the company upon Strong's death in 1919.

Eastman was committed to bringing photography to the greatest number of people at the lowest possible price. As his company grew and production of both the camera and film increased, manufacturing costs decreased significantly. This allowed the firm to introduce a number of new cameras, including the Folding Pocket Kodak Camera in 1898. It also brought out the first of a complete line of Brownie cameras, an easy-to-operate model that sold for $1 and used film that sold at 15 cents per roll, in 1900.

Over the next 20 years, the company continued to introduce photographic innovations. In 1902 Kodak brought to market a new developing machine that allowed film processing without benefit of a darkroom. The 1913 introduction of Eastman Portrait Film provided professional photographers with a sheet film alternative to glass plates.

In 1912 George Eastman hired Dr. C. E. Kenneth Mees, a British scientist, to head one of the first U.S. industrial research centers. Based in Rochester, this lab was where various tools and manufacturing processes that provided the company with a continuing stream of new products in the 1920s were invented. These new products, which included 16-millimeter Kodacolor motion picture film, the 16-millimeter Cine-Kodak motion picture camera, and the Kodascope projector, were targeted at the mass market and priced appropriately.

Kodak developed other new products to support the country's involvement in World War I. In 1917 the company developed aerial cameras and trained U.S. Signal Corps photographers in their use. It also supplied the U.S. Navy with cellulose acetate, a film product, for coating airplane wings, and produced the unbreakable lenses used on gas masks.

George Eastman had always been civic-minded; even as a struggling bank clerk he donated money to the Mechanics Institute of Rochester. As Kodak grew, his philanthropy extended to such institutions as the Massachusetts Institute of Technology, the Hampton and Tuskegee institutes, and the University of Rochester. He was instrumental in starting numerous dental clinics around the world, and he enjoyed a reputation as a paternalistic employer because of his profit-sharing programs and insurance benefits for workers. In 1932 George Eastman committed suicide at the age of 77, leaving a note that read, ''To my friends. My work is done. Why wait? G.E.''

That same year, the company introduced the first eight-millimeter motion picture system for the amateur photographer, consisting of film, cameras, and projectors. Three years later, it made available 16-millimeter Kodachrome film, the first amateur color film to gain commercial success. Similar film products for 35-millimeter slides and eight-millimeter home movies were introduced in 1936.

New photographic products continued to be introduced over the next decade, even as the company devoted a portion of its manufacturing capability to the production of equipment and film for the military during World War II. Following the war, Kodak focused its total attention once again on amateur photography with the introduction of a low-priced Brownie eight-millimeter movie camera in 1951 and the accompanying projector one year later.

In 1953 the company formed Eastman Chemical Products, Inc. to market alcohols, plastics, and fibers for industrial use. These substances were manufactured by Tennessee Eastman and Texas Eastman, two subsidiaries that had been formed in 1920 and 1952, respectively. The company had begun to manufacture these items because of its own use of chemicals in film manufacturing and processing.

Until this point, the company had always included the cost of film processing in the cost of film. A consent decree filed in 1954 forced Eastman Kodak to abandon this practice, but it also provided an opportunity for the company to serve a new market, independent photo finishers, with its film-developing products. Kodak acquired several photo finishing laboratories, including Fox Photo and American Photographic Group, to form an independent joint venture known as Qualex with Colorcraft Corp., owned by Fuqua Industries.

By 1958 the company had made significant advances in 35-millimeter color slide technology and introduced the first completely automatic projector, called the Kodak Calvalcade. A line of Kodak Carousel projectors introduced three years later became highly successful.

In 1963, one year after astronaut John Glenn had used Kodak film to record his orbit of the earth, the company introduced the Instamatic camera. Using a film cartridge instead of film roll, the Instamatic revolutionized amateur photography and became a commercial success because it was easy to use. Two years later, Kodak brought out a similar cartridge system for super-eight format Instamatic movie cameras and projectors. In 1972 five different models of a pocket version of the Instamatic camera were launched and proved immediately popular.

That same year, the company acquired Spin Physics, a San Diego, California-based producer of magnetic heads used in recording equipment. This purchase was completed in 1973.

In the early 1970s, Eastman Kodak became the defendant in a series of antitrust suits filed by several smaller film, camera, and processing companies. These legal actions alleged that Kodak illegally monopolized the photographic market. The most widely publicized suit, filed by Berkey Photo, charged that Kodak had violated the Sherman Antitrust Act by conspiring with two other companies, Sylvania Companies—a subsidiary of GTE Products Corporation—and General Electric Company, to develop two photographic flash devices. Berkey requested that Eastman Kodak be divided into ten separate companies and asked for $300 million in damages. The case was settled in 1981 for $6.8 million.

In 1975 Kodak introduced the Ektaprint Copier-Duplicator, putting itself into direct competition with two firmly entrenched rivals, Xerox and IBM. Kodak considered this market to be a good fit with its existing microfilm business. In addition, the company had already established a foothold with a similar product, the Verifax machine, which had been introduced in 1953. This copier used a wet process like that used in photography, but it had become obsolete when Xerox introduced a technological advancement called xerography, which was less messy and produced better-quality copies than previous systems. After careful research and planning, the Ektaprint copier was developed to serve businesses with large-scale duplicating needs. Not only could the Ektaprint produce numerous copies at high speed, but it could also collate them while duplicating, a unique feature at the time.

In 1976 Kodak took on another well-established firm when it challenged Polaroid Corporation's 30-year lock on instant photography with a new line of instant cameras and film that developed pictures outside the camera within a few minutes. Kodak had missed an opportunity to get in on the ground floor of this technology in the 1940s when it declined an offer to market an instant camera invented by Polaroid founder Edwin Land. The general feeling among Kodak's management at the time had been that Land's camera was a toy and the quality of its pictures not up to the company's accepted standards. Kodak had, however, also gained from Polaroid's success. It had become the exclusive supplier of negatives for Polaroid's instant, pull-apart color film in 1963. In 1969 Polaroid elected to take over this part of its film manufacturing itself. At the same time Polaroid cut prices drastically to bring its instant cameras more in line with the Kodak Instamatics. Kodak was convinced that Polaroid's instant photography products posed a threat to the company's market leadership. However, the company's methodical product-development process, which emphasized long-term product quality over quick market entry, as well as Polaroid's ownership of hundreds of related patents, proved to be major obstacles to an immediate competitive response. When Kodak finally introduced its own instant camera four years after the decision was made to develop it, the company was plagued by production problems and a Polaroid lawsuit alleging patent infringement. Although the company captured about 25 percent of the U.S. instant camera market within its first year, reports of quality flaws with the camera's instant photographs and Polaroid's response with another new instant camera stifled sales. Polaroid successfully exploited the business applications of instant photography—identity cards, for example—and retained its strong position in the market.

During this period, Kodak's President and Chief Executive Officer Walter A. Fallon and Chairman Gerald B. Zornow oversaw product development. When Zornow retired in 1977, Fallon assumed the chairmanship and was succeeded as president by Colby H. Chandler. Employed with Kodak since 1941, Fallon had worked his way up from production to direct the U.S. and Canadian photographic division. He had been responsible for the launch of the pocket Instamatic camera line. Chandler had joined the company in 1951 and, as Fallon's successor in the U.S. and Canadian photographic division, he was directly responsible for both the instant camera and the Ektaprint copier.

Upon becoming president, Chandler faced a challenge to Eastman Kodak's dominance in the photographic paper market by several Japanese competitors and U.S. suppliers, including Fuji Photo Film Company and 3M Company. These firms undercut Kodak's prices for a paper product of similar quality. Fuji also had the advantage of competing against a strong U.S. dollar, a factor that conversely reduced Kodak's profits significantly in foreign markets. The company responded with price reductions of its own, but suffered lower earnings and a decreasing level of investor confidence. Losing the title of official film of the 1984 Summer Olympics to Fuji added further insult to injury.

As the U.S. economy entered a recession in the late 1970s and sales growth in the company's consumer photographic products slowed, higher sales in other areas such as chemicals, business systems, and professional photo finishing pushed profits back on an upward trend. Several prior years of flat earnings across product areas were attributed largely to a lack of strategic planning. At the end of 1978 company operations were reorganized to consolidate the U.S., Canadian, and international photographic areas into one division. The company's first director of corporate planning was also hired to speed the product-development process and institute the controls needed to enable new products to become profitable more quickly.

The year 1980 marked the company's 100th anniversary. That year Kodak introduced the Ektachem 400 blood analyzer. This entry into the health sciences field represented a natural application of the company's film-manufacturing technology and rein-

forced its already strong presence as a supplier of x-ray film to hospitals and other health-care facilities.

During the 1980s the company faced intensifying Japanese competition in photography and a continuing decline in product demand. Rapid technological breakthroughs by other firms threatened to replace Kodak's core product line with more advanced equipment. The company instituted several measures to improve its performance. These included a stronger emphasis on nonphotographic products with high profit potential, a more aggressive approach to protecting its chemical imaging capabilities, a broader international marketing strategy, and a sharper focus on making acquisitions to bring the company up to speed technologically, particularly in electronics.

In 1981 the company purchased Atex, a major supplier of electronic text-editing systems used by publishers. Formed as an entrepreneurial venture in 1972 and the leader in its field at the time of the acquisition, Atex later lost ground to fast-changing computer technology as Kodak's traditionally slow-moving product development process was unable to keep pace with the industry.

Despite its shift in priorities to other areas, Kodak continued to support its bread-and-butter line of photographic products. In 1982 it introduced a line of small cameras that used film discs instead of cartridges and was considered a replacement for the pocket Instamatic camera.

Since the company's founding, Kodak had maintained a policy of treating its employees fairly and with respect, earning the nickname of the "Great Yellow Father." It was George Eastman's belief that an organization's prosperity was not necessarily due to its technological achievements, but more to its workers' goodwill and loyalty. As a result, company benefits were well above average, morale had always remained high, and employees never felt the need to unionize. This protective culture came to an end in 1983, however, when the company was forced to reduce its work force by 5 percent to cut costs. Competitive pressures from the Japanese and domestic and international economic problems had slowed product demand. Even the widely publicized disc camera failed to sustain its initial "hot" sales rate.

Upon Fallon's retirement in 1983, Colby Chandler took over as chairman and, in an attempt to keep up with the pace of change, pointed Kodak toward the electronics and video areas in earnest. During the 1970s the company had brought out products that either lacked quality or important features, or arrived too late on the scene to capitalize on new opportunities. Of all the products introduced during Fallon's tenure, only the Ektaprint copier was considered a success, although it gradually lost its marketing advantage to competitive offerings with greater speed and more features. Neither the instant nor the disc cameras had met original expectations. The company's x-ray film business also took a beating as hospital admissions dropped and attempts by medical institutions to control costs increased.

The company's new electronics division consisted of its Spin Physics subsidiary, a solid-state research laboratory, and another facility dedicated to the production of integrated circuits. Many of the products later introduced by the division, however, resulted from acquisitions or joint ventures with other companies. For example, in 1984 Kodak launched its first electronic product, a camcorder that combined an eight-millimeter video camera and recorder, in conjunction with Matsushita Electric Industrial Company of Japan. This represented a major departure for Kodak, which historically had been self-reliant in everything from manufacturing cardboard boxes to maintaining its own fire department.

Also in 1984 Kodak introduced complete lines of videotape cassettes for all video formats and floppy discs for use in personal computers. It bolstered the latter area in 1985 with the purchase of Verbatim Corporation, a floppy disc manufacturer. After five years of disappointing sales, Verbatim was sold to Mitsubishi Kasei Corporation of Japan.

Kodak underwent another major reorganization at the beginning of 1985 to capitalize more quickly on growth opportunities. Seventeen business units and a new Life Sciences Group were formed, the latter division to be involved in developing biomedical technology. Each of the 17 operating units, which had previously existed as a centralized group under the photographic division, were given more autonomy and flexibility to run their businesses as independent profit centers.

The company re-entered the 35-millimeter camera market in 1985 with a product made by Chinon Industries of Japan. Fifteen years earlier, it had withdrawn from the market because of doubts about the 35-millimeter camera's mass appeal.

In 1986, ten years after Polaroid filed its patent-infringement suit over Kodak's instant camera, a federal appeals court upheld a lower court ruling and ordered the company to leave the instant camera business. Kodak voluntarily offered its customers trade-in options for their obsolete cameras and was forced to make a somewhat different offer as a result of a class action lawsuit. The financial implications of this development and the continuing struggle to boost earnings led the company to institute another work force reduction in 1986, this time by 10 percent. Although the domestic picture was somewhat grim, the fact that nearly 40 percent of the company's sales came from overseas helped produce strong bottom-line gains over the previous year. A weakening U.S. dollar blunted the impact of foreign competition and allowed Kodak to reclaim lost ground in its core businesses while also entering new ones. An employee's suggestion to apply the company's manufacturing capabilities to the production of lithium batteries resulted in the successful introduction of a complete line of alkaline battery products under the Supralife brand.

Kodak also formed the Eastman Pharmaceuticals Division to establish an even stronger presence in health care. Joint venture agreements and licensing arrangements with existing pharmaceutical companies initially occupied division management's attention. In 1988 Kodak acquired Sterling Drug Inc., a manufacturer of prescription drugs and such consumer products as Bayer aspirin and Lysol cleaners, to make the company more competitive in the pharmaceutical industry. The acquisition, however, was viewed unfavorably by the company's shareholders, in part because Sterling had a second-rate reputation as a pharmaceutical manufacturer. One year later, this negative perception seemed correct. Intense competition had reduced the sales of Sterling's existing pharmaceuticals while new products

under development showed questionable effectiveness during testing.

In 1988 evidence came to light indicating that toxic chemicals from the company's Rochester plant had leaked into the area's groundwater, posing a possible health hazard to local residents. In April 1990 the company admitted that it had violated New York's environmental regulations and was fined $1 million. It also agreed to clean up the site of its Kodak Park manufacturing facility and reduce chemical emissions from the plant.

Under the direction of Mr. Kay Whitmore, who became chairman and CEO in 1990, profits of the goliath company grew steadily. However, the positive results that emerged from the company's restructuring of 1985 were eroded by the recession of the early 1990s. Coupled with the recession came the Persian Gulf War, which seriously dampened the tourist and travel industry and hurt sales of photographic equipment.

Once again, Kodak embarked on a path of restructuring and cost cutting. As a cost cutting incentive, management in 1990 devised an early retirement plan that would trim approximately 5,800 from the work force. One year later, however, the plan backfired somewhat when 6,600 decided to retire early. With a shortfall of employees, the company was forced to hire 1600 new workers. Management also was trimmed. Only three managers were replaced out of the 12 who retired in 1991.

Of the four business segments that had been in place since the previous restructuring—photographic, information, health, and chemicals—management merged photographic and information into a single group named Imaging. Three group presidents were appointed to head the three divisions. Downsizing, cost cutting, restructuring, and a ''suspicion of red tape,'' as one market analyst described it, injected new growth into Kodak and returned the company slowly to profitability.

The largest business segment and the one generating the most sales (approximately 57 percent) is Imaging. This division includes Kodak's core business of photography and photofinishing, as well as copying machines, computer printers, and software. The division is also exploring the various possibilities of new technologies, including digital photography. In 1992 the division developed a camera able to store photographic shots on a compact disc that can be displayed on a CD player. Such advances, including Kodak's introduction in the fall of 1992 of a writable compact disc publishing system (enabling the consumer to write, store, and retrieve information on a CD), have enabled Kodak to retain its position as the world leader in electronic imaging. To maintain this lead, the company established a small Center for Creative Imaging in Camden, Maine, an artistic haven, to encourage imaging innovations in a creative atmosphere.

Kodak's Health Product Division achieved record profits in 1991, accounting for approximately 24 percent of the company's sales. This testifies to the wisdom of broadening the company's scope beyond its traditional core business. Within this segment, restructuring has also taken place with the 1991 merger of two pharmaceutical companies into one entity, Sterling Winthrop, which manufactures not only pharmaceuticals but non-pharmaceutical consumer products. Sterling Winthrop in turn formed a joint venture with the French firm Sanofi in

1991, enabling it to penetrate the European pharmaceutical market more easily than before. The joint venture places Kodak's Health Division among the top twenty pharmaceutical concerns in the world. European customers will be serviced in turn by a new manufacturing plant in Strasbourg, France, that will also provide customer support.

Included within Kodak's Health Division is the Clinical Products Division, which originated in 1984 when Kodak introduced its Ektachem blood analyzer machine. Generating no sales when it first came out, by the early 1990s sales of the Clinical Products Division had topped a half billion dollars and were growing at a rate of 20 percent, twice the growth rate of Kodak overall. Other businesses within the Health group include x-ray machines and electronic imaging, sales of which contributed to making the Health Division Kodak's most promising and profitable in recession-plagued 1991.

The third division of Kodak, Chemical Product, generated approximately 18 percent of company sales in 1991. This group manufactures and markets chemicals, fibers, and plastics. In the 1990s Eastman Chemical Company has become the 15th largest chemical firm in the United States. The new focus of the Chemical Division has been on expansion and overseas sales. As a result, the Chemical Division has become a global enterprise, with joint ventures in many foreign countries. In 1991 Eastman Chemical entered the propylene business with the purchase of propylene interests as well as the urethane polyols business of ARCO Chemical Company. The Tenite Plastics division of Eastman Chemical is the largest plastic bottle and container supplier in the world.

Kodak has weathered many difficult economic times. In reasonable financial health at this time, the company is increasingly concerned with establishing an important presence in the global marketplace. Approximately 45 percent of the company's annual sales are generated overseas. Kodak was one of the first U.S. companies to take advantage of the fall of communism in Eastern Europe, setting up subsidiaries in Hungary and Poland and planning further penetration of that long deprived, but eager market. The company also has established a subsidiary in Turkey, numerous joint ventures with European firms, and a new headquarters in The Hague (Eastman Chemical).

Principal Subsidiaries: Eastman Kodak International Finance B.V. (Netherlands); Eastman Kodak International Sales Corporation (U.S. Virgin Islands); Eastman Technology, Inc.; Torrey Pines Realty Company, Inc.; Cyclotomics, Inc.; Datatape Incorporated; Electronic Pre-Press Systems, Inc.; Interactive Systems Corp.; Northfield Pharmaceuticals Limited; Ultra Technologies, Inc.; Eastman Chemical Products, Inc.; Holston Defense Corporation; Eastman Gelatine Corporation; Mustang Pipeline Company; Pinto Pipeline Company of Texas; Eastman Chemical International Ltd.; Eastman Chemical International, A.G. (Switzerland); Eastmanchem, Inc. (Canada); Eastman Canada, Inc.; Kodak Argentina, Ltd.; Kodak Brasileira C.I.L. (Brazil); Kodak Chilena S.A.F. (Chile); Kodak Colombiana, Ltd.; Kodak Mexicana, Ltd.; Kodak Panama, Ltd.; Kodak Export Limited; Laboratorios Kodak Limitada; Foto Interamericana de Peru, Ltd.; Kodak Caribbean, Limited; Kodak Uruguaya, Ltd. (Uruguay); Kodak Venezuela, S.A.; Kodak (Near East), Inc.; Kodak (Singapore) Pte. Limited; Kodak Philippines, Ltd.; Kodak Limited (U.K.); Kodak Ireland Limited (U.K.); Kodak Pathe (France); Kodak A.G. (Germany); Eastman Kodak International Capital Company, Inc.; Kodak Ges. m.b.h. (Austria); Kodak Oy (Finland); Kodak Nederland B.V. (Netherlands); Kodak S.p.A. (Italy); Kodak Portuguesa Limited; Kodak S.A. (Spain); Kodak AB (Sweden); Eastman Kodak (Japan) Ltd.; K.K. Kodak Information Systems (Japan); Kodak Japan Ltd.; Kodak Imagica K.K. (Japan); Kodak Far East Purchasing, Inc.; Kodak New Zealand Limited; Kodak (Australasia) Proprietary Limited; Kodak (Kenya) Limited; International Biotechnologies Inc.; Kodak (Egypt) S.A.; Komal S.B. (Malaysia); Kodak (Export Sales) Ltd. (Hong Kong); Kodak Taiwan Limited Inc.; Kodak Korea Ltd.; Sterling Drug Inc.

Further Reading: Chakravarty, Subrata N., and Ruth Simon, "Has the World Passed Kodak By?," *Forbes,* November 5, 1984; *Journey into Imagination: The Kodak Story,* Rochester, New York, Eastman Kodak Company, 1988; Annual Report: Eastman Kodak Company, 1991; Leib, Jeffrey, "Kodak Colorado Peddles Injection-Molding Expertise," *Denver Post,* March 6, 1992; Johnson, Greg, "Kodak Device Places Images of Film on Disc," *Los Angeles Times,* July 31, 1992; Perdue, Wes, "Eastman Kodak and BioScan Inc. Form Alliance," *Business Wire,* August 10, 1992; Astor, Will, "Huge Pioneer-Kodak Project Marks Progress," *Rochester Business Journal,* September 25, 1992; Burgess, John, "Firms Plan Multimedia Consortium," *Washington Post,* October 1, 1992; Weber, Jonathan, "Top High-Tech Firms Team Up on 'Multimedia,' " *Los Angeles Times,* October 7, 1992.

—Sandy Schusteff
updated by Sina Dubovoj

ENCYCLOPEDIA BRITANNICA, INC.

310 S. Michigan Ave.
Chicago, Illinois 60604-4202
U.S.A.
(312) 347-7000
Fax: (312) 347-7135

Private Company
Incorporated: 1943
Employees: 1,505
Sales: $586 million
SICs: 2731 Book Publishing

Encyclopaedia Britannica, Inc., has published one of the world's finest encyclopedias for more than two centuries. The *Britannica* is respected throughout the world for its combination of breadth and thoroughness in its treatment of everything from the Punic Wars to quantum mechanics, and many of its articles, written by outstanding scholars in their respective fields, are masterpieces of compact erudition unlike anything else in the field of learning. Today, Encyclopaedia Britannica, Inc., markets the *Britannica* in more than 100 countries around the world and is also the parent company of Merriam-Webster, Inc., publishers of the famed dictionaries; Compton's MultiMedia Publishing Group, Inc.; Evelyn Wood, Inc.; and Encyclopaedia Britannica Educational Corporation, which markets audio-visual and electronic learning aids as well as books to schools and libraries. Encyclopaedia Britannica, Inc., is owned in turn by the William Benton Foundation of Illinois, a charitable foundation supporting programs in journalism and the media at the University of Chicago.

The *Encyclopaedia Britannica* was first published between 1768 and 1771 "by a society of gentlemen in Scotland, printed in Edinburgh for A. Bell and C. Macfarquhar, and sold by Colin Macfarquhar at his printing office in Nicolson-street," as the First Edition's title page informed its readers. The idea of uniting in a single publication all aspects of human knowledge went back at least to Roman times, but it was in the eighteenth century, the "age of enlightenment," that encyclopedias in the modern form began to appear in Europe. The French *Encyclopedie,* first published in 1751, became the symbol of French radical humanism and generated international controversy for its allegedly blasphemous philosophy, but there is no evidence

that the creators of the *Encyclopaedia Britannica* were directly inspired by the fame of the *Encyclopedie* (which in fact was begun as a translation of an earlier work by the Englishman Ephraim Chambers).

Andrew Bell, a prosperous engraver of Edinburgh, and the printer Colin Macfarquhar were convinced that the English-speaking world could use a reference work featuring substantial treatises on the arts, sciences, and trades combined alphabetically with shorter entries defining important terms and concepts. The two men engaged William Smellie, a twenty-eight-year-old scholar at the University of Edinburgh, as general editor of the First Edition of their proposed *Encyclopaedia Britannica,* which was published and sold in one hundred parts between 1768 and 1771. The *Encyclopaedia* contained 2,659 pages, including articles borrowed from such luminaries as Benjamin Franklin (on electricity) and John Locke (on human understanding). The editors themselves wrote many of the shorter articles, while the longest pieces ("Surgery" and "Anatomy") were treatises of well over one hundred pages each. The new encyclopedia sold well, and its editors began immediate preparations for a second, much larger edition.

James Tytler succeeded Smellie as editor of the Second Edition, which was published between 1777 and 1784 in ten volumes totaling 8,595 pages and 340 copperplates engraved by Bell. The Second Edition was among the first encyclopedias to include articles on history and biography, two subjects which have since become standard. It was followed by a Third Edition of eighteen volumes completed in 1797, edited by Macfarquhar and George Glieg, later a bishop and Primus of the Scottish Episcopal Church. (Macfarquhar died in 1793 at the age of forty-eight, "worn out," as later publisher Archibald Constable put it, "by fatigue and anxiety of mind.") By this time the *Britannica* was well known and widely sought after; the Third Edition sold between 10,000 and 13,000 copies and is said to have returned the substantial profit of £42,000 to Andrew Bell, its sole proprietor after the death of Macfarquhar.

Bell remained the owner and manager of the *Britannica* until his own death in 1809, after which his heirs sold the company's stock and copyrights for £13,500 to Archibald Constable, an Edinburgh publisher. Constable was an able promoter and manager, and under his direction the *Britannica* made important advances in the quality of its writing and increased sales both in Great Britain and the United States. Constable's Fifth Edition of 1817 was criticized as little more than a reprint of Bell's Fourth, but soon afterward a six-volume Supplement appeared which cemented the reputation of the *Britannica* as the premier encyclopedia of the English-speaking world. Constable was the first *Britannica* publisher to solicit new articles from the leading scholars and artists of his day, and among the contributors to the Supplement and the Sixth Edition, both completed in 1824, were such distinguished men of letters as William Hazlitt, Walter Scott, David Ricardo, and Thomas Malthus. Constable died in 1827, before he could make a start on the planned Seventh Edition.

Copyrights to the essays were bought at auction by Adam Black, an Edinburgh bookseller, who collaborated with his relative Charles Black and their sons to publish the *Britannica* for the next seventy years as A & C Black Ltd. The Seventh

Edition, edited by Macvey Napier, appeared between 1830 and 1842 and included a set of introductory essays intended to describe the progress of human knowledge since medieval times in four fundamental classifications—metaphysical, moral, and political philosophy; mathematics and physics; chemistry; and zoology, botany, and mineralogy. Similar attempts to organize all knowledge under a handful of rubrics had been common among encyclopedists from Roger Bacon in the thirteenth century to the French *philosophes,* but the increasing scope and complexity of science in the nineteenth century discouraged the *Britannica* from making any further efforts in this direction. Indeed, so rapid was the progress of scientific and historical knowledge in the age of Charles Darwin and Karl Marx that by the 1860s the children of Adam Black were eager to publish a totally new *Britannica* in tune with the startling changes of their age. The resulting Ninth Edition (completed in 1889) has since been acknowledged as one of the most impressive collections of scholarship ever produced, its articles written by outstanding experts in every domain of the arts and sciences. Thomas Henry Huxley, the distinguished biologist, served as general advisor for the scientific articles; typical of the contributors' excellence was the example of Prince Pyotr Kropotkin, the famed Russian political theorist, who wrote his essay on "Anarchism" from his prison cell in Clairvaux, France.

The Ninth Edition sold about 10,000 sets in Great Britain between 1875 and 1898, but it found a far larger market in the United States, where its authorized publisher, Charles Scribner's Sons, sold no fewer than 45,000 sets during the same period. Unfortunately, international copyright laws had not been agreed upon between the two countries and several hundred thousand other, pirated *Britannicas* were sold in the United States, many of them incomplete or mutilated. Such marketing problems discouraged the Black family, which in 1897 agreed to turn over promotion of the *Britannica* to an American company led by Horace E. Hooper and Walter M. Jackson. The two men negotiated an agreement with the *Times* of London whereby that paper—the most respected in England, but also in financial trouble—would advertise, sell, and receive commissions for the latest reprint of the Ninth Edition. Although the scheme appeared improbable to many Englishmen, it succeeded in keeping the *Britannica* alive until Hooper and Jackson could purchase all copyrights and plates of the encyclopedia in 1901, thus bringing the symbol of England's cultural dominance into American hands at about the same time as the Empire lost its economic and political leadership to the United States.

Hooper and Jackson formed companies in both the United States and England to market their unique product. Both men were experienced publishers and booksellers, and in their efforts to find outlets for the *Britannica* they were aided in no small measure by the genius of Henry Haxton, a free-wheeling advertising executive who devised all manner of ad campaigns, games, and contests to generate popular interest in the formerly staid *Britannica.* After the publication in 1902 of a revised and supplemented version of the Ninth Edition marketed as the Tenth, Horace Hooper began work in earnest on a completely new Eleventh Edition. His enthusiasm was not matched by Walter Jackson and the two men gradually dissolved their partnership, but the Eleventh Edition sailed on under the editorial guidance of Hugh Chisholm in London and Franklin Hooper (the brother of Horace) in America. To reassure London

bankers of the new edition's salability, Horace Hooper negotiated an arrangement with Cambridge University by which the latter would lend its prestigious name to the encyclopedia in exchange for a degree of editorial control and royalties on sales. Suitably impressed, London financiers provided the capital needed to support publication of the twenty-nine volume Eleventh Edition in 1910 and 1911. Among its contributors were Matthew Arnold, R. L. Stevenson, and Alfred North Whitehead, and, like the Ninth Edition, the Eleventh would be long remembered as a treasure of world scholarship. The edition was the first to be dedicated to the American president as well as the British monarch, and the first to be printed by the large American printing firm of R. R. Donnelley and Sons. Despite its wealth of distinguished contributors and the imprimatur of Cambridge University, sales of the Eleventh were slowed by the First World War and the *Britannica* found itself once again in severe financial difficulty.

American marketing provided the solution again, this time via the retailing giant Sears, Roebuck & Co. Horace Hooper had long been the friend and golfing partner of Julius Rosenwald, the president of Sears and a well-known philanthropist in his own right. Rosenwald took an interest in the fortunes of the *Britannica,* and in 1915 Sears agreed to market a new, less expensive version of the Eleventh Edition designed to appeal to the middle-class buyer throughout the English-speaking world. Sales remained weak, however, and in 1920 Sears bought Encyclopaedia Britannica Company outright, retaining Horace Hooper as publisher and his brother Franklin as editor in New York, with Hugh Chisholm remaining London editor. Sears's purchase of the *Britannica* was a philanthropic gesture rather than a business decision, as it was clear by this time in its history that the encyclopedia would be chronically short of cash. Indeed, after three years of operation Sears reported a loss of $1.8 million at the *Britannica,* and in 1923 sold the company back to the widow of Horace Hooper (who had died in 1922) and her brother, William J. Cox.

The Twelfth and Thirteenth editions were published in 1922 and 1926, but these were merely reprints of the Eleventh edition along with supplementary material. Since the publication of the Eleventh edition in 1910, the First World War had profoundly altered the shape of western civilization, and in the late 1920s William Cox began the laborious process of raising the $2.5 million needed for a completely rewritten Fourteenth Edition. Rosenwald and Sears offered to contribute a million dollars if the University of Chicago could be persuaded to take over the role of general editor formerly filled by Cambridge. Chicago—and later Harvard—refused, however, and Sears was saddled with nearly all of the new Edition's cost, reassuming ownership in 1928 just prior to publication. Sales were good until the Great Depression paralyzed economies around the world in October 1929, when it became obvious that the *Britannica* would require radically new marketing techniques if it were not to prove a permanent liability for Sears. After the death of Julius Rosenwald in 1932, the company replaced William Cox as president with Elkan H. "Buck" Powell, a Sears secretary and treasurer.

Powell completely restructured Britannica. On the sales side, he scrapped the attempt to market the encyclopedia via Sears outlets and instead built a nationwide network of sales representatives who went door to door and also staffed booths at conventions, shopping centers, and the like. Of greater importance was Powell's decision to publish the *Britannica* continuously by revising a portion of its articles each year, thus keeping the entire work in print and relatively up to date at the same time. Previously, the financial health of the encyclopedia had been made unpredictable by its long publication cycle, which over a fifteen- to thirty-year period called first for a massive editorial effort with virtually no sales followed by an intensive sales program with no need for editors, until the growing obsolescence of the current work made a new edition necessary and the cycle began again. Powell recognized that such a pattern was inherently inefficient and in 1938 introduced the new system of continuous revision and publication, which has remained in effect ever since.

Although sales picked up during the 1930s under Powell's leadership, Sears chairman General Robert E. Wood was not comfortable with the company's ownership of the *Britannica.* In 1941 a vice-president of the University of Chicago named William Benton suggested that Sears again try to interest the University in running the *Britannica.* Benton was the remarkable co-founder of the advertising agency Benton and Bowles; after amassing a comfortable fortune he retired in 1935 (at the age of 35) and soon became active at the University of Chicago. Believing passionately in the importance of the *Britannica,* he urged the University to accept General Wood's offer to give it the company's stock, but the University's board of trustees balked at the financial risk. Benton thereupon offered to put up needed working capital if the University would agree to lend its name and editorial advice to the venture. An agreement was reached in 1943 by which Benton acquired two-thirds of the stock in a new company, Encyclopaedia Britannica, Inc., of which he became chairman, while the University received one-third of the company stock, a royalty on sales, and an option to buy another third of the company. Robert Maynard Hutchins, president of the University of Chicago, was named chairman of the Board of Editors of the *Britannica,* but the University assumed neither financial responsibility nor managerial control of the company.

In 1938 Britannica began publishing the *Britannica Book of the Year* (now called the *Britannica World Data Annual),* a yearly synopsis of world events, and in 1952 it brought out the 54-volume *Great Books of the Western World.* Edited by Hutchins and Mortimer Adler, who also wrote its two-volume index known as the *Syntopicon,* the *Great Books* attempted to trace the development of Western thought from the ancient Greeks to Sigmund Freud by collecting 443 critically important texts by 74 different authors. *Britannica* revised the *Great Books* in 1990 to include many twentieth-century authors as well. In 1943 Britannica branched into the world of film with the acquisition of ERPI, a division of Western Electric that owned the nation's largest collection of films for the classroom. Known first as Encyclopaedia Britannica Films, Inc., the company became Encyclopaedia Britannica Educational Corporation in 1966 and eventually expanded into filmstrips, video, and laser-disc technology as well as conventional films and reference books for school markets.

Under the continued leadership and financial support of William Benton, Encyclopaedia Britannica, Inc., was able to buy out the University of Chicago's share of stock in 1952 and begin preparations for the radically new Fifteenth Edition that would appear in 1974. Not only did Encyclopaedia Britannica survive, but thanks to the generosity of Benton it became the parent company of a host of other reference publishers, including Merriam-Webster, publisher of the famous dictionaries by that name, and F. E. Compton Company, fellow makers of encyclopedias. Encyclopaedia Britannica, Inc., went international in 1957 with the publication of the sixteen-volume *Enciclopedia Borsa* in Spanish, a joint venture that would later distribute Britannica products throughout Latin America under the name Encyclopaedia Britannica Publishers. *Britannica* went on to publish native-language encyclopedias in countries including Japan, the People's Republic of China, France, Italy, and Korea, all of them after 1974 under the management of Encyclopaedia Britannica International. The latter oversees all of Britannica's foreign business, which by 1990 included offices in 130 countries and operating companies in 17 countries.

William Benton died in March 1973, just before the *Britannica's* new Fifteenth Edition was published. *Britannica 3,* as the new edition was christened, incorporated the most radical changes in the encyclopedia since its founding two hundred years before. *Britannica 3* was composed of a ten-volume *Micropaedia* for handy reference use, a nineteen-volume *Macropaedia* for reading in depth, and a one-volume *Propaedia,* or guide to the encyclopedia's use. This hybrid creation was the subject of a front-page article in the *New York Times* and has been a source of considerable debate between those readers who prefer the traditional format and those who favor the innovative Fifteenth Edition. In 1985 a two-volume index was added, as well as other refinements. Britannica launched an extensive public relations campaign to promote its experiment; the results were excellent as measured by sales, but dissatisfaction with the *Britannica 3* remains more widespread than the parent company would likely admit.

Succeeding Benton as publisher and chairman of Encyclopaedia Britannica, Inc., was Robert P. Gwinn, a University of Chicago graduate, member of the board of directors of Encyclopaedia Britannica, and at that time chairman of Sunbeam Corporation. It was Gwinn who decided on the division of the company's operations into Encyclopaedia Britannica USA (now EB North America) and Encyclopaedia Britannica International in 1974, in addition to the Merriam-Webster, Compton's, and Educational divisions. Under the leadership of Gwinn, Encyclopaedia Britannica, Inc., increased total revenues every year between 1974 and 1990 (with the single exception of 1980), with sales more than doubling during the 1980s alone. A large portion of the parent company's revenue is contributed by Encyclopaedia Britannica North America, which sells the *Britannica* in thousands of display booths located at shopping malls, fairs, trade shows, and rail terminals, among other venues; its representatives also visit private residences upon appointment.

In 1980 all shares of Encyclopaedia Britannica, Inc., were transferred to the William Benton Foundation of Illinois, created as a non-profit supporting organization of the University of Chicago. By placing Encyclopaedia Britannica, Inc., in the hands of a foundation the Bentons hoped to ensure the company's long-term independence, both in its editorial philosophy and as a financial entity protected from hostile takeovers. Robert Gwinn was also named chairman of the Benton Foundation.

Recent developments at Encyclopaedia Britannica, Inc., have included the 1985 publication of a revised version of the Fifteenth Edition (with the number of articles in the Macropaedia reduced from 4,200 to only 681); the formation of Britannica Software (now Compton's New Media, Inc.) as a separate division working on the design of educational computer programs; acquisition of two reading-skills enterprises, American Learning Corporation and Evelyn Wood Reading Dynamics; publication in 1990 of a revised and expanded *Great Books of the Western World,* including six additional volumes and 20th-century authors; and the 1989 release of Compton's MultiMedia Encyclopaedia, a version of that encyclopedia transferred to compact disc for computer use. Encyclopaedia Britannica, Inc., also created a new Far Eastern Pacific Region in its international division, and in 1990 announced that it was embarking on a joint venture with Soviet publishers to produce a Russian-language encyclopedia. While Encyclopaedia Britannica, Inc., appears well prepared for survival in the age of global electronics, the company says there are no plans to publish the *Encyclopaedia Britannica* in any format other than its traditional, hardbound print volumes.

Principal Subsidiaries: Encyclopaedia Britannica North America; Encyclopaedia Britannica International; Merriam-Webster, Inc.; Encyclopaedia Britannica Educational Corporation; Compton's MultiMedia Publishing Group, Inc.; Evelyn Wood, Inc.

Further Reading: ''Encyclopedia,'' *Encyclopaedia Britannica,* Chicago, Encyclopaedia Britannica, Inc., 1963; Haase, Roald H., *The Story of Encyclopaedia Britannica,* Chicago, Encyclopaedia Britannica, Inc., 1990; Parr, J., ''Low Tech Lives,'' *Forbes,* November 17, 1986.

—Jonathan Martin

EXXON CORPORATION

225 East John Carpenter Freeway
Irving, Texas 75062
U.S.A.
(214) 444-1000
Fax: (214) 444-1348

Public Company
Incorporated: 1882 as Standard Oil Company of New Jersey
Employees: 101,000
Sales: $116.49 billion
Stock Exchanges: New York
SICs: 2911 Petroleum Refining; 1311 Crude Petroleum &
 Natural Gas; 1094 Uranium, Radium & Vanadium Ores

As the earliest example of the trend toward gigantic size and power, Exxon Corporation and its Standard Oil forebears have earned vast amounts of money in the petroleum business. The brainchild of John D. Rockefeller, Standard Oil enjoyed the blessings and handicaps of overwhelming power—on the one hand, an early control of the oil business so complete that even its creators could not deny its monopolistic status; on the other, an unending series of journalistic and legal attacks upon its business ethics, profits, and very existence. The uproar over the *Exxon Valdez* oil tanker spill in 1989 put the corporation once more in the position of embattled giant, as America's largest oil company struggled to justify its actions before the public.

The individual most responsible for the creation of Standard Oil, John D. Rockefeller, was born in 1839 to a family of modest means living in the Finger Lakes region of New York State. His father, William A. Rockefeller, was a sporadically successful merchant and part-time hawker of medicinal remedies. William Rockefeller moved his family to Cleveland, Ohio, when John D. Rockefeller was in his early teens, and it was there that the young man finished his schooling and began work as a bookkeeper in 1855. From a very young age John D. Rockefeller developed an interest in business. Before getting his first job with the merchant firm of Hewitt & Tuttle, Rockefeller had already demonstrated an innate affinity for business, later honed by a few months at business school.

Rockefeller worked at Hewitt & Tuttle for four years, studying large-scale trading in the United States. In 1859 the 19-year-old Rockefeller set himself up in a similar venture—Clark & Rockefeller, merchants handling the purchase and resale of grain, meat, farm implements, salt, and other basic commodities. Although still very young, Rockefeller had already impressed Maurice Clark and his other business associates as an unusually capable, cautious, and meticulous businessman. He was a reserved, undemonstrative individual, never allowing emotion to cloud his thinking. Bankers found that they could trust John D. Rockefeller, and his associates in the merchant business began looking to him for judgment and leadership.

Clark & Rockefeller's already healthy business was given a boost by the Civil War economy, and by 1863 the firm's two partners had put away a substantial amount of capital and were looking for new ventures. The most obvious and exciting candidate was oil. A few years before, the nation's first oil well had been drilled at Titusville, in western Pennsylvania, and by 1863 Cleveland had become the refining and shipping center for a rail of newly opened oil fields in the so-called Oil Region. Activity in the oil fields, however, was extremely chaotic, a scene of unpredictable wildcatting, and John D. Rockefeller was a man who prized above all else the maintenance of order. He and Clark therefore decided to avoid drilling and instead go into the refining of oil, and in 1863 they formed Andrews, Clark & Company with an oil specialist named Samuel Andrews. Rockefeller, never given to publicity, was the "Company."

With excellent railroad connections as well as the Great Lakes to draw upon for transportation, the city of Cleveland and the firm of Andrews, Clark & Company both did well. The discovery of oil wrought a revolution in U.S. methods of illumination. Kerosene soon replaced animal fat as the source of light across the country, and by 1865 Rockefeller was fully convinced that oil refining would be his life's work. Unhappy with his Clark-family partners, Rockefeller bought them out for $72,000 in 1865 and created the new firm of Rockefeller & Andrews, already Cleveland's largest oil refiners. It was a typically bold move by Rockefeller, who although innately conservative and methodical was never afraid to make difficult decisions. He thus found himself, at the age of 25, co-owner of one of the world's leading oil concerns.

Talent, capital, and good timing combined to bless Rockefeller & Andrews. Cleveland handled the lion's share of Pennsylvania crude and, as the demand for oil continued to explode, Rockefeller & Andrews soon dominated the Cleveland scene. By 1867, when a young man of exceptional talent named Henry Flagler became a third partner, the firm was already operating the world's number-one oil refinery; there was as yet little oil produced outside the United States. The year before, John Rockefeller's brother, William Rockefeller, had opened a New York office to encourage the rapidly growing export of kerosene and oil by-products, and it was not long before foreign sales became an important part of Rockefeller strength. In 1869 the young firm allocated $60,000 for plant improvements—an enormous sum of money for that day.

The early years of the oil business were marked by tremendous swings in the production and price of both crude and refined oil. With a flood of newcomers entering the field every day, size and efficiency had already become critically important for survival. As the biggest refiner, Rockefeller was in a better position than anyone to weather the price storms. Rockefeller and Henry Flagler, with whom he enjoyed a long and harmonious business relationship, decided to incorporate their firm to raise the capital needed to enlarge the company further. On January 10, 1870, the Standard Oil Company was formed, with the two Rockefellers, Flagler, and Andrews owning the great majority of stock, valued at $1 million. The new company was not only capable of refining approximately ten percent of the entire country's oil, it also owned a barrel-making plant, dock facilities, a fleet of railroad tank cars, New York warehouses, and forest land for the cutting of lumber used to produce barrel staves. At a time when the term was yet unknown, Standard Oil had become a vertically integrated company.

One of the signal advantages of Standard Oil's size was the leverage it gave the company in railroad negotiations. Most of the oil refined at Standard made its way to New York and the eastern seaboard. Because of Standard's great volume—60 carloads a day by 1869—it was able to win lucrative rebates from the warring railroads. In 1871 the various railroads concocted a plan whereby the nation's oil refiners and railroads would agree to set and maintain prohibitively high freight rates while awarding large rebates and other special benefits to those refiners who were part of the scheme. The railroads would avoid disastrous price wars while the large refiners forced out of business those smaller companies who refused to join the cartel, known as the South Improvement Company.

The plan was immediately denounced by Oil Region producers and many independent refiners, near-riots breaking out in the oil fields. After a bitter war of words and a flood of press coverage, the oil refiners and the railroads abandoned their plan and announced the adoption of public, inflexible transport rates. In the meantime, however, Rockefeller and Flagler were already far advanced on a plan to combat the problems of excess capacity and dropping prices in the oil industry. To Rockefeller the remedy was obvious, though unprecedented: the eventual unification of all oil refiners in the United States into a single company. Rockefeller approached the Cleveland refiners and a number of important firms in New York and elsewhere with an offer of Standard Oil stock or cash in exchange for their often-ailing plants. By the end of 1872, all 34 refiners in the area had agreed to sell—some freely and for profit, and some, competitors alleged, under coercion. Due to Standard's great size and the industry's over-built capacity, Rockefeller and Flagler were in a position to make their competitors irresistible offers. All indications are that Standard regularly paid top dollar for viable companies.

By 1873 Standard Oil was refining more oil—10,000 barrels per day—than any other region of the country, employing 1,600 workers, and netting around $500,000 per year. With great confidence, Rockefeller proceeded to duplicate his Cleveland success throughout the rest of the country. By the end of 1874 he had absorbed the next three largest refiners in the nation, located in New York, Philadelphia, and Pittsburgh. Rockefeller also began moving into the field of distribution with the purchase of several of the new pipelines then being laid across the country. With each new acquisition it became more difficult for Rockefeller's next target to refuse his cash. Standard interests rapidly grew so large that the threat of monopoly was clear. The years 1875 to 1879 saw Rockefeller push through his plan to its logical conclusion. In 1878, a mere six years after beginning its annexation campaign, Standard Oil controlled $33 million of the country's $35 million annual refining capacity, as well as a significant proportion of the nation's pipelines and oil tankers. At the age of 39, Rockefeller was one of the five wealthiest men in the country.

Standard's involvement in the aborted South Improvement Company, however, had earned it lasting criticism. The company's subsequent absorption of the refining industry did not mend its image among the few remaining independents and the mass of oil producers who found in Standard a natural target for their wrath when the price of crude dropped precipitously in the late 1870s. Although the causes of producers' tailing fortunes are unclear, it is evident that given Standard's extraordinary position in the oil industry it was fated to become the target of dissatisfactions. In 1879 nine Standard Oil officials were indicted by a Pennsylvania grand jury for violating state anti-monopoly laws. Though the case was not pursued, it indicated the depth of feeling against Standard Oil, and was only the first in a long line of legal battles waged to curb the company's power.

In 1882 Rockefeller and his associates reorganized their dominions, creating the first "trust" in U.S. business history. This move overcame state laws restricting the activity of a corporation to its home state. Henceforth the Standard Oil Trust, domiciled in New York City, held "in trust" all assets of the various Standard Oil companies. Of the Standard Oil Trust's nine trustees, John D. Rockefeller held the largest number of shares. Together the trust's 30 companies controlled 80 percent of the refineries and 90 percent of the oil pipelines in the United States, constituting the leading industrial organization in the world. The trust's first year's combined net earnings were $11.2 million, of which some $7 million was immediately plowed back into the companies for expansion. Almost lost in the flurry of big numbers was the 1882 creation of Standard Oil Company of New Jersey, one of the many regional corporations created to handle the trust's activities in surrounding states. Barely worth mentioning at the time, Standard Oil Company of New Jersey, or "Jersey" as it came to be called, would soon become the dominant Standard company and, much later, rename itself Exxon.

The 1880s were a period of exponential growth for Standard. The trust not only maintained its lock on refining and distribution but also seriously entered the field of production. By 1891 the trust had secured a quarter of the country's total output, most of it in the new regions of Indiana and Illinois. Standard's overseas business was also expanding rapidly, and in 1888 it founded its first foreign affiliate, Anglo-American Oil Company Limited of London. The overseas trade in kerosene was especially important to Jersey, which derived as much as three-fourths of its sales from the export trade. Jersey's Bayonne, New Jersey, refinery was soon the third largest in the Standard family, putting out 10,000 to 12,000 barrels per day by 1886. In addition to producing and refining capacity, Standard also was extending gradually its distribution system from pipelines and bulk wholesalers toward the retailer and eventual end user of kerosene, the private consumer.

The 1890 Sherman Antitrust Act, passed largely in response to Standard's oil monopoly, laid the groundwork for a second major legal assault against the company, an 1892 Ohio Supreme

Court order forbidding the trust to operate Standard of Ohio. As a result, the trust was promptly dissolved, but taking advantage of newly liberalized state law in New Jersey, the Standard directors made Jersey the main vessel of their holdings. Standard Oil Company of New Jersey became Standard Oil Company (New Jersey) at this time. The new Standard Oil structure now consisted of only 20 much-enlarged companies, but effective control of the interests remained in the same few hands as before. Jersey added a number of important manufacturing plants to its already impressive refining capacity and was the leading Standard unit. It was not until 1899, however, that Jersey became the sole holding company for all of the Standard interests. At that time the entire organization's assets were valued at about $300 million and it employed 35,000 people. John D. Rockefeller continued as nominal president, but the most powerful active member of Jersey's board was probably John D. Archbold.

Rockefeller had retired from daily participation in Standard Oil in 1896 at the age of 56. Once Standard's consolidation was complete Rockefeller spent his time reversing the process of accumulation, seeing to it that his staggering fortune—estimated at $900 million in 1913—was redistributed as efficiently as it had been made.

The general public was only dimly aware of Rockefeller's philanthropy, however. More obvious were the frankly monopolistic policies of the company he had built. With its immense size and complete vertical integration, Standard Oil piled up huge profits ($830 million in the 12 years from 1899 to 1911). In relative terms, however, its domination of the U.S. industry was steadily decreasing. By 1911 its percentage of total refining was down to 66 percent from the 90 percent of a generation before, but in absolute terms Standard Oil had grown to monstrous proportions. Therefore it was not surprising that in 1905 a U.S. congressman from Kansas launched an investigation of Standard Oil's role in the falling price of crude in his state. The commissioner of the Bureau of Corporations, James R. Garfield, decided to widen the investigation into a study of the national oil industry—in effect Standard Oil.

Garfield's critical report prompted a barrage of state lawsuits against Standard Oil (New Jersey) and, in November of 1906, a federal suit was filed charging the company, John D. Rockefeller, and others with running a monopoly. In 1911, after years of litigation, the U.S. Supreme Court upheld a lower court's conviction of Standard Oil for monopoly and restraint of trade under the Sherman Antitrust Act. The Court ordered the separation from Standard Oil Company (New Jersey) of 33 of the major Standard Oil subsidiaries, including those which subsequently kept the Standard name.

Standard Oil Company (New Jersey) retained an equal number of smaller companies spread around the United States and overseas, representing $285 million of the former Jersey's net value of $600 million. Notable among the remaining holdings were a group of large refineries, four medium-sized producing companies, and extensive foreign marketing affiliates. Absent were the pipelines needed to move oil from well to refinery, much of the former tanker fleet, and access to a number of important foreign markets, including Great Britain and the Far East.

John D. Archbold, a long-time intimate of the elder Rockefeller and whose Standard service had begun in 1879, remained president of Standard Oil (New Jersey). Archbold's first problem was to secure sufficient supplies of crude oil for Jersey's extensive refining and marketing capacity. Jersey's former subsidiaries were more than happy to continue selling crude to Jersey; the dissolution decree had little immediate effect on the coordinated workings of the former Standard Oil group, but Jersey set about finding its own sources of crude. The company's first halting steps toward foreign production met with little success; ventures in Romania, Peru, Mexico, and Canada suffered political or geological setbacks and were of no help. In 1919, however, Jersey made a domestic purchase that would prove to be of great long-term value. For $17 million Jersey acquired 50 percent of the Humble Oil & Refining Company of Houston, Texas, a young but rapidly growing network of Texas producers which immediately assumed first place among Jersey's domestic suppliers. Although only the fifth-leading producer in Texas at the time of its purchase, Humble would soon become the dominant drilling company in the United States and was eventually wholly purchased by Jersey. Humble, now known as Exxon Company USA, remained one of the leading U.S. producers of crude oil and natural gas, with drilling rigs in 19 states including Alaska's Prudhoe Bay, in 1991.

Despite initial disappointments in overseas production, Jersey remained a company oriented to foreign markets and supply sources. On the supply side, Jersey secured a number of valuable Latin American producing companies in the 1920s, especially several Venezuelan interests consolidated in 1943 into Creole Petroleum Corporation. By that time Creole was the largest and most profitable crude producer in the Jersey group. In 1946 Creole produced an average of 451,000 barrels per day, far more than the 309,000 by Humble and almost equal to all other Jersey drilling companies combined. Four years later, Creole generated $157 million of the Jersey group's total net income of $408 million and did so on sales of only $517 million. Also in 1950, Jersey's British affiliates showed sales of $283 million but a bottom line of about $2 million. In contrast to the industry's early days, oil profits now lay in the production of crude, and the bulk of Jersey's crude came from Latin America. The company's growing Middle Eastern affiliates did not become significant resources until the early 1950s. Jersey's Far East holdings, from 1933 to 1961 owned jointly with Socony-Vacuum Oil Company—formerly Standard Oil Company of New York and now Mobil Corporation—never provided sizable amounts of crude oil.

In marketing, Jersey's income showed a similar preponderance of foreign sales. Jersey's domestic market had been limited by the dissolution decree to a handful of mid-Atlantic states, whereas the company's overseas affiliates were well entrenched and highly profitable. Jersey's Canadian affiliate, Imperial Oil Ltd., had a monopolistic hold on that country's market, while in Latin America and the Caribbean the West India Oil Company performed superbly during the second and third decades of the 20th century. Jersey had also incorporated eight major marketing companies in Europe by 1927, and these too sold a significant amount of refined products—most of them under the Esso brand name introduced the previous year. Esso became Jersey's best known and most widely used retail name both at home and abroad.

Jersey's mix of refined products changed considerably over the years. As the use of kerosene for illumination gave way to electricity and the automobile continued to grow in popularity, Jersey's sales reflected a shift away from kerosene and toward gasoline. Even as late as 1950, however, gasoline had not yet become the leading seller among Jersey products. That honor went to the group of residual fuel oils used as a substitute for coal to power ships and industrial plants. Distillates used for home heating and diesel engines were also strong performers. Even in 1991, when Exxon distributed its gasoline through a network of 12,000 U.S. and 26,000 international service stations, the earnings of all marketing and refining activities were barely one-third of those derived from the production of crude. In 1950 that proportion was about the same, indicating that regardless of the end products into which oil is refined, it is the production of crude that yields the big profits.

Indeed, by mid-century the international oil business had largely become a question of controlling crude oil at its source. With Standard Oil Company and its multinational competitors having built fully vertically integrated organizations, the only leverage remained control of the oil as it came out of the ground. Though it was not yet widely known in the United States, production of crude was shifting rapidly from the United States and Latin America to the Middle East. As early as 1908 oil had been verified in present-day Iran, but it was not until 1928 that Jersey and Socony-Vacuum, prodded by chronic shortages of crude, joined three European companies in forming Iraq Petroleum Company. Also in 1928, Jersey, Shell, and Anglo-Persian secretly agreed to limit each company's share of world production to their present relative amounts, attempting, by means of this "As Is" agreement, to limit competition and keep prices at comfortably high levels. As with Rockefeller's similar tactics 50 years before, it was not clear in 1928 that the agreement was illegal, because its participants were located in a number of different countries each with its own set of trade laws. Already in 1928, Jersey and the other oil giants were stretching the very concept of nationality beyond any simple application.

Following World War II, Standard Oil was again in need of crude to supply the resurgent economies of Europe. Already the world's largest producer, Standard Oil became interested in the vast oil concessions in Saudi Arabia recently won by Texaco and Socal. The latter companies, in need of both capital for expansion and world markets for exploitation, sold 30 percent of the newly formed Arabian American Oil Company (Aramco) to Standard Oil and ten percent to Socony-Vacuum in 1946. A few years later, after Iran's nationalization of Anglo-Persian's holdings was squelched by a combination of CIA assistance and an effective worldwide boycott of Iranian oil by competitors, Jersey was able to take seven percent of the consortium formed to drill in that oil-rich country. With a number of significant tax advantages attached to foreign crude production, Jersey drew an increasing percentage of its oil from its holdings in all three of the major middle-eastern fields—Iraq, Iran, and Saudi Arabia—and helped propel the 20-year postwar economic boom in the West. With oil prices exceptionally low, the United States and Europe busily shifted their economies to complete dependence on the automobile and on oil as the primary industrial fuel.

Despite the growing strength of newcomers to the international market such as Getty and Conoco, the big companies continued to exercise decisive control over the world oil supply and thus over the destinies of the Middle East producing countries. Growing nationalism and an increased awareness of the extraordinary power of the large oil companies led to the 1960 formation of the Organization of Petroleum Exporting Countries (OPEC). Later, a series of increasingly bitter confrontations erupted between countries and companies concerned about control over the oil upon which the world had come to depend. The growing power of OPEC prompted Jersey to seek alternative sources of crude. Exploration resulted in discoveries in Alaska's Prudhoe Bay and the North Sea in the late 1960s. The Middle Eastern sources remained paramount, however, and when OPEC cut off oil supplies to the United States in 1973—in response to U.S. sponsorship of Israel—the resulting 400 percent price increase induced a prolonged recession and permanently changed the industrial world's attitude to oil. Control of oil was largely taken out of the hands of the oil companies, who began exploring new sources of energy and business opportunities in other fields.

For Standard Oil Company (New Jersey), which had changed its name to Exxon in 1972, the oil embargo had several major effects. Most obviously it increased corporate sales; the expensive oil allowed Exxon to double its 1972 revenue of $20 billion in only two years and then pushed that figure over the $100 billion mark by 1980. After a year of windfall profits made possible by the sale of inventoried oil bought at much lower prices, Exxon was able to make use of its extensive North Sea and Alaskan holdings to keep profits at a steady level. The company had suffered a strong blow to its confidence, however, and was soon investigating a number of diversification measures which eventually included office equipment, a purchase of Reliance Electric Company (the fifth-largest holdings of coal in the United States), and an early-1980s venture into shale oil. With the partial exception of coal, all of these were expensive failures, costing Exxon approximately $6 billion to $7 billion.

By the early 1980s the world oil picture had eased considerably and Exxon felt less urgency about diversification. With the price of oil peaking around 1981 and then tumbling for most of the decade, Exxon's sales dropped sharply. The company's confidence rose, however, as OPEC's grip on the marketplace proved to be weaker than advertised. Having abandoned its forays into other areas, Exxon refocused on the oil and gas business, cutting its assets and work force substantially to accommodate the drop in revenue without losing profitability.

Exxon also bought back a sizable number of its own shares to bolster per-share earnings, which reached excellent levels and won the approval of Wall Street. The stock buy-back was partially in response to Exxon's embarrassing failure to invest its excess billions profitably—the company was somewhat at a loss as to what to do with its money. It could not expand further into the oil business without running into antitrust difficulties at home, and investments outside of oil would have to be mammoth to warrant the time and energy required.

Exxon is no longer the world's largest company, nor even the largest oil group—Royal Dutch/Shell took over that position in the 1990—but with the help of the March 24, 1989 *Exxon*

Valdez disaster it has heightened its notoriety. The crash of the *Exxon Valdez* in Prince William Sound off the port of Valdez, Alaska, released about 260,000 barrels of crude oil. The disaster cost Exxon $1.7 billion in 1989 alone, and the company and its subsidiaries were faced with more than 170 civil and criminal lawsuits brought by state and federal governments and individuals.

By late 1991 Exxon had paid $2.2 billion to clean up Prince William Sound and had reached a tentative settlement of civil and criminal charges that levied a $125 million criminal fine against the oil conglomerate. One hundred million dollars of the fine was forgiven and the remaining amount was split between the North American Wetlands Conservation Fund (which received $12 million) and the United States Treasury (which received $13 million). Exxon and a subsidiary, Exxon Shipping Co., were also required to pay an additional $1 billion to restore the spill area.

Since the accident, Exxon has worked to bring environmental issues to the front of its marketing schemes through cleaner burning gasolines, oil recycling programs, and other product improvements.

Although the *Valdez* disaster was a costly public relations nightmare, Exxon's financial performance actually improved in the opening years of the last decade in the twentieth century. The company enjoyed record profits in 1991, netting $5.6 billion and earning a special place in the *Fortune* 500. Of the annual list's top ten companies, Exxon was the only one to post a profit increase over 1990. *Business Week*'s ranking of companies according to market value also found Exxon at the top of the list, with a value of $69 million.

The company's performance was especially dramatic when compared to the rest of the fuel industry: as a group the 44 fuel companies covered by *Business Week*'s survey lost $35 billion in value, or 11 percent, in 1991. That year, Exxon also scrambled to the top of the profits heap, according to *Forbes* magazine. With a profit increase of 12 percent over 1990, Exxon's $5.6 billion in net income enabled the company to unseat IBM as the United States' most profitable company. At 16.5 percent, Exxon's return on equity was also higher than any other oil company.

Like many of its competitors, Exxon has been forced to trim expenses in order to maintain such outstanding profitability. One of the favorite methods in recent years has been to cut jobs. Citing the globally depressed economy and the need to streamline operations, Exxon eliminated 5,000 employees from its payrolls between 1990 and 1992.

With oil prices in a decade-long slide, Exxon also cut spending on exploration from $1.7 billion in 1985 to $900 million in 1992. The company's exploration budget constituted less than one percent of revenues, and played a large part in Exxon's good financial performance. But some fuel industry observers warn that such drastic cuts overlook the competition's search for new oil reserves. Royal Dutch/Shell spent almost twice as much as Exxon on exploration over the same period. In the event of an international crisis that cut off oil supplies, would Exxon be prepared to fill the gap? With ten percent of the United States' petroleum reserves, Exxon is confident of its future.

Principal Subsidiaries: Esso Aktiengesellschaft (Germany); Esso Eastern Inc.; Esso Australia Resources Ltd.; Esso Exploration and Production Norway Inc.; Esso Holding Company Holland Inc.; Esso Holding Company U.K. Inc.; Esso Italiana S.P.A. (Italy); Esso Norge a.s. (Norway); Esso Sociedad Anonlma Petrolera Argentina; Esso Société Anonyme Française (France; 81.548%) Esso Standard Oil S.A. Limited (Bahamas); Exxon Capital Holdings Corporation; Exxon Insurance Holdings, Inc.; Exxon Overseas Corporation; Exxon Rio Holding Inc.; Exxon San Joaquin Production Company; Exxon Yemen Inc.; Imperial Oil Limited (Canada, 69.56%); International Colombia Resources Corporation (100%); Societe Francaise Exxon Chemical (France, 98.64%); Exxon Engergy Ltd.; Esso Production Malaysia Inc.; Esso Sekiyu Kabushiki Kaisha; Esso Singapore Private Ltd.; Exxon Chemical Trading Inc.; Friendswood Development Co.

Further Reading: Nevins, Allan, *Study in Power: John D. Rockefeller—Industrialist and Philanthropist,* 2 vols., New York, Charles Scribner's Sons, 1953; Hidy, Ralph W., and Murrel E. Hidy, *History of Standard Oil Company (New Jersey): Pioneering in Big Business, 1882–1911,* New York, Harper & Brothers, 1955; Gibb, George Sweet, and Evelyn H. Knowlton, *History of Standard Oil Company (New Jersey): The Resurgent Years, 1911–1927,* New York, Harper & Brothers, 1956; Larson, Henrietta M., Evelyn H. Knowlton, and Charles S. Popple, *History of Standard Oil Company (New Jersey): New Horizons, 1927–1950,* New York, Harper & Row, 1971; Sampson, Anthony, *The Seven Sisters: The Great Oil Companies and the World They Made,* New York, The Viking Press, 1975; Wall, Bennett H., *Growth in a Changing Environment: A History of Standard Oil Company (New Jersey),* New York, McGraw-Hill, 1988; Rogers, Alison, "The *Fortune* 500: It Was the Worst of Years," *Fortune,* April 20, 1992; Cropper, Carol M. et al., "The *Forbes* 500's Annual Directory," *Forbes,* April 27, 1992; Finch, Peter, "The *Business Week* 1000," *Business Week,* special issue, 1992; "Oil Majors Make Tough Decisions on Jobs, Assets," *Chemical Marketing Reporter,* July 13, 1992; Norman, James R., "A Tale of Two Strategies," *Forbes,* August 17, 1992.

—Jonathan Martin
updated by April Dougal

FARMLAND FOODS, INC.

P.O. Box 7305
Kansas City, Missouri 64116-0005
U.S.A.
(816) 459-6000
Fax: (816) 459-6979

Subsidiary of Farmland Industries, Inc. (99%)
Incorporated: 1970
Employees: 2,600
Sales: $850 million
SICs: 2011 Meat Packing Plants

Farmland Foods is the largest subsidiary and the third-largest business segment of Farmland Industries, Inc., which in turn ranks as the largest agricultural food marketing and manufacturing cooperative in the United States. Although Farmland Industries' Petroleum and Fertilizer-Chemicals segments cumulatively posted nearly $1.9 billion in 1992 revenues, Farmland Foods represents a crucial portion of the co-op's activity, especially as it moves toward a greater emphasis on earnings through value-added products and international distribution. Like its parent company, Farmland Foods serves a large owner-producer network spanning 19 midwestern states. Primarily a processor and marketer of pork products to retail and food service outlets, Farmland Foods and the Farmland label are complemented by Massachusetts-based Carando Foods, the largest U.S. producer of Italian specialty meats. With the 1991 addition of Carando, Farmland Foods operates eight processing plants spread across the country. Annual hog-processing capacity for the subsidiary is approximately five percent of the total U.S. output.

Farmland Industries began in 1929, under the name Union Oil Company, as a farm supply organization. As the company expanded its ventures, it altered its name to Consumers Cooperative Association in 1935 and to its present title in 1966. The company began experimenting in 1959 with pork production and marketing when it purchased a struggling plant in Denison, Iowa, and launched Farmbest, Inc. and the Farmbest label. In 1963 the co-op established another pork-processing plant in nearby Iowa Falls; sales for the year totaled $21 million. From that time until 1970 Farmland's food business developed into a $200-million industry, encompassing not only pork-packing, but beef-packing, turkey-processing, egg production, and swine-testing. Meat margins were then, as they are now, dangerously thin; yet Farmland committed itself wholeheartedly to the industry.

Under the direction of Farmland Industries' then vice-president, W. Gordon Leith, the foods branch of the co-op was officially launched as Farmland Foods in 1970. Central to its operations at the time were its line of hams, bacon, and sausages marketed under the Farmbest, Country Manor, and Farm-King labels.

Although primarily regional in focus, Farmland Foods had already marketed to major cities around the country and even entered the European and Japanese markets. According to a corporate news release that year, Farmland "undertook the marketing of meat at a time when other farmer-owned organizations were hesitant to face the uncertainties and pressures of the meat industry. The beef and pork operations under Farmland Foods are the largest that have ever been developed under farmer ownership and control." In addition to the Iowa plants, the original Farmland Foods consisted of a beef-packing plant in Garden City, Kansas; a turkey-processing plant in Cheraw, Colorado; egg plants in Hutchinson, Kansas, and Eagle Grove, Iowa; and swine-testing stations in Iowa and Nebraska.

During the 1970s the Farmland Foods label gradually supplanted Farmbest and the subsidiary entered the ranks of the nation's foremost meat packers. In 1976 it expanded its hog-processing capacity with a new plant in Crete, Nebraska, capable of high-speed skinning of 3,500 hogs per day. Overall hog-slaughtering capacity for Farmland now surpassed three million per year. During the decade the company also expanded its role as a beef processor through its participation in the boxed beef business. Farmland would later temporarily exit the beef-packing business to concentrate full-time on pork production. By 1989 Farmland Foods was the nation's tenth-largest pork processor. Farmland's parent company was at the same time entertaining the possibility of a historical merger with two Minnesota-based co-ops, Land O'Lakes and Cenex. The result would have been the creation of a $6 billion agribusiness. A tentative agreement between the three was signed in 1988, but by January 1989 merger talks had ceased due to a host of problems surrounding the proposed consolidation.

Farmland Foods entered the next decade committed to long-term growth. Beginning in 1990 it inaugurated a large-scale financing program. Improvement and operational loans of up to $1 million each were now being awarded to hog farmers in 19 midwestern states. In at least two of these states, first-ranking hog-producer Iowa and third-ranking Minnesota, controversies have arisen because of the financing, which some fear will destroy small hog-farming ventures in the name of big business. BCH Enterprises, a hog-breeding project established in Minnesota with Farmland resources, stalled in November 1991 due, ostensibly, to environmental questions. However, according to Sharon Schmickle in the *Star Tribune,*, the real issue revolves around "the very nature of farming and reveals a future that many farmers find frightening because bigger and fewer farms seem inevitable." The whole business of hog-contracting has become especially fierce in north central Iowa, according to Betsy Freese in *Successful Farming.* Not only is there ongoing disagreement among farmers about the merits of big business financing, there is also pressure between the firms themselves, including Murphy of Iowa, Swine Graphics's Pig Weighs and Means, Land O'Lakes's Swine Risk Sharing, and Farmland to become increasingly competitive in their deal-structuring. Better facilities, better technology, higher quality meat, and lower prices are the expected outcomes from such partnerships, but the future of small livestock farming remains far from certain.

"Perpetual white water" was the phrase applied by Farmland Industries' chairman and president in 1990 to the swift-moving field of agriculture. Farmland Foods' losses that year were $5.5 million, attributable to high live hog prices as well as higher processing costs. Other discouraging news included estimates that up to 25 percent of U.S. pork producers might vacate the industry within five years, sending prices even higher. The foods subsidiary, however, holds the key to the parent company's growth as a value-added producer, a goal it set for itself. In 1991 the company purchased Carando, headquartered in Springfield, Massachusetts. Sales volume for Carando prior to the sale totaled $68 million. Carando's Italian specialty meats, with strong markets in the Northeast and Florida, provided new opportunities for Farmland, as did its Riegel Foods division, specializing in quality hams and ham products.

Because of such attention to niche marketing, as well as the development of new products and a commitment to a $2 million annual advertising budget, Farmland Foods had strengthened its position by 1992. According to the company's 1992 annual report, "The long-term strategy to take Farmland Foods from a commodity business to a value-added marketing business is paying off. Farmland Foods, posting the highest sales volume in its history last year, became the fastest growing food company in the United States during 1992, according to *Meat and Poultry* magazine. Income before taxes for the subsidiary was $17.4 million, an increase of $14.4 million over 1991. In July 1992 the company broadened its "output" segment with the acquisition of Union Equity Co-Operative Exchange and Hyplains Beef. The purchases signify Farmland Industries' reentry into the grain and beef businesses and should provide a higher profile for Farmland as a major world food concern (Union's 1991 grain sales through its terminals in Houston and Galveston exceeded $1 billion). "Better Farming, Better Food" is the Farmland motto, and it can be expected that as the cooperative continues to serve its heartland members it will also continue on its high growth trajectory.

Principal Subsidiaries: Hyplains Beef, L.C.; Yuma Feeder Pig LTD, Inc.

Further Reading: "News Release," Farmland Foods, Inc., April 23, 1970; Grimm, Art, "Farmland Foods: Nation's Largest Co-op Meat Producer," *Co-op Report,* July/August 1970; "Farmland Foods," *Leadership,* January 1977; "Farmland's Annual Report Shows Numerous Steps to Boost Future Financial Returns," *Feedstuffs,* December 31, 1984; Marcotty, Josephine, "Land O'Lakes May Renew Merger Talk," *Star Tribune,* March 30, 1989; "Farmland Buys California Pork Producer," *Feedstuffs,* July 31, 1989; Phelps, David, Steve Gross, and Josephine Marcotty, "Marketplace Pulse," *Star Tribune,* October 11, 1989; "Credit Shopping Getting Easier," *Successful Farming,* February 1990; Smith, Rod, "Farmland Could Help Buy Farmstead Plant," *Feedstuffs,* November 26, 1990; Lofstrom, Joyce, "Farmland Foods Adds 'Carando Classic Italian' to Its Value-Added Meats," *Farmland News,* June 1991; Freese, Betsy, "Making Their Move," *Successful Farming,* September 1991; Schmickle, Sharon, "A Barnyard Dispute," *Star Tribune,* February 10, 1992; "Farmland Taps Anderson as Agency," *Nation's Restaurant News,* March 16, 1992; Lofstron, Joyce, "For 'Lean' and 'Light' Serve Farmland Meats," *Farmland News,* June 1992; Butcher, Lola, "Farmland Gets Fight over Pig Project: Vertical Pork Production Becomes Battle of Family vs. Corporate Farming," *Kansas City Business Journal,* July 3, 1992.

—Jay P. Pederson

FIGGIE INTERNATIONAL INC.

4420 Sherwin Road
Willoughby, Ohio 44094
U.S.A.
(216) 953-2700
Fax: (216) 951-1724

Public Company
Incorporated: 1963 as Automatic Sprinkler Corp. of America
Employees: 3,700
Sales: $1.17 billion
Stock Exchanges: NASDAQ
SICs: 3569 General Industrial Machinery Nec; 3556 Food
    Products Machinery

Figgie International Inc. is an international diversified operating company comprising more than 30 divisions. The company sells fire protection and safety equipment, technical (largely U.S. military) equipment, machinery and allied products (bottling, labeling, and packaging systems), consumer sports equipment, insurance and real estate services, and safety products.

The Figgie empire was built largely through acquisitions of small companies. Harry E. Figgie, Jr., its chairman and chief executive officer, launched Figgie in 1963 with the purchase of a failing Youngstown, Ohio, fire sprinkler company, Automatic Sprinkler Corp. of America. More acquisitions (53 in all) were to follow in the company's first five years. Figgie, a management consultant turned executive, bought Automatic Sprinkler with almost no money of his own, having persuaded bankers and investors to provide $7.2 million in purchase funds and another $2 million for capital investment.

He had prepared for this move to highly leveraged ownership by an intense program of business education (engineering master's degree, law degree, Harvard MBA) and experience, including nine years with the consulting firm Booz, Allen & Hamilton, where he specialized in acquisition.

The company nearly went bankrupt in its first year and, in a desperate move, even secretly moved one of its strike-bound manufacturing operations to another state while Figgie himself was ill with a high fever. After staving off bankruptcy, the new company began a whirlwind five years of acquisitions, following Figgie's "nucleus" theory. Figgie's theory involved bunching companies within promising markets for the sake of market

penetration and increased management expertise. Around Automatic Sprinkler he bunched fire protection and safety companies such as American LaFrance, the historic maker of fire engines, and Badger Fire Extinguisher Co. Around baseball equipment maker Rawlings Corp. he bunched consumer recreation companies such as hockey equipment maker Sherwood-Drolet Corp. Ltd. and Fred Perry Sportswear Ltd. Around Interstate Electronics Corp. he bunched electrical electronics firms; around Geo. J. Meyer Manufacturing Co., packaging machinery and material handling companies; and around Kersey Manufacturing Co. Inc. and Safway Steel Products Inc., construction and mining companies.

In one month, Figgie looked at 50 companies. In one 25-day period he closed five deals, all for small companies with an average $7 million in sales. The whole fire protection group had only $40 million in combined sales when purchased, including Automatic Sprinkler's $20 million. The debt-equity ratio was six to one at one point, all in 90-day rollover money. In November 1965 the company went public, Over-the-Counter, where it remained into the 1990s. Early in 1968 it was trading at 50 times earnings. But a promised $2.75 earnings per share did not materialize; instead it paid nine cents. "It was time to slow down," Figgie said later.

After survival and acquisition came consolidation. Figgie likened his company's growth to the one-room schoolhouse that grew to 40 rooms. By 1970 sales were at $365 million; profit was $8.6 million. The company expanded its international business, acquiring Fred Perry Sportswear, a British firm, in 1973. Its domestic divisions exported more and by 1980 offshore sales were almost $150 million. The company also moved into service operations. The company's data processing department became its Systems Management Group; its insurance department became Waite Hill Holdings—both free-standing profit centers still responsible for internal service but expected to take on outside clients too. Later an acceptance division and an international licensing division were formed, both on the same internal-external model.

There were valleys as well as peaks. Figgie stock dropped to three in 1974, from a high of 74. Harry Figgie was accused of neglecting management for the sake of acquisitions. He later admitted that developing management and installing needed financial controls were two "major problems" he dealt with in the 1970s. But while other conglomerates reduced themselves to a few top performers, Figgie International (so renamed in 1981) stayed the diversified course.

A big boost to Figgie's technical segment came in 1982 when it landed a $433 million U.S. Navy contract for electronic test instrumentation on the Trident II submarine weapons system. By 1984 this segment was to produce almost one-fourth of both revenues and profits; three-fourths of this segment's business was with the U.S. government.

The early 1980s were a time of difficulty, but by the mid-1980s the company was registering record sales in the neighborhood of $750 million. *Barron's* commended Figgie for the various restructurings and cost cutting measures that had helped achieve these gains. Figgie's debt-equity ratio was down to 0.84-to-one. Harry Figgie was looking for two or three more "respectable" years before re-entering the acquisition phase. He figured this move would be necessary to realize his goal of a multibillion dollar company.

The 1980s also saw the company move its headquarters from Harry Figgie's native Cleveland to a splendid Georgian-style building on 1,200 acres in Richmond, Virginia. After six years in Virginia, the company returned to Cleveland to create a new 630-acre commercial development.

By 1987 revenues had topped $919 million and profits were more than $42 million, for a four-year rise of over $200 million and $17 million, respectively. This was achieved not by selling less profitable divisions but by making them more profitable. Nonetheless, Harry Figgie was ready to make what he called "tuck-in" acquisitions with product lines related to Figgie's existing divisions. Largest of these was still the fire protection and safety products group, which now included a security service.

One of the major success stories was the restructuring of St. Louis-based Rawlings Sporting Goods, ball and equipment supplier to the baseball major leagues, the National Collegiate Athletic Association, and the National Football League.

Harry Figgie was building a reputation not only as an astute company builder but as "one of America's toughest bosses," according to Fortune magazine. He had served under General George S. Patton in World War II, he told Fortune in 1989, and apparently had taken on some of the general's demeanor. Sixty-five years old and with no intention of retiring, he was considered demanding, volatile, and not known to pull punches when dealing with his employees. He didn't deny his ability to bawl people out but contended that "ungodly" pressures of running a conglomerate had contributed to his volatility. Figgie International had bought "small companies with no management depth" over the years and that had left "no room for error."

A perhaps more serious problem, noted by commentators, was that he was running the company in his own style without training a successor, or so it appeared to a Forbes writer in 1988. By 1991, however, Harry Figgie, Jr., had brought his son, Dr. Harry E. Figgie III, a successful orthopedic surgeon who had been president of the family-owned Clark-Reliance Corp., of Cleveland, on as vice-chairman of technology and strategic planning. Dr. Figgie's four-page commentary on "Retooling the Corporation" appeared right after his father's four-page letter to shareholders in the 1991 annual report.

As for ownership, Figgie International has been viewed by some analysts as so dependent on Harry Jr.'s leadership, as well as underpriced on the stock market, that its value in sold-off bits and pieces would make it an attractive takeover target. To fend off takeover, the company issued a second class of common stock carrying more voting power. Then it sold more of the first, Class A stock, to pay for its purchase of more Class B stocks, thus strengthening management's hold on ownership. Financial World called it "an insider's crafty move" and said Wall Street feared it would "erode shareholder equity" and dilute earnings.

Meanwhile, acquisitions had gone apace. Figgie bought 24 companies between 1985 and 1988—makers of scissor lifts, dairy equipment, and thermometers, among other companies,

each with $20 million to $100 million in sales. Net income tripled in four years, reaching $65 million. Cash flow per share doubled since the early 1980s restructuring.

There were still problems. The Navy found fault with smoke protection gear supplied by Figgie's Scott Aviation division after a former Scott employee said he had been ordered to destroy test results that showed them defective. Later, during the Gulf War, Figgie found itself "at odds with the Army on its chemical warfare masks," Harry, Jr. reported in the 1991 annual report, managing a shot at the "military-political complex," which he implied was at the heart of the disagreement. Nonetheless, he "breathed a sigh of relief" that U.S. troops had encountered no chemical warfare in that conflict. He also was pleased to report the company's success in overturning the Army's decision to end its Figgie contract "for default" and make it instead a termination "for convenience of the government." Another flap had to do with working conditions in Rawlings's manufacturing operations in Haiti and Costa Rica; the Haiti operation was closed down because of political instability.

Through it all, Figgie International remained a textbook case of successful diversification. Its six operating segments, unrelated to each other but consisting of companies closely related within segments, had combined sales of $1.36 billion in 1990. It had been the only way to grow, according to Harry Figgie. "We'd identify growth industries and buy really sick companies in them," he told Across the Board magazine. It was "a high-risk strategy" in which "we should have failed," he said, presenting himself as a "dirty-fingers-type guy" who didn't know enough about finances to quit.

But he knew "manufacturing economics," said Across the Board, citing a Paine Webber Inc. analyst who praised Harry Figgie for his "terrific record of buying small [companies], tearing them apart to learn the business as [he and his employees] go along, and learning from the competitors." At least six "stellar turnarounds" resulted, among them Interstate Electronics Corp., the nucleus of the Figgie technical group; Scott Aviation, maker of high pressure oxygen systems; Rawlings Sporting Goods, the sole surviving U.S. sporting goods manufacturer; and Automatic Sprinkler, by then the number two U.S. installer of fire protection sprinklers, earning each year five times the $7.2 million that Harry Figgie paid for it in 1963.

In line with his acknowledged expertise in such matters, Harry Figgie has a sort of adjunct career in progress: he is a well received author of several books on management and economics, including Cutting Costs: An Executive's Guide to Increased Profits and Bankruptcy 1995, which was on best seller lists for several months beginning in October 1992.

But Figgie International, weathering another recession, faced "a tough, rugged, and hard year" in 1992, said Harry Figgie in the 1991 annual report. Only cost-cutting measures had saved the situation in 1991. Ahead was another "sobering year" which Figgie International was entering "buttoned down with a very cautious approach." One could only hope, said Harry Figgie in his usual pointed fashion, that in the election year 1992 "the politicians [would] not do too much damage to the weak recovery."

As for what lay ahead, Figgie International stands ready to profit from market improvements in all of its six major business areas. The company's past achievement, uniquely engineered by Harry Figgie, Jr., gives indication of survival and growth even through rugged years.

Principal Subsidiaries: American LaFrance; Figgie Fire Protection Systems; "Automatic" Sprinkler Corporation of America; Figgie Packaging Systems; Figgie Power Systems; Fred Perry Sportswear (U.K.) Ltd.; Interstate Electronics Corporation; Rawlings Sporting Goods; Safway Steel Products; Scott Aviation; Sherwood-Drolet Corp., Ltd.; Snorkel-Economy; Taylor Environmental Instruments; Waite Hill Holdings Inc.

Further Reading: Figgie, Harry E., Jr., "A Dream Comes True: The Story of Figgie International," Newcomen Society (U.S.),

1985; Maturi, Richard J., "Rebound Continues: Figgie International Profits from Recession Moves," *Barron's,* September 16, 1985; Marcial, Gene G., "Figgie Relives the Go-Go Years," *Business Week,* June 22, 1987; Maturi, Richard J., "Looking for 'Tuck-Ins': That's Figgie International's Acquisition Strategy," *Barron's,* July 13, 1987; "Figgie: Insiders Get Richer, Poor Get . . . ," *Financial World,* June 28, 1988; Hannon, Kerry, "There He Goes Again," *Forbes,* October 31, 1988; Nulty, Peter, and Karen Nickel, "America's Toughest Bosses," *Fortune,* February 27, 1989; "Casualties of Peace: The Navy Checks Its Safety and Finds Some Faulty Gear," *Time,* November 27, 1989; Thackray, John, "Diversification: What It Takes To Make It Work," *Across the Board,* November 1991.

—Jim Bowman

FINA, INC.

Fina Plaza
8350 North Central Expressway
301 Grant Street
Dallas, Texas 75206
U.S.A.
(214) 750-2400
Fax: (214) 890-1876

Public Company
Incorporated: 1956 as American Petrofina, Inc.
Employees: 3,665
Sales: $3.4 billion
Stock Exchanges: AMEX
SICs: 2911 Petroleum Refining; 1311 Crude Petroleum &
    Natural Gas; 5541 Gasoline Service Stations

FINA, Inc. is a medium-sized holding company whose chief operating subsidiary, FINA Oil and Chemical Co., Inc., produces, refines, markets, and transports petroleum products and natural gas, as well as engages in the manufacture and sale of petrochemicals. FINA is one of 166 companies in 34 countries affiliated with Belgium's largest corporation, Petrofina S.A. Established by the Belgian firm in the mid-1950s as American Petrofina, Inc., FINA quickly became an American success story. By 1990 the company achieved significant (10 to 14 percent) shares of the chemical products market with its sales of styrene monomer, polystyrene, and polypropylene, and was building the second-largest polystyrene plant in the world.

When Petrofina S.A. paid $10 million to establish American Petrofina, Inc. (APF) in 1956, it entered its first American business venture. The American company became one of many affiliates of this giant Belgian petroleum refining corporation, headquartered in Brussels. Several Belgians would always serve on APF's board of directors, and the Belgian firm would own the majority of stock. However, the president and CEO of APF would be American, and the company would operate independently. For many years Harry A. Jackson, Jr., would preside over the firm as president, and Walter C. Teagle, Jr., would serve as director of the company until his untimely death four years later. Together they would oversee the crucial early steps of APF that would transform it into a multi-billion dollar petroleum company.

When APF purchased the Panhandle Oil Company, incorporating it in April 1956, the company actually began to manufacture and market petroleum and natural gas. Panhandle had been a minor oil company based in Texas, but with diverse holdings in oil wells and natural gas reserves. Until oil was discovered in Alaska, the Southwest was the richest oil-producing region in the United States. The 1950s also were characterized by the discovery of vast natural gas deposits in Texas and Louisiana that would become an important energy source, as the gas was piped to all regions of the country. With ample cash flow, Jackson and Teagle negotiated the acquisition of the American Liberty Company of Dallas, which took place in January 1957. The American Liberty Company also was a small but diverse petroleum company which held significant natural gas reserves. After these purchases, APF's total assets stood at $88 million.

APF thereupon expanded continuously. Favoring the new company was its affiliation with an international conglomerate of oil companies, the Petrofina Group, which gave it advantages in terms of markets and raw materials. Throughout the 1950s, the company had an annual growth rate of 4 percent, with earnings in 1960 alone up 21 percent over the previous year. APF's profits derived not only from the manufacture and sale of petroleum from its 1,174 oil wells (by 1960, its refineries processed 36,207 barrels of crude oil daily), but increasingly from natural gas. The company's assets had grown in four years' time to nearly $94 million.

The 1970s would present challenges as well as enormous growth. Increasingly stringent and costly environmental-protection laws and regulations adversely affected the company—in particular those requiring the production of lead-free gasoline. The OPEC oil embargo of 1973 sent crude oil prices skyrocketing, cutting deeply into company profits. Nonetheless, APF's international connections enabled it to overcome the oil shortage quickly from other sources, as it would do in the equally trying months following Iraq's invasion of Kuwait seventeen years later. Meanwhile, its Cosdan Oil and Chemical Division was processing six percent of the crude oil into petrochemicals and plastics, offsetting somewhat the volatility of the oil market. With the completion of its modern new polystyrene plant at Calumet City, Illinois, in May 1970, Cosdan became the third-largest domestic manufacturer of the high-impact plastic. As to the growing environmental challenges in the 1970s, APF's management decided to install costly equipment in its refineries for the removal of lead alkyls in gasoline, and to promote the sale of the up-and-coming lead-free gasoline.

The constant fluctuations of the petroleum market—due to international crises, fires in oil refineries, or downturns in the economy—as well as continuous expansion and modernization of the company, were the chief themes in APF's history in the 1970s and 1980s. By 1980 APF's assets had climbed to $1.2 billion, and the company was still growing in diverse ways, particularly in the manufacture of chemicals and plastics. Despite the downturn in the economy during the recessionary 1970s, by 1980 APF had achieved the highest earnings in its history to date, thanks in part to the new Reagan administration's emphasis on free marketing and decentralization. Operating profits from APF's production of crude oil alone were 25 percent higher than in the previous year. In the new atmosphere of deregulation and elimination of price controls, so many exploratory wells were dug that an oil rig shortage resulted, while lands previously off-limits to oil drilling, especially in the Outer Continental Shelf, were leased to oil companies. The result was that by the end of 1980, the United States had reduced its dependency on foreign oil to 38 percent.

Previous investment in equipment to produce lead-free gasoline paid off handsomely, and APF in 1980 discontinued altogether its manufacture of high-octane leaded gas. Environmental regulations continued to increase in the 1980s, with the result that ever newer and costlier equipment was installed in APF's refineries to produce less-polluted air and water discharges. By 1990 APF was one of 23 oil companies whose assets totalled over $1 billion. The company's historic trends—expansion, modernization, and volatility with changes in the economic and political spheres—were never more apparent.

The first year of the new decade was the company's most prosperous to date. Benefitting from deregulation and other market incentives, the company proceeded with its modernization and streamlining of operations. At one of its two refineries (Port Arthur, Texas), a 770,000 pound catalytic cracking unit was assembled, controlled by state-of-the-art computers. With the capacity to refine up to 140,000 barrels of oil daily, the new facility was one of the most modern in the world. Exploration for oil in the new deregulated atmosphere proceeded at a rapid pace, especially in the Terrebonne Parish of Louisiana, which added nearly 21 million barrels of oil to company reserves. A new gasoline product called Genesis, which contained a chemical that would clean dirty engines, had been successfully introduced on the market. Meanwhile, company researchers were developing a method of making clean-burning compressed natural gas available for transportation. APF's new polystyrene plant was the largest in the United States, and the second-largest in the world; its polypropylene manufacturing facility was the third-largest in the world. Despite increasing environmental regulations, company profits that year were at a new peak: APF's petrochemical products, including styrene monomer, commanded 10 to 14 percent shares of the U.S. market, while revenues from oil exploration and production and natural gas marketing had increased 39 percent over the previous year.

However, expansion and modernization plans were abruptly upset by the other perennial theme in APF's history: volatility to major external crises. In August 1990 Iraq invaded Kuwait and the supply of crude oil from the region suddenly was interrupted, sending crude oil prices skyrocketing and nearly wiping out the gains made by APF's refining and gas-marketing segment the preceding seven months. On August 2 the U.S. government put an embargo on all crude oil supplies emanating from Iraq and Kuwait. APF already had bought 9.5 million barrels of crude oil from both, only half of which became obtainable. Costs of obtaining crude oil from other sources rose precipitously. Sharp public criticism of a steep increase in gasoline prices forced APF and other oil producers to keep the price of gas artificially low. During such crises, APF's constant streamlining and product diversity paid off: chemical sales remained strong, and crude oil supplies were rapidly secured from other sources, especially Saudi Arabia, in part through

APF's international connections as a member of the Petrofina Group.

While the challenge of the invasion and resulting Persian Gulf War was met successfully, profits and sales from oil and gas had barely recovered when a severe economic recession began. Net earnings fell from a peak of $126 million in 1990 to $42 million in 1991. Natural gas prices continued their plunge, mainly because of warmer winter temperatures. Oil exploration/production and natural gas earnings fell 56 percent, due to the downturn in crude oil and natural gas prices. The normally resilient chemicals sector of the company declined dramatically because of the recession, with earnings falling 35 percent from the previous year. Oil refining/production earnings in turn fell 83 percent from the previous year. On the positive side were the prospects for oil exploration, which promised good future results provided no new oil crisis erupted. Exploratory drilling, on the other hand, declined steeply. Intense competition among oil producers resulting from the public's pressure to lower gasoline prices led to a downturn in revenues for purveyors of FINA gasoline.

Grim as the financial scenario looked during the recession, CEO Rod Haddock and Chairman of the Board Paul D. Meek initiated some important steps that would bode well for the future. In the spring of 1991, the company changed its name to FINA, Inc. In July 1992 FINA purchased the high-density polyethylene (HDPE) business of the German chemical firm Hoechst-Celanese, located in Bayport, Texas. In part because the international Petrofina Group already was Europe's second-largest manufacturer of HDPE, the acquisition left FINA poised to become a leader in the HDPE market in America. FINA also planned to license its polypropylene technology internationally. In another lucrative deal, a popular chain of gasoline stations, operating the Good Time stores in the greater El Paso area, contracted to market approximately 26 million gallons of FINA fuel per year.

Nonetheless, the future of the oil production and refinery business of FINA was still volatile and uncertain. Perhaps because of this fact, negotiations proceeded in 1992 for the sale of FINA's downstream business and hundreds of its service stations to a Saudi Arabian oil firm. The arrangement would form a joint venture between FINA and Arabian Petroleum Company in which the business would be owned by the Saudi Arabian firm but operated by FINA. The more solid and lucrative chemical business would not be included in the Saudi deal. Management predicted the transfer of ownership would radically alter the identity and possibly reduce the size of FINA, but also make it more profitable and competitive in the long run.

Principal Subsidiaries: Fina Oil and Chemical Co., Inc.

Further Reading: FINA, Inc. Annual Reports, 1956, 1960, 1970, 1980, 1990, 1991; Petrofina, S.A. Annual Report, 1991; Snow, Nick, "Top U.S. Chemical Concerns Try to Avoid Over-Expansion," *Oil Daily,* April 3, 1989; Savage, Peter R., "Taking the Pulse of Petrochemicals," *Chemical Week,* April 12, 1989; "American Petrofina, Inc. (Executive Changes)," *New York Times,* August 29, 1989; "Fina, Others Press Exploration of Eastern S. Louisiana Region," *Oil and Gas Journal,* March 25, 1991; "American Petrofina Inc. Changes Name to FINA,"

New York Times, April 27, 1991; "Energy Feast, or Fuel Famine?" *Chief Executive,* June 1991; "Ten Major Oil Companies Hit New Asset Peaks," *National Petroleum News,* June 1991; "Fina Chairman 'Trapped' in Political Appointment," *Dallas Business Journal,* January 31, 1992; "FINA to Enter High-Density Polyethylene Business," *PR Newswire,* July 6, 1992; "Hoechst Celanese Agrees to See HDPE Business to FINA," *Chemical Week,* July 15, 1992.

—Sina Dubovoj

FOSTER'S BREWING GROUP LTD.

1 Garden St., South Yarra
Victoria 3141
Australia
(03) 828 2424
Fax: (03) 828 2556

Public Company
Incorporated: 1962 as Elder Smith Goldsbrough Mort Ltd.
Employees: 15,000
Sales: A$10.37 billion (US$7.13 billion)
Stock Exchanges: Adelaide New Zealand London Amsterdam
    Frankfurt Tokyo Montreal New York Toronto
    Luxembourg Zürich Basel Geneva
SICs: 2082 Malt Beverages; 5159 Farm-Product Raw
    Materials, Nec; 5154 Livestock; 5099 Durable Goods,
    Nec; 6719 Holding Companies, Nec

Foster's Brewing Group Ltd. is Australia's largest beer producer and the fourth largest beer maker in the world. Since
1990, Foster's has shifted its interests away from several areas
in which it was previously active, including banking and agency
for agricultural products, in order to concentrate its holdings on
beer production, distribution, and service.

The emergence of Foster's as a major force in Australian
business can be traced to the activities of one man, John Elliott.
Through an astonishing series of acquisitions over the course of
over a decade, Elliott assembled a major conglomerate using a
moderately sized jam company as its nucleus. At about the age
of 30, Elliott returned to Australia after a brief stay in the United
States, where he had worked as a consultant. Beginning in the
early 1970s, with his only significant business experience consisting of a short stint at Australia's largest corporation, Broken
Hill Proprietary Co. (BHP), and a six-year engagement at the
American consulting firm of McKinsey & Co. (two of those
years in Chicago, the rest in Australia), Elliott set out to conquer
the business world from the top, running his own company
rather than working his way up from within one. After rounding
up about A$30 million in backing from a collection of Austra-
lian business leaders, Elliott purchased Henry Jones (IXL) Ltd.,
a company whose main businesses were making jam and canning fruit. Henry Jones grew during the rest of the 1970s
through a series of acquisitions of companies that could provide

necessary auxiliary services, including canning, packing, milling, and freezing operations.

One of the companies that had helped finance Elliott's takeover
of Henry Jones was Elder Smith Goldsbrough Mort Ltd., Australia's leading stock and station agency business. This type of
business provided a wide range of agricultural services, including livestock and wool auctioning, real estate services, and
farming supply merchandising. The company had been in operation since about 1839. In 1981 Elder Smith became the target
of a takeover attempt by the Bell Group, a company controlled
by corporate raider Robert Holmes a Court. Elder Smith's management turned for help to Elliott, who suggested a merger to
stave off a hostile takeover. What took place was essentially a
reverse takeover, with the larger Elder Smith buying out Henry
Jones (IXL), creating Elders IXL, and the Jones management
team assuming the new company's leadership positions. The
"IXL" part of the name was derived from the name of the most
popular brand in Sir Henry Jones's jam line.

One important asset that Elder Smith brought into the merged
company was its fledgling banking operation, in which it provided farmers with a variety of financial services that included
advances, acceptance of deposits, and mortgages. The company's work in the world of finance was expanded in 1982,
when, a mere month after the merger's official completion, the
company acquired the Wood Hall Trust, a British company with
financial interests throughout the Far East and Australia. Elders
also diversified into the oil business in 1982, with the purchase
of a 19.9 percent interest in Bridge Oil Limited, a large publicly
held company.

The next event of great importance for Elders was the 1983
takeover of Carlton & United Breweries Ltd. (CUB), best
known as the makers of Foster's, Australia's most popular beer.
CUB had already purchased a 33 percent stake in Henry Jones
in 1980, much of which was Elder Smith's pre-merger holding
in that company. CUB had then helped the merger progress by
buying Holmes a Court's share of Elder Smith, eliminating the
specter of further takeover attempts by him. Between these two
actions, CUB had become Elders IXL's major shareholder at
over 49 percent by 1983. Toward the end of that year, a bid to
take over CUB was launched by New Zealander Ron Brierley,
head of Industrial Equity Ltd., an investment holding company.
Once again Elliott responded quickly, raising US$720 million
in two days with which to start buying up CUB stock. Within a
couple of weeks, Elliott had taken control of over half of the
brewery's stock, and by the middle of 1984, he had gained full
ownership.

The rest of the 1980s was marked by a non-stop series of
acquisitions in a variety of industries, including mining operations and more beer companies. One result of this period was a
reputation for Elliott as one of a rising breed of Australian
takeover artists, a group whose members included Holmes a
Court, media mogul Rupert Murdoch, and Alan Bond (also
known as the man who took America's Cup out of America).
The takeover of CUB, the largest in Australia up to that time,
also created a substantial debt for Elders. The strategy for
reducing the debt was to sell off the unprofitable parts of the
various acquired companies at the same time new ones were
being sought. For example, by the middle of the decade, there

was no longer a food division at Elders, whereas food was once the company's core industry. By 1986 the old jam factory in the suburbs of Melbourne, now housing the company's headquarters, was nearly the only remnant of the old version of Elders. Also dumped were the 350 pubs once controlled by Carlton & United. Among the company's purchases during the mid-1980s were a 40 percent stake in Roach Tilley Grice & Co., a major Australian stock brokerage, and a 20 percent interest in Kidston Gold Mines Ltd., both in 1984.

In 1985 Elliott launched a takeover bid for Allied-Lyons PLC, a company four times the size of Elders. Elliott's initial bid for Allied, a British brewery and food conglomerate in which he already held a 6 percent share, totalled $2.3 billion, the money coming from a multi-national banking syndicate led by Citicorp. The move for Allied reflected a desire on the part of Elders' management to expand substantially into European markets, prompted by the limitations of Australia's population of only 15 million. The bid for Allied eventually reached $2.7 billion, but it was allowed to lapse without achieving its goal. One reason for the failure of the takeover attempt was Allied's merger with the Canadian liquor company Hiram Walker, which was itself fending off a takeover bid. Meanwhile, Elliott once again became involved in a raid orchestrated by Holmes a Court, this time saving BHP, Australia's largest corporation, from a hostile takeover. With Holmes a Court's Bell Resources in control of 18 percent of BHP in the midst of its unfriendly bid, Elliott suddenly came up with about 19 percent of that company over the course of just a few hours and was invited to join BHP's board. Though grateful for Elliott's assistance in warding off the raid, BHP in turn purchased 19 percent of Elders in order to preclude the possibility of that company launching a BHP takeover attempt of its own. Before 1986 was over, Elders became the first foreign company to own a major British brewery when it acquired not Allied-Lyons, but Courage Brewing Ltd., England's sixth-largest brewer. Elders paid $2.1 billion for the brewery and the 5,000 pubs the company also controlled. This purchase greatly expanded the presence of Foster's beer in Europe. Previously there had been a licensing agreement with Watney's.

By the end of 1986, Elders was selling beer in about 80 countries around the world. The company's profit for that year was $143 million, a 73 percent increase over the previous year, on revenues of $5.4 billion. In 1987 Elders made its first North American beer acquisition, purchasing Carling O'Keefe Breweries, the third-largest brewer in Canada, for about $300 million. By that year, Elders was the world's number six beer maker. Once again company records were set for both revenue and profit. Elders reported operating profits of $350 million, a 132 percent jump, on $7.6 billion in revenues in fiscal 1987. It was a big year for Elliott in other ways as well. He was a rising star in Australia's Liberal Party, and his Carlton Football Club won the Australian equivalent of the Super Bowl.

In 1988 Elders bought the remaining 60 percent of Roach & Co. Ltd., the stock brokerage into which it had bought five years earlier. That year there was widespread speculation that Elders would mount a takeover bid for Anheuser-Busch, which controlled about 40 percent of the beer market in the United States. These rumors were fuelled in part by the fact that the Bond group, the company's chief rival in its home country, with

whom it virtually split in half the Australian beer market, had recently purchased G. Heileman Brewing Co. of Milwaukee, establishing a strong American base of operations. Although Elders held about 1 percent interest in Anheuser-Busch, no action was taken toward a takeover at that time. For the year, sales at Elders once again grew substantially, reaching $11.74 billion.

In 1989 Elders merged its North American beer operations (Carling O'Keefe) with Toronto's Molson Breweries. At the time of its creation, the joint venture controlled 53 percent of the beer market in Canada. Other events of 1989 reshaped the company's future and ultimately led to Elliott's departure from the company he had built into an international empire. Harlin Holdings Group, a private investing firm owned mainly by Elders managers and led by Elliott, bought a 17 percent stake in Elders to secure the company from bids for control by outsiders. Australian regulators ruled that Harlin had to extend its $3 per share offer to all shareholders. As a result of this decision, Harlin embarked on what amounted to a takeover campaign for Elders, and ended up with a 56 percent holding in the company. This was a far greater share than the group had intended to purchase, and the Harlin group found itself A$2.8 billion in debt.

The solution to this situation proposed by Elliott was to spin off the company's agricultural business as a public company, carry on strictly as a beer operation, and sell off everything else, with proceeds going to the shareholders, the largest of which was Harlin. Harlin would also sell a portion of its holdings in both the remaining and spun-off corporations. In 1990 Elders began actively disposing of its non-beer enterprises. The company's paper, mineral, oil, and gas investments were divested in June of that year with the sale of Elders Resources NZFP to Carter Holt Harvey. Other properties that were sold off included the company's stockbrokerage and investment banking businesses, its North American grain operations, and its holdings in Scottish & Newcastle Breweries Plc. In addition, over 80 subsidiaries were liquidated that year.

While this streamlining process was taking place, Peter Bartels replaced Elliott as chief executive officer of Elders in May 1990. Elliott retained his chairmanship of the company's board. For the fiscal year ending in June 1990, Elders reported the largest loss in the history of Australian business, A$1.3 billion. Much of the loss was attributable to huge write-offs associated with the company's ongoing structural overhaul. The losses were particularly disastrous for Elliott's Harlin Holdings, which had come to rely entirely on dividends from its shares of Elders to make the interest payments on its huge bank debts. Harlin moved to alleviate some of its financial pressure by selling about 20 percent of its holdings in Elders for A$960 million to Japan's Asahi Breweries Ltd.

In December 1990, the name of Elders IXL was changed to Foster's Brewing Group Ltd., which better reflected the company's increasing focus on the beer part of its business. Throughout 1991, the divestment of non-brewing properties continued. Elliott was succeeded as chairman by Neil Clark. Elliott continued as a board member, holding one of the three seats controlled by International Brewing Holdings Pty., the new name for the Harlin Group. International Brewing was still the largest Foster's shareholder at 38 percent in the early part of 1992, but its dependance on dividends from these shares as its sole source of revenue proved problematic. In March 1992 Bartels resigned as chief executive of Foster's. His resignation, according to the March 3 issue of the *Wall Street Journal*, came about because of his opposition to increased dividends, for which Elliott and Clark had been lobbying. Bartels was replaced by Ted Kunkel, head of the company's joint venture with Molson.

In June 1992 International Brewing was put into receivership by BHP, to whom it owed over A$1 billion. In September of that year BHP became the largest shareholder in Foster's, with a 32 percent stake in the company. BHP acquired this share from two sources, the security on its own defaulted loans to International Brewing, and by buying the shares controlled by the Vextin syndicate, a group of banks to whom International Brewing had also owed in excess of A$1 billion. Elliott, along with the other representatives of International Brewing, made his final exit from the Foster's board of directors in that month as well. Foster's reported a net loss for the third year in a row in the fiscal year ending in June 1992. The company lost A$951 million in that year, once again due largely to substantial write-downs, many of which were the results of unsound property loans made by the company's defunct investment banking branch. Foster's entered the calendar year 1993 a pared-down version of its former self. As beer makers of good international repute, with markets in hand on at least three continents, Foster's may very well emerge from a difficult period intact, once the consequences of its 1980s excesses have been minimized.

Principal Subsidiaries: Carlton & United Breweries Ltd.; Courage Ltd.; Carling O'Keefe Breweries; Elders Ltd.; Elders Finance Group.

Further Reading: "Elders IXL Acquires Over Half of Shares of Australian Brewer," *Wall Street Journal,* December 13, 1983; Debes, Cheryl, "An Aussie Raider's Heady Bid to Buy a British Brewer," *Business Week,* September 23, 1985; Hemp, Paul, "Elders Cleared to Again Seek Allied-Lyons," *Wall Street Journal,* September 4, 1986; Foster, Geoffrey, "How Elders Grew Up," *Management Today,* May 1986; "Our Turn Now," *Economist,* April 19, 1986; Maremont, Mark, "Foreign Beermakers Go Pub-Crawling," *Business Week,* October 6, 1986; Kraar, Louis, "John Elliott: Australia's Apostle of Beer and Business," *Fortune,* January 5, 1987; "Can Foster's Become the Real Thing?" *Economist,* September 12, 1987; Debes, Cheryl, "An Unquenchable Thirst for Breweries," *Business Week,* October 19, 1987; McMurray, Scott, "Elders IXL Has 1% of Anheuser-Busch," *Wall Street Journal,* September 28, 1988; Crabbe, Mathew, "The Beer Baron Goes Banking," *Euromoney,* November 1988; Maher, Tani, "Molson-Elders: A Case of Deja Vu," *Financial World,* March 7, 1989; "Sell, Sell, Sell," *Economist,* May 5, 1990; "The Brewers' Fight for Survival," *Euromoney,* May 1990; Witcher, S., "Elders IXL Posts $1.08 Billion Loss for Fiscal Year," *Wall Street Journal,* September 26, 1990; Witcher, S., "Foster's Brewing of Australia Names New Chief," *Wall Street Journal,* March 11, 1992; Witcher, S., "Era Ends at Foster's," *Asian Wall Street Journal Weekly,* June 8, 1992; Witcher, S., "Australia's Foster's Brewing Posts Loss for Third Consecutive Year," *Wall Street Journal,* September 16, 1992.

—Robert R. Jacobson

FREEPORT-MCMORAN INC.

1615 Poydras Street
New Orleans, Louisiana 70112
U.S.A.
(504) 582-4000
Fax: (504) 585-3265

Public Company
Incorporated: 1981
Employees: 7,250
Sales: $1.5 billion
Stock Exchanges: New York
SICs: 1479 Chemical and Fertilizer Mining, Not Elsewhere
    Classified; 1475 Phosphate Rock; 2874 Phosphatic
    Fertilizers; 2819 Industrial Inorganic Chemicals, Not
    Elsewhere Classified; 1021 Copper Ores; 1041 Gold Ores

Freeport-McMoRan Inc. (FMI) is engaged in exploring, mining, producing, processing, and marketing natural resources. Commodities include phosphate rock, phosphate fertilizers, sulfur, oil, natural gas, copper, gold, and other natural resources. It ranks as the largest U.S. producer of phosphate fertilizer and one of the largest independent companies involved in oil and natural gas production. FMI also is recognized as a cost-effective producer of copper. FMI was incorporated in 1981 through a merger of Freeport Minerals Company and McMoRan Oil & Gas Company. Each company became a wholly owned subsidiary of Freeport-McMoRan Inc.

Freeport Minerals Company (FMC) was incorporated in 1912 under the name of Freeport Sulphur Company. It pioneered the use of the Frasch invention in the United States as an engineering method to mine sulfur. Prior to the Frasch invention, Italy monopolized the sulfur market because of its cheap labor. Herman Frasch's invention, which utilized machinery rather than manual labor, allowed U.S. companies to produce the element at competitive world prices. The process involved flushing large quantities of hot water into pipelines sunk inward toward the sulfur find. As the ore melted, it was pumped to the surface in liquid form. The process initially had been engineered on a find near Lake Charles, Louisiana, in 1894. Frasch, along with a group of financiers, established the Union Sulphur Company in 1896 and acquired title to the Lake Charles site, as well as mineral rights and control over the Frasch patents.

Subsequently, sulfur was discovered at the Bryanmound site on the gulf coast of Texas near the Brazos River. Francis R. Pemberton, an entrepreneur, together with other investors, took an option on leases covering the Bryanmound property. Because the expiration of the patent that covered the major components of the Frasch process was imminent, Pemberton brought the find to the attention of several investors. Eric P. Swenson, vice-president of National City Bank in New York and a native Texan who retained strong financial ties throughout Texas, showed interest and visited the find in 1911. When Swenson saw the site, he realized that he could also develop a duty-free port nearby. Upon returning to New York, he formed the Vanderlip-Swenson-Tilghman Syndicate. He pooled capital of $700,000 to finance the project and purchased Bryanmound and the surrounding area.

Frasch's Union Sulphur Company sued to bar the syndicate from using the Frasch engineering method at Bryanmound on the grounds that supplementary unexpired patents were crucial to the process. After lengthy litigation, a U.S. circuit court of appeals ruled that the remaining unexpired patents did not provide needed insight to the invention. As a consequence, the syndicate founded Freeport Sulphur Company in 1912, as well as the Freeport Townsite Company to develop a city on the west bank of the Brazos River and the Freeport Terminal Company to maintain train facilities to the port. In 1913 Freeport Texas Company was chartered as a holding company for Freeport Sulphur Company; Freeport Townsite Company; Freeport Asphalt Company; Freeport Sulphur Transportation Company; Freeport Terminal Company; South Texas Stevedore Company; and La Espuela Oil Company, Ltd. Headquarters for the holding company were located in New York City and Eric Swenson served as the company's first president, remaining in that office until 1930.

New mining methods were introduced at Bryanmound during its early years of operation. Elevated pipes carrying the molten sulfur from the well to the storage vats were replaced with three-inch-wide sulfur lines encased in six-inch-thick pipes through which steam could circulate to protect the lines from inclement weather and reduce clogging. During World War I demand for sulfur rose sharply. Approximately 1,500 tons were generated daily at Bryanmound to cover shipments sent to U.S. factories producing combat weapons. Before its closure in 1935, the find yielded more than five million long tons of sulfur.

The company began exploration on a second mine in 1922 when it acquired sulfur rights to Hoskins Mound, 15 miles from Bryanmound. Unfavorable geological formations in the mound prompted innovative drilling methods that later were used at other sites. Company engineers checked the escape of hot water into sedimentary deposits of sand by pumping large quantities of mud into the formation, thus making the find a successful venture. They also developed a process to heat water with water boiler gases. The plant at Hoskins Mound closed in 1955 after producing more than ten million long tons of sulfur.

A growing opposition to Eric Swenson's attitude as president of FMC led to his deposal by stockholders, who felt Swenson was insensitive to their concerns. In 1930 Eugene Norton was named president and under his leadership the company became the first sulfur-producing firm in the United States to diversify its interests. In 1931 FMC purchased controlling interest in Cuban-American Manganese Corporation and, through its Cuban subsidiary in Oriente Province, gained access to rich deposits of low-grade manganese oxide ores. FMC's research department developed a process to refine manganese from low-grade ore for use in the manufacture of steel. As a result, between 1932 and 1946, when the find was exhausted, the company produced more than one million tons of manganese oxide. In 1936 the corporate name was changed from Freeport Texas Company to Freeport Sulphur Company.

Langbourne M. Williams was associated with FMC for many years. He was elected president of the company in 1933 and chairman in 1957, and served on the board of directors until 1977. When he became president in 1933, company operations began at Grand Ecaille, a sulfur dome in the Mississippi delta region, 45 miles south of New Orleans, Louisiana. Because the dome was located beneath marshlands, engineers drove thousands of wooden pilings into the land and built reinforced concrete mats over them to provide transportation to and from the mine. Company workers also dug a ten-mile canal between the plant and a site near the Mississippi River where they shipped the product to market. The site was later named Port Sulphur. Grand Ecaille served as a model in developing engineering solutions that would be applied in the future. When the plant at Grand Ecaille closed in 1978, more than 40 million tons of sulfur had been produced. During World War II company plants at Hoskins Mound and Grand Ecaille received army and navy "E" awards from the U.S. government for outstanding wartime production. Another FMC subsidiary, Nicaro Nickel Co., chartered in 1942, was under contract to the U.S. government and contributed more than 63 million pounds of nickel to the war effort. The plant closed in 1947 when it became unworkable to cover production costs and sell the ore at competitive peacetime prices.

Charles Wight became a director of FMC in 1948 and president in 1958. During the 1950s new mining discoveries allowed for continued product diversification. Discoveries of substantial finds of potash in New Mexico and Canada prompted FMC to establish the National Potash Company in 1955, in partnership with Consolidated Coal Company. Production began in 1957, and in 1966 FMC acquired full ownership of the successful operation.

At the same time, FMC's research center developed several technological advances, some resulting in lower mining production costs. In 1952 the company pioneered a process substituting seawater for fresh water in sulfur mining. This process eliminated the need to transport fresh water to sites located near sources of seawater. Another process developed at FMC's research center produced pure nickel and cobalt from nickel ore and rekindled company interest in mining Cuban ores. In 1955 FMC chartered the Cuban American Nickel Company and a subsidiary, the Moa Bay Mining Company. The company invested $119 million in constructing plant facilities and a town at Moa Bay, Cuba, as well as a refinery at Port Nickel, Louisiana.

In 1960, however, the government of Fidel Castro confiscated the Cuban facility. In all, FMC produced more than 3 million pounds of nickel, 310,000 pounds of cobalt, and more than

7,000 tons of the by-product ammonium sulfur before the plant closed. FMC eventually listed the Cuban facility as a tax loss.

Although FMC began oil exploration in 1913 when it chartered La Espuela Oil Company, Ltd. to handle fuel requirements for its operation at Bryanmound, it was not until 1948 that the company began a sustained program of oil and gas exploration. In 1956 it formed Freeport Oil Company to handle ventures in Louisiana, Kansas, Texas, and New Mexico. In association with two other interests, it discovered oil and gas reserves at Lake Washington, Louisiana, and set a record, at the time, by producing oil from the world's deepest well, which extended 22,570 feet below the ground. In 1958 Freeport Oil Company sold its interest at Lake Washington for approximately $100 million to Magnolia Petroleum Company. Throughout the 1960s and 1970s the company participated in various joint oil and gas discoveries throughout the United States.

Robert C. Hills became president of FMC in 1961 and remained in office for six years. During his administration FMC produced a record two million tons of sulfur and became the world's largest sulfur producer for 1963. At the same time, FMC launched several new subsidiaries to meet company needs. It formed Freeport Kaolin Company in 1963 after purchasing the main assets of Southern Clays Inc. Included in the sale were white clay reserves used as filler and coating materials in the manufacture of paper. From 1964 through 1981 Freeport Kaolin Company underwent a major expansion program designed to increase mining and processing capacity and to upgrade its products.

In addition, FMC organized Freeport of Australia in 1964 to oversee its mineral exploration, development, and production activities in Australia as well as in the surrounding Pacific Ocean region. In 1967 Freeport of Australia, in a joint venture with Metals Exploration, located large Australian nickel deposits near Greenvale, Queensland.

In 1966 FMC established Freeport Chemical Company to embark on a phosphate chemical project, for which it constructed a plant in Uncle Sam, Louisiana. The plant produced its first shipments of phosphoric acid and sulfur acid in 1968. In the 1970s plant facilities were expanded at Uncle Sam and a plant to produce sulfuric acid was added in Port Sulphur, Louisiana. A research project undertaken at FMC led to the recovery in 1988 of uranium oxide, commonly referred to as yellowcake, from phosphoric acid. Subsequently two uranium-recovery plants were opened: one at Uncle Sam and the second one at Agrico Chemical Company's phosphoric acid facility in Donaldsonville, Louisiana.

In 1966 FMC founded Freeport Indonesia, Inc., to mine copper in the province of Irian Jaya. Because the find, known as Grasberg Prospect, was located in a remote, mountainous region, open-pit mining operations did not begin until late 1972. The first copper shipment was made the following year, however, and was valued at $2 million. Gold and silver also were mined at the find.

During the 1970s through 1982, significant changes occurred in the company. In 1971 the company name changed from Freeport Sulphur Company to Freeport Minerals Company to reflect its role as a diversified mineral producer. Paul W. Douglas became president in 1975. FMC continued a policy of diversification in 1981 when it formed Freeport Gold Company to operate a gold find located in Jerrit Canyon, Nevada.

In 1980 FMC reported a record of $147.4 million in company earnings. Over the years FMC had worked in joint mining ventures with McMoRan Oil & Gas Company and acquired three million shares of its convertible preferred stock. In 1981, when the companies merged, it became one of the leading natural-resources companies in the country.

W.K. McWilliams, Jr., and James R. (Jim Bob) Moffett, both geologists, started a privately owned company, McMoCo, during the mid-1960s. McMoCo became the forerunner of McMoRan Oil & Gas Company. It began as a consultant for oil and gas exploration programs, but soon added personnel to enable it to handle entire projects, from locating finds to drilling and producing the product. Because the company had limited funds, outside sources provided risk capital. In return for its work, McMoCo received 25-percent interest in each find. B. M. Rankin, Jr., a specialist in land-leasing and sales operations, joined as an associate in about 1967. With his arrival, McMoCo was liquidated and the three owners formed McMoRan, the company name combining portions of their surnames. In order to secure necessary funding for its many drilling programs, the company decided to become a public company. In 1969 it merged with Horn Silver Mines Company, a public firm incorporated in 1932 and controlled by television personality Art Linkletter and several associates, that was listed on the Salt Lake City Stock Exchange. As a consequence, a new public firm, named McMoRan Exploration Company, emerged, with Linkletter as a board member. One of the firm's earliest oil explorations was on the gulf coast of Louisiana in LaFourche Parish; McMoRan owned 50 percent of the successful find.

During the 1970s, the company acquired a reputation as an aggressive petroleum explorer with cost-efficient drilling programs. It formed drilling partnerships with several organizations. In 1972 it signed an agreement with Geodynamics Oil & Gas Inc. and Comprehensive Resources Corporation and bought working interests in several oil- and gas-producing properties in Texas and Louisiana. In 1973 it formed a joint petroleum-exploration program with Dow Chemical Company. In this venture, Dow Chemical Company received 50-percent interest in all exploration finds, while McMoRan Exploration Company's interest varied from 25 percent to 38 percent per find. In 1975 the company began a $36 million onshore oil and gas exploration and development program with Transco Exploration Company. During its first year of operation, McMoRan Exploration Company successfully completed five of the 17 wells drilled. As a result, budgets for the second and third year of operation were expanded from $8 million to $14 million.

While many exploration programs were in progress, administrative and operational changes took place within the organization. In 1970 stockholders voted to de-list the company from the Salt Lake City Stock Exchange. In 1977 a four-member operating committee headed by Moffett was named to assume the duties of McWilliams and Rankin, who stepped down as cochairmen. Moffett became president and chief executive officer, while McWilliams and Rankin remained as consultants, directors, and stockholders. In 1978 the company was reincorporated in Dela-

ware and was listed on the New York Stock Exchange. In 1979 the name was changed from McMoRan Exploration Company to McMoRan Oil & Gas Company.

Other operational changes included the creation of subsidiaries to separate distinct operations within the organization and provide the company with additional exploration exposure. In 1977 McMoRan Offshore Exploration Company (MOXY) began operation to manage and expand oil and gas explorations in federal waters off the Gulf of Mexico. Interests in federal offshore lease blocks were acquired through sublease arrangements. In 1980 MOXY entered a three-year program with several organizations, including Transco Exploration Company and Freeport Minerals Company. Under the agreement, MOXY provided 25 percent of exploratory expenses in exchange for 35 percent working interest in the finds.

Another subsidiary, McMoRan Exploration Company (MEC), was formed in 1979 to handle exploration and production of oil and gas properties located primarily along the gulf area of Texas and Louisiana, both onshore and in waters owned by these states. In 1980 MEC began an exploration and development program for oil and gas operations in the gulf region with several organizations. MEC provided 25 percent of total exploration funds in return for a 37.5 percent working interest in the finds.

In 1981 McMoRan Oil & Gas Company merged with Freeport Minerals Company. The new company, Freeport-McMoRan Inc., elected Paul Douglas as president and Benno C. Schmidt as chairman of the board. James R. Moffett became vice-chairman but remained president of McMoRan Oil & Gas Company, directing all combined oil and gas activities. FMI's policy put greater emphasis on domestic oil and gas exploration programs yet sustained interest in growth programs in minerals and chemical products.

In 1982 Freeport Gold Company completed its first full year of operation. It held the record as the largest gold producer for the year, reporting an output of 196,000 ounces of gold. In 1983 FMI created Freeport-McMoRan Oil and Gas Royalty Trust to afford shareholders direct participation in the income from selected U.S. offshore oil and gas properties held by McMoRan Oil & Gas Company. Although the company was unable to put a value on these properties, its annual report for 1982 listed entire oil and gas assets at $1.06 billion.

FMC in 1983 purchased Stone Exploration Corporation, a company engaged in gas exploration, development, and production, primarily in south Louisiana. At the time, Stone Exploration had estimated proven reserves of 57 billion cubic feet of gas and gas equivalents.

In 1983 Paul W. Douglas resigned as president and chief executive officer. Schmidt, chairman of the company, assumed the additional position of chief executive officer but the position of president remained vacant. In 1984 Moffett succeeded Schmidt as chairman and chief executive officer. Schmidt became executive committee chairman and a director. Richard B. Stephens replaced Moffett as president of McMoRan Oil & Gas Company. Milton H. Ward assumed the duties of president and chief operating officer of FMI. At the time, FMI's asset base was valued at $1.4 billion.

In 1984 FMI enjoyed a 133 percent increase in its oil and gas reserves when it purchased a 50 percent working interest in Voyager Petroleum Ltd. of Canada and Midlands Energy Company, operating in the midwestern and western United States. Freeport-McMoRan Oil & Gas Company, a fully owned subsidiary of FMI, also became managing general partner of Freeport McMoRan Energy Partners, Ltd., which it incorporated in 1984.

In 1985 FMI sold certain assets to reduce its long-term debt. It sold Freeport Itaolin Company for more than $95 million to Engelhard Corporation, a manufacturer of specialty chemical and metallurgical products and a trader in precious metals. In June 1985 it sold a 25-percent interest in Midlands Energy Company to Bristol PLC, a British energy company, for $73 million. The 25-percent interest included natural gas and oil reserves, exploration land, and a stake in three processing plants. It sold 14 percent of its domestic oil and gas business for more than $125 million on the New York Stock Exchange in the form of depository receipts representing limited partnership units in its Freeport-McMoRan Energy Partners, Ltd. Additionally, it sold approximately 11 percent of its common shares in Freeport-McMoRan Gold Company, formerly known as Freeport Gold Company, to the public for more than $39 million.

Also in 1985, FMI acquired two new companies and announced a program to repurchase up to ten million common shares of its stock depending on market conditions. (By August 1991 FMI had spent over $1 billion to buy back common stock.) It bought Geysers Geothermal Company (GGC), a producer of steam for electric power generation, for $216.7 million. The purchase allowed FMI to extend the use of the hot-water technology it had developed while operating its sulfur reserves. It also bought most of the assets of Pel-Tex Oil Company for $74 million, thereby acquiring its oil and gas properties located in the gulf area of Louisiana and Texas.

Operational costs of the organization were significantly reduced beginning in 1985 when corporate headquarters in New York City were moved to New Orleans, Louisiana, and combined with FMI's office there. Oil and gas and certain mineral functions were also moved to the new Freeport-McMoRan Building built to serve as headquarters for the organization.

In 1986 FMI formed Freeport-McMoRan Resource Partners (FRP), whose operations included the production of phosphate, nitrogen fertilizer products, sulfur, and geothermal resources, and the recovery of uranium oxide from phosphoric acid. FRP stock was placed on the New York Stock Exchange. The same year, in partnership with Kidder, Peabody & Company, FMI reached an agreement to buy Petro-Lewis Corporation and an affiliate, American Royalty Trust Company, for $440 million. The acquisition increased FMI's domestic oil and gas production.

In 1987 FRP acquired a chemical-fertilizer plant located in Taft, Louisiana, from Beker Industries for $22.5 million. It also bought Agrico Chemical Company from The Williams Companies for more than $250 million. Agrico assets included phosphate rock mines, production facilities for phosphate and nitrogen fertilizers, and a large sales and distribution network.

During the year FMI changed its interests in Australia. It sold most of its holdings in the Greenvale Nickel project in Queens-

land in two transactions for a total of $26 million in cash and a deferred payment of $11 million. It set up Freeport McMoRan Australia Ltd. in 1987 to handle its gold and diamond projects in that country. Late in 1988 the new subsidiary merged with Poseidon Ltd., an Australian mining concern, and a new company emerged called Poseidon Exploration Ltd.

In November 1989 Moffett outlined a plan to sell between $1.2 billion to $1.5 billion in assets to reduce long-standing debts. Future company focus would be concentrated on developing two mammoth mining discoveries: the sulfur find in the Gulf of Mexico off Louisiana (Main Pass project), and the copper and gold finds in Indonesia (the Grasberg and Ertsberg projects). Moffet felt that the asset sales would also free up capital for the development of the fields, which had emerged as extremely valuable resources. The extension of the Grasberg ore body in Indonesia had transformed that operation into the largest single gold reserve in the world, and propelled it to a ranking as one of the top five copper reserves worldwide. In 1991 Freeport set up new subsidiaries to control operations in both Indonesia and the Gulf of Mexico.

The Main Pass Line was revealed as the first significant Frasch sulphur discovery on the North American continent since the 1960s, and one of the most productive oil fields in the Gulf of Mexico. Developers estimated that 67 million long tons of sulfur, 39 million barrels of oil, and seven billion cubic feet of natural gas lay beneath the Gulf near the Mississippi Delta. Extraction of these natural resources will cause settling on the Gulf floor, precluding super-strong framing inside the underwater mine.

Moffett liquidated $2 billion of FMI's assets to finance the projects. The 1989 sales included Freeport-McMoRan Gold Company and about $85 million of its oil and gas properties; Voyager Energy; geothermal energy assets; and an interest in an Australian mining company.

In 1990 the company sold its nitrogen fertilizer business to Agricultural Minerals Corporation for $275 million. It divested itself of Freeport-McMoRan Gold Company, sold to Minorco South Africa for about $705 million. At the end of 1990, FMI stated that it planned to auction an additional $750 million of its assets, again as part of its debt-reduction goal.

Despite the poor performance of most commodities, Freeport-McMoRan (and its investors) continued to prosper into the 1990s. The 1987–1990 divestments lowered FMI's debt to just over $1 billion by the end of 1991, down $500 million from the previous year. Moffett announced in mid-1991 that a preliminary agreement had been signed to market sulfur produced in the Soviet Union, including operation of a terminal with a capacity to handle 1.5 million tons of sulfur annually. In 1991 capital expenditures were expected to total $700 million, with most of the money to be spent on the Indonesian and Gulf of Mexico capital projects. The conglomerate also recapitalized the debt and equity of its properties in the fall of 1992 to provide even more capital to invest in its promising projects.

In the spring of 1992 FMI created a new subsidiary, Freeport Spain, to operate two new acquisitions: Fesa-Enfersa, a producer of fertilizer, and Rio Tinto Minera, a metal miner/smelter. Both of the companies were previously subsidiaries of Ercros, a company based in Barcelona, Spain. FMI purchased 51 percent interests in the companies in order to gain control of them.

At the same time, Freeport joined many of its primary competitors in international oil and gas exploration and production by targeting Thailand as its first oil and gas undertaking outside the United States. The paucity of exploration options in the United States pushed many mining companies, large and small, to explore international options.

Principal Subsidiaries: Freeport-McMoRan Resource Partners, Limited Partnership (62%); Freeport-McMoRan Copper & Gold, Inc.; Freeport-McMoRan Oil & Gas Co.; Freeport Uranium Recovery Co.; FMI Hydrocarbon Co.; Freeport Exploration Co.; Freeport Research and Engineering Co.; Freeport-McMoRan Business Enterprises, Inc.

Further Reading: Haynes, Williams, *The Stone That Burns; The Story of the American Sulphur Industry,* Princeton, New Jersey, Van Nostrand, 1942; Haynes, Williams, *Brimstone; The Stone That Burns, The Story of the Frasch Sulphur Industry,* Princeton, New Jersey, 1959; *First in Sulphur, First in Service:*

Freeport Sulphur Company, New York, Freeport Sulphur Company, 1961; "Freeport Says it with Sulfur," *Business Week,* November 4, 1967; "A Freeport First?" *Forbes,* May 1, 1970; *Freeport-McMoRan,* New Orleans, Freeport-McMoRan Inc., 1980; Mullener, Elizabeth, "Jim Bob Moffett: The Style of a Hot Shot, the Heart of a Wildcatter and the Soul of an Entrepreneur," *Dixie,* April 13, 1986; "Highlights of the Freeport Story," Freeport-McMoRan Inc., 1986; "Freeport's Flexible Focus," *Oil & Gas Investor,* July 1991; Pratt, Tom, "Mining the Capital Markets," *Investment Dealers Digest,* August 12, 1991; Wilder, Clinton. "CIO challenge: Managing EDS," *Computerworld,* November 11, 1991; Price, Robin B., "U.S. Independent Operators Step up the Pace of Non-U.S. Exploration, Development," *Oil & Gas Journal,* April 27, 1992; Zellner, Wendy, "Freeport-McMoRan, a Rare Commodity," *Business Week,* April 27, 1992; Plisner, Emily S., and Debbie Jackson, "Freeport to Control Two Ercros Units," *Chemical Week,* May 6, 1992; Moore, Gordon H., and Juan J. Campo, "Offshore Challenge," *Civil Engineering,* October 1992.

—Beatrice Rodriguez Owsley
updated by April Dougal

GANNETT CO., INC.

1100 Wilson Boulevard
Arlington, Virginia 22234
U.S.A.
(703) 284-6000
Fax: (703) 276-5548

Public Company
Incorporated: 1923
Employees: 36,700
Sales: $3.38 billion
Stock Exchanges: New York
SICs: 2711 Newspapers; 4832 Radio Broadcasting Stations;
  4833 Television Broadcasting Stations; 7312 Outdoor
  Advertising Services

Gannett Co., Inc., is the United States's largest newspaper
group. In 1991 the company owned 81 daily newspapers (including its flagship *USA Today*), more than 50 nondaily publications, and the weekly newspaper magazine *USA Weekend,*
among other holdings. Gannett's dailies boast a total average
paid circulation of over 6.2 million, more than any other newspaper group. The company also has owned and operated ten
television stations, eight FM radio stations, and seven AM radio
stations, many of which are in major markets. In addition, its
Gannett Outdoor was the largest outdoor-advertising group in
North America.

Gannett has been a leader in the application of technology and
in media issues since its founding in 1906. It continues to be a
leader today—albeit a more controversial one—largely because of *USA Today* and former chairman Allen Neuharth.
Current chairman John Curley wants to maintain the company's industry leadership role but takes a less flashy approach
than his predecessor. He is also focusing more on the bottom
line.

Gannett is the brainchild of Frank Gannett, who paid his way
through Cornell University by running a news-correspondence
syndicate; when he graduated he had $1,000 in savings. Gannett
got into the media business in 1906 when he and several
associates bought the *Elmira Gazette* in Elmira, New York,
with $3,000 in savings, $7,000 in loans, and $10,000 in notes.
They bought another local paper and merged them to form the
Star-Gazette, beginning a pattern of mergers to increase advertising power that the company would follow throughout its

history. Six years later, in 1912, Gannett bought the *Ithaca
Journal,* beginning his toehold in upper New York state. The
company gradually built up a portfolio of 19 New York dailies
by 1989.

In 1918 Gannett and his team moved to Rochester, New York, a
city whose papers would turn out to be among the company's
strongest. Many of Gannett's rising executives were groomed at
the Rochester papers. The group purchased two newspapers
upon their arrival and merged them into the *Times-Union.* The
papers' holdings were consolidated under the name Empire
State Group. In 1921 the *Observer-Dispatch* of Utica, New
York, was acquired. In 1923 Gannett bought out his partners'
interests in the Empire State Group and the six newspapers the
group then owned, and formed Gannett Co., Inc. Gannett
appointed Frank Tripp general manager. Tripp helped run the
everyday business of the papers, and the two were close allies
for years. The Northeast was Gannett's focus for the next 25
years, and the company expanded aggressively with acquisitions there. Another key executive, Paul Miller, joined the company in 1947, becoming Gannett's executive assistant. By then,
the company operated 21 newspapers and radio stations.

The company's role as a leader in technology began in 1929,
when Frank Gannett co-invented the teletypesetter. Gannett
newsrooms were among the first to use shortwave radios to
gather reports from distant sources. In 1938, before color was
used much in newspapers, many Gannett presses were adapted
for color; with its *USA Today,* the company would continue to
be a leader in color use. Other advantages included a corporate
plane that helped reporters get to the site of news quickly. Frank
Gannett died in 1957, but not before he saw Miller named
president and chief executive officer. Miller oversaw the company's expansion from a regional chain to a national one in the
next decade.

Gannett News Service, as it became known as, was founded in
1942 as Gannett National Service. The wire service subsidiary
provides the company's local papers with national stories from
Washington, D.C., and 13 bureaus. The stories often have a
local angle or local sources. A television news bureau was
added in 1982. Through all these years, Gannett grew by buying
existing newspaper and radio and TV stations. In 1966 it
founded its first newspaper, *Florida Today.* It was the work of
Allen Neuharth, who later was to become the founder of *USA
Today.* Neuharth brought the new paper to profitability in 33
months, an incredible feat in the newspaper business, according
to analysts. Because the paper was near the National Aeronau-
tics and Space Administration (NASA), it was dubbed "Florida's Space Age Newspaper." The paper has since been redesigned to emphasize state and local news and is promoted and
sold with *USA Today,* which provides national and international
coverage.

Gannett went public in 1967. In 1970 Miller assumed the title of
chairman, and Neuharth was promoted to president and chief
operating officer from executive vice-president, making him the
heir-apparent to the top position in the company. Neuharth went
on an acquisition spree, leading the company to its current size
and status in the media world. He became chief executive
officer in 1973 and chairman in 1979.

Two notable mergers were those with Federated Publications in 1971 and with Speidel Newspaper Group in 1977. Two years later, Gannett merged with Combined Communications, the biggest such merger in the industry at that time, for $400 million. The Evening News Association joined the Gannett family later when Gannett bought it for $700 million. One near-merger was with Ridder Publications. That company's president, Bernard H. Ridder, Jr., was a golfing mate of Miller. Ridder had concluded that the only way his small, family-held company's stock would ever reach its full potential was for Ridder Publications to merge with a big media company. The two talked, but Ridder proved to be more interested in Knight Newspapers because it had less geographic overlap with Ridder than did Gannett. But in 1989 Gannett and Knight-Ridder implemented a joint operating agency to combat the decline in newspaper advertising revenues in Detroit, Michigan. The cooperative venture was the largest-ever merging of two competing newspapers' business operations. The arrangement called for the Knight-Ridder's *Free Press* and Gannett's *Detroit News* to divide revenues equally. Since Gannett held more of Detroit's market share before the merger, it took a loss during the venture's first year, 1990.

Some industry critics have warned that media consolidation, such as Gannett's 1970s acquisitions, thwarts open debate and the exchange of ideas. Gannett defenders, however, claim that chain newspapers can be just as vigorous in promoting and defending the rights of a free press as independent newspapers. In an effort to illustrate that point, Gannett started its "News 2000" project to preserve and advance First Amendment rights and develop a more positive image for newspapers in the process.

In 1986 Neuharth retired as chief executive officer, passing the baton to John Curley. Curley had been president and chief operating officer since 1984; he joined Gannett in 1970. Curley took on the title of chairman in 1989 and still headed the company in 1993. Curley, a newsman, as most of Gannett's heads have been, was editor and publisher of several Gannett papers and was founding editor of *USA Today*.

Neuharth continued as chairman of the Gannett Foundation, which was established in 1935 by Frank Gannett to promote free press, freedom of information and better journalism, adult literacy, community problem-solving, and volunteerism. Neuharth spent as freely at the foundation as he had at the company, giving $28 million to various programs in 1989 alone. Despite criticism from some Gannett newspaper executives, Neuharth also oversaw the Foundation's move from Rochester, New York, to Arlington, Virginia, where *USA Today*'s offices are located. Interior design of the charity's new headquarters ran at $15 million.

With expenses rising faster than assets, Neuharth sold the Foundation's ten percent share of Gannett Co. back to the company for $670 million. On July 4, 1991, the philanthropy's name was changed to the Freedom Forum, and its mission was changed to focus on First Amendment and other strictly journalistic issues. Gannett Co. created a $5 million fund to replace money withdrawn from the Gannett Foundation's more community-oriented charities. Other accomplishments of the company in the early 1990s include: increasing the company's use

of recycled newsprint to 20 percent of total usage, over 180,000 tons; being named one of the United States' top 20 places for African-Americans to work; and becoming the first news service to syndicate a weekly newspaper column dedicated exclusively to gay and lesbian issues.

Neuharth had said in 1982 when he started *USA Today* that it would begin making annual profits in three to five years. By 1990 the paper had had quarterly profits but never a full year of profitability. Between 1982 and 1990, *USA Today* sapped the company of an estimated $500 million. And September of 1992 marked ten unprofitable years for *USA Today*. But with 6.6 million readers daily, the United States' most widely read newspaper also celebrated record advertising and circulation revenues. *USA Today* executives claim that had the U.S. economy not been in recession, the paper would have been in the black by 1990. Fortunately, the rest of Gannett's business was strong enough to offset *USA Today*'s annual losses. Curley, the paper's president and publisher, hoped that cost-containment measures, lower newsprint prices, and other savings in the production-distribution process would bring *USA Today* into profitability.

1991 was Gannett's most difficult year since the company went public in 1967. The company slipped from second to third in rankings of the United States' top media concerns as a result of Time Warner's leapfrog to first place. Annual revenues dropped 2 percent and net income was down 20 percent from the year before. Fifty-five of Gannett's 86 local dailies raised circulation prices, and circulation barely rose.

Yet the national daily newspaper was another demonstration of Gannett's leadership role in the use of technology, as well as journalism. The paper has also been an innovator in graphics, especially in the use of color. Media observers credit *USA Today*'s use of color as the spur for industry-wide interest in color graphics. The copy for the paper is composed and edited at *USA Today*'s Arlington, Virginia, headquarters, then transmitted via satellite to 36 printing plants in the United States, Europe, and Asia.

After the firm's buying binge under Neuharth, analysts say it is likely that Gannett will take a slower pace in the next several years. In 1990 it purchased Montana's *Great Falls Tribune* from Cowles Media for $41 million, making it the company's 83rd daily paper. There are fewer great deals to be made on newspaper acquisitions in recent years, however, so Gannett has been working to improve the profitability and journalistic performance of its current holdings.

In the 1990s Gannett has sought to improve its financial performance by catering to both ends of the media spectrum: consumers and advertisers. For consumers raised on television who say they find newspapers "boring," Gannett's flagship, *USA Today,* offers concise stories. The company also has been encouraging its local dailies to use more graphics and briefer stories. Advertisers are drawn to the print media's comparatively low costs and to *USA Today*'s 1.7 million week-day and 2.2 million weekend circulation.

Principal Subsidiaries: Gannett Direct Marketing Services, Inc.; Gannett News Service; Gannett Outdoor; Louis Harris &

Associates; Gannett National Newspaper Sales; Gannett Tele-marketing, Inc.; USA Today Update; USA Today Books.

Further Reading: Mott, Frank Luther, *American Journalism: A History, 1690–1960,* New York, Macmillan, 1962; Cose, Ellis, *The Press,* New York, Morrow, 1989; "Gannett: USA's Tomorrow," *Economist,* November 25, 1989; Calabro, Lori, "Douglas McCorkindale: Confessions of a Dealmaker," *CFO: The Magazine for Senior Financial Executives,* March 1991; Powell, Dave, "Technology and Imagination Are the Stuff from Which Businesses Can be Built," *Networking Management,* March 1991; Garneau, George, "Gannett Foundation's Revised Mission," *Editor & Publisher, the Fifth Estate,* June 8, 1991; Donaton, Scott, "Media Reassess as Boomers Age," *Advertising Age,* July 15, 1991; Foust, Dean, "Patching the Cracks in the House that Al Built," *Business Week,* December 16, 1991; Garneau, George, "A Flat Year Expected for 1992," *Editor & Publisher, the Fifth Estate,* January 4, 1992; Case, Tony, "Life from a Gay Perspective," *Editor & Publisher, the Fifth Estate,* July 11, 1992; Garneau, George, "Newspaper Financial Reports," *Editor & Publisher, the Fifth Estate,* August 8, 1992; Kerwin, Ann Marie, "Advice for the Next Century: Future Role of Newspapers Discussed by Panel," *Editor & Publisher, the Fifth Estate,* August 8, 1992; Endicott, R. Craig, "100 Leading Media Companies," *Advertising Age,* August 10, 1992; Fisher, Christy, "A Decade of 'USA Today': Color It Red," *Advertising Age,* August 31, 1992; Crain, Rance, "Readers Find Newspapers 'Boring . . . Dull,'" *Advertising Age,* September 14, 1992.

—Lisa Collins
updated by April Dougal

GENEVA STEEL

10 South Geneva Road
Vineyard, Utah 84058
U.S.A.
(801) 227-9000
Fax: (801) 227-9431

Public Company
Incorporated: 1987
Employees: 2,400
Sales: $420 million
Stock Exchanges: New York Pacific
SICs: 3312 Blast Furnaces & Steel Mills

Geneva Steel is the only integrated steel mill operating west of the Mississippi River. The mill's principal products are hot-rolled steel sheet, plate, and pipe products which are used for a variety of applications, including industrial and agricultural machinery, gas and water pipelines, ships and barges, storage tanks, railroad cars, and a variety of construction materials. They are primarily sold in the western and central United States. The company also produces semi-finished slabs and non-steel materials that are by-products of its steel-making operations. The company's properties consist of a 1400-acre site in Vineyard, Utah, 45 miles south of Salt Lake City, on which the steel mill is located, plus a lease on a 300-acre site nearby.

Geneva was originally designed as a single-line plate mill when it was built by the U.S. government in 1942 as part of the war effort. When the government no longer had need of it, the mill was sold to the United States Steel Corporation, a unit of USX Corporation, and modified into a single-line plate/sheet mill. USX operated the mill from 1944 until 1986 when it decided to close down the mill.

USX suspended operation of the mill from July 1986 to August 1987 but kept it on "hot idle" status hoping to sell it. In August 1987, the mill was acquired by a group of investors for $44 million (less than a third of its estimated liquidation value). USX's original asking price was $58 million.

The group was headed by Joseph Cannon, a native of Utah who was then working at a Washington, D.C. law firm, and Robert Grow, a real estate lawyer in Salt Lake City. Cannon was previously the associate administrator for policy and resource management with the Environmental Protection Agency (EPA)

during the Reagan administration. Other members of the group included one of Cannon's brothers, an uncle, and several other attorneys—none of whom had any appreciable experience in the operation of a steel mill.

It seemed the deal was going to fall through when one of the committed lenders—a Texas savings-and-loan institution—balked at providing financing. Adding more fuel to the fire, USX decided at that point to shut off the gas in the coke ovens, which would have destroyed the ovens and put the mill completely out of operation. It took a personal phone call from Joseph Cannon to Utah Senator Orrin Hatch (Republican) who, in turn, prevailed upon USX's chairman, David Roderick, to delay shutting down the coke-ovens for the time being. Finally, the financing was secured and Geneva Steel went into business on August 31, 1987. Within days after the signing of the papers, the mill start-up began. The coke ovens were put back into production in record time and Geneva Steel was shipping out product 33 days later.

The acquisition agreement between the new owners and USX stipulated that USX would retain liability for life insurance, health care, and pension benefits for those employees on the payroll prior to the acquisition. This agreement made it possible for the new Geneva Steel company to start out with a clean slate. Joseph Cannon would soon become chairman and chief executive officer, and Robert Grow would serve as president and chief operating officer. Also stipulated in the agreement was that all prior obligations regarding the mill, including cleaning up of the environmental conditions that existed before the company was purchased, were to be the responsibility of USX. However, Geneva volunteered to share equally in the cost of the first $20 million of environmental expenditures.

Geneva adopted a program to modernize the plant after the mill operations got under way. The existing technology was outdated, operating costs needed careful scrutiny, and equipment needed replacing—especially if management intended to avoid future pollution liability.

One of the first orders of business for Geneva was to negotiate a new labor agreement. The company offered worker incentives and profit sharing in exchange for a wage package of $20 per hour (versus an industry average of $27 per hour). The workers accepted this offer.

After laying the groundwork, Geneva Steel showed a profit in its first month in business and continued to do so through 1991. In 1989 they shipped 1,368,000 tons of steel; in 1990 they shipped 1,375,000 tons. After the mill became operational, Geneva put its modernization program into effect. It was specifically geared towards reducing operating costs, strengthening and adding to its product lines, increasing its efficiency, and bringing the company into compliance with environmental regulations. The estimated modernization cost, when completed, is expected to be in the neighborhood of $320 million—more than seven times the purchase price.

Although the steel market was not strong, it seemed a good time to buy a steel mill for the buyers. At the time of its purchase, prices for steel plate and sheet were on the rise. Suppliers were willing to negotiate favorable contracts with Geneva. Even so, improving cash flow and cost-savings became a top priority for the company. One approach they employed was to change the generally accepted inventory practice used by steel producers. While USX regularly kept $100 million inventory on hand and up to a 60-day supply of various items, Geneva began operating with a ten-day inventory, trimming their inventory leads by more than $40 million. Also, by producing a product mix of plate and sheet, Geneva was able to accommodate changing market conditions faster and still operate at capacity. Even during the recent recessionary period, Geneva was able to operate at over 85 percent capacity. Union grievances also fell considerably.

Being novices in the industry, Cannon and Grow chose to keep most of USX's managerial staff. It turned out to be a sound decision and a learning experience for them. The managers knew the mill, they knew the problems that existed, and so were able to suggest cost-effective solutions that could make the mill run more efficiently. Of the former USX managers Geneva Steel retained, only three left by the end of 1988.

Geneva Steel's earnings totaled more than $100 million in its first two years in business. Most of the profits, according to Joseph Cannon, went back into modernization. Cannon made it very clear in a November 4, 1991, *Industry Week* article that Geneva Steel would be around for a very long time, citing the fact that Geneva's iron ore mine in southern Utah had about 150 years worth of iron ore in it and they intend to use it all.

Geneva started out from a "no customer" base to more than 350 customers in 42 states. When the company was under the control of USX, no shipments of product were made west of Denver. But this changed; Geneva's steel destinations included San Francisco to rebuild the broken bridges and highways after the 1989 earthquake and Alaska to repair the *Exxon Valdez*.

In November of 1989, the shareholders agreed upon plans to recapitalize the company and to earmark the proceeds towards their modernization program. Their common shares were redesignated class A common stock, and approximately 2.75 million class A shares were converted into 27.5 million class B shares. This concentrated the voting power and control of the company in the hands of Joseph Cannon and Robert Grow. On January 1, 1990, ten class B shares were convertible into one class A share. On March 27, 1990, Geneva Steel went public and the underwriters, Merrill Lynch Capital Markets and Salomon Brothers Inc., sold 7,750,000 GNV class A common shares at ten dollars each in the initial public offering. The company is listed as "GNV" on both the New York and Pacific Stock Exchanges. The directors and officers of the company owned approximately 67 percent of the outstanding stock. Because they originally paid an average of 7.5 cents per share for their stock, they realized a 133-fold gain. Their plan was to put all the money back into a modernization program from 1990 to 1994 that would cost approximately $320 million.

The first step of their modernization commitment was the installation of two state-of-the-art Q-BOP furnaces (bottom-blown basic oxygen process furnaces) to replace the existing open hearths—the last ones still in operation in the United States. These new furnaces increased yields and quality and cut costs. Most importantly, with the Q-BOP, a batch of steel only took 45 minutes to produce, whereas an open hearth oven took 5.5 hours to do the same job.

Geneva purchased their two Q-BOPs for their scrap value ($4 million) from an idled Republic Steel facility near Chicago. It took five barges to move the parts down the Mississippi River, a convoy of 92 trucks to transport the pieces over the Rocky Mountains, and 67,000 man hours to install the furnaces, but it was considered a genuine bargain. If they were purchased and installed at the going price, it would have cost Geneva approximately $300 million to $400 million. To make the Q-BOPs fully operational cost the company an additional $73 million, plus additional costs for refinements and other improvements to make them environmentally efficient. By late September 1991, the furnaces were up and working and were far exceeding their expectations. Another time saver was the 1992 installation of in-line slab conditioning, or "hot scarfing," which eliminated hand scarfing to remove surface defects. Before the installation, the slabs had to be cooled before the scarfing could be done. The cost of the installation represents an investment of $13 million, but, according to Robert Grow, in a July 13, 1992, *American Metal Market* article, "We now do in four minutes what used to take us a week to do." Also, as part of their modernization program, the company installed continuous-casting technology and coil box equipment, which enabled them to roll large steel coils.

Geneva installed a biological waste-water treatment plant, at the cost of $8 million. This was the first of its kind in America and an environmental achievement. It uses microorganisms—or "bugs"—to eat ammonia from the plant's waste-water, converting it into harmless nitrogen. The "bug plant" operation served to improve the quality of water released into Utah Lake. They also installed a new benzene gas blanketing system that helped to reduce benzene emissions from Geneva's coke plant to below the detectable limit. Geneva received an Outstanding Achievement Award from the U.S. Environmental Protection Agency for these modifications.

Geneva was one of only two of the top 12 North American integrated steel mills to show a profit during the 1990–91 recession. The falloff continued into 1992 and steel prices declined more than 30 percent. Geneva's prices were down $90 per ton. The company experienced significant price competition due to reduced demand for steel products. Although the company still made a profit, their net income for fiscal 1990 was approximately 31 percent less than fiscal 1989. And the company's net income for fiscal 1991 was approximately 54.1 percent less than for fiscal 1990.

To maintain a reasonable cash flow, the company took on significant amounts of debt in the early 1990s. In March 1990 Geneva issued over $110 in fixed-rate long-term debt. Of that $110 million, the company repaid its entire outstanding balance of $62 million. In April 1991 the company obtained a three-year revolving credit facility of up to $50 million from a syndicate of banks (later the company's credit line came through Citibank). In addition, in June 1992 the company laid off about five percent of its work force and for the first nine months of its 1992 fiscal year the company reported a loss of $9.7 million.

As the economies in Europe and Japan turned down in 1992, exports of steel into the United States started to go up again. This was due in part to the expiration of the U.S. government's Voluntary Restraint Agreements on March 30, 1992, which had been in place for 11 years. Before that time, the United States had become a virtual dumping ground for excess steel production. In 1981 the U.S. government established Voluntary Restraint Agreements whereby foreign governments put a cap on their steel exports. In return, the government agreed to prevent anti-dumping suits by domestic steelmakers. Since March 1992, at least 85 anti-dumping suits were filed by domestic steel producers. They are currently being handled by the U.S. International Trade Commission.

In July 1991, shortly before the Q-BOPs finally became operational, Joseph Cannon stepped down from directing the mill's operations and assumed a less strenuous position with the company in order to be able to devote more of his time to seeking the Utah U.S. Senate seat that was vacated by the incumbent, Republican Jake Garn. Cannon was unsuccessful in his bid for the U.S. Senate, and on October 1, 1992, he resumed his former position as chief executive officer of the company.

At this time, Geneva began improving its rolling mill operation. This allowed the company to increase the size of its hot-rolled coil to 1,000 pounds per inch of width (PIW), or about 50,000 pounds per roll, approximately doubling its prior coil weights. The ability to produce coils of up to 1,000 PIW made it possible for Geneva to enter markets previously unreachable to them.

The steel industry is cyclical in nature and, according to Dean Witter Reynolds Inc., all signs point to steel price increases for the industry as well as for Geneva in the coming year. For the last four quarters, the company's prices have remained in the $315 to $319 per ton price range. In spite of this bottoming out, Geneva's cash position has improved so that the company should have little trouble in financing planned capital expenditures.

Although the steel industry is always affected by recessions, Geneva's cost structure remains competitive in the face of mounting international competition. In addition, Geneva will undoubtedly bid for work that develops from the federal government's plan to rebuild the nation's infrastructure. The government has earmarked $140 billion of highway trust funds to pay for those repairs. Finally, most of the steel service centers, which represent the bulk of the Geneva's sales, have reduced inventories to the straining point; these companies will have to start ordering again. All of these factors put Geneva in a strong strategic position for recovery.

Further Reading: "And They Say Americans Can't Compete," *Reader's Digest,* January 1993; "Making Hay from Nuts and Bolts," *Forbes,* May 2, 1988; "Steel Man May Alloy Clean Air, Politics," *Washington Post,* July 31, 1991; "Utah's Geneva Steel, Once Called Hopeless, Is Racking Up Profits," *Wall Street Journal,* November 20, 1991; "Joe Cannon's Unorthodox Journey," *Industry Week,* November 4, 1991; *Metals and Mining,* December 4, 1992.

—Ron Schultz

GERBER PRODUCTS COMPANY

445 State St.
Fremont, Michigan 49413-0001
U.S.A.
(616) 928-2000
Fax: (616) 928-2723

Public Company
Incorporated: 1901 as Fremont Canning Company
Employees: 12,871
Sales: $1.26 billion
Stock Exchanges: New York Midwest
SICs: 2032 Canned Specialties; 2361 Girl/Children's Dresses
& Blouses; 3069 Fabricated Rubber Products Nec; 3089
Plastics Products Nec.

A longtime giant of the baby food industry, Gerber Products
Company enjoys a solid reputation as the largest supplier of
baby products in the world. Gerber has dominated this market
since its introduction of the first commercially successful baby
food in 1928, establishing a 71 percent U.S. market share
despite serious and recurrent competition, such public relations
crises as the glass scares of 1984 and 1986, various management transitions and takeover threats, and several failed diversification strategies. The strong, steady growth from fiscal 1988
through fiscal 1992 of Gerber and its most important subsidiaries, including Gerber Childrenswear, Inc., and the Gerber Life
Insurance Company, is the result of the firm's realignment with
the slogan "Babies are our business . . . our only business!"
Under the recent direction of Alfred A. Piergallini, Gerber has
promised to pursue a "superbrand" strategy of both domestic
and international expansion within this one market that it
arguably understands and can capitalize on as none of its
competitors can.

Gerber traces its origins to the Fremont Canning Company, a
small packager of peas, beans, and fruits in rural Michigan
begun by Frank Gerber (1873-1952) and his father in 1901. At
that time, Gerber also served as a partner in his father's tannery.
When the tannery closed in 1905, Gerber focused all his efforts
on building the canning company. By 1914 he had expanded his
plant to permit year-round production. Three years later, with
the death of his father, Gerber became president of the company
and saw its sales exceed $1 million for the first time. Following

a brief postwar dip in profits, Fremont Canning experienced
steady growth during the 1920s.

By 1926 Frank Gerber's son Daniel (1898–1974) had risen to
assistant general manager of the company. A year later Daniel's
wife, Dorothy, made a monumentally significant suggestion:
that Dan persuade his father to begin manufacturing and selling
strained baby foods in order to end the tedious chore of cooking,
mashing, and otherwise preparing solid foods for infants. Frank
and Daniel undertook extensive preliminary research before
launching the concept, thoroughly testing the products, contact-
ing nutrition experts, distributing thousands of samples, and
conducting follow-up market research interviews. The baby
food line was introduced successfully in 1928, and the Gerbers'
careful implementation of the idea, relying on both professional
and public endorsement, established the foundation upon which
the present-day business rests.

The key to Gerber's successful marketing plan for baby food
was the advertisement placed in *Good Housekeeping,* which
enlisted mothers of young children to participate directly in a
coupon redemption program. The introductory offer—six cans
of Gerber's soup and strained vegetables for $1.00 and the name
of a favorite grocer—stressed the nutritional and time-saving
value of Gerber's foods and sought to generate enough re-
sponses that the canning company could offer proof to grocers
of the new demand for stocking baby food on their shelves. The
campaign was overwhelmingly successful, resulting in national
distribution within six months and first-year sales of 590,000
cans with gross revenues of $345,000. In effect, the Gerbers had
created a new industry, served previously only by pharmacists,
and then only under special circumstances and at a high cost to
the consumer. (Pharmacies typically priced 4.5 oz. cans at 35
cents each; the Gerbers, through mass production and marketing, were able to sell their cans at just 15 cents each, still a
premium price given the cost of adult foods but nonetheless
now well within the reach of the average American household.)

The company's monopoly on the market did not last long. By
1935 more than sixty other manufacturers had introduced their
own vitamin-rich, pressure-cooked, sealed baby foods. However, Fremont Canning held its commanding lead because of the
widely held and well-earned perception that the Gerber name
was synonymous with quality and expert-backed research. In
addition, no other company possessed a logo approaching the
appeal of the "Gerber Baby," which was already famous; or a
research and education department that flooded the market with
useful pamphlets on parenting, feeding, and child psychology;
or such a model spokesperson as Dorothy Gerber, whose newspaper column "Bringing up Baby" held sway with thousands
of mothers nationwide. During the difficult years of the Great
Depression, the Gerbers underscored their strength and vision
for the future by implementing a state-of-the-art agricultural
program, expanding into the Canadian market, doubling their
line of foods, and topping $1 million in annual sales.

The 1940s marked the full maturation of the baby food producer. By 1941 the company, which was meeting a demand for
a million cans of baby food each week, was renamed the Gerber
Products Company. Two years later the company abandoned
production of adult foods altogether and opened a second baby
food plant in Oakland, California. Given the post-World War II

baby boom, Gerber's timing could not have been better: by 1948 it was poised to channel all its resources toward satisfying a domestic demand that had swelled to 2 million cans daily. That same year, the company adopted its trademark slogan: "Babies are our business . . . our *only* business."

The 1950s saw the addition of three new plants—in Asheville, North Carolina; Rochester, New York; and Niagara Falls, Ontario—and an official changing of the guard that occurred with the death of Frank in 1952. Under the leadership of Dan Gerber, the company embarked on a new mission of expansion and diversification. Highlights of this era, which extended until Gerber's relinquishment of the CEO position in 1971, included the launching of the Gerber toy line in 1955, a listing on the New York Stock Exchange in 1956, the opening of a Mexican subsidiary in 1959, and the introduction of a large line of baby-related products in 1965. At the time of Daniel Gerber's death in 1974 the company could boast that it was the world's largest baby-food manufacturer, with sales of $278 million and an enviable domestic market share of nearly 70 percent. This was all the more remarkable since Gerber Products was just concluding a five-year price war with its competitors, at the beginning of which it held only a 53 percent share.

Ironically, at this high point the company had amended its slogan to read simply, "Babies are our business," a reflection of the company's slow drift away from the formative philosophy of the 1940s. In 1977 the company faced down a major threat when Anderson, Clayton, and Company, a food products firm based in Houston, launched a serious takeover attempt. Fortunately, the probability of a long legal battle dissuaded Anderson from further action and preserved Gerber's independence. Within two years, Gerber began in earnest a major campaign of diversification—in part to offset expected declines in birth rates—with the acquisition of CW Transport, a freight carrier based in Wisconsin. Although furniture, toy, and other subsidiaries followed, by 1989 Gerber had divested itself of many of these fringe ventures in order to refocus on its more profitable baby food, baby care, and clothing lines.

Perhaps the most serious threat to Gerber during the 1980s arose not from its broad policy of acquisition but from the public relations crises of 1984 and 1986. Gerber responded to the first of these two crises—involving reports alleging the presence of glass fragments in jars of baby juice—by recalling some 550,000 jars in a 15-state region. This cautionary action was viewed favorably by the public, and financial damage incurred by the company was limited to only a short-term, 4 percent drop in sales. The second glass crisis—which, like the first, sparked investigations that ultimately exonerated Gerber—involved some 645 complaints spread over 40 states. This time Gerber, headed by William L. McKinley, chose to remain silent and to take no action other than offer its cooperation with federal investigators. The decision proved unpopular and contributed at least in part to a drop in profits from $69 million in 1985 to $54 million in 1987; McKinley departed shortly after the resolution of the glass scare and was replaced by Leo D. Goulet.

Goulet's sudden death in 1987 forced the company's board of directors to seek new management from outside the company. Their search culminated in the hiring of David W. Johnson, who was perceived by many as a much-needed antidote to the com-pany's apparent lack of direction and vitality. Johnson's aggressive reemphasis, through advertising and product development, on Gerber as a major food company resulted in a 46 percent improvement in earnings from 1987 to 1988. However, with Gerber at the threshold of $1 billion in annual revenues, Johnson left the company to become CEO of Campbell Soup. Johnson's replacement, former Carnation senior vice-president Alfred A. Piergallini, has effectively sustained the Gerber reorientation through a "superbrand" development and marketing strategy, most notably with the introduction of the 16-product Tropical line of baby foods in 1991 and the 23-item Gerber Graduates line in 1992. As Piergallini wrote in the company's 1991 annual report, "Our ability to offer food, clothing, and care items for children from birth through three years of age under a single major brand sets us clearly apart from our competitors. We will leverage this advantage by expanding into new channels of distribution domestically and, over time, internationally, through the development of an infant and children's category approach for our retail customers." In 1991 Gerber entered foreign markets including the USSR, Thailand, Brazil, Chile, and Sweden, and in February 1992 purchased 60 percent of Alima, S.A., a Polish producer of food and juices. Of special significance to Gerber was the fact that although 98 percent of the world's births occur outside the United States, only 10 percent of Gerber's sales derived from this still largely untapped market.

Curiously, although 1992 marked a record year of sales and earnings for Gerber, punctuated by a strong performance of its insurance subsidiary and a prudent streamlining of Gerber Childrenswear, the company approached 1993 with uncertainty. Since July 1992 Gerber had been attempting, unsuccessfully, to unload Buster Brown Apparel, a once-profitable supplier of high-fashion clothing that had shown a trend toward declining sales. More importantly, Gerber was experiencing heavy competition in the form of a "discounting blitz" from H. J. Heinz Co. and Ralston Purina Co.'s Beech-Nut unit, which was undercutting Gerber's prices by as much as 28 cents per jar. Although the price-cutting storm had shown signs of abating by the end of 1992, Gerber's stock nonetheless suffered in December due to lowered earnings and food sales volume estimates for fiscal 1993. Commentators noted that Gerber might also have difficulty recapturing its baby food market share, which had fallen in September to 67.6 percent.

On the positive side, Gerber stood by its pledge to vigorously promote itself both at home and abroad. With its line of more than 240 food products in 58 countries, the largest research facility of its kind in the world, and the realistic expectation that birth rates would remain high rather than decline, the Gerber Products Company was expected to weather the 1990s far ahead of the competition. The billion-dollar baby care industry, of which Gerber controlled less than a 10 percent market share, was just one of several areas in which the company planned to expand its presence. Domestic and foreign acquisitions, as well as the full utilization of Alima as a European base of operations, were other likely possibilities for fueling Gerber's future growth. Gerber also showed signs of resorting to one of its earliest and most successful strategies: that of creating new perceptions of nutritional needs for infants. Piergallini's 1992 message to shareholders stated: "We will employ strategies to increase consumption of baby food, build baby food market share, and expand the baby care and apparel businesses. U.S. consumption of baby food begins at about 5–6 months of age and falls off at about 16 months. This is not good. Babies' special nutritional and developmental needs are not met with adult foods and breast milk or formula alone.'' While experts might debate this last contention, Gerber will no doubt move toward accomplishing the task it has set itself with all the verve and studious planning its founders first displayed more than sixty years ago.

Principal Subsidiaries: Alima-Gerber, S.A. (60%); Buster Brown Apparel, Inc.; Gerber (Canada) Inc.; Gerber Childrenswear, Inc.; Gerber Family Services, Inc.; Gerber France, S.A.R.L.; Gerber Life Insurance Company; Gerber Polska; Gerber Products Company of Puerto Rico, Inc.; Gerber Products Company Singapore (PTE.) LTD.; Productos Gerber de Centroamerica, S.A.

Further Reading: ''Daniel F. Gerber Is Dead at 75; Brought Baby Foods to Millions,'' *New York Times,* March 18, 1974, p. 32; ''Why Gerber Makes Such an Inviting Target,'' *Business Week,* June 27, 1977, pp. 26–7; *Fifty Years of Caring: Our Golden Anniversary Year, 1928–1978,* Fremont, MI: Gerber Products Company, 1978; Cleary, David Powers, ''Gerber Baby Foods,'' *Great American Brands: The Success Formulas that Made Them Famous,* New York: Fairchild Publications, 1981, pp. 112–19; Ingham, John N., *Biographical Dictionary of American Business Leaders,* Westport, Connecticut: Greenwood Press, 1983; Brown, Paul B., ''Unloved but Not Unworthy,'' *Forbes,* November 19, 1984, p. 286; Fucini, Joseph J., and Suzy Fucini, ''Dan Gerber: Gerber Baby Food,'' *Entrepreneurs: The Men and Women behind Famous Brand Names and How They Made It,* Boston: G. K. Hall & Co., 1985; Mitchell, Russell, and Judith H. Dobrzynski, ''Why Gerber Is Standing Its Ground,'' *Business Week,* March 17, 1986, pp. 50–51; Pick, Grant, ''Gerber's Baby under Stress,'' *Across the Board,* July–August 1986, pp. 9–13; Fannin, Rebecca, ''High Stakes at the High Chair,'' *Marketing & Media Decisions,* October 1986, pp. 62–72; McGill, Douglas C., ''Making Mashed Peas Pay Off,'' *New York Times,* April 9, 1989, p. F4; Baldo, Anthony, ''Gerber: The Baby Is About to Burp,'' *Financial World,* July 25, 1989, p. 16; Gershman, Michael, ''Gerber Baby Food: Strained Relations,'' *Getting It Right the Second Time,* Reading: Addison-Wesley Publishing Company, 1990, pp. 119–23; Moskowitz, Milton, Robert Levering, and Michael Katz, eds., ''Gerber,'' *Everybody's Business: A Field Guide to the 400 Leading Companies in America,* New York: Doubleday, 1990, pp. 48–9; Woodruff, David, ''Gerber: Mush Ado . . . ,'' *Business Week,* February 5, 1990, p. 30; Strnad, Patricia, ''Gerber Seeks 'Superbrand' Role,'' *Advertising Age,* April 9, 1990, p. 26; Gerber Products Company Annual Reports, Fremont, MI: Gerber Products Company, 1991–92; Loewy, B. A., Food Conference Summary Notes—Industry Report, S. G. Warburg & Co., Inc., April 10, 1992; Hanes, Phillis, ''Baby Food Goes Multicultural,'' *Christian Science Monitor,* June 18, 1992, p. 14; Turcsik, Richard, ''Gerber Sees Opportunity for Toddler Food Category,'' *Supermarket News,* August 24, 1992, p. 26; Berss, Marcia, ''Limited Horizons,'' *Forbes,* October 12, 1992, p. 66; Shapiro, Eben, ''Gerber Shares Drop 5% on Weakened Outlook,'' *The New York Times,* October 15, 1992, p. D5; Gibson, Richard, ''Gerber Products Expects Drop in Fiscal '93 Net,'' *Wall Street Journal,* December 16, 1992, p. A5.

—Jay P. Pederson

GILLETT HOLDINGS, INC.

5555 17th Street #3300
Denver, Colorado 80202
U.S.A.
(303) 292-0045
Fax: (303) 292-9603

Private Company
Incorporated: 1978
Employees: 4,800
Sales: $790 million
SICs: 2011 Meat Packing Plants; 4833 Television
Broadcasting Stations; 7011 Hotels & Motels

Once one of the largest communications conglomerates in the United States, Gillett Holdings, Inc. (GHI) is a highly volatile private company with interests in television broadcasting, ski resorts, and the meatpacking industry. The once-mammoth company has recently undergone dramatic, drawn-out restructuring as a consequence of its reliance on junk bond financing in the 1980s.

The history of Gillett Holdings is inextricably tied to the company's founder and namesake, George Gillett, Jr. Gillett was raised in Racine, Wisconsin, the son of a prominent surgeon. After high school, Gillett attended Amherst College in Massachusetts and Dominican College in Racine. He spent the next six years as a salesman for Crown Zellerbach and as a management consultant with McKinsey & Company. At McKinsey & Company, Gillett discovered the ideal attributes of the businesses he would later own and operate: low capital and labor requirements, an inherent franchise, easy promotability, and easy liquidation.

In 1966 Gillett invested in the Miami Dolphins and became the team's business manager. Two years later, he and two partners bought the Harlem Globetrotters from founder Abe Saperstein. The Globetrotters' popularity had begun to wane by the time Gillett acquired the part-sports, part-entertainment team, and he looked for ways to turn that trend around. Gillett began to realize and capitalize on the power of television when he teamed up with CBS programming executive Fred Silverman to develop an animated children's show based on the Globetrotters. The *Harlem Globetrotters* premiered in 1970 and became the most popular children's show that season. The show brought fans back to live Globetrotter appearances, enhanced CBS's

programming schedule, and helped advertisers sell their products.

Gillett used the Globetrotter franchise to build his first firm, Globetrotter Communications, which included the basketball team, the animated children's television show, a marketing division, and a golf equipment manufacturer. In 1969 Gillett bought his first broadcast interests, radio stations WIXY(AM) and WDOK(FM) in Cleveland. When Globetrotter Communications went public in 1971, Gillett used the proceeds to acquire three other radio stations, WVON(AM) and WNUS(FM) in Chicago and WDEE (AM) Detroit. But the recession of the 1970s stymied Gillett's expansion plans, and he liquidated these properties by 1975. Gillett sold out his stake in the Globetrotters for $3 million and began scouring the financial terrain for companies that could be turned around rapidly.

Two years later Gillett joined forces with Ed Karrels to purchase three UHF stations in the small markets of Sioux Falls, South Dakota; Erie, Pennsylvania; and Bakersfield, California, for $7 million. In 1978 Gillett took over Packerland Packing Company, a failing beef plant in Green Bay, Wisconsin. The beef industry of the late 1970s was plagued by overproduction and a market hampered by increasingly health-conscious Americans, so Gillett shifted the focus of the company toward production of lean, low-cholesterol meats. Packerland became the first company to win the U.S. Food and Drug Administration's "light" beef classification, largely as the result of Gillett's efforts. Packerland's sales skyrocketed, which impressed both the competition and Gillett's bankers, who provided Gillett with a steady source of cash for acquisitions elsewhere. The Gillett Group, as it was then known, was born.

Early in 1981 Gillett and Karrels successfully bid for their first major television station, WSMV-TV in Nashville, Tennessee. The station was top-ranked locally and, even though competition for the purchase was high, Gillett used his "seller's approach" to secure the deal. He and Karrels were among the minority of bidders willing to meet a firm condition of the owner, who insisted that the buyer move to Nashville and operate the station locally. The WSMV deal was also one of Gillett's first strategic buys—he convinced the owner, an insurance company, that it would save on taxes and net a higher profit by simply giving him the station in exchange for $42 million in notes that would not pay principal until 1986.

The purchase price was 21 times the station's annual earnings, but within five years it was worth $180 million. Gillett was lauded not only for his deal-making savvy, but for his loose-reined management style. In Nashville, Gillett kept two key executives on and, as one of those executives put it, "compelled them to overachieve." Gillett began his overhaul of WSMV by hiring a new sales manager, revising advertising rates, and courting regional advertisers. Gillett's ownership of WSMV was marred when an investigative news series critical of government meat inspections mentioned three supermarket chains that did $100 million annual business with Packerland. But the series did little to either of Gillett's interests: Between 1980 and 1986 WSMV's operating cash flow increased from $2 million to $11.2 million, and Packerland had become a steady source of revenue for other acquisitions, providing over $100 million cash by 1987.

Gillett's success in the mid-1980s bought him a prestigious piece of property. In 1985, at the urging of his wife and children, he purchased Colorado's huge Vail and Beaver Creek ski resorts. Gillett was soon found spending his summers and winters at Vail, yet maintained the family residence at Nashville, where his children attended school and frequently commuted by private jet between the homes.

The next year, Gillett sought the assistance of junk bond king Michael Milken of Drexel Burnham Lambert to raise over $650 million through the Drexel investment network. Over the next 12 months, Gillett acquired 12 television stations in the wake of liquidations and mergers throughout the broadcast industry. The stations included network affiliates and independents in such major markets as Baltimore, Richmond, Oklahoma City, and Tampa.

By 1986 Gillett was riding high on a cresting wave of entrepreneurial success. During the previous decade he had parlayed a $3 million nest egg into one of the most successful private companies in the United States. He had built his multi-faceted conglomerate during a time of deregulation and junk bond financing, and was on the verge of his biggest and most precariously financed deal yet.

He had been planning to purchase Storer Communications' six stations for several years, having known the company's chairman, Peter Storer, since the late 1970s. Rival investment groups Conniston Partners and Kohlberg Kravis Roberts (KKR) wrangled over control of the company throughout the mid- to late 1980s. But by the time Conniston forced Storer Communications into KKR's hands, KKR's plan to then hand over the broadcasting group to Lorimar-Telepictures had fallen through.

Despite warnings from Milken that, at 15 times cash flow, the price for Storer Communications was too high, Gillett made arrangements to purchase the Storer stations in partnership with KKR. The structure of the arrangement, like Gillett's WSMV-TV deal in Nashville, was unique in broadcasting. Gillett Holdings and Kohlberg Kravis Roberts each contributed $100 million in equity, and the remaining $1.1 billion of the purchase price was financed by $550 million in junk bonds (most of them paying no interest for seven years, but maturing at an astounding 17.5 percent) and $600 million in bank loans. The six stations were held by a new company, SCI Television, of which Gillett Holdings owned 51 percent and KKR the remaining 49 percent. George Gillett ran the stations and collected a management fee.

The deal soon had an impact on the holding company's operations. With the acquisition of the Storer stations, Gillett's local television holding grew to 17, five more than the Federal Communications Commission (FCC) allowed. In order to meet the FCC's standards, Gillett transferred ownership of five television stations to Busse Broadcasting, a company jointly owned by Lawrence A. Busse, a former Gillett Broadcasting officer, and, on a non-voting basis, the Gillett family trust. Despite the transfer, however, the FCC held up the Storer transaction over a month pending an investigation. In the end, the FCC approved the deal, providing that "neither Gillett nor any member of his family can serve as a trustee of the Gillett family trusts that partially own Busse Broadcasting or interfere in any way with the management of Busse." Gillett was not allowed to communicate with Lawrence Busse or a trustee except as required by state law and terms of the non-voting preferred stock held by Gillett's four children.

With the consummation of the Storer Communications deal in November 1987, Gillett Holdings and the broadcast television industry peaked. As viewers and advertisers were siphoned off by video and cable television, other major station owners, like Scripps-Howard, Capital Cities/ABC, and Lin Broadcasting also reported flat or falling earnings. In 1987 operating cash flow for Storer stations declined by 13 percent. Advertising slumped, and Gillett Holdings junk bonds plunged to as low as 80 percent of their original value.

By late 1989, Gillett Holdings was in trouble: George Gillett sold WSMV-TV for $125 million and used most of the proceeds to pay down bank loans. He astutely avoided capital gains taxes by selling the station to a minority-controlled entity, Cook-Inlet, but the transaction left $27 million due on the company's financing by August 1990. Meanwhile that fall, Storer Communications defaulted on $153 million in interest on public debt. But rather than force Storer Communications into bankruptcy, Gillett managed to convince bondholders to restructure the subsidiary's more than $500 million bonded debt. The creditors forced Gillett to cut his equity stake in the company from 55 percent to 41 percent, but Gillett maintained control of Storer Communications. He also postponed interest and principal payments on the refinanced debt until 1995, at which point bondholders would be paid in kind, not cash. Gillett considered selling some of the Storer stations, but prices for even the highest-rated affiliates had fallen 30 percent since their purchase.

Storer Communications' financial troubles reflected upward onto Gillett Holdings, which had problems of its own brewing. By 1990 the company's bonds had become so insecure that some traded as low as 17 cents on the dollar. Then, in August, Gillett Holdings defaulted on over $450 million in debt. By February 1991, bondholders frustrated with Gillett's half-hearted attempts at restructuring filed an involuntary bankruptcy petition. When the company failed to meet the resulting court-imposed restructuring deadline of June 25, the company was forced into Chapter 11 bankruptcy. In the meantime, Leon Black, a former director of Storer Communications and co-engineer of the Gillett takeover, purchased large blocks of Gillett Holdings stock through his investment vehicle, Apollo Advisers. The purchases gave Black the leverage to block any restructuring schemes of which he didn't approve.

Wrangling over restructuring of Gillett Holdings between Black and Gillett culminated in a January 1992 plan. Ownership of Gillett Holdings' three remaining television stations was transferred to the bondholders and Gillett himself lost control of the company, although he maintained a 40 percent nonvoting stake in Storer Communications. The plan also stipulated that George Gillett would continue to manage the television stations at a minimum salary of $30,000 weekly. The restructuring plan proposed to cut Gillett Holdings' $1.2 billion debt in half, as Leon Black offered to forgive debt in his control and contribute $40 million cash to jumpstart the floundering operation in exchange for 52 percent ownership of the new company.

At that point, however, yet another takeover mogul stepped into the picture. Carl Icahn had purchased $65 million in low-ranking junk bonds, and had earned a small voice in the restructuring plans. Unhappy with the 10 cents on the dollar he and other bondholders in his class were offered in the original plan, Icahn made public and private complaints that eventually earned him 16 cents and at least 15 percent of the restructured Gillett Holdings' equity.

By April 30, 1992, a plan was submitted to Federal Bankruptcy Court that was revised to reduce Gillett Holdings' debt by $75 million and rescind George Gillett's options to repurchase stock and buy back specified corporate assets. That same day, lawyers for Gillett Holdings filed 44 bankruptcy cases, placing nearly all of the conglomerate's subsidiaries under court protection.

By late 1992, as Gillett Holdings looked forward to its emergence from bankruptcy court, Storer Communications defaulted on a $140 million principal repayment that threatened to cast the subsidiary into Chapter 11 as well. George Gillett himself was not immune to the "bankruptcy bug," either: In August he filed for personal bankruptcy, losing his collection of 30 sports cars and a 235,000-acre Oregon ranch in the process. However, the still-savvy entrepreneur managed to protect his $1.5 million annual salary, $5 million in Gillett Holdings securities, and $125,000 per year in life insurance premiums.

Principal Subsidiaries: Vail Associates; Packerland Packing Company; Gillett Broadcasting; SCI Television, Inc.

Further Reading: "Gillett Moving to Buy Stake in Storer," *Broadcasting,* April 13, 1987; Buck, Rinker, "George Gillett's Private World," *Channels,* September 1987; "Storer TV Sale Under Attack by Hill," *Broadcasting,* October 5, 1987; "With Strings, FCC OK's Gillett Buy of Storer TV's," *Broadcasting,* November 2, 1987; "Gillett Stations Back in Trading Marketplace," *Broadcasting,* July 11, 1988; Foust, Dean, and David Lieberman, "Buying in Prime Time Has George Gillett in a Bind," *Business Week,* October 31, 1988; Flinn, John, "Losing Viewers? Maybe It's a State of Mind," *Channels,* November 1988; "George Gillett: Dynamic Dealmaker," *Broadcasting,* November 21, 1988; Morgenson, Gretchen, "On the Edge," *Forbes,* April 16, 1990; "Gillett Again in Talks With Creditors," *Broadcasting,* May 21, 1990; Giltenan, Edward, "Nail-biting Time," *Forbes,* April 29, 1991; "SCI Television Has Trouble With Loan Payment," *Broadcasting,* July 1, 1991; "Gillett Holdings Agreement," *New York Times,* January 23, 1992; Berman, Phyllis, "Warming Up For the Big Ones," *Forbes,* March 2, 1992; Bianco, Anthony, "Nasty Encounter of the '90s Kind," *Business Week,* May 11, 1992; "Gillett Holdings Puts Most Subsidiaries in Bankruptcy," *New York Times,* May 20, 1992; "SCI Television Again Defaults on Debts, a Sign of Weaker TV-Station Business," *Wall Street Journal,* August 10, 1992; "Crying All the Way to the Bank," *Forbes,* September 14, 1992.

—April S. Dougal

GRAND UNION COMPANY

201 Willowbrook Blvd.
Wayne, New Jersey 07470
U.S.A.
(201) 890-6000
Fax: (201) 890-6671

Wholly Owned Subsidiary of Grand Union Holdings
  Corporation
Incorporated: 1928
Employees: 20,000
Sales: $3.00 billion
SICs: 5411 Grocery Stores

When Grand Union began as a one-store operation in Scranton, Pennsylvania, the shelves were stocked with coffee, tea, spices, baking powder, and flavoring extracts. Today the $3 billion company's supermarkets carry thousands of items in more than 250 stores.

Cyrus, Frank, and Charles Jones founded what was to become Grand Union in 1872. They called the business the Jones Brothers Tea Co. The brothers expanded the business steadily, branching out with new stores in eastern Pennsylvania, Michigan, and New York. By the time it built its headquarters and warehouse in Brooklyn, New York, the company was known as the Grand Union Tea Co.

In 1912 Grand Union was a 200-outlet chain store with operations across the country. In addition to its business establishments, the company supported a small army of 5,000 door-to-door salesmen and delivered goods in horse-drawn wagons. The brothers incorporated the Jones Brothers Tea Co. in 1916.

Grand Union used its financial strength through the 1920s to acquire other food businesses, including Progressive Grocery Stores, the Union Pacific Tea Co., and Glenwood stores. After merging with the Oneida County Creameries Co. in 1928, the Jones brothers reincorporated under the Grand Union name.

During the 1930s Grand Union grew to be one of the country's most thriving food chains. In 1931 the company had 708 small stores and $35 million in sales.

The next decade saw the development of the "supermarket" concept. The idea was to house a range of groceries, including meat, dairy products, and inedible packaged goods, under one roof. When Lansing P. Shield took over as Grand Union president in the early 1940s, he embraced the supermarket format and plunged the company forward into a new era of food marketing. Grand Union was one of the first companies to utilize the format.

Shield helped evolve the supermarket concept by demanding that the spacious supermarkets be designed carefully so as not to overwhelm customers used to smaller shops. Shield suggested breaking down the open spaces by building more walls and dispersing special product displays throughout the aisles. By the mid-1950s, Grand Union operated about half the number of stores it did in the 1930s, but the stores turned out nearly seven times the volume of sales. By then the company had outgrown its Brooklyn headquarters. It opened a new facility in Elmwood Park, New Jersey, in a red brick tower that was later to become a community landmark.

When grocery stores became involved in the discounting business, Grand Union was again one of the first in the food business to welcome the idea. The first Grand Union general merchandise discount store, called Grand Way, opened in 1956 in Keansburg, New Jersey. After the Keansburg store proved a success, the company opened another in Albany, New York. By 1962 Grand Union was operating 21 discount stores. To keep the stores running smoothly, Chairman Thomas Butler hired Joseph L. Eckhouse, formerly the head of the Gimbel Bros. department store in New York, to oversee them. Eckhouse envisioned the Grand Way stores as a place to buy quality goods and fashionable clothing at lower prices than department stores. Eckhouse died, however, before his vision could be fully realized.

Grand Union, which reached $1 billion in sales in 1968, continued to open additional Grand Way stores and enter new retail businesses, including convenience food stores, trading stamps, and catalog showrooms for discounted general merchandise. As competitive pressures increased in the early 1970s, Grand Union entered another phase of supermarketing: the so-called superstore. These shopping emporiums sought to provide customers with myriad products of every kind at one locale. A Grand Union superstore, for example, offered consumer items in such diverse areas as prescription drugs, auto parts, clothing, shoes, and household gadgets, as well as the usual mix of groceries. By 1973 Grand Union was operating 10 such superstores. While these new businesses were not failures, they did not contribute enough to the company's bottom line to justify their continued existence. By the early 1970s they had begun to lose their luster and Grand Union began divesting itself of many of them.

In 1973 Grand Union stock was trading at less than half of book value and the company seemed to be stagnating. The company's status attracted the interest of Cavenham Ltd., a British food conglomerate, which made a $19 a share tender offer for control of the company. The move by Cavenham, which was owned by financier James Goldsmith, marked the first significant foreign investment in U.S. food retailing. When the $64 million deal was finalized in December 1973, Cavenham quickly appointed Englishman James Wood as president. Wood wasted little time in shaking up what was then the ninth-largest supermarket chain in the country.

Wood sparked the divestment of Grand Union's nonfood businesses, reorganized its management structure, and established a new image for the store based on low prices. Wood oversaw a Grand Union that had 534 supermarkets in New York, New Jersey, Connecticut, Massachusetts, Vermont, New Hampshire, Pennsylvania, Maryland, Virginia, West Virginia, Florida, Puerto Rico, and the U.S. Virgin Islands. The company's nonfood operations consisted of 23 Grand Way stores, 18 Grand Catalog discount stores, 18 E-Z shop convenience stores, a food equipment subsidiary, and the Stop & Save Trading Stamp division. After only a year Cavenham stripped Grand Union of 31 supermarkets, pulled back its trading stamp operations, and closed nine Grand Way outlets. Grand Union's performance for fiscal year 1974 was $2.3 million in net income, down from $8.4 million the year before. Sales, however, climbed for the year from $1.4 billion in fiscal 1973 to $1.5 billion in fiscal 1974. The following year Grand Union sold its E-Z shop division and closed five of its catalog showrooms.

The divestitures did have their price. In 1975 Wood stated that phasing out trading stamps completely would result in a $5,750,000 charge against earnings. In addition, the elimination of the nine Grand Way stores cost the company a $10 million pre-tax write-off. By 1978, however, Grand Union was ready to expand again. The company started opening new stores and acquired several regional supermarket chains in the Southeast and Southwest, including Colonial Stores in 1978. Three years later, Grand Union merged with J. Weingarten Inc., a Texas supermarket chain, which became an affiliate of the company. By 1982 the chain boasted 856 stores with outlets as far west as Texas, as far north as Canada, and as far south as Florida. The expansion was a gamble that eventually cost Grand Union more than it bargained for. In the fiscal year 1982 the company reported a record sales level of $4.1 billion, twice as much as what was recorded just three years ago. The drain on earnings proved to be just as drastic, with a drop of 30 percent to $24 million. "We screwed it up," said James Goldsmith in an article for *Business Week.*

After that calamitous financial performance, Grand Union again entered a phase of heavy consolidation. The biggest drop in the number of stores came in the fiscal year 1982, when it closed 150 stores. By November 1982 another 62 units were gone, leaving the company with just 671 supermarkets. The revamped organization was centered in New England and New York, with a few sites in Virginia, Georgia, and the Carolinas.

By ridding itself of money-draining nonfood operations and trimming the number of its outlets, Grand Union showed a renewed devotion to food marketing. In 1979 it introduced its Food Market prototype, a 45,000-square-foot supermarket with specialty departments featuring gourmet foods such as stuffed artichokes, specially blended coffees and teas, baked goods, and imported cheese. The company planned to spend the bulk of its $700 million capital improvement budget over six years to convert most of its units to the Food Market prototype.

Food Markets were a hit with shoppers. Imported wines and ready-to-cook dinners like fish and poultry were finding steady buyers, but the conversion project proved to be very expensive. The average cost of turning a store into a Food Market was $1.5 million. By 1982 70 stores had been converted at a cost of $100

million. The project contributed to another poor performance for the fiscal year ended April 1983. The store reported operating losses of $20 million, although it posted a $226,000 bottom-line profit. As Goldsmith put it in the *Business Week* profile, "We managed to turn a dull but fairly profitable chain into an exciting loss-maker." Some rivals blamed Grand Union for not doing enough research before converting a store to a Food Market. The converted sites that did well were located in areas with higher incomes rather than working class neighborhoods.

Other supermarkets were selling gourmet foods, but they covered the cost with profitable general merchandise departments, a business Grand Union abandoned after Cavenham Ltd. bought the company. Nonetheless, Goldsmith hoped that the expensive luxury food items would eventually make the store some money.

Ever on the lookout to maintain and improve upon the slim profit margins of the supermarket industry, Grand Union introduced another marketing innovation in 1983 to help increase its business. To help convince shoppers they were getting the lowest prices at Grand Union, the store began publishing a free booklet listing prices on some 9,000 products. The company hoped that shoppers would use the booklet if they found themselves in a competitor's store and could see for themselves that Grand Union's prices were cheaper. If a shopper found an item at a cheaper price, Grand Union promised to match it. Despite the expense of the new program, which cost about $80 million to create and promote, some stores reported an increase in sales as high as 25 percent.

Meanwhile, the company was still struggling in its efforts to return to profitability. In the fiscal year ended in April 1984, it posted a $115.2 million loss due to store closings concentrated in Florida, Washington, D.C., and Texas, a strike at its New Jersey stores, and the start-up costs of the new pricing program. Sales for the year dropped 2 percent from the previous year's $3.52 billion to $3.44 billion.

All efforts to put the supermarket giant back on track were not enough to keep Goldsmith from finally deciding to sell it. In 1989 Grand Union was bought for $1.2 billion by an investor group headed by Salomon Brothers Inc. and Miller Tabak Hirsch & Company, two New York investment banking firms. At the time, Grand Union was the 11th largest supermarket chain in the country with $2.7 billion in sales, 306 Grand Union and Big Star stores, and 21,000 employees. The two buyout partners each received a 40 percent interest in the company, with the remaining 20 percent held by senior management. The buyout of Grand Union added another $325 million to the company's $300 million in high-yield debt and another $545 million in bank loans.

Under its new owners, Grand Union set another course to improve its business. This meant offering more items in bulk and larger sizes and more competitive pricing through discounting, price freezes, and buy-one, get-one-free offers. In 1991 the company introduced its own line of environmentally-sound paper products.

Three years after the 1989 deal Grand Union's ownership shifted again when Salomon Bros. sold its interest in the company to Miller Tabak Hirsch & Company's affiliate, GAC Holdings L.P., which owns 41 percent of the GND Holdings Corp., the parent company of Grand Union. In fiscal 1991 Grand Union's numbers were still disappointing, with a loss of $53.8 million on $2.92 billion in sales. Grand Union was sold again in 1992 when a group led by Gary Hirsch, a principal of Miller Tabak, bought GND Holdings and formed a new holding company, Grand Union Holdings Corp.

Further Reading: Zimmerman, M. M., *The Super Market: A Revolution in Distribution*, New York, McGraw-Hill Book Company, Inc., 1955; Lebhar, Godfrey M., *Chain Stores in America, 1859–1962*, New York, Chain Store Publishing Corporation, 1963; Bralove, Mary, "Superstores May Suit Customers to a T: A T-Shirt or a T-Bone," *Wall Street Journal*, March 13, 1973; Bralove, Mary, "Grand Union Becomes a Much Tauter Ship Under British Captain," *Wall Street Journal*, January 31, 1975; "Grand Union Expects a $5,750,000 Charge From Stamp Phaseout," *Wall Street Journal*, June 19, 1975; "The Bargain That Wasn't," *Forbes*, August 21, 1978; "Grand Union Converts to Full-Service," *Chain Store Age Executive*, November, 1982; "Grand Union's Grand Scheme," *Progressive Grocer*, October, 1983; "Grand Union: Jimmy Goldsmith's Maverick Plan to Restore Profitability," *Business Week*, May 14, 1984; "Grand Union's Loss More Than Doubled in Fiscal 4th Quarter," *Wall Street Journal*, June 11, 1984; "Tough Times Lead to Tougher Posture," *Progressive Grocer*, October, 1984; Bartlett, Sarah, "$1.2 Billion Buyout of Food Stores," *New York Times*, April 11, 1989; Klepacki, Laura, "Grand Union Unveils Plans for Tough Times," *Supermarket News*, October 14, 1991; Brennan, Robert J., "Salomon to Sell Grand Union Stake to Miller Tabak," *Wall Street Journal*, April 14, 1992; *A Brief History of the Grand Union Company*, Wayne, NJ, Grand Union Company, 1993.

—Julie Monahan

GULFSTREAM AEROSPACE CORP.

P.O. Box 2206
500 Gulfstream Rd.
Travis Field
Savannah, Georgia 31402-2206
U.S.A.
(912) 964-3000
Fax: (912) 964-3775

Private Company
Incorporated: 1978
Employees: 4,800
Sales: $887.00 million
SICs: 3721 Aircraft

Gulfstream Aerospace Corporation, a private, medium-sized company located in Savannah, Georgia, is a world leader in the manufacture of business aircraft. The history of Gulfstream began in the 1950s, when the huge Grumman Corporation of New York, largely a manufacturer of military aircraft and parts, evolved an airplane for the use of big business as well as government. In 1959 the company unveiled the world's first business plane, the Gulfstream I. Two hundred of them sold quickly. When Grumman introduced the Gulfstream II in 1966, a record 256 of them were sold quickly at home and abroad. The GS II could fly faster than commercial jets and was the first business aircraft capable of carrying a full crew and seating up to sixteen passengers. This unique business jet caught the imagination of the monied public. Soon versions of the corporate jet were created by other companies, including Canada's Canadair and France's Dassault-Breguet, Gulfstream's chief competitors. In 1967 Grumman set up an assembly plant in Savannah, Georgia, for the manufacture of GS IIs.

Despite the popularity of the corporate jet, the business jet fell on hard times during the recession of the late 1970s, prompting Grumman to sell off its business jet assets and concentrate on its main industry, the manufacture of military aircraft. Allen E. Paulson, head of his own holding company in California, American Jet Industries (a company that converted planes into propjets), had longed for the moment when he could become owner of his own aircraft manufacturing company. Paulson had grown up in humble circumstances. As an adult he became an aircraft mechanic for TWA and eventually learned enough about avia-

tion to do business in aircraft parts, the basis of his early fortune. In 1978 he seized the opportunity to buy the Gulfstream plants and offices from Grumman for $52 million, forming the Gulfstream Aerospace Corporation. Despite recessionary times, plans were in the works to create an even better, more sophisticated business jet, the Gulfstream III.

Paulson's entrepreneurial daring paid off, and the early years of his company were surprisingly profitable. Revenues climbed from $187 million in 1980 to $582 million two years later. Under its dynamic new owner, Gulfstream transformed itself in the first year and a half from what had been largely an aircraft assembly plant to a major manufacturing center. Aircraft parts that had formerly been purchased from numerous vendors were manufactured by Gulfstream, increasing the company's production capacity. Paulson saw to it that the company transformed itself into a high-tech establishment with state-of-the-art manufacturing equipment and the latest computers. The company also expanded outside of Savannah, acquiring in 1981 a large (400,000 sq. ft.) plant in Oklahoma City, the Gulfstream Aerospace Technologies. Company morale was high, and the new GS III had a backlog of sales that the company raced to meet. The new corporate jet was in such demand that its production continued until 1987. Its popularity was due to many factors, including its long flight capability. It earned the distinction of being the first business jet to fly over both poles nonstop.

Times were changing for aircraft manufacturers, however. Over the previous ten years, the cost of developing a new jet had risen nine fold, and competition from foreign companies—whose aircraft industries were often government subsidized—was keen. In the mid-1980s, despite boom economic times, the aviation industry stagnated; 1982 was perhaps the worst year in the industry. Gulfstream's profits shrank, and Paulson offered eight million shares of the company's common stock for sale (out of 33 million shares, 70 percent of which he still owned). These were quickly snapped up, raising $152 million for the company.

At the same time, the domestic auto industry was experiencing flush times. The nation's third largest auto maker, Chrysler Corporation, headed by Lee Iaccoca, was casting about for ways to diversify. Chrysler Corporation bid $637 million for ownership of Gulfstream Aerospace in 1985, keeping Allen E. Paulson as chair of the new subsidiary. That same year, General Dynamics Corporation acquired Cessna Aircraft (an even bigger company than Gulfstream), which had been suffering financially for some of the same reasons.

Production of the GS III was brisk and plans were in the works for the premier business jet of the twenty-first century, the GS IV, yet Paulson chafed under what he considered to be Chrysler's ignorance of the aviation industry. Nonetheless, Chrysler's purchase of Gulfstream enabled the subsidiary to move forward and prosper, establishing record profitability in the years of Chrysler ownership. In 1987 production of the GS III ended and the GS IV was on the market, sleeker, faster, and practically noiseless, with a $15.8 million dollar price tag ($3 million more than its predecessor). In that year the GS IV set a world record for speed as it flew around the world. Gulfstream Aerospace had a backlog of 100 orders for the new GS IV, the biggest backlog in company history. In 1986 the company again expanded, acquiring a plant at Long Beach, California.

However, with the onset in 1990 of another recession, Chrysler decided to divest its non-automaking subsidiaries. A major effort had to be made to streamline the company to counter the onslaught of Japanese automobile competition, which had resulted in a $664 million loss in revenue for Chrysler that year. Once again, Gulfstream was for sale to the highest bidder, and Paulson was eager to repurchase the company and develop it.

With the assistance of Forstmann Little & Company, Paulson purchased all 25 million shares of Gulfstream's common stock from Chrysler to the tune of $825 million. Gulfstream Aerospace Corporation once more was an independent private company under Paulson's ownership, and again he purchased the company, as in 1978, at the height of a recession.

Paulson had big plans for the now-independent company. He envisioned the development of a supersonic world class corporate jet (which could reduce flying time from New York to California to less than three hours) in cooperation with the Sukhoi Design Bureau of the Soviet Union, as well as successors to the GS IV (now on the market: the GS V and the "expanded" version of the GS IV, the GS IV-SP). William C. Lowe was named president and CEO of the company, while Paulson retained his position as chair of Gulfstream.

While the joint project with the Soviet Union fell through and the supersonic jet was placed on the back burner, Paulson's other plans materialized under Lowe's management. Lowe was highly experienced, having served more than 25 years as a manager at IBM and as president for development and manufacturing at the Xerox Corporation. At Gulfstream, Lowe endeavored to diversify and streamline the company, although aircraft and aircraft parts continued to be Gulfstream's chief manufactures. It entered the international military market in its production of the SRA, or Special Requirements Aircraft. The company also concentrated on upgrading its older GS IIs and IIIs, for the more cost-conscious customer, to comply with FAA noise regulations, and to extend their life span into the twenty-first century. The international market became increasingly important to Gulfstream Aerospace; by the fall of 1991, well over 60 percent of GS sales were abroad.

Gulfstream evolved after its inception in 1978 from an aircraft assembly plant in Savannah, Georgia, to a major manufacturer of highly sophisticated jet aircraft, a world pacesetter. The company downsized in terms of employees from 5,500 to 4,900 while at the same time expanding its facilities considerably. It grew to include not only the original plants in Savannah, but also its engineering support center, Gulfstream Technologies in Oklahoma City, and assembly plants in Long Beach, California. In the fall of 1992, the new Gulfstream V, complete with computer workstation aboard and state of the art telecommunica-

tions, was unveiled at the National Business Aircraft Association Conference in Dallas; featured also was the upgraded GS IV-SP (Special Performance) business jet. Both aircraft were designed with advanced collision-avoidance features, and both promised to do well in the future.

As it entered the 1990s, Gulfstream looked ahead to the next century with more than its share of problems. Marketing luxury business jets in an era of budget cutting was becoming ever more difficult and challenging. Gulfstream Aerospace, although a flourishing company with excellent future prospects internationally, especially in the Asian and eastern European markets, was perennially cash strapped. An attempt in the spring of 1992 to duplicate the sale of common share stock of two years earlier fell through, with few buyers. Skepticism about Gulfstream's ability to pay its huge debt of nearly one billion dollars was a chief factor in the lack of interest to buy stock in the company. This forced Gulfstream's management to postpone its stock offering for a more propitious time.

Further Reading: Laws, Margaret, "Poised for Take-Off: The Clouds Are Finally Lifting for Private Plane Makers," *Barron's,* April 11, 1983; Marcial, Gene G, "Gulfstream May Be Ready to Soar Again," *Business Week,* September 10, 1984; "Takeovers," *Industry Week,* October 14, 1985; Goldwater, Leslie, "Gulfstream Aerospace: Smooth Flight From Role of Assembly to Total Manufacture," *Production,* July, 1987; Ticer, Scott, "Why Gulfstream's Rivals Are Gazing Up in Envy," *Business Week,* February 16, 1987; Baldo, Anthony, "Barrier Breaker," *Financial World,* April 18, 1989; Brown, David, "Sukhoi, Gulfstream to Study Supersonic Business Jet," *Aviation Week & Space Technology,* June 26, 1989; Levin, Doron P., "Gulfstream to be Sold by Chrysler," *New York Times,* December 7, 1989; Deutschman, Alan, "Flying Free?" *Fortune,* January 29, 1990; Risen, James, "Chrysler Sells Unit After Loss of $664," *Los Angeles Times,* February 14, 1990; Phillips, Edward, "Gulfstream Offers Business Jet Owners Upgrades to Meet Expanding Noise Limits," *Aviation Week & Space Technology,* November 12, 1990; Phillips, Edward, "Service, International Sales to Spur Business Flying in '90's," *Aviation Week & Space Technology,* March 18, 1991; Clow, Robert, "Gulfstream Sets Reverse LBO Despite Lagging Projections," *Investment Dealers Digest,* February 10, 1992; Anders, George, "Gulfstream Drops Proposal to Offer Stock to the Public," *Wall Street Journal,* April 2, 1992; "BMW Venture with Rolls-Royce Nets Gulfstream Order," *New York Times,* September 9, 1992; "Super Long Range Gulfstream V Mockup Shown at NBA 1992," Savannah, Gulfstream Aerospace Corporation, 1992; "The Story of: Gulfstream Aerospace," Savannah, Gulfstream Aerospace Corporation, 1992; "New Gulfstream IV-Special Performance Announced at Farnborough," Savannah, Gulfstream Aerospace Corporation, 1992.

—Sina Dubovoj

HANSON PLC

1 Grosvenor Place
London SWlX 7JH
United Kingdom
(071) 245-1245
Fax: (071) 235-3455

Public Company
Incorporated: 1950 as Wiles Group Limited
Employees: 70,000
Sales: £7.69 billion (US$11.15 billion)
Stock Exchanges: London New York Zürich Basel Geneva
    Paris
SICs: 6719 Offices of Holding Companies, Not Elsewhere
    Classified; 2111 Cigarettes; 2121 Cigars; 2131 Chewing
    and Smoking Tabacco and Snuff; 3271 Concrete Block
    and Brick; 2499 Wood Products, Not Elsewhere Classified

Hanson PLC (Hanson) is a British/American industrial conglomerate, or, as its founders prefer to describe it, an industrial
management company whose manufacturing subsidiaries are
located principally in the United Kingdom and the United
States. Sales are divided almost equally between the U.S. and
the U.K. companies, while the United States employs slightly
more than half of the total work force. The group's portfolio of
operating companies has been built up by acquisition between
1965 and the 1990s and includes three broad groups: consumer,
building, and industrial products. Its most recently acquired
subsidiary is Beazer USA, Inc., the largest sand and gravel
business in America.

In the United States the group's activities, carried on by some
150 companies, are coordinated by its major subsidiary, Hanson
Industries, and again fall into three categories: industrial products, which include chemicals, mobile hydraulic cranes, leather
supplies, office furniture and supplies distribution, and Gold
Fields Mining Corporation; building products, which include
Kaiser Cement and a number of companies in the Hanson
Lighting Group as well as Jacuzzi, market leader in whirlpool
baths and spas; and consumer products such as vacuum
cleaners, cookware, plastic housewares, and textiles. The group
also has substantial interests in associate companies in the
United States and Australia. In 1988, with market capitalization
at £7.3 billion, Hanson was fifth in the rankings and thus

achieved one of its stated goals, a place in the top ten U.K.
companies before 1988.

The origins of Hanson go back to 1964. In March of that year a
small City (London financial district) merchant bank, Dawnay
Day, floated the Wiles Group on the stock exchange. The group
was an animal byproducts, sack hire, and fertilizer business
created by George Wiles and based in Hull, Yorkshire. In
August of 1964 Wiles started to diversify through the acquisition of Oswald Tillotson Ltd., a company operating in the field
of commercial vehicle sales and distribution. James Hanson and
Gordon White were on the board of Oswald Tillotson Ltd. and
held a controlling interest in the company.

James Edward Hanson and Vincent Gordon Lindsay White
were both born in Yorkshire and, after war service, started their
early careers in their respective family businesses. The Hanson
family road-haulage business was 100 years old when it was
nationalized in 1948. James Hanson then spent some years in
Canada building up a transport business with his brother. In the
late 1950s he joined Gordon White—a family friend, whose
own family publishing-and-printing business, Welbecson, was
acquired by Wiles in 1965—in a venture importing U.S. greeting cards. Thus, the partnership that has underpinned the development of Hanson was already formed when the two men
joined first Tillotson and then Wiles.

Between 1965, when James Hanson became chairman of
the Wiles Group, and 1969, when the company was renamed the
Hanson Trust, further acquisitions were made to develop the
group into an industrial holding and management company. Its
principal objective was defined by James Hanson as ''. . . to
expand profitability while achieving careful expansion through
acquisitions.'' The purchase of Scottish Land Development in
1967 for £700,000 took Wiles into the hire and distribution of
earth-moving and construction equipment and pumps. In 1968
the group paid £3.2 million for West of England Sack Holdings,
which expanded its existing business in that field. In the same
year it bought the Butterley Company for £4.7 million, an
acquisition that took it into a new field of operations, the manufacture of bricks for house construction.

Hanson was by no means the only company then searching for
under-performing and asset-rich companies to target as prospective acquisitions. In 1968 the conglomerate Slater Walker
took a large shareholding in the Wiles Group. Hanson and
White over the years consistently pointed out the difference
between the takeovers made for financial reason—the fast
track—and those, like Hanson's, for industrial reasons: ''We
are the work horses.''

Between 1971 and 1973 Hanson expanded its brick-making
activities with the acquisition of the National Star Brick & Tile
Company for £2.1 million, British Steel Brickworks for £2.7
million, and NCB Brickworks for £2.2 million. It also bought a
majority interest in a property development company, City and
St. James. The changing scope of its activities led to a restructuring of its operations first in 1970, when it sold the commercial vehicle distribution operation, and then again in 1972, when
the expansion of brick manufacturing warranted the creation of
a separate division.

In 1973 the Bowater Corporation, eager to diversify out of the low profit-making newsprint and pulp activities and fresh from its merger with Ralli International (master-minded the previous year by Jim Slater), made an agreed bid for Hanson. But when the bid was referred to the government's Monopolies and Mergers Commission, Bowater withdrew. This experience, combined with the prevailing uncertain economic climate in the United Kingdom, led Hanson and White to look further afield for development prospects, more particularly because White, "in disgust at socialism," wished to leave Britain. In that year, therefore, White went to the United States. From the 1950s until the mid-1970s, merger activity in the United Kingdom was high and encouraged by governments, particularly the Labour government of Harold Wilson, which established the Industrial Reorganization Corporation specifically to promote mergers such as that of General Electric Company and Associated Electrical Industries Ltd. On the other hand, reference to the Monopolies Commission of mergers that might operate against the public interest sometimes brought a negative response. Even when the commission's verdict was not unfavorable, changing conditions in the period of consideration could lead to the breaking-off of the engagement, as happened with Hanson and Bowater. The commission was generally neutral on the matter of industrial conglomerates, although it pointed to the risks of the creation of stock to finance the purchase and to the danger of a failure to increase efficiency after the merger. More damning criticisms of the merger movement and its results in the United States were made by a U.S. congressional report in June of 1971.

In the United Kingdom the asset-stripping activities of other companies tarnished the public image of the industrial conglomerate in the late 1970s. Hanson has insisted that it is an industrial management company. In the United States Hanson Industries was formed as a holding company in 1973, with White as executive chairman. His first major acquisition came the following year when, at a cost of $32 million, Hanson Industries bought Seacoast Products, a Florida-based company manufacturing animal foodstuffs, fish meal, and edible oils that remained part of Hanson until 1986.

In the 1970s, against the background of a turbulent world economy shaken by two large increases in world oil prices, Hanson's growth on both sides of the Atlantic was steady rather than spectacular. In the United States in 1976, Hygrade Foods, the second-largest seller of hot dogs in ballparks, was acquired, along with other purchases in the food servicing and vending and textile industries. In the United Kingdom, Hanson acquired Rollalong, which manufactured mobile accommodation units. In addition, Hanson purchased two flour milling and cereal companies and acquired yarn and thread manufacturers.

All these acquisitions fell into what is now recognized as the Hanson pattern. Hanson looks for and buys companies manufacturing basic, low technology products. By introducing a system of centralized and strong financial controls combined with decentralized operating management, Hanson increases profitability both for shareholders and for the holding company, thus building up its resources for further acquisitions. Some acquisitions have required further financing with bank debt, and the Hanson gearing has risen sharply at various times in the 1980s, to be quickly reduced in part by disinvestment. The

diversity of Hanson's portfolio spreads the risk with the steady demand for food and other consumer products balancing the upswings and downturns in demand for building-industry supplies. The caution of the two founders is well-documented. James Hanson said, "I've always thought about the down-side risk on a take-over rather than the upside potential—we don't gamble." It was this approach, according to White, that led to the decision in 1974 not to buy 51 percent of Avis, the U.S. car rental business. White recalled, "I told him it could put us straight in the big league but that if it went wrong it would bust us."

Hanson's purchase, for £25 million, of Lindustries in the United Kingdom in 1979 was its largest to date and presaged a decade of even greater spending and growth, taking Hanson very definitely into the big league. In 1980 Hanson Industries acquired McDonough, which included footwear manufacturing and retailing and cement manufacturing interests, for an agreed bid of $180 million. In the following year, in what was to become a typical Hanson activity, it recouped $49 million by selling the concrete and cement business. In the United Kingdom there were two major acquisitions in 1982, the Berec Group, manufacturers of Ever Ready batteries, for £95 million and United Gas Industries, makers of gas meters and of gas and electric fires, for £19 million. In the following year Hanson bought United Drapery Stores (UDS) for £250 million and immediately recovered almost three-fifths of the purchase price by selling Richard Shops and some of the other UDS subsidiaries. Allders Stores, a department store chain, and Allders International, which owned and operated duty-free shops at U.K. airports and on ferries and cruise ships, remained part of Hanson until 1989 when it was sold for £210 million.

By 1984, with turnover up to over £2 million, Hanson was increasingly seen on both sides of the Atlantic as a predator, a reputation it enhanced in that year with the acquisition of the London Brick Company for £247 million, making Hanson the world's largest brick manufacturer. At the same time in the United States it paid $535 million for U.S. Industries (USI), stepping in with a brisk offer to replace a management buyout. This acquisition gave Hanson interests in diverse fields ranging from clothes to lighting manufacture, and subsidiaries in office and domestic furniture-making as well as heavy engineering. By doubling the size of the U.S. operation, the USI acquisition put Hanson Industries among the top 150 companies trading in the United States. In the following year in the United Kingdom, the attempt to increase its interests in the engineering industry failed when Powell Duffryn successfully resisted Hanson's takeover bid; in the United States Hanson Industries sold the food service management company Interstate United for more than three times the price it had paid in 1978.

1986 was marked by two major acquisitions. In the United States Hanson Industries won control of and paid $930 million for SCM Corporation, a typewriter, food, and chemical concern described by Fortune International as "sluggish." The chemical division, which is the world's second largest producer of titanium dioxide, has a successful sales and profits record under Hanson. In the two years after the acquisition of SCM, disposal of parts of the conglomerate raised more money for Hanson than it had paid for the purchase. On top of that, 52 percent of the typewriter business Smith Corona was sold by flotation on the New York Stock Exchange in 1989. The Smith Corona sale helped offset the price of SCM, but entangled Hanson in a legal battle lasting more than two years. Investors who bought shares in Smith Corona Corp. claimed that Hanson officials knew of the impending layoffs and falling sales the company announced shortly after the stocks were purchased, and disposed of the property with that knowledge. Hanson and White denied the accusations. Much of the purchase price of Hanson's 1986 U.K. acquisition, the Imperial Group, bought for £2.5 billion after United Biscuits had failed to gain control of the group, was also covered by divestments. Hanson disposed of the Imperial diversifications—the Courage Brewery and off-license chains, Golden Wonder crisps, the hotels and restaurants, and the food interests where the brand names of Ross Young and Lea & Perrins brought a premium price—while retaining the original Imperial tobacco business.

The increasing importance of and value put upon brand names in a multinational business world was reflected in the purchase in 1987 by Hanson Industries of the U.S. conglomerate Kidde, an acquisition regarded at the time in New York as one for which White had, at US$1.7 billion, grossly overpaid; 18 months later Kidde's return on capital was up by more than 8 percent, and the acquisition had come to be seen as an "excellent purchase." With over 100 different businesses, including such diverse products as kitchenware and Jacuzzi whirlpool baths, the Kidde acquisition took Hanson Industries into the top 60 U.S. companies. The Hanson investment criteria required that an investment must contribute to profits within one year and pay for itself within four years.

By the beginning of 1989, financial journalists and Hanson watchers were openly speculating about when or where the next takeover would come. The previous year had, for the first time in the 1980s, passed without a Hanson acquisition while disposals had enriched its war chest, giving the company disposable cash of £12 billion. The 1980–1981 recession had been a powerful stimulus to corporate slimming. The increasing application of "hansonization"—the combination of tight financial control with subsidiary autonomy on operational management—had played a part in reducing the number of badly managed candidates for acquisition. Within Hanson, expenditure of more than £500 over budget in the United Kingdom and US$3,000 in the United States required head office authorization.

In August of 1989, when Minorco was obliged to admit defeat in its attempt to take over Consolidated Goldfields PLC, Hanson stepped in with a successful bid of £3.5 billion. Following its usual post-acquisition policy, Hanson closed down Goldfields's London head office and sold its South African gold-mining interests and the U.S. aggregates business, Amey Roadstone Corporation, America (ARC).

Despite the worldwide recession in the early 1990s, Hanson continued to be "expansion-minded," as the chairman phrased it in his 1990 letter to the company's shareholders. In May of that year Hanson spent $240 million to buy a 2.8 percent stake (20 million shares) in Britain's largest industrial company, Imperial Chemical Industries (ICI). (ICI's pension fund was one of the largest holders of Hanson stock.) Just two months later, Hanson Industries acquired Peabody Holding Co., America's

largest coal producer. After a brief fight over the coal giant with AMAX, Hanson paid US$1.25 billion for Peabody, which upset some U.S. coal officials who resented the foreign ownership. Beazer Plc., one of Britain's largest home construction companies, found itself deeply in debt in a seriously depressed housing market; it also found itself to be a subsidiary of Hanson by the end of 1991.

A 1991 study of Hanson's history of takeovers found that the company made most of its profits by improving the performance of the companies it acquired. The finding refuted accusations that Hanson made most of its money by buying and selling assets. The analysis of the period from 1986 to 1990 showed that, of Hanson's total earnings of £4.16 billion, only 18 percent came from asset sales. During the same period, 55 percent of the company's £821 million pre-tax profits gain came from the improved performance of Hanson businesses. Despite strong trends in the United States, none of the deals utilized junk bond financing.

But in 1991 external and internal forces came to bear on Hanson's long history of growth through acquisition. The Persian Gulf war and worldwide recession slowed down mergers and acquisitions in the United Kingdom. There were fewer big deals made, but nearly the same number of smaller concerns changing hands. At the same time, Lords Hanson and White began slowly to pass leadership to Derek C. Bonham, who had been with Hanson 20 years, and David H. Clarke, a former director of Smith Corona. Bonham was appointed chief executive of Hanson in early 1992 and Clarke was the president of Hanson Industries, but Hanson and White—as executive chairmen of Hanson PLC and Hanson Industries, respectively—have maintained overall direction.

At that time Hanson PLC had more than $30 billion in assets, $13 billion in revenues, and 70,000 employees, but had neglected some of its core businesses, such as chemicals and coal mining. The company also faced a net deficit of about £1.5 billion, with loans of £9.5 billion and cash of £8 billion. Bonham and Clarke hoped to dispense with many of Hanson's consumer-related companies and make long-term investments in the key businesses.

In April of 1992 Hanson sold Ever Ready Ltd. to Ralston Purina Co. for £132 million, generating a £108 million profit. One month later, Hanson and White confounded financial analysts by selling the conglomerate's interest in ICI at a 17 percent pretax profit. The sales fueled speculation on which businesses would next join Hanson's roster. Observers thought Trafalgar House PLC, Pilkington PLC and Allied-Lyons PLC in Britain, and Solvay & Cie of Belgium were candidates for takeover. In October of 1992 the conservative strategy seemed to have been thrown out the window. Hanson announced its hostile £780 million cash bid for Ranks Hovis McDougall (RHM), a move that was quickly repulsed by RHM's board of directors.

Since 1964, Lord Hanson, who was knighted in 1976 and made a peer in 1983, and Lord White—knighted in 1979—have built up a company that is one of the largest in the United Kingdom and the United States. Their partnership, relying on Lord Gordon's creativity and Lord Hanson's administrative ability, by their own accounts is sustained by daily telephone calls and the assistance of small head office staffs of about 120 in the United States and 100 in the United Kingdom, and of senior managers, many of whom have been with Hanson for 20 years. Both believe in maximum delegation of responsibility, adhering to a view stated more than 50 years ago by John Crabtree, founder of Crabtree Electricals, since 1982 one of Hanson's subsidiaries: "There are far too many Managing Directors and Presidents of companies who fancy themselves as experts in some minor phase of the business and who drive their subordinates to desperation by riding their personal hobbies." Lord Hanson expressed his business philosophy in Dominic Lawson's article in the *Spectator* in 1989: "Many companies here are not rewarding their shareholders sufficiently and are more concerned with management stability and welfare than they are with the welfare of shareholders, which is all that matters. We don't run this business for ourselves." The company gave second priority to customers, and third importance to employees. This philosophy is reflected in the fact that Hanson operating managers are not offered high basic salaries but are rewarded with performance-related bonuses. Without looking for synergy or economies of scale and without the creation of a Hanson corporate culture or loyalty to the parent company, Hanson has achieved the objectives of its founders.

Principal Subsidiaries: Imperial Tobacco Ltd; Lindustries Ltd.; Hanson Amalgamated Industries; ARC Ltd.; London Brick Company Ltd.; Butterley Brick Ltd.; Hanson Housewares (U.S.A.); Hanson Recreation and Leisure (U.S.A.); SCM Chemicals Inc. (U.S.A.); Hanson Office Products (U.S.A.); Weber Aircraft Inc. (U.S.A.); Hanson Lighting (U.S.A.); Kaiser Cement Corporation (U.S.A.); Peabody Holding Co. (U.S.A.); SCM Glidco Organics (U.S.A.); Grove Worldwide Co. (U.S.A.); Hanson Industrial Services; Beazer USA, Inc. (U.S.A.); Cavenham Forest Industries, Inc. (U.S.A.); Beazer Homes Ltd.; Jacuzzi, Inc. (U.S.A.).

Further Reading: Campbell-Smith, D., "Much More than a Predator," *The Financial Times,* December 23, 1983; Fay, Stephen, "The Rise and Rise of Hanson and White," *Business,* March 1986; Lawson, Dominic, "The Hard Man from Huddersfield," *Spectator,* October 7, 1989; Bowen, David, "Secrets of a Big Game Hunter," *The Independent on Sunday,* July 29, 1990; "Hanson Assumes Total Ownership of Peabody Holding Co.," *Coal,* August 1990; "Hanson Likes the Look of ICI," *Economist,* May 18, 1991; House, Richard, and Lenny Glynn, "Harbingers and Hopes," *Global Finance,* June 1991; "Hanson Finds a True Friend in Need," *Management Today,* August 1991; Norman, James R., "Don't Rush Us," *Forbes,* October 14, 1991; Reier, Sharon, "Europe's CEO of the Year: Lord Hanson of Hanson plc," *Financial World,* October 15, 1991; "Hanson Sells Its Stake in ICI to Goldman," *Wall Street Journal* (Eastern), May 11, 1992; "Studying an ADR: Hanson PLC," *Canadian Shareowner,* May/June 1992; Melcher, Richard A., "Can This Predator Change Its Stripes?," *Business Week,* June 22, 1992; Powell, Scott, "Quality Credits: Hanson's Sterling Efforts," *Euromoney* (Credits Supplement), September 1992; "Hanson Offers $1.35 Billion for Bread Baker," *Wall Street Journal* (Eastern), October 6, 1992; "Hanson: Hunter's Return," *Economist,* October 10, 1992.

—Judy Slinn
updated by April Dougal

HARLEY-DAVIDSON INC.

1700 West Juneau Ave.
P.O. Box 653
Milwaukee, Wisconsin 53201
U.S.A.
(414) 342-4680
Fax: (414) 935-4806

Public Company
Incorporated: 1903 as the Harley-Davidson Motor Company
Employees: 5,300
Sales: $939.80 million
Stock Exchanges: New York
SICs: 3751 Motorcycles, Bicycles & Parts; 3711 Motor
    Vehicles & Car Bodies; 3443 Fabricated Plate Work—
    Boiler Shops

The only motorcycle manufacturer in the United States, Harley-Davidson Inc. has been designing heavyweight machines for bike enthusiasts for almost a century. The company is legendary for the great loyalty its vehicles have inspired in generations of cyclists.

The first Harley-Davidson motorcycle was built in Milwaukee, Wisconsin—still the location of the company's headquarters—in the early 1900s. The Davidson brothers—William, Walter, and Arthur—along with William S. Harley, designed and developed the bike and its three horsepower engine in their family shed. The machine went through many refinements until 1903 when the men established the Harley-Davidson Motor Company and produced three of their motorcycles for sale. Over the next several years both demand and production grew at a healthy rate, and by 1907 the company had begun to advertise.

Two years later the company produced a new model featuring a V-twin engine that produced a low, deep rumble now identified as the signature Harley-Davidson sound. The revolutionary engine—still a company standard—enabled riders to reach speeds of 60 miles-per-hour, which until that time had been believed impossible. Such capabilities served to set the company's motorcycles apart from the competition; by 1911 there were 150 other companies manufacturing the vehicles.

The onset of the First World War was actually a boon for Harley-Davidson. The motorcycle, having done well in its utilization by police, was commissioned for use by the military. It proved especially useful on the U.S.-Mexican border, which was suffering incursions by the forces of Mexican revolutionary leader Pancho Villa. In all, 20,000 of the company's machines were employed by the U.S. infantry during the war.

The battlegrounds of the war also served as proving grounds for the motorcycles. After resuming normal production, Harley-Davidson was able to begin incorporating improvements into its new machines. The 1920s saw the company taking the lead in innovative engineering with such features as the Teardrop gas tank and the front brake. In 1921, the winner of the first race in which motorists reached average speeds of more than 100 miles-per-hour was riding a Harley-Davidson machine.

The motorcycle industry was not immune to the financial difficulties of the Great Depression; only Harley-Davidson and Indian survived those years. However, a strong dealer network, continued use by the military and police, as well as the U.S. Postal Service, and strong exports to Canada and Europe allowed Harley-Davidson to weather the economic disaster.

Henry Ford's introduction of the assembly line, on which he could quickly and inexpensively produce his Model T automobile, had a profound effect on the motorcycle industry. While motorcycles had traditionally been used by workers and businesspeople, the more affordable car became their vehicle of choice. The motorcycle, in the meantime, was gradually becoming a recreational vehicle.

Military procurement during the Second World War, however, proved as helpful to Harley-Davidson as it was during World War I. In 1941 the company turned its entire manufacturing effort toward supplying U.S. and Allied troops going into battle, shipping nearly 100,000 machines overseas. Harley-Davidson's efforts earned them the Army-Navy "E" award, an honor bestowed upon companies that excelled at production during wartime. The healthy post-war economy found consumers with money to spend. To meet burgeoning demand, the company purchased additional manufacturing capacity in 1947.

As the second generations of the founding families began moving into management positions at the company, Harley-Davidson found itself "king of the road"—with the shutdown of Indian in 1953, the company became the sole American motorcycle manufacturer. Continuing to prove itself, the company introduced its Sportster model in 1957, heralding the era of the all-powerful, throaty "superbikes."

An entire subculture began to grow up around these motorcycles, and leather jackets and riding boots became as much a statement of one's desire for a life of freedom on the open road as a necessity for motorcycling. However, the film *The Wild One,* starring Marlon Brando, depicted bikers riding Harley-Davidson motorcycles as packs of lawless renegades. The stereotype that grew out of this is one the company still actively strives to dispel.

In 1965 Harley-Davidson went public when the two families decided to give up control and put the company's shares on the market. Four years later the company was bought by the American Machine and Foundry Co. (AMF), a leisure equipment manufacturer headed by Harley-Davidson fan Rodney C. Gott. The arrangement proved, at least initially, to be a good one for

Harley-Davidson for it was also in the 1960s that the company experienced its first competition since Indian went out of business. The financial resources and stability that AMF were able to provide helped the company battle Japanese motorcycle manufacturers who had begun exporting their vehicles around the world, placing themselves in direct competition with Harley-Davidson.

Demand for motorcycles continued to grow through the early 1970s, and, in an effort to keep up, the company opened an assembly plant in York, Pennsylvania, in 1974. While engines would still be made in the Milwaukee facilities, the bikes themselves would be assembled in the new plant.

In 1975 AMF put Vaughn Beals at the head of Harley-Davidson, and Jeff Bleustein was named chief engineer. Bleustein was charged with making manufacturing improvements, which were becoming increasingly necessary as production grew.

These efforts added an extra $1,000 in costs to each bike, however, and the profit line suffered as a result. To compensate, AMF management began to apply pressure for greater sales volume, with the result that quality began to suffer. The production standards that customers had come to count on were being lowered, and there were chronic shortages of parts, with the result that as many as 30 percent of the vehicles coming off the assembly line were incomplete. This, in turn, meant extra manpower searching for spare parts to finish outfitting the machines, a task that even fell to dealers on those occasions when incomplete bikes were accidentally shipped.

Such problems took their toll on the company, especially in light of rising Japanese competition. In 1969 Harley-Davidson had enjoyed an 80 percent share of the U.S. motorcycle market for super heavyweight machines—bikes with engines over 850 cubic centimeters (cc). Ten years later, just when Honda Motor Co. was opening a plant in Marysville, Ohio, that share had dropped sharply to 20 percent. While there were still some riders who would settle for nothing but a Harley-Davidson motorcycle, newcomers to the motorcycle market were opting for Japanese affordability and dependability.

To make matters worse, the 1981 recession severely threatened Harley-Davidson's share of the market for heavyweight bikes—motorcycles with engine capacities of 700 cc and higher—nearly finishing the company off as a manufacturer. Soon AMF began to lose interest in keeping the struggling business afloat. To save the company, and to effect a turnaround, 13 Harley-Davidson executives, led by Vaughn Beals, put together a plan for a leveraged management buy-out. With the financial support of Citicorp, the management team succeeded in taking control of Harley-Davidson from AMF on June 16, 1981, at a cost of $81.5 million.

Their turnaround strategy called for getting back on the quality track through new management and manufacturing techniques. Unable to beat them, Harley-Davidson instead decided to join their Japanese competition, adopting such management techniques as decentralized quality discussion groups and "just-in-time" inventory control. After the company's top management toured Honda's Marysville plant in 1981, Vaughn Beals noted in *Fortune,* "We were being wiped out by the Japanese because they were better managers. It wasn't robotics, or culture, or

morning calisthenics and company songs—it was professional managers who understood their business and paid attention to detail." In an effort to do likewise, management at the York plant developed three principles for change: worker involvement, manufacturing materials available as needed, and statistical operator control.

One of the first steps Harley-Davidson took was to group the employees in a plant-wide network to ensure their input in improving the manufacturing process. The York plant management met with workers' representatives for months in 1981 to achieve a consensus on what was sought and also to ease skepticism. The increases in productivity stemming from these measures were deemed to be the effects of effective communication, shop floor enthusiasm, and increased rewards and recognition.

The second point of the revitalization program involved managing the company's inventory. A program of just-in-time inventory control called MAN—Material As Needed—was developed, based on Toyota Motor Corporation's Toyota Production System. The plan called for the use of expanded communication in monitoring the flow of inventory.

Harley-Davidson also introduced a statistical operator control system to improve quality control. The aim was to reduce defects and scrap by reworking machines right on the assembly line. The process began with the operators, who established parameters for quality using statistical methods. Then workers along the assembly line would chart actual quality and introduce improvements where warranted.

During the early 1980s, the company began making cosmetic changes to their motorcycles, prompted by vice president William G. Davidson, grandson of the founder. Davidson, who felt it was important to remain close to the bike maker's customers and their needs, would often mingle with Harley devotees at gatherings, sporting his own beard, black leather, and jeans. As he explained in *Fortune,* "They really know what they want on their bikes, the kind of instrumentation, the style of bars, the cosmetics of the engine, the look of the exhaust pipes, and so on. Every little piece on a Harley is exposed, and it has to look right. A tube curve or the shape of a timing case can generate enthusiasm or be a turn-off. It's almost like being in the fashion business." In addition to changing the look of established models, the company began to design new motorcycles to appeal to a broad range of consumers.

Meanwhile, the competition was moving ahead. Though the recession of the early 1980s had depressed demand for heavyweight bikes, Japanese manufacturers swamped the U.S. market with their surplus inventory, driving average market prices down still further. In 1982, however, the company won an anti-dumping judgement from the International Trade Commission (ITC). This led then-U.S. president, Ronald Reagan, to impose additional tariffs on imported heavyweight Japanese models, as allowed by the ITC.

The additional tariffs—45 percent on top of an existing 4.4 percent measure—were meant to decrease gradually over five years, until April 1988. These measures would give Harley-Davidson the opportunity to effect their revitalization plans. Predictably, as the company's market share began to increase, so, too, did their profits. Harley-Davidson had lost $25 million in 1982, but rebounded into the black again in 1983 before posting $2.9 million in profits on sales of $294 million in 1984. Though Japanese bike makers were able to elude some of the tariffs by building more machines in the United States, by 1986 Harley-Davidson's share of the U.S. super heavyweight market had crept back up to 33.3 percent, ahead of Honda for the first time since 1980.

During this time, Harley-Davidson began placing more emphasis on their marketing efforts. In a 1983 public relations move, the company established the Harley Owners Group, a club with its own newsletter for fans of the motorcycle. By the end of the 1980s, membership in HOG had grown to 100,000 members.

In 1984 the company developed the SuperRide promotion, which was designed to attract large numbers of new buyers. Television commercials were aired, inviting people to visit one of Harley-Davidson's 600 dealers across the United States to test ride a new bike. Over 40,000 people took Harley-Davidson up on its offer. Though immediate sales did not cover the promotion's $3 million price tag, the effort did result in increased sales over the course of the next several years, and many of the new buyers were owners of rival Japanese models.

Although Harley-Davidson was making great strides, the company suffered yet another blow in 1984. Citicorp—nervous that the economy was headed back into a recession, especially in light of the 1988 deadline on import tariffs—informed Harley-Davidson that in future years they would no longer provide overadvances—money over and above the conservative lending limits set as part of the company's business plan.

Taking this as an indication that Citicorp wanted out of its arrangement with the company, Beals and Richard Teerlink, who was then the finance officer, began searching for another lender. Once word concerning Citicorp's plans got out, however, other banks showed little interest in making the commitment. By October of 1985 Beals and his management team had approached the investment firm Dean Witter Reynolds in order to begin Chapter 11 bankruptcy proceedings.

Fortunately, before those plans were finalized, Beals and Teerlink were linked with an interested lender. After weeks of hard bargaining, Heller Financial Corporation—whose second in command, Bob Koe, was a Harley buff—agreed to supply Harley-Davidson with $49 million to buy out Citicorp's stake in the business. Thus Citicorp was forced to take an $18 million write-down on their original investment.

Heller Financial Corporation's faith in Harley-Davidson paid off handsomely. The company's market share began to climb steadily, and profits for 1986 topped $4.3 million on sales of $295 million. That year a revived Harley-Davidson went public, offering 2 million shares of stock worth $20 million and $70 million worth of unsecured subordinate notes that would mature in 1997.

With the capital raised from these offerings Harley-Davidson purchased the motor home maker, Holiday Rambler Corporation. By December of 1986 the company had acquired all outstanding Holiday Rambler stock for approximately $156 million, enabling Harley-Davidson to diversify its manufactur-

ing efforts. The company further broadened its business in 1986 when the U.S. government awarded Harley-Davidson a contract to produce military hardware, including casings for 500-pound bombs and liquid-fueled rocket engines for target drone aircraft.

The previous year had proven to be such a successful one for Harley-Davidson that in March of 1987 the company asked the ITC to remove the tariffs imposed on Japanese superbike imports a year earlier than scheduled. Even so, Harley-Davidson's share of the super heavyweight market by the end of 1987 had climbed to 47 percent. In recognition of the company's turnaround, then-president Reagan toured Harley-Davidson's York plant, praising the employees for their hard work.

The changes in management philosophy at Harley-Davidson were quite significant. As associate purchasing agent Dave Gurka maintained in a 1988 *Labor-Management Cooperation Brief* published by the U.S. Department of Labor: "When AMF ran the company, in spite of its help in the continued existence [of Harley-Davidson] in bad times, it was . . . like a dictatorship, compared with today. The emphasis was on high volume—AMF wanted the parts and bikes out the door, now. Now the emphasis is on everyone working together and working on quality. It's quality or nothing."

In 1989 Harley-Davidson established a wholly-owned subsidiary in Britain and a joint venture in Japan to take advantage of emerging global markets for its product. In October of the same year, the company sold the assets of Parkway Distributors, a recreational vehicle parts and accessories distributor, for $3.5 million.

Despite the recession taking hold in 1990, Harley-Davidson saw its sales for that year increase to $864.6 million, up from $790.6 million a year earlier. The company also had a 62.3 percent share of the U.S. heavyweight motorcycle market, far and above Honda, their closest competitor with 16.2 percent. Holiday Rambler's sales were somewhat affected, however, by lower consumer spending.

Richard Teerlink, who had become president and CEO of Harley-Davidson, warned in the company's 1990 annual report that "maintaining Harley-Davidson's growth through a recessionary period will be a difficult, but not impossible task. We could easily exploit our worldwide motorcycle popularity for quick profits, a near-fatal mistake we made in the 1970s, but we are committed to a corporate vision that discourages short-term thinking."

The early 1990s brought the company some minor setbacks. Though sales in 1991 rose to $939.8 million, profits fell slightly, marking the first decrease since the 1986 refloatation. In addition, the company's motorcycle division experienced a work stoppage at the York plant, and sales and profits at the Holiday Rambler Corporation continued downwards. However, Harley-Davidson has learned from past mistakes and proven itself to be a survivor. Their products are again associated with quality, and the company continues to attract the loyalty of customers around the world.

Principal Subsidiaries: Holiday Rambler Corporation; Utilmaster Corporation; B&B Molders; Creative Dimensions; Nappanee Wood Products.

Further Reading: "Why Milwaukee Won't Die," *Cycle,* June 1987; "Riding the Road to Recovery at Harley-Davidson," *Labor-Management Cooperation Brief* No. 15 (April 1988), Washington, DC, U.S. Department of Labor; "Maintaining Excellence Through Change," *Target,* Spring 1989; "How Harley Beat Back the Japanese," *Fortune,* September 25, 1989; Peter Reid, *Well Made in America: Lessons from Harley-Davidson on Being the Best,* New York, McGraw Hill, 1990; "The Success of Harley-Davidson: 89 Years in the Making," *Harley-Davidson News,* Milwaukee, WI, Harley-Davidson Inc., 1992.

—Etan Vlessing

HER MAJESTY'S STATIONERY OFFICE

St. Crispins
Duke Street
Norwich NR3 1PD
United Kingdom
(603) 622 211
Fax: (603) 695 582

State-Owned Company
Incorporated: April 5, 1786
Employees: 3,500
Sales: £400 million (US$580 million)
SICs: 2731 Book Publishing, 2711 Newspapers, 2721
   Periodicals, 5112 Stationery & Office Supplies

Her Majesty's Stationery Office, or HMSO, is an unusual type of company that, although owned and operated by the British government, is basically commercial in nature. Because HMSO has no guarantee of business from the British government, it must compete with private print and office supply companies. Although it did not become commercially independent until recently, HMSO has been in existence for more than 200 years, providing every manner of documentary support to the British government, including passports, parliamentary records, manuals, forms, computers, and office equipment.

HMSO came into being during the 1780s when, as the costs of maintaining its empire began to mount, the British Parliament undertook a study of redundant costs in the administration of the government. Among the study's conclusions was that the government used too much paper. Naturally, those who most benefited from this abuse were the stationers who provided the parchment, ink, wax, and other supplies at public expense.

The government therefore set out to establish an official stationer who would be singularly accountable to the Treasury. On April 5, 1786, the government authorized John Mayor of the Treasury to create such an agency at New Palace Yard under the name His Majesty's Stationery Office. Gradually, the government's paper supply purchases were shifted to this office as the government's contracts, or "patents," with private suppliers expired. By August 15, 1787, the officially sanctioned Stationery Office supplied 11 agencies, the House of Lords, and the House of Commons. The business of the Stationery Office—

and its staff—continued to grow with the expiration of additional independent contracts, the last of which was terminated in 1800.

Lewis Wolfe ran the Office as comptroller from 1798 until 1802, when he was succeeded by George Dickins. Although all employees, and especially the comptroller, were subject to strict prohibitions against bribery and kickbacks, Dickins allowed discipline to erode. He came under suspicion after moving to new offices in New Scotland Yard in 1812, but it was not until ten years later that the government began an investigation into his activities.

The probe revealed that the Stationery Office's business had grown too large for its system of management and that, because of this, many agencies had returned to private suppliers. The Lords of the Treasury later agreed that the Office should receive a fixed annual stipend for its services, and that it should be divided into separate purchasing and issuing arms. Further, while the staff was cut from 40 to 32, the Lords instructed all government agencies to direct their business to the Stationery Office.

Dickins died of apoplexy in 1824 and was replaced by the 29-year-old Alexander Spearman, who had authored the Treasury's reorganization of the Office. Spearman held the post of Comptroller for only a year and was succeeded by John Church.

Church was considerably more aggressive in running the Stationery Office than his predecessors had been. In 1830 he boldly suggested that the Office take over the duties of printing that had been reserved for an enterprise run by Luke Graves Hansard. But while Hansard managed to hold on to the printing job, Church's suggestion that work for the government be awarded under competitive bid took hold. The Office, which had evolved into a clearinghouse rather than a simple supplier of stationery goods, began to demand that its suppliers bid competitively.

With the dissolution of separate King's stationers in Ireland in 1830 and in Scotland in 1833, the business of the Stationery Office continued to expand. In 1837, upon the death of King William IV and the ascension of Queen Victoria, Church ensured that all stationery items were changed to "Her" rather than "His" Majesty's Stationery Office.

John McCulloch, a 49-year-old literary Scotsman, succeeded Church in 1838. Noting that the government was obliged, for no good reason, to publish and distribute every public petition to Parliament (numbering more than 15,258 between 1801 and 1834), McCulloch suggested that considerable savings would be realized with a simple rule change. Attributing the Office's avalanche of paper to a rise in the activity of long-winded lawyers, McCulloch limited print runs to 1000 copies.

Also, having discovered that there was a profitable market for waste paper, McCulloch won the right to have excess paper returned to the Office for disposal. While the HMSO profited from resale of the paper, the task proved even more ominous than providing the paper in the first place.

The division of the Stationery Office into two units—a purchasing and an issuing division—never worked properly, and in 1856 the departments were reunited. In addition, some years earlier, HMSO created its own binding operation, eliminating costly subcontractors.

Hansard, meanwhile, ran a popular business printing records of Parliamentary debates. While technically a violation of secrecy rules, the records gained official status in 1855, when the Treasury instructed the Stationery Office to distribute 100 copies to public departments and colonial offices. Also that year, McCulloch and the HMSO's staff of 55 relocated to Queen Anne's Royal Stables at Storey's Gate on Princes Street.

McCulloch died in 1864, and was succeeded as Comptroller by another literary man, William Greg. Greg continued the practice of choosing suppliers by competitive bid. But, determined to keep HMSO ''nontechnical,'' he incorrectly judged the utility of new inventions, including the typewriter and the telephone.

Greg, however, died in 1877. Consistent with the wishes of the Commons, he was replaced not by another aristocrat, but by an experienced clerk with a facility for physical labor named Thomas Digby Pigott. Pigott's appointment was called into question because his father, a friend of Prime Minister Benjamin Disraeli, had maneuvered him into the job. Disraeli, however, defended Pigott, who proved an able administrator of HMSO. Within two years of taking the job, Pigott reorganized HMSO to better cope with the increasing demands the government was putting on it. By 1882, having taken on the production of numerous gazettes and acting as ''printer to Her Majesty and all Acts of Parliament,'' HMSO became a publisher as well as a stationer.

Concerned with the finances of the growing enterprise, the Treasury appointed yet another study of the Stationery Office. But Pigott demonstrated that the rise in his office's expenditures was, in fact, low when compared to the demands placed upon it. The Treasury recommended the creation of an in-house reporting staff. Queen Victoria meanwhile expanded the Office's publishing duties, effectively ending the private monopolies maintained by independent printers.

With the death of Queen Victoria and the ascension of a new king in 1899, the Stationery Office reverted to ''His Majesty's.'' Pigott, who retired in 1905 with a knighthood, was succeeded as controller of the Office by Rowland Bailey, an absorbed, meticulous planner from the Office of Works.

Bailey's first action was an appeal to bureaucrats to curtail the volume of their unnecessarily wordy paperwork. He led the Stationery Office's takeover of the government's *Votes and Proceedings* in 1907, and what remained of the Hansard record in 1909. The Office also saw increased demands because of the South African War, the National Insurance Act of 1911 and the Old Age Pensions Act. To supplement the Office's income, Bailey established a series of book stores that were open to the public.

Sir Rowland (knighthoods had become customary for Office controllers) retired in 1913. He was succeeded by the calmer Frederick Atterbury, whose skills were immediately tested by the outbreak of World War I in 1914, when the Treasury was forced to recall all gold coinage to finance war preparations. Having abandoned the gold standard, the government directed the Stationery Office to arrange for the printing of one pound and, later, 10 shilling notes. Using penny stamp paper—the only secure quality available—and working from a design purportedly sketched by Atterbury himself, the Office arranged for several million notes to be printed and numbered by Waterlow Brothers, delivering them to banks within days.

The war put incredible strains on the Stationery Office, with increased requisitions for typewriters, calculating equipment, registers, and rotary duplicators. Although wartime shortages forced bureaucrats to reduce the flow of voluminous ramblings they had previously considered necessary, orders for millions of ration books and public notices far surpassed any decrease in the Office's routine work. The stress was too much for subcontractors to handle, and many were forced to turn over their operations to the Stationery Office. To better handle distribution, the Office was divided into two regional branches, with the northern office located at Manchester, and numerous depots were established.

A new reinforced-concrete headquarters building, Cornwall House, was requisitioned by the army as a military hospital in 1918, before the Stationery Office could occupy it. That year, with a staff of more than 2,500 people, Atterbury resigned due to ill health. He was succeeded briefly by Ulick Wintour, and then by the assistant controller William Codling, who had risen through the Office hierarchy.

With the end of the war in 1919, Codling's Stationery Office took over the operations of the India Office Press and, in 1922, the War Office Press. A year earlier, to reduce the Office's burden on the public, Codling approved the inclusion of advertising in official documents. After its reorganization during the war, the structure of the Stationery Office remained intact for many years, proving economic and efficient in peacetime as well as wartime.

Continuing to expand its operations, the Stationery Office began publishing telephone directories in 1922, and in 1925 took on an ill-fitted cinematography section. But the Office had its difficulties. As an official state printer, HMSO had authority that many viewed as unfair in the marketplace. In 1926, a ten-day strike illustrated the depth of these feelings among the company's workers.

But at that time, the Office underwent yet another government review, revealing that it was very efficiently and responsibly managed. Unlike the days under William Greg, the Office had become a modern operation, applying the latest technologies, including offset lithography, copiers, dictation machines, and mechanical calculators. Rising costs, it was determined, were attributable to the rapid expansion in the size of the government. By the mid-1930s, the Stationery Office itself employed more than 3,000 people, two-thirds of whom were laborers and tradesmen.

By the end of the 1930s, with growing hostilities in Europe, the government undertook secret precautions to prepare Britain for another war. The Stationery Office was instructed to supervise the printing of 78 million ration books and instruction manuals on everything from cooking to air raids. With the evacuation of London a distinct possibility, Sir William Codling established a second press facility in Manchester. But after the war began and London came under attack, Sir William and his staff remained in London with Prime Minister Winston Churchill and the Royal family. In 1942, after 43 years with the Stationery Office, and 23 years as its controller, Sir William retired.

His successor was ex-lawyer and deputy controller Norman Scorgie, who knew exactly how to get things done under the circumstances of war. In addition to the Stationery Office, Scorgie was pressed into service planning for the reconstruction of Germany. Fortunately, this inappropriate request of the Stationery Office was lost in the flurry of activity during 1945.

Under Scorgie, the postwar Stationery Office expanded its sales organization and mail order service. But while Sir Norman proved highly capable, he remained only until 1949, and was replaced by Sir Gordon Welch.

Sir Gordon dealt with the transition of the Ministry of Information into the Central Office of Information and guided it into a postwar relationship with the Stationery Office. He also oversaw another relocation of the head office, this time to Atlantic House on Holborn Viaduct in 1951. Queen Elizabeth's coronation in 1953 was Sir Gordon's swan song, as he retired from his job as controller that year and Sir John Simpson took over.

Sir John believed that the Stationery Office had clearly overstepped its bounds of authority when private printers pointed out that the Office had begun selling items such as Christmas cards. These, the printers charged, were being produced under state subsidies. Sir John could not deny, however, that profits from these sales were made necessary by losses sustained on publications such as *The Highway Code, Horse Flies of the Ethiopian Region, The Measurement of Small Holes* (translated from Russian), and *The Rent Act and You.* Indeed, the Stationery Office even served as a distributor for United Nations publications. A government investigation in 1957 recommended that the work of the Stationery Office be streamlined and limited only to service to the central government. Later, the Office was relieved of its reprographic duties.

During the 1950s, the Stationery Office operated eight production factories, and subcontracted work to an additional 1,700 private firms. Concentrated in London, the Stationery Office had been asked to move with other government agencies to new locations outside the city. The task of moving fell to Sir Percy Faulkner, who succeeded Sir John in 1961. After considering Basingstoke, Swindon, and Norwich, Sir John deferred to the vote of his senior managers and chose the latter.

The move to Norwich marked several important changes for the Stationery Office, which had begun using the acronym HMSO. It greatly expanded its business by delving headlong into computerization. The proliferation of telephony in England dictated thicker phone books, which necessitated a larger printing facility at Gateshead on Tyneside in 1968. In addition to that and millions of government documents, HMSO had responsibility for Yellow Pages directories, pension books, Girocheques, and passports.

By 1972, HMSO was again under review. This time it was suggested that the Office revamp its management system to a system of accountability. It was also suggested that HMSO modernize its accounting methods, requiring the installation of

virtually all its existing production accounting equipment. In labor issues, the government asked HMSO to open an industrial relations office, and the company engaged in formal personnel management for the first time in its history.

The period also saw a parade of several short-time controllers, including Harry Pitchforth, who served from 1967 to 1969, Clifford Baylis, who served until 1974, and Harold Glover, who continued until 1977 when Bernard Thimont was appointed.

Although he served only until 1981, Thimont was instrumental in recreating HMSO as a business, using commercial-style accounting methods and even issuing annual reports. Under pressure from the new conservative government of then Prime Minister Margaret Thatcher to reduce expenses in the Civil Service, Thimont cut HMSO's staff by 10 percent in 1980. That same year, hoping to fully convert HMSO, Thimont won the right to charge government clients for their orders, shifting the budgetary burden from HMSO to customers, who found new incentives to cut waste.

Thimont left HMSO at the beginning of 1981 and Bill Sharp, a former controller of The Crown Suppliers, became its controller. Taking Thimont's goals a bit further, Sharp sought employees "with the spirit of businessmen rather than the spirit of bureaucrats." Sharp pressed for early retirements, reducing the HMSO work force from 6,000 in 1981 to 4,360 in 1983. He also reinstated board meetings and introduced corporate-style five-year business plans.

The preparations were necessary, as the government planned to remove HMSO from its annual stipend and lift the stipulation that government departments buy only from HMSO. After April 1, 1982—"Untying Day"—any agency that could find a better deal elsewhere was free not to patronize HMSO.

Sharp, who had brought about a similar business conversion at The Crown Suppliers, oversaw the reorganization of HMSO in 1984. The business was divided into four operations: supply, print procurement, publications, and production. In the process of reorganization HMSO spun off a telephone directory business. The company was left to stand on its own feet and compete on a purely commercial basis.

The first few years after "untying," HMSO fared quite well, maintaining, and even expanding its volume of business. Its primary promotional campaign was a numerical comparison of price efficiencies that demonstrated to the agency's customers exactly how much they had saved by using HMSO.

As part of an effort to continue driving down costs, HMSO began modernizing its production processes. In 1987, under John Dole, a new Parliamentary Press facility was opened, the Manchester plant was updated, and a new computer-assisted print ordering system was introduced.

The following year, the Chancellor of the Exchequer conferred upon HMSO a broader liberalization of its operating procedures, further enabling it to behave as a commercial operation. The Executive Agency status gave HMSO the freedom to establish a more decentralized organization and establish pay scales that were more in line with the market environment. This caused great concern on the part of several unions, but by 1990 a series of new labor agreements was in place that preserved employee harmony and, for the moment, eliminated the threat of strikes. The agreement also validated HMSO's transformation from a civil service employer to a real business.

Paul Freeman, who was named controller of HMSO in 1988, established a corporate quality council, whose job it was to implement a total quality management scheme, using the Juran project-by-project methodology. This enabled HMSO to gain government BS5750 accreditation—a government endorsement of methods and quality—at several of its facilities. To mark the significant changes that had occurred at HMSO at this time, the organization took a new logo in April of 1990.

HMSO is not likely to make the final bound to privatization. The nature of its business, which includes numerous highly sensitive documents, is perhaps too vital to entrust to private enterprise. But the overwhelming majority of HMSO's work is commercial in nature, so it must remain a commercially competitive organization, albeit one that is an agency of the government.

Further Reading: Her Majesty's Stationery Office, The Story of the First 200 Years, 1786–1986, Hugh Barty-King, Her Majesty's Stationery Office, Norwich, England, 1986; Annual Reviews, HMSO, Norwich, England, 1987, 1988, 1989, 1990, 1991, 1992.

—John Simley

HINO MOTORS, LTD.

1-1 Hinodai, 3-chome
Hino-shi, Tokyo
Japan
(425) 86-5011
Fax: (425) 86-5038

Public Company
Incorporated: 1942
Employees: 8,347
Sales: ¥637.4 billion ($5.34 billion)
Stock Exchanges: Tokyo
SICs: 3711 Motor Vehicles and Car Bodies; 3714 Motor
    Vehicle Parts and Accessories

Hino Motors is Japan's largest truck manufacturer—leading a field that includes Mitsubishi, Isuzu, and Nissan Diesel—and is second in the world only to Daimler-Benz. Built on just a few product lines, such as medium and heavy trucks, buses, and specialty vehicles, Hino has maintained strong, steady growth, in both domestic and export sales. Hino is closely associated with the Toyota Motor Corporation, for whom it assembles pickup trucks on a large scale, and Toyota controls 11.2 percent of Hino's outstanding shares.

Hino Motors was founded in 1910 as part of the Tokyo Gas Industry Company. The unnamed division was set up to build trucks for the burgeoning Japanese industrial economy. After turning out only a limited number of handmade vehicles, Tokyo Gas began mass production in 1918 with its TGE ''A-Type'' truck. The ''A-Type'' was popular and remained the company's primary model for many years.

As other automotive manufacturers were established in Japan, the Tokyo Gas concern remained a modest operation, dealing mainly in local niche markets. As the pace of industrialization increased during the 1930s, many other Japanese automobile companies consolidated their operations through complex mergers. These mergers were made necessary by the growing need to rationalize production by maximizing economies of scale. Such mergers also reduced the field of competitors.

A similar consolidation occurred at Tokyo Gas in 1937, when it combined its automotive division with two other companies, the Automobile Industry Company, Ltd. and Kyodo Kokusan K.K.

The combined enterprise was given the new name Tokyo Automobile Industry Company.

By 1941 Japan's occupation of China had created vast new markets for industrial products. It had also prompted a strict and debilitating trade embargo from the United States. Rather than backing down when faced with this American pressure, the Japanese government continued a massive armament program that benefitted many industrial companies, including Tokyo Automobile. That year, reflecting further specialization and consolidation in the industry, the company changed its name to the Diesel Motor Industry Company, Ltd.

In 1942, with Japan at war with the United States and Britain, Diesel Motor was split into two companies. The larger of the two retained the original company's name (and later became Isuzu Motors), and the smaller was reincorporated as the Hino Heavy Industry Company, Ltd.

Hino's suburban Tokyo facilities were spared from the effects of the war until its final week. On August 1, 1945, during a massive American bombing raid, a single incendiary bomb hit the Hino factory. Employees on the site doused each other with water before running into burning buildings to fight the fire; their efforts prevented the fire from spreading to the main production facility.

By September, with the war over, the Hino plant had been converted into a military barracks for occupation forces. Plant director Shoji Okubo learned that, with Japan's railroads in ruins, the occupation authority had approved the construction of 1,500 trucks per month. He gathered what few employees remained and boldly laid out plans for the production of a new heavy truck, which he felt would be necessary for Japan's reconstruction.

Surprised by Okubo's grand plans for development in the midst of Tokyo's devastation, Hino employees called 300 fellow workers back from the rural towns to which they had moved to escape bombing. Able to muster only 16 designers, and lacking parts suppliers and subcontractors, Okubo nevertheless had soon developed a concept for a new truck. At 6.5 tons and 7 meters in length, the Hino T10-20 exceeded all Japanese size regulations. However, Okubo protested that occupation trucks twice that size were crawling all over Japan, and he was able to effect a change in the law.

Before production could commence, the company had to secure financing. Hino's accountant Ryoichi Takada personally gave bank officers plant tours. Impressed by the facility's size and lack of damage, and by Takada's warm personality, they approved massive loans to Hino.

The company then established a national sales network and found subcontractors, including Sawafuji Electric, Takebe Tekkosho, and Goto Gokin. Only a year after the war had ended, the first prototype rolled out of the factory and across Japan for a sales tour. Because it was equipped with a highly efficient diesel engine (and fuel was still strictly rationed), the T10-20 proved extremely popular. With the capacity to produce only 20 trucks per month, Hino was unable to keep pace with demand.

On the strength of the T10-20, Okubo laid plans for the development of a large diesel trailer bus. A prototype of the 96-passenger T11B-25 was completed in July of 1947. Supported by a highly effective public relations campaign, orders for the bus exceeded sales projections and provided pressure to expand the plant.

During this time, Hino was denied entry into the bond market by the government Bank of Japan, which argued that the automotive industry was speculative and had no future in Japan. During the intense effort to raise funds, Takada fell ill for several months with appendicitis, and Masashi Arakawa was left to appeal the company's case to the government, which he did successfully. The company began trading shares on over-the-counter markets on February 21, 1948, gaining a listing on the Tokyo Stock Exchange on May 16, 1949. Through successive share issues, Hino succeeded in quadrupling its capitalization.

In 1948, in an effort to improve customer service, Hino separated its marketing and engineering departments into two entities, the Hino Diesel Industry Company and Hino Diesel Sales. In May of 1950, with only ten percent of the domestic market share for trucks, Hino rolled out its new 7-liter TH10, a 10-ton single cab truck. Perfectly suited to meet increased demands for road freight capacity, the TH10 nearly doubled Hino's market share in only one year.

The outbreak of the Korean War in June of 1950 caused the United Nations command to deplete Japan's stocks of gasoline powered vehicles. Hino was persuaded by the government to help satisfy public demand for these vehicles by opening a new production line. This experience led Okubo to seriously consider production of an automobile of foreign design. Confident of the eventual emergence of an "automobile society" in Japan, Okubo was highly impressed by the utilitarian Volkswagen. As demand for foreign cars clearly was rising, Okubo put out the call for a foreign partner.

The call was answered by Renault, which proposed that Hino assemble its 4CV model in Japan. The partnership would prove ideal for Hino, which had hoped to build a strong export business on just such a car, but which had no experience in anything smaller than large diesel vehicles. The 4CV assembly plant went into operation in March of 1953. Intended as a family car, the 4CV soon became popular with taxi drivers, police, and the business community.

In December 1952 Hino introduced a new single-unit bus, the BD10/30 "Blue Ribbon," based on European designs featuring engines placed beneath the vehicle's floor. Sales increased steadily from 225 in 1952 to 1,385 in 1956.

During this time, Okubo was struck by the absence of Japanese heavy dump trucks on several large construction jobs. Concerned that Japan was being rebuilt with expensive foreign machinery, he ordered the development of a comparable dump truck that would cost half as much as foreign models.

After personally testing four different prototypes, Okubo settled on the 13.5-ton model ZG. He lobbied the Bank of Japan for a special bond issue to finance production. Again, he was forced to justify his case, and succeeded only after convincing the examiner that Hino's trucks would prevent the loss of precious foreign exchange. The ZG later became the most popular construction dump truck in Japan. In an effort to downplay the diesel side of its business, Hino changed its name to Hino Motors, Ltd. in 1959.

In 1961, after 16 years as head of Hino, Shoji Okubo retired. He was succeeded by Masanobu Matsukata, who immediately encountered a series of currency- and trade-related economic shocks. Hino, however, was largely insulated from the effects of these shocks by broad demand for its products.

Japanese demand for automobiles began to escalate in 1960, as massive nationwide highway projects were nearing completion. In addition, the government estimated that seven million of its country's licensed drivers did not own a car. It was this strong and little publicized domestic demand that prepared Hino and other manufacturers for expansion into export markets.

Matsukata knew that Hino would never become a leader in the automobile industry as long as it was relegated to building another company's designs. In 1961, with an eye toward abandoning the Renault model, Hino introduced its own design, the rear-engine Contessa 900, and began to study new mass production methods. The Contessa entered an extremely competitive market, proving to Matsukata that Hino was not yet prepared to go it alone.

During a tour of a Toyota plant, Matsukata noted that fewer Toyota workers were turning out more varieties of products than Hino. Consequently, he began a relationship with Toyota to adopt its methods and cooperate on the production of its new cars. In 1966, at the beginning of Japan's Izanagi economic boom, Hino formally linked its operations to Toyota. Having learned low cost pressing technology from Renault, Hino began producing parts for Toyota on a large scale.

Hino carefully studied the development of Japan's highway network, betting that highway freight traffic was bound to grow rapidly. It began development of larger 8-ton, and then 10- and 12-ton trucks, including the TC30 and KF series. In 1964, to shore up its product range, Hino introduced the smaller 3.5-ton KM series truck, known as the "Ranger."

In 1968, Hino held just over 17 percent of the Japanese truck market. That year, the company initiated Strategy V, an effort to increase its market share to 30 percent. Having achieved this level in 1971—collecting the Deming Prize in the process—Hino put forth another challenge, Strategy D, the aim of which was to increase market share to 35 percent. Hino also built several new facilities, including a new headquarters office and a car factory at Hamura.

In the early 1970s, the Japanese economy was buffeted by two economic crises that directly affected Hino. The first, in 1971, stemmed from the American abandonment of the gold standard. Then in 1973, as the economy began to recover, the Arab oil embargo quadrupled the price of gasoline. In 1974, at the height of the crisis, Matsukata retired from Hino. He was succeeded by Masashi Arakawa, whose first action was to implement cost reduction policies and press for completion of a new, more fuel efficient engine.

The "Red" engine (named for the engine blocks, which were painted red) was a completely redesigned diesel engine with better fuel economy. Later models featured fuel injection systems based on designs from the German company MAN. Hino also developed a new micro mixing system that sharply reduced harmful emissions. But despite these efforts, Japan's truck market remained extremely weak.

Noting that Japanese trucks were already more efficient than many European and American models, and believing that Hino models would be considerably more competitive in foreign markets, Arakawa laid plans for a massive export program. The company established a sales network mainly in Southeast Asia and a parts depot in Europe and Latin America and set a goal of exporting 30,000 trucks.

During the export boom, Hino began assembling pickup trucks and compact cars for Toyota on a large scale. Having abandoned its own consumer designs, Hino experienced strong growth from its subcontractor arrangement with Toyota, particularly as its models gained popularity in Southeast Asia for their high quality and reliability.

In 1977, building on its previous experience with buses, Hino began production of a new touring coach. Bus sales, however, remained only a small part of the company's business.

To meet increased demand for its trucks, Hino opened a new production facility at Nitta in 1980. New market conditions dictated that Japanese manufacturers offer broader product lines with smaller production lots. In addition to higher fuel efficiency and lower maintenance, customers were also demanding more environmentally safe engines. These challenges to designers were achieved slowly through the introduction of electronic controls and systems in Hino vehicles. But the process of uniting microengineered electronics with the larger systems on massive trucks proved, at first, difficult.

These problems were generally resolved in time for the introduction of Hino's newest truck model, the Super Dolphin, in May of 1981. This new truck featured a highly efficient EP100 engine, greatly improved aerodynamics, and a spring suspended cab that afforded drivers a much smoother ride. While these features added to the price of the model, strong sales soon justified the improvements, and allowed Hino to surpass its export goal with 31,000 units.

In 1982, Hino manufactured its one millionth vehicle. The company also laid plans to establish new offices in Pakistan and the United States. Amid rising labor costs, and unable to move truck production offshore as quickly as automobile manufacturers, Hino opted to establish a kit assembly plant in Taiwan, in conjunction with Kuozui Motors.

Although domestic sales continued to suffer from the effects of another oil shock in 1979, losses were offset by strong sales in Thailand, China, and Saudi Arabia. For the first time, export sales exceeded domestic sales. Meanwhile, in 1983, Toshio Fukazawa replaced Arakawa as president of Hino Motors. After only a short tenure, Fukazawa was succeeded by Tomio Futami.

Beginning in 1986, the appreciating value of the yen—from ¥240 to ¥120 on the dollar—seriously damaged previously reliable export demand. New Japanese economic policies helped Hino to stimulate domestic demand and, finally, this market began to recover strongly.

Recognizing that drivers had gained a strong voice in recommending purchases, and that the public had grown concerned with the inherent ugliness of large diesel vehicles, Hino began to steer toward the development of more user friendly, aesthetically appealing models. The effort to build a "beautiful truck" culminated with the introduction of the Super F series truck in July 1989.

During the early 1990s, however, with the Japanese and American economies in recession and slower growth in Asian markets, Hino encountered difficult times. Forced to implement another cost reduction strategy, the company managed to avoid layoffs and the cancellation of new projects, including its S'Elega touring bus and a heavy-duty truck, Super Dolphin PROFIA. Furthermore, strong business from Toyota helped Hino's financial situation to remain firm.

Principal Subsidiaries: Thai Hino Industry Co., Ltd.; Thai Hino Motor Sales, Ltd.; Pilipinas Hino, Inc. (Philippines); Hino Motors (Malaysia) Sdn. Bhd.; Hino Diesel Trucks (U.S.), Inc.; Hino Engine Service (U.S.) Corporation; Kuozui Motors, Ltd. (Taiwan; affiliate); P.T. Hino Indonesia Manufacturing; Hino Diesel Trucks (Canada) Ltd.; Hinopak Motors Limited (Pakistan).

Further Reading: "On the Road Again," *The Economist,* November 26, 1988; "Hino Motors," *Diamond's Japan Business Directory,* 1991; "Hello Hino—Challenge of the Times," *Hino Forum,* vols. 84–88, Company Publications, 1992; *Hino Today,* Company Publication, 1992; *Corporate Profile,* Company Publication, 1992; Hino Motors Annual Report, 1992.

—John Simley

HOME BOX OFFICE INC.

1100 Avenue of the Americas
New York, New York 10036
U.S.A.
(212) 512-1000
Fax: (212) 512-5517

Public Company
Incorporated: 1972
Employees: 1,500
Sales: $800 million
Stock Exchanges: Boston Midwest New York Philadelphia-
   Baltimore
SICs: 4841 Cable & Other Pay Television Services; 7812
   Motion Picture & Video Production

Home Box Office Inc. (HBO) is the largest pay-TV channel in
the United States, with a subscriber base of about 17 million and
programming that includes sports events, comedy, Hollywood
films, and self-produced films. It is a subsidiary of Time Warner
Inc.

Home Box Office was founded by Time Inc. in 1972 to offer
cable television service. HBO bought the rights to recent films
and transmitted them to local systems via satellite and microwave relays. Its service was distributed by the local cable
operators, typically costing subscribers $6 a month, of which
HBO received $3.50. HBO management thought of themselves
as editorial marketers, selling its programming the way Time
sold magazines.

HBO grew slowly in its first years, as the nascent cable industry
struggled to get off the ground. Cable was hampered by market
fragmentation, lack of infrastructure, and tough federal regulations, some of them sponsored by the major television networks, which feared that cable could eventually steal much of
their audience and revenue.

During the mid-1970s the cable industry laid the groundwork
for rapid growth: it expanded its infrastructure through such
populous areas as New York City and the suburbs of Boston,
won a series of court victories that removed many Federal
restrictions, and won rate increases from local governments.
Pay-TV customers, those buying additional cable services such
as HBO, grew from 50,000 in 1974 to about l.5 million in 1978.
HBO won greater latitude in pursuing customers in 1977 when a

federal ruling lifted restrictions on the choice of movies and
sports available on pay-TV. HBO quickly became one of the
primary engines driving the growth of the cable industry. Cable
systems operators hooked up thousands of people for basic
services who were primarily interested in getting HBO.

HBO made its first profit in 1977. It lost tens of thousands of
customers in 1978, however, as a result of a move by its chief
rival, Showtime, which was challenging HBO head on for the
cable film audience. Showtime struck a deal with Teleprompter,
the largest cable systems operator in the United States, which
resulted in Teleprompter's customers receiving Showtime instead of HBO.

HBO worked hard on its programming, lining up enough films
to make it the premiere pay-TV outlet for commercial films. It
also began its *On Location* comedy series and *The Young
Comedians Show,* one of the first television spots for comedians
such as Robin Williams and Pee-wee Herman.

In 1978 Time spent $145 million to buy American Television &
Communications Corp., the second-largest cable systems operator in the United States, hoping a large number of its 675,000
customers would subscribe to HBO. HBO continued to expand,
and as it did it was able to pay higher prices per film than its
competitors, winning better films and more subscribers. Its
financial resources allowed it to purchase a block of 40 MGM/
United Artists films all at once, for instance, paying about $35
million. It also began investing in the preproduction financing
of movies in exchange for exclusive pay-TV rights. This pre-
buying was risky; HBO was paying in advance for the rights to
movies that might prove unpopular. Nonetheless, the practice
angered movie studios, which felt that HBO was intruding on
their turf, and some of them began looking for a way into the
cable TV industry. Some studios warned that HBO would drive
many film studios out of business and control the film industry.
Though such fears later proved unfounded, they demonstrated
the depth of concern attached to a new medium whose ultimate
potential remained a mystery.

In 1980 HBO introduced a second channel called Cinemax. It
was priced lower than HBO and was geared to compete with
Showtime. Viacom, Showtime's parent company, later charged
that Cinemax was priced below cost as a way to drive Showtime
out of business.

By 1982 HBO had 9.8 million subscribers, nearly 50 percent of
all pay-TV subscribers, and earned $100 million on sales of
$440 million. It was about three times as big as its nearest
competitor, Showtime. This size advantage contributed to
HBO's bottom line. For example, it paid about $1.4 million for
the hit film *Raging Bull,* or about 15 cents per subscriber.
Although Showtime paid less for the film, $1 million, that
worked out to more than 30 cents per subscriber. When *Star
Wars* went on the block in 1982, it matched a Showtime offer of
$1 per subscriber, but insisted on price concessions on less
popular films made by Twentieth-Century Fox.

At the end of 1982 HBO worked out a deal with Columbia
Pictures and CBS to create Tri-Star Pictures, the first major new
U.S. film studio in 40 years. Each company was to contribute up
to $100 million to the venture and HBO received the pay-TV
rights. By 1983 HBO was producing made-for-television mov-

ies and working on its own comedy programs, and had 13.4 million subscribers. Some observers wondered if it was becoming a fourth television network. But at the beginning of 1984, the growth of the cable industry as a whole slowed dramatically. Part of the cause was lingering infrastructure problems. New cable systems had not yet been built in such major markets as Chicago, Philadelphia, Detroit, and Baltimore. Other causes cited were rising cable rates at a time when more and more consumers owned video cassette recorders and could rent their own films. HBO had also become complacent in negotiating contracts, while competitors moved quickly. As a result, HBO's share of the pay-TV market slipped from 50.4 percent in June 1983 to 48.1 percent in June 1984, while its profit margins began eroding.

Parent Time Inc. responded by forcing out HBO chairman Frank J. Biondi, replacing him with Michael J. Fuchs. Fuchs cut HBO's staff by 125 employees and embarked on a $20 million advertising campaign by BBOO, New York, to polish HBO's image. He also renegotiated contracts with Columbia Pictures and Tri-Star for the broadcasting of films and cut expense accounts and other costs.

As a result of the contract renegotiations, HBO gave up exclusive rights to many films. Rival Showtime, meanwhile, was trumpeting its new policy of showing films exclusively or not showing them at all. Previously the two firms had both showed some films exclusively, but shared many others. As a result of this policy, Showtime won exclusive rights to several popular films. HBO management was angered, feeling that they had already learned that exclusive rights cost more than they were worth and that Showtime's move had increased the prices of acquiring even limited rights. Showtime's strategy also pushed HBO into negotiating for exclusive rights for more films than it otherwise would have done. Some industry analysts felt that the price of buying films for pay-TV should be decreasing, since the popularity of video cassette recorders had lowered their worth.

Despite the cable television slump, HBO had 14.6 million subscribers in 1985 and sales of about $800 million. Early the following year it began to scramble the signals it used to broadcast its programming to cable-system operators. Until then anyone with a satellite dish could tune in HBO for free.

Continuing to stock its film library, HBO bought the rights to 125 Warner Brothers films for five years for $600 million in 1986, also buying the rights to 72 films by MGM/UA Entertainment for four years. In 1987 it bought the rights to 85 Paramount Pictures films over a five-year period.

In 1989 Viacom filed a $2.4 billion antitrust lawsuit against HBO. Viacom's Showtime alleged that HBO was trying to put it out of business by intimidating cable systems that carried Showtime and trying to corner the market on Hollywood films to prevent rivals from showing any. The suit attracted wide attention, generating negative publicity for the cable industry at a time when the U.S. Congress was considering the re-regulation of cable. Part of the reason the anti-trust charges attracted so much attention was because they were being delivered by former top HBO employees. Frank J. Biondi had gone on to become Viacom's president and chief executive officer, while

Showtime's president, Winston H. Cox, was also a former HBO executive.

In 1989, hoping to branch out, HBO announced plans for a 24-hour all-comedy channel. Comedy was experiencing a popularity boom in the United States, and polls of cable subscribers showed enthusiasm for the idea. The Comedy Channel began with 6 million subscribers in November 1989, though industry analysts felt it would need 20 million to attract enough advertising to survive. Critics offered harsh appraisals of Comedy Channel's fare, citing in particular the way HBO strung together excerpts from stand-up routines, sitcoms and movie clips. Many cable operators were resistant to offering Comedy Channel at all. HBO moved quickly to entice them into buying ownership stakes as incentive to get the new channel wider availability. In April 1991 Comedy Channel suffered another setback when Viacom's HA! began broadcasting old sitcoms in their entirety, eschewing Comedy Channel's practice of showing excerpts. Most industry analysts believed that only one of the channels would survive. Many cable operators did not sign up for either, waiting to see which would get more support.

HBO invested heavily in advertising to win subscribers to its new and existing services, spending about $38 million in 1990 alone. However, both Comedy Channel and HA! were struggling, and in a surprise move, HBO and Viacom agreed to merge them into Comedy Central late in 1990.

In the meantime, Broadcast Music Incorporated, a performance-rights society, sued HBO over the rates it was paying for the use of BMI-protected music. The suit was settled in January 1991 when HBO agreed to raise the rate it paid for its blanket license to 15 cents per subscriber per year, up from 12 cents.

One of the most common complaints subscribers had about pay-TV channels was that they only showed one film at a time, so that if one had already seen it, one had nothing to watch. The cancellation rate for HBO was about four percent a month, or about 850,000 of its 17 million subscribers per year, and this lack of options was believed to be an important factor. To hang on to subscribers, HBO announced in 1991 that it would convert HBO and Cinemax to multichannel services. Each network would broadcast different programming simultaneously on three different channels. Many cable systems had no extra channels to offer, but HBO management hoped new technologies would expand the number of channels available. Because it had to wait for fiber-optic lines to be installed and data-compression techniques to become more widely available, however, some industry observers estimated it would be three to five years before these multiple channels were widely available.

In August 1992 the Viacom suit was finally settled out of court, having cost both sides tens of millions of dollars in legal fees. Time Warner, HBO's parent company, agreed to pay Viacom $75 million and buy a Viacom cable system in Milwaukee for $95 million, $10 million more than it was worth at the time according to the *Wall Street Journal.* Time Warner agreed to more widely distribute Showtime and the Movie Channel on Time Warner's cable systems, the second-largest in the United States. The two sides also agreed to a joint marketing campaign to try and revive the image of cable, which was again in a slump. HBO lost about 300,000 subscribers in 1991, leaving it with a total of 17.3 million. Cinemax had 6.3 million subscribers.

Further Reading: "Cable-TV Dangles New Lures," *Business Week,* December 1, 1973; "Pay-TV: Is It a Viable Alternative?" *Forbes,* May 1, 1978; "The Race to Dominate the Pay-TV Market," *Business Week,* October 2, 1978; "How HBO Dominates Pay-TV," *Business Week,* September 20, 1982; "A New Shooter in Tinseltown," *Newsweek,* December 13, 1982; Waters, Harry F., "Can HBO Change the Show?" *Newsweek,* May 23, 1983; Lindsey, Robert, "Home Box Office Moves in on Hollywood," *New York Times Magazine,* June 12, 1983; "Pay-TV: Even HBO's Growth Is Slowing," *Business Week,* July 9, 1984; "Can a New Chief Change the Picture at HBO?" *Business Week,* October 29, 1984; Trachtenberg, Jeffrey A., "Changing Reels," *Forbes,* May 20, 1985; Trachtenberg, Jeffrey A., "Mea Culpa, Mea Culpa," *Forbes,* December 16, 1985; Block, Alex Ben, "Shoot-Out Time in Pay TV," *Forbes,* September 22, 1986; Waters, Harry F., "Talk about a Running Gag," *Newsweek,* May 29, 1989; Kneale, Dennis, "HBO Vows to Stick with Comedy Channel and Seek Operators Willing to Buy Stake," *Wall Street Journal,* March 6, 1990; Cox, Meg, "Time Warner's HBO, Broadcast Music Settle Suit over Performance Rights," *Wall Street Journal,* January 11, 1991; King, Thomas R., "HBO to Offer Multiple Choice for Tuning In," *Wall Street Journal,* May 9, 1991; Roberts, Johnnie L., "Time Warner, Viacom Settle HBO Suit, Clearing a Cloud from Cable's Horizon," *Wall Street Journal,* August 21, 1992.

—Scott M. Lewis

HUFFY CORPORATION

7701 Byers Road
Miamisburg, Ohio 45342
U.S.A.
(513) 866-6251
Fax: (513) 865-2811

Public Company
Incorporated: 1928 as Huffman Manufacturing Company
Employees: 6,300
Sales: $680 million
Stock Exchanges: New York
SICs: 3751 Motorcycles, Bicycles & Parts; 3949 Sporting &
Athletic
Goods Nec; 7389 Business Services Nec

Huffy Corporation, a diversified manufacturer of bicycles, bicycle equipment, infant carriers and strollers, basketball equipment, and lawn and garden tools, grew out of the Huffman Manufacturing Company, which was founded in 1924. Founder Horace M. Huffman, Sr., learned the manufacturing business from his father, George P. Huffman, who owned the Davis Sewing Machine Company from 1887 to 1925. Taking advantage of the growing automotive industry, Horace Huffman's young company made equipment that could be used in service stations. Working out of a factory on Gilbert Avenue in a noisy section of Dayton, Ohio, near the Pennsylvania Railroad tracks, the first Huffman employees are credited with inventing a rigid spout that could be used to dispense motor oil from 50-gallon drums. The company grew quickly through the 1920s and 1930s and its line of service station equipment expanded. When it incorporated in 1928, the company posted earnings of $3,000.

In 1934 Horace Huffman announced plans to manufacture bicycles after sensing that they would become a popular mode of transportation during the Depression. In the beginning, production rates hovered at 12 bikes per day. Within two years, this rate increased to 200 daily. However, the company was still not producing fast enough to keep up with its competition and Huffman suffered several setbacks in the beginning. The Firestone Tire and Rubber Company was a primary bike customer, but in 1938 Huffman lost a major portion of the account because it could not keep up with Firestone's demand.

But the solution was not far away. Two years earlier, Horace Huffman, Jr., who was known by the diminutive ''Huff,'' had

joined the company on a full-time basis. After short stints as service manager and sales manager, he became works manager and converted the production process to a straight-line conveyerized assembly line. It was just the edge the company needed, and by 1940, bicycle production doubled and sales figures were nearing the $1.5 million mark. Huffman's improved production rate caught the eye of the Western Auto Company, which became a major customer, and also brought Firestone back into the fold.

The outbreak of World War II necessitated a shift in production. The company joined the thousands of other businesses that were vying for government contracts, and was able to secure an order for primers, an artillery shell part. The increased business brought Huffman's sales to nearly $2.8 million in 1942. The following year, the federal government placed an order for 4,000 bicycles. At this point, much of the work was being done by women who were filling the void left by the vast numbers of men who had been inducted into the armed forces. The later part of the war period proved to be difficult as the production of consumer products in all industries virtually ceased and Horace, Sr., suffered a fatal heart attack in 1945.

The younger Huffman was elected president and immediately had to face the challenge of sustaining production in the postwar period with limited supplies. The government's allocation program, he knew, would not provide enough materials to allow the company to compete at its pre-war levels. After attending a seminar on ''Work Simplification,'' Huff taught the procedure to his managers and then held a similar workshop for the company's major suppliers. By meeting the problem head-on, Huffman was able to help suppliers increase their own output and to raise its production levels. For two years, the company was able to run two shifts a day without experiencing the traditional slowdown during the winter months. Sales for each of the two years exceeded $10 million.

Then, in 1949, the company ran into the postwar recession. However, two developments allowed the company to survive. First, the Huffy convertible bicycle was introduced and was instantly popular. The bike also brought the name Huffy to the forefront of the bicycle industry. The second development occurred as a result of the company's search for a product that could be manufactured during the winter months. The decision to produce lawnmowers was announced in December of 1949.

As a result, the company quickly outgrew its physical plants, and in the early 1950s Huffman acquired a building in Delphos, Ohio, and moved the Automotive Service Equipment division to that location. New facilities were built in Celina, Ohio, to house the bicycle and lawnmower divisions. The Dayton manufacturing plant on Gilbert Avenue was closed and the general offices were moved to Davis Avenue. In 1959 Huffman opened its bicycle plant in Azusa, California.

By 1960 Huffman was the third largest bike manufacturer in the United States. In 1962 Horace Huffman, Jr., was named chairman and Frederick C. Smith became president and CEO. Smith had been materials manager during the crucial postwar period and was credited with strengthening the company's relationship with its suppliers.

In 1964 Huffman expanded its Outdoor Power Equipment division with the acquisition of Diele & McGuire Manufacturing. It was not an entirely successful expansion, however, and the division continued to lose money over the next decade. That same year, the Huffman corporate offices were moved to their current location in Miamisburg.

Huffman went public with its listing on the American Stock Exchange in 1968 and sales reached $42 million the following year. Stuart Northrup, a former Singer Sewing Machine executive, replaced Smith as president in 1972. By 1973 Huffman employed 2,500 workers at five locations.

Throughout the 1960s and early 1970s, Huffman enjoyed continued growth as the market for adult bicycles grew. More and more adults were turning to bikes for exercise and as a means to cut energy costs. Until the end of the 1960s, nearly half of all bicycles in the United States were sold through small independent bike shops that offered personal customer service. In the 1970s, the introduction of mass merchandise retail chains that stocked large quantities of consumer goods and sold them at discount prices opened up a new market for bike sales. Because British-owned Raleigh Cycle was firmly entrenched as the leading supplier to the independent shop owner, Huffman set its sights on the retail chains and developed a 10-speed that required the bare minimum of assembly and service.

The company's growth trend hit a snag in 1974, however, as a new recessionary period brought on an industry-wide slump. From its peak in 1973, bicycle sales dropped 50 percent by 1975. Huffman was forced to close its Celina plant for two months and lay off 25 percent of its workers.

Prior to the recession, foreign competition was also putting pressure on American bike makers. In 1972 foreign imports accounted for 37 percent of the U.S. market. The devalued U.S. dollar, however, cut this share to 15 percent by the end of the 1970s. New federal regulations setting safety standards for bicycles also cut into the sale of foreign models. As the industry revived itself toward the end of the 1970s, Huffman decided to take an aggressive marketing stance. Children again became the primary focus of the bike industry and Huffman introduced a new flashy, motocross-style bike called Thunder Trail. Designed to look like a motorcycle with waffle handle-grips, knobby tires, and racing-like number plates on the front, the new models also sported bright, jazzy colors and decals. Not content to settle for what they hoped *might* sell, Huffman held focus groups in shopping centers to determine which features were the most popular. In addition, a greater portion of advertising dollars was spent on television commercials, particularly during the hours when children's programs aired.

The popularity of the Thunder Trail bike made Huffman was the number one producer of bicycles in the United States by 1977 and all of the laid-off workers were called back. Net sales for 1977 were $130 million, a 21 percent increase from the previous year.

Although Huffman was still the leading producer of gasoline cans, oil can spouts, oil filters, and jack stands, the Automotive Equipment Division was only accounting for 10 percent of the company's sales. Bikes and bike accessories accounted for an overwhelming 90 percent. The Outdoor Power Equipment division, which had been struggling for years in the lawnmower market, was finally sold in 1975. The sale brought in a much-needed $10 million in cash. Realizing the need to diversify, Huffman acquired Frabill Manufacturing, a maker of fishing and basketball equipment, in 1977.

Until now, half of Huffman's bicycles were sold under private labels. By the end of the 1970s, however, the company decided to devote more energy to promoting its own brand name. Part of this effort included the decision, in 1977, to change the company name to Huffy Corporation. During this period, Huffy's management also opted not to enter the moped-manufacturing field because of doubts about the motorized bike's potential in the United States. Instead, $5 million was spent to expand existing production facilities.

In 1980 Huffy posted its fifth straight year of record earnings and announced plans to open a third plant in Ponca City, Oklahoma. However, despite its strong financial position, Huffy was not immune to the problems that most American businesses experienced in the 1980s. For one thing, production costs were rapidly increasing. In 1982 Harry A. Shaw III was named CEO and immediately embarked on the unpopular road to plant closings and layoffs. Shaw spearheaded the consolidation of all bike manufacturing operations into the Celina plant and sold the Automotive Products Division for cash. Huffy then invested more than $15 million in advanced robotics and new production equipment. The changes resulted in an increase in production capacity by 5,000 bikes a day and a 14 percent cut in production costs. Another $15 million was earmarked to improve computer-generated manufacturing in the bike plant by 1991.

A licensing, sales, and manufacturing agreement with Raleigh Cycle was also cemented in 1982, giving the company the opportunity to tap the high-specification bike market. However, the venture did not prove to be an asset and Huffy sold its rights in 1988.

With bike sales still accounting for 90 percent of the company's sales, the need to diversify was as evident as ever. In 1982 Huffy acquired Gerico, a maker of infant car seats and strollers, and YLC Enterprises, a provider of product assembly services for retail consumer purchases. The former now operates as Gerry Baby Products and the latter as Huffy Service First. Washington Inventory Service, a nationwide inventory-taking service, was acquired in 1988. By the end of the 1980s, bike sales dropped to 66 percent of the company's total sales revenues.

Throughout the 1980s, Huffy's engineers in the company's U.S. Cycling Federation Technical Development Center continued to develop innovations that would keep Huffy on the cutting edge of the racing industry. One development was to use composites to make disc wheels for racing bikes. Disc wheels are often preferred by racers because they eliminate the air turbulence caused by spoke wheels and can cut drag by 30 percent. The use of composite materials resulted in an even lighter-weight wheel. Refinements made by Huffy engineers allowed them to reduce the wheel weight from 5.5 lbs. to 2.5 lbs.

In 1990 Huffy acquired Black & Decker's stake in True Temper Hardware and capital stock in True Temper Ltd. in Ireland for $55 million. A manufacturer of garden and lawn tools, the company claims approximately 30 percent of the market.

Huffy plans to achieve $1 billion in annual net sales by the mid-1990s by devoting approximately 50 percent of its efforts to recreation and leisure time products, 20 percent to juvenile products, 20 percent in services to the retail industry, and 10 percent to other new consumer products. A commitment to diversification is evident in its pledge that no single business should contribute more than 50 percent of total operating profit.

Principal Subsidiaries: Huffy Bicycles; Huffy Sports; Huffy Service First; Gerry Baby Products Company; Snugli; Washington Inventory Service; True Temper Hardware.

Further Reading: ''Fifty Years of Growth Took Teamwork,'' *Huffman Highlights,* Miamisburg, The Huffman Manufacturing Company, 1973; ''Motocross, New Type Bicycle Puts Huffman Mfg. in High Gear,'' *Barron's,* August 23, 1976; ''Huffy Pedals Into First Place,'' *Sales & Marketing Management,* January 1978; ''Huffy Puts New Spin in the Bicycle Business,'' *Business Week,* October 10, 1977; Hannon, Kerry. ''Easy Rider,'' *Forbes,* November 16, 1987.

—Mary McNulty

HUNT OIL COMPANY

1445 Ross Ave.
Dallas, Texas 74202
U.S.A.
(214) 978-8000
Fax: (214) 978-8888

Private Company
Incorporated: 1934 as Hunt Production Company
Sales: $900 million
Employees: 1,900
SICs: 1311 Crude Petroleum & Natural Gas; 2911 Petroleum
Refining

Hunt Oil Company is among the nation's largest privately owned oil and gas producers. Known as the company that made its founder and original owner, H. L. Hunt, one of the wealthiest men in America in the 1940s, it has continued to make news in the 1980s with its success in high-risk overseas exploration at a time when other independent oil companies were staying closer to home.

H. L. (Haroldson Lafayette) Hunt was already one of the most successful independent oilmen before founding Hunt Oil. Originally a real estate speculator, he first became involved in the oil business in Arkansas and then Louisiana in the 1920s. His strategy was to drill in already known areas, jumping into lease-buying action immediately after a discovery was made. Hunt achieved historic success in November 1930 at age 41 when, together with a partner, Pete Lake, he bought 5000 acres in East Texas belonging to wildcatter Columbus ''Dad'' Joiner, shortly after a single-well oil discovery of which big oil companies were skeptical. Hunt secretly employed an oil scout to monitor test results at a nearby well and, before Joiner realized the full extent of the discovery, persuaded the wildcatter to sell all his leases for $1.34 million. Hunt paid Joiner $30,000 in cash with the rest to be paid out future production. Subsequent wells proved that Hunt had purchased rights to not only some of the richest ground in the new East Texas oil field, but to the largest single oil deposit in the continental United States (and, at that time, in the whole world), totaling 140,000 productive acres. This business deal made Hunt the largest independent in East Texas and became the financial cornerstone of Hunt Production Company, which would soon become Hunt Oil, based in nearby Tyler, Texas.

With the newly acquired valuable property, Hunt was able to secure a bank loan to expand and upgrade his equipment to make the land productive. Within a month after the Joiner deal, he founded Panola Pipeline Company and was already supplying crude petroleum from his new oil wells. By 1934, Hunt Production Company, which already had 229 wells and was still drilling on its 5000 acres, had produced 7.5 million barrels. In 1935, the company was grossing $3 million a year. At this time, Hunt's lead over the smaller independents widened, as his company was large enough to reap the benefits of the Connolly Hot Oil Act of 1935, which regulated pumping output in order to conserve oil reservoirs and ground pressure. Hunt Production, like the major companies, had sufficient acreage leased so that it could pump oil from wells spread apart.

In 1936, Hunt split with Lake, who had held 20 percent from the Joiner deal, and incorporated his holdings under the new name of Hunt Oil Company. With assets at the time worth about $20 million, Hunt Oil was henceforth solely owned by H. L. Hunt and other members of his family. Hunt soon started a subsidiary, Penrod Drilling, composed of a fleet of eleven steam-powered land rigs to both provide his own drilling needs and to be contracted out to others. He also diversified into the refining business by buying 50 percent of the nearby Excelsior Refinery for $150,000 and renaming it the Parade Gasoline Company.

At the end of 1937, Hunt Oil moved its headquarters to downtown Dallas. The East Texas oil field no longer the company's only center of activity, Hunt Oil managed operations in Louisiana and Arkansas in addition to other parts of Texas. During this time, the company also became involved in international marketing, making a barter deal with Germany of oil for steel drill pipe and exporting oil to Japan through a California trading company. Closer to home, H. L. Hunt purchased 7000 acres of farmland, launching Hunt Oil's continual sideline of agricultural enterprises, which have included a cattle ranch.

During World War II, the increased demand for oil led to the opening of new offices for Hunt Oil, which produced a total of over 100 million barrels during the period from 1941 to 1945, averaging 60,000 barrels a day. Following the war, Hunt Oil was able to maintain high output through expanded operations. It opened a refinery in Tuscaloosa, Alabama, and started a chain of gasoline stations in Alabama and Louisiana under the name Parade. Hunt Oil explored for oil under the names Hunt Oil and its subsidiary Placid Oil Company, drilled for oil under the name Penrod, and transported oil under the name of the Panola Pipeline. The company also acted as an umbrella corporation that provided accounting and other services for the rest of the Hunt family enterprises, which encompassed scores of separate entities, companies, partnerships, and trusts in several states, and which were spread out among the members of H. L. Hunt's families. ''A maze of interlocking and interdependent relationships, the Hunt corporate structure was confusing even to employees hired to help operate it,'' wrote Hunt biographer Harry Hurt.

Beginning in the 1950s, H. L. Hunt began to entrust more responsibility to top associates and to his sons from his first marriage. Ownership of Penrod Drilling, which possessed about 25 drilling rigs and was worth over $25 million by the 1960s, had been transferred to three of his sons in 1948. Placid Oil also came to be managed by the children of Hunt's first marriage, and, in the early 1960s, had production double that of Hunt Oil. As H. L. Hunt became less involved with the oil business, he began devoting more energy to a food and drug subsidiary of Hunt Oil, HLH Products, which he started in 1960—partly as a means to integrate his vast farmland holdings. This food division continuously lost money, however, partly due to being overextended with too many product lines (up to 1340), but also because of problems with salesmanship, management, sponsorship ties to conservative political media, and even embezzlement.

In the early 1960s, Hunt Oil's production began to level off. Although by the early 1960s production was estimated at 65,000 barrels a day—the same it had been in the late 1940s—the increase in the price of oil meant that revenues were still climbing. Wells 20 to 30 years old were declining in production, while additional production from new wells was barely offsetting the depletion of the old fields. Moreover, these new wells were being drilled by subsidiary companies and not Hunt Oil itself. For the first time since Hunt Oil's inception in 1936, the company's income was based solely on wells that had been found in past years. One reason for decreased drilling by Hunt Oil was its financial obligation to cover the losses of HLH Products, which by 1969 had totaled more than $30 million—averaging $4 million per year.

Consequently, in early 1971, H. L. Hunt auctioned off nearly all of the property of HLH Products for $9 million, leaving only the drug and cosmetics plant in Dallas which continued to do business under the name H. L. Hunt Sales. As a result of the sale, Hunt Oil could afford to resume drilling and made a recovery. Another revenue boost at the beginning of the 1970s was the company's participation in the five-member consortium headed by Getty Oil, which in 1969 won a lease on Alaska's North Slope. Hunt Oil invested $50 million for a one-fifth share, thus becoming partial owner of one of the last great oil fields in North America. Its original investment was returned many times over. These successes, however, were no longer under H. L. Hunt's leadership. For some time already his sons Herbert and Bunker, as vice-presidents, and his nephew Tom Hunt, production manager, had become the real operators of Hunt Oil.

Upon H. L. Hunt's death in November 1974, his share of Hunt Oil—80 percent—passed to his second wife, while its management went to their son Ray, leaving the children from his first marriage with 18½ percent. Two of the latter, Herbert and Bunker, who were still vice-presidents of Hunt Oil, were already becoming increasingly involved in their own business operations, while Ray, who had been employed by Hunt Oil since graduating from college in 1965, had become the one most involved with the management of Hunt Oil. Herbert and Bunker decided to form their own independent oil company, Hunt Energy, from the subsidiaries of Hunt Oil they owned, leaving Ray to become president of Hunt Oil in February 1975. Two years later, Ray obtained the remaining shares of Hunt Oil owned by his half-brothers in exchange for a specified cluster of Hunt Oil properties, including oil leases, a pipeline in North Dakota, and Florida timberlands.

After his half-brothers split off from Hunt Oil, Ray Hunt modernized the company, hiring new managers and consolidating the diverse enterprises that remained with his branch of the family: oil and gas, timber and farm properties, H. L. Hunt Sales, and his own real estate companies of Hunt Investment and Woodbine Development Company. He introduced new methods of management and operating efficiency, instituted new medical benefits and pension plans for employees, and elevated salary scales.

Concentrating once again on the oil business, Ray Hunt hired new geologists and gave Hunt Oil a bigger exploration budget. The headquarter's staff increased from 50 to 200 by the end of the 1970s, and within a few years of taking control, Hunt had increased the area of offshore drilling leases from 100,000 to 1 million acres. The value of domestic oil reserves under Hunt's control increased from $100 million to $300 million in five years, also due in part to the sudden increase in oil prices caused by the Arab oil embargo of 1973. He also became involved in other facets of the energy business by making a deal with Dallas-based Energy Resources to provide drilling technology for uranium mining. Under Ray Hunt, Hunt Oil increased its annual revenue by 300 percent to $750 million by 1990.

The main contributor to this phenomenal regrowth of Hunt Oil from the late 1970s onward was its good luck with new overseas drilling ventures. Up to this point, all of Hunt Oil's production, unlike that of its former subsidiary Placid Oil, had been only in the United States. Although previous attempts at foreign ventures had been made, it was not until 1976 that Hunt Oil got involved in foreign exploration. A representative of the Sabine Corporation, a small Dallas-based oil company, was seeking a buyer for its 15 percent stake in a British North Sea exploration led by Mesa Petroleum for a price of $50,000. The representative first tried to approach Bunker Hunt at Hunt Energy but, not finding him in, went instead to the neighboring office of Ray Hunt, who decided to buy the stake. The Beatrice Field in the North Sea turned out to contain a total of 150 million barrels, more than doubling the reserves belonging to Hunt Oil. With oil prices rising in the late 1970s the value of this holding grew to more than $500 million. "We were in the club now. It allowed us the vehicle to quickly establish ourselves in the international arena," Ray Hunt told the New York Times Magazine.

By 1980, Hunt Oil's leases overseas had reached 21.9 million acres, including interests in Australia, Portugal, and South Korea. The company was even trying to gain an offshore lease from China, although talks broke off without an agreement. Hunt Oil's strategy with foreign exploration has been to look for oil in less-developed regions of the world, even if politically unstable, focusing on high-risk, high-return investments. Then, after a discovery is made, the company forms joint-venture partnerships to absorb the cost of drilling development wells. Hunt Oil has been one of the few companies to do well in out-of-the-way foreign sites, due to several factors. First, it is large enough to finance its own exploration operations without help from the larger oil corporations. Second, its private ownership structure allows it to pursue higher risk, longer-term investments which shareholders of a publicly traded company might not tolerate. In yet another advantage over major corporations, foreign governments in some cases may be reluctant to work with large corporations perceived to represent the "Western monopoly."

Hunt Oil's most profitable success of the 1980s was in Yemen, where it was responsible for the country's first oil discovery. In 1981 Hunt Oil received a production-sharing contract from the government of North Yemen to drill for oil within a 5000 square-mile concession. According to the contract's terms, the Yemeni government would initially keep half of the oil, its share increasing as production increased. With its first well, Hunt Oil in January 1984 discovered the Alif Field, an oil basin measuring more than four million acres in a vast desert containing estimated reserves of 400 million barrels of recoverable oil. "North Yemen will mean as much to Hunt in the 1980s and beyond as the purchase of Dad Joiner's oil rights in East Texas meant to H. L. Hunt in the 1930s," Jim Oberwetter, Hunt Oil government affairs director, told the *Dallas Business Courier* in 1986.

While Hunt Oil acted alone in the exploration and drilling of the Yemeni find, it signed on partners to help with the production. Sales of shares allowed Hunt to recover almost all of its investment costs by early 1988. In 1985, Exxon bought a 49 percent share in a venture to build a refinery and a pipeline, while a consortium of South Korean companies purchased another 24.5 percent share. The following year, Hunt Oil began construction on a $300-million, 263-mile pipeline from the Alif Field refinery to the port of Hodeida on the Red Sea, across three mountain ranges and through territory controlled by sometimes unruly tribes. The line, with a 200,000-barrel-per-day capacity, was completed in December 1987, whereupon Hunt Oil made the first oil shipments out of the country after an investment of more than $600 million. By the following year, Hunt Oil was delivering an estimated 150,000 barrels a day to tankers. By December 1990, Hunt produced more than 100 million barrels of oil from Yemen, and in 1991 had a staff of 220 that produced $100 million for the year. Although the refinery and pipeline operated by Hunt and financed by Exxon will eventually revert to the Yemeni government, Hunt Oil has drilled subsequent successful wells in Yemen beyond the Alif Field and offshore in the Red Sea.

Hunt Oil hoped to duplicate its success in North Yemen with two new oil and gas exploration programs in Jordan and Chile in 1988, signing production sharing agreements with authorities in each country. Although no oil was found in either country by 1992, Hunt Oil continued to drill in new places near the border of Bolivia and Peru into 1993. Elsewhere in South America, Hunt Oil obtained exploration rights to property in Guyana in 1991 after a Canadian competitor actually found oil but withdrew, believing the jungle site lacking commercial potential. In another distant country and after several years of negotiations, Hunt Oil received exploration rights with a production sharing agreement to more than 7 million acres in southern Laos.

In response to Hunt Oil's rapidly expanding oil exploration activities, a reorganization of the company was announced in July 1986. The restructuring included the formation of a new holding company, Hunt Consolidated, under which all the firm's profit centers, including Hunt Oil, became subsidiaries. A new president was named for Hunt Oil—the first non-member of the Hunt family—while Ray Hunt, owner of Hunt Consolidated, remained as chairman. In a press release, Ray Hunt stated that the growth of the company "necessitated a streamlining of our corporate holdings" in order "to operate efficiently." In 1991, as part of a strategy to shed businesses not related to its core real estate and energy exploration and production units, Hunt Consolidated sold off its health and beauty products subsidiary, Hunt Products, Co., which had been purchased by the Hunts in 1962.

In the early 1990s, Hunt Oil increased emphasis on exploration in the United States as well as overseas. Previous drillers, believes the company, have overlooked major fields that modern technology can uncover, particularly in natural gas. The new Oryx Gulf of Mexico offshore platform, of which Hunt Oil owns one-third, started producing 26 million cubic feet of gas and 720 barrels of condensate per day in January 1991. A year later, the company drilled a deep wildcat well to 25,000 feet in western Texas. Gas prices and the potential to drill deeper than before were the key to developing such gas fields.

Thus Hunt Oil continues to grow, both domestically, where it operates in 11 states, and overseas. In 1992, the company was ranked 35th out of the 469 U.S. companies (public, private, or subsidiaries) engaged in crude petroleum and gas production, and was the fourth-largest private petroleum company. Larger than most independents, yet distinct from the major corporations, Hunt Oil is almost in a class of its own.

Principal Subsidiaries: Hunt Refining Company

Further Reading: Hurt, Harry III, *Texas Rich: The Hunt Dynasty from the Early Oil Days through the Silver Crash,* New York, W. W. Norton, 1981; Lampman, Dean, "Hunt Oil's Bonanza in North Yemen," *Dallas Business Courier*, July 21, 1986; Cook, James, "Yemen: Felix Redux?," *Forbes*, February 22, 1988; Lampman, Dean, "Hunt Oil Hopes for Big Overseas Strikes," *Dallas Business Journal*, May 30, 1988; Blanton, Kimberly, "Hunt Oil Selling Health, Beauty Unit," *Dallas Times Herald*, May 23, 1991; Petzet, Alan G., "Delaware-Val Verde Gas Drilling Busy," *Oil & Gas Journal*, January 13, 1992; Bancroft, Bill, "Hunting Elephants around the World," *New York Times Magazine*, March 24, 1992.

—Heather Behn Hedden

HYUNDAI
Cars that make sense.

HYUNDAI GROUP

140-142, Chongno-gu
Seoul
Republic of Korea
(02) 746-1114
Fax: (02) 741-2341

Public Company
Incorporated: 1947 as Hyundai Engineering & Construction
   Company
Employees: 170,000
Sales: W5.70 trillion (US$8.41 billion)
Stock Exchanges: Seoul
SICs: 1796 Installation or Erection of Building Equipment,
   Nec; 3519 Internal Combustion Engines, Nec; 3561 Pumps
   and Pumping Equipment; 3569 General Industrial
   Machinery and Equipment, Nec; 3711 Motor Vehicles and
   Passenger Car Bodies; 3713 Truck and Bus Bodies; 2449
   Wood Containers, Nec; 3441 Fabricated Structural Metal;
   3714 Motor Vehicle Parts and Accessories; 3592
   Carburetors, Piston, Piston Rings, and Valves

Hyundai Corporation is the trading arm of Hyundai Group, one
of South Korea's largest *chaebols,* or conglomerates. The corporation integrates the group's sales and marketing strategies,
imports natural resources through overseas investment and joint
ventures, and provides assistance to overseas operations. The
corporation leads the numerous member companies of the
group in sales. Since the companies belonging to the Hyundai
Business Group are closely linked, the history of Hyundai
Corporation must be viewed as part of the story of the group.

Hyundai Business Group has displayed spectacular growth
since it was founded in 1947. The group's rapid expansion—to
a point where its interests include car manufacturing, construction, shipbuilding, electronics, and financial services—reflects
the achievements attained during South Korea's economic miracle. The company has grown to a formidable strength in
several areas, and its rise to prominence in the construction,
shipbuilding, and automotive sectors has taken the world by
surprise. The specialized divisions are now run as independent
affiliated companies.

Hyundai's growth was linked inextricably to South Korea's
reconstruction programs following World War II and the Korean War, and to the state-led capitalism that resulted in a

polarization of the country's corporate structure and the domination of the economy by a number of conglomerates. World
War II left the country devastated, and the small recovery Korea
had been able to make following this conflict was reversed
during the Korean War, which lasted from 1950 to 1953. The
chaebols, which are similar to Japan's *zaibatsu,* worked with
the government in rebuilding the economy and formed an integral part of Korea's economic strategy and its drive to build up
its industrial base.

One man, Chung Ju Yung, has been at the center of Hyundai's
progress since 1950. Chung, honorary chairman in 1990, left
school at an early age and developed what has been described as
an autocratic and unconventional management style. He noted
those areas of industry that the government had selected as
crucial to economic development, and structured the group
accordingly.

The foundation of Hyundai was laid before the Korean War, in
1947, when Chung set up Hyundai Engineering & Construction
Company. The company was involved in the early stages of the
country's recovery following World War II. After the Korean
conflict, development intensified, and Hyundai was quick to
take on a key role, working on civil and industrial projects as
well as housing programs. In 1958 it set up Keumkang Company to make construction materials, and four years later, when
the first of Korea's five-year development plans was launched,
Hyundai was well placed to win a range of infrastructure
contracts. This plan and its successors aimed to lay the foundations for an independent economy by targeting sectors of industry for expansion.

Against this background Hyundai expanded its construction and
engineering operations as the economy's momentum increased.
In 1964 it completed the Danyang Cement plant, which in 1990
produced well over one million tons of cement. In 1965 the
company undertook its first overseas venture with a highway-
construction project in Thailand. Hyundai expanded rapidly
overseas, developing a market with particular success in the
Middle East. Its projects in this region included the US$931
million Jubail industrial harbor project in Saudi Arabia.

In 1967 the group took one of its most significant steps, setting
up the Hyundai Motor Company and thus sowing the seed for
what was to become the country's leading domestic car manufacturer. Initially the company assembled Ford Cortina cars and
Ford trucks. Two years later Hyundai took another step abroad
with the establishment of Hyundai America, incorporated in
Los Angeles, to work on housing complexes and other civil
projects. In 1970 it further enhanced its position in the construction sector by setting up Hyundai Cement Company to deal with
increased demand at home and overseas.

Toward the end of the 1960s the government had begun to
promote the heavy and chemical industries. Oil and steel were
both targeted. The planners then turned their attention to the
consumption of indigenous steel and focused on shipbuilding,
which was then relatively backward (producing only coastal
and fishing vessels), and on the automotive industry. The ambitious plans for these industries were to be of great significance
both to Hyundai and the nation as a whole, and the 1970s
proved to be a period of rapid development.

Hyundai's entry into shipbuilding was to provide the country with a sharp increase in shipbuilding capacity and eventually take Korea's shipbuilding industry to second position in the world, behind Japan. In 1971 Chung decided to begin shipbuilding, and by the following year the company's shipyard had held its ground-breaking ceremony in Mipo Bay, Ulsan, on the southeastern tip of the Korean peninsula. In the following year the yard was incorporated as Hyundai Shipbuilding and Heavy Industries Company.

The Ulsan yard was still at the planning stage when Hyundai won its first contract, for two oil tankers, from Livanos, a Greek shipowner. The order paved the way to a loan from Barclays Bank of the United Kingdom. Chung had to borrow capital from foreign banks to build the yard, which was opened in 1974. In the following year, the Hyundai Mipo Dockyard Company was set up to do conversions and repairs.

This sector developed rapidly throughout the 1970s, but the group was hit by the first oil crisis and the consequent decline in demand for large tankers. Hyundai, however, quickly won four orders for large tankers from the Japanese, its main competitors, and concluded technical cooperation deals with Kawasaki Heavy Industries of Japan and Scott Lithgow of the United Kingdom. Before the market collapsed, 12 large tankers were built at the yards.

This collapse forced Hyundai to turn to the building of medium-sized vessels. It also took steps to remain abreast of technological developments in the industry and to develop spin-offs. In 1975 Hyundai Shipbuilding and Heavy Industries created an industrial-plant and steel-fabrication division, and in the following year began to produce marine engines carrying famous names such as Sulzer and B&W.

A further collaboration was clinched in 1977 with Siemens, of West Germany, which led to the creation of the electrical-engineering division. In the following year the company changed its name to Hyundai Heavy Industries Company (HHI) to reflect its diverse operations. At the same time it incorporated its engine and electrical engineering divisions into Hyundai Engine and Machinery Company and Hyundai Electrical Engineering Company, respectively.

One of the most significant moves in Hyundai's relatively short history was made in 1975, when the group began constructing an integrated car factory adjacent to its heavy-industry complex at Ulsan. It was to be the foundation of Korea's largest auto company, one that was to dominate Korea's home and export markets. By the late 1980s UBS Phillips and Drew Global Research Group ranked Hyundai 13th in the world auto industry, with the production of 819,000 vehicles and 1.9 percent of the world retail market.

The aim of this ambitious project was to move away from car assembly only and to produce, with government backing, a Korean car, a four-seat sedan called the Hyundai Pony. To this end, it called on overseas expertise and finance, a policy used not only by Hyundai but by other Korean industrial groups as well. George Turnbull, a former managing director of British Leyland, who was then vice-president of Hyundai Motors, was in charge of the project. The car was styled by the well-known Italian designer Giorgetto Giugiaro, was powered by a Mitsubi-

shi Motor engine, and used U.K. components. The project was financed largely by U.K. and Japanese sources.

The vehicle was launched in 1975. By the following year, Hyundai was producing 30,000 cars, and by 1979 the total had risen to 110,000. Although Hyundai could sell every vehicle it produced in the protected home market, it soon sought to attack export markets by reserving approximately one-fifth of its production for overseas sale. The company first tested the European market, and its potential for sophisticated markets, by setting up a network of dealers in the Benelux countries, where there were no dominant local manufacturers.

Other areas of the group saw intense activity throughout the 1970s. In 1975 Dongsu Industrial Company, a construction-material manufacturer, was created, followed in the same year by Seohan Development Company, a welding and electrode carbide maker. Since it was so heavily reliant upon exports and several essential imports, the group in 1976 set up Hyundai Corporation, its trading arm. At the same time it created Hyundai Merchant Marine Company, which concentrated on cargo services, chartering, brokerage, and related services. The trading arm has proved to be an important source of revenue and has grown into one of the country's top exporters.

In the same year, on the construction side, Hyundai formed Koryeo Industrial Development Company and Hyundai Housing and Industrial Development Company, whose operations included construction design and property development. Hyundai Precision and Industry Company was created in 1977. Its activities include auto parts, container manufacture, and locomotive parts.

A year later the group turned its attention to the timber industry with the formation of Hyundai Wood Industries Company, which makes wood products and furniture. In 1978 the group expanded its heavy and chemical industries to include iron and steel manufacturing when it absorbed Incheon Iron & Steel Company and Aluminum of Korea.

The 1980s brought problems for HHI. Two of its key businesses, shipbuilding and overseas construction (the development of which had been actively encouraged by the government in the 1970s), encountered worldwide decline during the decade. Korean shipbuilders saw new export orders in 1985 slump to only US$522 million, compared with US$2.3 billion the year before, while profits plummeted. Overseas construction orders also fell away quickly after reaching a peak of more than US$13 billion in 1981 and 1982.

In both cases Korean industry had to discard its policy of growth at any price. There were job cuts and a move toward more sophisticated projects such as industrial plant construction and improved technology. In addition, the company had to contend with damaging labor strikes, which hit its shipyards and other parts of the group, notably the car factories. HHI instituted major productivity improvements at the beginning of the decade and stepped up its diversification with the creation of the Offshore & Steel Structure Division in 1980. Through this division it launched a major drive into the offshore market, into which it had broken in the late 1970s with orders for the Jubail project in Saudi Arabia. The division initially operated one yard, but, as demand increased, a second was added in 1983.

In 1982 HHI took over three dry docks from Hyundai Mipo Dockyard Company, which brought the total it operated to seven. Hyundai Mipo, which looked after the company's ship repair and conversion business, was reorganized and moved to a new repair yard two kilometers away from HHI. A year later HHI undertook further reorganization by turning its maritime-engineering division into the special and naval shipbuilding division, which now concentrates on building naval craft such as destroyers, frigates, and patrol boats.

The increased emphasis on new technology and innovation was reflected in the setting up of Hyundai Welding Research Institute in 1983—whose work has since been extended to take in factory automation—and the creation of a research-and-development center, the Hyundai Maritime Research Institute, a year later. Work continued on developing products such as the new generation of very large crude carriers, the world's first semi-submersible drilling rig, delivered in 1987, and a mixed container-passenger vessel for a Norwegian operator in 1988. The company also broke into the gas-carrier market in 1986.

The latter part of the decade was clouded by strikes, which were to tarnish the Korean shipbuilding industry's image. In addition, the company had to contend with higher wage costs that blunted the competitive edge it had over its Japanese rivals. HHI also became embroiled in a legal wrangle with Sir Yue-Kong Pao's World-Wide Shipping Group in 1988. The dispute was over an order for very large crude carriers, which it had agreed to build in 1986 when the market was in a trough.

The strikes that affected the Ulsan yard in the latter part of the 1980s hit production and sales, and in 1988 HHI was to record its first-ever loss, that of W29 billion on sales that declined slightly to W945 billion; this came after breaking even the previous year. In 1990 the yard was hit by further strikes, although it managed to land a US$600 million order for ten combination vessels from a Norwegian shipping group.

The 1980s were to prove equally eventful for Hyundai Motor Company. After the oil shock of 1979 the government took steps to protect the industry, which had by then made large investments in plants and equipment. It kept a tight grip on the development of this sector and in 1981 divided the market, restricting Hyundai to car and large commercial vehicle manufacture. These regulations were revised in 1986 following the recovery of the market, and Hyundai was able to resume manufacture of light commercial vehicles.

By the middle of the decade, Hyundai had taken Canada by storm. Its Pony subcompact vehicle became Canada's top-selling car less than two years after entering the market. Hyundai's sales in Canada, where it was also selling the Stellar, shot from none in December of 1983 to 57,500 units in the first nine months of 1985, topping those of Honda and Nissan combined. Total production in 1985 had risen to 450,000.

In 1985 the company announced plans to build a car assembly plant at Bromont, near Montreal, and at the same time decided to enter the U.S. market. The entry into the U.S. market, begun in 1986, proved an immediate success. Its low-priced Excel model was well received, and of the 302,000 cars exported in that year, 168,000 were sold in the United States, where sales were to increase to 263,000 the following year. Hyundai's

initial success in the United States, though, faded before the end of the decade when sales began to flag. Its problems in its key overseas market were attributed to the lack of new models, increasing competition in the weakened U.S. car market, and the severe strikes that hit the company in the latter part of the 1980s and in 1990.

Hyundai decided to move up market with the introduction of the Sonata, a four-door sedan, in late 1988; initial sales, though, proved disappointing. A year later this car was being manufactured at the Bromont plant, following the opening of the factory in 1989. In the same year Hyundai signed a deal with Chrysler Corp. to build 30,000 midsize, four-door cars for the U.S. company, starting in 1991. Chrysler is linked to Mitsubishi Corporation, which in turn is affiliated with Hyundai, in which it holds a 15 percent stake.

Hyundai planned to increase production at the Canadian plant to 100,000 by the time the Chrysler deal came into effect. Export sales, which were also hit by the appreciation of the won and the depreciation of the yen, have remained sluggish. Increased wage costs also affected the group but had the advantage of boosting domestic sales that, for the industry as a whole, increased 50 percent to 356,000 units in 1989.

The group became intent on reducing its dependence on the U.S. markets. By 1990, the domestic market was proving increasingly important to the essentially export-oriented group. Both the car and construction markets were enjoying strong demand at the end of the decade. This situation helped Hyundai Engineering & Construction, like the vehicle operations, to take up the slack created by declining markets abroad, particularly in the Middle East. The group had accumulated experience in a broad range of plant construction, including Korea's first nuclear power plant. Meanwhile exports in the shipbuilding sector were showing a marked improvement.

Following the creation in 1983 of Hyundai Electronics, Hyundai stepped up its presence in the electronics field and produced semiconductors, telecommunication equipment, and industrial electronic systems. The company, which focused on industrial markets, was seeking to increase its presence in consumer electronics, despite formidable competition from domestic companies such as Samsung and Goldstar.

The group as a whole has shown itself capable of taking diverse markets by storm and is determined to maintain and expand its markets by stepping up research-and-development spending. However, the country's drive towards democracy has brought new uncertainties. In the changing economic and political environment, the group faces a labor force seeking higher wages, a less competitive currency, and increasing competition in the all-important overseas markets.

Faced with this changing political scene and a less favorable international rate of exchange, Hyundai shifted gears in the early 1990s. In automaking, its largest enterprise, it worked to regain lost ground in the United States, where demand for its low-priced Excel and somewhat higher-priced Sonata models slumped in the wake of widespread consumer complaints and a depressed entry-level market. Hyundai's new Elantra sedan, selling for $9,000, was to be its lead item in the U.S. market. The group's chairman at that time, Chung Ju Yung's son,

Chung Se-yung, was expecting a new day for the group, as Korea itself matured with new labor and political freedoms.

As Korea's second-largest conglomerate, with 1990 revenues estimated at $35 billion, Hyundai Group was clearly to play an important role in the new Korea. Indeed, the Hyundai founder and chairman, Chung Ju Yung, chose personally to play a new, political role in that development, founding a new political party early in 1992 with a view to promoting open-market policies. This Unification National Party (UNP) promptly won ten percent of National Assembly seats; and Chung himself, then retired from his Hyundai chairmanship, set his sights on the Korean presidency. The Hyundai conglomerate, already forced by the government to pay billions in back taxes, came under even more severe government pressures after Chung formed his party. Regulators charged illegal political contributions by one Hyundai company and accused others of tax evasion. In addition, Hyundai's ability to finance its operations was threatened by other government actions. In return, Hyundai, at this time headed by Chung Se Yung, threatened to withhold huge investments planned for the coming year. In 1993, having finished third in South Korea's presidential election, Chung Ju Yung reportedly has said that he will resume chairmanship of the Hyundai Group and will reorganize the corporation into many specialized, independently run companies.

In auto and personal-computer sales, Hyundai companies moved aggressively. In mid-1992 Hyundai's new Motor America president, Dal Ok Chung, took over in the Fountain Valley, California, headquarters. Among other marketing devices, Hyundai offered generous rebates and free two-year service warranties that covered even windshield wiper blades. By early 1993, Hyundai was offering the first auto engine it had designed and made itself, as opposed to the Japanese-made Mitsubishi engines that were used in its earlier models. More than ever committed to the smaller vehicle, Hyundai was selling autos in more than 100 countries.

In personal computers, Hyundai in mid-1992 took a drastic step when it moved its entire electronics operation to the United States, the world's largest computer market. Hyundai Information Systems had already entered the direct personal-computer market, cutting prices and offering toll-free telephone support and sales. The new operation, based in San Jose, California, had entirely American leadership, headed by IBM veteran and former CompuAdd president Edward Thomas. The California advantage was mainly proximity to the market, which meant lessened inventory requirements. These developments showed the Hyundai Group to have the same innovative and energetic approach that had characterized its earlier ventures.

Principal Subsidiaries: Hyundai Heavy Industries Co. Ltd; Hyundai Motor Company; Hyundai Engineering and Construction Co. Ltd; Hyundai Corporation; Hyundai Petrochemical Co. Ltd; Incheon Iron and Steel Co. Ltd.

Further Reading: Woronoff, Jon, *Asia's "Miracle" Economies,* Seoul, Si-Sa-yong-o-sa Inc., 1986; James, H., *Korea—An Introduction,* London, Kegan Paul International, 1988; *Hyundai,* Seoul, Hyundai Business Group, 1989; "Hyundai: The Gloves Are Off," *The Economist,* April 25, 1992.

—Bob Vincent
updated by Jim Bowman

IMO INDUSTRIES INC.

3450 Princeton Pike
P.O. Box 6550
Lawrenceville, NJ 08648
U.S.A.
(609) 896-7600
Fax: (609) 896-7688

Public Company
Incorporated: 1901 as De Laval Steam Turbine Company
Employees: 7,400
Sales: $928 million
Stock Exchanges: New York
SICs: 3829 Measuring & Controlling Devices Nec; 3511
   Turbines & Turbine Generator Sets; 3566 Speed Changers,
   Drives & Gears; 3826 Analytical Instruments; 3714 Motor
   Vehicle Parts & Accessories

Imo Industries, Inc. is a leading producer in a number of domestic and international industrial, defense, transportation, commercial aviation and marine, utility, and process, oil, and gas markets. Imo's Instruments and Controls Business manufactures a wide range of analytical and optical instruments and electronic and mechanical controls, while its Power Systems Business provides an array of engineered power products and services to customers around the globe.

Imo Delaval, Inc., renamed Imo Industries, Inc. in 1989, was created as a public company in December 1986, when Transamerica Corporation, which had acquired the De Laval Steam Turbine Company in 1962, distributed Imo stock to its shareholders on a one-for-ten basis. (Since then the stock has been traded on the New York Stock Exchange with the symbol IMD.) In 1986 Imo Delaval, with 21 plants in North America and Europe and close to 3,500 employees, had revenues of $358 million. The newly independent company launched an aggressive strategy on several fronts. Through the late 1980s and early 1990s, Imo actively sought to acquire companies involved in related business areas to strengthen and enhance existing product and service lines. Continuing the company tradition, resources were dedicated to development of engineering applications and solutions in a number of areas, including efforts to respond to worldwide environmental concerns.

Imo's long-established reputation and stability have been grounded in the success of its turbines, compressors, pumps, and motion control equipment, which are still produced by Imo companies, including Delaval Turbine, Imo Pump, Warren Pumps, Boston Gear, and Delroyd Worm Gear, and still account for almost two-thirds of its operations. The energetic acquisitions campaign of the late 1980s has effected a greater diversity in current activities. Revolutionary night vision and laser systems produced by new subsidiaries Baird (acquired in 1987) and Varo (acquired in 1988) have made Imo a major force in electro-optical systems. A one-piece door lock developed by Roltra, a major supplier to Fiat and 100 percent Imo-owned since 1991, has attracted attention in European and other automobile markets. Other products such as sensors and pressure switches from Gems Sensors (acquired in 1969) and Barksdale (acquired in 1964), respectively, have been redesigned for detecting leaks in underground storage tanks and piping systems. A Gems electronic liquid level switch has been instrumental in revolutionizing Freon gas recycling and recovery systems. In the 1990s, with billion dollar sales, Imo Industries management sees its role as providing strategic direction and support for its some two dozen quasi-independent operations.

The history of Imo Industries begins in Stockholm, Sweden, in March 1890, when Dr. Carl Gustaf Patrik de Laval—called the "Thomas Edison of Sweden"—founded Gustaf de Laval Angturbin Fabrik to produce his single stage geared turbine. The motivation behind his steam-turbine invention was to find a way to power large versions of the automated cream separators that he had introduced a number of years before and which were being produced in Sweden and, since 1883, in America by the De Laval Separator Company in Poughkeepsie, New York.

Dr. de Laval's geared steam turbine generator was the first of its kind in the United States when it was exhibited at the 1893 World's Fair in Chicago. The finished design incorporated an expanding nozzle, flexible shaft, and double helical gears, and initially could be produced in different-sized units ranging from five to 200 horsepower. (This unit and a Baird spectrometer are two Imo Industries products on permanent display at the Smithsonian Institution in Washington, D.C.) Realizing the potential of his invention to increase industrial efficiency while reducing power-generation costs, Dr. de Laval wanted to introduce his turbine to industries in America as well as in his home country. His continuing experiments quickly led to new industrial applications for the turbine, including powering outdoor lighting and shipping.

In 1896, in what was possibly the first commercial application of a steam turbine for electric power generation in the United States, the New York Edison Company imported and installed two 300 horsepower De Laval turbines, establishing the first electric generating stations in New York City. While financial setbacks delayed Dr. de Laval's plans to manufacture the steam turbine engines in the United States, other companies such as Westinghouse and General Electric acquired patents and gained a valuable head start.

On December 9, 1900, an article in the Trenton *Sunday Advertiser* announced that the De Laval Steam Turbine Company would be opening a new plant the following May and was expecting to employ "a large number of skilled mechanics" in the manufacture of steam turbine engines. A group of American investors (who were 30 percent owners) was led by Francis J.

Arend, director of the De Laval Separator Company. By the end of 1902, the Trenton plant was producing gears, centrifugal pumps and compressors, and allied high-speed equipment in addition to the steam turbines. The company originated and became a major supplier of city waterworks pumping equipment.

In application after application, high-speed centrifugal turbines were replacing steam driven equipment, and De Laval was an industry pacesetter. Year after year the De Laval engineers made notable advances in engineering achievements in response to the needs of American industry. During World War I, the company was a key supplier of power generating equipment to the U.S. Navy. And during the postwar building program the company supplied precision reduction gearing for 60 destroyers and 11 cruisers. At this time, requirements of the U.S. defense industry led to the lessening of ties between the American manufacturing company and its Swedish parent. Arend was made the company's first American president in 1916; he served until his death in 1942.

In the 1920s, instead of retooling to provide large turbines to drive the central power station generators that were needed to supply power to communities across America, De Laval chose to concentrate on marine sales and industrial power generation. By the end of the decade and during the next few years, as the company weathered the Depression, sales decreased and operations were pared down.

In 1932 the company acquired a license to sell three-screw positive displacement pumps manufactured by the Swedish firm AB Imo-Industri. Some of De Laval's most important achievements in the coming years came from efforts to design, produce, and expand applications of these pumps and the design and production of precision gears for marine propulsion. Pump orders took off following the events in Europe in 1939, and when the U.S. Navy began building its Mahan class destroyers, the De Laval double-reduction geared turbines were on board. Those not manufactured in the Trenton plant were produced elsewhere using De Laval designs. One of the few U.S. manufacturers with the experience, staff, and machinery to build the large, complex propulsion equipment needed to power warships and freight carriers, De Laval was awarded the Navy's "E" award for excellence for these vital contributions to the war effort.

Continuing research and development after the war and through the 1950s concentrated on products for peacetime markets, such as the centrifugal compressor for high-pressure gas pipeline transmission needed to pump natural gas from wellheads to consumers. Domestic and worldwide marketing efforts were expanded to increase sales and to offer licenses to manufacture selected products in remote locations. The Imo pump was still strong, and worm gear products, whose sales had declined, were strengthened through a partnership with the John Holroyd & Co. of Great Britain, known for its worm gearing made to involute helicoid thread form. In the 1960s, Delroyd (a combination of the names De Laval and Holroyd), with some of the most advanced worm gear manufacturing equipment in the world, began operations in a new addition to the greatly expanded Trenton plant.

Two World Wars, the Depression, the Korean conflict, and other world events and trends, such as a worldwide shipbuilding boom in the mid-1950s, had caused De Laval's operations to rise and fall and had influenced product decisions. Swedish control of the De Laval Steam Turbine Company by AB Separator had been diminished although the financial tie remained. By the late 1950s the Swedish firm needed additional funding to grow with Europe's dynamic peacetime economy and began looking for a buyer for its 70 percent of De Laval. It was not until several years later, in April 1962, that an investment group headed by Lehman Brothers became full owners of the newly named De Laval Turbine Company. The following year Lehman Brothers found a buyer for the company: Transamerica Corporation, a large insurance and financial services firm based in San Francisco. Transamerica was looking for a business to complement General Metals, a manufacturing subsidiary that was one of its many industrial holdings.

Although Transamerica's acquisition of De Laval was not unanimously approved, once accomplished the advantages were capitalized upon and turned into assets. Realizing that De Laval's sales and professional personnel (experienced in targeting the marine and utility markets) could benefit General Metals's Enterprise diesel engines (to date a mediocre performer) and Barksdale valve and switch lines as well as De Laval products, Transamerica decided in 1964 to merge General Metals and all of its industrial holdings into one manufacturing operation: De Laval. Fortunately, the new management also recognized that product development was fundamental to the De Laval enterprise and kept it a priority. In fact, within the next few years, as De Laval concentrated on marine, electric utility, gas transmission, municipal, process, and general industrial markets—in other words, not only military—Transamerica saw earnings increase over 90 percent to account for 7.3 of the parent company's reported earnings. Under W. J. Holcombe, who became De Laval president in 1965 after having managed Transamerica's western manufacturing companies, sales continued to increase each year and by 1970 had more than doubled, with net income increasing nearly twelve-fold. As the company entered 1971 with a $113 million backlog, the future looked bright.

In 1971, to accommodate some of its manufacturing divisions' growth, the De Laval corporate offices were moved from Trenton to nearby Princeton. At this time, the company comprised three product divisions (aero components, industrial components, and heavy equipment) and more than a dozen companies. Growth continued through the 1970s, particularly in the area of aero components, with the acquisition of E.B. Wiggins (1975) and Red-Lee Metal Finishing (later Airfoil) (1978) and expansion of production capability. Diverse new products included Imo's geared twin screw pump and, from Wiggins Connectors, a fuel service system that permitted rapid refueling of racing cars and off-road vehicles without contamination-causing leakage. By 1976 De Laval's $22 million net income accounted for almost 20 percent of Transamerica's consolidated income.

Beginning in the 1970s, and extending into the next decade, continuing company growth was accompanied by global outreach. Early milestones included: the opening of a compressor plant in Toronto, Canada; joint ventures in Mexico (EPN-Delaval, SA) and the Netherlands (Delaval-Stork); and the procurement of orders for utility and petrochemical applications from Poland and Yugoslavia. Sales offices were established around the world, from London and Paris and the Hague to Athens and Saudi Arabia to Singapore and Hong Kong. The 1986 acquisition of Imo AB, in Stockholm, the original Swedish patent holder, brought the company full circle as well as supporting its leadership in the worldwide screw pump market.

The growth period of the 1970s and 1980s was also marked by changes in company leadership. W. J. Holcombe moved to an executive position in Transamerica and assumed De Laval chairmanship in 1972 before leaving the company in 1975. Ivan Monk, who had joined De Laval in 1961, presided over the company for two years, followed by Donald T. Bixby, who served as president from 1974 to 1983 and chairman of the board until his retirement in 1985. It was Bixby who broke ground in Lawrenceville, New Jersey, for the new company headquarters in 1979. In 1983 Truman W. Netherton moved from Westinghouse to become De Laval's president. Three years later, in 1986, W. J. Holcombe returned to the newly independent company as chief executive officer and was named president the following year.

Independence from Transamerica in 1986 brought with it many fundamental changes. A loss of $21.8 million—the first in 25 years—occasioned the divestment of several divisions (Enterprise, Texas Forge, and Pumptron) whose business depended on depressed markets like oil, gas, agricultural, and nuclear utilities. At the same time, focusing on companies involved in the manufacture and sale of complementary profit-making product lines, the company began a strategic acquisition campaign. As a means of delimiting the company's course, Imo was reorganized to form its two current primary businesses: Instruments and Controls, and Power Systems. Management was restructured to better coordinate sales and operations and to accommodate future business opportunities. More attention was directed to serving the extensive aftermarket needs of the energy marketplace.

Beginning in 1987, the newspapers bristled with accounts of Imo acquisitions, large and small. Among the largest were Baird Corporation (1987, $55.8 million), manufacturer of spectrometers and optical systems; Incom International Inc. (1987, $145.8 million), a group of manufacturers of electronic controls and power transmission devices; and Varo (1988, $117 million), a major supplier of night vision equipment to the military. Less costly but important acquisitions included Warren Pumps and Roltra (1989), Quabbin Industries (1990), an aftermarket service company and producer of retractable seals to increase

turbine efficiency, and Opto-Electronic Corp., which was merged with Varo.

Earnings in the early 1990s were depressed. Gross profit margins slipped from 29.1 percent in 1989 to 25.8 percent in 1991. Paying down accumulated long-term debt from its acquisition program and lessened potential recovery momentum. However, the company expects to offer some long-term protection from up-and-down behavior in various markets with its carefully developed multiple-niche strategy. W. J. Holcombe continues as chief executive officer and chairman of the board.

Company-wide efforts remain directed toward increasing the competitive advantage through marketing initiatives and manufacturing efficiencies and diminishing the effects of market fluctuations. The year 1991 saw a nine percent workforce reduction as manufacturing processes designed to increase productivity and reduce lead times were implemented. Streamlining strategies have also resulted in the integration of like operations such as the combining of Varo and OEC (Electro-Optical Systems) and the consolidation of a new Turbo-Care group. Multi-division marketing such as the recent Pacific-area program based in Singapore exemplifies the company's efforts to reach expanded global markets.

One-third of operations are attached to military contracts, including ongoing programs such as night vision and laser equipment. Aerospace product development has been increasingly targeted to commercial aviation customers. And there is a recent focus on products for transportation, industrial, utility and cogeneration, and oil, gas, and process markets that stress efficiency and environmental initiatives that may underscore stability and contribute to long-term profitability and recovery.

Principal Subsidiaries: Adel Fasteners; Aeroproducts; Baird; Barksdale Controls; Boston Gear; CEC Instruments; Controlex; Delaval Condenser; Delaval Turbine; Delroyd Worm Gear; Fincor Electronics; Gems Sensors; Heim Bearings; IMO Pump; Morse Controls; Roltra Morse; TransInstruments; TurboCare, comprising Airfoil, Centrimarc, Deltex/Pro Mac, Quabbin, and Turboflex; Warren Pumps; Wiggins Connectors; Varo.

Further Reading: De Laval IMO 1890–1990, An Industrial Evolution; Imo Annual Report 1991; *Moody's Industrial Manual,* 1992, Vol. 1; *Value Line Investment Survey Ratings and Reports,* 1988, 1989, 1990, 1992.

—Margaret Barlow

INTERNATIONAL DATA GROUP

One Exeter Plaza
Boston, Massachusetts 02116
U.S.A.
(617) 534-1200
Fax: (617) 262-2300

Private Company
Incorporated: 1964
Employees: 5,000
Sales: $880 million
SICs: 2721 Periodicals; 6719 Holding Companies Nec

With a global network of more than 190 computer publications in more than 60 countries, International Data Group (IDG) is a leader in information-technology publishing. In addition to its publishing divisions, IDG has top-performing research divisions and an exposition management subsidiary which runs computer-related conferences and exhibitions worldwide.

The roots of this enterprise reach as far back as IDG founder Patrick J. McGovern's high school newspaper route. In 1953, with $20 saved from his route, McGovern combined carpet tacks, plywood boards, bell wire and flashlight bulbs into a computer that was unbeatable at tic-tac-toe. When he found people didn't enjoy playing the machine if they were obliged to always lose, McGovern programmed it to make a mistake every 40th move, so contenders could occasionally win. This computer tic-tac-toe champion won McGovern a full scholarship to the Massachusetts Institute of Technology (MIT).

McGovern had gotten the computer bug from reading a book, *Giant Brains: Or, Machines That Think,* while in the 10th grade. McGovern later edited a Boston-based computer magazine put out by the author of *Giant Brains.* It was after MIT, while associate publisher of *Computers and Automation,* that McGovern began to witness the information gap between the companies making computers and the people who bought and used them. This was 1964, still fairly early in the computer age and the blooming field of artificial intelligence.

McGovern was tapped by rivals of IBM to conduct a market research program to determine where computers were heading and how they were being used. Firms such as Univac, Xerox, and Burroughs paid McGovern for his research and soon International Data Corporation (IDC) was born. He hired high school students across the country to help count computers and collect information. Within three years, IDC was grossing $600,000 and growing. Today IDC oversees worldwide market research services supported by the world's largest database of computer sites and systems.

With his experience as associate editor and publisher of *Computers and Automation*—the country's first computer magazine—and with a strong market research arm in place, the next logical step was publishing. McGovern got the idea when his research showed that computer systems managers were not aware of what others were accomplishing with computers, nor were they keeping up with products. In 1967 McGovern launched *Computerworld,* the flagship weekly that is now the cornerstone of IDG's publishing empire. Introduced before the computer boom, the publication's intent was to provide rapid-access information about new products and applications to computer department managers. It went from eight-page issues to 72-page issues within the first year; within five years, *Computerworld* had become the largest specialized business publication in the United States. Its readership today tops 650,000, claiming 25 percent of the computer publications market.

The launching of *Computerworld* led to the establishment of CW Communications, Inc., which was to become IDG Communications, Inc. when IDG was founded in 1967. IDG Communications, the publishing arm of International Data Group, produces newspapers, magazines, and books around the world. With the research arm of IDG locating computer vendors and users as well as potential advertisers and subscribers, IDG was able to pinpoint market opportunities for healthy publications. As early as 1972 McGovern began responding to the need for computer information outside of the United States. Recognizing that each country has its own information needs and application problems, McGovern sought to establish local publications in native languages. His first venture was *Shukan Computer,* a Japanese publication that drew on *Computerworld* while attuned to regional needs. IDG has a reputation for responding to new markets as they emerge. It has a current global network of more than 190 publications in more than 60 countries, covering 92 percent of the worldwide computer market.

The company boasts the largest editorial staff in the world—800 people linked by IDG's International News Service. Success of the individual publications has been helped by IDG's decentralized management structure. With mission and values defined at the top, the success or failure of individual publications depends on decisions made at the unit-level. This allows them to be responsive to their immediate market quickly. The staff at IDG headquarters in Boston has always been remarkably small and founder and chairman McGovern is said to spend most of his time on airplanes. Only financial control is centralized; each unit reports monthly and performances are shared to spur competition as well as cooperation. Another advantage of IDG's structure is that articles can be shared by publications in different countries.

The third arm of IDG dates to 1976, when McGovern developed "Communications Networks," in response to the rapid growth of telecommunications technology. IDG now offers the premier trade show for large users of communications technology. The IDG World Expo Corporation today runs 65 computer-related exhibitions and conferences in 21 countries, including Korea, Hong Kong, Japan, and Australia. World Expo produces conferences, seminars and trade expositions for the information technology industry worldwide, ranging from small regional programs to industry-wide conferences.

In keeping with its ear-to-the-ground timing, IDG announced the publication *Macworld Magazine* on the same day that the Macintosh computer was introduced. In 1980 it initiated *China Computerworld,* a joint venture with the People's Republic of China. Within five years it had 100,000 paid subscribers and a 40 percent profit margin. The Beijing-based weekly was China's first computer publication.

IDG is currently private; 35 percent of the company has been sold to a profit-sharing employee trust. McGovern has long made the claim that when the company reaches the $1 billion mark, IDG employees will become majority shareholders. In 1985 the billion dollar mark appeared to be on the horizon and McGovern was expressing a fascination with Japan. Since then, two publishing slumps have moved back the timetable for reaching the $1 billion mark.

The reasoning behind the company's promise, according to McGovern, is that too many other businesses, after losing a founder or owner, find loyal staff and team members—those who have built the company—replaced. According to an in-house interview, McGovern has said that "What we try to do is build a global community of talented people who share a common vision of providing information services on information technology. And we want to have this community control its own destiny."

Having started a stampede, IDG found itself in a crowded computer research market by 1984. The first shakeout in the computer publishing field hit. Magazines were folding or merging on a weekly basis. This was partly a reflection of what was happening in publishing as a whole: in recessions, advertising budgets are often among the first cuts and that immediately affects magazines. But it was also the result of a market glut. By 1985 there were roughly 120 larger computer publications fighting over limited readers and ads. Neck and neck with IDG through most of the 1980s was fellow publishing titan Ziff Communications Company. Ziff publishes industry staples, *PC Magazine* and *PC Week,* among others and, like IDG, has a research division. In IDG's case, there are three separate research companies: International Data Corporation, Technology Investment Strategies Corporation, and LINK Resources. LINK tracks the demand side of the PC market, working to anticipate market acceptance of new technologies, as well as developing strategies for assessing growth of the home office market. LINK serves an international client base, providing research reports and proprietary studies. International Data Corp. monitors the supply side, gathering data from vendors and serving nearly 4,000 corporate clients worldwide. The research companies serve to provide the best computer-marketing information for clients. Naturally the corporate parent also benefits.

While the market slumped at home, changes abroad opened new doors. The same saturation was reflected in the United Kingdom, which went from a small number of computer magazines in 1981 to a high of more than 150 in 1985. The glut killed off 30 magazines that year alone. So IDG began looking to other parts of the world. In 1985 IDG began its first joint publishing venture with Hungary, producing *Computerworld SZT* and *PC Mikrovilag.* Here again, IDG was ahead of the trend. McGovern recognized the hunger of newly democratized countries to enter the Information Age. "In the former Soviet Union, and in the other Eastern European countries, they see high-tech as their ticket to making their future much brighter," he said in an in-house interview. He claimed that unsold copies of IDG publications are unheard of in Eastern Europe. In nations that had been without political and economic freedoms, the urge to catch up with the computer world was fierce. Between 1986 and 1989 IDG's revenues doubled as they entered new markets worldwide, including Japan, Taiwan, and the U.S.S.R. In April of 1988 IDG forged the first publishing joint venture agreement with the Soviet Union to publish the quarterly *PC World USSR.* It was the first Soviet magazine on computer technology.

There was another computer magazine industry shakeout in 1989. In that year IDG had folded or merged previously robust publications and closed *80 Micro* and *Macintosh Today.* The culprit was flat ad spending again, but this time it was tied not only to the economy; readers were caught between generations of personal computers. Many publications were tied to aging computer systems such as the Commodore 64 or the Apple II, which were being eclipsed by newer systems. With the dramatic drop in the cost of personal computers in the early 1990s, many new users came into view, bringing with them different application needs. In 1989 the vast technological change within the industry meant consolidation and fallout, taking publications along. The worsening recession was an additional blow to ad revenues.

That same year ended with the fall of the Berlin Wall and the floodgates to a new market were opened. IDG launched new publishing operations in Yugoslavia, Czechoslovakia, Poland, Bulgaria, and Romania—in 1990 alone. Another magazine, *Manager,* was added to its USSR operations. Later, ventures were started up in Turkey, Slovenia, and Vietnam. In June of 1990 IDG and Nigeria-based WENCA Technology began *PC World Africa.* It appeared on newsstands in 20 African nations, none of them in South Africa. At that time, it was estimated that 15 percent of African businesses owned at least one personal computer. Also in 1990, IDG purchased the largest chain of PC-training schools in the United States, an expansion move away from the magazine market.

Much of IDG's success was attributed to its decentralized management and its tradition of starting up magazines in-house, rather than by acquiring them, which is how many publishers grow quickly. In the 1990s IDG began buying publishing units. The first of these was Lotus Publishing Corporation, with estimated annual revenues of $10 million. Publications included *Lotus magazine,* a monthly for Lotus customers with a circulation of 368,000, and a line of books published in conjunction with Simon & Schuster. *Electronic News* was acquired by IDG from Chilton Co. Inc. in 1991. Again the sale's figure was not disclosed. *Electronic News,* launched in 1957, became the leading publication for corporate and operational management in the $100 billion worldwide electronics industry. Its strength in covering key developments in microcircuits and electronic technology—a burgeoning aspect of the industry—was a solid addition to IDG's family of publications and shared information.

In 1992 IDG purchased *Electronics International,* a 32-page weekly covering China's electronics industry. The publication began in 1986 with only four pages an issue. The electronics industry in China had been growing at ten percent a year since 1989. Also in 1992, IDG announced it would be folding *Lotus* into *PC World,* claiming it would create the "nation's largest computer magazine," a claim disputed by other publications. Since its acquisition, *Lotus* had not been performing well due to its limited readership. This announcement stiffened the competition between Ziff and IDG for the dominant position in computer-magazine publishing. The claim was made that IDG was losing parts of its core market in the United States for the same reason it was successful abroad, and that it did not spend enough money to make its titles competitive. Though IDG was ranked ahead of Ziff in 1992, Ziff's market share was increasing.

Still, McGovern was very persuaded of the potential for growth in the computer publishing industry in late 1992. A drop in costs meant an increase in sales and users he argued, and "now there are more people regularly reading computer publications than there are people reading general business publications." The increase in mail order computer sales, bypassing dealers and distributors, also translated into a boost for publications.

As it stands, McGovern expects his empire to be majority owned by its employees by the mid to late 1990s, when he hopes to hit the $1 billion in sales mark.

Principal Subsidiaries: IDG Communications; International Data Corporation; LINK Resources; Technology Investment Strategies Corporation; IDG World Expo Corporation; IDG Books Worldwide.

Further Reading: Behar, Richard, "As You Give," *Forbes,* April 29, 1985; Howard, Majoria, "Paper Gold," *Boston Magazine,* July 1988; Reilly, Patrick, "More Shakeouts Hit Computer Magazines," *Advertising Age,* May 29, 1989; Cuff, Daniel, "Vice Chairman to Head International Data Unit," *New York Times,* January 19, 1990; "If Nigeria Gets a PC Magazine, Can PCs be Far Behind?" *Business Week,* February 12, 1990; "International Data Acquires Lotus Unit," *Wall Street Journal,* January 14, 1991; "Publisher Buys A Lotus Unit," *New York Times,* January 14, 1991; "Rich and Titled," *Economist,* March 30, 1991; Lewis, Peter, "The Executive Computer," *New York Times,* June 23, 1991; "Electronic News Acquired by IDG," *Electronic News,* November 4, 1991; "Western Eye on China's Electronics Industry," *Christian Science Monitor,* February 25, 1992; Johnson, Bradley, "Computer Magazines Take Advertising On-Line," *Advertising Age,* August 31, 1992; Johnson, Bradley, "IDG and ZIFF Debate Who's Got Top PC Title," *Advertising Age,* September 14, 1992; Hume, Scott, "Playing the Separation of Powers Game," *Advertising Age,* November 9, 1992.

—Carol Keeley

INTERNATIONAL MULTIFOODS CORPORATION

Multifoods Tower
P.O. Box 2942
Minneapolis, Minnesota 55402
U.S.A.
(612) 340-3300
Fax: (612) 340-3338

Public Company
Incorporated: 1892 as New Prague Flouring Mill Company
Sales: $2.28 billion
Employees: 8,231
SICs: 2038 Frozen Specialities Nec; 2053 Frozen Bakery
    Products Except Bread; 2041 Flour & Other Grain Mill
    Products; 2045 Prepared Flour Mixes & Doughs

International Multifoods Corporation was once known as one of the "Big Three" in U.S. flour milling, along with General Mills and Pillsbury. But in the past two decades the company has undergone sweeping restructuring strategies—first diversifying heavily into consumer foods and animal feeds in the 1970s and early 1980s, then divesting itself of such interests (including its original product, Robin Hood flour) and fortifying its stake in the food vending industry in the late 1980s and early 1990s—to focus primarily on its U.S. Foodservice division and secondarily on its Canadian Foods and Venezuelan Foods divisions. To emphasize its most recent strategy, the company has adopted the abbreviated signature of "Multifoods." The U.S. Foodservice division, which accounts for 75 percent of all Multifoods sales, is driven by Vendors Supply of America, Inc., (VSA), the domestic leader in vending distribution, with nearly $1 billion in annual sales. Since its acquisition in 1984, VSA has grown rapidly in what remains a highly fragmented market; its continuing health is welcome news to Multifoods shareholders, many of whom consider the bold move by Archer Daniels Midland to acquire, in 1990, a 9.4 percent investment in the once floundering company as a singularly auspicious development.

Multifoods traces its roots to the Polar Star Milling Company, an initially prosperous southern Minnesota business that was unable to weather the soaring railroad freight rates and plunging flour prices of the early 1890s. When the Faribault company declared bankruptcy in 1891, owner Francis Atherton Bean was destitute but not despairing. The following year, with a loan

from his brother-in-law, the fifty-year-old Bean rented a mill located in New Prague that had also gone out of business. Due to a close-knit, cooperative atmosphere, and the wheat-buying and accounting expertise of Bean's son, F. A. Bean, Jr., the New Prague Flouring Mill Company became a success within a few short years. In 1896 the former owner decided to reclaim and manage the mill; again undaunted, Bean attracted more than $30,000 in capital from local investors and constructed a new mill, which operated under the same name. Increased production and storage capacity as well as an improved location were among the key factors that allowed Bean to expand in the next few years and purchase additional mills in Blue Earth and Wells, Minnesota.

In 1908 the company launched its first, and one of its most successful, international ventures with the purchase of the Mc-Lean Mill in Moose Jaw, then the largest city in Saskatchewan, Canada. Given a growing population, rich agricultural land, and dependable railway lines, Bean, Sr., saw considerable potential for the business, which opened the following year as Saskatchewan Flour Mills Ltd.; the parent company now became International Milling and thus commanded heightened status at home, despite its still primarily regional thrust. Bean's vision was confirmed three years later when the company purchased another mill in Calgary, Alberta. Expansion continued and the Canadian operations were soon renamed Robin Hood Flour Mills, Ltd., a designation reflecting the rising popularity of the company's brand name flour, first introduced around 1910 exclusively for the Canadian markets.

According to several accounts, perhaps the high point for the company's founder came at Christmas time in 1911 when Bean decided to secretly visit, over a two-week period, all the yet unpaid creditors of the failed Polar Star business from back in 1890. Although he had no legal obligation to do so, Bean resurrected and satisfied all the old bills in full, paying both principal and interest for what amounted to more than $200,000. In so doing, he not only ensured himself an unforgettable Christmas, he also secured his place as one of the most loved and respected of all Minnesota entrepreneurs.

In 1923 the company moved its headquarters to Minneapolis in order to become a major national competitor in the flour-milling industry. To accommodate the northward flow of Kansas winter wheat, the company acquired mills in Sioux City and Davenport, Iowa. It also realized that other similar-sized Minnesota "interior mills," including the Commander group (later Commander-Larabee Corporation), centered in Montgomery, were quickly gaining a foothold in the Minneapolis flour district. By the mid-1920s, at least 17 such companies had entered this industry center. Equally important to millers, particularly those interested in establishing a presence in the East and a gateway to the European export trade, was Buffalo, New York, which International Milling succeeded in entering by the end of the decade.

In Canada, meanwhile, under the leadership of Charles Ritz, Robin Hood Flour was attaining national distribution, promoting itself as a high quality, "milled from washed wheat" flour and successfully pricing itself above the competition. By 1945 Robin Hood would become the leading consumer flour in Canada, a position it has never since relinquished. This marketing-success-in-the-making inspired Bean's successor, W. L. Harvey, to bring the Robin Hood name to the United States, along with its chief architect. Beginning in 1937, Ritz replaced the company's several regional brands with Robin Hood and then launched a full-scale media blitz, going head-to-head with two chief competitors, Pillsbury's Best Flour and General Mills's Gold Medal Flour. Because of Robin Hood's late entry into the market, results of the long-running campaign were disappointing. As Atherton Bean, grandson of the founder and the company's fifth president later remarked, "There is an adage in the industry. You can be first or second and be confident of success, but if you're third or fourth you're at risk." Unfortunately, that was the position of Robin Hood Flour in the United States. International Milling, nevertheless, became a formidable foe in the industrial flour market, and from the war years through the 1950s, with the purchase of 15 mills, the company spread into a number of new markets in the central and eastern regions of the country. Beginning in 1951, the company also entered the formula feed business and became a major supplier of enriched grains to livestock farmers in the Upper Midwest.

In 1958 International Milling, which had been exporting not only to Europe, but also Africa, the Middle East, the Orient, and South America, made a momentous decision: to extract itself from markets with political and economic difficulties and focus on one that promised both stability and lucrative returns. The obvious choice at the time was Venezuela, a solid export market—of which the company controlled more than a third—that remained virgin territory for North American investment. The decision was aided by the Venezuelan government's threat in 1956 to close off the import trade; by promising to establish its own wheat mill within the country, the company circumvented the potential loss of market. Located in the Caribbean port city of Puerto Cabello and christened Molinos Nacionales C.A. (MONACA), the mill became a subsidiary of Robin Hood Flour Mills, Ltd., of Canada. Under the early direction of Andre Gillet, MONACA quickly became a leading Venezuelan food corporation, branching out into rice processing, corn milling, spices, bakery mixes, oat cereals, and animal feeds. Most importantly, MONACA was eminently profitable from the beginning, typically contributing 20–30 percent of total earnings on only eight to ten percent of net sales.

Gillet's tenure at MONACA, which extended until his return to Minneapolis in 1968, coincided with Francis Atherton Bean's presidency and chairmanship of the company. The 1960s saw considerable shifts in domestic eating habits and International Milling—with the extra capital supplied by going public in 1964—responded by aggressively entering the consumer foods markets. This policy of expansion and diversification, which was common in the industry, was officially implemented by William G. Phillips, a former president of Glidden-Durkee who Bean hand-picked to restructure the company. Phillips oversaw some 43 acquisitions during the next decade and soon had a multi-faceted company (signified by its new name of International Multifoods, adopted in 1970), operating more than 900 Mister Donuts stores, the Boston Sea Party restaurant chain, a meat-processing plant, several decorative products manufacturers, and a score of small, niche-market food products.

By 1980 the company reported revenues exceeding one billion dollars. Throughout this time, during a fifteen-year period stretching until 1984, the company reported uninterrupted growth in earnings. Yet such signs were misleading. Long before the 1984 decline, the company had become aware of its lagging market shares in nearly all its consumer products; only Kretschmer Wheat Germ represented a market-leading product. Multifoods' ability to compete with the major food corporations was hampered not only by its relative anonymity among consumers but also by its many indiscriminate purchases.

A new restructuring was in order and Phillips appointed Gillet to handle the daunting task of reshaping the now ungainly corporate giant. Complicating matters was the looming threat of an unfriendly takeover and the disgruntlement of shareholders, obliged to accept a less than ten percent return on equity while the industry average was close to 20 percent. The metamorphosis that Gillet effected during the next several years was, according to analyst Jim McCartney, "one of the deftest sleight of hand tricks in corporate America's history. By quietly selling off pieces and buying new ones, Gillet gradually transformed [Multifoods] from a flour milling and consumer foods company into a food service distribution and manufacturing company." Gone was Robin Hood Flour, the cornerstone of the company (the U.S. trademark rights were sold to General Mills and the mills themselves to ConAgra, though international Robin Hood operations remained), as well as a host of other less substantial enterprises. In their place was a list of food purveyors that promised a new synergy and direction for the company. The single most important purchase Multifoods made at the time was the 1984 acquisition of Denver-based Vendors Supply of America. A vending distributor with $200 million in annual sales, VSA was bought for $15 million and then carefully developed into a convenient one-stop supplier to vending operators, with 19 warehouses serving 48 states. The foodservice industry that VSA caters to has blossomed into a $262 billion market, an ever-increasing proportion of which the subsidiary plans to dominate.

Since 1989, Gillet's visionary lead has been strengthened by the cost-conscious programs of CEO Anthony Luiso, a former executive of Beatrice and a veteran of the food trade. Luiso joined Multifoods in 1986 as head of restaurant supply operations and contributed to a 21 percent rise in revenues, which totaled $1.7 billion; profits for the same year vaulted an astonishing 82 percent to $33 million. One of the toughest decisions facing Luiso is deciding the fate of MONACA. Despite outstanding earnings in 1990 (25 percent of total operating earnings on only nine percent of net sales), or for that matter a lengthy record of strong performance, MONACA is continually vulnerable to the inflation-prone economy of Venezuela. In addition, several analysts have come to view the flour- and feeds-processor as a cumbersome appendage for the new Multifoods, even given MONACA's number one and two positions in its three primary businesses.

Looking ahead to the 1990s, Multifoods can be expected to focus increasingly on its domestic operations. According to Luiso, more than 70 percent of company revenues are now derived from U.S. ventures that have only been in place since the mid-1980s. Such rapid and dynamic change may cause investors to be wary, yet any fears may not be justified given

Multifoods' wholesale capture of leading positions in virtually every market it has entered, from surimi (imitation seafood) and bakery mixes to burritos and specialty meats. Once tagged "the wallflower of Wall Street," Multifoods is a rejuvenated company, promising a solid commitment to its shareholders. Luiso, voluntarily one of the lowest paid of all Fortune 500 chief executives, has gambled a sizeable chunk of his own money to ensure this. In a now notorious 1989 agreement, he pledged to purchase, within a five-year period, some 153,000 shares of IMC stock at a price near its 52-week high. As he told Eric Wieffering in August 1990, "Three years from now, we plan to be the best at being responsive to our customer base. If we do that, then we can more than double the size of this company in the next five years. Remember, I'm betting a million bucks, and, to me, that is real money."

Principal Subsidiaries: Fantasia Confections, Inc.; JAC Creative Foods, Inc.; Mexicana de Inversiones FEMAC, S.A. de C.V. (45 percent); Mixco Intl., S.A. de C.V. (49 percent); Molinos Nacionales, C.A. (MONACA); Multifoods Bakery Distributors, Inc.; Multifoods Bakery International, Inc.; Prepared Foods, Inc.; Robin Hood Flour Ltd. (Canada); Vendors Supply of America, Inc.

Further Reading: Kuhlmann, Charles Byron, "The Growth of the Milling Industry After 1890—The Minneapolis District," *The Development of the Flour-Milling Industry in the United States,* Boston and New York, Houghton Mifflin Company, 1929; "Once Bankrupt Firm Now Second in Field," *Minneapolis Tribune,* October 17, 1954; Mason, Ralph, "City Firm Building Mill in Venezuela," *Minneapolis Star,* February 28, 1958; Hobart, Randall, "Multifoods Changes Symbol to Reflect Increasing Diversity," *Minneapolis Star,* June 23, 1971; Youngblood, Dick, "Multifoods Buys Largest Maker of Wall Accessories," *Minneapolis Tribune,* October 27, 1972; Johnson, Ken, "Mixing It Up at Multifoods," *Corporate Report,* March, 1975; "Corporate Identity Program Increases Awareness of Multifoods," *Impact (for Multifoods Employees Worldwide),* November 18, 1975; Larson, Don W., "Grain and Flour Milling," *Land of the Giants: A History of Minnesota Business,* Minneapolis, Dorn Books, 1979; "William Phillips and Andre Gillet Head up International Multifoods," *Skyway News,* April 5, 1983; "Multifoods Beginnings Weren't International," *Skyway News,* May 31, 1983; Houston, Patrick, "Multifoods Is Ditching Its 'Mishmash of Little Businesses'," *Business Week,* September 22, 1986; Madden, Stephen, "On the Rise: Anthony Luiso, 44," *Fortune,* August 15, 1988; McCartney, Jim, "Repackaging International Multifoods," *St. Paul Pioneer Press,* August 14, 1989; Wieffering, Eric J., "Multifoods Makeover," *Corporate Report Minnesota,* August, 1990; "Burritos, Anyone?" *Forbes,* March 18, 1991; "Multifoods Attributes 39 percent Increase in Earnings to Improving Businesses," *Star Tribune,* April 18, 1991; Carideo, Anthony, "Food Firm Serves up a Menu of Good News," *Star Tribune,* July 1, 1991; Egerstrom, Lee, "Multifoods Misunderstood Despite Its Improvements," *St. Paul Pioneer Press,* September 30, 1991; *Multifoods Today: Building Tomorrow Together, 1892–1992,* Minneapolis, International Multifoods, 1992; "International Multifoods Corporation," *Corporate Report Minnesota,* February, 1992; Kennedy, Tony, "Multifoods Buys Frozen Products Firm in Canada," *Star Tribune,* April 28, 1992; Kennedy, Tony, "Multifoods Unveils New Corporate Logo," *Star Tribune,* May 14, 1992; Kennedy, Tony, "Multifood Stockholders Want Company to Get Rid of 'Poison Pill'," *Star Tribune,* June 27, 1992.

—Jay P. Pederson

ipcmagazines

IPC MAGAZINES LIMITED

Kings Reach Tower, Stamford Street
London SE1 9LS
United Kingdom
(071) 261-5000
Fax: (071) 261-1138

Public Company
Incorporated: 1968
Employees: 5,300
Sales: £280 million ($406 million)
Stock Exchanges: London

A division of Reed Elsevier, the world's second largest publisher (created in 1993 when Reed International merged with the Dutch company Elsevior), IPC Magazines Limited is the largest consumer magazine publisher in Europe. It has more than 50 magazines in circulation, with its market leaders in the notoriously competitive women's magazine category. While the company continues to explore new readerships, introducing new titles in the science and youth segments in the late 1980s, many of its most popular titles, such as *Country Life, Horse and Hound,* and *Melody Maker,* have a long and respected tenure. Sales of IPC magazines comprised just over one-third of the £700 million the U.K. spent on consumer titles in 1991.

Many of the magazines IPC produces were created through the efforts of three English companies, the George Newnes Company, William Odhams Ltd., and Amalgamated Press (later renamed Fleetway), which merged during the late 1950s to form what is known as IPC Magazines Ltd. The George Newnes Company was founded in 1881, when Newnes, inspired after reading a story about a runaway train in a Manchester newspaper, put together the magazine *Tit-bits* comprised of similar dramatic stories. The endeavor was a great success, and, in order to continue publishing, Newnes opened a restaurant for further financing. *Tit-bits* circulation rose to 200,000 in two years, the rise fueled by new marketing techniques.

Newnes went on to publish *Review of Reviews* and *Strand,* which featured the cases of Sherlock Holmes. *Country Life,* established in 1897 by Newnes and Edward Hudson, covered culture in rural England and remained a British favorite throughout the twentieth century. Two other Newnes magazines published by IPC are *Woman's Life* and *Woman's Own.* Founded in 1932, *Woman's Own* was given significant media

coverage for its role, as described in Reed International's *Chapters from Our History,* in "campaigning to improve the role of women in the community." The magazine remained popular, selling a remarkable average of 1.5 million copies a year in 1991.

Another IPC predecessor originated with William Odhams, who first published the *Guardian*—a paper whose primary audience was high church officials—in 1890. Odhams's sons took over in 1896, and renamed the business William Odhams Ltd. Ten years later the well-known financier and publisher Horatio Bottomley suggested the idea for a magazine called *John Bull,* which became quite popular. In 1920, John Bull Ltd. merged to form Odhams Press Ltd. The company produced several popular titles that were still being published by IPC more than seventy years later.

Odhams' most notable titles were *Woman, Ideal Home,* and *Horse and Hound.* Founded in 1937, *Woman* was launched soon after Britain's women had gained the right to vote and discussed "any and every subject for the domestic and career woman." Furthermore, *Woman* was Britain's first full color weekly printed by Odhams's high speed printworks. *Ideal Home* was founded in 1920 by poet and artist William Morris and Captain G.C. Clark, who served as its first editor. In Clark's words, the magazine's mission was to reach "the wide circle of the middle class" and "to strive against the erection of hideous houses." *Ideal Home* continued providing decorating ideas for each successive generation; the magazine sold nearly half a million copies in 1991. *Horse and Hound* was founded in 1884, for a true niche market. The magazine strove to use a contemporary approach to a traditional topic, and has maintained the largest circulation of any equestrian weekly, selling an annual average of 160,000 copies in the early 1990s.

Another IPC predecessor was the Amalgamated Press, founded by Alfred Harmsworth in 1888. The publisher initially produced *Answers to Correspondents,* the first magazine of its kind dedicated to answering readers' questions on any possible subject. Other Amalgamated publications included *London Magazine, Woman and Home, Woman's Weekly,* and several children's magazines. Created in 1911, *Woman's Weekly* is the oldest women's magazine produced in the U.K. and sold an average of 1.8 million copies in 1991.

Amalgamated Press, George Newnes, and Odhams Press Ltd. were all acquired by the United Kingdom's largest newspaper publisher, the Mirror Group, during the period from 1958 to 1961. In 1963, the International Publishing Corporation Ltd. was formed as a holding company for the Mirror Group. In addition to owning and operating 29 printing companies, IPC Ltd. produced hundreds of magazines, three London daily newspapers, and several journals.

During the 1950s, several new publications were introduced. The weekly *New Musical Express (NME),* founded by Morris Kinn in 1952, was the first to print the first top-selling record charts. Following music trends over the decades, *NME* sold an average of over 200,000 copies a year forty years after its launch. *New Scientist* was founded in 1956 with Percy Cudlipp as editor. IPC sales of the weekly title in 1991 averaged 200,000 copies a year. In 1958 *Women's Realm* was introduced with the aim to provide more practical information and advice than any other women's weekly. The goal was met; by 1991 the title sold nearly a million copies a year.

In 1970, the Reed Group—a publisher in the business, commercial, and consumer sectors—and Reed International acquired IPC, retaining the name IPC Magazines Ltd. for their consumer magazines division. According to the Reed International publication *Chapters from our History*, the group was "a potent force with important leverage over advertisers and sales outlets alike."

Reed's goal for the newly formed IPC was to dominate the consumer magazine market. The firm achieved its aim, especially in the women's weekly magazine sector, receiving little serious competition for twenty years. Competitors generally viewed the costs of financing an entry into IPC territory as too high and the risks as far too great. Some challengers did eventually emerge, however; by the 1980s the publishers National Magazine Company and EMAP created some successful monthly magazines in the women's and youth markets.

Some effects of the IPC virtual monopoly began to surface in the late 1980s. As columnist Harold Lind commented in *Marketing*, June 21, 1990, "the major drawback of a monopoly is that it tends to be painfully inefficient and slow moving, hurting the public less by its extortionate demands than by the use of its dominant position to keep out desirable innovation."

Whether or not IPC was deliberately keeping out desirable innovation was debatable. One measurable outcome following the company's twenty-year dominance, however, was the decline in women's weekly magazine sales. According to Lind, consumer sales fell by just over 50 percent, while advertising decreased by an even greater amount. Ironically, although many of IPC's women's magazines had been founded in the early 1900s to meet the changing values and needs of its readership, the overall cultural upheaval of the late 1960s and 1970s, and the changing roles of women in particular, probably played a part in the women's magazine market drop. Some U.K. observers and consumers began to think that the entire sector of the industry was in a terminal descent.

Publishing began to change rapidly in the mid-1980s as various European magazine publishers moved into the U.K. to test their marketing skills in a different venue. Though it took large scale financing, publishers successfully moved into IPC territory and by the late 1980s effects were apparent. After a brief overall sales increase in all consumer magazines, the high profile titles soon gained buyers while the lesser known magazines suffered losses. IPC, like other publishers, began scrambling to find more niche markets to control.

IPC's biggest threat was the German company Gruner + Jahr (G & J), a heavy hitting publishing concern with a great deal of capital. In 1986 Gruner and Jahr successfully introduced *Prima* into the British market, a magazine already successful in a number of European countries. The entrance of German companies into the British market was a preview of future conditions under the then developing European common market. IPC entered a challenging phase in it history, undergoing a series of changes some of which the company initiated, others of which were necessary defensive reactions to stiff competition.

The company introduced a number of new titles testing out a variety of market niches. IPC hoped that its new *Essentials* publication would rival Gruner & Jahr's *Prima* magazine for an extended European readership. When IPC scheduled the magazine's introduction for the end of January 1988, G & J responded by changing the sale date of *Prima* to compete directly with IPC's entry. IPC then moved up its new magazine's launch date to the second week of January.

IPC moved aggressively to purchase Thompson Magazines in March of 1988 for £28 million. While the British publisher National Magazines Company was invited to bid, Germany's G & J was not. The Thompson acquisition gave IPC two mass market magazines, *Family Circle* and *Living*, with a combined circulation of close to one million. More importantly, however, as reported by David Reed in *Marketing*, "The acquisition of *Family Circle* and *Living* by IPC is almost certain to change the way magazines are sold, and therefore read."

Reed referred to two changes. First, he noted, the two new acquisitions were the only magazines in the U.K. to have an exclusive contract for sale in supermarkets. If IPC chose to make its other magazines available to supermarket buyers, a potentially huge consumer audience, company sales could rise well beyond those of its competitors. Second, the move of acquiring two mass market titles hinted that IPC intended to enter the larger European market. The earlier a publisher gained a foothold in European markets, the more prepared that company would be for the common market.

IPC's next move was to give *Family Circle* and *Living* a trial period of marketing via news agents in addition to supermarket distribution. The magazines had been offered exclusively through supermarkets since 1965, and although IPC's move was intended to achieve a larger market, it also allowed for the possibility that supermarkets would react by selling competing mass market magazines.

As competition in the women's magazine market heated up, IPC made several decisions. The company acquired Carlton Magazine's *Look Now* and merged it with IPC publication *19* in July 1988, displaying both magazine names on the cover for the first several issues. IPC and Carlton were both owned by Reed International, a relationship IPC considered incidental to the merger.

The IPC/Carlton magazine *Riva* was introduced in late spring 1988 and promptly cancelled in mid-October. The budget for *Riva's* launch was the largest ever, and the magazine was cut before half of the funds were used. IPC publishing director Nigel Davidson had spoken accurately when quoted in the July 28, 1988, *Marketing*: "The market in the past 18 months has changed dramatically and everything we do has to be reassessed." The year 1989 posed more changes and once again IPC brought out a new title. *Me* was designed to compete with the German weeklies *Best* and *Bella*, which were aimed at women of an average age of 29.

One advantage IPC had over its competitors was loyal advertisers who had been with the women's titles for years. Such a relationship was subject to change, however, as IPC's weeklies had been experiencing a twenty-year decline in sales. Circulation of *Woman* and *Woman's Own* was still strong in February of 1989 at just under one million for each title, but the competitive pressure was not lifting.

IPC reacted to competition in 1989 by redesigning all of its "big four" titles. *Woman* was given a practical emphasis to distinguish it from *Woman's Own*. Both magazines appealed to a younger woman consumer. At the same time IPC restyled *Woman's Realm* to attract a segment other than the more mature reader of IPC's *Woman's Weekly*. The *Women's Journal* logo, design, and typeface were changed to capture the older, more glamorous market.

At this time IPC Magazines took a step noted industry wide. The company, which rarely hired outside advertisers, chose one for *Women's Journal*. The once dominant magazine had dropped in circulation by nearly 25 percent over the previous five-year period. As Liz Levy wrote in *Marketing*, "the magazine environment is changing fast. A blitz of new titles has knocked that company's big four out of the comfortable knowledge that they are habit purchases."

A front page story in the February 15, 1990, *Marketing* featured the headline "Sales Plummet for IPC Titles." The decline in circulation came from titles across the board, including the women's big four, *Essentials,* and *Chat,* a popular gossip magazine acquired in 1989. Even the old standbys *Country Life* and *Country Homes* felt the hit. IPC quickly decided to revamp *Chat* as well as *Ideal Home,* the market leader in its segment. By May 1990 the company cancelled its monthly title *Women's World*, launched in 1978, due to declining ad revenues. Once again IPC turned some energies toward new titles, creating *Vox* to appeal to the 20- to 30-year old male, and by mid-1991 it was redesigning *Women's Realm,* which had become the company's lowest circulation women's weekly.

In its extensive efforts to sell magazines, IPC's group incentive department tried an innovative promotion which was a great success. Commissioning a company to develop an attractive and practical packaging solution, IPC enclosed imitation pearl earrings as a free gift in a special issue of *Women's Weekly*, which sold out quickly.

With the appointment of John Mellon as chief executive officer in 1987, IPC hoped to address some of its marketing problems. By 1991 the company was regarded as having kept in step with—or even a step ahead of—the industry changes. A revamped classified advertising department increased revenue, and new accounting technology helped boost company profits as well.

IPC continued its drive through the 1990s to control carefully defined markets in the U.K. and internationally. In the United Kingdom, IPC's *Puzzle Weekly* was a good example of exploiting a niche market. The company also entered in a joint venture with German publisher Burda to produce *Practical Parenting* and other magazines as well. IPC's *Essentials* was the first U.K. magazine to be licensed in overseas markets. By the early 1990s, *TV Times* sold an average of 2.5 million copies a year. As Mellon summed up in the July 4, 1991, *Marketing,* "It's difficult for us to expand in the U.K., but with Europe we've only scratched the surface."

IPC maintains two subsidiaries. IPC Telemarketing is a leading U.K. provider of Audiotex services in the categories of Information, Entertainment, Direct Marketing, and Transactions. Through joint venture agreements with print and broadcast media, marketing, and advertising clients, IPC Telemarketing works weekly to update its portfolio of Audiotex services. IPC Marketforce is the U.K.'s largest distributor of consumer magazines, delivering 54 IPC magazines as well as 121 titles for 20 other publishers. IPC Marketforce pioneered the use of Electronic Data Interchange (EDI) with its suppliers and customers and aims to be the best circulation management firm in the business.

The IPC Classifieds division, a recent addition to the IPC fold, has, according to a June 1992 company publication, "developed the most sophisticated operation of its kind in European consumer publishing." Using state-of-the-art telephone and advertising systems, IPC Classifieds sells 33 titles, and has opened up new marketplaces for its parent publisher.

Magazine divisions at IPC are divided into four categories. The IPC Weeklies Group produces six leading women's weeklies, two television guides, and a coupon insert published seven times a year. The division sells seven million copies weekly, reaching an audience of 22 million, and employs approximately 500 people. SouthBank Publishing Group, with a staff of 400, produces ten monthly magazines and one bimonthly title in the women's and home sectors. The Holborn Group publishes 19 titles, evenly split between weeklies and monthlies, as well as one bimonthly title for the youth, music, and various niche markets. The Specialist and Leisure Group, with over 200 on staff, produces twelve highly regarded magazines in the weekly and monthly sectors.

Principal Subsidiaries: IPC Telemarketing; IPC Marketforce.

Further Reading: Simpson, Rachel, "Essentials Jumps the Gun on Gruner Spoiler," *Marketing,* January 7, 1988; Reed, David, "IPC snaps up Thomson mags in £28m deal," *Marketing,* March 10, 1988; —"IPC Gets a Foot in the Supermarket Door," *Marketing,* March 17, 1988; —"IPC Breaks its Bond," *Marketing,* May 26, 1988; —"Look Now is Casualty in Dogfight for Space," *Marketing,* July 28, 1988; —"IPC Tries Outsider for 'Big Five' Push," *Marketing,* July 28, 1988; "Riva's Collapse a Sinister Omen for New Titles," *Marketing,* October 27, 1988; "IPC Restyles Woman with a Practical Edge," *Marketing,* January 12, 1989; "Fortress IPC Fails to Repel the Challengers," *Marketing,* February 16, 1989; Brierley, Sean, "IPC Pushes into Germans' Weekly Niche," *Marketing,* May 18, 1989; Levy, Liz, "IPC Picks Outsider to Stop Women Straying," *Marketing,* July 27, 1989; Brierly, Sean, "IPC Woos Mature Women in Move away from Young Crowd," *Marketing,* August 17, 1989; Fry, Andy, "Sales Plummet for IPC Titles," *Marketing,* February 15, 1990; "Women's World Folds," *Marketing,* May 3, 1990; "IPC Homes in on the Ideal Magazine Mix," *Marketing,* May 10, 1990; Lind, Harold, "As IPC Loses its Monopoly, Competitors are Faring Well," *Marketing,* June 2, 1990; Fry, Andy, "IPC Tries to Keep in Tune with Launch of Music Title Max," *Marketing,* June 28, 1990; "Agencies Hit out at IPC," *Marketing,* August 23, 1990; Oliver, Brian, "Harnessing the Power Premiums," *Marketing,* November 11, 1991; Hoggan, Karen, "Revamp for Women's

Realm to Halt Decline,'' *Marketing,* May 2, 1991; Fry, Andy, ''IPC Takes Legal Action against BBC Advertising,'' *Marketing,* May 23, 1991; ''The Me-too Success Story,'' *Marketing,* July 4, 1991; Syedain, Hashi, ''IPC to Launch German Title,'' *Marketing,* January 16, 1992; ''Female Touch Works in Recession,'' *Marketing,* February 27, 1992; Low, Jack, ''IPC Magazines, Europe's Largest Consumer Magazine Publisher,'' London: IPC Magazines Ltd., June 1992; ''Chapters from Our History,'' London: Reed International PLC, 1992; Low, Jack, and Fiona Baker, eds., ''IPC News,'' London: IPC Magazines Ltd., December 1992–January 1993.

—Frances E. Norton

NHK 時代をあつく伝えたい。

JAPAN BROADCASTING CORPORATION (NIPPON HOSO KYOKAI)

2-2-1 Jinnan
Shibuya-ku, Tokyo
Japan 150-01
(3) 3465-1111
Fax: (3) 3469-8110

State Administered Company
Incorporated: 1926
Employees: 13,600
Operating Revenues: ¥553.67 billion (US$4.64 billion)
SICs: 4833 Television Broadcasting Stations; 4832 Radio Broadcasting Stations

The Japan Broadcasting Corporation, better known as NHK, is Japan's national public broadcasting network, as established under the 1950 Broadcast Law. The company is administered by a board of governors appointed by the prime minister and is supported by public fees, which are collected from viewers through a funding arrangement called "receiving fees." Everyone in Japan with a television set within range of NHK broadcasts is required by the Broadcast Law to pay the company a fee. Through programming that is similar to that of the United States's Public Broadcasting System, NHK airs a variety of educational, cultural, entertainment, and news programs.

In addition to operating two terrestrial and two satellite television channels, NHK operates three conventional radio networks and Japan's shortwave radio service. The company also conducts broadcast media-related research through the NHK Technical Research Laboratories and the NHK Broadcasting Culture Research Institute.

NHK traces its origins to the Tokyo Broadcasting Station, which aired Japan's first radio transmission on March 22, 1925. Tokyo Broadcasting was established with a license from the Ministry of Posts and Telecommunications. The radio station was then incorporated under government charter in August of 1926 as Nippon Hoso Kyokai, the Japan Broadcasting Corporation. As Japan's national broadcaster, NHK was in a unique position to reach the Japanese people, spread over four, large, mountainous islands, roughly all at the same time. Through NHK the country as a whole was able to hear live broadcasts of such important events as the special programs aired to celebrate the enthronement of Emperor Hirohito in November, 1928.

In June of 1930, the company formed a research laboratory in order to explore technological advances that would further the broadcasting industry. That same year, the first international radio transmission was received successfully from London, England, setting the stage for regularly scheduled overseas broadcasting. Under the name Radio Tokyo, broadcasting of daily English- and Japanese-language programs to the Pacific Coast of North America began on June 1, 1935.

After establishing a second radio network in April of 1931, NHK became more involved in current events, providing newspaper-format news programming and coverage of the 1932 Olympic games in Los Angeles. Three years later NHK began broadcasting school lessons, as part of a national effort to standardize the country's educational curriculum and extend learning to remote areas.

However, with the rise of militarism in Japan, NHK, as well as other media, eventually fell under the control of the government. Through the late 1930s, NHK gradually lost its impartial tone and soon was dominated by imperialist rhetoric. It was through the network that Japanese public opinion was effectively galvanized against European imperialists who, it was charged, had colonized Asia.

At this time, experimental television broadcasting was being carried out at NHK's laboratories. Before any regular application could be established, however, the Japanese became distracted by the country's war in China and, later, the war in the Pacific. Virtually all technological development was diverted to military projects, including the establishment of military communications throughout Japan's theater of war operations.

NHK, in the meantime, had become largely an instrument of government propaganda, though efforts were also made to provide the people with helpful information. For example, toward the end of the war, when Japan was suffering from shortages, NHK broadcast directions on how to produce food from common plants, and even tea, so that people could avoid starvation.

When Emperor Hirohito addressed the nation in August of 1945, he did so over NHK. It was the first time anyone but a small circle of advisors had ever heard his voice. He announced the surrender of Japan to Allied forces.

No longer under the control of the government, NHK broadcasted important news to the Japanese people about the occupation, the formation of a new government, and the establishment of new laws. One of those new laws, enacted in June of 1950, was the Broadcast Law, which established NHK as a special corporation under the direction of a board of governors. This law laid out special provisions designed to guarantee the impartiality and journalistic integrity of NHK, so that it could never again be used as a propaganda device.

Resuming work on technological development, NHK conducted a successful trial of color television broadcasting in March of 1952. The first rudimentary stereo radio broadcasts were also tried that year, using two different AM frequencies.

Experiments with FM broadcasts commenced five years later in Tokyo, and regular FM programming began in 1969.

The shortwave station, Radio Tokyo—having suspended transmission at the end of World War II—resumed operation on February 1, 1952, under the name Radio Japan. Its new mission, in the postwar era, was to promote better understanding of Japanese culture and to provide Japanese people living abroad with news and entertainment from their homeland. The station broadcasted in several languages, including English, Russian, Chinese, Arabic, and Indonesian.

NHK entered a new era in February of 1953 when the broadcaster began providing television services, initially aired four hours per day. Though there were few commercial reasons to start a television station—Tokyo could only claim about 900 television sets—NHK forged ahead. The company provided a catalyst for other television broadcasters to enter this new medium, spurring growth in the industry. Only months after hitting the airwaves, NHK provided a live telecast of the coronation of Queen Elizabeth II in England. The next year, the company began recorded programming with kinescopes, enabling it to repeat broadcasts and produce fully-rehearsed programs.

The television service became immensely popular, particularly after the entry of Fuji Television, Nippon Television, and Tokyo Broadcasting. The rapid commercialization of the new medium enabled these television services to quickly incorporate new technologies, including color broadcasting, which NHK introduced in August of 1960. Nationwide color broadcast capability was completed in 1966, and by 1971 all General TV programs were being broadcast in color.

While NHK began educational television programming with the opening of a second network, Educational TV, in January of 1959, another network, Nippon Educational Television, began broadcasting to a similar audience only a few weeks later. NET and NHK continued to operate educational programs in tandem for several years until 1973, when NET formally became the commercial network TV Asahi.

NHK was an early pioneer of satellite transmission technology. Virtually as soon as the first public circuits were opened, NHK began news feeds from the United States, Europe, and Africa. The first use of live satellite coverage came on November 22, 1963, when reports on the assassination of President John F. Kennedy were carried live on NHK.

With the proliferation of television broadcasting in Japan, particularly within the heavily populated urban areas, the airwaves were soon depleted of available frequencies. Therefore, NHK began experimental transmissions in the new UHF frequencies. The first of these put to practical use were on special NHK stations in Tokyo and Osaka during 1971.

NHK's charter in the Broadcast Law mandated the company's responsibility for airing programs of a more culturally complex nature than commercial television could afford to support. Aside from educational programming, NHK carried symphonies, opera performances, interviews, and documentaries. This programming, however, needed an appropriate venue, and NHK obliged in 1973, with the construction of a massive broadcasting complex and a theater, NHK Hall.

While culturally enriching, these programs did not draw tremendous audiences, though the shows did serve to make these subjects more popular than they might have been. To provide some variety in their programming format, NHK began airing baseball games—extremely popular in Japan—boxing, soccer and the Olympic games.

NHK was one of the first networks to try direct broadcasting, that is, beaming a signal directly to viewers' televisions from a satellite. DBS, as it was called, provided several advantages over the terrestrial network, the most important of which was high quality reception throughout Japan. Since 70 percent of Japan is mountainous, it had thus far been difficult for many viewers living in valleys and less populated areas to receive quality radio and television transmissions. Even NHK, with the most complete network in Japan, covering approximately 95 percent of the country, would benefit from DBS, which would enable huge areas to receive high-quality signals at a much lower cost than a network of ground-based relay stations.

NHK's first DBS tests took place in July of 1978. Based on these tests, NHK developed the MUSE system, designed for the transmission of high-definition television (HDTV) signals. Hi-Vision, as HDTV is called in Japan, was demonstrated at the Tsukuba Science Expo in 1985. Using its research facility, NHK became a participant in a Japanese consortium, the Hi-Vision Promotion Association (HPA), working to broadcast HDTV.

Two DBS satellites were launched in January of 1984 and February of 1986, aboard Japanese N-2 and H-1 rockets, allowing NHK, among other users, to begin experimental DBS broadcasts in May of 1984. A regular 24-hour service began three years later and had about 150,000 viewers. When the second DBS channel went on line on June 3, 1989, there were more than 1.5 million viewers. The service was available to anyone with a television and a parabolic antenna. Two more satellites were launched in 1990 and 1991. These satellites beamed two NHK channels—by 1992 the number of viewers had grown to 6 million—and a third operated by the commercial consortium, Japan Satellite Broadcasting Corp.

In October of 1983, NHK began teletext broadcasting, which delivers subtitles to hearing impaired viewers, in Tokyo and Osaka. An improved service was introduced two years later, and by 1986, the entire network was equipped for teletext service. In addition, in 1985, the company also started an Emergency Warning Broadcasting System. Intended for use in the event of natural or other disasters, the system was employed several times to warn viewers of severe weather, tsunamis, and, on one occasion, a volcanic eruption.

In addition to NHK's two terrestrial television stations, General TV and Educational TV, the broadcaster operates two DBS stations, Satellite Television Channel One and Channel Two. Some of the more popular programs on NHK television are *Asia Now, NHK Morning Magazine,* and American NFL football games. NHK also operates news-oriented Radio 1 and the educational Radio 2 on medium wave (AM), an FM music network, and the shortwave-frequency Radio Japan. NHK operates shortwave relay stations in Canada, Singapore, French Guiana, Sri Lanka, Gabon, and Britain.

Since its establishment under the Broadcast Law of 1950, NHK has been administered by a board of governors chosen by the prime minister and approved by both houses of Parliament. The 12-member board is responsible for appointing the president and a group of auditors, who survey the president's business practices. In addition, NHK's strategic and operating policies, including the annual budget and programming plans, are determined by the board. The budget and operational plans are then submitted to the Minister of Posts and Telecommunications, who reviews the material, which is passed on to the Cabinet and, finally, to Parliament for approval.

Accepting governmental financial support only for overseas shortwave services, NHK's operating budget is financed through receiving fee contracts with television owners, originally collected door-to-door or through bank transfer. In the 1970s, however, automatic bank transfers were introduced and in the early 1990s represented the method of payment used by more than 60 percent of the contracted households. NHK charges ¥1,320 each month for regular channels and an additional ¥930 for DBS reception.

Through this unusual funding mechanism, NHK operates Japan's largest broadcast network, completely without commercial support. In addition the company has always been at the forefront of technological advancements in the industry. NHK is more than a broadcaster, it is in many ways a broadcast laboratory.

Principal Subsidiaries: NHK Enterprises, Inc.; NHK Educational Corporation; NHK Creative Co., Ltd.; NHK Software, Inc.; NHK Joho Network, Inc.; NHK Promotion Co., Ltd.; NHK Art, Inc.; NHK Technical Services, Inc.; Japan Broadcast Publishing Co., Ltd.; NHK Kinki Media Plan, Inc.; NHK Nagoya Brains, Inc.; NHK Chugoku Software & Planning, Inc.; NHK Kyushu Media, Inc.; NHK Tohoku Planning, Inc.; NHK Hokkaido Vision, Inc.; NHK Sogo Business, Inc.; NHK Integrated Technology, Inc.; NHK Culture Center, Inc.; NHK Computer Service, Inc.; NHK Business Service, Inc.; Print-Center, Inc.; NHK Service Center, Inc.; NHK International, Inc.; NHK Engineering Service, Inc.

Further Reading: "The Changing Face of Television," *Look Japan,* March 1993; *NHK Factsheet,* Tokyo, NHK, 1993; *NHK in Focus,* Tokyo, NHK, 1993.

—John Simley

JOHN FAIRFAX HOLDINGS LIMITED

235-243 Jones Street
Broadway, New South Wales 2007
Australia
(02) 282-2833
Fax: (02) 282-3133

Public Company
Incorporated: April 9, 1955 as John Fairfax Limited
Employees: 4,340
Sales: A$359.1 million (US$247 million)
Stock Exchanges: Sydney
SICs: 2711 Newspapers; 2721 Periodicals; 6719 Holding
   Companies, Nec

John Fairfax Holdings Limited is the holding company for an Australian publishing enterprise established more than 150 years ago. Family owned and operated until the 1990s, Fairfax is the oldest publishing group in Australia, and one of its largest. Its operations are centered around three publications—the *Sydney Morning Herald,* the *Age* and the *Australian Financial Review.*

The Fairfax family originated in Warwickshire, England, where the patriarch of the family publishing empire, John Fairfax, was born in 1805. At the age of 12 he went to London to work as an apprentice bookseller, librarian, and printer. Returning to Warwickshire in 1827, he started his own printing business and later established a small newspaper, the *Leamington Spa Courier.* In 1835, having converted to a "dissenter's church," he turned his energies to a less conservative paper, the *Leamington Chronicle.*

But after being sued twice, Fairfax decided to emigrate with his family to Australia, then an English penal colony. Arriving in Sydney in 1838, he found work as a typesetter for the *Commercial Journal and Advertiser.* After a short stint as a librarian, he purchased an interest in the daily *Sydney Herald* and in 1841 purchased the paper with a partner, Charles Kemp, for £10,000.

With the closure of the rival *Australian* in 1848, the *Herald* dominated local journalism. By 1852 "Granny *Herald,*" as the paper had become known, had a circulation of more than 4,000. The following year, Kemp sold his interest in the paper to Fairfax, who enlisted his son Charles as a partner.

A leader in his community, John Fairfax stood for election in 1856, but lost. Still, with circulation now over 6,600—third in the British Empire only to London's *Times* and *Telegraph*—Fairfax exercised considerable influence over public opinion.

Bringing his second son, James Reading Fairfax, into the partnership, the enterprise became John Fairfax & Sons. The company launched a second paper, the *Sydney Mail,* and installed new, more efficient Richard Hoe rotary presses.

Charles Fairfax died after being thrown from a horse in 1863 and was replaced in the partnership by a third son, Edward. The business continued to expand, particularly after the demise of another competitor, the *Empire.* John Fairfax died in 1877, leaving the business to his two sons.

James Reading Fairfax strengthened the *Herald's* reputation for evenhandedness and authority and, with his large build and Edwardian beard, was an imposing figure. It was his bold decision to turn over daily operation of the business to a capable former rival, Hugh George. Under George, the appearance of a competitor, the *Sydney Daily Telegraph,* cut into circulation but not into advertising revenue.

After George died in 1886, Edward grew openly weary of the business and sold his interest to James, who in turn brought his three sons into the company. Meanwhile, Samuel Cook, a parliamentary reporter for the *Herald,* replaced George as general manager.

Cook oversaw the conversion of the *Herald* to mechanical typesetting in 1895, an important move that lowered labor costs and sped production. Such an investment was risky, as the economy was plagued by depression, but soon paid off. Cook left the company in 1907 and was replaced by William George Conley, a former reporter.

James Reading Fairfax, now in his seventies, began to delegate more authority to his sons James Oswald and Geoffrey. James Oswald was more domineering than his lighter spirited brother. Due to a weak voice, though, he was forced to precisely punctuate his sentences—a habit that most found annoying.

In 1916, with the outbreak of war in Europe, Australia's involvement as member of the British Empire brought hardship to the *Herald's* readership. The Fairfax company, too, had grown beyond effective family administration. So, to limit the family's liability from litigation and facilitate the transfer of interests between family members, John Fairfax & Sons was registered as a limited corporation.

The cost of newsprint increased dramatically during World War I, forcing the company to declare its first operating loss in 1919. This was remedied by raising the sale price of the paper from 1d to 1.5d. With the end of the war, however, came the death of the elder James Fairfax at the age of 85.

Within years, both Geoffrey, who had no children, and William Conley also died. The principal heir to the family business was James Oswald Fairfax's son Warwick; he had held only brief tenure on the board. When his father died in 1926, Warwick found himself in control of more than a third of the company's shares.

The young Warwick Fairfax placed tremendous trust in his managing director, Rupert Henderson, despite an often acrimonious relationship. A previous director, Charles Harris, was fired after four years for drinking and gambling to excess. Another, Athol Hugh Stuart, fared better, involving the Fairfax enterprise in a collaboration with Sir Keith Murdoch's *Herald and Weekly Times* (HWT) company to form the Australian Associated Press and a newsprint operation in Tasmania. He also oversaw Fairfax's reversion to proprietary status, eliminating the obligation to publish its balance sheet. But Stuart's demeanor grew violent, and in 1938 he too was fired.

After successive years of declining profit, Henderson reorganized Fairfax. He was so successful in shoring up the bottom line that the company's profits—when compared to the low figures of the previous years—became a source of embarrassment, especially during World War II, when after-tax profits more than doubled.

Warwick, who often wrote for the paper under pseudonyms, was frequently ill during World War II. In 1944 one of his articles so enraged Henderson that he accused Warwick of developing ''an evangelical fervor'' and threatened to resign. The two made amends, however, and Henderson stayed on.

Warwick Fairfax had a troubled personal life, which led to his first divorce. While he remarried in 1948, he and Henderson became concerned about the possible loss of family control of the enterprise. They convinced some family members to relinquish their interests in the company to them and virtually ran the company as a committee of two until 1949, when Angus Henry McLachlan was promoted to general manager.

Fairfax fought numerous battles for niche markets during this period, substantially expanding its publishing empire in and around Sydney with such papers as the *Australian Financial Review*. When rival Frank Packer made a bid to acquire several papers run by the independent Associated Newspapers, Henderson beat him to the punch, in effect merging that business with Fairfax. Later, several of the papers and their operations were consolidated into one facility, a new production house on Sydney's Broadway.

In 1955 Fairfax also acquired a license for Sydney's ATN7 television. The expansion stretched Fairfax's financial resources so thinly that the company was forced to go public on April 9, 1956.

Warwick Fairfax, meanwhile, had become embroiled in another matrimonial debacle when, it was charged, he forced the break-up of a friend's marriage. He divorced a second time, married his friend's wife, and was forced to leave the company temporarily to settle litigation. Warwick renewed his waning interest in the company, which, under Henderson's managerial direction, had obtained a second television station, QTQ in Brisbane. The company also took over its number two rival in Sydney, the Mirror Newspapers, through a shell company.

The *Mirror,* however, was a poor fit and was sold in 1960 to Keith Rupert Murdoch, who had inherited his father's publishing group. Murdoch used this entree into Sydney wisely, utilizing the *Mirror'*s publishing facilities to launch a rival national paper, the *Australian.* In 1972 Murdoch also snapped up

Packer's *Daily Telegraph* and *Sunday Telegraph,* which competed directly with Fairfax.

Fairfax, however, had also been busy during the 1960s, acquiring the *Newcastle Morning Herald, Newcastle Sun,* and *Canberra Times,* an interest in Canberra television station CTC, and the Australian share of the British television group ATV. Six radio stations that came with ATV were later spun off as Macquarie Broadcasting Holdings Ltd.

Henderson retired in 1964 but retained his seat on the board. He was succeeded as chief executive officer by McLachlan. Under McLachlan, Fairfax acquired the Melbourne-based Syme company, which published the *Age* and, beginning in 1969, the 114-year-old *Illawarra Mercury.* Later that year, McLachlan suffered a coronary occlusion that forced his retirement. Unwilling to return managerial control of the paper to the 68-year-old Warwick, McLachlan, Henderson, and Warwick's cousin Vincent nominated R. P. Falkingham as the company's treasurer. Outraged, Warwick put up a good fight and later won, though from the ceremonial position of chairman. At last, he had direct editorial control and the power to fire people.

However, after the company launched a nationwide weekend paper, the *National Times,* in 1971, Fairfax's directors and other employees grew increasingly irritated by the arch-conservative views of Warwick. The situation came to a head in July of 1976, when the directors asked Warwick to resign in favor of his son, James Fairfax, who had distinguished himself at the helm of Amalgamated Television. This time, they succeeded.

While relegated to a minor position in the company, Warwick mounted an ill-conceived attempt to take over Fairfax and was forced to cede even more power as a result. R. P. Falkingham, meanwhile, finally assumed the position of chief executive officer. He was properly suited for the job, showing no bias for Fairfax's newspaper business over its other important mediums.

All aspects of the Fairfax Group, though, were suffering reverses in the marketplace. Falkingham responded by adopting more realistic rates and prices and, in 1977, placed D. N. Bowman in charge of the flagship *Sydney Morning Herald.* Bowman made several changes, including the implementation of the computer-based Arsycom cold type press system, which drastically reduced production costs.

In 1979 Rupert Murdoch surfaced again with a bid to take over Fairfax's other rival, the *Herald and Weekly Times.* Determined to thwart Murdoch, Fairfax began amassing a ''friendly'' holding in its competitor. In the end, however, the government compelled Murdoch to abandon his bid on antitrust grounds. The defense of the HWT cost Fairfax dearly, causing it to sell off its interests in CTC and QTQ television.

In addition, sales of Fairfax's *Herald* and *Sun* were stagnant, the company's Sungravure magazines—acquired with Associated Newspapers during the 1950s—were in trouble, and its interest in Macquarie Broadcasting showed no gains. Perhaps out of desperation, Falkingham recommended that he be replaced as general manager by 36-year-old Gregory John Gardiner, and that Fairfax's five Sydney papers be put under the editorial direction of Maxwell Victor Suich.

Warwick Fairfax, still offering his opinions, opposed the appointment of Suich and Gardiner, whom he considered too young. Nevertheless, under the direction of the two men, the tenor of the *Herald* and its sister papers became decidedly cynical, even sensational. While this was extremely distasteful to the aging board, they could not deny that circulation, if not yet profits, was rebounding strongly.

Despite attempts to modernize Fairfax, much of the company's labor-intensive production capacity was outdated and increasingly uncompetitive. A decision to overhaul several facilities led to serious labor trouble, particularly at Sungravure Magazines, where workers were already on strike for higher pay. Gardiner championed the cause of upgrading the facilities and, in the end, succeeded, resulting in the lay off of 375 Sungravure employees. The division subsequently changed its name to Fairfax Magazines Pty. Limited.

Opposing Gardiner in this and many other matters was Falkingham, who quickly fell out of favor with the board and was forced to resign. Rather than replace him, the board split Falkingham's responsibilities between Gardiner and Fred Benchley, a veteran of the magazine group.

The pressure for consolidation in the Australian publishing industry hit a fever pitch in the mid-1980s. Financiers such as Rupert Murdoch, Robert Holmes à Court, and Alan Bond swarmed over the market, raiding smaller companies to consolidate their operations with other papers they controlled.

After Murdoch's aborted attempt to enter Fairfax's Sydney market in 1979, Holmes à Court launched an unsuccessful bid for Fairfax in 1981. Far more serious, however, was Murdoch's second attempt at the *Herald and Weekly Times* in 1986. This time, the company's board advised its shareholders to accept the buyout offer from Murdoch's News Corporation. A combined HWT/News organization was capable of dominating advertising rates throughout Australia through network advertising.

Fairfax Group was determined to foil Murdoch; so, however, was Holmes à Court, who offered nearly A$2 million for HWT. Murdoch countered with a A$2.3 million bid for HWT and its Queensland Press subsidiary. Although Fairfax offered a bid of its own, it was too low to be taken seriously. Fairfax could do little but watch. Sir Warwick was by now gravely ill, which only complicated matters.

In January of 1987 Murdoch struck a deal with Holmes à Court, in which Holmes à Court would sell all of his existing shares in HWT to Murdoch, increasing his control of HWT to 44 percent. Later, he arranged to purchase Advertising Newspaper's 11 percent share in HWT and emerged with a majority.

In order to stay ahead of regulators and make his deal work, Murdoch was forced to reorganize his television properties. In a complex deal involving Murdoch, Fairfax, Bond, Holmes à Court, and HWT's Kerry Packer, virtually every major station changed hands. Fairfax emerged with the Melbourne television station Murdoch had promised to Holmes à Court, and thus held television, radio, and newspaper interests in Sydney and Melbourne.

Warwick Fairfax died in 1987, but the battle for supremacy in Australian journalism was not over. Later that year, fearing that Holmes à Court would bid for Fairfax, Warwick's 26-year old son, Warwick, Jr., launched a surprise bid for control of the company, under the belief that many of the 150 Fairfax family members would not sell their shares to Holmes à Court.

Warwick's takeover, launched through a shell company called Tryart Pty. Limited, succeeded in taking the company private. But in the process, he deeply split the family and placed Tryart A$1.7 billion in debt. In order to service the company's heavy debt, Tryart was forced to sell off several assets of the Fairfax Group.

In December of 1990 the leveraged buyout failed when Tryart proved unable to meet its debt service obligations and was forced into receivership. Warwick Fairfax, Jr.'s bid to protect the company had only made it more vulnerable for a takeover. Almost immediately, a bid was made for the company, not from the Australians Murdoch or Holmes à Court, but by Canadian newspaper financier Conrad Black, in partnership with Kerry Packer, whose paper the Fairfaxes had once endeavored to rescue from such a takeover.

Black was widely despised in world banking and publishing circles, but had distinguished himself some years earlier by turning London's *Daily Telegraph* into a highly profitable venture. Upon news of the bid in 1991, Fairfax's employees went on strike, protesting Black's antilabor record and right-wing political views.

Despite the opposition, Black ironed out a deal with Tryart's creditors and assembled a consortium called Tourang Limited, which consisted of Black's Telegraph PLC, Hellman & Friedman, and Consolidated Press Holdings. Consolidated Press was forced to withdraw from Tourang after Australian regulators questioned the legality of its participation under media cross-ownership regulations.

Tourang succeeded in taking over all the assets of Tryart, including John Fairfax Pty. Limited. On January 7, 1992, Tourang changed its name to John Fairfax Holdings Limited and gained a listing on the Australian Stock Exchange.

The ill-fated attempt to save Fairfax Group Pty. Limited from nonfamily interests only speeded the family's loss of its patriarch's company. But it may have happened soon enough to save Fairfax from several years of poor performance under what many considered to be inept "newspaper man" management. Black restored financial strength to the Fairfax organization and ensured that, if nothing else, at least the company didn't fall into the hands of Rupert Murdoch.

In Black's first year as nominal head of the resuscitated Fairfax group, the company's publications garnered numerous awards and marked respectable financial performances, in spite of the depressed Australian economy. It remains to be seen what efficiencies Black may extract from John Fairfax Holdings Limited if the company's profitability begins to lag.

Principal Subsidiaries: Associated Newspapers Ltd.; AAV New Zealand Ltd. (95%); David Syme & Co., Ltd.; Dysford Pty. Ltd.; Fairfax Community Newspapers Pty. Ltd.; Fairfax

Corporation Pty. Ltd.; Fairfax Finance Pty. Ltd.; Fairfax Ian Ltd.; Fairfax Investments Pty. Ltd.; Fairfax Letterbox Australia Pty. Ltd.; Fairfax Newspaper Holdings Pty. Ltd.; Homes Pictorial Publications Ltd. (80%); Homes Pictorial Unit Trust (80%); Illawarra Newspapers Holdings Pty. Ltd.; Intercity Hire Pty. Limited; John Fairfax Group Pty. Ltd.; John Fairfax Group Finance Pty. Ltd.; John Fairfax Group Inc. (United States); John Fairfax Ltd.; John Fairfax & Sons Ltd.; John Fairfax Ltd. (New Zealand); John Fairfax Ltd. (United Kingdom); John Fairfax Ltd. (United States); Joynton Ave No. 2 Pty. Ltd.; Magazine Promotions Australia Pty. Ltd.; Magazine Properties Pty. Ltd.; Magdiss Pty. Ltd.; Manoa Investments Pty. Ltd.; Morisset Courier Unit Trust (80%); Newcastle Newspapers Pty. Ltd.; Rozelle Terminal Handling Company Pty. Ltd.; Ridge Publications Pty. Ltd.; S. Richardson (Newspapers) Pty. Ltd.; Suburban Investments Pty. Ltd.; Syme Communications Ltd. (New Zealand); Syme Electronic Communications Pty. Ltd.; Syme Media Pty. Ltd.; Syme Travel & Entertainment Pty. Ltd.; Suburban Community Newspapers Pty. Ltd.; The Rockwood Pastoral Company Pty. Ltd.; Votraint (No. 297) Pty. Ltd.; Votraint (No. 427) Pty. Ltd.; Wattle Street Properties Pty. Ltd.

Further Reading: ''John Fairfax Board Moves to Put Firm Into Receivership,'' *Wall Street Journal,* December 11, 1990; Souter, Gavin, *Heralds and Angels: The House of Fairfax, 1841–1990,* Melbourne University Press, 1991; ''Conrad Black Likes a Good Fight, and He's Getting One,'' *Business Week,* December 2, 1991; John Fairfax Holdings Limited Prospectus, 1992; Fairfax Annual Report, 1992.

—John Simley

JOSTENS

JOSTENS INC.

5501 Norman Center Drive
Minneapolis, Minnesota 55437-1088
U.S.A.
(612) 830-3300
Fax: (612) 830-0818

Public Company
Incorporated: 1906 as Jostens Manufacturing Company
Employees: 8,000
Sales: $876.4 million
Stock Exchanges: New York
SICs: 3911 Jewelry & Precious Metals; 2741 Miscellaneous
   Publishing; 7372 Prepackaged Software; 2329 Men/Boys'
   Clothing Nec

A giant in the education products industry, Jostens is best known as a manufacturer of high-quality class rings for high school and college students. Since 1960, the company has also produced specially commissioned rings for contestants in the World Series, the Super Bowl, the NBA Championship, and the NHL Stanley Cup. Despite such high-profile coups, however, Jostens' core ring business (as well as its yearbook, photo, and awards segments—all part of the $546 million School Products Group) has experienced declining growth as a direct result of enrollment decreases throughout the 1980s and early 1990s. Fueling hopes for the future is Jostens Learning Corporation (JLC), a wholly owned subsidiary, created through a continuing chain of acquisitions, that leads the field of computer-based instructional technology. In fiscal 1992 revenues for JLC totaled $172 million, or approximately 20 percent of all corporate gross income. An agreement to merge chief competitor Wicat Systems into JLC promises to further speed growth in this area, in which CEO H. William Lurton expects to see an increase of about 25 percent annually. Lurton is often accorded most of the credit for maintaining the health and profitability of the company in a difficult market through savvy decision-making, diversification as well as divestment, and operational cost-cutting. Expectations that enrollment figures will rebound and show small but steady increases through the remainder of the 1990s further support the prevailing opinion that Jostens will continue to remain healthy with Lurton at the helm.

Begun in 1897 by Otto Josten, Jostens was originally a small jewelry and watch repair business located in Owatonna, Minne-

sota. In 1900 the founder began manufacturing emblems and awards for nearby schools and in 1906, the year of incorporation, Josten added class rings to his product line, to be sold to schools throughout the Midwest. The company remained small and relatively inconspicuous until Daniel C. Gainey, a former teacher and football coach, was hired in 1922 as the first full-time Jostens ring salesman. The rings at the time carried no gemstones and were all one size. Yet Gainey, with his dynamic and winning personality, secured sales of $18,000 within his first year. The amount was so large that he was forced to return to Owatonna to personally ensure that production demands could be met. By 1923 Gainey had enlisted four more sales representatives—all part-time—and revenues quickly rose to $70,000. Thus class rings became the central concern for the Jostens Manufacturing Company. In 1930 the watch-making and repair business was sold and the capital used to construct the company's first ring manufacturing plant. Three years later, with sales approaching the $500,000 mark, Gainey was elected chairman and CEO, positions he held until his retirement in 1968. According to several accounts, Gainey's greatest contribution to the company was his establishment and motivation of a nationwide sales force. Direct sales through independent representatives remain the primary source for the company's virtually uninterrupted growth.

During World War II Jostens contributed to the war effort by adapting its plant and equipment to manufacture precision parts and other materials. Major expansion came following the end of the war. In 1946 the company added graduation announcements to its offerings; in 1950 Jostens launched the American Yearbook Company. Both moves further tapped the education market and made the company less dependent on seasonal sales from rings. In 1958 the company made its first acquisition, purchasing the Ohio-based Educational Supply Company, a manufacturer of school diplomas. Jostens went public the following year and a seemingly unending series of acquisitions, which fortified the company's dominance of the high school and college products markets, characterized the next ten years. Sales for 1962 totaled $26 million; three years later the company obtained its listing on the New York Stock Exchange. In 1968 the company expanded into the Canadian photography market with the purchase of Winnipeg-based National School Studios. By this time Jostens was the undisputed domestic leader in both class ring and yearbook sales. Gainey's retirement, however, coupled with Jostens' relocation to Minneapolis in 1969, triggered a tumultuous period that nearly shipwrecked the then nearly $100-million-dollar company.

Star Tribune columnist Dick Youngblood, reflecting back on this period, wrote: "Jostens had been in turmoil since the late 1960s, when company patriarch Daniel C. Gainey, a major stockholder, pretended to retire as CEO. The trouble was, Gainey remained active enough over the ensuing four years to force the resignation of three chairmen and a president, including his own son." In 1970, amidst the turmoil, a top-performing Jostens salesman and division manager was appointed executive vice-president and effectively became the company's chief operating officer. His name was Bill Lurton. Unbeknownst to senior management, however, including Lurton, Gainey had begun negotiations with acquisition-hungry Bristol-Myers. Once Gainey's plan surfaced, several top Jostens officials tendered their resignations; Lurton was among the few who remained. Although Bristol-Myers halted negotiations after the management fallout, Jostens remained in peril under the leadership of replacement CEO Richard Schall. A former top official at General Mills and Metro Goldwyn Mayer, Schall, according to *Corporate Report* editor Terry Fiedler, "presided over Jostens for about 18 months before the advent of what amounted to a palace coup." An outsider with little knowledge of the business, Schall had brought in his own management team and had radically disrupted the friendly, teamwork-oriented corporate culture and threatened to move the company too quickly into new, uncharted territory. "The Lurton-led old guard demanded that Schall leave, threatening to leave themselves if he didn't. The directors sided with the old guard and in February 1972 Lurton became CEO of Jostens."

Twenty-one years later, Lurton remains in the position, well-liked by his employees and greatly esteemed by his fellow Minnesota CEOs. During his early tenure he moved quickly to reestablish Jostens as a thriving, focused company. Diversification beyond educational products, thought to be the key to the company's future, was renewed only for a short time before being largely curtailed. In 1974 Lurton divested Jostens of a greeting cards manufacturer and a men's accessories business. Five years later he also rid the company of interests in wedding rings and library supplies. Jostens Travel, first organized in 1972, was also dissolved before the end of the decade. Jostens did keep at least one peripheral acquisition, Artex Enterprises, for the long term. A manufacturer of custom-imprinted athletic and casual wear, the Artex label survives within the Jostens Sportswear division and is marketed primarily through mass merchants.

Aside from the aftermath of the Gainey debacle, Lurton's greatest challenge as a CEO came in the late 1970s and early 1980s, when demographic studies clearly showed that the last of the baby boom generation had graduated from high school and therefore beyond the core products line. According to Jackey Gold in *Financial World,* "Lurton's worry was that declining high school enrollments would shake Wall Street's faith in the company's ability to perform. Jostens' board of directors, too, became infected by such concerns and in August 1982 approved Lurton's proposal for a management buyout." The decision to go private was, for lack of financing, never realized; neither, however, was the company's forecasted decline.

Instead, Lurton launched a concerted campaign to impress Wall Street and counteract potential downswings in profits by boldly entering the proprietary schools business. Beginning in 1983, he acquired San Gabriel Colleges of California and Metridata Education Systems of Kentucky. Three additional private, vocational schools were acquired in 1984. That same year Jostens also entered the audio-visual learning and educational software fields by acquiring the Educational Systems Division of Borg-Warner Corporation, which it later renamed Jostens Learning Systems. The new flurry of purchases carried sales to over $400 million in 1985, when Jostens was accorded Fortune 500 status for the first time. In 1986 the company acquired Illinois-based Prescription Learning Corporation (PLC). A developer of customized computer hardware, software, and support services for the educational market, PLC was merged with Education Systems Corporation three years later to form JLC.

Meanwhile, to the consternation of several analysts, Jostens divested itself of its burgeoning list of proprietary schools, all 36 of them. The company sold the schools to CareerCom Corp. in 1987 for a sizeable profit. As then Education Division spokesperson Gary Buckmiller explained, "We didn't view the sale as getting out of the proprietary school business, but rather as changing the way we're involved in the business." The involvement, through JLC, has become one of support and service for, rather than management of, instructors and curriculum. Jostens' one remaining non-educational venture, the Business Products Division, was also sold in 1987, for a gain of $40 million. Now 90 years old, the company had returned to its roots in its service emphasis. By this time Jostens boasted an employee work force of some 9,000, in addition to an independent sales force numbering approximately 1,400.

Jostens' nearly 27 percent average return on investment between the years 1983 and 1989 brought kudos from all corners for the CEO. *Fortune* magazine highlighted Jostens among its 500 in 1989 as one of the "Companies That Compete Best." In 1990 Lurton was accorded the honor of "Executive of the Year" by *Corporate Report Minnesota*; further recognition came the same year from *Industry Week,* which celebrated Lurton as one of "America's Unsung Heroes." Until fiscal 1992 the news regarding Jostens and Lurton continued to be highly favorable. The 1990 purchase of Gordon B. Miller & Co. (the oldest recognition products company in North America) and Lenox Awards augured well for the company, as did its multi-media agreement with Western Publishing's Little Golden Books. Even the 1992 performance reports were respectable, considering the lingering effects of a recession: net sales increased two percent, while net income showed a four percent decline. The announced consolidation of jewelry manufacturing and photo processing operations are expected to contribute to a quick rebound. The Jostens organizations hopes that rising school enrollment, an improving economy, and a new management team for the Sportswear group will improve the company's performance.

Whether or not the company can meet Lurton's goal of returning to "double-digit growth in sales and earnings," it is likely the company will continue to prosper through its customary reliance on both acquisitions and service-oriented sales and marketing. JLC, operating in a marketplace that experts estimate is only 15 percent tapped, appears poised for fast-paced growth, especially considering its August 1992 purchase of Wicat Systems and its arrangement with Texas-based Dell Computer to market a Jostens line of 386 and 486 systems. Jostens' intention is to emerge as a leading, full-service provider in its selected markets. In any event, Jostens Inc. enters the 1990s securely entrenched as a leading manufacturer in the education product industry.

Principal Subsidiaries: American Yearbook Company, Inc.; Artex Manufacturing Company, Inc.; Jostens Canada, Ltd.; Jostens Engraving, Inc.; Jostens Learning Corporation; Jostens/Massachusetts, Inc.; Jostens Photography, Inc.; S. C. Cap & Gown, Inc.; Wayneco Enterprises, Inc.

Further Reading: Greenbaum, Jessica, "Lord of the Rings," *Forbes,* May 21, 1984, pp. 108–10; "Jostens Moves to Head of the Class," *St. Paul Pioneer Press & Dispatch,* October 14,

1985; Fierman, Jaclyn, and Jeffrey Rayport, "How to Make Money in Mature Markets," *Fortune,* November 25, 1985, pp. 46–50; *Josten's Today* (special 90th anniversary issue: "90 Years of People, Progress and Pride"), August 1987; Raley, Marcia A., "Dain Bosworth Research Capsule: Jostens," January 25, 1988; Saporito, Bill, "Companies That Compete Best," *Fortune,* May 22, 1989, p. 36; Fiedler, Terry, "H. William Lurton: Modesty That Rings True," *Corporate Report Minnesota,* January 1990, pp. 45–51, 92; Gold, Jackey, "How to Make a Cash Cow Dance," *Financial World,* June 12, 1990, pp. 38–9; Benson, Tracy E., "America's Unsung Heroes," *Industry Week,* December 3, 1990, pp. 12, 22–23; Youngblood, Dick, "In a Shrinking Market, He Gently Led Jostens to New World of Growth," *Star Tribune,* March 18, 1991; Moylan, Martin J., "Jostens Learning Gives Stock an Edge," *St. Paul Pioneer Press & Dispatch,* August 12, 1991; Byrne, Harlan S., "Jostens Inc.: Demographics Offer an Earnings Kick," *Barron's,* October 14, 1991, p. 38; "Highlights from Josten's History," Minneapolis: Jostens, 1992; Foster, Jim, "Jostens Plans Consolidation Moves," *Star Tribune,* January 29, 1992, p. 3D; Gross, Steve, "Jostens Learning Expanding PC Line," *Star Tribune,* April 15, 1992, p. 3D; "Jostens Has Lower Earnings, Sales," *Star Tribune,* January 19, 1993.

—Jay P. Pederson

KELSEY-HAYES GROUP OF COMPANIES

38481 Huron River Drive
Romulus, Michigan 48174-0098
U.S.A.
(313) 941-2000
Fax: (313) 941-2230

Wholly Owned Subsidiary of Varity Corporation
Incorporated: 1927
Employees: 7,447
Sales: $1.35 billion
Stock Exchanges: New York Toronto
SICs: 3714 Motor Vehicle Parts & Accessories

The Kelsey-Hayes Group of Companies, a division of the Varity Corporation, comprises the Kelsey-Hayes Corporation, Dayton-Walther, and Kelsey Parts. The Kelsey-Hayes Corporation is a major supplier of wheels, brakes, and other components to the world automobile industry. Originally a supplier of wooden wheels to the fledgling automobile industry in the early 20th century, Kelsey-Hayes has evolved into a major international corporation. Kelsey-Hayes is the leading producer of electronically controlled antilock brake systems.

Kelsey-Hayes was originally formed in 1927 as the result of a merger of the Kelsey Wheel Company and the Hayes Wheel Company. The parallel wheel-making history of founders John Kelsey and Clarence B. Hayes began much earlier.

John Kelsey formed the K. H. Wheel Company (with partner H. J. Herbert) in 1909 with the hopes of developing a spring wheel. Advised by Henry Ford to focus instead on the production of traditional wheels made of hickory wood, Kelsey took his advice and by 1919 his company was producing wooden wheels at a rate of 2 million per year and in 1915 the Kelsey Wheel Company was reincorporated for $13 million. Ford gave Kelsey his flying start, buying more than three quarters of the company's wheel production in 1909. Afraid of becoming too dependent on Ford, Kelsey diversified, giving Ford less than a third of his business in 1910 and, following a disagreement with Ford, less than 10 percent in 1912. While still selling to Ford, by 1915 the company's business had grown to $3.5 million in total revenues and had 15–20 percent of the wheel market, supplying not only Ford but also Hudson, Paige, Chalmers, and Stude-

baker. Government demand for artillery type wheels provided a further boost to profitability—in 1918 80 percent of production was devoted to defense type wheels—and by the end of World War I the company was solidly profitable.

A major cost cutting innovation was a wheel with a metal felloe band that cut the amount of wood needed in the production of wheels. This enabled Kelsey to capture a larger market share and, coupled with the boom in car and truck sales, Kelsey's wheels were on 70 percent of Ford's cars by early 1920. Kelsey Wheel was on its way and growing.

While John Kelsey was achieving great success, Clarence B. Hayes was building a company of his own. Beginning with a one year stint at the Kalamazoo Wheel Company, which built wooden buggy wheels, Hayes quickly moved on to become the vice-president, then president and general manager of the Imperial Wheel Company where he worked with W. C. Durant, who later founded General Motors.

In 1909 Hayes formed the Hayes Wheel Company. After buying out the National Wheel Company plant in Jackson, Michigan, he began to phase out the production of buggy wheels and switched exclusively to the production of wooden car wheels. Hayes would expand his operations to five more plants during the decade and by 1920 he had 60 percent of the American automobile wheel business.

While both the Kelsey Wheel Company and the Hayes Wheel companies got their start with the production of wood wheels, by the 1920s both were expanding into the production of wire wheels. Wire wheels were cheaper to produce and they were replaceable and transferrable from one axle to another (while wood wheels came as part of the entire axle assembly). Wire wheels were on one-quarter of all new vehicles by 1927 and clearly represented the wave of the future. This competitive pressure, a threat to the very existence of wooden wheel makers, was certainly a major motivating force behind the 1927 Kelsey-Hayes merger. The Kelsey-Hayes Wheel Company was born.

John Kelsey's wheel company had been producing wire wheels throughout the 1920s but had been accused of violating a patent for wire wheels that had been issued to Edward Cole of the Wire Wheel Corporation of Buffalo, New York. This company was primarily involved with patent licensing. The nature of the patent dealt with the critical issue of mountability of the wheel and Wire Wheel refused a license to Kelsey and threatened to sue for patent infringement. John Kelsey died early in 1927 and George Kennedy became the company's president. Kennedy's solution to this legal imbroglio was to purchase the Wire Wheel Company to get control of the patent but this wasn't the end of the problem: the patent was actually owned by the Packard Co., which had been receiving royalties from Wire Wheel. Kennedy paid $500,000 to Packard and production of wire wheels was now fair game. By 1929, the new Kelsey-Hayes Corporation was producing 10,000 wire wheels a day. The company also entered the brake field, supplying brakes for Ford's Model A.

During the lean years of the Great Depression the company solidified its hold on its General Motors market by purchasing the General Motors subsidiary Jaxon Steel Products Company of Jackson, Michigan. Kelsey-Hayes also provided the wheels for Henry Ford's invasion of the European market. By 1931, with the depression in full swing, the company lost $667,000 and in 1932 it lost $1.1 million. George Kennedy's Kelsey-Hayes corporation had accumulated massive amounts of short-term debt, mostly owed to banks and to General Motors. After the losses in the early to mid-1930s, Kelsey-Hayes went through a financial restructuring and cost-cutting campaign which resulted in small but growing profits in 1938 and 1939. Ever conscious of the need for new product development, Kelsey-Hayes began supplying standard-equipment hydraulic brakes to Ford and developed a new brake drum. Kelsey-Hayes had weathered the storm and would be prepared for the coming war production effort.

In 1940, Kelsey-Hayes began producing machine guns for the mounting war effort, first for the British and then for the United States. It made tank components, wheels and accessories for ordnance vehicles, aircraft wheels, brakes and other parts. In anticipation of the transition to a post-war economy, Kelsey-Hayes acquired French & Hecht, Inc., a leader in the agricultural and construction industry wheel business.

Although the period following the war was a time of massive innovation, the road out of the government regulated war economy was not completely peaceful. With unemployment on the rise and real wages of workers falling, the United States experienced a wave of strikes that shut down much of American industry for at least some part of 1946. Kelsey-Hayes was not immune. A wildcat strike by 4500 members of the United Auto Workers in 1946 closed the company down for 46 days.

With the strike settled, Kelsey-Hayes looked to cost-cutting measures and product diversification. In 1946 the company also began supplying power brakes to Buick and Chrysler and in 1947 Kelsey-Hayes acquired Lather Company, which also made brake components. The innovation and product diversification continued through the early 1950s as the company reached the highest profit margins in its history. During the Korean War the company made inroads into the aircraft industry.

In recognition of the diversification and expansion, the company changed its name, becoming simply the Kelsey-Hayes Corporation. Kelsey-Hayes was now at the front of new product innovation, introducing chrome-plated wheels, the first aluminum wheels, and power brakes, and was the leading producer of auto wheels, brakes, and other components. The strategy was to diversify in order to grow, both through research and development and through acquisition of other promising companies. To move into research and development for the burgeoning aircraft industry, Kelsey-Hayes acquired Control Specialists, Inc. The company also moved into the production of wheels and brakes for truck trailers, buses, and agricultural equipment.

In 1958 the company began explorations into the development of antilock brake systems for automobiles. Though the technology had been developed much earlier, antilock brake systems had only been employed as a safety measure on commercial aircraft. This basic technology eventually resulted in the development of electronic sensors that could read wheel speeds and send the information to a computer to prevent wheel lock on large automobiles. This evolving technology would be a mainstay of Kelsey-Hayes's business for years to come.

The product innovations continued into the boom years of the 1960s when Kelsey-Hayes was a pioneer in the development of disc brake systems. Kelsey-Hayes disc brake systems beat out the competition and became standard equipment on Lincoln Continentals and Thunderbirds, and by the time the 1970s rolled around, 85 percent of American cars came with Kelsey-Hayes disc brakes. Kelsey-Hayes replaced Bendix as the number one brake supplier to Ford. Not only had Kelsey-Hayes become a leading brake producer, but there were also Kelsey-Hayes parts in virtually every jet engine.

While the 1960s were years of expansion and diversification, the 1970s were extremely volatile. As was often the case for Kelsey-Hayes, as goes the automobile business, so goes the business of automobile suppliers. The challenge for Kelsey-Hayes following the oil crunch of the early 1970s was to develop products tailored to the new lighter, more fuel efficient, cars of the future. Towards this end, Kelsey-Hayes opened a research and development center in Ann Arbor, Michigan, designed to accelerate new product development, intensify the application of new manufacturing processes and search for new material applications for new and existing products. At the same time that the company was implementing this longer term strategy its sales continued to expand, topping the half billion dollar mark in 1973.

By 1973, however, in the face of a severe economic downturn, Kelsey-Hayes found itself over-extended in credit markets and, with its stock value plummeting, takeover loomed. In 1973 Kelsey-Hayes Corporation became a wholly owned subsidiary of Fruehauf Corporation, a leading producer of truck trailers. The takeover was only a small bump in the road for Kelsey-Hayes, however. The new financial support provided from Fruehauf enabled Kelsey-Hayes to continue its growth and by 1975 Kelsey was supplying disk brakes for all new subcompact cars including Volkswagen in Germany. Fruehauf commented in its 1975 annual report: "Kelsey-Hayes recognized the trend toward smaller cars several years ago. All of its automotive manufacturing plants have the flexibility to manufacture the required smaller components." Kelsey-Hayes was also maintaining its market share in wheels, brake components, and axles, as well as in helicopter transmissions, parts for jet engines, and hydraulic brake systems for the military. Kelsey-Hayes had become Fruehauf's shining star, accounting for 60 percent of Fruehauf's corporation revenues and becoming the company's only profitable business.

By 1978 Kelsey-Hayes was in full development of aluminum wheels as a cost cutting improvement over the traditional steel wheels. In addition, with the auto market in a severe slump beginning in 1978, Kelsey began to increase its share of the automobile replacement parts market. Since the auto makers were selling less new cars, older cars were staying on the road longer and hence the demand for replacement parts was rising. Thus, the replacement parts market buffered the negative effects of declines in automobile production.

In the late 1970s Kelsey-Hayes also began looking toward new production processes and, through its purchase of Compositek Engineering Corporation, the company had a new expertise in fiber-reinforced plastics that allowed substantial weight savings in wheel production. By 1979 the company could manufacture every type of wheel, from the traditional steel wheel to a light weight, low-alloy steel wheel. This technological breakthrough, of course, allowed Kelsey-Hayes to make lighter weight die castings and other lighter, stronger, parts.

The success of Kelsey-Hayes following its merger with Fruehauf was not without controversy. Fruehauf's acquisition of Kelsey-Hayes was ruled by the Federal Trade Commission, in 1978, to violate anti-trust laws in three Kelsey-Hayes product lines: heavy-duty wheels, anti-skid braking devices, and truck trailers. The argument was that these markets were serviced by few suppliers and the buyout would reduce effective competition through the possibility that Fruehauf would deny other suppliers the opportunity to sell to Fruehauf. Since Fruehauf had, in the past, attempted to make some of the same products as Kelsey-Hayes, a merger of the two companies was ruled to be a restraint on trade. Fruehauf was ordered to divest itself of some of its Kelsey-Hayes assets in order to enforce competitive behavior. The legal battle dragged on into the 1980s.

Further complicating the matter was the flurry of leveraged buyouts that affected many businesses in the United States in the 1980s. Following a protracted unfriendly takeover bid, Fruehauf was divested and Kelsey-Hayes became the remaining operation. This new successor to Fruehauf became the K-H Corporation, selling its trailer division and the Fruehauf name to the Terrex Corporation. K-H became the holding company for the Kelsey-Hayes Corporation. For the first time in a long time, K-H became a publicly traded, independent corporation. Thanks to booming sales of its antilock brake systems, aluminum wheels and electronic sensors its profits grew by more than 10 percent in fiscal year 1987.

But the independent K-H Corporation did not last long. At the time, some experts believed that K-H could make a go of it as an independent company. But, saddled with interest payments on a debt load of over $600 million, which drained its growth potential, the K-H Corporation went looking for a suitor. In 1989 the Varity Corporation, a Toronto-based farm equipment and auto parts manufacturer, purchased K-H Corporation for $577 million in cash and securities.

Since the buyout, Kelsey-Hayes has evolved into the Kelsey Hayes Group of Companies, reorganized into business units in order to focus on individual product lines: anti-lock brake systems, brakes, aluminum wheels, steel wheels, and others. The Group remains solidly profitable and an integral component of Varity's operations: Kelsey-Hayes's revenues of $1 billion in fiscal year 1990 were nearly a third of Varity's total revenues. Despite relatively weak markets, Kelsey-Hayes continues to compete aggressively in a global market. The company has introduced a four-wheel anti-lock brake system line (that many experts believe will be standard on all cars by the end of this decade) that is compatible with virtually every car and light truck made anywhere in the world. Hand-in-hand with the development of the antilock brake systems is the development of electromechanical products. Aluminum wheels, originally developed by Kelsey-Hayes in the 1950s, has become one of the company's fastest growing markets. These innovations and continued refinement of new products and processes, along with expansion of overseas production in the Asian-Pacific region, including a joint manufacturing venture with Japan's Topy Industries Ltd., indicate that Kelsey-Hayes will remain a dominant force in the global economy.

Principal Subsidiaries: Brembo/Kelsey-Hayes, Sp.A (Italy); FPS/Kelsey-Hayes, Sp.A (Italy); Western Wheel Corp.; Pacoma (Germany).

Further Reading: May, George S., *A Most Unique Machine: The Michigan Origins of the American Automobile Industry*, Grand Rapids, Michigan, Eerdmans, 1975; *A Billion Wheels Later*, Romulus, Michigan, Kelsey-Hayes Company, 1984; Callahan, J. M., "Life After Buyout," *Automotive Industry*, August 1987; "Canada's Varity Agrees to Buy K-H For Reduced Price," *Wall Street Journal*, October, 5, 1989.

—John A. Sarich

KENNECOTT CORPORATION

10 E. South Temple
Salt Lake City, Utah 84133
U.S.A.
(801) 322-7000
Fax: (801) 322-8181

Wholly owned subsidiary of RTZ Corporation PLC
Incorporated: 1915 as Kennecott Copper Corporation
Employees: 3,500
Sales: $942 million
SICs: 1021 Copper Ores; 1041 Gold Ores

Kennecott Corporation, a wholly owned subsidiary of the huge British metals and mining company RTZ Corporation PLC, is one of the largest and most efficient producers of copper in the world. Kennecott's mine at Bingham Canyon in Utah was the source of 265,000 tons of copper in 1991. Kennecott is also a major gold producer as well; with the Bingham site producing 450,000 troy ounces, and the company's other U.S. mines accounting for another 232,000 troy ounces. These mines include Barneys Canyon in Utah, South Carolina's Ridgeway mine, and the Rawhide mine in Nevada. Bingham Canyon puts out significant quantities of molybdenum and silver as well. Kennecott's Greens Creek mine in Juneau, Alaska produced over 4,000 troy ounces of silver in 1991, and also contributed over 20,000 tons of zinc. Kennecott was the world's leader in copper output through most of the twentieth century. It is part of RTZ, a global metals empire that has few, if any, rivals, employing about 73,000 people.

The chain of events that would lead to Kennecott's founding began in 1901. With financial backing from the Havemeyer family, a young mining engineer named Stephen Birch acquired mining rights on a sizeable chunk of promising copper property near the Kennicott Glacier in Alaska (the difference in spelling between the glacier and the company was the result of a clerical mistake). Birch returned East to seek additional investors in the venture, and was introduced by the Havemeyers to J. P. Morgan and to members of the Guggenheim family the following year. At that time, the Guggenheims were the most powerful force in the industry, controlling the vast majority of copper reserves and nearly all of the smelting capacity in the western United States. These two financial giants formed the Kennecott Mines Company to develop mining operations on the claims purchased

from Birch, and Birch was named general manager of the organization. In 1907, Morgan and the Guggenheims, calling themselves the Alaska Syndicate, purchased the Alaska Steamship Co., a large fishing fleet, the Beatson Copper Co. of LaTouch Island, Alaska, and, most importantly, 200 miles of right-of-way on which they completed a $25 million railroad that led to the copper mine. The Alaskan ore proved to be very rich in copper, and with the railroad and shipping line in place to transport the ore to civilization, the operation was quite profitable for the syndicate.

The mine at Kennicott, however, appeared to contain only about twenty years' worth of copper ore. In addition, the high cost of building the Copper River and Northwestern Railroad had required the sale of millions of dollars in stocks and bonds. In 1915, in order to both dilute the railroad's cost and find new ventures for the capital produced by the Alaskan mine, Kennecott Copper Corporation was incorporated out of the various financial interests involved, with Stephen Birch as President. The Guggenheims were by this time already actively working copper mines in Chile and Utah. Upon Kennecott's creation, they decided to merge their Braden Copper Co. property in Chile, as well as 25 percent of the Utah Copper Co., into Kennecott, concentrating on the smelting end of the industry as the family's primary business interest. These moves gave Kennecott possession of Braden's El Teniente, the world's largest underground mine, in the Chilean Andes. In 1936 Kennecott acquired the remainder of Utah Copper Co. and its huge Bingham copper pit, which would become the heart of Kennecott's operations for decades to come.

The Bingham pit was developed by Daniel Cowan Jackling, the metallurgical engineer who pioneered the mass mining of low-grade ores from open pit mines. Jackling also used his revolutionary methods at mine locations in Nevada, Arizona, and New Mexico, all of which were eventually bought by Kennecott.

Unlike many new companies, Kennecott made money every year in its early history. The company did not suffer its first operating loss until 1932, at the bottom of the Great Depression. World War I had created high demand for all metals, and when it ended, the copper industry found itself stuck in high gear, overproducing in the face of slowed demand. Kennecott was able to remain profitable mainly because production at the Alaskan site was among the cheapest in the industry, including extremely low labor costs. The trend among copper companies in the 1920s was toward vertical integration. Companies such as Anaconda and Phelps Dodge created their own fabricating operations in order to guarantee outlets for the products of their copper mines. Kennecott participated in this trend, but to a far lesser extent than did its main competitors. The company's only significant non-mining acquisitions during this period were the Chase Companies Inc. (which became Chase Brass and Copper Co.) in 1929, and American Electrical Works (changed to Kennecott Wire and Cable Co.) in 1935.

In 1933, following Kennecott's first unprofitable year, Birch was succeeded as president and chairperson by E. T. Stannard, a director of J. P. Morgan and Company. Around that time, the market was beginning to show the effects of a new flood of copper from Rhodesia. Since Kennecott was set up as a high-production outfit, and also had to keep Chase Brass operating full tilt, cutting back production was not a practical strategy. Stannard instead sought out new markets. Although this policy made no significant gains, Kennecott was bailed out in the late 1930s, as was the copper industry in general, by greatly increased demand for copper in preparation for entry into World War II.

Stephen Birch died in 1940, leaving management of the company firmly in Stannard's hands. Through the first half of the 1940s, the war kept production moving at a healthy pace, and Kennecott's operating revenues reached a peak of $265 million in 1943. When the war ended, however, Stannard saw that Kennecott's continued growth would depend upon its willingness to diversify and explore new geographical and geological arenas. In 1945, Stannard allotted half a million dollars for exploration, a figure comparable to that spent by its main competitors Phelps Dodge and Anaconda. Oil, gold, and titanium were the principal commodities on which Kennecott began to focus. In 1945, the company teamed up with Continental Oil for a joint prospecting and drilling venture. By this time, Kennecott was already a major U.S. gold producer, since that metal is often a natural byproduct of copper mining. But not until 1947 did the company go looking for gold directly. That year, Kennecott's exploration chief, Anton Gray, was sent gold-hunting in South Africa. This action resulted in the creation of the Kennecott-Anglovaal Exploration Co., Ltd., a joint gold-exploration firm.

More important was the company's entry into the titanium business. Titanium is found in ilemite, one of the most abundant minerals in the earth's surface. Ilemite had been discovered in parts of Quebec in the early 1940s, and Kennecott began its search in the region in 1944. Two years later, Kennecott's explorers, led by Gray, discovered the largest ilemite deposit in the world, over 100 million tons, at Lake Tio in eastern Quebec. Kennecott spent a half million dollars finding, claiming, and measuring the mine. In 1948, Quebec Iron and Titanium Corp. (Q.I.T.) was formed, with Kennecott controlling two-thirds interest and New Jersey Zinc Co., which had been exploring the area as well, owning the remaining share.

An airplane crash in September 1949 claimed the lives of three important company officers: the retiring president; his designated successor, Arthur D. Storke; and R. J. Parker, a vice-president. The executive vacuum created by the disaster was quickly filled by Charles Cox, formerly head of Carnegie-Illinois Steel.

By 1952, Kennecott was easily the biggest copper producer in the United States; 46 percent of the nation's primary copper output was produced by Kennecott that year. With addition of the Braden mine in Chile, the company accounted for about 25 percent of the entire copper production of the free world. Kennecott was still far less integrated than Anaconda or Phelps Dodge, with only 25 percent of the company's copper production used by its fabricating subsidiaries, Chase Brass and Kennecott Wire & Cable. The Bingham mine in Utah alone provided about two-thirds of Kennecott's domestic copper output in 1952, and 29 percent of the entire nation's production. Braden represented about 30 percent of the company's copper volume. Kennecott's operating revenue reached $470 million that year.

Expansion into other metals and oil continued into the 1950s under Cox. In 1952, three test wells were drilled in western Texas as part of the joint program with Continental Oil. About $42 million was invested in the two South African gold mining ventures by 1956. Kennecott purchased the Kaiser Aluminum and Chemical Corp. in 1953, as well as 76 percent interest in a Nigerian firm, Tin and Associated Minerals Ltd. In 1957, the company joined forces with Allied Chemical and Dye Corp. to launch Allied-Kennecott Titanium Corp., formed to build a North Carolina plant to produce and sell titanium. This venture proved to be short-lived, and the company dissolved seven years later. An attempt was made in 1958 to vertically integrate further into the wire and cable fabricating field, with the purchase of Okonite Co. This idea was also thwarted, however, when in 1966 Kennecott was forced to sell Okonite at a loss due to perceived antitrust violations, just as modernization investments were beginning to pay off in increased earnings.

During Cox's tenure as Kennecott's president from 1950 to 1960, difficulties were encountered finding areas in which to expand. In that timespan, the company's copper production actually decreased. Kennecott's domestic copper output dropped from about 418,000 tons to 339,000 tons in the first half of the decade alone. Only $12 million was invested in the Chilean operations between 1946 and 1956, compared to over $200 million invested by Anaconda in that country. Furthermore, Q.I.T. had problems processing the titanium that was mined in Canada, and the South African gold mines turned out to be busts, losing about $36 million. Nevertheless, Kennecott's earnings remained solid throughout the decade, thanks largely to a steady flow of cheaply produced copper from the seemingly bottomless Bingham mine. In 1956, it cost only 12 cents to mine a pound of copper at Bingham, which was the lowest cost per pound in the United States. About half of the company's copper was used to make some type of wire. 30 percent of the output was used by electric companies, 12 percent by the military, and about 13 percent by automotive companies.

Cox retired in 1961. Frank Milliken, an engineer and metallurgist, was promoted from executive vice-president to take his place. The following year Milliken launched a $110 million program to expand domestic copper production capacity by 28 percent over five years. A new corporate division was organized in 1964, the purpose of which was to develop new mining properties. These new operations included a lead, zinc, and silver mine in Utah, a lead mine in Missouri, and a Canadian molybdenum mine. In 1967, Kennecott sold 51 percent of the El Teniente mine to the government of Chile for $80 million. The company then lent $93 million to Chile as part of an expansion program at the mine.

In 1968, Kennecott undertook its most aggressive diversification project yet, the acquisition of Peabody Coal Co., the largest producer of coal in the United States. The purchase price for Peabody was $622 million, about 70 percent greater than Peabody's market value. Three years later, however, the Federal Trade Commission (FTC) ordered Kennecott to divest itself of Peabody, on the grounds that the company should have diversified by either starting up its own coal operation or by acquiring a smaller one. The FTC argued that purchasing Peabody eliminated a potential competitor from the field. Kennecott fought the ruling for several years, investing over $500,000 in Peabody. However, Peabody did not prove to be especially profitable for Kennecott. Between 1968 and 1976, Peabody's profits were less than one-sixth as high as the $431 million earned by Continental Oil's Consolidation Coal Co., Peabody's nearest competitor in steam coal production. After a number of failed legal challenges, Kennecott finally complied with the FTC in 1977, selling Peabody to a group headed by Newmont Mining for around $1 billion.

In 1971, Chilean President Salvador Allende nationalized that country's copper mines, stripping Kennecott of its partial ownership of El Teniente, the largest underground copper mine in the world. Aware of growing nationalistic sentiment in the 1960s, company leadership had foreseen the possibility of Chile's appropriation of the mines, and the sale a few years earlier of 51 percent interest in El Teniente to the government of Chile turned out to be a very wise move. By the time of the takeover, the share of Kennecott's income that came from Chile had been reduced to 11 percent from 25 percent in the 1960s, and though the event was certainly unsettling, Kennecott suffered far less than Anaconda, which had continued to invest heavily in that country. In 1972 an agreement was reached with the Overseas Private Investment Corp. (OPIC), the U.S. government agency that had insured Kennecott's 1967 loan to Chile. Under the terms of the settlement, Kennecott received $66.9 million from OPIC, taking a $9.8 million loss on the loans, on which Chile had made only two payments.

The 1970s were sluggish for Kennecott. The copper market was at its most depressed state since the 1930s, with prices down due to an abundant supply from new mines in Africa and elsewhere. New competition arose in the United States from growing companies such as Magma Copper Co. and Cyprus Mines Corp. These developments contributed to a $10.9 million loss for Kennecott in 1976, excluding Peabody, on $956 million in sales. Kennecott's annual capital investments were just over half those of Anaconda or Phelps Dodge during the mid-1970s, even though the production capacities of those two companies was smaller. While Kennecott was losing money in 1976 and 1977, both of those main competitors recorded profits.

Late in 1977, Kennecott acquired the Carborundum Co., a manufacturer of industrial products such as abrasives and pollution control equipment. Although Carborundum was a profitable company, with sales growing at a pace of about 15 percent a year, some stockholders felt that the $568 million Kennecott paid, about half the money from the sale of Peabody and twice Carborundum's market value, was too high. A group of Kennecott stockholders filed a suit to block the acquisition. Though no action came about as a result of the suit, criticism of Kennecott's management began to simmer, focusing on Milliken in particular.

With dissatisfaction growing, a proxy fight was launched in 1978, led by T. Roland Berner, chief executive of Curtiss-Wright Corp., a maker of aircraft engines. Berner promised that, if successful in taking over control of Kennecott, he would immediately sell off Carborundum and use the proceeds to pay out $20 a share to stockholders. By March of 1978, Curtiss-Wright owned 9.9 percent of Kennecott's stock. After much complex legal wrangling, Milliken managed to fight off the challenge. One result was the integration of several Carborun-

dum executives into top Kennecott management positions. Another result of the struggle was the occupation by Berner and two associates of seats on the Kennecott board of directors.

Following the proxy battle, Milliken retired. Thomas D. Barrow, a senior vice-president at Exxon, was named Kennecott's new chief executive. Barrow, upon accepting the position, immediately bought over three-quarters of a million dollars of Kennecott stock, making him the company's largest single stockholder. In 1981, Barrow negotiated the sale of Kennecott to Standard Oil Company of Ohio (Sohio) for $1.8 billion. Although Kennecott was still the nation's largest copper producer, it had been severely weakened by the industry-wide problems of the 1970s. With copper shortages expected in the 1980s, Kennecott needed to find hundreds of millions of dollars with which to modernize its facilities in order to take advantage of the elevated copper prices created by the new cycle of short supply. Sohio, flush with cash from its huge oil field at Prudhoe Bay in Alaska, came forward to supply the necessary funds. The purchase in turn gave Sohio an insurance policy against the depletion of its oil reserves.

In 1985 the Bingham Canyon mine was temporarily shut down because of depressed copper prices. During that time, the company invested $400 million to modernize the Utah Copper operations, including construction of an in-pit crushing and conveying system. A few months later, Kennecott purchased part of Anaconda's copper mine at Carr Fork, Utah. Kennecott had been trying to acquire the property, which bordered Bingham Canyon, for several years, and the mine had been closed since 1981. The following year, Sohio decided to focus all of its copper efforts on Bingham Canyon. With that decision, Sohio sold all of its other copper mines, dealing its Ray Mines division in Arizona to Asarco, and selling New Mexico's Chino Mines division to Phelps Dodge.

Kennecott became a subsidiary of BP Minerals in 1987, when BP purchased an outstanding minority interest in Standard Oil In June of 1989, BP Minerals was acquired by RTZ Corporation PLC, Britain's largest mining company. In July of that year, construction began on Kennecott's Denton-Rawhide gold mine in Nevada's Mineral County. A joint venture was launched in 1990 with U.S. Energy Corp. to mine uranium in southern Wyoming.

In December of 1991, the Environmental Protection Agency (EPA) issued a complaint charging Kennecott with 217 counts of mishandling hazardous wastes and chemical byproducts. In April 1992 the company reached an agreement in principle with federal and state environmental agencies on establishing a pilot program to clean up the wastes in the area of its Utah copper operations over a 10-year period. President G. Frank Joklik stated that the agreement's framework was "the product of a Kennecott concept brought to the U.S. EPA and the Utah DEQ over a year ago."

The Fourth Mill Line at Bingham Canyon began operating in January of 1992, adding an additional 32,000 tons of copper and 84,000 ounces of gold to the company's production capacity annually. Plans were also made in 1992 for the construction of a new $880 million smelter west of Salt Lake City. The new smelter will enable Kennecott to process all of its own concentrate, rather than send 40 percent elsewhere to be refined. While Kennecott's future success will depend largely on the fluctuations of a historically volatile copper market, the company seems to have settled into a comfortable niche. The reliability and efficiency of Kennecott's operations at Bingham Canyon are a large part of what has enabled it to survive through periods of depressed prices and questionable management. It is also this reliability that will probably make Kennecott a valuable asset to its parent company, and it is equally possible that membership in RTZ's empire will moderate the negative impact on Kennecott of future situations that prove harmful to companies throughout the copper industry.

Principal Subsidiaries: Kennecott-Utah Copper Corporation; Kennecott-Ridgeway Mine; Denton-Rawhide Mine (51%); Greens Creek Mine (53%); Barneys Canyon; Flambeau Mining Company.

Further Reading: McDonald, John, "The World of Kennecott," *Fortune,* November 1951; Clark, C. A. Jr., "Kennecott Copper," *Barron's,* March 16, 1953; Thurlow, Bradbury, "Kennecott Copper," *Barron's,* February 20, 1956; "Where Copper is Not Quite King," *Business Week,* December 7, 1968; Loving, Rush Jr., "How Kennecott Got Hooked With Catch-22," *Fortune,* September 1971; "Kennecott Copper," *Forbes,* April 15, 1972; "Kennecott Collects on Its Insurance," *Business Week,* December 23, 1972; Welles, Chris, "The Kennecott Blunders," *Financial World,* March 1, 1978; "The Battle of the Lightweights," *Forbes,* May 1, 1978; Ehbar, A. F., "Kennecott After the Battle," *Fortune,* June 5, 1978; Cook, James, "A Man Who Knows Where He's Going," *Forbes,* April 30, 1979; Moskowitz, Milton, *Everybody's Business: An Almanac,* Harper & Row, 1980; Argall, George, "Takeovers Shake USA Mining Companies," *World Mining,* May, 1981; "Kennecott Renews Itself With Sohio's Oil Money," *Business Week,* April 26, 1982; Jordan, Carol, "Anaconda Sells Part of Mine to Kennecott," *American Metal Market,* October 3, 1985; Zipf, Peter, "Kennecott Output Capacity Sale Seen Having Little Effect on Copper Mart," *American Metal Market,* September 16, 1986; "Excellence and Style," *Engineering and Mining Journal,* August, 1989; Abrahamson, Peggy, "Kennecott Agrees On Cleanup," *American Metal Market,* April 8, 1992; "Big Plan in Copper Country," *ENR,* April 20, 1992; *RTZ Corporation Annual Report,* RTZ Corporation PLC, 1992.

—Robert R. Jacobson

KFC CORPORATION

P.O. Box 32070
Louisville, Kentucky 40232
U.S.A.
(502) 456-8300
Fax: (502) 454-2195

Wholly Owned Subsidiary of PepsiCo, Inc.
Incorporated: 1955 as Kentucky Fried Chicken
Employees: 160,000
Sales: $6.70 billion
SICs: 5812 Eating Places

KFC Corporation is the largest fast-food chicken operator, developer, and franchiser in the world. KFC, a wholly owned subsidiary of PepsiCo, Inc., operates over 5,000 units in the United States, approximately 60 percent of which are franchises. Internationally, KFC more than 3,700 units, of which two-thirds are also franchised. Among the 65 countries where KFC conducts business, Australia, Canada, Japan, Mexico, and New Zealand are its strongest markets. In addition to direct franchising and wholly owned operations, the company participates in joint ventures, and continues investigating alternative venues to gain market share in the increasingly competitive fast-food market.

Kentucky Fried Chicken was founded by Harland Sanders in Corbin, Kentucky. Sanders was born on a small farm in Henryville, Indiana, in 1890. Following the death of Sanders's father in 1896, Sanders's mother worked two jobs to support the family. The young Sanders learned to cook for his younger brother and sister by age six. When Mrs. Sanders remarried, her new husband didn't tolerate Harland. Sanders left home and school when he was twelve years old to work as a farm hand for four dollars a month. At age fifteen he left that job to work at a variety of jobs, including painter, plowman, streetcar conductor, ferryboat operator, insurance salesman, justice of the peace, and service-station operator.

In 1929 Sanders opened a gas station in Corbin, Kentucky, and cooked for his family and an occasional customer in the back room. Sanders enjoyed cooking the food his mother had taught him to make: pan-fried chicken, country ham, fresh vegetables, and homemade biscuits. Demand for Sanders's cooking rose; eventually he moved across the street to a facility with a 142-seat restaurant, a motel, and a gas station.

During the 1930s an image that would become known throughout the world began to develop. First, Sanders was named an honorary Kentucky colonel by the state's governor; second, he developed a unique, quick method of spicing and pressure-frying chicken. Due to his regional popularity, the Harland Sanders Court and Cafe received an endorsement by Duncan Hines's *Adventures in Good Eating* in 1939.

Sanders Court and Cafe was Kentucky's first motel, but the Colonel was forced to close it when gas rationing during World War II cut tourism. Reopening the motel after the war, Sanders's hand was once again forced: in the early 1950s, planned interstate 75 would bypass Corbin entirely. Though Sanders Cafe was valued at $165,000, the owner could only get $75,000 for it at auction—just enough to pay his debts.

However, in 1952 the Colonel signed on his first franchise to Pete Harman, who owned a hamburger restaurant in Salt Lake City, Utah. Throughout the next four years, he convinced several other restaurant owners to add his Kentucky Fried Chicken to their menus.

Therefore, rather than struggle to live on his savings and Social Security, in 1955 Sanders incorporated and the following year took his chicken recipe to the road, doing demonstrations on-site to sell his method. Clad in a white suit, white shirt, and black string tie, Sanders's white mustache and goatee—and the cane he carried—belied the young man's energy he threw into his work. In 1956 Sanders moved the business to Shelbyville, Kentucky, 30 miles east of Louisville, to more easily ship his spices, pressure cookers, carryout cartons, and advertising material. And by 1963 Sanders's recipe was franchised to more than 600 outlets in the U.S. and Canada. Sanders had seventeen employees, and travelled more than 200,000 miles in one year promoting Kentucky Fried Chicken. He was clearing $300,000 before taxes, and the business was getting too large for Sanders to handle.

In 1964 Sanders sold Kentucky Fried Chicken for $2 million and a per-year salary of $40,000 for public appearances; that salary later rose to $200,000. The offer came from an investor group headed by John Y. Brown, Jr. a 29-year-old graduate of the University of Kentucky law school, and Nashville financier John (Jack) Massey. A notable member of the investor group was Pete Harman, who had been the first to purchase Sanders's recipe 12 years earlier.

Under the agreement, Brown and Massey owned national and international franchise rights, excluding England, Florida, Utah, and Montana, which Sanders had already apportioned. Sanders would also maintain ownership of the Canadian franchises. The company subsequently acquired the rights to operations in England, Canada, and Florida. As chairman and CEO, Massey trained Brown for the job; meanwhile, Harland Sanders enjoyed his less hectic role as roving ambassador. In *Business Week,* Massey remarked: "He's the greatest PR man I have ever known."

Within three years, Brown and Massey had transformed the "loosely knit, one-man show . . . into a smoothly run corporation with all the trappings of modern management," *Business Week* described. Retail outlets reached all fifty states, plus Puerto Rico, Mexico, Japan, Jamaica, and the Bahamas. With

1,500 take-out stores and restaurants, Kentucky Fried Chicken ranked sixth in volume among food-service companies—it trailed such giants as Howard Johnson, but was ahead of McDonald's Corporation and International Dairy Queen.

In 1967, franchising remained the foundation of the business. For an initial $3,000 fee, a franchisee went to "KFC University" to learn all the basics. While typical costs for a complete Kentucky Fried Chicken start-up ran close to $65,000, some franchisees had already become millionaires. Tying together a national image, the company began developing pre-fabricated red-and-white striped buildings to appeal to tourists and residents in the United States.

The revolutionary choice Massey and Brown made was to change the colonel's concept of a sit-down Kentucky Fried Chicken dinner to a stand-up, take-out store emphasizing fast service and low labor costs. This idea created, by 1970, 130 millionaires, all from selling the colonel's famous pressure-cooked chicken. But such unprecedented growth came with its cost, as Brown remarked in *Business Week:* "At one time, I had 21 millionaires reporting to me at eight o'clock every morning. It could drive you crazy." Despite the number of vocal franchisees, the corporation lacked management depth. Brown tried to use successful franchisees as managers, but their commitment rarely lasted more than a year or two. There was too much money to be made as entrepreneurs. For example, multiple franchisee Richard Thomas sold his stores to the company for cash, took a 30-day vacation, then returned to Brown looking for a challenge. Thomas was put in charge of the newly acquired H. Salt Fish & Chips and did so well, he decided to return to the franchise business.

Several observations about franchise arrangements noted by stock market analysts and accountants in the late 1960s became widespread news by 1970. First, Wall Street noticed that profits for many successful franchisers came from company-owned stores, not from the independent shops—though this was not the case with Kentucky Fried Chicken. This fact tied in with a memorandum circulated at Peat, Marwick, Mitchell & Company, and an article published by Archibald MacKay in the *Journal of Accountancy* stating that income labeled "initial franchise fees" was added when a franchise agreement was signed, regardless of whether the store ever opened or fees were collected. Such loose accounting practices caused a Wall Street reaction: franchisers, enjoying the reputation as "glamour stocks" through the 1960s, were no longer so highly regarded. Kentucky Fried Chicken stock hit a high of $55.50 in 1969—then fell to as low as $10 per share within a year.

In early 1970, following a number of disagreements with Brown, Massey resigned. When several other key leaders departed the company, Brown found the housecleaning he planned already in progress. A number of food and finance specialists joined Kentucky Fried Chicken, including R. C. Beeson as chief operational officer and Joseph Kesselman as chief financial officer. Kesselman brought in new marketing, controlling, and computer experts; he also obtained the company's first large-scale loan package ($30 million plus a $20 million credit line). He affected a style change as well, convincing Brown to stop wearing a string tie to work.

By August 1970 the shake-up was clear: Colonel Harland Sanders, his grandson Harland Adams, and George Baker, who had run company operations, resigned from the board of directors. Colonel Sanders, at 80, knew his limits. In a 1970 *New York Times* article, Sanders stated, "(I) realized that I was someplace I had no place being . . . Everything that a board of a big corporation does is over my head and I'm confused by the talk and high finance discussed at these meetings."

CEO Brown spent the rough year of 1970 shoring up his company's base of operations. By September, Kentucky Fried Chicken operated a total of 3,400 fast-food outlets; the company owned 823 of these units. The company, once too large for the colonel to handle, grew too mammoth for John Y. Brown as well. In July 1971 Kentucky Fried Chicken merged with Connecticut-based Heublein Inc., a specialty food and alcoholic beverage corporation. Sales for Kentucky Fried Chicken had reached $700 million, and Brown, at age 37, left the company with a personal net worth of $35 million. Interviewed for the *Wall Street Journal* regarding the company's 1970 financial overhaul, Brown commented, "You never saw a more negative bunch . . . If I'd have listened to them in the first place, we'd never have started Kentucky Fried Chicken." Article author Frederick C. Klein included closing parenthetical remarks in which observers close to the company noted that "in engineering Kentucky Fried [Chicken]'s explosive growth, Mr. Brown neglected to install needed financial controls and food-research facilities, and had let relations with some franchise holders go sour."

Heublein planned to increase Kentucky Fried Chicken's volume with its marketing know-how. Through the 1970s the company introduced some new products to compete with other fast-food markets. The popularity of barbecued spare ribs, introduced in 1975, kept the numbers for Kentucky Fried Chicken looking better than they really were. As management concentrated on overall store sales, they failed to notice that the basic chicken business was slacking off. Competitors' sales increased as Kentucky Fried Chicken's dropped.

For Heublein, acquisitions were doing more harm than good: Kentucky Fried Chicken was stumbling just when the parent company had managed to get United Vintners, bought in 1969, on its feet. In 1977 the company appointed Michael Miles, who was formerly responsible for the Kentucky Fried Chicken ad campaign at Leo Burnett and had joined Heublein's marketing team in 1971, to chair the ailing Kentucky Fried Chicken. Richard Mayer, vice-president of marketing and strategic planning for Heublein's grocery products, took charge of the Kentucky Fried Chicken U.S. division.

Mayer found that the product mainstay, fried chicken, wasn't up to the high quality Colonel Harland Sanders would expect. Miles and Mayer also faced the same problem John Y. Brown had not managed to surmount: relations with franchisees were sour. In the mid-1970s, the franchisees sold more per store than company-owned stores. Faring better without Heublein's help, they resented paying royalty fees to the ineffective corporate parent. To top that off, the stores were looking out of date.

Having unloaded well over 300 company-owned stores in the early 1970s, by the end of the decade Heublein began to buy some back from the franchisees. Renovation of the original red-and-white striped buildings began in earnest, with Heublein putting $35 million into the project. On the outside, Kentucky Fried Chicken facades were updated, while on the inside, cooking methods veered back to the colonel's basics. Sticking to a limited menu kept Kentucky Fried Chicken's costs down, allowing the company time to recoup. Timing was fortunate on Kentucky Fried Chicken's turn-around; it happened just in time for Colonel Sanders to witness. After fighting leukemia for seven months, Harland Sanders died on December 16, 1980.

Miles and Mayer's work culminated with the highly successful 1981 ad campaign, "We Do Chicken Right." A year later, in step with the fast-paced 1980s, R.J. Reynolds Industries Inc. acquired Heublein, giving Kentucky Fried Chicken another lift; the company had expansionary vision, capital, and the international presence to tie it all together. Kentucky Fried Chicken sales that year reached $2.4 billion. By 1983 the company had made impressive progress. With 4,500 stores in the U.S. and 1,400 units in 54 foreign countries, no other fast-food chain except McDonald's could compete. But while many industry insiders were crediting the team with victory, Mayer wasn't so quick to join in. As he noted in *Nation's Restaurant News*, "People keep talking about the turn-around at KFC. I'd really rather not talk about it. The turn-around is only halfway over."

With the entrance of R. J. Reynolds came the exit of Michael Miles, who resigned to become CEO of Kraft Foods; Mayer took over as chairman and CEO. Mayer continued on a cautious line for the next several years, refusing to introduce new products as obsessively as its competitors. "In the past two years," Mayer said in a KFC company profile in *Nation's Restaurant News*, "people have gone absolutely schizoid ... A lot of chains have blurred their image by adding so many new menu items." In further commentary, he added, "We don't roll out a flavor-of-the-month."

Mayer's conservatism gained him the respect of Wall Street and his peers in the fast-food industry. In 1986 soft-drink giant PepsiCo, Inc., bought Kentucky Fried Chicken for $840 million. Reasons cited were KFC's superior performance and its 1980–85 increase in worldwide revenue and earnings. The successful operator of the Pizza Hut and Taco Bell chains, PepsiCo did quite well introducing new products through those restaurants. It was just a matter of time before Kentucky Fried Chicken would be expected to create new products.

To foster new product introduction, in 1986 Kentucky Fried Chicken opened the $23 million, 2,000,000-square-foot Colonel Sanders Technical Center. In addition, the company began testing oven-roasted chicken through multiple-franchisee Collins Foods; further test-marketing of home delivery was undertaken using PepsiCo's successful Pizza Hut delivery system as an example. By late 1986 Donald E. Doyle, succeeding Mayer in the post of Kentucky Fried Chicken's U.S. president, inherited the task of developing new menu items.

The overall market for fast food seemed glutted by the late 1980s. PepsiCo CEO D. Wayne Calloway saw Kentucky Fried Chicken's national niche as secure for two reasons: first, with competition spurred by the large number of fast-food suppliers, weaker chains would inevitably leave the market; second, Ken-

tucky Fried Chicken still had room to grow in the Northeast and Mid-Atlantic regions. Internationally, the company planned 150 overseas openings in 1987. Japan, a major market, had 520 stores, Great Britain had 300, and South Africa had 160. KFC International, headed by Steven V. Fellingham, planned to concentrate on opening units in a handful of countries where its presence was limited. The People's Republic of China was the most notable new market secured in 1987; KFC was the first American fast-food chain to open there.

Imperative to the success of Kentucky Fried Chicken was the establishment of successful relations with the numerous franchisees. Most of them lauded parent PepsiCo's international strength and food-service experience; KFC had its own inherent strength, however, according to franchisees, which the parent company would do well to handle with care. That strength was the sharing of decision-making.

In 1966, for instance, the Kentucky Fried Chicken Advertising Co-op was established, giving franchisees ten votes and the company three when determining advertising budgets and campaigns. As a result of an antitrust suit with franchisees, in 1972 the corporation organized a National Franchisee Advisory Council. By 1976, the company worked with franchisees to improve upon contracts made when Brown and Massey took over. Some contracts even dated back to when Colonel Sanders had sealed them with a handshake. The National Purchasing Co-op, formed in 1979, ensured franchisees a cut of intercompany equipment and supply sales. All of these councils had created a democratic organization which not only served the franchisees well, but helped keep operations running smoothly as Kentucky Fried Chicken was shifted from one corporate parent to another. As time passed, however, PepsiCo's corporate hand seemed to come down too heavily for franchisee comfort.

In July 1989, CEO and Chairman Richard Mayer resigned to return as president to General Foods USA, where he had begun his career nearly thirty years earlier in sales and product management. Mayer, who together with Mike Miles was credited for bringing Kentucky Fried Chicken out of the 1970s slump, departed as the company battled over contract rights with franchisees. John M. Cranor, an executive who had joined PepsiCo twelve years earlier, took over as CEO. Kyle Craig, formerly with Burger King, Steak & Ale, and Bennigan's, began in an advisory role, later stepping up to become president of KFC-USA.

Within months Cranor was meeting with franchisee leaders in Louisville to defend parent PepsiCo's contract renewal. Among the issues debated was PepsiCo's plan to revise the franchisee-renewal policy, which guaranteed operators the right to sell the business, and an automatic ten-year extension on existing contracts with reasonable upgrading required. It was in KFC's long-term interest to settle the dispute without litigation, Cranor believed—and with good reason. In August of 1989 franchisees had established a $3.6 million legal fund, averaging $1,000 per unit, to fight the battle in court if necessary. Cranor remained optimistic, relying on the history of positive relations with franchisees.

Despite contract battles and communication troubles, in the fall of 1990 Kentucky Fried Chicken called a one-day truce to celebrate in honor of Colonel Sanders's 100th birthday. Meanwhile, fast-food competitors with stricter organization were keeping up with changes in consumer demand and introducing new products at a dizzying rate. KFC, in contrast, had difficulty creating new products linked to the cornerstone fried chicken concept, and getting them out quickly through franchisee stores. Hot Wings, brought out in 1990, was KFC's only hit in a number of attempts, including broiled, oven-roasted, skinless, and sandwich-style chicken.

In late September 1990, Kentucky Fried Chicken increased its holding of company-owned stores by buying 209 U.S. units from Collins Foods International Inc.; Collins retained its interest in the Australian KFC market. The acquisition boosted Kentucky Fried Chicken's control of total operating units to 32 percent, versus the franchisees' 68 percent. The corporation also added Canada's Scott's Hospitality franchises to its fold, an increase of 182 units.

To update its down-home image and respond to growing concerns about the health risks associated with fried foods, in February 1991 Kentucky Fried Chicken changed its name to KFC. New packaging still sported the classic red-and-white stripes—but this time wider and on an angle, implying movement and rapid service. While the colonel's image was retained, packaging was in modern graphics and bolder colors. New menu introductions were postponed, as KFC once again went back to the basics to tighten up store operations and modernize units. A new $20 million computer system not only controlled fryer cooking times, it linked front counters with the kitchen, drive-thru 'window, manager's office, and company headquarters.

Though KFC may have had problems competing in the domestic fast-food market, those same problems did not seem to trouble them in their international markets. In 1992 pre-tax profits were $92 million from international operations, as opposed to $86 million from the U.S. units. Also, in the five year span from 1988 through 1992, sales and profits for the international business nearly doubled. In addition, franchise relations, always troublesome in the domestic business, ran smoothly in KFC's international markets. To continue capitalizing on their success abroad, KFC undertook an aggressive construction plan—an average of one non-U.S. unit is built per day, and it is expected that by 1995 the number of international units will exceed those in the U.S.

Non-traditional service, often stemming from successful innovations instituted in the company's international operations, was seen as a way for KFC to enter new markets. Delivery, drive-thru, carry-out, and supermarket kiosks were up and running. Other outlets in testing were mall and office-building snack shops, mobile trailer units, satellite units, and self-contained kiosks designed for universities, stadiums, airports, and amusement parks. To move toward the twenty-first century, executives believed KFC had to change its image. "We want to be *the* chicken store," Cranor stressed in a 1991 *Nation's Restaurant News.* Cranor's goal was total concept transformation, moving KFC to a more contemporary role. With nearly 8,500 restaurants in operation worldwide, KFC Corporation was well on its way.

Further Reading: "Success Story: Potential Ruin is Turned to Boom," *New York Times,* March 22, 1964; "Cooking up Profits, Southern Style," *Business Week,* June 24, 1967; "Franchising: Too Much, Too Soon," *Business Week,* June 27, 1970; "Colonel Sanders Bowing Out," *New York Times,* August 8, 1970; "Heublein May Buy Kentucky Fried Via Stock Swap," *Wall Street Journal,* January 22, 1971; "Heublein Merger Plan with Kentucky Fried Is Ratified by Holders," *Wall Street Journal,* July 9, 1971; Klein, Frederick C., "John Y. Brown, Rich and Taking It Easy," *Wall Street Journal,* April 1, 1975; "The Education of Hicks Waldron," *Forbes,* December 8, 1980; Hume, Scott, "KFC to Stick with What It's Finally Doing Right," *Advertising Age,* June 27, 1983; Jeffrey, Don, Peter Romeo, and Rick Van Warner, "KFC Company Profile" (a multiple-article series), *Nation's Restaurant News,* December 15, 1986; Prewitt, Milford, "Mayer Flies KFC Coop; PepsiCo Names Cranor," *Nation's Restaurant News,* July 31, 1989; Prewitt, Milford, "Cranor Answers KFC Critics," *Nation's Restaurant News,* November 27, 1989; Koeppel, Dan, "The Feathers Are Really Flying at Kentucky Fried," *Adweek's Marketing Week,* September 3, 1990; Martin, Richard, "Collins to Sell 209 KFC Units to PepsiCo for $123 Million," *Nation's Restaurant News,* September 24, 1990; Keegan, Peter O., "KFC Shuns 'Fried' Image with New Name," *Nation's Restaurant News,* February 25, 1991; Keegan, Peter O., "KFC Takes Step Back to Move Forward," *Nation's Restaurant News,* November 18, 1991; " 'Corporate' Meets the Colonel in KFC's Entrepreneurial Cranor," *Nation's Restaurant News,* November 18, 1991.

—Frances E. Norton

KOHLER.

KOHLER COMPANY

44 Highland Drive
Kohler, Wisconsin 53044
U.S.A.
(414) 457-4441
Fax: (414) 457-1271

Private Company
Incorporated: 1873 as Kohler & Silberzahn
Employees: 14,000
Sales: Not Published
SICs: 3432 Plumbing Fixtures Fittings & Trim; 3519 Internal
   Combustion Engines Nec

Kohler Company is one of the largest privately operated firms in the United States. Unlike others that were once public companies but were taken private through debt-ridden leveraged buyouts, Kohler has always been owned and run by a circle of family members who descended from the founder. One of Wisconsin's largest employers, Kohler is best known for its line of baths, sinks, toilets, and other bathroom fixtures. The company is also a leading producer of electric generators and internal combustion engines, owns two distinguished furniture manufacturers, and operates successful hospitality and real estate businesses in Kohler, Wisconsin, where it has its corporate headquarters and largest manufacturing facilities.

The Kohler Company was established in 1873, at the beginning of a debilitating five-year economic depression. That year the company's founders, John Michael Kohler and Charles Silberzahn, purchased an iron foundry from Kohler's employer and father-in-law, Jacob Vollrath, for $5000. Kohler, a 29-year-old Austrian immigrant, was the senior partner in the business, which was located on Lake Michigan in Sheboygan, Wisconsin.

In their first year, Kohler & Silberzahn were hit hard by the depression. But, as manufacturers of agricultural implements, such as watering troughs and scalding vats (to remove hair from animal carcasses), they had a good market: people had to eat, and farmers had to feed them.

In November 1878, at the end of the depression, Silberzahn sold his interest in the business to Herman Hayssen and John H. Stehn, who were employees of the enterprise. In 1880, with improved business prospects, the company established a newer, larger machine shop; however, this plant was destroyed by fire only months after opening, forcing the operation to move to a new location.

Rebounding from this costly setback, the small company introduced a line of unique enameled plumbing fixtures in 1883. While its significance was not yet fully realized, this line would propel Kohler into a period of strong growth. The company sold thousands of enameled sinks, cuspidors, stove reservoirs, kettles, and pans, as well as the first Kohler bathtubs, fashioned from one of the company's watering troughs. By 1887, the year the company was formally incorporated, these products accounted for 70 percent of Kohler's revenues.

The Kohler Company encountered its first labor difficulties in March 1897, when 21 members of the AFL Iron Molder's Union struck over new pay rates. After some of the molders returned to work and others were replaced, the strike ended without any formal settlement.

By 1900 Kohler employed more than 250 people, with 98 percent of its revenues coming from enameled iron products such as tubs, sinks, and water fountains. The factory in Sheboygan had become too small to meet growing production needs. Because it was not practical to expand the plant, which was now surrounded by homes, John Michael Kohler began building a new factory four miles west of Sheboygan in the small community of Riverside. The company entered a period of extraordinarily bad luck when John Michael Kohler died in November 1900 at the age of 56. Less than three months later, before a new chairman could be selected, the company's new iron foundry and machine and enamel shops burned down. Herman Hayssen and John Stehn's widow sold their interests in the company to the Kohler family, and in February 1902 the company was reorganized as the J. M. Kohler Sons Company under the leadership of Robert, Walter, and Carl Kohler, the oldest sons of John Michael Kohler. Two years later Carl died at the age of 24, and in 1905 Robert died at the age of 35, leaving the entire company to Walter Kohler.

Walter Kohler was a strong believer in corporate responsibility. As most of his employees were newly arrived immigrants, Kohler built the American Club, a stately boarding hotel where employees could live until they had enough money to purchase housing and send for their families. He established a benefit organization to provide employees with sickness and death benefits, and even provided lessons in civics, English, and American history so they could pass citizenship exams.

Kohler also laid plans to establish an entirely new community built around the company. He commissioned architects, city planners, and landscape architects, including the Olmsted Brothers (who designed New York's Central Park), to develop a city plan.

In 1911, after some years of stability, the work force had grown to 950 and the company had 10 sales offices, including one in London. That year the company introduced a revolutionary one-piece enamelware built-in bathtub with integral apron that was more sanitary than conventional two-piece tubs. The village of Kohler, meanwhile, had grown to 40 houses, and was incorporated in 1912 with a population of 254. In 1917 the Kohler Improvement Company began building houses in the planned community, selling them to Kohler Co. employees at cost. A second development was started in 1923, and others have followed until the present day.

By the mid-1920s Kohler had become the third largest plumbing products company in the United States, adding such sales boosters as vitreous china toilets and wash basins and brass faucets, shower heads, and other fittings. The company also introduced a revolutionary new product called the "electric sink." Essentially a dishwasher, but 20 years ahead of its time, the device did not catch on. Shortly afterward, Kohler introduced a slightly more successful novelty, the electric clothes washer.

In 1929 the company's products were chosen on the basis of their excellent design for inclusion in an exhibition at New York's Museum of Modern Art celebrating "the artistic qualities of the bath." The following year Kohler began manufacturing cast iron boilers and radiators for increasingly popular hot water and steam heat systems.

As one of the leaders in Wisconsin industry, Walter Kohler held substantial political power. In 1929 he ran successfully as a Republican for governor of Wisconsin. Distinguished for his administrative acumen rather than his political instincts, he was termed a "poor politician." He vigorously supported the unpopular President Herbert Hoover in 1932, a move that undoubtedly caused him to lose re-election to a second term.

Inspired by the growth of electrical appliances but faced with poor electrical distribution, Kohler began developing small electrical generators. The first unit, introduced in 1920 as the "automatic power and light," provided 1500 watts of 110-volt DC power from a generator driven by a four-cylinder gasoline engine. The small generator marked a significant improvement over existing generators, which merely charged batteries at 32 volts and were not as portable.

While the generators were intended for farm electrification, they were pressed into service by maritime and railroad companies, European castle owners, and others in need of portable power sources. Admiral Richard Byrd later took five Kohler generators with him on his first expedition to the South Pole in 1926, and took seven Kohler generators with him on his return in 1933. Revisiting his original base station on the frozen continent, his team found the generators from the first expedition in perfect working order. Byrd named an Antarctic mountain range for Kohler and later became a close friend of the family.

By 1932, however, residential building had fallen to just 11 percent of their 1928 levels, and Kohler was facing the prospect of massive employee layoffs. Because the company was not in debt and retained favorable terms for raw materials, Kohler resolved to keep the company in operation, and to stockpile whatever products could not be sold. This full employment policy had the effect of saving the local economy from ruin.

The company was revisited by labor unrest in July 1934 when a portion of the work force struck Kohler for the right to be represented by the Federal Union. The strike was cancelled later that year when the Union lost an employee vote to represent all of Kohler's production and maintenance employees. In arbitration, however, the National Labor Relations Board instructed the company to recognize a smaller, independent union, the Kohler Workers' Association.

In 1940 Walter Kohler died, and a battle for control of the firm broke out between Walter's children and their father's younger brother, Herbert Kohler, who was running the company. While the children argued for strict hereditary succession, the situation was further complicated by the fact that Herbert's mother and Walter's mother were sisters. In the end, Herbert prevailed.

When the United States became involved in World War II, much of Kohler's commercial operations ground to a halt. Iron, brass, and chrome supplies were diverted for war use by the government, which asked Kohler to resume production of military wares (during World War I Kohler had made mine anchors, projectiles, and shells). The company's first military products were precision valves and fittings for use in aircraft, such as the DC-3 and B-29. Kohler also built a variety of electric generators for the armed forces.

Based on its experience in precision crafted metallurgy, the government asked Kohler to produce 105mm and three-inch artillery shells, as well as forgings for rockets and other shells, fuses, torpedo tubes, piston rings, shell rotating bands, and engine bearings. After the war, Kohler discontinued much of its military production, but resumed building 105mm shells during the Korean War. The company did, however, continue to manufacture precision products and generators, albeit for different markets.

Given the occasional unreliability of utility-supplied power, many hospitals, banks, and other offices had to have their own emergency standby power, but required larger capacities than the 10 megawatt models Kohler manufactured. Eager to supply this market, Kohler began development of 100 kilowatt diesel-powered systems. As the market continued to grow, Kohler introduced a 230 kilowatt model and, some years later, a massive 500 kilowatt system. Today, Kohler generators are available in models ranging from a 2,250-watt portable to a 1.6 megawatt standby/prime power model. Kohler also makes generators, transfer switches, switchgear and accessories for the standby, prime power, marine, recreational, mobile, and portable markets.

Kohler also manufactures small gasoline engines, which were first built to power the company's electric generators. During the 1950s, the small engines found an explosive market in Thailand and Vietnam, where they were used to power boats, pump water on rice paddies, and drive air compressors. Virtually all the air-cooled engines in Southeast Asia at this time were made by Kohler and sold through a distributor in Hong Kong.

In 1951 Walter Kohler, Jr., a former officer and director of the company, followed in his father's footsteps to become the governor of Wisconsin. He was re-elected twice, serving until 1957. At the company, labor trouble arose again in April 1954 when the UAW-CIO local called a walkout to protest changes in union shop rules, seniority, and pay increases without regard to merit. Seeing these demands as unfair and potentially crippling to the profitable operation of the corporation, the company resisted. The strike continued until September 1960, when bargaining resumed, and a new contract was concluded two years later. The strike earned a place in the *Guinness Book of World Records* as the longest strike in American history.

Entering the 1960s, the company's engine, still strong in Asia, gained momentum in the United States, where Kohler motors were used to power lawn mowers, garden tractors, construction equipment, and even snowmobiles. International Harvester, John Deere, Wheel-Horse, Jacobsen, and Bombardier (inventor of the snowmobile) incorporated Kohler engines in their products. By 1963 Kohler was one of the leading small engine suppliers in the industry.

In order to keep pace with this growing demand, Kohler established two new production facilities, in Mexico City and Toronto. However, the company ran into strong competition from Japanese and German manufacturers who had extensive experience with two- and four-stroke engines. Kohler suffered market share loss, but won back a significant share of the market by introducing higher technology two-cycle engines in 1968. It later won a suit against market leader Briggs & Stratton, which had tried to coerce its distributors to stop handling Kohler engines.

The company experienced another leadership crisis in 1968 when Kohler's president, J. L. Kuplic, died unexpectedly. Only six days later, Herbert Kohler, Sr., chairman and CEO of the company for 28 years, also died. Herbert Kohler, Jr., heir to the company, was at the time a self-described "hippie," pursuing a career outside the company. He later told *Supply House Times,* "By preplanning my life, my father removed my right to fail. As a result, for a portion of my life I experienced nothing but failure. That led me to become a substantial rebel."

Company directors elected to pass over the younger Kohler, and named an interim chairman. In an unusual departure from company traditions, the directors named non-family members Lyman Conger and Walter Cleveland as chairman and president, respectively. When Conger retired in 1972, Herb Kohler was appointed chairman, and two years later he succeeded Cleveland as company president.

Under Herb Kohler's leadership, the Kohler company doubled in size to an estimated $700 million in annual sales (official figures are not published). After 110 years of strictly internal growth, much of the expansion came from the company's new venture into acquisitions. In 1984 the company acquired the Schaumburg, Illinois–based Sterling Faucet Company. Two years later, Kohler purchased Baker, Knapp & Tubbs, a high-end furniture manufacturer headquartered in Grand Rapids, Michigan, and Jacob Delafon, a plumbing products manufacturer headquartered in Paris. The company also established a Japanese subsidiary. In 1989 Kohler purchased the McGuire Furniture Company, a San Francisco-based manufacturer, Oakland-based Kallista, Inc., Portland-based Ann Sacks Tile and Stone, and Dupont Sanitaire-Chauffage, in Paris. Kohler also planned to expand into the leisure industry, based on its experience in turning the company's one-time workers' hotel, the American Club, into a successful full-scale convention and recreation resort hotel.

Principal Subsidiaries: Baker, Knapp, & Tubbs, Inc.; McGuire Furniture Company; Sterling Plumbing Group, Inc.; Kallista, Inc.; Ann Sacks Tile and Stone, Inc.; Kohler de Mexico, S.A. de C.V.; Kohler Japan, K.K.; Dupont Sanitaire Chauffage (France); Jacob Delafon (France); Kohler Ltd. (Canada); Kohler Sanimex, S.A. de C.V. (Mexico); Helvex, S.A. de C.V. (Mexico).

Further Reading: Bold Craftsmen, Company Document, 1973; "This Is Herb Kohler, Like Him or Not," *Supply House Times,* November 1986; "Kohler Company," *Forbes,* December 11, 1989; *Kohler Company,* Company Document, 1991.

—John Simley

KRAFT GENERAL FOODS, INC.

Three Lakes Drive
Northfield, Illinois 60093
U.S.A.
(708) 646-2000
Fax: (708) 646-2922

Wholly owned subsidiary of Philip Morris
Incorporated: 1989
Employees: 100,000
Sales: $28.2 billion
SICs: 2022 Cheese—Natural & Processed; 2035 Pickles,
  Sauces & Salad Dressing; 2099 Food Preparations Nec

Kraft General Foods was formed in March of 1989, following Philip Morris's acquisition of Kraft, Inc. in December of the previous year. The diversified tobacco giant's first major push into the food industry came in 1985 when it acquired General Foods Corporation. After completing the Kraft acquisition, Philip Morris combined the two food companies to create one subsidiary called Kraft General Foods, Inc. This subsidiary was divided into seven major groups: General Foods USA; Kraft USA; Kraft General Foods International; Kraft General Foods Canada; Oscar Mayer; Kraft General Foods Frozen Products; and Kraft General Foods Commercial Products. Although the two companies operate under a united name, each has a long and rich history.

GENERAL FOODS

General Foods has been in many ways the prototypical American food processor. The company was a pioneer in the acquisition and assimilation of smaller food companies and built a huge multi-national, multi-product corporation. It has also historically applied leading-edge technology to its product development. For example, General Foods snatched up Clarence Birdseye's company well before the food industry recognized the potential of frozen foods. Later innovations, including Tang instant breakfast drink, Pop Rocks carbonated candy, and Cool Whip nondairy dessert topping, all originated in the laboratories of General Foods. General Foods also stands as the largest coffee producer in the world. The company's Maxwell House, Sanka, Brim, Yuban, and General Foods International Coffees brands make up roughly 25 percent of total sales. General Foods is the nation's number-three producer of breakfast cereals

(Post), the leader in powdered drink mixes (Kool Aid, Country Time, Crystal Light, and Tang), and the nation's top producer of gelatin dessert products (Jell-O).

The groundwork for General Foods was laid by Charles W. Post, a health enthusiast who tried to seduce America's coffee drinkers away from the caffeinic drink with a cereal beverage he called Postum. Post built the company that would become General Foods with a number of promising products and the marvel of modern marketing.

In 1891 Post checked into the Kellogg brothers' renowned sanitarium in Battle Creek, Michigan, in hopes of revitalizing his frail health. Post, ill for several years, was weak and confined to a wheelchair. The stay proved propitious; while at the Kelloggs' sanitarium, Post came up with several ideas which would eventually be profitable.

Post later opened the La Vita Inn in Battle Creek, where he experimented with healing through mental suggestion and special diets. A few years later Post began marketing a cereal beverage similar to the one he had received as a coffee substitute at the Kelloggs's. He began marketing this blend of wheat, bran, and molasses called Postum cereal beverage in 1895. Post incorporated the Postum Cereal Co., Ltd. in 1896 with a paid-in capital of $100,000.

In 1897 Post introduced a new cereal, made from whole wheat and malted barley flour, called Grape-Nuts. Grape-Nuts were baked for 20 hours, turning the starch into dextrose and creating an easily digested cereal. In 1904 Post marketed a corn flake cereal under the name "Elijah's Manna." Not immediately successful, the new cereal was renamed "Post Toasties" and subsequently became a big hit with American consumers. Post continued to bring new products to the market, including Post's bran flakes, Post's bran chocolate bar, and Post's wheat meal.

Within five years of its incorporation, Postum Cereal Company's capital had risen to $5 million. The company's Battle Creek facility was the largest of its kind in the world. Postum employed 2,500 people and its factories covered more than 20 acres. Charles W. Post had amassed a personal fortune and spent his money freely to propagate his own views. Post was an outspoken critic of closed shops and labor unions, spending thousands on advertisements attacking organized labor. This crusade against unions resulted in occasional boycotts of Post products and incurred the personal enmity of union organizers throughout the nation. Carroll Post once told an interesting tale about his brother Charles in a letter. One day the two Post brothers sat at a lunchroom counter where two brands of corn flakes—Post Toasties and Krinkle—were for sale. While the two men were eating, a railroad worker came in and asked for corn flakes. When the waitress asked which brand he wanted, the man said, "give me Krinkle. That man Post is always fighting our union." But the Posts had the last laugh: Krinkle was merely another name for Post Toasties, marketed as a reduced-price corn flake.

Despite Post's stance against organized labor, the Postum Cereal Company did not have trouble with labor in its own factories. It paid the highest wages in the industry, emphasized safe working conditions, and implemented accident and sickness benefit programs. The company also built about 100 homes for its workers which were sold on very favorable terms.

In May of 1914, Charles W. Post committed suicide at his winter home in Santa Barbara, California. The day-to-day operations of the Postum Cereal Company had been run by a group of managers—C. W.'s ''cabinet''—for several years. Upon his death, Post's daughter, Marjorie Merriwether Post, took over the company and helped launch the expansion that would create the company known as General Foods.

Marjorie Post was well acquainted with the Postum business. She had often accompanied her father on business trips and frequently sat in on meetings. In 1920 she married Edward F. Hutton, an investment broker. Two years later the Postum Cereal Company went public, and Marjorie Post stepped down from active management of the company. Her husband, who became chairman of the company in 1923, and Colby M. Chester, who became president in 1924, ran the company's day-to-day operations. Majorie remained a key policymaker, however, and was critical to the company's acquisition strategy and transition into General Foods.

That transition began in 1925 with the acquisition of the Jell-O Company. Before frozen pies, cakes, and novelties entered the market, Jell-O was the premier dessert brand. In 1926 the company absorbed Swans Down cake flour and Minute tapioca. Baker's coconut, Baker's chocolate, and Log Cabin syrup were acquired in 1927. The company also shortened its name to Postum Company that year.

In 1928 the Postum Company acquired Maxwell House Coffee, whose roots dated back to 1892 when Joel Cheek perfected the coffee blend served at the famous Maxwell House hotel in Nashville, Tennessee. President Theodore Roosevelt visited Nashville in 1907 and was served Maxwell House coffee. When asked if he wanted a second cup of coffee, Roosevelt answered, ''Yes, indeed, it's good to the last drop.'' This reply became the company's famous slogan.

In 1929 the Postum Company made another significant acquisition when it paid $22 million for a controlling interest of the General Foods Company, owned by Clarence Birdseye. Birdseye perfected new techniques for freezing vegetables and meat. An adventurer by nature, Birdseye had gotten the idea for his freezing technique while on an expedition to Labrador. Birdseye noted that the Eskimos routinely froze caribou and fish, and that these products retained their flavor even when stored for months before thawing. He hypothesized that the bitterly cold air contributed to fresh taste and this method might be superior to the commonly practiced slower freezing. Birdseye returned in 1917 to begin research and eventually perfected a process that could be used commercially. In 1924 Birdseye founded the General Seafoods Company in Gloucester, Massachusetts.

Marjorie Merriwether Post had noticed Birdseye's operations in 1926, but it took her three more years to convince Postum executives to acquire the company. The price had increased tenfold in that time, but Postum nevertheless happily acquired the company. The enlarged Postum Company also adopted the name General Foods in 1929, and Clarence Birdseye became head of the new General Foods laboratory, where he continued his work on frozen foods.

While the Great Depression affected all parts of the economy, food was a relatively stable industry. After record profits in 1929, General Foods' spent its energy in 1930 on consolidating its recent acquisitions. As a result, earnings dropped slightly that year. In 1932 the company acquired the remaining 49 percent of General Foods. It expanded quickly, adding six new plants that year to freeze nearly 100 different products. In 1932 General Foods also purchased the Sanka Coffee Corporation, makers of decaffeinated coffee. General Foods had been distributing Sanka since 1927 through an agreement with the company's European owners.

General Foods's earnings, which had reached $19.4 million in 1929, dropped to $10.3 million in 1932. In 1933, however, they began to rise again as consumer purchasing power strengthened. In 1935 E. F. Hutton resigned as chairman of the company and C. M. Chester assumed the post, where he remained until 1946. Marjorie Post returned to the company as a director the next year, a position she retained until 1958.

During World War II, General Foods, like other food companies, achieved record sales, despite food shortages and other wartime exigencies. Sales in 1943 were more than double those of 1929. During the war, the company's Denver plant produced ten-in-one rations for the U.S. Army. General Foods also began developing an instant coffee for the army in 1941. In 1943 General Foods acquired the Gaines Dog Food Company, and the next year it added Yuban premium coffee to its already strong coffee line. Instant Maxwell House coffee—one of the first postwar consumer products—was introduced in 1945.

In May of 1953, General Foods acquired the Perkins Products Company of Chicago. Perkins manufactured a variety of powdered beverage mixes to which the consumer added sugar and water for a fruit-flavored drink. Kool-Aid has been a favorite of kids across the nation ever since. Years later General Foods added a number of other products to its beverage division, including Tang, Country Time, and sugar free Crystal Light. In 1954 the company entered the salad dressing market with its purchase of the Hollywood manufacturer 4 Seasons, Inc., and in 1960 Open Pit barbecue sauce was acquired.

Acquisitions of established companies continued as General Foods diversified outside of the food industry. In 1957 the company bought the SOS Company, a leading scouring-pad manufacturer. Ten years later, however, the Federal Trade Commission ruled that the acquisition violated antitrust laws and forced General Foods to sell the company. In 1968 General Foods entered the fast-food business by purchasing the Burger Chef chain for more than $15 million. In December of 1969, General Foods added the Viviane Woodard Cosmetic Corporation, a door-to-door operation, for $39 million. And in 1970, toy company Kohner Brothers and the nation's largest seed company, W. Atlee Burpee Company, were both acquired.

Because General Foods did not have as much luck with its nonfood subsidiaries as it did with food businesses, it disposed of most of them. Kohner Brothers was sold to Gabriel Industries after just five years; the Viviane Woodard cosmetics business was closed in 1975; Burpee was sold in 1979; and, after consistently losing money, the Burger Chef chain was sold in 1982.

In the late 1950s and early 1960s General Foods aggressively branched out into international markets. In 1956 the company acquired a controlling interest in the La India Company, Venezuela's number-one chocolate company. In 1959 the company's Canadian subsidiary purchased the Hostess snack-food company of Canada; in 1960 it purchased the Kibon ice cream company of Brazil and the French coffee-roaster Etablessements Pierre Lemonnier S.A.; in 1961 it bought Krema Hollywood Chewing Gum Company S.A. of Paris; and General Foods of Mexico S.A. was formed in 1962. Numerous other food processors throughout the world were purchased as well. At the end of the decade General Foods had major subsidiaries operating in Canada, the United Kingdom, Australia, France, Mexico, Brazil, Venezuela, Denmark, Sweden, Spain, and Italy.

By the mid-1960s General Foods was an established giant in the industry. Chairman C. W. Cook, who took over in 1965, ran a company whose outstanding successes were based on new-product development, sweeping market research, and enormous advertising budgets.

During the 1970s international acquisitions continued at a furious pace, but domestic operations settled down a bit. Frozen foods became increasingly popular as more double-income families found less time to cook and had extra cash for quick meals. The company's BirdsEye frozen-food division also enjoyed a boost in earnings. But not all of General Foods units benefited from such favorable demographic changes. Jell-O, for example, suffered as new products such as frozen novelty desserts came to the market. In 1979 the Jell-O unit pushed to recapture the dessert market, employing an advertising campaign to reverse Jell-O's steady decline. In the early-1980s the company introduced Jell-O Pudding Pops—frozen pudding on a stick—to capitalize on its well-known name and expand its share of the market.

Nonetheless, at the end of the 1970s General Foods was not performing up to expectations. The company was overly dependent on coffee for its revenues—its various coffee brands accounted for 39 percent of General Foods' entire revenues in 1980.

In 1981 General Foods made its largest acquisition to date when it bought the Oscar Mayer company, the leading American hot dog maker, for $470 million. Oscar Mayer, founded in 1883 by a Bavarian immigrant, was a family-held company until the purchase and had a reputation for high-quality products. General Foods was trying to reduce its dependence on the coffee trade, but Wall Street critics charged that with the purchase of Oscar Mayer, the company was opening itself up to the wildly cyclical, low-margin packaged-meat business.

Regardless, the merger did give General Foods access to an extensive refrigerated supply network. In addition, the acquisition afforded General Foods a high profile in the refrigerated meat section at the supermarket—Oscar Mayer was the largest national brand of lunch meats, and its Louis Rich turkey products unit was top in that growing segment of the market.

In 1984 the company agreed to sell its Gaines Pet Food division for $157 million. General Foods' overall performance went down as coffee sales dipped, and the Post Cereals unit, too, began to slide.

In November of 1985 Philip Morris purchased General Foods for $5.6 billion. Philip Morris had long been known as an aggressive marketer. Its chairman, Hamish Maxwell, planned to turn around General Foods and, at the same time, decrease Philip Morris's reliance on the shrinking tobacco market. In January of 1987, Philip Smith became CEO of General Foods. Smith began a massive reorganization of the company in 1987, splitting its three core product lines—coffees, meats, and assorted groceries—into separate units.

KRAFT

Kraft is one of the oldest and best-known food brands in the world. Many of Kraft USA's products, such as Velveeta pasteurized process cheese spread, Parkay margarine, Miracle Whip salad dressing, and Philadelphia Brand cream cheese, have become integral parts of the American diet. In addition, Kraft products are sold in 130 countries around the world. Such stability seems enviable, yet it has been a mixed blessing. Kraft has long sought a proper balance between the traditional products on which its reputation is based and the development of new endeavors aimed at sustained growth.

One of Kraft, Inc.'s primary predecessor companies was established by James L. Kraft, the son of a Canadian farmer. In 1903 Kraft started a wholesale cheese distribution business in Chicago. Kraft hoped to relieve grocers of the need to travel daily to the cheese market by delivering cheese to their doors. Business was dismal at first, and it was later reported that Kraft lost $3,000 and his horse the first year.

But the business eventually took hold and James was joined by his four brothers, Fred, Charles, Norman, and John. In 1909 the business was incorporated as J. L. Kraft & Bros. Company. New-product development and innovative advertising fueled the company's growth. As early as 1911, Kraft mailed circulars to retail grocers and advertised on elevated trains and billboards. Later, he was among the first to use color advertisements in national magazines. In 1912 Kraft opened a New York office to develop an international business. By 1914 the company sold 31 varieties of cheese throughout the country, and that year it opened its own cheese factory in Stockton, Illinois.

Before the advent of refrigeration, cheese was sold in large wheels which spoiled quickly after being cut open. Kraft developed a blended, pasteurized cheese that did not spoil and could be packaged in small tins. Kraft began producing what it called process cheese in 1915 and received a patent in 1916. Six million pounds of this cheese were sold to the U.S. Army during World War I.

In 1919 Kraft placed its first advertisements in national magazines. The next year, Kraft acquired a Canadian cheese company. In 1924 Kraft's name was changed to Kraft Cheese Company and the company offered its shares to the public. That year Kraft also opened its first overseas sales office, in London, which led to the establishment of Kraft Cheese Company Ltd. there in 1927. The same year Kraft moved into Germany by opening a sales office in Hamburg. In 1928 Kraft merged with Phenix Cheese Corporation, the maker of Philadelphia Brand cream cheese. The newly formed Kraft-Phenix Cheese Corporation had captured 40 percent of the nation's cheese market by

1930 and boasted operations in Canada, Australia, Britain, and Germany.

The 1920s spawned another growing dairy concern, the National Dairy Products Corporation, whose fortunes were soon to be linked with Kraft-Phenix. National Dairy was the product of a 1923 merger between the Hydrox Corporation of Chicago, an ice cream company established in 1881 and purchased in 1914 by pharmacist Thomas McInnerney, and the Rieck-McJunkin Dairy Company of Pittsburgh. Throughout the remainder of the 1920s, National Dairy acquired other small dairy concerns in the East and Midwest, including the Breyer Ice Cream Company and Breakstone Bros., Inc., the sour cream and cottage cheese company. In 1929 National Dairy set out to acquire Kraft-Phenix. The merger was completed on May 12, 1930. The group of companies assembled by McInnerney prior to the Kraft-Phenix merger eventually formed the core of Kraft's Dairy Group.

The merger did not radically affect the way in which the two companies operated. McInnerney's strategy had always been to provide essentially autonomous subsidiaries with the resources needed for growth. Consequently, Kraft functioned independently from New York-based National Dairy, which acted primarily as a holding company.

After the merger, Kraft settled down to introduce many of the brands that now form the heart of its consumer product line; Velveeta pasteurized process cheese spread had been introduced in 1928; Miracle Whip salad dressing and Kraft caramels came in 1933; the famous macaroni and cheese dinner in 1937; and Parkay margarine in 1940. Again, innovative advertising—this time on radio—encouraged quick public acceptance of the new products. In 1933 the company sponsored the "Kraft Musical Revue," a two-hour musical variety show. Later the program was shortened to one hour and was broadcast weekly as the "Kraft Music Hall," hosted by Bing Crosby. Overseas operations expanded, guided by a policy that mandated local control and products tailored to meet the needs and tastes of foreign consumers. Meanwhile, in 1935, National Dairy introduced Sealtest ice cream, named after a quality-control system for its dairy products.

Kraft was a major food supplier during World War II. By the end of 1941, four million pounds of cheese were shipped to Britain weekly. Many Kraft products, including field rations of cheese, were produced for the U.S. government. Kraft's labs researched better methods of food production while home economists at Kraft Kitchens, a division established in the home economics department in 1924, developed recipes to ease wartime shortages.

In 1945 the Kraft Cheese Company became Kraft Foods Company. In the postwar years, Kraft resumed the formula of new-product development and advertising that had helped build the company. In 1947 Kraft created and sponsored the first commercial network program on television, the "Kraft Television Theatre." Along with the new advertising vehicle new products, such as sliced process cheese in 1950 and Cheez Whiz pasteurized process cheese spread in 1952, were introduced.

In 1951 the postwar economic boom drove National Dairy's sales over the $1 billion mark for the first time. Thomas McIn-

nerney died in 1952 and J. L. Kraft died the following year. Kraft's death marked the end of the Kraft family's leadership of the business. National Dairy began to reorganize along more centralized lines soon after its founders died. The autonomous subsidiaries became divisions of a single operating company in 1956 and 1957. Meanwhile, the company took its first cautious steps toward diversification with the acquisition of Metro Glass, a maker of glass packaging, in 1956.

During the late 1950s and the 1960s, Kraft continued to expand its product line, adding new products such as jellies and preserves in 1956, "jet-puffed" marshmallows in 1959, barbecue sauce in 1960, and individually wrapped cheese slices in 1965. During the 1960s, Kraft also introduced many of its products in foreign markets.

In 1969 National Dairy renamed itself Kraftco Corporation and in 1972 it transferred its headquarters from New York to the Chicago suburb of Glenview. The company name changed in 1976 to Kraft Inc. to emphasize the company's focus on food processing and to more clearly identify it with the internationally known Kraft trademark. Reorganization accompanied the name change; the movement toward a more centralized structure—begun in the 1950s—was accomplished by partitioning the company into divisions according to specific markets or products.

Kraft manifested a decidedly conservative business strategy during the 1970s. Unlike other major food companies, Kraft did not seek acquisitions to shore up sagging profits. New-product introductions also slowed somewhat; after the introduction of Light n' Lively yogurt and ice milk in 1969, squeezeable Parkay margarine came in 1973 and Breyers yogurt in 1977. The difficult business climate of the 1970s may have encouraged a defensive posture as inflation increased costs and cut into profits.

John M. Richman, who began at Kraft as a lawyer at the National Dairy Products Corporation, became Kraft's chairman and CEO in 1979. Richman planned to strengthen the company's position in its traditional markets while diversifying into higher-growth industries. His first move—a truly bold stoke—was a merger with Dart Industries, a Los Angeles-based conglomerate headed by the flamboyant Justin Dart.

Dart Industries was established in 1902 as the United Drug Company. Dart began his career in the retail drug business and built Rexall Drugs into one of the largest chains of drugstores in the country. With Rexall as his base, Dart began an aggressive acquisition campaign, diversifying into chemicals, plastics, glass, cosmetics, electric appliances, and land development. In 1969 the company name was changed to Dart Industries to reflect this diversity. At the time of the merger, the flagship of Dart Industries was its successful Tupperware subsidiary that sold plastic food containers through direct sales by independent dealers using a "home party" plan.

The aggressive, innovative, and rapidly growing Dart Industries fit perfectly into Richman's plan; it offered Kraft instant diversification. The merger also offered advantages for Dart and his company. Richman's boldness appealed to Dart, who thought that Kraft would give Dart Industries some stability. Thus, Dart & Kraft was launched on September 25, 1980 with John Richman as its chairman and CEO and Justin Dart as chairman of the executive committee. Kraft and the subsidiaries of Dart—Tupperware, West Bend appliances, Duracell batteries, Wilsonart plastics, and Thatcher glass—continued to operate independently. However, some analysts doubted that such a diverse company would succeed.

As in many restructurings, there were some early rough spots, but major changes in operating procedure were confined to top managers. Middle managers were left in their familiar roles to ease the transition. Altogether, management apparently succeeded in unifying two very different firms with a minimum of friction.

Industry analysts, nonetheless, felt compelled to ask which partner would dominate the merger. Although Kraft was the larger of the two companies, the consensus was that the more aggressive and growth-oriented Dart would be the dominant party. The reasoning was that Dart had been given preference in the new company's name and it was Kraft's desire to become more like Dart that initially led to the merger. On the first anniversary of the merger, Richman himself commented that "in terms of organization and outlook, we're more a Dart than a Kraft."

Indeed, Dart & Kraft's initial activities bore out this assessment. Soon after the merger, the company bid $460 million for the Hobart Corporation, a manufacturer of food-service equipment. The deal was completed in April of 1981. And even while the Hobart deal was being negotiated, Dart & Kraft announced that it was considering further acquisitions.

Although several smaller acquisitions followed in the next two years, diversification slowed because several subsidiaries experienced managerial problems or proved vulnerable to the recession of the early 1980s. Poor performers included Kraft's European operations and its food-service business, and Dart's plastics unit and its West Bend appliances. Even Hobart was troubled by sagging profits and declining market share in its Kitchen Aid division, which produced top-of-the-line kitchen appliances. Company efforts to get these businesses back on track were beginning to show results when trouble struck Tupperware.

Tupperware had been a phenomenal success; it doubled sales and earnings every five years prior to 1980. But in 1983 sales slipped seven percent and profits were down 15 percent. Tupperware's slide was attributed to attrition among its dealers—as more women took jobs outside the home, there were fewer people to sell and buy Tupperware.

In 1984 the company planned to increase returns from 13.3 percent to 18 percent, and thus place Dart & Kraft in the top fifth of the consumer-products industry. This ambitious goal was to be attained by adding new products, extending existing lines, and using aggressive marketing and advertising.

Michael A. Miles, the man who had revived Kentucky Fried Chicken, was brought in to direct the new effort. Miles first cut costs by overhauling the European division. Many of Kraft's brands competed in mature markets. Additions to these lines—for example, bacon and cream cheese-flavored salad dressings—boosted sales. The company also acquired promising new brands that appealed to the upscale consumer. Among these were the import-style cheeses of Churny Company, Inc., Celestial Seasonings herb teas, Lender's bagels, and Frusen Glädjé premium ice cream.

The company pursued similar tactics in Dart & Kraft's nonfood businesses, but when sales continued to lag into 1986, the company decided, in effect, to dissolve the six-year-old merger. Hobart, Tupperware, Wilsonart, and West Bend were spun off into a new company called Premark International, Inc. Kraft retained all of the product lines it had brought to the 1980 merger and also gained Duracell batteries.

Kraft followed through on its plan to expand its product lines and market them aggressively, a strategy that won visible gains. The company's management seemed to have rediscovered J. L. Kraft's approach that combined the stability of well-known brand names with creative marketing and the continuous development of new products aimed at changing American tastes.

Philip Morris's designs on the packaged-foods industry became clear when the company purchased Kraft in 1988. In March of 1989 Philip Morris merged the Kraft and General Foods units into one giant entity called Kraft General Foods, Inc. At the helm was Kraft's Michael Miles.

As a result of the merger, the company became the largest food marketer in the United States. Profits at Kraft General Foods grew at an average rate of more than 20 percent in its first two years. Early on, the company's size proved to be a competitive advantage; it saved $400 million through initial consolidations and its purchasing power multiplied. Size had its drawbacks, however. The company was slow to respond to demand in some markets. For example, Kraft waited until 1990 to introduce Touch of Butter, well after other food producers responded to the public's growing concern about excess cholesterol. Tensions existed between the Kraft and General Foods forces within the company as well. One notable failure during this period was Kraft microwave entrees, originally developed by General Foods, but marketed under the Kraft name as a result of internal politics. The product was discontinued after only six months.

In 1991 Miles became CEO of Philip Morris. He was replaced at Kraft General Foods by Richard Mayer. The company's sales in the North American market grew only one percent in 1991. Several of the company's most important product categories lost market share that year, including cheese, processed meats, and frozen dinners. In the $5.2 billion retail cheese market, Kraft General Foods's drop to 42 percent control cost the company approximately $125 million in profits. The company's Oscar Mayer line of processed meat products was hurt by the rising tide of health-consciousness among consumers. To combat this trend, healthier-sounding items such as "light" bologna and turkey bacon were introduced. In addition, close to 300 products with lagging sales were eliminated. Demand for Louis Rich processed turkey products was slipping as well. Kraft General Foods responded by closing its Tulare, California plant, thus cutting the payroll by more than 1,000 employees. Another market share loser was BirdsEye frozen vegetables, which fell behind Pillsbury's Green Giant brand in share of sales.

An area in which Kraft General Foods achieved positive results in 1991 was in its Post cereal unit. Honey Bunches of Oats, introduced in 1989 (when Post registered an all-time low market share of 10.9 percent), snared one percent of the $7.5 billion breakfast cereal market by 1991. This was the company's first gain in that area in more than ten years. Coffee also performed well for Kraft General Foods in 1991. During the year the Maxwell House brand regained market leadership over Procter & Gamble's Folgers.

In 1992 KGF Marketing Services was formed. The purpose of this unit was to assist in coordinating marketing strategies and bridge the gaps between the different operating units. Late in 1992 the operating units of Kraft General Foods were realigned. The company eliminated two of its seven original operating groups, KGF Frozen Products and Oscar Mayer Foods. In January of 1993 Kraft General Foods completed the $450 million purchase of RJR Nabisco's cold cereal business.

Despite the difficult business climate of recent years, a company the size of Kraft General Foods will undoubtedly continue to have a major impact on the packaged-foods industry. As further adjustments are made, the company will likely become increasingly able to take advantage of its stronger products while, at the same time, recapturing market share in the areas in which it has been losing ground.

Principal Subsidiaries: General Foods USA; Kraft USA; Kraft General Foods Canada.

Further Reading: Dudley, Charles Eaves, *Post City, Texas,* Austin, Texas, State Historical Association, 1952; *Kraft, Inc.— Through the Years,* Glenview, Illinois, Kraft, Inc., 1988; Liesse, Julie, and Judann Dagnoli, ''Goliath KGF Loses Steam after Merger,'' *Advertising Age,* January 27, 1992; Warner, Fara, ''Kraft General Foods Move to Mend Its Floundering Marriage,'' *Adweek's Marketing Week,* February 24, 1992; Sinisi, John, ''KGF's New Dressing,'' *Brandweek,* September 28, 1992.

—updated by Robert R. Jacobson

LITTLE CAESAR INTERNATIONAL, INC.

2211 Woodward Avenue
Detroit, Michigan 48201
U.S.A.
(313) 983-6000
Fax: (313) 983-6197

Private Company
Incorporated: 1959
Employees: 90,000
Sales: $2.05 billion
SICs: 5812 Eating Places; 6794 Patent Owners & Lessors

Using the same pizza recipe it started with in 1959, this family-run business has grown to become the third largest pizza chain in the United States. Little Caesar International, Inc.'s interests include Little Caesar Enterprises, Inc.; Olympia Arenas, Inc.; the Detroit Red Wings hockey team; Blue Line Distributing; the Detroit Tigers Baseball Club; and the historic Fox Theatre. The primary business, a chain of carry-out pizza restaurants, has been built on the concept of "two pizzas for the price of one" and other innovative production and marketing techniques. Little Caesars has over 4,500 franchise units in the United States, Canada, England, and Puerto Rico.

The business was established in 1959 in Garden City, Michigan, by Michael and Marian Ilitch. Born during the Great Depression, Michael served in the United States Marine Corps from 1947 to 1951 and played on the Detroit Tigers baseball club's farm team from 1951 to 1955; a leg injury cut his professional sports career short. Ilitch sold awnings for the next four years, then founded Little Caesars in 1959.

At the time, the restaurant offered spaghetti, fried chicken, and french fries, as well as pizza. Little Caesars found a niche in retail pizza by offering quality at low prices, and opened a second restaurant in just two years. In 1962 the first franchise was opened in the Detroit metropolitan area.

By the end of the 1960s, Little Caesars had built or franchised over 50 restaurants, including one in Canada. During that decade, delivery was a service of most Little Caesars restaurants, but in 1971 the chain moved to carry-out only. The restaurant set itself apart from many competitors by using only natural ingredients, including high-gluten flour in the pizza dough, specially grown California tomatoes, and grade A cheese. Little Caesars still prides itself on the use of all-natural spices, as opposed to the synthetic flavorings used throughout the pizza industry.

The 1970s were years of innovation and phenomenal growth for Little Caesars. In 1971 the company began its two-for-one "Pizza! Pizza! (Two Great Pizzas! One Low Price.)" concept and made it a permanent feature of the company's marketing campaigns in 1975. The marketing strategy has forced competitors in some heavily saturated areas to mimic the two-for-one offer. In 1977 Little Caesars also introduced drive-through windows at its quick-serve locations, and in 1979 developed a pizza conveyor oven that sped up the production of pizza and other baked items.

During the 1980s Ilitch continued Little Caesars's rapid growth and marketing innovation. In 1980 the chain had 226 units with sales of $63.6 million. By mid-decade annual sales had grown more than five-fold to $340 million. The company achieved successful expansion through an emphasis on several simple concepts: market saturation, two pizzas for the price of one, and carry-out only. Approximately 98 percent of Little Caesars units were 1,200- to 1,800-square-foot units offering take-out only—overhead and maintenance on these shops is considerably lower than that of competitors who offer sit-down or even delivery-only service, because the restaurants don't require waiters, waitresses, busboys, dishwashers, or delivery personnel.

In 1984 the company built its 500th restaurant, then saw the 1,000th Little Caesars just two years later. By that time, the company was not only well established in 38 states and parts of Canada, but had also built an outpost in Great Britain. Marketing innovations included the first college campus restaurant, at the University of Oklahoma, and the first hospital restaurant, in Detroit at Mt. Carmel Mercy Hospital.

The Ilitches also began to develop peripheral interests in the 1980s. They purchased the Detroit Red Wings hockey club in 1982. Then in a slump, the Red Wings club improved markedly after the Ilitch family acquired it. The team captured the Norris Division Championship in the 1986–87, 1987–88, and 1991–92 seasons. In 1992 *Financial World* magazine reported that the Red Wings were the most valuable franchise in the National Hockey League (NHL). The percent of capacity attendance at Joe Louis Arena (the Red Wings' home ice) has been among the highest in the NHL.

The Ilitches also own the Red Wings' farm team, the Adirondack Red Wings of Glens Falls, New York. The family's sports/entertainment holdings were augmented in 1988 with the purchase of the Detroit Drive arena football team. The team won three out of four Arena Football League championships between 1989 and 1992.

The family acquired the Red Wings' home ice as well in 1982. Olympia Arenas, Inc., the management company for Joe Louis, Cobo, and Glens Falls arenas and Detroit's Fox Theatre have been successful business ventures for the family. In the 1980s Olympia established itself as a trend-setter among arenas when it brought in Little Caesars and Everything Yogurt concessions and separated beer service from all other concessions for speedier service. In 1992 the Meadow Brook Music Festival, an outdoor entertainment center at Oakland University in Rochester Hills, Michigan, was added to the Olympia Arenas group.

The Fox Theatre has become a special Ilitch family project. They purchased the 5,000-seat historic theater in 1987 and invested $50 million in its restoration. The theater was reopened in November 1988 and was ranked the nation's top grossing theater—in sales and attendance—by *Performance* magazine that year. The theater's schedule includes a variety of concerts, the annual Variety Broadway series, and restored classic films. The Fox expects to reach the 4-million-patron mark during the 1992–93 season. The theater's success is also measured by the other businesses its restoration has drawn to the formerly declining area of Detroit in which it is located.

Little Caesars moved its corporate headquarters to the Fox Office Centre, adjacent to the Theatre, in 1989. The 10-story office building houses over 500 employees, a child development center, a gift shop, a small convenience shop, and two restaurants. Both restaurants were opened in 1990. America's Pizza Cafe, created by Michael Ilitch, features thin-crust pizzas baked in a wood-fired oven, gourmet pastas, and desserts. Tres Vite, a bistro-style restaurant, was conceived by Ilitch and nationally known chef Jimmy Schmidt. Ilitch and Schmidt have also collaborated on Cocina del Sol, with a Southwestern menu, and Buster's Bay, a seafood restaurant, both in the Detroit metropolitan area. Their fourth restaurant, a northern-Italian eatery called Stelline, was set to open in Troy in May 1993.

In recent years Little Caesars has experimented with the basic carry-out, two-for-one pizza concept. Variations on the basic unit include restaurants with limited seating, drive-through units, and arena concessions. In a joint venture with Kmart Corp., Little Caesars built over 400 Pizza Stations in Kmart stores in 1992. The self-serve restaurants featuring pasta and vegetable salads, soups, fresh fruits, and the standard pizza, sandwich, and hot pasta, constituted almost half of Little Caesars's 1992 unit growth. The company has also introduced new items like Crazy Bread, Chocolate! Chocolate! Ravioli! Ravioli!, Caesars Sandwiches, and Baby Pan! Pan! lunch pizzas.

Little Caesars marketing and promotion efforts have focused on value ("Pizza! Pizza! Two Great Pizzas! One Low Price!") and quality ("When you make pizza this good, one just isn't enough."). According to Rona Gindin writing in *Restaurant Business,* the company invests a minimum of five percent of its sales on advertising, and franchises (which constitute 75 percent of all units) spend a comparable percentage on local and corporate promotions.

In 1988 the company dropped W. B. Doner and Co. as its advertising agents and awarded the account to Cliff Freeman's division of Saatchi & Saatchi DFS Compton. Freeman had already made a name for himself with Wendy's International, Inc.'s "Where's the Beef?" ads. Freeman's seven 30-second spots constituted the company's first network television campaign. The ads featured comical situations that have become a hallmark of Little Caesars promotions.

A spot called "Yes, But" employed a carload of non-English-speaking characters who learned the phrase "Yes, but" by discovering the hidden costs behind the competition's two-pizza deal. Ads in the early 1990s used outrageously long, rubbery "cheese pulls" (melted cheese that stretches between two pieces of pizza) to accentuate the quality and quantity of cheese on a Little Caesars pizza. In one ad, when "big brother" hands his high-chair-bound little sister a piece of Little Caesars "Cheeser! Cheeser!" pizza that has been stretched to its limit, she's yanked from the room, down the hall, around the kitchen table and out the door into the waiting arms of her grandparents. The ads have been credited with Little Caesars's sales' doubling from 1988 to 1991 to $1.7 billion.

Little Caesars's marketing and promotion are also accomplished through community programs sponsored by the company. Ilitch himself has volunteered time to such organizations as the Easter Seal Telethon, the Michigan Special Olympics, the National Association for the Advancement of Colored People, and a variety of organized children's sports.

In 1985 Ilitch established the Little Caesars's Love Kitchen Foundation, two mobile restaurants that serve pizza to the needy. The two units travel throughout the United States and Canada feeding over 100,000 people annually. In 1988 the Love Kitchen received President Reagan's Citation for Private Sector Initiatives, and a Presidential Citation for Volunteerism was awarded to the program under the Bush administration.

In 1992 the Ilitches became the sole owners of the Detroit Tigers Baseball Club. Although some observers predict that the team will lose money for several years, the family notes that the acquisition "fulfilled a lifelong dream."

The Little Caesars empire has strong family ties throughout. Ilitch's wife, Marian, and several of the children are involved with the family business. The Ilitches say that all seven of their children have had a role in the success of the company. The family ties extend beyond the Ilitches: Mike Ilitch estimates that 85 percent of Little Caesars franchisees are relatives, with as many as three generations involved in the business. Ilitch also claims that over half of the company's corporate vice-presidents started out at work in the restaurants. He credits this close-knit network with Little Caesars's rapid growth.

In the early 1990s, Little Caesars's sales outpaced the industry's growth by 24 percent; the company remains locked in a closely fought battle with its two largest competitors, Pizza Hut Inc. and Dominos Pizza Inc. Little Caesars was named "Best Value in America" by *Restaurants & Institutions* magazine for the third year running in 1992.

Principal Subsidiaries: Little Caesar Enterprises, Inc.; Blue Line Distributing; Olympia Arenas, Inc.; Detroit Red Wings; Detroit Tigers.

Further Reading: Gindin, Rona, "A Fight to Stay on Top," *Restaurant Business,* July 1, 1986; Maki, Dee Ann, "Ilitch-Lites is Helping Growth Plans Pan Out for Little Caesar Pizza," *Advertising Age,* May 2, 1988; "New Little Caesars Ads Make Pan! Pan! Comical," *Restaurant Business,* June 10, 1988; Garfield, Bob, "Little Caesars' Cheesy Ad Really Pulls in Audience," *Advertising Age,* November 25, 1991; Weinstein, Jeff, "Pizza/Italian Shows Strong Growth Curve," *Restaurants & Institutions,* July 8, 1992; Oneal, Michael, " 'Pizza Pizza' and Tigers, Too," *Business Week,* September 14, 1992.

—April S. Dougal

THE LOUISIANA LAND AND EXPLORATION COMPANY

909 Poydras Street
P.O. Box 60350
New Orleans, Louisiana 70160
U.S.A.
(800) 351-1242
Fax: (504) 566-6891

Public Company
Incorporated: 1926 as Border Research Corporation
Sales: $825.3 million
Employees: 763
Stock Exchanges: New York Toronto London Basel Geneva
    Zürich
SICs: 1311 Crude Petroleum & Natural Gas; 2911 Petroleum
    Refining

The Louisiana Land and Exploration Company (LL&E) is one of the largest independent oil and gas exploration companies in the United States. Headquartered in New Orleans, it operates a crude oil refinery near Mobile, Alabama, and conducts exploration and production operations in the United States and selected foreign countries. Of the company's 225 million barrels of oil equivalent reserves, nearly 60 percent are garnered from domestic sources. Foreign reserves are located in the U.K. and Dutch sectors of the North Sea, Canada, and Columbia.

LL&E traces its roots to the 19th century, when midwestern businessman Edward Wisner moved to Louisiana for his health. Wisner was struck by swampy southern Louisiana's resemblance to the low-lying Netherlands, where industrious farmers had reclaimed millions of acres for farming. Envisioning farming on a grand scale, Wisner bought hundreds of thousands of acres, built levees, and drained the land.

Wisner's plans, however, were thwarted by southern Louisiana's severe weather. A 1915 hurricane destroyed many of the levees that Wisner had constructed. The venture's finances faltered and in time there were foreclosures. Much of the land was eventually taken over by a group of midwesterners led by Henry Timken, who owned an Ohio ball bearing company. Timken hoped to lease the land to fur trappers.

In 1925 speculator Edward Simms approached Timken with an idea for a company that would explore for oil in the almost 600,000 coastal acres Timken then controlled. Timken agreed and in 1926 exchanged his acres for shares in the Border Research Corporation.

It soon became apparent that the land owned by Louisiana Land and Exploration, as the company was renamed in 1927, was rich in petroleum resources. In 1928 LL&E signed a contract with Texas Co. (now Texaco) in which that company agreed to lease all of LL&E's acreage around ten productive salt domes. (A salt dome is a raised central area of salt or rock, around which beds of sedimentary rock dip in all directions. Oil and gas often become trapped in the pockets that form around these structures.) In the contract, which was very generous for its time, Texaco agreed to pay LL&E a 25-percent royalty on production and $8\frac{1}{3}$ percent of its net profits on a dome-by-dome basis. The contract would remain in effect for as long as Texaco continued to drill on the acreage. "It was a very unusual contract for 1928," LL&E president Ford Graham told *Dun's Review* in 1965. "The normal royalty was one-eighth ($12\frac{1}{2}$ percent). And profit sharing on top of the royalty was unheard of."

In 1930 Texaco also agreed to pay LL&E's $1.8 million funded indebtedness. In exchange for this, Texaco would retain one-half of the royalties and profits payable to LL&E up to the amount of $800,000. In 1935, after Texaco had been fully reimbursed, LL&E paid its first dividends.

On November 7, 1938, LL&E and Texaco amended their contract. Texaco released the fee lands belonging to the company not located on or near the domes or structures which were then being operated by Texaco. This released acreage amounted to approximately 557,000 acres.

Through the 1930s and 1940s, LL&E collected royalties on oil and minerals extracted from the land it owned and controlled. In addition to Texaco, which was still its major leaseholder, LL&E secured royalty agreements with Phillips Petroleum Co., Stanolind Oil & Gas Co., Alder Oil Co., and Plymouth Oil Co., among others. In February 1943, President E. B. Tracy signed a contract with Duval Texas Sulfur Co. that gave that company sulfur exploration, development, and production rights on LL&E's land and leased interests in Louisiana's Terebonne Parish.

During these years, LL&E did virtually no operating of its oil projects. The company had few employees and operators shouldered the major expenses of exploration and development. As a result, LL&E enjoyed low expenses and high profits. In 1943, for instance, LL&E employed only 24 people, yet earned $1.8 million on sales of $3.4 million.

In the 1950s, CEO Robert M. Youngs began to guide LL&E into other exploration, both on its own lands and on land it leased in other U.S. areas of production. As on previous occasions, LL&E's involvement was a financial one. It held working interests but did not actively manage projects.

As LL&E operations grew, both sales and revenues increased. In 1955 it reported $13.4 million in profits on sales of $22.4 million. In 1960 Youngs signed a second contract with Texaco that subjected 275,625 additional acres to six years of exploration and development. Under the agreement, LL&E retained a 25 percent working interest and a 20 percent royalty in Texaco's share of production. "We pay 25 percent of the cost," Ford Graham enthusiastically told *Dun's Review* "and get 40 percent of the income. Texaco pays 75 percent and gets 60 percent. And they paid us a $4 million bonus on the lease!"

The early 1960s proved very successful for LL&E. In 1964 the company reported profits of $32.1 million on sales of $64.1 million. In addition to the Texaco royalties, which were still significant (of 25 Lake Barre Field wells Texaco completed in 1964, 21 produced oil, two produced gas and only two were dry), LL&E had signed royalty agreements with Union Oil of California, Signal Oil, Amarada Hess, and Humble Oil and Refining. Moreover, because of varied corporate exploration philosophies and changes in drilling and seismic forecasting techniques, LL&E was constantly leasing and re-leasing the same acreage to different operators.

Outside of Louisiana, Youngs acquired mineral rights and royalty interests on 152,870 acres in Texas, New Mexico, North Dakota, South Dakota, Montana, Colorado, Florida, and Mississippi. By 1964, non-royalty, working-interest or joint-venture income had increased to 45 percent of LL&E's total sales.

As the company expanded into working interests, it hired geologists, geophysicists, and engineers. It continued, however, with its policy of contracting other firms to perform seismic surveys and other exploration and development tasks. In 1965 LL&E had only 145 employees. Graham worked hard to keep expenses down. "Our organization," he told *Dun's* "is the non-rigid, non-army type. For example, we don't hesitate to use consultants. When we have a project we'll go to Houston, rent a computer and run it through. And when we're finished we don't own the computer or have the people on our permanent payroll."

But while Graham focused on controlling costs, he, like other CEOs of that era, also sought profits in new businesses. In 1966 he acquired Jacintoport Corporation, an industrial real estate firm with Gulf Coast holdings such as the Houston Ship Channel. *Forbes* later criticized the Jacintoport purchase, maintaining that LL&E had gotten into industrial real estate, "just at the time when the play was going out of it along the Gulf Coast."

Continuing to diversify, in 1968 Graham obtained the rights to participate in the resort development of approximately 50,000 acres on the western half of Molokai Island, Hawaii—an island previously best known for its leper colony.

LL&E continued to do quite well in the late 1960s and early 1970s, reporting income of $51.9 million on 1970 sales of $114 million. In the early 1970s, however, its Louisiana reserves began their natural decline. To make up for this, LL&E participated in additional working interest wells and in 1970 discovered a major reserve estimated at 720 million barrels of oil in the Jay Field in Santa Rosa, Florida. In 1971 revenues from working interests exceeded those from royalty interests for the first time.

The company continued to look for new sources of oil and in October 1972 newly named CEO John G. Phillips announced a $75 million offering to finance a new subsidiary, Louisiana Land Offshore Exploration Co. (Lloxy), that would explore for oil and gas in the Gulf of Mexico. *Forbes* criticized the offer, charging that the company had waited too long to get into explorations and would be left with expensive deeper water wells. This criticism was borne out in December of that year when Lloxy paid $60 million for Gulf leases covering land under 300 feet of water.

As LL&E expanded its exploration efforts (by 1974 it was exploring in southern Louisiana, the Rocky Mountain area, a geological stratum from northern Louisiana to Florida, and off the coasts of Louisiana and Texas) it began to act as operator in an increasing number of its working interest efforts. In 1975 the company opened a small refinery in Mobile, Alabama, to process 30,000 barrels a day of Jay Field crude.

Phillips, meanwhile, continued to diversify. In 1974 Jacinport reported $2 million in real estate sales. In 1975 the Kalua Koi Corporation, LL&E's 50-percent-owned Hawaiian operation, began construction on the first phase of a 298-unit hotel condominium complex. In addition, in December 1976 LL&E acquired the Warrior River Coal Company, owners of a small surface mine in Tuscaloosa, Alabama. The following June a wholly owned subsidiary of LL&E, the Sun Fire Coal Company, began to develop an underground mine near Hazard, Kentucky.

Seeking new profit sources and seeing links between fossil fuels and mineral extraction, Phillips laid out $51 million for the Copper Range Company in May 1977. The Copper Range Company owned a copper mine in White Pines, Michigan; refined and fabricated copper bars, strips, plates, and sheets; owned 185 thousand acres of mixed hardwood timber; enjoyed extensive mineral rights in upper Michigan; and owned a one-half interest in a Nevada gold mine.

The Copper Range acquisition did not please the financial community. *Forbes* called Copper Range "a company so bad that some analysts wondered whether it was acquired to make Louisiana Land unattractive as a takeover candidate." As if to bear out this description, LL&E's mining operation lost $7.8 million in 1977 and $6.6 million in 1978.

Phillips, however, remained committed to Copper Range. Construction began on a new catalytic reformer that would provide more highly valued refined products. Due to higher prices for refined copper, the mining operation even turned a profit of $9.7 million in 1979.

These diversification adventures were possible in part because of high profits in the oil industry. Between 1978 and 1980 LL&E's sales jumped from $549.4 million to $1.075 billion while earnings increased from $94.8 million to $180.2 million, despite $64 million in 1980 windfall profits taxes.

But while business was very good in the late 1970s there were doubts about LL&E's future. With no more than 4.4 years of proven reserves on hand in 1980, Phillips needed to find new reserves at a reasonable cost if he was to insure the company's continued profitability. To do this, he committed major amounts of capital to new exploration initiatives. In 1980 he formed CLAM Petroleum, a 50 percent owned unconsolidated affiliate through which LL&E would invest $250 million in the U.K. North Sea's South Brae Field. In 1981 he budgeted a still-record $653 million for exploration and development. This figure included $181 million for 215 wells; $64 million for leases in Wyoming, the Gulf of Mexico, Australia, Indonesia, Columbia, and the North Sea; and $286 million for construction at Brae Field, platforms in the Gulf of Mexico, and a tertiary recovery project at Jay Field.

In the early 1980s, industry economics changed LL&E's fortunes. Deteriorating economic conditions, windfall profits taxes, high dry hole costs, narrower profit margins, and declining demand all pressured earnings. In 1981 earnings fell to $145.2 million despite revenues of almost $1,277.5 million. To make matters worse, copper revenues declined and precious metals margins shrank.

In 1982 matters continued to deteriorate as a recession caused a downturn in prices for liquids, lower demand and prices for copper, a halving of refinery margins, and reduced demand for natural gas. Responding to these problems, Phillips curtailed and then suspended copper mining, reduced staff, eliminated high-risk exploration ventures, cut back on capital expenditures, and in November reduced the cash dividend. At year's end, he was able to salvage earnings of $76.3 million despite mining operations that sustained a pretax loss of $38 million.

The company's troubles climaxed the following year as investor Delo Caspary mounted a proxy fight to remove Phillips and the rest of management. Supported by the Hunt family, which boasted a 12.3 percent block of LL&E stock, Caspary attacked LL&E's record since the mid-1970s, pointing to declining earnings, reduced dividends, falling reserves, and the copper acquisition.

Caspary's charges had some legitimacy. *Business Week* called Louisiana Land's record "dismal" and noted that despite spending $1.4 billion over the previous four years Phillips had failed to increase oil and gas reserves. The magazine went on to comment that LL&E's finding and developing costs were among the industry's highest and noted that the company had closed its Michigan copper mine after completing work on a $78 million dollar copper smelter. Management trumped Caspary, however, when it pledged to spin off to stockholders a tax-sheltered royalty trust holding oil and gas properties that generated $30 million a year.

After winning the proxy fight in 1983, Phillips sold LL&E's coal properties and bought back 71 million shares for $212.8 million. That year the company also saw initial returns from both the tertiary recovery project at Jay Field and the "A" platform of the Brae Field in the North Sea. By year's end, Phillips could boast of $94 million in profits on sales of $1.25 billion.

In 1984 Phillips was replaced by E. L. Williamson, who worked to sustain profit margins and increase reserves. In 1986 Williamson rid LL&E of the Copper Range Company—taking a $91 million charge in the process. The same year he paid $486 million for Inexco Oil Co., an oil company with reserves that

included 9.9 million barrels of liquids and 392.7 million cubic feet of domestic natural gas reserves. These moves strengthened LL&E's overall position, but plunging oil prices and the Copper Range charge took their toll. LL&E reported 1986 losses of $20.6 million.

In 1987 the company began to acquire newly opened low cost leases in the shallow waters of the Gulf of Mexico. Given narrow margins, however, LL&E's major interest was in purchasing additional interests in proven properties.

In 1988 crude prices fell by more than $3 a barrel and newly named CEO and chairman H. Leyton Steward was forced to take an $81.8 million restructuring charge and a $33.3 million loss. Steward announced that LL&E would sell nonstrategic oil and gas properties and use the proceeds to repay long-term debt and repurchase up to 10 percent of outstanding stock.

Earnings recovered in 1989 as oil prices rose while replacement costs remained low. Steward used excess cash flow—including $198 million from asset sales—to repurchase nearly 2.6 million shares and reduce LL&E's total debt by one-third. That year also marked Steward's conclusion of a property exchange that substantially increased LL&E's interest in the Madden Field in Wyoming.

As the largest owner of environmentally sensitive wetlands in the continental United States, LL&E had long been careful to protect its investment. It insisted that drillers bury pipe so as to not disrupt grasses or aquatic life, and it constructed pumps and water control structures to prevent erosion or saltwater intrusion. In 1989 the Department of Interior recognized this effort and awarded LL&E its Conservation Award for Respecting the Environment.

LL&E enjoyed a good exploration year in 1990. It replaced 203 percent of expended reserves, adding 55 million equivalent barrels of oil and natural gas, 46 percent of which came from the East Brae Field. Costs were low at $3.23 per barrel and by year's end, LL&E's reserve life index stood at 8.4 years, nearly double that of 1980.

LL&E's company earnings, $54.9 million in 1990, fell to $20.9 million in 1991 as falling oil and natural gas prices combined to make the year a difficult one. Nevertheless, the company budgeted $200 million for capital and exploration and continued to drill in the Gulf of Mexico, Madden Field in Wyoming, the gas-rich Anadarko Basin of Western Oklahoma, the North Sea, southeastern Alberta, and Columbia, where it was garnering positive results from a drilling program begun in 1978. It also sought to expand riskier but potentially more lucrative foreign exploration. To this end, in 1991 LL&E acquired two interests in Australia and applied for a concession in Papua New Guinea.

Founded as the Border Research company in 1926 and renamed Louisiana Land and Exploration a year later, LL&E, for its first twenty years, essentially collected royalties from fossil fuels extracted from nearly 600,000 acres it controlled in southern Louisiana. During the 1950s, CEO Robert M. Youngs began investing in working interest wells. During the 1960s, CEO Fred Graham began a process of diversification that would eventually include a Hawaiian resort, a coastal industrial real estate operation, and coal, gold, and copper mines. During the early 1980s, lackluster exploration results and fluctuating prices destabilized the company's finances and forced it to sell its non-oil and gas efforts and concentrate on finding new low-cost reserves.

Principal Subsidiaries: CL&E Corp.; Inexco Oil Co.; Wilson Bros. Drilling Co.; Molokai California Ltd.; LLOXY Holdings, Inc.; White Pine Leasing, Inc.; LL&E Properties, Inc.; Westport Utilities Systems Co., Inc.; LL&E (Netherlands) Inc.; CLAM Petroleum Co.; MaraLou Netherlands Partnership (50%).

Further Reading: Weiner, Jack B., ''Look at Louisiana Land!'' *Dun's Review,* October 1965; ''The 1983 Battle of New Orleans,'' *Business Week,* May 16, 1983; Reier, Sharon, ''Unlikely Champion,'' *Financial World,* January 23, 1990.

—Jordan Wankoff

MACMILLAN, INC.

55 Railroad Avenue
Greenwich, Connecticut 06830-6302
U.S.A.
(203) 862-7500
Fax: (203) 862-7712

Private company
Incorporated: 1896 as The Macmillan Company
Employees: 9,400
Sales: $1,070 million
SICs: 2731 Book Publishing

Macmillan has been a distinguished name in publishing for more than 150 years. Macmillan, Inc. is the American offspring of the British publishing house founded in 1843 and now known as Macmillan & Co., Ltd.; the two firms have been entirely separate since 1951, sharing only the names of their Scottish founders and a hundred years of book publishing history.

Macmillan, Inc. has prospered mightily in the years since its independence, building especially strong positions in the text-book and children's book markets in the United States. After assembling a diverse portfolio of subsidiaries in the 1960s Macmillan fell victim to the machinations of rogue publishing baron Robert Maxwell shortly before the latter's death and the resulting collapse of his empire in 1991. A profitable and well-managed company, Macmillan is likely to be sold intact by Maxwell's bankruptcy administrators and resume its place among the leading American publishers.

Macmillan, Inc. had its origins in the English publishing firm established in 1843 as D. & A. Macmillan. Daniel and Alexander Macmillan were brothers born to the family of a Scottish farmer in 1813 and 1818, respectively. After completing their primary school education the two boys were set to work, Daniel for a bookseller and binder in Irvine, Scotland, while Alexander taught school for several years before joining a firm of Glasgow booksellers. In 1833 Daniel Macmillan went to work at a book-store located near Cambridge University that specialized in classical authors. He soon gained a reputation among university students as a well-read, reliable guide to recent publications. After a brief stint with a London bookseller, during which time Daniel was joined by his younger brother, the Macmillans opened their own shop in London and in 1843 published their first book, *The Philosophy of Training*, a tract that called for the establishment of additional teachers' colleges in Britain.

As the title of their initial volume might suggest, the Macmillan brothers were young men of sober and religious tastes. Daniel in particular considered publishing to be much more than a business venture. "You surely never thought you were merely working for bread!" he once wrote to a fellow book dealer. "We booksellers, if we are faithful to our task, are trying to destroy ... all kinds of confusion, and are aiding our great Taskmaster to reduce the world into order, and beauty, and harmony." On the other hand, the Macmillans were also practical men who earned a living from the sale of books, and they operated their publishing firm with a judicious mixture of idealism and market savvy. As Charles Morgan noted in *The House of Macmillan*, Alexander once commented of one of the firm's more high-minded authors, "had we had only such books as his we could not have lasted three years."

Before that lesson could be learned, however, D. & A. Macmillan found itself near bankruptcy. The brothers closed their London business after only a year and with borrowed money managed to buy a retail shop back in Cambridge. The source of this borrowed capital was Archdeacon Hare, a Cambridge churchman with whom Daniel Macmillan had become friends during his first tenure in Cambridge. Through Hare and the latter's brother-in-law, the theologian F. D. Maurice, the Macmillans became supporters of a reform movement known as Christian Socialism. Most of their early publications reflected the liberal sentiments of that group with respect to education and church reform. In particular, the Macmillans shared the Christian Socialist commitment to universal education in Great Britain. The firm, as a consequence, soon became (and remains to this day) a leading publisher of textbooks and other educational material. This pedagogic emphasis was also encouraged by Macmillan's location near Cambridge University, many of whose students and famed scholars frequented the Macmillan shop on Trinity Street and were later published by the firm.

The first noteworthy success of Macmillan & Co. (the name adopted in 1850) was the 1855 publication of a novel by Charles Kingsley, *Westward Ho!*. Equally important was *Tom Brown's School Days* by Thomas Hughes, published in 1857; both authors were reform-minded writers introduced to the Macmillans by Archdeacon Hare. After Daniel Macmillan's early death in 1857 his brother Alexander assumed the direction of Macmillan & Co., a position he would retain for the next 32 years. Encouraged by the firm's success in the fiction market, Alexander opened a second branch in 1858 at 23 Henrietta Street, London. Alexander Macmillan was a considerably more sociable individual than his brother had been, and the shop in Henrietta Street became the setting for "feasts of Talk, Tobacco and Tipple" held every Thursday night and attended by a number of England's most brilliant writers. Tennyson, T. H. Huxley, and Herbert Spencer were among the regular guests at these intellectual "feasts," and many of them would later contribute to the success of *Macmillan's Magazine*, a monthly journal begun by Alexander Macmillan in 1859 that remained a pillar of mid-Victorian culture until its demise in 1909.

Macmillan & Co. prospered under Alexander's astute guidance. Its stable of authors comprised an exceptional gallery of late nineteenth-century English novelists, including Lewis Carroll, Matthew Arnold, William Gladstone, George Meredith, Walter Pater, Christina Rossetti, Lord Tennyson, Thomas Hardy, W. B. Yeats, and Rudyard Kipling. Macmillan & Co. continued its tradition of providing inexpensive educational texts with a number of long-running series, including the *Science Primers*, edited by Huxley, *English Men of Letters*, and *Literature Primers*. In addition to *Macmillan's Magazine*, the company also published *The Practitioner* for the medical profession and *Nature*, the prestigious science journal still read around the world. To edit and publish these many projects, Alexander Macmillan called on the help of his son, George A. Macmillan, and the two sons of his brother Daniel, Frederick and Maurice. Upon Alexander's retirement in 1889 it was Frederick Macmillan who succeeded him as chairman of the limited partnership.

In the meantime, the seeds of the American branch of Macmillan had been sown. Alexander Macmillan recognized the potential importance of the American market as early as 1859, when he retained Scribner & Welford as agents for Macmillan books in the United States. In 1867 he spent eight weeks in the United States, where he met President Grant as well as distinguished men of letters. During his visit he wrote back to a colleague that "a great international publishing house is possible, and would be a good plan to be realized." He therefore set up a New York branch office as headquarters in the United States, hiring as its director George Edward Brett, a young Englishman then working for a London distributor. Brett opened the Macmillan office at 63 Bleecker Street in August of 1869, acting primarily as a marketing and sales director for Macmillan titles throughout the United States. (The New York office did no publishing of its own until the late 1890s.) In 1874 Brett's son, George Platt Brett, joined the firm as a traveling salesman, where he acquired the experience that enabled him to effectively lead the firm after the death of his father in 1890. Remarkably enough, the Bretts remained in control of the American offices of Macmillan from its creation in 1869 to the early 1960s, a span matched by few other families in the history of United States business.

George P. Brett was an ambitious as well as capable man. After his father's death he was asked by the Macmillans to assume direction of the New York office, but he refused to do so, proposing instead that he be made partner in a new American corporation. Brett's position as the key man in their American markets left the Macmillan family with little room to maneuver, and in 1896 the Macmillan house was divided into two newly established entities, The Macmillan Company in New York and Macmillan & Co., Ltd., of London. The two companies were both controlled by the Macmillan family (which retained about 61 percent of the American company's stock until the 1951 split); they freely shared titles and authors and made use of the company's worldwide network of sales branches established in the early twentieth century in such ports of call as Bombay (established 1901); Toronto (1904); Calcutta (1907); Melbourne (1912); and Madras (1913). Nevertheless, the creation of a separate company in New York was destined to have profound implications for the house of Macmillan, as the American organization outstripped its parent and eventually required complete independence at mid-century.

Fueled by George Brett's inexhaustible energy and detailed knowledge of every aspect of the book business, The Macmillan Co. grew steadily to a position of prominence in American publishing by the 1930s. The publication of Winston Churchill's novel *Richard Carvel* in 1899 was the first of many successes in the general (or trade) market for Macmillan, fol-

lowed soon after by Jack London's *The Call of the Wild* and F. Marion Crawford's *Sacracinesca*. More typical of the Macmillan tradition was its continuing commitment to the educational field, where it published both textbooks for general school use and reprints of classic works for the growing college market. The standardized nature of educational texts made it possible for Macmillan to become the first American publisher to open branch offices across the country, each of which was provided with its own warehouse inventory of titles. (Previously, publishers had shipped directly to bookstores from a single national warehouse.) Between 1895 and 1909 such semi-independent branches were established in Chicago, Boston, Atlanta, Dallas, and San Francisco.

In addition to its trade agreements with Macmillan of London, the Macmillan offices in the U.S. built a vigorous business in the Far East prior to the second World War, where it sold upwards of $750,000 of books annually before the commencement of hostilities in the Pacific.

A third George Brett assumed the leadership of Macmillan in 1936. George Platt Brett, Jr., who started work at Macmillan in 1913, became president in 1931 and, upon the death of his father (then chairman) in 1936, became the company's chief executive officer. Brett found it difficult to duplicate his father's success; Macmillan was vying for the lead in United States publishing in terms of both titles and sales (approximately $5 million) in the mid-1930s, and the loss of its business in Asia was a significant blow.

The publishing industry as a whole was undergoing rapid change. The introduction of cheap paperbound books vastly increased the potential market for books and placed an emphasis on high-volume, low-cost publishing methods. To this new environment, both larger and more specialized than in years past, Macmillan brought a number of assets and certain decided liabilities. Its strength in the educational and college markets would provide the company with a solid revenue base for years to come, as America's growing population increasingly considered higher education to be a necessity rather than a luxury. Further, the company's 1919 creation of a children's books department gave Macmillan a head start in this important market as well. On the other hand, Macmillan was slow to appreciate the impact of paperbacks on the publishing landscape and in general did not adapt well to the mass merchandising techniques required by the newly enlarged market for "trade" books (those sold in retail bookstores).

As a result, after a brief period of preeminence in the trade market (highlighted by the publication of the 1936 blockbuster *Gone with the Wind*) Macmillan soon returned to its traditional position in the middle of the field of United States trade publishers. Of its $13.2 million in sales in 1950, approximately two-thirds were generated by the educational and college departments, with trade and medical books making up the remainder. In the following year Macmillan of London agreed to sell its 61 percent share of The Macmillan Co.'s stock on the open market, thus completing the American company's separation from its English parent. The two companies continued for some years to use a common international sales force but at present have no formal ties.

The booming 1950s should have been a decade of tremendous growth for Macmillan. The American population grew wealthier and younger, and great numbers of its young people not only finished high school but went to some institution of higher learning as well. While the company's primary strengths lay in educational texts, however, Macmillan's sales increased from 1950's $13.1 million to $19.1 million in fiscal 1960, a relatively modest increase given the circumstances. Feeling the pressure of intense competition on all fronts, Macmillan did not object when Crowell-Collier Publishing Company began buying up its shares in late 1959, and in December 1960 the two companies were merged under the Crowell-Collier name. Crowell-Collier, incorporated in 1911 but active since 1883 as the publisher of *Collier's* magazine, was then about twice Macmillan's size in terms of revenue, the bulk of it from radio stations and *Collier's Encyclopedia*. The merger provided Macmillan (the name was reassumed within a few years) a much needed infusion of cash and, more importantly, the leadership of Raymond C. Hagel, who became CEO in 1963. Hagel replaced Bruce Y. Brett, the last of that family to serve as president of Macmillan.

In his 17-year tenure as Macmillan's chief, Raymond Hagel engineered the company's transformation from a sleepy publisher of textbooks to an enormous conglomerate with additional interests in retail sales, language schools, musical instruments, printing, and information services. Macmillan's growth was startling when compared with that of previous decades: from the merged companies' 1960 sales of $54 million, Macmillan went over the $400 million mark a mere twelve years later and boasted sales of about $600 million annually by 1980. Among its numerous acquisitions were the Brentano's chain of retail bookstores; the myriad language schools of Berlitz Inc.; Standard Rate & Data Service; C. G. Conn, maker of musical instruments; and Gump's, the San Francisco-based specialty store. The diverse portfolio was typical of conglomerates built in the 1960s and 1970s and, also typically, did not enjoy a long life span. Macmillan's patchwork creation was dismantled by the next generation of executives, T. Mellon Evans and his son E. P. Evans.

When Evans gained control of Macmillan in 1980 (via the purchase of stock) he was dissatisfied with the rate of return earned by the company's far-flung assets. He fired Hagel and sold off most of Macmillan's businesses outside the areas of publishing, instruction schools, and the fast-growing information services division. After the painful recession of 1981–82, which brought company revenues down as far as $430 million, the company responded to Evans' strategy. Both sales and net income rose briskly throughout the 1980s, with publishing entrenched as the backbone of corporate revenue (about 46 percent) and most of the publishing dollars garnered in the educational markets. The instructional schools were also solid, averaging around 20 percent of revenue. The star of Macmillan's line-up, however, was unquestionably its cluster of information service companies, which by 1987 were contributing profits equal to the publishing division ($62 million) on half the revenue dollars. The information services segment included firms engaged in direct marketing, trade journal publishing, industry directories, and Standard Rate and Data Service.

In mid-1988 Macmillan became entangled in one of the stranger episodes of twentieth-century business history. As happened so often in the 1980s, Macmillan and its attractive assets became the object of a bidding war between three heavyweight corporate raiders—the Barr brothers, Kohlberg Kravits Roberts & Co., and the Czech-born British media mogul Robert Maxwell. After three months of struggle Maxwell succeeded in gaining control of Macmillan for $2.6 billion—about $1 billion more than the company was generally thought to be worth. Macmillan executives threatened to quit en masse rather than work for Maxwell, the mysterious proprietor of scores of companies in Europe and North America, including the Mirror Group newspapers in England, several huge printing firms, and the Official Airline Guide, bought for $750 million at about the same time as the Macmillan deal.

Maxwell then died under mysterious circumstances, further muddying the future course of Macmillan. Shortly after Maxwell's body was found floating in the ocean near his yacht in late 1991, a long line of creditors discovered that his mighty empire was a kind of financial optical illusion, a labyrinth of publicly traded companies owned or controlled by Maxwell's private family concerns, which in turn had used loans and pension funds from the public corporations (such as Maxwell Communications Corporation-MCC, the parent company of Macmillan) to secure loans of their own. In the end, it appears that among other bizarre maneuvers Maxwell was siphoning money from MCC to help his private companies buy MCC shares in the hope that such purchases would bolster the public company's weak stock price and thereby calm his bankers, to whom he had pledged MCC stock as collateral.

As the authorities continue to try to untangle the financial and legal mess uncovered by Maxwell's death, Macmillan's future status remains unclear. MCC was placed under the joint administration of United States and English bankruptcy courts acting with the help of Price Waterhouse, the accounting firm, and was to be sold off piecemeal to repay some of its $2.5 billion in debt and the hundreds of millions of dollars fraudulently transferred by Maxwell. From this debacle Macmillan, Inc. should emerge in good order and nearly whole. Although reliable figures are not available, there is no reason to think that Macmillan's core of educational publishing and information service companies is not as strong as it was in the late 1980s. One possible buyer is K-III Holdings, a Kohlberg Kravits Roberts investment company headed by William F. Reilly, the last pre-Maxwell president of Macmillan. Whoever ends up with control of Macmillan, however, will probably have to do without its profitable Berlitz subsidiary—57 percent of that company's stock was pledged as collateral for Maxwell family loans and is now part of the international squabble over who gets what of the Maxwell empire.

Further Reading: Morgan, Charles, *The House of Macmillan (1843–1943)*, New York, The Macmillan Company, 1944; Maremont, Mark, and Mark Landler, "An Empire Up for Grabs," *Business Week*, December 23 1991; Bower, Tom, *Maxwell: The Outsider*, New York, Viking, 1992.

—Jonathan Martin

MAGMA COPPER COMPANY

7400 N. Oracle Road
Suite 200
Tucson, Arizona 85704
U.S.A.
(602) 575-5600
Fax: (602) 575-5674

Public Company
Incorporated: 1910
Employees: 4,548
Sales: $819 million
Stock Exchanges: New York
SICs: 1021 Copper Ores

Magma Copper Company is one of the largest copper producers in the United States. The company's 1992 copper output of 566.8 million pounds included its two primary products, high-quality copper cathode and high-quality copper rod from both magma mines and custom sources. Copper rod, about half of Magma's copper production, is the fundamental raw material of the copper wire and cable industry. Magma owns and operates three copper mines in southeastern Arizona: an underground copper sulfide mine and open pit copper oxide mine at San Manuel; an open pit copper sulfide mine at Pinto Valley; and an underground copper sulfide mine at Superior. The San Manuel and Pinto Valley sites are home to facilities for leaching and solvent extraction-electrowinning (SX-EW), a chemical method for processing copper. At San Manuel, Magma operates the largest flash furnace in the world. This smelting and refining complex, operated by the company's Magma Metals Company subsidiary, is the most modern in the United States and represents close to one-fourth of the nation's smelting capacity. The smelter is capable of processing more than one million tons of copper concentrate per year, enabling Magma to process not only all of its own copper output, but also copper from outside sources, either purchased or on a custom basis. In addition to copper, Magma produced 5.2 million pounds of molybdenum, a metal used in strengthening steel, and residues containing 106,000 troy ounces of gold and 2.7 million troy ounces of silver in 1992.

In 1877, production began at the Silver Queen Mine in the Hastings Pioneer Mining District in the Arizona territory. This district later became Superior, and it was here that Magma

Copper Company was organized in 1910, holding the Silver Queen mining property. The company's founder was Colonel William Boyce Thompson, a mining engineer turned Wall Street trader, who went on to create Newmont Mining Corporation eleven years later as a holding company for his collection of mining investments, his holding in Magma prominent among them. Magma's underground mine at Superior first went into production in 1912. In 1914, the Magma Arizona Railroad Company was founded, linking the Superior site with the Southern Pacific Railroad system about 28 miles away. Magma's first smelter was constructed at Superior in 1924.

Magma gradually rose through the ranks during the 1930s and 1940s, and by 1950 was the eighth largest copper producer in the United States. The company was working only the Superior mine during this period, and its ascent was possible because of the exceptional richness of Superior's ore, which was 6.0 percent copper. It was Magma's acquisition and subsequent development of San Manuel over the next several years, however, that truly launched Magma into a position of prominence in the copper industry. The area around San Manuel had been a center of mining activity since late in the nineteenth century. In 1879, gold and silver mines had been started in the Old Hat District around Mammoth, and molybdenum and vanadium mines appeared at Tiger between 1915 and 1920. The Tiger mines were purchased in 1934 by St. Anthony Mining Company, which soon began producing lead and zinc there. During the early 1940s, the federal government began to take an interest in the area, hoping to address war-time copper needs. The War Production Board in 1942 investigated for copper in the Mammoth area, and exploration drilling was undertaken at Red Hill in the San Manuel region by the U.S. Bureau of Mines from 1943 to 1945.

In 1944, Magma consolidated and purchased the bulk of the San Manuel mineral claims, and began its own program of drilling and exploration. Underground exploration and development at San Manuel began four years later. It soon became clear that San Manuel was a major copper discovery, containing what was estimated at the time as 480 million tons of copper ore, with the existence of further orebodies nearby suspected. The cost of developing the mine, plant, community, and railroad was estimated at $111 million, and to help offset this, Magma borrowed $94 million from the U.S. government in 1952. Construction on the surface plant began the following year.

Magma's assets by the end of 1952 were $6.2 million. The company's capital structure in the first half of the 1950s was simple, consisting entirely of just under one million shares of outstanding common stock, 40 percent of which was owned by Newmont Mining, Lazard Freres, and company management. Magma's activities during this period were almost entirely confined to two pursuits, copper production at Superior and development of the San Manuel mine. In 1953, the development of a new ore bed in the Superior mine allowed Magma to increase its production by about 50 percent over the previous year. This increase in output, accompanied by record copper prices, led to earnings that year of $3.48 per share, compared to 58 cents per share in 1952.

Production at San Manuel began in 1956, with the first stopes undercut and the start-up of smelting operations there. With the flow of copper from San Manuel's 500 million-ton reserves, Magma soon jumped from eighth to fourth-largest among copper producers in the United States. Nevertheless, because of the vast sums being poured into the development of San Manuel, Magma's potential as a big money-earner appeared to be years away from fruition. Dividends had been suspended in 1949, shortly after the acquisition of San Manuel, and their reinstatement did not seem likely until the huge government loan could be retired, an event not scheduled to occur until 1973. Between 1956 and 1962, the value of Magma common stock was cut in half.

Nevertheless, Magma's potential was recognized by the management of Newmont Mining. In 1962, Newmont acquired 784,842 additional shares of Magma stock, offering Magma stockholders three-fourths of a share of Newmont preferred stock for each Magma share. Added to the 285,961 Magma shares that Newmont already owned, this gave Newmont 80.6 percent ownership of Magma. The acquisition was part of Newmont president Plato Malozemoff's strategy of domestic investment, thereby reducing the company's reliance on foreign holdings, particularly those in southern Africa. Over the years, the share of Newmont's income originating abroad had grown to well over 50 percent. As part of the deal, Malozemoff was able to refinance Magma's government loan, enabling Magma to resume paying dividends. Following the acquisition, the Justice Department charged Newmont, Magma, and Phelps Dodge with antitrust violations, based on interlocking directorships and Magma's 3 percent interest in Phelps Dodge. Newmont was ordered to divest Magma. This order was successfully dodged, however, and Newmont satisfied the Justice Department by getting rid of its Phelps Dodge holdings and removing the Phelps Dodge directors from its own board.

Magma continued to increase its production capacity throughout the 1960s. In 1965, expansion at San Manuel raised its daily ore output from 30,000 to 40,000 tons. In 1968, Magma purchased the Kalamazoo, Arizona copper property of the Houston-based Quintana Minerals Ltd. for $27 million. The purchase of the Kalamazoo orebody roughly doubled the size of Magma's copper reserves up to one billion tons. The Kalamazoo mine was located about a mile west of San Manuel, and although its size and composition were much like those of San Manuel, its ore lay much deeper, beginning at about 2,500 feet below the surface. The acquisition was a three-way deal, with Quintana receiving about 42,000 shares and $15 million from Magma, plus about $5 million and 72,000 shares from Newmont. Newmont in turn received 170,000 shares of Magma common stock. Magma's net income was $10.9 million in 1968, lower than expected due to strikes in the copper industry.

Magma was fully merged into Newmont Mining Corporation in 1969. In return for each share of Magma, minority stockholders received .85 share of newly issues Newmont convertible preferred stock valued at $4.50 per share. The merger, which made Magma a wholly owned subsidiary of Newmont, contributed to Newmont's shift toward reliance on domestic income. By 1970, 65 percent of Newmont's net income originated in the United States and Canada, and also thanks to Magma, three-fourths of its revenues were provided by copper. Magma's 1969 earnings jumped to $26.2 million, more than double the previous year. The company's copper output for that year was 113,000 tons.

In March of 1970, construction was started on a new electrolytic copper refinery at San Manuel. The refinery's capacity was to be 200,000 tons per year, and construction and engineering on the $30 million project were to be provided by Bechtel Corporation. Meanwhile, an additional $100 million was being poured into the expansion of San Manuel's smelting and concentrating facilities, as well as upgrades at the Superior site. In 1971, Magma president Wesley P. Goss announced that the Superior smelter, which had closed in July of that year due to a strike, would not be reopened. As expansion at San Manuel progressed, larger amounts of copper concentrate produced at Superior were shipped to San Manuel for processing. By consolidating smelting operations at San Manuel, Magma saved the cost of altering the aging Superior smelter to meet antipollution regulations.

Magma made the transition beginning in 1972 from producing only anode copper to producing commercial cathode and continuous copper rod, and also became fully integrated, processing all of the copper that it produced. The company's ore processing capacity was expanded in 1972 from 40,000 to 60,000 tons per day. Under company president Wayne Burt, who took over in 1972, the sum invested in San Manuel, including mining costs, processing facilities, company town, and six-mile railroad from the mine to the mill, had reached a total of $460 million by the end of 1977. A world record 300 million tons of copper ore hoisted from underground had been produced at San Manuel through Magma's deep-level block caving system by 1978. By that year, mining at San Manuel, which had begun at 1,475 feet, had reached a depth of 2,375 feet. And two-thirds of the mine's reserve had not yet been tapped, not to mention the nearby Kalamazoo orebody which was still in the early stages of development. In 1978, with worldwide copper consumption at a record pace, Magma's earnings rose to $13 million, up from $701,000 the previous year, on sales of $274 million, compared to $236 million in 1977. Magma sold 172,000 tons of copper in 1978, an increase of 18.6 percent. The Superior division, reopened since 1973 with a new mine plant in operation, was operating at capacity, and San Manuel slightly below capacity throughout 1978. By 1980, Magma had captured seven to ten percent of the domestic copper rod market. Magma's position in the industry was somewhat unique, in that it sold its entire production to outside users on annual contracts, while competitors such as Phelps Dodge and Kennecott were selling theirs to fabricating subsidiaries, and others such as Asarco were smelting and refining copper produced elsewhere. Magma's major customers included GK Technologies' General Cable Co. and Western Electric Co., a unit of AT&T. These two companies combined accounted for about 16 percent of Magma's sales in 1979.

By 1980, Magma was among the lowest-cost producers of copper in the United States, with a net cost, adjusted for byproduct credits, of about 70 cents a pound. These byproducts included over 44,000 ounces of gold, 1 million ounces of silver, and 3.3 million pounds of contained molybdenum sold in 1979. In 1980, Magma's production was slowed by a four-month labor strike beginning in July, as well as 16 days of lost production at San Manuel due to an underground mine fire. Nevertheless, by 1981, copper production at Magma was back up to over 65,000 tons per day, working the mills to capacity and keeping the refinery operating at 85 percent of its 215,000 ton per year capacity. About three-fourths of Magma's refined copper output was converted to copper rod at the company's continuous cast mill.

The Superior Division of Magma was shut down once again in 1982 for economic reasons. This time the mine would remain idle until 1990. In 1983, Gordon Parker succeeded Burt as Magma's president and chief executive officer. Burt retained his positions as chair of Magma's board and senior vice-president of operations at Newmont. Parker had been a Newmont vice-president since 1981, and had been with the company since 1959, primarily working in the company's southern African operations. In 1984, Magma purchased the Hawthorne Works continuous cast copper rod mill in Cicero, Illinois from AT&T Technologies. The purchase increased Magma's rod capacity to about 300,000 tons per year.

Development began in 1985 on the open pit oxide mine at San Manuel, and operations there commenced the following year. These operations included dump leaching of waste and a solvent extraction/electrowinning (SX-EW) plant. Newmont recapitalized Magma in 1986, and the Pinto Valley operation was contributed to Magma as an operating division. Pinto Valley, located five miles west of Miami, Arizona, was an open pit sulfide mine, with facilities capable of producing 260,000 tons of concentrates containing 80,000 tons of copper per year.

In 1987, Newmont spun off Magma to its stockholders. One share of Magma common stock was issued for each outstanding Newmont share. Newmont, which retained 15 percent interest in Magma, was in the process of selling off properties in the aftermath of a failed takeover attempt. By spinning off Magma, Newmont accomplished two things. It saved itself the cost of bringing San Manuel up to environmental standards, an ongoing struggle that had contributed to operating losses at Magma since 1980; and it essentially removed Newmont from the volatile copper industry, allowing the company to concentrate almost exclusively on its gold operations.

Magma recorded its first profit in nine years in 1988, as copper prices rebounded to $1.50 a pound from a low of 60 cents the year before. The company earned over $56 million, after posting a $41 million loss in 1987. Revenue grew about 50 percent to $607 million. The company's new flash furnace at San Manuel, the largest in the world, went into production in 1988. With a capacity of over one million tons of copper concentrate per year, the smelter represented about 21 percent of the smelting capacity in the United States. In April of 1988, Magma's CEO Brian Woolfe died suddenly. His successor was J. Burgess Winter, formerly a senior vice-president at BP Minerals America. In 1989, Magma bought back its remaining shares held by Newmont as part of a recapitalization plan.

Magma set company records in several areas in 1990. Net income was over $84 million, a 44 percent increase over 1989. The company's refined copper output for the year was 469.8 million pounds, not including custom smelting. Another record was set by the production of 115.7 million pounds of copper using the SX/EW process, 24 percent higher than the 1989 figure. 1990 also brought the formation of Magma Gold Ltd., a subsidiary for the possible expansion into gold mining activities, particularly at the McCabe mine in Humboldt, Arizona.

Operations were also resumed at the Superior mine in 1990, ending eight years of closure due to high operating costs and low productivity.

In 1991 Magma gained 100 percent ownership of the Robinson mining district, an operating copper and gold orebody containing large copper reserves located near Ely, Nevada. Magma gained 100 percent ownership the following year. Magma had purchased a majority interest in Robinson late in 1990. The more recent purchase gave Magma the 41 percent share previously held by minority partner Alta Gold Co., based in Salt Lake City, for $29 million. A January 1992 feasibility study indicated that Robinson could potentially contribute 125 million pounds of copper and 86,500 ounces of gold per year at a relatively low cost over 16 years of mine life. In October of 1991, Magma management and ten labor unions representing its work force signed a new agreement that was revolutionary both in its content and in the process that led to its creation. The most notable aspect of the contract was its length, fifteen years, including a guarantee of eight years with no work stoppages. The contract negotiations utilized a unique worker participation program, in which work-redesign teams composed of both workers and managers were organized to address specific problems.

The new labor agreement gives Magma an edge over its competition as the twentieth century draws to a close. With ore reserves in place sufficient to carry the company into the next century, Magma's position in the industry appears secure, thanks largely to its gigantic smelting and refining facility at San Manuel. Much will depend upon Magma's ability to develop international sources for concentrate feed for the smelter as well as bring the Robinson property on line and proceed with other ore reserve development projects.

Principal Subsidiaries: Magma Metals Co.; Magma Gold Ltd.; Magma Nevada Mining Co.; Magma Arizona Railroad Company; San Manuel Arizona Railroad Company; Magma Limited Partners Co.

Further Reading: "San Manuel Development Will Make Magma 4th Largest U.S. Copper Mine," *Barron's,* January 4, 1954; "Newmont Mining Boosts Magma Holdings to 80.6% Through Exchange Offer," *Wall Street Journal,* May 10, 1962; "Fair Exchange," *Forbes,* May 1, 1963; "Newmont Mining Enjoys a Richer Dividend Take," *Barron's,* September 28, 1964; "Magma Copper Agrees to Buy Arizona Tract of Quintana Minerals," *Wall Street Journal,* March 19, 1968; "Acquisition by Newmont of the Rest of Magma is Approved by Holders," *Wall Street Journal,* May 6, 1969; "Magma Starts Building $30 Million Gopper Refinery in Arizona," *Engineering and Mining Journal,* April 1970; "Newmont Mining a Sound Value," *Financial World,* July 1, 1970; "Magma Copper Co.," *Engineering and Mining Journal,* September 1971; Jackson, Dan, "Block Caving Keeps San Manuel Competitive," *Engineering and Mining Journal,* June 1978; "Magma Sales, Earnings Increase in '78," *American Metal Market,* April 6, 1979; Crown, Judith, "Magma Garners 7–10% of US Copper Rod Market," *American Metal Market,* June 3, 1980; "Efficiency, Byproducts Ease Magma's Costs," *American Metal Market,* April 24, 1981; "Gordon Parker Elected Magma President, CEO," *American Metal Market,* December 20, 1983;

Jordan, Carol, "Magma Buys AT&T's Copper Rod Facility," *American Metal Market,* October 4, 1984; Bair, Karen, "Newmont Spin Off of Magma Becomes Effective March 20," *American Metal Market,* March 12, 1987; Slovak, Julianne, "Magma Copper Co.," *Fortune,* December 5, 1988; "Magma Posts Turnaround in '88," *American Metal Market,* February 8, 1989; Ray, Keith "Magma Copper Sets Up Gold Mining Subsidiary," *American Metal Market,* October 30, 1990; "Magma Copper Sets '90 Net Mark," *American Metal Market,* February 4, 1991; "Magma Buys Alta Shares," *American Metal Market,* October 2, 1991; Miller, William H., "Metamorphosis in the Desert," *Industry Week,* March 16, 1992; Magma Copper Company 1991 Annual Report, Tuscon, Arizona: Magma Copper Company, 1992.

—Robert R. Jacobson

MANVILLE CORPORATION

Post Office Box 5108
Denver, Colorado 80217
U.S.A.
(303) 978-2000
Fax: (303) 978-2440

Public Company
Incorporated: 1901 as H. W. Johns-Manville Corporation
Employees: 16,000
Sales: $2.02 million
Stock Exchanges: New York
SICs: 2621 Paper Mills; 2631 Paperboard Mills; 3296
  Mineral Wool; 6719 Holding Companies Nec.

Manville Corporation is an international manufacturing and natural-resources supplier operating in three areas: forest products such as paper, cartons, and plywood; fiberglass products such as home insulation; and specialty products that include lighting fixtures and industrial filters. Until the mid-1980s, Manville mined and sold asbestos for use in insulation, building, aerospace, automotive, and other industries. The company has divested itself of its interests in all asbestos-related businesses, but remains enmeshed in substantial litigation brought by asbestos workers with claims based on the effects of working with the material. While business operations continue, Manville's future may hinge on the decisions issued by the courts in these cases.

In 1858, at the age of 21, Henry Ward Johns founded the H. W. Johns Manufacturing Company in New York City. The company specialized in the manufacture of asbestos textiles, roofing, and insulation materials. Over the next 40 years, until his death in 1898 of "dust phthisis pneumonitis," believed to be asbestosis, Johns discovered a number of the applications of asbestos, which became known as the "mineral of a thousand uses." In 1886 Charles B. Manville founded the Manville Covering Company in Milwaukee, Wisconsin, and managed the company until 1900. In 1901 H. W. Johns and Manville merged to create H. W. Johns-Manville (J-M), a corporation engaged primarily in the mining, manufacturing, and supply of asbestos fibers and products to industry and the government.

The management of J-M has been relatively stable over the years. The Manville family remained active in the management of the company through most of the twentieth century. From

1921 to 1923, Thomas F. Manville headed the company as president, treasurer, and a member of the board. In 1924 he became chairman; H. E. Manville was elected president and T. F. Manville, Jr., joined the board of directors. By 1928 H. E. Manville and Thomas Manville, Jr., sat on the board, while T. F. Merseles served as the company's president. In 1930 H. E. Manville was named chairman of the executive committee and L. H. Brown became president. This hierarchy continued until 1939.

In 1927 J-M became a publicly held corporation. During the 1920s and 1930s, J-M acquired several mining and manufacturing operations in the United States and Canada. Purchases included the Celite Company of California, miners and processors of diatomaceous earth—diatomite is a filtering agent—in 1928 and, in 1930, the Stevens Sound Proofing Company of Chicago, owners of patents for sound insulation.

As early as 1929, J-M was defending itself against lawsuits for asbestos-related deaths. Asbestosis is a nonmalignant scarring of the lungs caused solely by exposure to asbestos. The incidence of the disease seems to be related to the duration and intensity of exposure. It may take decades for evidence of the disease to appear. Mesothelioma is a form of cancer associated with asbestos that affects the linings of the chest or abdominal cavities and that usually kills its victims within a year of its appearance. The legal issues in asbestos cases centered on the following two questions. When did the health hazards of working with asbestos become foreseeable? When warnings were issued, did they communicate adequately the danger?

From the beginning, J-M claimed that employees were contributorily negligent, because they knew or should have known the dangers associated with asbestos and taken precautions. Manville used this defense, often successfully, in cases filed during the next four decades. In addition, Manville continued to argue into the 1980s that until 1964 there was no known reason to warn insulation workers of the dangers of working with asbestos. Plaintiffs countered that warning labels should have been in use as early as the 1950s.

In 1930 Dr. A. J. Lanza of the Metropolitan Life Insurance Company began a four-year study, "Effects of Inhalation of Asbestos Dust upon the Lungs of Asbestos Workers." Based on his findings, in late 1933 Lanza recommended that J-M perform dust counts at its plants. Vandiver Brown, who served as Manville's vice-president, corporate secretary, and chief attorney, wrote Lanza to request changes in his report. Specifically, Brown requested that he downplay the negative implications of asbestos exposure. In his book, *Outrageous Misconduct: The Asbestos Industry on Trial*, Paul Brodeur described a memo Brown wrote in 1935 to company colleagues in which he noted a speaker who said, " 'the strongest bulwark against future disaster for the industry is the enactment of properly drawn occupational-disease legislation,' which would 'eliminate the jury' as well as 'eliminate the shyster lawyer and the quack doctor since fees would be strictly limited by the law.' " Later that year, Brown wrote that the company's best interests would be served by having asbestosis receive minimal publicity. Brown's correspondence would be entered as evidence in trials almost a half century later by plaintiffs who, in efforts to win punitive as well as compensatory damages against the company, contended that J-M deliberately downplayed the effects of exposure.

British studies concurrent with Lanza's encouraged Parliament to pass legislation to protect asbestos workers in 1931. In the United States, three years passed before asbestosis was considered for classification as a disease under workmen's compensation laws.

Beginning in 1936 J-M and nine other asbestos companies funded a study of the effects of asbestos on animals. Dr. LeRoy U. Gardner reported significant changes in the lungs of guinea pigs within a year after exposure to asbestos dust. Gardner died in 1946 before formally reporting his findings.

In 1939 L. H. Brown became president of J-M, a position he held until 1948, and H. E. Manville stepped down as chairman. The year 1940 was significant as the only year in which the name Manville did not appear in the list of company officers. In 1941 H. E. Manville, Jr., joined the board of directors, a post he held into the 1960s.

At the start of World War II, J-M was among the world's leading suppliers of asbestos, and 1939 through 1945 were strong years for J-M financially. During those years, tens of thousands of workers in U.S. government shipyards and other installations used thousands of tons of asbestos in building ships and airplanes. In 1943 the Navy Department and the U.S. Maritime Commission published a study that outlined the risks to insulation workers of high asbestos dust levels. In "Minimum Requirements for Safety and Industrial Health in Contract Shipyards," the study reported that asbestosis could arise from breathing asbestos in any job that created dust. Many of the workers and seaman exposed to asbestos during this period would bring suit against J-M years later.

In 1947 J-M signed the first in a series of policies with the Travelers Insurance Company, the company's insurers for the next 30 years. The extent of the insurers' liability in the asbestos suits would be debated and litigated into the 1990s.

In 1948 L. H. Brown became chairman of the board. R. W. Lea was named president. Three years later, L. M. Cassidy, formerly vice-president of sales, assumed the position of chairman; a second vice-president, A. R. Fisher, became president and a third, C. F. Rassweiler, was named vice-chairman. These men controlled the company until 1957.

From 1950 through 1970 J-M's sales grew at an average annual rate of four percent. While sales of asbestos and other raw materials represented only 13 percent of J-M's volume, they contributed between 30 percent and 40 percent of earnings.

In 1951 John A. McKinney joined the company as a patent lawyer; he was to become president 25 years later. By 1952 the staff included Fred L. Pundsack, Chester E. Shepperly, Monroe Harris, and Chester J. Sulewski, all of whom, along with McKinney, figured prominently in the bankruptcy court protection program some 30 years later. In 1958 J-M acquired L-O-F Glass Fibers Company, which then became and operates today as the Manville Sales Corporation. Francis H. May, Jr., of Libbey-Owens-Ford Glass Company, joined Manville and became executive vice-president for finance and administration. Fisher was named chairman as well as president.

During the 1950s J-M workers who came into contact with insulation on job sites began filing workmen's compensation claims against the company. The company's first-hand knowledge of the dangers of asbestos would become a factor in future suits in which it would be a defendant.

In 1960 Clinton Brown Burnett became president of J-M, a post he held for a decade. Burnett headed the company during a period of rising production costs and price declines. In response, he trimmed operations by closing plants and assembly lines. He led the company through cautious diversification into fiberglass, carpeting, and gypsum; opened a building materials research and development center in New Jersey; and expanded vigorously overseas.

During the 1960s asbestos received increasing attention from the medical community. In 1963 Dr. I. J. Selikoff of Mount Sinai Medical Center in New York reported to the American Medical Association the findings of his study of the effects of asbestos on workers. Selikoff estimated that 100,000 U.S. workers and their family members would die of diseases associated with asbestos in the twentieth century. That study, coupled with the news coverage that followed, brought the problem to the public's attention. In 1964, for the first time, J-M agreed to place warning labels on its products. The labels read, "Inhalation of asbestos in excessive quantities over long periods of time may be harmful."

By 1969 Burnett, now 62, and the board of directors were looking for solutions to two problems: J-M's slow growth over the preceding ten years, and the lack of an heir apparent to succeed the president when he retired. William C. Stolk, a director since 1951, recommended W. Richard Goodwin, a 45-year-old management consultant with a doctorate in experimental psychology, for help in solving the first problem and, potentially, the second. Goodwin began counseling J-M in June 1968. He joined the company as vice-president for corporate planning in April of 1969, and was named president in December of 1970. Burnett became chairman of the board, only to retire in about a month. He left Goodwin with a solid company, having $145 million in working capital, no long-term debt, and a leading position in environmental control, building materials, and asbestos.

Goodwin immediately implemented the changes he had recommended during his consultancy. He formed a three-man management team, composed of himself and J-M veterans Francis May and John B. Jobe, executive vice-president for operations. May and Jobe ran the company while Goodwin concentrated on growth. He led the company into real estate development, recreation, irrigation systems, and construction. Sales rose 91 percent from 1970 to 1975; profits rose 115 percent between 1970 and 1974, and earnings in 1976 set a company record. In 1974 J-M's international division, with 22 plants and four mines in 12 countries and sales offices worldwide, generated 32 percent of corporate net profit on 14 percent of gross sales.

In 1973 Manville and its codefendants lost their final appeal in *Clarence Borel v. Fibreboard Paper Products Company, et al.* The case would be a turning point in asbestos litigation, for the jury found the defendants guilty of contributory negligence. It also awarded the plaintiff damages based on the contention that the companies knew of the dangers inherent in working with the product. In upholding the verdict, the U.S. Appeals Court wrote what was described in *Strategic Management* as a scorching indictment of the defendants.

One of Goodwin's major contributions to J-M was his decision to move the company from Madison Avenue in New York. Goodwin selected the Ken-Caryl cattle ranch, 15 miles from downtown Denver, Colorado, as the site for the new headquarters. When completed, the new building was described in *Business Week* as "ultramodern . . . [the building] juts out like a landlocked ocean liner in a mountain canyon." The building was a tangible reminder that J-M's style had changed drastically.

Goodwin never worked at the new location. Just two weeks prior to its completion, he was summoned to New York to meet with the board of directors. On September 1, 1976, Goodwin, Francis May, and other aides flew in and were met by John A. McKinney, a senior vice-president and the company's top legal officer by this time. The next evening, William F. May, John P. Schroeder, and Charles J. Zwick, members of the board of directors, met with Goodwin. Schroeder explained that they represented the nine outside directors on J-M's 12-member board, and that they all wanted his resignation. Goodwin was surprised but acquiesced. The terms of his separation agreement prevented him from ever discussing his departure or the reasons for it. Industry observers speculated that Goodwin's management style was too casual or flamboyant for the conservative board, and that once he got the company moving in the right direction, the directors replaced him. The next morning, John A. McKinney, who did not know in advance that the board sought to remove Goodwin, was appointed the new president of J-M. *Fortune* quoted McKinney as saying, "It happened so fast, I almost missed it."

Under Goodwin, J-M had stressed growth. Under McKinney, J-M stressed profits. During his first year as president, McKinney eliminated unprofitable diversification and expanded asbestos and fiberglass capacity. One of his early acts as president was to elevate Fred L. Pundsack, a 24-year J-M veteran, to executive vice-president of operations, on equal footing with Francis May. Pundsack's directive was to maximize profits.

McKinney quickly earned a reputation as a tough negotiator. In 1977 Quebec threatened to nationalize the company's Jeffrey mine, the world's largest asbestos mine. McKinney put J-M's $77 million expansion plan on hold and took a hard line with Premier René Levésque. Levésque withdrew his proposal and J-M resumed its expansion plans. Later in the year, J-M's fiberglass production suffered from a 102-day strike at its Defiance, Ohio, plant. The strike cost the company $7.5 million in lost revenues. McKinney stood his ground and in October workers accepted the same offer they had rejected in September, by a two-to-one margin. In May 1977 McKinney was named chairman of the board and chief executive officer. Pundsack became president and chief operating officer.

In 1977 J-M estimated that the $16 million available through primary coverage to settle outstanding asbestos suits would be depleted within two years. New case filings rose from 159 in 1976 to 792 in 1978. Cases were being settled at a faster pace as well, with an average cost to the company of $21,000, of which $15,400 was awarded to the plaintiff and the balance going for legal fees. As Travelers was unable to predict the scope and number of future suits, it refused to renew its policy for the 1977 fiscal year. J-M was forced to insure itself.

By 1979 McKinney was spending half of his time on the asbestos problem. He continued to be a tough negotiator. In May 1979 a writer for *Fortune* stated, "Asbestos litigation is almost a separate business at J-M." The company was a co-defendant in about 1,500 lawsuits brought by insulation workers who handled J-M's products while working for other companies in construction or in the shipyards. At McKinney's insistence, J-M sued the government to force it to indemnify the company against the suits from shipyard workers, as many of the claimants had worked with asbestos insulation during World War II and the Korean War in defense-related capacities.

In January 1979 J-M completed its acquisition of Olinkraft Inc., a $447 million forest-products company, for about $600 million. W. Thomas Stephens, who was to have a lead role in J-M's later bankruptcy reorganization, moved to J-M from Olinkraft. Olinkraft, now operating as Manville Forest Products Corporation, owned 600,000 acres of timberlands in Louisiana, Arkansas, and Texas. It owned or leased another 100,000 acres in Brazil. Unexpectedly high start-up costs for Olinkraft, combined with a currency devaluation and tax increases in Brazil, caused J-M's net income to fall 20 percent in the fourth quarter of 1979. Although its stock price fell 40 percent, Manville surpassed the $2 billion mark in sales for the first time.

Revenues in 1980 were on a par with those in 1979, with earnings dropping sharply in a weak construction market. The company remained heavily involved with asbestos. McKinney noted that asbestos and Manville were virtually synonymous and told *Forbes* in May 1980, "The day asbestos isn't good business for us, we'll get out of it." At the same time, he felt that Olinkraft, once past its initial problems, would shape the future of J-M. In 1980 McKinney reported that the company remained optimistic in the face of mounting lawsuits, as the firm had been victorious in the majority of the cases that had thus far proceeded to trial.

Effective October 30, 1981, J-M's shareholders approved a reorganized corporate structure consisting of a new parent company, Manville Corporation, and five wholly separate operating subsidiaries: Manville Building Materials Corporation, Manville Forest Products Corporation, Manville International Corporation, Manville Products Corporation, and Johns-Manville Corporation. Johns-Manville shareholders retained their stock, which was converted to Manville Corporation stock on a share-for-share basis.

As of December 31, 1981, Manville was a defendant or co-defendant in approximately 9,300 asbestos suits brought by 12,800 individuals. Juries were making large awards in punitive damages, which were not covered by insurance. By 1982 settlements approximated $40,000 per case, including legal fees. Manville's consultants estimated that over the course of the next 20 years the company could be liable for 32,000 cases in addition to the 16,500 that had already been filed. Possible litigation costs were estimated at $2 billion, twice the company's assets at the time. By 1985 19,750 claims had been filed against the company. In addition, Manville was alleged to be liable for asbestos-removal property-damage claims. Manville repeatedly filed appeals to postpone payments in suits it had lost. McKinney continued to assert that the government must pay a portion of the claims arising from exposure in the ship-yards and other government jobs.

On August 26, 1982, in light of the asbestos litigation and posted losses in the first and second quarters of the year, Manville filed for protection under Chapter 11 of the U.S. Bankruptcy Code. While under bankruptcy court protection, Manville's earnings for the first nine months from continuing operations improved from $10 million to $59 million. Legal expenses, however, increased apace: in one year, 1982–1983, legal costs rose from $1 million for a period of nine months to $11 million for the same period a year later.

After a dozen court-granted postponements, Manville proposed its reorganization plan on November 21, 1983. The plan was produced unilaterally, since attempts at a negotiated settlement with asbestos victims' representatives had failed. At that time, Manville proposed to split itself into two companies: the first would handle the business and the second would possess few assets yet all of the liability for the asbestos claims. Manville would be insulated from any and all claims. All cash, after operating expenses, would be funnelled to the second company. Suits would be settle by the company out of court. Concurrently, Manville left the asbestos business, selling its last plant in 1985.

Leon Silverman, court-appointed attorney for unknown future asbestos claimants, helped orchestrate the final reorganization plan, filed on February 14, 1986. This plan resembled the earlier proposal with these amendments: the second company became two trusts, for personal injury—the health fund—and for property-damage claims. The trusts would be funded through cash, future earnings, stock, bonds, and insurance payments worth at least $2.5 billion. Initially, the health-fund trust was to receive $1 billion. Beginning in 1992, Manville would have to pay the health fund $75 million a year. The property-damage trust was to be funded initially with $125 million, with additional funds available. In addition, plaintiffs retained the right to a jury trial if they disagreed with the determination made by the trusts. The plan seemed to satisfy the claimants, but at considerable expense to Manville common stock owners, who saw their investment becoming virtually worthless under the plan. On neither side was there agreement that the trusts were viable solutions. Michael L. Goldberg, attorney for 700 asbestos claimants, estimated in 1988 that the trusts would be almost $200 million short by 1992.

In 1986 McKinney resigned and Josh T. Hulce, who had been president since 1984, abruptly quit. George Dillon, a Manville director for 17 years, became chairman and W. Thomas Stephens was tapped to become president and chief executive officer. Stephens, formerly an industrial engineer with Olinkraft and Manville's chief financial officer during the preceding three years, was credited with playing a pivotal role in bringing Manville out of bankruptcy. One of Stephens's first moves as

president was to establish small meetings with Manville employees, who, like the public and the stockholders, had lost faith in the company. Stephens reassured them that Manville would continue to operate much as it had in the past. He intended to concentrate on its core businesses and generate enough cash flow over the next years to fund the trust. Profits doubled in 1987 to a record $164 million.

In 1988 Manville emerged from bankruptcy. The Chapter 11 filing forced Manville to reexamine the way it conducted its business. Extensive in-house restructuring resulted in a policy of encouraging more decision-making from the company's various components. Incentive programs were also instituted.

After three full years of trimming operations, Manville was again a healthy company with new product lines. It moved out of its headquarters into smaller spaces in Denver and reinvested the concomitant savings in plant upgrading. In the November 1988 *Business Month* Stephens stated, "Two back-to-back years of record performance should send out a signal pretty loud and clear that we're stronger than ever."

One of Manville's subsidiaries, Atlanta-based Riverwood International, is a rising star in the paper industry stock market. A producer of lumber, containerboard, and clay-coated paperboard for the beverage and food industries, Riverwood makes 50 to 60 percent of the paper beer cartons in the United States. The company also manufactures 20 to 30 percent of all paper containers made for soft drinks. Riverwood became a public company in June 1992 when it sold 12.1 million shares of stocks. Manville, however, still controls 80 percent of the company.

By 1990 almost 130,000 claims had been filed and the Manville Personal Injury Settlement Trust ran out of funds. The dearth of cash was due to the rapid pace of claims settlement, many of which were delayed during Manville's bankruptcy. The Fund trustees, headed by Director Marianna Smith, proposed three cost-cutting measures. First, the Fund would refuse to pay post-judgment interest whenever plaintiffs contested their trust settlements. Second, settlements and court-order judgments would be paid in installments rather than in lump sums. Third, the Trust would declare that funds were not subject to attachment or levy by the court. Attorneys for the plaintiffs argued that the Fund trustees did not have the authority to implement such restrictions and called for Manville to liquidate the Trust's 24 million shares, worth approximately $1 billion. Although the company accelerated a $50 million payment to the trust, it was revealed that the claims that had been settled would not be paid for almost 20 years, long after many of the claimants had died. In July 1990 the court imposed a payments freeze while the company tried to determine how to handle the situation. In September 1990 Manville agreed to add up to $520 million to the asbestos fund during the next seven years.

Manville suffered great public relations losses as a result of the asbestos lawsuits. In an annual *Fortune* magazine poll of America's most admired companies, Manville finished last for five consecutive years, from 1987 to 1991. In an effort to regain the public's trust, Manville now regularly monitors the health of its employees with a computer tracking system. In addition, Manville places cautionary labels on any of its products that have been found to contain possible carcinogens. This procedure has particularly hurt sales in Japan, where packages with cancer warnings were initially refused entry into the country. As litigation continues into the 1990s, the future of the company seems predicated on the resolution of the asbestos issue.

Principal Subsidiaries: European Overseas Corporation; Glaswerk Schuller G.m.b.H. (Germany); International Manville Corporation; Johns-Manville Corporation; Johns-Manville India Limited; Ken-Caryl Ranch Corporation; Manville Canada Inc.; Manville Sales Corporation; Rocky Mountain International Insurance Ltd.; Manville de France S.A.; Manville Deutschland G.m.b.H. (Germany); Manville do Brasil Isolantes Termicos Ltda. (Brazil); Manville Española S.A. (Spain); Manville Europe Corporation; Manville Forest Products Corporation; Arkansas & Louisiana Missouri Railway Co.; Pine Pipeline Inc.; Manville (Great Britain) Inc.; Manville h.f. (Iceland); Manville Investment Corporation; Manville International B.V. (Netherlands); Manville Italiana S.p.A. (Italy); Manville Japan Ltd.; Manville Mexicana S.A. de C.V. (Mexico); Manville Produtos Florestais Ltd. (Brazil); Lages Reflorestamento Ltda. (Brazil); Igaras-Servicos Agro-Florestais Ltd. (Brazil); Manville Remedtech, Inc.; New Materials Inc.; New Materials, Ltd. (U.K.).

Further Reading: Solomon, Stephen, ''The Asbestos Fallout at Johns-Manville,'' *Fortune*, May 7, 1979; Brodeur, Paul, *Outrageous Misconduct: The Asbestos Industry on Trial*, New York, Pantheon Books, 1985; Pearce, John A., II, and Richard B. Robinson, Jr., ''Case 18: Manville Corporation (1987),'' *Strategic Management: Strategy Formulation and Implementation*, Homewood, Illinois, Irwin, 1988; Adler, Stacy, ''Manville Proposes Steps to Preserve Claims Fund Cash,'' *Business Insurance*, January 22, 1990; Roach, John D. C., ''Reshaping Corporate America,'' *Management Accounting*, March 1990; Adler, Stacy, ''Manville Trust Officials Defend Management,'' *Business Insurance*, June 18, 1990; Galen, Michele, ''Back in Jeopardy at Manville,'' *Business Week*, June 25, 1990; Adler Stacy, ''Judge Sets a Deadline for Manville Trust Reform,'' *Business Insurance*, July 16, 1990; Dillon, George C., ''Does It Pay to Do the Right Thing?'' *Across the Board*, July/August 1991; Zepser, Andy, ''The Asbestos Curse,'' *Barron's*, October 14, 1991; McNaughton, David, ''Manville Corp. Unit Prospers in the Paper Industry,'' *Denver Post*, February 17, 1993.

—Lynn M. Kalanik
updated by Mary McNulty

MARK IV INDUSTRIES INC.

MARK IV INDUSTRIES, INC.

P.O. Box 810
One Towne Centre
501 John James Audubon Parkway
Amherst, New York 14226-0810
U.S.A.
(716) 689-4972
Fax: (716) 689-6098

Public Company
Incorporated: 1970 as Mark IV Homes, Inc.
Employees: 11,900
Sales: $1.15 billion
Stock Exchanges: New York
SICs: 3714 Motor Vehicle Parts & Accessories; 3052 Rubber
   & Plastics Hose & Belting; 3651 Household Audio &
   Video Equipment

Mark IV Industries, Inc., is a conglomerate of small manufacturing companies with operations in three major areas: professional audio equipment, power transfer and fluid handling, and mass transit and traffic control. But its greatest asset may be CEO Salvatore H. Alfiero's's propensity for finding and acquiring small technical or industrial companies that are undervalued but are leaders in specialized or niche markets. Mark IV owns more than 60 plants in the United States and abroad.

Alfiero and president Clement R. Arrison have been responsible for the spectacular development of Mark IV and have remained its principal shareholders since the company began. For the most part Alfiero is involved in finances and growth while Arrison is more involved in operations, but they consider themselves a team, with each able to function well in both areas. The 1980s were a particularly successful time for Mark IV. Between 1985 and 1991 the company bought more than 40 properties for a total of $1.25 billion dollars, and sales exploded from $38.6 million to almost $1.2 billion. *Insiders Chronicle* called it "one of the flashiest corporate growth performers of the 1980s."

Alfiero, with an undergraduate degree in aerospace engineering from Rensselaer Polytechnical Institute and an MBA from Harvard, and Arrison, a graduate of the University of Michigan with a degree in electrical engineering, met in 1967 when they both worked for Radatron, a Buffalo company manufacturing automatic radar detectors.

After two years, they invested in Glar-Ban International, a small company in Cheektowaga, New York, that manufactured non-glare instrumentation panels for aircraft. Both Alfiero and Arrison took leadership positions with the company. At the same time, Alfiero and a partner started Mark IV Homes, Inc., a mobile-home manufacturer in Pennsylvania. They were planning to call the company Cardinal Homes but they needed an alternate name in case their first choice was taken. Alfiero's associate happened to notice a cigar box on the desk; the name on the box was Mark IV. When they found out that the name Cardinal was, indeed, already in use, Mark IV Homes, Inc., was born.

In 1970 Glar-Ban bought Radatron, Alfiero's and Arrison's former employer, for $400,000. Glar-Ban continued to buy small companies for the next few years: in 1971, T. James Clarke Box & Label Corp., a drug and health-care packaging manufacturer in Jamestown, New York; in 1972, E. N. Rowell Co., another box and packaging manufacturer in Batavia, New York; in 1974, Metal Awning Components Inc., in Clawson, Michigan; and in 1975, Nuclear Radiation Developments (NRD), a manufacturer of smoke detection and static elimination equipment in Grand Island, New York.

Mark IV Homes grew steadily from 1969 to 1973, building six plants and acquiring Roycroft Industries, Inc., a mobile-home manufacturer in Chesaning, Michigan. Then a recession hit and the company's sales dropped from $29 million in 1973 to $19 million the next year. Interest rates were too high for potential buyers to finance housing purchases, and to make matters even worse, consumers were also turning away from mobile and manufactured homes. Mark IV showed a loss of almost $2 million in 1974 and posted losses for the next two years as well. Alfiero knew he had to get out of the mobile home business.

In 1976 Alfiero bought out his Mark IV Homes partner. Alfiero and Arrison merged Glar-Ban and Mark IV, moved their headquarters to Williamsville, near Buffalo, and changed the name of the company to Mark IV Industries, Inc. In 1977 Mark IV, now the owner of several small, diverse manufacturing companies, showed a profit of $787,000, its first profit in four years, and sales increased from $18 million to $30 million. Still, it took several years for the company to find its direction. Alfiero and Arrison bought a few more small companies, but as Alfiero told the *New York Times,* "we were a company looking for what we wanted to be."

In the early 1980s, they knew they wanted to become a miniconglomerate and play the acquisitions game. They sold unprofitable or marginal enterprises, including Rowell, Radatron, and their remaining mobile home plants. They bought polystyrene foam producer Toyad Corp. of Latrobe, Pennsylvania, for more than $5 million and Pacemaker Plastics, Inc., for a quarter of a million dollars.

The two chief officers felt confident about their company because they had a solid base and a healthy balance sheet, but they still did not have a firm sense of where they were going until 1983, when they bought Protective Closures, the nation's top manufacturer of plastic caps, seals, and plugs. Arrison told *Western New York* magazine, "Over the years, we have become more sure of the areas where we do well and the areas we should avoid. In the beginning, we would try most anything. Today, we are much more selective in the industries where we'll participate and the types of companies we'll let go.''

Acquisition of Protective Closures did not come easily. Mark IV finally acquired it for $10 million only after a bidding war with another company. But Protective was a clear moneymaker. With the addition of Protective Closures Mark IV's sales shot up from $21.5 million in 1983 to almost $39 million in 1984, and the company earned close to $2 million, nearly doubling its profits in a year. Mark IV executive vice-president and former chair of Gulton Industries E. Maclin Roby told the *New York Times* that purchase of Protective Closures ''was a pivotal event.'' He called it the ''cash machine that allowed them to go off on a wider acquisition program.'' Not only was purchase of Protective Closures a monetary success, but Mark IV finally found its direction: it would buy small undervalued companies that were already the leaders in their own specialized markets.

Alfiero and Arrison called this first phase of the new Mark IV its ''build and prune'' phase. The company was using debt to buy manufacturing companies in three core areas, and acquired companies had to be leaders in their niche markets. If some operations of the acquired company did not fit the product or profitability objectives of Mark IV, they were sold, enabling Mark IV to buy other companies or buy down its debt.

Following this ''build and prune'' strategy, in 1985 Mark IV bought LFE Corp. of Clinton, Massachusetts, a manufacturer of hydraulic, process control, and environmental control products. It also happened to be almost twice the size of Mark IV. Mark IV borrowed $37 million to buy LFE, and this acquisition also paid off in a big way. Mark IV's annual sales tripled to $120 million with its purchase of its first diversified company. In 1986 Mark IV purchased Gulton Industries Inc., a New Jersey company making electronics products for defense, audio, graphic display, and industrial uses.

Both LFE and Gulton perfectly fit Mark IV's criteria for acquisition. As Alfiero outlined in the *New York Times,* Mark IV's strategy was to target companies with a strong market position, a wide array of proprietary products, and less than 25 percent of its sales to aerospace or military industries. Perhaps most important, company insiders could not be in control of a substantial share of the company's stock.

Acquisition of both LFE and Gulton started as hostile takeovers since neither company probably would have taken Mark IV's acquisition quest seriously because of its relatively small size. But after Mark IV began to purchase a substantial number of shares, it got the attention it wanted. Before long hostile takeovers turned into friendly acquisitions.

Mark IV allowed a great deal of autonomy to the divisions it bought. Although management remained decentralized and division managers continued to run their own companies without day-to-day interference from Mark IV, the Mark IV corporate staff grew quickly, and in 1986, the company moved from its cramped offices in the Buffalo suburb of Williamsville to the nearby town of Amherst.

Mark IV did not have to worry about not being taken seriously after buying LFE and Gulton. According to *Financial World,*

Mark IV was the fastest growing company in the United States in 1986. Mark IV continued to follow its ''prune and build'' strategy, buying Conrac Corp., an electronics displays manufacturer; Eagle Signal Controls, a traffic signal manufacturer; and Cetec and Electronic Counters and Controls, both audio equipment manufacturers. In five years, Mark IV's assets had skyrocketed from $19 million to $612 million. Investors who had paid less than $2,000 each in 1969 owned stock worth more than $2 million in 1987.

In the fall of 1988 the company paid $625 million for Armtek of Jamestown, New York, a manufacturer of automotive and industrial products, in the biggest acquisition in Mark IV's history. Alfiero told *Forbes* magazine, ''The biggest thing we had going for us was that nobody thought we could pull it off.''

With this purchase of another company twice its size, Mark IV's debt was more than $1 billion, and Alfiero and Arrison sought to reduce that debt quickly. Within a year, Mark IV sold two of Armtek's divisions—Copolymer, a chemicals producer, and Blackstone, a manufacturer of original equipment heat exchange systems for cars. Using those net proceeds, Mark IV paid off money borrowed to finance the Armtek purchase and ended up paying only $37 million for the Dayco Products, which had been responsible for half of Armtek's sales and profits. Dayco was a definite moneymaker. With sales of $425 million, it was the nation's leading supplier of original equipment automobile accessory drive systems and the second leading supplier of aftermarket accessory drive systems.

Alfiero also began buying Mark IV's junk bonds at a heavily discounted rate when the government began pushing companies to put them on the market. Alfiero eliminated another $250 million in debt this way.

In 1991 Mark IV purchased F-P Electronics, a Canadian manufacturer of electromagnet information display devices; Anchor Swan, maker of garden hoses and flexible hoses for cars; Vapor, the world's largest maker of door systems for trains and buses; and two foreign companies, Dynacord of Germany and Klark-Teknik of the United Kingdom, both adding to Mark IV's audio line.

The company's largest core business in 1992 was Power Transfer and Fluid Handling. Mark IV's Dayco was the leading manufacturer of industrial belts and hoses used in home appliances, diesel engines, snowmobiles, and gardening, and a leading supplier of coolant hoses, power steering hoses, fuel hoses, transmission oil cooler hoses, and belts to the U.S. Big Three automakers. This core business also benefited in the 1990s from increased public concern about the environment since Dayco manufactured gasoline dispensing hoses, including the vapor recovery hose used at gasoline pumps to return gas fumes. This hose was also introduced in Europe in response to the European Clean Air Act.

In 1992 the Mass Transit and Traffic Control division worked with AT&T to develop and distribute an automatic electronic toll collection system that would allow drivers to pay their tolls with their AT&T ''Smart Card'' without stopping at toll booths. Mark IV also supplied traffic lights, electrical controls, interior lighting, and passenger information systems for buses, trains, and airplanes. The Americans with Disabilities Act also brought new opportunities to Mark IV, which had developed information display systems with enhanced audio and video display. Mark IV also looked forward to increased sales related to more government funding of mass transit systems.

Mark IV's third core area, professional audio equipment, produced recording studio equipment, systems for live performances, and products for permanently installed sound systems. Its products included amplifiers, microphones, mixing consoles, signal processors, and loudspeakers. Consolidation of the audio industry in the early 1990s was a boon to Mark IV because it could acquire companies that were well known and respected. Mark IV's audio equipment was sold under its division names, Electro-Voice, Altec, Vega, Dynacord, Gauss, Klark Teknik, and University Sound. Mark IV sound systems were used in the 1991 "Monsters of Rock" tour in England, Europe, and Russia, as well as at Euro Disneyland, which had the largest computer-controlled sound system in the world when it opened in 1992.

Mark IV retained several companies, particularly instrumentation companies, that did not strictly fit into its core areas but were leaders in niche markets in the aerospace, defense, and plastics industries. It also kept one of its earliest acquisitions, Clarke Container, a maker of child-resistant prescription bottles.

While the 1980s were a period of acquisition and growth, with Mark IV's products holding market-leading positions in the United States and the world, the recession in the early 1990s called for a different growth strategy. Mark IV focused on debt reduction, improved operations and continued selective acquisition, changing its acquisition strategy from purchase of public companies that would establish core businesses to purchase of private companies that would bolster Mark IV's core businesses. Because of its very diversified product lines and markets, Mark IV Industries was much better equipped to weather recession than its predecessor Mark IV Homes.

Alfiero and Arrison anticipated that the last half of the 1990s would bring a return to more aggressive growth, especially in the international arena, and that by the year 2000, half of its revenues would come from markets outside the United States.

Principal Subsidiaries: Altec Lansing Corporation; Anchor Swan, Inc.; Clarke Container Company, Inc.; Dayco Europe AB (Sweden); Dayco Products, Inc.; DDA (England); Dynacord Electronic und Geretebau GmbH & Co.KG (Germany, 80%); Eagle Signal Controls and Automatic Signal; Electro-Voice, Incorporated; FCD Corp.; Femco; F-P Electronics (Canada); Gauss and Electro Sound; Glar-Ban Incorporated; Graphic Instruments; Gulton Data Systems; Interstate Highway Sign; Kirkhof/Goodrich; Klark Teknik PLC (England); LFE Industrial Systems Corporation; LFE Instruments; LLE (Germany); Luminator; Lustreprint Incorporated; Mark IV Audio AG (Switzerland); Mark IV Audio, Inc.; Mark IV Instruments Limited (England); Mark IV IVHS (Canada); Mark IV Transportation Products Corp.; Mokon; NRD, Inc.; Protective Closures Co., Inc.; Servonic; Statham; University Sound, Inc.; Vapor; Vapor Canada Inc.; Vega. The company also has other subsidiaries with Mark IV, Dayco, Lunkoflex, or Klark-Teknik in titles.

Further Reading: Zremski, Jerry, "Mark IV Industries Is Growing into Big Conglomerate," *Buffalo News,* June 15, 1986; Wiener, Daniel P., "Mark IV: The Making of a Miniconglomerate," *New York Times,* August 9, 1987; English, Dale C., "Profile: Sal H. Alfiero, Clement R. Arrison," *Western New York,* August 1989; Mehlman, William, "Asset Juggling Skills Keep Mark IV on High Curve," *Insiders' Chronicle,* January 29, 1990; Norman, James R., "Quick Reflexes," *Forbes,* March 2, 1992; Annual Report, 1992, Mark IV Industries, Inc.

—Wendy Stein

MARS, INC.

6885 Elm Street
McLean, Virginia 22101
U.S.A.
(703) 821-4900
Fax: (703) 448-9678

Private Company
Incorporated: 1911 as Mar-O-Bar Co.
Employees: 28,000
Sales: $13 billion
SICs: 2064 Candy & Other Confectionery Products; 2024 Ice
   Cream & Frozen Desserts; 2047 Dog & Cat Food; 2044
   Rice Milling

Mars, Inc. is a diversified international company ranked in 1992 as the leading manufacturer of candy and confectionery products. Mars is known for its famous brands—such as Snickers, Milky Way, M&M's, Kal Kan, Whiskas, and Uncle Ben's Rice—as well as for its leaders' preoccupation with privacy and its unconventional office structure. Mars, Inc. is controlled by the Mars family, and the secrecy surrounding the company and the family is legendary. The company maintains that Mars should be known for its brands, not the personalities of its executives; therefore, photographs and interviews with insiders are rarely permitted. The company does not publish any financial information.

Mars's primary businesses are branded snack foods, accounting for approximately 43 percent of sales; pet-care products, comprising 44 percent of sales; and main meal, electronics, and drinks, accounting for the remaining 13 percent of sales. By region, about half of sales are in Europe, 40 percent in the Americas, and 10 percent in Australia, Japan, and the West Pacific. Snack foods, pet food, and main meal divisions have their origins before mid-century. The electronics and Dove International divisions represent the more recent Mars businesses.

Mars began in 1911 as the Mar-O-Bar Company, a snack food business founded by Frank C. Mars of Tacoma, Washington, who made a variety of butter cream candy in his home. Quality and value were the foundations of his first candy factory, which employed 125 people. In 1920 Frank Mars relocated to larger quarters in Minneapolis, where Snickers (without the chocolate coating) and Milky Way bars were created. The company posted a loss of $6,000 in 1922, but by 1924, sales exceeded

$700,000. Mars changed his company's name to Mars Candies in 1926. With the rapid growth of the company, Mars sought larger quarters and built a new plant in suburban Chicago in 1928. Sales actually quadrupled during the lean years of the Depression and new products were introduced, including Mars Almond Bar, Snickers Bar (now sporting a chocolate covering), and 3 Musketeers.

Frank Mars hired his son Forrest E. Mars to work in the candy operation after his graduation from Yale, but the two reportedly had a stormy relationship. In the early 1930s, Frank, giving Forrest some money and the foreign rights to manufacturer Milky Way, ordered his son to start his own business abroad. Moving to England, Forrest established a confectionery and a canned pet food company, which met with great success.

In 1940 Forrest Mars returned to the United States and founded M&M Limited in Newark, New Jersey, to manufacture chocolate candies in a sugar shell. At that time, stores reduced their stock of chocolate in the summer because of the lack of air conditioning, and Forrest hoped to capitalize on the unique construction of M&M's to sell the candy year round. The name of the candy was derived from the initials of Mars and an associate, Bruce Murrie. M&M's Peanut Chocolate Candies were introduced in 1954, the same year the famous slogan "the milk chocolate melts in your mouth—not in your hand" was first used.

Frank Mars's business was also experiencing great success. In 1943 Mars ventured into the main meal business, which includes a wide selection of rice products, including whole grain, savory, boil-in-bag, fast cook, instant, and frozen rice as well as other products. Uncle Ben's rice utilizes a rice processing technology called parboiling, which was developed in England and was first used in the United States by a Texas food broker with whom Forest E. Mars, Sr., formed a partnership. Several months after their first production facility was completed, they began selling rice to the U.S. Army, which they continued to supply throughout World War II.

After the war, the company introduced converted rice to the American public, and by 1952 it sold the country's number one brand of rice. Around this time, the company adopted the name "Uncle Ben" for a locally famous rice grower known for producing high quality rice crops. Uncle Ben's is now the leading brand of rice worldwide, sold in more than 100 countries, with manufacturing facilities in the United States, Australia, Belgium, German, the Netherlands, and the United Kingdom. Other popular brands include Country Inn rice, Dolmio spaghetti sauces, pasta, and oriental dishes named Suzi Wan, primarily sold in Europe and Australia.

Because of increased production, Mars constructed a new plant in Hackettstown, New Jersey, in 1958. In the early 1960s, facilities were extended to Europe with a factory at Veghel in the Netherlands. In 1967 Forrest merged his business with the Mars Company owned by his father and took over operation of the new company. He established a radically egalitarian system at the company in which workers were called associates and everyone—from the president down—punched a time clock. Offices were eliminated and desks were arranged in a wagon-wheel fashion, with the higher ranking executives in the center, to facilitate communication between individuals and functional areas. Notoriously demanding, Forrest rewarded his associates with salaries that were substantially higher than those in other comparably-sized companies.

In 1968 Mars—already the largest dog food packer in the world, with subsidiaries in Europe, South America, and Australia—acquired Kal Kan Foods, Inc., a dog food company founded in 1937 that later supplied food for dogs in the U.S. military during World War II. With assistance from Mars, Kal Kan expanded by adding a second canned pet food plant in Columbus, Ohio, and a dry pet food plant in Mattoon, Illinois, while expanding into midwestern and eastern markets. New product development of Mars pet-care products has been aided by the creation of the Waltham Centre for Pet Nutrition in the United Kingdom, which was formed to study the nutritional preferences and needs of pet animals. Nutritional studies are published regularly in scientific and veterinary journals, and Waltham has become a world authority on pet care and nutrition.

Mars Electronics International (MEI) began operating in Britain in 1969 and expanded to the United States in 1972. MEI was responsible for the introduction of electronics to the vending machine industry, and today has millions of coin mechanisms installed worldwide. In 1985 MEI expanded its product line to include advanced bill technology and cashless payment systems. In addition to serving the vending industry, MEI also provides products for use in pay phones and amusement parks. MEI's electronics technology has also been applied to data acquisition and laser scanning devices. In 1987 the company's British and American operations were merged to form the largest international manufacturer of electronic coin machines. In addition to its two manufacturing facilities, MEI has marketing and sales offices throughout the United States, Europe, Australia, and the Far East.

Forrest, Sr., retired from Mars in 1973. His elder sons, Forrest E. Mars, Jr., and John Mars, took over Mars as co-presidents—joined in 1983 in the Office of the President by their sister Jackie, who takes a lesser role in running the company. In his retirement, Forrest, Sr., started a candy business named Ethel M. Chocolates (after his late mother) to produce premium boxed chocolates. Around 1988 Ethel M. Chocolates was purchased by Mars.

Despite its unorthodox corporate culture, the Mars company has thrived. Hershey Foods Corp. and Mars, Inc. have historically fought a battle to hold the number one spot in the U.S. candy market, an honor which passes between them. Mars took over the top spot in the early 1970s and by late in the decade had pushed its market share 14 percentage points ahead of Hershey. According to an industry executive quoted in *Fortune,* "it took the Hershey people seven or eight years to realize that Mars was not going to go away. . . . Then it took them another five years to get their act together." Hershey responded with a flurry of new product introductions, heavy advertising, and innovative marketing efforts. In the mid-1980s Mars tried to combat this by creating a new image for candy as a sweet snack, not just junk food. Mars paid $5 million to have M&M's and Snickers named "the official snack foods of the 1984 Olympic Games." Commercials featured athletes getting quick energy from sugary

snacks. By 1985 industry analysts noted that the two companies were neck and neck, with Mars's recent brands including Bounty Bars, Combos, Holidays M&M's, Kudos, Starburst, Skittles, and Twix Cookie Bar.

Mars added frozen snacks to its repertoire when it acquired Dove International in 1986. The Dove Bar, a hand-dipped ice cream bar with a thick chocolate coating, was created in 1956 by Leo Stefanos, the proprietor of a Chicago candy shop. For many years, the bar was only available in the Chicago area, and it became a gourmet treat when it appeared in selected U.S. markets during the early 1980s. Doveurope was established in 1988. Other Mars frozen treats include Dove miniatures and ice-cream versions of 3 Musketeers, Milky Way, and Snickers bars.

In 1988 Hershey Foods Corp. surpassed Mars as the largest U.S. candy maker when it acquired Cadbury Schweppes's U.S. division, boasting the Mounds and Almond Joy brands. In 1989 Mars received another setback when it tried to launch Sussande chocolate bars, a high priced European-style bar, which, according to a report in *Forbes,* was a costly failure.

The company rivalry between Mars and Hershey reversed itself in 1991, when Mars increased its percentage of the total candy market from 16.7 percent to 17.9 percent while Hershey's market share remained flat at 17 percent, according to the *Wall Street Journal.* Mars was very successful with its 1990 introduction of peanut butter M&M's, which took a toll on Hershey's number two–ranked Reese's peanut butter cups. Mars launched 12 new products in 1991, including a dark chocolate candy bar under the Dove name, mint and almond M&M's, Milky Way Dark, and Peanut Butter Snickers.

Also in 1991 Mars introduced Expert, a superpremium dog and cat food line meant as an alternative to Hill's Science Diet and Iams, which are sold only in pet stores and feed shops. An industry analyst noted in the *New York Times* that "people are feeding their pets like they feed their children. The nutrition kick has moved over to our pets." To meet customer demand, Mars quickly moved into the specialty pet food area, but made the product accessible by selling it in supermarkets. Mars's other pet-care lines continued to do well. According to company literature, Kal Kan is the fifth largest pet food manufacturer in the United States. Other top sellers in Australia, Europe, and the United States include Pedigree and Partners dog foods; Whiskas, Sheeba, and Brekkies cat food; and Winergy Horsesnacks.

Mars also explored healthier alternatives for its traditional snack products when, in 1992, the company became the first customer of Proctor and Gamble Co.'s caprenin, a low-calorie cocoa butter substitute. Mars used caprenin in Milky Way II bars, launched on the West Coast in April 1992. Made of fatty acids naturally found in other fats such as peanut oil, cheese, and milk, caprenin is not subject to Food and Drug Administration approval as fat substitutes are. Some of the sugar in Milky Way II is replaced with polydextrose, a low-calorie carbohydrate. The resulting candy bar is 25 percent lower in total calories and has 50 percent fewer calories from fat than the original Milky Way. By introducing Milky Way II, Mars became the first candy manufacturer to try to gain or retain calorie- and fat-conscious customers.

The company did not ignore its strengths, however. In late 1992, Mars began testing Mahogany, a line of premium chocolates, in Germany. These candies include truffles, bars, and boxed chocolates in reddish-brown and gold packaging with such South American motifs as palm trees and colonial style houses. The candy is relatively expensive, with a small box of eight truffles costing almost $4 and a 50-gram chocolate bar selling for more than $1.

Analysts have questioned Mars's future stability, particularly in light of the Mars brothers' reputed inability to share power with top managers who do not carry the family name, and it is unclear who will assume control of the company when they retire. For now, though, the company continues to rest near the top of the confectionery products, dog and cat food, and rice milling industries. With numerous internationally recognized brands, including the perennially top-ranked Snickers, Kal Kan, and Uncle Ben's, Mars is enjoying its unique recipe for success.

Further Reading: "Our Most Important Ingredient is Quality," McLean, VA: Mars, Inc., 1980; Fucini, Joseph J. and Fucini Suzy, *Entrepreneurs: The Men and Women behind Famous Brand Names and How They Made It,* Boston: G.K Hall & Co., 1985; Lawrence, Steve, "Bar Wars: Hershey Bites Mars," *Fortune,* July 8, 1985; "Mars Acquires the Dove Bar," *New York Times,* August 12, 1986; Saporito, Bill, "Uncovering Mars' Unknown Empire," *Fortune,* September 26, 1988; Katayama, Frederick H., "Snickers Ice Cream Bar," *Fortune,* August 13, 1990; Johnson, Bradley, "Kal Kan Goes Upscale," *Advertising Age,* September 24, 1990; Noble, Barbara Presley, "Will the American Pet Go for Haute Cuisine?," *New York Times,* December 16, 1990; "On the Wings of a Dove," *Washington Post,* May 13, 1991; Steinhauer, Jennifer, "America's Chocoholics: A Built-In Market for Confectioners," *New York Times,* July 14, 1991; "Mars Merger Talks Denied by Nestlé," *New York Times,* September 20, 1991; "A Little Illustrated Encyclopedia of M&M/Mars," Hackettstown, NJ, M&M/Mars, 1992; "P&G Sells Caprenin to Mars, Achieving Product's First Sale," *Wall Street Journal,* January 20, 1992; Fisher, Christy, "Milky Way Cuts Calories," *Advertising Age,* January 20, 1992; Cantoni, Craig J., "Quality Control from Mars," *Wall Street Journal,* January 27, 1992; Sprout, Alison L, "Milky Way Light," *Fortune,* February 24, 1992; Brenner, Joël Glenn, "Planet of the M&M's," *Washington Post Magazine,* April 12, 1992; Hwang, Suein L., "Peanuts and Caramel Combine to Create Sticky Competition," *Wall Street Journal,* April 14, 1992; Kitt, Janette, "Securing a Foothold for Confectionery," *Candy Industry,* July, 1992; Rutherford, Andrea C., "Candy Firms Roll Out 'Healthy' Sweets, but Snackers May Sour on the Products," *Wall Street Journal,* August 10, 1992; Koselka, Rita, "Candy Wars," *Forbes,* August 17, 1992; Mussey, Dagmar, and Laurel Wentz, "Mars Tries Premium Chocolate in Europe," *Advertising Age,* December 14, 1992.

—Janet Reinhart Hall

Applying Intelligence for Amenity Environments

Matsushita Electric Works, Ltd.

MATSUSHITA ELECTRIC WORKS, LTD.

1048, Kadoma
Osaka 571
Japan
(06) 908-1131
Fax: (06) 908-7053

Public Company
Incorporated: 1935 as Matsushita Electric Industrial
Employees: 25,200
Sales: ¥1.07 trillion (US$8.29 billion)
Stock Exchanges: Osaka
SICs: 2499 Wood Products, Nec; 3641 Electric Lamp Bulbs
   and Tubes; 3645 Residential Electric Lighting Fixtures;
   3699 Electrical Machinery, Equipment, and Supplies, Nec

Matsushita Electric Works (MEW) is the industrial counterpart of the better-known Matsushita Electric Industrial Co., Ltd. (MEI), makers of consumer electronic products under brand names including Panasonic and National. MEW's six operating divisions manufacture a wide variety of electrical, lighting, and building products in relative anonymity, with most observers assuming incorrectly that MEW is a subsidiary of MEI. While MEI retains 28 percent of MEW's stock, the latter operates independently, and its mix of products is probably closer to the original interests of Konosuke Matsushita, the charismatic founder and builder of the Matsushita business group.

Konosuke Matsushita was born in 1894 to a farming family. When his father was ruined by commodities speculation, Matsushita, who was nine years old at the time, went to work in a bicycle shop. He became interested in the growing number of uses for electricity in Japan, and worked for several years in an Osaka light bulb factory. In 1918, at the age of 23, Matsushita founded his own company in Osaka to manufacture electric plugs.

Matsushita's company survived its difficult first years and soon was benefiting from the robust economy of the 1920s. He added bicycle lights and electric heaters to his product line and aggressively cultivated clients in Japan's complex network of retailers, usually unwilling to do business with smaller, independent suppliers. Despite the onset of the Depression in 1929, Matsushita continued to add products to his catalog—radio sets and

dry batteries in 1931 and electric motors four years later. Matsushita delivered his products more cheaply than other suppliers, using volume and efficiency to keep his costs low. He also built a reputation as a generous and fair employer, able to inspire loyalty and hard work among employees. His popularity continued unabated until his death in 1989 at the age of 94.

On December 15, 1935, Matsushita incorporated his growing business as Matsushita Denki Sangyo—or Matsushita Electric Industrial—the name later applied solely to the consumer products group. The company prospered during World War II, when the Japanese economy required both innovative technology and maximum production from all manufacturers.

Matsushita and other Japanese industrialists eventually watched their factories destroyed and the Japanese economy reorganized according to the plans of General Douglas MacArthur and his occupying officials. Like many other business leaders, Konosuke Matsushita was marked for early retirement by the Allies for his support of the Japanese war effort, but a threatened strike on the part of loyal trade unions convinced the occupation authorities otherwise: Matsushita remained as chairman.

It was at this point, when many of the country's largest conglomerates were being broken into smaller pieces by the authorities, that Matsushita was forced to spin off Matsushita Electric Works, to produce industrial complements to MEI's consumer products. In 1947 Masaharu Niwa was named president of the new company, which concentrated on wiring devices for both residential and commercial structures. Given Japan's massive demand for new construction, MEW needed only to survive the first few chaotic postwar years in order to win a virtually unlimited market for its basic products. With Konosuke Matsushita backing MEW by means of his substantial equity holdings, the young company was soon prospering.

In 1951 MEW was listed on the Osaka Stock Exchange, an indication of its need for fresh capital to fund further growth. The following year the company introduced a line of fluorescent lighting fixtures, the beginning of its extensive involvement in lighting systems of all kinds. As the Japanese economy picked up steam during the mid-1950s, MEW continued to add a variety of products to its collection, most of them related to the construction industry but some aimed at the growing consumer markets usually handled by its sister company. In 1953, for example, MEW introduced electric hair dryers and shavers, creating an appliance division to which a healthy portion of the company's sales can be attributed. More typical was its 1958 offering of plastic gutters for the residential housing market, a market for which MEW would eventually develop scores of products ranging from kitchen and bath fixtures to exterior siding.

In the 1960s the Japanese economy came into its own as a global industrial leader. Both of Konosuke Matsushita's creations grew at a prodigious pace, and MEW further strengthened its position in industrial electrical components. Not as dependent on international sales as its parent, MEW waited until the 1970s before making substantial overseas investments. In 1974 it established MS-Relais GmbH in West Germany to manufacture electric relays for sale in Europe, a market that became very important for MEW. Also in 1974, MEW ventured for the first time into the U.S. market with the establishment of Aromat Corporation. Since then, MEW has increasingly emphasized local production rather than export, adding other plants in Taiwan and Thailand as well as sales corporations in seven countries. To support these growing international facilities, MEW created a Dutch finance company, Matsushita Electric Works Netherlands.

In 1977, after serving for 30 years as the company's president, Masaharu Niwa was elected chairman of MEW. Zenichi Kozaki became president, while the 82-year-old Konosuke Matsushita remained a very active director and executive advisor. Matsushita had by this time become something of a prophet of Japanese business methods, authoring nearly 50 books promoting "the peace and happiness of society through business." MEW became active in the growing high-technology electronics field when it added an electronics and plastic materials group. Along with another addition, the automation controls group, this electronics initiative gave MEW a foothold in a segment of an industry certain to benefit from Japan's always-advancing technological expertise.

The majority of the company's business, however, remained basic lighting, wiring, and building-material products, which together have accounted for approximately 75 percent of corporate revenue. With the death of Konosuke Matsushita in 1989, MEW in a sense launched into a new era, though the venerable Masaharu Niwa remained as honorary chairman until his death in January of 1992. Still 28 percent owned by its sister company, MEW remained firmly in the Matsushita group, though the company had demonstrated its ability to develop and market an increasingly wide array of high-tech and consumer goods on its own.

MEW's strides in these areas continued into the 1990s as the company set new sales records—for fiscal year 1991 the figure reached just over ¥1 trillion, up 4.5 percent over 1990. While lighting sales remained about the same, and automation controls recorded a 6.8 percent drop, substantial improvement was recorded in home appliances and building projects, which experienced increases of 12 and 8 percent, respectively. In addition, net income hit a record ¥34.8 billion.

Since fixtures and appliances account for more than three-fourths of MEW's product line, the company naturally turned to large showrooms as sales venues; in 1991 there were 47 such showrooms scattered throughout Japan. With an eye toward the company's future, MEW also invested in projects that would pave the way for good contractor relations and technological

advancements. Among these was the NAiS Techno Plaza in Tokyo, which provided a place for architects, contractors, and other building professionals to highlight their services. The company also operated 21 research-and-development laboratories—to which 4.2 percent of MEW's expenditures were apportioned—and a sales and marketing computer network called SIS (Strategic Information System) that was largest in use by any Japanese manufacturer. In the construction arena, MEW joined with other companies in the development of large housing units, factory automation, and communications networks. In addition, MEW entered into a joint venture with Mitsui and Co. and the Kinden Corporation to participate in the "intelligent," or automated-service building market. MEW has also won awards for its systems and designs, including two for its fire alarm systems.

Overseas operations, at 6.2 percent of total sales, continued to grow. Matsushita Electronic Materials Inc. was established in Forest Grove City, Oregon, to manufacture multi-layer printed circuit-board materials. On the other U.S. coast, in New Jersey, Aromat Corporation made automation-control components like those manufactured for the European market by MS-Relais.

With the support of its sister company, as well as its growing presence in foreign markets—38 manufacturing and sales operations in 17 countries—Matsushita Electric Works, Ltd. should soon enjoy much greater recognition.

Principal Subsidiaries: National Wood Products Co., Ltd.; Meiji National Co., Ltd.; Matsushita Gaiso Kenzai Co., Ltd.; Kitakyushu Matsushita Electric Works, Ltd.; Tatsuno Matsushita Electric Works, Ltd.; Obihiro Matsushita Electric Works, Ltd.; Mohka Matsushita Electric Works, Ltd.; NTP Co., Ltd.; Oki Denki Bohsai Co., Ltd.; National Electric Clock Co., Ltd.; Owari Matsushita Electric Works, Ltd.; Aromat Corporation (U.S.A.); Aromat Canada Inc.; SDS-Relais AG (Germany); SDS-Relais (Schweiz) AG (Switzerland); SDS-Relais Austria Ges.mbH; SDS-Relais Limited (U.K.); SDS-Relais Italia S.R.L. (Italy); SDS-Relais France SARL; MS-Relais GmbH (Germany); Matsushita Electric Works (Thailand) Ltd.; NPL Taiwan Co., Ltd.

Further Reading: "History of Matsushita Electric Works, Ltd.," Osaka, Matsushita Electric Works, Ltd., 1989; Matsushita Electric Works, Ltd. Annual Report, 1991.

—Jonathan Martin
updated by Jim Bowman

MATTEL, INC.

333 Continental Boulevard
El Segundo, California 90245-5012
U.S.A.
(310) 524-2000
Fax: (310) 524-4443

Public Company
Incorporated: 1948
Employees: 15,000
Sales: $1.85 billion
Stock Exchanges: New York
SICs: 3944 Games, Toys & Children's Vehicles; 3942 Dolls
    & Stuffed Toys

Mattel, Inc. designs, develops, manufactures, markets, and distributes a wide variety of toy products worldwide. The company's products comprise a number of core toy lines, including Barbie fashion dolls, doll clothing, and accessories, Hot Wheels toy die cast vehicles, Disney toys, See 'N Say talking toys, a line of large dolls including Li'l Miss, Magic Nursery, P. J. Sparkles, and various new product introductions. Most of Mattel's toys are made overseas in manufacturing facilities in China, Malaysia, Italy, Indonesia, and Mexico. Today, Mattel represents the world's second largest toy company.

Mattel was founded in 1944 by Elliot and Ruth Handler. The youngest of ten children of Polish immigrants, Ruth Handler was a secretary for Paramount Pictures in Los Angeles when she married Elliot Handler, an industrial engineer. Handler started out designing light fixtures but soon began making furniture for sale out of his garage. The business attracted four partners and quickly rose to become a $2 million enterprise making giftware and costume jewelry. By 1945 Elliot Handler grew restless and wanted a new business approach to remain competitive in the fast-changing postwar world. Handler's plans led to a dispute with his partners and he sold his interest in the company at a loss. Meanwhile, in 1944 Ruth hooked up with an old friend, Harold Matson. They started Mattel Creations with Elliott designing products. The name Mattel was formed by combining Matson's last name with Handler's first name. Ill health soon forced Matson to sell out.

Mattel first entered the picture frame business using scrap plastic and wood. With the leftover wood slats and plastic,

Handler designed doll house furniture. Matson manufactured and Ruth Handler then formed a simple sales organization, and the company was off to a winning start. In its first year, the company pulled in $100,000 and netted $30,000.

The Handlers had little business experience and even less capital, but the demographics of a huge baby boom plus a virtual toyless market place immediately after World War II gave them a unique opportunity to make their mark. Even so, it took them a couple of years to begin to see profits. In 1946, another low cost line of molded furniture with meticulous detail put the Handlers out of the doll furniture business. Because of their introduction of a "birdy bank" and a "make believe makeup set," however, they managed to break even, and in the following year the Handlers introduced the first in a long string of hits in the toy industry. The "Uke-a-Doodle," a miniature plastic ukelele, was an immediate success and drew large orders. In 1948, the Handlers introduced another hit—a new all-plastic piano with raised black keys. Although a winner, the company lost ten cents for each piano it sold because of quality problems relating to the die-cast sound mechanism breaking loose from the plastic.

These early business experiences taught the Handlers some poignant lessons in the necessities of avoiding obsolescent products, ruinous price competition, poor cost control, and product quality problems. They realized that a successful business had to produce unique and original products of superior quality and strength that could not be easily copied by competitors.

In 1948, the company incorporated in the state of California. At the same time, the Handlers and an outside inventor began developing a music box employing a unique mechanism. A shortage of capital and the refusal of banks to gamble on the struggling young firm put the project on hold. However, with a $20,000 loan from Ruth Handler's brother-in-law, Mattel completed the project and produced another winner. As Elliot Handler later recalled, "our music box had a patented mechanism which had continuous play value because it operated only when the child turned the crank. It was different, it was well made, and because we were able to mass-produce it, the price was lower than the imports." By taking an old world idea and adapting it to modern production techniques, the Handlers beat out their Swiss competition, which up to then had dominated the domestic market for music boxes. By 1968, Mattel had sold more than 50 million of the toy music boxes.

The success of the music box taught the Handlers a few other lessons. First, they discovered that child participation was essential for any quality toy, and that children should be able to interact with a toy and want to play with it often and for extended periods of time. Second, the Handlers recognized that a toy with lasting appeal is preferable to short-lived faddish products and can serve as a basis for other toys to follow.

The year 1955 brought other important firsts for Mattel. Sales reached $5 million a year, the company introduced another hit—Burp Guns—and the Handlers decided to make a gamble that would forever change the toy business. In what seemed a risky venture, the Handlers agreed to sponsor a 15 minute segment of Walt Disney's Mickey Mouse Club on the ABC Television Network. The Handlers signed for 52 weeks at a cost of $500,000, equal to Mattel's net worth at the time. Up until this time, toy manufacturers relied primarily on retailers to show and sell their products, and advertising occurred only during the holiday season; never before had a toy company spent money on advertising year-round. With television, however, toys could be marketed directly to children throughout the country. Thus with the slogan "you can tell its Mattel, it's swell," the Handlers began a marketing revolution in the toy industry that produced an immediate payoff. The company sold many toy Burp Guns and made their brand name well known among their viewing audience.

In 1957, the company, exploiting the popularity of television Westerns, introduced toy replicas of classic Western guns and holsters. From the basic Burp Gun mechanism, Mattel developed the "Fanner 50" Western pistol and a toy version of the Winchester rifle, complete with ejecting bullets. Mattel's sales reached $9 million and the following year hit $14 million.

Then in 1959, Mattel made toy industry history with the introduction of the Barbie Doll, the best-selling toy of all time. The idea for the doll originated with Ruth Handler, who had observed that their daughter favored adult-looking paper dolls to baby dolls. So the Handlers set to work designing a teenage fashion model doll and, despite a cool reception at the 1959 New York Toy Fair, the result was a smash hit that propelled Mattel into the national spotlight. Barbie, the famed doll named after the Handlers' own daughter, soon prompted official fan clubs across the United States, which by 1968 had a total membership of about 1.5 million. Mattel marketed Barbie as an insatiable consumer of clothes and accessories, which were sold separately, and soon they provided her a boyfriend, the Ken doll.

After the phenomenal success of Barbie, Mattel entered the competitive large doll market in 1960 with another winner—Chatty Cathy, the first talking doll. That year, Mattel made its first public stock offering, and, by 1963, its common stock was listed on the New York Stock Exchange. Mattel's sales skyrocketed from $26 million in 1963 to more than $100 million in 1965.

Throughout the 1960s, the company continued to introduce popular toys: Baby First Step (the first doll to walk by itself), live action dolls with moving eyes and mouths, See 'N Say educational toys, the Vac-U-Form machine, and an entire line of Thingmaker activity toys including Creepy Crawlers, Fun Flowers, Fright Factory, and Incredible Edibles. Another spectacular hit was introduced in 1968—Hot Wheels miniature model cars.

During this time, the company began aggressively diversifying its operations into a worldwide enterprise with a host of acquisitions: Dee and Cee Toy Co., Toronto (1962); Standard Plastics, New Jersey, a producer of vinyl cases (1963); Hong Kong Industrial Co., Ltd. and Precision Moulds, Ltd., Hong Kong (1966); Rosebud Dolls Ltd., a British doll manufacturing firm (1967); Monogram Models (1968); A & A Die Casting Company (1968); Ratti Vallensasca and Mebetoys, Milan, Italy

(1969); Ebiex S.A. Brussels, Belgium (1969); H & H Plastics Co., Gardena, California (1969); Metaframe Corp., Maywood, New Jersey (1969); Ringling Bros. and Barnum and Bailey (1970); and others. In 1968, Mattel reincorporated in Delaware and by the end of the decade it was the world's number one toy maker.

But the good times soon soured. In 1970, Mattel's plant in Mexico was destroyed by fire, and the following year a shipyard strike in the Far East cut off their toy supplies. To maintain the appearance of corporate growth Seymour Rosenberg, executive vice president and chief financial officer, fixed the books by reporting orders as sales, although many of the orders had been canceled and shipments had not been made. For two years Mattel issued false and misleading financial reports until 1973, when the company reported a $32 million loss just three weeks after stockholders had been assured that the company was in sound financial condition. Mattel's stock plummeted and the Security and Exchange Commission (SEC) stepped in to investigate. Before Judge Robert Takasugi of the federal district court in Los Angeles, Ruth Handler and Rosenberg pleaded no contest to the SEC charges.

Rosenberg was fired, the banks pressured the Handlers to resign, and the court ordered Mattel to restructure its board so that the majority would be company outsiders. Furthermore, the court fined Ruth Handler and Rosenberg each $57,000 and gave them 41-year sentences, which were suspended on the condition that they both perform 500 hours of charitable work annually for five years. Finally, in 1980 the Handlers cashed in most of their Mattel stock, ending their involvement in the company they had founded. Comprising approximately 12 percent of the company, the stock was worth about $18.5 million. Ruth Handler then went on to start Nearly Me, a company producing prosthetic breasts for mastectomy patients.

A new management team under Arthur S. Spear, a Mattel vice president, replaced the Handlers in 1975 and by 1977 the company had returned to profitability. By 1980, Mattel was running a slew of other businesses, including the Ringling Bros., Barnum & Baily Circus, Shipstad & Johnson's Ice Follies, Western Publishing—the largest publisher of children's books—and an entire line of electronic toys, most notably Intellivision video games.

But Mattel stumbled badly for much of the 1980s. Many of their business acquisitions turned out to be unprofitable and had to be sold. Also, a big slump in video game sales in the early 1980s drove Mattel out of the video game business with a $394 million loss, putting the company on the edge of bankruptcy. The company might have gone under if the New York venture capital firms E. M. Warburg, Pincus & Co. and Drexel Burnham Lambert had not stepped in with $231 million in 1984 to save the company from the video game debacle. Still, in 1985 the company fell behind Hasbro as the world's largest toymaker. Two years later it took another $113 million loss when the market for its Master of the Universe toy line for boys evaporated. As a result of Mattel's troubles, its stock plummeted from a peak of 30⅝ in 1982 to 10¼ in 1987.

That year, however, Mattel's fortunes took a dramatic upswing when John W. Amerman was appointed as the new chairperson. Amerman had joined the company in 1980 as head of Mattel's international division. Under his direction the division's sales had quadrupled, far outpacing the profitability of Mattel's domestic operations. In his new role, Amerman moved quickly to cut Mattel's overhead by closing 40 percent of the company's manufacturing capacity, including plants in California, Taiwan, and the Philippines. He slashed the payroll by 150 at Mattel's corporate headquarters in California, saving an estimated $30 million annually. Mattel also refinanced high-cost debt and curbed advertising costs. (Mattel had been the first to pioneer in the early 1980s the development of television programming based on a toy line—a 30 minute promotional show disguised as entertainment.) Most important, Amerman turned the company around by focusing on core brand names with staying power such as Barbie and Hot Wheels, and by making selective investments in the development of new toys.

Despite a lackluster economy and generally flat sales in the toy industry, Amerman's strategy has paid big dividends for Mattel. The Barbie line was bolstered and expanded to include approximately 50 different dolls per year and about 250 accessory items, including everything from shoes and clothing to linens, backpacks, furniture, and a cosmetics line. A promotional campaign in honor of Barbie's 30th birthday in 1989 propelled her onto the cover of *Smithsonian Magazine,* confirming her status as a true American icon. By 1991, Mattel estimated that 95 percent of all girls in the United States aged three to 11 owned Barbie dolls. In fact, Barbie has been so good for Mattel that between 1987 and 1992, sales shot up from $430 million to nearly $1 billion, accounting for about half of the company's $1.85 billion in sales. As a result of this phenomenal growth, Mattel opened a new state-of-the-art Barbie manufacturing plant in 1992 just outside Jakarta, Indonesia. Mattel's emphasis on other core brands including Hot Wheels die cast vehicles, large dolls, Disney products, and See 'N Say educational preschool toys have also provided a string of continuous hits. The company captured a majority share of the large doll market with winning lines in Li'l Miss and Magic Nursery. A popular new line of Disney infant and preschool toys featuring such animated stars as Mickey Mouse and Donald Duck was introduced in 1988.

Mattel has also pushed aggressively into other areas of the toy business, including the plush toys, games, boys' action toys, and activity toys categories, which comprise 46 percent of the total toy market. By entering these areas, Mattel has increased its participation in the total industry business from 34 to approximately 80 percent to become a full-line toy company. The company has made a particularly strong move into the toys for boys market, where it has been traditionally weak. Since 1991 Mattel has introduced a host of new products including Bruno the Bad Dog, a monster truck that changes into a ferocious dog, action figures based on the upcoming Arnold Schwarzenegger movie, *Last Action Hero,* and Gak, a gooey substance that stretches and oozes.

A strengthened strategic alliance with The Walt Disney Company in 1991 allows Mattel to sponsor attractions and to develop and sell toys at three Disney theme parks. The agreement is anticipated to give Mattel unparalleled exposure as more than 50 million children, parents, and grandparents visit the parks each year. Mattel also negotiated the exclusive rights to sell dolls, stuffed characters, and preschool toys based upon such movie favorites as *Cinderella, Beauty and the Beast,* and *Aladdin.* The agreement produced approximately $200 million in revenue for Mattel during 1991. Moreover, Mattel has the exclusive rights, once held by Hasbro, to sell stuffed Mickeys and other top Disney characters starting in 1993. Amerman predicts that by the year 1995, sales for the Disney line will produce volume of $500 million.

Beyond Disney, Mattel reached an agreement with Hanna-Barbera in November 1991 to market toys based on the cartoon characters Yogi Bear, Boo-Boo, Cindy Bear, and the Flintstones. Another agreement with Turner Broadcasting allows Mattel to develop and sell Tom and Jerry products. The company also entered the activity toy area with the acquisition in 1991 of Aviva Sports, Inc., a developer of sport toys, and through an agreement with the children's cable network, Nickelodeon, to sell a new line of activity toys, including its Gak and the Color Writer. A push into the game market led Mattel in 1992 to acquire International Games, Inc., the producer of such profitable core franchises as the UNO and Skip-Bo card games.

Mattel sees its best growth opportunities overseas. Currently, the company has 30 affiliate organizations around the world, more than any other toy company. Fifty percent of Mattel's sales volume is achieved in international markets. Since 1982, sales for its international division have exploded from $135 to $825 million in 1992. The company believes that there are sound reasons to be optimistic for dramatic sales growth in the international markets in the future. Almost twice the number of children live in Europe as in the United States, and sales growth is anticipated to be bolstered in Europe by the arrival of Toys 'R Us and other toy superstores. Mattel expects that by 1995 sales volume in Europe will outpace sales in the U. S. market.

Mattel is also counting on its superstar toy lines—Barbie, Hot Wheels, and other core products—to capture a large share of the world's second largest toy market, Japan. Mattel is the only U. S. toy company with a wholly owned marketing organization in Japan, giving it an advantage over other U. S. toy companies among the Japanese. Thus, with its expanding product line in both the domestic and international markets, Mattel appears well positioned to take advantage of new growth opportunities in the future.

Principal Subsidiaries: Arco Toys, Ltd; Aviva Sports, Inc.; International Games, Inc., Mattel Pty., Ltd. (Australia); Mattel Belgium; Mattel Canada, Inc.; Mattel Chile S.A.; Mattel Scandinavia A/S; Corolle Anselme (France); Mattel France S.A.; Mattel GmbH (Germany); Mattel Greece S.A.; Mattel B.V. Holland; Mattel (HK) Ltd. (Hong Kong); Precision Moulds Ltd. (Hong Kong); Mattel Toys KFT (Hungary); PT Mattel Indonesia; Mattel Toys (India); Mattel Italy SRL; Mattel K.K. (Japan); Mattel (K.L.) SDN BHD (Kuala Lumpur, Malaysia); Mattel Malaysia SDN BHD (Penang, Malaysia); Mabamex, S.A. de C.V.; Montoi, S.A. de C.V.; Matco (Puerto Rico); Mattel Toys PTE Ltd. (Singapore); Mattel España S.A.; Mattel A.G. (Switzerland); Mattel Asia Ltd. (Taiwan); Mattel U.K. Ltd.; Mattel Corgi (U.K.).

Further Reading: Everybody's Business, 1st ed. (1980); *Guide to Company Profiles,* (New York: Doubleday, 1990); ''The Impossible Is Really Possible: The Story of Mattel,'' *Newcomen Address,* 1968; ''Mattel Has to Play Harder Than Ever,'' *Business Week,* May 25, 1987; ''Barbie at 30,'' *Forbes,* November 1988; ''Playing Favorites,'' *Marketing & Media Decisions,* March 1990; ''Barbie Does Budapest,'' *Forbes,* January 7, 1991; ''Looking For A Few Good Boy Toys,'' *Business Week,* February 17, 1992.

—Bruce P. Montgomery

MAXUS

MAXUS ENERGY CORPORATION

717 North Harwood St.
Dallas, Texas 75201-6594
U.S.A.
(214) 953-2000
Fax: (214) 953-2996

Public Company
Incorporated: 1910 as Diamond Alkali Corporation
Employees: 1,939
Sales: $718.4 million
Stock Exchanges: New York Pacific Basel Geneva Zürich
SICs: 1311 Crude Petroleum & Natural Gas; 1381 Drilling
   Oil & Gas Wells

Maxus Energy Corporation is an independent crude oil and
natural gas exploration and production company based in Dallas, Texas, with international activity in Indonesia and 13 other
countries and domestic activity primarily in the mid-continent
and Gulf of Mexico regions of North America.

Maxus was created in April 1987 from the domestic and international exploration, production, and geothermal operations of
Diamond Shamrock Corporation, which traced its history to the
Diamond Alkali Corporation, a chemical operation founded in
1910. However, Maxus bears little if any resemblance to that
earlier organization due to the restructurings, acquisitions, and
divestitures of the 1970s and 1980s.

The Diamond Alkali Corporation was founded in 1910 by four
Pittsburgh-based glass makers who wanted to manufacture their
own soda ash, the major raw material in glass production. They
incorporated the Diamond Alkali Corporation on March 21,
1910, and with a capitalization of $1.2 million built a soda ash
plant in Painesville, Ohio, on the Lake Erie shore. They planned
to sell the plant's excess capacity to large glass producers, but
before the Painesville plant began operation in 1912 they were
blocked by the established soda ash manufacturers, who signed
long-term, lucratively priced contracts with the major glass
manufactures. This action might have bankrupted Diamond Alkali but for World War I which dramatically increased the
demand for glass.

After the war, the company, under the direction of president T.
R. Evans, the son of two of the company's founders, expanded.
This expansion seemed at times haphazard but it usually took
into account synergies in different industrial processes. The
company began making bicarbonate of soda in 1918. In 1920 it
built a silicate of soda plant in Cincinnati and in 1925 it expanded the Painesville plant to produce calcium carbonates,
cement, and coke. Diamond waltzed successfully through the
Depression. In 1929 it inaugurated chlorine production and in
1933 it reported profits of $3 million on sales of about $13
million.

The company continued to be profitable after T. R. Evans died
suddenly in 1931. Even so, Evans's son, Raymond F. Evans—
then a senior chemistry major at Princeton and a major stockholder—was worried that Diamond was stagnating and without
a research department would eventually lose its place in the
market. He moved to address these concerns. In 1936 he organized—with the help of sympathetic directors—a project to
substitute dolomitic limestone for ordinary limestone in soda
ash production and produce a new by-product, magnesium
oxide. The project was a success, and when World War II
increased magnesium demand for use in incendiary bombs,
Evans was recruited to run a government magnesium plant. In
1942 he established Diamond Alkali's first research laboratory.
The following year he was named the company's general manager and shortly thereafter executive vice-president and then
president and CEO.

As CEO Evans decentralized the company. In 1946 he broke
ground for a second chlorine/caustic soda plant in Deer Park in
Houston. He added detergents to Diamond's product mix and in
1948 moved its headquarters from Pittsburgh to Cleveland. In
the decade that followed, Diamond Alkali entered several new
markets, producing chromic acid, perchlorethelyne and chlorinated methanes like carbon tetrachloride. It entered the agricultural chemicals market with the acquisition of Kolker Chemical
Works, established itself in the production of methylchloride,
methylenechloride, and chloroform by acquiring Belle Alkali
Company in West Virginia, and built an agricultural chemicals
plant in Mexico. Most importantly, it also launched itself into
the plastics business with the manufacture of polyvinyl chloride
(PVC) at Deer Park.

Evans continued to back this expansion with a strong commitment to research. In 1951 he inaugurated the Technical Center
at Painesville and in 1961 inaugurated the Diamond Research
Center at Concord.

In the 1960s Diamond made several major acquisitions and
expanded into new operations. It acquired Chemical Process
Company, Fiber Chemical Corporation, Harte & Company, and
Nopco Chemical; it bought and then sold iron ore manufacturer
and Great Lakes shipper Piclands Mather. It organized a specialty chemical division and expanded its production of bulk
industrial chemicals and plastics and built a new chlorine/
caustic and PVC plant in Delaware City, Delaware.

In the mid-1960s, Evans recognized that petrochemical combines were the wave of the future. Since he did not want
Diamond Alkali, like so many other mid-sized chemical companies, to be acquired by an oil colossus, he approached Shamrock
Oil & Gas with a merger plan and in 1967, the two companies
joined.

Like Diamond Alkali, Amarillo-based Shamrock Oil & Gas had been nourished by Pittsburgh money. Banker Henry Fownes had provided financial stability while engineer and oil economist J. Harold Dunn had guided the company into becoming a sizable petroleum producer and refiner with its own string of service stations in the Southwest. Before its merger with Diamond Alkali, Shamrock had been too small to diversify into chemicals but profitable enough to be a takeover target for the major oil producers.

Raymond F. Evans ran the renamed Diamond Shamrock Corporation with help from C. A. Cash of Shamrock Oil & Gas. In the first half of the 1970s, the company expanded its oil and gas exploration efforts, built a manganese dioxide plant in Baltimore and a chrome chemicals facility in North Carolina.

But while the company was quite successful—it earned $140 million on sales of $1.4 billion in 1976—its leadership was aging. In 1976 senior management selected 44-year-old William H. Bricker to lead Diamond Shamrock into the 1980s and beyond. Trained as a horticulturist, Bricker had joined the company in 1969 after a brilliant sales career with California Spray and Chem-Agro. Once on board at Diamond Shamrock, he had risen quickly, first turning around the company's ag-chemicals business and then becoming a group vice-president in 1971, president of Diamond Shamrock in 1974, and CEO in 1976.

Before becoming CEO, Bricker had been well liked and perceived as a team player. That perception soon changed. In 1979 he set out to make Diamond a major energy company. Over Evans's objection, he acquired Falcon Seaboard Inc., a coal producer, for $250 million. When, that same year, he moved the corporate headquarters to Dallas from Cleveland, Evans resigned in protest. "I had the feeling from personal contact," Evans later told *Business Week*, "that he wasn't going to listen to anyone." Diamond Shamrock was still doing very well at this time. In 1981 when Bricker laid out $220 million for Amherst Coal, the company posted record earnings of $230 million on sales of $3.4 billion. An impressed market boosted Diamond's stock near its all-time high of $40 per share.

The events of the following year, however, were a portent of things to come. Though recession and lower energy prices caused earnings to fall 35 percent, the company spent $161 million to buy drilling rights in Alaska's Beaufort Sea. By year's end the price of a Diamond share had fallen to $17. In 1983 Bricker made what both *Business Week* and *The Wall Street Journal* called one of the worst oil acquisitions of the decade. He acquired Natomas, a struggling San Francisco-based oil company, for $1.5 billion. According to *Business Week,* that price amounted to $12.50 a barrel for Natomas's oil, twice what reserves were fetching in the open market. Later it was discovered that Natomas's price was being manipulated by arbitrager Ivan Boesky and Diamond Shamrock's investment advisor Kidder, Peabody. At year's end a dry hole in Diamond's Beaufort Sea drilling venture led to a big write-down and its first ever loss of $60 million.

After retrenchment in 1984, Bricker tentatively agreed to sell Diamond to Occidental Petroleum in 1985 for Oxy stock worth $28 a share. Bricker later backed away from the deal. Instead, he restructured the company and instituted a massive stock buyback which he financed by jettisoning whole divisions, including the chemical business. Falling energy prices, which had devalued Natomas, led the company to take $891 million in write offs. Losses for the year totaled $605 million.

Dogged by losses and debt caused both by poor investment and by falling energy prices, Bricker struggled to maintain share prices through buybacks. In 1986 he refused a $16-per-share acquisition offer from T. Boone Pickens. After Pickens offered to buy 20 percent of Diamond stock for $15 a share early in 1987, he announced a last reorganization and then resigned. The company would split into Maxus Energy and Diamond Shamrock. Maxus would hold oil, natural gas, and coal production assets while Diamond Shamrock would include refining and marketing. Prudential Insurance agreed to buy $300 million in Diamond convertible preferred stock for which it would get an annual dividend of 9.75 percent, three seats on Diamond's board, and veto power over takeover. Diamond would use Prudential's investment to buy back 20 million shares of common stock.

After Bricker resigned, *Business Week* published an article which laid Diamond Shamrock's troubles squarely at his feet. The article questioned many of his decisions—especially the Natomas deal—explored the possibility of conflicts of interest, gave evidence of his inability to listen to directors or other senior management, and described a lavish corporate culture out of step with a debt-ridden company.

Charles L. Blackburn, a Shell Oil executive who had recently joined Diamond Shamrock, became Maxus Energy's chairman, president, and CEO. Blackburn aimed to make Maxus lean and profitable and to set clear goals: divest non-exploration and production operations, cut $20 million in overhead costs, eliminate non-essential activities, confine North American exploration to proven basins, and broaden international exposure commensurate with resources.

Maxus took the first steps toward all of these goals in Blackburn's first year. It sold its coal company for $135 million, signed a letter of intent to sell its geothermal assets and divested several non-oil and gas businesses. It sold its British North Sea properties as part of an effort to divest properties it had little control over. It cut more than $20 million in administrative costs—closing offices, eliminating non-essential activities, and consolidating departments such as oil trading and natural gas marketing.

Divestment of the coal company led to a $51.1 million first quarter loss while a write-down of geothermal assets and Alaskan coal reserves caused a second quarter non-cash charge of $380 million. For 1987, Maxus reported a loss of $539.6 million, compared to a restated $115 million in 1986. The 1987 loss without discontinued operations and write-offs was $106.9 million compared to $193.1 million in 1986. Cash flow rose while long-term debt declined. At this point Maxus's activities encompassed four North American divisions, including: holdings in the Anadarko Basin of the Texas Panhandle and western Oklahoma; the Williston Basin of North Dakota and Montana; the Powder River Basin in Wyoming and Montana; the Permian Basin in west Texas and eastern New Mexico; the Texas and Louisiana Gulf coast areas; and the Western Canadian Sedimentary Basin. Its international operations were primarily in Indonesia and the Dutch North Sea, with ongoing exploration activities in Africa, Asia, Europe, and South America.

Early in 1988, Blackburn outlined a plan for the future which included continued cost cutting, aggressive sales, sales of non-strategic assets, and most importantly the application of new conceptual plays in proven basins in order to reduce risks and operations costs while exposing the company to the possibility of finding reserves that went beyond replacement of production. This strategy proved successful despite accounting changes and weak oil prices which led to a 1988 loss of $131.6 million. To cut costs, Blackburn refinanced some debt and reorganized the U.S. exploration and production staff, closing offices and relocating approximately 120 employees to Dallas. He sold its Dutch North Sea holdings for more than $22 million and selected U.S. properties for $38 million. Most importantly, a new conceptual play rewarded Maxus with its largest oil discovery ever in the Intan and Widuri fields of the Southeast Sumatra area of Indonesia.

Clearly Blackburn was on the right track. The *Wall Street Transcript* gave him its 1988 Gold Award in the Oil & Gas Industry and described him as a ''nonconformist executive with the conviction and confidence that inspires creativity and enthusiasm.'' Regarding the Indonesian discoveries the paper's analyst commented that he ''took a subbase that had been condemned and went back with a new and different geological concept and made two significant discoveries. I think it takes a person like Blackburn at the top of an exploration company to give the people in the field the freedom to take a whole different look at the property.''

In 1989 Blackburn made significant progress toward rectifying Maxus's balance sheet problems. He sold oil and gas assets (including its Canadian operations and a 10 percent share of its leases in Northwest Java) for $310 million and used some of the proceeds to reduce debt balance by $123 million and replace $80 million of senior debt with a subordinated zero-coupon convertible debt issue.

With Maxus's balance sheet problems behind it, Blackburn turned to the company's basic business—finding and selling oil and gas. He sped exploitation of Intan production and created the Frontier Group, a team of geologists and geophysicists dedicated to developing new plays worldwide. In North America, he narrowed the focus to the Gulf Coast and mid-continent areas and confined exploration to prospects with at least 12 billion cubic feet of gas and finding costs of $2 per barrel of oil equivalent. Finally, he focused marketing efforts and aggregated supplies to realize premium prices for volatilely priced natural gas.

In 1990 higher Indonesian production combined with lower debt and depreciation costs carried Maxus to its first ever profitable year when it earned $7.3 million on revenues of $685 million. Revenues continued to grow in 1991 when they reached a record $791 million. But because of falling energy prices the company lost $11.2 million. Blackburn continued to focus the company on areas which could be most profitable. He sold Maxus's Rocky Mountain and Permian Basin assets and acquired reserves that made it the second largest natural gas producer in the Texas Panhandle. International revenues exceeded domestic revenues for the first time. In terms of production Maxus had become a domestic natural gas producer and an international oil producer.

In 1992 the company continued to strengthen its position despite the unpredictability of energy prices. In October of that year Maxus and Kidder, Peabody & Company settled a suit in which Maxus alleged that Kidder executive Martin A. Seagal had provided inside information that arbitrager Ivan Boesky had used to run up Natomas's price before Diamond Shamrock had purchased that company. Kidder agreed to pay Maxus $125 million in cash plus an additional $40 million for warrants to buy Maxus stock.

Further Reading: Bricker, W. H., *Diamond Shamrock Corporation,* Newcomen Society Number 1064, 1977; Mason, Todd and G. David Wallace, ''The Downfall of a CEO,'' *Business Week,* February 16, 1987.

—Jordan Wankoff

MAXWELL COMMUNICATION CORPORATION PLC

33 Holborn
London EC1N 2HB
United Kingdom
(071) 822-2345
Fax: (071) 353-3398

Public Company
Incorporated: 1964 as British Printing Corporation
Employees: 14,360
Sales: £996.90 million (US$1.45 billion)
Stock Exchanges: London Paris Brussels Antwerp Frankfurt Toronto Montreal New York Tokyo
SICs: 2711 Newspapers: Publishing, or Publishing & Printing; 2721 Periodicals: Publishing, or Publishing & Printing

Maxwell Communication Corporation plc (MCC) was formerly one of the world's ten largest media groups, with interests in information services and electronic publishing, school and college publishing, language instruction, and reference book and professional publishing. An aggressive, controversial player in the international business world throughout its history, the company's dissolution in the early 1990s was an astonishing one. The mysterious death of MCC's founder and chairman, Robert Maxwell, in 1991 triggered one of the most spectacular corporate collapses in modern-day business history.

Maxwell was born Jan Ludvik Hoch in the village of Slatina Solo in the Czechoslovakian province of Ruthenia in 1923. His family was part of the prewar Hungarian Jewish community that had lived in this region since the 16th century. After the outbreak of World War II, Maxwell succeeded in escaping to the United Kingdom, where he enlisted in the British army. By the end of the war he had been promoted to the rank of captain and had been awarded the Military Cross for bravery. In 1946 Maxwell became a naturalized U.K. citizen. Most members of Maxwell's family in Ruthenia were victims of the Holocaust.

The origins of MCC can be traced to Maxwell's early postwar career in occupied Berlin. Shortly after the war Maxwell made contact with Ferdinand Springer, who before the war had been Germany's leading publisher of scientific books. Maxwell agreed to act as Springer Verlag GmbH & Co. KG's representa-

tive outside Germany. Maxwell's new U.K. company, European Periodicals, Publicity and Advertising Corporation (EPPAC), was granted the exclusive worldwide distribution rights for Springer's journals and books. In 1949 Maxwell helped form a new company called Lange, Maxwell & Springer (LMS) in which the Springer interests took a 49 percent stake. LMS took over the distribution of Springer's books outside Germany on behalf of EPPAC.

A year earlier Springer Verlag had formed a joint venture with the British publisher, Butterworth & Co. (Publishers) Ltd., under which LMS would distribute Springer's scientific journals for them. This venture proved to be unprofitable. In 1951 Maxwell bought Butterworth's stake in the joint venture. Maxwell also acquired half of the German interest in the joint venture, thus gaining 75 percent of the company. The former joint venture was renamed Pergamon Press Ltd. In 1954 Maxwell was forced to break with Springer. He agreed to dissolve LMS and operate under the name I. R. Maxwell & Co. Ltd. Springer gave Maxwell exclusive rights until 1959 in the British Empire, France, China, and Indonesia. Maxwell broke completely with Springer at the beginning of 1960.

In the meantime, Maxwell had decided to transform Pergamon into a major world publisher of scientific journals. By the end of 1957 Pergamon was publishing over 100 journals and books. In 1961 Maxwell sealed a five-year agreement with Macmillan Inc. of New York for the exclusive distribution of Pergamon books. The arrangement was terminated in August 1964 because of disappointing sales. In July 1964 Pergamon became a public company, although Maxwell retained majority control. In the following several years, Pergamon acquired a number of diverse publishing firms and merged its encyclopedia interests with the encyclopedia subsidiary of the British Printing Corporation (BPC). The new joint venture was called International Learning Systems Corporation Limited (ILSC).

In January 1969 Maxwell reached an agreement with Saul Steinberg, chairman of Leasco Data Processing Equipment of the United States, whereby Leasco would launch a formal bid for Pergamon subject to Maxwell's permitting a team of accountants appointed by Leasco to have full access to all of the Pergamon business records. Maxwell was to become president of Leasco's European division. On August 21 Leasco withdrew its bid because of doubts about Pergamon's accounts and ILSC. Maxwell disputed Leasco's right to take this course of action and had the dispute referred to the Takeover panel. On August 27 the panel decided Leasco had the right to withdraw and recommended a full Board of Trade inquiry over the objections of Maxwell. A shareholders' meeting was called at Pergamon for October 10. The meeting voted to dismiss Maxwell as company chairman and remove him from the board. Leasco gained control of Pergamon with 61 percent of the vote. However, Leasco decided not to proceed with its takeover bid, but retained its 38 percent stake in the company.

Maxwell retained control of Pergamon's U.S. subsidiary, Pergamon Press Inc. (PPI), even though the U.K. parent company controlled 70 percent of its stock. In April 1971 he reached an agreement with Leasco over PPI, thus ending their dispute.

In July the Board of Trade issued its report on Pergamon. The board alleged that there had been irregularities in the accounting practices of the company, and in particular in its subsidiary, ILSC. It concluded that "notwithstanding Mr. Maxwell's acknowledged abilities and energy, he [was] not in [their] opinion a person who can be relied on to exercise proper stewardship of a publicly quoted company." Stung by the report, Maxwell unsuccessfully took legal action to get the report overturned.

Frustrated in his attempts to regain full control of Pergamon, on January 9, 1974, Maxwell launched a £1.5 million takeover bid for Pergamon. On January 23 he won the support of Pergamon's board, and by late February Reliance (formerly called Leasco) had agreed to sell its 38-percent holding in Pergamon to Maxwell for £0.12 a share, receiving just over £600,000 in return for its original £9 million investment. Maxwell's new U.S. company, Microform International Marketing Corporation, now owned 90.7 percent of Pergamon. Maxwell subsequently purchased the remaining Pergamon shares. By 1977 Pergamon's sales had risen from £7 million to £20 million and its net annual profits had increased from £27,000 to £3.3 million.

In 1980 Maxwell began a major expansion program. He began to purchase shares in the once-powerful British Printing Corporation, his former partner in ILSC. BPC had been formed in February 1964 from the merger of Purnell & Sons Ltd. with Hazell Sun Ltd. Purnell & Sons had been established in 1849. In July 1980 Maxwell launched a dawn raid—the acquisition of a large number of shares—on BPC and acquired 29.5 percent of its shares. In February 1981 Maxwell launched a takeover bid for BPC with the agreement of the National Westminster Bank, BPC's most important creditor. Later in the month the Pergamon Press agreed to inject £10 million into BPC in return for a controlling interest in BPC. Maxwell became deputy chairman and chief executive of BPC. By May of 1981 Pergamon owned 77 percent of BPC and Maxwell had become chairman.

Maxwell battled early and often with the BPC trade unions. Although the trade unions signed an agreement with Maxwell to reorganize working practices as part of his survival plan for BPC the workers at the Park Royal printing works conducted two years of strikes between 1981 and 1983. BPC closed facilities and transferred production as part of this struggle and took full advantage of the trade union reforms introduced by the Thatcher government during the 1980s.

Maxwell changed BPC's name to the British Printing and Communications Corporation (BPCC) in March 1982. This change reflected his wish to expand into areas such as cable and satellite television, computers and data banks, electronic printing, and communications high technology that were being developed in the 1980s. In 1984 he became the publisher of the United Kingdom's Mirror Group Newspapers Ltd. In 1986 Maxwell began a further expansion of BPCC. He began with the takeover of Pergamon's crown jewels, its 361 scientific journals, for £238.65 million in March of 1986. In October 1987 BPCC changed its name to Maxwell Communication Corporation; the name BPCC was reassigned to one of MCC's subsidiaries. In December MCC completed another "reverse takeover," this time of Pergamon's books division for £100 million.

In 1987 Robert Maxwell attempted to transform MCC into a major publisher in the United States as part of his plan to make the company one of the top ten international media and communications corporations. At that point the company already had publishing businesses in more than 15 countries. In May 1987 Maxwell launched a US$2 billion hostile cash bid for Harcourt Brace Jovanovich (HBJ), the leading American publisher of school textbooks. HBJ responded with a comprehensive US$3 billion recapitalization plan in order to defend itself against MCC. MCC pursued legal action in support of its takeover bid for HBJ. The failure of several lawsuits in the U.S. courts, however, led the company to withdraw its takeover bid in late July. Maxwell also failed in 1987 with his bid to acquire 50 percent of Bell & Howell, the U.S. educational publisher and manufacturer of information storage equipment.

On July 21, 1988, MCC launched a bid for Macmillan Inc., a large U.S. publishing group. Macmillan and its attractive assets became the object of a bidding war eventually won by MCC after three months of struggle. On November 4 MCC acquired Macmillan for US$2.6 billion—about $1 billion more than the company was generally thought to be worth. A few days earlier MCC had also acquired the Official Airline Guides division (OAG) of Dun & Bradstreet, a leading provider of airline schedule information and related services in North America, for $750 million.

In order to finance MCC's huge U.S. acquisitions, Maxwell abandoned most of the printing side of MCC's business to concentrate on publishing. In January 1989 MCC began to dispose of over US$1.4 billion worth of MCC's printing and noncore subsidiaries. In September 1989 MCC secured US$3 billion in medium-term debt to refinance the borrowings taken on at the time of the purchase of Macmillan and OAG. MCC used some of the borrowings to acquire Merrill Publishing, the U.S. educational books group, for $260 million in the same month. At the same time MCC's disposals continued with the flotation of 44 percent of Macmillan's former language instruction subsidiary, Berlitz International, in December 1989, raising $130 million. An agreement was made at the end of March 1991 to sell Pergamon Press to Elsevier for £440 million. The company's efforts to reduce its debts, which had reached serious proportions, continued into the beginning of the next decade.

Maxwell Communication Corporation's debt load, exacerbated by its appetite for acquisition and expansion as well as the economic climate, was known to be significant. But it was not until Maxwell's death in November 1991 that the true dimensions of MCC's fiscal sickness became known.

The recession, coupled with widespread skepticism among brokers about the ability of MCC to pay its debt, depressed the company's share price. Maxwell thus set in motion a series of increasingly desperate maneuvers to push the stock price back up. He bought massive amounts of MCC stock, which he was using as credit collateral, via a plethora of trusts and holding companies owned or controlled by Maxwell family concerns. He also raided the bank accounts and pension funds of MCC and Mirror Group Newspapers Ltd., his other publicly traded company, to make further purchases of MCC stock, all to no avail. Estimates of the amount stolen by Maxwell from his public companies now range as high as $1.4 billion.

On November 5, 1991, Maxwell was found dead, floating off the stern of his yacht. Creditors, already suspicious of MCC's fiscal health, soon discovered that the company was in utter financial ruin. Authorities are engaged in sorting through the labyrnthine remains. MCC was placed under the joint administration of United States and English bankruptcy courts acting with the help of Price Waterhouse. Of MCC's subsidiaries, Macmillan and Official Airline Guides are likely to be sold more or less intact by the bankruptcy administrators. MCC itself was hopelessly insolvent and will be liquidated to repay some of its $2.5 billion in debt.

Further Reading: Haines, Joe, *Maxwell,* London, Macdonald, 1988; Snoddy, Raymond, "Monday Interview," *Financial Times,* August 6, 1990; Maremont, Mark, and Mark Landler, "An Empire Up for Grabs," *Business Week,* December 23, 1991; Bower, Tom, *Maxwell: The Outsider,* New York, Viking, 1992.

—Richard Hawkins
updated by Jonathan Martin

McCORMICK & COMPANY, INC.

MCCORMICK & COMPANY, INCORPORATED

18 Loveton Circle
P.O. Box 6000
Sparks, Maryland 21152-6000
U.S.A.
(410) 771-7301
Fax: (410) 771-7462

Public Company
Incorporated: 1903
Employees: 8,000
Sales: $1.47 billion
Stock Exchanges: NASDAQ
SICs: 2099 Food Preparations Nec; 2087 Flavoring Extracts
   & Syrups Nec

McCormick & Company, Incorporated is the largest U.S. seller of spices, seasonings, and flavorings. Its estimated 43 percent market share is more than double that of its closest competitor, Durkee Foods. From the early 1960s through 1989, the company also gained a reputation as a real estate developer, primarily in the Baltimore area. However, a core revitalization campaign and the sale of this business segment have directed the company back to its roots. McCormick now operates four divisions: consumer products, industrial and food service, packaging, and international. Although all segments are prosperous, the international division holds the most promise for McCormick's future growth. Conducted by means of joint ventures and licensing arrangements around the world, the international division posted sales in fiscal 1991 of $225 million, up nearly 15 percent over 1990. Profitability from joint ventures approached $9 million, a 140 percent increase over the previous year.

A 25-year-old Baltimore man named Willoughby M. McCormick founded the company in 1889 when he began making fruit syrups, juices, flavoring extracts, and root beer in his home. McCormick enlisted three young assistants to help with production and with door-to-door sales. Early marketing techniques included the use of the Bee Brand and Silver Medal labels and the adoption of the motto: "Make the Best—Someone Will Buy It." The company earned a reputation not only for its condiments and other consumables but also for such household and medicinal products as Iron Glue ("Sticks Everything But the Buyer") and Uncle Sam's Nerve and Bone Liniment ("For Man or Beast").

Within a year, the company was profitable enough to move to larger quarters. At this time, McCormick added a number of new products, including food colorings, cream of tartar, liver pills, castor oil, talcum powder, witch hazel, blood purifier, cold cream, bay rum, tooth powder, and toilet water. Three years later, after McCormick's brother, Roberdeau A. McCormick, had joined the business, the company again moved. Soon even more everyday products—bluing compound, ammonia, roach traps, flypaper, and bird seed—were added to the line. By 1894, the company had begun to export overseas. The following year the corporation was dissolved so that a partnership could be formed between Willoughby and Roberdeau (the two ultimately incorporated in 1903). This year the Clover Brand made its debut. In 1896 the company took a crucial step forward by acquiring Philadelphia-based F. G. Emmett Spice Company and firmly committing itself to the spice industry. Promotions that coincided with this event included the sale of the first McCormick cookbook and a novelty premium offer.

At the turn of the century the company opened an export office in New York City and began shipping its products to and from the East and West Indies, South Africa, Europe, and Central and South America. In 1902 the company acquired a four-story plant and unveiled the Banquet Brand for its line of spices and mustards. Promotions continued apace. With such slogans as "McCormick Means Merit" and the title of "Manufacturing Chemist, Drug & Spice Millers, Importers and Exporters," McCormick was fast becoming the East Coast leader in its selected fields. Although in 1904 a great fire in Baltimore destroyed the majority of the company's assets and records, temporary quarters were quickly established, and the company eventually regained its foothold through new product introductions. These included Clover Blossom spices and Banquet teas. The company gained welcome publicity in 1907 at the Virginia Exposition in Jamestown, when it received gold medals for a number of its branded products.

The next two decades were characterized by more rapid growth and the company's rise to national prominence. In 1910 the company was among the first in the country to introduce gauze-pouch tea bags. This same year Willoughby was chosen to preside over the newly formed Flavoring Extracts Manufacturing Association, the purpose of which was to ensure uniformity in materials and packaging while elevating the status of regional spice companies. Willoughby's nephew, Charles P. McCormick, joined the company as a part-time shipping clerk in 1912; years later, Charles would prove instrumental in resuscitating the business following Willoughby's death. At the onset of the Roaring Twenties, the company was manufacturing over 800 products, embracing the national mood of prosperity and optimism. In 1921 it started construction of a new corporate headquarters: a nine-story building, replete with printing plant, analytical lab, machine shop, cafeteria, and railroad siding, overlooking the inner harbor of Baltimore. Five years later, McCormick stock was offered to wholesale grocers for the first time. Although the company would not achieve coast-to-coast distribution until after World War II, it hired Scotch bagpipers (the symbol for the company's Bee Brand) to advertise its products on the streets of large cities across the United States.

Sales reached $5 million in 1928, prompting the company to schedule office openings in Houston and San Francisco within the next few years. However, the stock market crash and the Great Depression placed the company in serious peril by 1930. Willoughby McCormick's initial response to plummeting sales was to drastically reduce wages. Within two years, he was forced to seek outside capital from New York investors to sustain the company's operations. McCormick died of a heart attack before accomplishing his mission, and it was left to his nephew, 36-year-old Charles P. McCormick to turn the business around.

As the new president and chair of a floundering company, the potential for expansion of which was still enormous, Charles instituted a new business philosophy, which he termed "Multiple Management." McCormick's guiding belief was that a company, whatever its products or services, was nothing without its workforce, and an empowered workforce made for an empowered, efficient, and successful company. He established junior boards of directors to implement this philosophy and to provide regular forums for the exchange of ideas which might ultimately lead the company to become more productive and to seek new directions for growth. A radical departure from established business practices at the time, McCormick's plan also included a ten percent increase in general wages and a reduction in weekly hours from 56 to 45, all steps which would seem to preclude the company's downfall. Nevertheless, McCormick's leadership and his emphasis on employee productivity enabled the company to return to profitability within a year. Pioneering programs in profit sharing and medical benefits were among the company's rewards to its dedicated employees. The Multiple Management system became ingrained in the McCormick corporate culture and soon found hundreds of adherents in businesses across the United States, Canada, and Great Britain. McCormick's unique views and experiences were published in book form in 1938 as *Multiple Management* (reprinted as *The Power of People*) and *The McCormick System of Management*. A corporate pamphlet commemorating 50 years of the McCormick system declared that: "C. P. McCormick understood human nature and respected people. That was one of the reasons he got good results. Those who knew him and worked with him testify that he valued the opinions of others, didn't feel threatened by contrary ideas and was willing to change when a better idea came along."

Within the first five years under the new McCormick system, some 2,000 separate ideas were generated and implemented by the junior boards. Among the company's most visible innovations were a spoon-sift top and new metal containers for its spice line. In 1938 a McCormick research team developed a spice fumigation process called "McCorization" that produced the highest grade spices available without any detectable flavor loss. The early 1940s were distinguished by McCormick's undisputed rebirth as the East Coast's largest seller of spices. It was at this time that the company also began consolidating its product line under the McCormick name and the big "Mc" trademark.

Finally, in 1947, McCormick gained coast-to-coast distribution with the acquisition of A. Schilling & Company of San Francisco. A spice, coffee, and extract concern with a history older than that of McCormick, Schilling's house brand was so popular that it was retained for domestic spice sales west of the Mississippi. "United to Serve the Nation's Good Taste" became the new corporate slogan, and sales surpassed $25 million during the first full year of consolidation. Because of McCormick's growing presence overseas, with exports to 44 countries, the company opened the 1950s with yet another slogan: "From All the World—Known the World Over." Acquisitions, joint ventures, and the formation of new subsidiaries have since become an area of concentration for McCormick. Highlights of the company's early acquisitions include the 1959 purchase of Canada's largest spice company, Gorman Eckert & Co. (whose name was later changed to Club House Foods); the 1961 purchase of California-based Gilroy Foods, a producer of dehydrated onions, garlic, and other vegetables; the 1962 purchase of Baker Extract Co., a venerable New England competitor; and the 1968 purchase of Tubed Chemicals Corporation, a packer and manufacturer of plastic tubes.

McCormick remained busy on other fronts as well. In 1959 it introduced its Gourmet line of spices. Four years later, it modified its spice tins with a plastic duo-flip top and also established the industrial products division to provide custom service for food processors. However, McCormick's most dynamic move occurred outside the food and spice industry. In 1962, while searching for a 50-acre plot near Baltimore to satisfy its needs for expansion, the company learned of a much larger piece of commercial property whose developers were in financial trouble. Guided by then president John Curlett and chairperson C. P. McCormick, the company decided to form a real estate company, Maryland Properties, Inc. (later renamed McCormick Properties), to purchase and bring the Greater Baltimore Industrial Park project to completion. Through various leasing arrangements, the subsidiary made money during its first year, and soon it began acquiring and developing other properties in the Washington D.C. and Baltimore areas. From 1973 until 1988, McCormick's real estate arm operated as an unconsolidated subsidiary. In one of its best years, 1983, it reported a strong profit of $13 million on revenues of $86 million. Three years later, a *Financial World* article recorded chairperson Harry Wells's plans to build the subsidiary, with operating assets of close to $300 million, into a $1 billion operation by 1991. Shortly after that, new leadership determined that the company's long-term health would be best served by a concentrated refocus on its food-and-spice businesses.

Despite the regular introduction of new products, new slogans, new subsidiaries, and new distribution arrangements, McCormick's core industry had suffered from slowing growth almost since the time of C.P. McCormick's death in 1970. Depressed stock values during the late 1970s enhanced the possibility of a takeover, and one company, Sandoz Ltd., appeared as though it might become the majority shareholder in McCormick. An immense Swiss chemical and pharmaceutical firm, Sandoz succeeded in acquiring almost five percent of McCormick's nonvoting stock in 1979 at $19 a share; it then offered to buy the remainder of the company for $37 a share. Nearly a year later, McCormick succeeded in buying its shares back, at $28 apiece, amidst wild rumors on Wall Street and rollercoaster speculative trading. Sandoz had made a profit, but McCormick, more importantly, had recovered its equilibrium, at least for a time. In 1982, trouble reappeared within the company's grocery division. It was found that for a four-year period, from 1977 to

1980, expense accounting had been delayed in order to satisfy corporate profit goals. Stockholder suits quickly followed. Because of this dereliction, the heretofore exclusive board of directors now decided to open its doors to outside executives.

This change alone was not enough to deflect further setbacks related to profits. During the first half of the 1980s, domestic spice consumption dropped an alarming 20 percent. The company unveiled a new gourmet line of spices in 1985, supported by a massive consumer education campaign and the slogan: "McCormick/Schilling Gourmet. Quite simply, the best spices on earth." Two years later, the company planned another major rollout with the biggest marketing budget in its history. Saturation of this sort had been atypical of the venerable company, and, according to Janet Novack in an article in *Forbes*, "McCormick had always figured that in the spice business it was enough to woo retailers, and consumers would follow. After all, its full line of 103 gourmet and 107 regular spices takes so much space . . . that once established, it leaves little room for competitors' products." By Wells's admission, the company was slow to react to changing consumer trends—so slow that, "for a while there," writes Novack, "an alert and strong competitor, had there been one, could have knocked it right off its lofty perch." Despite its increased attention to marketing, however, McCormick's profits and market share were still crumbling at the end of 1986.

The spice company's modern rebirth came with the ascension of Charles P. McCormick, Jr., grandnephew of the founder, to the positions of president and CEO in 1987. Assisted by then chief operations officer Bailey Thomas (elected chairperson and CEO in 1993), McCormick sold off the real estate and underperforming food divisions and sunk some $200 million into consumer marketing and product development. The revitalization campaign, known as Project One, involved shelving the traditional red-and-white spice tins in favor of elegantly labeled clear plastic bottles, produced by a corporate subsidiary. Other product rollouts included a line of dehydrated sauce mixes. The company also began fortifying its relations with the industrial and food service businesses and by the early 1990s counted at least 80 of the 100 largest American food processors as its clients.

McCormick's strategy for future growth includes increasing domestic market share to around 50 percent. Steps toward meeting this goal included the 1993 acquisition of the Golden Dipt Division of DCA Food Industries. The company's other primary strategy is to increase its international presence, which it hopes to do through a series of joint ventures and through expansion of its foreign subsidiaries. As the spice supplier for such expanding global chains as McDonald's and Burger King, McCormick should also stand to grow in this area. After a long and complex history, the new McCormick remains much the same as the McCormick of early Multiple Management days in its committment to employees, innovations, and product excellence worldwide.

Principal Subsidiaries: Festin Foods Corp. (50%); Gilroy Foods, Incorporated; Golden West Foods, Inc.; Kancor Flavours and Extracts Limited (40%); Lukcor, S.A. (50%); McCormick & Wild, Inc. (50%); McCormick Canada, Inc.; McCormick de Centro America, S.A.; McCormick de Mexico, S.A. de C.V. (50%); McCormick de Venezuela, C.A.; McCormick Foods Australia Pty. Ltd.; McCormick Ingredients Southeast Asia Private limited; McCormick GmbH; McCormick-Lion Limited (49%); McCormick S.A.; McCormick U.K. plc; Sesaco Corporation (22.5%); Setco, Inc.; Shanghai McCormick Seasoning & Foodstuffs Company, Limited (35%); Stange (Japan) K.K. (50%); Tubed Products, Inc.

Further Reading: Miles, Christine, "Spice and Sugar," *Forbes*, September 29, 1980; "Step Back into the Future: Fifty Years of Multiple Management, 1932–1982," Hunt Valley, Maryland, McCormick & Company, 1982; Levering, Robert, Milton Moskowitz, and Michael Katz, "McCormick & Company, Inc.," *The 100 Best Companies to Work for in America*, Reading, Massachusetts, Addison-Wesley Publishing Company, 1984; "This Is McCormick," Hunt Valley, Maryland, McCormick & Company, 1984; Brown, Paul B., "Unlikely Landlord," *Forbes*, February 27, 1984; Dodds, Lynn Strongin, "Well Seasoned: Spices and Real Estate Do Mix," *Financial World*, September 2, 1986; Novack, Janet, "A Close Call," *Forbes*, January 26, 1987; *100 Best Recipes for 100 Years from McCormick*, Hunt Valley, Maryland, and Elmsford, New York, McCormick & Company and The Benjamin Company, 1988; Cochran, Thomas N., "McCormick & Co.: Cogeneration Project Adds Spice to Profit Prospects," *Barron's*, July 4, 1988; Clark, Kim, "McCormick Turns 100 with Zest," *The Sun*, September 27, 1989; Abelson, Reed, "Spicy Days at McCormick," *Fortune*, January 15, 1990; Bangsberg, P. T., "Pepsi and McCormick Launch China Spice, Seasoning Venture," *Journal of Commerce and Commercial*, April 11, 1990; Linden, Dana Wechsler, "Hot Stuff," *Forbes*, November 26, 1990; Oliver, Joyce Anne, "Spice in His Life Comes from Motivating His Workers," *Marketing News*, February 17, 1992; Levering, Robert, and Milton Moskowitz, "McCormick," *The 100 Best Companies to Work for in America*, Doubleday, New York, 1993; "McCormick & Co. Elects Bailey A. Thomas and H. Eugene Blattman to Executive Positions," *Milling & Baking News*, January 19, 1993; "McCormick & Co. Posts Record Results in Fiscal 1992," *Milling & Baking News*, January 19, 1993; "McCormick Buys Consumer Product Line of Golden Dipt from DCA," *Milling & Baking News*, January 19, 1993.

—Jay P. Pederson

MCDONALD'S CORPORATION

McDonald's Plaza
Oak Brook, Illinois 60521
U.S.A.
(708) 575-3000
Fax: (708) 575-5814

Public Company
Incorporated: 1955
Employees: 169,000
Sales: $19.93 billion
Stock Exchanges: New York Midwest Pacific Toronto
   Frankfurt Munich Paris Tokyo Zürich Geneva Basel
SICs: 5812 Eating Places

Since its incorporation in 1955, McDonald's has not only become the world's largest quick-service restaurant organization, but has literally changed Americans' eating habits. On any given day, nearly seven percent of the American population will eat a meal at a McDonald's restaurant; in a year, 96 percent of Americans will visit a McDonald's. The company stands head and shoulders above its competition, commanding by far the leading share of the fast-food market. The company's growth is best described as phenomenal; McDonald's has recorded increasing sales and earnings every quarter since it went public in 1965.

In 1954 Ray Kroc, a seller of Multimixer milkshake machines, learned that brothers Richard and Maurice (Dick and Mac) McDonald were using eight of his high-tech Multimixers in their San Bernardino, California, restaurant. His curiosity was piqued, and he went to San Bernardino to take a look at the McDonalds' restaurant.

The McDonalds had been in the restaurant business since the 1930s. In 1948 they closed down a successful carhop drive-in to establish the streamlined operation Ray Kroc saw in 1954. The menu was simple: hamburgers, cheeseburgers, french fries, shakes, soft drinks, and apple pie. The carhops were eliminated to make McDonald's a self-serve operation, and there were no tables to sit at, no jukebox, and no telephone. As a result, McDonald's attracted families rather than teenagers. Perhaps the most impressive aspect of the restaurant was the efficiency with which the McDonalds' workers did their jobs. Mac and Dick McDonald had taken great care in setting up their kitchen. Each worker's steps had been carefully choreographed, like an assembly line, to ensure maximum efficiency. The savings in preparation time, and the resulting increase in volume, allowed the McDonalds to lower the price of a hamburger from 30 cents to 15 cents.

Believing that the McDonald formula was a ticket to success, Kroc suggested that they franchise their restaurants throughout the country. When they hesitated to take on this additional burden, Kroc volunteered to do it for them. He returned to his home outside of Chicago with rights to set up McDonald's restaurants throughout the country, except in a handful of territories in California and Arizona already licensed by the McDonald brothers.

Kroc's first McDonald's restaurant opened in Des Plaines, Illinois, near Chicago, on April 15, 1955. As with any new venture, Kroc encountered a number of hurdles. The first was adapting the McDonald's building design to a northern climate. A basement had to be installed to house a furnace, and adequate ventilation was difficult, as exhaust fans sucked out warm air in the winter, and cool air in the summer.

Most frustrating of all, however, was Kroc's initial failure to reproduce the McDonalds' delicious french fries. When Kroc and his crew duplicated the brothers' method—leaving just a little peel for flavor, cutting the potatoes into shoestrings, and rinsing the strips in cold water—the fries turned into mush. After repeated telephone conversations with the McDonald brothers and several consultations with the Potato and Onion Association, Kroc pinpointed the cause of the soggy spuds. The McDonald brothers stored their potatoes outside in wire bins, and the warm California breeze dried them out and cured them, slowly turning the sugars into starch. In order to reproduce the superior taste of these potatoes, Kroc devised a system using an electric fan to dry the potatoes in a similar way. He also experimented with a blanching process. Within three months he had a french fry which was, in his opinion, slightly superior in taste to the McDonald brothers' fries.

Once the Des Plaines restaurant was operational, Kroc sought franchisees for his McDonald's chain. The first snag came quickly. In 1956 he discovered that the McDonald brothers had licensed the franchise rights for Cook County, Illinois (home of Chicago and many of its suburbs) to the Frejlack Ice Cream Company. Kroc was incensed that the McDonalds hadn't informed him of this arrangement. He purchased the rights back for $25,000—five times what the Frejlacks had originally paid—and pressed on.

Kroc decided early on that it was best to first establish the restaurants and then to franchise them out, so that he could control the uniformity of the stores. Early McDonald's restaurants were situated in the suburbs. Corner lots were usually in greater demand because gas stations and shops competed for them, but Kroc preferred lots in the middle of blocks to accommodate his U-shaped parking lots. Since these lots were cheaper, Kroc could give franchisees a price break.

McDonald's grew slowly for its first three years; by 1958 there were 34 restaurants. In 1959, however, Kroc opened 67 new restaurants, bringing the total to more than 100.

Kroc had decided at the outset that McDonald's would not be a supplier to its franchisees—his background in sales warned him that such an arrangement could lead to lower quality for the sake of higher profits. He had also determined that the company should at no time own more than 30 percent of all McDonald's restaurants. He knew, however, that his success depended upon his franchisees' success, and he was determined to help them in any way that he could.

In 1960 McDonald's advertising campaign, "Look for the golden arches," gave sales a big boost. Kroc believed that advertising was an investment that would in the end come back many times over, and advertising has always played a key role in the development of the McDonald's Corporation—indeed, McDonald's ads have been some of the most identifiable over the years. In 1962 McDonald's replaced its "Speedee" the hamburger man symbol with its now world-famous golden arches logo. A year later, the company sold its billionth hamburger.

In the early 1960s, McDonald's really began to take off. The growth in automobile use that came with the suburbanization of America contributed heavily to McDonald's success. In 1961 Kroc bought out the McDonald brothers for $2.7 million, aiming at making McDonald's the number one fast-food chain in the country.

In 1965 McDonald's Corporation went public. Common shares were offered at $22.50 per share; by the end of the first day's trading the price had shot up to $30. A block of 100 shares purchased for $2,250 in 1965 was worth, after nine stock splits, more than $400,000 in 1989. McDonald's Corporation is now one of the 30 companies that make up the Dow Jones Industrial Index.

McDonald's success in the 1960s was largely due to the company's successful marketing and flexible response to customer demand. In 1965 the Filet-o-Fish sandwich, billed as "the fish that catches people," was introduced in McDonald's restaurants. The new item had originally met with disapproval from Kroc, but after its successful test marketing, he eventually agreed to add it. Another item that Kroc had backed a year previously, a burger with a slice of pineapple and a slice of cheese known as a "hulaburger," had flopped. The market was not quite ready for Kroc's taste; the hulaburger's tenure on the McDonald's menu board was short. In 1968 the now-legendary Big Mac made its debut, and in 1969 McDonald's sold its five-billionth hamburger. A year later, as it launched the "You Deserve a Break Today" advertising campaign, McDonald's restaurants had reached all 50 states.

In 1968 McDonald's opened its 1,000th restaurant, and Fred Turner became the company's president and chief administrative officer. Kroc became chairperson and remained CEO until 1973. Turner had originally intended to open a McDonald's franchise, but when he had problems with his backers over a location, he went to work for Kroc in 1956. As operations vice-president, Turner helped new franchisees get their stores set up and running. He was constantly looking for new ways to perfect the McDonald's system, experimenting, for example, to determine the maximum number of hamburger patties one could stack in a box without squashing them and pointing out that

seconds could be saved if McDonald's used buns that were presliced all the way through and weren't stuck together in the package. Such attention to detail was one reason for the company's extraordinary success.

McDonald's spectacular growth continued in the 1970s. Americans were more on-the-go than ever, and fast service was a priority. In 1972 the company passed $1 billion in annual sales; by 1976, McDonald's had served 20 billion hamburgers, and system wide sales exceeded $3 billion.

McDonald's pioneered breakfast fast food with the introduction of the Egg McMuffin in 1973 when market research indicated that a quick breakfast would be welcomed by consumers. Five years later the company added a full breakfast line to the menu, and by 1987 one-fourth of all breakfasts eaten out in the United States came from McDonald's restaurant.

Kroc was a firm believer in "putting something back into the community where you do business." In 1974 McDonald's acted upon that philosophy in an original way by opening the first Ronald McDonald House, in Philadelphia, to provide a "home away from home" for the families of children in nearby hospitals. Twelve years after this first house opened, 100 similar Ronald McDonald Houses were in operation across the United States.

In 1975 McDonald's opened its first drive-thru window in Oklahoma City. This service gave Americans a fast, convenient way to get a quick meal. The company's goal was to provide service in 50 seconds or less. Drive-thru sales eventually accounted for more than half of McDonald's system wide sales.

In the late 1970s competition from other hamburger chains such as Burger King and Wendy's began to intensify. Experts believed that the fast-food industry had gotten as big as it ever would, so the companies began to battle fiercely for market share. A period of aggressive advertising campaigns and price slashing in the early 1980s became known as the "burger wars." Burger King suggested that customers "have it their way"; Wendy's offered itself as the "fresh alternative" and asked of other restaurants, "where's the beef?" But McDonald's sales and market share continued to grow. Consumers seemed to like the taste and consistency of McDonald's best.

During the 1980s McDonald's further diversified its menu to suit changing consumer tastes. Chicken McNuggets were introduced in 1983, and by the end of the year McDonald's was the second largest retailer of chicken in the world. In 1987 ready-to-eat salads were introduced to lure more health-conscious consumers. The 1980s were the fastest paced decade yet. Efficiency, combined with an expanded menu, continued to draw customers. McDonald's, already entrenched in the suburbs, began to focus on urban centers and introduced new architectural styles. Though McDonald's restaurants no longer looked identical, the company made sure food quality and service remained constant.

Despite experts' claims that the fast-food industry was saturated, McDonald's continued to expand. The first generation raised on restaurant food had grown up. Eating out had become a habit rather than a break in the routine, and McDonald's relentless marketing continued to improve sales. Innovative promotions, such as the "when the U.S. wins, you win" give-aways during the Olympic games in 1988, were a huge success.

In 1982 Michael R. Quinlan became president of McDonald's Corporation and Fred Turner became chairperson. Quinlan, who took over as CEO in 1986, had started at McDonald's in the mailroom in 1963, and gradually worked his way up. The first McDonald's CEO to hold an MBA degree, Quinlan was regarded by his colleagues as a shrewd competitor. In his first year as CEO the company opened 600 new restaurants.

McDonald's growth in the United States was mirrored by its stunning growth abroad. By 1991, 37 percent of system wide sales came from restaurants outside of the United States. McDonald's opened its first foreign restaurant in British Columbia, Canada, in 1967. Since then the company established itself in 58 foreign countries and now operates more than 3,600 restaurants outside of the U.S., through wholly owned subsidiaries, joint ventures, and franchise agreements. Its strongest foreign markets are Japan, Canada, Germany, Great Britain, Australia, and France.

While western Europe's population far exceeded that of the United States in 1992, it had only 1,300 restaurants. Latin America, with twice the population of the United States, sufficed with 200 restaurants. China's first McDonald's restaurant, located in Shenhen, made a profit in its first year of operation. Beijing and Shanghai restaurants soon followed, giving China's 1.1 billion people three places to find the golden arches. In March of 1992, two native Czechoslovakians opened a McDonald's in Prague, and it took three years of bureaucratic red tape to open the Jakarta, Indonesia, restaurant.

In the mid-1980s, McDonald's, like other traditional employers of teenagers, was faced with a shortage of labor in the United States. The company met this challenge by being the first to entice retirees back into the workforce. McDonald's has always placed great emphasis on effective training. It opened its Hamburger University in 1961 to train franchisees and corporate decision makers. By 1987, more than 30,000 people had received "Bachelor of Hamburgerology" degrees from the 80-acre Oak Brook, Illinois, facility. The corporation opened a Hamburger University in Tokyo in 1971, in Munich in 1975, and in London in 1982.

The McDonald's Corporation operates only 20 percent of its restaurants. It receives 20,000 franchise inquiries a year. In 1991, 350 new licensees joined the corporation's extensive training program, and of these more than 60 percent were women and minorities. By the end of 1991, there were more than 12,000 system wide restaurants.

Braille menus were first introduced in 1979, and picture menus in 1988. In March of 1992, Braille and picture menus were reintroduced to acknowledge the 37 million Americans with vision, speech, or hearing impairments.

Quinlan continued to experiment with new technology and to research new markets to keep McDonald's in front of its competition. Clamshell fryers, which cooked both sides of a hamburger simultaneously, were tested. New locations such as hospitals and military bases are being tapped as possible sites for new restaurants. In response to the increase in microwave oven usage, McDonald's, whose name is the single most advertised brand name in the world, has stepped up advertising and promotional expenditures stressing that its taste is superior to quick packaged foods.

McRecycle USA began in 1990 and included a commitment to purchase at least $100 million worth of recycled products annually for use in construction, remodeling, and equipping restaurants. Chairs, table bases, table tops, eating counters, table columns, waste receptacles, corrugated cartons, packaging, and washroom tissue are all made from recycled products. McDonald's worked with the U.S. Environmental Defense Fund to develop a comprehensive solid waste reduction program. Wrapping burgers in paper rather than plastic led to a 90 percent reduction in the wrapping material waste stream.

Although it took McDonald's 33 years to open its first 10,000 restaurants, the company plans to open the next 10,000 by 2005, mainly by taking advantage of strong opportunities overseas. The company's ability to adapt to the changing tastes and habits of its customers has made it the virtually unassailable leader in the fast-food industry. McDonald's commands $13 billion of America's $93 billion quick-service food industry, but considers its area of national sales growth to be the $200 billion "eat out" market. Providing more "loose" seating, rather than the conventional bolted down tables and chairs, has been considered as one way to relax the atmosphere and attract more families as dinner patrons. Pizza, chicken, and pasta menu additions also have been tested.

By the spring of 1992, the company was testing MenuVision television network in 12 eastern U.S. restaurants. Computer-generated images of menu items and promotional deals were displayed on monitors. McNews, a closed network of live entertainment provided by Turner Broadcasting, also was tested.

In July 1992, the corporation announced a new program for investors who own less than 50 shares, which would allow them to purchase additional McDonald's shares or donate the new issues to selected charities without incurring brokerage commissions. During the 30-day offer, McDonald's made matching donations equal to the value of all shares donated, up to a combined maximum of $100,000 worth of stock—all to attract and retain small individual investors. New challenges will undoubtedly arise, but the company seems to have plenty to look forward to.

Principal Subsidiaries: McDonald's Deutschland GmbH; McDonald's Development GmbH; McDonald's Hamburgers Limited; McDonald's Italia Srl.; McDonald's Restaurants of Canada Ltd.; McDonald's Restaurants (Hong Kong) Ltd.; McDonald's Sistemas de España; McDonald's System of Australia Ltd.; McDonald's System of France SARL; McDonald's System of New Zealand Ltd.

Further Reading: Kroc, Ray. *Grinding It Out: The Making of McDonald's,* Chicago, H. Reguery, 1977; Love, John F., *McDonald's: Behind the Golden Arches,* New York, Bantam Books, 1986.

—updated by Anne C. Hughes

MCKEE FOODS CORPORATION

P.O. Box 750
Collegedale, Tennessee 37315-0750
U.S.A.
(615) 238-7111
Fax: (615) 238-7127

Private Company
Incorporated: 1957 as McKee Baking Company
Employees: 4,250
Sales: $525 million
SICs: 2051 Bread, Cake & Related Products; 2052 Cookies
    & Crackers; 2043 Cereal Breakfast Foods

Family-owned and operated, McKee Foods Corporation is the David to such Goliaths as Nabisco Brands, Continental Baking Co., and Interstate Bakeries. McKee Foods' threat to these and other food giants is the niche of snack cakes, the driving force behind the company's 400 percent growth in sales since 1982. This figure is all the more remarkable when one considers the company's comparatively low profile, lack of full-scale national distribution, and cautious approach to expansion. The secret to McKee's success is its Little Debbie snack cake line which, in 1992, accounted for 52 percent of all snack cakes sold in the United States. By comparison, McKee's closest competitor, Ralston-Purina's Continental Baking, posted only an 18 percent market share. Nutty Bars, Figaroos, Oatmeal Creme Pies, Caravellas, Golden Cremes, Devil Cremes, Swiss Rolls—some 38 varieties in all grace the regular Little Debbie snack cake line. McKee Foods also markets granola bars, granola cereals, and other bakery products under the Sunbelt label.

The company was born during the heart of the 1930s depression. A young North Carolina couple, O. D. and Ruth McKee, lost their savings after a bank failure and moved from their home in Hendersonville to Chattanooga, Tennessee, in 1933. O. D. found work as a bakery salesman, selling Virginia Dare Cakes from Becker's Bakery, a local establishment, for five cents each. By 1934 O. D. had purchased his own delivery truck. He then found out that Jack's Cookie Company, another Chattanooga bakery, was up for sale. O. D. cashed in his truck and he and Ruth became owners and operators of their first business. According to the company publication *The Story behind Little Debbie Snack Cakes,* the two ''were ideal business partners because her cautious, conservative nature was the perfect complement to his risk-taking, adventuresome spirit.''

In 1935 O. D. moved the business to a new location and began making soft cookies and cakes. A year later they handed the business to Ruth's father, Symon D. King, and returned to North Carolina to launch a new bakery. Located in Charlotte and named Jack's Cookie Company like its predecessor, the business was highly successful. In 1946, O. D., who ''always had a gift for innovation and automation,'' built a new, state-of-the-art plant. During this period he also invented a soft oatmeal creme pie, ''the company's oldest continuous product,'' according to *Milling and Baking News.*

The McKees sold their Charlotte business in the early 1950s and considered retiring. However, they decided instead to return to Chattanooga and manage the original Jack's, now called King's Bakery and owned by Ruth's brother, Cecil King. In 1954 O. D. and Ruth purchased the company stock and the foundation for the McKee Baking Company was born. As he had previously, O. D. served as salesman, inventor, and production manager while Ruth operated as purchaser, personnel manager, and office manager. In 1957, when they outgrew the Chattanooga bakery, the operation moved to nearby Collegedale. It was at this location that the company established its headquarters and grew into a major private corporation. The original Collegedale plant was expanded more than a dozen times before a sister plant was added. In 1982 the McKee family launched a third plant in Gentry, Arkansas; a fourth followed eight years later in Stuarts Draft, Virginia. By this time Ruth had passed away and O. D. had transferred management to his sons, Ellsworth and Jack, while retaining his chairmanship.

In 1960 the company made history in two ways. First, after having led the industry in mass production of small snack cakes, it conceived the ''family'' pack of twelve individually wrapped cakes sold as one multipack unit. Second, it began affixing the Little Debbie brand, named after Ellsworth's daughter Debra, to its products. Both Little Debbie and the family pack remain the company's most significant generators of sales. A proliferation of snack cake varieties since that time—including the introduction of the Sunbelt line in 1981—has only fueled the momentum of these two landmark events.

By 1982 McKee Baking, with $130 million in sales, ranked 22nd in the industry, behind such billion-dollar giants as Continental and Interstate. Sales at the time were concentrated principally in the Midwest, Southwest, and West. By 1987 the company was able to boast annual sales growth of ten to 15 percent since the advent of Little Debbie, a product line that had now expanded to 32 varieties available in 41 states. McKee succeeded in conquering Continental's Hostess, Interstate's Dolly Madison, and other major national brands through its low pricing. According to *Forbes* writer William Stern, the feisty competitor sells its products through supermarkets for 50 percent to 70 percent less than other comparable items. More surprisingly, the company's net margins after such heavy undercutting are approximately six percent, while the average for the industry is 5.5 percent. ''What's to stop McKee's giant competitors from matching its low prices?'' queries Stern. ''Common sense.... They are giant corporations with giant overhead, while McKee is a family business. And, even with lower prices, it would take them years to get the economies of scale McKee gets from its overwhelming market share.'' McKee maintains its low overhead by employing an independent distribution system and by expanding production only to keep pace with demand. Another advantage it has over the competition is the long shelf life of its naturally preserved products—some three to four times as long as that of Hostess Twinkies.

Since 1980 McKee has enhanced its market share by selling to convenience stores as well as supermarkets and by periodically rolling out national television campaigns, the most memorable of which was launched in 1985 featuring impersonator Rich Little. New products, including Little Debbie Fancy Cakes and the Little Debbie Snack Favorite line, also serve as powerful inducements to buyers, at least half of which are age 15 and under. Now named the McKee Foods Corporation, the company markets to 44 states and has achieved sales of $525 million. Under chief executive officer Ellsworth McKee, the Tennessee bakery has preserved its highly private identity and strong family management (many third generation McKees hold high positions within the company). Although investment houses and bakery competitors, especially Continental, have hoped for the family to sell, Ellsworth has responded: ''There's no way we can be forced to.'' With its present highly profitable status as the largest independently owned company of its kind in the country, and with consumer demand and snack cake share still rising, there would be little sense in doing so.

Further Reading: ''The Bakery Top 40,'' *Bakery Production,* June 1983; *Milling and Baking News,* February 10, 1987; ''McKee Plans 'Little Debbie' Plant in Virginia,'' *Bakery Production,* May 1987; ''Family Clout Backs Philosophy of Independence in Era of Mergers,'' *Milling & Baking News,* November 11, 1988; ''McKee Baking Sets July Start for Production at New Virginia Plant,'' *Milling & Baking News,* May 8, 1990; ''McKee's New Snack Plant Begins Production,'' *Bakery Production,* August 1990; Stern, William, ''Mom and Dad Knew Every Name,'' *Forbes,* December 7, 1992; *The Story behind Little Debbie Snack Cakes,* McKee Foods Corporation.

—Jay P. Pederson

MDU RESOURCES GROUP, INC.

400 North Fourth Street
Bismarck, North Dakota 58501-4092
U.S.A.
(701) 222-7900
Fax: (701) 222-7606

Public Company
Incorporated: 1924 as Minnesota Northern Power Company
Employees: 1,800
Sales: $352.5 million
Stock Exchanges: New York
SICs: 1311 Crude Petroleum & Natural Gas; 1221
    Bituminous Coal & Lignite—Surface; 4923 Gas
    Transmission & Distribution; 4911 Electric Services

MDU Resources Group, Inc. (MDU) mines coal, participates in oil exploration, generates and distributes electricity, and transports and delivers natural gas. The company operates in Montana, North Dakota, South Dakota, and Wyoming and holds energy leases in Canada and on the Gulf Coast. Among its subsidiaries, the Fidelity Oil Group takes part in oil and natural gas ventures; Knife River Coal Mining Company mines over 4.7 million tons of lignite coal annually; Montana-Dakota Utilities Co. distributes natural gas and supplies electricity to 253 communities; Prairielands Energy Marketing, Inc. provides services to diverse energy markets; and Williston Basin Interstate Pipeline Company operates a natural gas pipeline system.

R. M. Heskett founded MDU as Minnesota Northern Power Company in 1924. Heskett was an engineer who began his career building electric streetcar systems in Wisconsin. After the automobile put the streetcar industry in decline, he entered the electric utility business with the financial backing of Wausau, Wisconsin, investors Cyrus C. Yawkey, Aytch Woodson, and the Alexander brothers. Heskett's first venture was in the teens and early 1920s, when he built and then sold the Minnesota Utilities Company. After this he retired briefly, but at the age of 53 he began the company that would become MDU Resources Group, Inc.

On March 14, 1924, he and his Wausau backers incorporated the Minnesota Northern Power Company. Heskett ran the company from Minneapolis and served as vice-president and general manager. Cyrus C. Yawkey and Walter Alexander served as president and secretary but had no operational responsibilities.

Minnesota Northern began its operational life by purchasing three utilities: Minnesota Electric Light and Power Company in Bemidji, Minnesota; the Glendive Heat, Light and Power Company in Glendive, Montana; and the electric utility at Sidney, Montana.

In 1926, Heskett bought 80 acres near Cabin Creek, in Eastern Montana, and drilled for natural gas. Drillers found enough gas for Heskett to commission a report on the site from Hope Engineering. Hope claimed it held enormous reserves, so Heskett quickly bought up the surrounding property. In 1927 Heskett hired Montana gas wildcatter Harry V. Mathews to run Gas Development Company, a subsidiary that would explore for and develop gas, and build pipelines. Gas Development set up four wells in 1927 and 18 wells in 1928. It acquired development interests in the Bowdoin Dome in northeastern Montana and the Pondera Field outside of Conrad, Montana.

Minnesota Northern sold this gas to an increasing territory of homeowners and businesses in the upper Midwest. It built pipelines to Marmarth, North Dakota, and Miles City, Montana, and it laid pipe southeast into the Black Hills of South Dakota. In 1929 the company committed $8 million for a 90-mile line to connect Glendive, Montana, with Williston, North Dakota, and a 220-mile line from the Baker Field to Bismarck, North Dakota. Besides this geographic expansion, the company also pursued acquisitions as another method of increasing business. In January 1929 Heskett acquired the Havre Natural Gas Company, and in 1930 he bought Montana Cities Gas Company, Northern Natural Gas Development Company, and the manufactured gas properties at Sheridan, Wyoming.

Through the late 1920s, Heskett's electric business followed a similar path of acquisition and extension. In 1925 alone Minnesota Northern acquired electric plants in seven North Dakota towns and seven Montana communities. In most cases, Heskett built long transmission lines, closed inefficient isolated plants, and dropped rates. In 1926, he acquired the Terry, Montana, power plant, installed a 600-kilowatt generator at Fairview, Montana, and hung several transmission lines between Montana and North Dakota, including a line from Bainville, Montana, to Williston, North Dakota.

Such acquisitions and line extensions continued, but the most significant activity of the late 1920s was a successful battle with Montana Power Company for the Miles City, Montana, electric franchise. Both companies organized publicity campaigns which urged Miles City residents to vote for their interests. Minnesota Northern also worked to expand per-customer electrical usage by selling refrigeration equipment to businesses and appliances to homeowners. Consumers could buy an automatic washer through their electric bill for one dollar down and a dollar a month. According to the official company history, *The Mondakonians—Energizers of the Prairies,* Minnesota Northern promoted the offer as "a copper washer for a silver dollar."

The Depression struck Minnesota Northern's territory in the late 1920s, when drought and depressed farm prices affected the Dakotas and eastern Montana. Following the stock market crash in 1929, conditions became even worse. Heskett committed $5 million to capital projects at the urging of President Herbert Hoover for American utility executives to continue major construction projects in an attempt to aid the ailing U.S. economy. It soon became apparent, however, that business could not spend its way out of the Depression. Credit tightened and Minnesota Northern's income fell from $4 million in 1930 to $3.2 million in 1934. Longtime employee H.N. Elvig noted in *The Mondakonians* that the company's financial structure "was held together by such slender financial threads as to require the founders of the company to guarantee its debts with their own assets." Heskett refinanced troublesome short-term debt, cut wages across the board, inaugurated a sales campaign led by merchandise manager W.L. "Bill" Hayes, and perhaps most importantly relied on the essential financial soundness of Minnesota Northern's Wausau-based backers.

In 1935, Minnesota Northern was faced with another type of threat when Congress passed the Public Utility Holding Company Act (PUHC), which limited utility holding companies to one operating subsidiary. The law was a reaction to the abuses of several giant electric utility holding companies who then dominated the industry, but it applied to all utility companies. Heskett opposed the bill. Nevertheless, he consolidated all Minnesota Northern's subsidiaries into one operating utility called the Montana-Dakota Utilities Co. Montana-Dakota conformed to the PUHC and was able to continue operations without interruption.

Growth returned in the later half of the 1930s. The needs of natural gas and electric customers expanded, especially around Fort Peck, where the U.S. Army Corps of Engineers was damming the Missouri River. Between 1935 and 1939 revenues fluctuated between $4.4 million and $4.6 million, finally breaking the $5 million mark in 1940. Economic conditions improved further as Europe went to war. In the spring of 1941, Heskett told shareholders that "the year 1940 was one of the most satisfactory in the history of the company. . . . For the first time in its history, total operating revenues of the company exceeded $5 million and net income after all deductions exceeded $1 million," according to *The Mondakonians*.

Also in 1940, the company acquired the gas franchise of Crookston, Minnesota, and completed a 117-mile pipeline from Fort Peck to Glendive, which added six communities to its customer base and connected the Bowdoin Field reserves to its growing pipeline system. By year's end sales of equipment and appliances were up 25 percent and MDU had 23,757 gas customers and 18,052 electric customers.

As the nation geared up for war, many Mondakonians, as Montana-Dakota employees called themselves, joined up, were drafted, or left the region. By June of 1942, close to 10 percent of the company's prewar work force was in the service. During the war itself, labor and materials shortages made repairs difficult and expansion nearly impossible. After the war, Montana-Dakota expanded and took its present shape.

On the electric side, MDU made two key acquisitions. In October 1945, it paid $7 million for the Dakota Public Service Company, an electric and mining firm whose subsidiaries provided electricity to 91 communities, including Bismarck, North Dakota, and had yearly revenues close to $2 million. Two years later, Montana-Dakota paid $1.8 million for the Sheridan County Electric Company, its first electric utility in Wyoming.

The company took a variety of steps to secure electricity for its new customers. It bought power from the federal government's Fort Peck dam, and agreed to transport power to area electric cooperatives in exchange for 5,000 kilowatts of firm power from the Bureau of Reclamation's Fort Peck dam along the Missouri River. In terms of generating capacity, Montana-Dakota constructed several small diesel and coal-fired generators in the 3,400–8,500 kilowatt range and completed its first large steam generator, the 25,000-kilowatt, coal-fired R.M. Heskett Station. Overall generating capacity increased from 14,837 kilowatts to 68,270 kilowatts between 1945 and 1951. Transmission mileage was up from 973 to 2,616. Kilowatt-hour sales grew from 40.5 million to 221.6 million, and electric revenues skyrocketed from $1.5 million to $6.88 million.

In the gas business, Montana-Dakota's primary postwar aim was to firm up supplies, which had begun to run short in 1944 and 1945. In the summer of 1947, Montana-Dakota began storing gas for winter usage in Carter Oil Company's Billy Creek Field south of Buffalo, Wyoming. In 1948 it started buying gas from Pure Oil Company's Worland, Wyoming, field, and in 1950 it built a 334-mile, 12-inch gas transmission pipeline from the Worland field to the gas storage field at Cabin Creek.

With established supplies, the gas business again began expanding. In May 1951, Montana-Dakota acquired Billings Gas and the Rocky Mountain Gas Company. Billings Gas owned natural gas properties in Billings, Montana, and eight other Montana towns, while Rocky Mountain owned the Big Horn Pipeline and held the gas franchises in four Wyoming communities. Billings and Rocky Mountain increased Montana-Dakota's natural gas customer roles by 16,000 and helped push its 1951 gas revenues to $9.1 million. Montana-Dakota's total revenues for 1951 were $16.8 million.

Montana-Dakota also explored new business areas after the war. It acquired the Knife River Coal Mining Company—which switched from underground to surface mining—in the 1945 deal for Dakota Public Service. Then in the 1950s, oil reserves in eastern Montana were tapped. Rather than exploit the oil themselves, Montana-Dakota executives signed a net proceeds agreement with Shell Western E & P. Shell Western operated the company's 90,000-acre leased properties, which by 1958 were producing more than 860,000 barrels and paying $300,000 to Montana-Dakota.

By the mid-1950s, growth in electrical usage demanded further generating capacity. On June 6, 1956, the company broke ground for the Lewis & Clark Station, a 44,000-kilowatt, lignite-fired unit on the Yellowstone River outside Sidney, Montana. Completed in 1959 for $12 million, Lewis & Clark was succeeded a scant two years later by ground-breaking on a $10.5 million, 66,000-kilowatt addition to Heskett Station.

As electrical demand continued to increase (kilowatt-hour sales would more than double in the 1960s), Montana-Dakota looked for innovative ways to increase capacity. In 1962, it proposed a seasonal swap of electricity with the Bureau of Reclamation's Pick-Sloan dams but was turned down. In January 1963 it joined the 20-member Mid-Continent Area Power Planners, an organization which worked to strengthen transmission ties in the upper Midwest. In 1965, Mid-Continent members agreed to build a 5,400-mile grid of high-voltage transmission lines across a state region, enabling members and others to buy and sell excess capacity.

In 1964, R. M. Heskett, then in his nineties, stepped down after 30 years at the head of the company. Cecil Smith was named chairman of the board, while his nephew and R.M. Heskett's son, David Heskett, was named Montana-Dakota president and CEO. David Heskett reorganized the company according to modern management practices. He delegated authority to department heads, installed a conventional chain of command, and brought in new outside directors. Two years after R. M. Heskett's death in 1966, David Heskett moved the company headquarters from Minneapolis, Minnesota, to Bismarck, North Dakota.

In the late 1960s, Montana-Dakota experienced continued customer and usage growth. To satisfy electric demand, in 1969 David Heskett and officials of Minnesota's Otter Tail Power Company and South Dakota's Northwestern Public Service Company announced a joint venture to construct a 400,000-kilowatt, lignite-powered generating station near Big Stone Lake in eastern South Dakota. Montana-Dakota would contribute $20 million to the $100 million project, which would break ground in 1971 and be completed in 1975. The plant, whose construction marked the end of a long rivalry between Montana-Dakota and Northwestern Public Service, would be fueled by coal mined at Knife River Coal Mining Company's Gascoyne Mine in Bowman County in southwestern North Dakota.

In the early 1970s, the company expanded its natural gas distribution system in two "Progress" projects. "Progress '70" extended gas pipelines 227 miles eastward across North Dakota, bringing service to 12 new communities at a cost of $18.5 million. "Progress '72" extended the gas system north to the U.S. Army's Perimeter Acquisition Radar (PAR) site near Cavalier, North Dakota, and led the way to gas service for five North Dakota communities. To supply these new customers, Montana-Dakota explored for gas in the five sedimentary basins of the Rocky Mountain High Plains Region, and in 1974 acquired gas from the Rapelje Lake Basin northwest of Billings.

The major event of 1972 was the Rapid City, South Dakota, flood. On June 9, Rapid Creek overflowed, killing 238 people and damaging or destroying more than 2,000 dwellings. Montana-Dakota crews worked through the night for the next two weeks restoring service to the Black Hills and rebuilding much of the devastated gas transmission system.

The Big Stone Plant was finished on time in 1975, but at a higher cost than anticipated. A major component in its $160 million price tag was $30 million for pollution abatement. Pollution control was becoming a major cost throughout the Montana-Dakota system. Between 1973 and 1975, the company spent $8.7 million on electrostatic precipitators, scrubbers, and new smokestacks at existing generators. At Knife River, surface mining was subject to increasingly stringent North Dakota reclamation laws. Pollution control was not the only area where costs rose in the mid and late 1970s. Inflation, high interest

rates, and increasingly expensive natural gas squeezed finances and forced the company to repeatedly seek rate relief.

Despite these pressures, Montana-Dakota again needed new generating capacity by the mid-1970s. In 1977, Montana-Dakota and four regional partners announced they would build a 410-megawatt, lignite-powered generating station at Beulah, North Dakota. Situated adjacent to the Beulah Mine of the Knife River Coal Mining Company, Coyote Station would be a mine-mouth plant, cooled by piped-in Missouri River water.

Montana-Dakota also needed new gas. In the late 1970s, a nationwide natural gas shortage exacerbated the problems the company faced in the cold winter of 1977–1978. Because it stored gas in underground formations, Montana-Dakota survived the winter without any major mishaps. It did, however, interrupt service to industrial customers.

On January 1, 1978, David Heskett retired, and Montana-Dakota's chief financial officer, John A. Schuchart became president. Schuchart aimed to reorganize Montana-Dakota in ways which would exploit its technical know-how. In the early 1980s, however, the company faced natural gas supply problems brought about by changing policies. To meet a growing demand for gas, Montana-Dakota contracted for supplies of deregulated gas. Deregulated gas proved too pricey for customers, however. Consumers conserved and industrial customers switched to cheaper alternate fuels, leaving Montana-Dakota with multimillion dollar contracts for gas it could not use.

On the electric side, Schuchart spent the 1980s rearranging Montana-Dakota's supply structure. He retired several older plants and in 1985 acquired further shares of the Big Stone and Coyote generating stations. In June 1986 he bought capacity at Basin Electric Power Cooperative's Antelope Valley II plant.

By the mid-1980s, Schuchart was able to institute his reorganization plan. In 1985, he created MDU Resources Group, Inc., structured like a holding company under which he grouped the individual lines of business, though still operating within the bounds of the PUHC. Schuchart explained in *The Mondakonians* that the reason for the restructuring, begun in 1985 "was to better enable us to develop the individual assets which prior to that time had really been embedded and lost in the Montana-Dakota Utilities Co. structure."

Among the new subsidiaries, Williston Basin Interstate Pipeline Company faced a difficult time in the gas supply, production, and transmission business. Under deregulation, the role of the pipeline company changed from merchant to transporter. Rates fell, which was good news for the consumer but bad news for MDU, whose overall gas business suffered as deregulation and warmer than normal winters caused a downward spiral in prices.

The Fidelity Oil Group took proceeds from the Shell-run Cedar Creek Anticline property and invested them in oil and gas operations in the western half of the U.S. and Canada. From the beginning of the program in 1986, when reserves totaled 12 million barrels, Fidelity increased reserves to 17 million barrels by the end of 1991.

At Knife River Coal Mining Company, the late 1980s saw business suffer for two reasons: coal was in oversupply, and sales volume dropped sharply in 1987 after a crack in the rotor shaft caused a shutdown of the Big Stone Plant. After the reorganization, Knife River executives began looking at mineral mining and clean coal technology as new ways to exploit their expertise. This effort intensified during the early 1990s, when clean air legislation put the future of the lignite coal business in doubt. In June 1992 it acquired KRC Aggregate, Inc., a sand and gravel mining company based in Lodi, California, and the company also considered buying cleaner-burning coal operations in the West.

The last element in Schuchart's reorganization was Prairielands Energy Marketing, which expanded markets for the corporation's energy products. In 1991, Prairielands signed a 17-year capacity agreement with the Northern Border Pipeline system. The agreement provided a link between regional natural gas reserves and major national markets. In 1992, Prairielands began utilizing the natural gas futures market.

From its beginning in 1924 as an investment project of utility executive R. M. Heskett, MDU grew into a $367 million company by acquiring existing electric and gas utilities around the upper Midwest and extending pipelines. MDU eventually confined its operations to a four-state area, where it also maintained a pipeline system, drilled for gas, and mined coal. After reorganizing as a holding company in the mid-1980s, MDU Resources Group, Inc. continued to experience success through decentralization and modernization of its diversified holdings.

Principal Subsidiaries: Fidelity Oil Group; Knife River Coal Mining Company; Montana-Dakota Utilities Co.; Prairielands Energy Marketing, Inc.; Williston Basin Interstate Pipeline Company.

Further Reading: Beck, Bill, *The Mondakonians: Energizers of the Prairie,* Duluth, Minnesota, MDU Resources Group, Inc., 1992.

—Jordan Wankoff

MEDIA GENERAL, INC.

333 Grace Street
Richmond, Virginia 23219
U.S.A.
(804) 649-6000
Fax: (804) 649-6865

Public Company
Founded: 1879 as Dispatch Co.
Employees: 6,900
Sales: $595.6 million
Stock Exchanges: American
SICs: 2711 Newspapers; 2621 Paper Mills; 4833 Television
   Broadcasting Stations; 4841 Cable & Other Pay Television
   Services

Media General, Inc. is a diversified media company with interests in daily and weekly newspapers, cable and broadcast television, radio, and newsprint production, mostly in the southern and eastern United States.

The precursor to Media General began in 1879 as the Dispatch Co., which published the *Richmond Dispatch* and was run by the Bryan family. In 1896 the Bryans bought the *Richmond Leader*, and seven years later they merged it with a competing newspaper to create the *News Leader*. In 1937 the company started an AM radio outlet in Richmond. In 1949 an FM radio station was also launched. The FM station reached a larger area but had a much smaller audience, especially in its first few decades when FM technology was in its infancy.

By 1940 the company's newspapers had the widest circulation in Virginia, and the Dispatch Co. changed its name to Richmond Newspapers Inc. During the 1950s and 1960s the *News Leader* was known for its conservative editorials that strongly supported segregation, and some critics blamed it for splitting Richmond along racial lines. In 1964, the company began a $8.3 million three year modernization program. New technologies were rapidly changing the way newspapers could be produced, and Richmond decided to take advantage of them. The company bought computer typesetting equipment, new presses, and photocomposition machinery, which set advertising on photographic film instead of in type. The equipment was expected to save $300,000 to $400,000 a year. The company also added a 42,780 square foot, five floor addition to its main office.

By the mid 1960s the Richmond area had grown to about 1.2 million people, and the company's newspapers were read by 90 percent of the community's households—the highest rate of readership in a major U.S. media market. With a circulation of 275,000, Richmond Newspapers not only had the highest circulation of Virginia newspapers, but was 34th in the United States. The *Times-Dispatch* had 12 news bureaus. The AM radio station was reaching a million listeners during the day by the late 1960s, and nearly 500,000 at night. The firm also owned both daily newspapers in Winston-Salem, North Carolina and a cable television system in Virginia.

In 1966 the company went public and set about transforming itself from a small newspaper publisher into a media conglomerate. That year it bought a 52.2 percent interest in the Tribune Co. for $17.5 million, plus an exchange of stock. Based in Tampa, Florida, this media company had 1965 revenues of $18.9 million and owned the *Tampa Tribune* and the *Tampa Times*, as well as radio stations WFLA AM and FM and the television station WFLA. The television station, an NBC affiliate started in 1955, was the fastest growing part of the operation, with income jumping from $416,000 in 1961 to $1.4 million in 1965. Its broadcasts had a 75-mile radius and reached 1.7 million people. Furthermore, Tampa was one of the fastest growing cities in the United States and was considered a good environment in which to build a media business.

In 1969 Media General Inc. was formed as a public holding company for Richmond Newspapers and the Tribune Co. Media General then bought an additional 29 percent of the Tribune Company's stock for $9 million. Alan S. Donnahoe, a former statistician and research director who had been with Richmond Newspapers since 1950, was appointed president of Media General. In 1970 the new company bought New Jersey's *Newark News* and Garden State Paper's newsprint recycling plants from Richard B. Scudder for $50 million in Media General stock. The newspaper was soon closed for a year by an extended strike, however, and when it reopened it was severely weakened. *The Newark News* lost $3 million in five months before Media General closed it down. The company's loss was mitigated by the fact that it had earlier sold the Sunday edition to the rival *Newark Star-Ledger* for $20 million. Media General also kept $8 million worth of the *News*'s presses.

Garden State Paper's reprocessing mills in California, New Jersey, and Chicago sold recycled newsprint to 160 newspapers and had patents on its recycling processes. Its cash flow was $27 million in 1970, growing to $32 million in 1971. With recycling becoming increasingly popular, it was expected to continue that growth rate. The recycling plant was so successful that some industry analysts felt that it was the paper plant, not the newspaper, that Media General had been after in the deal.

One of the primary functions of the company's computers and phototypesetters was preparing the *News Leader*'s financial section. In 1971 the company decided it could use those data to start a strictly financial newspaper. The *Financial Daily* was printed weekday afternoons in Richmond and flown to major cities along the east coast. It included financial data on 9,000 securities and 4,000 stocks as well as news centering on financial interests. When the printers union struck over wages and control of the automated typesetting equipment, Donnahoe bought more computers and the automated printing continued.

However, the *Financial Daily* continued to lose money; it lost $1.5 million during its first months of operation. Although the company spent $300,000 on an ad campaign for the *Financial Daily* and mailed 400,000 subscription offers, it found only 2,500 people interested in the $165 per year subscription. Rather than continue to support the newspaper, hoping it would eventually break even, Donnahoe soon decided to turn it into the *Financial Weekly*, lowering the price to $50 a year. When the daily paper went to a weekly format, management transferred the automated printing techniques to the other Richmond newspapers. About 200 printers were replaced by 140 clerks, who were paid an average of $50 a week less than the printers. Impressed with the $750,000 per year the new automation saved in production expenses, the company spent $24 million to automate the Tampa newspapers. It also began selling financial data to money managers, though the *Financial Weekly* was still losing money in 1973. Garden State Paper was contributing 20 percent of Media General's revenue, and in mid-1973 the firm announced plans to boost its recycling capacity 25 percent to 325,000 tons a year.

In the mid-1970s advertising fell and newsprint costs rose. Many newspaper chains were pinched by these trends, but Media General was able to profit because of its newsprint recycling operations. Not only did they hold down its own costs, but the firm made money selling newsprint to such customers as the *New York Times*, the *Washington Post*, and the *Los Angeles Times*. Garden State Paper accounted for about 40 percent of Media General's $170 million in total revenues. The biggest user of waste paper was the residential construction market, which used tons of fiberboard made from recycled paper. Demand from a homebuilding boom lead to a doubling of the price of waste newsprint in 1973 and 1974, and to ensure Garden State's supply, Media General bought one of the biggest waste paper dealers in New York and signed contracts with several West Coast brokers.

In 1977 Media General, along with Knight-Ridder Newspapers, Inc. and Cox Enterprises, Inc., built a $125 million newsprint mill in Dublin, Georgia. The mill had an annual capacity of 156,000 tons, of which Media General took 20,000. Media General earned $18 million in 1978 on sales of $243.7 million. In 1980 the firm bought Golden West Publishing Corp., a chain of weekly newspapers in Southern California, for $8 million. It bought another weekly newspaper publisher, Highlander Publications, for $12.7 million.

In 1982, with afternoon newspapers in steep decline throughout the United States, Media General stopped publication of the *Tampa Times* evening paper. It also sold WFLA AM and FM to John Blair & Co. for $14 million. Cable television was becoming a huge market, however, and Media General won a 15-year cable franchise in affluent Fairfax County, Virginia, near Washington, D. C. The cable system was a $120 million investment. In 1982, newspapers and publishing accounted for 42 percent of company profits, while newsprint accounted for 45 percent and broadcasting 13 percent.

Also in 1982, Media General bought William B. Tanner Co., a Memphis-based media buying service, for $36 million. The Tanner Co. served 200 large advertisers and about 6,000 broadcast outlets. In 1983, William Tanner was charged with income tax fraud, mail fraud, and accepting kickbacks, and federal law enforcement agents searched Tanner's premises for documents relating to the charges. Consequently, Tanner stepped down, and Media General took direct control of the company, renaming it Media General Broadcast Services. Tanner eventually pleaded guilty and went to jail, but Media General was cleared of any wrongdoing. Nevertheless, the broadcast unit was seriously hurt by the episode. Sales plummeted, and Media General Broadcast began losing between $2 million and $6 million a year.

In 1983 Media General bought television stations in Jacksonville, Florida, and Charleston, South Carolina. In 1984 Donnahoe, who was 68, retired and was succeeded by James S. Evans, who joined the firm in 1973 as a vice-president. Revenue for 1984 was $507.8 million.

In 1985 the company ceased publication of the afternoon *Winston-Salem Sentinal*. Its sister paper, the profitable morning *Journal*, expanded its coverage, started a new weekly business section, and absorbed most of its staff. Also in 1985, Media General acquired 40 percent of Garden City Newspapers Inc., the troubled newspaper publisher that the firm hoped to turn around.

After the stock market crash of 1987 a group of investors lead by Hollywood producer Burt Sugarman bought about ten percent of Media General's stock. In 1988 the group offered first $1.57 billion and then about $2 billion for the company shares they didn't already own. Media General management was able to refuse the takeover offer, because the company had been created with two kinds of stock. The owners of the Class B stock, mostly the company's management, were given veto power over any takeover attempts. Sugarman challenged the legality of the A and B structure, but a judge upheld it, and, in the end, Sugarman sold his stake back to Media General for $100 million. Of this, $44 million was in cash and $56 million was represented by interest in the Pomona, California, paper mill.

In 1988, the company sold Media General Broadcast Services to its management. Broadcast was still losing money, and Media General took a charge against earnings to cover the sale. In 1989, five Media General insiders sold about 50 percent of their stake in the company. The five said that they were selling for tax purposes, but some industry analysts felt that the move was related to a downturn in advertising and media, as well as the recent loss of the Pomona paper mill. The company also sold its recently acquired weekly newspapers at Highlander Publications and Golden West Publishing. The company made $20.7 million in 1989 on sales of $595 million.

Newsprint operations accounted for 47 percent of company profits in 1987. Although in 1990 the company decided to sell Garden State's recycling mill in Garfield, New Jersey, as part of a strategy to concentrate on its communications properties, management soon changed its mind and took the mill off the auction block before it was sold. The company had a difficult year in 1991, losing $62 million, partly due to a decline in sales prompted by the recession, and partly due to a sharp increase in capital expenditures. The recession hampered advertising sales at the company's own newspapers and also hurt sales of recycled newsprint, since other newspapers were printing fewer pages. The recession seriously hurt the debt laden Garden City Newspapers, and Media General wrote off its investment and took a $78.3 million charge against earnings.

In May 1992 publication of the 104-year-old Richmond *News Leader* ceased. An afternoon paper, its circulation had sunk to under 100,000, while the morning *Times-Dispatch* was thriving. The *News Leader* was merged into the *Times-Dispatch*, and 44 of the two newspapers' 1,100 employees were laid off.

Further Reading: "Richmond Newspapers Presses Ahead." *Barron's,* January 16, 1967; "Media General to Start a Financial Newspaper," *Wall Street Journal,* May 17, 1971; "Media General's Fortunate Misfortune," *Business Week,* November 25, 1972; "The Old Newspaper Man," *Forbes,* January 15, 1976; Cuff, Daniel F., "A Jolt to Media General Image." *New York Times,* September 15, 1983; Harris, Roy J., "Barris Industries, Giant Group Offer $1.57 Billion to Buy Media General," *Wall Street Journal,* March 1, 1988; Dorfman, John R., "Five Media General Insiders Sell Close to 50% of Shares," *Wall Street Journal,* May 8, 1989; "After 104 Years, Richmond Newspaper Closes," *New York Times,* May 31, 1992.

—Scott Lewis

MEIJER INCORPORATED

2929 Walker Avenue N.W.
Grand Rapids, Michigan 49504-9428
U.S.A.
(616) 453-6711
Fax: (616) 791-2572

Private Company
Incorporated: 1934
Employees: 48,000
Sales: $3 billion (estimate)
SICs: 5411 Grocery Stores; 5141 Groceries—General Line

Meijer Incorporated is a retailer operating more than 70 food and general merchandise stores as well as 55 gas stations throughout Michigan and Ohio; the company also owns and operates four office centers, two divisions of property services, and more than ten distribution centers. Meijer entered the wholesale shopping segment in 1992 with the development of SourceClub, warehouse-shopping designed for the individual shopper, as well as the more traditional targeted customers from small businesses and affiliated groups. In business since 1934, Meijer has created up to 10,000 private-label brands.

Hendrik Meijer emigrated from the Netherlands to the United States in 1907, settling in Michigan. In 1914 he opened a barbershop, expanding it to a double storefront by 1923. When the Depression hit, Meijer had trouble finding a tenant to rent the new space in his Greenville, Michigan, location. He decided to open a grocery store, hoping to cover the building rent and operating costs from store profits. With $338.76 of goods bought on credit, Hendrik Meijer opened his food store in 1934, competing with a grocer across the street as well as more than 20 competitors in town.

With his son Frederick, born in 1919, Hendrik Meijer traveled as far as necessary to find the best goods for his grocery at the lowest prices available. In keeping with the needs of 1930s America, Meijer's goal was to help customers of his Thrift Market store save money. To speed shoppers' progress through the store, Fred built a space designed to display twelve hand-held baskets. Above the baskets was a hand-written sign inviting customers to take one and help themselves. This "self-service" innovation of 1935 increased the number of customers Meijer could serve, thus aiding the growth of the business. By 1937 Hendrik Meijer had doubled the size of his original store.

As the grocer across the street from the original Meijer store mowed his neatly-kept lawn, Hendrik noticed the more trampled path to the front door of his shop with pride. In 1942 Meijer opened a second store. With the help of wife Gezina, daughter Johanna, and son Fred, Hendrik Meijer's business succeeded through the 1940s. In the 1950s the family built four new stores and opened a supermarket chain in western Michigan. After a fire leveled Meijer's first Greenville store, the company relocated to its present Grand Rapids, Michigan, headquarters.

Meijer had more than ten stores in operation in Grand Rapids, Muskegon, and Holland, Michigan, by the late 1950s. Trading stamps became popular in supermarkets across the country through the next two decades. Meijer, though offered a stamp program from some of the major vendors, declined. Then the company, with some trepidation, initiated its own Goodwill stamp campaign in 1956 at a cost of $10,000 a week. While gross sales increased, overhead costs increased as well, keeping Meijer's profits steady.

In 1961, with 14 supermarkets in operation, Meijer decided to drop the stamp program. According to the owner, there was neither profit nor reputation to be gained from doing what nearly all other retailers were doing at the time. With a thorough campaign planned, Meijer began a series of advertisements designed to promote its singular position as a supermarket that maintained a strong customer base simply by offering below-average prices. Beginning with a week-long newspaper series, Meijer ran ads with no identification to spark the interest of readers.

A picture of a baby and the statement, "It's about time somebody wakes up!" was followed with another infant photo and the words, "Nobody, but nobody gets nothin' for nothin'." In the following Sunday paper, Meijer identified itself and announced that it was closing stores the following Monday to lower hundreds of prices. Banners urged buyers to "Save U.S. Green Currency—Redeemable Anywhere for almost Anything!" Finally, Meijer revealed its plan to drop stamps. When shoppers arrived at Meijer on Tuesday, they found shelves lined with a profusion of tags listing "Typical Stamp Store Price" as compared with "Meijer No-Stamp Price." The company continued its barrage, with circulars detailing price lists, comparing as many as 540 items with competitors' prices. While the competition offered double- and triple-coupon savers, Meijer nonetheless increased its market share as a result of the campaign it waged to keep its image as a different kind of supermarket.

By 1961 Meijer had 14 supermarkets in the Grand Rapids area, with more on the way. In 1962 the company opened its first Thrifty Acres Discount Department Store, a combination food/retail item store similar to a hypermarket which had opened in Belgium the previous year. Within two years Meijer had three Thrifty Acres built, and had two more in the planning stages. These large capacity discount markets vastly increased Meijer's lead in the retail segment. The growth of Meijer was overshadowed, however, by the death of founder Hendrick at age 57 in 1964. Fred continued expansion after his father's death, building Meijer's reputation as a low-cost retailer.

Extending further into Michigan through the late 1960s, Meijer entered the Ohio market as well. The Meijer one-stop shopping theme, which the company claims to have pioneered, gave the customer a chance to buy these items in addition to food, checking all of the following merchandise out at one counter: garden and pet supplies, small appliances, jewelry, sporting goods, clothing, and home fashions. Growth remained steady through the 1970s. Meijer had more than 20 stores open, some set up with gasoline pumps as well. Though Meijer planned to build more retail/gas station combination stores, its plans were stalled by a 1978 law prohibiting a business from selling both gasoline and alcohol unless it was in a village, town, or municipality with a population less than 3,000.

By the 1980s the hypermarket was a concept destined to remain. On the national scene, retail giants like Kmart and Wal-Mart dominated; locally, competitors increased advertising and low-price wars. As more and more stores increased their square footage and challenged Meijer in the discount retail segment, the company had to more aggressively carve out its niche. There was no way around it; Meijer increased advertising dramatically. In 1984 the business bought 880 inches of page space in the Grand Rapids Press; by December 1985, Meijer had increased space to 2,800 inches.

The company introduced in-store delis, bakeries, and fresh meat and fish departments in the mid-1980s, promoting the changes under the slogan "Rediscover Meijer's." An example of the low-price wars was the December, 1985 scuffle over banana sales. Meijer advertised them at 14 cents a pound. When an independent offered bananas for 11 cents, Meijer countered with a ten cents a pound offer. Another competitor planned on selling the fruit for five cents a pound. The goal was to get more and more customers in the door, the price of bananas simply a sideshow. As Grand Rapids market owner David Daane, quoted in the January 20, 1986 trade journal Supermarket News, commented: "You know what they say in the grocery business: One guy jumps off the cliff and the others follow." Important to note is how Meijer resembled its competitors in strategy, and when, and if, it differed from them.

In February of 1987 Meijer marched into the Columbus, Ohio market, claiming more than 20% of the shopping public with only one store open in the area. The company planned at least one more unit in Columbus, which was gaining other wholesale club stores as well at the time.

A major change in Meijer's practices occurred a year later when the company announced it would keep most of its Michigan and Ohio stores open 24 hours after March 7, 1988. Forty-three of 46 stores were designated to be open round the clock, and—departing from the previous policy of closing Meijer stores for Thanksgiving and Easter—on every day except for Christmas Day and a half day on Christmas Eve. Employees sent a letter to Fred Meijer, requesting that he reconsider the change and allow them the chance to spend holidays with families and friends. Meijer chose instead to present the new hours as an opportunity for employees to be promoted from part time to full time, or to move up to management ranks.

In an effort to sell alcohol in its Michigan stores, in March 1988 Meijer pushed passage of a state bill to change the ten-year-old law prohibiting the sale of alcohol and gasoline from the same location. The bill would allow gas pumps on a site where liquor was sold provided the shopping center had 50,000 square feet of space or an inventory of at least $250,000. Opponents included the Associated Food Dealers of Michigan and the Package Liquor Dealers Association. The latter group stated that the bill was discriminatory and served the interests of the big chains only.

Meijer had reason enough to compete at any level possible; by 1988 the company, still unknown outside its Michigan/Ohio retail segment, ranked number 42 in the Fortune 400 private companies. Fred Meijer, son of the founder, had an estimated wealth over $400 million. After 50 years in business, company sales were estimated at $2 billion. Meijer proved a serious challenge to any small retailers in its market, and could even go up against the mega-retailers K mart and Wal-Mart. In addition to its Meijer stores, the company owned 36 Sagebrush casual clothing stores, 16 Tansy women's clothing stores, and either owned or leased various in-store services such as postal stations and dry-cleaning units.

By year-end 1988, Meijer phased out its Sagebrush and Tansy facilities as leases expired. Meijer stores increased to 53, and the company put $20 million into the construction of its tenth distribution center, its largest to date, near Detroit. Since construction was delayed at the distribution center, a halt was called on the progress of four new stores slated for the Dayton, Ohio region, and one in Columbus. Four other store constructions, at the prototypical size of 225–250,000 square feet, were on target schedules. Two were in Detroit suburbs, one near Ann Arbor, and one in Springfield, Ohio, which could replace the Meijer store already there (49,000 square feet, one of the smallest the company operated).

A Meijer innovation in early 1989 was an electronic checking system. The Meijer 1 Card allowed customers to withdraw from their checking accounts automatically, with no paperwork or identification verification necessary. Patrick Gavin, vice president of pharmacy, service, and retail technology, stated in the Grand Rapid Press that Meijer would be "the first in the world to set up a paperless software system through [its] cash registers." The company and banking institutions could save money, up to a total of $1.75 per check, on processing fees.

By mid-1989, sales for the entire Meijer chain were estimated at $65 million per week, bringing the annual sales figure to approximately $3 billion. Store sales were not the only indicator of Meijer's success, however; each new Meijer store cost $18 million to put up, and Meijer was opening up to five per year during the 1980s. The company researched expansion possibilities in new markets such as Toledo, Ohio, and both South Bend and Indianapolis, Indiana.

In keeping with its growth, Meijer decided to make a historical advertising shift, moving from Grand Rapids' Johnson & Dean to Southfield, Michigan-based W.B. Doner & Company. Near Detroit, Doner had national marketing expertise, something Meijer looked for in a changing marketplace. Johnson & Dean had had the Meijer account for 33 years, a record time period in advertising, producing 200 radio and 150 television ads per year. In the Advertising Age, Patricia Strnad commented that, historically "Meijer appear[ed] to have relied on copying other advertising ideas rather than creating new ones."

Two months after Wal-Mart advertised its environmentally friendly stance, and at the same time as two unrelated supermarket chains in San Diego and Pittsburgh promoted similar concepts, Meijer initiated its environmental awareness program in late 1989. In-store posters, grocery bags, and shopping cart signs stated, "We Care About the Earth We Share." Videos, pamphlets, and other educational publications were slated for distribution as well. Grand Rapids-based D&W Food Center, a long-time Meijer competitor, had established an environmental program years before; the chain considered making its efforts more public in response to consumer interest in the issue.

Meijer awarded an advertising package to the Nappies biodegradable diaper manufacturer, Ontario-based Dafoe & Dafoe, in response to that company's efforts. While experts questioned whether the plastics used in the product were indeed biodegradable, Meijer countered by stating that the emphasis of its program was on consumer education. As quoted in *Supermarket News*, Meijer stated, "We're not interested in debating the specific merits of each manfacturer's claim. We're just trying to make it easier for customers to research these issues." The trade journal went on to observe that environmental issues would move to the forefront of retailers' agendas through the 1990s and into the next century.

Early in 1990—as it had done 30 years earlier—Meijer once again led its peers in abandoning double-coupon promotions. Beginning in its metropolitan Detroit stores, Meijer dropped the promotion in February. Ryan Mathews, Detroit-based editor of the journal Grocery Marketing, was quoted in the *Detroit Free Press*, describing such campaigns as "the most senseless act of marketing that [stores] can engage in." Luckily for Meijer, the retailer was known for its excellent customer service. The company could then use advertising to emphasize that aspect of its image, rather than concentrate on prices only, as most competitors did. Drawing from founder Hendrik Meijer's steady, practical approach to retailing, Meijer's ad agency W. B. Doner & Company planned television spots based on that theme, with the slogan: "Meijer. The store built on common sense."

Meijer store openings planned included three in Michigan in 1990 and seven in 1991, with three planned for the Dayton, Ohio market and four slated for Toledo. Wal-Mart confronted Meijer in its own backyard, moving into the Ohio market with the construction of a new distribution center there. Industry analysts noted Meijer's traditionally loyal customer base as a hedge against the Wal-Mart presence. Digging its heels in, Meijer took advantage of the exit of retailers Ames and Hills from the Cincinnati area to re-enter a market it had pulled out of in 1987. (After six years of operating eight stores offering general merchandise only, Meijer had sold its stores to Zayre, which Ames acquired in 1988. Both Ames and Hills filed Chapter 11 bankruptcy in 1991.)

Management changes in April of 1990 paved the way for Fred Meijer's eventual retirement. His sons Doug and Hank Meijer were named co-chairmen, while Fred became chairman of the executive committee, with plans to work with senior management on the company's day-to-day operations. Other key executives included Mark Meijer, a member of the "Office of the Chairman," and Earl Holton, president and chief operating officer. Vice-Chairman Harvey Lemmen retired during the changeover.

Meijer continued researching expansion possibilities, usually with five years' lead time. Indiana and Kentucky were areas with growth potential. The company continued growing through the early 1990s as a premier discount retailer in the Midwest, maintaining a low profile and high profit margins. With sales at $3 billion, Meijer led in the field of hypermarket supercenters. The company viewed the challenges of the twenty-first century with its reputation as a consumer-oriented, progressive organization intact.

Further Reading: "Don't Just Drop Stamps—Give Customers Something Better," *Progressive Grocer*, February, 1963; Kaplan, Rachel, "Meijer Ads Heat Up Grand Rapids Market," *Supermarket News*, January 20, 1986; Kelly, Mary Ellen, "Traditional Columbus Chains Brace for Superstore Assault," *Discount Store News*, February 16, 1987; Couretas, John, "Most Meijer Stores to Open 24 Hours," *Grand Rapids Press*, February 6, 1988; Strnad, Patricia, "Meijer Hyper in Midwest Markets," *Advertising Age*, February 15, 1988; "Longtime Super Store Meijer Poised for Growth after Completion of DC," *Discount Store News*, December 19, 1988; Radigan Lohr, Mary, "Meijer Stores to use Electronic Checking System," *Grand Rapids Press*, March 12, 1989; "Meijer Finds Right Combination for Midwest," *Discount Store News*, July 17, 1989; Radigan Lohr, Mary, "Meijer Inc. Switching to Detroit-area Ad Agency," *Grand Rapids Press*, August 8, 1989; Strnad, Patricia, "Hypermarket Pioneer Changes Tack," *Advertising Age*, September 25, 1989; "Forbes 400," *Forbes*, October 23, 1989; DeNitto, Emily, "Meijer Breaks Store-Wide 'Earth Friendly' Program," *Supermarket News*, November 6, 1989; Muller, Joann, "Meijer First Store to Cut Double Coupons," *Detroit Free Press*, February 20, 1990; Strnad, Patricia, "Meijer Shapes Ads on Common Sense," *Advertising Age*, April 16, 1990; "Meijer Faces Challenge from Wal-Mart Thrust," *Discount Store News*, July 16, 1990; Halverson, Richard C., "Meijer to Re-enter Cincy after Hills, Ames Exit," *Discount Store News*, June 17, 1991; "Meijer Leads Field as Hyper/Supercenter Challengers Take Aim," *Discount Store News*, July 22, 1991; Cipriano Pepperl, Jo-Ann, "Meijer: Serving Customers an Array of Choices," *Greater Lansing Business Monthly*, February 1, 1992.

—Frances E. Norton

MERCURY COMMUNICATIONS, LTD.

New Mercury House
26 Red Lion Square
London WC1R 4HQ
United Kingdom
(071) 528-2000
Fax: (071) 528-2577

Subsidiary of Cable & Wireless PLC and BCE Ltd
Incorporated: 1982
Employees: 9000
Sales: £915 million (US$1.33 billion)
SICs: 4813 Telephone Communications, Except Radio

Mercury Communications, Ltd. is one of the largest providers of telephone services—local, long distance, and international—in the United Kingdom. Both an ambitious business venture and an experiment in telecommunications competition, Mercury was created in 1982 and competes chiefly with British Telecommunications plc, the British telephone company, recently privatized after nearly 100 years as a division of the general post office.

Soon after the first telephone exchange in England was established in 1879, the British government placed the Postmaster General's office in charge of licensing telephone companies. In 1898 the Postmaster General issued licenses to 13 new telephone companies, hoping that they would break the near monopoly on telephone service held by the then dominant National Telephone Company. But by 1913 five of the six competitors that succeeded in building networks had been taken over by the post office or National Telephone. The following year the post office took control of National and created a state-run monopoly that would run nearly all of Britain's telephone services for the next 70 years. The British government determined that telephone networks were "natural monopolies," and ended its experiment with telecommunications competition.

In 1981, however, the British government under Prime Minister Margaret Thatcher undertook an effort to privatize nearly all the country's state-run industries, including British Airways, British Steel, British Aerospace, and the post office's telephone monopoly. The British Telecommunications Act that year reincorporated the telephone company as British Telecom in preparation for its sale to the public. The act also began the privatization of Cable & Wireless, the state-run offshore telephone company, which did most of its business in Hong Kong.

During this time, the British Department of Trade & Industry invited newcomers to file for licenses to compete with British Telecom. Cable & Wireless, Barclays PLC, and British Petroleum (BP) applied for one of these licenses after setting up a joint subsidiary called Mercury Communications, through which they planned to go head-to-head with BT.

The launch document describing Mercury proposed establishing a digital trunk network aimed only at high volume corporate users. The proposal specifically dismissed the notion of offering nationwide switched services, which would enable virtually any customer to bypass the BT network.

In February 1982, after no other companies applied for permission to challenge BT, Mercury received an interim operating license. The consortium named Sir Michael Edwardes, renowned for his success in turning around British Leyland, as Mercury's new chairperson.

At this time, three other companies applied for and received permission to operate as Public Telecommunications Operators, or PTOs. But because the government did not want to complicate the emerging "duopoly," the licenses for these companies, Vodaphone and Cellnet, were limited to cellular telephony. The third, Kingston Communications, was an independent local service provider.

Mercury began constructing its primary network, and in 1983 completed a microwave link between London and Birmingham. The following year Mercury began laying fiber optic cable along British Rail tracks, completing what became known as the "Figure of Eight," a double loop network extending north to Manchester, Leeds, and Nottingham, and south to Milton Keynes, London, and Bristol. At the center was Birmingham, where Mercury established its National Operations Center.

After Mercury negotiated an agreement to interconnect its network with BT, it encountered serious difficulties from the monopoly's workforce. Members of the Post Office Engineering Union (now the National Communications Union) refused to build the links between the two networks out of fear that Mercury would destroy BT's profitability, forcing large-scale employee layoffs.

The union hit Mercury from every side, at one point inciting fear that microwave radiation was potentially lethal. But, after mollifying the public with a scientific explanation of the nature of microwaves, and pointing out that BT operated a microwave network far more massive than anything Mercury had proposed, the union abandoned the issue. The media later chastised the union for failing to recognize that competition could cause the market to expand. Mercury, meanwhile, won a settlement with the union after threatening to take the matter to court.

During this time, the companies involved in the Mercury venture were often at odds and had great difficulty cooperating. In May 1984 Barclays suddenly withdrew from the consortium, claiming it had achieved its investment goals, but also apparently tired of battling BP. Consequently, Cable & Wireless and BP split Barclays 20 percent share of the venture. Then in August BP announced that it too would leave the consortium, offering no explanation. It was rumored at the time that BP was involved in negotiations to establish a rival network in cooperation with Pacific Telesis, but this was never substantiated.

Now in complete control of the company, Cable & Wireless installed Gordon Owen as Mercury's new managing director, instructing him to re-establish order. A month later, the government passed the 1984 Telecommunications Act, which privatized BT and certified Mercury to operate as a PTO for 25 years. The license was nearly identical to BT's but did not oblige Mercury to serve every customer who requested service.

Owen was known as a demanding manager, and he was appropriately suited to the task of making Mercury work. The company invested heavily in its network during 1984 and 1985, when it made a fundamental change in strategy. Instead of limiting itself to dedicated lines for high-volume business users, Mercury elected to build a switched network that would enable any caller, even residential customers, to use Mercury.

This strategy posed a new, more ominous threat to BT. Moving well beyond the lucrative but limited private line market, Mercury's entry into switched services stood to bring choice to millions of Britons who had been captive to BT. When Mercury began offering switched services in 1986, BT was obligated to handle any call traffic routed from Mercury and was restricted from discriminating against that traffic in terms of handling priority.

In this one bold step, Mercury placed itself at the forefront of the world telecommunications competition curve. The company was not only able to compete for private line services, but stood ready to handle literally millions of local, long distance, and international calls.

By contrast, while the U. S. government had succeeded in breaking up AT&T's monopoly, introducing long distance competition, local calls remained under smaller local monopolies, operated mostly by former Bell System companies.

In order to use Mercury service, customers had to instruct their local BT exchange that the call should be handed off to Mercury. This was done by dialing a special touch tone code. Seeing this extra button-pushing as a potential competitive disadvantage, Mercury arranged for the manufacture of special telephones equipped with a blue button. By pressing this button, the special code was entered automatically.

Mercury introduced switched international services in May 1987. The following year, it installed its first 26 public telephones at London's Waterloo train station. This number later grew to more than 4,500, supplanting BT's traditional red phone booths and other more modern public phones.

Between 1986 and 1988, Mercury had amassed a three-year operating loss of more than £66 million. A year later, however, the company recorded a profit of £18 million. This grew to £66 million in 1990, and doubled a year later.

Leadership at Mercury rotated quickly during the late 1980s. Gordon Owen was replaced by Peter van Cuylenburg, a former executive at Texas Instruments. Thoroughly steeped in modern electronic technology, van Cuylenburg treated the public network as a computer, rather than as a collection of switching centers. He also is credited with building the company's marketing and customer service operations, seeing them as one area where Mercury could clearly excel over BT.

In 1992, after only a short tenure, however, van Cuylenburg left Mercury and was replaced by Mike Harris, a former head of First Direct Bank. Harris emphasized financial strength in Mercury, and helped to keep the company's costs down during its initial years of heady growth. Under Harris, Mercury acted upon its desire to operate a network completely separate from BT.

Until this time, Mercury was forced to route the first and last leg of each call over BT facilities. These "local loops" (essentially the cable from a switching center to a customer's telephone) were far too expensive for Mercury to replicate. The cheaper alternative was to use the loops that BT had already established, and pay for that access. This arrangement kept Mercury at the mercy—and thoroughly under the thumb—of BT.

During the 1980s, however, a new industry began to grow in Britain that also required loops, albeit very different loops. Transmission of cable television signals required a thicker coaxial cable with sufficient bandwidth to carry as many as 30 different channels. Even occupied with 30 channels, these cables left sufficient bandwidth to carry a simple voice signal.

By connecting customers' telephones to cable loops, Mercury could switch and route calls over its network without ever having to cross BT's doorstep. Of course, the call would have to be handed off to BT if the receiver was a BT customer. Similarly, BT would have to hand off any calls from its customers to a Mercury customer.

Mercury entered into alliances with 16 cable companies throughout the U.K., who were then able to offer telephone as well as television services to their customers. At the end of January, 1993, Mercury had supplied over 117,000 telephone lines to cable operators. Cable operators, already licensed for telecommunications, benefited greatly by being able to offer two services on one network infrastructure. The cable industry was also promised favorable government regulations over the next decade.

In November of 1992, Cable & Wireless sold a 20 percent share in the enterprise to the Canadian company BCEbc, the parent company of Bell Canada, for about £480 million. In addition to bringing more than 100 years of telecommunications expertise to Mercury, BCE owns two large cable television systems in the United Kingdom.

Mercury then began work on personal communications networks, or PCNs, that will be able to handle a call anywhere it is taken. PCNs improve upon cellular phone technology by giving the customer total portability, able to make or take calls in the home or car, in an airplane, or even while on vacation thousands of miles from home. PCN technology will use smaller phone sets that operate at cheaper airtime rates than cellular phones.

Because PCNs are likely to replace conventional land-based and even cellular telephones, many companies waged heated competitions for the highly coveted rights to build PCN networks. Mercury's sister company, Mercury Personal Communications, was awarded a PCN license by the government in July 1991.

With a quarter million registered residential customers and more than 60,000 business customers, Mercury controls about ten percent of the British telecommunications market.

Principal Subsidiaries: Mercury Link 7500 Limited; Mercury Data Networks Limited; Mercury Communications (Enterprises) Limited; Mercury Payphones Limited; Direct Call Limited (trading as Adlink); TR Financial Communications plc (trading as Mercury Dealing Systems).

Further Reading: "Back Page Interview," *Connexion*, February 6, 1991; "Mercury Switch," *Connexion*, November 27, 1991; "BT Beater," *Business Magazine*, April, 1992; "Back Page Interview," *Connexion*, November 25, 1992; "Canadian Deal Equips Mercury to Challenge BT," *The Observer*, November 25, 1992; *Mercury Communications: The Facts, Company Document,* September, 1992; *Report and Accounts,* 1992.

—John Simley

METROMEDIA COMPANY

One Meadowlands Plaza
Sixth Floor
East Rutherford, New Jersey 07073
U.S.A.
(201) 804-6400
Fax: (201) 804-6432

Private Company
Employees: 19,000 full-time; 33,000 part-time
Sales: $2 billion
SICs: 4813 Telephone Communications Except
    Radiotelephone; 7312 Outdoor Advertising Services; 7011
    Hotels & Motels; 4812 Radiotelephone Communications;
    5812 Eating Places

Metromedia Company has emerged over the past decade as one of the largest private concerns in the United States, with varied interests in fields of technology, entertainment, telecommunications, and the restaurant industry. Guided by its founder and president, billionaire John W. Kluge, Metromedia has grown from a minor player in broadcasting to a major force in many areas of business. Throughout its history, the company's philosophies and business strategies have reflected the instincts and interests of Kluge, who is generally regarded as one of the richest individuals in the world.

John Kluge was born in Chemnitz, Germany. He and his family moved to the United States when he was eight years old, settling in Detroit. After a brief stint at Wayne State University, Kluge received a scholarship from Columbia and finished his schooling there. Even in college, Kluge's ambitious and risk-taking character was in full bloom. Kluge supplemented his scholarship money with income from three different jobs and skillful card playing. He graduated in 1937 and returned to Michigan, where he accepted a position with the Otten Brothers Company. He quickly acquired part-ownership of the company's paper conversion business.

With the advent of World War II, Kluge joined the U.S. Army, where he quickly rose to the rank of captain with the War Department General Staff in Military Intelligence. After the war, Kluge sold his interest in Otten Brothers and remained in Washington.

In 1946 Kluge purchased a radio station in Silver Spring, Maryland, for $15,000. Over the course of the next dozen years he acquired a number of additional FM radio stations, which at the time were regarded as an unappetizing alternative to AM stations. Over time, however, FM radio became the preferred medium for popular music and other programming and advertising revenue for FM stations rose in corresponding fashion.

By the mid-1950s Kluge's business activities began to take on a level of diversification that would be a hallmark of his for decades to come. In 1956 he and former competitor David Finkelstein merged their food brokerage businesses in Baltimore. In 1959 Kluge delved again into the field of broadcasting, acquiring a minority interest in the Metropolitan Broadcasting Corporation (formerly the Dumont Broadcasting Corporation), taking control and changing the company's name to Metromedia in 1960. Again, Kluge defied conventional wisdom, purchasing a number of independent VHF stations and ignoring stations affiliated with the three major networks. As Kluge's long-time business associate Stuart Subotnick noted in *Electronic Media,* "we do have a penchant for making passed-over visibles valuable." Operating under the banner of Metromedia, Kluge purchased and sold stations in progressively larger markets, trading up on a tax-deferred basis. Innovative programming, coupled with a lean operating style, enabled Metromedia to achieve operating margins that far outpaced those of stations associated with the major networks. At its height, the company boasted television stations in many of the country's major media markets, including New York, Los Angeles, Chicago, Dallas, Boston, Houston, and Washington, D.C.

In the 1960s Metromedia entered the realm of outdoor billboard advertising. The company acquired Foster & Kleiser, a regional outfit based in the western United States, as well as businesses in Chicago and New York. Metromedia's initial investment of $14 million in the industry enabled it to consolidate a variety of fragmented markets into an established national company. By the early 1980s Metromedia owned approximately 45,000 outdoor advertising displays in 19 major metropolitan areas.

Under the direction of Kluge, Metromedia also established a presence in a wide array of other areas of business and entertainment. Metromedia business interests have included music publishing companies; recorded music; direct mail advertising; television production and syndication, including the syndication of the Merv Griffin Show; *Playbill* magazine; the Harlem Globetrotters; and the Ice Capades.

The 1980s marked a dramatic shift in emphasis for Metromedia, as it divested itself of long-held concerns in advertising and broadcasting and launched itself into the new territories of telecommunications and the restaurant industry. This change in direction was due in no small part to a major change in the company's status. In 1984 Kluge took the company private through a leveraged buyout of the company's stockholders, a maneuver that cost him $1.6 billion. Armed with more than 90 percent ownership of Metromedia, however, Kluge was free to take the company in whatever direction he pleased.

Kluge sold his outdoor advertising interests in 1986 for more than $700 million in cash and preferred stock, a significant return on his initial investment of $14 million. He also sold his six independent television stations and one network station in 1986 for more than $2 billion. These stations, primarily purchased by Rupert Murdoch, served as a cornerstone of his fledgling Fox Broadcasting Company. In addition, Metromedia disposed of its radio broadcast holdings, divesting itself of nine stations and the Texas State Networks system through a management buyout of approximately $285 million.

During the early 1980s Metromedia began exploration of the cellular telephone industry. Intrigued by the business potential of the industry, Metromedia spent $300 million in the purchase of paging companies. The company quickly moved to consolidate its holdings, creating the country's largest paging and cellular business. Metromedia sold the majority of its holdings in the cellular industry to Southwestern Bell in 1986 for $1.3 billion, but Kluge remained a significant player in the industry. In 1990 and 1992 Metromedia sold its remaining cellular holdings for an additional $2.2 billion.

John Kluge also established a presence in the film industry during the 1980s, acquiring majority ownership of Orion Pictures Corp. in 1988. This was done at the behest of Orion cofounder Arthur B. Krim, a friend of Kluge's. Krim and the rest of the Orion group were concerned about the takeover threat of Viacom and its chairman, Sumner Redstone. As Kluge himself has admitted in *Electronic Media*, the investment in Orion was not exclusively a business decision: "This was an investment that was made as a personal favor in a white knight situation."

Orion remains a troubled studio, however, despite significant contributions from Kluge. The company filed Chapter 11 bankruptcy proceedings in December 1991. In 1992 the company emerged from bankruptcy with a debt of approximately $400 million, and the terms of the bankruptcy reorganization, which earmarks all excess cash after expenses to creditors for the next three to six years, have hamstrung the company in its efforts to create new product. Despite the company's need for capital, most observers feel that Kluge is reluctant to sink any more cash into Orion.

Metromedia made several key acquisitions in the late 1980s, purchasing the Ponderosa, Bonanza, Steak & Ale, and Bennigans chains. Ponderosa and Bonanza are operated by Metromedia Steakhouses Company, L.P., and Steak & Ale and Bennigans are operated by S&A Restaurant Corp. While the Steak & Ale and Bennigan's chains have remained profitable (if susceptible to decreasing market share), the Metromedia Steakhouses chains have lost $190 million since 1989.

Both Ponderosa and Bonanza had historically served as low-priced alternatives to other restaurants, offering customers low prices in exchange for cafeteria atmosphere and cheaper grades of beef. Industry trends, however, indicated that both chains were losing customers. Moreover, Kluge's almost simultaneous purchases of the two long-time competitors aroused fears on both sides of forced conversions, territorial disputes, and second-class treatment. After a tense period of time, more than 100 former Bonanza franchise owners have voluntarily converted to the Ponderosa scheme. Metromedia has subsequently embarked on an expensive effort—$29 million over two years—to upgrade the chains. Metromedia's interest in its restaurant holdings was also indicated by the abrupt departure of Ponderosa

president and chief executive Mike Jenkins in March 1992. As Jenkins himself stated in *Nation's Restaurant News,* "restaurants have become a major part of the company, and John [Kluge] and his staff probably want to get more personally involved." Indeed, Metromedia's restaurant holdings currently account for approximately 60 percent of its annual earnings.

Metromedia remained a major force in the telecommunications industry throughout the 1980s and into the 1990s, despite its 1986 divestment of cellular and paging interests. Kluge created the Metromedia Communications Corp., which currently ranks as one of the leading second-tier, national long-distance carriers in the United States with $400 million in annual revenues. Hoping to increase its market share, Metromedia announced in February 1993 that a letter of intent providing for the merger of Metromedia Communications Corporation, Resurgens Communications Group, based in Atlanta, and LDDS Communications, Inc., based in Jackson, Mississippi, has been signed. According to the *Wall Street Journal,* the merger would create "the fourth largest long-distance company, with annual revenues of 1.5 billion."

Metromedia has also become heavily involved in several high-technology ventures. Axon Systems Inc. is a profitable medical technology company that produces advanced brain-wave monitors for medical use. Stanadyne is a producer of state-of-the-art diesel fuel injectors. Finally, Metromedia Technologies, which utilizes computer printer technology to create billboards and theatrical stage sets, boasted revenues of $25 million in 1992.

Kluge is also examining the business possibilities that have presented themselves with the changed political landscape of Russia and Eastern Europe. As part of the International Telcell Group consortium, Metromedia is poised to establish itself as a major provider of wireless cable, cellular and paging services throughout Russia and Eastern Europe. Metromedia hopes to recoup its initial investment in Telcell's first full year of operation.

Metromedia remains a healthy company, with a variety of profitable interests in many different industries. John W. Kluge, commonly viewed as the richest man in the United States—he has donated $110 million to his alma mater, Columbia University—continues to guide the company on a daily basis.

Principal Subsidiaries: Metromedia Steakhouses Company, L.P.; S&A Restaurant Corp.; Metromedia Technologies Inc.; Metromedia Communications Corporation.

Further Reading: "The Man Who Buys Red Ink," *Forbes,* February 15, 1967; "Metromedia Presents 'Over Their Dead Bodies,' Starring John Kluge," *Forbes,* April 1, 1971; Kluge, John, *The Metromedia Story,* The Newcomen Society, New York, 1974; Rudnitsky, Howard, "The Play's the Thing," *Forbes,* June 8, 1981; Sloan, Allan, "The Magician," *Forbes,* April 23, 1984; Stevenson, Gelvin, "Metromedia's Blockbuster Bid to Stretch out its Debt," *Business Week,* November 26, 1984; "Rupert Murdoch's Big Move," *Business Week,* May 20, 1985; Maremont, Mark, "A Daring Gamble on Mobile Phones," *Business Week,* July 8, 1985; Anderson, Kevin, "No. 1 Kluge Treasures Taking Risks," *USA Today,* October 9, 1991; Coleman, Lisa, "What's Up, John?" *Forbes,* November

25, 1991; Mermigas, Diane, "Behind the Billions," *Electronic Media*, February 10, 1992; Carlino, Bill, "Bonanza franchisees seek direction; urge parent Metromedia Steakhouses to take action on chain's future," *Nation's Restaurant News*, May 25, 1992; Sawaya, Zina, "Overcooked?" *Forbes,* June 8, 1992; Weber, Joseph, "The Millstones at Metromedia," *Business Week*, March 1, 1993.

—Scott M. Lewis

MID-AMERICA DAIRYMEN, INC.

3253 East Chestnut Expressway
Springfield, Missouri 65802-2584
U.S.A.
(417) 865-7100
Fax: (417) 865-9176

Cooperative
Incorporated: 1968
Employees: 4,800
Sales: $1.75 billion
SICs: 2021 Creamery Butter; 2204 Ice Cream & Frozen
  Products

Mid-America Dairymen, Inc. is one of the largest dairy cooperatives in the United States and is the country's second largest producer of mozzarella cheese. It serves more than 12,500 dairy farmer members via a vast network of manufacturing plants and such centralized services as marketing, research and development, and legislative lobbying. The co-op sells a large line of dairy goods—including Italian and American cheeses, butter, sour cream, coffee creamer, infant formula, whey, and dehydrated products—to wholesalers, retailers, restaurants, and other foodservice outlets under the Mid-America Farms and other labels. Recently, the company entered the value added consumer market with Sport Shake, a dairy-based beverage available in several flavors; the product symbolizes an attempt by Mid-America to recapture consumers it lost to the booming soft drink and juice markets during the 1980s. Future plans for this market include reduced fat cheeses, light butter, and a light version of Sport Shake. The company also supplies most of the nation's major food companies with custom-processed dairy ingredients.

Like industry leader Associated Milk Producers Inc. (AMPI), Mid-Am was formed through a series of mergers of smaller dairy cooperatives. In the late 1950s, the National Milk Producers Federation began to struggle against divisiveness in its ranks; according to historian James L. Reeves, ''dairy leaders in the central United States were beginning to realize that there were regional problems that could only be attacked by a special organization. Superpool prices, intermarket movements of milk, health department regulations and other regional relationships needed to be addressed on a regional basis.'' In April 1964, a federated cooperative called Associated Dairymen was formed.

This umbrella co-op consisted of 30 smaller co-ops, which together represented 35,000 dairy farmers in the Midwest and Southwest. For the next ten years, Associated provided a number of important services to its members; its greatest role, however, was as a forum for dialogue between local and regional dairy farmers, which led to the establishment of regional dairy cooperatives in the late 1960s and early 1970s.

In 1966 the St. Louis-Ozarks Marketing Agency (SLOMA) was formed by three co-ops in southwest Missouri: Sanitary Milk Producers, Producers Creamery Company, and Square Deal. SLOMA addressed pricing and marketing problems on a smaller scale than Associated Dairymen. By March of 1968 the SLOMA co-ops were close to an official merger. However, in light of their ongoing discussions with Producers Creamery Company of Chillicothe, Missouri, as well as with newly formed Mid-America Dairymen of Kansas City, the SLOMA merger was delayed until July in order to include all five co-ops. At that time, Mid-America Dairymen, rather than SLOMA, was adopted as the new regional co-op's title. This 15,000-member organization had several initial objectives. These included: ensuring a reasonable income for its farmers; bargaining with milk handlers for prices above the status quo; marketing customary and specialized products; developing member information programs; and initiating research and development practices to ensure the long-term health of the cooperative.

In addition to these tasks, Mid-America also focused on further mergers and acquisitions. The most important of these was the agreement between Omaha-based Central States Dairy Cooperative and St. Paul-based Twin City Milk Producers Association to merge with Mid-America in December 1969. Upon final approval in April 1970, the newly strengthened Mid-America could boast annual sales of $355 million. Twin City Milk's proximity to the North Star Marketing Cooperative of St. Paul generated another large merger that would give Mid-Am a solid marketing structure in Minnesota, Wisconsin, and North and South Dakota. North Star, consisting of 22 member co-ops with a combined $81 million in annual sales, was especially important to Mid-Am's future due to its specialty drying plant located at Bruce, Wisconsin, which produced dried cheese, dried butter, dried sour cream, and dried dairy mixes. A new state-of-the-art dehydration facility was underway at Zumbrota, Minnesota, while the North Star merger was being completed from mid-1970 through 1971. All told, more than a dozen mergers of varying sizes occurred during this early period of growth.

Because of such expansion—all brought about by the impetus of Associated Dairymen—Mid-America spent the next several years dealing with problems of internal restructuring. Adverse developments in farm legislation, as well as a 1973 antitrust suit filed by the U.S. Justice Department, also took a toll on the co-op. 1974 represented a singularly burdensome year for Mid-America. Record high feed prices, a weak economy, declines in consumer spending power, and a drastic downward tilt in cheese, butter, and nonfat dry milk prices all contributed to massive inventory losses for the cooperative. Mid-Am lost nearly $8 million that year on revenues of $625 million. At the beginning of 1975, price supports were still at a minimum and Mid-Am was faced with the difficulty of fairly allocating its recent losses among its members.

Amid the turmoil, Gene Baldi, then executive vice president and general manager, tendered his resignation; numerous farmers also left the cooperative. President William A. Powell and the other board members then elected senior corporate vice president Gary Hanman to oversee Mid-Am's day-to-day operations and effect a turnaround. "Within three months," according to historian Reeves, Hanman "had sold the company aircraft, withdrawn company vehicles from management and supervisory staff personnel, accepted the resignations of four top administrative management people and restructured the operating divisions." Hanman's goal in restructuring was to redirect much of the operational management to the six membership divisions: Central States, Kansas City, Iowa, St. Louis, Northern, and Southern. Mid-Am ended the year with earnings of over $1 million. More importantly, it had decided to act upon the marketing committee's recommendation to form a marketing subsidiary to increase name brand sales and reduce Mid-Am's dependency on commodity sales (commodities then represented around 82 percent of sales but contributed only 30 percent to the overall gross margin). The subsidiary was called Mid-America Farms, and it proved successful from its beginning in 1976, despite heavy competition in the branded products arena from Kraft, Land O'Lakes, Carnation, and others. A later move away from national to niche marketing, and a greater emphasis on food ingredient sales solidified Mid-America Farms' role for the cooperative.

A new array of problems faced dairy farmers during the 1980s, particularly the replacement of milk by soft drinks as the leading American beverage. Nevertheless, the decade was begun auspiciously, with sales exceeding $1 billion for the first time and net savings up 44 percent from 1979. Furthermore, in 1982, Mid-America was named dairy processor of the year by the industry's foremost journal, *Dairy Record;* Mid-America was the first co-op ever to receive the honor. Although the number of dairy farms in the nation continued to shrink during the decade, Mid-America's membership losses were less severe, in part due to several new acquisitions. The co-op also entered into joint arrangements with other large dairy producers, including East Coast leader Agway. One of Agway's subsidiaries, H. P. Hood, agreed in 1982 to sell a half-interest in its Clearfield Cheese Company to Mid-America. In 1985 Mid-America bought H. P. Hood's remaining interest but then quickly sold the processor to Schreiber Food Company, the nation's second largest cheese business, in order to realize a $1.2 million gain on the investment. Other expansions into cheese-processing, however, continued to preoccupy Mid-America. Around this time, the cooperative also began to increase its fluid milk processing capabilities.

During the mid-1980s, cost-cutting and profit enhancement became key to the survival of farmers in general, and the dairy industry in particular. Among cooperatives with a national rather than regional focus, it was apparent that considerable overlap in manufacturing, distribution, and marketing existed. If such co-ops were to compete with the large corporate food producers—and there was no reason they shouldn't—further consolidations were necessary. The problem with consolidation, of course, was the complexity of most co-op arrangements: large boards, large memberships, varying systems for financial remuneration, and varying obligations to suppliers and purchasers. In 1986 AMPI and Mid-Am discussed a possible merger, but soon agreed that their structural differences posed too great an obstacle to consolidation.

Land O'Lakes, however, whose corporate headquarters were based in Arden Hills, Minnesota, the same city as those of Mid-Am's Northern Division, seemed amenable to such a joint venture. Although a far more diversified agribusiness than Mid-Am, Land O'Lakes was and is a powerhouse in the dairy industry and, because of its high profile and leadership in joint-marketing, represented an important potential ally for the smaller Missouri-based co-op. In January 1987 the two agreed to link plant operations in southeastern Minnesota for the production and marketing of milk and whey. Cost savings for the joint venture were supposed to have approached $1.5 million. Because of the venture's success, Land O'Lakes and Mid-Am entered into discussions of further mergers which, had they been ratified, would have created a $4 billion food and dairy company. Proper capitalization for the proposed consolidation became the primary stumbling block, however, and all discussions were halted in October 1989.

By the early 1990s Mid-Am was successfully operating no less than 16 joint ventures in the Midwest—four alone in Wisconsin, the nation's number one dairy state. Its service territory effectively covered all of North Dakota, South Dakota, Wisconsin, Iowa, Illinois, and Missouri as well as portions of Kentucky, Tennessee, Arkansas, and Texas and much of Oklahoma, Kansas, and Nebraska.

Yet, as in all commodity-oriented businesses, Mid-Am still suffered from production and pricing swings. During the first half of 1990, the cooperative lost $6.1 million due to a market saturated by such products as milk and cheese. Part of the problem could be traced to a federal herd buyout program initiated in 1988 which engendered higher prices and, ultimately, overproduction. Mid-Am closed 1991 with a $2.5 million loss before the cost of a litigation settlement. A huge decrease in selling and administrative expenses for fiscal 1991 allowed Mid-Am to recoup its momentum and report net savings of $11.5 million (after an antitrust settlement with the National Farmers Organization). At the core of Mid-Am's increased profitability was a consolidation of its six divisions into two: the Western and Eastern Groups. The elimination of 122 positions, the disposal of surplus real estate, and the sale of certain operating facilities also contributed to Mid-Am's lowest year for capital expenditures since 1986. Other important developments for the company included a merger with Glenn Milk Producers Association of Willows, California, and the launching of a joint marketing venture with Southern Milk Sales to handle some two billion pounds of milk annually. In addition to these businesses, Mid-Am's current joint ventures—several of which fall outside Mid-Am territory—include those with Golden Valley Cheese, Raber Foods Inc., Spring Valley Cheese, Western Food Processing, Golden Harvest Popcorn, Hiland Dairy, Roberts Dairy, and Sinton Dairy.

In his President's Message for 1991, Ivan Strickler reiterated the company's commitment to profitability and growth: "Dairy cooperatives must increase their scale of operations through consolidations, mergers, joint ventures and marketing agencies in common, in order to more effectively and more efficiently market fluid milk and manufactured dairy products."

Strickler's "mixed picture" for the future also pointed out Mid-America's need to enter the global market. Operating in a competitive industry and faced with the unpredictability of new legislation, Mid-America nonetheless has its high reputation to rely upon. The cooperative received a Select Supplier Award from Campbell Soup Company in December 1991 as well as several quality awards from the National Milk Producers Federation. An attention to developing new products, such as D-Lite, a low-fat, low-cholesterol American cheese made with the fat substitute Simplesse, should also aid Mid-Am as it faces an uncertain future. The challenges, though, are much the same as they were when Mid-Am was first born: to "grow with the food industry; inform the public and consumers about our products, the unique nature of cooperatives as businesses and the need for stability in agriculture."

Principal Subsidiaries: Mid-America Farms.

Further Reading: Menninger, Bonnie, "Zardas End 78-Year Family Milk Run," *Kansas City Business Journal,* June 8, 1987; Brandt, Steve, "Land O'Lakes, Mid-America Plan Deal," *Star Tribune,* July 22, 1987; Reeves, James L., *The First 20 Years: The Story of Mid-America Dairymen,* Republic, Missouri, Mid-America Dairymen, 1989; Marcotty, Josephine, "Land O'Lakes May Renew Merger Talk," *Star Tribune,* March 30, 1989; Phelps, David, Steve Gross, and Josephine Marcotty, "Marketplace Pulse," *Star Tribune,* October 11, 1989; Marcotty, Josephine, "Cheese Price Caught in Squeeze," *Star Tribune,* November 2, 1990; 1991 Annual Report, Kansas City, Missouri, Mid-America Dairymen, Inc., "First American Cheese with Simplesse Debuts," *Supermarket News,* July 20, 1992.

—Jay P. Pederson

MIRROR GROUP NEWSPAPERS PLC

P. O. Box 160
The Mirror Building
Holborn Circus
London EC1P 1DQ
United Kingdom
(071) 353-0246
Fax: (071) 822-2144

Public company
Incorporated: 1971
Employees: 1520
Sales: £460 million (U.S.$667 million)
Stock exchanges: London
SICs: 2711 Newspapers: Publishing, or Publishing &
  Printing;

For much of the twentieth century London's *Daily Mirror* has been one of the world's most popular newspapers, a pioneer of what has been characterized variously as New Journalism, the popular press, or, less charitably, the scandal sheet. Founded in 1903 by Alfred Harmsworth (Lord Northcliffe), "unquestionably the greatest journalist of his time" in the words of *The Times* of London, the *Daily Mirror* is today the anchor of the Mirror Group's holdings, which include seven major daily newspapers and a variety of printing, leasing, and graphics companies. As recently as 1991 the Mirror Group was itself a part of the media conglomerate owned by Robert Maxwell. Upon his mysterious death in November of that year it was discovered that the Group's bank accounts and pension funds had been pilfered for use by Maxwell and his sons in a last ditch attempt to save their tottering financial empire. It is still too early to gauge the enduring effect of Maxwell's crimes, which cost the company a £421 million write-off in 1992, but the Group's newspapers continue to show a healthy operating profit and its new management team has embarked on a concerted effort to erase the damage inflicted by Maxwell.

The creation of the *Daily Mirror* was only one episode in the revolution in British journalism wrought by Alfred Harmsworth and his brother Harold (later Lord Rothermere). Until the end of the nineteenth century, British newspapers and magazines had been written by and for the aristocracy and professional middle class, a relatively small percentage of the country's total popu-

lation. Compared to most of the industrialized nations Britain had developed a vigorous and often vitriolic press, but not until the last half of the nineteenth century did anyone propose seriously to publish a newspaper for the lower-middle and lower classes. Alfred and Harold Harmsworth, born to the family of an impoverished schoolteacher, would eventually amass fortunes, wield enormous political power, and become members of the House of Lords.

Alfred Harmsworth exhibited his gifts for writing and self-promotion at an early age. As a grammar school student outside London he founded and edited the school newspaper. The young man pursued a career in journalism and began to contribute short pieces to the popular periodicals then coming into their own. From minor journals such as *Comic Life* and *Young Folk Tales* Harmsworth soon graduated to *Tit-Bits*, a hugely successful national magazine composed of excerpts from other, longer works. In 1887 he founded his own popular periodical called *Answers to Correspondents*. The magazine's title suggested its format, a collection of letters to the editor and his answers; it also suggested the nature of the New Journalism as a whole. England's advanced economy had created a large middle class whose members, such as Alfred Harmsworth himself, were literate and curious about the world at large but uninterested in the higher arcana of politics, theology, and *belles lettres*. These readers, Harmsworth felt, hungered for publications that reflected and commented on their own middle-class lives, free of cultural pretensions, informative but simply written, and spiced with stories of love and violent crime. Such were the "Answers" that Alfred Harmsworth would return to the growing number of "Correspondents" in fin de siecle England.

In 1894 Harmsworth bought the moribund *London Evening News* for £25,000 and completed the triumph of popular daily journalism, aided by a talented young editor named Kennedy Jones and by his brother Harold, who would remain the financial and administrative director of the Harmsworth syndicate. Two years later the Harmsworth brothers founded the *Daily Mail*, the first of the "halfpenny" morning papers in England and an astonishing success from its initial publication date, when it already boasted the world's largest daily circulation. The secret of Harmsworth's success was summed up in his phrase, "explain, clarify, simplify," or perhaps more frankly in the formula articulated by Kennedy Jones: "crime, love, money and food." In truth, the *Mail* (and later the *Mirror*) did not seem to follow any particular editorial philosophy. It did combine elements of ultranationalist politics, sex and violence, sports, cartoons, and advice columns, all written in brisk humorous prose and framed by bold black headlines.

These were papers for the plain-speaking common man, a market long associated with the United States but largely unrecognized in England until Harmsworth provided the "daily mirror" in which they could recognize themselves. Nor were women excluded from this democratic awakening; the *Daily Mirror* owed its origin to Alfred Harmsworth's rare sensitivity to women as a newly emerging force in the political and cultural life of England. In 1903 Harmsworth established a paper written entirely by and for women. This enlightened experiment lasted about a year, the women of England for unknown reasons failing to rally around the *Mirror* as anticipated. The *Mirror*'s weekly losses of £3,000 soon convinced Harmsworth that ''women can't write and don't want to read.'' He dismissed the female staff, replacing them with the usual gang of cigar-smoking men, and relaunched the paper in 1904 with a lead story entitled ''How I Dropped £100,000 on the *Mirror*.''

The success of the new *Mirror* was not predicated on the gender of its editors, however. Harmsworth took advantage of recently evolved technology to make the *Daily Mirror* the first half-penny paper in England illustrated with photographs, which until that time had appeared in newspapers rarely and at substantial cost. The *Mirror*'s photographs were sharp and clear and inexpensive, and the paper was soon known for its front-page photos of the royal family, war scenes, and famous criminals. The liberal use of photographs, combined with the usual Harmsworth mix of letters, gossip, contests, and short news articles, proved to be a powerful lure for the English working class. Circulation shot upward to 350,000 in 1905 and six years later topped the one million mark, making the *Mirror* the world's first daily to reach that figure.

The *Mirror* was edited in these years by Alexander Kenealy, an Irishman whose instinct for sensational news had been honed by years of work with publishing magnate William Randolph Hearst in the United States. Under Kenealy, the *Mirror* took a further turn towards the journalism of titillation and sensationalism, eventually going too far to suit Alfred Harmsworth himself. The publisher, who was made a baronet in 1905, wanted to exercise power in the political as well as commercial sphere and he found the *Mirror* something of an embarrassment. In 1908 Harmsworth bought *The Times* of London and rapidly lost interest in the *Mirror*, which he sold to his brother Harold in 1914. The elder Harmsworth went on to a career of frustrated political campaigns and a growing megalomania; he was remembered by Lloyd George, the distinguished Prime Minister, as ''far and away the most redoubtable figure of all the Press barons of my time. He created the popular daily, and the more the other journals scoffed . . . the more popular it became.'' More typical of upper-class feelings, however, were the words of Lord Salisbury, who charged that Harmsworth had ''invented a paper for those who could read but could not think, and another for those who could see but could not read.''

Harold Harmsworth (Lord Rothermere to be) was a businessman of talent and for some years the *Mirror* prospered under his ownership, helped especially by the public's hunger for photographs of the fighting in the First World War. By 1917 the *Mirror* was the most popular daily in Great Britain, but Rothermere's obsessive criticism of governmental waste eroded the paper's circulation base in the 1920s. Like his brother, Rothermere could not resist trying to play the power broker in his nation's political life. The *Mirror* remained essentially conservative, as it had always been, but Rothermere used the paper as a vehicle for voicing his private feelings about the leaders of the Tory Party, for years attacking the government for alleged inefficiency and corruption. The culmination of this campaign was Rothermere's founding of the United Empire Party in the late 1920s, a short-lived far right-wing party whose jingoistic statements presaged Rothermere's later support for fascism. Rothermere's fulminations were politically ineffectual and eventually proved to be bad for business as well. With the *Mirror*'s circulation sinking quickly Rothermere sold his shares in 1931, his reputation permanently damaged by the rebukes of

fellow conservatives such as Stanley Baldwin. ''What the proprietorship of these pages is aiming at,'' said Baldwin in a famous 1930 speech, ''is power, and power without responsibility—the prerogative of the harlot through the ages.''

The politically turbulent 1930s witnessed the birth of a new, radical *Daily Mirror*. While Lord Rothermere formally adopted the fascist philosophy of Hitler and Mussolini, his former paper became one of England's leading advocates of democratic rights and armed resistance to Hitler's growing power in the east. Of the four men chiefly responsible for the new *Mirror*, three of them—editors H. G. Bartholomew and Hugh Cudlipp, and columnist William Connor (pen name 'Cassandra')—were by birth and temperament sympathetic to the working classes; the fourth, Cecil Harmsworth King, was the nephew of founder Alfred Harmsworth. Together these four men created the *Daily Mirror* of which historian A. J. P. Taylor would later remark, ''The English people had at last found their voice.'' It was an irreverent, loud voice, in which could be heard elements of both high principle and low culture, semi-pornographic cartoons side by side with early and accurate warnings about the menace of Hitler. In 1934, years before most of England's high-brow papers gave up the rhetoric of ''appeasement,'' the *Daily Mirror* characterized the German dictator with startling prescience as ''the hysterical Austrian, with his megalomania, based on an acute inferiority complex, his neurasthenia, his oratorical brilliance . . .'' The *Mirror*'s enthusiasm for confrontation would vary in the years following, but from 1937 onwards it was England's leading proponent of the rearmament needed to deal with ''the gangsters'' of Europe.

In this sentiment it found an ally in none other than Winston Churchill, one aristocrat whom the *Mirror* supported during the 1930s and the first years of war. As the symbol of embattled Britain Churchill could rely on the applause of the *Mirror*, which if nothing else had always identified itself with the interests of England. The *Mirror*, though, was an essentially iconoclastic journal with leftist leanings and soon it was criticizing the coalition government for various failings, in 1942 nearly suffering censorship for publishing what Churchill believed were demoralizing statements. By war's end the *Mirror* had fully resumed its pre-war support for the Labour Party, helping defeat Churchill in the 1945 election. As always, the *Mirror* reflected and amplified the beliefs of its two million-plus readers, who in 1945 were overwhelmingly pacifist and neo-Socialist in their feelings.

In 1951 Cecil Harmsworth King deposed H. G. Bartholomew as chairman of the *Mirror*. The paper was probably then at the peak of its influence, the leading daily in all of Great Britain (possibly in the world) and the voice of the New Left that would dominate the country's politics for the next thirty years. Cecil King took the paper several steps further, however; it was under King's leadership that the *Mirror* expanded from newspaper to ''Group.'' For years the *Mirror* had published a successful weekend edition called the *Sunday Pictorial*, and to this core King added a vast collection of magazines by taking over the Amalgamated Press in 1958 and Odhams Press a few years later. The holdings from the latter deal included a leading Labour newspaper, the *Daily Herald*. Along with the *Daily Record* and *Sunday Mail*, both of Glasgow, Scotland, the *Mirror* and its newly acquired magazine empire were all merged in the early 1960s into the International Publishing Corporation (IPC), described by Hugh Cudlipp in his 1962 book *At Your Peril* as "the greatest publishing operation the world has ever seen."

IPC owned the leading publications in virtually every category of British journalism, its power so great that in 1961 a parliamentary committee was formed to determine whether the *Mirror* takeover of Odham should not be prohibited by the government for reasons of free trade and the general good. The merger went through anyway, and IPC became one of the world's first "media conglomerates," as they would later be called, and Cecil King, like his uncle Alfred Harmsworth, established himself as a "media baron."

King's long and remarkable career ended abruptly in 1968 with his resignation under pressure from the board of directors. IPC's profits were apparently suffering from the entrenched power of its printing unions, power fought for and won with the help of newspapers like IPC's own *Daily Mirror*. The English printers union was a strong one and it adamantly opposed new technologies that would cut costs at the expense of union jobs. Cecil King despaired of the situation, and two years after his departure IPC was merged with Albert E. Reed & Co. Ltd., one of the largest paper products companies in Europe. IPC had long been the largest shareholder in Reed (the Harmsworth brothers became involved in the Canadian paper business as early as 1906) and in 1970 the two firms banded together in the interests of vertical integration under the name of Reed International.

Reed had no more luck with the printing unions than had IPC, and one by one the pieces of its publishing empire were sold off during the 1970s, starting with the magazines. Last to go were the *Mirror* newspapers, which then as now consisted of the *Daily Mirror, Daily Record, Sunday Mirror, The People* (a glossy Sunday spread), the *Sunday Mail, The Sporting Life*, and *The Sporting Life Weekender*. Reed could find no buyer for the *Mirror* newspapers, however, and a plan to float the group on the public exchange was ruined when Price Waterhouse discovered gross union laxities and described them in its prospectus statement. At the last minute an unlikely white knight appeared in the form of Robert Maxwell, Czech-born business dealer extraordinaire, who purchased the *Mirror* papers for about £90 million in 1984.

Mirror Group Newspapers Ltd. (MGN) became a pillar of Robert Maxwell's incredibly tangled business empire, a mysterious world in which the distinction between private and public companies was regularly ignored by Maxwell and his sons Ian and Kevin. A former MP for the Labour Party and a professed friend of the working man, Maxwell in truth had little regard for anything beyond his own insatiable desire for fame, and he had long coveted a public platform such as MGN offered. He took over MGN editorial policy while denying that he would even be interested in doing so, and by threat of company closure persuaded the unions to cut their employee levels and relinquish a host of archaic union rules.

For the same reason, Maxwell did not hesitate to break the law when his financial network began unraveling in the late 1980s. His 1988 purchase of Macmillan, Inc., the American publisher, and Official Airline Guides, Inc., for which he borrowed a combined $3.35 billion, pushed his empire further into precarious territory. The anemic economy in 1989 sent the price of stock at Maxwell Communications Corporation (MCC) spiraling downwards. MCC was the holding company for Maxwell's American interests and the collateral for many of the huge loans made to Maxwell's private holding companies at the top of the pyramid. To bolster MCC's falling share price Maxwell engaged in a blur of desperate transactions, including the use of Mirror Group pension funds and other cash accounts to buy MCC shares and provide collateral for further new loans. Shortly after the first signs of imminent personal bankruptcy appeared in November 1991, Maxwell's body was found floating off the stern of his yacht, at which point his conglomerate fell to pieces in a welter of bankruptcy filings and criminal investigations.

Of all of Maxwell's holdings, MGN was probably the soundest at the time of his death, but the company sustained serious losses due to Maxwell's illegal business dealings. In its 1992 annual report MGN noted a one-time extraordinary loss of £421 million to cover the cost of repairs, but the company also showed a healthy operating profit of £91 million on revenues of £460 million. Bankruptcy administrators are expected to eventually float MGN on the public market, where its inherent strengths will probably enable the group to survive intact.

Principal Subsidiaries: MGN Limited; Scottish Daily Record & Sunday Mail Limited (Scotland); Mirror Colour Print Limited; Mirror Group, Inc. (United States).

Further Reading: Escott, T. H. S., *Masters of English Journalism,* London, T. Fisher Unwin, 1911; Edelman, Maurice, *The Mirror: A Political History,* London, Hamish Mailton, 1966; Maremont, Mark, and Mark Landler, "An Empire Up for Grabs," *Business Week,* December 23 1991; Bower, Tom, *Maxwell the Outsider,* New York, Viking, 1992.

—Jonathan Martin

MITCHELL ENERGY AND DEVELOPMENT CORPORATION

P.O. Box 4000
The Woodlands, Texas 77387-4000
U.S.A.
(713) 377-5500
Fax: (713) 377-5802

Public Company
Incorporated: 1946 as Roxoil Drilling, Incorporated
Employees: 2,900
Sales: $874 million
Stock Exchanges: New York Pacific Boston Philadelphia
SICs: 1311 Crude Petroleum & Natural Gas; 1321 Natural
   Gas Liquids; 6552 Subdividers & Developers Nec

Mitchell Energy & Development Corporation is one of the Houston-Galveston area's leading real estate developers and one of the nation's largest independent natural gas and liquid hydro-carbons producers. Its largest real estate development project is The Woodlands, a 25,000-acre community with a population of more than 33,000. Among energy related activities, it produces natural gas liquids, operates intrastate pipelines and explores for and produces natural gas and crude oil. In 1991 it produced 60.5 billion cubic feet of natural gas and approximately 18 million barrels of oil, condensate, and natural gas liquids.

Financier H. Merlyn Christie first incorporated the company as Roxoil Drilling on February 5, 1946. That December, the firm changed its name to Oil Drilling, Incorporated, when a share of the company was bought by geologist George P. Mitchell.

Mitchell, the son of a Greek goatherd who immigrated to Arkansas, would eventually become the company's CEO and guiding light. Mitchell's family gained an American name after a railroad timekeeper who couldn't pronounce Savva Paraskivopoulis decided to call his father Mike Mitchell. Born in Galveston in 1919, the younger Mitchell worked his way through Texas A & M University's renowned petroleum engineering school. Despite his lack of experience, he got work as a consulting geologist, taking a small fee and a percentage of any oil found.

In the late 1940s, Oil Drilling put together prospects for others and drilled as investors. It discovered or developed production in a score of Texas fields and in 1951 it began exploration and production operations in Alberta and on the Ontario side of Lake Erie.

In 1952 a Chicago bookie called George Mitchell, trying to sell him a 10,000-acre lease in North Texas, an area known as "the wildcatter's graveyard." Going against the conventional wisdom, Mitchell bought the lease and drilled near Bridgeport, where he opened what would become Mitchell Energy's extraordinarily successful North Texas holdings. During 1953, the company drilled 13 consecutive producing development wells there and by year's end, it had more than 300,000 North Texas acres under lease—an area which in the early 1990s was still the heart of Mitchell Energy's production.

Also in 1953, George Mitchell's older brother, engineer Johnny Mitchell, joined the firm. Johnny Mitchell had worked with his brother as a consulting geologist and was remembered by a *Forbes* correspondent as a flamboyant man who walked about Houston in jungle shorts and a pith helmet, and who wrote a potboiler war novel, *The Secret War of Captain Johnny Mitchell*. By year's end, George Mitchell, Johnny Mitchell, and Merlyn Christie had bought out Oil Drilling's other shareholders and formed a new operating subsidiary—Christie, Mitchell & Mitchell (CM&M).

CM&M expanded operations through the mid-1950s. In 1954 it opened a Western Canada field office in Calgary, where in 1955 it discovered the Alvord 3000' Strawn and Tidwell 4600' Strawn fields.

All was not completely rosy for the new firm, however. In 1956 royalty owners in North Texas's Wise County—where CM&M had drilled 57 oil wells and 103 gas wells in 34 separate fields—began to grow impatient with CM&M which, because of low gas prices, was keeping gas shut-in. George Mitchell decided to deal with the disgruntled royalty owners publicly. He invited the entire county to a barbecue, where he told 3,000 residents that though it had not seen a penny of revenue from gas sales, the company was willing to spend another $7 million to drill 40 wells in the area in 1956 and another 170 wells in 1957. Given the company's financial commitment, residents agreed to wait for satisfactory prices before demanding royalties.

It was not as if the company was not trying to market its gas. As early as 1954 it had negotiated with Natural Gas Pipeline Company of America for a pipeline spur that would transport Wise County gas to Chicago. The Federal Power Commission had rejected this first deal and did not approve a spur into Wise County until 1957. Through the late 1950s and early 1960s, the company expanded and reorganized. It became part owner of the GM&A Gas Products Plant at Bridgeport, which opened in 1957. In 1959 George Mitchell became CEO. And in 1961 the company, which had just discovered the Alvord South Caddo Conglomerate Field in Wise County, formed CM&M Equilease to lease oil field equipment.

In 1962 the Mitchell brothers bought out Merlyn Christie's remaining stock and changed the company's name to Mitchell & Mitchell Gas & Oil. The following year they acquired their first intrastate gathering and transmission business—Southwestern Gas Pipeline, which owned 200 miles of pipeline in Palo Pinto County, Texas. In 1963 George Mitchell bought the

Grogan-Cochran Land Company, whose 50,000-acre tract in Montgomery and Grimes Counties would later figure prominently in Mitchell Energy's real estate developments.

By 1964 Mitchell & Mitchell had over 1,000 producing wells. In 1965 its gas reserves surpassed 400 billion cubic feet, and in 1966 it became Texas's top independent gas producer and the nation's third-ranked independent interstate gas marketer.

In the mid-1960s, George Mitchell continued the process of integrating into Mitchell & Mitchell services that the company had previously paid for. In 1965 he purchased pulling (workover) units for the North Texas division and began to buy out the other investors in the GM&A Gas Products Plant. Also, when a gas and oil surplus forced Texas authorities to limit production to ten days a month, he bought Houston real estate as an investment and a tax shelter.

Through the remainder of the decade, Mitchell continued to acquire assets, even as Mitchell & Mitchell became the nation's second largest independent producer of gas moving in interstate commerce. In 1966 he purchased the remaining interest in 53,250 Lake Erie acres from Livingston Oil and Gas and bought a controlling interest in Gulf Gas, which owned 100 miles of pipeline in Texas's Eastland, Callahan, Brown, and Coleman Counties. In 1967 he increased Mitchell & Mitchell's GM&A ownership to 80 percent and on January 1, 1968, the company acquired R. E. (Bob) Smith and Company's oil and gas leaseholds in Texas, Louisiana, and Canada.

In 1969 Mitchell formed Brazos Gas Compressing to provide compression service for the company's Southwestern and West Cen-Texpipeline systems. At the same time, Southwestern Gas Pipeline completed the company's first underground gas storage facility, at Lone Camp, Texas. And at year's end, Mitchell & Mitchell discovered 100 billion cubic feet of gas in Lafitte's Gold Field on Galveston Island.

By the early 1970s, the company was beginning to act like a major player in natural gas, which in 1971 accounted for almost two-thirds of its activities. In 1970 it leased its first acreage off the Texas shore through a joint venture with Diamond Shamrock, Inc. and the Natural Gas Pipeline Company of America. In 1971 it changed its name to Mitchell Energy & Development Corporation and went public in February of that year, issuing 770,000 shares of common stock (about 4.5 percent of total) to finance long-term growth prospects.

Parallel with Mitchell's growth as an energy company, George Mitchell, who owned almost 71 percent of the company, saw a future in land development. Using land assets acquired in the 1960s, he planned a new community—The Woodlands—25 miles north of Houston. The project would in part be financed by $50 million in loan guarantees provided by the Department of Housing and Urban Development's "New Communities" project and would, it was hoped, provide a stable long-term income stream.

It seemed that the company could grow both as an energy concern and as a land development business. In 1973 Mitchell expanded its gas gathering systems, acquiring 25 percent of the Ken-Ohio Pipeline in Ohio. In 1974 he entered the contract drilling business by forming MND Drilling to support his North Texas operations; he also acquired Butler Drilling's assets to support Gulf Coast operations for $9.3 million.

In 1974 George Mitchell also opened his ambitious real estate development, The Woodlands, and the project was widely criticized. Certain commentators thought it was consuming capital that would be better used in drilling. Others, like *Forbes*, essentially laughed at an oil man like George Mitchell getting into real estate.

The Woodlands was in fact consuming capital and hurting drilling operations. Between 1972 and 1974, interest costs on the land went from $6.6 million to $19 million. And between 1972 and 1977, the company spent $60 million on roads, buildings, golf courses and other infrastructure. According to *Forbes*, Mitchell drilled 311 wells between 1973 and 1974 but only 182 wells between 1975 and 1976. During the same period crude reserves fell 2 percent and natural gas reserves fell 7 percent.

In Mitchell's defense, his strategy was one that required major front-end investments and planned for long-term return. Only the future would tell what the project's success would be. Moreover, the land's value was appreciating (the appraised value of The Woodlands had risen from $99 million in January of 1972 to $123 million in August of 1973), so there was already a paper profit from the venture.

Although Mitchell Energy's previous rates of growth did not return until the late 1970s, the company did continue to reach new milestones in the mid-1970s. In 1975 its Texas Intrastate pipeline system topped 1,000 miles. In 1976 it participated in drilling its 3,000th well, and in August of 1977 it began production in Arkansas County, Texas's Mesquite Bay Field.

As The Woodlands crossed the break even point, earning $8.7 million (about 10 percent of Mitchell's net) in 1978, the company returned to acquisitions. That year, it acquired the drilling assets of Jack Houston Exploration Company and purchased 80 percent of the 300-mile Winnie Pipeline System, 34 percent of the 500-mile Tejas Gas network and 50 percent of the 79-mile Tejas-Southwestern Pipeline. These new pipelines brought the company's total intrastate pipelines to more than 2,200 miles.

Gas processing had long been an important activity for the company but in 1979—when the government lifted controls on natural gas liquids—operating earnings from the company's gas processing segment soared from $27 million in 1979 to $99 million two years later.

The company first entered the field of natural gas liquids when George Mitchell hired Bruce M. Withers, Jr., in 1974. Withers, a young former Tenneco employee, convinced Mitchell to buy five small, portable, highly efficient gas processing plants called turbo expanders. Using cryogenics, an available but not widely used technology, these plants condensed a very high proportion of liquids out of natural gas. The company would then sell these natural gas liquids (NGLs)—after fractionating them into ethane, propane, butane, and natural gasoline—to manufacturers of plastics, paints, solvents, synthetic rubber, gasoline, and a wide variety of other products. The dry residue gas—mainly methane—was sold as fuel for homes and industry.

By the early 1980s, Mitchell's NGL operation had become both admired and profitable. "They got an innovative thinker when they hired Withers," D. N. McClanahan, a Houston NGL consultant, told *Business Week*, "and really beat everybody to the punch with cryogenics." Mitchell Energy's 35 natural gas processing plants made it one of the nation's top 15 NGL producers. And in 1980 its daily NGL production of 35,500 barrels accounted for 28 percent of its $696 million in sales and 45 percent of its $221 million in operating earnings.

Mitchell Energy continued making acquisitions and in 1982 reported revenues topping $1 billion and net income of $115.2 million. These were growth years. The company extended its gas gathering system past 3,200 miles in 1981, acquired a 50 percent interest in its 54th gas processing plant in 1982, and reached the 45,000 barrels per day level in NGL sales for the first time in 1983.

Both the oil industry and Texas real estate faltered in the mid-1980s, however, as oil and gas prices declined from their 1982 peaks. Lot sales at The Woodlands fell by two-thirds, and Mitchell Energy kept gas shut in rather than sell assets at below replacement costs. Revenues fell to $595 billion, and profits fell to a relatively infinitesimal $8.4 million in 1986. Even so, Mitchell Energy was one of the few independents to stay in the black.

The company responded to a market that had suddenly turned hostile by cutting drilling expenditures to extremely low levels and, insulated to some degree by the relative strength of NGL prices, managed to remain in the black through the remainder of the decade. The company drilled its 5,500th well in 1988 and in 1989 it acquired a 50 percent interest in a 235-mile gas pipeline running from Robertson County to an interchange near Katy, Texas. In 1989 the company made $30.4 million on revenues of $658 million.

After another difficult year in 1990, when oversupply sent gas prices plummeting, Mitchell Energy recovered somewhat in 1991 when new home sales at The Woodlands improved. But natural gas prices plummeted again in 1992, and the company reorganized its exploration and production division to reduce staff and focus on both a substantial backlog of undrilled wells in proven areas such as North Texas, Southeast New Mexico, East Central Texas, and the Texas Gulf Coast. It also acquired natural gas fields being sold by energy companies who were focusing on overseas exploration. "The cutbacks are being undertaken," George Mitchell told the *Oil & Gas Journal*, "as a result of today's abysmally low prices, which make it unprofitable to explore for natural gas in higher risk areas."

In the summer of 1992, the enormous gas bubble which had kept prices low for so long began to shrink. Mitchell Energy joined Conoco in acquiring Oryx Energy's interest in 14 processing plants in Texas and Oklahoma. This acquisition increased Mitchell's NGL production capacity by 10,000 barrels a day to between 55,000 and 60,000 barrels a day, and made the company a top 10 gas liquids producer.

Mitchell Energy and Development Company began in 1946 as a packager of energy investments. Under the leadership of geologist George Mitchell it grew into a successful driller of natural gas and oil and expanded into gas gathering systems and natural gas processing plants. In the early 1970s, the company invested heavily in The Woodlands, which has been sporadically profitable while adding immensely to the company's paper worth. Profits soared during the energy crisis of the 1970s and after the deregulation of natural gas liquids in 1979, but fell with gas prices during the mid- and late 1980s. Ever expanding in its gas gathering and processing capabilities, Mitchell is set to profit if gas prices rise.

Principal Subsidiaries: MND Energy Corp.; Mitchell Energy Corp.; Brazos Gas Compressing Co.; Liquid Energy Corp.; Oilworld Supply Co.; Southwestern Gas Pipeline, Inc.; Mitco Pipeline Co.; Northeastern Gas Pipeline, Inc.; Southeastern Marketing Co.; Mitchell Marketing Co.; Winnie Pipeline Co.; Acacia Natural Gas Corp.; Woodlands Corp.; Mitchell Catamount, Inc.; Mitchell & Mitchell Investment Corp.; Woodlands Communications Network, Inc.; MND Hospitality, Inc.; Mitchell Mortgage Co.; MND Finance Co.; Woodlands Venture Capital Co.; MND Service, Inc.

Further Reading: Coggeshall & Hicks Inc. "Mitchell Energy and Development Corporation," *Wall Street Transcript*, December 25, 1972; Mitchell, George P., "Mitchell Energy & Development Corp.," *Wall Street Transcript*, September 24, 1973; Rauscher Pierce Refnes, Inc. "Mitchell Energy and Development Corp.," *Wall Street Transcript*, July 9, 1979; "Nobody's Laughing Now," *Forbes*, March 2, 1981; "Mitchell Energy: Pumping Up Profits With Portable Natural Gas Processors," *Business Week*, July 20, 1981; Byrne, Harlan S., "Mitchell Energy & Development: A Houston Survivor Stays in the Black, Looks For an Uptrend," *Barron's*, July 16, 1990; Mack, Toni, "Staying Power," *Forbes*, January 21, 1991; "Mitchell Energy Says It Is Cutting Staff, Selling Assets, Looking for Acquisitions," *Wall Street Journal*, April 7, 1992; Byrne, Harlan S., "Mitchell Energy: A Cautious Cheer as "Bubble" Floats Away," *Barron's*, October 5, 1992.

—Jordan Wankoff

MITSUBISHI HEAVY INDUSTRIES, LTD.

5-1, Marunouchi 2-chome
Chiyoda-ku, Tokyo 100
Japan
(03) 3212-3111
Fax: (03) 3201-6258

Public Company
Incorporated: 1964
Employees: 45,000
Sales: ¥2.6 trillion (US$21.7 billion)
Stock Exchanges: Tokyo Osaka Nagoya Kyoto Hiroshima
  Fukuoka Niigata Sapporo
SICs: 3731 Ship Building & Repairing; 3721 Aircraft

Since the 1880s the diversified collection of industrial manufacturers now known as Mitsubishi Heavy Industries (MHI) has constituted the heart of the vast Mitsubishi group. Essentially all of Mitsubishi's many industrial offspring were developed as adjuncts to its shipbuilding business, begun in 1884. After suffering several dissolutions in the 20th century, MHI reemerged in 1964 as the world's leading shipbuilder and a powerful competitor in several related engineering fields. Since the disastrous mid-1970s slump in shipping—caused principally by the OPEC oil crisis—MHI has accelerated its investment in other fields and reduced shipbuilding to a comparatively minor 11 percent of sales. Its heavy-machinery, power-plant, and construction-equipment divisions are all larger than the original shipbuilding business. With the addition of aircraft production, rocket design, and countless other engineering projects, MHI ranks as one of the world's foremost heavy industrial manufacturers.

The Mitsubishi interest in shipping and shipbuilding extends back to the group's founding in 19th-century Japan. Yataro Iwasaki, born in 1834 to a rural samurai family, early in his life became an official with the Kaiseken, the agency responsible for regulating trade in his native Tosa domain, on the island of Shikoku. By adroitly straddling the roles of public official and private entrepreneur, Iwasaki was able to start a small shipping company in the late 1860s. In 1875 the Japanese government gave Iwasaki the 13 steamships that he had operated on its behalf during a brief military engagement with Formosa, making his newly named Mitsubishi Shokai—or Three-Diamond

Company, the source of the firm's logo—the dominant shipping agent in Japan.

With extensive mining interests and a talent for currency speculation, Iwasaki became so successful that the government created a rival shipping firm, the KUK, to foster competitive pricing. After a short fare war that threatened the ruin of both firms, Mitsubishi's shipping assets were merged with those of the KUK in 1885 to form a single, state-sponsored company. Mitsubishi retained a small amount of stock and exercised some control in the new firm, but its interest shifted to land-based industries, in particular mining and shipbuilding. In 1884, unable to make a go of shipbuilding, the Japanese government had loaned and then transferred outright its two leading shipyards to the private sector. Mitsubishi took control of the best of these, located in Nagasaki, and became Japan's premier builder of ships and the only one capable of competing in the international marketplace.

Japan's shipbuilding industry was still relatively primitive, however, and remained so until the 1896 Shipbuilding Promotion Law combined with the Sino-Japanese War to spur domestic demand. Mitsubishi, by this time known as Mitsubishi Goshi Kaisha, became the favorite supplier of large ocean-going vessels to the state shipping company NYK, building 43 percent of all ships ordered between 1896 and World War I. Despite the close ties between the two companies, it appears that Mitsubishi did not receive preferential treatment. Indeed, although Mitsubishi gained fame in 1898 as the supplier of Japan's first ocean-going steamship—the 6,000-ton Hitachi Maru—its delivery was so tardy that the NYK awarded a second, similar contract to a British firm.

From 1896 through 1904, the eight years between Japan's wars with China and Russia, Mitsubishi's shipbuilding business increased by nearly 300 percent. In 1905 it acquired a second dockyard, in Kobe, and by 1911 employed some 11,000 workers at Nagasaki alone. Mitsubishi's shipbuilding division was not yet especially profitable—a disproportionate amount of the parent company's profits still came from mining and stock dividends—but it soon gave rise to a panoply of subordinate industries that supplied the yards with raw materials and parts. For example, in 1905 the Kobe yard spawned what would eventually become Mitsubishi Electric Corporation, a leading manufacturer of generators and electric appliances. Other shipbuilding divisions grew into power plants and independent producers of airplanes, automobiles, and heavy equipment. Bolstered by its highly profitable mining interests, Mitsubishi was able to afford the vast sums of money and years of work required to transform its subsidiaries into world leaders.

When World War I began in 1914, Japanese shipping lines were unable to procure a sufficient number of foreign ships to maintain their booming business, and so turned to local manufacturers such as Mitsubishi. Japanese production increased more than tenfold between 1914 and 1919, with Mitsubishi leading the field. So great was the surge in business that the Iwasaki family, still in control of Mitsubishi Goshi Kaisha—the group's holding company—decided to spin off a number of its leading divisions into separate, publicly held companies, thereby gaining access to outside capital without substantially weakening the company's dominant position. In 1917 the Mitsubishi Shipbuilding Company (MSC) was created, along with Mitsubishi Bank, Ltd., Mitsubishi Iron Works, and a trading company for the entire group, now called Mitsubishi Corporation. The major components of the Mitsubishi *zaibatsu,* or conglomerate, were thus in place by 1920, although the ensuing years would bring many modifications to its structure.

As is generally the case, the wartime buildup in ship orders was followed by a severe depression. As business declined below prewar levels many shipbuilders were bankrupted and all were forced to make drastic layoffs. The slump continued throughout the 1920s, merging into the Great Depression. Mitsubishi's lack of shipbuilding contracts continued until the beginning of World War II. In the meantime, however, MSC was actively pursuing a number of other technological developments, most notably the airplane and the automobile. Having made its first airplane in 1916 and first auto in the following year, MSC grouped these products under the name Mitsubishi Internal Combustion Engine Manufacturing Company in 1920. This offshoot went through several changes before taking the name of Mitsubishi Aircraft Company in 1928, at which time it was already one of Japan's leading manufacturers of military aircraft. After six years of independence, however, the aircraft and automobile facilities were once again united with MSC to form Mitsubishi Heavy Industries in 1934. It is not clear why this strategy was adopted, but the imminent prospect of war with China may have suggested the need for a more unified industrial force.

To stimulate the moribund shipping industry, the Japanese government instituted the Scrap and Build Scheme in 1932. This policy called for shipowners, aided by government subsidies, to replace their older vessels with a smaller number of new, more efficient ships. In this way Japan's excess capacity could be reduced while simultaneously modernizing its fleet and promoting new shipbuilding technology. As the leading Japanese builder, Mitsubishi Heavy Industries (MHI) greatly benefited from this program, and even more so from the program's successor, the 1937 Superior Shipbuilding Promotion Scheme. This campaign was clearly prompted by Japan's preparations for war, as it subsidized the construction of large cargo ships with an eye to their eventual use for the transportation of troops and supplies. In the years following, government intervention in shipbuilding escalated to outright control, as the Imperial Navy placed all dockyard facilities under its direct command in 1942. The MHI yards at Nagasaki and Kobe produced a wide range of government warships, including the world's largest battleship, the Musashi. In addition, MHI used its aircraft experience to build 4,000 bombers and some 14,000 of the famous Zero fighters, widely recognized as the finest flying machine in the Pacific during the war's early years. The Zero provided an early example of the cost efficiency and quality that marked Japanese industrial design. A lightweight machine, the Zero could be produced quickly and economically, yet it boasted superior aerobatic abilities and heavy firing power. The Zero made Mitsubishi infamous in the West, discouraging postwar marketers of other Mitsubishi products from highlighting the company name in advertising.

At the end of the war in 1945, an estimated 80 percent of Japan's shipyards were still in usable condition. Mitsubishi's main yard at Nagasaki, however, did not escape the effects of the world's second atomic explosion. At war's end the occupying Allied forces halted all shipbuilding activity, restricting the heart of Japan's industrial economy. During the two years in which this ban remained in effect, MHI kept busy by repairing damaged vessels and even using its massive plants for the manufacture of furniture and kitchen utensils.

With the growing realization that Japan could be a strategic asset in the postwar battle against Asian communism, the Allies relaxed the more stringent limitations, and many Japanese companies resumed production. For MHI, occupation forces waited until 1950 to chop its mighty assets into three distinct and geographically separated firms: West Japan Heavy Industries, Central Japan Heavy Industries, and East Japan Heavy Industries. Part of an effort to destroy the Mitsubishi *zaibatsu* as a recognizable entity, the division of MHI was intended to force the three companies to compete against each other for contracts, thus hindering their growth.

The rest of the Mitsubishi group was similarly fragmented, and although it gradually reassumed its former shape, the Iwasaki family no longer controlled the various subsidiaries by means of a single holding company. Instead, each of the major Mitsubishi companies acquired stock in its fellow companies, and a triumvirate composed of the former MHI companies, Mitsubishi Bank, and the group's trading company became the unofficial head of what remained a voluntary economic entity. It is remarkable that this loosely connected portfolio of war-ravaged corporations should then have proceeded to outperform its global competitors over the next few decades. The three heavy-industry companies, in particular, faced an almost impossible situation. Forced to compete with one another, forbidden from pursuing the military contracts that had formerly provided a huge portion of its business, and confronted by international competitors whose technological progress had not been interrupted by the war, the new MHI trio appeared destined for failure.

Several factors combined to help MHI get past this critical period. The 1947 Programmed Shipbuilding Scheme provided low-interest government loans to the shipping companies that needed but could not afford new vessels. In effect, the government decided which ships should be built and helped pay for them, injecting the capital needed to restart a business cycle that had nearly ground to a halt. Secondly, the three companies were able to use some of their idle aircraft facilities in the manufacture of motor scooters and automobiles. Under the direction of the head designer of the Zero, Kubo Tomyo, the rejuvenated auto division sold about 500,000 scooters before the government asked it to resume making small autos in 1959. Thirdly, Japan's shipbuilders realized that the Japanese economy depended on ships and their manufacture, and that if Japanese ship producers could not compete in the postwar international market the entire nation would suffer.

Driven by such a threat to its existence, the former MHI companies hired an increasing number of highly competent engineering graduates from Japan's leading universities and set them to work emulating the advanced technology of the United States and Western European countries. Able to rely on trade unions that were loyal and flexible in the extreme, they were soon producing ocean-going vessels equal in quality to but less expensive than anything made in the West. The Korean War of 1951 to 1953 triggered a huge increase in orders and, after surviving the short depression following the Korean War, the companies were able to exploit the rapidly developing worldwide demand for oil tankers. The tanker market was in turn given a tremendous jolt by the Suez Canal crisis of 1956, since the canal closing sparked a surge of orders for larger, more efficient ships able to complete the long journey around Africa. Between 1954 and 1956 total orders at Japanese builders more than tripled to 2.9 million gross tons, of which at least two-thirds were placed by foreign shipping companies.

The post-Suez depression in shipbuilding was severe enough to prompt fresh diversification at MHI. Increased research financing was devoted to civil engineering, plant construction, and automobiles, all of which MHI's years of experience in heavy industry had well prepared it to undertake. In 1958, in cooperation with 23 other Mitsubishi Group corporations, Mitsubishi Heavy Industries created Mitsubishi Atomic Power Industries. MHI continues to dominate contemporary Japanese production of atomic power. Automobile production rose steadily, if not as quickly as at rivals Toyota and Nissan, and by 1964 the Nagoya plants were manufacturing 4,000 cars per month. Even aircraft production had been resumed by the early 1960s.

With the world increasingly dependent on imported oil and Japan's construction skills honed to perfection, Mitsubishi was hit by an avalanche of orders for tankers during the 1960s and early 1970s. To accommodate this extraordinary boom, the three parts of MHI were once again united, resulting in the 1964 rebirth of Mitsubishi Heavy Industries. This giant's 77,000 employees and $700 million in sales were spread among a handful of the most important heavy industries, but ship-building utilized the bulk of MHI's resources. A new dock with 300,000-gross-ton capacity was built at Nagasaki in 1965, followed by the 1972 completion of a mammoth 1-million-gross-ton supertanker facility at the same yard. This ultra-efficient dock enjoyed only a short life, however—the oil crisis of 1973 and 1974 soon brought tanker orders to a near standstill, permanently crippling the entire Japanese shipbuilding industry.

The economic downturn was devastating. By 1975, the last of the peak tanker years, 40 percent of MHI sales and one-third of its workers were involved in shipbuilding. By 1985 those numbers were 15 percent and 17 percent, respectively, and they have since continued to decline. Once again, the Japanese were confronted with a catastrophic loss of business, but MHI managed to shift its assets quickly enough to survive. Having already spun off its automobile division to form Mitsubishi Motors Corporation in 1970, MHI aggressively pursued clients in the power-plant and factory-design fields. It also resumed its position as the top supplier of military hardware to Japan's growing defense force. MHI has streamlined its production facilities by shifting employees from older industries such as shipbuilding to newer ones such as machinery and power-plant production, at the same time allowing natural attrition to shrink its overall labor bill.

The result is a very diversified company. Mitsubishi Motors is no longer a consolidated subsidiary of its parent. In 1990 MHI owned less than 26 percent of the automaker's stock. Given

MHI's traditionally poor marketing and consumer sales skills this separation will likely prove a boon for each company.

MHI eventually emerged successfully from the disastrous downturn of the shipbuilding industry, and has become Japan's industrial leader in other areas as well. While there were minor sales losses during the weakening of the global economy in the early 1990s, MHI's diversified manufacturing interests quickly rebounded. On the eve of the 21st century, MHI is Japan's largest, most important, manufacturing concern.

At present, MHI consists of five principal divisions, with associated branches and joint ventures worldwide: shipbuilding and steel structures; power generation equipment and facilities; heavy machinery; aerospace and defense; general (multifunction) machinery and air conditioners.

The shipbuilding and steel structures manufacturing segment presently accounts for approximately 14 percent of MHI's sales, a figure likely to increase significantly. MHI is Japan's leading shipbuilder, while shipbuilding (passenger, merchant, naval vessels) accounts for approximately 65 percent of sales for this division. One reason for MHI's successful recovery from the severe downturn in the shipbuilding recession is the company's transfer of thousands of highly skilled shipbuilding workers to other MHI divisions; when shipbuilding orders began to increase in the 1980s, these workers were shifted back to shipbuilding. Hence MHI does not suffer from the quandary of other leading shipbuilding industries in Japan and elsewhere: a severe shortage of skilled labor. The outlook for shipbuilding remains highly positive, in large part because of the need to overhaul the world's leaky oil tankers and other aged and increasingly unsafe and inefficient merchant vessels. In addition, MHI is the world leader in liquid natural gas carriers, which could emerge as the dominant fuel-powered vessel of the future.

MHI has also benefited from the Japanese government's commitment in the 1990s to engage in massive public works projects such as building and repairing roads, bridges, tunnels, smokestacks, and parking and leisure facilities. The steel structures industry of MHI, formerly a drag on the company, is growing and likely to expand into the next century.

MHI's power generation division is extremely strong and likely to remain so. Accounting for approximately 27 percent of sales, the division's principal customers are utility companies. Major products manufactured by this division include low-polluting, large gas turbines, electric power boilers, diesel engines, and nuclear power equipment. With the rise of the standard of living in southeast Asia overall, MHI sales in this division are expected to increase. In Japan, the shift to nuclear power continues, with the consequent growth in demand for nuclear power equipment. MHI is a leading company in developing alternative power technologies and in coal gasification techniques.

One MHI division that has not fared especially well has been heavy machinery. Most of the sales of this division (24 percent of total MHI sales) for years were centered on printing machinery. Demand for paper and pulp products has been stagnant for many years. The division, as a result, has been forging ahead in the development of environmental equipment, especially garbage incinerators, flue gas treatment products (to reduce noxious emissions in the atmosphere), and in gas engineering. MHI hopes that this division, mired in a perennial slump, improves its performance in the future.

Twenty-one percent of MHI's sales derive from its aircraft/defense component business. Although sales of defense-related equipment have slowed, MHI remains Japan's largest manufacturer and marketer of civil aircraft. Lastly, the general machinery/air conditioning segment accounts for 14 percent of company sales revenues. While sales of forklifts and construction machinery are stagnant, demand for air-conditioning equipment is growing, even in the depressed car manufacturing sector. Currently, air conditioning constitutes 57 percent of sales in this division.

MHI's five well-integrated manufacturing sectors, coupled with its attention to new technologies, have enabled the company to ensure that its major business segments remain growth industries. Nearly half of MHI's sales derive from its international markets, reflecting its reliance on a customer base that is worldwide.

Principal Subsidiaries: Mitsubishi Heavy Industries America, Inc. (U.S.A.); MHI Corrugating Machinery Company (U.S.A.); Mitsubishi Engine North America, Inc. (U.S.A.); MHI Forklift America, Inc. (U.S.A.); Bocar-MHI S.A. de C.V. (Mexico); Mitsubishi Brasileira de Industria Pesada Ltda. (Brazil); CBC Indústrias Pesadas S.A. (Brazil); ATA Combustao Tecnica S.A. (Brazil); Mitsubishi Heavy Industries Europe, Ltd. (U.K.); MHI Equipment Europe B.V. (Netherlands); Saudi Factory for Electrical Appliances Company, Ltd. (Saudi Arabia); Bohai & MHI Platform Engineering Co., Ltd. (China); Mitsubishi Heavy Industries (Hong Kong) Ltd.; MHI-Mahajak Air-Conditioners Co., Ltd. (Thailand); Thai Compressor Manufacturing Co., Ltd. (Thailand); Highway Toll Systems Sdn. Bhd. (Malaysia); MHI South East Asia Pte. Ltd. (Singapore).

Further Reading: Lubar, Robert, "The Japanese Giant That Wouldn't Stay Dead," *Fortune*, November 1964; Tindall, Robert E., "Mitsubishi Group: World's Largest Multinational Enterprise?," *MSU Business Topics*, Spring 1974; "Mitsubishi: A Japanese Giant's Plans for Growth in the U.S.," *Business Week*, July 20, 1981; Wray, William D., *Mitsubishi and the N.Y.K., 1870–1914: Business Strategy in the Japanese Shipping Industry*, Cambridge, Harvard University Press, 1984; Chida, Tomohei, and Peter N. Davies, *The Japanese Shipping and Shipbuilding Industries: A History of Their Modern Growth*, London, The Athlone Press, 1990; Smith, Maurice, "A Touch of the Mitsubishis (Mitsubishi Heavy Industries)," *The Accountant's Magazine*, January, 1991; Bates, Daniel, "Systems Modeling in Distribution Pact with Tokyo Goliath," *Pittsburgh Business Times & Journal*, March 9, 1991; "Airbus and the Japanese," *New York Times*, November 21, 1991; "Westinghouse Electric Corp.," *Wall Street Journal*, March 24, 1992; Blustein, Paul, "High-Tech's Global Links: Industry's Huge Costs Unite Former Rivals," *Washington Post*, July 16, 1992; "Mitsubishi Heavy Industries Pact," *Wall Street Journal*, November 2, 1992; "Mitsubishi Heavy Industries Ltd.," *The Oil and Gas Journal*, November 23, 1992.

—Jonathan Martin
updated by Sina Dubovoj

MOBIL CORPORATION

3225 Gallows Road
Fairfax, Virginia 22037
U.S.A.
(703) 846-3000
Fax: (703) 846-4669

Public Company
Incorporated: 1931 as Socony-Vacuum Corporation
Employees: 67,500
Sales: $63.23 billion
Stock Exchanges: New York
SICs: 2911 Petroleum Refining; 1311 Crude Petroleum &
   Natural Gas; 6719 Holding Companies Nec; 8711
   Engineering Services; 1382 Oil & Gas Exploration
   Services; 1381 Drilling Oil & Gas Wells; 4612 Crude
   Petroleum Pipelines; 4613 Refined Petroleum Pipelines

Mobil Corporation is America's second-largest oil company and a vocal representative of the oil industry. Its sophisticated public relations is in keeping with Mobil's background in the financial, marketing, and administrative aspects of the oil business. Neither of the two companies whose 1931 merger created Mobil—Standard Oil Company of New York (Socony) and Vacuum Oil Company—had significant experience in the production of crude oil. Both were refiners and marketers, and it is in those two areas that Mobil has achieved its considerable success.

Of Mobil's two progenitors, Socony was the larger and more generalized oil company, while Vacuum's expertise lay in the production of high-quality machine lubricants. Vacuum got its start in 1866 when Matthew Ewing, a carpenter and part-time inventor in Rochester, New York, devised a new method of distilling kerosene from oil using a vacuum. The process itself proved to be no great discovery, but Ewing's partner, Hiram Bond Everest, who had invested $20 in seed capital in the project, noticed that its gummy residue was suitable for lubrication, and the two men took out a patent on behalf of the Vacuum Oil Company in 1866. Ewing sold his interest in Vacuum to Everest shortly thereafter. The heavy Vacuum oil was soon much in demand by manufacturers of steam engines and the new internal-combustion engines. In 1869 Everest patented Gargoyle 600-W Steam Cylinder Oil, which was still in use into the 1990s, and the firm continued to prosper.

Within a decade Vacuum had expanded sufficiently to catch the eye of John D. Rockefeller's Standard Oil Company. Beginning in 1872, Standard had bought up scores of refineries and marketing companies around the country, and in 1879 it added Vacuum Oil to its list of conquests, paying $200,000 for 75 percent of Vacuum's stock. By that date Standard Oil had achieved an effective monopoly on the oil business in the United States. Despite its small size, Vacuum was given latitude by the Standard management, who respected its excellent products and the acumen of Hiram Everest and his son, C. M. Everest.

The Everests pursued an independent course in foreign sales. As early as 1885 Vacuum had opened affiliates in Montreal and in Liverpool, where its staff included 19 salespeople, and within the next decade the company added branches in Toronto, Milan, and Bombay. Vacuum became the leader among Standard's companies in the use of efficient marketing and sales techniques, packaging its lubricants in attractive tins, pursuing customers with a well-organized, efficient sales team, and, when necessary, bringing in a lubricants specialist to help customers choose the oil best suited to their needs. Company oils were made according to a secret formula, and by 1911 the Vacuum marketers had made the name Mobil oil known on five continents. In the United States, Vacuum products were sold nationwide by the Standard chain of distributors and in the northeast by Vacuum's own agents.

In 1906 Vacuum added a second refinery to its original Rochester plant, and in 1910 Standard Oil Company of New Jersey (Jersey Standard), the holding company for the Standard interests, invested $500,000 to enable its big Bayonne, New Jersey, refinery to manufacture some of Vacuum's lubricants for export. In 1911 the Standard companies were ordered to break up by the United States Supreme Court, and among the 34 splinters were Vacuum Oil and Standard Oil Company of New York (Socony). Socony, the second-largest of the newly independent companies, had been created along with Jersey Standard in 1882, both as a legal domicile for Standard's New York assets and to serve as the administrative and banking center for the entire Standard Oil Trust. William Rockefeller, John D. Rockefeller's younger brother and long-time business partner, remained the president of Socony from its inception until 1911.

From the first it was planned that in addition to serving as Standard's headquarters, Socony would handle the great bulk of the trust's growing foreign sales. It took over from Standard Oil Company of Ohio ownership of the merchant firm of Meissner, Ackermnn & Company, with offices in New York and Hamburg and agents around Europe. At first Standard relied exclusively on such brokers for its foreign business, but as the years went on the company set up its own foreign subsidiaries around the world. By 1910 the Standard subsidiaries had usurped almost all of the foreign sales, with Socony's affiliates handling about 30 percent, while Vacuum Oil, which had also built a small but widespread sales group, contributed six percent to the total. In addition to the sales it made itself, Socony also bought and then resold all Standard products leaving New York, and even for a time those shipped out of California to Asia. Bolstered by its double role, Socony's sales were among the largest of any Standard company, and as Standard's official overseas representative, it became a familiar name in many countries.

Another of Socony's important functions, especially prior to 1899, when Jersey Standard began assuming such duties, was to administer most of the Standard group's internal affairs. In the New York City office building at 26 Broadway were housed not only Socony's own corporate leaders, but also the small group of men who ran Standard Oil. Some individuals, such as William Rockefeller, served on both boards, and the interplay between Socony and the Standard group was intimate and complex. Socony also assumed banking functions for the group. After 1899 Jersey Standard became the sole holding company for all of the Standard interests, but Socony continued much as before in its various key roles.

By the time of the dissolution of Standard in 1911, Socony had established its position in Europe and Africa and built a thriving business in Asia as well. China became an important market for Socony. Socony eventually built a network of subsidiaries from Japan to Turkey that by 1910 was handling nearly 50 percent of the kerosene sold in Asia. In the United States, Socony's five refineries turned out kerosene, gasoline, and naptha for sale in New York and New England, through jobbers and a growing number of the new roadside stores known as "gas stations."

In 1911 the Supreme Court upheld a lower court's conviction of Jersey Standard for violation of the Sherman Antitrust Act and ordered the organization dissolved. Each of the 34 new companies created by the order was allotted varying proportions of the three basic oil assets—crude production, refining, and marketing—but neither Socony nor Vacuum Oil ended up with any sources of crude. Both companies were strong marketers and refiners, and both became occupied by the search for enough crude oil to keep their plants and salesmen busy. Socony's need for its own crude supplies was greater since it produced a large volume of oil-based fuels and lubricants, while Vacuum's business was more limited in both volume and variety. Socony set out to secure ownership of its own wells.

At that point in the history of U.S. oil production, the natural area in which to explore was Texas, Louisiana, and Oklahoma. In 1918 Socony bought 45 percent of Magnolia Petroleum Company, which owned wells, pipelines, and a refinery in Beaumont, Texas, and did most of its marketing in Texas and the Southwest. After buying the rest of Magnolia in 1925, Socony purchased General Petroleum Corporation of California to help supply its large market in Asia. Then it entered the Midwest for the first time with a 1930 purchase of White Eagle Oil & Refining Company, with gas stations in 11 states. Socony now needed even more crude oil to supply these additional market outlets, and like most of the other big international oil concerns, Socony looked to the Middle East.

World War I had demonstrated the crucial role of oil in modern warfare and prompted the U.S. government to encourage U.S. participation in the newly formed Turkish Petroleum Company, operating in present-day Iraq. A consortium of U.S. oil companies was sold 25 percent of Turkish Petroleum. By the early 1930s only Jersey Standard and Socony were left in the partnership, with each eventually holding 12 percent. Oil was first struck by the company, renamed Iraq Petroleum, in 1928, and by 1934 the partners had built a pipeline across the Levant to Haifa, Palestine. From Haifa, Socony could ship oil to its many European subsidiaries.

In the meantime, Vacuum Oil had made a number of important domestic acquisitions and had strengthened its already far-flung network of foreign subsidiaries, but continued to share Socony's chronic shortage of crude. The two companies, similar in profile and complementary in product mix, joined forces in 1931 when Socony purchased the assets of Vacuum and changed its name to Socony-Vacuum Corporation. The union was the first alliance between members of the former Jersey Standard conglomerate and created a company with formidable refining and marketing strengths both at home and abroad. To supply its joint Far East markets more efficiently, in 1933 Socony-Vacuum (SV) and Jersey Standard created another venture called Standard-Vacuum Oil Company (Stan-Vac). Stan-Vac would ship oil from Jersey Standard's large Indonesian holdings to SV's extensive marketing outlets from Japan to East Africa. By 1941 it was contributing 35 percent of SV's corporate earnings.

In 1934 Socony-Vacuum Corporation changed its name to Socony-Vacuum Oil Company, Inc. (SVO). The company's growth made SVO the second-largest U.S. oil concern by the mid-1930s, with nearly $500 million in sales, exclusive of Stan-Vac. From warehouses and gas stations in 43 states and virtually every country in the world, SVO sold a full line of petroleum products, many of them sporting some variety of Vacuum's famous Mobil brand name or its equally familiar flying red horse logo. With 14 refineries in Europe alone and a fleet of 54 ocean-going tankers, by 1941 SVO's holdings were truly international in scope and balance—a situation that caused growing anxiety as World II approached. When the Nazis stormed across Western Europe they found working SVO refineries that they promptly put into the service of the Third Reich. The largest prize, a huge refinery at Gravenchon, France, was destroyed by the retreating French in a blaze that lasted for seven days. Similarly, the $30 million Stan-Vac refinery at Palembang, Indonesia, was kept out of Japanese hands by burning it to the ground. The war also cost SVO some 32 ships and the lives of 432 crew members, lost to German submarines. Throughout this period, increased military sales generally made up for SVO's wartime capital losses and declining civilian revenue.

Socony-Vacuum Oil Company's search for crude oil continued. In the immediate postwar years SVO completed a transaction that would provide the company with oil for many years to come. In the 1930s, Standard Oil Company (California) and the Texas Company—later known as Chevron and Texaco, respectively—had bought drilling rights to a huge chunk of Saudi Arabia, and when they realized the extent of the fields there the two companies sought partners with investment capital and overseas markets. SVO and Jersey Standard had ample amounts of both, and they agreed to split the offered 40 percent interest in the newly formed Arabian American Oil Company (Aramco). SVO had second thoughts about so large an investment and settled for ten percent instead. This miscalculation was rendered less painful by the truly enormous scale of the Arabian oil reserves. In the coming decade of economic growth and skyrocketing consumption of oil, SVO would develop and depend upon its Arabian connection even more strongly than the other major oil concerns.

In the United States a new culture based on the automobile and abundant supplies of cheap gasoline spread the boundaries of cities and built a nationwide system of interstate highways. SV's long use of its Mobil trade names and flying red horse logo had made these symbols known around the country, and in 1955 the company capitalized on this by changing its name to Socony Mobil Oil Company, Inc. (SM). In 1958 sales reached $2.8 billion and continued upward with the steadily growing U.S. economy, hitting $4.3 billion five years later and $6.5 billion in 1967. In 1960 a subsidiary, Mobil Chemical Company, was formed to take advantage of the many discoveries in the field of petrochemicals. Mobil Chemical manufactures a wide range of plastic packaging, petrochemicals, and chemical additives. In 1989 it contributed 32 percent of Mobil's net operating income—generated on sales representing less than seven percent of the corporate total.

Egypt's nationalization of the Suez Canal in 1956 was one of many indications that SM's Middle Eastern dependence could one day prove to be problematic, but there was little the company could do to reduce this dependence. Even significant new finds in Texas and the Gulf of Mexico were not able to keep pace with America's oil consumption, and by 1966 the Middle East, principally Saudi Arabia, supplied 43 percent of SM's crude production. Also in 1966 Socony Mobil Oil Company changed its name to Mobil Oil Corporation, using "Mobil" as its sole corporate and trade name and de-emphasizing the use of the Pegasus logo in favor of a streamlined "Mobil" with a bright-red "o." Still constantly searching for alternative sources of crude, Mobil got a piece of both the North Sea fields and the Prudhoe Bay region of Alaska in the late 1960s, although neither would be of much help for a number of years. In the meantime, world consumption had slowly overtaken production and shifted the market balance in favor of the Organization of Petroleum Exporting Countries (OPEC), which would soon take advantage of the relative scarcity to enforce its world cartel.

During the 1960s Mobil Oil's nine percent annual increase in net income was the best of all major oil companies, and it continued as a major supplier of natural gas and oil to the world's two fastest-growing economies, West Germany and Japan. In 1973, however, OPEC placed an embargo on oil shipments to the United States for six months and began gradual annexation of U.S.-owned oil properties. The price of oil quadrupled overnight and a new era of energy awareness began, as the international oil companies lost the comfortable positions they had held in the Middle East since the 1920s. On the other hand the immediate result of OPEC's move was to boost sales and profits at all the oil majors. Mobil Oil's sales nearly tripled between 1973 and 1977 to $32 billion, and 1974 profits hit record highs, prompting a barrage of congressional and media criticism that was answered by Mobil Oil's own public relations department. Mobil Oil quickly became famous as the most outspoken defender of the oil industry's right to conduct its business as it saw fit.

Despite its apparent ability to make money in any oil environment, Mobil Oil was concerned about the imminent loss of its legal control over the Middle Eastern oil on which it depended. Under the special guidance of President and Chief Operating Officer William Tavoulareas, Mobil Oil chose to strengthen its ties with Saudi Arabia, spending large amounts of time and money courting the Saudi leaders, investing in industrial projects, and in 1974 acquiring an additional five percent of the stock in Aramco from its partners. In 1976 Mobil Oil Corporation again changed its name, to Mobil Corporation. In the early 1990s it enjoyed one of the closest relationship with the Saudis of any oil firm, a bond whose value increases sharply when oil is scarce but is a liability when plentiful supplies make Mobil's purchases of the expensive Saudi crude less than a bargain. In addition, Mobil has considerably increased its budget for oil exploration, concentrating mainly on the North Sea and Gulf of Mexico regions. Although these efforts have largely succeeded in replacing Mobil's reserves as fast as they are used up, the company bought Superior Oil Company in 1984. Mobil paid $5.7 billion for Superior, mainly for its extensive reserves of natural gas and oil.

By that time the oil market had once again changed course. Conservation measures and a generally sluggish world economy reversed the price of oil in 1981, and it continued to drop throughout the decade. Mobil thus found itself locked into contracts for expensive Saudi crude and burdened with the debts incurred in the Superior purchase at a time of falling revenues. To make ends meet, Chairman Rawleigh Warner, Jr., and his 1986 successor, Allen E. Murray, made substantial cuts in refineries and service stations, upgrading Mobil's holdings of both to a smaller number of more modern, efficient units. By 1988 Mobil had pulled out of the retail gasoline business in 20 states and derived 88 percent of its retail revenue from just 14 states, mostly in the Northeast. It had also cut its oil-related employment by 20 percent as well as getting rid of its Montgomery Ward and Container Corporation of America subsidiaries, holdovers from a move toward diversification in the mid-1970s.

The $6 billion sale of assets was used to reduce debt, and Mobil's financial performance improved accordingly as the decade drew to a close, although not enough to please Wall Street analysts. The 1980s were generally not a good period for Mobil, which continued, on paper at least, to show a worrisome decline in proven oil reserves.

World events in the early 1990s had contradictory repercussions for Mobil and the petroleum industry as a whole. The Persian Gulf War in particular, and instability in the Middle East in general, heightened the importance of Mobil's carefully cultivated friendship with Saudi Arabia. But a recession in the United States and the worldwide economic slowdown lowered the demand for energy and chemicals, thereby weakening prices.

The corporation marked its 125th anniversary in 1991, but there was little cause for celebration. As earnings across the gas and oil industry dropped, Mobil's profits fell by only one-half percent, but the corporation braced for a deepening recession with restructuring and internal investment. Asset sales of $570 million in 1991 included a Wyoming coal mine and hundreds of wells in western Texas. Capital and exploration spending crested that year at over $5 billion, up almost 16 percent from the previous year.

The recession deepened in 1992, and Mobil Chairman and CEO Allen E. Murray continued restructuring as earnings plunged precipitously across the industry. By the end of the year, Mobil had divested itself of a polyethylene bread bag manufacturing business, a polystyrene resin business, and its interests in nine oil fields in west Texas and southeast New Mexico. Mobil also cut its domestic work force by more than 2,000 in 1992 and slashed $800 million from that year's capital and exploration budget. It may have seemed that even nature moved against the oil industry: August's Hurricane Andrew forced the evacuation of oil and gas rigs and platforms on the Gulf of Mexico, in Alabama, on Mobile Bay, and even as far inland as Beaumont, Texas. Gulf operations began the return to normal within a week of the devastating storm.

The company notes that environmental and philanthropic efforts have been a hallmark of Mobil's operations. In 1991 Mobil started the industry's first nationwide used oil collection program, and it continued to contribute to such cultural and educational projects as "Teach for America," a nonprofit teacher corps. But Mobil's otherwise good environmental record was marred in 1992 when, after three years of litigation, an environmental manager at Mobil Chemical proved that his superiors attempted to force him to falsify the findings of environmental audits. A jury awarded the former employee $1.75 million in damages and interest in his wrongful discharge suit against Mobil.

Mobil's worldwide influence, with strong positions in Saudi Arabia, Nigeria, and Asia's Pacific Rim, included a commanding presence in Indonesia. In the early 1990s, Mobil was the largest U.S. firm extracting natural gas in Indonesia, which was one of the world's largest producers of that resource. Natural gas constituted 50 percent of Mobil's worldwide resources at that time, making the Indonesian activities doubly important.

The corporation hoped to emerge from the lingering recession with a strong balance sheet that would allow management to make acquisitions and invest in product development, which have historically been Mobil's strengths.

Principal Subsidiaries: Mobil Exploration & Producing U.S. Inc.; Mobil Exploration & Producing North America, Inc.; Mobil Land Development Corporation; Mobil Natural Gas Inc.; Mobil Oil Corporation; Mobil Oil Exploration & Producing Southeast Inc.; Mobil Producing Texas & New Mexico Inc.; Tucker Housewares Inc; Mobil International Finance Corp.; Mobil Administrative Services Co., Inc.

Further Reading: Hidy, Ralph W., and Muriel E. Hidy, *History of Standard Oil Company (New Jersey): Pioneering in Big Business 1882–1911,* New York, Harper & Brothers, 1955; Sampson, Anthony, *The Seven Sisters: The Great Oil Companies and the World They Made,* New York, Viking Press, 1975; *A Brief History of Mobil,* New York, Mobil Corporation, 1991; "Industry Earnings Plunge from 1990 Level," *Oil & Gas Journal,* December 2, 1991; "Irani: Oxy Winds up Restructuring Program; Murray, Mobil Discussing More Moves,"*Oil & Gas Journal,* March 23, 1992; "Oil Companies Report Sharply Lower Earnings," *Chemical Marketing Reporter,* April 27, 1992; Kopp, Wendy, "The ABCs of Raising Millions," *Working Woman,* June 1992; "Indonesia—Looking for Oil and Gas: As Explorations Step up So Do Equipment Imports," *East Asian Executive Reports,* June 15, 1992; "Oil Majors Make Tough Decisions on Jobs, Assets," *Chemical Marketing Reporter,* July 13, 1992; "Restructuring Still Rampant in U.S.," *Oil & Gas Journal,* July 13, 1992; "More U.S. Production Changes Hands," *Oil & Gas Journal,* July 20, 1992; Koen, A. D., "Hurricane Shuts Down Gulf Activity," *Oil & Gas Journal,* August 31, 1992; "Environmental Manager's Ethical Stand Vindicated," *Environmental Manager,* September 1992; Caney, Derek, "Ethylene Snaps Back after Andrew," *Chemical Marketing Reporter,* September 7, 1992; "Hurricane Slams Gulf Operations," *Oil & Gas Journal,* September 7, 1992.

—Jonathan Martin
updated by April Dougal

MORRISON KNUDSEN CORPORATION

Morrison Knudsen Plaza
P.O. Box 73
Boise, Idaho 83729
U.S.A.
(208) 386-5000
Fax: (208) 386-7186

Public Company
Incorporated: 1932 as Morrison-Knudsen Company, Inc.
Employees: 12,850
Sales: $2.28 billion
Stock Exchanges: New York Boston Pacific Midwest
SICs: 3743 Railroad Equipment; 1623 Water, Sewer &
    Utility Lines; 1629 Heavy Construction Nec; 6719
    Holding Companies Nec

Morrison Knudsen Corporation (MK) has long stood as one of the world's largest engineering and construction organizations. A 1954 feature article in *Time* identified co-founder Harry Morrison as ''the man who has done more than anyone else to change the face of the earth.'' Such words reflect the magnitude and scope of the company's projects, ranging from work on the superconducting super collider to wartime building initiatives in South Vietnam to construction of portions of the trans-Alaska pipeline.

The company's origin dates back to Idaho's Boise Valley at the turn of the century, when Morris Hans Knudsen and Harry W. Morrison teamed up to exploit business opportunities introduced by the National Reclamation Act of 1902. The U.S. government was subsidizing projects to irrigate vast tracts of desert. Knudsen, a native of Denmark, moved to Idaho with his wife in 1905. He became well known for his skill using horses and basic scrapers to haul dirt. Morrison, a native of Illinois, moved to Idaho in 1904 as a concrete superintendent for water reclamation projects. In 1912 Morrison and Knudsen collaborated on their first job, a subcontract for approximately $14,000 worth of work at a pumping station along the Snake River near Grand View, Idaho. This and other early jobs generated little, if any, profit. The first financially successful endeavor for the duo was the 1914 construction of Three-Mile Falls Dam in Oregon. In addition to yielding a profit, the Three-Mile job established the company as a legitimate player in dam construction, which

became one of the company's hallmarks. (By the 1980s MK had built more than 150 dams, including Brownlee, one of three dams built across the Snake River in Hells Canyon for Idaho Power; Karadj, near Teheran, Iran; San Luis, in California, with a crest length of more than three miles; and Hungry Horse and Yellowtail, both in Montana.)

One of the most significant milestones in the growth of Morrison-Knudsen Company was, in fact, construction of yet another dam, the Hoover (Boulder) Dam, contracted in 1931. The magnitude of the job led to the incorporation of Morrison-Knudsen Company, in 1932. The project was massive, drawing on 5,000 workers. It called for 4.5 million yards of concrete (enough to pave a four-lane highway from Seattle to Miami, according to company sources) and reached a height of 726 feet upon completion. To handle such a formidable task, Morrison brought together a consortium of different companies, Six Companies, Inc., thus introducing the now-commonplace practice of joint-venture construction. The dam was completed in 1935, two years ahead of schedule.

Having survived the depression, due, in part, to its success with the Hoover Dam project, MK was prepared to meet the business demands of World War II. The company joined other contractors in a joint venture known as Contractors, Pacific Naval Air Bases. Building airfield facilities on Midway and Wake islands in late 1941, more than 1,200 company workers were captured by the Japanese. On the Hawaiian island of Oahu, MK was also engaged in the construction of 20 huge naval fuel-storage vaults, each 250 feet high and 100 feet in diameter. MK launched its company magazine, the *eMKayan*, in March 1942, a strategic time to reinforce public relations.

These and other World War II projects established ties that have kept MK entrenched in military contracting to the present. In addition to extensive building contracts in Vietnam, the company procured a substantial amount of business outside of active battle zones. The Distant Early Warning (DEW) Line, a chain of bases and radar installations, was constructed and maintained across northern Canada, as was the ''White Alice'' communications system in Alaska. In the 1960s MK became a leading builder of missile facilities, including the first U.S. underground Titan missile installation at the Lowry Air Force Base in Colorado. More recently, the company sponsored a joint venture for the Aeropropulsion Systems Test Facility, an advanced jet engine center for the U.S. Air Force (completed in 1984). Finally, the company also was involved in the reconstruction of Kuwait following the 1991 Gulf War. According to *U.S. News & World Report*, such an expensive national reconstruction effort had not been launched since the Marshall Plan molded a new Europe after the Second World War.

While World War II initiated new business, the war's end also brought reconstruction projects and expansion opportunities in new domains. In 1950 MK bought the Cleveland-based industrial builder H. K. Ferguson Company, which aided greatly in the trend toward rebuilding the American infrastructure. The 1950s also marked the establishment of the company's engineering subsidiary, International Engineering Company, Inc., which was designed primarily to implement public works in less industrialized nations (its first project was a dam in India). By the mid-1950s, the firm had been commissioned by 10 foreign governments. The company had by this time established a notable presence in a number of international markets, working on projects in such distant lands as Afghanistan, China, Iran, and Saudia Arabia. A *Time* Magazine article in May 1954 titled "Builders Abroad—Ambassadors with Bulldozers" emphasized the impact of the construction industry on world economy. The magazine cover featured a portrait of Harry Morrison with the subheading, "To tame rivers and move mountains."

The company further diversified in the 1960s, establishing itself as one of the major contractors to the developing space program. In addition to other contracts for the American space program, in 1966 the company contracted the Vehicle Assembly Building (VAB) in Florida. The world's largest building at the time, it was used to assemble the Apollo and Saturn V rockets, for which MK also constructed the launching pads.

The Vietnam War in the 1960s and early 1970s also stimulated business, as the U.S. government engaged the company as the sponsor of a joint venture—called RMK-BRJ—that consisted of MK International, Raymond International, Brown & Root, and J. A. Jones Construction Company. Under the command of the U.S. Naval Facilities Engineering Command, RMK-BRJ constructed bridges, highways, jet airfields, hospitals, deepwater ports, communications facilities, water supply systems, power plants, supply depots, and other facilities from 1962 to 1972. The venture, which employed more than 50,000 people, resulted in roughly $1.9 billion of business.

The challenges of the Vietnam era forged the business skills of William H. McMurren, who was elected president and chief executive officer in 1970. McMurren served for 14 years and carried the company into the 1980s under a new program of expansion and diversification. McMurren first established his abilities as a manager while directing missile site construction during the early 1960s. From 1970 to 1984, when he died at the age of 57, McMurren enhanced the traditional construction abilities of MK and extended activities to engineering, construction management, mining, real estate, manufacturing, and shipbuilding.

Indeed, the late 1970s and early 1980s marked a period of unprecedented growth for MK. The company expanded into mining, a logical offshoot of its heavy civil engineering operations. MK explored for precious metals, coal, lignite, and limestone mines throughout the United States and in various foreign countries. Notable examples included the 1973 Rio Blanco Copper mine in Chile, hewn out of solid rock in the forbidding landscape of the Andes Mountains; the Cerrejon Coal Project, a $2-billion turnkey project in northeastern Colombia; and the 1989 joint venture with Eastmaque Gold Mines, Ltd. to operate and develop the Cargo Muchacho Project in southeastern California (known as the American Girl Joint Venture). MK also delved into shipmaking, acquiring full ownership of National Steel and Shipbuilding Company (NASSCO) of San Diego in 1979. One of its first projects was the construction of a fast-combat support ship for the Navy, with an open contract for further orders.

MK also moved into environment-related industries of hazardous waste handling and storage and energy plant repair, modification, and improvement. By 1987 the company had carried out design and construction management of remedial actions programs at 24 abandoned uranium processing sites nationwide for the Department of Energy. It also worked on waste-to-energy plants in Florida; Charlotte, North Carolina; and Fayetteville, Arkansas.

Also chartered to broaden MK's base was the new venture, Morrison-Knudsen Services, designed to maintain and operate military facilities in Alabama, Arizona, and California. Finally, the company focused particular energy on its railroad business, rebuilding transit cars and, by the late 1980s, serving as the sole domestic manufacturer of the cars). By the early 1980s MK's varied initiatives, fostered by McMurren, had bolstered the company's potential on numerous fronts.

The firm's growth, however, was hampered by a harsh economic climate in the mid-1980s, prompting the company to restructure its operations. On May 3, 1985, stockholders approved a plan of reorganization and agreement of merger wherein Morrison-Knudsen Co., Inc. became a wholly owned operating subsidiary of Morrison Knudsen Corporation. Other subsidiaries included Morrison-Knudsen Engineers, Morrison-Knudsen International Company, and MK-Ferguson Company (National Steel and Shipbuilding Company remained a subsidiary of Morrison-Knudsen Company). The new company structure was designed to accommodate growing complexities in the engineering and construction industries. The short-term result of the reorganization bordered on disaster. In 1988 MK suffered a loss of $3.35 per share from continuing operations and $8.17 per share loss from discontinued operations, in part because of a $42 million pretax loss on the disposition of its interest in the shipbuilding operation of NASSCO.

Due, in large part, to such slippage, the company initiated another round of reorganization in 1988, appointing William J. Agee to replace W. J. Deasy as chairman and CEO. Agee's principal responsibility was to reverse the negative trend in MK earnings while at the same time resuscitate his own business reputation, which had suffered in the media since the early 1960s.

As chief financial officer at Boise Cascade Corporation, Agee had been instrumental in heading the company in the direction of urban renewal, an area that was trendy, though not especially prudent, according to Richard Stern in a June 1992 *Forbes* article. Boise Cascade's financial woes, which included defaulted real estate sales and inadequate reserves for South American bonds owned by a subsidiary, did not reach their peak, however, until after Agee had left the company. In 1972 he joined Bendix Corp. as chief financial officer, becoming chairman in 1977. In 1980 he drew criticism for his relationship with a young protegee, Mary Cunningham, who rose to the position of vice-president of strategic planning at Bendix before the age of 30. In 1982 Agee and Cunningham married. In that same year, Agee launched a hostile bid to take over Martin Marietta Corporation, the missile and technology company. Marietta fought back by buying Bendix shares in what was called a "Pac-Man defense," a reference to the video-game character that defends itself by swallowing its enemies to become stronger. Finally, Allied Corp. intervened, absorbing Bendix and dismissing the Agee couple.

Upon joining MK, Agee effected an immediate strategy to rescue the company from debt and heavy losses. He cut the payroll, stopped bidding for small projects, and rebuilt the company's international business. He made MK's transportation-construction business the top-ranked company in the United States, while other main lines improved, but less dramatically. Agee also strengthened MK's balance sheet, cutting debt from $300 million to almost nothing and amassing $100 million in cash. Other financial figures also looked promising: in February of 1990, the company reported 1989 net income of $32.2 million, or $2.81 per share, on revenue of $2.2 billion, representing an all-time record for net income from continuing operations of the engineering and construction and rail systems segments, and surpassing the 1981 record by over $3 million. 1990 net income rose to $34.5 million ($2.90 primary earning per share) on revenue of $1.7 billion. By 1991 the company reported a second quarter backlog of $4.1 billion, up from $3.4 billion for the same period during the previous year. Agee's restructuring, however controversial, had dramatically transformed MK's financial fortunes.

A large part of the change was attributable to MK's emphasis on the transportation sector, especially design and construction of transit cars. Ken Fisher, president and CEO at Fisher Investments, identified excellent investment opportunities in a 1992 portfolio letter, recognizing that MK had built up its rapid transit system business from less than one percent of its total revenues to 40 percent. The company's success in its emphasis on the transportation industry was further illustrated by the position it assumed at the forefront of a revival of interest in rail transportation in the United States. Sensitive to current trends, Agee envisioned not only high-speed rail between cities, but also commuter transit in every major U.S. city.

To that end, the company won various contracts around the country. It contracted the construction of tunnels and substations for the Bay Area Rapid Transit system in northern California and tunnels and underground stations for the Washington D.C. "Metro" subway system. In November 1991, MK was approved by the Honolulu City Council to design, build, operate, maintain, and supply vehicles for a $1.7-billion, 15.6-mile elevated rapid transit system serving Honolulu. In January 1992 the company became managing director for a consortium to develop a high-speed rail system linking Houston, Dallas-Fort Worth, Austin, and San Antonio. Progress has been slowed, however, by negotiations over several issues: whether to employ French TGV or German FasTrac technology; whether to seek federal (or public) funds, or remain funded by private capital; and whether, once funded, the project would pay for itself. A less high-tech, though considerably more realized project, was the Hornell plant, located near Elmira, New York, that started remanufacturing 750 transit cars in the early 1980s. The plant lost significant earnings that year, but subsequently managed to improve profits. In March 1992 MK announced an agreement with Caterpillar, Inc. to use state-of-the-art Caterpillar engines in its generation of new locomotives.

MK was also involved in the controversial bidding for a Los Angeles transit project in 1992. The bidding pitted MK and the Japanese-based Sumitomo Corporation against each other for a Los Angeles County transportation contract to build the $122-million Green Line Cars. Although the MK bid was approxi-

mately $5 million cheaper for the County of Los Angeles, Sumitomo won the bid, allegedly due to greater experience in the industry. Ray Grabinski of the transportation commission explained to ABC News that "this wasn't the difference between a Honda and a Ford Taurus. This was the difference between a Honda and a mechanic saying he can build you a car." A national uproar ensued, arguing in favor of American jobs and fueling a rash of anti-Japanese sentiments. In January county transportation officials canceled their contract and convened a special panel to standardize rail car design and build the vehicles locally, possibly drawing on a multi-company venture to implement it. Though MK did not win back that contract, it found business further north, in San Francisco, where it contracted with the Bay Area Rapid Transit (BART) to renovate an abandoned steel warehouse in the area as a manufacturing site for 88 Caltrans cars by 1994. The so-called "California car" was designed as a double-decker model for commuter systems and longer-distance routes inside the state.

A less controversial, though highly publicized, deal was also made with Metra, the Chicago area commuter rail agency, in January of 1992. The contract called for MK to build 173 new rail cars and to refurbish 140 existing cars. The tab, worth $378 million, constituted the largest transit-car order for the company and one of the biggest in U.S. history. According to the contract, MK was to reopen one section of the Pullman freight car plant on Chicago's South Side and begin hiring in late 1992, with final deliveries scheduled for late 1995. Since employment was particularly low on the South Side, where USX Corp. South Works steel mill had recently closed, skilled workers were in abundance. Nevertheless, labor disputes erupted when MK won the contract over Montreal's Bombadier, Inc.; Bombadier had committed itself to a United Auto Workers' facility, while MK had not promised union ties. Despite these and other problems to overcome, the general outlook was hopeful. A May 24 article in the *Washington Post* linked the MK initiative back to the Pullman Standard Co.'s pioneering work in the luxury couchette industry: "The U.S. passenger car business apparently is being reborn in the very birthplace of the sleeping car."

Despite Agee's reorganization of the company and his revival of the transportation industry, the profit turn-around he promised MK was far from certain. Earnings between 1985 and 1987 remained between $33 million and $36 million. In September 1992 Agee announced write-offs amounting to roughly $27 million for accounting changes, recall of substantial debt, and loss of the Honolulu rapid-transit contract. In order to build an organization big enough for his plans, Agee also began capitalizing development costs instead of expensing them, according to *Forbes'* Richard Stern, who warned that such procedures could become time bombs waiting for capitalized projects to fail. In addition, fears that MK was underbidding on some projects and risking its own capital on others led First Boston analyst Deborah Thielsch to recommend selling the stock in February of 1992, according to Stern. Nevertheless, in May of the same year, Agee confidently announced to a *PR Newswire* correspondent that "our excellent market position across the board is a clear sign that our strategy and hard work are paying off."

Morrison Knudsen Corporation is encouraged by the success of its rail systems segment. The company's rail interests enjoyed its best ever earnings in the fourth quarter of 1992 and garnered several significant orders from customers such as the Metra commuter line that services Northeast Illinois, the California Department of Transportation, and Amtrak. Amtrak also chose a joint venture led by MK to design and build a high-speed-rail electrification system from New Haven, Connecticut, to Boston for $296 million. MK also enhanced its standing in the rail industry through its 1992 acquisitions of TMS, Inc., a leading manufacturer of turbochargers for locomotive engines, and Power Parts Company, which distributes locomotive engine parts.

Principal Subsidiaries: Morrison-Knudsen Company, Inc.; Morrison-Knudsen International Company, Inc.; Morrison-Knudsen Engineers, Inc.; MK-Ferguson Company

Further Reading: "Builders Abroad; Ambassadors with Bulldozers," *Time*, May 3, 1954; *eMKayan*, Morrison Knudsen Corporation, Boise, ID, March 1987; "Morrison Knudsen Makes Management Changes," *PR Newswire*, September 12, 1988; "Morrison Knudsen Broadens Earning Base, Sustains Earnings Trend," *PR Newswire*, October 18, 1989; "MK 1990 Earnings Up Seven Percent," *PR Newswire*, February 8, 1991; "Honolulu City Council Vote Affirms Selection of MK-Led Team," *PR Newswire*, November 15, 1991; Krueger, Bob, "Dream of Texas High-Speed Rail May be Dying," *Houston Chronicle*, January 12, 1992; Dobbs, Lou, "Interview with Morrison-Knudsen CEO William Agee," *CNN Moneyline*, January 21, 1992; Fritsch, Jane, "Axing of Sumitomo Paints County into Corner," *Los Angeles Times*, January 24, 1992; Maturi, Richard, "Revived Morrison Knudsen Focuses on the Environment," *The Denver Business Journal*, February 21, 1992; "MK Signs Agreement with Caterpillar for Locomotive Engine," *PR Newswire*, March 31, 1992; Phillips, Don, "Getting U.S. Back on Track; Transit Agency Uses Economic Muscle to Revive Pullman Rail Car Legacy," *Washington Post*, May 24, 1992; Stern, Richard L., and Reed Abelson, "The Imperial Agees," *Forbes*, June 8, 1992; Yang, Dori Jones, and Kevin Kelly, "Why Morrison Knudsen is Riding the Rails," *Business Week*, November 2, 1992.

—Kerstan Cohen

MUELLER INDUSTRIES, INC.

2959 N. Rock Road
Wichita, Kansas 67226
U.S.A.
(316) 636-6300
Fax: (316) 636-6390

Public Company
Incorporated: 1893 as H. Mueller Manufacturing Company
Employees: 2,055
Sales: $517.30 million
Stock Exchanges: New York
SICs: 3351 Copper Rolling & Drawing; 3363 Aluminum
    Die-Casting; 3088 Plastic Plumbing Fixtures; 3491 Valve
    & Pipe Fittings; 3498 Fabricated Pipe & Fittings; 3469
    Metal Stampings, Nec

Headquartered in Wichita, Kansas, Mueller Industries, Inc. is a leading manufacturer of brass, bronze, copper, plastic, and aluminum products in the United States. The company operates eight factories and owns a short-line railroad in Utah. Mueller also holds various natural resource properties in the United States and Canada.

Mueller Industries traces its history back to 1852 when 20-year-old Hieronymous Mueller migrated to the United States. Mueller was an inventor with an interest in plumbing—particularly plumbing using copper. In 1872 he patented an improved water tapping machine. In 1877 he became the first to pour castings using brass, an alloy of copper and zinc. Mueller parlayed these inventions into manufacturing facilities, and in 1893, with $68,000 in capital, he incorporated his business in Michigan as the H. Mueller Manufacturing Company.

The firm prospered throughout the next two decades. In 1913, as Great Britain entered World War I, Mueller completed its first Canadian plant. With the United States's entrance into the war, Mueller, like many industrial companies, participated in a general increase in manufacturing. In order to produce munitions, the company began construction, in Port Huron, Michigan, of the first commercial forging facility in the United States. When that plant opened on December 17th, 1917, the business was reincorporated as Mueller Metals Company.

After the war, Mueller continued to make technological advances, key to the growth of significant industries. For the nascent mechanical refrigeration industry, the company provided brass forging which did not leak refrigeration gas like the porous castings previously in use. In addition, the Port Huron plant pioneered high-strength brass forging for gears, bearings, and pumps used by manufacturers of mechanical devices.

Mueller was still directing its primary efforts at the plumbing supply business, however. In 1923 the company introduced soft copper tube for underground water supplies and, in 1924, hard copper tube for indoor water supplies. By 1927, Mueller was firmly established in the plumbing business and was producing a full line of fittings and valves produced in its own foundry.

Perhaps Mueller Brass's—having changed its name in 1925—most important innovation came in 1930 when the company introduced the revolutionary Streamline solder-type fitting. Previously, fittings—which joined pieces of tube—had been the weakest sections of pipes. However, the new solder-joined fittings were actually stronger than the tubes they connected. It was due to this development that all-copper plumbing and heating systems were established as industry standards.

After the stock market crashed in 1929, Mueller fell victim to the same types of pressures other industrial companies were experiencing. Moreover, as a company that provided supplies to industrial firms, especially in the area of housing construction, Mueller experienced sales that generally reflected the low level of economic activity in the country. This being the case, Mueller canceled dividends and tightened its belt during the first half of the 1930s.

Surprisingly, Mueller returned to profitability by the mid-1930s, reinstating dividends in 1935. Toward the end of the decade, the war in Europe and a reviving economy at home spurred production. Mueller became highly profitable, a fact borne out by generally increasing dividends, including the record $2.25 dividend the company paid in 1941.

After the war, Mueller remained profitable, especially during the 1950s when earnings fluctuated between $2.50 and $5.50 per share, and sales averaged around $59 million. Given positive economic conditions, president and chief executive officer F. L. Riggin decided to expand the company. In December of 1951 he paid $1.25 million for Valley Metal Products Co. of Plainwell, Michigan. He bought, and later sold, Sheet Aluminum Corporation, of Jackson, Mississippi, and in March of 1958, he acquired American Sinteel Corporation, a Yonkers, New York, manufacturer of powder metal parts.

Along with acquisitions, Riggin upgraded existing facilities and built new ones. In 1954 he launched an eight-year program to expand and diversify the production of fabricated goods. In this effort, he placed particular emphasis on specially-engineered, copper-based alloys. In addition, Riggin opened an impact extrusion facility in Marysville, Michigan, in 1958. The plant, which shaped aluminum and copper by forcing it through a die, adapted the inherent strength and minimal weight of extrusions to specialized needs of customers who ranged from aerospace manufacturers to home appliance suppliers.

During the early 1960s, Mueller continued to do well, adding a larger proportion of defense subcontracting to its mix of customers. At this time the company was producing rods, forgings, tubes, and castings made from aluminum, copper, brass, bronze, and other alloys. Among the many semi-finished and fabricated items the company produced were powdered metal, screw machine parts, machined castings, forgings and impact extrusions, refrigeration valves and fittings, chromium- and nickel-plated fabricated items, electrotinned and hot dipped fabricated items, and copper pipes, tubes, and fittings used in plumbing, heating, and air conditioning.

Mueller continued to grow, reporting profits of $2.35 million on sales of $80.8 million in 1963. The company also acquired the assets of the Bay Engineering Company of Bridgeport, Michigan, the following year. Management, however, did not cling to the idea of a large, independent Mueller with an indefinite future.

For some time, U.S. Smelting Refining and Mining (USSRAM) had been acquiring Mueller stock and by 1965 had amassed a 72 percent share of the company. That year USSRAM made an offer to acquire the remainder of Mueller through a stock swap—a proposal which was approved overwhelmingly by both companies. Technically, Mueller Brass and USSRAM merged to become a new Mueller subsidiary called Mueller Brass Corp. Upon completion of the consolidation, however, the subsidiary's name was changed to U.S. Smelting, Refining, & Mining Company and USSRAM's management took over the new company, in effect absorbing Mueller.

USSRAM was a mining company whose primary products were gold, silver, lead, and zinc. Founded in 1906, the company was relatively stable until the early 1960s when a proxy fight led to the ascension of Martin Horwitz to the offices of president and chief executive officer in 1964. Under Horwitz, USSRAM had followed an aggressive path of acquisitions and had begun to develop the Continental Copper Mine in New Mexico. In acquiring Mueller, Horwitz was looking to join copper mining and smelting with the production of copper products.

The merger proved to be profitable from the start. In 1969, after Horwitz invested $17 million in Mueller's interests and $16 million in the copper mine, USSRAM's sales reached an all time high of $170 million, while income hit a record $12 million.

In fact, the merger provided Mueller with the capital to introduce new products, modernize old facilities, and build new plants. In 1967 the company began to offer plastic pipe and fittings. The Port Huron rod mill was modernized in 1971—doubling its copper alloys capacity. That same year construction of a Fulton, Mississippi, tube mill—including a 6,300 ton automated extrusion press—was completed. In a speech reprinted by the *Wall Street Transcript,* Horwitz called the Fulton plant "possibly the most efficient tube mill in the United States." He concluded that given the plant's low cost operation, it had "enabled Mueller to report profits when other mills were reporting losses and still others were closing down."

In the early 1970s, USSRAM changed its name to UV Industries, Inc. to better represent an increasingly diverse product mix that, by then, also included electrical equipment. Mueller, in the meantime, continued to expand, though not quite at the pace it did in the late 1960s. In 1973 the company purchased plants in Hartsville, Tennessee, to produce refrigerator and air condition-

ing components. By 1976, however, slow housing starts had led to a performance that, while acceptable, was nowhere near what it might be in a boom economy.

In 1977 Victor Posner, chairman of Sharon Steel Corp., offered to buy UV Industries. Posner was a Miami Beach businessman who had dropped out of high school and made a fortune in real estate by the time he was 30. He got involved in mergers and acquisitions and eventually used his NVF Company to gain control of Sharon, then the 12th largest steel company in the United States. One of Posner's tactics was to use subordinate debentures—bonds subordinate to other claims and backed by the general credit of the issuer—rather than a specific lien on particular assets in order to fund his activities.

This was the means of payment he proposed in the acquisition of UV Industries. UV, however, was wary of Posner and the two sides went back and forth with extensive negotiations. Finally, on November 26, 1979, it was agreed that Sharon would acquire UV for an interim note worth $517 million and the assumption of UV's liabilities. However, they also agreed that Sharon could not sell any UV assets until the interim note was exchanged for cash. This particular clause was important because it was widely assumed that Posner would pay for the deal by selling UV's large portfolio of investments and marketable securities. According to the *Wall Street Journal,* some analysts thought that cash would be hard to come by and that Posner had "erred badly in trying to swallow UV."

Under the Posner regime, Mueller remained profitable, and in 1983 the company's Canadian subsidiary in Strathroy, Ontario, began manufacturing metric fittings. Sharon, however, had difficulties. The company's debts were too high, and in 1985, Sharon defaulted on $33 million in interest payments. Bondholders could have forced the business into bankruptcy immediately; instead, they negotiated with Posner, who wanted them to swap their subordinated debentures for a package of common shares and low-interest and zero-coupon notes.

The largest bondholder was Quantum Overseas N.V., an investment fund based in Curacao. Quantum and the other holders allowed payments on the debentures to be extended more than 20 times while they tried to negotiate a settlement. In 1986 it was rumored that Sharon would sell Mueller to Quantum for $55 million, but that exchange never took place.

Finally in 1987, Quantum called in the $96.9 million in Sharon securities it held and in April of that year, Sharon filed for Chapter 11 bankruptcy. Over the next two years, Quantum officials and Sharon's other creditors worked to hammer out a plan to divide Sharon's assets and help the company emerge from bankruptcy.

During this time, Mueller was not static. The company had never filed for Chapter 11 and remained a viable enterprise. In 1990 Mueller acquired U-Brand Corporation, an Ashland, Ohio, company whose plants in Ashland and Upper Sandusky, Ohio, manufactured plastic valves, pipe couplings, steel pipe nipples, malleable iron pipe fittings, iron castings, and plastic pipe fittings for wholesalers and hardware stores. In addition, Mueller continued to innovate, bringing out—coincident with new strict EPA regulations—the SRD-1 (tm) which allowed customers in the refrigeration and climate control industries to capture and recover fluorocarbons during repair operations.

The issues surrounding Sharon were finally resolved on December 28, 1990, when negotiators, headed by Raymond Wechsler, an advisor to the Quantum Fund, hammered out a plan to divide up the company. After 25 years as a subsidiary, Mueller reemerged as an independent company called Mueller Industries, Inc. The new Mueller was an industrial concern which held its traditional plumbing and flow control equipment operation as well as natural resource holdings. This new sector of the business included the Utah Railway Co.—a short-line that carried coal to Provo, Utah, for transshipment by major rail carriers—Alaskan gold mining operations, and a variety of mining interests in Canada and the West.

In its first year as an independent company, Mueller announced a loss of $43.7 million on sales of $441 million. Almost all of the 1991 loss was due to a revaluation of assets, coupled with costs related to the bankruptcy proceeding and restructuring of the business following the reorganization. Harvey L. Karp, who became chairman and CEO on October 8, 1991, moved quickly to shape up the company. He enhanced the balance sheet by selling $25 million worth of investment grade notes and negotiated for expanded borrowing capabilities that provided $40 million. In an effort to focus on the company's core manufacturing business, the sale of the malleable iron business—which had not been profitable for Mueller—was arranged in 1992. To help upgrade operations neglected for many years, Karp made a commitment to allocate more capital and undertake improvement projects. He also negotiated settlements of litigation which asserted a $16.5 million guarantee obligation for the Sharon Steel business. This settlement turned out to be very favorable when Sharon filed Chapter 9 in the fourth quarter of 1992. Finally, among other key executives, Karp recruited William D. O'Hagan, who had 32 years experience in the industry, to be Mueller's chief operating officer and president.

Karp's efforts paid off handsomely—for the year ended 1992, earnings were up significantly, reaching $16.6 million on sales of $517.3 million. As Karp stated in *PR Newswire,* "We are optimistic that housing starts, the principal leading indicator of our business will increase in 1993. If they do, we are ready to take advantage of the market opportunities."

Principal Subsidiaries: Alaska Gold Company (85%); Mueller Brass Co.; Itawamba Industrial Gas Co., Inc.; Streamline Copper & Brass, Ltd.; U-Brand Corp.; Arava Natural Resources Co., Inc.; U.S. Fuel Co.; King Coal Co.; Utah Railway Co.; Washington Mining Co.; Canco Oil & Gas Ltd.; Aegis Oil & Gas Ltd.; Bayard Mining Corp.; Mining Remedial Recovery Co.; USS Lead Refinery, Inc.; Carpentertown Coal & Coke Co.; Amwest Exploration Co.; USSRAM Exploration Co.; Richmond Eureka Mining Co. (81%); Ruby Hill Mining Co. (75%); White Knob Mining; Kennet Co., Ltd.

Further Reading: "Mueller Brass Co. Lowers Copper Water Tube Price," *Wall Street Journal,* April 15, 1963; "Mueller Brass Expects Record Fiscal '63 Sales Above $75 Million Mark," *Wall Street Journal,* September 30, 1963; "Mueller Tube Mill Nears Completion," *American Metal Market,* June 25, 1970; Mari, Albert, "Chase, Mueller Reduce Their Brass Rod Prices Initiating New Decline," *American Metal Market,* September 30, 1976; "UV Industries, Inc.," *Wall Street Transcript,* December 13, 1976; Harrigan, Suhan, "Victor Posner Faces Hair-Raising Month as Exchange for UV Note Is Postponed," *Wall Street Journal,* July 21, 1980; "Sharon Steel Is in Talks to Sell Its Mueller Unit," *Wall Street Journal,* December 2, 1986; "Plan for Sharon Steel to Leave Chapter 11 Is Set by Co-Sponsors," *Wall Street Journal,* October, 26, 1989; Norman, James R., "Pulling Sharon Steel off the Scrap Heap," *Forbes,* August 20, 1990; *Mueller Industries, Inc. 1991 Annual Report,* Wichita, KS, Mueller Industries, Inc., 1992; "Mueller Industries Announces Higher Third Quarter Earnings on 34 Percent Increase in Sales," *PR Newswire,* October 21, 1992.

—Jordan Wankoff

MURPHY OIL CORPORATION

200 Peach St.
El Dorado, Arizona 71730-5836
U.S.A.
(501) 862-6411
Fax: (501) 862-9057

Public Company
Incorporated: 1950 as Murphy Corporation
Employees: 3,991
Sales: $1.69 billion
Stock Exchanges: New York Philadelphia Pacific Boston
    Chicago
SICs: 1311 Crude Petroleum & Natural Gas; 0762 Farm
    Management Services; 0851 Forestry Services; 6719
    Holding Companies Nec

Murphy Oil Corporation is the corporate parent of a consolidated group of enterprises that conducts onshore and offshore exploration activities in 11 countries and produces oil and natural gas liquids in the United States, Canada, Spain, Gabon, and the North Sea. Murphy owns two U.S. oil refineries and shares ownership in a U.K. refinery. Along with wholesale and retail sales in the United States, Western Europe, and Canada, Murphy is engaged in farming, timber and land management, and lumber manufacturing operations, primarily in Arkansas and Louisiana, and in real estate development in Little Rock, Arkansas.

The Murphy story began in the early 1900s in El Dorado, Arkansas, where Charles H. Murphy, Sr., started a lumber company with thousands of acres of timberland along the Arkansas-Louisiana border. Although he drilled his first oil well in the Caddo Pool of northern Louisiana in 1907, his primary efforts in oil exploration did not actually commence until 1936–37, when he and his associates discovered two large oil fields in southern Texas and Arkansas. At this time Murphy realized his land holdings were worth more for oil than for timber.

Murphy's business interest gradually expanded into a loose collection of partnerships, corporations, and individual holdings. In 1944, after he and his associates discovered their largest deposit near Delhi, Louisiana, they brought their diverse entities together as C. H. Murphy & Company.

Charles H. Murphy suffered a stroke late in the decade, and his son, 21-year-old son Charles H. Murphy, Jr., was put in charge during his subsequent illness. With his new role in the company the younger Murphy wasn't able to attend college but eventually educated himself by reading the classics and learning foreign languages, and his ambitions grew with the goals of the company. He saw that corporate status would be necessary to achieve company objectives, so, in 1950, he reincorporated C. H. Murphy & Company as Murphy Corporation, the predecessor of the current corporation.

During the early 1950s, Murphy continued to explore for oil on the more than 100,000 acres of company-owned land, which also contained timber and farming operations. In 1956, two years after Charles H. Murphy, Sr., died, his son brought the company public, offering shares on the New York Stock Exchange.

Toward the end of the decade Murphy began the expansion program that would ultimately lead to the Murphy Oil of today. He helped found the 51 percent owned Ocean Drilling and Exploration Company (ODECO), an outfit one reviewer called "one of the true pioneers and innovators in the off-shore drilling industry." In 1958 he exchanged 71,958 shares for Murphy's first refinery—Lake Superior Refining Company's Superior, Wisconsin, installation.

In 1960, Murphy continued to grow, acquiring Amurex Oil Co., River States Oil Co., and National Petroleum Corp. Most importantly, that year a merger took place with Spur Oil Co., an outfit whose extensive service station network would become Murphy's own.

After acquiring a second refinery in 1961—Ingram Oil and Refining Company's Meraux, Louisiana, installation—Murphy began expanding the company's drilling network. In 1962 he obtained the Western Natural Gas Company's Venezuelan properties and production. In the following years the company would begin exploring the Persian Gulf, Libya, the North Sea, the Louisiana shore, and other lands in the continental United States. It would also take large land positions in British Columbia, off the shore of Nova Scotia, in New Zealand's Tasman Sea, and off the coast of New South Wales in Australia.

As a result of this overwhelming concentration on fossil fuels, Murphy reorganized the company as Murphy Oil Corporation on January 1, 1964, placing the company's farm and timber interests—which now included 200,000 owned acres and 100,000 acres managed for others—into a wholly owned subsidiary, Deltic Farm & Timber Co., Inc.

In the mid-1960s, the company scored large successes in Iran's Sassan Field and in Libya. Between 1964 and 1969 the company's production of crude oil and liquids increased from 16 thousand barrels per day to 37 thousand barrels per day, while refinery intake rose from 43 thousand barrels per day to 90 thousand barrels per day. Much of the gasoline refined by the company went to owned or independently operated gas stations using the SPUR name. By 1969 there were 942 leased and owned SPUR stations and 1,332 SPUR stations operated by others. Of these, 548 were in the United Kingdom, 315 in Eastern Canada, and 127 in Sweden.

ODECO also grew during the late 1960s. Between 1964 and 1969, its revenues more than doubled from $12.4 million to $28.5 million. Of all drilling contractors ODECO was in a unique position to help its corporate parent. The company contracted work for itself in addition to farming some jobs out, and therefore received portions of successful leases on their proceeds, adding to Murphy's total reserves. By 1968 ODECO was operating 12 drilling barges and according to the *Wall Street Transcript* was considered "one of the best growth stocks in the oil industry."

About the only Murphy product which did not grow during the 1960s was natural gas production, which fell from a record 65.6 million cubic feet per day in 1962 to 60.3 cubic feet per day in 1969. However, rising production did not always translate into rising profits. Steep transportation costs, high exploration costs, weak refined products prices, and losses in Europe led to declining profits for 1967 through 1969 when net income fell from $8.2 million to $6.2 million.

Despite these losses, Murphy—who still controlled 51 percent of the stock—continued to expand the company. In 1969, he created Murphy Eastern Oil Company in London, to monitor diversified overseas operations. The same year he signed off on ODECO's formation of Sub Sea International, Inc. to operate various undersea systems such as diving bells and underwater welding chambers.

In 1970, a year in which profits rose to $9.3 million, reflecting higher prices and lower ocean freight costs, Murphy Oil began drilling in the British North Sea through an eight percent participation with Burmah Oil and Williams Bros. To finance this project as well as drilling barges for ODECO and additional acreage in the Gulf of Mexico, the company sold $34 million in convertible debentures in 1969 and 800,000 shares of common stock in June of 1971.

By 1971, the company as a whole was reporting revenues of $300 million. While two-thirds of its crude reserves were in Iran, Libya, and Venezuela, it had also created Murphy Oil Company, Ltd., which oversaw exploration, production, and marketing operations in Canada and was headquartered in Calgary, Alberta.

The OPEC oil embargo of 1973 was a boon for Murphy Oil. Sales shot up from $377.6 million in 1972 to $499 million and $862 million in 1973 and 1974, respectively. At the same time profits ballooned from $14.3 million to $48.5 million and $60.9 million. And in 1977 the company surpassed $1 billion in sales for the first time, selling $1.11 billion worth of fossil fuel products and services.

Prices remained high at the end of the decade. In 1979, after North Sea drilling paid off in the huge Ninian Field (the United Kingdom's third largest), the company racked up three consecutive years of record sales and income. Revenues surpassed $2 billion for the first time in 1980 while in 1981 profits reached $163 million despite a total $119 million increase in American, Canadian, and British crude oil excise taxes.

Throughout the industry, high prices made higher cost and higher risk exploration activities economically viable. Murphy invested heavily in prospects in Alaska and off the coast of Spain, and although he balanced these more risky plays with leases near established properties in the Gulf of Mexico, the company's activities reflected those of an industry that was taking more chances and using more drilling rigs. This was good news at ODECO where executives ordered several new platforms to satisfy demand.

On February 15, 1982, the company experienced a tragedy inherent in the ocean drilling business. During a severe storm off the coast of Newfoundland, ODECO's semisubmersible Ocean Ranger sank. Eighty-four persons were on board and all were lost.

Although margins, particularly for refined products narrowed in the early 1980s, Murphy remained highly profitable. In 1983, the company began pumping oil from the Gaviota field off the north coast of Spain. The same year, it reorganized as a holding company creating Murphy Oil USA, Inc. to oversee U.S. domestic oil interests and selling its Canadian marketing division, consisting of 100 owned or leased SPUR stations, a dealer network, and three product terminals.

In 1984, Charles H. Murphy, Jr., while retaining his role as the company's chairperson, turned the positions of CEO and president over to Robert J. Sweeney, an engineering physicist with a long career at Murphy. Sweeney faced an industry in which overcapacity and conservation had begun to pressure crude prices, and, consequently, refining and drilling margins. For example, as crude prices fell from $34 a barrel to $27 a barrel, there were periods in which the cost of products refined at company facilities were $2 higher than the same products on the spot cargo market.

In the fourth quarter of 1985, crude prices fell into the $15 to $20 range. Given reasonable returns for much of the year, Sweeney was able to salvage profits of $79.7 million, but in 1986 continued low prices forced him to take drastic economic measures. He slashed exploration budgets, terminated scientist positions, reduced support personnel by 15 percent, and let hundreds go at ODECO. Overall, he laid off over 1,600 employees—almost 30 percent of the company's total. Despite these efforts, the company lost $194.7 million, in what Sweeney in his annual report called "a terrible year."

Prices began to rise again in 1987, and all of the company's sectors rebounded except for ODECO, which suffered in a generally poor drilling climate. Since ODECO's capital costs were very high, underutilization of rigs meant heavy losses. In 1987 ODECO lost $61 million and at one point during the year was using only 29 percent of capacity. Excluding ODECO's figures, Murphy made $18 million that year; taking ODECO's losses into account, the company lost $44 million.

During these low years, management retained its credibility with stockholders by maintaining a $1-per-share dividend. Moreover, Sweeney did make some moves toward growth. He used company land holdings to enter the real estate business in Little Rock, Arkansas, where the company was building homes and a PGA quality golf course. In 1986, he bought ten drilling rigs, reasoning that a shakeup was underway and that ODECO might profit from being one of the few surviving firms. In 1987, he bought out the 23 percent minority interest in Murphy Oil Company Ltd., Murphy's London based subsidiary. That year the company also replaced its oil and gas reserves on an energy equivalent basis.

In 1988, Jack W. McNutt succeeded Sweeney as CEO. Like Sweeney, McNutt presided over a basically profitable company whose drilling subsidiary was what the *Arkansas Gazette* called the "monkey" on its back. ODECO was one of the nation's top three drilling companies, but like the industry as a whole, it had overbuilt and was carrying too many underutilized rigs.

During his first year, McNutt tried to gain more leverage in ODECO by buying out its minority owners. Though unsuccessful in this endeavor, Murphy reported a net income of $39 million in 1988—the first profit in three years. Murphy's outlook continued to improve in 1989, and the company made a major rebound in 1990 when because of higher prices induced by Iraq's invasion of Kuwait, sale of the Sub Sea International (ODECO's diving segment), and divestment of a share of its interest in Ninian Field, Murphy reported 1990 net income of $114 million, the best overall result since 1983.

1990 was also marked by an industry-wide trend toward increased production of natural gas, a fuel whose environmental benefits many believed would prove valuable to utility and automotive companies in the future. At Murphy this trend was evidenced by record production and by the fact that for the first time natural gas production exceeded liquid hydrocarbon production on an energy equivalent basis.

In 1991, McNutt finally disposed of Murphy's ODECO problem. After several unsuccessful attempts, he acquired the minority interest in ODECO through a tax free exchange of shares and then sold ODECO for $372 million. Though the deal was not actually consummated until January 30, 1992, it was reported in 1991 as an $83.9 million charge against earnings and resulted in a loss for the year of $11 million.

Principal Subsidiaries: Murphy Oil USA, Inc.; Murphy Eastern Oil Co.; Deltic Farm & Timber Co., Inc.; Murphy Oil Co. Ltd.; Murphy Exploration & Production Co.

Further Reading: A Brief History of Murphy Oil USA, Inc., Murphy Oil Company.

—Jordan Wankoff

NABISCO FOODS GROUP

7 Campus Drive
Parsippany, New Jersey 07054
U.S.A.
(201) 682-5000
Fax: (201) 428-4584

Wholly owned subsidiary of RJR Nabisco, Inc.
Incorporated: 1898 as the National Biscuit Company
Employees: 39,000
Sales: $6.45 billion
SICs: 2064 Candy & Other Confectionery Products; 2041
   Flour & Other Grain Mill Products; 2043 Cereal Breakfast
   Foods; 2047 Dog & Cat Food; 2052 Cookies & Crackers;
   2079 Shortening, Table Oils, & Other Edible Fats & Oils;
   2099 Food Preparations

For nearly a century, Nabisco has been one of the most widely recognized names in the American food industry. Today Nabisco Foods Group (formerly Nabisco Brands, Inc.) is among the world's largest manufacturers of cookies and crackers, featuring such famous brands as Oreo, Fig Newtons, and Premium Saltines.

Nabisco Brands was formed in 1981 through a merger of Nabisco and Standard Brands. In 1985 R. J. Reynolds Industries, Inc.. acquired Nabisco Brands in one of the largest takeovers in business history. The origins of Nabisco, however, date back to the formation of the National Biscuit Company at the end of the 19th century. In its early years, the company was usually called N.B.C. In 1941 the company adopted Nabisco, already a popular nickname, as the preferred abbreviation, but it was not until 1971 that Nabisco became the official corporate name.

The National Biscuit Company resulted from the 1898 merger of the midwestern American Biscuit Company, itself the result of the merger of 40 midwestern bakeries, and the eastern New York Biscuit Company, formed from eight bakeries and a smaller firm, the United States Baking Company. Thus, N.B.C. represented the culmination of decades of amalgamation within the biscuit industry. With 114 bakeries and a capital of $55 million, the Chicago-based company held a virtual monopoly on cookie and cracker manufacturing in the United States.

The chief architect of the 1898 merger and the first chairman of the new company was Adolphus Green. Green, a Chicago law-

yer and shrewd businessman who had negotiated the American Biscuit Company merger, remained the guiding force at N.B.C. during the first 20 years of its existence. It was Green who was responsible for N.B.C.'s legendary emphasis on standardized, brand name products. Every N.B.C. bakery adhered to exact recipes and uniform standards of production, and N.B.C. developed products that could be nationally identified with the company. All of its merchandise was marked with the company's distinctive emblem: an oval topped by a cross with two bars. (Green found the symbol in a catalog of medieval Italian printers' marks, where it was said to represent the triumph of good over evil.)

Green decided to launch the National Biscuit Company by introducing a new line of biscuits. He chose the ordinary soda cracker, but gave N.B.C.'s an unusual octagonal shape and packaged it in a special protective container. Until then, crackers had been sold in bulk from cracker barrels or large crates, which did little to retard sogginess or spoilage. N.B.C. took crackers out of the barrel and put them into small cardboard boxes with the company's patented "In-er-Seal" waxed paper lining to retain freshness.

Novelty packaging was not enough. Green also commissioned the Philadelphia advertising agency N.W. Ayer & Son to come up with a catchy name for the new cracker. The Ayer agency suggested "Uneeda Biscuit" and also helped promote the product with illustrations of a rosy-cheeked boy clutching a box of Uneeda Biscuits. The boy was dressed in a rain coat and galoshes to call attention to the packaging's moisture-proof nature. The Uneeda Boy became one of the world's best-recognized trademarks.

N.B.C. was a pioneer in company advertising, spending an unprecedented $7 million in its first decade to promote its products. Across the country, newspapers, billboards, and posters queried, "Do you know Uneeda Biscuit?" By 1900, sales of Uneeda Biscuits surpassed 100 million packages, prompting Green to remark that Uneeda was the most valuable word in the English language.

A host of imitators attempted to cash in on the popularity of Uneeda, and the company's attorneys were kept busy defending N.B.C. trademarks against infringement. The company won injunctions against rival bakeries marketing "Iwanta," "Uwanta," and "Ulika" biscuits. By 1906 N.B.C. had successfully prosecuted 249 cases of copyright infringement.

The National Biscuit Company built its reputation on securing customer loyalty to recognized brands such as Uneeda. In the early years of the 20th century, the company concentrated on expanding its line of cookies and crackers. Older products originally created by Nabisco's precursor bakeries that continued to be successful included Fig Newtons and Premium Saltines. In 1902 N.B.C. introduced Barnum's Animal Crackers in the famous decorative box resembling a circus cage filled with animals. In 1912 both Lorna Doones and Oreos were created, the latter eventually becoming the world's best-selling cookie.

N.B.C. moved its headquarters from Chicago to New York in 1906, where the company's factory on Manhattan's lower west side was the world's largest bakery. Yet Adolphus Green still managed the biscuit conglomerate as if it were a small family business. Green disliked delegating power. He personally inspected every company bakery once or twice a year, and most local managers communicated directly with Green. Green's authoritarian style annoyed many of his colleagues and led to frequent resignations from the board of directors. As a result, when Green died in 1917, few of the original directors remained and company management was in disarray.

The most pressing task for Green's successor, Roy E. Tomlinson, was reorganizing N.B.C.'s administrative network. Tomlinson had worked his way up the corporate ladder and was sensitive to the various levels of command. He delegated greater authority to other directors and to middle management, and remained company head until the 1940s.

The year Tomlinson took over was the year America entered World War I. During the war N.B.C. produced a special bread ration for soldiers and Tomlinson acted as advisor to the United States Food Administration. Wartime rationing of wheat flour and sugar also meant that cookies were less sweet and crackers were made of corn meal and rye. Company advertisements at the time depicted Uncle Sam holding boxes of N.B.C. products with the patriotic caption "made as he says."

The 1920s were a period of great prosperity for N.B.C. The company built a number of new bakeries and, in 1925, established its first foreign subsidiary, in Canada. N.B.C. also expanded its product line to include pretzels, breakfast cereal, and ice cream cones. Much of this diversification came about through acquisitions of other companies. In 1928 N.B.C. purchased the Shredded Wheat Company for $35 million. That same year N.B.C. acquired the McLaren Consolidated Cone Corporation, the world's largest manufacturer of ice cream cones.

The Depression years slowed company growth, but despite failing profits. N.B.C. managed to maintain and even raise dividend payments through a policy of severe wage reductions. The price of shareholder satisfaction, however, was labor unrest. In the early 1930s serious strikes broke out at Nabisco plants in New York, Philadelphia, and Atlanta, where angry picketers proclaimed "U-Don't-Needa biscuit!"

Some new Nabisco products helped bolster company sales during the Depression. In 1931 Nabisco took over the Bennett Biscuit Company and concentrated on its most popular product line, Milk-Bone Dog Biscuits, originally marketed as "a dog's dessert." N.B.C. boosted sales by advertising the product's breath-sweetening properties. In 1934 Nabisco met with great success when it launched Ritz Crackers as a new prestige item. Throughout the 1930s, N.B.C. relied heavily on radio advertising, promoting its products on the company-sponsored "Let's Dance" radio program featuring the orchestras of Xavier Cugat and Benny Goodman.

In 1941 the letters "N.B.C." in the official trademark were exchanged for the word "Nabisco," a popular nickname which had first appeared as a possible name for Uneeda Biscuits. The change was made in part to reduce confusion with the recently established National Broadcasting Company.

During World War II the company was again faced with the problem of rationed flour, sugar, butter, and oil. Recipes were altered and substitute ingredients used. Nabisco also developed an emergency field ration for pilots and paratroopers and even supplied the canine corps with dog biscuits.

The immediate postwar years were a troubled time for Nabisco. The company's longtime leadership in the biscuit industry had led to a certain complacency. During the Depression Nabisco had neglected to make capital improvements, and many bakeries were now outdated and in dire need of renovation. In 1945 the Nabisco board elected the young and energetic George Coppers as president. The inertia of the 1930s gave way to an expansive new attitude as Coppers undertook the modernization of Nabisco's antiquated bakeries. Within ten years he had spent more than $150 million renovating old plants and building new ones. The reconstruction program culminated in 1958 with the opening of an ultra-modern bakery and research center in Fair Lawn, New Jersey.

The 1950s also marked the beginning of overseas expansion for Nabisco. In 1950 the company formed a manufacturing partnership with La Favorita Bakery in Venezuela, and in 1953 it established another partnership with the Famosa Bakery in Mexico. From this foothold in Latin America, Nabisco has grown to become a major supplier of baked goods to the region.

In 1960 Lee S. Bickmore succeeded Coppers as president and the company accelerated acquisitions and overseas expansion. In 1961 Nabisco acquired the Cream of Wheat Corporation and the French firm Biscuits Gondolo. The next year, the company purchased the English bakery Frears, as well as New Zealand's largest biscuit firm, Griffin and Sons. In 1963 Nabisco acquired Biscuits Belin of France, the Danish baking concern Oxford Biscuit Fabrik, and the James O. Welch Company, makers of Junior Mints and Sugar Babies. The following year, Nabisco bought Harry Trueller, one of West Germany's largest confectioneries. Overseas acquisitions continued apace in 1965 with the addition of the Italian biscuit company Saiwa and the Spanish bakery Galletas.

By the end of the 1960s, Nabisco was the leading manufacturer of crackers and cookies not only in the United States, but in Canada, France, and the Scandinavian countries, and was a major supplier to many other European and South American countries.

The 1970s were a period of continued growth. Nabisco sales reached the $1 billion mark for the first time in 1971, and the $2 billion mark only five years later. In 1970 the company made its first Asian investment by establishing a joint venture with the Yamazaki Baking Company of Japan. Nabisco also upgraded its facilities in 1975 with the construction of a modern flour mill in Toledo, Ohio, and a computerized bakery in Richmond, Virginia. That same year the company moved its headquarters to a specially designed complex in East Hanover, New Jersey.

During the 1970s Nabisco made its first acquisitions outside of the food industry, buying the toy maker Aurora Products and the drug company J. B. Williams, manufacturer of Geritol and Sominex, in 1971. Here, the company was in unfamiliar territory, and the results were not always satisfactory. Aurora proved largely unprofitable and was sold in 1977. The J.B. Williams unit was frequently at odds with the Federal Trade

Commission, and in 1982 Nabisco sold Williams to the Beecham Group for $100 million.

Eventually the inflation and mounting energy costs of the 1970s led Nabisco to consider the possibility of a merger with another large food concern. Early in 1981, Nabisco Chairman Robert Schaeberle and Standard Brands Chairman F. Ross Johnson announced plans for a merger between their companies.

Standard Brands was formed in 1929 when the Fleischmann Company, the maker of products as diverse as yeast and gin; Chase & Sanborn, a coffee roaster; and the Royal Baking Powder Company all merged. The resulting company prospered through the Depression, finding new markets for its products ("Yeast for Health") and expanding existing product lines. Between 1929 and 1981, when Standard Brands merged with Nabisco, Standard Brands acquired several more important businesses, including Planters Nut & Chocolate Co. in 1961 and the Curtiss Candy Company, makers of the Baby Ruth candy bar, in 1964.

Nabisco Brands wasted no time in demonstrating its enhanced potential for growth. In 1981 the company paid $250 million to buy the Life Savers Company. That same year the company bought a controlling interest in the Mexican cookie firm Gamesa for $45 million. In 1982 Nabisco Brands purchased the English biscuit company Huntley and Palmer Foods for $140 million. In 1985 the company formed a partnership with the Yili Food Company in China to produce Ritz Crackers and Premium Saltines for the Chinese market.

The nation's growing health consciousness was a new concern for Nabisco Brands during the 1980s. To this end the company marketed low salt versions of Ritz Crackers, Saltines, and Triscuit Wafers. Nabisco also introduced Wheatsworth Crackers, made with whole wheat flour and containing no artificial flavors or colors.

In a friendly takeover in 1985, Nabisco Brands was purchased by R. J. Reynolds, a worldwide manufacturer and distributor of tobacco, food, and beverage products, for $4.9 billion, creating the nation's largest consumer-products company, with annual sales of more than $19 billion. Nabisco had sought the merger in part to avoid hostile takeover attempts, while Reynolds was interested in diversification. Later in the year R. J. Reynolds changed its name to RJR Nabisco, Inc. F. Ross Johnson, the president of Nabisco and the former chairman of Standard Brands, became RJR Nabisco's new president.

In 1988 Johnson and a management group at RJR Nabisco attempted to take the company private in a $17.6 billion leverage buyout. The buyout was an attempt on Johnson's part to boost stock prices, though he soon lost control of the situation as other firms entered the fray. The brokerage house of Kohlberg Kravis Roberts (KKR) upped the bidding for RJR Nabisco to $20.3 billion. The broker Forstmann Little, along with Procter and Gamble and Ralston Purina, became the third bidder. KKR ultimately won with a record $24.5 billion in cash and debt securities, and replaced Johnson with Louis V. Gerstner Jr., the former president of American Express.

KKR and Gerstner have pledged not to dismember the company but to manage it for the long run. Nonetheless, in order to cover the company's monumental debt, RJR Nabisco does plan some asset sales; the first was its European cookie and cracker business to BSN, France's largest packaged-food group, for $2.5 billion.

New products provided ten percent of 1991 North American sales—about double the industry average. This was due in part to the introductions—ranging from salty snacks to line extensions—doing well on their own, instead of stealing sales from other Nabisco brands. One of the most popular existing-brand ad-ons has been miniature versions of Oreo, the number-one cookie in the United States. To accommodate the smaller sandwich cookies, the company's Chicago bakery added computer-supported production lines costing millions of dollars. However, Mini Oreo cookies could not fully meet national distribution until mid-1992 due to high consumer demand in midwestern and southern states.

Mr. Phipps pretzel chips was named 1991 "New Product of the Year" by *Food & Beverage Marketing* magazine. Other new products included Fat-Free Mister Salty pretzels, Gummi Savers candy, LifeSavers Holes candy, Made 'Em Myself cookie kits, and Zings cracker chips. The LifeSavers brand is the United State's best-selling line of hard-roll candy.

The Fig Newtons' franchise has steadily grown throughout the years to include raspberry, apple, and strawberry flavors. The cookie's 100th anniversary in 1991 allowed Nabisco to launch a new promotional campaign that increased the brand's visibility. By 1992 a fat-free version came out and helped to place Fig Newtons as the third-best selling cookie in the United States—after Oreo and Chips Ahoy!, also Nabisco mainstays.

Aggressive advertising, promotion, and new biscuit product introductions also allowed Nabisco to expand its Latin American market—its primary international focus. For example, in Brazil, cookie and cracker sales increased by 39 percent in 1991.

Planters and LifeSavers were combined with Nabisco Brands as part of a total reorganization plan in 1991. With the Planters business revolving primarily around buying nuts at the best price and persistent merchandising, and the LifeSavers focus on keeping point-of-sale racks full, executives realized that they were two completely different entities. Similar blurred-priority situations were discovered, resulting in decentralized marketing, manufacturing, and new product development. Fleischmann's Division was created to focus on refrigerated products. The company's most marketing-intensive brands, like Grey Poupon dijon mustard and Milk-Bone dog biscuits, were reorganized into a Specialty Products Division. And a Food Service Division began marketing to restaurants, fast-food chains, airlines, schools, and others. Nabisco Brands was renamed Nabisco Foods Group.

In contrast, U.S. warehouse sales and logistics were consolidated. Nabisco Foods claims this move was not primarily to save money, but to allow sales representatives the ability to offer retailers a wider array of products at one time. By 1992, some supermarket industry analysts noticed that unit volume growth had become more difficult and that top managers would have to become more involved in the selling process in order to meet retailers' growing power.

By October of 1992, the Nabisco Foods Group had acquired Plush Pippin Corporation and Stella D'Oro Company. Plush Pippin, the Kent, Washington-based manufacturer of premium frozen pies, had $22 million in sales for 1991. Stella D'Oro, marketer of bread sticks and baked specialty treats, reported $65 million.

As Nabisco Foods Group tries to maximize profitability, it must face the fact that most Nabisco bakeries are 30 to 35 years old and in need of modernization. Since the major reconstruction phase of the 1950s, the company has neglected capital improvements. On the other hand, Nabisco's famous brand names are a tremendous strength. Ritz, Oreo, Triscuit—few companies can claim so many products that are household words. These brands, along with Nabisco Brand's recent reorganization and string of acquisitions, should keep the company in the forefront of the food industry.

Principal Subsidiaries: Fleischmann's Division; LifeSavers Division; Nabisco Biscuit Co.; Nabisco Brands Ltd. (Canada); Nabisco International Incorporated; Planters Division; Specialty Products Division.

Further Reading: Cahn, William, *Out of the Cracker Barrel: The Nabisco Story from Animal Crackers to Zuzus,* New York, Simon and Schuster, 1969; *42 Million a Day: The Story of Nabisco Brands,* Nabisco Brands, East Hanover, New Jersey, 1986; Lampert, Hope, *True Greed: What Really Happened in the Battle for RJR Nabisco,* New York, New American Library, 1990.

—updated by Anne C. Hughes

NACCO Industries, Inc.

NACCO INDUSTRIES, INC.

5875 Landerbrook Drive
Mayfield Heights, Ohio 44124
U.S.A.
(216) 449-9600
Fax: (216) 449-9561

Public Company
Incorporated: 1925 as North American Coal Corporation
Employees: 9,474
Sales: $1.4 billion
Stock Exchanges: New York
SICs: 1221 Bituminous Coal & Lignite—Surface; 3537 Industrial Trucks & Tractors; 6719 Holding Companies Nec

NACCO Industries, Inc. is a medium-sized, diversified holding company consisting of four major operating subsidiaries: the oldest, the North American Coal Corporation, is the tenth-largest producer of lignite (surface-mined) coal in the United States; Hyster-Yale Materials Handling, Inc., which designs and manufactures forklifts for domestic and foreign markets, is the largest forklift manufacturer in the nation; Hamilton Beach/Proctor-Silex, Inc., is one of the nation's leading producers of electric home appliances; and The Kitchen Collection is a highly successful nationwide retailer of home electric products and kitchenware. Because of its great diversity, NACCO Industries, according to *Donaldson, Lufkin and Jenrette,* is "one tough company to analyze." The subsidiaries appear to have nothing in common, and yet NACCO has emerged as a quirky American business success story.

NACCO's story is very much the story of its founder, Frank E. Taplin, who founded the North American Coal Corporation in 1925. A native of Cleveland, Ohio, which today is still the headquarters of NACCO Industries, Taplin was born in 1875 with obvious entrepreneurial talents. When he was only seventeen he became an office boy, then salesman, for the Standard Oil Company in Cleveland. He went on from there to become a salesman for the Pittsburgh Coal Company, and finally, at age twenty-five, he became the sales manager of the Youghiogheny and Ohio Coal Company.

Coal was king in the United States at the turn of the century. Virtually all of the country's energy needs were met by it. Not surprisingly for an enterprising young American who had started his career in an oil company, Taplin would turn his energies to the coal industry, and especially to establishing a coal business of his own.

His sales experience paid off: in 1913 he bought the Cleveland and Western Coal Company, an imposing name for a small business that as yet only sold rather than manufactured coal. With war breaking out in Europe, however, business boomed in the United States, and soon Taplin's firm was in a position to expand its business and enter coal mining on its own. With the U.S. in the war by 1917, the demand for coal was high and the time ripe for Cleveland and Western to acquire three mines, to be followed by others. Postwar recession and a national coal miners' strike in 1919 did not make a serious dent in the company's fortunes. In 1925, with the incorporation of the Powhatan Mining Company, operator of Ohio's largest mechanized deep mine, the Cleveland and Western Coal Company changed its name to the North American Coal Corporation, or NACCO.

As long as Frank Taplin was president and chairman of the privately owned company, NACCO expanded, despite labor and legal disputes that troubled the company during its early years. More ominous than these problems was the steady decline in the use of coal as an energy source, even though the country's vast coal reserves were second in the world only to the Soviet Union's.

The company's steady growth continued under Taplin's leadership even during the hard-hit 1930s. Although the company suffered financial losses during the Depression, Taplin was in the forefront in the fight to extend NRA codes to the coal industry that would raise coal miners' wages and reduce their hours of work. Unfortunately, his death in 1938 left NACCO rudderless as well as mired in legal disputes.

The outbreak of World War II signalled an end to the Depression and started the upswing of many private fortunes, but NACCO's circumstances were still grim. By 1942, however, a new president had taken the helm: the energetic, able Henry G. Schmidt, who left his engineering position at Goodyear Tire and Rubber Company to guide NACCO back to prosperity during the war years, and to postwar expansion thereafter.

At the end of the war, the future of coal seemed locked into permanent decline. Not only did imported oil become the main American energy source, but so did natural gas, initially abundant but finite in the long run. Significant demand for coal in the postwar years, however, came from utility companies, which were expanding at a dizzying rate to meet Americans' increasing electricity needs. In 1946, only ten percent of NACCO's coal was used by utility companies; by the late 1950s, this figure rose to over fifty percent. The rest of the coal demand came from the steel, cement, and chemical industries. In the postwar period, NACCO mirrored the tendency of other large mining companies toward increasing consolidation and expansion. This occurred in part because of the few large corporations, primarily giant industries and utility companies, that constituted the company's major customers.

By 1952 NACCO consisted of four large coal-mining subsidiaries that engaged in underground mining. Since the late 1930s, however, bituminous coal extracted from underground mines was giving way increasingly to lignite coal extracted from strip mines. Extraction from strip mining was not only more efficient but also more economical and far less dangerous than deep coal mining. As a result, NACCO acquired its first lignite field in North Dakota in 1957. Indian Head Mine, which contained the richest lignite coal deposits in North America, would be NACCO's most productive mine for decades to come. Five years after the acquisition of Indian Head Mine and other mining properties in North Dakota as well as in West Virginia, NACCO became the ninth-largest coal producer in the United States, with 70 percent of its coal purchased by utility companies.

Throughout the 1960s, NACCO expanded its coal production and business opportunities with utility companies in New York, Pennsylvania, and Ohio, as well as with the United Power Association in the Great Plains states. In this agreement, NACCO would provide one million tons of coal annually to the power company from its Indian Head Mine. In 1972 NACCO committed itself to provide the Michigan Wisconsin Pipeline Company with billions of tons of coal from its North Dakota reserves, which would be turned into liquified gas. Turning coal into gas for use as a liquid fuel was done successfully by the petroleum-starved Germans in World War II; with natural gas levels in the U.S. reaching a plateau in the early 1970s, gasified coal seemed to have a promising future. In anticipation, NACCO pledged to build the first major coal gasification plant in the nation, to be completed in 1981. With lignite coal mining playing an increasingly important role, NACCO turned its North Dakota and Texas operations in 1974 into a separate operation, the Western Division. In the early 1970s, NACCO's Western Division acquired the Falkirk Mining Company and Coteau Properties Company in North Dakota as wholly owned subsidiaries.

While profits could not have seemed better in the late 1970s, despite the passage of strict federal mine safety laws as well as frequent strikes and walkouts by the United Mine Workers, doubts were growing as to whether NACCO could remain profitable in the future. The replacement of coal with nuclear power, and the certainty of stricter environmental legislation that could raise costs even further, made the future of coal seem dim. By then, Henry Schmidt had long since retired, and a new team of managers, headed by Chairman Otes Bennett, Jr. and President/CEO Ward Smith, were at the helm to oversee a drastic alteration of their company.

In May 1986 the alteration was complete: the company would no longer be a coal-mining company with its entire profit derived from the manufacture and sale of coal, but instead would become a holding company. Renamed NACCO Industries, Inc., the new structure enabled the company to diversify. The North American Coal Corporation became a wholly owned subsidiary; although it was the oldest component of NACCO Industries, it would within a few years cease to be the biggest or most important (in 1990 it generated only 23 percent of NACCO's operating profit). The second subsidiary became the newly acquired Yale Materials Handling Corp., a top-of-the-line forklift truck manufacturer with factories in the United States, Great Britain, and Japan (a joint venture with Sumitomo Heavy Industries, Ltd.).

Market analysts had expected NACCO to diversify into energy-related businesses and, surprised by the dissimilarity of its subsidiaries, forecasted negative consequences. Instead, by 1990 the *Journal of Corporate Finance* reported that NACCO Industries had become ''one of the top performers'' on the New York Stock Exchange. No doubt part of the reason for its success was the company's emphasis on decentralization, with each subsidiary operating on its own, with only target-setting and incentives from above.

Only a few years after restructuring, NACCO's coal-mining subsidiary sold off its bituminous coal-mining operations in the East, and concentrated instead on the mining of billions of tons of lignite, surface-mined coal in North Dakota and Texas. Through its long-term contracts with utility companies, the North American Coal Corporation proved to be recession resistant, generating a modest but important cash flow for the holding company's other business ventures. By 1990 the coal company, consisting of its own wholly owned subsidiaries Falkirk Mining Co., Coteau Properties, Sabine Mining Company, and the newest, Red River Mining Company, trimmed its staff by 30 percent and decentralized its operations to its individual mines. With full or partial interest in most of the 37 billion tons of North Dakota's coal reserves, the North American Coal Corporation was the tenth-largest coal-mining firm in the United States, despite trimming off its bituminous operations.

NACCO Industries continued to diversify beyond these two subsidiaries. In 1989 and 1990, the holding company acquired the market leader in forklift truck manufacturing, the Hyster Company, as well as Proctor-Silex, a leader in the manufacture of home electrical appliances. In 1990 NACCO's managers announced the combination of Hyster and Yale to form a wholly owned subsidiary, Hyster-Yale Materials Handling, Inc., which became the biggest industrial lift truck manufacturer in North America (under separate brand names) and a serious competitor on the world market. Hyster-Yale became NACCO's biggest subsidiary, generating 67 percent of operating profit in 1990. The move was hailed on Wall Street as a sign of increased efficiency and long-term profitability. The downside of the merger of the two top-of-the-line lift truck companies was its vulnerability to the vicissitudes of the market: in 1991, profits of the subsidiary fell 14 percent from the previous year, due to 1990's recession.

The year 1990 also saw bold moves on the part of NACCO in the merger of Proctor-Silex, manufacturer of heat-generating electrical appliances such as toasters and coffee makers, with Hamilton Beach, maker of kitchen items such as blenders, mixers, and food processors. NACCO's third subsidiary, Hamilton Beach/Proctor-Silex, became the leader in small kitchen appliances in the United States and, unlike Hyster-Yale, remained very profitable throughout the recession.

NACCO's fourth subsidiary, The Kitchen Collection, acquired in 1988, was a chain of 72 stores (with more planned in the 1990s) located throughout the United States. The Kitchen Collection sold primarily factory-outlet Hamilton Beach/Proctor-Silex appliances and other kitchen items. Though small, The Kitchen Collection expanded continuously and proved to be recession resistant. Together, housewares (Hamilton Beach/

Proctor-Silex and The Kitchen Collection) generated 10 percent of NACCO's profit in 1991.

With three subsidiaries acquired in the space of one-and-a-half years, NACCO Industries planned to concentrate on development rather than further business acquisitions. From a venerable coal company to a vibrant and dynamic holding company with dissimilar businesses and global interests (in which coal mining held only a backseat), NACCO became a new company. President and CEO Alfred M. Rankin, Jr., together with Chairman of the Board Ward Smith, acted as the strategists and target setters of the decentralized corporation. Their goal continued to be turning NACCO Industries subsidiaries into the top market leaders in their respective enterprises and globalizing the company. While the 1990s recession dampened profits and resulted in many job layoffs, the worldwide recovery of the market should offset these losses. The North American Coal Corporation already was planning to mine billions of tons of bituminous coal outside of Anchorage, Alaska, for the Japanese market; Hyster-Yale had important interests in Great Britain, Germany (Jungheinrich), and Japan (Sumitomo Heavy Industries), with growing interests in other Far Eastern countries. Cost-cutting and incentive measures resulted in NACCO becoming an aggressive new competitor on the global market.

Principal Subsidiaries: North American Coal Corp.; The Kitchen Collection; Hyster-Yale Materials Handling, Inc. (97%); Hamilton Beach/Proctor-Silex, Inc. (80%).

Further Reading: "The North American Coal Corporation, Western Division and Subsidiaries," North American Coal Corporation; "The North American Coal Corporation and Subsidiaries," North American Coal Corporation, 1977; *Coal Age,* October 1977; Oihus, Colleen, *A History of Coal Mining in North Dakota, 1873–1982,* Bismarck, 1983; *Annual Report: NACCO Industries, Inc.,* Cleveland, Ohio, 1986, 1990, 1991; Luxenberg, Stan, "Unearthing Profits from Cleaner Coal: Strikes and Surpluses Have Stung the Mining Companies," *New York Times,* December 17, 1989; Lappen, Alyssa A., "A Chip Off the Old Block (NACCO President A. M. Rankin)," *Forbes,* April 16, 1990; "Forging a Synergistic Portfolio from a Diverse Combination," *Journal of Corporate Finance,* Summer 1990; Levkovich, Tobias M., "NACCO Industries," *Smith Barney,* October 3, 1990; "NACCO Industries, Inc.," *Wall Street Journal,* March 18, 1992; "NACCO Industries, Inc.," *Business Journal-Portland,* July 13, 1992; "Research Bulletin, NACCO Industries," *Donaldson, Lufkin & Jenrette,* August 19, 1992.

—Sina Dubovoj

372 NATIONAL CONVENIENCE STORES INCORPORATED

NATIONAL CONVENIENCE STORES INCORPORATED

100 Waugh Drive
Houston, Texas 77007-5829
U.S.A.
(713) 863-2200
Fax: (713) 880-0579

Public Company
Incorporated: 1959
Employees: 5,000
Sales: $1 billion
Stock Exchanges: NASDAQ
SICs: 5411 Grocery Stores; 5541 Gasoline Service Stations

National Convenience Stores Incorporated (NCS) operates retail convenience stores and gasoline service stations in the Sun-Belt states of Texas, California, and Georgia.

NCS's early growth parallels that of the convenience store industry. Established in 1959 as U-Tote'M of San Antonio, Texas, the business made most of its major acquisitions, beginning in California, in the 1970s and 1980s. By the 1990s the market was glutted, and the three largest convenience store chains filed for bankruptcy, including National Convenience Stores Inc.

In 1959 F. J. Dyke, Jr., an executive with U-Tote'M in San Antonio, formed a partnership to buy five convenience stores in the city from Sommers Drug Stores. The Sommers stores, operating under the name Stop N Go, were changed to U-Tote'M stores. In February 1961 the partnership acquired all U-Tote'M California stores of the same name. The following year the company changed its name temporarily to the National Drive-In Grocery Corporation. By 1965 National Drive-In had moved its corporate offices to Houston and was operating 260 stores in seven states.

In the early 1960s convenience stores offered nearly every product supermarkets sold. New multi-shelved refrigerators gave operators the opportunity to offer a large variety of products in smaller space. The big sellers, sold in all convenience stores at that time, included packaged lunch meats, health and beauty items, tobacco, soft drinks, milk, butter, eggs, cheese, and bread. Ice cream, frozen foods, light bulbs, beer, bulk produce, and toys were sold by most operators as well.

In the mid-1960s the state of Texas alone boasted fourteen multi-unit convenience store headquarters; the new National Drive-In Grocery Corporation certainly faced competition. By 1967 the convenience store industry was selling $1 billion in products, with the total number of stores reaching 8,000 nationwide. The growth of the industry was attributed to the increase in working mothers, as well as shifting living patterns—more people either lived in the suburbs or used their cars to get around. The general economic health of the period also spurred the use of convenience stores that, with higher prices, had previously been considered a luxury by some segments of the population in the early 1960s.

One in three convenience stores was franchised by year-end 1969; fast foods and self-service gasoline pumps were viewed as growth segments for store operators. More than 2,000 new stores were opened in the industry as a whole, with total sales in the market at $2 billion.

The present name of National Convenience Stores, Inc., was adopted in 1968 as the company anticipated large-scale growth. NCS acquired the Austin, Texas-based Town & Country stores the same year. The following year was a banner year for NCS; the company acquired Handee Food Mart's 35 Houston-area stores, Sanitary Farm Dairies, Inc., and the Baskin-Robbins Ice Cream Stores chain, as well as the franchise to manufacture and distribute Baskin-Robbins ice cream in the eastern half of Texas. Within two years NCS sold the Baskin-Robbins franchise for $2.5 million. NCS then bought 23 PDQ Food Stores in 1973 for undisclosed terms.

V. H. Van Horn, who had joined the company in 1966 as a management trainee and steadily risen through the ranks, was named CEO in 1975. Van Horn faced a big challenge early on. In October 1977 General Host, a diversified company in food services, baking, meat packing, and convenience stores, acquired a 14 percent stake in NCS from former NCS president F. J. Dyke. NCS subsequently sued General Host for alleged securities violations. The NCS suit, filed in federal court, sought to block purchases by General Host, any of its directors, or F. J. Dyke. The following month NCS came to an agreement with the corporation that stated that General Host would not buy more than 21 percent of NCS common shares until after December 2nd of the same year.

In December 1977 National Convenience Stores announced it agreed to be acquired by Circle K Corporation in a stock exchange worth approximately $36 million. Van Horn was to assume the position of president and chief operating officer of the new merger. The merger was soon called off; according to an account in the February 6, 1978, issue of the *Wall Street Journal,* a spokesman for NCS stated, "It is unlikely that the merger, given the current conditions, could be consummated."

By 1979 the company acquired nearly all the common stock of Texas Super Duper Markets, Inc., for a total of 68 convenience stores. NCS also bought Super Quick, Inc., including 19 stores equipped with self-serve gasoline facilities, and Jay's Washateria, Inc., an operator of ten laundromats.

National Convenience Stores posted record earnings for fiscal year 1980. President Van Horn attributed the rise to increased product sales per store and higher gasoline sales in a larger number of operating stores. Quoted in the August 25, 1980, *Supermarket News*, Van Horn commented that "We have well exceeded our announced goal of doubling 1977 net earnings of $3.4 million in 1980."

In December 1981 NCS acquired 116 stores operating under the name Mr. M Food Stores in San Antonio and Houston from McCombs International, Inc., for $14.5 million in cash. The company became the largest convenience store operator in Houston with the purchase. While the company's acquisitions increased the total number of stores to 834, the push for new stores really began in 1982. NCS made plans to open 75 that year, 70 the following year, and 100 in fiscal 1984, up to a total of perhaps 400 by 1986 (not including stores gained through acquisition). Yet NCS management was closing nearly as many stores as it was opening. In 1981 57 stores opened, while 42 low performers were shut down. The results were positive; sales per store doubled over a five-year period. To generate cash for overall debt reduction, the company sold 850,000 shares for a total of $10.3 million in February 1982.

NCS planned layout changes in its stores to reflect changes in product demand, profitability, and its changing customer profile. Grocery items were pushed back into the store while higher margin general merchandise—health and beauty aids, cigarettes, automotive supplies, magazines—were brought up front. NCS concentrated on fast foods as well, where profits margins were as high as 40 percent. The company noticed that its average customer was not the typical convenience store customer—a 35-year-old male, making a purchase of less than two dollars. Instead, at National Convenience Stores the average customer was a single 18-year-old male, with less responsibility and more discretionary income. In response to this new data, and in an overall effort to re-energize marginal stores, NCS created the Quik Store, which would feature "Top 40" records and tapes, magazines and newspapers, and coin-operated video games.

Beginning in May 1983, National Convenience Stores, Inc., began a series of acquisitions: for $18 million NCS bought 125 stores in western Texas under the name Colonial Food Stores; in December the company completed the purchase, for cash and stock, of 15 Stop 'N Serve stores in the Houston area, and six Super Stop stores. The acquisitions were separate buys.

To complement the number of acquisitions, President Van Horn initiated a major plan for growth, emphasizing marketing and merchandising strategies. The Stop N Go logo was updated and a plan to rename all National units Stop N Go was devised. A new store layout was designed that utilized a hexagonal shape to make the most of both indoor and outdoor space. Planners reasoned that with six sides, the interior of the stores would have no dead space; front door parking would be increased as well. Of the 3,100 square feet of total area, 600 were designated for fast-food sales. A sitting area was included in the new design as well, to emphasize the fast-food service. Large canopies outside over the gas pumps both drew attention and sheltered customers from bad weather; the pumps were also situated close to the front door for quick payment.

Van Horn's general strategy was to take the lead in retailing and merchandising tactics to stay ahead of the imposing crowd of convenience store competition. By December 1984 there were approximately 50,000 convenience stores across the United States, with more being built. Drug stores and supermarkets joined in the rush to provide convenient shopping for customers. Jerry Welch, senior vice-president of stores, was behind the change in store design and also advised a change in product mix. Since the single male shopper (aged 18 to 35) was already a mainstay, Welch planned to woo the female shopper, who preferred products in the nonfood category, such as health and beauty aids, housewares, and hardware. In a move similar to his methodology in upgrading NCS's fast food category, Van Horn recruited executives from the drugstore industry (whose primary customer is female) to gain expertise in that market.

National Convenience Stores increased its advertising budget significantly to sell its new image. As Welch, quoted in the December 3, 1984, *Advertising Age*, put it: "We want to have a warm, friendly image. We want to make our stores more attractive for women and senior citizens."

As the convenience store industry moved toward fast foods, it tried to veer away from its dependence on gasoline sales. By year-end 1986 a typical store gained 50 percent of revenues and 25 percent of profits from gasoline. While profit margins were historically high, the trend would not last. Another factor affecting the convenience store industry as a whole was the "open 24-hours" policy, which began to attract robbers as well as customers. Many convenience store operators installed brighter lighting both inside and outside stores to fight the problem.

More specific to NCS fortunes, however, was the stumbling southwestern economy. The combination of Houston's hard times and the cost of financing its new image sent NCS sliding. NCS's net profits for fiscal 1986 were $3.6 million; the previous year, profits were $15.5 million, and in 1984, $18.4 million. As reported in the February, 1987, *National Petroleum News,* "This [was] the first time in the company's 26-year history to experience such a dramatic downturn in its fortunes."

NCS enjoyed 38 consecutive quarters of record earnings until December 1984. The fall in oil prices hit NCS particularly hard, since one-third of its stores were in the Houston market. At first, the company misinterpreted the problem and offered price-cutting promotions, which were successful for only a month. But the recession hitting Houston was a problem far larger than any promotion NCS could devise. As the real-estate market collapsed, strip malls and other shopping centers began to offer store space rent-free for the first two years. New convenience stores sprouted all over the city at locations that, fortunately for NCS, Van Horn considered marginal. The new store operators wouldn't get the traffic of prime NCS stores, which were often at high-visibility corner locations.

Quick to react, NCS underwent a major restructuring effort in 1986. The company sold 186 operating stores in nine markets to the Circle K Corporation for $51.2 million. The total number of NCS stores went from 1,130 in mid-1985 to 960 in early 1987; the states in which NCS operated, concentrated in the southern and southwestern region, dropped from eleven to six.

As important as the sell-offs was the company's reorganization at both the field and district levels. Instead of four geographic divisions, with a different vice-president handling store operations and marketing, Van Horn consolidated into two regions of coverage. The result was a more centralized marketing campaign, with all stores focused on the same advertising and merchandising schemes. Field personnel were reduced by 20 percent.

At the district level, NCS's rapid growth had created an excess of management positions. The company had one district office for each 30 stores; in Houston, there were ten offices. Each office employed a personnel manager, five store supervisors, and two to three of both maintenance and administrative staff. NCS tightened up Houston operations by eliminating the personnel positions and cutting administration from thirty to four positions. District managers were set up in store offices, and training was offered in three locations, rather than in ten. The reorganization in Houston saved the company $5 million a year.

NCS also concentrated on the Hex store, which offered more fast foods, general merchandise, and gasoline, to appeal to a broader customer base. Hex stores were larger and had more gasoline pumps than traditional stores, upping the volume of sales and allowing the company to hire higher quality staff and pay them well. The company also remodeled more than 200 of its existing stores in 1986, with plans to redo 150 in 1987 and all older units by mid-1989.

In August 1987 National Convenience Stores sold 40 operating and 3 closed stores in Midland-Odessa, Texas, to Southland Corporation (the operators of the 7-Eleven store chain) for $12.5 million. The company then followed that up with a purchase of 400 properties from Southland in the greater Houston market, including 269 operating stores, for approximately $75–80 million. The acquisition doubled the NCS presence in Houston, an area where the company had been losing money for three years. As reported in the April 17, 1988, *Houston Chronicle,* it appeared "as if NCS capitalized on an opportunity to lose twice as much." But viewed within a larger framework, the acquisition enabled NCS to rid the Houston market of its competition—therefore eliminating lower profit margins due to price wars with competing stores. In the same *Houston Chronicle* article Montgomery Securities analyst Bo Cheadle, commenting on the NCS purchase price of $92,000 per store, stated: "They didn't buy them, they stole them." NCS, for example, had sold marginal units to Circle K a year earlier—many without gasoline pump facilities—for $125,000 a store.

CEO Van Horn believed the Houston economy hit its lowest point in the spring of 1987. With more than 500 stores in the country's fourth-largest market, Van Horn banked his company's fortunes on an economic turnaround. Armed with that philosophy, the company initiated a veritable property swap with Southland Corporation. In August 1988 NCS sold 52 properties in the Las Vegas market, including 43 operating convenience stores, for $25.6 million. By April of the following year NCS bought 102 properties in San Antonio from Southland, including 79 convenience stores, for $28 million.

The purchase brought the company's San Antonio store base to 208, nearly 37 percent of the market. San Antonio became NCS's second-largest stronghold; trailing it were Dallas/Fort Worth, with 142 stores, and Los Angeles, with 105. The National Convenience Stores' plan was to concentrate in fewer markets with a stronger presence. For example, in 1986 NCS had approximately 1,100 stores in 21 markets; by mid-1989 the store number remained constant, but was focused in only 10 markets.

During this period, NCS was burned by two costly promotional pushes that went awry. A successful NCS promotion involving coupons redeemable for Black & Decker appliances got out of hand. The company posted a $2.1 million loss for the fiscal quarter ending December 31, 1988, due to $7 million in costs related to the ill-conceived promotion. Another promotion the company engaged in—selling beer and soft drinks below supermarket prices—lost money as well. Van Horn fired the executive in charge of the campaigns, and the company brought prices back to where they were previously. Quoted in the August 18, 1989, *Forbes,* the NCS chief said, "We've returned to our basic premise that convenience has value." NCS hoped the larger number of customers it garnered from the ill-fated promotions would continue frequenting its stores.

Another change in emphasis for NCS became evident in 1989, as the company began tailoring merchandise to more closely match the neighborhoods in which the stores were situated. Stores in higher income areas began to stock high-priced wines, gourmet pasta sauces, and magazines such as *Vanity Fair* and the *New Yorker;* in black neighborhoods, black health and beauty displays were added; in core middle-class markets more bottled waters and frozen and quick-to-prepare foods were stocked. In Hispanic areas, stores stressed Mexican cooking items and Spanish-language magazines; NCS also translated signs into Spanish and hired bilingual employees. A related move was the installation of in-store scanning equipment, which provided NCS with marketing data to assess its new product mix. The company budgeted $12 million to advertise its new strategy.

In August 1989 NCS decided to move out of the Nashville market, selling 37 operating and 14 closed convenience stores to Mapco Petroleum, Inc., for $21.8 million. The funds would be used to repay $100 million in debt that NCS borrowed to fund its significant Houston and San Antonio acquisitions. It was an irony of the business that NCS sold to Mapco, since the oil companies entering the convenience store industry posed a threat to all convenience store operators.

The total number of convenience stores peaked at 83,000 in the late 1980s. Industry profits, however, dropped by an alarming 75 percent. The fallout in the convenience store industry was inevitable. The market was overcrowded; from a high of 83,000 units in the late 1980s, the number of convenience stores fell to 71,200 in several years. In May 1990 Southland Corporation, the largest convenience store chain, posted an annual loss of $1.3 billion (notwithstanding the fact that it gained $52 million in tax credits following the sale of a 50 percent stake in Citgo Petroleum). Circle K, the number-two chain, filed for Chapter 11 bankruptcy status. NCS claimed a slim profit of $383,000 for the quarter ending March 31, 1990. The company's extraordinary $7.1 million profit, for the nine-month period ending on the same date, was due to $6.6 million gained from a stock swap with shareholders.

Van Horn's revised plans to reinvent the convenience store business—with targeted product mixes, point-of-sale scanners, and redesigned stores—was one method to try and overcome the industry downturn. The first NCS unit that opened with the changes listed boasted an increase in sales of 20 percent. In the first redesigned Hispanic store, sales rose more than 20 percent as well.

But by early 1991, fewer than 150 stores out of 1,071 were restyled; the cost, in the tens of thousands of dollars, was far too high for NCS to afford at a time when the company's long-term debt was near $190 million. NCS experimented with several new ventures, including selling Pizza Hut and Taco Bell products at five Houston-area stores in June 1991. The company also sold 24 operating stores in the El Paso area to Diamond Shamrock, Inc., for cash.

On December 9, 1991, National Convenience Stores was forced into a voluntary reorganization under Chapter 11 of the United States Bankruptcy Code as the company struggled with the combined effects of the sagging U.S. economy, low gasoline prices, and increased competition in the convenience store industry. The company had little cash and its creditors had grown increasingly concerned about NCS's posted losses four out of the previous five years. For the quarter ending December 31, 1991, NCS reported a net loss of $177.7 million; the Persian Gulf crisis negatively affected prices and volume of gasoline for the company.

In contrast to Dallas-based Southland and Phoenix-based Circle K, which owed billions when they entered bankruptcy, NCS's long-term debt as of the bankruptcy filing date was $162 million. The company had managed to pare the debt an average of $10 million a year since 1987. Though the picture was positive, J. Christopher Brewster, chief financial officer for NCS, resigned in April 1992; the company did not fill the vacant position.

By mid-year 1992 NCS had closed nearly 200 stores; well over 800 were still in operation in Texas, California, and Georgia. The company's new venture—offering Taco Bell and Pizza Hut products—was limited to fifteen stores; the original plan was to involve nearly 100 NCS Stop N Go stores.

NCS filed its first reorganization plan in Houston in late July 1992, with plans to pay creditors in full in periods ranging from 30 days to 15 years. When one creditor (not on the creditors committee) objected to the plan, NCS Vice President F. R. Daily, Jr., quoted in *The Wall Street Journal*, July 27, 1992, responded: "The court expects you to prepare the plan and file it when it's ready. It's stretching the point to say it's premature and unexpected. "An alternative plan was presented one month later for confirmation by the bankruptcy court pending creditor approval. NCS had reason to be optimistic about repaying its

debts; net income for the quarter ending June 30, 1992 was $4.4 million, as compared to a net loss of $5.6 million a year earlier. The Fourth Amended and Restated Joint Plan of Reorganization was confirmed February 25, 1993, and became effective March 9, 1993.

Principal Subsidiaries: Kempco Petroleum Co.; National Money Orders, Incorporated; NCS Realty Co.; Stop N Go Markets of Georgia, Inc.; Stop N Go Markets of Texas, Inc.; Texas Super Duper Markets, Inc.; Schepps Food Stores, Inc.

Further Reading: Mehlman, William, "National Convenience Stores Rides High in Rough Market," *Insiders' Chronicle,* August 30, 1982; Lawrence, Jennifer, "National on the Go in Convenience Market," *Advertising Age,* December 3, 1984; Reid, Marvin, "Can New 'Hex' Stores Plus Cutbacks Restore NCS' 'Stop N Go' Revenues?" *National Petroleum News,* February 1987; Mack, Toni, "A Six-Pack of Cabernet, Please," *Forbes,* September 18, 1989; Smith, Donald M., "NCS Regroups, Develops New Marketing Strategies to Revitalize Operations," *National Petroleum News,* March 1990; Prewitt, Milford, "A Tale of Three C-Stores: Slim Profits, Big Losses and Chapter 11," *Nation's Restaurant News,* May 28, 1990; Helliker, Kevin, "Stop N Go's Van Horn Wants to Reinvent the Convenience Store," *Wall Street Journal,* February 6, 1991.

Other Sources: "Accord by National Convenience Stores is Reached in Suit," *Wall Street Journal,* November 7, 1977; "Circle K Corporation Set to Acquire National Convenience Stores," *Wall Street Journal,* December 9, 1977; "National Convenience Acquires Three Houston Chains," *Wall Street Journal,* May 21, 1979; "NCS Has Record Sales, Earnings," *Supermarket News,* August 25, 1980; Gubernick, Lisa, "Stores for Our Time," *Forbes,* November 3, 1986; Benedict, Daniel, "NCS, 7-Eleven Deal a Calculated Risk," *Houston Chronicle,* April 17, 1988; Freeman, Diane, "Houston's NCS Buys 79 7-Elevens in S.A.," *Houston Post,* November 3, 1988; Blumenthal, Karen, "Food Retailer Finds Promotional Success is Bottom-Line Bust," *Wall Street Journal,* January 18, 1989; Carr, Paul H., "NCS to Dominate Convenience Store Market," *San Antonio Business Journal,* April 10, 1989; Saponar, R.C., "Mapco to Purchase 37 Stop-N-Go Markets," *Nashville Business Journal,* August 7, 1989; Blumenthal, Karen, "All Stop 'N Go Stores Plan to Rearrange Merchandise to Cater Better to Localities," *Wall Street Journal,* October 26, 1989; Beachy, Debra, "NCS Reveals Marketing Strategy," *Houston Chronicle,* October 26, 1989; "Posner Buying into NCS," *Houston Chronicle,* December 21, 1989; "Stop N Go's Parent Reports $6.3M Loss," *Nation's Restaurant News,* June 3, 1991; Helliker, Kevin, "National Convenience Stores Petitions Bankruptcy Court for Chapter 11 Status," *Wall Street Journal,* December 11, 1991.

—Frances E. Norton

NERCO, INC.

500 N.E. Multnomah St., Suite 1500
Portland, Oregon 97232-2045
U.S.A.
(503) 731-6600
Fax: (503) 230-9045

Public Company
Incorporated: 1977
Employees: 2,200
Sales: $919.9 million
Stock Exchanges: New York Toronto
SICs: 1041 Gold Ores; 1044 Silver Ores; 1221 Bituminous
   Coal & Lignite—Surface

NERCO, Inc., is a *Fortune* 500 company that produces and markets low-sulfur coal, oil, and natural gas. NERCO had also been involved in gold and silver mining, though the company was working to divest its precious metals holdings.

Pacific Power & Light Company—later PacifiCorp Inc.—created NERCO in 1977 when federal laws mandated the development of federal coal leases, forcing PP&L to dispose of 1.4 billion tons of Wyoming and Montana coal reserves. PP&L chairman Don C. Frisbee appointed utilities lawyer Gerard K. Drummond president of NERCO and charged him with developing PP&L's uncommitted coal reserves and reinvesting cash flows.

The assets Drummond had to work with at that time were a 50 percent nonoperating share of the Decker mine in southeastern Montana, a two-thirds interest in the Jim Bridger mine near Rock Springs, Wyoming, and management of the David Johnston mine near Glenrock, Wyoming. NERCO also had several long-term contracts with major coal burning utilities in the Midwest and Southwest.

Drummond reorganized NERCO into a holding company with four operating companies: NERCO Mining Company, the company's center piece and over the long term its most stable component; NERCO Coal Company, which would invest in eastern coal; NERCO Minerals Company, which would invest in minerals and precious metals; and NERCO Oil & Gas, Inc., set up to explore for oil and gas reserves.

"Our diversification strategy is intended in part to overcome the reality that a natural resource company faces in eventually depleting finite resources," Drummond explained in NERCO's 1984 annual report. "More important, this strategy allows us to apply our technical knowledge and management abilities to other businesses that offer attractive growth opportunities."

Drummond's first attempt at diversification did not prove to be a success. He bought heavily into a Wyoming-based uranium exploration and development company. Two years later he joined with Union Carbide Corporation to explore and develop uranium resources in New Mexico. When the bottom dropped out of the uranium market in 1980, NERCO ended those activities.

Coal was the next area on which Drummond concentrated. In 1978 NERCO acquired surface mines in Indiana, Alabama, and Tennessee. In 1980 the company completed the Spring Creek Mine, a southern Montana facility with an annual capacity of 10 million tons.

Drummond also decided to diversify into precious metals. NERCO acquired gold and silver rights in eastern Oregon in 1980. The next year the company purchased Resource Associates of Alaska, Inc., an expertise-laden exploration company that held mineral rights to five million acres in Alaska. In addition, in December of 1982 NERCO agreed to buy Occidental Petroleum's Occidental Minerals Corporation, an outfit which held half interest in the Alligator Ridge Gold Mine—one of the country's ten largest—and a controlling interest in the Candelaria silver and gold mine—the country's largest open-pit primary silver mine—in Hawthorne, Nevada.

NERCO did well in the first years after its organization. Revenue rose from $72.1 million in 1977 to $215 million and $372.1 million in 1980 and 1981, while income rose from $12 million to $46.1 million and $29.1 million, respectively. The one cloud on the horizon was a dispute about a long-term coal contract. A subsidiary of Houston Industries, Inc. sought to halt deliveries from Spring Creek. Houston claimed they were having combustion problems, though the coal met contract specifications. NERCO temporarily provided replacement coal, but the dispute remained.

In 1982 NERCO entered the oil and gas business when they acquired Clements Energy, Inc. (CEI), a small exploration company based in Oklahoma City. Almost immediately CEI ran into financing problems. Before the company could redirect its fund-raising efforts, it lost much of 1983 to the problem. NERCO officials later stated in the company's 1984 annual report that their "timing was poor" in buying CEI.

Already the country's fifth-largest coal producer, according to *Coal Age,* NERCO added reserves, people, and barge and rail loading facilities to its eastern coal operation in 1983. Its strategy was to discover customer needs, then develop products and services to meet those needs.

In its minerals business, NERCO moved away from risky exploration. Its new strategy was to buy undervalued properties and improve their operating efficiencies. To this end, the company acquired two open-pit Nevada silver and gold mines and

077Bs

lowered Candelaria's silver production costs 16 percent to under $6.00 per ounce.

Though 99 percent of revenues still came from the coal business, at the end of 1983 company officials were happy to report progress in diversification. Total revenue for the year reached $415.4 million, while income topped $38 million.

1984 proved to be another good year. NERCO made a major metals acquisition; went public in August, selling ten percent of its shares; and signed several new coal contracts. Overall earnings topped $54 million, and return on equity reached 20 percent.

At NERCO Minerals, low metals prices made long-term investment properties available. For a total of $40 million, the company purchased interests in the Taylor Silver Mine in Nevada, the DeLamar Silver Mine in Idaho, and the Victor Gold Mine in Colorado—acquisitions that made NERCO a top five U.S. silver producer and one of the top ten U.S. gold producers. Unfortunately, low prices also kept the company's metals off the market, forcing NERCO Minerals to store, rather than sell, 3.5 million ounces of silver and 40,000 ounces of gold.

NERCO's western coal operation landed several long-term utility contracts and broke into the industrial market with four new sales contracts, including a 550,000 ton-per-year contract with American Crystal Sugar Company. Overall, the western operation sold 21.3 million tons of coal, two-thirds of which it mined itself.

In the East, NERCO acquired mines, reserves, and coal handling facilities in West Virginia, Kentucky, and Indiana. The company began to make headway in the area, signing supply contracts with Ford Motor Co., Alabama Power Company, and the Tennessee Valley Authority. Sales of 3.4 million tons of coal in 1984 nearly doubled 1983 levels, while revenues increased to about $98 million from $48 million the previous year.

At NERCO Oil & Gas, exploration results improved, following a rough start-up period. The company lowered finding costs and secured a higher level of industry participation. Of 48 wells in which the company participated, 24 were expected to be productive.

Drummond faced several problems in 1985. Total earnings dropped a disappointing 20 percent to $43.4 million. Oil and gas operations lost $35 million on exploration; low prices kept mineral production off the market; a new gallium arsenide—used in the electronics industry—operation turned in unspectacular results; and the western coal operations were hit with lawsuits from long-term coal customers. The City of Austin in Texas and the Lower Colorado River Authority jointly sought to void a two million ton-per-year agreement with the Decker mine, while Detroit Edison sought restitution and damages for amounts overpaid in prior years.

Drummond and other executives took what actions they could. The measures included replacing the oil and gas management, cutting personnel, and reducing exploration in favor of development drilling and production purchases. In minerals, they reduced operating costs, hedged prices, and began selling inventory to provide cash for operations. To make the coal operations more efficient and reduce overhead, they combined the western and eastern subsidiaries into NERCO Coal Corp., headquartered in St. Louis, Missouri.

There was some good news in 1985, however. Despite lawsuit-related contract terminations, NERCO Coal sold 27.9 million tons of the product, up from 24.7 million tons the previous year. The company also signed multi-year contracts with American Crystal Sugar Company, Western Sugar Company, and Wisconsin Public Service Corp.

NERCO also continued making strategic acquisitions and investments. It purchased the remaining interest in the DeLamar silver and gold mine and opened the Antelope Mine—its tenth surface coal mine—on the southern edge of Wyoming's Powder River Basin. In addition, a joint operating agreement was formed with Mitsubishi, creating the MitNer Group to market coal and coal services internationally.

In 1986, NERCO Coal resolved one of its legal disputes. For a $29 million payment, the company agreed to lower rates to the financially-strapped Platte River Power Authority in Colorado. Wrangling continued, however, in other cases, including a dispute in which Utility Fuels withheld approximately $35 million. Despite these problems, yearly coal sales increased, driven in part by the newly opened Antelope Mine.

Flagging prices kept NERCO's minerals business in the red during 1986. It continued to expand, however, obtaining new reserves and lowering costs. The company paid $47 million for the Con gold mine in the Northwest Territories of Canada. Operating costs throughout its system were lowered with such measures as dropping the cost of an ounce of Candelaria silver from $5.95 in 1984 to $4.84 in 1986.

The oil and gas business also lost money in 1986. Management cut costs by putting the subsidiary under the direction of the minerals division and cut risk by moving from exploration to development. It also acquired undeveloped reserves in West Virginia and participated in a joint venture with its parent company, PacifiCorp Inc., to encourage cogeneration.

1987 was a good year for NERCO. The coal arm of the business resolved its legal disputes, minerals were profitable, and although both the oil and gas and advanced materials operations lost money, the company as a whole increased revenue six percent to $632.3 million, while income rose five percent to $60.1 million.

NERCO Coal cut deals with most of its legal adversaries. It lowered prices to Utility Fuels in exchange for a $106 million payment, replaced Louisiana Power & Light's 20-year coal contract with a 25-year natural gas agreement, and early in 1988 settled with the Lower Colorado River Authority/City of Austin for a cash payment. In February of 1988 the company agreed to let Commonwealth Edison of Chicago purchase in-ground reserves rather than take delivery.

The *Wall Street Transcript* gave Drummond and NERCO its 1987 Coal Industry Bronze Award. Editors concluded, "Despite the fact that this company has faced some very difficult contract negotiations and litigation, management has responded calmly and decisively, maintaining a clear focus on operation and profitability.''

Rising commodity prices led NERCO Minerals to its first profitable year since 1983. Overall gold sales were up 39 percent to 153,000 ounces and silver sales were up almost 74 percent to 9.1 million ounces. In addition, the company lowered it's extraction cost for silver eight percent to $4.06 per ounce and added reserves by exploring at mine sites and building a carbon-in-leach plant at Alligator Ridge.

On the downside, gallium arsenide wafers were a small drain, and oil and gas lost $6.7 million on $14.1 million in revenues. Despite losses, the oil and gas subsidiary continued acquiring reserves, spending $65 million on production and low-risk properties on the Gulf Coast.

In 1988 NERCO's oil and gas business finally recorded a profit, earning $9.5 million on revenues of $88.9 million. Much of the jump came from $284 million in natural gas acquisitions. Included among the acquisitions were a 55 percent interest in Northern Louisiana's Black Lake Field for $150 million, as well as more of the same field purchased from Hunt Petroleum for $35 million, and Enron's interests in Louisiana and Texas acquired for $90 million.

Despite the fact that coal was still king—70 percent of NERCO's revenues were generated from the coal business— losses of volume from contract settlements meant the company had to intensify marketing efforts. It sold its first steam coal to Japan, began constructing a new dragline at Antelope, and exploited a Venture Fuels joint venture with Detroit Edison to deliver Spring Creek coal to Minnesota Power & Light and other new customers. Minerals also remained profitable in 1988, but because of lower silver sales, revenues fell 24 percent to $100.1 million while income fell to $5.3 million.

The company continued to grow in 1989. Newly-appointed NERCO Inc. president Lawrence E. Heiner, formerly president of NERCO Minerals, could be proud of revenues which reached $711 million. In addition, income hit $68.1 million, and return on equity—earnings per share plus stock appreciation—hit a fantastic 63.5 percent, chiefly because of share appreciation.

The appreciation was caused by three factors. A 5.16 million share offering made the stock more visible. Investors expected natural gas prices to rise—NERCO was among the top 40 U.S. producers—and company watchers anticipated pending air quality legislation would increase demand for low-sulfur coal.

NERCO's three main businesses were all up over the previous year. Gas sales jumped 94 percent, while oil sales rose 16 percent. Combined oil and gas revenues of $151.1 million were 70 percent above 1988, while income of $31.1 million tripled the previous year's. In December of 1989 the company announced a $162 million purchase of natural gas and oil interests off the shores Louisiana and Texas.

At NERCO Minerals sales were up—43 percent for gold and 22 percent for silver. Increased sales and lower extraction costs— especially at the underground Con mine, where gold extraction costs fell 23 percent to $230 per ounce—pushed revenues up 21

percent to $121.1 million and boosted operating income 8 percent to $9 million.

NERCO Coal Company—which still accounted for 61 percent of earnings and represented stability for the company—paid $35 million for the Bright Coal Group's rights to 44 million tons of low-sulfur West Virginia coal. The company also completed a 75 cubic yard dragline at Antelope and replaced a fleet of haul trucks with a coal conveyor system at the Jim Bridger Mine.

The one down side of 1989 was the closure of non-core businesses. These included the short-lived Cascade Information Resources, Inc., and the gallium arsenide operation, Spectrum Technology, Inc., for which it took a $7.9 million pre-tax charge.

In 1990, NERCO had another excellent year, reaping $827.7 million in revenues and $167.5 in income. Coal sales increased 13 percent to 36.1 million tons, natural gas production rose to a record 69.2 billion cubic feet, and gold production reached 181,100 ounces. Despite these results, however, NERCO's stock price fell 16 percent due to the market's belief that decreased prices for some of NERCO's commodities—particularly natural gas and silver—would negatively effect the company's earnings potential. In fact, during 1990, natural gas prices were soft, gold prices fell to their lowest point in 4 years, and silver reached a 15-year low, falling below $4 per ounce, prompting the suspension of mining at NERCO's primarily silver operation.

The situation worsened in 1991 as spot prices weakened for the company's products, and the recession and weather reduced market demand. Compounding these factors, NERCO incurred substantial debt, funding an acquisition that led to increased interest expense. Though both revenue and income continued to rise, the market, in light of these developments, sent stock prices down another 13 percent.

Faced with this tough operating environment, Lawrence E. Heiner—who had been elected chief executive officer that year—restructured NERCO in order to reduce costs. In an effort to lower debt and future risk, he also sold or transferred several assets. The main problem the company had to deal with was falling prices for both gold and silver. NERCO cut silver sales in half as mineral revenues fell 18 percent to $91.4 million and income fell 96 percent to $.4 million. Management considered selling the precious metals operation but continued to increase capacity, commencing production in the Colorado Cripple Creek District, beginning an autoclave project at the Con mine, and initiating a new cyanide recycling system at DeLamar.

At this point, the other business concerns seemed basically healthy. NERCO Coal set a production record for the third consecutive year and retained a healthy $135.9 million in profits from revenues of $530.5 million. It settled a labor dispute at Decker and a contract dispute with a Wisconsin utility. It increased international sales and transferred ownership of Bridger Coal Company and Glenrock Coal Company to PacifiCorp. Since Federal air quality legislation was making low-sulfur coal the country's preferred fuel, NERCO Coal also sold two of its higher sulfur operations in Indiana.

NERCO Oil & Gas made a major acquisition in 1991, paying approximately $500 million for the offshore assets of Union Texas Petroleum Holdings, Inc. These new holdings—which increased natural gas production 44 percent and added 41 percent in proved reserves—made NERCO a top 20 U.S. independent natural gas producer and one of the largest independent producers in the Gulf of Mexico. The acquisition also raised revenues 39 percent to $297.7 million, while boosting income 22 percent to $62.4 million. To reduce delivery exposure, NERCO also sold its 25-year gas supply contract with Louisiana Power & Light for $75 million.

Early in 1992 conditions worsened for NERCO as high reserves, a week domestic economy, and the warmest winter weather in more than 100 years drove natural gas prices to a 12-year low. The situation caused a downgrade in NERCO's credit rating, which in turn resulted in higher credit costs.

In the first quarter of 1992, the company reported a net loss of $172.8 million and was forced to take a non-cash, after-tax $150 million write-down of the carrying value of its oil and gas assets. The company worked to reduce debt, strengthen its balance sheet, and position itself to improve its credit rating.

Selected assets in all three of its business units were divested, and the sale of the entire minerals subsidiary was under consideration.

Prices recovered strongly during the second quarter, but in the third quarter the company reported a loss of $25.7 million associated with the sale of several non-core oil, gas, and coal assets at depressed prices. In addition, NERCO had finally decided to divest its minerals operations and was working toward that end. Due to the depressed minerals market, the company's third quarter report predicted such a sale could result in a pre-tax loss in excess of $150 million.

Principal Subsidiaries: NERCO Coal Corp.; NERCO Oil & Gas, Inc.; NERCO Minerals Company.

Further Reading: Green, Peter, Dan Jackson, and Paul C. Merritt, ''Nerco Tops 20-Million-tpy Mark,'' *Coal Age,* October 1982; ''NERCO Says Profit Fell in 4th Period on Unit's Loss From Operations,'' *Wall Street Journal,* January 30, 1986; Annual Reports, 1986–91, Portland, OR, NERCO Inc.; ''NERCO, Inc.,'' *Wall Street Transcript,* December 12, 1988.

—Jordan Wankoff

NESTLÉ S.A.

Avenue Nestlé 55
CH-1800 Vevey
Switzerland
(021) 924-2526
Fax: (021) 921-1885

Public Company
Incorporated: 1866 as Anglo-Swiss Condensed Milk
    Company
Employees: 218,000
Sales: SFr 54.50 billion (US$36.22 billion)
Stock Exchanges: Zurich Geneva Paris Frankfurt Dusseldorf
    Amsterdam Vienna London Tokyo Brussels Basle
SICs: 2066 Chocolate and Cocoa Products; 2023 Dry,
    Condensed, and Evaporated Dairy Products; 2024 Ice
    Cream and Frozen Desserts; 2026 Fluid Milk; 2064 Candy
    & Other Confectionery Products; 2043 Cereal Breakfast
    Foods; 2037 Frozen Fruits, Fruit Juices & Vegetables;
    2038 Frozen Specialties; 2087 Flavoring Extracts and
    Flavoring Syrups; 2095 Roasted Coffee; 2834
    Pharmaceutical Preparations; 2048 Dog and Cat Food

Nestlé is the largest food company in the world. With more than 400 manufacturing facilities on five continents, Nestlé has often been called ''the most multinational of the multinationals,'' largely because only 2 percent of its sales are made in its home country. Nestlé S.A. is a holding company for some 200 operating units that manufacture and sell a wide variety of products, including coffee, juices, chocolate and malted beverages, chocolates and confectionery, culinary and refrigerated products, dairy products, baby food, frozen foods and ice cream, pet foods, and pharmaceutical products.

While serving as the American consul in Zurich, Charles Page decided that Switzerland, with its abundant milk supply and easy access to the whole European market, was the perfect location for a condensed milk factory. The first canned condensed milk had been produced in the United States by Gail Borden some ten years before, and originally Page planned to produce and sell ''Borden Milk'' in the European market as a licensee. The plan fell through, however, so in 1866 he established the Anglo-Swiss Condensed Milk Company as a limited company in Cham, Switzerland.

The company's name was meant to flatter the British, to whom Page hoped to sell a great deal of his condensed milk. Anglo-Swiss first expanded its operations beyond Switzerland's borders in 1872, when it opened a factory in Chippenham, England. Condensed milk rapidly became a staple product in European cupboards—the business downturn in 1872 and the depression of 1875 did not affect the firm's sales. Charles Page died in 1873, leaving the company in the hands of his brother George and Anglo-Swiss's other investors. The next year, Anglo-Swiss undertook further expansion in England by purchasing the Condensed Milk Company, in London. By 1876 sales were almost four times their 1872 level.

Meanwhile, in Vevey, Switzerland, in 1867 Henri Nestlé began selling his newly developed cow's-milk food for infants who could not be breast fed. Demand for his Farine Lactee Nestlé soared; between 1871 and 1873, daily production more than doubled, from fewer than 1,000 tins a day to 2,000. Nestlé's goal was to bring his baby food within everyone's reach, and he spared no effort in trying to convince doctors and mothers of its benefits. But while his energy and good intentions were nearly endless, his financial resources were not. By 1873, demand for Nestlé's product exceeded his production capabilities, resulting in missed delivery dates. At 61, Nestlé was running out of energy, and his thoughts turned to retirement. Jules Monnerat, a former member of parliament who lived in Vevey, had long eyed the business, and in 1874 Nestlé accepted Monnerat's offer of SFr 1 million. Thus, in 1875, the company became Farine Lactee Henri Nestlé with Monnerat as chairman.

In 1877 Nestlé faced a new competitor when the Anglo-Swiss Condensed Milk Company—already the leading manufacturer of condensed milk in Europe—decided to broaden its product line and manufacture cheese and milk food for babies. Nestlé quickly responded by launching a condensed milk product of its own. George Page tried to buy the competing company outright, but he was firmly told that Nestlé was not for sale. Turning his attention elsewhere, he purchased the Anglo-Swiss Company's first factory in the United States in 1881. The plant, located in Middletown, New York, was built primarily to escape import duties, and it was soon successful enough to challenge Borden's supremacy in the American condensed milk market. It also presented a drawback: George Page spent so much time there that Anglo-Swiss began to lose its hold on Europe—much to the delight of Nestlé. After George Page's death in 1899, the Anglo-Swiss Condensed Milk Company decided to sell its American business to Borden in 1902 so that it could concentrate on regaining market share in Europe.

Until 1898 Nestlé remained determined to manufacture only in Switzerland and export to its markets around the world. But that year the company finally decided to venture outside Switzerland with the purchase of a Norwegian condensed milk company. Two years later, in 1900, Nestlé opened a factory in the United States, and quickly followed this by entering Britain, Germany, and Spain. Early in the 1900s, Nestlé also became involved in chocolate, a logical step for a company based in Vevey, the center of the Swiss chocolate industry. Nestlé became a partner in the Swiss General Chocolate Company, the maker of the Peter and Kohler brands. Under their agreement, the chocolate company produced the first Nestlé brand milk chocolate, while

Nestlé concentrated on selling the Peter, Kohler, and Nestlé brands around the world.

In 1905 Nestlé and the Anglo-Swiss Condensed Milk Company finally quelled their fierce competition by merging to create the Nestlé and Anglo-Swiss Milk Company. The new firm would be run by two registered offices, one in Vevey and one in Cham, a practice it continues today. With Emile-Louis Roussy as chairman, the company now included seven factories in Switzerland, six in Great Britain, three in Norway, and one each in the United States, Germany, and Spain.

In response to an increase in import duties in Australia—Nestlé's second-largest export market—the company decided to begin manufacturing there in 1906 by buying a major condensed milk company, the Cressbrook Dairy Company, in Brisbane. In the next few years production and sales continued to increase as the company began to replace sales agents with subsidiary companies, particularly in the rapidly growing Asian markets.

Most of its factories were located in Europe, however, and when World War I broke out in 1914, Nestlé's operations, particularly in such warring countries as Britain and Germany, were seriously affected. Although production continued in full force during the early months of the war, business soon grew more difficult. By 1916 fresh milk shortages, especially in Switzerland, meant that Nestlé's factories often sold almost all of their milk supplies to meet the needs of local towns. Shipping obstacles, increased manufacturing and operating costs, and restrictions on the use of production facilities added to Nestlé's wartime difficulties, as did a further decrease in fresh milk supplies due to shortages of cattle.

To deal with these problems and meet the increased demand for its products from governments supplying their troops, Nestlé decided to expand in countries less affected by the war and began purchasing existing factories, particularly in the United States, where it established links with several existing firms. By 1917, Nestlé had 40 factories, and in 1918, its world production was more than double what it was in 1914. Nestlé pursued the same strategy in Australia; by 1920 it had acquired a controlling interest in three companies there. That same year, Nestlé began production in Latin America when it established a factory in Araras, Brazil, the first in a series of Latin American factories. By 1921, the firm had 80 factories and 12 subsidiaries and affiliates. It also introduced a new product that year—powdered milk called Lactogen.

It didn't take long for the effects of such rapid expansion to catch up with the company, however. Nestlé and Anglo-Swiss reported its first loss in 1921, to which the stock market reacted with panic, making matters worse. The company explained that the SFr 100 million loss was due to the rising prices of raw materials such as sugar and coal, and a trade depression that had caused a steady fall in consumer purchasing power, coupled with falling exchange rates after the war, which forced the company to raise prices.

To battle the storm, the company decided to reorganize both management and production. In 1922 it brought production in line with actual sales by closing some of its factories in the United States, Britain, Australia, Norway, and Switzerland. It

also hired Louis Dapples, a banking expert, to put the company back in order. Dapples directed Nestlé with an iron fist, introducing stringent financial controls and reorganizing its administration. By 1923, signs of improvement were already evident, as Nestlé's outstanding bank loans had dropped from SFr 293 million in 1921 to SFr 54.5 million in 1923. Meanwhile in France, Belgium, Italy, Germany, and South Africa, production facilities were expanded. By consolidating certain operations and expanding others, Nestlé was also able to widen its traditional range of products.

Overall, the late 1920s were profitable, progressive times. In addition to adding some new products of its own—including malted milk, a powdered beverage called Milo, and Eledon, a powdered buttermilk for babies with digestive disorders—the company bought interests in several manufacturing firms. Among them were butter and cheese companies, as well as Sarotti A.G., a Berlin based chocolate business that began manufacturing Nestlé, Peter, Cailler, and Kohler chocolate. In 1928, under the direction of Chairman Louis Dapples, Nestlé finally merged with Peter, Cailler, Kohler, Chocolats Suisses S.A.—the resulting company of a 1911 merger between the Swiss General Chocolate Company and Cailler, another leading firm—adding 13 chocolate plants in Europe, South America, and Australia to the growing firm.

Nestlé was becoming so strong that it seemed even the Depression would have little effect on its progress. In fact, its U.S. subsidiary, Nestlé's Food Company Inc. of New York, barely felt the stock market crash of 1929. In 1930 Nestlé created new subsidiaries in Argentina and Cuba. Despite the Depression, Nestlé added more production centers around the world, including a chocolate manufacturer in Copenhagen and a small factory in Moravia, Czechoslovakia, to manufacture milk food, Nescao, and evaporated milk. Factories were also opened in Chile and Mexico in the mid-1930s.

Although profits were down 13 percent in 1930 over the year before, Nestlé faced no major financial problems during the Depression, as its factories generally maintained their output and sales were steady. Though Nestlé's New York-based subsidiary, renamed Nestlé's Milk Products Company, was more affected than those in other countries, U.S. sales of milk products were steady until 1931 and 1932, when a growing public frugality began to cause trouble for more expensive but established brands like Nestlé's. Profit margins narrowed, prices dropped, and cut-throat competition continued until 1933, when new legislation set minimum prices and conditions of sales.

The markets, such as the United States, that were among the first to feel the effects of the Depression were also the first to recover from it. The Depression continued in Switzerland, however. Nestlé products manufactured there could no longer compete on international markets since Swiss currency exchanges were made especially difficult from the early 1930s, when many major countries devalued their currencies, until 1936, when Switzerland finally did likewise. The company decided to streamline production and close several factories, including its two oldest, in Cham and Vevey.

Decentralization efforts begun during the Depression continued to modify the company's structure gradually. By 1936, the industrial and commercial activity of the Nestlé and Anglo-Swiss Condensed Milk Company itself was quite limited in comparison with the considerable interests it had in companies manufacturing and selling its products. More than 20 such companies existed on five continents. In effect, the firm had become a holding company. Consequently, the Nestlé and Anglo-Swiss Condensed Milk Company Limited was established to handle production and marketing on the Swiss market; the parent company officially became a holding firm, called the Nestlé and Anglo-Swiss Holding Company Ltd.; and a second holding company, Unilac Inc., was created in Panama by a number of Nestlé's overseas affiliates.

In 1937 Louis Dapples died, and a new management team, whose members had grown up with the organization, took over. It included Chairman Edouard Muller, formerly managing director; Carl J. Abegg, vice-chairman of the board; and Maurice Paternot, managing director. In 1938 Nestlé introduced its first non-milk product: Nescafé. The revolutionary instant coffee was the result of eight years of research, which had begun when a representative of the Brazilian Coffee Institute asked Louis Dapples if Nestlé could manufacture "coffee cubes" to help Brazil use its large coffee surplus. Although coffee crystals and liquid extracts had been tried before, none had satisfactorily preserved a coffee taste.

Nestlé's product took the form of a soluble powder rather than cubes, allowing users to control the amount of coffee they used. Although Nestlé originally intended to manufacture Nescafé in Brazil, administrative barriers were too great, so Nescafé was first manufactured in Switzerland. Limited production capacity meant that it was launched without the elaborate marketing tactics usually used for products with such potential.

Nescafé quickly acquired a worldwide reputation, however, after it was launched in 1939 in the United States, where it did exceptionally well. Nestea, a soluble powered tea, also made a successful debut in the early 1940s.

World War II had a dire effect on Nestlé. In 1939 profits plummeted to $6 million, compared to $20 million the year before. As in the last war, the company was plagued by food shortages and insufficient supplies of raw materials. To wage its own battle against the war, the company decided to split its headquarters at Vevey and transfer part of the management and executive team to an office in Stamford, Connecticut, where it could better supervise distant markets. Nestlé continued under control of dual managements until 1945.

But the war was not all bad for Nestlé. When the United States became involved in 1941, Nescafé and evaporated and powdered milk were in heavy demand from American armed forces. Nestlé's total sales jumped from $100 million before the war to $225 million in 1945, with the greatest increase occurring in North America, where sales went from $14 million to $60 million. With the end of the war, Nestlé's European and American branches were able to discuss future plans without fear of censorship, and the company could begin to face the challenge of rebuilding its war-torn subsidiaries. Nestlé also re-launched Nescafé and baby foods and began to research new products extensively. Researchers focused on the three areas Nestlé considered most likely to affect the food industry's future: an

increase in world population, rising standards of living in industrialized countries, and the changing social and economic conditions of raw-material-producing countries.

In 1947 Nestlé merged with Alimentana S.A., the manufacturer of Maggi seasonings, bouillon, and dehydrated soups, and the holding company changed its name to Nestlé Alimentana Company. Edouard Muller became the first chairman of Nestlé Alimentana, but he died in 1948, before the policies he helped formulate put the company on the road to a new future. Carl Abegg assumed leadership of the board.

In 1950 Nestlé acquired Crosse and Blackwell, a British manufacturer of preserves and canned foods. Nestlé hoped its $24 million investment would serve as a marketing outlet for Maggi products, but the plan was less than successful, primarily because Crosse and Blackwell could not compete in the United Kingdom with H.J. Heinz Company. Similar setbacks occurred in 1963, when Nestlé acquired Findus frozen foods in Scandinavia for $32 million. Although the company performed well in Sweden, it encountered difficulties in other markets, where the British-Dutch giant Unilever reigned. While parts of the Findus operation eventually became profitable, Nestlé merged its German, Italian, and Australian Findus branches with Unilever. The development of freeze-drying in 1966 led to Taster's Choice, the first freeze-dried coffee, as well as other instant drinks.

In 1971 Nestlé acquired Libby, a maker of fruit juices, in the United States, and in 1973 it bought Stouffer's, which took Nestlé into the hotel and restaurant field and led to the development of Lean Cuisine, a successful line of low-calorie frozen entrees. Nestlé entered the nonfood business for the first time in 1974 by becoming a major shareholder in the French company L'Oreal, a leading cosmetics company. Nestlé diversified further in 1977 with the acquisition of Alcon Laboratories, a Forth Worth, Texas, pharmaceutical company that specialized in ophthalmic products. Then, two years later, Nestlé purchased Burton, Parsons and Company Inc., an American manufacturer of contact lens products. The company also adopted its present name in 1979—Nestlé S.A.

The 1970s saw Nestlé's operations in developing countries increase considerably. Of Nestlé's 303 manufacturing facilities, the 81 factories in developing nations contributed 21 percent of Nestlé's total production. In the mid-1970s, however, the firm faced a new problem as a result of its marketing efforts in these countries, when a boycott against all Nestlé products was started in the United States in 1977. Activists claimed that Nestlé's aggressive baby food promotions made mothers in developing countries so eager to use Nestlé's formula that they used it any way they could. The poverty-stricken areas had high rates of illiteracy, and mothers, unable to read and follow the directions, often mixed the product with local polluted water or used an insufficient amount of the expensive formula, unwittingly starving their infants. Estimates of Nestlé's losses as a result of the boycott, which lasted until the early 1980s, ranged as high as $40 million.

In 1981 Helmut Maucher became managing director of Nestlé and made this controversy one of his top priorities. He met with boycott supporters and complied with the World Health Organization's demands that Nestlé stop promoting the product through advertising and free samples. His direct confrontation of the issue contrasted with Nestlé's earlier low-profile approach and was quite successful in allaying its critics' fears.

Maucher also reduced overhead by turning over more authority to operating units and reducing headquarters staff. In addition, he spearheaded a series of major acquisitions. In 1985 Nestlé acquired Carnation, a U.S. manufacturer of milk, pet, and culinary products, for $3 billion, at the time one of the largest acquisitions in the history of the food industry. This was followed in 1985 by the acquisition of Hills Brothers Inc., the third-largest American coffee firm, which added ground roast coffee to Nestlé's product line. In the late 1980s, as food companies around the world prepared for the integration of the European Economic Community in 1992, Nestlé continued to make major acquisitions. In 1988 the company paid £2.55 billion for Rowntree Mackintosh PLC—a leading British chocolate manufacturer—marking the largest takeover of a British company by a foreign one to date. That same year Nestlé also purchased the Italian pasta maker Buitoni SpA.

Capital expenditures reached SFr 2.8 billion in 1991. Half was devoted to installation improvements, including data processing and automation, particularly in North America and Europe. The other half was spent expanding plants, primarily in Latin America and the Far East, areas where products were often based on local raw materials, tastes, and habits. That year Nestlé made 31 acquisitions, also adding a new factory in the People's Republic of China. Among the companies purchased were Alco Drumstick, a U.S. ice cream manufacturer with many European activities; Indra, a Swedish frozen-food maker; La Campiña, a Mexican evaporated-milk producer; and 97 percent of Intercsokoládé, a Hungarian chocolate maker.

In September of 1991 Nestlé and the Coca-Cola Co. formed an equally split joint-venture concern, Coca-Cola Nestlé Refreshment Company, to produce and distribute concentrates and bases for the production of ready-to-drink coffee and tea beverages. With an initial capitalization of $100 million, the products, to be sold under the Nescafé and Nestea brand names, would be marketed worldwide—with the exception of Japan—primarily through Coca-Cola's international network of businesses.

Nescafé, sold in more than 100 countries by 1991, was launched in the Republic of Korea—Coca-Cola and Nestlé's first joint endeavor—as was Nescafé Cappuccino in Europe. Hills Bros. "Perfect Balance," a 50 percent-decaffeinated coffee, began selling in the United States, as did Nestea in cans at the beginning of 1992. By early 1992, a joint venture allowed the company to obtain a majority interest in Cokoladovny, a Czechoslovakian chocolate and biscuit producer. In addition, Nestlé battled for and won, with a bid of $2.3 billion in cash, the French mineral water producer Source Perrier. The company had also set its sights on acquiring the balance of the L'Oreal cosmetics company in order to make it a wholly owned subsidiary. Nestlé S.A. reported a 17 percent increase in profits for the first 6 months of 1992.

A series of geographical efforts to form more or less integrated economic blocs in coming years should bode well for a company as multinational as Nestlé. A single European Community market; the extension of the North American Free Trade Agreement (NAFTA) to Mexico; the Treaty of Asunción, which should organize a free trade area and coordination of Latin American sector policies; integrated economic union among some Southeast Asia countries; and, in general, a more receptive attitude in many countries toward investment by foreign businesses may indeed help Nestlé increase sales and manufacturing efficiency, as well as achieve economies of scale.

With 438 factories in 63 countries and sales of more than SFr 50 billion on its 125th anniversary, Nestlé is the undisputed leader in the food industry. Its long history of international operations should stand it in good stead, but the giant will have to stay nimble to maintain its place as trade barriers crumble in Europe and its competition grows large and strong enough to challenge Nestlé around the world.

Principal Subsidiaries: Alcon Canada, Inc.; Carnation Foods Company Ltd. (Canada; 50%); Clintec Nutrition Company (Canada; 50%); Laura Secord, Inc. (Canada); Nestlé Canada, Inc.; Alcon Laboratories, Inc. (U.S.A.); Clintec Nutrition Company (U.S.A.; 50%); L. J. Minor Corporation (U.S.A.); Nestlé Beverage Company (U.S.A.); Nestlé Brands Foodservice Company (U.S.A.); Nestlé Dairy Systems, Inc. (U.S.A.); Nestlé Food Company (U.S.A.); Nestlé Puerto Rico, Inc. (U.S.A.); Nestlé Refrigerated Food Company (U.S.A.); Nestlé Trading Corporation (U.S.A.); Owen/Galderma Laboratories, Inc. (U.S.A.; 50%); Stouffer Foods Corporation (U.S.A.); Stouffer Hotel Company (U.S.A.); Stouffer Restaurant Company (U.S.A.); Sunmark, Inc. (U.S.A.); Wine World, Inc. (U.S.A.); Alcon Laboratorios Argentina S.A.; Nestlé Argentina S.A.; Alcon Laboratorios do Brasil S.A. (Brazil); Companhia Produtora de Alimentos (Brazil); Industria de Sorvetes Ltda. (Brazil; 50%); Nestlé Industrial e Comercial Ltda. (Brazil); Centenario S.A. (Chile; 99.5%); Nestlé Chile S.A. (99.7%); Productos Alimenticios Savory S.A.I.C. (Chile); Nestlé de Colombia S.A.; Productos Nestlé (Costa Rica) S.A.; Productos Nestlé (El Salvador) S.A.; Nestlé Ecuador S.A. (74.7%); Productos Nestlé (Guatemala) S.A.; Nestlé Hondureña S.A. (Honduras); Nestlé-JMP Jamaica Ltd.; Alcon Laboratorios S.A. de C.V. (Mexico); Alimentos Findus S.A. de C.V. (Mexico); Café Continental S.A. de C.V. (Mexico); Compañía Nestlé S.A. de C.V. (Mexico); Industrias Alimenticias Club S.A. de C.V. (Mexico); Productos Alimenticios La Campiña S.A. de C.V. (Mexico); Productos Carnation S.A. de C.V. (Mexico); Productos Nestlé (Nicaragua) S.A.; Nestlé Caribbean, Inc. (Panama); Nestlé Panamá S.A.; Nestlé Perú S.A. (89.3%); Sociedad Dominicana de Conservas y Alimentos S.A. (Dominican Republic; 70%); Nestlé Trinidad and Tobago Ltd. (80.6%); Caramelos Royal C.A. (Venezuela); Chocolates Nestlé S.A. (Venezuela); Nestlé Venezuela S.A.; Saudi Food Industries Co. Ltd. (Saudi Arabia; 51%); Nestlé China Ltd. (Hong Kong); Nestlé India Ltd. (40%); P.T. Food Specialties Indonesia (57%); Alcon Japan Ltd.; Buitoni Japan K.K. (70%); Nestlé K.K. (Japan); Nestlé-Mackintosh K.K. (Japan; 66%); Société pour l'Exportation des Produits Nestlé S.A. (Lebanon); Nestlé (Malaysia) Sdn. Bhd. (51%); Malaysia Cocoa Manufacturing Sdn. Bhd. (49%); Milkpak Ltd. (Pakistan; 40%); Nestlé Philippines, Inc. (55%); Nestlé Foods Co. Ltd. (Republic of Korea; 99.1%); Nestlé Korea Ltd. (72%); Nestlé Shuangcheng Ltd. (People's Republic of China; 64%); Nestlé Singapore (Pte) Ltd.; Ceylon

Nutritional Foods Ltd. (Sri Lanka; 52%); Nestlé Lanka Ltd. (Sri Lanka; 93.7%); Anping Distributors Ltd. (Taiwan); Nestlé Products (Thailand), Inc.; Nestlé (South Africa) (Pty) Ltd.; Société Camerounaise de Produits Alimentaires, Diététiques et Autres CAMAD-Nestlé (Cameroon); Compagnie Africaine de Préparations Alimentaires CAPRAL-Nestlé (Ivory Coast; 70.7%); NOVALIM-Nestlé (Ivory Coast; 92.2%); Industrie du Froid S.A.E. (Egypt; 86%); Société Gabonaise de Produits Alimentaires—SOGAPRAL (Gabon; 90%); Nestlé Ghana Ltd. (45%); Nestlé Foods Kenya Ltd. (87.5%); Nestlé's Products (Mauritius) Ltd.; Nestlé Foods Nigeria PLC (40%); Nestlé Sénégal; Nestlé Tunisie (Tunisia; 59.2%); Nestlé Zimbabwe (Pvt) Ltd.; Alcon Laboratories (Australia) Pty Ltd.; Friskies Pet Care Pty Ltd. (Australia); Nestlé Australia Ltd.; Nestlé Confectionery Ltd. (Australia); Nestlé New Zealand Ltd.; Food Specialties (PNG) Ltd. (Papua New Guinea); Alcon Pharma GmbH (Germany); Alois Dallmayr Kaffee oHG (Germany; 48.6%); Blaue Quellen Mineral-und Heilbrunnen AG (Germany; 90.6%); Clintec-Salvia GmbH (Germany; 50%); Heimbs & Sohn GmbH & Co. KG (Germany; 48.6%); Nestlé Deutschland AG (Germany; 97.2%); Trinks GmbH (Germany; 90.6%); Vittel Mineralwasser GmbH (Germany; 52.5%); Nestlé (Ireland) Ltd.; Alcon Laboratories (U.K.) Ltd.; Cereal Partners U.K. (50%); Gray, Dunn & Co. Ltd. (U.K.); Multisnack Ltd. (U.K.); Rowntree Mackintosh Ltd. (U.K.); The Nestlé Co. Ltd. (U.K.); Indra AB (Sweden); Lars Jönsson AB (Sweden; 50%); Svenska Nestlé AB (Sweden); Zoégas Kaffe AB (Sweden; 90.8%); Alcon Pharmaceuticals Ltd.; Dyna S.A.; Food Ingredients Specialties S.A.; Frisco-Findus AG (98.7%); Frismat AG; Leisi AG Nahrungsmittelfabrik; Maggi AG; Nespresso S.A.; Nestlé World Trade Corporation; Société des Produits Nestlé S.A.; Thomi & Franck AG; Nestlé Prodalim Gida Mamulleri Imalat Ve Pazarlama Anonim Sirketi (Turkey; 97.2%); Österreich-ische Nestlé GmbH (Austria); Alcon-Couvreur N.V. (Belgium); Friskies Service Merchandising S.A. (Belgium); Nestlé Belgilux S.A. (Belgium); Refrifood Benelux S.A. (Belgium); Vittel Import S.A. (Belgium; 52.5%); Nestlé Danmark A/S (Denmark); Alcon Iberhis S.A. (Spain); Derivados Lácteos y Alimenticios S.A. (Spain); Granja Castelló S.A. (Spain; 50%); Productos del Café S.A. (Spain); Sociedad Nestlé AEPA (Spain); Nestlé-Findus Oy (Finland); Cereal Partners France (50%); Chambourcy S.A. (France; 99.9%); Clintec Nutrition Clinique S.A. (France; 50%); Davigel S.A. (France; 99.9%); France Glaces-Findus S.A.; Gloria S.A. (France); Herta S.A. (France); Laboratoires Alcon S.A. (France); Loumidis S.A. (Greece); Nestlé Hellas S.A.I. (Greece; 51%); Nestlé-Rowntree S.A. (France); Société de Produits Alimentaires et Diététiques, SOPAD-Nestlé S.A. (France); Société Générale des Eaux Minérales de Vittel S.A. (France; 52.5%); Source Perrier (France); Alcon Italia S.p.A. (Italy); Berni Industrie Alimentari S.p.A. (Italy); Clintec S.r.l. (Italy; 50%); Nestlé Italiana S.p.A. (Italy); Intercsokoládé Kft (Hungary; 97.1%); A/S Nestlé Norge (Norway); Artland Nederland B.V. (Netherlands); Nestlé Nederland B.V. (Netherlands); COMCAFE Comercial de Café, Ltda. (Portugal); Nestlé Portugal S.A.

Further Reading: Heer, Jean, *World Events 1866–1966: The First Hundred Years of Nestlé,* Vevey, Switzerland, Nestlé, 1966; *Historical Highlight,* Vevey, Switzerland, Nestlé, 1991; Nestlé Annual Report, 1991; Heer, Jean, *Nestlé: 125 Years, 1866–1991,* Verey, Switzerland, Nestlé, 1991; "Nestlé Consolidating its Chocolate Production," *New York Times,* February 5, 1993; Templeman, John, Stewart Toy, and Dave Lindorff, "Nestlé: A Giant in a Hurry," *Business Week,* March 22, 1993.

—updated by Anne C. Hughes

Newmont Mining Corporation

NEWMONT MINING CORPORATION

One United Bank Center
1700 Lincoln St.
Denver, Colorado 80203
U.S.A.
(303) 863-7414
Fax: (303) 837-5873

Public Company
Incorporated: 1921 as Newmont Corporation
Employees: 2,550
Sales: $623 million
Stock Exchanges: New York Paris Zürich
SICs: 1041 Gold Ores

Newmont Mining Corporation, primarily through two subsidiaries, is engaged in the exploration, mining, and processing of gold. The bulk of Newmont's revenue is generated by Newmont Gold Company (NGC), of which parent Newmont controls a 90.1 percent interest. Operating in Nevada along a 38-mile stretch of the Carlin Trend, NGC is North America's leading producer of gold. NGC controls a 58-square-mile area of mineral rights in the Carlin region, while Newmont owns rights to a surrounding additional 420 square miles. In 1991, NGC accounted for about $573 million of Newmont's $623 million total sales, mining 132 million tons of gold ore and selling 1.58 million ounces of gold. Newmont's other main subsidiary is the wholly owned Newmont Exploration Limited (NEL) whose role is to discover new gold deposits in NGC's areas of interest and to determine the minable ore reserves in these deposits by drilling. In exchange for a 10 percent royalty, NGC has rights to any gold discovered by NEL in the 2,300-square-mile area around its Carlin property. Newmont's cost to produce an ounce of gold in 1991—$203—was a more efficient rate than 75 percent of the Western world's gold production.

Newmont was founded in 1921 as Newmont Corporation by Colonel William Boyce Thompson as a type of holding company for his varied financial interests. Thompson was born in 1869 in Alder Gulch, Montana, and grew up in Butte. An overweight, cigar-smoking man with a penchant for gambling (a telling hobby for someone in his line of work), Thompson eventually landed at the Columbia School of Mines, after which he made some money in the coal business. Upon selling stock in a copper mine he had bought on installments, Thompson arrived around 1905 on Wall Street where he became a successful trader, making gains in several industries, including oil, steel, and minerals. Newmont's early strategy was to establish development companies and then to sell off much of their stock. The remaining stock was accumulated in a portfolio whose income was used to finance further mining projects. Thompson had a hand in launching several companies, including Magma Copper and Texas Gulf Sulphur, but his standard policy was to make a quick profit on a new venture and to move on to the next one.

Newmont stock reached a peak of 236 in 1929, but crashed with the rest of the stock market and dropped to 37 in 1930. Thompson died the same year, never fully recovering from surgery to reduce his obesity. His personal attorney, Charles F. Ayer, took over as head of Newmont, and the company began to retain its acquired properties rather than perpetuating its earlier cycle of trading them off. Among the companies Newmont acquired in the years prior to World War II were O'okiep Copper Compny, Ltd., of South Africa, and Colorado's Idarado Mining Corporation. Also launched during this period was Newmont Oil Company, whose aim was to explore Texas and Louisiana for oil reserves.

By 1940, Newmont existed as an interesting hybrid of holding company and operating company. As a holding company, Newmont's investments were primarily in well-known metal and mining companies, with copper leading the way. These investments included hundreds of thousands of shares of Kennecott, Phelps Dodge, and Hudson Bay Mining and Smelting. Gold represented about 19 percent of the company's total investments. Among the significant ventures that Newmont was actively developing were O'okiep, in which Newmont held a two-thirds interest; Getch Mine, Inc., a Nevada gold mine, 18.6 percent held by Newmont; and Alder Oil Company, a wholly owned subsidiary.

Through O'okiep, Newmont launched successful ventures in southern Africa. Abandoned by its British owners, O'okiep was acquired by Newmont for the modest investment of $2 million, and Newmont subsequently took advantage of the increased demand for copper during World War II. After the war, due to high costs and a labor shortage in the United States, Newmont decided to concentrate its prospecting abroad. The result was the acquisition of an abandoned copper-lead-zinc mine at Tsumeb in the former German colony of South-West Africa. The German owners had collected an extremely rich ore at the mine, and when the site was seized in 1939 by South Africa's Custodian of Enemy Property about 800,000 tons of the ore had been left at the surface. Newmont teamed with American Metal Company and five other partners for a bid of just over $4 million, with Newmont's share at 29 percent. Tsumeb's ore reserves turned out to be much greater than anyone—including its former German operators—had imagined, and the purchase price was covered by merely processing the ore that had been dumped at the surface.

By 1950, Newmont was led by Fred Searls who, like Thompson, was a recognizable figure on Wall Street. Known for his red bowtie and yellow-topped boots, Searls disliked publicity and preferred ore exploration to sitting in an office. During this time, Newmont became involved with lucrative Sherritt Gordon

Mines of Canada. In 1951, John Drybrough, president of the Newmont Mining Corporation of Canada subsidiary, informed Newmont officials that a company run by his brother-in-law had discovered nickel deposits in Manitoba, as well as a new, more efficient method for processing the ore. With the backing of J. P. Morgan and Company, Metropolitan Life, and several other insurance companies, Newmont went ahead with the project and invested $10 million in the mining company. Eventually Sherritt Gordon became one of the largest producers of nickel in the world.

Plato Malozemoff became Newmont's president in 1954. The son of a mining engineer, Malozemoff was born in 1909 in St. Petersburg, Russia, where his father was managing director of British-owned Lena Goldfields, Ltd., the largest gold-mining company in Russia until its seizure by the Soviets in 1920. The Malozemoff family eventually landed in San Francisco, where Plato earned a degree in mining engineering at Berkeley in 1931. After receiving his master's degree from the Montana School of Mines, Malozemoff assisted his father in the management of gold and copper mines in Argentina and Costa Rica. He was first noticed by Newmont executives around 1943 while working for the Office of Price Administration's minerals branch in Washington, D.C., and was hired by Newmont in 1945. One of the driving forces behind the Sherritt Gordon deal, Malozemoff was made a vice-president as the project successfully unfolded.

Under Malozemoff's leadership, Newmont entered a period of steady growth by acquisition and diversification, often through joint ventures with other well-established companies. In 1955, Newmont joined Phelps Dodge, American Smelting and Refining, and Cerro de Pasco in forming the Southern Peru Copper Corporation. That same year, a uranium oxide mine was opened in Washington State with the company's majority interest in the Dawn Mining Company. Newmont also bought a 28.8 percent share in the development of a South African copper mine with Rio Tinto in Transvaal, South Africa. In 1955, a particularly active year, investments were also made in the Philippines, Canada, and Algeria. In 1957, Empire Star Mines Company, Ltd., was merged into Newmont.

At the end of the 1950s, Newmont began to reverse its trend toward reliance on foreign investment. In 1959, $8.2 million of the company's $13 million dividend income came from foreign holdings, primarily the mines of Tsumeb and O'okiep. Newmont took action to remedy this imbalance in 1962 by trading some of its own preferred stock for a large block of stock in Magma Copper. With this deal, Newmont's interest in Magma was raised to 80.6 percent, and suddenly the company's income from domestic holdings surpassed its foreign-generated total. Following the acquisition of additional Magma shares, Newmont was forced by the U.S. Justice Department to divest its 2.9 percent interest in Phelps Dodge on the grounds that holdings in both large copper companies violated antitrust laws. Newmont complied, and also removed two Phelps Dodge representatives from its own board of directors.

By the middle of the 1960s, over half of Newmont's income originated in North America. Most of this was in the United States, largely due to the 1965 opening of the company's new mine at Carlin, Nevada. The mine, operated by Carlin Gold

Mining Company (a wholly owned subsidiary of Newmont), began operations in April 1965, producing 128,500 ounces of gold by year-end. The output was doubled the following year and Carlin quickly became the second-largest gold producer in the nation, trailing only the 90-year-old Homestake Mine, also in Nevada. More amazing than Carlin's size was the technology used to collect its difficult-to-obtain riches. In 1966, 12 tons of overburden had to be removed and 3 tons of ore milled to retrieve an ounce of gold at Carlin. Furthermore, the gold particles were the smallest yet ever mined, requiring an electron microscope to be seen. Despite these obstacles, Carlin became the lowest-cost gold mine in the Western world, a fact reflected in Newmont's earnings figures which rose to $5.15 a share in 1966.

Malozemoff became Newmont's chairman of the board in 1966, reinforcing his position as the company's main visionary force. Between 1965 and 1967, Malozemoff and Newmont quadrupled the sum spent by the company on exploration, reaching $4.4 million in 1966. The company's Palabora Mine in South Africa also came into production in early 1966 and began paying dividends by the end of the year. Between Palabora, Tsumeb, and O'okiep, Newmont realized dividends approaching $20 million from its southern African properties. Toward the end of 1966 and into 1967, Newmont acquired a 33 percent interest in Foote Mineral Company, a major producer of iron alloys and lithium products. This purchase enabled Newmont to place three representatives (one of them Malozemoff) on Foote's board of directors. Several Newmont ventures in the 1960s, however, were unsuccessful. A lead-zinc mine in Algeria became nationalized by the government; Granduc Mine, an underground copper project in Canada, encountered a series of costly construction and development delays, including an avalanche that dumped 50,000 tons of snow on the work camp and killed 26 laborers; and a joint venture with Cerro Corporation, Atlantic Cement Company, failed to turn a profit for several years, running into alternating problems with machinery and labor.

In 1969 Newmont merged completely with Magma Copper, of which it already owned 80.6 percent. Magma's minority stockholders were issued Newmont convertible preferred stock in exchange for their shares. With earnings of over $26 million at the time of the merger, Magma was the fourth-largest domestic copper producer, and by 1970 about three-fourths of Newmont's revenue came from copper. The company's strategy of shifting away from reliance on foreign sources continued; by 1970, U.S. and Canadian investments accounted for 65 percent of Newmont's net income. Many in the industry considered this a positive development, since the early 1970s were a period of increased mine nationalization as well as political machinations that made foreign investments riskier than usual.

Newmont's direction in the 1970s was toward becoming more of an operating company and less of a holding company. An ambitious expansion program was undertaken at Magma, which quickly became Newmont's chief source of revenues, accounting for about 36 percent in 1972. This expansion was largely accomplished by investing around $90 million in 1971 in two Arizona locations, Superior and San Manuel, including $18 million for a new electrolytic copper refinery at San Manuel. The expansion raised the combined output of San Manuel and

Superior to 145,000 tons of copper in 1972. By that same year, 78 percent of Newmont's net income was generated by companies operating inside Canada and the United States. Foreign interests contributed about 28 percent of the company's revenues, with Tsumeb, O'okiep, Palabora, and Southern Peru Copper leading the way.

The 1970s were a roller-coaster decade for Newmont. Technical problems plagued the new smelter at San Manuel in 1972, and new anti-pollution laws required the installation of another $30 million worth of equipment. By 1973, however, these and other problems were largely solved. Labor problems at Granduc improved, and Newmont's other Canadian mine, Similkameen, enjoyed a smooth first year of operation, producing near its capacity. In 1974, Newmont set a net earnings record of $113.6 million. That same year, the company paid $28.5 million to increase its interest in Foote Mineral Company to 83 percent of voting shares. The Foote acquisition gave Newmont control of the non-communist world's largest deposit of spodumene ore (used to produce lithium), located at Kings Mountain, North Carolina.

Between 1975 and 1978 copper prices plummeted, dropping from $1.55 a pound in 1974 to as low as 50 cents—resulting in the selling price of copper falling below its production cost in the United States. In 1977, Newmont led a consortium of six companies in purchasing Peabody Coal Company from Kennecott, which had been ordered in 1971 by the Federal Trade Commission to divest itself of what was the largest coal producer in the United States. Newmont's share in the consortium, which called itself Peabody Holding Company, was 27.5 percent. With copper prices in free-fall, however, Newmont's net income declined to $5.1 million in 1977, a drop in earnings also affected by a $15-million strike at Peabody and the closing of the Granduc mine.

Newmont recovered somewhat toward the end of the 1970s. Costs were cut by suspending operations at Idarado Mining Company of which Newmont owned 80 percent, as well as at the Gamsberg zinc project, a South African joint venture. In April 1978, the end of the nationwide coal strike also allowed Peabody to become profitable once again. The Newmont Oil subsidiary began to benefit from the price deregulation of new natural gas, and higher gold prices were beneficial to the wholly owned Carlin operation. Even the often sluggish Atlantic Cement Company showed a profit in 1978 after losing about $400,000 the previous year. By 1979 gold was beginning to play an increasingly important role for Newmont. With high gold prices, it took only 30 months for the Telfer gold mine (70 percent owned by Newmont) in Australia's Great Sandy Desert to pay back the $23.5 million laid out in development costs. In fact, Newmont earned more from gold in 1979 than it had from all its operations the year before.

In 1980, Newmont began processing gold ore from its Maggie Creek mine, 14 miles south of the main area of the Carlin operation. The open pit orebodies at Maggie Creek were estimated at 4.8 million tons of ore containing about 440,000 ounces of gold. Then, less than a mile from Maggie Creek, Newmont discovered Gold Quarry—the twentieth century's most important gold strike—which was estimated to contain over 8 million ounces of gold. In 1981, while Newmont was still assessing the importance of the Gold Quarry discovery, shares of Newmont were being acquired by Consolidated Gold Fields Plc. (CGF), a British mining company. Malozemoff was able to reach an agreement with CGF under which CGF would end up holding 26 percent interest in Newmont, but would not attempt to increase that share. This agreement was changed in 1983, allowing CGF up to a 33.3 percent interest in Newmont as well as a maximum of three representatives on Newmont's board instead of the previous limit of two.

Newmont purchased the Miami, Arizona, copper operations of City Service Company in 1983. The operations included the Pinto Valley open pit mine, whose annual capacity rated about 70,000 tons of copper contained in concentrate. Malozemoff ended his long tenure as Newmont's chief executive officer in September 1985 and was succeeded by Gordon R. Parker, who had been named company president ten months earlier as well as president and chief executive officer of Magma. Malozemoff, 75 years old at the time, retained his chairmanship of Newmont's board. In October, Newmont reorganized its management structure, consolidating its operations into four groups headed by executives with global responsibility: non-ferrous metals under David C. Ridinger; Carlin Gold Mining Company and the company's 70 percent interest in Telfer gold mine under T. Peter Philip; lithium and industrial minerals under Thomas A. Williams; and energy operations, including Peabody and Newmont Oil, under Edward P. Fontaine.

Carlin Gold Mining Company's name was changed to Newmont Gold Company in 1986. The following year, corporate raider T. Boone Pickens and his investment group, Ivanhoe Partners, attempted a takeover of Newmont, making an offer of $95-a-share for the 90 percent of Newmont they did not already control. The takeover attempt was thwarted, however, when in one day CGF hiked its share of the company up to 47.7 percent, a move made possible by Newmont's announcement of a $33-a-share dividend payment as part of a new restructuring plan. In order to compensate for the cash drain the payout created, Newmont began a series of selling off its properties. Magma Copper was spun off to Newmont shareholders, saving Newmont the costs of modernizing Magma's facilities. At the end of 1987, the company sold its 80 percent interest in Foote Mineral for about $74 million. Another $350 million was brought in by the sale of Newmont's 4.2 million shares of Du Pont stock. Finally, all four mines in South Africa held by Newmont were sold for $125 million.

The main consequence of Newmont's restructuring was the shift of the company's focus to gold exclusively. In 1988, the company sold its interests in Newmont Oil and in both Canadian ventures, Sherritt Gordon and Similkameen. With the 1990 sale of its 55 percent interest in Peabody, Newmont had shed virtually all of its non-gold holdings and was the largest gold producer in North America. In 1991, a merger was arranged, and then collapsed, between Newmont and American Barrick Resources. American Barrick had acquired a 49 percent interest in Newmont in a deal the previous year with Hanson Plc., which had acquired the shares when it took over CGF in 1989.

In 1992, Newmont continued to actively explore for gold, both in North America and abroad. A joint venture was agreed upon with the Republic of Uzbekistan for producing gold at Muruntau, and similar gold exploration ventures were initiated with Costa Rica, Thailand, Peru, and Indonesia. In the United States, Newmont acquired the rights to two prospective gold properties, Grassy Mountain in Oregon and Musgrove Creek in Idaho. In light of Newmont's record of flexibility and good timing with regards to various geographical and metallurgical factors, it seems likely that many of these upcoming ventures will prove to be successful.

Principal Subsidiaries: Newmont Gold Company (90.1%); Newmont Exploration Limited; Resurrection Mining Company; Idarado Mining Company (80.1%); Dawn Mining Company (51%).

Further Reading: Brandon, Keith, "A Diversified Investment in Minerals," *Barron's,* May 26, 1941; "Newmont Mining's Fourth Generation of Gamblers," *Fortune,* October 1965; MacRae, Robert M., "Resourceful Investor," *Barron's,* July 31, 1967; Sherman, Joseph V., "Over the Rainbow," *Barron's,* October 2, 1967; "Newmont Mining a Sound Value," *Financial World,* July 1, 1970; "From Shotguns to Rifles," *Forbes,* June 15, 1971; Anreder, Steven S., "Newmont Poised for '73 Recovery," *Barron's,* December 4, 1972; Staebler, Jonathon, "Peak Results on Tap for Newmont Mining," *Barron's,* November 5, 1973; "The Engineer Who's Domesticating Newmont," *Business Week,* October 5, 1974; "Peabody Terms Told," *Chemical Week,* December 8, 1976; Maresca, Stephen, "Bright Copper Outlook Adds Luster to Newmont Mining," *Barron's,* November 27, 1978; Berman, Phyllis, "Will Copper Outshine Gold?" *Forbes,* November 26, 1979; "Carl in Gold Mining Will Develop Its Maggie Creek Deposits," *Engineering and Mining Journal,* October 1980; Yafie, Roberta C., "Newmont Mining Agrees to Buy Cities Service Ariz. Copper Operations," *American Metal Market,* December 3, 1982; Guzzardi, Walter, "The Huge Find in Roy Ash's Backyard," *Fortune,* December 27, 1982; Botta, Mike, "Two Mining Firms Draw Closer," *American Metal Market,* November 3, 1983; Jordan, Carol L., "Newmont Mining Reorganizes and Consolidates Management," *American Metal Market,* October 3, 1985; Davis, Jo Ellen, "One Swallow Could Make Pickens' Summer," *Business Week,* September 14, 1987; Welling, Kathryn M., "After the Raid," *Barron's,* June 6, 1988; "Gold Fields or Mine Field?" *Forbes,* April 2, 1990; Rudnitsky, Howard, "Sir Jimmy's Golden Deal," *Forbes,* July 8, 1991; Rudnitsky, Howard, "Sir Jimmy's Busted Deal," *Forbes,* August 19, 1991; *Newmont Mining Corporation, 1991 Annual Report,* Denver, Newmont Mining Corporation, 1992.

—Robert R. Jacobson

NEWS CORPORATION LIMITED

2 Holt Street
Sydney, New South Wales 2010
Australia
(02) 288-3000
Fax: (02) 288-3424

Public Company
Incorporated: 1979
Employees: 30,700
Sales: A$8.76 billion (US$6.77 billion)
Stock Exchanges: Amsterdam Australia Hong Kong London
New York New Zealand Paris Tokyo
SICs: 2711 Newspapers: Publishing, or Publishing &
Printing; 2731 Books: Publishing, or Publishing &
Printing; 4833 Television Broadcasting Stations; 7812
Motion Picture and Video Tape Production; 4512 Air
Transportation, Scheduled

News Corporation Limited is the holding company for the range of enterprises created or acquired since the 1950s by the Australian-American businessman Rupert Murdoch. It is the largest publisher of English-language newspapers in the world, and its subsidiaries include HarperCollins Publishers, the world's largest publisher of English-language books, as well as television stations, film production companies, printing firms, and airlines.

Rupert Murdoch was born in Melbourne in 1931, the son of Sir Keith Murdoch, managing director of the Herald and Weekly Times newspaper group. Sir Keith did not own many shares in the group, but was the major shareholder in News Ltd., which published the Adelaide *News* and *Sunday Mail,* and in a Brisbane company whose two newspapers he amalgamated into one, the *Courier-Mail.*

Sir Keith died in 1952. After graduating that year, his son spent some months as a junior subeditor at the London *Daily Express* and returned to Australia in 1953 to take over the Adelaide newspapers. His father's executors sold the *Courier-Mail* to the Herald and Weekly Times group. In 1956 News Ltd. acquired the Perth *Sunday Times;* in 1957 it launched *TV Week*—inspired by the American *TV Guide*—which was to be the most profitable of all its Australian publications. In 1958 control of Channel 9, one of two TV channels in Adelaide, was awarded to Southern Television Corporation, in which News Ltd. had 60 percent of the shares. Murdoch's empire-building had begun.

The year 1960 was a watershed. News Ltd. bought Cumberland Newspapers, a group of local papers in the Sydney suburbs, then acquired the Sydney *Daily* and *Sunday Mirror* from the Fairfax group. Rohan Rivett, the editor of the Adelaide *News,* became the first of many editors to be fired from Murdoch newspapers. Five weeks before his dismissal he had been celebrating his acquittal on charges of seditious libel. These had arisen out of the *News*'s criticisms of a state government inquiry into the case of an Aborigine found guilty of a murder that Rivett, and Murdoch, thought he had not committed. His departure marked the end of Murdoch's leanings toward anti-establishment views.

In 1964 News Ltd. launched *The Australian,* Australia's first national newspaper, based in Canberra. Murdoch considered the venture prestigious enough to be worth a loss of A$30 million, over the course of 20 years, to keep going. Typesetting in Caberra and flying the matrices to Melbourne and Sydney for printing were difficult, and in 1967 the paper was moved to Sydney. In 1969 its latest editor oversaw its re-adoption of opposition to the Vietnam War, a return to the stance first espoused by the paper in 1965 when Australian troops were initially assigned there.

Murdoch, meanwhile, was in London. In October 1968 Robert Maxwell had offered to buy the United Kingdom's News of the World Organization (NOTW) for £26 million. The company owned the Sunday newspaper *News of the World,* the Bemrose group of local newspapers, the papermaker Townsend Hook, and several other publishing companies. It had been run since 1891 by the Carr family, which had now split into two factions, one led by NOTW's chairman, Sir William Carr, with 32 percent of the shares, the other by his cousin, Derek Jackson, whose decision to sell his 25 percent stake had precipitated the crisis. Maxwell, born in Czechoslovakia, was then a Labour member of Parliament. Maxwell's foreign origin, combined with his political opinions, provoked a hostile response to his bid from the Carrs and from the editor of the *News of the World,* Stafford Somerfield, who declared that the paper was—and should remain—as British as roast beef and Yorkshire pudding. News Ltd. arranged to swap shares in some of its minor ventures with the Carrs and by December it controlled 40 percent of the NOTW stock. In January 1969 Maxwell's bid was rejected at a shareholders' meeting where half of those present were company staff, temporarily given voting shares. Illness removed Sir William Carr from the chairmanship in June of 1969. Murdoch succeeded him. In 1977, just before his death, Carr wrote to Maxwell to express regret that he had spurned his original offer for NOTW. In 1990 the *News of the World* was the biggest-selling English-language newspaper in the world.

Murdoch next sought a British daily to accompany the *News of the World.* He found it in 1969, when IPC decided to sell off *The Sun,* which had been launched in 1964 but had never been profitable, with sales of about one million copies. Under Murdoch, by contrast, *The Sun*'s circulation reached two million in 1971 and three million in 1973.

NOTW had added television to its list of interests in 1969, when it bought eight percent of the voting shares in London Weekend Television (LWT), a company created in 1968 to run commercial television from Friday evening to Sunday night in a large and lucrative region centered on the capital city. The holding was rapidly built up to 36 percent of the voting shares and Murdoch became a non-executive director of LWT. He promptly saw to the dismissal of its managing director and took the chair of the executive committee in charge of scheduling, thus running the station without having been awarded a franchise. The Independent Television Authority ordered LWT to put its affairs in order without Murdoch in charge. The controversy over this incident was revived in 1977 when the government-appointed Committee on the Future of Broadcasting made severe criticisms of the authority's failure to enforce its own rules. By that time, however, Murdoch had moved to the United States, and NOTW's shares in LWT were sold in 1980.

Back in Australia, Murdoch found that *The Australian* had become too liberal for his liking. In 1971 he dismissed its editor, Adrian Deamer, who had been in the post for three years—a remarkable record, considering that the paper would have 13 editors in its first 16 years. In 1972 News Ltd. bought the Sydney *Daily* and *Sunday Telegraph* from Packer's Consolidated Press, which had been losing circulation to the three Fairfax papers, the *Sydney Morning Herald,* the *Sun,* and the Sunday *Sun-Herald.* The ailing *Sunday Australian* was absorbed into the *Sunday Telegraph* soon afterward.

Murdoch had become close to Gough Whitlam, then leader of the Australian Labor Party, and gave A$75,000 to the party's advertising campaign in 1972. If this was a return to Murdoch's earlier radicalism, it was short-lived. Within three years his papers were attacking the Labor Party again, with *The Australian,* for example, using raw figures, rather than seasonally-adjusted ones, to suggest, wrongly, that unemployment was rising. After the 1975 election, in which Whitlam was defeated, Murdoch himself, using a "special correspondent" byline, wrote a report for *The Australian* on the Labor Party's secret—and eventually fruitless—appeal to Saddam Hussein, the dictator of Iraq, for financial aid, which resulted in a meeting in Sydney between Whitlam and Saddam's nephew. Ironically, what appeared to be just more anti-Whitlam propaganda was true.

In 1973 the News group made its first American acquisitions, purchasing three newspapers in San Antonio, Texas. One of these, the *San Antonio News,* achieved brief but worldwide notoriety in 1976 with the striking but inaccurate headline "Killer Bees Move North." The next American acquisition, in 1976, was the *New York Post,* the city's only evening paper. This was swiftly followed, early in 1977, by the purchase of the New York Magazine Company, which published the magazines *New York* and *Village Voice.* The acquisitions were, in fact, accomplished so quickly that *New York*'s proposed comment on the *Post* purchase, a picture of Murdoch as a killer bee, had to be dropped.

Murdoch's personal supervision of the *Post* led to an increased circulation, most notably through a series of reports on the "Son of Sam" serial killings, culminating in the misleading headline "How I Became a Mass Killer" over a selection of old and innocuous letters from the murderer to a girlfriend. The *Post* did especially well in the summer of 1979 when, armed with separate agreements with the unions, a long-running strike kept its rivals closed. The paper continued to suffer from finan-

cial problems, caused partly by the reluctance of the large department stores to advertise in such a down-market publication.

Murdoch did not neglect the Australian sector of his growing empire. In 1978 News Ltd. joined forces with the Packer's group and the British football pools company Vernons to start a New South Wales lottery. In 1979 it built up a 48.2 percent stake in Channel TEN-10, a Sydney television station. At the Australian Broadcasting Tribunal hearings into its purchase, Murdoch praised the work of its chairman and promised that the station would retain total independence without interference. Two weeks after the tribunal approved the change of ownership, the chief executive was replaced by a News Ltd. director with no television experience; two months later the chairman resigned.

A much bigger acquisition followed, also in 1979, when News Ltd. gained control of ATI, a group of airlines and other transport firms. Its founder, Sir Reginald Ansett, stayed on as chairman of ATI, but Murdoch became chief executive. Murdoch agreed with Sir Peter Abeles, the chairman of the TNT transport group, that News Ltd. and TNT should have 50–50 ownership of ATI and that Abeles should become joint chief executive. There then followed lengthy public hearings before the Australian Broadcasting Tribunal on whether News Ltd. should be allowed to own a Melbourne television station, the original goal of the ATI/TNT dealings. The tribunal decided against granting approval, mainly on the grounds that a Sydney-Melbourne combination under one company would have too big a role in network operations. By the time of the ruling, however, News Ltd. had paid for the station and the statutory six months allowed for ordering divestment had passed; the tribunal's decision had no effect. The ruling was eventually reversed on appeal.

The current structure of Rupert Murdoch's group of companies also dates from the creation of News Corporation as the main holding company in 1979. In 1990 Murdoch owned only 7,200 shares in News Corporation itself, but he also had control of Cruden Investments Pty Ltd., which owned more than 116 million shares, about 54 percent of the total.

In 1981 News International, the British arm of the Murdoch group, acquired 42 percent of the voting shares in the British publishers William Collins and Sons and bought the London *Times,* the *Sunday Times,* the *Times Literary Supplement,* and the *Times Educational Supplement* from what is now The Thomson Corporation. Fifteen years earlier, Lord Thomson's own purchase of The *Times* and its supplements had been investigated by the Monopolies Commission, as Lonrho was to be investigated when it made a bid for the London *Observer* later in 1981. Yet the government of the day waived this requirement in News International's case.

At the same time as News Corporation's image was being pushed up-market by these ventures, its down-market newspapers were all engaged in attracting more readers with an adaptation of bingo. In Britain, *Sun* bingo cards were sent to every household, and rival papers all picked up the game. It then spread to the Sydney *Daily Mirror* and to the *New York Post,* where it had to be renamed Wingo for copyright reasons. The rival *Daily News* responded with its own version, Zingo. Murdoch has since disposed of the *Post,* but acquired the *Boston Herald*—formerly the *Herald-American*—in 1982 and the *Chicago Sun-Times* in 1984.

The Sun's editors—Larry Lamb and, from 1981, his successor Kelvin McKenzie—brought the paper into line with Murdoch's political views. Thus in 1982 the paper offered enthusiastic support to the British forces in the Falklands War (as almost all the national newspapers did), but characteristically went further, marking the sinking of the Argentine cruiser *General Belgrano* with the headline "Gotcha!" and calling the BBC's defense correspondent and two rival newspapers traitors. *The Sun* remains the biggest-selling daily newspaper in Britain.

Murdoch's up-market papers could be tempted by sensationalism as well. In 1983 News Corporation was severely embarrassed by the revelation that the much-publicized secret diaries of Adolf Hitler, which the *Sunday Times* planned to serialize under an arrangement with the German magazine *Stern,* were forgeries. Lord Dacre, better known as the historian Hugh Trevor-Roper, who served as one of the "national" non-executive directors of Times Newspapers, first declared that the samples he had seen were genuine, then told the editor of the *Sunday Times* that they were forgeries just as the printing of the world exclusive story began. Murdoch decided to go ahead with the printing; *Stern* had to return the money it had paid for the diaries, and the *Sunday Times* actually retained some of the extra readers the story had attracted to it.

The appointment of Andrew Neil as editor of the *Sunday Times* later in 1983 negated the guarantees exacted from News International by the British government two years before, since the required consultation with the newspaper's staff did not take place. Harold Evans had reluctantly resigned from the editorship of the *Times* in 1982, at Murdoch's request. Evans could have appealed over Murdoch's head to the "national" directors but chose not to do so, leaving the guarantees untested.

News Corporation first ventured into satellite television in 1983. It acquired majority holdings in Satellite Television PLC (SATV), which had been set up in 1980 to supply a U.K.-based service to northern Europe, and in the Inter-American Satellite Television Network, which was renamed Skyband Inc. and had its head office moved from California to New York. It was largely to gain access to a supply of feature films and television programs that News Corporation bought into the Twentieth Century Fox Film Corporation, also in 1983. Twentieth Century Fox has since become a wholly owned subsidiary. Within two years, with the News International papers all featuring articles attacking the BBC, SATV, renamed Sky Channel, had about three million subscribers in 11 European countries and was available in Britain on cable.

During 1985 Murdoch and his closest advisers planned the removal of all the News International papers from the Fleet Street area, the traditional base for national newspapers, to a plant at Wapping, in east London, where troubled relations with the print unions could be superseded by a single union agreement with the Electrical, Electronic, Telecommunications and Plumbing Union (EETPU). Electronic typesetting equipment was ordered, but kept hidden from the print workers; the

EETPU recruited new production staff, and then, when the plant was ready, the journalists on the four newspapers were given from one to three days to move or to leave the company and the plant began producing papers in January 1986. It was not only the 5,500 sacked print workers who felt somewhat betrayed after this dramatic move. The EETPU never did get a single union agreement, and News International does not recognize any trade unions. In 1987 the British company acquired a fifth newspaper, *Today,* from the company Lonrho—which had bought out the newspaper's founder, Eddy Shah—soon after its launch in 1986.

While 1986 was a year of triumph for Murdoch in Britain, in Australia it was a year of retreat. News Ltd. sold off both Channel TEN-10 in Sydney and ATV 10 in Melbourne, as well as radio stations, a record company, and three newspapers. However, 1987 was the year of the acquisition of the Herald and Weekly Times group once run by Murdoch's father. Shortly before the deal went ahead, Murdoch had a private meeting with the prime minister, Bob Hawke, and the treasurer, Paul Keating, and his Australian newspapers all switched political allegiance to Labor, the governing party. The purchase of the Herald and Weekly Times group cost A$2.3 billion, was the biggest single takeover of newspapers ever accomplished, and made News Corporation the largest publisher of English-language newspapers in the world. Shortly afterward the chairman of the Australian Press Council resigned in protest at the government's failure to invoke the Foreign Takeovers Act against Murdoch, for by this time Murdoch had become an American citizen. It was not until 1989 that newly released government documents revealed that the Foreign Investment Review Board had opposed the acquisition, although Prime Minister Hawke declared that it had not.

News Corporation ended 1987 with two more purchases, the *South China Morning Post,* the most important English-language newspaper in Hong Kong, and the American publishing house Harper & Row. It then sold 50 percent of Harper & Row to William Collins and Sons. This arrangement lasted only until April of 1989, when News International bought Collins outright. HarperCollins Publishers, created as a merger of these and other book and map publishers, is now the largest English-language publisher in the world.

In 1988, three decades after he had borrowed its format for his own publication on television, Murdoch bought the American magazine *TV Guide* and the company that published it, Triangle Publications, for $2.83 billion. Fox Broadcasting Company started up during the same year as the first new television network in the United States to challenge the long-established trio of ABC, CBS, and NBC. Its huge initial costs were reduced, fortuitously, when a Hollywood writers' strike allowed it to run a large number of repeats, and it broadcast at first only on Saturdays and Sundays.

In February 1989 Sky Television was launched in the United Kingdom as a four-channel service available at first only on cable but increasingly via satellite receiver dishes. By the summer of 1990 it was reaching 1.6 million households, but the losses incurred in its development were a major cause of declining profits for News Corporation, along with the eight-month-long airline pilots' strike in Australia. It was claimed that profits would have been higher than in the financial year 1988–1989 if these two factors were excluded. Profits were also being eroded by the rising cost of interest payments on the group's rising level of debts.

Murdoch had once said that he never gave anyone shares but just borrowed to finance expansion. The next year or two revealed the disadvantages of that policy, as the sale of his Australian book publishing and distribution companies in June of 1989 proved to be the start of a trend, though revenue and profits from most of News Corporation's subsidiaries continued to grow. In 1990 it sold 49 percent of South China Morning Post (Holdings) Ltd., parts of its minority holdings in the news agency Reuters and in the publishers Pearson plc, the American publishing firm J.B. Lippincott, the British papermaker Townsend Hook, the Fox subsidiary DeLuxe Laboratories and the American magazines *Star* and *Sportswear International.* Its acquisitions that year—25 percent of the Spanish publisher Grupo Zeta; the whole of F. F. Publishing and Broadsystem Ltd. in Britain; and 50 percent holdings, with Hungarian partners, in two publishing companies, Mai Nap Rt and Reform Rt—were relatively minor.

One way around the group's increasing financial problems was to juggle the figures in News Corporation's annual reports. For example, the 1988 losses by News Ltd., the Australian division of the group, were shown as A$202 million in the 1989 report but as A$83 million in 1990, although the overall impact on group profits was said to be the same in both reports. Another way was to restructure the subsidiaries so that a higher proportion of group profits could be made in tax havens, such as Bermuda. In 1989, 25 percent of profits were attributed to tax haven companies; in 1990 the proportion was 54.5 percent, and News Corporation's effective tax rate was 1.76 percent rather than the statutory 39 percent.

The merger of Sky Television with its smaller rival, BSB, in November 1990 did nothing to stem the continuing losses from satellite television, since it meant that BSB's £380 million loan facility was withdrawn. It also turned out that neither company had consulted the Independent Broadcasting Authority, which licensed BSB's operations, and had thus breached the contract. Once again, as with ATV 10 in Melbourne, Murdoch presented the regulatory body with a *fait accompli.* By mid-1991 Sky, now renamed BSkyB, had swallowed up £1.5 billion in investments from various shareholders, among whom News Corporation was the largest, with a 49 percent stake.

Between August and December 1990 the value of News Corporation shares fell by two-thirds. News Corporation's debts, to 146 banks, stood at more than US$8.2 billion, and Murdoch had to promise to repay US$1.2 billion by June 1992.

In 1990 Murdoch began a well-planned, controlled restructuring of News Corporation's massive debt. After months of foot-dragging, his banks arranged a refinancing package dubbed "Project Dolphin" that called for US$7.6 billion to be repaid by 1994. In return, the interest rate on the debts was raised by a full percentage point, and Murdoch agreed to a fire sale on many of his recent acquisitions. Between February 1991 and February 1992, Murdoch parted with $800 million worth of businesses, including most of News Corporation's United States maga-

zines—*New Woman, New York,* and *Premier*—and equity in recently acquired Group Zeta. In the process, Murdoch's equity in News Corp has been reduced to about 30 percent, thereby reducing his volatile influence on the company but retaining his marketing savvy.

As News Corporation's stock price rose, it sold $180 million of convertible preference shares (a type of equity) to three American companies, then divested itself of 55 percent of its Australian printing and magazine businesses. The resulting new company, called Pacific Magazines and Printing, took A$300 million in debt from News Corp's balance sheet and raised A$382 million from investors via a rights issue.

By the end of 1991, Murdoch had won back the confidence of his banks. They agreed to extend News Corp's repayment schedule by three years, allowing him to carry $3 billion of debt that had been due in February 1994 until 1997. The banks also permitted News Corp to pay some dividends and keep some of the proceeds of its asset sales.

Against all odds, and to the surprise of many observers, Murdoch and News Corporation not only survived the largest restructuring outside bankruptcy court in history, but went on to reach new highs in the early 1990s. By third quarter 1991, News Corporation's net profits had skyrocketed to A$107.5 million ($84.3 million). The 315-percent increase from the previous year may have salved the pain of Murdoch's divestment from the magazine business.

Although News Corp's British and Australian tabloids continue to bring in steady profits, Murdoch has turned his attention almost exclusively to movies and television, having sold nearly all the company's American newspapers and magazines except *TV Guide.* News Corp's Fox network has topped ratings charts with shows such as *The Simpsons* and *Beverly Hills 90210,* Twentieth Century Fox's *Home Alone* became one of the most popular movies in history, and even BSkyB began to show promise. By the end of 1992, BSkyB had subscriptions of 3.4 million households in Great Britain and Ireland, amounting to approximately 19 percent of the total population of the United Kingdom.

Although Murdoch was discouraged from going on another acquisitions spree, he did forge an alliance with French TV giant Canal Plus to develop pay television services throughout Europe. With only six percent of West European homes equipped with cable, the market for pay-TV is regarded as a largely untapped one. Analysts predict that News Corp/Canal Plus will be a formidable opponent in the battle for subscribers.

News Corporation's enormous commercial weight, coupled with its accompanying social influence, have made both the group and Murdoch, its chief executive, the subject of significant controversy. This is usually presented in personalized terms. For example, there are several biographies of Murdoch available, but no history of the group as such. This approach tends to distort the allocation of responsibility for the activities of a group that its admirers regard as a great achievement and its detractors as a dangerous concentration of power.

Principal Subsidiaries: News Ltd.; Nationwide News Pty Ltd.; The Herald and Weekly Times Ltd.; News International plc

(U.K.); News Group Newspapers Ltd. (U.K.); Times Newspapers Holdings Ltd. (U.K.); British Sky Broadcasting plc (U.K., 50%); South China Morning Post (Holdings) Ltd. (Hong Kong, 51%); HarperCollins U.S. Inc.; HarperCollins (UK) Ltd.; News Publishing Australia Ltd. (U.S.A.); News America Publishing Inc. (U.S.A.); Fox Inc. (U.S.A.); Twentieth Century Fox Film Corporation (U.S.A.); Access Securities Pty Ltd.; News Publishers Holdings Pty Ltd.; New U.S. Holding Pty Ltd.; News Securities B.V. (Netherlands); Newscorp Investments Ltd. (U.K.); Newscorp Securities Ltd.; The News Investments (Australia); News Publishing Australia Ltd. (U.S.A.); New Guinea Courier Pty Ltd. (62.5%); News Data Security Products Ltd. (60%); News Datacom Research Ltd. (60%); Post Courier Ltd. (62%); Rabaul Times Pty Ltd. (62.5%); Sky Radio Ltd. (51%); South Pacific Post Pty Ltd. (62.5%); South China Morning Post (Holdings) Ltd. (51%); Spectak Productions Pty Ltd. (51%).

Further Reading: Regan, Simon, *Rupert Murdoch,* London, Angus and Robertson, 1976; Leapman, Michael, *Barefaced Cheek,* London, Hodder and Stoughton, 1983; Munster, George, *A Paper Prince,* Ringwood, Penguin Books Australia, 1985; Harris, Robert, *Selling Hitler,* London, Faber and Faber, 1986; Wintour, Charles, *The Rise and Fall of Fleet Street,* London, Hutchinson, 1989; "100 Leading National Advertisers: Monsanto Co.; Montgomery Ward & Co.; Nestle SA; News Corp.; Nike Inc.," *Advertising Age,* September 25, 1991; "Back From the Brink," *Economist,* December 7, 1991; Michaels, James W., "Rapping With Rupert," *Forbes,* September 28, 1992; Williams, Michael, "Giant Tag Team for Pay-TV," *Variety,* October 12, 1992.

—Patrick Heenan
updated by April Dougal

NINTENDO CO., LTD.

60, Fukuine Kamitakamatsu-cho
Higashiyama-ku, Kyoto 605
Japan
(075) 541-6111
Fax: (075) 551-2722

Public Company
Incorporated: 1889 as Marufuku Company, Ltd.
Employees: 2,280
Sales: ¥471.42 billion (US$3.95 billion)
Stock Exchanges: Tokyo Osaka Kyoto
SICs: 3944 Games, Toys, and Children's Vehicles

Nintendo Co., Ltd. is a toy and home-entertainment concern
that is famous worldwide for its popular home video games.
Nintendo's products moved in the mid-1980s from the relative
obscurity of the amusement arcade to change the concept of
home entertainment in both Japan and the United States. Nintendo's main U.S. product, the Nintendo Entertainment System
(NES), and its Japanese counterpart, the Family Computer
(Famicom), were embraced by the consumers of both nations
with an enthusiasm normally granted to short-term fads. In
Japan one in three households bought a Famicom, and sales
trends in the United States pointed toward a similarly spectacular distribution rate for the NES. Nintendo's success proved to
be no mere fad. What kept Nintendo Mania, as it was known in
the United States, from going the way of other toy booms was
Nintendo's ability to maintain customer interest in its arcade-
quality home video games over a long period of time. Nintendo's products and its marketing methods—which featured
restraint, an obsessive interest in quality control, and an effective public relations scheme—gave it, according to a Nintendo
executive quoted in *Business Week* in 1987, "a boom with no
bust."

Nintendo was founded as the Marufuku Company, Ltd., in
Kyoto, Japan, in 1889 by Fusajiro Yamauchi, the great grandfather of the current president of Nintendo. Marufuku made
playing cards for the Japanese game of Hanafuda, which is said
to have had its origin in Tarot cards. In 1907 Marufuku introduced the first Western-style playing cards in Japan. Marufuku
first made the Western-style cards for Russian prisoners of war
during the Russo-Japanese War of 1904 to 1905 when the
soldiers wore out the decks they had brought from Russia.

Between 1907 and World War II Marufuku solidified its status
in the playing-card business. World War I, in which Japan
fought on the side of the Allies, did not affect business in any
remarkable way. In 1925, however, Marufuku began exporting
Hanafuda cards to Japanese emigre communities in South
America, Korea, and Australia. The years 1925 to 1928 also
saw Marufuku developing a new, more effective marketing
strategy that placed its products in tobacco shops. These marketing moves were complemented by Marufuku's aggressive
advertising, as Japan's business practices became more Wes-
ternized.

World War II devastated the Japanese economy and delivered a
hard blow even to the previously modest but stable home
amusement market. The playing card industry and Marufuku,
though, fared far better than most. In the austere postwar
climate, when entertainment had to be cheap and simple, the
demand for playing cards only decreased slightly. Marufuku,
whose physical plant had not been damaged much in the war,
thrived in the years following the war.

Hiroshi Yamauchi became Marufuku's president in 1949, embarking on a wide-ranging program to modernize and rationalize the way his family's company was run. In 1952 Marufuku
consolidated its factories, which had been scattered throughout
Kyoto. In 1951 Yamauchi changed the company name to one
more appropriate to the leisure industry; he called it the Nintendo Playing Card Company, Ltd. In Japanese, the word "Nintendo" has a proverbial meaning that loosely translates as,
"You work hard but, in the end, it's in heaven's hands."

Business boomed in the postwar era. In 1953 Yamauchi responded to a shortage in playing-card-quality paper by challenging his company to develop plastic playing cards. After
initial difficulties in printing and coating the plastic cards, Nintendo started mass-production. In 1959 Nintendo first showed
its sharp eye for the children's market when it released playing
cards in Japan that were printed with Walt Disney cartoon
characters. By 1962 business was so good that Nintendo decided to go public, listing stock on the Osaka and Kyoto stock
exchanges.

A year later Nintendo began the drive towards diversification
and innovation that eventually led it to the late-1980s boom that
made its name a household word. First, in 1963, Nintendo
augmented its product line by marketing board games as well as
playing cards. By 1969, the game department was so successful
that a new game-production plant was built in Uji city, a suburb
of Kyoto. The year 1970 saw Nintendo introducing electronic
technology for the first time in Japan with its Beam Gun Series.
An especially popular example of this technology was the laser
clay-pigeon shooting system, introduced in 1973, in which
arcade players aimed beams of light at targets projected on a
small movie screen. By 1974, Nintendo was exporting this and
other projection-based games to the United States and Europe.

In the next few years, arcade-game technology made remarkable strides, with Nintendo in the vanguard. In 1975, in cooperation with Mitsubishi Electric, Nintendo first developed a video
game system using a video player—a technology made more
complex the next year when a microprocessor was added to the
system. By 1977, this technology was being marketed as part of

the first, relatively unsophisticated generation of home video games.

In the amusement arcade Nintendo's games were beginning to feature higher levels of technology. In 1978 Nintendo developed and started selling coin-operated video games using microcomputers. This innovation, which in 1981 resulted in such arcade hits as Donkey Kong, gave to arcade video games the complex graphics and stereo sound that Nintendo would later market for home use.

As the 1980s began, Nintendo started selling the Game and Watch product line—a hand-held series of electronic games, such as football, with liquid crystals and digital quartz microhardware. By this time, Nintendo found that its export business required a firmer foothold in the United States and established Nintendo of America, Inc., a wholly owned subsidiary, in New York City. In 1982 the U.S. office was moved to Redmond, Washington, and established there with an operating capital of US$600,000. As the 1980s progressed, the company focused on the development and marketing of home video technology. A new plant was built in 1983 in Uji city to meet the production requirements of Nintendo's new flagship product, the Family Computer. Famicom, which allowed arcade-quality video games to be played at home, came to be played in more than 35 percent of Japan's households.

With Famicom swiftly selling in Japan, Nintendo began exporting it to the United States. In 1985, however, when Nintendo was ready to go into U.S. homes, the home video market there seemed all but tapped out. The United States had experienced a dramatic home video boom in the late 1970s and early 1980s, but by mid-decade this boom had ended, leaving the U.S. industry with hundreds of millions of dollars in losses. The sales of the U.S. home video industry had plummeted from a $3 billion peak in 1983 to a $100 million trough in 1985. These figures did not daunt Nintendo. Nintendo quietly test marketed its games during the darkest depths of the U.S. slump. The U.S. response was quite enthusiastic. Nintendo concluded that the problems in the U.S. home video market were caused by an excess of uninspiring, low-quality games with which an undisciplined industry had flooded the market, losing the trust and patience of its customers as it went after quick profits.

Nintendo came to the United States in full force in 1985 with its American version of the Famicom, renamed the Nintendo Entertainment System. First year profits were astounding, and the skillfully managed demand of the U.S. market showed few signs of softening from its introduction to the end of the decade. According to Yamauchi, Nintendo owed its success to its ability to control the quality and amount of game software being sold for its NES systems. The NES hardware was similar to its Japanese precursor, the Famicom, consisting of a Nintendo control deck, hand controls, and the game cartridges themselves. The control deck sported an eight-bit computer that generated stereo sound and images in 52 colors. It hooked up with the purchaser's television set to allow the viewer to play a complex video game—which could take up to 70 hours to complete—by manipulating a joy stick that controlled movement in two dimensions.

The NES control deck was sold at close to cost, about US$100, to place it in as many homes as possible. Nintendo then made a profit by selling its own game cartridges at US$25 to US$45 apiece, and by arranging lucrative licensing agreements with the numerous computer software manufacturers who were eager to get a piece of Nintendo's pie by creating software for Nintendo's games.

From the very beginning of its U.S. home video foray, Nintendo gained customer loyalty and enthusiasm by producing or licensing sophisticated, challenging, and surprising software for its NES. By 1989, this practice had translated into a 75 percent to 80 percent share of a US$3.4 billion home video game market. But the business strategies that brought Nintendo to its position of dominance soon came under intense scrutiny. Stymied competitors, the U.S. government, and Nintendo's own licensees—who found that Nintendo's mode of granting licenses for game software could soak up as much as 50 percent of their profits—all came to regard Nintendo's trade practices with a suspicion that led to widely publicized litigation.

Nintendo and most industry analysts maintained that a lack of quality control killed the first home video craze in the early 1980s. To avoid making the same mistake, Nintendo erected a demanding series of market controls. Each of its licensees was limited to developing only six new game titles a year. Nintendo manufactured its own patented game cartridges and required would-be software programmers to buy the cartridges in batches of 10,000 and then to assume full responsibility for reselling the game cartridges after they had been programmed by the licensee. To make certain that hardware competitors and software licensees would not try to circumvent Nintendo's control, Nintendo included a security chip in each game cartridge. Games programmed on cartridges lacking this microchip appeared scrambled when one tried to play them. Nintendo reserved the right to modify games or to forbid a licensee's attempts to market a game that had been deemed unsatisfactory in evaluations conducted by the company. When a licensee's game gained approval, the developer had to wait two years before selling a version of its game to Nintendo's competitors. Because of these safeguards, the quality of Nintendo-compatible software remained high. Yet dissatisfaction developed in the U.S. industry with Nintendo's control.

In December of 1988 Tengen Incorporated, a subsidiary of Nintendo's arch-rival Atari and a Nintendo software licensee, filed an antitrust suit. Tengen wished to make games that would run on Nintendo's NES without having to go through Nintendo's series of quality-control measures. Having cracked the code programmed into the microchip in Nintendo's cartridges, Tengen released a game without Nintendo's approval. Nintendo filed a countersuit in February of 1989 claiming patent infringement. By then Tengen's parent company, Atari, had jumped into the fray, filing a separate US$100 million antitrust suit against Nintendo. As the litigation piled up, it became apparent that cultural differences in business practices were near the heart of the conflict.

The 1980s were otherwise a successful decade for Nintendo. It concentrated on popularizing its existing products and developing new ones. In Japan Nintendo developed and started to sell a Family Computer Disk Drive System, which hit the mature

Japanese market in 1986. The way this new product expanded communications capabilities of the Famicom was dramatically showcased in 1987, when Nintendo in Japan organized a nationwide Family Computer Golf Tournament. Players throughout Japan used modems, public telephone lines, and disc facsimile technology to compete against each other from their own living rooms in Nintendo's home video game version of golf. Nintendo looks to the day when nationwide tournaments can be conducted with contestants comfortably ensconced in their living rooms. The network, which Nintendo soon hoped to duplicate in the United States, allowed people throughout Japan not only to play Nintendo games against each other but enabled people to download information from stock companies and trade in stocks, shop, or make ticket reservations.

In 1989 Nintendo announced a deal with Fidelity Investment Services, Boston, to bring this technology to the United States. For about US$200, American owners of Nintendo's NES could buy a modem, a controller/joy stick, and a Fidelity-designed software cartridge that would allow the use of their home-entertainment hardware for a more serious purpose: managing stock portfolios. A US$3 million grant in 1990 to MIT's Media Lab was earmarked for researching the possibility of making video games more educational.

Despite such serious uses of its equipment, Nintendo remained synonymous with high-technology home fun, largely due to its expert marketing techniques and customer support. In 1988 Nintendo began publishing *Nintendo Power* magazine for its U.S. customers. This magazine, aimed at adolescents, was filled with game-playing tips and announcements concerning recently developed games and hardware. For those times when Nintendo Power could not help a frustrated game player, Nintendo introduced a 20-hour telephone bank with advice from 300 game counselors.

Further public-relations efforts included a deal with Ralston Purina Company in May 1989 to market a citrus-flavored Nintendo Cereal System, featuring edible versions of the heroes from Nintendo's video games. In 1989 Nintendo also teamed up with PepsiCo and the nationwide toy retailer Toys 'R' Us for special joint promotions and in-store displays. Nintendo spent $60 million on U.S. advertising that year.

In 1989 Nintendo also returned to the hand-held electronic game market it had created a decade earlier. The battery-operated Game Boy, about the size of a paperback book, featured interchangeable game cartridges, stereo sound, and complex dot-matrix graphics. In Japan Nintendo unveiled a new 16-bit advanced version of the Famicom, dubbed the Super Family Computer. Its more complex electronics meant more challenging games, more interesting graphics, and more realistic sound. Nintendo waited to release the U.S. version of the 16-bit machine until it felt the American market was ready.

The company's leader, Yamauchi, is one of the richest men in Japan, and yet he does not own a car or a television. He professes a disinterest in electronic games, saying he prefers chess-like board games. A frugal and cautious businessman, Yamauchi is known for his reserved demeanor. It is said that his personality matches the minimalist architecture of the company's headquarters in Kyoto. Despite Yamauchi's disciplined management style, the company is still able to create an environment in the research and development division that is conducive to creativity.

In reality, only ten percent of Nintendo's games originate under Nintendo's roof. The bulk of the company's products are created by independent designers, some of whom have become millionaires in their own right in spite of Nintendo's strict guidelines. Designers must build a game on speculation, pay Nintendo to produce the game cartridge, and then pay for the necessary marketing and advertising. These rules and Nintendo's near-monopoly of the video game market have lead many in the industry to characterize Yamauchi as a tyrant.

Developments in the early 1990s may threaten Nintendo's hold on the market. Several anti-trust cases, including one brought by a U.S. Senate subcommittee and the continuing one brought by Time Warner's Atari Games, could change the look of the video game industry. And the continued success of Sega Enterprises, Ltd., could mean that Nintendo has met its first real competitor. It was Sega's 16-bit Genesis System that led Nintendo to upgrade its eight-bit machinery. Sega's growing product line and state-of-the art programs rival those of Nintendo and offer buyers an alternate when they are considering the purchase of a video game system.

Nintendo will not be easily vanquished, however. Indeed, many industry observers see Nintendo as the "next Disney," and a survey of school children found that the Mario character is more popular than Mickey Mouse. Although video game sales slowed in 1990, growing less than half as fast as they had the previous year, Nintendo's sales increased by 63 percent. When U.S. videogame sales reached $4.2 billion by 1991, Nintendo products accounted for $3.2 billion.

In the summer of 1992 Japan's Capcom Co. released Street Fighter II for Nintendo, and the game met with immediate success. For 1992 Nintendo plans to produce Super Mario Paint, a drawing program featuring the company's star character, and a game based on the Road Runner cartoon character. Also in the works is a compact disk package that can play both music CDs or live-action video software. Nintendo hopes eventually to raise its U.S. household penetration rate from 17 percent to the 35 percent it has achieved in Japan. Once Nintendo gets the hardware in place, Yamauchi wants to mirror in the United States the profit-producing ten-to-one software-to-hardware ratio that Nintendo has achieved in Japan.

Principal Subsidiaries: Nintendo of America, Inc. (U.S.A.); Nintendo of Canada, Ltd.

Further Reading: McGill, Douglas C., "Nintendo Scores Big," *New York Times,* December 4, 1988; Moffat, Susan, "Can Nintendo Keep Winning?," *Fortune,* November 5, 1990; "Now, the Latest Beepings from Video-Game Land," *Money,* July 1991; Brandt, Richard, "Clash of the Titans," *Business Week,* September 7, 1992.

—Rene Steinke
updated by Mary McNulty

NORANDA INC.

P.O. Box 45
Commerce Court West
Toronto, Ontario M5L 1B6
Canada
(416) 982-7111
Fax: (416) 982-7423

Public Company
Incorporated: 1922 as Noranda Mines Ltd.
Employees: 51,000
Sales: C$11.86 billion (US$9.43 billion)
Stock Exchanges: Toronto
SICs: 1031 Lead and Zinc Ores; 1041 Gold Ores; 1044
   Silver Ores; 2411 Logging; 2421 Sawmills and Planing
   Mills

In 1922 Noranda was simply a word used to describe northern Canada. Today, the word Noranda conveys images of one of the largest companies in Canada and one of the largest mining companies in the world. The firm has three industry segments with activities throughout the world: mining and minerals (copper, zinc, nickel, and aluminum metallurgical facilities, and aluminum and steel wire rope manufacturing), forest (pulp, paper, and lumber products), and oil and gas.

The history of Noranda begins with the story of a prospector named Edmund Horne, and a hunch. During the early 1920s, at a time when northern Canada was unchartered—the area was mostly wilderness, and prospectors preferred to stay on the familiar grounds of Ontario—Horne was drawn to the Rouyn district in northeastern Quebec. He visited Rouyn repeatedly, because he believed it "didn't seem sensible that all the good geology should quit at the Ontario border!" Horne could reach Rouyn only by way of a chain of lakes and rivers.

His enthusiasm was contagious, and soon a group of 12 men had raised C$225 to finance further explorations. The effort paid off when word of Horne's first strike made it to S. C. Thomson and H. W. Chadbourne, two United States mining engineers with a syndicate of investors interested in exploring Canadian mines. In February of 1922 the syndicate bought an option on Horne's mining claims in Ontario and Quebec and exercised it. Noranda Mines Ltd. was incorporated in 1922 to acquire the U.S. syndicate's mining claims.

The next task was to make the area more accessible to miners. Roads were cut through the forests, and travel often required skis and sleds. Some equipment arrived by barge and ski-equipped plane, both of which could travel the lakes and rivers with relative ease. The mine began producing gold, copper ore, sulfur, and iron, and Noranda convinced the Canadian government to lay roads, railways, and power lines. Eventually, Noranda Mines Ltd. constructed a mill and a smelter, and a city began to take shape in what was once untamed wilderness.

Not satisfied with this initial success, Noranda Mines began to acquire other holdings. In 1927 it bought 80 percent of the stock in Waite-Ackerman-Montgomery Mines, which changed its name six years later to Waite Amulet Mines Ltd. Also that year Noranda acquired a majority interest in Aldermac Mines Ltd., of Rouyn.

Because it believed strongly that Canadian ore should be processed in Canadian plants, Noranda Mines eventually acquired or built several processing companies. Canadian Copper Refiners, Ltd., a company in which Noranda Mines held majority interest, was constructed in eastern Canada in 1929 as a joint effort of Noranda Mines, London's British Metal Corporation, and Nichols Copper Company of New York City. The following year, Noranda Mines purchased a rod and wire mill just east of the copper refinery and bought a substantial interest in Canada Wire & Cable Company, Ltd., of Leaside, Ontario.

In the early 1930s Noranda Power Company, Ltd., a new subsidiary, was formed. In 1934 this company took over the parent firm's power rights and leases on the Victoria River, only to transfer the rights to the government's National Electricity Syndicate under a new agreement four years later.

The 1930s set the stage for a decades-long tradition of growth through acquisitions, as Noranda made its climb to the ranks of Canada's largest companies. In 1935 the firm bought a substantial interest in Pamour Porcupine Mines, Ltd., located in the Porcupine district of Ontario. A few years later, it also acquired a 63.75 percent interest in Compania Minera La India for its gold mines in Nicaragua. In 1939 Noranda bought the controlling interest in Aunor Gold Mines, Ltd., which was formed earlier that year to take over additional Porcupine property. The late 1930s also saw the creation of Noranda Exploration Company, Ltd., a subsidiary formed in 1938 to undertake exploration work in Quebec.

By 1936 output of metals in the province of Quebec totaled well over C$30.6 million, thanks to the development sparked by Noranda Mines. From 1926 to 1936 Noranda stimulated the nation's economy by pouring into it approximately C$71 million in supplies, transportation, salaries, and taxes. By the end of World War II, the area's mineral production had climbed to C$150 million annually.

Perhaps due to the events of World War II, however, the 1940s—and even the 1950s—saw less corporate activity than earlier decades. Still, the company made two major acquisitions, including Castle Tretheway Mines Ltd.'s Omega Gold Mines, which Noranda Mines bought jointly with Anglo-Huronian Ltd. in 1944. Four years later, Noranda Mines and a subsidiary, Waite Amulet Mines, bought more than 500,000 shares of Mining Corporation of Canada Ltd. In 1956 Noranda acquired a sizable interest in Bouzan Mines Ltd.

By the early 1960s the company began to see a flurry of activity, beginning with the acquisition of Western Copper Mills Ltd., located near Vancouver, in 1963. The new acquisition joined with Noranda Copper & Brass Ltd., a Noranda Mines subsidiary, to form Noranda Copper Mills Ltd. Also that year, the company acquired the remaining shares of Mining Corporation of Canada, which continued the firm's exploration efforts. In addition, Anglo-Huronian, Bouzan Mines, Kerr-Addison Gold Mines, and Prospectors Airways—all Noranda affiliates—merged to form Kerr-Addison Mines Ltd.

In December of 1964 Noranda Mines made its most important acquisition when it merged with Geco Mines Ltd. The new company retained the name Noranda Mines Ltd. Based in Manitouwadge, in northwestern Ontario, Geco was a major producer of copper, silver, and zinc. The following year, Canada Wire & Cable, in which Noranda Mines had an interest since 1964, became a wholly owned subsidiary. In 1966 the firm also bought 80 percent of Norcast Manufacturing Ltd., which then purchased shares in Wolverine Die Cast Group. Also that year, Noranda Mines formed Noranda Manufacturing, Ltd., a holding company for its various manufacturing subsidiaries. Noranda Mines also acquired a controlling interest in Pacific Coast Company in 1967.

By 1968 Noranda Mines had become a widely held mining company with most of its activities centered around Quebec. Employees numbered 5,000. It was also in 1968 that 37-year-old Alfred Powis became president of Noranda Mines. Formerly a financial analyst in Montreal with Sun Life Assurance Company of Canada, Powis joined Noranda Mines in 1955 as an assistant to the firm's treasurer. Under Powis's leadership, the company began its evolution from a regionally based mining firm to an industry leader with subsidiaries involved in energy and forestry, in addition to mining.

It seems that Powis's aggressive tactics, including a chain of takeovers, were key contributors to the company's success. Powis's success did not come overnight, however. The company first had to weather the impact of several large investments made in the late 1960s.

In the early 1970s the mining industry, as a whole, was depressed. Consequently, Noranda Mines had limited earnings from 1966 to 1972, increasing in that period by only 21 percent. In addition, gross capital employed rose from C$500 million in 1967 to C$1.5 billion in 1973. The rate of return on that capital dropped from 16 percent in 1966 to only 9 percent in 1972. Powis worked through the cyclical, industry-wide recession, and finally, in 1973, investments began to pay off; Noranda's sales climbed 75 percent to C$121 million, a company record.

Additional investments made in the early 1970s included Tara Exploration and Development Ltd., which owned lead and zinc properties in Ireland, and Belledune Fertilizer Ltd., acquired from Albright & Wilson Ltd. in 1972. The year 1974 saw even more acquisitions, including a 55 percent stake in Fraser Companies Ltd. and Alberta Sulphate Ltd., and 38.5 percent of Frialco, a Cayman Island firm with controlling interest in Friguia, a bauxite mining company in the Republic of Guinea.

In addition, Noranda Sales Corporation of Canada Ltd., a subsidiary, bought in the spring of 1971 a 50 percent interest in Rudolf Wolff & Company, a British trading firm dealing with metals and other commodities.

The mining industry, known for caution, watched Powis march on this unusual acquisition path, then witnessed Noranda sales climb from C$60 million in 1972 to C$155 million two years later. It was during this era that a *Canadian Business* contributor referred to Powis as "the Houdini of the Canadian mining industry."

What goes up, however, must come down, and in 1976, earnings dropped to C$47 million. Demand for the two biggest contributors to the company's sales—copper and zinc—began to lag. The automobile industry was replacing zinc die castings with plastics. Copper, too, was being supplanted by various substitutes, from aluminum for power lines to glass fibers for communication cables.

In addition, many of the firm's earlier investments had been financed with short-term loans, which seemed like a good idea when business was booming. Although Powis acknowledged that money was tight at Noranda Mines in 1977, he defended his decision to load up on short-term debt, telling *Canadian Business,* "We put restraints on at the end of 1974 when we could see that things were getting grim. Those clamps have stayed on." Powis also indicated he was prepared for the tight zinc market.

To help wait out the cyclical downturn in the mining industry, the company diversified, concentrating on other business segments, such as manufacturing and forestry. As Powis stated in the July 22, 1974, issue of *Iron Age,* the future of Noranda would be "where our nose takes us. . . . We originally got into manufacturing so we could have a home for our products." In addition, the company invested millions of dollars in efforts to convert some old saw mills into profitable lumber plants. That marked its entry into the forestry industry.

In 1981 Powis lost a long-running, highly publicized battle with Brascan, Ltd., a Toronto holding company owned by Edward and Peter Bronfman. Brascan became Noranda Mine's largest stockholder, and Powis, who became accountable to the Bronfmans, stayed on as chief executive officer. Brascan added C$500 million to Noranda Mines's bankroll, and set the company back on its acquisition path.

In 1981 Noranda Mines first picked up Maclaren Power and Paper Company, a newsprint, pulp, and wood-products enterprise located in Buckingham, Quebec. The following year it bought 49.8 percent of MacMillan Bloedel, Canada's largest paper company. The minority shareholding was sufficient to give Noranda Mines control of the company. While the acquisitions were intended to decrease the company's concentration on the lagging copper market, the expansion of the early 1980s initially resulted in decreased profits: in 1980 the firm had record earnings of C$408 million, while in 1983 it lost C$117 million due to interest payments on the acquisitions and expansion loans, which totaled C$169 million in 1983.

Powis and Adam Zimmerman, president of Noranda Mines, shared an optimism that began to pay off in the mid-1980s.

Sales of zinc, fine paper, and other products began to recover, and, just as Noranda Mines finished a C$300 million addition to its aluminum smelter, demand for the element skyrocketed. Diversification was paying off, and to reflect its expanded activities, the company changed its name from Noranda Mines Ltd. to Noranda Inc. in 1984.

In 1986—after a C$253,900 loss caused by strikes and other labor problems in 1985—the firm's net income stood at C$43,300, and total revenue was C$3.55 billion. In 1987, as various labor strikes were resolved, company officials predicted the firm would see its highest earnings since 1980. Also in 1987, the company was restructured, dividing its various business segments into four subsidiaries: Noranda Energy, Noranda Forest, Noranda Minerals, and Noranda Manufacturing.

In October of 1989, after a heated battle between Powis and former protegé William James—who had left Noranda and become chairman of Falconbridge, Ltd., a rival mining company—Noranda bought 50 percent of Falconbridge. Ownership of the multibillion dollar company is shared by Trelleborg A.B., a Sweden-based conglomerate. The move not only gave Noranda half of Falconbridge, but also ownership of Kidd Creek, a Timmons, Ontario, copper and zinc mine that Noranda had long coveted.

Although most of Noranda's assets are located in North America, Noranda markets its products globally. The firm's goal is to be a premier diversified natural resources company. Under the leadership of President David Kerr, the company remains committed to a sensitive environmental policy, a pledge necessary for any business to be well received in the 21st century. But the company's professions of environmental responsibility and the public's perception of its efforts often diverge. Noranda's Forest division has been a frequent target of criticism. While environmental groups decry clear-cutting, Noranda Forest officials cite reseeding programs that plant twice as many seedlings as are cut. Although the company has been unable to meet environmentalists' demands in some areas, Noranda Forest has been compelled to meet consumer demands for recycled paper.

Noranda Forest Recycled Papers was established in 1989 and operates at a mill with a 50-year history of recycled paper production. The mill was the first to receive the Canadian Standards Association's Environmental Choice designation for its inclusion of more than 50 percent recycled paper and 5 percent postconsumer fiber in its fine paper. The operation has been very successful, and Noranda has raised the postconsumer content of its recycled paper to 10 percent in line with 1991 federal guidelines.

Noranda made halting progress in its handling of labor relations in the 1990s. When officials at a subsidiary, Brenda Mines Ltd. in British Columbia, realized that the mine's ore vein would be exhausted within three years, the company took steps to ensure a more stable transition for its workers. With the cooperation of the Canadian government's department of Employment and Immigration, the provincial Ministry of Advanced Education

Training and Technology, representatives of management, and hourly and salaried employees, a job placement center was created to help employees recognize and prepare for new job prospects. The program earned an award from the Canadian Mental Health Association for "excellence in addressing the personal issues" related to the closure.

The Brenda Mines scenario, however, did not necessarily characterize labor relations in the late 1980s and early 1990s. A 94-day strike at the Noranda Aluminum smelter in New Madrid, Missouri, capped a 20-year adversarial relationship at that Noranda division. And a ten-month strike that started in July of 1990 at Brunswick Mining and Smelting's huge zinc/lead mine near Bathurst, New Brunswick, threatened to shut down that division. Noranda executives admitted that management-labor relations were never lower, but agreements in 1991 at both subsidiaries focused on more open communications at all levels.

The lingering recession of the early 1990s hit Noranda hard in 1991, when it posted a C$133 million loss for the year. Although the mining and metals and oil and gas groups posted net gains, a C$75 million loss in the forest division cut into those profits. The balance of the losses was blamed on overproduction and the high level of the Canadian dollar relative to the U.S. dollar. The poor financial performance inspired management throughout the conglomerate to focus on cash conservation, cost containment, and asset sales. In 1991 the Canada Wire and Cable division was sold to Alcatel Cable for more than C$400 million.

In the early 1990s, Noranda's Alfred Powis and David Kerr were cautiously optimistic about the conglomerate's future. Encouraging forecasts of persistently low interest rates and a weakening of the Canadian dollar had been offset by lingering low levels of demand for Noranda's products. The company's leadership hoped to merely ride out the financial storm.

Principal Subsidiaries: Noranda Minerals Inc.; Noranda Forest Inc. (82%); Canadian Hunter Exploration Ltd.; North Canadian Oils Ltd. (51%); Norcen Energy Resources (33%); Noranda Aluminum, Inc.; Wire Rope Industries Ltd. (90%); Falconbridge Limited (50%).

Further Reading: Roberts, Leslie, *Noranda,* Toronto, Clarke-Irwin, 1956; Beizer, James, "Metal Mining Troubles Loom Large in Canada," *Iron Age,* July 22, 1974; Daly, John, "The Final Victory: Falconbridge May Prove to Be Too Expensive," *Maclean's,* October 9, 1989; Francis, Diane, "Alfred Powis as Corporate Superman," *Maclean's,* November 27, 1989; Antoniak, Jane, "Profile: Green Giant," *CA Magazine,* March 1991; Young, Jim, "Noranda Meets New Fine Paper Postconsumer Waste Standards," *Pulp & Paper,* March 1991; Zuehlke, Mark, "The Right Way to Handle a Closure," *Canadian Business,* August 1991.

—Kim M. Magon
updated by April Dougal

NUCOR CORPORATION

2100 Rexford Road
Charlotte, North Carolina 28211-0000
U.S.A.
(704) 366-7000
Fax: (704) 362-4208

Public Company
Incorporated: 1955 as Nuclear Corporation of America
Employees: 5,600
Sales: $1.46 billion
Stock Exchanges: New York
SICs: 3312 Blast Furnaces & Steel Mills; 3441 Fabricated
Structural Metal; 3316 Cold-Finishing of Steel Shapes

The bane of big steel companies and a recurrent favorite of Wall Street, Nucor Corporation ranks as the seventh-largest steel manufacturer in the United States. Its approach to steel production is predicated upon drastically undercutting both foreign and domestic competition, a feat it has accomplished through no small amount of hard work, risk-taking, and visionary thinking. For all practical purposes, Nucor launched the steel minimill industry in the late 1960s. Since that time, minimills have increasingly edged the large integrated steel companies out of most niche markets, capturing some 15 percent of domestic production. As king of the minimills, Nucor's share of the $39 billion industry in terms of sales is now close to four percent. This low percentage is deceptive because Nucor has remained eminently profitable in a difficult economy and in a virtually non-growth industry: in 1991 the minimill earned $95.8 million before taxes while the six top companies cumulatively lost an estimated $1.5 billion. What has truly shaken the industry, however, is Nucor's bold entry into the flat-rolled steel market, the last domain of Big Steel. In 1991, flat-rolled steel accounted for approximately 47 million of the 90 million tons produced nationwide. Nucor currently has two flat-rolled steel mills and has plans to build two additional plants, raising its capacity in this area to some eight million tons by the year 2000. Several analysts (as well as Nucor's maverick CEO, F. Kenneth Iverson) have speculated that if Nucor accomplishes its goals for expansion while continuing to outperform the competition, it may very well become the number one steelmaker in the country.

Nucor traces its origins to the turn of the twentieth century, when automobile inventor Ransom Eli Olds founded the Olds Motor Works in Lansing, Michigan, with the considerable aid of venture capitalists. In 1904, Olds, dissatisfied with his lack of control over the business, abandoned it to found a new company, R. E. Olds Company; the name was quickly changed to Reo Motor Car Company to avoid a lawsuit over the use of the ''Olds'' name. From 1904 until 1924 Olds served as president of the company, before turning to real estate speculation, an unfortunate business move that ultimately led him to sell most of his Reo stock. When demand for the luxury cars manufactured by Reo plummeted during the Great Depression, the plant began making a number of other products, including lawn mowers and the Reo Speedwagon delivery truck. Olds died in 1950 and his namesake company, which had survived one bankruptcy, was now headed toward another. By December 1954 the company was all but dead; however, when stockholders were informed of plans for liquidation in 1955, a small contentious group found a glimmer of hope in a tiny Reo business property, Nuclear Consultants, Inc. According to Nucor biographer Richard Preston, what followed was ''a forced takeover, an unusual move in corporate finance, wherein the dissidents forced Reo to take over Nuclear Consultants against Reo's wishes.'' When the paperwork was complete, Reo was reborn as Nuclear Corporation of America and became the first publicly traded nuclear company. Various publicity stunts and the power of the word ''nuclear'' propelled the company and its stock skyward. Yet its business endeavors in nuclear instrumentation, nuclear energy, chemicals, and electronics bordered on the illusory. A series of largely unrelated acquisitions, funded through stock offerings, sustained the company. One of these subsidiaries, Vulcraft, led to the establishment of Nucor.

In 1962 Iverson, then a young mechanical engineer, became general manager of Nuclear's Vulcraft division in Florence, South Carolina. It soon became apparent that Vulcraft, a metal fabrication business specializing in steel joists and girders, was virtually the only healthy division within the conglomerate. A string of money-losing years led the Nuclear Corporation to the verge of bankruptcy in 1965. By this time Iverson had been elevated to group vice president and transferred to the parent company's headquarters in Phoenix. Essentially, Nuclear was a business with $20 million in sales and $7 million in assets that was losing $400,000 annually. Two major loan defaults that year caused the president to resign and the board to appoint Iverson as the new president and CEO; the logic governing the decision was that Iverson had been in charge of the only divisions within the company that were profitable.

Taking over at mid-year, Iverson dumped half the divisions, reduced management positions from 12 to 2, and posted the last loss ever for the company, some $2.2 million. Now came decisions regarding Nuclear's future operations. At this point, Vulcraft, with its South Carolina plant and another in Norfolk, Nebraska, held the greatest promise for growth. In 1966 Iverson committed himself to Vulcraft's steel joist industry, relocating to Charlotte and establishing corporate headquarters in a modest 2,000 square foot office. During the first three years under his management, Nuclear's net sales rose from $21 million to $35 million, largely on the virtue of Vulcraft's dominant 20 percent share of the joist market. Although profits kept pace with this growth, Iverson was concerned with Vulcraft's dependency on others for its steel. Until Vulcraft graduated from steel fabricator to steel producer, its earnings were entirely dependent on steel prices outside its control.

In 1968 Iverson, in the first of several momentous decisions for the company, prepared Nuclear to become a minimill steel producer. His initial goal was to manufacture bar steel at a price competitive with foreign producers, who had been supplying up to 80 percent of the company's raw material. The goal was perhaps unrealistic, for Iverson would also be taking on such giants as U.S. Steel, a chief Vulcraft supplier. Furthermore, the construction cost for a traditional coke-and-iron steel mill was prohibitive. However, steel could be created another way: by melting scrap steel in electric-arc furnaces. Iverson took the gamble by effectively mortgaging the company for a loan of $6 million. The money was used to erect a plant in rural Darlington, South Carolina, and purchase the necessary equipment, a furnace, a continuous casting machine, and a rolling mill. According to *Success,* Iverson "recruited farmers, sharecroppers, and salesmen to do the dirty, often dangerous work of making steel. High technology and untrained troops made for a volatile mix, and delays and catastrophes caused stock prices to drop to pennies. But a legendary company culture was born: inventive, resourceful, team oriented, inspired by impossible challenges."

The delays and catastrophes centered around the plant's casting machine, which experienced regular breakouts of hot steel from the time production began in June 1969 until late 1970, and the newness of the venture in general. Depressed earnings finally rebounded spectacularly in 1971, jumping 140 percent. In 1972, they leaped another 70 percent. This same year, Iverson dropped the company's outmoded title and renamed the business Nucor Corporation. Nucor was now at the brink of the so-called golden era of the minimills. It had two successful operations: Vulcraft, which supplied joists to the construction industry, and Nucor Steel, which produced low-cost bar steel, largely for Vulcraft. Both posed a threat to the big steelmakers, but they were slow to respond. A flurry of minimills arose during the 1970s, following Nucor's lead and producing bar steel for the joist business at prices that eventually drove Bethlehem, Republic, and others out of the market.

In 1977 Nucor launched its second assault on Big Steel by branching out into steel decking, for use in floors and roofs supported by its Vulcraft joists. Two years later the company again led the minimills by manufacturing cold-finished bars, employed in shafts and precision parts. By the end of the decade, Nucor ranked among the top 20 steel companies in the country, with sales of $430 million and net earnings of $42 million. Within a five-year span, it had more than tripled production through a series of new mill constructions. Its core business, Vulcraft, had also expanded through new plant openings and had virtually secured its position as the biggest steel joist producer in the United States. The one blemish on these years of fast-paced growth was a mill fire accident in 1974 which killed four Nucor employees.

The company would later face criticism from its competitors, the media, and community leaders that its operations were needlessly dangerous. Much of the criticism stemmed from the fact that Nucor's workforce remains nonunion and therefore subject to lower wages and less assurance that a certain working environment will be maintained. Nevertheless, the dynamic Nucor work ethic and corporate culture, shared by management and employees alike, offered something unions would find impossible to provide during the 1980s: job security. In an industry plagued with plant closings, cutbacks, and layoffs, Nucor stands out as one company firmly committed to its steel-workers. No Nucor employee has ever been laid off; to hold down costs during difficult downswings, Nucor instead asks its workforce to reduce hours. As for wages, the company's stringent team performance standards offer incentives to employees to exceed production goals and, as a result, receive bonuses that can more than double their annual wages. The employees have also benefited from such unusual policies as guaranteed college scholarships for their children, a policy first established when Iverson wanted to help the families affected by the 1974 accident. Nucor attributes much of its success to its nonunion, nonurban employees. As its brochure *The Nucor Story* states: "A major ingredient in Nucor Corporation's success has been its commitment to locate its diverse facilities in rural locations across America. As a result of deliberately selecting non-urban locations, Nucor has been able to establish strong ties to its local communities and its work force. The ability to become a leading employer and pay a leading wage has been a key to attracting hard-working, dedicated employees."

Such simple, effective strategies have become the trademark of the company and its CEO. Another important ingredient in the company's success is its sparse management staff. Only four management layers exist inside the company, beginning with Iverson and current president, John Correnti, and leading directly down through general managers, department heads, and foremen, to the general laborers. All wear identical hard hats, as a tribute to teamwork and as a further sign of differentiation from unionized companies. The small staff, inornate headquarters, and Iverson's relentless drive to become a world-class competitor have all made for a supremely cost-conscious corporation in which new technologies are seized, decisions made swiftly, and production encouraged apace.

Iverson's races into new steel industries and new technologies during the 1980s were necessitated not by Big Steel, which was floundering, but by other American minimills and by the new world leader, Japan. In 1986 the CEO decided to tackle the last frontier, sheet steel—an expensive and prized market that no minimill had dared to consider. Start-up costs for manufacturing sheet steel were enormous, more than a quarter of a billion dollars. At the time, Nucor's assets amounted to little more than twice that figure. Annual revenues stood at just $755 million. Nonetheless, Iverson took the plunge, first by exploring possibilities within the company to produce a state-of-the-art casting machine whose efficiency would trounce the competition. Although the in-house project held promise, Iverson was anxious to be the first to acquire and implement the technology, and an invention already in progress, by West German engineering firm SMS Schloemann-Siemag A.G., was chosen as the best candidate for Iverson's plans. Called the compact-strip-production machine (CSP), the invention was over 1,000 feet long and composed of some one million parts. Most experimental and most crucial to its success was a casting tower, supposedly capable of producing sheet steel just two inches thick instead of the conventional ten inches. According to Preston, "Inventors had been trying to invent a machine that would make an endless strip of steel since 1856, when Sir Henry Bessemer had tried it and failed. . . . Any company that could solve the problem would by definition become the global leader in the manufacture of steel." Assembly of the machine began in 1988 at a new plant site in Crawfordsville, Indiana; by mid-1989 the first experiments were begun. Throughout the period, the Crawfordsville Project and the CSP attracted a shower of criticism from the big steel companies, as well as a jumble of stock trading and public speculation.

Under plant managers Keith Busse and Mark Millett the CSP was eventually completed, and despite delays, breakouts, and one fatal explosion in January 1990, the Crawfordsville plant was soon operating near capacity, producing flat-rolled steel in one-fourth the time of its competitors at $45 less per ton. Busse had said, "What we're doing in Crawfordsville is like taking a Conestoga wagon for the first time across the plains." Iverson, looking to the future, had remarked, "We are going to leapfrog Japan." Neither was overstating the enormity of the Nucor gamble. The freak accident, caused by a broken cable which sent a ladle of molten steel crashing to the plant floor, left one dead. In the aftermath of the explosion, it was feared that dozens more may have perished. Nucor was fortunate, however, for had the calamity been any greater it might have endangered the company's survival. OSHA (Occupational Safety and Health Administration) inspectors poured over the evidence before levying a $30,000 fine. The victim's family also sought settlement with the company. What arose from the tragedy was a renewed commitment to plant safety; a Nucor study undertaken a few years later showed that the company ranked in the top third among steel mills in terms of safety.

The Nucor of the 1990s remains committed to aggressive growth. The corporation now consists of eight businesses (Nucor Steel, Nucor-Yamato, Vulcraft, Nucor Cold Finish, Nucor Fastener, Nucor Bearing Products, Nucor Building Systems, and Nucor Grinding Balls) operating 15 plants in North Carolina, South Carolina, Alabama, Indiana, Arkansas, Texas, Nebraska, and Utah. Products from Nucor's mills include steel joists and joist girders; steel deck; cold finished steel; grinding balls, fasteners and bearings; carbon and alloy steel; and metal building systems. The Nucor joint venture with Yamato Kogyo, which employs Japanese casting technology to produce wide-flange construction beams, is emblematic of the company's ongoing commitment to excellence on all manufacturing fronts within the industry. Among Nucor's most recent developments are the September 1992 opening of its second thin-slab sheet mill in Hickman, Arkansas, and its proposal to open an iron-carbide plant in Trinidad. The Trinidad project involves a new conversion process for iron ore, which in its finished state could be used to replace a portion of the steel scrap used in Nucor's sheet steel mills. Most appealing to investors is Nucor's clean balance sheet, which shows regularly high cash flow and no debt. As Birmingham, U.S. Steel, and others announce their own plans for building minimills, Nucor appears well-positioned to maintain its lead.

When Iverson was asked by *Inc.* magazine whether Nucor had plans to diversify, as the steel giants have done, he responded, "No, we're going to stay in steel and steel products. The way we look at it, this company does only two things well, and that is it builds plants economically and it runs them efficiently. That's the whole company. We don't have any financial expertise, we're not entrepreneurs, we're not into acquisitions. Steel may not be the best business in the world, but it's what we know how to do and we do it well."

Principal Subsidiaries: Nucor Machined Products, Inc.; Nucor-Yamato Steel Company (51%).

Further Reading: Schriber, Jon, "The Solution That's Not a Solution," *Forbes,* January 5, 1981; Kirkland, Richard I., Jr., "Pilgrims' Profits at Nucor," *Fortune,* April 6, 1981; Rohan, Thomas M., "The 'Other' U.S. Steel Industry Is Booming," *Industry Week,* July 13, 1981; "Minimills, Maxiprofits," *Time,* January 24, 1983; Metzger, Mark K., "F. Kenneth Iverson of Nucor: Man of Steel," *Inc.,* April 1984; Love, Martin, "Steel from the Workshop," *Forbes,* April 30, 1984; Karmin, Monroe W., "Where Shift to High Tech Already Pays Dividends," *U.S. News & World Report,* September 3, 1984; Scredon, Scott, "Iverson: Smashing the Corporate Pyramid," *Business Week,* January 21, 1985; Clifford, Mark, "Like Big Steel, Like Little Steel," *Forbes,* May 20, 1985; Fortney, David L., "The Little Steel Mill That Could," *Reader's Digest,* August 1985; Gendron, George, "Steel Man Ken Iverson," *Inc.,* April 1986; Simon, Ruth, "Nucor's Boldest Gamble," *Forbes,* April 3, 1989; Preston, Richard, *American Steel: Hot Metal Men and the Resurrection of the Rust Belt,* New York, Prentice Hall Press, 1991; Armel, Anne Lobel, "Competition Thins out as Iverson Casts Nucor's Lot," *Iron Age,* August 1991; "Nucor Advantage: A New Way of Thinking," *The Inland Steelmaker,* January 31, 1992; "Strike the Underbelly," *Success,* January/February 1992; Milbank, Dana, "Minimill Inroads in Sheet Market Rouse Big Steel," *Wall Street Journal,* March 9, 1992; "Nucor Annual Meeting Report," May 14, 1992; Wrubel, Robert, "The Ghost of Andy Carnegie?" *Financial World,* September 1, 1992; C. J. Lawrence Market Report, October 6, 1992; Oliver, Regina, "F. Kenneth Iverson of Nucor Corp.: Forging a New Steel Age," *North Carolina,* November 1992; Milbank, Dana, "Nucor to Build Iron-Carbide Plant to Aid Minimills," *Wall Street Journal,* January 7, 1993; Beirne, Mike, "Nucor Sets Iron Carbide Plant," *American Metal Market,* January 8, 1983; Baker, Stephen, "Striking While the Iron Is Hot," *Business Week,* January 11, 1993; "Nucor Ups Sheet Tags by $10 to $15 Per Ton," *American Metal Market,* January 29, 1993; *The Nucor Story,* company publication, n.d.

—Jay P. Pederson

OCEAN SPRAY CRANBERRIES, INC.

One Ocean Spray Drive
Lakeville-Middleboro, Massachusetts 02349-0001
U.S.A.
(508) 946-1000
Fax: (508) 946-7704

Cooperative
Incorporated: 1930 as Cranberry Canners, Inc.
Employees: 2,200
Sales: $1.09 billion
SICs: 0171 Berry Crops; 2033 Canned Fruits and
 Vegetables; 2037 Frozen Fruits, Fruit Juices & Vegetables;
 2099 Food Preparations Nec

A leader in the marketing of shelf-stable juice drinks, Ocean Spray Cranberries, Inc. is responsible for 80 percent of the cranberries sold worldwide. Since its beginning, the company has functioned as a grower-owned agricultural cooperative; however, its strong emphasis on new product introduction, advertising, and packaging places it in direct competition with many publicly owned companies. Once known only as a seasonal cranberry sauce business, Ocean Spray now markets blended juice drinks, juice concentrate, fresh fruits, and several other items to both retail and food service outlets year-round. Ocean Spray's Cranberry Division, with $852 million in 1992 sales, still accounts for the bulk of the company's operations. However, since the addition of grapefruit growers to the cooperative in 1976, the company has displayed an increasing tendency to develop a broad fruit-oriented product line to fortify its presence in the consumer market. Preserving a strong brand image, perfecting production forecasting techniques, and promoting operational efficiency have all led the cooperative into the ranks of the Fortune 500. Ocean Spray's stock is held by some 150 grapefruit growers in Florida and nearly 750 cranberry growers in Massachusetts, New Jersey, Wisconsin, Oregon, Washington, and Canada.

The history of Ocean Spray is naturally tied to the history and lore of the cranberry, an unusual native American wetland fruit. Small, reddish, and distinguished by a strong, bitter flavor, the cranberry was first used by various native American tribes in the New England area to make dyes as well as a high-energy food called pemmican: a concentrated mixture of dried venison, fat,

and cranberries shaped into cakes. Cranberries were believed to have been present at the first Thanksgiving feast in 1621. The first cranberry juice recipe dates back to 1683. Throughout colonial times, cranberries also became widely used in tarts, preserves, and sauces. Exports to Europe also began during this era. However, commercial cultivation of cranberries did not commence until the early 19th century, when Captain Henry Hall began experimenting with cranberry vines in East Dennis, Massachusetts. As many already knew, the Cape Cod marshland, with its high concentration of peat, was particularly conducive to cranberry growing. Hall, however, made the singularly important observation that when sand from the nearby dunes blew into the marshes, or bogs, the cranberries thrived. He began applying sand manually and found he could grow cranberries that were larger and juicier than those found elsewhere. Growers from another state in which the cranberry was native, New Jersey, soon followed Hall's lead. Among such pioneers were Benjamin Thomas and John Webb. During the 1850s, cranberry cultivation spread to Wisconsin; three decades later, farmers in both Washington and Oregon began establishing cranberry bogs of their own. By the mid-twentieth century, mechanical pickers were invented to replace manual procedures, and soon wet-harvesting techniques were developed to take advantage of the cranberry's natural buoyancy.

The Ocean Spray name was conceived by a Boston lawyer named Marcus L. Urann, who gained a reputation as the "Cranberry King" for a cranberry sauce he packaged in tins and marketed under the brand as early as 1912, as well as for his later promotions. Urann headed the Ocean Spray Preserving Co. of South Hanson, Massachusetts, and was one of the principal proponents behind a merger of similar companies to form a large, powerful cooperative. Urann reasoned that a merger would erase the stiff competition he faced from the Makepeace Preserving Co. of Wareham, Massachusetts, and The Enoch F. Bills Co. of New Egypt, New Jersey, and also allow for greater marketing clout. John C. Makepeace and Elizabeth F. Lee, the other two owners involved in Urann's proposed merger, joined Urann in signing a certificate of incorporation in June 1930. A delay by Urann in transferring the Ocean Spray trademark jeopardized the merger for a short time; however, by August, Cranberry Canners, Inc. had been formed and Ocean Spray's survival was thus ensured.

Urann, as president and general manager, assumed responsibility for advancing the cooperative by meeting with and encouraging growers and by enlarging the demand for cranberries. Among the products introduced by Cranberry Canners during the 1930s were Cranberry Juice Cocktail and Ocean Spray Cran, both tart-tasting forerunners of later, sweetened juice and juice concentrate products. With the 1940s and the addition of Wisconsin, Oregon, and Washington growers to the cooperative, the product line expanded to include dehydrated cranberries (for U.S. troops) and cranberry-orange marmalade. By 1943 the co-op controlled 15 facilities for production, storage, and distribution. Because of the rising prominence of the cranberry and the Ocean Spray label, the cooperative renamed itself the National Cranberry Association (NCA) in 1946. During this same year, the company also began marketing fresh cranberries, in cellophane packaging, for the first time.

The NCA, with a membership nearly double that of its modern-day variant, continued to sustain itself throughout the 1950s principally as a seasonal business that revolved around the Thanksgiving and Christmas holidays. Highlights of this decade were numerous and included the incorporation and then formal assimilation of Canadian growers; the first Ocean Spray television commercials; the retirements of Urann in 1955 and Makepeace (who had served as secretary-treasurer) in 1957; the introduction of frozen cranberry-orange relish and frozen cranberries; and the final renaming of the cooperative in 1959 to reflect the central importance of the Ocean Spray brand. On November 9, 1959, Ocean Spray Cranberries, Inc. was faced with its first and only major crisis. On that day the Secretary of the Department of Health, Education and Welfare announced that residue from the potentially cancer-causing weed killer aminotriazole had been found in cranberries produced in Washington and Oregon. Because of the ill-timed announcement—just prior to Thanksgiving—Ocean Spray's entire cranberry business was in jeopardy. Cranberries quickly became known as ''cancer berries'' and hopes for any profits from that year's holiday sales were dashed. Although the co-op's new president, George C. P. Olsson, rightly asserted that the purported danger was nonexistent, it was too late to avert the widespread fear that had been raised. Grocers were forced to take all suspect products off their shelves. Ironically, ''The History of Ocean Spray Cranberries'' records that a membership newsletter dated December 1957 had actually alerted growers to the dangers of aminotriazole, then an unapproved weed killer which, if used, could ''cause needless expense to your cooperative and result in the condemnation of your crop.'' The Department of Agriculture had actually approved the compound in 1958 for use after harvests, but the linkage to cancer and the tests for detecting residues were not established until the following year.

For a time, the co-op was in danger of folding, but a partial comeback in sales for 1960, as well as a government subsidy for unsold cranberries found to be free of residue, kept the business going. However, Ocean Spray's earlier successes had now created the problem of over production. New marketing avenues needed to be explored if the high demand for cranberries were to be revived. Edward Gelsthorpe, an executive with experience at both Colgate Palmolive and Bristol Myers, was brought in to develop a new, long-term marketing plan for the company. Gelsthorpe's answer, unpopular at the time, was to emphasize juice drinks under the Ocean Spray brand. Between 1963 and 1968 the company committed itself to the consumer drinks market with Cranberry Juice Cocktail, Cranapple, and Grapeberry (later changed to Crangrape). The guiding philosophy was to compete against both the large soft drink and orange juice markets not through product imitation but through product diversity. As consumers became more health conscious during the 1960s and 1970s, the Ocean Spray formula for success struck a responsive chord. By the mid-1970s the cooperative was on the fast track to achieving Fortune 500 status and appeared all the more healthy after its bold expansion into grapefruit growing. A minor setback occurred in 1979 when the Federal Trade Commission, as part of an investigation of all agricultural cooperatives, threatened an antitrust action against Ocean Spray. No suit was launched, however, and so the company began the 1980s with its $235 million in annual revenues intact.

In 1981 the company made packaging history with its introduction of the block-shaped juice container with attached drinking straw. The innovation captured a new segment of the juice-drinking public, children, and has since become a staple of the Ocean Spray product line. This same year Ocean Spray achieved its ranking as the largest domestic seller of canned and bottled juice drinks. The co-op fought vigorously to retain the title during the decade—as new competitors entered the fray—with a growing number of product introductions, including Mauna-La'i, a guava-lemon drink; Firehouse Jubilee, a tomato drink; Ocean Spray Liquid Concentrates; and Cranberry Fruit Sauces. By the mid-1980s, the company had reached annual revenues in excess of $500 million. The company also improved its distribution system, expanded its marketing to food services, and capitalized on the Cape Cod tourist industry by attracting millions of visitors each year to its headquarters and museum near Plymouth Rock.

One of the most important developments for Ocean Spray came in 1985 with its acquisition of Milne Fruit Products of Prosser, Washington. A manufacturer of fruit concentrates and purees, Milne was once primarily a grape business but has grown under Ocean Spray to process cherries, blueberries, blackberries, plums, raspberries, strawberries, and cranberries. Milne's largest customer is Ocean Spray, but the subsidiary also serves such major food companies as Kraft General Foods, Gerber Products, Nestlé, Sunkist, Welch, and Baskin-Robbins. Most importantly for its parent company, Milne has tripled in size since acquisition and has become a significant generator of non-patronage revenue, which is reinvested in the cooperative for future expansion.

The only blight on the company during the eventful 1980s occurred in 1988, when it was charged under the Clean Water Act with illegally dumping insufficiently treated effluent from its Middleboro plant into the town's sewer system. Ultimately, Ocean Spray was fined $400,000; the company also donated $100,000 in water-treatment equipment to the town of Middleboro. Since this time, Ocean Spray has become an industry leader in promoting environmentally sound operations and has spent some $26 million upgrading waste-treatment facilities.

While the cooperative reformed itself environmentally, it was also in the process of analyzing all of its internal operations. A program called Right Turn Only (RTO), dedicated to quality improvement, problem-solving, and teamwork, was adopted to aid Ocean Spray in remaining competitive while fostering an open working environment. In the area of market research, crucial in a brand-driven industry, Ocean Spray decided to take advantage of new database technologies by entering into a joint venture with Information Resources of Chicago. The result was a state-of-the-art software program called CoverStory that offered market information from universal product code (UPC) figures and trends. Other innovations include techniques to boost crop yields and forecast harvest results.

Under John S. Llewellyn, Jr., Ocean Spray recently became a billion-dollar company and continues to build on its strong brand image. The cooperative's most important new development involves a joint arrangement with PepsiCo to distribute individual cans and bottles of Ocean Spray juices and drinks. This agreement offers Ocean Spray a relatively inexpensive opportunity to increase its individual serving segment, which accounts for roughly $100 million in sales, through vending machine, convenience store, and related outlets. According to reporter Jon Berry, ''The logic behind the New Age partnership is forceful. During the past decade, Ocean Spray has burst from obscurity to become one of the acknowledged innovators in the beverage industry. But its strength has been notable only in supermarket aisles. To become an equal power in single-serve sales, Ocean Spray would have to spend millions building a distribution system.''

Although fiscal 1991 was marred by flat sales, lower than expected harvests, heavy competitive pressures, and a Wisconsin freezer storage fire, the company had reason to look optimistically to the future. Foodservice sales were up 19 percent, citrus revenues increased 21 percent, and Refreshers Fruit Juice Drinks and Ruby Red Grapefruit Juice Drink came on line. Single-serve sales, representing ten percent of the company's revenues, showed the potential for tripling in size during the decade. In 1990, Christopher Daly wrote: ''The cranberry. . .is in many ways an American success story.'' One could say the same of its biggest supporter, Ocean Spray.

Principal Subsidiaries: Milne Food Products, Inc.

Further Reading: ''Cranberry Growers Reel under Pre-Holiday Blow,'' *Business Week,* November 14, 1959; Skilnik, Rayna, ''Ocean Spray's Canny Marketing,'' *Sales & Marketing Management,* August 18, 1980; Ling, Flora S. H., ''The Little Man's Monopoly,'' *Forbes,* December 8, 1980; *The History of Ocean Spray Cranberries, Inc.,* Lakeville-Middleboro, Massachusetts, 1981; Buell, Barbara, ''How Ocean Spray Keeps Reinventing the Cranberry,'' *Business Week,* December 2, 1985; ''Crushed Cranberries,'' *Time,* February 8, 1988; Donahue, Christine, ''Can Ocean Spray Sell Cranberry Sauce Off-Season?'' *Adweek's Marketing Week,* June 26, 1989; Hanson, Peter D., ''How Ocean Spray Trims the Risks of Seasonal Borrowing,'' *Corporate Cashflow,* May 1990; Daly, Christopher B., ''Squeezing the Humble Cranberry into a Success Story,'' *Washington Post,* November 21, 1990; Schmitz, John D., Gordon D. Armstrong, and John D. C. Little, ''Cover Story—Automated News Finding in Marketing,'' *Interfaces,* November/December 1990; Eichinger, Mark S., ''Empowerment: A Blue-Collar Perspective,'' *Personnel Journal,* October 1991; Pace, Eric, ''George Olsson, 88, Head of Cooperative Built on Cranberries,'' *New York Times,* November 16, 1991; Berry, Jon, ''Ocean Spray Joins the Pepsi Generation,'' *Adweek's Marketing Week,* March 9, 1992; ''How Ocean Spray Gave Cranberries Some Sparkle,'' *New York Times,* November 26, 1992.

—Jay P. Pederson

ONEIDA®

ONEIDA LTD.

Sherrill Rd.
Oneida, New York 13421
U.S.A.
(315) 361-3100
Fax: (361) 829-3963

Public Company
Incorporated: 1880 as Oneida Community, Limited
Employees: 5,100
Sales: $479.4 million
Stock Exchanges: New York
SICs: 3914 Silverware & Plated Ware; 3262 Vitreous China
  Table & Kitchenware; 3231 Products of Purchased Glass;
  3643 Current-Carrying Wiring Devices

Oneida Ltd. is the world's largest stainless steel and silver-plated flatware maker. Its operations in the United States, Canada, Mexico, the United Kingdom, and Italy manufacture and market sterling, silver-plated, and stainless products, commercial china tableware, and industrial wire. Oneida also markets tableware and crystal gift items. The company originated in a utopian community established in the mid-nineteenth century, and has had a strong reputation for quality since that time.

The Oneida Community was founded by John Humphrey Noyes in upstate New York in 1848. The Community was founded on Noyes's theology of Perfectionism, a form of Christianity with two basic values: self-perfection and communalism. These ideals were translated into everyday life through shared property and work as well as "complex marriage"—monogamous marriage was abolished, and children were raised communally from their second year until age 12.

This child care system freed the women as well as the men to take part in the Community's manufacturing of animal traps, chains, silk items, and silver knives, forks, and spoons. The Oneida Community soon became known not only for the unconventional lifestyle of its members, but also for the quality of its goods. The Newhouse trap invented by a founding member of the community was known around the world.

The Oneida Community existed longer than most other utopias of the nineteenth century in part because of the solvency of its businesses, and the members of the group lived and worked together from 1848 until the late 1870s. Prosperity didn't shield

the organization from conflict, however, and in 1879 the Community split into two factions. Unable to resolve their differences, the members voted to transform the group's businesses into a joint-stock company, the Oneida Community, Limited, which would be owned and operated by former members of the society. The Community was valued at $600,000 and stocks were distributed according to each member's original contribution and length of service. The stock was divided among 226 men, women, and children, the majority of whom received between $2,000 and $4,999 in shares. The progressive nature of the new company was reflected in, among other things, the presence of a woman, Harriet Joslyn, as superintendent of the silk mill and a member of the board of directors.

During the fifteen years following Oneida's reorganization, the company's financial standing deteriorated. A severe depression in the 1890s, inadequate leadership, and emigration from the community plagued the new company. Some have speculated that the failure of the utopian community contributed to demoralization of the worker/stockholders, further eroding the company's prospects for success.

But in January 1894, Pierrepont Burt Noyes (P. B. Noyes), the son of Oneida's founder, rejoined the company after working as an Oneida wholesaler in "The World," as many Oneidans referred to the world outside their community. At only 23 years old, P. B. Noyes replaced an uncle on Oneida's board of directors. His experience outside the Community enabled him to see and criticize weaknesses that threatened the company's existence. Within two months Noyes led a proxy fight to oust directors who clung to old-fashioned business strategies. Nearly 24,000 shares were voted, and Noyes's side won by just 16 shares. Noyes was offered the position of superintendent at Oneida's Niagara Falls Plant, and soon raised the operation's standards of quality to their former levels. In 1899 the company announced its largest profits to date and paid its stockholders a dividend of seven percent.

By the time he reached the age of thirty, Noyes had risen to de facto control of Oneida. The board nominated him to the newly created post of general manager with authority to oversee all of the company's divisions—canning and manufacturing of tableware, traps, chains, and silk thread. Noyes's rise to prominence at Oneida marked the company's emergence into the industrial world of the twentieth century. Before the turn of the century Oneida had relied on its managers' creativity, thrift, and diligence and the excellent reputation of its products. Noyes introduced the new production methods, competitive strategies, large-scale distribution methods, and promotional efforts that were beginning to typify American industry. In 1904 he established Oneida's emphasis on marketing and brand recognition by increasing the company's promotion budget from $5,000 to $30,000 per year. Noyes financed this move by diverting profits from the trap business that would otherwise have been used to expand trap manufacturing, which he saw as a dying business.

From that time on, even during the Depression, advertising remained a major item on Oneida's balance sheet. Oneida's earliest advertising campaigns established many of the trademarks that would characterize the company's advertising for decades to come. The print ads typically appeared in widely circulated women's magazines. Rather than describe all of its tableware at length, Oneida used most of its advertising space for a picture of one or two pieces of silver plate, which it often associated visually with someone or something attractive. Oneida was also one of the first companies to employ celebrity spokespeople to promote its products. Ten years before the practice was widely accepted, Oneida commissioned Irene Castle, a famous dancer and fashion plate to promote Community ware.

Despite Noyes's aggressive move to gain control of Oneida, he still sought to maintain the communal harmony and idealism on which the Community was founded. Managers who lost positions on the board of directors retained positions with the company, and many came to respect the new management. In addition, Kenwood, a private community built around the company, gave Oneida a sense of family that remained strong through the early decades of the twentieth century; well into the 1920s, descendants of Oneidans held almost 90 percent of company stock. Noyes sought to make Oneida and the community of Kenwood "modern utopias" by increasing wages, improving work conditions, providing welfare and recreational benefits, and improving the physical environs of Kenwood.

Noyes attracted children of Oneidans who had gone off to college and careers in "The World" back to the company by appealing to their sense of ambition: the modern utopia he described meant intellectual challenge, reasonable pay, and self-improvement. The corporate culture was based on the sense of inventiveness and labor/management cooperation that has distinguished the company throughout its history. Oneida's silverware operations have never suffered a work stoppage due to labor disagreements.

In 1904 Noyes proposed voluntary salary reductions for management when the company encountered financial difficulties. The proposal was enforced in 1914, when all salaried personnel took a 10 percent pay cut until early 1916. In 1921 larger cuts were necessary—Noyes reduced his own salary by half, the directors took a 33 percent cut, and other officials took smaller cuts corresponding to their salaries. The Depression required similar cuts.

Oneida's chain business was sold in 1912 and the silk industry was liquidated in 1913, when man-made substitutes for silk were invented. The company's canning business was discontinued in 1915 because it was unable to compete with large-scale modern production methods. But the consolidations enabled Oneida to open its first international factory, in Niagara Falls, Ontario, in 1916.

Noyes resigned from the general managership in 1917 to let younger people into Oneida's management. Three months after he resigned, the United States entered World War I. Oneida joined the wartime effort with the production of ammunition clips, lead-plated gas shells, and combat knives. The company also served as the principal source of a wide range of surgical instruments used in military hospitals. In 1919 Noyes returned briefly to Oneida after serving with the U.S. government's Fuel Administration. He later served in Europe on the post-World War I Peace Conference and the Rhineland Commission to decide the particulars of Allied occupation of Germany.

Noyes resumed the general managership of Oneida in 1921 amid financial crisis. After steering the company through that predicament, he gave the general manager position to a son-in-law, Miles E. Robertson, in 1926, retaining the post of president and de facto control of the company. Oneida's trap business was sold in 1925, which left the company entirely dependent on the silverware manufacture. By 1930, 33 percent of the board of directors was composed of people from outside the community.

In 1935 the company's name was changed to Oneida Ltd. to differentiate tableware produced by Oneida from that of lower quality subsidiaries of the company, such as Wm. A. Rogers. The name change signaled a new era at Oneida. Noyes ceded control of Oneida to Miles Robertson, although he didn't formally hand over the presidency until 1950. Robertson was known for his "toughness": despite the rigors of the Great Depression, Oneida made a profit in 1933, when no other company in the silverware industry could. By this time, Oneida had subsidiaries in Canada and Great Britain.

Robertson began to recruit outside Oneida and Kenwood during that decade as well. After the mid-1930s, Noyes's ideological influence gave way to more worldly viewpoints. Oneida became less community-oriented and more like a typical corporate culture with few family ties and less of a social utopian bent. Before World War II, new members of Oneida's management knew that they would never become wealthy at the company, but would gain personal satisfaction through the successes of the company. But with the arrival of more and more "outsiders," increasing competition for quality personnel, and increasing segregation of Oneida from the Community, management salaries slowly grew to meet prevailing wages in the industry.

World War II brought about other changes at Oneida as well. The company's contribution to the war effort included production of silverware for the Army and Navy and surgical instruments for military hospitals. Oneida also produced products for the battlefield: rifle sights, parachute releases, hand grenades, shells, survival guns, bayonets, aircraft fuel tanks, and chemical bombs, among other things. The company even purchased a separate factory in Canastota, New York, that produced army trucks, aircraft survival kits, and jet engine parts. That plant stayed in operation for several years after the war.

Although the Oneida of the 1950s had accepted the wage scales of the outside world, it continued to operate by Noyes's principle that management should take salary cuts in tough financial times. However, the employees of the 1950s had changed along with the times, and a 1957 cut in directors' salaries was perceived by employees not as a demonstration of management's vested interest in the welfare of the company, but as a drastic measure indicating impending financial disaster.

The directors restored their pay, but Oneida's financial problems continued until 1960, when the company posted its first annual deficit. That same year Pierrepont Trowbridge ("Pete") Noyes replaced his father as president of Oneida. Oneida had trouble adjusting to the loss of government orders that had supplemented silverware sales during World War II and the Korean War. The work force declined from a high of 3,800 in 1949 to 2,000 in 1960. Oneida responded by developing new lines with new products, reorganizing production, and introducing new advertising and marketing strategies. By the end of the decade, the work force had grown to more than 3,000 employees.

In 1977 Oneida moved to diversify its interests through the purchase of the Camden Wire Co., Inc. Camden Wire was one of the principal U.S. manufacturers of industrial wire products. One year later Oneida acquired Rena-Ware, a cookware manufacturer with operations in 34 countries and the majority of sales outside the United States. That year the company also got a new president, John Marcellus, Jr., who had joined Oneida in 1946. Pete Noyes continued as chairman until 1981, when Marcellus also assumed that position.

By 1983 the company sold over half of all flatware purchased in the United States. The company sought to purchase other companies in order to infiltrate the total tableware market. Oneida purchased Buffalo China Inc., one of the nation's largest volume producers of commercial chinaware, and Webster-Wilcox, a producer of expensive hollowware (silver serving platters). In 1984 the company acquired D. J. Tableware, maker of high quality flatware, hollowware, and china for the food service industry. Oneida also began to market a line of crystal stemware and gift ware in the mid-1980s.

The company's marketing campaigns were similar to its earliest promotional efforts. Spare but elegant advertisements in *Brides* and *Vogue* featured single items, and were so popular that Oneida sold some of the ads as posters. The recession of the early 1980s, however, saw Oneida's earnings plummet 65 percent in 1982. As primarily a consumer products company (industrial wire sales only constituted 24 percent of Oneida's profits in the mid-1980s and less than 30 percent in 1991), Oneida suffered more than expected. The company's problems were exacerbated when Japanese and other importers flooded American housewares departments with inexpensive flatware.

Oneida attempted to compete by taking the high road—emphasizing the superiority of its products and leaving the low-end manufacturers to fight among themselves. The strategy was unsuccessful, and Oneida's market share plummeted to 39 percent in 1986. The company laid off workers and lost more than $1 million between 1985 and 1986.

In 1986 the board of directors moved to revive Oneida using a new strategy, based not on marketing and new products, but on thrifty production. John Marcellus resigned, and the company named William Matthews as chairman and CEO and Samuel Lanzafame, formerly of the Camden Wire subsidiary, as president. Lanzafame had made Camden Wire Oneida's most profit-able division, and the board hoped that he could do the same with the parent company. Lanzafame worked to enhance Oneida's economies of scale—when he became president, the company's two flatware plants operated at only 60 percent to 70 percent of capacity because they were concentrating on expensive flatware alone. The company began importing more inexpensive flatware to market under its name until it could bring its own factories up to speed on production of lower-quality (but higher volume) merchandise.

Matthews, the new chairman of the board, sold off the company's fleet of limousines and its corporate jet, then trimmed the management staff by 15 percent. He encouraged worker loyalty by offering an Employee Stock Option Plan in 1987 that put 15 percent of the company's stock in the employees' hands. Late in the decade, he oversaw the investment of more than $26 million into plant improvements, including computer design and manufacturing systems, plant consolidation, and machinery upgrades. By the end of the 1980s, Oneida had regained its 52 percent share of the flatware market. Lanzafame resigned as president in 1989. Gary Moreau was named president in 1991, joining Matthews at the helm of the company.

Throughout the economic, social, and political changes that Oneida has seen during its 150-year history, the company's reputation for excellence and brand recognition have remained unshakable. In 1992 an independent national consumer study revealed that 87 percent of consumers name Oneida as the first company they think of when asked about stainless steel flatware—and there was no close second.

Principal Subsidiaries: Camden Wire Co., Inc.; Oneida Canada Limited; Oneida Mexicana, S.A.; Kenwood Silver Company, Inc.; Oneida Distribution Services, Inc.; Buffalo China, Inc.; D.J. Tableware, Inc.; Oneida International, Inc. (70%); Sant'Andrea S.r.l.; Oneida, S.A.

Further Reading: Carden, Maren L., *Oneida: Utopian Community to Modern Corporation,* Baltimore: The Johns Hopkins Press, 1969; McGough, Robert, "Too Much of a Good Thing," *Forbes,* November 17, 1986, 68–70; Robertson, Constance, "The Oneida Community," Oneida Ltd., 1985; Rosen, Daniel, "Big-Time Plugs on Small-Company Budgets," *Sales & Marketing Management,* December 1990, 48–54; Sutor-Terrero, Ruthanne, "Oneida: Making Stainless Shine," *Financial World,* July 25, 1989, 14; Taub, Stephen, "First a Strikeout, Now a Triple Play," *Financial World,* August 31, 1983, 34–35.

—April S. Dougal

ONEOK INC.

100 West Fifth Street
P.O. Box 871
Tulsa, Oklahoma 74102-0871
U.S.A.
(918) 588-7000
Fax: (918) 588-7273

Public Company
Incorporated: 1906 as Oklahoma Natural Gas
Sales: $677 million
Employees: 2,229
Stock Exchanges: New York Chicago
SICs: 1311 Crude Petroleum & Natural Gas; 4923 Gas
   Transmission & Distribution; 6719 Holding Companies
   Nec

ONEOK Inc. (pronounced "one oak") is a diversified energy company headquartered in Tulsa, Oklahoma. Among its utility subsidiaries, Oklahoma Natural Gas Company serves three-quarters of Oklahoma and, in terms of the number of customers it serves, is the twentieth-largest gas utility company in the United States. ONG Transmission Company, another utility division, leases pipeline capacity and provides the link for interstate gas transportation. ONEOK's non-utility division, the Energy Companies of ONEOK, is an important natural gas liquids processor and a mid-sized gas and oil exploration and production company.

ONEOK began as Oklahoma Natural Gas (ONG) and was formed in an era when natural gas was treated as a nuisance in the oil fields. In 1906 Territorial Congressman Dennis T. Flynn and businessman C. B. Ames decided to pipe gas from north-eastern Oklahoma to Oklahoma City, which at the time was served by a manufactured gas facility. To do this, on October 12, 1906, they formed the Oklahoma Natural Gas Company with backers Theodore N. Barnsdall of the Barnsdall Oil Company and former Standard Oil officer Glen T. Braden.

Flynn, who was ONG's first president, signed contracts to supply local distributors, and on December 28, 1907—a month after Oklahoma was admitted to the union as the 46th state—a 100-mile pipeline, costing $1.7 million, was completed from Tulsa to Oklahoma City.

Braden replaced Flynn after the pipeline's completion, and managed the nascent company in an Oklahoma that had no highways and few schools, but more than its share of "high noon" law that was enforced by the fastest gun. This was the period when state legislators were expected to check their side-arms with the Sergeant at Arms in each legislative body. During World War I, Braden increased the company's capitalization to $10 million and reduced the price of its stock from $100 to $25 per share.

In 1921, Harry Heasley replaced an ill Braden as president. Heasley soon created two oil companies to exploit the extensive oil-bearing properties ONG had found while seeking natural gas. The second of these, Oklahoma Eastern, was later merged with Devonian Oil through an exchange of stock.

In the mid-1920s, the American economy boomed and the oil and gas business boomed with it. With such increased economic activity, ONG became a takeover target. On July 31, 1926, the company was sold to New York investment bankers White, Weld, and Company.

White, Weld, and Company promptly renamed the company Oklahoma Natural Gas Corporation, and sold it to Phillips Petroleum, which wanted it as an outlet for its vast Texas Panhandle gas holdings. Phillips elected a new board, named R. C. Sharp as president, and moved the company's headquarters to Tulsa, which was rapidly becoming a center of the nation's oil and gas industry. In Tulsa, Phillips also arranged for the building of a new ten-story, $600,000 headquarters.

Phillips used ONG until it could complete its own pipeline to the Midwest and then, on October 15, 1927, sold it to the American Natural Gas Corporation, a holding company subsidiary of utility company financiers G. L. Ohrstrom and Company, Inc.

Ohrstrom's aim, like that of many utility holding companies, was to extract cash from its holdings. It used a variety of methods to do this, including taking a profit from brokered acquisitions. For instance, it purchased and then sold to ONG the Southern Kansas Gas Company, the Western Gas Service Company of Texas, and the gas properties of Oklahoma Gas and Electric Company.

At this point, ONG's shares were moving up sharply because of the large dividends it was paying in the form of preferred stock. As was common, ONG's dividends bore no relation to its true rate of growth. What revenue increases the company did experience came from stock sales rather than productivity. In fact, during this period, employees sold stock house to house. It was inevitable that the situation would correct itself and it did. On October 29, 1929, the stock market crashed and the company and Ohrstrom were plunged into turmoil along with the rest of American industry.

At ONG, management changed rapidly. In June, 1930, Oklahoma Natural Gas Corporation president Thomas R. Weymouth resigned and was replaced by E. C. Deal, who traded the company's Texas properties for the Oklahoma Natural Gas Corporation in eastern Oklahoma. Then, through arrangements with Tri-Utilities, which was an Ohrstrom holding company,

Deal constructed a pipeline from the Quinton field in eastern Oklahoma to Sand Springs, just west of Tulsa.

In October 1931, Deal resigned as president and was elected chair of the board of directors. To meet obligations, his successor, retired army colonel E. A. Olsen, interrupted dividends on common stock, paid little or no dividends on preferred stock, cut salaries, canceled vacations, and laid off employees.

In 1932, Olsen resigned and was replaced by Robert W. Hendee. Within a year, the company brought in A. E. Bradshaw, executive vice president of the First National Bank and Trust Company of Tulsa, to reorganize its finances. Bradshaw dissolved the Oklahoma Natural Gas Corporation and reincorporated it in Delaware as the Oklahoma Natural Gas Company. He exchanged stock, extended short-term debt, and honored current bonds. After the company completed Bradshaw's $30 million refinancing program in 1936, it shed its holding company and contracted Stone and Webster Service Corporation for management advisory services previously provided by the holding company.

Service had suffered during the Ohrstrom years, and the public was so dissatisfied that it almost built a municipal gas plant in Oklahoma City. To make matters worse, the Oklahoma legislature, responding to the demands of retailers, prohibited ONG from merchandising appliances. A return to normalcy began on June 1, 1936, when Joseph ''Jos'' Bowes gained the ONG presidency. Smart and tough, Bowes improved customer relations and emphasized that as an Oklahoma company, ONG owed allegiance to its customers and shareholders only.

Bowes fostered ONG's financial health through the late 1930s, and by 1940, when a sustained cold spell froze wells and threatened to interrupt service, he was able to initiate a heavy construction program to upgrade major lines and build additional ones. That year ONG also paid $4.7 million for Central States Power and Light Corporation, a gas utility that served Stillwater, Henryetta, Holdenville, and what was to become the Clinton area of western Oklahoma.

World War II drew many employees into the military and increased demands on ONG's distribution system. In fact, the necessity of supplying eight major military installations in Tulsa, Oklahoma City, Enid, Norman, and Muskogee led the company to build a 96-mile high-pressure pipeline from the Cement and Chickasha fields to the Stroud junction, halfway between Tulsa and Oklahoma City.

During the war, ONG also began storing gas in depleted gas formations. In the late 1930s, the company pioneered research and development of what became a widely used technology in which gas was injected into formations that effectively became underground storages. The injections would take place principally in the summer months when there was low customer demand. The gas was withdrawn later, usually in the winter, to meet high demand. The process subsequently alleviated the demands on the transmission system to transport large amounts of gas long distances if underground storages could be located near population centers. The company continued to develop underground storages and created five of them strategically located throughout the system.

Following the war, ONG acquired distribution operations in the Oklahoma communities of Sand Springs, Crescent, Dover, Guthrie, Hennessey, and Kingfisher, bringing its 1950 customer total to 270,000. That year it also renovated its Tulsa office building and purchased the five-story Key Building in Oklahoma City. Both buildings were provided with gas air-conditioning, which was a relatively new innovation.

In the early 1950s the company acquired an interest in a natural gas gathering system and in three gasoline plants in Oklahoma's Garvin and McClain counties. It spent $10 million annually on capital improvements as it linked its Depew underground gas storage facility with Oklahoma City and Tulsa, constructed service centers in Oklahoma City and Tulsa, built a gas processing plant in the Ringwood Field of Major County, and installed an advanced microwave and VHF radio communications system.

Bowes reported to shareholders that 1954 had been the company's best financial year. Earnings rose to $1.62 a share from $.94 a year earlier, and for the first time gas-fired central heating installations in homes edged out floor furnaces as a means of residential heating.

The company grew internally through the mid-1950s, and in the late 1950s and early 1960s returned to acquisition and expansion. It expanded its Garvin County gasoline plant, and in 1959 bought an interest in the Laverne gas processing plant in northwestern Oklahoma. In 1960, it acquired the Northern Oklahoma Gas Company, the Standard Gas Company, and the State Fuel Supply Company, gaining distribution operations in Ponca City, Newkirk, Perry, Madill, Tishomingo, Anadarko, Wewoka, and Lindsey.

In 1964, H. A. ''Tex'' Eddins replaced Bowes as chair of the board. Eddins, who had become president in 1955, had already made his mark on ONG, creating, in June 1962, the company's first wholly owned subsidiary, Oklahoma Natural Gas Gathering Company (ONGGC). ONGGC gathered gas from around the state and sold it in interstate commerce. Unlike its parent, ONGGC operated interstate and was therefore subject to federal regulation.

Eddins was concerned with ensuring an adequate long-term gas supply. He began a program of securing reserves in the Red Oak Field of southeastern Oklahoma. In 1965, he acquired Zenith Natural Gas Company and converted Zenith's Kansas properties into a second subsidiary. In 1966 he formed Oklahoma Natural Gas Transmission Company, which built and operated a 93-mile transmission pipe from Red Oak in eastern Oklahoma to Sapulpa, southwest of Tulsa.

Tragically, Eddins died suddenly on April 26, 1966, while attending an employee service awards meeting. He was replaced by Executive Vice President C. C. ''Charlie'' Ingram, an engineer who had joined the company in 1940 as an engineer trainee following his graduation from the University of Oklahoma.

Ingram emphasized exploration and gas purchases and reacted quickly to changing economic conditions and technologies. In his first two years as CEO, he began the process of computerization, adopted plastic pipe for distribution systems, embraced new and less expensive techniques of laying pipe, and launched a major sales campaign to combat the electric industry's "total electric home" promotional program. In 1968, he formed Thermal Systems, Inc., which built central cooling and heating plants in Tulsa and Oklahoma City and, eventually, a cold storage warehouse.

In 1970, with gas supply as a primary concern, Ingram reorganized ONG's operating department, established a gas supply department, and formed Oklahoma Natural Development Corporation.

Gas supply was a problem everywhere. But while oil was encountering foreign interruptions, in the natural gas industry the federal government itself was the cause of shortages. Wellhead prices for gas transported across state lines was set at politically attractive but economically unrealistic levels, and interstate gas companies found it increasingly difficult to compete for new supplies. Being an intrastate gas utility and not subject to federal regulation of what price it could pay, ONG was able to acquire adequate gas supplies in the midst of shortages throughout the rest of the industry.

In 1971, ONG served 500,000 customers and generated more than $100 million in revenues. But Ingram and newly named president Wayman E. Humphrey remained focused on supply. In 1972, they formed ONG Exploration Company and encouraged customers to conserve. In 1973 the company's intrastate status allowed it to remain competitive for new gas supplies even as the Arab oil embargo tightened energy supplies and many companies within the U.S. energy industry were caught short.

To insure access to new supplies, Ingram in 1973 created ONG Western Inc. to build a 200-mile, $20 million pipeline into the gas-rich Anadarko basin of western Oklahoma. He incorporated ONG of Norway, Inc., to bid on oil and gas leases in the North Sea, and by 1974 was spending a yearly $9 million for exploration and production, including a $3 million wildcat program.

The mid-1970s was a time of customer growth for ONG, despite real and threatened shortages. In 1974, it began making large deliveries to the first of five large new fertilizer plants. Its 1976 earnings increased by 51 percent, and in 1977 it extended pipelines 500 miles and installed a computerized customer information system.

Nevertheless, an overall solution to the continuing shortages in the interstate market was needed. Although Oklahoma Natural survived without interruption in service to its customers and sold emergency deliveries to interstate companies, pressure was building on Congress to act.

Congress provided a solution when it passed the Natural Gas Policy Act of 1978. The NGPA deregulated wellhead prices for newly found gas and therefore provided incentive for exploration. But the act, which eventually released vast supplies, caused price fluctuation during the 1980s, which resulted in major changes in the industry.

In December 1980 ONG changed its corporate name to ONEOK Inc. Pronounced "one oak," the new name was meant to change perceptions. "What we've become," ONG's annual report stated, "is a company with a good, solid foundation in the utility business and increasing success and growth in non-utility areas."

The company had indeed grown and diversified. Oklahoma Natural Gas had become a major player in the industry. It distributed gas to 215 communities, wholesaled it to distributors serving 47 states, and had some 600,000 residential customers. Within ONEOK's non-utility division, the ONEOK Energy Companies, ONEOK Exploration Company explored for oil and natural gas, while Smart Drilling Company, acquired in 1979, was a contract-drilling operation.

In 1981 and 1982, sales reached record $1 billion levels. Revenues were also reaching record heights, as was capital spending, which topped $181 million in 1982. This spending included subsidiary TransTex Pipeline Company's share of the new Red River Pipeline, and Caney River Transmission Company's share of the new Ozark Gas Transmission System, which crossed the Arkoma Basin from Oklahoma to Arkansas.

But despite these records, by 1982 the company was feeling the pinch of recession-caused weaknesses in the industrial market. This market was especially important because ONEOK had signed take-or-pay contracts with its own suppliers and was therefore obliged to pay for gas even when it had no customers. Since 1982 take-or-pay claims amounted to some $108 million, Ingram and newly named CEO J. E. Tyree were faced with the necessity to economize. They cut costs, reduced ONG's capital budget, and fought these claims in court. Nevertheless, a weak economy, sparse contract-drilling demand, lower investment tax credits, increased interest costs, and a $12.8 million drilling write-off in Malta all cut 1983 earnings per share to $2.51 from 1982's $4.88.

To make matters worse, even though executives did what they could to keep industrial deliveries high by cutting prices to ONG's five fertilizer plant customers to keep them in business, deliveries continued to fall from 1982's 281 billion cubic feet (bcf) to 242 bcf. The erosion of deliveries exposed ONEOK to heavy take-or-pay claims.

Weather and rate increases helped the company recover to a degree in 1984. But while ONEOK tried to look optimistic as it opened a new 17-story company headquarters in downtown Tulsa, it cut capital expenditures, moved away from natural gas exploration, and reduced the number of rigs in its contract-drilling operation.

Events of 1985 continued to be sobering. Earnings per share continued to fall, as did demand. New federal regulations allowed industrial users to purchase gas from the wellhead and transport it through pipeline-capacity leases. On the energy side, ONEOK drilling company reported a net loss of $5 million, about half of which was attributable to a three-rig write-down.

On the positive side, executives instituted a long-range planning strategy, moved strongly into oil production by acquiring Imperial Oil for $9.4 million, and formed ONG Transmission Company to handle opportunities in pipeline capacity leases. These opportunities were made more lucrative by the fact that Oklahoma was the nation's third most prolific gas-producing state.

In 1986, a sluggish economy, warm weather, and unrecoverable take-or-pay settlements of almost $6.2 million forced ONEOK into drastic economies. It consolidated offices, cut down on drilling, and through early retirement policies, reduced its work force by 380, or nearly 15 percent. Things continued to deteriorate in 1987. After a jury awarded Forest Oil $50 million in a take-or-pay suit, banks withdrew an $85 million line of credit and ratings services downgraded ONEOK's debt.

To get ONEOK back on its financial feet, J. D. Scott, who had become president and CEO in 1986, interrupted regular dividends, appealed the Forest Oil verdict, and established reserves of $112.3 million for unresolved take-or-pay disputes. In 1988, he continued downsizing by providing an early retirement package and incentives for 113 employees to resign or retire. He also sold slightly more than 50 percent of the company's exploration leases. A light at the end of the tunnel began to appear in 1989, when earnings per share rose 71 percent, dividends were restored, and exploration and production activities became profitable for the first time in five years. In 1990, Standard and Poors and Duff and Phelps upgraded ONEOK's debt to A- from BBB+.

Scott evidenced his own confidence through acquisitions and expansions. He committed to a major expansion of the Ozark Gas Transmission System, announced a ONEOK Exploration strategy committed to riskier plays with bigger payoffs, acquired the Lone Star Gas Company in central Oklahoma, and continued a research, development, and demonstration project, begun in 1980, that used natural gas as an alternative fuel for vehicles.

By 1991, Harlan S. Byrne of *Barrons* commented that "for the first time in several years, most things that count were starting to click for ONEOK." In 1992 ONEOK remained optimistic despite a significantly warmer than normal winter and unprofitable spot market prices. The company formed ONEOK Gas Marketing to pool and market the products of Oklahoma's independent producers, and ONEOK Technology Company to develop and market a new meter-setting device. Looking to the future, ONEOK planned to introduce a natural gas-fired heat pump and to promote compressed natural gas fleet vehicles in a state that already has more natural-gas fueled vehicles than any state in the union.

Principal Subsidiaries: Caney River Transmission Company; ONG Red Oak Transmission Company; ONG Sayre Storage Company; ONG Western, Inc.; TransTex Pipeline Company; OkTex Pipeline Company; ONEOK Services, Inc.; ONEOK Technology Company; ONEOK Drilling Company; ONEOK Exploration Company; ONEOK Products Company; ONEOK Resources Company; ONEOK Gas Marketing Company; ONEOK Leasing Company; ONEOK Parking Company.

Further Reading: Wheeler, Ed, "Oklahoma Natural Gas Company: A Profile," Oklahoma Natural Gas Company *Gasette,* October 1974; "Looking Back," Oklahoma Natural Gas Company *Gasette,* October 1981.

—Jordan Wankoff

ORYX ENERGY COMPANY

P.O. Box 2880
Dallas, Texas 75221-2880
U.S.A.
(214) 715-4000
Fax: (214) 715-3870

Public Company
Incorporated: 1971
Employees: 1,500
Sales: $1.39 billion
Stock Exchanges: New York
SICs: 1311 Crude Petroleum & Natural Gas; 1382 Oil & Gas
    Exploration Services

Oryx Energy Company, headquartered in Dallas, Texas, is one of the world's largest independent oil and natural gas companies. The company's main activities include finding, acquiring, developing, and producing oil and gas throughout the world, chiefly in the Gulf of Mexico, the North Sea, Indonesia, and Ecuador.

A relatively young company, Oryx emerged from a reorganization of the Sun Oil Company in 1988. Sun Oil's earlier roots date back to 1882 when Joseph Pew and E. O. Emerson began the Penn Fuel Company to supply the city of Pittsburgh, Pennsylvania, with energy. Two year later, they sold Penn Fuel and established the People's Natural Gas Company as new competition in the market.

In 1886, Pew's nephew, Robert, traveled to Lima, Ohio, to investigate possible oil deposits. A discovery was made, and by 1889 the company was bringing Ohio crude oil to refineries near Lima and Toledo, from which the oil could be shipped to markets in the northeast. During this time, in 1887, the company was renamed the Sun Oil Company, marking the first time the word Sun appeared in the company's register. In 1894, Sun formed the Diamond Oil Company and purchased for $22,000 the refinery belonging to the failed Crystal Oil Company, based in Toledo, Ohio. Robert Pew became refinery manager.

In 1899, Emerson sold his share in the company to Pew. Two years later, Pew moved quickly to investigate Texan oil fields following the discovery of the famous Lucas Well in the Spindletop oil field near Beaumont, Texas. Once again, Robert Pew was dispatched to investigate business possibilities. A month later, he was joined by younger brother J. Edgar. They reported back that abundant, cheap oil was available, and, in 1901, the Pews formed The Sun Company in New Jersey. This new venture was to join in partnership with the United Gas Improvement Company, based in Philadelphia, to ship crude oil from Texas to Pennsylvania. The first shipment arrived aboard a tanker in March 1902 and was unloaded at a refinery on the Delaware River.

Pew's business strategy was simple and endured for many years in his company: discover new oil deposits and develop economical ways to ship the crude to refineries built near populous areas. In 1911 the Sun Company moved to absorb the Sun Oil Company. Joseph Pew became president, while Arthur E. Pew, J. Howard Pew, and Robert Pew all served as vice-presidents. Frank Cross was secretary-treasurer.

On October 10, 1912, Joseph Pew died of a heart attack. He was succeeded by his son, J. Howard Pew, who would lead the company for the next 35 years. The outbreak of World War I two years later saw the company increase its shipbuilding operation to supply the U. S. military. Sun Ship-Building Company, based in Chester, Pennsylvania, launched its first vessel in October 1917.

By 1918 the United States had 6.1 million cars on the nation's highways, and the company entered the motor oil business. Sunoco Motor Oil brand products were introduced the following year, and subsidiaries in Canada and the Netherlands were formed to market them overseas. In 1920, the company's first service station opened in Ardmore, Pennsylvania. Many more openings would follow, and Sunoco products would be advertised nationally in magazines and newspapers. In 1922, the company's name was changed back to the Sun Oil Company. Additional oil products available in the Sunoco line in future years included Sun Red, a quality lubricant.

On November 12, 1925, 15 percent of stock in the Sun Oil Company was first listed on the New York Stock Exchange. The proceeds of the issue would help build more bulk plants and enlarge distribution facilities. Two years later, the company added a marketing department, headed by Samuel Eckert, to its front office operation. Walter C. Pew became general sales manager. Also during this time, the company's research and development department came up with a single grade of unleaded, high octane gasoline, which it called "Blue Sunoco."

The Great Depression hit the Sun Oil Company hard. Sales for the company tumbled from $98 million in 1930 to $69 million a year later. Profits in those years fell to $3.1 million in 1931, against $7.75 million a year earlier. Nevertheless, the company deemed it wise to move ahead with an ambitious capital expenditure program worth $9.5 million in 1931 alone. A pipeline from the Marcus Hook refinery near Cleveland, Ohio, to Syracuse, New York, was completed. The company's tanker fleet was modernized, and the Sun-Yount-Lee crude pipeline in Texas was built.

By 1939, the Sun Oil Company was producing more than 12.3 million barrels of oil a year, up from 6.7 million barrels a decade earlier. During the Second World War, the company produced fuel for use by the U. S. Air Force and saw four of its ships sunk during wartime service. During the first six months of 1945, the

Marcus Hook Refinery was refining and shipping more than 1.1 million barrels of oil a month to the allied effort.

Intensified wartime oil production served the company well after 1945. Oil fields in Louisiana and Texas had been discovered and drilled. Such discoveries were crucial to Sun; without them, their production have would declined.

In 1947, J. Howard Pew stepped aside as president of the company. While remaining a director on the board, he was replaced by the company's comptroller, Robert G. Dunlop. Joseph Pew, Jr., became the company's chairperson.

On the transportation side, Sun Oil Company joined with the giant Standard Oil Company, based in Ohio, in 1949, to build the 1,000-mile Texas to Ohio mid-valley pipe line, which provided a new source of crude for the Toledo refinery. In December 1951, all company pipe lines were brought under the umbrella control of the Sun Pipe Line Company, a wholly owned subsidiary to be run by William Kinsolving.

Regarding production, in 1954, Sun Oil Company looked overseas for new crude oil sources. Oil from the Arab Gulf was secured and exploration for added sources was ongoing in Latin America, Pakistan, and the Bahamas. Two wells, pumping 6,000 barrels of oil daily, were successfully drilled in Venezuela in 1957. The company also began drilling for natural gas reserves in the American Midwest.

By 1960, the company was producing more than 54 million barrels of oil annually, some of which came from wells in Canada overseen by a subsidiary office in Calgary. Crude reserves held by Sun totalled nearly one billion barrels. Overall company sales that year topped $755.4 million, producing net profits of $14.7 million.

Committed to product research and development, Sun built an applied physics center at Newton Square, Pennsylvania, in 1956. This center aimed at developed modernized refining processes and applying physics to solving problems in the production and distributions of company products. To develop new oil and petrochemical sources, the company built a $2.5 million research laboratory at the Marcus Hook refinery the following year. By 1958, Sun Oil Company service stations throughout North America offered six grades of Sunoco motor oil to customers.

Attempts at finding natural gas reserves in the North Sea off of Scotland were rewarded in the early 1960s. Similar natural gas finds were made in the Arab Gulf off the coasts of Iran and Dubai. In 1964, work began on the Great Canadian Oil Sands Ltd. plant in northern Alberta. The plant would make synthetic crude from the Athabasca tar sands.

The company's total net assets topped $1 billion in 1967. Profits that year reached $108.6 million. Sun Oil Company entered a merger with the Tulsa-based Sunray DX Oil Company. The combined operation—employing two divisions, one for manufacturing, marketing, and transportation and the other for exploration and production—began with more than $2 billion in net assets, and profits of $164.4 million in its first year of operation.

The two divisions in 1971 became separate legal companies, Sun Oil Company of Pennsylvania and Sun Oil Company, registered in Delaware. Also that year, J. Howard Pew died and his position on the board was filled by Robert Dunlop. In addition to his new responsibilities as company chairperson, Dunlop continued as chief executive officer until 1974 when he was succeeded by Robert Sharbaugh.

In 1973, the oil industry was shocked by the OPEC oil scandal. Sun and other companies began to operate amid public suspicion of the huge profits they were apparently reaping amid shortages at the gas pump. The price of gas rose, skyrocketing 12-fold by the end of the decade, and the climate produced widespread changes at Sun. In 1975, the company went through a wide ranging restructuring. A new corporate headquarters was built and opened in July 1976. Operations were divided into 14 units, and two property companies were established to watch over the company's vast real estate holdings. Each operating unit was to be a separate entity, with its own management structure. Thus the company was given flexibility at a time when industry change had become commonplace. Robert Sharbaugh commented at the time that restructuring for Sun would become a "constant."

In 1976, the company's name was changed to Sun Company Inc., to reflect the fact that it planned to become more than just an oil company. Sun positioned itself for wider petrochemical and natural gas business opportunities in the years ahead.

Then, in 1979, the oil industry suffered its second shock of the decade when, after the Shah of Iran's fall from power, the country's revolutionary government cut off all oil supplies to major oil companies, including Sun. In the mid-1980s the company began developing a 14,000 acre southern Texas oil field called the Pearsall field on the Austin Chalk. Although many rival oil companies had found that their wells in the region were drying up, and, by 1985, Sun's own wells were producing on average of only five barrels of oil daily, Sun engineers and geologists persisted, developing a horizontal drilling technique working parallel to the oil platform surface. That way, they found natural reservoirs of oil in vertical fractures.

By 1989, the average Pearsall field well was producing 1,300 barrels a day. In November of that year, the Heitz #1 discovery well pumped nearly 3,300 barrels daily and 2.2 million cubic feet of natural gas. At the same time, the falling price of oil led the company to make a $260 million writedown in 1988 on the value of its energy assets. That produced a net loss that year for the company of $305 million, against net earnings of $158 million a year earlier.

On November 1, 1988, Sun Company Inc. spun off the Sun Exploration and Production Company (Sun E&P), which became an independent, publicly owned company. But inevitable confusion resulted between Sun E&P and the Sun Oil Company of Pennsylvania, which refined, marketed, and distributed company products. So, in May of 1989, Sun E&P became Oryx Energy Company in an effort to distinguish the independent operation. Robert Hauptfuhrer, Sun Company president between 1984 and 1986, and now Oryx chair and chief executive officer, argued at the time: "Since Sun markets branded gasoline in the District of Columbia, we have often encountered confusion amidst legislators on Capitol Hill. We are mistakenly being linked with major integrated companies, whose policy views could be different from ours.''

In 1990, Oryx applied its horizontal drilling technology to the Ellenburger field in central Texas, the Bakken shale in North Dakota, and the Californian Midway Sunset field. With only five percent of the world's oil reserves in the United States, Oryx was also eager at this time to expand its international energy reserves. In January 1990, Oryx paid British Petroleum Plc $1.1 billion for a portfolio of international oil and gas properties. The reserves were found mainly in the North Sea just off the British coastline as well as in Indonesia, Ecuador, Gabon, and Italy.

Also in the 1980s, in response to consumer demand in North America, the company expanded its exploration for natural gas deposits, which it hoped would provide a less expensive and more environmentally sound alternative to oil, coal, and nuclear energy.

By 1986, the company was actively looking in the Gulf of Mexico for natural gas reserves. All in all, 235 offshore blocks and 40 producing platforms were drilled. A year later, the company began to employ a geological exploratory tool using high resolution 3-D seismic soundings to discover deposits. The procedure was able to help Oryx get at reserves previously obscured by features of natural terrain, such as rocky overhangs.

The 1990 Persian Gulf conflict temporarily increased the price of oil worldwide. This was shortlived, however, as was reflected in Oryx's share price, which opened the year at $44 but slipped back 20 percent at year end to $36. Profits in 1990 for Oryx, however, were favorable. They were posted at $225 million, up from $139 million a year earlier. New drilling for natural gas

deposits that year took place in the Mississippi salt domes, the Anadarko and Arkoma basins in the Midwest, and the gas rich Gulf Coast.

In 1991, James McCormick retired as president of Oryx after 38 years with the company. Consequently, Robert Keiser became president and chief operating officer of the company, while Robert Hauptfuhrer remained CEO and chairperson.

That year, company profits fell sharply to $19 million as the world price for oil and natural gas continued under pressure after the end of the Gulf War. As part of a restructuring of Oryx, nonstrategic assets were sold to raise $400 million, much of which went towards easing long-term debt to around $2 billion. In a further attempt to bring down operating costs, 40 percent of the company's workforce was let go.

Oryx's difficult trading climate was reflected in its share price, which fell 29 percent during 1991 to $22. The crisis in the oil market did have one benefit for Oryx. A slump in the Dallas property market allowed the company to secure a new headquarters building in the city at an attractive rent level.

For the future, much depends on the price of a barrel of oil, a measure difficult to forecast. The costcutting measures and honing of core activities at Oryx ought to serve the company well as it adjusts to changing operating conditions in the 1990s.

Further Reading: Challenge and Response: The Evolution of Sun Company, 1976; *Our Sun,* Sun Oil Company Public Relations, Spring 1961; ''Oryx Energy Company: New Name Proposed By Sun E&P Board'', Sun E&P news release, March 21, 1989.

—Etan Vlessing

OSHKOSH TRUCK CORPORATION

P.O. Box 2566
Oshkosh, Wisconsin 54903
U.S.A.
(414) 235-9150
Fax: (414) 233-9624

Public Company
Incorporated: 1917 as Oshkosh Motor Truck Manufacturing
   Company
Employees: 2,400
Sales: $641 million
Stock Exchanges: NASDAQ
SICs: 3710 Motor Vehicles & Equipment

Oshkosh Truck Corporation is a major manufacturer of specialized truck and transport equipment. Based in Oshkosh, Wisconsin, the company produces a broad range of products designed to meet the needs of specific market niches. The three major markets to which Oshkosh sells its products, both domestically and internationally, are defense, municipal, and commercial. Included among the heavy-duty vehicles Oshkosh produces are military transport vehicles, aircraft fire-fighting equipment, snow removal vehicles, stripped chassis for motor homes, buses, and walk-in delivery vans, and various types of trailers. The company's main Oshkosh plant houses its corporate headquarters, as well as machining, fabricating, and subassembly facilities. Also located in Oshkosh are an engineering test and development center, a truck subassembly and final assembly plant, a parts distribution center, and a paint and final test plant. Oshkosh operates one of the world's most modern chassis manufacturing plants, which is located in Gaffney, South Carolina. The chassis plant features a 650-foot-long moving assembly line. The company's trailer division's headquarters and manufacturing plant division are located in Bradenton, Florida and Mansfield, Texas.

Oshkosh Truck was founded by William R. Besserdich and Bernhard A. Mosling in 1917. The two men had received patents in 1914 and 1915 for improvements on four-wheel-drive capability. Besserdich and Mosling approached several established automobile manufacturers—including Ford, Packard, and Studebaker—about using their designs to produce a four-wheel-drive vehicle. After a series of rejections, they decided to

start their own company. Handling the business end of the operation, Mosling sold stock in the new company, raising $250,000 in capital. Meanwhile, master engineer Besserdich was busy coming up with a prototype vehicle design. In May of 1917, the Wisconsin Duplex Auto Company, located in Clintonville, Wisconsin, was incorporated. Besserdich was the company's president, and Mosling was listed as its manager and secretary. The prototype vehicle was a four-cylinder, three-speed, 3,000-pound truck called Old Betsy. The success of Old Betsy's four-wheel-drive components attracted investors. Since many of the investors were based in Oshkosh, 47 miles south of Clintonville, the company relocated there toward the end of 1917 and changed its name to Oshkosh Motor Truck Manufacturing Company.

The first Oshkosh truck to hit the market was the two-ton capacity Model A, at a price of about $3,500. After the Model A, Oshkosh began offering the Model B, which could carry 3.5 tons, and soon afterward, the five ton Model F. The four-wheel-drive ability of the Oshkosh trucks quickly set them apart from conventional trucks already on the market. Sales grew from seven trucks in 1918 to 54 in 1919, to 142 in 1920. The company, however, hit a slump immediately following World War I. A postwar depression, combined with a government program that donated surplus trucks to municipalities, resulted in sales that shrank from 62 trucks in 1921 to 16 in 1923. In 1922 Mosling replaced Besserdich as company president.

In 1925 Oshkosh introduced the Model H, a powerful truck with a six-cylinder engine. The Model H proved to be useful for road construction and snow plowing, and therefore sold well to municipalities. Sales of the Model H kept Oshkosh in business through the second half of the 1920s. The company fell victim to the Great Depression, however, and in 1930 was forced to reorganize. It re-emerged as Oshkosh Motor Truck Company. R. W. Mackie was president of the company's new incarnation, while Mosling concentrated on improving the company's sales. Oshkosh introduced two new trucks in 1932, Models FC and FB. Both new models had six-cylinder gasoline engines. Their transmissions ranged from four- to twelve-speed, and their hauling capacities were as high as 44,000 pounds. In 1933 Oshkosh unveiled Model TR, the first earthmover to appear with rubber tires. The four-wheel-drive TR was designed to be used with dozer blades, bottom-dump trailers, or self-loading scrapers. Major buyers of the truck included airport construction contractors, dam and canal builders, and mining companies.

Oshkosh diversified its product line further with the introduction of the J-Series in 1935. The J-Series trucks had capacities from two to three-and-a-half tons, and they had the classic rounded styling of 1930s automobiles. Oshkosh experimented in the 1930s with rear-wheel-drive vehicles, but the fierceness of competition from mass-production companies forced a quick withdrawal from that market, leaving Oshkosh to continue focusing on four-wheel-drive equipment. Many of Oshkosh's best customers in the 1930s were located in dairy states such as New York and Wisconsin, as well as parts of New England. In those areas, prompt plowing of roads was required throughout the winter to enable delivery from remotely located dairy farms. In 1930 the prices of Oshkosh trucks ranged from $2,885 to $13,500.

In 1939 Oshkosh introduced its W-Series truck, which marked Oshkosh's first significant entry into production for military use. The Army Corps of Engineers selected the company's Model W-700 for a variety of operations, including snow removal from Air Corps runways and general wrecker work. Toward the end of World War II, production began on Model W-1600. The W-1600, driven by all three of its axles, was designed for off-road use in oil fields and for pulling heavily laden trailers. Mosling stepped back into the company's presidency in 1944. Under Mosling Oshkosh continued developing the W-Series of trucks, introducing the W-2200 in 1947. The W-2200 could run on either a gasoline or diesel fuel and was virtually unmatched in the size of plows or wings with which it could be equipped. Large numbers of the truck were purchased by mining companies for hauling ore and by sugar companies for plantation to processor transportation.

Production of the W-2200 ended in 1955. The same year, Oshkosh began making the Model 50–50, the first truck specifically built to carry concrete. It was an immediate hit in the ready-mix concrete industry on account of its four-wheel-drive ability at work sites and its greater capacity compared to previous models. The postwar building frenzy helped fuel brisk sales of the 50–50, particularly in the major ready-mix concrete markets of Florida, Indiana, Michigan, and Ohio. The truck's immediate success led to the creation later that year of a diesel-powered version, the Model 45–55, with a rear axle capacity of 23,000 pounds, slightly higher than the 18,000 pound capacity of the 50–50.

Bernhard Mosling was succeeded as president of Oshkosh by his son John Mosling in 1956. Oshkosh came out with Model 1832 that year. Model 1832 was the company's first tandem-axle ready-mix truck and was based on the design of the 50–50. During the 1960s, variations of Model 1832 were created to better contend with federal brake standards and certain state's weight distribution requirements for bridges. In the early 1960s the F-Series was developed by pushing the front axle forward, in contrast with the "long-nose" appearance of the 1832. Models with set-back axles evolved into the C-Series. As demand increased for larger concrete carriers to accommodate the booming construction industry, F-Series trucks were made available in 6x6, 8x6, 10x6, and 10x8 drives. Eventually, a need arose for a variation with tandem driving front axles, and this became the D-Series.

Oshkosh's first major defense contract after World War II was for more than 1,000 WT-2206 vehicles. The WT-2206 was a large, heavy-duty truck capable of plowing snow at much higher speeds than conventional equipment. The Air Force purchased the trucks for clearing runways at its northern-most bases. Their ability to plow while moving at 55 miles-per-hour was well-suited to the quick-response needs of the Distant Early Warning system that was created in the thickest period of Cold War tensions. In 1968 Oshkosh began building the U.S. Navy MB-5, an aircraft rescue and fire-fighting (ARFF) truck capable of carrying 400 gallons of water. The water could expand to 5,000 gallons of extinguishing foam when combined with a special concentrated form of the foam.

The U-30 was also designed and built by Oshkosh for the Air Force in 1968. The U-30 was an aircraft tow tractor designed to tow the C5A cargo aircraft. Another tow tractor, the smaller MB-2, went into production that year as well. Forty-five of the U-30 and 72 of the MB-2 were built in all. In 1971 the Navy ordered 73 MB-1s. The MB-1 was an ARFF similar to the MB-5, but had a capacity of 1,000 gallons. These were followed throughout the 1970s by a progression of larger crash-rescue trucks. These included the P-4, a 6x6 truck with a 1,500 gallon capacity; a variation of the P-4 called the P-4A; and the gigantic 66-ton P-15. The U.S. Air Force bought more than 500 P-4s in the early 1970s. P-4As were also purchased by both the U.S. Navy and the Australian Air Force. The P-15, which first appeared in 1977, could carry 6,000 gallons of water, expandable to 60,000 gallons of foam fire-suppressant. Oshkosh received its first U.S. Army contract in 1976. The contract called for 744 tractors to be built that could pull trailers full of heavy equipment or tanks. Oshkosh responded with the M-911 Heavy Equipment Transporter (HET). The M-911 MET design was based on the company's F-Series truck, and was still being produced 15 years after the initial contract was awarded. In 1979 the Air Force contracted Oshkosh to deliver more than 100 aircraft loaders. The aircraft loader designed and built by Oshkosh was called the 40K because of its ability to lift 40,000 pounds.

Meanwhile, on the civilian side, Oshkosh was introducing a number of new trucks in the 1970s. The B-Series, first produced in 1975, was a forward placement concrete carrier. The B-Series truck allowed the operator, seated in a one-person cab over the front axle, to drive to the precise location the concrete was to be discharged, and control the chute without leaving the cab. As the ready-mix business provided increasing revenue for Oshkosh throughout the decade, products were presented for other uses as well. In 1974 a new J-Series (which was not related to the J-Series of the 1930s) emerged as heir to the F-Series legacy. Two models, the Desert Prince and the Desert Knight, were built for use in oil-field operations. The two six-wheel-drive trucks had 325 to 485 horsepower diesel engines and large balloon tires to travel over sand. A large number of these trucks saw action in the Middle East and in China. The R-Series was also launched during this period. The R-Series was a line of heavy-duty 6x4 trucks and tractors designed to withstand the more challenging road conditions of the Middle East, Africa, and Australia. The E-Series was also designed for the international over-the-road truck market. The E-Series cab was located over the engine. Both the E- and R-Series trucks were powered by Caterpillar engines.

Despite the company's civilian products, defense contracts continued to provide the majority of Oshkosh's growth through the 1980s. In 1981 Oshkosh was awarded its largest contract yet, a five-year deal from the U.S. Army to produce Heavy Expanded Mobility Tactical Trucks (HEMTT). The contract called for delivery of 2,140 trucks, valued at $242 million, with an option on the further production of 5,350 additional vehicles, good for another $600 million. The HEMTT came in five different eight-wheel-drive models: two cargo trucks, a wrecker for vehicle recovery, a tractor, and a fuel tanker. The HEMTT continued to be produced and delivered to the Army into the 1990s. Its role in the 1990 Persian Gulf War included pulling the Patriot missile launcher.

Oshkosh improved its concrete line in 1982 with the appearance of the S-Series. This series made a mixer and a chassis available as a single unit, allowing the ready-mix producer to purchase and receive fuel support from one source. Meanwhile, defense contracts poured in, including a 1984 deal to provide the U.S. Air Force with 715 P-19 ARFF vehicles. The following year, John Carroll became the company's president. That year, Oshkosh delivered 1,400 Logistics Vehicle Systems (LVS) trucks to the U.S. Marines. Like the HEMTT, the LVS was a multipurpose vehicle. It had a variety of rear sections that could be detached and interchanged. In 1986 the Air Force ordered 787 R-11 aircraft refuelers from Oshkosh, a contract worth $78 million over three years. Spurred by this steady stream of military contracts, Oshkosh saw its revenues soar during this period. From $86 million in 1982, sales climbed remarkably steadily each year to $400 million in 1986. The company's net income advanced even more impressively, from $3.4 million to $24.8 million in the same span. Oshkosh had not had a losing year since 1930.

In 1985 Oshkosh went public. By 1987 Oshkosh employed 1,700 workers at six plants throughout Oshkosh. Stephen Mosling and Peter Mosling own approximatley 85 percent of the company's class A stock, which elects three quarters of the board of directors. The portion of Oshkosh's revenues derived from government contracts had reached 85 percent by 1987, compared to 40 percent five years earlier. At the end of the 1980s, efforts were made to restore the balance between civilian and military manufacturing. In 1989 Oshkosh acquired the motor home chassis business of Deere and Co. The Deere division had sales around $100 million. Oshkosh diversified further in 1990 with the purchase of Miller Trailers Inc. and Miller Ventures, Inc. for about $14 million.

Military contracts did not entirely dry up for Oshkosh. In January of 1990 the U.S. Army awarded Oshkosh the contract for more than 1000 M-1070 Heavy Equipment Transporters, whose main function is hauling tanks. In September of 1990 Oshkosh won another Army contract, this one for 2,626 Palletized Load System (PLS) vehicles. The PLS truck is ten-wheel driven and can carry 16.5 tons of cargo. In 1990 Oshkosh lost $2.8 million on revenue of $453 million. Sales were down in every segment of the business except for chassis, while operating expenses rose 41 percent. Oshkosh was affected dramatically in 1991 by Operation Desert Storm. In both 1990 and 1991 earnings were held back by the costs associated with starting up new projects, most of them military. For 1991, however, Oshkosh did manage to turn a profit of $755,000 even though revenue dropped to $420 million. The company was also hurt by the ongoing recession in the construction industry, slowing sales of ready-mix concrete equipment.

Under company chairman and chief executive R. Eugene Goodson, Oshkosh rebounded somewhat in 1992. Without product development costs, sales jumped to $641 million, and net income for the year was $8.8 million. As reductions in the defense budget of the United States government become increasingly likely, Oshkosh Truck's future growth will most likely depend on its ability to more actively shift focus to its commercial markets. The company introduced a refuse/recycling truck to lessen its dependence on military business. Yet an overall revival of the building industry would be the most convenient way for such a shift to take place, ensuring future customers for Oshkosh's large, nonmilitary vehicles.

Further Reading: "Dragon Wagon Joining Marines for Test Run," *Automotive News,* December 29, 1980; Thornton, Jack, "Army Pact to Oshkosh Truck," *American Metal Market,* June 1, 1981; Maturi, Richard J., "In the Fast Lane," *Barron's,* April 20, 1987; Dubashi, Jagannath, "Designer Trucks," *Financial World,* May 19, 1987; Luxenberg, Stan, "A Truck Maker's Transition," *New York Times,* October 22, 1989; "Oshkosh Truck Corp.: A Bright Outlook Despite Pentagon Cutbacks," *Barron's,* January 20, 1992; *Oshkosh Truck Corporation: 1991 Annual Report,* Oshkosh, Wisconsin: Oshkosh Truck Corporation, 1992; Wright, David and Clarence Jungwirth, *Oshkosh Trucks: 75 Years of Specialty Truck Production,* Osceola, Wisconsin: Motorbooks International, 1992.

—Robert R. Jacobson

PENTAIR

PENTAIR, INC.

Waters Edge Plaza
1500 Country Road B2 West
St. Paul, MN 55113-3105
U.S.A.
(612) 636-7920
Fax: (612) 639-5203

Public Company
Incorporated: 1966 as Pentair Industries Incorporated
Employees: 8,300
Sales: $1.23 billion
Stock Exchanges: NASDAQ
SICs: 3981 Diversified Conglomerate; 3553 Woodworking
   Machinery; 3482 Small Arms Ammunition; 2678
   Stationery Products

A diversified manufacturer of industrial equipment, water pumps, power tools, sporting ammunition, and premium-grade paper, Pentair, Inc. is a top-performing *Fortune* 500 company that holds from 10 to 30 percent market share in many of its businesses. Its enviable record of growth (since 1969, return on common equity has averaged 17 percent) is due to its highly distinctive, corporate strategy of buying underperforming— even floundering—concerns and then implementing capital and management improvements to effect quick turnarounds. In the early years of the company's history, the plan was adopted for purposes of sheer survival; as the company prospered despite periods of debt load, it became apparent that regular acquisitions through leveraged financing would be the company's mainstay. Firmly committed to both shareholders and employees, Pentair has rebuffed three takeover attempts during its history and has pledged to remain independent and devoted to long-term growth. Pentair divides its ten subsidiaries into three groups: Specialty Products, General Industrial Equipment, and Paper. Autonomously operated, subsidiaries in these groups (which include market leaders Cross Pointe Paper Corporation, Delta International Machinery Corporation, and Hoffman Engineering Company) maintain 24 locations in the North America and Europe.

Pentair was founded in July 1966 in Arden Hills, Minnesota, as a five-person partnership for the purpose of manufacturing high-altitude research balloons. The partners, three engineers, a foreman, and a salesman—all former employees of a local

branch of Litton Industries—incorporated as Pentair Industries, Inc. in August and completed an initial public offering in January 1967 to sustain their seriously undercapitalized business. Further complicating matters at the time was the lagging market for inflatables. Following the guidance of cofounder and acting manager Murray Harpole, the company decided to purchase a neighboring, virtually bankrupt business for the small sum of $14,500. With some modest engineering applications this new venture, the American Thermo-Vac Company, promised at least one saleable product: vacuum-formed, high-quality canoes. By the fall of that year red-and-white ''Penta Craft'' canoes were being successfully manufactured and sold. However, both the canoe and inflatables businesses were fraught with problems; by the end of 1967, the company had few assets, zero profits, and little direction.

As Del Marth later reported, ''By June, 1968, before Pentair was two years old, the corporate dream had become a nightmare. The company had no product to speak of, it was nearly out of money, one cofounder had died and three others had abandoned the venture.'' What sustained the company was Harpole's pledge to commit himself entirely to the business for at least five years—this and the entry of high-risk investor Ben Westby. Although Westby did not formally join the company until May 1968, he had been in close contact with Harpole for some time and had accompanied the founder on a business trip to Wisconsin, to consider the purchase of then debt-ridden, privately-owned Peavey Paper Mills, Inc.

A manufacturer of absorbent tissue paper, Peavey was acquired in June and became Pentair's first wholly owned subsidiary. The deal that Westby and Harpole had arranged was important for two reasons. First was the low cost: $10,000 down, $20,000 due in one year, and an additional five percent of after-tax profits for the first five years. Second, and most importantly, was the paper mill's potential: annual sales of $4 million in its current state of disrepair and mismanagement. Of course, with this ostensibly one-of-a-kind deal came a particularly painful and hidden price: Peavey's $1.5 million in debt. Despite this preventable surprise, a lesson in cautious and thorough research, the acquisition was made profitable within three months due primarily to Harpole's management and labor-negotiation skills. The purchase also left Pentair free to divest itself of its first two, nonproducing businesses. Now a viable paper company with substantial assets, Pentair began attracting considerable notice from the investment community and, with both a three-year Procter & Gamble contract and a preliminary agreement to acquire a Trinidad paper mill, Pentair closed the year on a high note.

In 1969, due to Pentair's new status as an acquisition-oriented, ''international corporation,'' company stock soared from $2 per share to $25 and a 3-for-1 split was declared. Before the end of the year, however, operations at the Trinidad paper mill were halted due to social and political unrest in that country. The contract with Procter & Gamble to produce absorbent wadding for use in its disposable Pampers fueled the company's growth for the next few years. Still Harpole and Westby considered Pentair's position was still tenuous. Ensuing diversifications into leather goods, meat-rendering, and computer software by and large failed to give the company the stability required for uninterrupted long-term growth. Then came the acquisitions of

Niagara of Wisconsin Paper, Miami Paper, and Flambeau Paper Corporations, in 1972, 1974, and 1978, respectively. Initial annual sales for the three totaled some $90 million. Although Pentair had sold Peavey in 1976 due to plant and market limitations, it had now affirmed itself as a major supplier of coated groundwood, book grade, and commercial printing papers, producing some 350,000 tons annually. The company signaled its arrival as a major corporation by declaring its first quarterly cash dividend in 1976. Four years earlier it had sustained a debt-to-equity ratio of greater than 7-to-1, but by 1979, after paying down debt with paper profits, it had more than reversed the numbers and gained some valuable banking partners in the process.

The 1970s were also notable for several management developments, including the departure of Westby in 1974 and the hiring of D. Eugene Nugent, an ITT executive, as vice president of operations in 1975. Harpole, singularly aware that tenacious and disciplined management had become the key to Pentair's success, handpicked Nugent as his likely successor. Both agreed that maintaining a lean corporate staff, which then numbered only ten despite more than 1,000 employees and widespread operations, would be a continuing goal for the company. (Management actually became proportionally leaner as employee levels continued to rise.) As Jeffrey Trachtenberg stated, reporting on Nugent's management style for *Forbes* in 1984, "big corporation management stifles risk-taking at the operational level. Pentair's setup is that of a slim holding company running herd over a pack of operating subsidiaries. . . . It pushes decision-making out where it belongs, among the operating managers."

The "pack" Trachtenberg referred to was the early fruition of a carefully thought out strategy by Harpole and Nugent to diversify into industrial products manufactured primarily for industrial users. As early as 1978 the two had commenced their search for such businesses to offset the capital-intensive paper group, which, led by Niagara, nonetheless represented a fairly consistent source of cash flow. According to Harpole, whose *Living the American Dream* recounts the corporation's history, he and Nugent "had to be successful on their first venture because the investment community was skeptical of our ability to expand beyond paper." The initial goal was for a company with annual sales of $25 to $100 million, preferably floundering and consequently available at a bargain price. Unfortunately, the realization of the goal was postponed, largely due to a time-consuming battle against a takeover threat by Steak and Ale founder Peter Wray, an attempt which ended only after Pentair agreed to a $4.5 million settlement in early 1981. By the middle of that year Pentair had researched and considered more than 125 manufacturers before deciding in October to acquire Porter-Cable Corporation (the portable power tools division of Rockwell International) of Jackson, Tennessee, for $16 million. Another debt-laden—but revenue-heavy—paper mill acquisition in 1983 and the 1984 purchase of Rockwell's woodworking machinery division renamed Delta International, boosted earnings to $21 million on annual sales of $545 million, vaulting the paper-and-tools company into the *Fortune* 500 rankings. The company had flourished beyond anyone's expectations.

With Nugent established as CEO and Harpole imparting a legacy stretching well beyond his retirement as chairperson in

1986, Pentair fortified itself for years to come with additional forays into industrial products, beginning with the acquisition of McNeil Corporation and its two major divisions: Lincoln, a St. Louis-based maker of lubricating products and automotive service equipment, and F. E. Myers, an Ohio-based producer of water pumps. Lincoln was eventually split into Lincoln Automotive and Lincoln Industrial. The transaction expanded the industrial group considerably, so that it now accounted for 32 percent of sales and 43 percent of operating profits. In 1988 Pentair completed one of its largest purchases, that of Federal-Hoffman Corporation (FC Holdings, Inc.), a Minnesota-based manufacturer of sports ammunition as well as metal and composite electrical enclosures. Divided into Federal Cartridge and Hoffman Engineering, FC Holdings commanded $300 million in annual sales, or nearly 40 percent of Pentair's total sales for the previous year. Now, a decade after its stated objective to strengthen through diversification, the company had reduced its dependency on paper sales to just 30 percent while multiplying its total equity tenfold.

Late in 1985, the company announced an ambitious $400 million joint venture between Pentair and Minnesota Power of Duluth to form Lake Superior Paper Industries (LSPI). The venture was to be the company's first sustained "ground floor up" business, with the culmination of years of technical expertise, industry-specific knowledge, and financial clout put to the test. LSPI, the newest and most efficient paper mill in North America, began start-up operations in late 1987 and, by March of 1988, was producing supercalendered, publication-grade paper (SCA) for a highly competitive U.S. market. The difficulty of the market and the huge capital outlay worried investors from the start. However, "while others either wrung their hands or snickered," wrote Alyssa Lappen for *Forbes,* "Nugent pressed ahead with a capital investment project that now claims customers ranging from Sears and J. C. Penney to *Rolling Stone.* Foreign competitors like West Germany's Haindl Papier and Feldmühle have been squeezed, while more customers line up for Pentair's paper every day." In its second year of operations, LSPI was operating at 87 percent of its 245,000 ton-per-year capacity and had positioned itself as the domestic leader of SCA. By the end of 1991, production had risen to 93 percent and earnings had increased 58 percent over 1990 levels.

In 1992 Winslow Buxton, former president of Niagara of Wisconsin, succeeded Nugent as CEO. One of his short-term goals, inherited from Nugent, is to acquire another manufacturing company (with sales from $200 to $500 million) while elevating overall corporate sales to $2 billion by 1996. Sales growth in 1990 of only 1 percent and a fractional sales loss in 1991 make such an acquisition a near imperative, given Pentair's history. In a June 1992 article "Pentair on the Prowl," Susan E. Peterson reported that "the company has investigated more than 150 possible candidates in the past 18 months but has had a tougher time finding a suitable match than during past acquisition searches." The search continues into 1993, past Nugent's target date of late 1992. For investors, the delay will no doubt be worth it: Pentair, with a 17.7 percent compounded dividend return since 1976, has earned high esteem from shareholders and analysts alike. Market-maker Piper Jaffray raised its opinion of Pentair stock (PNTA) to "buy" in January after determining that current trading levels were low, especially given a projected 8.5 percent growth in earnings for 1993. "We believe,'' the report states, ''that as PNTA continues to de-emphasize its coated paper businesses and report significant gains in its industrial businesses, the analytical focus and price/earnings ratio will reflect the underlying performance of the core, non-paper businesses.''

Regardless of whether divestitures of one or more of the company's paper mills will result from the impending industrial acquisition, Pentair maintains its commitment to its trademark leverage strategy. ''There's a lesson to be learned,'' writes Jill Fraser, ''from Pentair's highly disciplined approach to leverage. It has adhered rigidly to five basic principles: buy cheap; raise productivity fast; utilize cash flow from existing businesses to pay down debt; shun junk bonds; and above all, protect existing relations with bankers.'' This is the strategy that will sustain Pentair well into the 21st century. The markets it serves—industrial, construction, woodworking, automotive, recreation, consumer, and printing—may change, but its hard-won policies will undoubtedly remain much the same.

Principal Subsidiaries: Cross Pointe Paper Corporation; Delta International Machinery Corporation; Federal Cartridge Company; Hoffman Engineering Company; F. E. Myers Co.; Niagara of Wisconsin Paper Corporation; Porter-Cable Corporation; Lincoln Automotive; Lincoln Industrial; Lake Superior Paper Industries (50%).

Further Reading: Trachtenberg, Jeffrey A., '' 'It's Not Glamorous, But It Works,' '' *Forbes,* May 21, 1984; Jaffe, Thomas, ''Paper Profits,'' *Forbes,* August 25, 1986; Marth, Del, ''Friendly Takeovers,'' *Nation's Business,* May 1986; Lappen, Alyssa A., ''Gene's Dream,'' *Forbes,* May 30, 1988; ''Pentair Agrees to Buy Anoka Holding Firm,'' *Star Tribune,* November 15, 1988; Fraser, Jill Andresky, ''The Five Rules of Debt,'' *Corporate Finance,* December 10, 1991; ''Paper Losses Mean a Real Income Drop for Pentair,'' *Star Tribune,* February 5, 1991; Carideo, Anthony, ''Many Are Expecting a Turnaround in '92,'' *Star Tribune,* August 26, 1991; Harpole, Murray J., *Living the American Dream: Pentair, Inc.—The First Twenty-Five Years,* St. Paul, Minnesota: St. Thomas Technology Press, 1992; Peterson, Susan E., ''Pentair's '91 Revenues Dip, But St. Paul Company Reports a 28.2 Percent Increase in Net Income,'' *Star Tribune,* January 31, 1992; Peterson, Susan E., ''Pentair on the Prowl: The Conglomerate Has Been Seeking a Major Acquisition for More Than a Year,'' *Star Tribune,* June 20, 1992; Analyst's Report, Piper Jaffray Inc., January 14, 1993.

—Jay P. Pederson

PERDUE FARMS INC.

P.O. Box 1537
Salisbury, Maryland 21802
U.S.A.
(410) 543-3000
Fax: (410) 543-3212

Private Company
Incorporated: 1920
Employees: 12,500
Sales: $1.2 billion
SICs: 2015 Poultry Slaughtering & Processing; 2048
Prepared Feeds Nec; 2075 Soybean Oil Mills

"My chickens eat better than you do." As one of the many snappy advertising slogans used by Perdue Farms since the late 1960s, this phrase helped Frank Perdue build his family poultry farm into a company that boasts annual sales of more than $1 billion. Perdue Farms is the fourth-largest producer of raw chicken in the United States, trailing only Tyson Foods subsidiary Holly Farms, Conagra Poultry, and Gold Kist.

When people think of Perdue Farms, the lean, creased features of longtime chief executive officer and advertising spokesman Frank Perdue usually come to mind. But the company was actually founded by Frank's father, Arthur W. Perdue. In 1920 the elder Perdue bought five dollars worth of laying hens and went into business selling eggs in Salisbury, Maryland.

For its first two decades, the company remained a tiny, family-run organization, in large part because of Arthur Perdue's unwillingness to borrow money to finance expansion. "He was a checkbook-balance man," his son would later say of him, as quoted in *Inc.* magazine. "If he had money in the bank and didn't owe any, it didn't matter how much we lost. But if he owed money, it didn't make any difference if we were making a million a week—we had to get that paid off before we expanded."

In the meantime, Frank Perdue went off to college, entering Salisbury State College in 1937, but left after two years to rejoin the family business. He kept his own flock of chickens on the side and had 800 hens of his own by 1941. The company grew in automatic response to improved economic conditions, as the nation pulled out of the Great Depression of the 1930s and demand for eggs increased. The Perdues found, however, that maintaining their sole focus on eggs also limited their profit potential. During the 1940s, they shifted their emphasis away from egg production and began turning out broiling chickens for resale to processors. Among their early customers were industry giants Swift & Company and Armour. By 1952, when Frank Perdue succeeded his father as president of the company, Perdue Farms was racking up annual sales of $6 million on a volume of 2.6 million birds.

Even still, the younger Perdue felt constrained by his father's conservative ways. Frank Perdue held a vision of turning the family business into a fully integrated breeding operation with its own hatcheries and feed mills. Finally, in 1961, the elder Perdue agreed to his son's plan to finance a soybean mill by borrowing money—the first time in his 40 years in the poultry industry that he had willingly gone into debt. "When we finally borrowed money, I was 41 years old and he was 76," Frank later recalled in *Inc.* "Knowing the nature of the individual, I have to be appalled in retrospect that he put his name to a $500,000 note."

During the 1960s, Frank Perdue built up a tall stack of vertical integration for Perdue Farms. By 1967 the company could boast of one of the largest grain storage and poultry feed milling operations on the East Coast, soybean processing plants, mulch plants, a hatchery, and some 600 farmers raising birds under the Perdue name.

The engine that drove Perdue Farms' rapid expansion during this time was, of course, Frank Perdue himself. And in later years, whether out of pride or simple desire to state the obvious truth, he would not hesitate to take credit for the company's success. "I wanted the company to grow to the maximum extent possible," he told an *Inc.* reporter in 1984. "I wouldn't be satisfied with number two. I have driven very hard to increase production." He also drove very hard to increase sales. During the early days of the company, he served his father as salesman, traveling up and down the Eastern Seaboard to meet with buyers. Once he became president, Frank Perdue continued attending supermarket openings to keep his company's profile as high as possible. "My father wouldn't do it," he commented in *Inc.*, "but I'll do anything it takes for this business because I consider it more my baby than it was his. I was totally into it without any letup for 20 to 30 years. I've been the principal force in its growth."

Indeed, by 1967 Perdue Farms was posting annual sales of more than $35 million. At about this time, however, the company faced a serious threat as processors began to buy chickens directly from farmers, cutting out middlemen like Perdue Farms. Processors were thus able to expand their profit margins and squeeze their outside suppliers by driving harder bargains with them. Perdue Farms responded to this challenge by becoming a processor itself, adding its own processing operations and delivering the processed birds to market on its own. The Perdue brand name made its debut in retail meat counters in 1968. The company chose New York City as its first target market because of the city's high concentration of people with above-average incomes and its reputation for having consumers who are hard to impress; Perdue figured that if its chickens sold there, they would sell anywhere.

Frank Perdue had his doubts about whether or not this move into retailing would succeed, but he would soon find himself pleasantly surprised. For one thing, Perdue Farms held a significant advantage over its major competitors: it had easy access to the major urban markets of the Eastern Seaboard. Salisbury is a several-hour truck ride away from New York, Philadelphia, and Washington, D.C., and an overnight drive from Boston and Hartford. Secondly, the company's redoubled efforts to produce high-quality chickens paid off. To ensure that he could grow birds that were more tender than the rest, Perdue hired two professors from North Carolina State University to write a computer program that would supervise the feeding of his chickens, establishing formulae that would keep the birds as healthy as possible at each stage of their growth.

Finally, and perhaps most importantly, advertising generated consumer awareness of the Perdue brand name beyond the company's fondest expectations. In 1972 the company hired Scali McCabe Sloves, a small New York agency, to handle its advertising; in turn, the agency made perhaps the most fateful decision in the history of Perdue Farms—putting Franklin Parsons Perdue himself on the air. In print, on radio, and on television, the voice and visage of Frank Perdue became a known presence in the northeastern United States almost from the very start. *Inc.* described him as a most unlikely corporate spokesman—"slender, laconic, whiny-voiced, balding, droopy-lidded, long-nosed"—but Perdue's earnest appeals based on the quality of his product proved to be effective. *Business Week* once wrote that he possessed "all the fervor and sincerity of a Southern preacher" in his television commercials.

Catchy slogans also helped; one print advertisement that ran in the early 1970s showed a stern visaged Perdue with his arms folded and standing beneath the words, "Everybody's chickens are approved by the government. But my chickens are also approved by me." In a lighter vein, another Perdue ad instructed housewives, "If your husband is a breast or leg man, ask for my chicken parts." Perdue may have uttered the most immortal of all his slogans, however, when he informed his audience that "it takes a tough man to make a tender chicken."

Perdue's success as a frontman for his own company in major media markets during the 1970s and 1980s, in fact, inspired advertising agencies to make pitchmen out of other chief executive officers, including Eastern Airlines' Frank Borman and Chrysler's Lee Iacocca. It also drew the attention of New York City Mayor Edward Koch, himself something of a Frank Perdue look-alike and no stranger to the value of publicity, who once called Perdue "an upper-echelon chicken guy."

But this transformation of a Maryland chicken farmer into a media icon would have meant nothing if it had not inspired more people to buy Perdue chickens. Between 1972 and 1984, Perdue Farms' sales doubled every two years. By the end of that period, the company was selling 260 million birds per year and generating revenues of more than $500 million. This success made Perdue Farms one of the 50 largest private companies in the United States.

Arthur Perdue died in 1977 at the age of 91. He had never really retired from the company that his son now ran; he retained the position of chairman and came to the office every day until the end of his life. Frank Perdue officially succeeded him as chairman in 1979.

While Perdue Farms was riding the increasing popularity of both its pitchman/chief executive officer and its chicken to success and fortune, the company did not by any means escape the notice of its competitors. Its main rival was North Carolina-based Holly Farms, which later became a subsidiary of Tyson Foods. Holly Farms was a much larger company than Perdue Farms and sold chicken to a nationwide market. Perdue Farms was its main competitor in the lucrative Northeast. As early as 1971, Holly Farms watched the Perdue experiment in selling at the retail level under its own brand name with great interest and concluded that Perdue Farms could be beaten—at least in part because Perdue Farms was pricing its broilers as high as ten cents per pound above other brands. That year, Holly Farms began selling under its own brand name.

The two companies competed neck and neck during the 1980s, introducing new products in an effort to spur sales growth and out-do the other. During the early eighties both were spending $6 million dollars a year for advertising. In 1983 Perdue Farms introduced chicken franks—hot dogs stuffed with chicken instead of pork or beef. In 1985 Holly Farms began selling fillets and bite-size nuggets—"all you do is dip 'em and do 'em," went their slogan—under the name Time Trimmer. In response, Perdue Farms launched a line of prepared chicken products called Perdue Done It!, which included breaded and precooked nuggets and cutlets. As it turned out, neither Perdue nor Holly Farms could quite out-do the other, but both succeeded well enough so that in 1985 the two companies together accounted for one-fourth of all the fresh chicken sold in the United States.

Frank Perdue resigned as chief executive officer in 1988 but remained as his company's chairman and advertising spokesman. He was 67 years old and, with 90 percent of Perdue Farms stock in his and his family's hands, his personal fortune was estimated to be at least $350 million. Perdue was succeeded by one of his longtime executives, Donald Mabe, who lasted only three years in that office, retiring in 1991.

Also in 1991, Perdue retired as chairman, although he remained the company's chief public relations asset. The ensuing vacuum at the top was partially filled by Perdue's 41-year-old son James, who became chairman upon his father's retirement. Perdue Farms' board decided to leave the chief executive officer spot open, hoping that it would serve as an incentive for both the younger Perdue and his second-in-command, company president Pelham Lawrence.

Unlike his father, James Perdue did not start out in life as an enthusiastic poultry man. He worked only informally for the family business while he was growing up. After graduating from college, he entered the marine biology program at the University of Washington and graduated with his Ph.D. in 1983. But James Perdue's departure from the family business was a matter of personal growth as much as it was an expression of differing interests. "The reason I left . . . was to find out more about myself, to get a better confidence level," he related in the *New York Times* soon after becoming chairman of Perdue Farms. "Although I am Frank Perdue's son, I wasn't born with confidence. That can only come with victories." By his own estimation, his graduate work gave James the self-assurance that he needed. Meanwhile, he kept abreast of company affairs through regular conversations with his father. As his graduate studies were coming to an end, Frank Perdue flew out to Seattle and asked James to come work for Perdue Farms.

Under James Perdue, Perdue Farms enacted subtle, but important changes in the way it produced chicken. The management process was opened up so that plant workers had more influence in decision-making. The company also sought to improve worker safety after the state of North Carolina fined it in 1989 for permitting unsafe working conditions at its four processing plants there. These changes in Perdue Farms' operating procedures were begun by Frank Perdue before he retired, but the task of carrying them out was left mostly to his son. By his own admission, the outspoken elder Perdue was less temperamentally suited to the task of selling the company's efforts to its own workers. ''Jim's style is different from mine,'' he confessed in the *New York Times*. ''He can sell the achievement of quality in a more palatable way. I am more demanding, he is more conciliatory.'' Low-key by nature, James Perdue announced no plans to appear in television commercials.

Perdue Farms' revenue growth began to level off in the late 1980s and early 1990s, but the poultry industry as a whole saw its 20-year sales boom come to an end at the same time. Chicken sales grew at a rate of four to five percent per year during the 1970s and 1980s, but in the early 1990s, per capita consumption of poultry declined while production continued to increase. For Perdue Farms, sales leveled off at $1.2 billion in 1991 and 1992.

Catchy slogans and appealing television commercials notwithstanding, it seems that how well Perdue Farms does is tied to the overall popularity of chicken with the American consumer. The continuing success of the company depends to a large extent on whether the taste of chicken and concerns over the relative healthfulness of poultry versus red meat can sustain growth in the industry as a whole. But it is certain that Perdue Farms has come down to its third generation of Perdues as a noteworthy success story, from which a significant portion of the American public learned that it takes a tough man to make a tender chicken.

Further Reading: ''Perdue Chicken Spreads Its Wings,'' *Business Week,* September 16, 1972; Mamis, Robert A., ''Frank Perdue,'' *Inc.,* February 1984; Giges, Nancy, ''Holly Farms, Perdue Face off in Chickie Run,'' *Advertising Age,* September 16, 1985; Barmash, Isadore, ''The Quieter Style of the New Generation at Perdue,'' *New York Times,* July 16, 1992.

—Douglas Sun

PERKIN ELMER

THE PERKIN-ELMER CORPORATION

761 Main Avenue
Norwalk, Connecticut 06859
U.S.A.
(203) 762-1000
Fax: (203) 762-6000

Public Company
Incorporated: 1939
Employees: 6,085
Sales: $911 million
Stock Exchanges: New York Pacific
SICs: 3826 Analytical Instruments; 3559 Special Industry
  Machinery Nec

The Perkin-Elmer Corporation is the world's leading producer of analytical instruments used in military operations, space exploration, and several areas of scientific research. A key contributor to the development of such optical tools as the infrared spectrometer, the spectrophotometer, and laser retrore-flectors, the company is also known for its work on NASA's Hubble Space Telescope, an ambitious and ultimately unsuccessful project that has nevertheless provided scientists with some valuable information through space photography. Having undergone a series of restructurings in the late 1980s and early 1990s, the company remains, in the words of CEO Gaynor N. Kelley, a "global, yet compact, coordinated and efficient" provider of instrumentation and technology.

Perkin-Elmer originated in the early 1930s when a common fascination with astronomy brought together an otherwise unlikely duo: Charles W. Elmer, the head of a firm of court reporters who was already not far from retirement age, and Richard Perkin, a young investment banker who had left Pratt Institute in Brooklyn, New York, after a year of studying chemical engineering to try a Wall Street career.

The two met when Perkin dropped in on an astronomy lecture Elmer delivered at the Brooklyn Institute of Arts & Sciences. They soon became friends and also recognized a common interest in turning their hobby into a business opportunity in precision optics. Deciding to set up shop in New York City, Perkin raised $15,000 in start up capital from his relatives, while Elmer was able to contribute in $5,000. They ordered equipment from

Europe, and on April 19, 1937 they formed Perkin-Elmer as a partnership.

Perkin and Elmer started their optical design and consulting business in a small Manhattan office, but within a year they were producing optical components in Jersey City, New Jersey. On December 13, 1939 they incorporated. The company moved to Connecticut's Fairfield County in 1941—initially to Glenbrook outside Stamford, later to Norwalk and Wilton—its home area ever since.

The onset of World War II made clear the importance of an American source for precision instruments, and Perkin-Elmer was able to operate at a profit from the start. In 1942, it became the first optical instrument maker to win a Navy "E" (for Excellence). The principal wartime products were instruments and components used in airplane range finders, bombsights, and reconnaissance systems. However, the company was also able to arrange for research that extended its optical know-how into a brand new field, coming out with its initial infrared spectrometer in 1944. Germany had also done work in infrared spectroscopy, but had put it aside to concentrate on more urgent military needs, enabling Perkin-Elmer to build a substantial lead. The production of a spectrometer, which uses infrared rays for quick and accurate analysis of chemical compounds, was the start of a whole array of analytical instruments such as gas chromatographs (which Perkin-Elmer introduced in 1955 as its second major analytical group) and atomic absorption spectrophotometers, collectively ushering in a new era in analytical laboratory operations. The equipment is used both for research and for production control, as well as several other activities including crime investigations.

After the war the company was chosen to design and build the 33-inch Baker Schmidt telescope, which Harvard University installed in 1950 at an observatory in South Africa. As part of its defense work, in 1955, it built a Transverse Panoramic Camera, the 12 by 14 foot frames of which could take precise horizon-to-horizon aerial reconnaissance pictures from 40,000 feet, a major achievement in those presatellite days. And from the early, unmanned satellite launchings on, Perkin-Elmer instruments were used regularly in spacecraft. Furthermore, the company remained a leading supplier of missile guidance equipment to the military.

During the 1950s Perkin-Elmer also moved energetically into foreign markets. It set up a manufacturing affiliate in West Germany in 1954 and in Britain in 1957, while sales units were established in several more countries. In 1960 a Japanese production unit, Hitachi Perkin-Elmer, was established, with Hitachi Ltd. holding a 51 percent interest.

Cofounder Elmer died at age 83 in 1954. A year later the company sold its first stock to the public and began trading over the counter. On December 13, 1960—21 years to the day since Perkin-Elmer incorporated—Dick Perkin bought the first 100 shares for $47.50 a share at the traditional New York Stock Exchange ceremonies as Perkin-Elmer was listed with the ticker symbol PKN. Since that time, Perkin-Elmer's stock has undergone four 2-for-1 stock splits. While PKN tends to be quite a volatile stock, prices have generally been well above that early level.

Perkin served as president and chairperson until June 1961, when he brought in Robert E. Lewis, who had been president of Argus Camera and Sylvania Electric, to take over as president and chief executive. Perkin remained chairperson, concentrating on long range plans and overseas development, until his death at age 62 in 1969.

Perkin-Elmer came early to the laser era in 1961. In fact, the whole concept was so new that the unit handling the development was called the Optical "Maser" Department, because when Dr. Theodore Maiman first came out with the beams at Hughes Aircraft in 1960, their name was derived from Microwave Amplification by Stimulated Emission of Radiation. Since light waves, shorter and with higher frequency than microwaves, can be concentrated into narrower beams and operate at higher speed, the technology quickly centered on the *optical* maser version, that is, light beams. It wasn't long before "l" for light replaced the "m" and the term became laser. Most of Perkin-Elmer's laser work in the 1960s was in defense and space applications. One triumph came in 1969 when the Apollo 11 astronauts, their helmet visors protected by a Perkin-Elmer coating, deployed Perkin-Elmer laser retroreflectors on the moon's surface; shooting beams from earth at these reflectors later permitted extremely accurate distance measurements.

During the 1960s, the company made some acquisitions supplementing internal expansion of its instrument line. Then, in the 1970s, in line with a trend in American corporate culture, Perkin-Elmer undertook a number of ambitious diversification moves. The foundation was laid for what Perkin-Elmer calls its material sciences business with the acquisition in September 1971 of METCO Inc. of Westbury, New York, the leading supplier of plasma and flame spray material and equipment. (After acquiring the corporation, Perkin-Elmer opted to lowercase the name to "Metco.") The Metco thermal spraying process applied a metal or ceramic coating to improve a part's wear, corrosion rate, or heat resistance. The improved surface provided by such spraying can permit the use of less expensive materials in all sorts of machinery and engine components.

Also during this time, Perkin-Elmer sought to take advantage of the transistor boom by entering the semiconductor equipment business. In 1973 it introduced the Micralign projection mask aligner, designed to facilitate the production of semiconductors. The company entered yet another popular field the following year, acquiring Interdata, Inc., active in super-minicomputers.

While building up its presence in these new areas, Perkin-Elmer also continued to enhance its analytical instrumentation and optical lines. Among major optical assignments, Perkin-Elmer received in 1977 the prime contract to develop the Hubble Space Telescope for NASA. This particular project proved to be a mixed blessing. After the $1.5 billion telescope was finally launched into space in 1990, it was discovered that the Hubble could not achieve its full mission because of some design and manufacturing flaws. Even so, it has been able to send back, as the *New York Times* put it, "valuable pictures of the near and far heavens."

In the instrumentation area, Perkin-Elmer has introduced increasingly computerized equipment. For instance, in 1975 it brought out an infrared spectrometer controlled by a micropro-

cessor; a decade later, the company offered augmented automation by use of robotics. Meanwhile, in 1977 Perkin-Elmer had further broadened its product base through the acquisition of Physical Electronics Industries, which specialized in surface science analytical instruments used to examine the chemical composition and bonding of the first few atomic layers of a surface. Later, the company began to explore biotechnology instrumentation.

Up until the mid-1980s, Perkin-Elmer's growth formula had resulted in generally rising sales to a record $1.3 billion in the July 1985 fiscal year, compared with only around $300 million by the mid-1970s and under $50 million in 1963. Profits, while more volatile, had also grown strongly from around $2 million in 1963. However, profits peaked at $82.6 million in fiscal year 1981. By the latter part of the 1980s, Perkin-Elmer determined that massive diversification no longer paid off. And—again like so many other corporations—it entered a series of divestitures and restructurings.

Even as it proudly celebrated the 50th anniversary of Perkin-Elmer's start as a partnership, management bluntly told stockholders in the 1987 annual report that in this "watershed year ... we faced the realities of a significantly changed marketplace. We recognized that markets for high technology goods ... have become much more competitive." The message was accompanied by a $95 million restructuring charge, which left the company $18 million in the red for the July 1987 year, its first recorded loss.

This first stage of restructuring consisted mainly of dropping unprofitable product lines, consolidating plants, and streamlining sales and service operations, as well as scaling back their workforce by six percent. The company maintained its six basic business lines: analytical instruments, semiconductor equipment, optical systems, materials and surface technology, minicomputers, and the German manufacturing unit called Bodenseewerk Geraetetechnik (BGT), which specialized in missile and other avionic systems for the United States as well as the German government.

Fiscal 1988 brought the anticipated rebound, with profits of $72 million. By the end of the year an agreement had been reached to withdraw from the computer business. Back in 1985, Perkin-Elmer had put its computer business into a new subsidiary called Concurrent Computer Corporation and had sold an 18 percent stake to the public. Now, the company arranged to sell its remaining 82 percent interest to Massachusetts Computer Corporation. The sale was completed early in fiscal 1989, with Perkin-Elmer realizing a moderate profit on the transaction.

As fiscal 1989 progressed, management decided on a far more drastic restructuring, dropping three more major business segments and leaving a company centered on just two basic fields: analytical instruments and material sciences. As a measure of the magnitude of these steps, the historically recalculated revenues from "continuing operations" for fiscal 1987 came to only $600 million or less than half the record $1.3 billion that all of the then-operating units had actually brought in. For fiscal 1989, both sales and profits from continuing operations showed healthy gains over the two preceding years, but an $82 million write-down of the businesses being dropped resulted in a net loss of $24 million.

Most of the actual divestitures took place between November 1989 and May 1990. BGT in Germany was sold to the Diehl Group. The Hughes Aircraft subsidiary of General Motors acquired most of the Government Systems (formerly called Optical Systems) operations, though some parts of this business were sold separately, in several instances to companies set up by former Perkin-Elmer subsidiary managers. Most of the semiconductor equipment operation was placed in a unit then acquired by Silicon Valley Group, while another portion went to a company formed by unit management. In three of the divestitures, Perkin-Elmer, at least temporarily, took a minority stake to facilitate the deal. While these dispositions had required a writedown of book value, the sales generated net cash inflow of nearly a quarter of a billion dollars. Perkin-Elmer used it to buy back some ten million common shares, more than 20 percent of the total outstanding.

The more narrowly focused Perkin-Elmer boosted sales and turned a $44 million profit in fiscal 1990, but the next year, with problems aggravated by worldwide weak economies, the Persian Gulf war, and other international turmoil, events proved that the company was not yet in the clear. Gaynor N. Kelley—who had started at Perkin-Elmer in 1950, became president in 1985, and added the titles of chairperson and CEO in October 1990—cited the "excellent potential" of the company's two remaining businesses, but told stockholders in the fiscal 1991 annual report that "our management team concluded that additional changes were necessary to achieve that potential." He added: "This was a sobering realization because our company had already experienced tremendous upheaval." Another $53 million was set aside for necessary restructuring, this time pushing fiscal 1991 results $15.6 million into the red.

Kelley had started on his task almost as soon as he was placed in full charge. In December 1990, he issued a call to action, noting that while the company was intent on "preserving the things we do that work well, and changing those things that do not," it needed to recognize that customers are increasingly "solution-oriented rather than technology-oriented." He solicited help from teams of employees from all sectors of the company to implement his goals and develop new products that customers would want.

While the United States is Perkin-Elmer's single largest market, it accounts for less than 50 percent of total company business; most of the foreign volume comes from Europe. Kelley is formulating steps to attract more Pacific business, but his basic principle is that the company's products generally have a worldwide rather than localized market. Consequently, he has instituted a switch from operating by geographical units to organizing around the product on a worldwide basis. The entire global instrument business has been divided into three major groups: life sciences, organic sciences, and inorganic sciences. At the same time, management of the materials sciences operation was overhauled. The July 1992 year saw recovery with revenues at a postdivestiture high of $911 million and profits of $59 million. In *Forbes*, Reed Abelson ventured that Perkin-Elmer "seems finally on the right track."

Nor has Perkin-Elmer's contraction of its business lines meant abandonment of aggressive search for new opportunities within its chosen fields. A prime example is the company's growing interest in biotechnology instrumentation. In 1986 Perkin formed a joint venture with biotech specialist Cetus Corp. Utilizing the polymerase chain reaction (PCR) technique developed by Cetus, the venture produced DNA instrumentation products that can amplify DNA from tiny samples. In December 1991 Cetus was acquired by Chiron Corp. after selling its PCR technology to major drug producer Hoffmann-La Roche. As a result the Perkin-Cetus venture was replaced by a long-term agreement with Hoffmann. In early 1993 Perkin acquired Applied Biosystems, an expert in DNA sequencing and synthesizing systems, which can become the base for Perkin-Elmer's total biosystems effort. It is in such ways that Perkin-Elmer counts on invigorating its business without straying from its instrument orientation.

Further Reading: "Perkin-Elmer Picks a Head," *Investor's Reader,* May 10, 1961; "Richard Scott Perkin," *Investor's Reader,* April 25, 1962; "The March of Science on Both Coasts," *Investor's Reader,* December 18, 1963; *Our Heritage,* Perkin-Elmer anniversary brochure, 1987; Abelson, Reed, "Getting its Act Together," *Forbes,* August 31, 1992.

—Henry Hecht

PET INCORPORATED

400 South Fourth Street
St. Louis, Missouri 63102
U.S.A.
(314) 622-7700
Fax: (314) 622-6525

Public Company
Incorporated: 1885 as Helvetia Milk Condensing Company
Sales: $1.8 billion
Employees: 7,200
Stock Exchanges: New York
SICs: 2023 Dry, Condensed & Evaporated Dairy Products;
2099 Food Preparations Nec; 2752 Commercial Printing—
Lithographic

Pet Incorporated, a specialty food producer with a number of familiar name-brands, operates 33 manufacturing plants internationally, two-thirds of them located in the United States. Pet produces and markets its products through two primary units, the Worldwide Mexican and International group and Pet USA, the latter of which comprises all frozen, refrigerated, and shelf-stable products with the exception of the company's Mexican food brands. A large percentage of its revenues comes from brands that hold the number-one or number-two market share in their categories.

Formerly the Pet Milk Company, Pet is the successor to the Helvetia Milk Condensing Company, organized in 1885 in Highland, Illinois, just across the river from St. Louis, Missouri. In November 1884, an article in the *Highland Union* announced that "a certain party in St. Louis intends to erect an establishment here for condensing milk." By February 1885, a committee of Highland citizens bought 150 shares of stock at $100 per share to fund the start-up of a condensing plant by a Swiss immigrant named John Meyenberg. By mid-June, the first unsweetened "Highland Evaporated Cream" was produced and, despite a steam-powered sterilizer explosion three weeks later that resulted in a month-long shutdown, the business continued. Two unrelated incidents by the end of 1885 gained recognition in the South for Helvetia's evaporated milk. The fledgling company donated 10 cases of its product to victims of a Galveston, Texas, fire, and an El Paso, Texas, grocer ordered 100 cases after successfully feeding the milk to his ill infant.

Troubles occurred the following year, however. In early 1886, after numerous cases of milk spoiled on grocers' shelves, the Helvetia shareholder committee recommended that the company halt operations before funds were depleted. Meyenberg, incensed with the committee's decision and criticisms of his method, left Highland and never returned. Following the brief stint of David Suppiger as president, Louis Latzer, a young farmer who had resigned from the board of directors within the first year of Helvetia's operations, agreed to head the company. Backed with a college degree and an education in chemistry, Latzer, aided by Dr. Werner Schmidt of Highland, spent years tracing the bacteria that had caused the earlier milk spoilage. Their efforts eventually succeeded and, in the process, Latzer had automated Helvetia's plants, introducing faster production as well as safer canning processes and lower consumer costs.

Notwithstanding the early setbacks, Helvetia won an award for excellence from the Mechanics Industrial Exposition in San Francisco in 1887, and blue ribbons from both the 1890 Paris Exposition and the 1893 Columbian Exposition in Chicago. The recognition gained from these awards was due to the marketing work of John Wildi, a founding director who promoted Helvetia's evaporated milk in several key markets: as a healthful baby food; as a recipe base; and as a milk-substitute for Southern areas with little refrigeration as well as for mining regions in the western United States.

Responding to the request of a New Orleans food broker for a "baby-sized" can to sell for a nickel, the company introduced "Our Pet Evaporated Cream," and registered the name as a trademark in 1895. Following a great marketing success at the 1904 World's Fair, Wildi went into the evaporated milk business himself, keeping nearly 33 percent of Helvetia stock. Upon his death in 1907, an agreement was reached that enabled Wildi's family attorney, William Nardin, to join Helvetia's board of directors.

During the Spanish-American and First World wars, the U.S. government ordered huge supplies of evaporated milk, spurring Helvetia to build a second plant in Greenville, Illinois. By 1918 the company had a total of ten production sites in the Midwest, Pennsylvania, and Colorado. As World War I ended, Helvetia closed plants due to oversupply, reluctantly pulling out of western markets. Latzer sold the excess milk to St. Louis businessmen, who turned to him in 1920 when a strike by the local milk producers association limited the brokers' supplies. The St. Louis strikers also convinced the Highland area farmers to strike, however, and Latzer was forced to close the plant.

By early 1921, Latzer's son John ran Helvetia from its reestablished headquarters in nearby St. Louis. In 1923, the company was renamed Pet Milk Company, after its best-selling evaporated milk brand. Within two years Pet Milk bought the Salt Lake City-based Sego Milk Products Company, giving Pet Milk more depth in milk supply, as well as a chance to reenter the western American market. In the late 1920s the company built new plants and made a number of acquisitions, including an ice cream plant in Greenville, Illinois, and a milk processing plant in Johnson City, Tennessee. In 1928 Pet Milk was first traded on the New York Stock Exchange, and the following year the Pet Dairy Products Company was established. By 1934 Pet Milk became the first company to add vitamin D to its dairy products via the process of irradiation.

Louis Latzer died in 1924 after 37 years with the company. John Latzer delegated sales and marketing to William Nardin, who in turn recruited his friend Erma Proetz for some modern advertising ideas. Proetz took over the Pet Milk account for Gardner Advertising, establishing Gardner test kitchens in the late 1920s as well as successful radio broadcasts that carried both the company and consumers through the tough days of the Great Depression and World War II. Proetz's shows eventually aired on nearly 200 American stations and led to other innovative Pet Milk promotions.

After World War II Pet Milk began a slight movement into other markets. The company became the first to offer nonfat dry milk, an advance over the powdered milk developed in the 1920s. Sales soared due to the postwar baby boom, making 1950 the all-time-high sales year for Pet Evaporated Milk. Soon thereafter, fresh milk became readily available, however, and sales began a steady decline.

When John Latzer died in 1952, after more than 30 years with Pet Milk, his brother Robert Latzer took over. While Robert continued in the Latzer tradition, emphasizing research and production, he knew the company needed to diversify. In 1955, as a result of the efforts of Louis Latzer's grandson Theodore Gamble, Pet Milk acquired its first nondairy operation: the Pet-Ritz Foods Company in Michigan. To initiate growth outside the United States, Pet Milk also established a Canadian subsidiary to produce and sell goods. The expansion plans were announced in 1959 by Gamble, elected president in February following Robert Latzer's move to chairman.

In preparation for a growth spurt, Gamble worked with the consultant Booz, Allen & Hamilton. Through restructuring, Pet Milk reduced committee numbers, initiated a profit-centered divisional structure, and recruited marketing professionals. The company also planned new product development to wean itself from the declining milk market (as late as 1960, 95 percent of Pet Milk sales were in dairy products). By the early 1960s, diversification had begun in earnest. Within two years Pet Milk bought a variety of food producers, including the C. H. Musselman Company, Laura Scudder's, Downyflake Foods, Stephen F. Whitman & Son, Inc., and R. E. Funsten Company, the largest U.S. pecan producer at the time. These acquisitions brought Pet Milk a total of approximately $90 million in sales. Through its Canadian subsidiary, Pet Milk also acquired Van Kirk Chocolate, Cherry Hill Cheese, and the Numilk Division of Dominion Dairies. In 1963 the company bought the Dutch-based C. V. Gebroeders Pel, a producer of jelly and other confections.

Gamble's plan was to move away from commodity products and toward specialty and snack foods, which were considered high-growth markets. In 1964 Pet Milk moved into the gourmet foods market, buying Reese Finer Foods, Inc., and D. E. Winebrenner Co., a fruit-juice maker. The following year, Pet Milk acquired George H. Dentler & Sons, a snack food company, and Stuckey's, Inc., the latter marking Pet Milk's first non-processing venture in the food industry. While Stuckey's pecan candy production fit with Pet Milk's earlier Funsten acquisition, Stuckey's also owned and operated 27 roadside stores.

Pet Milk created a new market with their 1962 introduction of Pet-Ritz frozen pie-crust shells. Another of Pet Milk's successful products at this time was Sego Liquid Diet Food, introduced in 1961. After competitors had opened up a market, Pet Milk brought in its own version, a thicker, high-protein drink available in a variety of flavors. By 1965 Sego brought in $22 million to the company's Milk Products Division sales. As Pet-Ritz frozen-pie products and Musselman applesauce met stiff competition, Pet Milk worked to carve its own position in the market by developing specialty items like quick-bake pies, no-bake pies, and chunky-spicy applesauce.

In 1966, in order to reflect its enlarged and diversified product line, Pet Milk changed its name to Pet Incorporated. Sales had increased 123 percent since Gamble had taken over, and he pushed for further growth, merging with the St. Louis-based Hussmann Refrigerator Company. Although Hussmann's market was fairly mature at that time, a fact Gamble was aware of, Pet bought a controlling interest in the Mexican-based American Refrigeration Products S.A, a company partially owned by Hussmann and which was expanding into Guatemala. Pet also acquired Atlanta-based Aunt Fanny's Bakery, and the following year bought Schrafft restaurants for $14 million. In 1968 the corporation made a key acquisition, purchasing the 50-year-old Texas-based Mountain Pass Canning Company, maker of the Old El Paso brand. Within two decades, Old El Paso products brought $170 million in sales to Pet.

Funding for these acquisitions came largely from a special credit Pet obtained through the sale of its portion of General Milk Co., a joint venture made with competitor Carnation Company in 1919. Pet gained $30.8 million on the sale, originally having paid $875,000. Also during this time, Pet arranged agreements in many foreign countries, including Spain, Sweden, Costa Rica, and Chile. Gamble had obviously increased volume at Pet through the early 1960s; his goal was to increase returns by the end of the decade on all the volume Pet had acquired. International expansion was clearly one way to do so.

As Pet eyed future expansion, problems arose. A teamster strike at the Hussmann refrigeration division came just as the corporation was moving from two old plants to a new $13 million site in St. Louis. In addition, a slowdown in housing and supermarket building put Hussmann in tough straits. Many new products launched earlier in the decade either failed entirely or were subject to competitors' new product introductions. For example, Carnation introduced a powdered instant diet food before Pet had its Sego version ready, thus chipping away at Pet's own strong contender.

A corporate sizing-up resulted in an overall downsizing. The president of the milk division resigned and was replaced by the successful head of frozen foods, John Bittner. Two milk plants were closed, and chairman Gamble cut corporate personnel by nearly 200. Quoted in the September 15, 1968, issue of *Forbes,* Gamble talked about further changes: "As important as eliminating jobs has been the realignment of responsibilities. We were going heavily in the direction of specialization. We've come back to more generalists in management.'' As a result, Gordon Ellis, formerly Pet's president and chief operating officer, resigned to become president of Fairmont Foods.

Upon Gamble's death in March 1969, Boyd F. Schenk became president and chief executive officer of Pet. Schenk, who first joined Pet Milk as a laboratory technician in 1947, had previously been named president of the fledgling frozen foods division in 1963, transforming it into one of Pet Milk's four largest divisions. By 1976, under Schenk's guidance, Pet enjoyed record earnings, clearing $23.7 million on record sales of $1.01 billion. The company devoted more money to advertising and promotions than ever before, budgeting over $30 million (the previous year's total) for fiscal year 1977. Products promoted included a range of nondairy-related foods: waffles, potato chips, canned shrimp, and Mexican foods. Pet also continued to introduce new products intended for niche markets, such as a natural, ''old-fashioned'' peanut butter, Old El Paso frozen Mexican pizzas, Pet-Ritz pizza crusts, Sego diet bars, and frozen donuts, a product attempted fifteen years earlier. While some in the food industry thought the public was no longer interested in convenience products, Schenk disagreed on the basis that the increasing number of two-income families created a continued demand for such products—provided the quality was high and the price was right.

In 1978, Chicago-based IC Industries Inc. (ICI)—a conglomerate that got its name from the Illinois Central Railroad—completed an unfriendly takeover bid for Pet. ICI had nearly tripled its revenue in the previous twelve years through a variety of takeovers intended to steer the company away from the railroad business. After two years of planning, secret purchases of Pet shares, and complex negotiations, ICI Chairman William B. Johnson summed up the experience in the Wall Street Journal (August 7, 1978): ''It was expensive, it was extraordinarily hard work, it was terribly intense and it can't be the best introduction to a future relationship. I hope we never do another one.'' Although Schenk made no public comment, the U.S. Justice Department did. Antitrust chief John Shenefield stated to a Senate panel in late July that the department disapproved of the excessive conglomerate mergers achieved through hostile takeover bids.

Complicating the acquisition were ongoing talks Pet had conducted with the fast-food chain Hardee's, which it had agreed to buy for $95 million in March 1978. ICI had no interest in Hardee's, and by July Hardee's sued both ICI and Pet, claiming that Pet's proposed merger was a defensive move. Before completing its takeover, ICI agreed to pay Hardee's $1.5 million for its troubles. Upon its acquisition, Pet became the largest unit of its parent company, and Hussmann Refrigerator Co. was established as a separate subsidiary of ICI.

By mid-1980, Pet had pared down more than 30 divisions into four groups: Grocery; Specialty; Frozen & Bakery; and International. Pet bought McGrew Color Graphics in 1982, adding it to the St. Louis Lithographing subsidiary to form a specialty printing division. Ray Morris, president of Pet's grocery group during the ICI takeover, was promoted to president of Pet in 1984. While at first many saw the ICI merger as the end of Pet, Morris and others on the executive team eventually viewed the change as a chance to reassess Pet's strategy. The company

divested itself of many businesses, totaling $750 million in volume, including the Musselman Company and some specialty retail liquor stores.

Pet once again launched acquisitions, maintaining its position as a premier food company. In 1982 Pet bought the William Underwood Company and its related products, including the B&M and Accent brands. A major advantage of the Underwood acquisition was the company's processing facilities in a number of foreign countries. By 1985 Pet sold its dairy division. In the June 15, 1987, issue of Forbes, Pet president Ray Morris admitted that evaporated milk was ''a declining business, but you don't want to sell your heritage.'' The company's largest acquisition was that of Ogden Food Products, in November 1986, which brought the Progresso, Las Palmas, Hollywood, and Hain brands to the Pet lineup. The same year the company also acquired Canada's Primo Foods Limited, a marketer of over 800 Italian items, including pasta, tomato sauce, specialty meats, and bakery goods, most imported from Italy.

Pet continued offering line extensions on products already familiar with the public, giving the company a product introduction success rate of 50 percent, as compared to the industry average of 10 percent. New products sales were close to $125 million in 1987, up 25 percent from the previous year. Pet's Downyflake frozen waffles remained first in a $200-million, and growing, breakfast foods market. The company cornered the high-end of the market whenever possible, following the lead of Gamble twenty years earlier. Commodity-based items weren't as profitable as specialty foods, and Pet's quality image allowed the company to charge higher prices for specialty items.

In 1988 Pet established a hold in the market of refrigerated foods through its acquisition of Orval Kent Food Company, Inc., a producer of salads for foodservice and supermarket delicatessens. Orval Kent controlled nearly a third of the market and, through its own series of acquisitions, had superior distribution capabilities in the United States and in Mexico, the latter where it had one plant. The following year Pet acquired Pillsbury's Van de Kamp frozen seafood line and, through its Canadian subsidiary, added the specialty meat producer Coorsh and Bittner.

Morris looked to the end of the 1980s with an increase in international sales, which were 13 percent of total sales in 1988. Through Underwood, Pet established bases from which to launch American-made Pet products in other nations. The Old El Paso brand was sold in 32 countries and continued to grow, illustrating the room for international expansion. To concentrate on the food industry, parent ICI changed its name to Whitman Corporation and sold its railroad and defense operations.

The next few years proved a bumpy ride for Pet, however. Morris retired in 1989 as planned, and Robert Copper was chosen to be president and CEO. Copper then resigned his position 11 months later, an action agreed upon with Whitman president Miles Marsh. In another minor skirmish, Pet incurred some costly legal problems following the sale of its former dairy operations in 1985. Pet was caught up in a nationwide antitrust investigation of the bidding practices of the dairy industry relating to the sale of milk to governmental agencies, primarily school districts. As of January, 1993, Pet had paid fines and civil damages aggregating approximately $7.5 million to the federal government and various states for the pre-1985 period.

A major turnaround occurred in April 1991, when parent company Whitman spun off Pet. Under Whitman, Pet had purchased fourteen companies; sales shot from $882 million to $1.9 billion during the 12-year relationship. Miles Marsh was appointed chairman and chief executive of Pet. Pet's stock value increased as the corporation was once again viewed as an independent food company—not merely part of a conglomerate. William Korab, president of Pet's grocery group, was quoted in the March 16, 1992, issue of *Forbes* as saying: "It's our company. It's us. If something goes wrong, someone else didn't do it. We did it to ourselves." Oddly enough, as the *Wall Street Journal* reported, Korab himself was replaced by Robert Tuckis, in a "management shakeup intended to streamline the company." Such changes, continued the *Journal*, "which follow a disappointing quarter, give Miles Marsh, chairman and CEO, more direct oversight of the company." Other changes during 1992 included Pet's intention to sell Whitman's Chocolates, a 150-year-old business. Robert L. Tuckis, president of Pet's Grocery Group, died September 4, 1992, and the company shortly thereafter announced the appointment of Raymond N. Felitto to a newly created position as president of Pet USA. Pet approached the twenty-first century like many of its competitors, more focused on marketing and global growth.

Principal Subsidiaries: Old El Paso Foods Company; Progresso Foods Company; Hain Pure Food Company, Inc.; Ramirez & Feraud Chile Company, Inc.; William Underwood Company; Orval Kent Food Company, Inc.; Orval Kent de Linares S.A. de C.V.; St. Louis Lithographing Company; Primo Foods Ltd.; C. Shippam Ltd.; Peck's Australia Pty. Ltd.; Diablitos Venezolanos, C.A.; Helvetia Redevelopment Corporation; Aktiebolaget Estrella (49%).

Further Reading: "Pet Milk Says It Plans Acquisitions, Expansion," *Wall Street Journal*, May 19, 1959; "Diversification Pays Off," *Financial World*, April 15, 1964; "Pet Milk Spills Over into Other Pastures," *Business Week*, July 31, 1965; "A Little Like a Russian," *Forbes*, June 1, 1967; "Pet's Playing Field," *Fortune*, June 15, 1967; "The Upward Stumble," *Forbes*, September 15, 1968; "Pet Names Schenk President," *Wall Street Journal*, March 21, 1969; "Pet Says Introductions of Products Will Hit a High in Fiscal 1977," *Wall Street Journal*, June 4, 1976; Wysocki, Bernard, "IC Bid to Gain Control of Pet Inc. Stirred Up Wide-Ranging Battle," *Wall Street Journal*, August 7, 1978; *Creating a Masterpiece*, St. Louis, Pet Inc., 1985; Flint, Jerry, "Take the High Ground," *Forbes*, June 15, 1987; Salvage, Bryan, "Pet Inc.: A Powerhouse in Specialty Foods," *Prepared Foods*, January 1988; Otto, Alison, "Orval Kent: Whitman's New Pet Project," *Prepared Foods*, April 1989; Liesse Erickson, Julie, "New Pet Chief Sets Shelf-stable Line," *Advertising Age*, September 11, 1989; "Whitman's Copper Quits Pet Unit Posts," *Wall Street Journal*, August 8, 1990; "Milk Price-Fixing," *Wall Street Journal*, August 27, 1991; Lubove, Seth, "On Their Own," *Forbes*, March 16, 1992; "Pet to Sell Whitman's Chocolates Unit as New Managers Fail to Revive Line," *Wall Street Journal*, June 22, 1992; "Pet Inc. Grocery Unit's Head Quits in Shake-Up," *Wall Street Journal*, July 8, 1992.

—Frances E. Norton

PILGRIM'S PRIDE CORPORATION

P.O. Box 93
Pittsburg, Texas 75686-0093
U.S.A.
(903) 856-7901
Fax: 903-856-7505

Public Company
Incorporated: 1963 as Pilgrim Feed Mills, Inc.
Employees: 10,700
Sales: $787 million
Stock Exchanges: New York
SICs: 2015 Poultry Slaughtering & Processing

Once a privately held business, Pilgrim's Pride Corporation is the fifth largest chicken processor in the United States (behind Tyson, ConAgra, Gold Kist, and Perdue) and the second largest in Mexico. The company is approximately 65 percent owned by its founder, chief executive officer, and "celebrity" spokesperson, Lonnie A. (Bo) Pilgrim.

As a completely integrated operation, Pilgrim's Pride superintends egg producing, contract growing, feed milling, animal rendering, and processing of its brand name foods for the retail, fast-food, food service, and food warehouse markets. Although its principal sales regions are the West, the Southwest, and Mexico, the company also sells selected chicken products to eastern European and Pacific Rim countries. Pilgrim's Pride entered the prepared foods market in 1986 to offset violent swings in chicken prices and profits and now ranks as the country's second largest supplier of prepared chicken products. Despite successes in these and other areas, increases in overall sales have slowed since 1989, and profits have steadily declined. By the end of fiscal 1992, the company was struggling under the weight of a $29.7 million loss, attributable to excess poultry production and sinking prices. The sudden naming of a new president at mid-year signalled the necessity for quickly stabilizing such volatility and effecting a turnaround, as did the entry of the Archer-Daniels-Midland Co., which now holds an 18 percent interest in Pilgrim's Pride. The company saw its sales for the first quarter of fiscal year 1993 increase 12.8 percent over sales for the same quarter of fiscal year 1992

According to Toni Mack in *Forbes,* when Pilgrim was a boy "and wanted a Coke, his father, who ran the general store in the

northeast Texas hamlet of Pine, would first make him sell six Cokes for a nickel apiece to the men working the nearby cotton gin." Such was the early business training of the chicken magnate who, by his own admission, "started from nothing." Because his father died abruptly from a heart attack, leaving the store in debt and the family with just $80, Bo was forced to labor from age 11 at several different jobs. At the age of 17, he and his brother Aubrey purchased a farm supply store in Pittsburg, Texas, with money borrowed from a bank and a local dentist. The first capital investment was a used cotton gin, which the brothers converted into a feed grinder. From 1945 until 1966, the year of Aubrey's death, the company—eventually incorporated as Pilgrim Feed Mills, Inc.—expanded into egg-hatching and broiler-processing. In 1968, Lonnie and Aubrey's heirs reincorporated the business as Pilgrim Industries, Inc.

Well into the 1980s, sales increases for the company averaged 20 percent annually. This growth was largely due to Bo's gutsy leadership and willingness to endure debt-to-equity ratios in excess of 4-to-1 in order to stay ahead of the competition. Jessica Greenbaum, in an article in *Forbes,* quotes one of Pilgrim's bankers as stating that Bo had "expanded as fast as he possibly could. The balance sheet couldn't sustain anymore." Pilgrim's strategy apparently paid off, for between 1960 and 1984, the number of broiler producers in the country shrank by more than 80 percent to just 55. Almost a decade later, the number stands at 45.

Beginning in January 1983, Pilgrim began promoting his company and the Pilgrim's Pride label through an award-winning television commercial, in which he appeared wearing a Pilgrim's hat as he affably related the superiority of his product line. The ads helped raise the profile of the Texas-based company, which posted sales that year of $268 million and profits of $2.1 million. The following year, Pilgrim's Pride had become the ninth largest chicken producer in the United States and the first to introduce fresh, whole, boneless chickens to the market. Yet, despite such advances, as well as a conscientious paring down of its debt, the business was perhaps as precarious during the mid-1980s as it had ever been. The reason for this, wrote Mack, was that "the company was almost entirely dependent on highly cyclical commodity chicken sales. Twice over the years, commodity chicken down-cycles had almost bankrupted Pilgrim's Pride." Pilgrim's solution to this problem came in January 1986, when the company began operating a state-of-the-art "further processed" facility at Mt. Pleasant, Texas. In November of the same year, the company went public with a listing on the New York Stock Exchange; however, Bo maintained ownership and control by retaining 80 percent of the company's shares.

Bo's gamble on prepared chicken for the retail market proved just as risky as the commodity business, due to strong competition from Tyson and ConAgra as well as heightened advertising and promotional costs totaling as much as $6 to $8 million a year. 1988 marked a low point for the company when it posted an income loss of nearly $8 million on $506 million in sales. A switch to the accrual method of accounting, however, allowed the business to report a final profit of $1.7 million.

Two well-timed decisions enabled Pilgrim's Pride to rebound dramatically in 1989. The first was Bo's surrender of the retail market (now a minuscule percentage of corporate sales) and full-scale assault on the food service industry. Although Tyson remains the leader, Pilgrim's Pride has been able to promote itself as a strong alternate through contracts with such frontrunners as Kentucky Fried Chicken, Kraft General Foods, and Wendy's restaurants. The second well-timed decision was Pilgrim's entry into the Mexican consumer market with the late 1987 acquisition of four fully integrated poultry operations serving the populous hub of Mexico City. The purchase price for the Mexican venture totaled $15.1 million. Largely because of these two moves, 1989 net sales shot up 30 percent, and net income rose above $20 million, for a profit-to-sales ratio of just over 3 percent. (Pilgrim's long-term goal is to boost this latter figure to around 4 percent.) The only blemish for the company that year was Pilgrim's involvement in a campaign contribution scandal with eight Texas lawmakers. Pilgrim's CEO was forced to defend himself before a grand jury, but he was not indicted and was able to return to the business of keeping the company in the black.

From 1987 to 1991, the company tripled the size of its Mexican operations, built a strong presence in frozen retail, established a dependable export business, and witnessed enormous increases in output for its further processed and prepared divisions. In addition, it entered into a number of joint marketing and advertising arrangements that kept down costs while increasing market share. All of this helped contribute to record sales of $786 million. Nevertheless, profits were down 21 percent and hovering at just 1.5 percent of revenues. Pilgrim's was a well-integrated agribusiness, twentieth in domestic egg production, fifth in broiler sales, and blessed with a solid brand name and rising per capita consumption of its leading product. It had anticipated and responded to consumer demand with a wide array of new food products, including fresh tray packs, party packs, chicken patties, nuggets, strips, and ready-to-eat gourmet entrees and appetizers. Furthermore, the company owned dozens of modern breeder and grow-out farms; several feed mills and processing plants; and 19 distribution facilities in the Southwest and in Mexico. The explanation for Pilgrim's slide was most likely twofold: the company had failed to distance itself enough from the cyclical price woes of plain processed chicken, and it had saddled itself with increasing debt.

In 1991, the company spent $34.4 million on improving the efficiency of its Mexican facilities and another $26.1 million on improving its domestic plants. The company entered 1992 hoping for the best and aiming at reaching sales of $1 billion by 1994, but while the year proved to be full of noteworthy events, few of them were good news for the company. In January a fire at the Mt. Pleasant plant left 21 injured following a full evacuation of some 1,200 employees. The cause of the fire was determined to be a loose hydraulic line near a burner. Fortunately, all injuries were minor. Then, in May, a debt restructuring was announced that would allow the company greater latitude in repaying its short-term obligations. The deal was completed in late June and served to extend Pilgrim's loan maturities until May 1, 1993. However, in order to arrange the waivers, the company was forced to sell five million common shares to Archer-Daniels-Midland (ADM) at six dollars per share. As a result, Bo Pilgrim's personal stake was effectively reduced from almost 80 percent to approximately 65 percent. A clause limiting ADM from acquiring more than a 20 percent interest and Pilgrim's indemnification of ADM against losses for an undisclosed period of time were also part of the deal.

Despite such warning signals, several analysts were surprised by a management reorganization announced in August, which involved the replacement of William Voss, president since 1988. Voss's successor, 11-year veteran Monty Henderson, was appointed to turn a declining earnings trend around. For the first nine months of fiscal 1992, ending June 27, the company sustained a net loss of $17.1 million. In the company's final quarter, another huge drop was added to the bottom line, resulting in one of its worst years ever. According to a *Wall Street Journal* article published just after this last piece of news, Pilgrim's year-long "financial funk" was in danger of worsening. Short-term debts still needed to be reduced and further loan negotiations seemed inevitable. In November the company announced that it would not pay its common stock dividend for the first quarter of fiscal 1993. In addition, it was reported that "Pilgrim's Pride is seeking waivers of financial covenants in loan agreements with major secured lenders to whom it owes $65 million." Discussions for extending the May 1993 deadline until October 1993 were in progress.

In a March 16, 1993, press release, Pilgrim's Pride announced that it filed a registration statement with the U.S. Securities and Exchange Commission regarding its proposed public offering of $100 million of Senior Subordinated Notes due 2003. According to the press release, "The offering is part of a refinancing plan designed to consolidate indebtedness, extend the average maturity of Pilgrim's Pride outstanding indebtedness and improve Pilgrim's Pride's operating and financial flexibility."

Pilgrim's Pride has pinned its hopes for a recovery on the areas where it has remained strongest: prepared foods for the foodservice industry and consumer sales to the Southwest and Mexico. Minimal increases in domestic chicken consumption should not deter the company, provided prices rebound and overproduction is avoided. Viewed in a historical context, the company's current problems might only be a small downturn in an overall trend of rising revenue and profitability, for Pilgrim's Pride still remains a major contender in chicken processing.

Principal Subsidiaries: Pilgrim's Pride de Mexico; Texas Egg Limited.

Further Reading: Greenbaum, Jessica, " 'Sell 'em or Smell 'em'," *Forbes,* July 16, 1984; Mack, Toni, "Pilgrim's Progress," *Forbes,* June 25, 1990; "History and Description: Pilgrim's Pride Corporation," Pittsburg, Texas, Pilgrim's Pride, 1991; "Lonnie 'Bo' Pilgrim," Pittsburg, Texas, Pilgrim's Pride, 1991; "21 Hurt in Texas Plant Fire," *New York Times,* January 9, 1992; "Pilgrim's Pride Corp.: Archer-Daniels-Midland Co. Agrees to Buy an 18% Stake," *Wall Street Journal,* May 13, 1992; "Pilgrim's Pride Ousts President, Chooses Henderson for Post," *Wall Street Journal,* August 10, 1992; Crispens, Jonna, "Pilgrim's Pride Has New President," *Supermarket News,* August 24, 1992; "Pilgrim's Pride Says Refinancing Delays Threaten Loan Pacts," *Wall Street Journal,* October 2, 1992; "Pilgrim's Pride Omits Dividend on Common for Fiscal 1st Period," *Wall Street Journal,* November 27, 1992; "Pilgrim's Pride Corp.," *Wall Street Journal,* January 13, 1993; Pilgrim's Pride press release, March 16, 1993.

—Jay P. Pederson

PIZZA HUT INC.

9111 East Douglas
Wichita, Kansas 67027
U.S.A.
(316) 681-9000
Fax: (316) 681-9869

Wholly Owned Subsidiary of PepsiCo Inc.
Incorporated: 1958
Employees: 260,000
Sales: $5.25 billion
SICs: 5812 Eating Places; 6794 Patent Owners & Lessors

Pizza Hut Inc., a subsidiary of PepsiCo Inc., oversees 7,200 pizza restaurants and delivery outlets in 68 countries worldwide.

Pizza Hut was founded in 1958 by brothers Dan and Frank Carney in their hometown of Wichita, Kansas. When a friend suggested opening a pizza parlor—then a rarity—they agreed that the idea could prove successful, and they borrowed $600 from their mother to start a business with partner John Bender. Renting a small building at 503 South Bluff in downtown Wichita and purchasing secondhand equipment to make pizzas, the Carneys and Bender opened the first Pizza Hut restaurant; on opening night, they gave pizza away to encourage community interest. A year later, in 1959, Pizza Hut was incorporated in Kansas, and Dick Hassur opened the first franchise unit in Topeka, Kansas.

In the early 1960s Pizza Hut grew on the strength of aggressive marketing of the pizza restaurant idea. In 1962, the Carney brothers bought out the interest held by Bender, and Robert Chisholm joined the company as treasurer. In 1966, when the number of Pizza Hut franchise units had grown to 145, a home office was established to coordinate the businesses from Wichita.

Two years later, the first Pizza Hut franchise was opened in Canada. This was followed by the establishment of the International Pizza Hut Franchise Holders Association (IPHFHA). It aimed at acquiring 40 percent of the company's franchise operations, or 120 stores, and adding them to the six outlets wholly owned by Pizza Hut.

The acquisitions, however, brought turmoil to the chain. Varied accounting systems used by the previous franchise owners had to be merged into one operating system, a process that took eight months to complete. In the meantime, sales flattened and profits tumbled.

In early 1970 Frank Carney decided that the company practice of relying on statistics from its annual report to inform its business strategy was inadequate, and that a more developed, long-term business plan was necessary. The turning point occurred when Pizza Hut went public and began growing at an unprecedented pace. Carney said in 1972: "We about lost control of the operations. Then we figured out that we had to learn how to plan."

Pizza Hut's corporate strategy, arrived at after much consultation and boardroom debate, emerged in 1972. Carney would later remark that the process of introducing a management structure did much to convince PepsiCo Inc. that the pizza chain was worthy of purchase.

The corporate strategy's first priority was increasing sales and profits for the chain. Continuing to build a strong financial base for the company to provide adequate financing for growth was the second priority. The strategy also called for adding new restaurants to the chain in emerging and growing markets.

In 1970 Pizza Hut opened units in Munich, Germany, and Sydney, Australia. That same year, the chain's 500th restaurant opened in Nashville, Tennessee. Further acquisitions that year included an 80 percent stake in Ready Italy, a frozen crust maker, and a joint venture, Sunflower Food Processors, formed with Sunflower Beef, Inc. The menus for all restaurants added sandwiches to the staple "Thin 'n Crispy" pizza offering.

In 1971 Pizza Hut became the world's largest pizza chain, according to sales and number of restaurants—then just more than 1,000 in all. This was followed a year later by the chain gaining a listing on the New York Stock Exchange. Pizza Hut also achieved, for the first time, a one million dollar sales week in the U.S. market.

At the end of 1972 Pizza Hut made its long-anticipated offer of 410,000 shares of common stock to the public. The company expanded by purchasing three restaurant divisions: Taco Kid, Next Door, and the Flaming Steer. In addition, Pizza Hut acquired Franchise Services, Inc., a restaurant supply company, and J&G Food Company, Inc., a food and supplies distributor. The company also added a second distribution center in Peoria, Illinois.

In 1973 Pizza Hut expanded further by opening outlets in Japan and Great Britain. Three years later the chain had more than 100 restaurants outside the United States and two thousand units in its franchise network. The company's 2,000th restaurant was opened in Independence, Missouri. It also established the 35 x 65 meter red-roof Pizza Hut restaurant building as the regulation size for all its new establishments. The new construction standard called for free-standing buildings built in a distinctive one-story brick design. The sites seated from 60 to 120 people.

Advertising played an increasingly influential role at Pizza Hut at this time, broadening the chain's public profile. Campaigns were run on both a national and local level in the U.S. market. Spending on local advertising increased from $942,000 in 1972 to $3.17 million in 1974.

In 1977 Pizza Hut merged with PepsiCo, becoming a subsidiary of the global soft drink and food conglomerate. Sales that year reached $436 million, and a new $10 million dollar headquarters office opened in Wichita. PepsiCo had clearly seen potential in Pizza Hut. People continued to eat outside their homes, especially as convenience and price-competitiveness in the fast food industry gained importance.

The 1980s brought new competitors to Pizza Hut, all challenging its number one position in the pizza restaurant trade, then worth $15 billion in sales annually in the United States alone. While in the 1970s the company's main competitors had been regional chains like Dallas-based Pizza Inn, Denver-based Shakey's, and Phoenix-based Village Inn and Straw Hat, fierce competition in the 1980s brought new entrants into the quick-service pizza category, including Little Caesar's, Domino's Pizza International, and Pizza Express.

To raise its profile, Pizza Hut introduced ''Pan Pizza'' in 1980 throughout its network. The product, with a thicker crust made in deep pans, soon became popular. The success of new additions to Pizza Hut's menu was facilitated by the marketing resources provided by PepsiCo.

For example, in 1983 Pizza Hut introduced ''Personal Pan Pizza,'' offering customers a five-minute guarantee their food would arrive quickly and steaming hot. The aim was to make a quick, affordable pizza the ideal lunchtime meal. Another addition to the chain's menu was ''Hand-Tossed Traditional Pizza,'' which would be introduced in 1988.

In 1984 Steven Reinemund was appointed president and chief executive officer of Pizza Hut. He oversaw a period of unprecedented growth for the pizza chain. In 1986 Pizza Hut opened its 5,000th franchise unit in Dallas, Texas and began its successful home delivery service. By the 1990s the delivery/carryout business had grown to account for approximately 25 percent of the company's total sales.

In 1990 Pizza Hut opened its first restaurant in Moscow. Russians' pizza of choice, ''Mockba,'' a pie topped with sardines, tuna, mackerel, salmon, and onion, became a favorite at the Moscow Pizza Hut. The Moscow location quickly established itself as Pizza Hut's highest volume unit in the world. Restaurants just behind in total volume served are found in France, Hong Kong, Finland, and Britain. Other favorite toppings for pizzas in countries other than the United States include sauerkraut and onion, and spinach, ham, and onion. In Hong Kong corned beef and Canadian bacon are favorites, while Asians and Australians seem to enjoy various curry pizzas.

Competition in the United States was heightened in 1991 when McDonald's, the world's largest hamburger fast food chain, put ''McPizza'' on its menu in several test markets and even offered home delivery to customers. Despite this challenge and the economic recession of the early 1990s, Pizza Hut continued to profit. Company sales at the pizza chain were up ten percent worldwide to $5.3 billion in 1991 as growing health awareness and the popularity of vegetarian lifestyles had prompted many people to reconsider pizza as a nutritious alternative. Pizza Hut Delivery, the home delivery side, provided $1.2 billion in sales alone, and overall Pizza Hut sales, added to those of subsidiaries Taco Bell and Kentucky Fried Chicken (KFC), gave parent company PepsiCo more than $21 billion in sales that year on its restaurant and fast food side.

Pizza Hut remains concerned with making itself more accessible. Drive-through units are available for customers' convenience, Pizza Hut Express units are being developed. The Express unit originated in shopping malls, where it provided customers with fast food at affordable prices made possible by lower operating overheads. Since that time, Pizza Hut has positioned Express units in school cafeterias, sports arenas, office buildings, and major airports. The company sees nontraditional locations as the fastest-growing sector of its operations in the 1990s.

PepsiCo's corporate sponsorship of Pizza Hut includes funding the BOOK IT! National Reading Incentive Program, which encourages higher literacy rates among young people. The reward for better reading ability is free pizza at any Pizza Hut. In 1992, the Book It! program involved more than 17 million students in North America alone, and Pizza Hut received letters of endorsement that year from President George Bush and Secretary of Education Lamar Alexander.

PepsiCo has taken advantage of changes in the world following the end of the Cold War, expanding Pizza Hut into new and emerging markets. In 1991 PepsiCo had restaurant outlets in 80 countries worldwide. Wayne Calloway, chairman of PepsiCo, indicated he wished to see continued growth with the approach of the 21st century. He commented, ''The major question for international restaurant growth is, 'How fast can we get there?' A steadily growing interest in eating away from home and the continued gravitation to convenience foods are creating an atmosphere of excitement for our restaurants.''

Further Reading: Gumpert, David, *How to Create a Successful Business Plan,* Inc. Publishing, 1990; *The Pizza Hut Story,* Wichita, Kansas: Pizza Hut, 1989.

—Etan Vlessing

POLAROID CORPORATION

549 Technology Square
Cambridge, Massachusetts 02139
U.S.A.
(617) 577-2000
Fax: (617) 577-5618

Public Company
Incorporated: 1937
Employees: 12,000
Sales: $2.15 billion
Stock Exchanges: New York Pacific
SICs: 3861 Photographic Equipment & Supplies; 3827
   Optical Instruments & Lenses; 3851 Ophthalmic Goods;
   3841 Surgical & Medical Instruments

Polaroid Corporation was founded on Edwin H. Land's belief that consumer markets should be created around inventions generated by scientific research. His philosophy resulted in scientifically innovative products, some of which were fantastically profitable and others that were not commercially viable. Instant photography products, introduced in 1948, saved Land's company from financial disaster and continue to be Polaroid's principal source of income. After Polaroid stock plummeted in the 1970s, and with Land's retirement in 1982, the succeeding team of managers, many of whom had built careers at Polaroid, began to reformulate Polaroid's corporate culture. While the company continues to be a scientific innovator, it also has cultivated an aggressive marketing department, which bases product development on market research.

In 1926 Edwin Land's desire to create useful products based on scientific invention prompted him to pursue independent research on polarization rather than to return to Harvard after his freshman year. After creating a prototype synthetic polarizer in New York, Land returned to Harvard in 1929. A polarizing material selectively screens light waves. It could, for example, block waves of light that create glare while allowing other waves through. With the help of George Wheelwright III, a young Harvard physics instructor, Land obtained access to a laboratory and began producing small sheets of polarizing material. Land applied to patent this process in 1929, and a patent was granted in 1934. In June of 1932, eager to explore the invention's practical applications, Land and Wheelwright abandoned their academic careers and founded Land-Wheelwright Laboratories, backed with Wheelwright's capital.

In 1933 the men incorporated their laboratory. Land-Wheelwright's staff—Land, Wheelwright, their wives, and a handful of other researchers—concentrated on developing polarizing material for no-glare car headlights and windshields. Enthusiasm for their work ran high, but commercial success eluded the Land-Wheelwright crew. Rebuffed by carmakers in Detroit, the company had no customers during the height of the Great Depression.

Photography giant Eastman Kodak provided the company's first financial break when it made a $10,000 order for photographic polarizing filters, later dubbed Polafilters. These plates, which consisted of a sheet of polarizing material sealed between two glass discs, increased contrast and decreased glare in photographs taken in bright light. Land-Wheelwright accepted the order and delivered the filters to Kodak. By this time, a friend, Professor Clarence Kennedy of Smith College, had dubbed the material "Polaroid," and the name was adopted. In 1935 Land negotiated with American Optical Company to produce polarized sunglasses. Such glasses could screen out glare rather than simply darken the landscape, and Land-Wheelwright contracted to begin production of Polaroid Day Glasses, a longtime source of revenue for Polaroid.

In 1937 Land formed Polaroid Corporation to acquire the operations that he and George Wheelwright had begun. Eight original shareholders fronted $375,000 to back Land and his projects. They invested in Land and his ideas, allotting him a voting trust of stock that gave him control of the company for the next decade. Wheelwright left the company in 1940 to become a navy lieutenant and never rejoined the company. Researchers had devised a number of commercial applications for Polaroid polarizing sheets—such as desk lamps, variable-density windows, lenses, and three-dimensional photographs called Vectographs—but most of these products never became significantly profitable.

Polaroid continued to court the major automakers, attempting to induce one of them to demonstrate its headlight system at the 1939 New York World's Fair. The carmakers all refused the project, but Chrysler agreed to run a Polaroid three-dimensional (3-D) movie at its display. Audiences dodged water that seemed to spray out of a garden hose into the crowd and gawked through Polaroid-made glasses of oppositely polarized lenses as an automobile appeared to dance itself together in the air above them. The public loved 3-D, but filmmakers were content with the magic of color and sound, and passed over the new technology.

In another unsuccessful marketing project, variable-density windows were installed on the observation car of the City of Los Angeles. Two polarized discs were mounted in the train wall; by means of a knob, passengers could turn the inner disk so that the window gradually became grayer until it was completely dark. As with the 3-D process, the novelty of polarized windows was not hugely successful.

In 1939 Day Glasses were the source of most of Polaroid's $35,000 profit. Although sales rose to $1 million in 1941, the company's 1940 losses had reached $100,000, and it was only

World War II military contracts that saved Land and his 240 employees. By 1942 the wartime economy had tripled Polaroid's size. A $7 million navy contract to work on the Dove heat-seeking missile project was the largest contract Polaroid had ever had, although the bomb was not used during World War II. Polaroid produced a number of other products for the armed forces, including a device that determined an aircraft's elevation above the horizon, an infrared night viewing device, goggles, lenses, color filters for periscopes, and range finders.

Also during the war, the 3-D technology was employed in a machine-gunner training unit. Polaroid designed a trainer in which the student operated a life-size anti-aircraft gun against the 3-D simulation of an attacking plane. Reconnaissance planes were equipped to take 3-D Vectographs, which provided relief maps of enemy territory. When viewed with polarized glasses, the 3-D pictures exposed contours of guns, planes, and buildings that camouflage obscured in conventional photographs. Vectographs were used in planning almost all Allied invasions, including that of Normandy. By the end of the war, in 1945, Polaroid's sales had reached $16 million. But as military contracts declined, so did staff, and Polaroid was down to about 900 employees, from a wartime high of 1,250. Sales fell to just $4 million in 1946 and were less than $2 million in 1947.

By 1946 Land had realized that Polaroid Corporation was in deep trouble. Land also had come to believe that instant photography was Polaroid's only research line with potential to save the company. Land had first considered developing instant photography technology in 1943, when, on Christmas day, his three-year-old daughter asked to see the photographs her parents had taken earlier that day. Prompted by his daughter's query, Land conceived, in a flash, an instant, self-developing film and a camera that would process it. By 1946, however, the research on the film was far from complete. Nonetheless, Land announced early that year that the instant camera system would be demonstrated at the February 21, 1947, winter meeting of the Optical Society of America. Working around the clock, Polaroid scientists developed a working model of the system, which allowed Land to take an instant picture of himself at the Optical Society meeting. The photograph developed itself within a minute. The image of Land peeling back the negative paper from an instantly produced picture of himself made front page news in the *New York Times,* was given a full page in *Life* magazine, and was splashed across the international press.

It was an additional nine months before the camera was offered to the public via Jordan Marsh, Boston's oldest department store. The original camera, which weighed five pounds when loaded, sold for $89.75; film cost $1.75 for eight sepia-toned exposures. On the first day the camera was offered, demonstrators sold all 56 of the available units, and the cameras kept selling as fast as the factory could produce them. First-year photographic sales exceeded $5 million. By 1950 more than four thousand dealers sold Polaroid cameras, when only a year earlier Kodak had virtually monopolized the U.S. photography market.

The 1950s were a decade of rapid expansion. Sales mounted, spurred on by an aggressive television advertising campaign. Instant photography could be demonstrated graphically on television. Black-and-white film was introduced in 1950 to an enthusiastic public. Enthusiasm quickly turned to ire, however, as the black-and-white images began to fade and disappear. Unable to develop a non-fading black-and-white film, Polaroid provided sponge-tipped tubes of a liquid polymer, which the consumers hand applied to each picture to set the image. This awkward process was not eliminated until 1963.

Despite the inconvenience, demand for instant photography held. To accommodate growing sales, Polaroid built a plant in Waltham, Massachusetts. The company's common stock was listed on the New York Stock Exchange in 1957. Polaroid formed its first international subsidiaries in 1959, in Frankfurt and Toronto. In 1960 it established Nippon Polaroid Kabushiki Kaisha in Japan and licensed a Japanese firm to produce two cameras for overseas sale.

During the 1960s Polaroid continued to offer improvements and variations on the original instant film and camera, although other products were also introduced. Polaroid's first color film was introduced in 1963, along with a pack-loading black-and-white film. In 1965 the inexpensive Swinger was pitched to teens. Selling for less than $20, the camera took only black-and-white pictures, sustaining the market for Polaroid black-and-white film. In 1966 the ID-2 Land Identification system was introduced. It produced full-color laminated cards in two minutes, allowing the company to provide instant driver's licenses and other photo identification cards. In 1967 Polaroid began construction on several new factories to boost production of cameras, film, color negatives, and chemicals. The company's stock split two for one in 1968. During the late 1960s Polaroid was outpacing other top stock market performers. In 1970 sales reached $500 million.

In October of 1970 two black workers at Polaroid called upon other black employees to leave their jobs until Polaroid ceased all business in South Africa. Polaroid had no subsidiaries or investments in the country, but its products were distributed through Frank & Hirsch and some items were sold directly to the government. South African commerce accounted for less than 0.1 percent of the company's annual profits. Polaroid sent two black and two white employees to South Africa to assess the situation, and in 1971 the company decided to stop selling its products to the South African government. In addition, black workers at Frank & Hirsch would receive equal pay for equal work and be educated for promotion. Polaroid established a foundation to subsidize black education in South Africa, and made $25,000 in contributions to black cultural associations. Polaroid ended its association with Frank & Hirsch in 1977.

In 1972 the October cover of *Life* magazine featured a cluster of children grasping after a photograph whizzing out of the new SX-70 wielded by inventor Land. The SX-70 was the first integrated camera and film system, and the pictures developed outside the camera by themselves. The public eagerly purchased the camera. Despite the fact that sales in the early 1970s continued to grow at a rate of 20 percent per year, the tremendous expense of research, manufacturing, and marketing for the SX-70 caused earnings to fall. Financial analysts began to question Polaroid's stability. In 1974 Polaroid executives admitted that the company did not expect to make more than $3 a share that year. Actually, earnings were only 86 cents per share. Polaroid stock plummeted. By July of 1974, just 26 months after the SX-70 was introduced, the stock had fallen from 149½ to 14⅛.

In 1975 Land turned the presidency of Polaroid over to Bill McCune, a senior vice-president who had been with the company since 1939 and had worked closely with Land on the development of the first instant camera and film. Manufacture of the SX-70 remained very costly, and numerous design features required modification. Yet Land was satisfied with the camera and wished to pursue research on Polavision, an instant motion picture system. McCune and others, however, favored improving the SX-70. Highly skeptical of Polavision, McCune wanted to base new product lines on market research, rather than following Land's method of creating a consumer demand for Polaroid's latest invention. Land introduced Polavision at the 1977 annual meeting, and a limited introduction followed. Although a scientific marvel, the instant films lasted only two and a half minutes and were silent. Videotaping was just hitting the market, and so Polavision was never a consumer success.

Land received his 500th patent and was inducted to the National Inventors Hall of Fame in 1977. Polaroid's corporate culture began to shift when McCune was voted chief executive officer in 1980. While Land's entrepreneurial drive had created the company, a more diversified, market-oriented management was needed to continue to propel it. In 1982 Land retired fully, devoting his attention to research at the Rowland Institute for Science, which he had founded in 1965.

In 1976 Polaroid entered a costly and lengthy patent-infringement battle with Eastman Kodak Company. Kodak had been producing the negative component of Polaroid's black-and-white film since 1944, and its color negative since 1957. With the introduction of the Polaroid SX-70, though, Kodak terminated its partnership with Polaroid, and began its own instant-photography research. In 1976 Kodak introduced the EK-4 and EK-6 instant cameras and PR-10 instant film. Polaroid filed suit within a week, charging 12 patent infringements in camera film and design.

Legal preparations dragged on for five years, until the trial began in October of 1981. Ten of the twelve original counts were pressed. After 75 days of testimony and three years of deliberation, U.S. District Court Judge Rya Zobel ruled that seven of the ten Polaroid patents were valid and had been infringed upon. As a result, Kodak's line of instant-photography products was terminated in 1986. When settlement talks began, Polaroid claimed about $6.1 billion in damages, lost sales, and interest. The case was not settled until 1991 and resulted in a payment by Eastman Kodak of $925 million.

In August of 1988 Shamrock Holdings offered to buy Polaroid at $40 a share plus 40 percent of the award from the Kodak settlement. Polaroid's board of directors rejected the offer, and soon after the company sold 14 percent of its outstanding shares to an employee stock ownership program (ESOP). Shamrock charged that the ESOP was a form of management entrenchment, and sued. Delaware courts upheld Polaroid's position, and Shamrock raised its offer to $45 a share. Polaroid's board again rejected the offer and subsequently announced a $1.1 billion common stock buy-back. Shamrock again sued Polaroid in February of 1989 for management entrenchment, but Polar-

oid's tactics were again upheld. The fight against Shamrock was led by Chairman McCune and I. MacAllister Booth, who had become president in 1983 and CEO in 1985. The pair pruned Polaroid staff in the early 1980s and reorganized the company into three divisions: consumer photography, industrial photography, and magnetic media.

The first success reaped from this new marketing strategy was the Spectra, introduced in 1986. The upscale Spectra came out of market research indicating that instant camera users wanted better picture quality. Again responding to this desire, Polaroid introduced Hybrid IV, an instant film of near 35-millimeter quality, during the early 1990s. Polaroid also introduced a line of conventional film and videotapes starting in 1989. Marketing strategies also continued to become more sophisticated. In 1990 a $60 million advertising campaign emphasized new uses for instant cameras. Suggested uses include recording household items for insurance purposes or keeping a visual record of properties when house-hunting. In addition, the company cultivated its non-consumer markets, which contribute at least 40 percent of photographic sales.

While Polaroid's product lines may be more fully guided by market demand, Polaroid continues to be a research-and-development driven company. It was Booth's hope that market research would generate stable, profit-making ventures, as Polaroid carries Land's creative scientific spirit into the 1990s. At the dawn of the 21st century, the Polaroid Corporation has become the world market leader in instant photography, electronic imaging, and a major world manufacturer and marketer of conventional films, videotapes, and light polarizing filters and lenses. Such a high proportion (approximately half) of Polaroid's revenues derive from international sales that the company survived the worst year of the U.S. recession, 1991, with flying colors, making the recession period one of the best ever in terms of sales. For the first time in Polaroid's history, the $2 billion dollar sales mark had been surpassed. With the resurgence of the domestic economy and the onset of recession in Europe and Japan, the company expects its global positioning to assist in its financial performance. By the mid-1990s, the company will have undergone the biggest plant expansion in its history that includes the construction of its first ever facility for the production of advanced films for Polaroid's new electric imaging products.

Along with major plant expansion, Polaroid has embarked on a new marketing and advertising strategy that targets market segments (business, health, industry, education, family) and promotes new products designed specifically for these segments. In fact, the blitz of new Polaroid products has surprised market analysts accustomed, over the past two decades, to criticizing Polaroid's stagnation and moribund sales.

Polaroid products fall under the categories of core photography and high resolution imaging. Polaroid clearly has shifted away from its total reliance on its historical mainstay, the instant camera. Gone forever are the days of focusing on a single product. The company's potentially most lucrative product is the Helios medical laser imaging system, which produces a medical diagnostic image without chemical processing. Another new and promising but far less expensive medical imaging product, the Polaroid EMS Photo Kit, is a camera specifically designed for the 35,000 emergency medical team (EMT) squads in the United States. A series of new electronic imaging products also have been developed for the business segment, including desktop computer film recorders, the Polaroid CI-5000 and CI-3000, and the CS-500i Digital Photo Scanner. In addition, Polaroid has developed the ProCam, an instant camera earmarked for the business customer.

For the nonprofessional or amateur consumer, the long awaited "Joshua" instant camera was introduced first in Europe in 1992, and then in the United States as "Captiva" in the summer of 1993. Captiva, indistinguishable in appearance from a 35 millimeter camera, takes high quality instant photos that are not ejected in the usual manner, but stored in the rear of the camera, which in turn contains a viewing window enabling the user to see the development of the last exposed frame. Because the photos are smaller than regular-sized 35 millimeter pictures, the camera appeals to those whose lifestyles favor a more compact and instant camera. "HighDefinition" instant film for the amateur photographer came on the market in 1992, further closing the gap in quality between 35 millimeter and instant film. Despite market analyst predictions, Polaroid Corporation has transformed itself into a company of the future: a streamlined, multinational, and diverse, multi-product company.

Principal Subsidiaries: Inner City, Inc.; Olint, Inc.; Polaroid Caribbean; Polaroid Foundation; Polaroid Ges.m.b.H. (Austria); Polaroid (Belgium) N.V.; Polaroid AS (Denmark); Polaroid (U.K.) Ltd.; Polaroid (France) S.A.; Polaroid GmbH (Germany); Polaroid (Italia) S.p.A.; Polaroid AB (Sweden); Polaroid AG (Switzerland); Polaroid Australia Pty. Ltd.; Polaroid Far East Ltd. (Hong Kong); Nippon Polaroid K.K. (Japan); Polaroid do Brasil Ltda. (Brazil); Polaroid Canada Inc.; Polaroid de Mexico, S.A. de C.V.; Polaroid Espana, S.A. (Spain); Polaroid (Europa) B.V. (Netherlands); Polaroid (Norge) A/S (Norway); Polaroid Oy (Finland); Polaroid Singapore Private Ltd. (Singapore).

Further Reading: Polaroid Corporation: A Chronology, Cambridge, Massachusetts, Polaroid Corporation, 1983; Dumaine, Brian, "How Polaroid Flashed Back," *Fortune,* February 16, 1987; Wensberg, Peter C., *Land's Polaroid,* Boston, Houghton Mifflin, 1987; Hammonds, Keith H., "Why Polaroid Must Remake Itself—Instantly," *Business Week,* September 19, 1988; "Edwin Land: Inventor of Polaroid Camera," *Los Angeles Times,* March 2, 1991; "Film Recorders (Overview of Four Evaluations of Desktop Film Recorders)," *PC Magazine,* May 14, 1991; Nulty, Peter, "The New Look of Photography: The Transition from Film to Electronic Imaging," *Fortune,* July 1, 1991; Palmer, Jay, "Spending Kodak's Money: Polaroid Uses Its Settlement Bounty to Sow Seeds of Future Growth," *Barron's,* October 7, 1991; "Polaroid Leads Peripherals Parade at Graphics Show," *PC Week,* March 16, 1992; "Polaroid Launches a Major Quality Initiative," *Modern Materials Handling,* April 1992; Rosenberg, Ronald, "Above Expectations: Strong Overseas Sales Lift Polaroid Income," *Boston Globe,* October 14, 1992.

—Elaine Belsito
updated by Sina Dubovoj

PUBLIX SUPER MARKETS INC.

1936 George Jenkins Blvd.
Lakeland, Florida 33801
U.S.A.
(813) 688-1188
Fax: (813) 680-5257

Private Company
Incorporated: 1930
Employees: 72,000
Sales: $6.2 billion
SICs: 5411 Grocery Stores

Publix Super Markets Inc. stands as one of the top eight chains of supermarkets in the United States by sales volume with more than 400 stores. Publix limited its sales to Florida until the 1990s, but is now moving into Georgia. For years the signs on the front of Publix have read, "Where shopping is a pleasure," reflecting the firm's early belief in the importance of customer satisfaction.

Publix was founded in 1930 by George W. Jenkins, the son of a rural Georgia grocer. Jenkins moved to Winter Haven, Florida, in 1927 and took a job as a stock clerk at the local Piggly Wiggly. He became the store's manager six weeks later at the age of 17. At the age of 20 he borrowed $2,000 and started his own 27-by-65-foot store across the street, with five employees. The store earned $500 its first year, in the midst of the Great Depression.

Jenkins was a natural manager and carefully observed how to best sell grocery store items. He was one of the first in the grocery business to stress courteous, friendly employees, high-quality goods and excellent service, while most of his competitors were focusing on price and productivity. He also treated his employees well, promoting almost entirely from within, and giving them a large amount of control over their section of a store. Most store managers throughout the chain's history started as baggers.

Jenkins was so successful that he had opened 18 more Publix stores by 1940, including some acquired with the purchase of the small All-American chain in 1939. In 1940 Jenkins opened his first supermarket, an 11,000 square foot space with a paved parking lot, air conditioning, wide aisles, electric doors, and frozen-food cases. Though large food stores had been opened

during the Depression, they were generally stark and ill-equipped. The aesthetics and features of Jenkins super stores were unique for American grocery stores and reflected his belief that shopping should be an enjoyable experience. By 1950, 22 of these supermarkets had been opened, with total sales of $12.1 million.

In 1949 Publix began its own one-person advertising department headed by R. William Schroter. Schroter soon began using local free-lancers who eventually grew into the W. M. Zemp & Associates advertising firm in St. Petersburg. The company advertised heavily in newspapers but avoided the weekly circulars used by many supermarkets.

In the early 1950s Publix began using S&H Green Stamps, a stamp program that gave shoppers a certain number of stamps per dollar spent and then enabled them to use completed stamp books to get discount merchandise. Publix decided that a 14 percent increase in sales would pay for the cost of the stamp program and found that the resulting sales increase easily exceeded that level. Publix quickly became the largest vendor of the stamps in the United States. Jenkins liked the stamps because he believed that they encouraged store loyalty, as well as the thrifty habits he grew up with. In the late 1950s Publix began selling stock to employees, eventually becoming 98 percent employee-owned.

Publix's success in less developed parts of Florida encouraged Jenkins to move into the lucrative, but highly competitive, Miami market. The first Publix in Miami opened in 1959. The Publix formula proved as successful in Miami as it had in other parts of Florida, and in 1963 the firm opened a warehouse to service the growing number of supermarkets it was opening there. The state of Florida itself contributed to the chain's expansion as it became one of the fastest-growing states in the United States. Fed partly by its move to Miami, Publix had grown to 114 stores by 1965, with sales of $262.9 million, and 157 stores, with sales of $465.7 million in 1970. The chain was expanding into new areas of Florida as well. In 1974 the firm opened a 200,000-square-foot warehouse in Jacksonville to supply Publix stores between Jacksonville and Tallahassee.

Publix management kept a careful eye on lifestyle trends. As more women began to work and more people remained single, stores were adjusted accordingly. One of the biggest changes came in 1966 when Publix stores moved from one small frozen-food display case to large, upright cases with glass doors. As frozen-food sales continued to grow, Publix added more freezers in and devoted more attention to how they were stocked, keeping brand name products together rather than sorting by food type. Frozen foods were updated regularly, and the firm spotted food trends such as yogurt and frozen pizza earlier than most of its rivals.

In setting up shelves, dairy cases, and freezers, the firm was careful to keep ease of shopping its top priority, but the company also kept high-margin items at eye level and made certain that items were arranged in a way that made it easy to restock quickly.

In the early 1970s, with a wave of discount stores taking hold in Florida, Publix opened its own discount chain. Publix opened 24 of them, called Food World, in ten years. In 1976 Publix introduced in-store photo-finishing, giving away a roll of film or an extra set of prints with each roll it developed. Within ten years the firm accounted for 12 percent of the total photo-finishing business in its marketing area.

In 1979 the company had reached nearly $2 billion in sales and had 234 stores and 26,000 employees. It was the eleventh-largest chain in national sales and had an after-tax net averaging 1.7 percent, far ahead of most of its rivals. Publix was the leading grocery chain in Daytona Beach, Palm Beach, and St. Petersburg, where it had 30.6 percent of the market. It was the second-largest chain in the Miami area, with 26 percent of the market. All Publix stores were similar inside and had in-store delis and bakeries. Publix supermarkets also took advantage of technology, using the second-largest number of price scanners in the United States.

Publix's skilled marketing and use of up-to-date technology had contributed to its success, but so had the stability of its work force. The firm had never experienced a strike, lockout or layoff, and had no union members in its work force. It also had the lowest employee turnover of any large chain. This was attributed to employment policies that included a profit-sharing plan that distributed 20 percent of net profits at each store to that store's full-time workers, a retirement plan funded by 15 percent of pre-tax profits, and the policy of heavily promoting from within the company. Employees were also given more responsibility than at most large chains. Publix was named as one of the top ten companies to work for in America by the 1993 edition of *The 100 Best Companies to Work for in America.*

Publix still limited its operations to Florida, but by 1980 it had a strong presence throughout the state, with the exception of the panhandle. Its operations were divided into three divisions: the Jacksonville division, which covered the northern third of the state; the Miami division, which covered the eastern coast south of Brevard County; and the Lakeland division, which covered the rest of the state. The company headquarters were located in Lakeland, where a 425,000-square-foot grocery warehouse stored a three-week supply of goods.

Publix spent about 0.75 percent of sales on advertising, amounting to about $15 million in 1980. Newspapers accounted for 68 percent of the advertising budget, television 24 percent, and radio five percent. The company had formerly used even less radio, but was increasingly turning to it to reach younger Floridians. Once at the stores, customers found theatrical merchandising displays that changed weekly. The displays were worked out by the employees of each store and at various times included a mannequin sitting in an old-fashioned bathtub, fountains, papier-mache volcanoes, model trains, and real cars. The displays were done without direction from the Publix central office since Jenkins believed that store managers best knew what would work in their own territory.

The 1980s brought considerable change to Publix. One of the first changes was automatic teller machines, which Publix began installing before many banks did. The firm was also the first supermarket chain to install bar-code scanners in every store. Jenkins had always refused to open his stores on Sunday, but in 1982, losing market share to stores that did open on Sunday, he relented. In 1985 all but three of the discount Food Worlds were

closed. With workers getting a percentage of their store's profits, a discount store lacked internal support. Sales for 1985 reached $3.2 billion, up from $2.8 billion in 1983, and Publix was the ninth-largest grocery chain by sales.

The 1980s also brought a change of management at Publix. In 1984 Joe Blanton, who had been president for ten years, died, and was replaced by Mark Hollis. Hollis represented a new generation of management at Publix.

Superstores, with 30,000 square feet or more, were another 1980s innovation. After its competitors successfully began opening them, Publix began opening its own superstores, with up to 39,000 square feet each. While industry analysts praised Publix's early use of new technologies, some criticized the firm for lagging behind its competitors in opening large stores that offered more services. Most Publixes were located in shopping malls where customers could also shop for goods other than food. By the beginning of the 1980s, however, consumers were moving towards single stores where they could buy most things they needed. Publix's competitors opened combination stores where customers could fill prescriptions in addition to buying groceries. In 1986 Publix followed, opening its first combination store in Orlando. The 55,000-square-foot, upscale space combined a grocery store with gourmet food and deli and bakery sections, with hardware, toys, and the firm's first pharmacy. The combination stores included a one-hour photo department, a counter where cameras and small electronics were sold, and an expanded cosmetics, health, and beauty aids section. The stores were intended to appeal to younger, professional, two-income families, and their sites had been carefully selected with an eye on demographics. Publix quickly opened two more Publix Food & Pharmacy stores in Tampa, one in Tamarac, near Fort Lauderdale, and three more in other parts of Florida. The firm also remodeled and expanded old supermarkets and opened new ones. Publix opened 28 stores in 1986 and more than 30 in 1987, often choosing sites where Florida's population had not yet exploded but was expected to.

To help support these new stores, Publix doubled the size of the Lakeland warehouse to 440,000 square feet, and planned a 660,000-square-foot perishables warehouse near Fort Lauderdale. To increase flexibility in merchandizing and marketing, Publix dropped S&H Green Stamps in the Lakeland and Jacksonville divisions in June 1987. In 1989 Publix again tried a new technology when it began moving toward automatic checkout machines. The machines allowed customers to scan their own groceries, and then pay a central cashier.

In January of 1990, after suffering a stroke, George Jenkins retired as chairman and chief executive and became chairman emeritus. He was succeeded by his son, Howard M. Jenkins, who was 38 years old. The younger Jenkins had begun at the retail level and worked his way up to management.

At the time of the leadership change, Publix had 370 stores, 60,000 employees, and profits of $128.5 million on sales of $5.386 billion. It was the 21st-largest retailer in the United States, behind Walgreen and McDonald's. Publix did not have concrete plans for a store outside of Florida however, until late in 1990, when it announced plans to build a 48,000-square-foot store in Kingsland, Georgia, about 80 miles south of Savannah.

Plans for a second store in a Savannah shopping mall were soon announced. In August of 1991, with 384 Publix stores in existence, the firm announced that it was looking for sites in Atlanta. Some industry observers felt that the firm would have a hard time finding desirable locations due to its late entry into the Atlanta market, though others were more optimistic. Publix was expected to encounter stiff competition from the Kroger chain, which also stressed customer service. It also faced the problem of securing supplies, with the nearest Publix distribution site being six hours away in Jacksonville. But with its years of experience—and constant flow of cash from its hundreds of existing stores—some analysts believed Publix would succeed in Georgia as it had in Florida.

Further Reading: Dietrich, Robert, Linsen, Mary Ann, et al. ''Publix, Where Pleasure is Profitable,'' *Progressive Grocer,* September, 1980; Bork, Robert H., Jr., ''Call Him Old-Fashioned,'' *Forbes,* August 26, 1985; Elson, Joel, ''Publix and the New Florida Market,'' *Supermarket News,* April 20, 1987; Zweibach, Elliot, ''George Jenkins Named Chairman Emeritus at Publix,'' *Supermarket News,* January 8, 1990.

—Scott Lewis

QUAKER STATE CORPORATION

P.O. Box 989
255 Elm Street
Oil City, Pennsylvania 16301
U.S.A.
(814) 676-7676
Fax: (814) 676-7030

Public Company
Incorporated: 1931
Employees: 4460
Sales: $813.6 million (1991)
Stock Exchanges: New York Pacific
SICs: 2911 Petroleum Refining; 1222 Bituminous Coal—
    Underground; 6351 Surety Insurance; 7549 Automotive
    Services Nec.

Quaker State Corporation is an independent refiner and marketer of Pennsylvania grade motor oil. It produces, refines, and markets petroleum and associated products to international markets. It also operates coal mining, gas drilling, and production facilities, truck and car lighting equipment companies, and insurance and quick oil change centers. Quaker State oil products are derived from a field on the western slope of the Appalachian mountains, comprising parts of western Pennsylvania, West Virginia, eastern Ohio, and southwestern New York. There are 1,300 wells of varying sizes throughout the region, producing 450,000 barrels of oil in total, as well as four refineries, allowing for easy access and keeping transportation costs low. Quaker State also operates 302 gas wells in the Pennsylvania area. Pennsylvania crude oil, generally free of sulphur, tar, asphalt, and other impurities, is noted for its stable paraffin base, particularly useful in engines running at higher than normal temperatures. Furthermore, Quaker State oil products have traditionally commanded a premium in price over other brands.

Quaker State's origins may be traced to the founding of Oil City, Pennsylvania, in the nineteenth century. Oil was first discovered there in 1859 by ''Colonel'' Edwin Drake, bringing instant prosperity to the region. As evidence of this growth, the census for Oil City registered 12 families in 1860; five years later, the town had a population of 6,000. Derricks were set up within a few feet of each other, and barges loaded with newly-drilled oil rushed en masse from the oil fields down the Pioneer

Run Creek, creating a traffic jam at Oil City on their way to the mouth of the Allegheny River. Such expansion and competition continued into the twentieth century.

The name ''Quaker State'' was coined in 1912 when T. G. Phinny of Phinny Brothers Oil Company of Oil City used the name to distinguish his product from that of rival marketers. The following year Phinny answered a call from the Franklin Automobile Company of Syracuse, New York, for a quality motor oil that would meet its vehicles particular lubricating needs; until Quaker State, no oil product could successfully lubricate the Franklin cars.

In 1914 Franklin signed a contract with Phinny and Eastern Refining, securing an exclusive supply of Pennsylvania grade crude oil for its vehicles. Soon thereafter, through a 1915 advertisement in the *Saturday Evening Post*, Quaker State became a nationally known brand. The advertisement read: ''The Franklin requirements were severe. Many oils were tested, but Quaker State alone met these requirements.'' The notice then went on to explain Quaker State's unique attributes, and asked Franklin owners to ask their nearest dealer for the product. It concluded: ''Quaker State is certified and guaranteed to be the highest known quality oil suitable for every engine purpose. It prolongs the life of the motor. Will not burn before lubricating. Gives practically double mileage. Prevents engine overheating. Cuts oil bills.''

In 1924, the Eastern Refining Company purchased the Quaker State brand name, and renamed itself the Quaker State Oil Refining Company. The Quaker State Corporation was formed seven years later on July 1, 1931, when Chicago stockbroker Charles Pape brought together 19 regional oil drillers, offering each company 55,000 shares in the new corporation they could form by merging their refining or marketing facilities to create a well balanced company. The firms participating in the founding of Quaker State Corporation included the Eastern Refining Company, Sterling Oil Company of West Virginia, Ohio Valley Refining Company, Enterprise Oil Company Inc., Independent Refining Company, Lake Erie Lubricants Inc., Iron City Oil Company, Gallagher Bros. Inc., and Appaline Oil Company.

Quaker State's first president was Harry Crawford, part owner of President Oil Company, and in his first year in this capacity, Quaker State ran up $6.8 million in sales. Its profit line of $1.7 represented a fine rate of return, and bode well for the company's future.

In 1936, Quaker State signed an agreement with the Standard Oil Company, today called Amoco, to act as the company's exclusive sales agents for the its oil products in 13 midwestern states. The new partner would later put all Quaker State products in its gas stations throughout the United States. Also that year the company was listed on the New York stock exchange, denoted by the trading symbol KSF, which remains in use to this day.

Quaker State's original charter said nothing about drilling and production of oil products, and until 1944, Quaker State bought its supply of oil from independent producers. But in that year, increased wartime demand for energy use led the company to buy the Forest Oil Company's crude oil drilling facilities situated around Bradford, Pennsylvania. Since that time, the company has drilled and produced around 20 percent of its oil supply.

Wartime demand led to the increased use of additives in Quaker State oil products. In 1940, the company introduced a motor oil with greater chemical stability, which it called Stabilized Quaker State Motor Oil. A year later, the company brought to the market Quaker State HD High Detergency Oil. After 1945, the growth of the U.S. car industry and the size of car engines themselves prompted innovations in oil products production. In 1954, Quaker State introduced an oil product with anti-wear, anti-rust, anti-corrosive and high detergency ingredients.

By 1960, sales for Quaker State were on average surpassing the $50 million mark, representing an eightfold rise on sales in the thirty years since the company was first established. Innovations during the 1960s included the introduction of Quaker State DeLuxe Motor Oil and Quaker Koat, an undercoating for cars. In 1964, Quaker State decided to diversify its business, and it purchased Truck-Lite Company, based in Falconer, New York, which made fancy lights fitted onto trucks, trailers, and tractors.

In 1970, sales for the company topped $120 million, with profits posted at $10.7 million. At this time, Quaker State expanded its production capacity to meet growing demand for its products. It opened the Congo Refinery at Newell, West Virginia, in 1972, which represented at the time the most modern, specialized, lubricant refinery on the continent. Providing a company-wide increase of 75 percent in refining capacity, the Congo refinery allowed sales for Quaker State to reach $300 million in 1975.

Increasing government regulation of the company's core motor oil and auto supply businesses prompted diversification yet again. In May 1976, the Valley Camp Coal Company, based in Cleveland, Ohio, was purchased for around $50 million, offering vast coal reserves in eastern and western U.S. regions. Also during this time, Quaker State built its current headquarters on Elm Street in Oil City and bought three additional car parts suppliers: Corn Brothers of Smyrna, Georgia; National Oil Company of Newark, New Jersey; and Texstar Automotive Corporation, based in St. Louis, Missouri.

By the early 1980s, Quaker State had taken the big step of marketing its motor oil products across North America in such mass merchandise and discount outlets as Woolco and K-Mart. Its products included air, gasoline, and oil filters as well as anti-freeze, specialty oils for high-performance cars, fuel additives, exterior and interior coatings, hand cleaners, and cooling system and air conditioning products. Moving into mass merchandising caused much debate within the Quaker State boardroom. As Quentin Wood, chair of the oil products company, recalled in 1986: "... finally everyone recognized that the ultimate choice was not to forsake the garage mechanics and auto dealers and service stations who had sold our products from the beginning, but to stay with them and move also into mass merchandising." The move allowed Quaker State to double its market share of the North American motor oil market from ten percent in 1980 to 20 percent by mid-decade.

Quaker State also diversified its business by purchasing the Heritage Insurance Group in 1984 in return for 2.4 million shares of the motor oil company's stock. Headquartered in Agoura Hills, California, Heritage sold life, health, and accident insurance to car owners.

In 1985, Quaker State purchased The Helen Mining Company, a coal producer headquartered in Homer City, Pennsylvania, and gained a 17-year contract to supply coal to a nearby utility plant. That year Quaker State also responded to the emerging environmental movement by replacing the traditional metal packaging of its retail motor oil products with resealable "Easy Flow" plastic containers which did not drip or leak, adding to consumer convenience. The container's clear side stripe along the edge functioned as a measurement gauge.

Also in 1985, Quaker State moved into the car aftersales market, bringing new products and services to car owners. Acquiring 1.4 million shares of the Salt Lake City-based Minit-Lube Inc., Quaker State proposed to operate quick oil-change centers under the Minit-Lube brand name. Up to 14 different services would be offered at these outlets—including oil change, chassis lubrication, and fluid and filter replacements—all performed in under ten minutes. As Quentin Wood said of this expansion in 1986: "We're working hard to take advantage of opportunities to leverage our brand name into a growing number of products and services. Quaker State intends to remain the market leader in motor oil, and intends to become a leader in other automotive products as well."

The following year, Quaker State raised its profile by sponsoring for the first time its own stock car on the U.S. NASCAR racing circuit. It also began running year-round advertising spots during televised sports programs, also intended to boost its profile among motor oil users.

For all its mid-1980s expansion, however, Quaker State did not anticipate the recession at the end of the decade. A marked reduction in sales and profits began in 1989, and the year was regarded by Jack Corn, vice chairperson and CEO, as "difficult and disappointing." While Quaker State purchased Sturdivant Life Insurance Company, to bolster the car insurance side of the corporation, and McQuik's Oilube Inc., to complement its Minit-Lube chain of outlets, the company was hit hard by price cutting in the fast lube business nationwide. A $1.7 million write-down of Minit Lube assets had to be made.

Quaker State also announced in 1989 a reorganization of the company to make five business units: Quaker State Oil Refining Corporation, Quaker State Minit Lube, Heritage Insurance Group, Truck-Lite Company, and an energy unit made up of The Valley Camp Coal Company and gas and oil development. Reorganization and costcutting enabled Quaker State to boost sales in 1990 by 6.7 percent to just under $875 million, and profits up 65 percent to $19.5 million, despite a poor market for motor oil products in general and the decline of new car and truck purchases adversely affecting the fast lube business.

In January of that year, the company's core petroleum business was spun off from the parent company, and given the name Quaker State Oil Refining Corporation. Four months later, Quaker State sold its McKean refinery and Emlenton wax plant for a profit of $5.4 million, relying more heavily on its Congo Refinery at Newell, West Virginia. Persistent problems with facilities at the company's Valley Camp Coal Company operation, including a major roof fall, in addition to start-up problems at the Shrewsbury Mine, caused an operating loss of $4.1 million on the coal mining side of operations.

The recession also produced disappointments for Quaker State in 1991. In fact, oil drilling and production was the only profitable area in the company's portfolio, and intense price wars between oil refiners during the late 1980s, especially after the Persian Gulf War began, eventually hit that part of the business. In 1991, the motor oil business produced 92 percent of operating profits for the company; all other sectors were either losing money or just barely profitable. Corn observed that "1991 as a year was a big disappointment. But we think we know what's ailing the units where we didn't do well and are correcting the problems." Nevertheless, the coal business has continued in a slump, and during the summer of 1992, Quaker State announced that not only would it seek a buyer for the Valley Camp Coal Company, but also that the unprofitable Shrewsbury Coal Company was to be closed down.

Regarding its future, Quaker State has proven willing and able to make all the cost-cutting and reorganizational measures necessary to survive the recession of the early 1990s. While this will serve as an advantage to the company, it will probably be a long time before Quaker State achieves sales as posted during the 1980s. A low debt load will allow it to expand, but growth will likely be organic for the most part. Meanwhile, Quaker State will continue to take full advantage of its brand name and its reputation for quality products in the next century.

Principal Subsidiaries: Quaker State Oil Refining Corp; Quaker State Minit Lube Inc.; The Valley Camp Coal Company; Heritage Insurance Group; Sturdivant Life Insurance Company; Truck-Lite Company Inc.; QS E&P, Inc.; Valley Camp Inc.; Great Lakes Coal and Dock Company; Quaker State Japan Co. Ltd.

Further Reading: Wood, Quentin, *Quaker State Roots Go Deep into the World's First Oilfield,* The Newcomen Society of the United States, 1986; *The Story of Quaker State,* Quaker State Public Relations, 1989.

—Etan Vlessing

REPUBLIC ENGINEERED STEELS, INC.

410 Oberlin Road S.W.
P.O. Box 579
Massillon, Ohio 44648-0579
U.S.A.
(216) 837-6000
Fax: (216) 837-6204

Private Company
Incorporated: 1989
Employees: 5,000
Sales: $750 million
SICs: 3325 Steel Foundries Nec

With eight plants in five states and annual sales of approximately $750 million, Republic Engineered Steels, Inc. is the country's largest integrated producer of high quality bar and specialty steels. The company operates plants in Chicago, Massillon and Canton, Ohio, and Gary, Indiana as well as in Beaver Falls, Pennsylvania and Willimantic, Connecticut.

Republic traces its history to the establishment of the Berger Manufacturing Company in Canton, Ohio in 1886. Over the next hundred years, a series of new companies and mergers shaped the evolution of the corporate entity. In 1930 financier Cyrus Eaton formed Republic Steel Corporation from a merger between the Interstate Iron and Steel Company and Central Alloy Steel Corporation. With the merger, Republic Steel became the third largest steel producer in the country, competing with United States Steel Corporation and the Bethlehem Steel Corporation. Republic Steel's research staff and skilled work force, as well as its concentration of electric furnaces suitable for making a new product—stainless steel—provided certain commercial advantages over its larger rivals.

Republic Steel's fortunes were affected by the conditions that influenced the development of all domestic steel producers in the years that followed: the economic constraints of the Great Depression, the growing movement to organize steelworker labor, the demands for steel by the military during World War II, capital and geographic expansion after the war, and finally, increasing competition from imported steel and steel products.

In 1984 Republic Steel was acquired by the LTV Corporation and merged with Jones & Laughlin to form LTV Steel Co. in an effort to compete more effectively with the threats that imported steel products were presenting. However, the merger did not resolve the companies' problems, and LTV declared bankruptcy in July 1986. Still in bankruptcy in October 1988, LTV management decided to concentrate on the flat rolled steel business. The other major area of business, the bar division, was offered for sale.

Management and employees of the bar division, concerned that a highly-leveraged buyer would be more likely to liquidate the division's assets than invest the capital needed to operate it as a going concern, tendered a formal bid to buy the bar division through an Employee Stock Ownership Plan (ESOP). LTV accepted the bid in May 1989, and the purchase was formally signed effective November 28, 1989. Russell W. Maier, who had been president of the bar division, became president and chief executive officer of the new Republic Engineered Steels, Inc.

Maier had been with Republic Steel since before the merger that formed LTV Steel. Starting in 1960 as an industrial engineer, Maier was promoted to a series of positions with increasing responsibility. In 1983, he was named chief operating officer, and after the merger, he served as executive vice president of LTV until becoming president and general manager of the bar division in 1985. According to the *New York Times,* Maier initially fought the idea of employee ownership, but has come to believe that a combination of employee ownership and full employee participation in decision making resulted in employee suggestions that led to significant cost savings.

The original initiative for the buyout is said to have come from the steelworkers union, the United Steelworkers of America (USWA). The complex ESOP was designed by New York investment bankers Lazard Freres, and the purchase price was set at $280 million. The bar division's 5,000 employees, union and management, contributed an average of $4,000 each or a total of $20 million. Another $190 million was borrowed from the Bank of Boston and Security Pacific Bank, and the remaining $70 million was borrowed from LTV. The transaction left the new Republic in a highly-leveraged position, but committed to its own operating future. Federal tax policies advantageous to the ESOP-owned Republic permitted greater use of cash generated from operations. Significant cash obligations for the young company included its debt service, contributions to its ESOP and a post-retirement health benefit fund. Since its formation, Republic has made a major reduction in its debt.

In conjunction with the purchase, a new labor agreement was reached between the USWA and Republic management. Appendix H-1 to the agreement acknowledged the need for the involvement of all employees in the success of the business. A committee, consisting of union representatives, salaried employees and management, and known as the H-1 committee, determined to develop a new corporate culture, conducive to respect and trust between the groups, and oriented toward the profitability of Republic.

The H-1 committee established a company-wide education program to enable the new employee-owners to understand the ESOP structure, to make sense of the financial statements, and to grasp the basic elements and goals of Republic's business plan. Republic provided most of the multi-million dollar cost of the program, which involved an hour of business instruction each month for each employee-owner for thirty months.

Republic's sales for its first stub year, through June 1990, were approximately $379 million. The next six months, from July 1990 through December 1990, saw a sharp drop to $310 million. Republic blamed the general economic environment and responded by reorganizing into four separate business centers, each with profit accountability: Steel Division, Rolling Division, Cold Finished Division, and Specialty Steel Group.

In addition, in June of 1991, Republic announced a target of $80 million in cost reductions. Employee suggestions on operations were actively sought as alternatives to job cuts. By February 1992, more than 1,000 suggestions had been submitted, valued by Republic at $60 million in savings. One suggestion alone which made dramatic savings, approximately $3.6 million, was a new plan for the separation of different types of scrap steel for more efficient and reliable use in recycling.

By including "Engineered" in its new corporate name, Republic signified its intent to meet demanding specifications from its customers, more than 50 percent of whom were in the automotive industry. The products of Republic's Rolling Division and Cold Finished Division could be produced in a wide variety of sizes, grades, shapes, and finishes. The Specialty Steel group produced precision bar steel which met critical requirements for aerospace as well as energy and defense applications.

Republic's principal competitors in these markets included U.S. Steel/Kobe joint venture, the Timken Co., MacSteel Co., Bethlehem Steel's bar division, Inland Steel's bar division and North Star. Low cost minimills like Koppel Steel and Nucor were an increasing threat to Republic as well.

As a privately-held company, Republic was not required to release its results of operations to the public. It does, however, disclose financial information on a quarterly basis—including operating income which has been positive for all but one quarter since its formation. In any event, within its first 13 months Republic was able to build a cash reserve of approximately $90 million, out of which it paid down $37 million of its debt.

Republic made only one stock dividend payment, shortly after the ESOP was formed. Since the stock was not publicly traded, employee-owners could only sell their stock back to the company, and then only upon retirement. A minimal gain of a few hundred dollars might be recognized by the individual. But to most of the employee-owners in the early days, job security was more critical than capital gains. While Republic was not the first U. S. steel company to respond to financial troubles with employee ownership, its experiment was conducted on a much broader scale than that of Weirton Steel, for instance, which preceded it. As CEO Maier looked to the future in the early 1990's, he was "cautiously optimistic." Maier recognized that the future of Republic was tightly bound with that of the automotive industry that it served and the U. S. economy as a whole.

Principal Subsidiaries: Nimiskillian and Fuscarawas Railway Company; Oberlin Insurance Company

Further Reading: Kilborn, Peter T., "New Paths in Business When Workers Own," *New York Times,* November 22, 1991; Drown, Stuart, "Republic Attempts Recasting," *The Beacon Journal,* August 26, 1991; Serrin, William, *Homestead: The Glory and Tragedy of an American Steel Town,* New York, Random House Inc., 1992.

—Marcia McDermott

RICH PRODUCTS CORPORATION

1150 Niagara Street
Buffalo, New York 14213
U.S.A.
(716) 878-8000
Fax: (716) 878-8266

Private Company
Incorporated: 1965
Employees: 6,000
Sales: $890 million
SICs: 2023 Dry, Condensed & Evaporated Dairy Products;
  2038 Frozen Specialties Nec; 4832 Radio Broadcasting
  Stations

Rich Products Corporation pioneered the nondairy industry with a soybean-based whipping cream, and later became known for Coffee Rich, a cream substitute used in coffee. Sold largely to the food service industry, both products continue to dominate their respective markets. Rich is also involved in the manufacturing of frozen foods.

Robert E. Rich, Sr., first learned about product substitution during World War II through the War Food Administration. After the war, he put that knowledge to use and directed a laboratory team to search for a vegetable-based replacement for whipped cream. His product was to be based on soybeans. In 1945 Rich was on his way to visit a distributor on Long Island and packed some of his soybean-based whipping cream in dry ice for the long train ride from Buffalo, New York. He had intended just to keep the cream cool, but it was frozen solid when he arrived in Long Island. When Rich mashed the frozen mass, he found that it still whipped up beautifully. The discovery launched the beginning of a frozen nondairy products industry.

Rich's innovation, named Rich's Whip Topping, was lauded as "the miracle cream from the soya bean." This was 1945, when the frozen food industry was burgeoning. Rather than marketing to supermarkets, Rich targeted his product to the food-service sector, reasoning that restaurants, schools, hospitals, and other cost-conscious operators seemed a likely audience for the product. Rich quietly built solid markets, carving a niche that remains unchallenged.

During its early years, Rich continued to create variations on its Whip Topping. In the 1950s the company came out with the first commercial line of frozen cream puffs and eclairs. Its next innovation came in 1961 with the development of Coffee Rich, the nation's first frozen nondairy creamer. Since its introduction, Coffee Rich has dominated the market, claiming a 90 percent share into the 1980s. The product was also ahead of its time in health considerations: along with Whip Topping, Coffee Rich is the only 100 percent cholesterol-free, low-fat cream product distributed nationally. As soybean oil is low in saturated fats, Coffee Rich meets American Heart Association guidelines where most other non-dairy creamers fail because they are made from high-fat tropical oils.

In the 1960s Rich Products began marketing frozen dough. While supermarkets wanted the aroma of fresh baked goods tempting shoppers, it was too much trouble for them to set up expensive bakeries on their facilities, and frozen dough met their needs perfectly. In the early 1960s, Rich began construction on a nondairy plant in Fort Erie, Ontario, just across the Niagara River from Rich's Buffalo headquarters. This plant is still in operation, producing both frozen dough and non-dairy products. By the mid-1980s, Rich was operating what is still the world's largest frozen dough plant in Murfreesboro, Tennessee. The dough—for breads, rolls, and pastries—was sold to supermarket chains throughout the country.

In 1969 Rich acquired Elm Tree Baking Company in Appleton, Wisconsin, adding frozen baked goods to their product line. Appleton is currently one of 11 Rich plants producing bakery products.

The 1970s were marked by spurts of growth for Rich. To keep up with product demand, Rich had to expand its production capabilities rapidly. During this time, Rich acquired nine plants, including Federal Bakers Supply in Garfield, New Jersey, and L. K. Baker Company in Columbus, Ohio. Other operations were purchased in Winchester, Virginia, and Claremont and Fresno, California. Rich also purchased Palmer Frozen Foods, a regional frozen bakery goods producer and distributor in eastern Pennsylvania.

Rich also expanded its product line to seafood specialties, soup bases, and gravy mixes. As late as 1975, however, about 71 percent of Rich's revenues were still coming from non-dairy replacement products.

Rich launched an aggressive campaign of growth through acquisition that saw its sales quadruple over the next eight years. Acquisitions included the H. J. Heinz Company of Lake City, Pennsylvania, contributing cream pies and cakes to Rich's line, and PREAM, a nondairy coffee powder, from Early California Foods of Los Angeles. By 1982 company sales were at $400 million, and sales of non-dairy replacement products accounted for about half of those revenues.

Succeeded by his son, Robert Rich, Jr., as president of the company, Rich, Sr., remained chairman. Together they developed an unusual acquisition strategy, giving preference to other father-and-son companies. Rich, Sr., contended that all the company's takeovers were friendly and that most of their acquisitions' owners stayed on afterward. Other acquisitions in the 1980s included the former Lloyd J. Harriss plant, a Saugatuck,

Michigan-based pie producer, and Casa Di Bertacchi of Vineland, New Jersey, a producer of frozen Italian pasta and meat specialties.

In 1980 the company introduced a process, called Freeze Flo, that allowed products to remain soft while frozen, spurring the development of products such as frozen pie fillings that could be eaten right out of the freezer. The process took seven years and nearly $5 million to develop. By 1983 it held 39 patents and was bringing in $2.5 million a year in licensing to 50 companies, mostly overseas. Rich incorporated Freeze Flo into many of its own new products, such as Rich's Grand America Ice Cream, the only ice cream on the market that can be shipped and stored at zero degrees Fahrenheit.

In 1983 Rich acquired Nashville's Tennessee Doughnut Company and Antionetta's Frozen Italian Specialties of Harleysville, Pennsylvania. The company also purchased the Class AAA Buffalo Bisons baseball franchise, based in Rich's headquarters city. The team went on to set new minor league attendance records into the 1990s, becoming the best-drawing minor league baseball team in the nation.

In 1986 Rich entered into a joint venture with J. R. Wood Inc., of Atwater, California. Together they launched Rich Fruit Pak, a frozen fruit processing plant in Escalon, California. The company formed Rich Communications Corporation in 1987. This served as the parent company to a pair of Western New York radio stations: WGR-AM Newsradio 550 and WGR-FM "97 Rock." These stations supply the area with broadcasts of the NFL Buffalo Bills, the NHL Buffalo Sabres, and the Bisons. In 1988 Rich's frozen food line added barbeque and specialty meats with the acquisition of Byron's, Inc., of Gallatin, Tennessee.

These additions notwithstanding, the company's plan to expand via acquisition of family owned food companies was slowed when the numerous leveraged buyouts of the 1980s pushed prices too high. Rich avoided the large debts that were often necessary to complete such transactions. Acquisitions slowed, and Rich concentrated on in-house development of a technology to make cholesterol-free frozen foods.

In 1990, in its 32nd acquisition since 1969, Rich acquired the Blue Bird Baking Company, a major producer of pies and cakes. Having virtually reached its operating capacity, Rich planned to increase the capacity in six of its nine bakery manufacturing plants by 35 percent in order to make room for new products. Rich launched a multimillion-dollar capital expenditure plan that included plant expansions and renovations in California, Ohio, Wisconsin, Pennsylvania, Tennessee, and Virginia. In the spring of 1990, Rich built a $17 million research and development center.

In 1992 Rich acquired the Seneau Baking Company of Marlborough, Massachusetts, which became Rich Marlborough, a state-of-the-art bakery products manufacturing plant. The company also acknowledged the strength of its Mexican market that year by opening a broker's office in Guadalajara, joining the Rich offices in Monterrey and Mexico City. Whipped toppings, fruit fillings, glazes, and Better Creme icings were some the company's best sellers in Mexico. Rich also has offices in Asia, Japan, Singapore, Australia, and the United Kingdom.

Principal Subsidiaries: Byron's, Inc.; Casa Di Bertacchi Corporation; Rich-SeaPak Corporation; Nanticoke Seafood Corporation; Rich Baseball Operations; Rich Communications Corporation; Rich Transportation Services; Stadium Services Inc.

Further Reading: Greenberg, Jonathan, "All in the Family," *Forbes,* April 25, 1983; Rosenbaum, Rob, "Freeze Flo Success Grounded in Skills of Rich Researchers," *Business First of Buffalo,* October 28, 1985; Cone, Edward, "The Best-Laid Plans," *Forbes,* July 24, 1989; Crispens, Jonna, "New Products Priority in Rich Project," *Supermarket News,* February 25, 1991; Malchoff, Kevin, "Frozen Food and Foodservice: The Perfect Match," *Frozen Food Digest,* July 1991; "Rich Products Names Recipe Contest Winners," *Nation's Restaurant News,* November 18, 1991; "Rich Products Opens Mexico City Office," *Nation's Restaurant News,* January 27, 1992; Riddle, Judith, "Rich Products Expanding Non-Dairy to Guadalajara," *Supermarket News,* February 17, 1992; "Executive Changes," *Supermarket News,* March 8, 1992; "Rich Brings Out Topless Pies," *Supermarket News,* April 20, 1992; "Rich Offers Filled Mini Doughnuts," *Supermarket News,* June 8, 1992; "Rich Furthers Growth Plans with Seneau Baking Purchase," *Nation's Restaurant News,* July 8, 1992; Lahvie, Ray, "Rich Products Acquires Seneau Baking Company," *Bakery Production and Marketing,* July 24, 1992.

—Carol Keeley

RICHFOOD HOLDINGS, INC.

2000 Richfood Rd.
P.O. Box 26967
Richmond, Virginia 23261-6967
U.S.A.
(804) 746-6000
Fax: (804) 746-6144

Public Company
Incorporated: 1937 as Richfood, Inc.
Employees: 1,047
Sales: $1.06 billion
Stock Exchanges: NASDAQ
SICs: 5141 Groceries—General Line; 5147 Meats & Meat
   Products; 5143 Dairy Products Except Dried or Canned;
   6719 Holding Companies Nec

Richfood Holdings, Inc. is the largest food wholesaler and distributor in the mid-Atlantic area and the 15th-largest such company in the United States. The company was run as a not-for-profit grocers' cooperative until the late 1980s, and although it had achieved over a billion dollars in annual revenues by that time, it was poorly managed, debt-heavy, and floundering. After the cooperative went public, the situation only worsened and soon Richfood was on the auction block. When no buyers could be found, veteran grocery distributor Donald Bennett agreed to become CEO and attempt the prodigious task of turning the company around. Since Bennett's entry in 1990, the company has improved dramatically, attracting the attention of investors as well as its competitors. Although overshadowed by industry giants Super Valu Stores and Fleming Companies, Richfood is now an aggressive regional market leader whose health has been restored.

The company began in 1937 as Richfood, Inc., a Virginia-based cooperative wholesaler formed and managed by its retailer members. The goal of the company was to ensure the survival of the small independent stores that were beginning to feel the pressures of competition from large supermarket chains. The supermarket concept—with its emphasis on service, name brands, and deep discounts—had gradually taken hold since the 1920s and was becoming the standard form of retailing even in rural areas. Unfortunately, at Richfood there was little need for accountability. Patronage rebates and guaranteed price controls on stock were the chief indices by which the company and its

members operated, and even thrived, for decades. Richfood's mission, according to Seth Lubove, "was simple: buy groceries from manufacturers, take a standard markup to cover costs and move the goods on to the retail grocers whenever they wanted them, and damn the costs."

Over the next several decades this cooperative system showed signs of failing. Its members began to realize that other, more efficient wholesalers provided better services, including capital loans which were necessary for expansion and renewed vitality. Fleming Foods of Virginia, a subsidiary of Fleming (which, through acquisition, was fast becoming the nation's largest wholesaler) was one company that contrasted sharply with Richfood. Asset rich and profit oriented, Fleming Foods was supported by a public company capable of offering its customers several advantages over the competition.

Finally, in 1987, to satisfy Richfood's disgruntled members, CEO W. C. Taliaferro and the board decided to bring the company public. Richfood Holdings was formed in order to subsume the business, which was accomplished in May 1988. The company's last full year as a cooperative was abysmal in terms of income versus sales. Although it had tallied revenues of $956 million, its overall margin was little more than a tenth of one percent, far below the traditional food industry target of 1 percent. The company was, in actuality, losing money, a trend that continued during its first year as a public corporation. After decades of operating as a cooperative, Richfood was ill-prepared to turn a profit and was still ruled by a board of grocery retailers interested primarily in their own businesses' welfare rather than Richfood's.

In July 1989, after the company lost an account with A & P Super Fresh, which had come to represent ten percent of its annual sales, the board decided to put Richfood up for sale. Because of a poor balance sheet and a declining reputation, no acceptable bids came. Taliaferro left the company at this crossroads in early 1990. Claude B. Owen, Jr., a board member since 1988, was elected chairperson, and Edward Villanueva was chosen to serve as acting president. However, Richfood faced several predicaments—most notably its technical default on a $39.5 million loan with Prudential—and it was felt that new management was needed to make the company profitable. Consequently, in May 1990 Donald Bennett was brought in as CEO. Bennett, former head of Wetterau's food distribution business, had studied Richfood as a possible acquisition and so was familiar with the company's numerous problems.

One of the few factors working in Bennett's favor was Richfood's distinction as the largest food distributor in its operating region. It had established a customer base, but this had suffered from neglect during the management upheaval. In several cases, Richfood pricing policies had caused its retail clients to lose market share to such aggressive, lower-priced competitors as Food Lion. Largely at fault were Richfood's existing contracts with food manufacturers; they had been poorly negotiated by former management and often resulted in stark pricing discrepancies on the supermarket end. Aggravating matters was the state of the company's giant Richmond warehouse, allegedly so disorganized that workers had difficulty locating items.

According to Elicia Brown, Bennett "swung into action immediately, booting out most of the top management, slashing inventories almost in half, revising trucking routes and schedules and enhancing advisory and financial programs for Richfood's retailers." His most important single move was facing down food manufacturers by unilaterally imposing pricing discounts. "There was an arena that raised holy hell about it," remembered Bennett, "but when we invited the manufacturers to sit down and talk with us, in the end we paid back less than ten percent of the deductions made."

The negotiations led to more sensible gross margins for Richfood and to greater credibility among its customer base, approximately 650 supermarkets in Virginia, West Virginia, Maryland, the District of Columbia, Delaware, and North Carolina. Bennett followed up by establishing a cost-plus pricing system tied to various incentive programs that make it enticing for clients to increase their dependency on Richfood as a distributor. Other early moves that improved Richfood's viability included the sale of a nonfood subsidiary, Garner Wholesale Merchandising, and the acquisition of Fleming's distribution center in Waynesboro, Virginia. The former provided proceeds for paying down the company's sizable debt and the latter added more than $100 million to the company's annual volume and, more importantly, made Richfood a distributor to numerous Independent Grocers Alliance (IGA) outlets. IGA is now Richfood's second-largest customer.

During Bennett's first year earnings shot skyward, increasing some 160 percent. Richfood's stock, likewise, appreciated dramatically. In February 1992, Brown stated, "analysts are now predicting that earnings will grow 30 percent a year over the next five years." A few months later, at the end of fiscal 1992, Richfood was still outperforming itself. Profits had risen 46 percent to $13.8 million on relatively flat sales. Richfood was proving that it could compete even as deflation hampered the entire industry. Better delivery service, automated on-line buying, joint marketing programs, and an expanded private label inventory all contributed to the bottom line. In addition, operating costs that two years earlier had sliced away eight percent of revenues were decreased to 5.77 percent, near Bennett's ultimate goal of 5.4 percent. Another goal of Bennett's, attaining a net profit margin of 1.3 percent, was also close to being realized in 1992.

Only a few doubts about Richfood have arisen since Bennett's arrival. One, voiced by Elliot Zwiebach of *Supermarket News*, was that the company had 37 percent of its sales concentrated in just two retail chains, Farm Fresh and Ukrop. Another, ventured in *Financial World* by Ryan Matthews, was the potentially short lifespan of "wholesale distributors whose bottom line depends on pressuring food manufacturers." Both doubts would seem to be quelled by Richfood's increasing customer base and continuing profitability. In March 1991 the company, hoping to fortify its presence in the Baltimore-Washington area, entered into a principal supplier agreement with a Leedmark hyperstore. Further growth in the area is planned. The company also hopes to bolster its stake in North Carolina through its warehouse format Pack'N Save stores, first introduced in August 1991. The stores, embodying an emerging trend in retailing, offer savings similar to those of a membership club without demanding bulk purchases or membership fees.

Richfood has also begun to play a major role in financing and buying arrangements. In 1992, Nick's Market, a 34-store chain, was sold through the aid of Richfood to interested independent retailers. Such deals are clearly in the company's interest; because of its financing and brokerage services, all of the stores remained Richfood customers under new management. Ongoing improvements for the company include expanding and updating its product line, which includes more than 20,000 items, 1,600 of which are private label products. The irony underlying all of Richfood's recent developments and successes is that the company is becoming a likely target for acquisition by the larger food distributors. In 1989 Richfood wanted and couldn't find a buyer. Since that time, with Bennett in charge, the situation has been completely reversed.

Principal Subsidiaries: Market Insurance Agency, Inc.; Market Insurance Co., Ltd.; Market Improvement Corp.; Richfood, Inc.

Further Reading: Turcsik, Richard, "Richfood Sale Offer Withdrawn," *Supermarket News,* January 8, 1990; Turcsik, Richard, "Bennett to Join Richfood as Its President and CEO," *Supermarket News,* May 14, 1990; Zwiebach, Elliot, "Richfood: Turning the Corner," *Supermarket News,* November 12, 1990; Byrne, Harlan S., "Richfood Holdings: Cost-Paring Puts Supplier on Solid Footing," *Barron's,* July 1, 1991; Brown, Elicia, "Squeezing the Turnip," *Financial World,* February 4, 1992; Zwiebach, Elliot, "Richfood Sales Rise, Profit Soars," *Supermarket News,* August 24, 1992; Zwiebach, Elliot, "Richfood CEO: Price Deflation Places Emphasis on Efficiency," *Supermarket News,* September 7, 1992; Lubove, Seth, " 'A' is for Accountability," *Forbes,* December 21, 1992.

—Jay P. Pederson

ROLAND MURTEN A.G.

Postfach 194
CH-3280 Murten
Switzerland
037 72 11 45
Fax: (0) 37 71 25 02

Private Company
Incorporated: 1938
Employees: 215
Sales: SFr51.3 billion (US$32.38 billion)
SICs: 2051 Bread, Cake, and Related Products; 2052
   Cookies and Crackers; 5141 Groceries—General Line;
   5149 Groceries and Related Products, Nec

As the manufacturer of Zwieback and brand name *pains croustillants,* Roland Murten is a household name throughout Switzerland and parts of Germany. Specializing in bread products with a long shelf life, Roland Murten has built a solid industry with a few popular staple products.

Two thirds of Roland's employees are production workers based in factories in Morat and Avenches. There are 28 representatives in charge of product promotion in all of Switzerland. Roland's products also sell well in Japan, Germany, and 40 other countries. Since 1978, Roland has been a subsidiary of Sandoz Alimentation SA. This is a division of food-product subsidiaries held by Sandoz A.G., a large chemical company based in Basel.

Although Switzerland is able to meet less than half of the domestic demand for grain—only about half of the country's land is available for farming, and of that, nearly 60 percent is fodder crops and grazing areas for the country's dairy and beef industries—Roland Murten uses domestic ingredients from the region as much as possible. In addition, to bake the *pain croustillant,* only the quantity of flour or meal necessary for the day's production is ground, which also helps to preserve vitamins and minerals.

The firm was founded in 1938 by Leopold Schoffler. At that time, Schoffler was a specialist in baked goods and was very well known for his innovations in the domain of products with a long shelf life. Schoffler's work in this regard was the catalyst for a whole new product line and related industries in Northern Europe and in Germany.

The 1930s were a tumultuous time in Switzerland's history. Though the small, mountainous country, bordered by France, Germany, Austria, Italy, and Liechtenstein, is famed for its tradition of neutrality and its role as guardian of Europe's trans-Alpine routes, this did not insulate Switzerland from world market fluctuations. The Great Depression did have an impact on the country, though the results were less severe than they were for Switzerland's neighbors. It was during this time that Schoffler set about choosing a spot for his new enterprise.

The town of Murten/Morat, situated near the French and German borders—hence the two versions of the city's name—in the canton of Fribourg, seemed the ideal place. At that time, Fribourg was an economically distressed district with a relatively large reservoir of workers. In addition, Murten/Morat was located in the center of a region that already produced rye bread and its related ingredients, so goods could be delivered from the surrounding countryside directly to the company's mill. A factory for Schoffler's proposed product line of crusty breads would fit in well.

The firm got its name from Schoffler's fondness for knights, combined with his desire to find a name that was somewhat whimsical, as well as easy to pronounce in both French and German. Although only one-fifth of Switzerland's population is French-speaking while two-thirds is German-speaking, the location of the firm necessitated a fluently bilingual name and identity. As Schoffler was inspired by the legend of the knight Roland, he decided to combine Roland with the name of the town. Thus the French version of the company's name is Roland Morat SA, and the German version is Roland Murten AG. The company's well-known logo depicts a knight standing within the outline of a castle.

The first line of production—initially only *pains croustillants,* or crusty, dry breads similar to the Melba Toast sold in the United States—was manufactured in 1939, the same year that Adolf Hitler and his forces occupied Czechoslovakia and invaded Poland. Soon World War II was consuming the continent, and times became difficult for the fledgling enterprise. Though Switzerland was neutral during the war, it did mobilize troops for border defense, and the economies of its neighbors, Germany, France, and Italy were disrupted. In addition, what had initially been an ideal location for the young company was becoming increasingly precarious. Situated as it was so close to the German border, the effects of pro-German propaganda flooding that region of the country after the fall of France were becoming increasingly apparent. For a time, there was serious division within Switzerland, as well as great economic difficulties.

Despite these problems, Schoffler and Roland's various investors struggled on, even producing the first line of Zwieback, which resembled Swedish crackers, in 1941. *Pain croustillant* and Zwieback were sold in vacuum-sealed packages to ensure a long shelf life. Especially popular in the German portions of Switzerland, they became part of nearly every restaurant's bread basket. In addition to the role Roland products garnered as a breakfast item, they continue to be, like Melba Toast, the staple of dieters. Beginning in 1949, Roland added another product to its line with its first Sticks and Bretzels. *Pain croustillant,* Zwieback, Sticks, and Bretzels continue to constitute the cornerstones of Roland's income.

After the death of Leopold Schoffler in 1949, his son, Heinz, took over direction of the company. From very early on, the company concentrated much effort and money on its marketing and advertising campaigns, and after World War II Roland began placing even more emphasis on the promotion of its products. It was under Heinz Schoffler's leadership, however, that Roland started to build a substantial market. Though the concept of marketing was still relatively new, the company systematically organized sales promotion measures, setting up thousands of in-store taste tests in 1953.

In a nation as remarkably diverse in language and cultural contact as Switzerland, products must be easily recognizable to all consumers. Every aspect of Roland's promotional efforts was fine-tuned to attract and keep their customers. The company paid a great deal of attention to such things as product packaging, making it very simple and homogeneous. Uniform packaging with blue and red bands of color and the company's logo made it easy for customers to identify Roland's products, regardless of what language they spoke.

Over the years, Roland has adapted its product line to meet market demands. New products have been launched and others retired, according to consumer preferences. In addition to the seven varieties of *pain croustillant,* three varieties of Zwieback,

Sticks Roland, and Bretzels Roland, the company's other products include Biscottes, Fit-Corn, Pancroc, Grissini, Snackers, Flutes de Morat, Chips au fromage, Apero-Pic, Noix, Coques de meringues, Tartelettes, and Eventails and Biscuits. Though these items are popular and well-known, they do not have the market-dominance of the incontestable leaders Roland has in its staple dry breads and Zwieback. However, the product line for retail commerce and such large consumers as hotels, hospitals, and restaurants is comprised of more than 80 products.

In recent years Roland has launched some successful new items in two different domains: products with a long shelf life, and *biscuits apéritifs.* Some of the dry bread products contained nuts and fruit; new Zwieback varieties featured crystalized sugar. The company is poised to take advantage of increasing interests in healthy and durable edibles.

While Roland enjoys great product recognition and market-share, the market volume of any product in Switzerland reaches a natural ceiling due to the country's size. For this reason, Roland continues to apply itself to varying its product line, but is especially attentive, of late, to the increasingly important foreign market. With the Swiss reputation for quality products, this seems a sure way for Roland Murten AG to keep growing.

Further Reading: Roland Morat SA (press release), Murten/ Morat, Switzerland, Roland Murten AG, 1993.

—Carol Keeley

ROLLS-ROYCE PLC

65 Buckingham Gate
London SW1E SAT
United Kingdom
(071) 222 9020
Fax: (071) 222 9020

Public Company
Incorporated: 1884 as F.H. Royce and Company
Employees: 61,000
Sales: £3.51 billion (US$5.09 billion)
Stock Exchanges: London
SICs: 3724 Aircraft Engines & Engine Parts; 3728 Aircraft
   Parts & Equipment, Nec; 3511 Turbines & Turbine
   Generator Sets; 3519 Internal Combustion Engines, Nec;
   3559 Special Industry Machinery, Nec; 3799
   Transportation Equipment, Nec

Rolls-Royce Plc is a British aero-engine maker supplying advanced engineering products for civil and military uses. The company's two main divisions are its aerospace group, producing gas turbine engines for civil and military aircraft, and its industrial power group, which designs and builds power generation, transmission, and distribution systems worldwide.

The origins of Rolls-Royce date back to its founder, Sir Frederick Henry Royce, born in March 1863 in Lincolnshire. His rags to riches story began when as a youth he went to London to sell newspapers for W. H. Smith on a street corner. In 1872, the year of his father's death, young Henry found himself in financial straits and augmented his newspaper selling job with work as a telegraph messenger. Five years later Royce got a job as an apprentice in a railway works near Peterborough, where he learned the basics of modern engineering. In 1880, he graduated to becoming a tester with the Electric Light and Power Company in London, and he studied the principles of electrical engineering in his spare time. In 1884 Royce and his friend Ernest Claremont began a small electrical and mechanical engineering workshop, F. H. Royce and Company, on Cooke Street in Manchester.

Business was slow and difficult at first. But before long, the company became known for its electrical dynamos and cranes. Sales for the company rose from £6,000 in 1897 to £20,000 in 1899. That year, the company's name was changed to the Royce

Company, and its capital base was increased to £30,000 to allow a new factory to be built at Trafford Park, Manchester.

By 1902, the nascent motorcar industry in Britain caught Royce's eye. He bought a secondhand French Decauville, stripped it down to its parts, and studied the vehicle. Then he set about building his own. The result was a two-cylinder, ten horsepower model not much different from the Decauville. The first model produced from the Cooke Street works emerged in 1904, in time to catch interest from another Decauville enthusiast of the day, Charles Rolls.

Born in 1877, Charles Stewart Rolls came from a more privileged background than Royce. After studying at Eton and Cambridge, he traveled around the Continent in the early 1890s, developing an interest in the motor car, which was then becoming popular in France. In 1903, once back in Britain, Rolls became a motorcar dealer. He sold mostly continental models, but with his dealership in fashionable Brook Street, London, and a repair shop in nearby Fulham, Rolls was coming to know the British car market well.

Rolls's interest in becoming a dealer of British automobiles led him to Royce's new line. The two men met, and a deal was finally struck for C. S. Rolls and Co. to become the exclusive dealer for Royce. An agreement between the two men, dated December 23, 1904, stipulated all cars sold by their arrangement were to be called "Rolls-Royce." Four models went into production: the twin cylinder, ten horsepower; the three-cylinder, 15 horsepower; the four-cylinder, 20 horsepower; and the six-cylinder, 30 horsepower. All the vehicle engines shared a series of parts—pistons and rings, valves, connecting rods, springs and bearings, among others.

In 1905, the first year of production, Rolls-Royce's four types of vehicles ranged in price from £395 to £890, and were therefore purchased only by the wealthy. Expansion of the motorcar market at this time tended to focus on innovations in engine design. In 1905, Rolls-Royce introduced its eight-cylinder, V-8 engine, regarded by motoring enthusiasts as innovative for the smoother, quieter ride it allowed.

In 1906 Rolls-Royce introduced the 40/50 model, or the Silver Ghost, named for its metallic appearance and its engine that was "quiet as a ghost." Orders for this and earlier models climbed steadily that year, and this brought about the expansion of the company to a new factory in Derby. To fund the new plant, a subscription of new shares worth £100,000 was completed on the stock market in December of 1906. The 1906 prospectus listed a new name: Rolls-Royce Limited. The subscription named Royce as chief engineer and works director, and Rolls as technical managing director. Ernest Claremont was appointed to chair the company.

The Derby factory opened on July 9, 1908 amid much pageantry. Proof that the new Silver Ghost was to be a success came in 1911 when the Indian government ordered eight new models for use by King George V and his entourage during the Delhi Durbar that year.

Around this time, Rolls began to distance himself from the car company as both his fame and outside interests grew. He resigned as technical managing director and became a consultant to Rolls-Royce in April 1910. Three months later, Rolls was tragically killed when his Wright biplane crashed. As a symbol of mourning, the intertwined "RR" logo on the Rolls-Royce radiator plate was changed from red to black. Soon thereafter Royce fell seriously ill from exhaustion, and he spent much of 1912 convalescing on the continent. In time, Royce took a home in the south of France and reduced his shop floor work at the Rolls-Royce factory in Britain to conserve his health.

Day-to-day responsibility of Rolls-Royce Limited then fell to Claude Johnson, who reaffirmed the long-time company commitment to producing and perfecting one model. For a company building luxury cars, the benefits of military procurement beginning at the outbreak of the First World War were not immediately apparent. But, in 1914, Rolls-Royce found itself in demand to produce chassis for armored fighting vehicles, and Rolls Royce cars soon became widely used as staff cars for the British Army.

During this time Rolls-Royce was also called upon to design aircraft engines to help with the war effort. The company's association with aviation propulsion had begun earlier. In fact, the original 1906 agreement between Rolls and Royce had mentioned in the first paragraph that the company had a wide mandate to provide propulsion on land, at sea, and in the air. Furthermore, Royce had served as a consultant to the Royal Aircraft Factory at Farnborough. However, outside of this early interest in aviation, which Royce shared with Rolls, actual production of aero engines didn't begin until the onset of the World War I.

In early 1915, Royce led a team of engineers, including A. G. Elliot, chief assistant, in working out a design. Within three days of the war's outbreak, Royce was pouring over plans for a 200 horsepower aero engine. Some of the technology—crankshaft, connecting rods, geartrains—were borrowed from the Silver Ghost motorcar engine. But more pistons were required; 12 in all. And so was born the 60 degree V12 engine that became the prototype for all machinery produced by Rolls-Royce after 1918.

Testing of a 225 horsepower aero engine had begun at Derby. By 1916, the engine went into production. It was named the Eagle and was put into wartime service beginning in 1916 at 250 horsepower in size. By 1918, the Mark VIII form had risen in size to 365 horsepower. Two other engines, the Hawk and the Falcon, had been designed by Royce from his home in the south of France and relayed to his production team in Derby for manufacture. In total, 5,000 Rolls-Royce aero engines were made during the First World War. By the late 1920s, the company derived more profit from continuing to make aero engines than it did from making cars.

Producing aero engines also had applications for developing motorcar engines. In 1924, for example, Rolls-Royce introduced front wheel brakes to its cars, as well as power assistance through a gearbox driven servo. The postwar years also signaled a departure from the company's practice of producing only one car model. In 1922, the 3.5 litre, 20 horsepower model was introduced. In 1925, the "New Phantom" succeeded the Silver Ghost. While its larger seven litre engine had overhead valves

rather than side valves, the chassis and the running gear were the same as those used on the Silver Ghost.

Over the next ten years, Rolls-Royce continued to manufacture automobiles for an increasingly exclusive and wealthy clintele. In 1931, the company purchased Bentley Motor Ltd., a consistently undercapitalized English manufacturer of high-performance automobiles. Royce, who was conferred a baronetcy in 1930, died in 1933.

Just before the outbreak of World War II, the Phantom II was replaced by the Phantom III. The new model was driven by a V12 engine, the most powerful yet. Without Royce to oversee its introduction, however, the Phantom III production had been expensive. This led in 1937 to the company's consideration of rationalizing its design and production facilities to contain expanding operating costs.

Before his death in 1933, Royce had set about designing a new generation of aero engines that surpassed 1,000 horsepower in size. The result was the PV12, a 27 litre engine eventually named the Merlin. The Merlin was first used by the Royal Air Force in 1937. Two years later, the aero engine could maintain 1,000 horsepower to 16,000 feet. Impressed with its design and output, the Royal Air Force agreed to help fund the development of three fighter planes designed around the Merlin—the Fairey Battle Bomber, the Hurricane, and the Spitfire. All performed with memorable accuracy in the famed Battle of Britain during the Second World War. Innovations to the engine during this time ensured it could attain 1,000 horsepower at twice the original altitude, 36,000 feet, by 1944. The engine's operating ceiling grew to 47,000 at the war's end as well.

During the war, Dr. A. A. Griffith at the Royal Aircraft Establishment was recruited by Rolls-Royce to design an innovative contrafan engine for the company. Other inventions by Rolls-Royce engineers included the early gas turbine engine for aerospace travel designed by Stanley Hooker and Frank Whittle in 1940.

In 1945, Ernest Hives, general manager of Rolls-Royce, decided that the future of the company lay in continuing to produce aero engines, and that the next frontier would lay in gas turbine engines, signaling an immediate cessation to the production of the piston turbine engine. Activity during the Second World War had greatly expanded Rolls-Royce. Factories at Crewe and Glasgow, Scotland had been opened. By 1945, the company employed well over 50,000 people, and car production was moved from Derby to Crewe, so that the Derby facilities could work almost exclusively on developing the gas turbine aero engine, particularly for the civil aviation industry.

An early customer of the Merlin engine was the Canadair DC4M, a Canadian-built aircraft. The introduction of a military engine in a civil aircraft took some tinkering before it was done successfully. Rolls-Royce used its experience to judge just how different commercial engine expectations were from military ones.

In 1953, Rolls-Royce introduced the Dart propjet engine for the Vickers Viscount. This new engine had a centrifugal design and had taken over from the Merlin 60 series of engines. The last Dart engine was built in 1986, producing nearly 40 years of production. The last Merlin, on the other hand, was built 16 years after the first one.

Rolls-Royce also introduced the turbojet engine in the form of the AJ65 model, or the Avon. Beginning in the 1950s, it powered such aircraft of the day as the Canberra, Hunter, and Lightning. The company's second wholly civil aero engine was the RB141, or Medway, launched in 1959. It served the BEA and BOAC airlines for a few years before it was replaced by the Spey, a smaller version. Besides being used in the BAC One Eleven, Fokker F28, and Gulfstream II and III, the Spey made its way across the Atlantic into the American LTV A7 military aircraft.

By the end of the 1960s, Rolls-Royce was facing increasing competition from American aero engine makers Pratt & Whitney and General Electric. To maintain its technological edge, Rolls-Royce introduced the Tay, successor to the Spey. Developing new aero engines, however, consumed much time and money. So much so that in February 1971 the company faced financial collapse and was subsequently nationalized by the British government.

To reduce costs, the company spun off its carmaking division into a separate company, Rolls-Royce Motor Cars Ltd., a subsidiary of Vickers Plc. The new company, operating under license to Rolls-Royce Ltd, continued the use of the Rolls-Royce name and the distinctive RR symbol.

At the same time, development of the RB211 engine under the engineering leadership of Sir Stanley Hooker, continued apace. By 1972, the RB211 went into production for use in the Tristar aircraft. It has since been utilized in Boeing 757s and 747-400s, the latest generation of civil aircraft, and through continued improvements provides 65 percent more thrust than the original engine model introduced in 1972. In 1987, Rolls-Royce announced that 75 percent of customers for the new Boeing 757 airliner had chosen the RB211 engines for propulsion.

On the military engine side of operations, Rolls-Royce took part in the three-nation Turbo-Union RB199 engine development for the Tornado aircraft during the mid-1980s. The company also provided Pegasus vectored-thrust engines for the British V-Stol Harrier aircraft, used primarily by the Royal Air Force.

Rolls-Royce engines have also been used in marine crafts. The year 1987 saw the 100th industry RB211 engine used in land-based and off-shore installations, mainly by the oil and natural gas industries in drilling operations. Furthermore, as of 1988, more than 25 naval forces worldwide were powering their vessels with Rolls-Royce gas turbine engines.

In May 1987, the British government refloated Rolls-Royce on the London stock market, securing more than two million shareholders in the process. Many were from overseas, primarily Americans.

By the end of 1988, a more hopeful business climate produced an order book for Rolls-Royce of £4.1 billion, compared with the £2.7 billion a year earlier. Sales for the company were slightly down, however, on 1987 figures, as was the operating profit at £333 million.

In 1988, the company launched the RB211-524L civil turbofan engine. In addition, Rolls-Royce signed an agreement to provide the European Fighter Aircraft, a three-member European military production project, with the EJ200 engine. The company had a 33 percent stake in the project.

After its refloatation, Rolls-Royce set about diversifying away from its sole emphasis on aero engines. To that end, in May 1989, the company merged with Northern Engineering Industries Plc (NEI), which designed and constructed capital plant and equipment, particularly for the power generation industry. The merger brought Terry Harrison, managing director of NEI, and Dr. Robert Hawley, managing director of operations at NEI, to the Rolls-Royce board.

That year Frank Turner, director of civil engineers at Rolls-Royce, welcomed the diversification from NEI which ensured the company would now derive 35 percent of its sales from non-aero engine business. He commented: "Through the sixteen years of state ownership, we were constrained . . . in obtaining approval for anything new. In effect, our gun arm was strapped. We found ourselves only able to react to the initiatives of our competitors, and then only when it was very late in the day."

The company announced in 1989 the formation of a joint venture between NEI and Asea Brown Boveri, the Swiss-based engineering group. The venture, NEI ABB Gas Turbines Ltd, was to be based in Newcastle in northern England. In the same year, Rolls-Royce launched its next generation of technology, the Trent engine, to pick up where the RB211 series left off. The first orders went to wide-body aircraft, such as the McDonnell Douglas-11 and the Airbus 330. Boeing subsequently announced it would carry the Trent engines on its 767-X aircraft.

In 1990 Lord Tombs, chairperson of Rolls-Royce, spoke of the possible consequences of the approaching world recession, and disruption to the global airline industry from the unfolding Persian Gulf conflict, commenting that "the industrial climate in the UK is a very difficult one. Much . . . depends on the international economic situation after the resolution of the Gulf conflict and upon the health of the airline industry." The next year saw a worsened economic climate for Rolls Royce. The worldwide recession deepened, and airline passenger travel fell, hitting the fortunes of airline carriers and causing a decrease in orders for aircraft. The mining and engineering industries also slumped, affecting the company's fortunes similarly.

Sales for Rolls-Royce in 1991 fell 4 percent to £3.51, but pre-tax profits fell more sharply to £51 million, compared with £176 million a year earlier. At the same time, the company's order book rose to a record £6.6 million. Additional orders were made for the Trent engines to go into new Boeing 777s bought by Thai Airways International and Emirates.

As Rolls-Royce looks to the future, an end to the world recession would naturally benefit the company's engineering endeavors. Regarding aerospace, reduced defence spending worldwide will adversely affect the sale of engines to military aircraft companies. Growth in the civil aviation industry remains uncertain. While the commercial airline industry has recovered from the effects of the Persian Gulf conflict, it remains ailing under the weight of excessive debt loads and forced restructurings. Nevertheless, the company's share of the civil aviation market grew from ten percent at the time of its refloatation in 1987 to 23 percent at the beginning of 1993. And its research and development side is gearing up to supply the market for second-generation supersonic travel anticipated to begin by the turn of the century.

Principal Subsidiaries: Deeside Titanium Ltd; Rolls-Royce Associates Ltd; Rolls-Royce Business Ventures Ltd; Rolls-Royce China Ltd; Rolls-Royce Far East Ltd; Rolls-Royce France Ltd; Rolls-Royce India Ltd; Rolls-Royce Leasing Ltd; Rolls-Royce Plant Leasing Ltd; Sawley Packaging Company Ltd; Stresswave Technology Ltd; Cooper Rolls Ltd; Rolls-Royce Turbomeca Ltd; Turbo-Union Ltd; Turbine Components Australia; Eurojet Turbo GmbH; IAE International Aero Engines AG; Cooper Rolls Inc.

Further Reading: Bird, Anthony, and Ian Hallows, *The Rolls Royce Motor Car,* London, B. T. Batsford Ltd, 1972; Turner, Frank, "Rolls-Royce in Perspective Past, Present and Future," 1991, R. J.

—Etan Vlessing

ROVER GROUP PLC

Ivy Cottage
Canley Road
Coventry CV5 6QX
United Kingdom
(20) 367 0111
Fax: (20) 371 4759

Subsidiary of British Aerospace Plc
Incorporated: J. K. Starley and Company Ltd., 1888
Employees: 33,500
Sales: £3.7 billion (US$5.37 billion)
Stock Exchanges: London
SICs: 3711 Motor Vehicles and Car Bodies

The Rover Group is Britain's leading car maker and exporter, producing approximately 500,000 models annually and accounting for roughly 45 percent of the nation's car exports. Since its beginnings in the mid-1800s, the company has maintained its market share while enduring both change—through groupings, mergers, and takeovers with various British car makers—and a 1988 sale to British Aerospace.

The foundation for Rover was established in 1861 when John Kemp Starley, an engineer by trade, and William Sutton established a firm in Coventry to make penny-farthing cycles and tricycles. In 1869 Starley broke with Sutton and took on another partner, Rowley Turner. They built and operated a factory in Coventry's Cheylesmere district to continue making pedal bikes, but that partnership lasted only one year. In 1870 Starley took William Hillman on as a foreman as he established the Coventry Machinists Company. The two men's partnership lasted six profitable years before Hillman set out on his own.

In 1884 Starley's business first used its future name when it produced a new bicycle model called The Rover. The name was intended to indicate how the cycle could wander, or rove, across great distances. Four years later, Starley changed the name of his company to J. K. Starley and Company Ltd. Also at this time, Starley began experimenting with a bicycle propelled by a battery. The company sold 11,000 bicycles in 1896, at an average price of £14.88. Sales for the company reached £160,000 that year, with profits pegged at £21,945.

The company had grown in size and sales to a point where a successful share offering on the London stock market could be made that year. The company would now be called The Rover Cycle Company Ltd., with a capital value after the offering of £150,000. Another £50,000 in five percent debentures were also placed on the company's books.

Despite his success with bicycles, Starley persisted in developing a two-wheeled vehicle that could power itself. The result was a motorcycle developed at the turn of the century. By 1904 Starley had produced his first car, an eight-horsepower vehicle. In 1906 his company became the Rover Company Ltd.

During the early 1900s, new car makers often made a name for themselves and their models by entering road race meetings. The first such meetings were staged in France. Britain, however, kept to a strict 12 m.p.h. speed limit for new cars, which disallowed road racing. By 1903, though, Parliament relented and allowed time trials for new cars to be held on the Isle of Man. Rover entered the road race annually and won the International Tourist Trophy race with its 20 horsepower model in 1907. One of the firm's most famous races took place in 1930 when the Light Six car model entry raced the Blue Train, a continental locomotive, across France. The Light Six reached the finish line 20 minutes before the train.

Rover continued producing bicycles, motorcycles, and motorcars through World War I. In 1914, however, the company devoted itself to the war effort by making military vehicles, mortars, gas shells, and other hardware for the British Army. The company's domestic car production picked up after the end of the war in 1918 and, two years later, the Rover eight-horsepower model rolled off the production line. More than 17,000 of these models were made and sold until 1925. Rover was also gaining positive recognition with other products; the Royal Automobile Club awarded the company's 14/15 horsepower model of 1924 the Dewar Trophy.

By 1939 and the start of World War II, Rover was employing more than 21,000 people who built aero engines, tank engines, and aircraft wings for the British Army. The company was also instrumental in developing a jet engine for the British Air Force. Coventry experienced heavy bombing from German fighter planes during the war, and Rover's plant in that city was not spared. Because of the damage, the company moved its manufacturing facilities to Solihull, Birmingham, in 1945. Here work continued on developing a top-secret small gas turbine engine. The reward came on March 8, 1950, when Rover engineers rolled out the first gas turbine propelled car.

After 1945, a large-scale reorganization of the British car industry took place. The companies that would eventually join Rover, the Austin and Morris companies, were rivals to Rover in the family car market.

Austin, led by Herbert Austin, had produced its first car, a three-wheel model, in 1896. While working for the Wolseley company, Austin built a four-wheeler which won its class in the Automobile Club of Great Britain 1000 mile trial in 1899. In 1905 Austin established the Austin Motor Company at Longbridge, Birmingham. A year later, the first "Austin" was unveiled. The 30 horsepower motorcar built with a four-speed gear box and chain drive rear axle was aimed at the affordable end of the car market. By 1910 just under 1,000 workers were making a range of Austin car models with engine sizes from 6.8 horsepower to 60 horsepower.

After World War I and the concentration on military production, Austin put its efforts in one model, a 20 horsepower car modelled on American tastes. Though this almost ruined the car company, it redeemed itself in 1922 with the introduction of the Austin Seven model. Small and lightweight, the Austin Seven could seat four people and appealed to families, becoming one of the most popular vehicles in its class. Again, the Austin company turned strongly to military hardware production during World War II, but resumed domestic car production at the war's conclusion. Its first postwar model was the Austin Sixteen. In 1951 Austin opened a new assembly building at its Longbridge plant and overhauled its production line. Austin also announced a pending merger with the Morris car company, a rival for decades and maker of the Morris and MG car models.

Morris Motors had been established in 1910 by William Richard Morris who designed his first car model, the Morris Oxford, that year. The first completed model was driven off the assembly line in Cowley on March 28, 1913. Morris's company suffered from the industry slump after World War I and he slashed prices on his car models in the early 1920s to save the company. Morris teamed up with U.S. steel manufacturer Edward G. Budd in 1926 to form the Pressed Steel Company. Morris's aim was to build the first British all-steel car body and, in 1928, the finished product was the Morris Isis Six, a medium sized salon car model. The popular eight-horsepower Morris Minor was also introduced in August of 1928.

During this time, Morris was taking ownership of his suppliers. The Hotchkiss factory, builders of the Cowley engines, came on board in 1922 and SU Carburetors was swallowed up in 1923. In addition, Wolseley Motors was acquired for £140,000 in 1937. Morris Motors continued launching new products after World War II; the Minor was a popular four-seater designed by Alec Issigonis, and both the Morris Six and Isis, the last six cylinder Morris models, were also introduced at this time.

The rivalry between Morris and Austin ended with their merger into the British Motor Corporation in 1952. The other side of Rover Group's expansion took part with commercial vehicle production. In 1961 the Leyland Group acquired Standard Triumph, makers of motorcycles and motorcars. A year later, Leyland merged with Associated Commercial Vehicles and the Leyland Motor Corporation was established. Then, in 1966, luxury car maker Jaguar and the British Motor Corporation joined their businesses to form British Motor Holdings. A year later the Leyland Motor Corporation expanded its car business by acquiring the Rover Company. A further shakeup of the British car industry took place in 1968 when the Leyland Motor Corporation and British Motor Holdings merged to form the giant British Leyland Motor Corporation, makers of family and commercial vehicles. The company changed its name to British Leyland Ltd. in 1975, BL Ltd. in 1978, and the Rover Group Plc in 1986.

Despite the turmoil of takeovers and mergers, Rover steadily continued to develop its trademark vehicles. A major postwar development for Rover was the Land Rover car model, unveiled at the 1948 Amsterdam Motor Show. Modeled after the four-wheel drive British War Department Jeeps, the Land Rover's production was a direct result of the postwar steel shortages—extensive use was made of easily obtainable aluminum alloy. Mechanical parts, on the other hand, were kept simple, yet sturdy. Land Rover production topped 500,000 models in 1960. That year new models included diesel engines, optional wheelbases, and a selection of body styles. Exports of the Land Rover—which was quickly becoming the backbone of the company—were made to all points of the world, where the vehicle became a familiar sight traversing deserts and jungles alike.

By 1970 Rover had introduced an upscale version of the Land Rover called the Range Rover. Incorporating a host of new design features, the Range Rover won the Don Safety Trophy for its new model that year. Other awards followed for the Range Rover, including the 1982 Design Council Award for the four-door version. Also during the 1970s, the Range Rover was exhibited at Paris's Louvre Museum. This showing served as a testament to the vehicle's timeless styling.

In 1979 Rover began a long-term relationship with Honda of Japan, a rival car maker then making inroads into the European car market. At the time Rover was looking for a partner with whom to develop a new car model. Honda agreed to a joint venture, and the two partners soon unveiled the Honda Ballade, built in Cowley and sold in Britain as the Triumph Acclaim. At the same time, Rover produced several new car models to head off increased competition from Japanese car makers in Europe. In 1984 the Rover 200 series, consisting of affordable, mid-size cars, was introduced. The series continued through the late 1980s.

Long known for mass car production at the bottom end of the market, Rover was now branching out into the luxury-car market. In 1986 Rover brought forth the Rover 800 series, executive cars with advanced styling and technology. Three years later, the company launched the luxury Rover 200/400 range of midsized executive cars. Rover had a tradition in Britain and the rest of Europe of supplying company cars. With its new line of luxury cars, Rover could now cater to top executives.

In July of 1988, the British government announced that it would sell Rover, then led by chairman Graham Day, to British Aerospace, Britain's largest manufacturing and engineering group. The sale, with a price tag of $255 million, did not pass without controversy. In 1989 the National Audit Office in Britain found the government had sold Rover for less than its true value and had paid more than $75 million to British Aerospace in hidden subsidies. The British government argued that in recent years it had paid more than $6 billion in taxpayer funds to support Rover. That was a cost it could no longer meet but, at the same time, it did not want to see the company broken up by a foreign buyer.

These fears were well founded because Rover had withstood an offer from General Motors of Detroit in 1986. Before making a deal, Rover also had to consider its partnership with Honda. In 1987 Honda agreed to fund a $2.5 billion investment program jointly with Rover. The British government hoped that selling Rover to British Aerospace would ensure that Honda would hold to its investment plans—something Honda might not do if the car company was being sold to a rival.

In 1989 Rover launched yet another four-wheel leisure car line, the Land Rover Discovery. This followed a £100 million investment program. The effort propelled Rover's four-wheel drive stable of cars to the top position in their class of cars in terms of market share. A year later, the Land Rover was relaunched under the name Defender. This followed Land Rover having attained 1.5 million in sales over the history of the four-wheeler, with one million models still on the road at the time. In 1990 Honda and Rover moved closer together with a 20 percent cross share holding arrangement giving both companies a share in each others' business.

The world recession of the early 1990s took its toll on the car maker. In early 1991, Rover announced it was to suspend sales of its upscale sedans in the U.S. car market. Sales had been less than projected, and the cost of marketing cars overseas outweighed prospects for profits. Yet, the Rover Group remains Britain's largest car maker and sales revenue for 1991 were nearly $8 billion. Rover's continuing cooperation with Honda of Japan should stand the motor car company in good stead as it continues facing up to Japanese competition in Europe through the 1990s. Yet Rover can draw upon its experience of handling change as it looks to meet the challenges of the next century.

Principal Subsidiaries: MG; Land Rover.

Further Reading: ''Making Rover Fly,'' *The Economist,* December 9, 1989, p. 61; ''A Brief History of the Rover Group,'' Rover Group, 1990; ''The Rover Revolution,'' *Management Today,* May 1992, p. 91.

—Etan Vlessing

SATURN CORPORATION

1420 Stevenson Highway
Troy, Michigan 48007-7025
U.S.A.
(313) 524-5721
Fax: (313) 528-6300

Wholly Owned Subsidiary of General Motors Corporation
Incorporated: 1983
Employees: 6,904 in 1992
Sales: $750 million
SICs: 3711 Motor Vehicles & Car Bodies

Saturn Corporation grew out of a project begun in 1982 within General Motors Corp. (GM) to explore the potential for building a small car of superior quality and value as efficiently as possible, combining the most advanced technology with the newest approaches to management. Saturn realized its product goal by producing a car ranked behind only the Lexus and the Infiniti (imported luxury cars produced by Toyota and Nissan) in the 1992 J.D. Power & Associates customer satisfaction survey. Saturn is regarded as more than simply a successful product, however; the company is seen as an embodiment of GM's vision of modern corporate ideals.

Saturn was the product of an extraordinary effort within GM to create a company from scratch, without any preconceived notions and combining the most advanced techniques and ideas in all areas. From community and employee involvement in decision making, to environmentally responsible plant design, to dealers trained to avoid the high-pressure sales techniques typical of traditional car salesmen, Saturn has sought to embody a 1990s model of corporate enlightenment. Recognized for its innovations in product design and production methodologies, the company has been the recipient of a great deal of positive publicity. While articles praising Saturn are plentiful, however, critics argue that its accomplishments have been achieved slowly and at great expense.

Saturn grew out of a particular climate within the car industry. At the time of the company's conception, the "Big Three" car makers (General Motors, Ford, and Chrysler) had traditionally built large cars, emphasizing quality and comfort. The industry began to change in the 1950s when foreign car makers (notably Renault and Volkswagen) offered American consumers smaller cars at lower prices. Imports had claimed a 10.1 percent market

share by 1959, but they were pushed back to a 4.8 percent share in 1962 after the introduction of the Corvair (GM), the Valiant (Chrysler), and the Falcon (Ford) in 1960.

By the late 1960s, the Big Three began to be challenged by Japanese car manufacturers. The Vega was GM's answer to the challenge. In 1968 GM announced that it would build the Vega from scratch rather than redesign another GM car. The finished product, introduced in 1970, proved disappointing. Vegas were prone to rust and their aluminum engines warped. The Chevette, GM's more successful small car introduced in 1975, was nearing the end of its 10-year product cycle when GM began to work on a replacement, code-named the S car. In 1981 GM determined that the S car could be built much less expensively by Isuzu (GM had bought 34.2 percent of Isuzu in 1971). Its next small car (the Chevrolet Spectrum) was built in Japan. This series of events confirmed in some people's minds the suspicion that the U.S. couldn't produce small cars competitively. As smaller cars were widely believed to represent the future direction of the industry, the episode called into question the likelihood of the long term survival of the Big Three car manufacturers. To address this concern, Ford initiated the "Alpha project" and Chrysler began work on "Concept 90".

At GM an internal project to build an affordable, high-quality, small car to compete with the imports was approved in May of 1982 by GM Vice-Chairman Howard Kehrl in conjunction with Alex Mair and Robert Eaton, Vice-Presidents in charge of Design and Engineering. On June 15 Alex Mair sat down with engineers Joe Joseph and Tom Ankeny to sketch out the plan. By July the project had been dubbed "Saturn," a reference to the Saturn rocket that propelled the American astronauts to the moon during the space race with the Soviets.

The project enjoyed strong sponsorship from the highest ranks of the company. In keeping with the emphasis on consensus throughout Saturn, no one in particular is considered the project's founding father. In the words of then-GM Chief Roger Smith, "I don't know who is the father of Saturn around here. I think all of us are promoting it and pushing it. I've been hot for it but I'm not going to tell you that I started it, because that wouldn't be true."

Although the project was to be kept confidential, press leaks began in early 1983. As cooperation with the union was vital to the success of the project, GM had begun behind-the-scenes discussions with Donald Ephlin, the UAW manager covering GM. By October, a joint GM-UAW Study Center was agreed upon.

Motivated in part by claims that the company was turning its back on the U.S. by building cars in Japan, on November 3, 1983, GM announced a new operating unit, the wholly-owned Saturn corporation, with an initial capitalization of $150 million. It would be the first nameplate added to the General Motors ranks since Chevrolet joined GM in 1918. Saturn would incorporate the latest technology available. The operations were to be completely computerized, with robots utilized to reduce direct labor, and flexible manufacturing techniques and just-in-time inventory systems introduced.

The importance of the project is evident in the wording of its announcement. Chairman Roger Smith announced Saturn as "the key to GM's long-term competitiveness, survival, and success as a domestic producer.... We expect it to be a learning laboratory," he said, "We also expect that what we learn with Saturn will spread throughout GM." He described Saturn as the key to improving every GM plant and product.

Key staff recognized for bringing the project to this point included Alex Mair of the Technical Staffs Group, Bob Eaton of Advanced Product & Manufacturing Engineering, Irv Rybicki of the Design Staff, and UAW leaders Don Ephlin and Joe Molotke. Executives appointed to take the company forward included the former head of the Oldsmobile Division, Joseph Sanchez, as President; the former executive director of Saturn project, Reid Rundell, as Executive Vice-President for Strategic Planning; John Middlebrook as Vice-President for sales, service, and marketing; Tom Manoff as Vice-President for finance; Jay Wetzel as Vice-President for engineering; and Guy Briggs as Vice-President for manufacturing operations. Sanchez died suddenly on January 26 and William E. Hoglund was appointed President on February 4. Hoglund served until Richard G. "Skip" LeFauve succeeded him on February 3, 1986.

The company was launched. On December 19, 1983, a joint GM-UAW study center was announced. The following February, 99 people ("the Group of 99") were designated to identify key founding principals for Saturn and to search the world for the best ideas in all areas. The group consisted of a functional cross-section of people, including plant managers, superintendents, union committee men, production workers, and skilled tradesmen, as well as UAW and GM staff from 41 UAW locals and 55 GM plants.

The group split into seven functional teams to explore stamping; metal fabrication and body work; paint and corrosion; trim and hardware; heating, ventilation, and air conditioning; and powertrain and chassis. In all, the Group of 99 visited 49 GM plants and 60 other companies around the world. They made 170 contacts, traveled 2 million miles, and put in 50,000 hours of effort.

The group's findings were presented in April 1984. The principle keys to success identified included ownership by all employees, the assumption of responsibility by all, equality and trust among employees, the elimination of barriers to doing a good job, giving staff the authority to do their job, and the existence of common goals. Specific recommendations included the use of a conflict resolution process that had been developed by the group and the formation of consensus driven partnerships within work teams as well as between the union and company management.

The search for a plant location began immediately after the company was announced. Two days later, Illinois Governor James Thompson became the first to visit GM advocating a site in his state. By the end of the search process, 24 governors had paid visits to GM and 38 states had expressed interest. Donald Avenson, the Speaker of Iowa's House of Representatives, offered to pay half of the first year's wages for workers ($140 million) if Saturn settled in Iowa. Spring Hill, Tennessee, was confirmed as the plant site on July 30, 1985, and in May 1986 construction began.

The plant is a mile long and half a mile wide, totalling 4 million square feet and consisting of four functional buildings: powertrain (engine and transmission systems), body systems (frames, exterior panels), vehicle interior systems (interior trim), and vehicle systems (final assembly). The facilities' core team, which designed the layout, included employees at all levels. The team considered unique lighting requirements in different areas; placed restrooms and cafeterias conveniently; and designed a sophisticated roadway that separates truck traffic from pedestrians, decentralizes loading docks so materials arrive where they are needed, and ensures that no one walks more than five minutes from parking lot to work.

As controlling labor costs was crucial to competing with the imports on a cost basis, cooperation with the UAW was an important factor. During the 1980s GM had suffered losses and had laid off 170,000 UAW workers. The competitive environment spurred both sides to work together on improving the prospects for American car manufacturing. Al Warren, Vice-President of GM's Industrial Relations Staff, and Donald Ephlin, UAW Vice-President and Director for the General Motors Department, were instrumental in creating a strong bond between Saturn and the UAW.

On July 26, 1985, the UAW executive board approved a unique labor agreement for Saturn. It reduced the number of job classifications, allowed unprecedented flexibility in job content, eliminated work rules, and set pay rates at 80 percent of the base rate at other GM plants with the difference made up in performance incentives. All Saturn workers are salaried and participate in a "risk-reward" system in which they lose 20 percent of their pay if the company does not reach common goals (e.g. sales goals) but earn proportional bonuses if goals are exceeded. Each team manages its own budget, inventory, and hiring.

Training is an important part of Saturn's human resource strategy. Workers spend from 250 to 750 hours in training to become "job-ready." On the job, they spend a minimum of five percent of each year in training. Workers are acclimated to Saturn's philosophy through core courses on conflict management, consensus decision making, and team dynamics. They also receive specialized technical training on machinery, parts quality, and working with vendors. The training program seeks to promote teamwork, self-direction, initiative, and responsibility. As of mid-1992, Saturn's success in the human resource area could be measured by the lowest absentee rates in the industry. Absenteeism at Saturn was 2.5 percent, a far cry from the 14 percent figure at other GM plants.

As other elements of the company were being developed, product development staff were working on the cars. The first demonstration vehicle was completed on September 15, 1984. Although Saturn was a "no year" project (it had no set launch date), GM chairman Roger Smith was determined to begin production before he retired. He drove the first car off the production line on July 30, 1990, one day before he retired and turned the reigns over to Robert Stempel.

The first truckload of Saturns was sent to dealers in California on October 11, 1990. By November the company garnered several awards, including *Popular Science*'s "1990 Best of What's New in Automobiles" and an award from the Society of

Plastics Engineers for its thermoplastic door panel. In June 1992 the first exports went to Taiwan. Annual production quickly reached 240,000 units and buyers were lined up on waiting lists, but the company was still losing money. By 1993 Saturn expected to raise production to 320,000, allowing the company to turn its first profit; the product line included seven models of sedans, coupes, and wagons.

In developing parts and manufacturing processes, Saturn employed Product Development Teams (PDTs) consisting of manufacturing engineers, finance staff, materials managers, quality engineers, and UAW technicians. The teams decide what materials to stock and evaluate prospective suppliers for quality, price, and efficient organization.

In keeping with the "complete job-focus" philosophy, a part is manufactured from start to finish in one place. Ergonomics is another important consideration. Equipment is "low-tech and people-oriented." It is chosen by its users and frequently adjusts to individuals. Whereas workers must crawl inside the vehicle to work on the cockpit of most cars, Saturn cockpits are assembled in a fixture that can be rotated for the comfort of the individual worker. A skillet system allows workers to ride on a moving platform with the car as it moves down the assembly line. While the basic system was copied from GM's Opel facility in Germany, Saturn widened the platform and turned the cars sideways, saving 40 percent in floor space.

In the engine and transmission area, lost-foam casting was used on a large scale for the first time, providing casting precision, flexibility, material savings, minimal tool wear, and reduced machining. In making trim, plastic colors are mixed at the injection molding machine, reducing change-over time and costs. Other innovative production methods include an environmentally sound waterborne paint process and a method of testing transmissions with air rather than oil.

Marketing has also been a central issue at Saturn. The first marketing customer clinic was held in San Francisco in March of 1985, five years before production began. The car itself is designed to be adaptable to changing consumer preferences. Whereas older cars depend on exterior panels for structural strength, Saturns are structurally based on a strong "space frame" to which the exterior "skin" is attached, allowing for quick style changes. Saturn's marketing philosophy was also concerned with bringing in "plus business" (non-GM buyers). Based upon the profile of imported car buyers, the targeted Saturn consumer would be an average of 38 years old, earning an average of $51,000 annually. A large percentage would live on the west coast and 50 percent would be college graduates.

The Saturn Marketing Planning Team incorporated the ideas of 16 dealers representing 25 manufacturers. Led by Donald Hudler, the team studied distribution methods of 30 major U.S. corporations and came up with Saturn's Market Area Approach (MAA) announced on May 26, 1987. MAA set up 300 "territories" to be handled by individual franchised dealers.

Saturn sought the consistency of service lacking in the GM dealer network. In early 1989 dealers were invited to apply for franchises. Saturn dealers are trained in low-pressure sales and are encouraged to pay salaries rather than commissions. The strong demand for the car, coupled with significant dealership

control over territory, has enabled Saturn dealers to average twice the unit sales volume of other car dealerships. In addition, the August 3, 1992 Business Week noted that a 17 percent gross margin is built into the "no-haggle" sticker price (other cars average 12 percent).

An important step in defining Saturn's marketing strategy was the selection of an advertising agency. Fifty agencies had applied for consideration by a review panel composed of two Saturn executives, two retailers, and a UAW representative, but the agency chosen was not among them. Thomas Shafer, Director of Marketing Services, felt that it was important to consider West Coast agencies since the small car market was most competitive there. As a result, the Hal Riney & Partners agency was named as Saturn's "communications partner" on May 24, 1988. Riney set about creating a "charismatic brand." He felt strongly that model names would detract from the Saturn name and insisted that the cars simply be called "Saturns" (numbers would distinguish various models). Dealerships would be called "Saturn of x" and colors would be "red" rather than the more pretentious "raspberry red". Saturn advertising was designed to be emotionally driven, with a focus on the human element rather than the product. In February 1989 the first print ad was released even though cars would not be available for more than a year.

In addition to external marketing work, Riney assisted the new company with internal communications. In April 1989 Riney produced "Spring, in Spring Hill," a documentary explaining the company to employees, suppliers, and the press. It was later aired as an infomercial. In the film team members explain what the project means to them. In the words of a Riney executive, "We wanted to get people rooting for Saturn, the company."

Saturn lost $800,000 in 1990 with calendar year sales of 1,881 units. 1991 calendar year sales were 74,493 units, and 1992 sales reached 196,126 units by December 31, with a substantial number of additional units back ordered. In the 1992 model year Saturn earned a 2.8 percent market share. It is estimated that the company needs to sell 300,000 cars per year to make a profit. Increasing capacity significantly would require further investment in new facilities or the retooling of an existing plant. Building new capacity is unlikely as GM continues to close old plants; retooling, however, also presents problems, as duplication of the innovations in the Spring Hill plant is a formidable task. In addition, there are few existing facilities large enough to accommodate the manufacturing of all necessary components at one site, as Saturn does in Spring Hill.

By mid-1992 Saturn cars had 95 percent domestic content and were ranked as the highest quality American car, with defect ratings rivaling those of top Honda and Nissan vehicles and customer satisfaction ratings second only to Lexus and Infiniti. On the negative side, the company was far from recouping the undisclosed billions that GM had invested in it and was not operating at full capacity. In addition, an average of 35 hours of labor were required per car compared to the stated company goal of 20 hours.

In an effort to transfer experience gained at Saturn throughout GM, the company has moved several Saturn executives to other divisions. GM President and CEO Jack (John F., Jr.) Smith, who succeeded Robert Stempel in 1992 after the latter's controversial ouster, talks about "Saturnizing" all of GM. Yet Donald Ephlin was quoted in the August 17, 1992, issue of *Business Week* saying, "One of the things GM does very poorly is spread improvements across the system."

The future of Saturn remains unclear. Its parent company, General Motors, is undergoing a painful series of layoffs and other cost-cutting measures in response to its well-documented financial woes. The uncertainty about GM's fiscal health has thus clouded speculation about the prospects of its fledgling subsidiary. Saturn's product line, however, has enjoyed a generally warm reception, and GM obviously has high hopes for the company.

Further Reading: Smith, Roger B., *Remarks by Roger B. Smith, Chairman General Motors Corporation*, Saturn Corporation, Troy, MI, January 8, 1985; Higgins, James V., "Saturn's Revolution: How GM Set the Course to Next Century," *Detroit News,* January 13, 1985; DeMott, John S., "Saturn Makes its Debut at GM," *Time,* January 21, 1985; Gruley, Bryan, and Ann M. Job, "Saturn Sets Off 'Civil War'," *Detroit News,* January 27, 1985; Whiteside, David, and others, "How GM's Saturn Could Run Rings Around Old Style Carmakers," *Business Week,* January 28, 1985; "Saturn Fact Sheet," Saturn Corporation, Troy, MI; White, Joseph B., and Melinda Grenier Guiles, "Rough Launch: GM's Plan for Saturn, To Beat Small Imports, Trails Original Goals," *Wall Street Journal,* July 7, 1990; "Forming the Future: The Marriage of People and Technology at Saturn," Saturn Corporation, Troy, MI, 1990; "Saturn Beats Benz, Acura in Survey," *Flint Journal,* Flint, MI, June 30, 1992; Woodruff, David, "Saturn: May We Help You Kick The Tires?" *Business Week,* August 3, 1992; Woodruff, David, "Saturn: GM Finally Has a Real Winner, but Success is Bringing a Fresh Batch of Problems," *Business Week,* August 17, 1992; "Building the 1993 Saturn," Saturn Corporation, Troy, MI; "Saturn: GM's Final Frontier," *Automobile Quarterly,* Fall, 1992; Butler, Lacrisha, "Sasser Praises Saturn Work," *The Tennessean,* Nashville, October 7, 1992; White, John R., "General Motors Should Build Everything As Well As It Builds Its Saturns," *Boston Globe,* November 15, 1992; Serafin, Raymond, "The Saturn Story: How Saturn Became One of the Most Successful Brands in Marketing History," *Advertising Age,* November 16, 1992; McGrory, Mary, "Saturn Gives U.S. Autos Some Get-Up-And-Go," *The Tennessean,* Nashville, December 1, 1992; O'Toole, Jack, and Jim Lewandowski, "Important Dates in Saturn History," Saturn Corporation, Troy, MI.

—Mary-Sophia Smith

SAVANNAH FOODS & INDUSTRIES, INC.

P.O. Box 339
Savannah, Georgia 31402-0339
U.S.A.
(912) 234-1261
Fax: (912) 232-3469

Public Company
Incorporated: 1916 as Savannah Sugar Refining Corporation
Employees: 2,137
Sales: $1.1 billion
Stock Exchange: New York
SICs: 2062 Cane Sugar Refining; 5149 Groceries & Related
    Products Nec; 2063 Beet Sugar; 4213 Trucking Except
    Local

Savannah Foods & Industries, Inc. is one of the largest sugar producers in the United States. Under the brand names Dixie Crystals, Evercane, Colonial, and Pioneer, Savannah markets both cane and beet sugar throughout the eastern part of the country. Among the facilities owned and operated by Savannah are its sugar refineries in Savannah, Georgia; Clewiston, Florida; and Gramercy, Louisiana. Through wholly owned subsidiaries, the company also produces beet sugar at several midwestern locations. Savannah's Michigan Sugar Company, which was purchased in 1984, operates processing plants in four Michigan cities: Carrollton, Caro, Croswell, and Sebewaing. Great Lakes Sugar Company, a wholly owned subsidiary of Michigan Sugar Company, has two facilities in Ohio, at Fremont and Findlay. Savannah also produces raw sugar from sugar cane at the Raceland, Louisiana mill of its Raceland Sugars, Inc. subsidiary. Additional subsidiaries include Savannah Foodservice, Inc., which produces packaged sugar and condiments for institutional use, and Food Carrier, Inc., a truckload carrier operation.

The Savannah Sugar Refining Corporation was founded by Benjamin Oxnard in 1916. Oxnard came from a family of sugar refiners. With his father and three brothers, he had operated the Fulton Sugar Refinery in Brooklyn, New York, and later he and partner Richard Sprague ran a 7,500-acre plantation and refinery called Adeline in St. Mary's Parish, Louisiana. Between about 1910 and 1915, the Louisiana operation encountered a series of setbacks. The complex was severely damaged by a fire, and then, after the factory was rebuilt and modernized, the plant's supply of sugar cane was affected by consecutive seasons of floods, droughts, and frosts. These problems were compounded by the passage of laws allowing free entry of foreign-produced sugar into the United States. This string of developments led Oxnard to investigate moving the operation to a more profitable location. While Oxnard sought to relocate in Virginia, James Imbrie, one of the major backers of the project, made his financing conditional: he would provide the necessary funding if the company moved to Savannah, where his family had land they wanted developed industrially. After consulting with his family, Benjamin Sprague (Richard's brother and the operation's engineer), and manager William Pardoner, Oxnard accepted the offer, and a site for the new refinery was chosen on the south bank of the Savannah River. At Ben Sprague's urging, the largely Cajun labor force from the Louisiana operation was imported to run the new plant. This meant a 700-mile migration for the community of workers and their families, about 300 people in all, many of whom had never been outside St. Mary's Parish.

Choosing the name Dixie Crystals for the new company's product, Oxnard set the Savannah Sugar Refinery into production in the summer of 1917. At the refinery's start-up, 19 million pounds of raw sugar were in store, selling at five cents a pound. The timing of Savannah's appearance was excellent. The onset of World War I created a sugar shortage, and with demand so high, the U.S. government took control of production. When the war ended, however, the government controls were entirely withdrawn, and the price of raw sugar from Cuba began to climb rapidly. A period ensued known in the sugar industry as "The Dance of the Millions," so called because of the millions of dollars that were said to have danced into oblivion. Raw prices were escalating at an artificially fast rate, supported by the mistaken assumption on the part of refinery management that there was a worldwide shortage. As prices gradually adjusted themselves back down, many companies were caught with huge orders of overpriced raws. Savannah, for example, lost a million dollars on 10,000 tons of raws from Java intended to keep the refinery running for about three weeks. Oxnard was forced to sell it at a substantial loss before the ship carrying it had even reached North America.

In 1924, Oxnard died, and William Pardonner was named president of Savannah. Oxnard's two sons, Thomas and Benjamin Jr., joined the company around that time. Thomas became assistant secretary of the company in 1924. The following year, Richard Sprague's son William joined the company as well. The Oxnard and Sprague families would go on to dominate the company's leadership ranks throughout its history. In the late 1920s, Savannah became a member in the Sugar Institute, which was essentially an organization set up to orchestrate price-fixing in the sugar industry. The government successfully sued to destroy the Institute, and the member companies left the battle with huge legal fees, half a million dollars of which were owed by Savannah.

Savannah remained in business during the Great Depression. Although raw sugar prices dropped to 1.04 cents a pound in 1930, an increase in consumption to some extent countered the losses, and by 1936, the company appeared to have emerged from the period largely intact. That year, stockholders received a four-for-one split on their shares, and employees were given a bonus equivalent to ten percent of their yearly salaries. In 1938, Savannah began marketing its sugar in paper bags. Their bagged sugar, new to the industry, came in three sizes, two-, five-, and ten-pounds. Company lore tells of an ambitious Dixie Crystals salesman who demonstrated the merits of the paper packaging to store owners by urinating on the bags, proving that paper bags were superior to cloth bags in repelling moisture.

The Oxnard and Sprague families retained their hold on the company's leadership after the death of Ben Sprague in 1944. Thomas Oxnard became Savannah's president, and Bill Sprague became executive vice-president at an identical salary to Oxnard's. Company records were set that year for both processing and deliveries, even though World War II was creating serious labor shortages and holding production below its potential. Following the war, Savannah undertook a program to keep producing at plant capacity while at the same time cutting operating costs. To assist in this process, the company enlisted the aid of Frank Chapman, a sugar engineer from Tate and Lyle, a prominent British sugar company. Chapman had by necessity become an expert at fuel conservation during the war. In 1949, Savannah's sales fell by $400,000 from the previous year, largely due to a decline in the market for blackstrap molasses, the company's primary by-product. This decline was offset, however, by the new cost-cutting measures, and therefore Savannah's earnings did not suffer significantly.

During the 1950s, the public image problem that has to this day plagued the sugar industry began to set in. For the first time, sugar began to be associated with bad health, and with obesity in particular. Savannah fought back with its own advertising. The company's own 1954 annual report pointed to sugar's role as an appetite suppressant, describing the relationship between hunger and blood sugar level. One advertising campaign of the era similarly stated, ''Sugar helps dieters to say no.'' Another emphasized sugar's ability to provide a quick burst of energy, asking the consumer, ''Why do mountain climbers carry sugar?''

Lawton Calhoun became the company's president in 1961, the beginning of a turbulent decade for Savannah. In the early part of the 1960s, worldwide consumption of sugar began to increase substantially. At the same time, extremely low prices around the world led many sugar producers to stop production. Meanwhile, Cuban sugar production dropped significantly, and two straight years of bad weather had decimated Europe's beet crop. In the face of a potential global sugar shortage, prices began to climb. Between January and May of 1963, the price of a pound of sugar doubled, from 6.6 cents to 13.2 cents. Before the year was over, prices rose and fell several times, creating havoc among U.S. sugar companies that were accustomed to relatively stable prices kept in check by a variety of Sugar Acts. Somehow, Savannah emerged as the only refinery in the United States to turn a profit in 1963.

While the sugar industry as a whole was in chaos in 1963, Savannah did not sit still. In December of that year, work began on a new refinery in Clewiston, Florida, which was completed and operational less than a year later. The Everglades Sugar Refinery, Inc., as the plant was called, was about one-eighth as large as the main plant in Savannah and had a production

capacity of 400,000 pounds of refined sugar a day. The sugar produced there was sold under the ''Evercane'' brand name. In the mid-1960s, Savannah found itself the target of several takeover attempts. One strategy Calhoun employed to ward off hostile attempts was to keep the company's cash till unattractively low. This is usually accomplished by purchasing other companies. Savannah followed this pattern with the 1968 purchase of Western Grain Company, a firm based in Birmingham, Alabama for just over $26 million. Western Grain produced a range of products that included grits, cornmeal, and livestock feeds, but its most attractive feature was its Jim Dandy line of dog food. The whole package was renamed the Jim Dandy Company, and its acquisition helped increase Savannah's total sales by 21 percent in 1968.

William Sprague, Jr., was named president at Savannah in 1972. The following year, the company's earnings were held back by a two-week-long strike at Jim Dandy, an early indication of a string of problems that would arise at that subsidiary. A price freeze on sugar prevented Savannah from passing its higher costs along to its customers. In 1975, Transales Corporation, Savannah's storage facility subsidiary—which was dissolved in May of 1992—was established. That year, Savannah was among twelve sugar companies in six states named in an antitrust suit that alleged conspiracy to fix sugar prices. Another similar suit was added two years later, charging fourteen companies with violating the Sherman Antitrust Act. Meanwhile, Savannah diversified further in 1976, with the launching of Food Carrier, Inc., its trucking subsidiary.

By the end of the 1970s, the Jim Dandy acquisition proved to have been a mistake. Although it was ranked second in the United States among brands of grits, Jim Dandy recorded an operating loss of $3 million in 1979, attributed by Savannah officials to poor management in Birmingham. Savannah finally managed to unload a good deal of Jim Dandy's assets in 1981, selling some to Martha White Foods Inc. of Nashville for around $5 million, and selling the company's dog food operation in Decatur, Alabama to an Atlanta company called Willmac Inc. for about $12 million.

In 1980, Savannah was named for the first time on *Fortune* magazine's list of America's 500 largest companies. In October of that year, Savannah acquired Sunaid Food Products for $750,000. Sunaid, based in Miami, manufactured single-serving packets of sugar, ketchup, and other condiments. This purchase paid off quickly, with profits exceeding the purchase price within two years.

Savannah was the second-largest sugar refining company in the United States by the early 1980s, trailing only Amstar Corporation. After good years in 1980 and 1981, the company was hurt by the imposition of import quotas in 1982. This led to artificially high sugar prices, which in turn gave a new competitive edge to high fructose corn syrup (HFCS) in the natural sweetener market. Within a week of one another Coca-Cola and Pepsi-Cola, both huge sugar users, announced a switch to HFCS, and by 1984 one sugar company and six refineries went out of business. Savannah, however, managed to thrive during this period by securing new territory in the Midwest to compensate for sugar's losses in the sweetener market. In 1983, the company shipped 900,000 tons of sugar, and its plants operated at 95 percent of capacity. In 1984, Savannah paid $66 million for the Michigan Sugar Co., a beet sugar producer with yearly sales of about $97 million.

In 1985, Savannah became more deeply involved in beet sugar with the purchase of the Ohio beet sugar operations of the Great Western Sugar Company for about $14.5 million. Great Western, a unit of Hunt International Resources Inc., had filed for Chapter 11 bankruptcy, and the purchase included a mill in Fremont, Ohio and a storage facility in Findlay, Ohio, along with a sizable amount of inventory. The following year, Savannah acquired Colonial Sugars, Inc., a cane sugar refiner with plants in Louisiana and Missouri. Savannah's sales for 1986 reached $634 million.

By the late 1980s, Savannah was the largest sugar producer in the United States, with sales of $1.1 billion in 1989. This company's share of the sugar market was 21 percent, about equal to the share held by the British company Tate & Lyle, which had in 1988 purchased Amstar, the former U.S. leader. Savannah was able to capture such a hefty portion of the market because of its ability to survive the 1980s while ten of the nation's 22 cane refineries did not. These companies were largely the victims of a 20 percent loss to HFCS in the market for natural sweeteners. Savannah's stability was also enhanced by its beet refinery acquisitions of the 1980s, although beets still provided only about 15 percent of company sales by the end of the decade.

Savannah set company records for both net income and sales in 1990. The company earned $48.6 million on sales of $1.2 billion that year. Both of these figures declined slightly in 1991. That year, Savannah Foodservice began operating on the west coast, opening a plant in Visalia, California. In October of 1991, Savannah purchased the 100-year-old South Coast Sugars, Inc. of Raceland, Louisiana. That company's name was changed to Raceland Sugars, Inc., and it was expected to generate about $25 million in annual sales. Savannah celebrated its 75th birthday in 1992, and as the 1990s continued, the company appeared to be on track to finish its first century as a frontrunner in the sugar industry.

Principal Subsidiaries: Everglades Sugar Refinery, Inc.; Savannah Sugar Refining Corporation; Colonial Sugars, Inc.; Michigan Sugar Company; Savannah Foodservice, Inc.; Food Carrier, Inc.; Great Lakes Sugar Company; Raceland Sugars, Inc.; Phoenix Packaging Corporation; Savannah Investment Company.

Further Reading: Aiken, Eric, ''Sweetness and Light,'' *Barron's,* April 1, 1974; ''12 Sugar Refiners Named in Lawsuit,'' *Journal of Commerce,* September 18, 1975; ''Suit Filed against 14 Sugar Refiners,'' *Journal of Commerce,* March 25, 1977; Stavro, Barry, ''Survival Hedge,'' *Forbes,* July 30, 1984; ''Sweet Stock,'' *Forbes,* September 5, 1988; Hackney, Holt, ''Savannah Foods: A Timely Sweetener?'' *Financial World,* August 22, 1989; Novack, Janet, ''Three Yards and a Cloud of (Sugar) Dust,'' *Forbes,* September 4, 1989; *Savannah Foods Annual Report 1991,* Savannah, Georgia: Savannah Foods & Industries, Inc., 1992.

—Robert R. Jacobson

SCHWAN'S SALES ENTERPRISES, INC.

115 West College Drive
Marshall, Minnesota 56258-1747
U.S.A.
(507) 532-3274
Fax: (507) 537-8143

Private Company
Incorporated: 1948 as Schwan's Dairy
Employees: 7,500
Sales: $1.1 billion (est.)
SICs: 2038 Frozen Specialties Nec; 2024 Ice Cream & Frozen Desserts

A highly successful dairy and frozen food company, Schwan's Sales Enterprises, Inc. holds 70 percent of the national school market for frozen pizzas and boasts one of the most extensive home delivery operations in the country. Since the 1960s, revenues for the holding company have doubled virtually every three to four years, due to a wise acquisition policy and a continually expanding truck fleet and sales force. According to a 1989 *Forbes* estimate, the company, entirely owned by Marvin Schwan, derived $350 million from pizza sales to institutions and $750 million in home delivery sales. Schwan is considered a consummate entrepreneur, and his devotion to customers, employees, and operational details is regarded as the driving force behind the company's long and healthy history. Schwan himself attributes his business's success to a carefully trained network of salespeople, truck drivers who serve primarily rural markets in 49 states providing diligent, personalized attention. Schwan's is comprised of some dozen operating divisions, the most successful of which is Tony's Pizza, whose chief competitors are the Pillsbury pizza lines Jeno's and Totino's.

Marvin's father, German immigrant Paul Schwan, entered the ice cream business following World War I when he accepted a delivery job with a creamery in the southwest Minnesota town of Marshall. In 1944 the elder Schwan was financially able to launch his own venture. That year he bought half interest in a milk bottling plant, which happened to be adjacent to the Marshall Ice Cream Company, his most recent employer. The new firm, Neisen and Schwan's Dairy, was a family enterprise from the start, founded on personalized delivery service to area homes. At the age of 14, Marvin accepted a milk delivery route and supplemented his income on weekends by packaging ice cream bars, fudgesicles, and popsicles. Realizing that he could boost his productivity by 25 percent, Marvin purchased a bag-opening machine with his own funds; his father recognized both the advancement in productivity and Marvin's initiative and reimbursed his son for the capital expenditure. By 1948 the business, which both supported local dairy farmers and provided a valuable service to households, was well known and respected. With the help of Marvin's own investment, Paul bought out his partner, renamed the business Schwan's Dairy, and opened a new plant in town. Paul's wife, Alma, assisted in the daily operations by running the Schwan's Dairy Store, a small restaurant that offered homecooked meals and Schwan's dairy products. Marvin left Marshall at this time to attend a two-year college, but returned on weekends to assist with the business. His father, meanwhile, had begun experimenting with surplus cream and perfected his own recipes for chocolate and vanilla ice cream, which he soon began manufacturing in 2½-gallon containers.

Marvin's decision to return full-time to the business in 1950 was perhaps the single greatest reason for the modest dairy's development into a national concern. After barely weathering a retail price freeze on milk during 1951–52, Schwan's swiftly rebounded when Marvin discovered that he could undercut the comparatively higher ice cream prices of neighboring towns. Experienced in home delivery and alert to the current rise in freezer purchases by rural families, he had only to purchase a truck and establish a route. Within a year, he added a second truck to his delivery operation and quickly began to promote the Schwan's name as synonymous with the best ice cream—now available in a dozen flavors—in southern Minnesota. Distinctive yellow trucks, the simple cursive logo, the round returnable ice cream containers, and the courteous assistance of the drivers helped attract a remarkably loyal and longstanding customer base.

By the mid-1950s Schwan, faced with the realities of high overhead for his growing fleet and sales force, positioned the company for greater profits and a greatly expanded market by adding first a depot in the southeast portion of the state and then a freezer-warehouse in the central portion. Schwan's faced its second major crisis in 1957 when the Redwood River reached flood stage in Marshall, severely damaging equipment in the central plant and halting operations for four days. A federal disaster loan allowed the business to recover, which it did rapidly under Marvin, who had effectively become the company's general manager. By the early 1960s sales had easily surpassed $4 million and the full-time workforce had swelled from the original five to well over 100. The company met the challenge of another crisis in 1962, that of a nearby fire which threatened to destroy the plant's north wall and with it a 10-ton condenser, and redoubled its efforts to grow into a stable, thriving company. The site of the auto dealership which was destroyed by the fire was soon purchased by Schwan's to allow for an expanded headquarters and by 1963, round-the-clock operations were initiated, elevating ice cream production to some 11,000 gallons daily.

In *Self-Made: The Stories of 12 Minnesota Entrepreneurs*, authors Carol Pine and Susan Mundale accord special significance to the year 1963 for the company. Aside from marking the fifteenth anniversary of the business as a solely owned family enterprise, 1963 was the year in which Marvin adopted a long-term acquisition policy to ensure that the company could experience aggressive growth while remaining profitable. Among the first acquisitions were a prepared sandwich company and a condensed fruit juice company, both of which were incorporated under the new holding name of Schwan's Sales Enterprises, Inc. Two years later, Schwan discovered that one of his Wisconsin salesmen had begun carrying Roma brand frozen pizzas on his route. With the rising popularity of prepared pizza, the small label promised additional diversity and sales for the delivery company and so Schwan signed a contract to market the pizzas in a four state region. By 1969—the year of Paul Schwan's death—pizza sales were approaching those of ice cream and, consequently, Schwan was eager to expand his territory. Prevented from doing so by Roma, Schwan placed an ad in the *Wall Street Journal* disclosing his interest in purchasing a complete pizza manufacturing plant. He received a response from Kansas-based Tony's Pizza. After determining that the Tony's pizza recipe required improvement, Schwan acquired the company in 1970, made the necessary alterations, and then launched the division with a somewhat new marketing scheme: selling the pizzas via a special fleet of trucks directly to retail stores rather than chain warehouses. As in his home delivery routes, the emphasis was on providing the customer with quality, freshness, and service. Each driver was given the latitude to enhance sales for his route and profits for each route were tallied daily, weekly, and monthly.

The pizza acquisition proved a resounding success and fueled much of the company's growth during the 1970s, despite heavy competition from Jeno's and Totino's. Another turning point for the company came in 1974, in the wake of a devastating fire at the ice cream plant. Schwan saw the tragedy as an opportunity to rebuild in a more suitable location and almost moved his business. Fortunately for the citizens of Marshall (25 percent of whom now work for him), Schwan decided to recommit himself to the community that had helped him to prosper. By 1979 he had built his delivery system into a 1,000-truck fleet. Ever conscious of the bottom line, he converted the entire fleet to LP gas at this time to combat the rising costs for conventional fuel. Finally, he ended the decade by diversifying beyond the food business with the acquisition of Syncom Magnetic Media, a computer tape and diskette manufacturer based in Mitchell, South Dakota.

As Schwan's entered the 1980s, roughly half of its sales came from pizza. The remaining half came from its line of home-delivered products, which had now expanded to include meats, frozen fish, bread, frozen fruit, and french fries in addition to a full line of dairy products. While the ongoing success of the latter half of operations was virtually ensured, the former—represented primarily by Tony's—was pitted against serious Minnesota rivals Totino's (acquired by Pillsbury in 1975) and Jeno's. Totino's, benefiting from the Pillsbury name and large sales apparatus, led the national market share with 22 percent, followed by Tony's and Jeno's, each with approximately 13 percent of the market. The competition between the big three had been fierce for several years, and in 1981 Schwan's launched a serious attack on the number one position with a highly controversial ad campaign, which playfully hinted that

the other leading pizza manufacturers employed a glue-like substance in their cheese while only Tony's contained 100 percent real cheese. Despite outcries from its competitors, Schwan's benefited from the exposure, and the campaign went on to win the top Minnesota advertising award of the year. However, 1981 was also the year in which the company sustained its greatest personal loss, the death of an employee and the injury of eight others following an anhydrous ammonia leak at the main plant.

By the mid-1980s, with sales approaching $500 million, Schwan entered the institutional pizza market and quickly carved out his own sizeable niche, thereby circumventing the need for competing head-to-head, at high cost, in the retail grocery market. Schwan had discovered that cheese surpluses were being delivered to the nation's public schools by the Department of Agriculture. He reasoned, correctly, that the schools would be willing to trade their allotments for discounted school lunch pizzas, to be manufactured by Schwan's with the government cheese. Schwan greatly strengthened his foothold in this new market with the acquisition in 1986 of his major school lunch competitor, Sabatasso Foods. In 1988 he established a virtual monopoly with the additional acquisition of Better Baked Pizza. During this same period of rapid growth, Schwan had instituted a portable pricing and inventory system that squeezed even greater profit margins from his home delivery business. As always, Schwan's intent was and is to maintain his business as a self-financing operation, ensuring the private company's longevity and eminent profitability.

In 1982, Pine and Mundale wrote that although "almost every other kind of home delivery system has gone the way of the dinosaur, Schwan's Sales Enterprises has grown and prospered." The statement remains just as true more than a decade later, due to Schwan's business acumen, the quality of his products, and, probably above all, the effectiveness of his drivers. Although the job of driving for Schwan's is notoriously rigorous, involving long hours and considerable physical labor, Schwan is known as an extremely fair boss and, with one-third of all executives drawn from the Marshall workforce, employee loyalty is notoriously high.

In 1992 Schwan's acquired two more companies, bringing its total to twelve. One, Monthly Market, is a for-profit food cooperative catering to fund-raising groups; the other, Panzerotti, is a stuffed pastry business. Although no annual revenues were disclosed with either of the sales, both businesses will likely benefit by their integration with the Schwan's delivery system. Other Schwan's businesses include a pastamaker, an egg roll company, and an equipment-leasing outfit. The only looming threat to the company is the mid-1992 entry of PepsiCo's Pizza Hut into the institutional pizza market. According to *Corporate Report Minnesota*, Pizza Hut "lobbied Congress to successfully get a waiver of required U.S. Department of Agriculture inspections of meat-topped pizzas." The waiver could place Schwan's at a distinct disadvantage, given its expensive labor union force and current compliance with USDA regulations. However, if history is any indication, Schwan's will undoubtedly fight back. Perhaps the greatest tribute paid to Schwan is that by former competitor and Duluth businessman Jeno Paulucci (who sold his pizza empire to Pillsbury in 1985). "I've never met a tougher competitor in my life, because you never know he's there,'' he told *Forbes.* ''I got to thinking that there is no use trying to build a frozen pizza business when this guy's got all of it that's profitable.''

Further Reading: McGrath, Dennis J., ''Schwan's Turns Ice Cream into Lots of Cold Cash,'' *Minneapolis Tribune,* October 29, 1978; Jones, Jim, ''3 State Frozen Pizza Firms Fight to Become Big Cheese,'' *Minneapolis Star,* November 13, 1978; Clark, Don, ''Stuck: Pizza Firm Scolded for Glue Comparison,'' *St. Paul Pioneer Press,* January 30, 1981; Jones, Jim, ''Tainted Pizza Ad Wins Top Award,'' *Minneapolis Star,* June 25, 1981; Kramer, Julie, ''1 Killed, 8 Hurt in Marshall Ammonia Leak,'' *Minneapolis Tribune,* August 22, 1981; Pine, Carol, and Susan Mundale, ''Marvin Schwan: The Emperor of Ice Cream,'' *Self-Made: The Stories of 12 Minnesota Entrepreneurs,* Minneapolis, Dorn Books, 1982; Pine, Carol, and Susan Mundale, ''Frozen Assets: How Marvin Schwan Led His Ice Cream Company along the Rocky Road to Success,'' *Corporate Report,* September 1982; Fritz, Michael, ''Schwan's Song,'' *Forbes,* April 3, 1989; Blemesderfer, S. C., and Eric J. Wieffering, ''Pizza Hut Delivers Blow to Schwan's,'' *Corporate Report Minnesota,* February 1992; Kennedy, Tony, ''Schwan's Buys Two State Food Firms, Including Tino Lettieri Pastry Business,'' *Minneapolis Star Tribune,* June 24, 1992; ''Schwan's Buys 2 Minnesota Food Firms,'' *St. Paul Pioneer Press,* June 25, 1992.

—Jay P. Pederson

SERVICE AMERICA CORP.

P.O. Box 10203
Stamford, Connecticut 06904
88 Gatehouse Road
Stamford, Connecticut 06902
U.S.A.
(203) 964-5000
Fax: (203) 964-5018

Private Company
Wholly Owned Subsidiary of Servam Corp.
Incorporated: 1960
Employees: 23,000
Sales: $1.09 billion
SICs: 5812 Eating Places

Service America Corp. is a leader in the highly competitive contract food service segment of the retail food industry. Service America has operations in 44 states and the District of Columbia and is ranked among the United States' top 20 retail food companies in annual sales. The company is the principal subsidiary of Servam Corp., and its operations are divided into three primary segments: vending, dining, and recreation services. The vending and dining segments provide food service to businesses, industrial and manufacturing plants, office buildings, hospitals, and educational, correctional, and government facilities. Vending and dining comprise 50 percent and 38 percent of company revenues, respectively. Recreation services make up about 12 percent of company revenues, providing concession operations primarily for convention centers and sports arenas.

When Service America was established in 1960 as United Servomation, there was no "contract food service segment" in existence. At that time, the vending industry, which later gave birth to the contract food service market, was hitting a ten-year peak. Vending machines had been introduced to Americans over 70 years earlier by Thomas Adams, who installed them on New York City's elevated train platforms to sell his Chicklets gum. After World War II the vending industry grew twice as fast as the gross national product, driven by three primary factors: rising labor costs made machines an attractive alternative to human laborers; technological advances in food preservation and dispensing equipment permitted service of hot meals, sandwiches, coffee, and soft drinks; and technological

advances were made in money-changing equipment. Vendors targeted "captive" markets in factories, offices, schools, and other institutions—a huge market with plenty of potential for growth and competition. The vending industry had achieved $2.5 billion in annual sales by 1960, and with statistics showing that Americans ate one in four meals away from home, vendors and stockbrokers foresaw a fine future for vending.

Headquartered in New York City, United Servomation was formed in late 1960 as a combination of eleven vending organizations. In its first year, the company had $18 million in sales and netted $800,000. At the time, most vending companies were still selling cigarettes, candy, soft drinks, and coffee in venues like bus stations, factories, offices, schools, and hospitals. Two of Service America's perennial competitors, Automatic Canteen and Automatic Retailers of America (ARA) were already established industry leaders.

By 1965 Servomation was a $100 million public company with over 70,000 vending units in 29 states coast-to-coast. Fifty independent vendors had joined Servomation's ranks, bringing the total number of affiliates to 89. The company was so decentralized that most affiliated companies kept their pre-Servomation names, so that the company was more like a confederation than a corporation.

Most machines were located in traditional institutional sites but United Servomation also operated some completely automatic restaurants, like its Realm of the Coin at Boston Massachusetts's Madison Hotel.

In the early 1960s, vending comprised the vast majority of Servomation's sales, bringing in 87 percent of company revenues. But during the middle of that decade, the vending industry began to reformulate its mission as a service not necessarily tied to vending machines.

This change came about, in part, as a result of research linking cigarettes to cancer and other health hazards. In the early 1960s, cigarettes comprised about 30 percent of Servomation's vending sales. By the end of the decade, cigarettes only accounted for about 15 percent of sales. Many vendors saw the changes on the industry's horizon and began to concentrate on food service.

The evolution from vending to contract food service came about in three phases. First came the addition of hot and cold prepared foods to traditional lines of snacks, candy, and cigarettes. Second, the building of cafeterias and break rooms for daily lunchtime customers in institutional and industrial settings set vending machines apart from the regular work area. Finally, many vending companies began to operate standard restaurants, snack bars, and coffee shops.

Servomation entered the new market in 1963 when the company purchased A. L. Mathias Co. and began to coordinate machine sales with manual (as opposed to mechanical) service in vending's traditional, captive markets. "Servomats," semi-automatic cafeterias with a bank of vending machines and a small grill for hot dishes, were introduced in 1963.

Servomation also entered the retail food industry in 1963, opening its Singing Waters restaurant in Philadelphia, PA, and two roadside Mr. Bill's restaurants. Both units featured frozen, precooked foods that would be reconstituted on-site using microwave ovens. The company also purchased Red Barn System, Inc., a limited menu, self-service restaurant with franchises from coast to coast. The acquisitions were impressive and attracted attention to the company, but they only constituted five percent of annual sales and earnings.

The company's mainstay was still vending, comprising 70 percent of sales at the end of the decade. In 1966 Servomation acquired Minnesota Acme Vending (Minneapolis), which increased the company's annual volume by $1 million. In the late 1960s, 36 percent of Servomation's contracts were with durable goods manufacturers. Other manufacturers made up 18 percent of the company's volume, commercial, financial, and communications companies comprised ten percent, and hospitals, government and military institutions contributed 11 percent. Servomation's reliance on contracts with cyclical businesses, especially durable goods manufacturers, meant that its well-being was tied to its contractors' well-being, which had a tendency to fluctuate dramatically.

In the latter half of the decade, Servomation tried to move away from durable goods to more dependable markets. In 1967 30 percent of the company's 300 new contracts involved colleges and universities, and 12 percent were made with hospitals and medical institutions. Both markets had built-in, perennial constituencies: students and sick people.

During its first decade, Servomation posted consistent annual sales and earnings gains. These gains were based primarily on acquisitions that opened expanding markets and a welcome industry-wide price boost in 1968. By the end of the decade the company had more than 190 operating centers and branches in 38 states, 118,400 vending machines, and 11,900 employees. The long-awaited price increase, from ten cents to 15 cents for beverages, came in 1968. The 50 percent increase was difficult to implement because of customer resistance and the overhaul of thousands of machines; but with sales of 6.2 billion cups of hot coffee and soft drinks (31 percent of vending machine sales) in 1967, Servomation welcomed the change.

By the early 1970s the company's reliance on sales to durable goods manufacturers made it particularly vulnerable. The company's earnings dropped in 1970 and 1971 when automobiles and other durable goods suffered sluggish sales. Layoffs and cutbacks in these industries directly affected Servomation's profits.

The company reacted by aggressively pursuing contracts in recreation and concession food service. By 1971 Servomation had major contracts with The Forum in Los Angeles, San Diego Stadium and Sports Arena, Del Mar Thoroughbred Club, Ontario Motor Speedway, and other recreational facilities. By 1973 hospital, school, and college business provided 21 percent of the company's sales.

Servomation also tried to move further into contract food service and away from vending. By 1973 vending constituted 63 percent of sales, a seven percent drop from the beginning of the decade, and a 36 percent drop from 1960. Servomation's services had broadened to encompass a wide variety of food-related services: full-service restaurants, fast-food restaurants, concession stands, cafeterias, and mobile catering trucks.

In 1973 the company also made an important change in its image by changing the names of all its operations, which had formerly kept the name they had when acquired, to Servomation Corporation. That year the company achieved the highest profits in its history, $11.2 million, or $2.07 per share. 1974's earnings fell from that high, due in part to rising food costs that were not immediately passed on to consumers.

By the end of the 1970s, Servomation's problems had mounted. The public company underwent an anti-trust investigation by the Federal Trade Commission late in 1974 and survived a takeover threat in 1977. By September 1978 the company merged with City Investing Co.'s GDV Inc. division, an acquisition of $188.7 million. Servomation's new parents were primarily concerned with real estate, construction, and financial services. The purchase brought the company into a new decade of leveraged buyouts and mounting debt.

In 1985 Allegheny Beverage Corp. purchased Servomation for $225 million and merged it with its Macke division. The new entity, renamed Service America Corporation, emerged as one of the United States' largest contract food service management and vending operations, with a value of $1.2 billion.

Allegheny Beverage borrowed heavily to finance the purchase of Servomation, but watched sales plummet over the next two years. Many observers blamed Allegheny's management style for Service America's poor performance, citing excessive price increases and several company-wide salary freezes, which led to lower employee morale and a high turnover rate. Per-unit sales dropped more than $200,000 between 1985 and 1987 because of lost accounts and decreased volume in existing accounts.

Led by Chief Executive Officer Carr Newcomer, a group of frustrated Service America senior managers teamed up with the New York investment banking firm of Morgan Lewis Githens and Ahn, Inc. (MLGH&A), and Merrill Lynch Interfunding to purchase Service America from Allegheny Beverage in 1987. The group of investors formed Servam Corp., a private firm, to facilitate the purchase process, which began in April. Allegheny Beverage became a motivated seller when its creditors demanded payment and threatened Chapter 11. When Servam's investors lowered the purchase price from $500 million to about $450 million, Allegheny Beverage's stockholders and managers had no choice but to accept the shrinking offer.

Newcomer led Service America until mid-1989, when Steven Leipsner became the company's CEO and president. Formerly head of Marriott Corp.'s Travel Plazas, Leipsner hoped to challenge Marriott, Canteen, and ARA Service for leadership of the contract food service industry. To do so, he first focused on using more brand-name items, expanding the full-service dining segment, and encouraging employee input at all levels.

Like his predecessors in the 1970s, Leipsner hoped to steer Service America away from an emphasis on vending, which still accounted for about 50 percent of the company's total revenue, toward full-service dining.

With an eye to changing that emphasis, Leipsner began in earnest to negotiate contracts for nationally-branded food items. Research showed that adding a popular retail name to an institutional menu meant sales increases of 100 percent when properly promoted. Service America made franchising agreements with Wendy's, Dunkin' Donuts, Little Caesars, and TCBY to use their products and brand names. It put Oscar Mayer hot dogs, Tyson chicken-breast sandwiches, and Hormel hamburgers in its vending machines, and hoped for sales increases of ten percent to 15 percent.

Since competition among the top four contract foodservice firms is high, Service America has also attempted to keep up with ever-changing customer demands. National dietary trends in the 1980s and 1990s, for example, prompted Service America to introduce its "Fitness Fare" menu, which featured low-sodium, low-fat, high-fiber, low-sugar, low-cholesterol, low-calorie, and decaffeinated items. Service America also began to feature ethnic foods, especially Italian and Chinese dishes, when research indicated increased consumer interest in those products.

The company also worked to make dining at many of its full-service, in-plant facilities more appealing through themed promotions with special menus, decorations, and music. Themes included Festa Italiano, Grecian Islands, Mardi Gras Rythms, and Nifty '50s.

In early 1990 Service America had won a major dining contract: a $13 million account with Ameritech, the parent company of AT&T's Midwest operations. The contract included feeding 65,000 people per day at 22 locations, the largest foodservice agreement in Service America's history. Other big accounts of the 1990s included the U.S. Supreme Court, the U.S. House of Representatives, several General Motors plants, NASA, Jack Murphy Stadium in San Diego, California, and New York's Jacob Javits Convention Center.

Despite many advances, Service America was unable to reverse financial trends that started during Allegheny Beverage's disastrous two-year reign. When Servam purchased Service America, it also took on debt related to Allegheny Beverage's leveraged buyout in 1987. The company was also hurt by nagging economic factors related to Service America's continuing dependance on contracts with durable goods manufacturers. A recession during the late 1980s and early 1990s caused many of the factories and businesses under contract with Service America to experience reduced employment levels and even closings. At 50 percent of annual sales, Service America's vending business, with its manufacturing sector contracts, felt particularly acute financial difficulties.

Many contractor companies also lowered or eliminated subsidies that had made eating at Service America's on-site cafeterias more attractive to employees. When Service America was forced to raise prices to compensate for lost subsidies, many customers ate elsewhere, further lowering revenues.

In October 1990 the company began a two-year struggle to restructure nearly $400 million in debt. The primary holder, with almost half the debt, was GE (General Electric) Capital Corp. Within a year, Service America had reached a deal with GE and other bondholders to trade approximately $100 million of the debt for equity in the company and reduce interest payments by about $20 million per year.

But just one year and a 1992 loss of $63 million later, Service America found itself in Federal Bankruptcy Court seeking protection from creditors owed a total of $312 million in long-term debt. In the course of the bankruptcy process, Service America filed for permanent debtor-in-possession financing that will permit it to continue operations while the debt reorganization proceeds. A reorganization plan submitted by Service America gives bondholders nearly 33 percent of the company in exchange for $50 million.

Steven Leipsner was named chairman, CEO, and president of Dallas Texas's S & A Restaurant Corp., and was replaced, after a brief transition period, by Robert Beeby (a member of the board). At the end of 1992, with Chapter 11 proceedings underway, Beeby assured "normal and uninterrupted" service in the immediate future.

Further Reading: "Star Fades Vending Issues," *Financial World,* July 12, 1961; Glenn, Armon, "Two Sides of the Coin," *Barron's,* January 6, 1964; "Vendors Outgrow Machines," *Business Week,* October 10, 1964; "Brighter Outlook for Vending," *Financial World,* May 5, 1965; Willatt, Norris, "Boarding-House Reach," *Barron's,* November 21, 1966; "Price Boosts, New Markets Help Servomation Prosper," *Barron's,* October 21, 1968; "Servomation Corp. Monthly Stock Letter," *Wall Street Transcript,* November 17, 1969; "Vendors Pull Out All Stops," *Business Week,* August 15, 1970; "Servomation Corp.," *Wall Street Transcript,* September 18, 1972; "Servomation Corp.," *Wall Street Transcript,* June 11, 1973; "Servomation Corp. Says Fiscal '74 Net Will Fall From Year Earlier High," *Wall Street Journal,* June 27, 1974; "FTC's Antitrust Study of Servomation Ends," *Wall Street Journal,* August 5, 1974; "Servomation Drops Suit Against Oakbrook, Others," *Wall Street Journal,* December 15, 1977; "Servomation in Switch, Sets GDV, Inc. Merger," *Wall Street Journal,* September 1, 1978; "Merged Companies Renamed," *Nation's Restaurant News,* July 8, 1985; Hays, Laurie, "Allegheny Beverage Agrees to Sell Unit and Is Discussing Sale of All Other Lines," *Wall Street Journal,* April 23, 1987; "Allegheny Beverage Corp.," *Wall Street Journal,* October 6, 1987; Freeman, Alan, "Proposed Sale by Allegheny Beverage Falters," *Wall Street Journal,* October 26, 1987; "Holders Approve the Sale of Service America Unit," *Wall Street Journal,* December 3, 1987; Beiswinger, George L., "In-House Foodservices Emphasize Good Health," *The Office,* July 1989; Carlino, Bill, "Service America Aims at Segment Leaders," *Nation's Restaurant News,* February 5, 1990; Leonard, Bill, "Food Services Discard Throwaway Image," *HR Magazine,* March 1991; Curry, Gloria M., "The Care and Feeding of Corporate America," *The Office,* June 1991; Lorenzini, Beth and Brenda McCarthy, "The Branding Evolution," *Restaurants & Institutions,* September 9, 1992; "Service America Eyes Plan to Help Clear Debt," *Nation's Restaurant News,* October 19, 1992; Allen, Robin Lee, "Service America Files for Ch. 11 Protection," *Nation's Restaurant News,* November 2, 1992; "Servam's Service America Unit," *Wall Street Journal,* November 10, 1992.

—April S. Dougal

SHONEY'S, INC.

1727 Elm Hill Pike
Nashville, Tennessee 37120
U.S.A.
(615) 391-5201
Fax: (615) 231-2621

Public Company
Incorporated: 1968
Employees: 34,600
Sales: $2 billion
Stock Exchanges: New York
SICs: 5812 Eating Places; 6794 Patent Owners & Lessors

Headquartered in Nashville, Tennessee, Shoney's, Inc. is one of the restaurant industry's most respected companies. The United States' tenth largest restaurant chain operates or franchises over 1,800 restaurants in 36 states and Canada, including Shoney's, Captain D's, Lee's Famous Recipe Chicken, and the Pargo's and Fifth Quarter specialty restaurants.

The company originated with a drive-in restaurant called "Parkette" in Charleston, West Virginia. Alex Shoenbaum opened the restaurant in 1947, then acquired a Big Boy franchise in 1951. Two years later, Shoenbaum renamed the Parkette "Shoney's Big Boy." During this time, Ray Danner was building a restaurant business in central Tennessee and opened his first Big Boy franchise in 1959 in Madison, Tennessee. He incorporated his privately owned company in 1968 as Danner Foods, Inc. One year later Danner Foods became a publicly traded company.

During its affiliation with the Marriott Corporation, the parent company of Big Boy restaurants, Shoney's restaurants doubled in size every four years. Based on a chain of family-style coffee houses along the busy highways of the Southeast, Shoney's restaurants featured a friendly, uniformed waitstaff that served from a "homestyle" menu adapted to the region.

In 1972 the company dropped "Big Boy Enterprises" from its name, and Ray Danner assumed the role of chairperson and chief executive officer, while Alex Shoenbaum became a senior chairperson. Danner took an active role in Shoney's management, building the company on a foundation of hands-on, operations-oriented management. His unique style became part of the corporate culture, and his managers become "Shoneyized"

or imbued with respect for efficiency and a sense of responsibility. "Danner's Way," as it came to be known, promoted simplicity, customer satisfaction, constant striving for perfection, and management by example. His management team worked in shirtsleeves in order to be prepared to pitch in whenever and wherever necessary. Danner himself monitored everything from corporate staff practices to food service through the use of "mystery shoppers" dispatched periodically to each unit. He was also known to visit restaurants in person, and to clean restrooms that didn't meet his standards during his spot checks. His willingness to roll up his sleeves both proved his point and embarrassed the responsible individual, who cleaned alongside him.

Although employee standards at Shoney's were uncompromising, the rewards were enticing. The company instituted a program in which the best hourly workers could be awarded college scholarships that would help pave the road to middle and upper management positions within the company. In exchange, trainees would work nights and weekends and take college courses recommended by Shoney's. The company provided students with plenty of opportunities for advancement, maintaining five to seven manager positions for each restaurant, area manager positions for every three to four restaurants, and divisional director positions supervising ten to twenty restaurants. Furthermore, Shoney's recruited more than half of its managers internally.

According to many observers, Danner's management style was the basis of Shoney's strong profits and steady growth.

Opportunities in the company were not limited to work in family-style restaurants. Danner had, in 1969, begun to market a new fast-food concept featuring batter dipped fish and related food products for sale in a chain of Mr. D's Seafood restaurants. By 1975, when the chain's name was changed to Captain D's, over 250 units were in operation. By 1980 there were more Captain D's than Shoney's, and by 1985 the seafood chain's sales constituted 30 percent of the company's total. Captain D's has consistently outproduced its competitors, including its primary rival, Long John Silver.

After discovering that its family restaurants located near motels earned over 30 percent more than stand-alone shops, Shoney's established Shoney's Inns, a lodging division which it paired with specialty restaurants called Fifth Quarter Steakhouses. The two enterprises complemented each other, and were managed separately. Within ten years the chain of inns had grown to 21, but two nagging problems with the venture had developed. First, the hotels did not return the high, quick profits of the food service operations, and second, the vastly different management requirements clashed with Shoney's (and Danner's) distinctive style. The chain was eventually sold to Gulf Coast Development, Inc. in 1991.

The Fifth Quarter concept has fared better as a growth vehicle for Shoney's. In a departure from the "family" concept, the dinner houses feature prime rib and alcoholic drinks on their menu. Despite its small size, providing less than four percent of company revenues, the Fifth Quarter chain has grown at a consistent 20 percent annually, and is represented in five Southeast and Midwest states.

By the end of the 1970s Shoney's began to feel the constraints of a franchising agreement that limited its growth to an 11-state territory. In 1979 the company began to phase "Big Boy" marketing elements from its image. This was Shoney's first step toward severing its 25-year tie to Marriott Corporation. Shoney's forced the break when it built a restaurant in another Marriott franchisee's territory. Although the new restaurant eliminated all vestiges of Big Boy from its signs and menus, the other franchisee sued, thereby starting the breakup process, which was accomplished in 1984.

Shoney's was able to capitalize on its increasingly identifiable name and shift its menu and image toward a healthier concept as a result of the breakup. Disenfranchisement has enabled the company to distance itself from the "Big Boy" character's physical image and remove the signature double-decker hamburger from its menu. Since the "divorce," Shoney's has expanded its family restaurants' territory to 29 states coast-to-coast.

In 1981 Danner stepped aside to make David K. Wachtel the chief executive officer of Shoney's, while he remained on the board of directors. Wachtel, a product of Shoney's management training program, had started with the company at age 16 as a dishwasher in Nashville, Tennessee, and had moved steadily through the ranks of busboy and cook, to become the manager of the first Captain D's in 1969 at age 28. Wachtel immediately began to make changes in the Shoney's equation. He ended the company's 14-year franchise relationship with Heublein's Kentucky Fried Chicken for the same reason that Danner broke away from Marriott Big Boy: territorial limitations that set boundaries on growth.

Soon thereafter Wachtel bought Famous Recipe, a struggling Midwestern chicken chain. The Famous Recipe chain consisted of 225 stores founded by Lee Cummings, a nephew of colonel Harland Sanders of Kentucky Fried Chicken fame. Shoney's worked to hone the Famous Recipe concept over the next few years by dropping unprofitable or mismanaged franchises, adopting a uniform "farmhouse" design, and diversifying the chain's menu. Management also gave the chain a more personal image by adding "Lee's" to the name and employing Cummings as concept spokesperson. By 1985 Lee's Famous Recipe had been "Shoneyized"; its sales rose 103 percent and the chain spanned 23 states.

During this time, Wachtel also introduced a restaurant innovation that revitalized Shoney's morning sales reports. The "all-you-can-eat" breakfast bar, brought on in 1981, reversed a ten-year decline in morning sales. By the end of the decade, the breakfast bar boosted morning sales at company owned restaurants to 25 percent of total sales.

Despite accelerated morning sales and a $3.4 million net profit made in selling Heublein and acquiring Famous Recipe, Danner and other board members and managers felt that Wachtel was expanding the company too quickly, and he resigned the position of chief executive officer after occupying it for less than one year. Danner then resumed the position of chief executive officer and spent the next seven years struggling to find a successor who would carry on his management ideals.

In 1986 he made J. Mitchel Boyd, a longtime franchisee and an originator of "Pargo's" specialty restaurant, chief executive officer and vice-chair. Boyd, his wife Betty, and Gerry A. Brunetts had founded Pargo's, a restaurant in Manasses, Virginia, that featured such light fare as appetizers, pasta, salads, and sandwiches, and was expanded to include nine restaurants in Tennessee and Virginia. This restaurant was made a part of Shoney's specialty group when Boyd assumed his role as vice-chair at Shoney's.

In 1988 Danner engineered a $728 million recapitalization that paid shareholders a $16 per share cash dividend and paid Danner, who owned 19 percent of the stock at the time, $111 million in cash. The recapitalization was a clear sign that Danner was ready to hand Shoney's over to new management, and in 1989 he gave Boyd the chair.

It only took six months for Boyd's emphases on marketing and experimentation with menus and overall company image to clash with Danner's obsession with the day-do-day operations of the company. As with Wachtel, financial success didn't earn Boyd any points. Leonard H. Roberts succeeded Boyd in December 1989 and has served as Shoney's chief executive officer and chairperson since that time. Roberts, known as something of a maverick in the restaurant industry, engineered Arby's Inc.'s five-year turnaround in the 1980s. But when his relationship with Arby's Victor Posner became strained over franchisee relations, Roberts accepted the chair at Shoney's. Roberts attempted to capitalize on Shoney's organizational and management strengths, while also developing its marketing and research and development.

Roberts faced a very different task at Shoney's than the Arby's situation had demanded: he was expected to continue the financial and organizational success that the company was long known for before the recapitalization. Shoney's had never had an unprofitable quarter and had in the mid-1980s been named "best managed restaurant company" in the United States by the *Wall Street Transcript*. At the same time, Roberts hoped to continue the territorial expansion that Danner and others had begun after the 1984 break from Big Boy. From 1984 to 1989, Shoney's had moved into Ohio and Florida, then Kentucky, Indiana, Texas, New Mexico, Oklahoma, and Maryland/Washington D.C. But the 1989 recapitalization hindered Shoney's ability to invest in expansion from within.

Roberts faced another challenge early in his career at Shoney's. In 1989 the Legal Defense and Education fund of the National Association for the Advancement of Colored People (NAACP) brought a discrimination suit against the company. The suit, which originated in Florida, charged that Shoney's systematically discriminated against African Americans by limiting employment opportunities and job selection, creating what it termed "a hostile, racist work environment."

Shoney's signed an agreement with the Southern Christian Leadership Council (SCLC) in 1989 to invest over $90 million in minority business development, community service, and other socially-responsible areas. The following year Shoney's launched an affirmative action strategy called "Workforce 2000." The program mandates equitable representation of minorities and women in Shoney's ranks. The company is using some programs that were already in place, like the scholarship program, and has added recruitment programs at 48 historically black colleges and universities to enhance its affirmative action efforts. Shoney's has also encouraged entrepreneurship among minority businessmen through its Minority Franchise Development Program; since 1989, the company has increased the number of minority franchisees from two to eleven. The company's Minority Purchasing Program uses minority suppliers for everything from children's menus to food processing; from 1989 to 1992 annual purchasing from minority suppliers has increased from under $2 million to nearly $14 million.

Although the NAACP case had not been settled in 1992, and the charges of racism still haunt the company's image, its efforts have met with some quantifiable success: minorities represent 30 percent of Shoney's employees. Moreover, the number of minority franchisees has increased since 1989 from two to 11. At the same time, the number of units owned and operated by minority franchisees has climbed from two to 14. Annual purchasing from minority business suppliers also increased from less than $2 million in 1989 to nearly $14 million in 1992.

Shoney's has also sought to polish its corporate image through philanthropic and community relations efforts. These include sponsorship of the Bootstrap Scholarship Awards, which honors Middle Tennessee high school seniors who have achieved despite serious obstacles; support of the Southern Christian Leadership Conference; and support of the Tennessee Minority Purchasing Council's Business Opportunity Fair.

Roberts began to focus on franchising, a skill he honed while managing Arby's, and his primary goals are to add 500 franchises to Shoney's roster and, by the end of the 1990s, to "dominate the family segment." The company added 48 franchisees in fiscal 1991, and will have to increase that per-year figure in order to reach its goal by the turn-of-the century. One franchising deal with Thompson Hospitality L.P., one of the largest minority-run food service operators in the country, has helped Shoney's further penetrate the Washington, D.C., area and keep its agreement with the SCLC. Shoney's financed the $17 million deal to convert 31 former Marriott Big Boy restaurants into Shoney's by the mid-1990s.

To that end, Roberts tripled the size of the company's research and development staff and made that department part of marketing rather than operations. One of research and development's primary concerns was menu development, a high priority on Roberts's list.

In the early 1990s the wisdom of the 1988 recapitalization became manifest. Shoney's stock nearly tripled from 1989 to 1991 and the company's value grew accordingly, from $273 million to $809 million. Additionally, the company made extraordinary progress on debt retirement, having exceeded its scheduled payments by $155 million and reduced the debt's maturity by 3.5 years. Declining interest rates haven't hurt the company, either; interest on debt dropped from a peak of 12.5 percent to 9 percent.

A primary financial objective for the 1990s is a 20 percent annual increase in earnings, which will increase cash flow and enable Shoney's to retire more of its debt. As the debt is diminished, the company will free up more capital to invest in company stores, research and development, and expand its specialty chain. In order to achieve that goal, Shoney's instituted Project 80/85, a plan to increase customer satisfaction by setting goals of 80 percent customer satisfaction in 1992 and 85 percent in 1993.

In early November 1992, Shoney's, Inc. received provisional approval of a settlement in the discrimination lawsuit filed by the NAACP in 1989. The settlement addressed possible monetary damages for applicants and employees of the company restaurant entities and corporate office between February of 1985 and November 3, 1992. It was estimated that between 20,000 and 40,000 current employees, former workers, and applicants would share in the settlement. Under the settlement, Shoney's made $105 million available to pay potential claims. The settlement resulted in a special charge of $77.2 million against earnings for the fourth quarter and fiscal year of 1992. The company states that it expects that substantially all of the funds will be paid over a five-year period. The lawsuit appeared to have little impact on Shoney's stock. In fact, the company's stock price rose in the days following the announcement of the settlement.

In December of 1992 Len Roberts resigned as chief executive officer and chairman of Shoney's, Inc. to pursue other interests. Taylor Henry, Jr., an 18-year Shoney's veteran who played a significant role in 1988's recapitalization plan, succeeded Roberts in both positions.

Although competition within the family dining segment is fierce, Shoney's continued in the 1990s to capitalize on diversification, service, new marketing strategies, and menu development. Shoney's moved towards decentralization of its franchising efforts, including Project 500, leaving franchising to the individual restaurant chains.

Principal Subsidiaries: Shoney's Restaurants; Captain D's; Lee's Famous Recipe; Mike Rose Foods; Pargo's; Fifth Quarter Steakhouses.

Further Reading: Engardio, Pete, "Shoney: Bursting Out of Its Dixie Boundaries," *Business Week,* April 15, 1985; Chaudhry, Rajan, "Shoney's Mulls Life After Debt," *Restaurants & Institutions,* May 20, 1992; Cheney, Karen, "Cater to Kids, Please Parents," *Restaurants & Institutions,* July 8, 1992; Cheney, Karen, "Food Bars, Light Items Wake Up Breakfast Patrons," *Restaurants & Institutions,* June 24, 1992; Feldman, Rona, "Market Segment Report: Family," *Restaurant Business,* August 10, 1992; Gindin, Rona, "Shoney's Shows Who's Boss," *Restaurant Business,* October 10, 1985; "Insights: Shoney's Expands A.M. Bar, Forecasts Unit Growth," *Restaurant Business,* January 1, 1988; Kochilas, Diane, "Leonard Roberts," *Restaurant Business,* May 20, 1991; Konrad, Walecia, "Shoney's Needs a Recipe for Succession," *Business Week,* December 25, 1989; "Leonard Roberts: Can He Put More Meat on Shoney's?" *Business Week,* October 8, 1990; Raffio, Ralph, "Market Segment Report: Family," *Restaurant Business,* October 10, 1991; Rudolph, Barbara, "Something Has to be Wrong," *Forbes,* July 19, 1982.

—April Dougal

SMITHFIELD FOODS, INC.

501 North Church Street
Smithfield, Virginia 23430-0000
U.S.A.
(804) 357-4321
Fax: (804) 357-1379

Public Company
Incorporated: 1936 as Smithfield Packing Company
Sales: $1.05 billion
Employees: 5,400
Stock Exchanges: NASDAQ
SICs: 2011 Meat Packing Plants

Smithfield Foods, Inc. is the largest pork processor in the eastern United States. In addition to North Carolina, the company operates production facilities in Virginia, Maryland, and Wisconsin. Its line of hams, hot dogs, bacon, sausage, and deli and luncheon meats is marketed wholesale, under private labels, and under such brand-name labels as Smithfield, Esskay, Gwaltney, Luter's, Jamestown, and Patrick Cudahy. Known as a leader in vertically integrated pork processing since 1987, Smithfield has strived to counter severe fluctuations in hog prices as well as high transportation costs by reducing its reliance on Midwest hog producers. The company's joint hog-producing venture with Carroll's Foods is instrumental in fulfilling this goal. Other southeastern U.S. suppliers, including giant Murphy Farms, have helped the company trim costs in the notoriously thin-margin, cyclical industry.

Many would agree that Smithfield's competitive edge is synonymous with the leadership of chief executive officer Joseph W. Luter III. After reclaiming in 1975 what was his own company, Luter has ushered Smithfield into the high-tech age by acquiring companies, forging partnerships, reducing overhead, and instituting capital improvements to boost efficiency. More importantly, he has elevated Smithfield to the elite ranks of those Fortune 500 companies offering the highest total returns to investors.

Since colonial times the small town of Smithfield, Virginia, has been known for its quality hams. Even today, under Virginia law, a ham may only be marketed as a "genuine Smithfield" if it has cured for six months within the confines of the town. One such marketer, family-owned Gwaltney Packing, was the employer of Luter's father and grandfather during the 1930s. In

1936 these two decided to establish their own ham business and succeeded in raising $10,000 from local investors. They opened across the street from Gwaltney and built their small private company into a multimillion dollar concern.

When Luter's father died suddenly of a heart attack in 1962, Luter, near graduation from college, shelved his plans to attend law school and returned to oversee the business. Seven years later the company, with annual revenues of $35 million, had attracted the interest of Washington, D.C.-based Liberty Equities, a small conglomerate. Luter sold the family company for $20 million but was retained as manager. After being summarily dismissed by the new owners six months later, Luter promptly launched a second career in real estate development.

The packing plant, now operating as Smithfield Foods, Inc., fattened itself through non-pork acquisitions and unnecessary staff expansion. By the mid-1970s Smithfield was floundering along with Liberty Equities and Luter saw an opportunity to repurchase the company at a fraction of its worth. Because of actions taken by the Securities and Exchange Commission, Liberty had essentially reduced itself to Smithfield Foods, a failing $100 million pork-processing and fish wholesale business, further hampered by a nonproductive chain of 27 seafood restaurants. Price inflation throughout the food industry, as well as poor management, had severely affected the company, whose debt had risen to $17 million while net worth had plummeted to $1 million. Creditors were demanding a management change and Luter agreed to a salary and stock options package that encouraged turnaround. As one analyst in a 1988 *Financial World* article claimed, "Essentially, Joe Luter got the company back for ten cents on the dollar."

Luter quickly reduced Smithfield's debt by selling the nonpork operations. He achieved profitability within seven months by slashing nearly $2 million in overhead through the elimination of middle managers and via sharp reductions in data processing costs. Thus streamlined and firmly back in the meat business, Smithfield began to expand through acquisition. In 1978 it purchased a plant in Kinston, North Carolina. In 1981 Smithfield snatched up Gwaltney (at 35 cents on the dollar) for $34 million. Luter derived special satisfaction from this acquisition because not only had Gwaltney been a longtime competitor, it had also succumbed to the trappings of conglomerate spending under ITT Corp. Luter continued to seek out and buy at bargain rates other underperforming pork companies throughout the 1980s. These included Hancock's Country Hams, Patrick Cudahy Incorporated, and Schluderberg-Kurdle Co. (renamed Esskay, Inc.). By 1988 annual revenues had skyrocketed to $864 million, well within striking range of the billion dollar mark.

In 1987, in a particularly prescient move, Luter launched a 50–50 partnership with Carroll's Foods, the country's fifth largest pork producer. Strategically located in North Carolina—within single-day transportation to half the U.S. population—Smithfield-Carroll's has helped the company lessen its dependence on Midwest hog farmers, the traditional source for the pork-packing industry. Coupled with hogs supplied by East Coast giant Murphy Farms, the partnership-generated pigs helped to account for 50 percent of Smithfield's annual requirements. In addition to saving on high transportation costs, Luter also benefitted from lower weight loss during shipment, thereby enhancing his product line's quality and marketability.

According to Sharon Reier, "what is remarkable about Luter's resurrection of Smithfield is that he did it in an industry plagued by plant overcapacity and a flat consumption pattern in pork product over the past ten years, and dominated by large, well-heeled conglomerates that could subsidize poor margins in meat-packing operations with profits from other divisions." Of course, even Luter's Midas touch has little control over four-year cycles in hog prices, which directly affect the company's profitability. When prices are high, more pigs are raised and the eventual oversupply results in falling prices and undersupply—a true, high-risk commodity business. As a consequence of this predictable cycle, net income for Smithfield totaled $7 million in 1990 but rose sharply to nearly $29 million in 1991. Net income for 1992 began cycling downward again to $21 million. Smithfield, necessarily, takes a long-term view of earnings performance through compound growth rates. In the 1991 letter to shareholders it explained that "an analysis of the Company's performance over the last 16 years provides some enlightening results. When the 16 years are divided into four, four-year segments, the Company's earnings fall into a consistent and predictable growth pattern.... The Company's sales, net income and net income per share have shown compound growth rates of 14 percent, 31 percent, and 33 percent, respectively, over the last 16 years." One distinct advantage of these cycles, both for the company and for investors, is that Smithfield stock prices have also followed a dip-and-rise pattern. With his extra profits, Luter has capitalized on downswings to buy back some 50 percent of the company's shares during the same 16-year period and has increased his individual stake to approximately 20 percent, according to a 1992 *Forbes* article.

To keep Smithfield on the cutting edge, Luter has concentrated on his niche markets, avoided high advertising budgets, and relegated more than half of his production to nonbranded commodity pork sales for the supermarket and food-service industries. Most promising for the future is Luter's quest for the genetically perfect pig: lean, hardy, and easy-to-process. An exclusive contract between Smithfield-Carroll's and National Pig Development Co. (NPD), a family-owned British firm, may prove to be the answer. The first generations of NPD's transplanted stock are being raised at the North Carolina facility. In July 1992, according to David Ress, "Mr. Luter ran some tests on a 265-pound hog ... comparing it with an especially lean American hog culled from the best of Smithfield's current stock. The American pig had an inch of fat on its back. The British pig had less than half that, Mr. Luter said. The raw, or 'green' ham from the American pig yielded 52 percent lean meat after boning and after the fat was trimmed. The British pig's yield was 62 percent." Development and marketing of the pigs is expected to continue, particularly through Smithfield's formation of Brown's of Carolina and its centerpiece, a state-of-the-art slaughtering plant located in Bladen County, North Carolina, which opened for production in September 1992.

The phasing out of a dated Baltimore facility the same month, the late 1992 acquisition of a John Morrell plant in Wilson, North Carolina, and the company's search for a plant situated to serve the West Coast all bode well for Smithfield. An analyst cited in Rita Koselka's *Forbes* article "expects Smithfield's earnings to double over the next four years, although not in a straight line." While other, larger meat-packers are struggling, Smithfield remains supremely poised and may yet corner the market for high quality hog-marketing.

Principal Subsidiaries: Brown's of Carolina, Inc. (86%); Esskay, Inc.; Gwaltney of Smithfield, Ltd.; Patrick Cudahy Incorporated (80%); The Smithfield Packing Company, Incorporated.

Further Reading: Jaffe, Thomas, "Pig Out," *Forbes,* December 1, 1986; McComas, Maggie, "Smithfield Foods Inc.," *Fortune,* February 16, 1987; Reier, Sharon, "High on the Hog," *Financial World,* June 28, 1988; Hinden, Stan, "Interest in Smithfield Stock Sparks a Flurry of Trading," *Washington,* April 10, 1989; Koselka, Rita, "$ Oink, $ Oink," *Forbes,* February 3, 1992; Stovall, Robert H., "Small Stocks with Big Names," *Financial World,* May 12, 1992; Ress, David, "Britain's Low-Fat Pigs Expected to Beef Up U.S. Pork Market," *Journal of Commerce and Commercial,* July 1, 1992; "Esskay, Inc. to Phase Out Production at Baltimore Plant," Company Press Release, September 30, 1992; Marbery, Steve, "Smithfield Foods Brainstorms Western Venture," *Feedstuffs,* November 16, 1992.

—Jay P. Pederson

SNAP-ON TOOLS CORPORATION

2801 80th Street
Kenosha, Wisconsin 53141-1410
U.S.A.
(414) 656-5200
Fax: (414) 656-5577

Public Company
Incorporated: 1920 as Snap-on Wrench Company
Employees: 6,800
Sales: $983.8 million
Stock Exchanges: New York
SICs: 3423 Hand & Edge Tools Nec; 3546 Power-Driven
Handtools; 3825 Instruments for Electrical Signal
Measurement; 3559 Special Industry Machinery Not
elsewhere classified

Snap-on Tool Corporation manufactures and distributes a line of approximately 14,000 hand tools and equipment. Snap-on tools are sold and distributed directly to end-users in over 100 countries via a network of approximately 5,100 franchised and nonfranchised dealers and employee sales representatives who visit prospective customers in an assigned territory on a regular basis. The corporation considers itself the originator of the mobile van method of marketing hand tools.

Snap-on was founded in 1920 by Joe Johnson and William A. Seidemann. Prior to Johnson's idea for "interchangeable sockets," the socket wrenches used by mechanics were one-piece units. Professional auto mechanics quickly recognized the efficiency and flexibility that resulted from pairing many sockets with few handles. From the beginning, sales were generated by demonstrating the benefits of the novel tool sets directly to the customers. New tools were added to the line, and a catalog was published in 1923. By 1925, 165 salesmen were demonstrating and distributing Snap-on tools.

Stanton Palmer, a former factory sales representative, served as president of the corporation from 1921 until his death ten years later. At that time, Snap-on sought financial help from one of its principal creditors, Forged Steel Products Company, whose owner, William E. Myers, became Snap-on's new president. When Myers died in 1939, Joe Johnson, the corporation's conceptual founder, became the president of both Snap-on and Forged Steel.

Under Johnson's leadership the sales force continued to grow. During World War II, when supplying the military's needs caused tool shortages in the civilian market, Snap-on began releasing available stock to its sales force, in an attempt to maintain goodwill with the civilian customer base. By 1945, all salesmen were carrying stock and making immediate deliveries to their customers. Shortly thereafter, Snap-on made each seller an independent businessperson in an assigned territory.

Subsidiaries in Canada and Mexico aided growth in the 1950s. The Snap-on product line was also expanded. Corporate acquisitions of specialized companies brought products which addressed the mechanic's need for increasingly complex diagnostic tune-up and maintenance equipment. During this period, Snap-on also acquired its system of branches (which had operated previously as independent outlets). Branch acquisitions permitted Snap-on greater control over the marketing and distribution systems.

Victor M. Cain became president upon Johnson's retirement in 1959. In 1965, a Snap-on branch was opened in the United Kingdom. An important patent on the "flank drive" design of wrenches was also awarded in 1965, after years of legal debate. The "flank drive" design produced wrenches with a superior grip, less likely to round the corners of 12-point fasteners under high torque conditions.

Snap-on's growth was dramatic in the period that followed. Sales increased from $66.2 million in 1969 to $373.6 million in 1979, while profits increased from $6 million to $42.6 million. Norman E. Lutz became president in 1974, overseeing growth in the worldwide sales force to over 3,000. In 1978, Lutz became chair and chief executive officer (CEO), and Edwin C. Schindler became president. That year Snap-on stock was first listed on the New York Stock Exchange.

The early 1980s saw rapid changes in the company's management. In 1982, Lutz retired and was replaced by Schindler as chairperson, while William B. Rayburn became president; the following year Schindler died, and Rayburn became the company's chairperson and CEO. A slight decrease in both revenue and earnings in 1982 was attributed to that year's recession. Snap-on examined operations and took measures to improve profitability through reducing expenses as well as marketing more aggressively. Even in this disappointing year, however, net earnings were significant at $37.3 million on $430.5 million in net sales, or 8.7 percent of sales.

Snap-on continued to cultivate its image as the foremost supplier of well crafted products and customer oriented service. During the 1980's, Snap-on became the sole supplier of tools to NASA for the space shuttles. In 1984, Snap-on acquired an equity stake of approximately 34 percent in Balco, Inc., a developer of engine diagnostic and wheel service equipment. The frequency of visits to customers had increased to weekly in some cases, and the vans carried $50,000 to $200,000 of hand tools and equipment inventory. Additional services provided by dealers, such as cleaning previously purchased Snap-on tools every six months, allowed dealers to identify and recommend replacement of worn out tools.

While Snap-on was beginning to face competition from a variety of sources, including Sears, Roebuck and Co., the Mac

Tools subsidiary of Stanley Works, the Matco Tools subsidiary of Chicago Pneumatic, and various Japanese companies, Snap-on was able to maintain its premium prices because of the services it offered and the customer relationships in place.

Snap-on has stated that its market share cannot be determined, but in October 1986, *Forbes* estimated that "with its long head start and 49 percent of the market, Snap-on has as many dealers tooling about as all of its competitors combined." At this time, Snap-on was distributing two million catalogs each year. The 350-page catalogs were considered Snap-on's "most valuable single marketing tool" by Rayburn, who told *Forbes* that "our industrial people leave them with buyers, purchasing agents and requisition people. Our dealers leave them with shop owners and mechanics. When there is a mechanical problem, they look in the catalog for a tool that can solve it."

In 1988, new chairperson Marion Gregory faced a new challenge for Snap-on. An increasing number of lawsuits were filed by former and current dealers in state courts around the United States. The claims included allegations of misrepresentation, contract violations, and causing emotional distress. In an early case, George Owens, a former dealer, claimed that he was pressured to divide his territory with another dealer. A California jury awarded $6.9 million in damages, an amount later reduced in settlement. Other lawsuits claimed misrepresentation of potential profits to dealers, automatic billing of dealers by Snap-on for certain tools provided to the dealers for promotional purposes, and pressure to extend credit.

Snap-on's general policy was to consider settlement as preferable to litigation; the company accrued or paid a total of $7.9 million, $16.6 million, and $16.2 million for litigation-related costs in 1989, 1990, and 1991, respectively, before "determining to pursue more cases to final determination and apply a more stringent policy toward settlement," per Snap-on's 1991 Annual Report. Snap-on also asserted claims of its own against its insurance carriers with respect to coverage on certain dealer claims.

In 1991 Robert A. Cornog, formerly the president of Macwhyte Company, became chairperson, president, and CEO of Snap-on, ending a long tradition of filling these positions from within the company. Also that year, Snap-on began to enroll all new U.S. dealers as franchisees and offered the option of applying for a franchise to existing dealers. Snap-on viewed the conversion to a franchise program as an opportunity to establish greater control over the marketing and business activities of its dealers. The program was not designed to increase revenues, and costs in new group insurance programs, stock purchase programs, and special volume-purchase discounts were expected to offset franchise fees. As an inducement to convert, Snap-on waived initial and some recurring franchise fees for existing dealers. Nonetheless, most existing dealers did not elect to apply for franchises.

Snap-on issued common stock valued at approximately $21.2 million to acquire the remaining interest in Balco, Inc. in 1991. The corporation also announced its intention to consolidate product inventories from 51 branch warehouses to four regional distribution centers. By this time, operations were conducted in subsidiaries located in Canada, the United Kingdom, Mexico, Germany, Australia, Japan and the Netherlands. Sales in other countries accounted for 17 percent of total revenue, though only 5 percent of operating income.

Net earnings, which had been down from earlier levels for three years in a row, were still $34.3 million on net revenue of $881.7 million or 8.3 percent of net revenue in 1991, despite the recession in the United States and Canada. This translated to an after-tax return on average shareholders' equity of 11.4 percent, considerably below the 18–23 percent level that Snap-on had enjoyed in the years 1983–89. In response, Snap-on reorganized its management structure to allow separate accountability for its three business areas: Finance, Manufacturing and Technology, and Marketing and Distribution.

As Snap-on management looked to the end of the twentieth century, management recognized that the corporation would have to adjust to fundamental changes in its business in order to achieve the high levels of return it sought. Believing that improved automotive quality and warranty programs had caused slower repair volume growth and had shifted work to the auto dealers, Snap-on determined to develop new products and services for existing customers while reaching out to the new markets as well.

Snap-on management began to consider whether other services, such as a credit card for general use, might profitably be offered to its credit-proven customers, who were in weekly contact with Snap-on dealers. Outside sourcing of products, which already accounted for 35 percent of Snap-on's manufacturing, was considered an opportunity for cost savings. International and industrial markets were seen as offering a possible means toward the growth to which Snap-on had always been accustomed.

With over 200 patents and 80 pending patent applications, Snap-on was also encouraging its research and development team to challenge the ordinary way of doing things. One of those young researchers might one day produce as powerful an idea as that of young Joe Johnson, who wondered in 1919 why a mechanic had to buy a different handle for every socket he used.

Principal Subsidiaries: Snap-on Tools of Canada Ltd.; Snap-on Tools Limited; Snap-on Tools International, Ltd. (F.S.C.); Herramientas Snap-on de Mexico, S.A.; Snap-on Tools GmbH; Snap-on Tools Import and Wholesale Pty. Ltd.; Snap-on Tools Netherlands B.V.; Snap-on Tools Japan, K.K.; Snap-on Tools (Europe) Limited; Snap-on AG; ATI Industries, Inc.; Balco, Inc.; Sun Electric Corp.

Further Reading: Smith, Geoffrey N., "Snap-on's Proprietary Ingredient," *Forbes*, October 6, 1986; Fanning, Deirdre, "Monkey Wrench at Snap-on Tools," *Forbes*, June 27, 1988.

—Marcia McDermott

elf aquitaine

SOCIÉTÉ NATIONALE ELF AQUITAINE

Tour Elf
2, place de la Coupole
Courbevoie (Hauts de Seine)
France
(1) 47 44 45 46
Fax: (1) 47 44 78 78

Public Company
Incorporated: 1976
Employees: 88,000
Sales: FFr201 billion (US$36.28 billion)
Stock Exchanges: Paris Brussels Luxembourg Frankfurt
   Düsseldorf Basel Geneva Zürich New York
SICs: 6513 Operators of Apartment Buildings; 6719 Offices
   of Holding Companies, Nec; 1311 Crude Petroleum and
   Natural Gas; 5169 Chemicals and Allied Products, Nec;
   5052 Coal and Other Minerals and Ores; 5051 Metals
   Service Centers and Offices

Société Nationale Elf Aquitaine, also known as Elf, is France's largest oil company, ranking among the top ten publicly traded oil companies in the world. It is a fully integrated oil and gas company, combining upstream production capacity from fields around the world with strong downstream refining and distribution facilities. The second-largest French chemicals producer, Elf Aquitaine also has holdings in human health care, biotechnology, and beauty product companies. Its size is all the more impressive in view of its youth. One of Elf's constituent enterprises, the Régie Autonome des Pétroles, first exploited modest gas reserves in 1939 at Saint-Marcet in the Haute-Garonne province of southwest France. But it was not until the 1950s that major gas and oil discoveries in France and the Algerian Sahara really started the future Elf Aquitaine on its rocket-like ascent.

Elf Aquitaine's origins could be said to go back further than the 1939 Saint-Marcet discovery to 1498, when Jacob Wimpfeling, a theologian from Alsace, was surprised to note mineral oil welling out of the ground at a place called Pechelbronn (fountain of pitch). Almost 500 years later, in 1970, the Antar group, which then owned Pechelbronn, was taken over by Elf. The company claims that the history of Elf Aquitaine "cannot be separated from history itself." A closer connection might be perceived between the history of Elf and the history of France's

energy policy as practiced by successive governments since World War II.

Elf Aquitaine was—and remains—controlled by the state. In 1992 this control was exercised through Entreprise de Recherches et d'Activités Pétrolières (ERAP), a 100 percent state-owned company, which in turn held 51.56 percent of Société Nationale Elf Aquitaine. The remainder of SNEA's shares were divided among some 400,000 private shareholders.

Elf thus represents a clear departure from the relationship between the state and private enterprise in France as seen in the case of its older rival, the Compagnie Française des Pétroles (CFP), which later became Total. CFP began in 1924 with the state holding no shares at all; since 1931, the state has contented itself with holding 35 percent of the company. The constituent companies of Elf Aquitaine have, in their time, been set similar objectives of "national interest" to those set by Prime Minister Raymond Poincaré for CFP in 1924. But in the case of Elf and its forerunners, the state has always held a majority of the shares.

The discovery of gas at Saint-Marcet in the summer of 1939 was made by a small exploration syndicate set up with public funding earlier in the decade to prospect for oil and gas in the region. It was one of a number of such organizations nationwide. The syndicate was created because the state realized that major oil companies had bigger and better interests in other oil-bearing parts of the world, such as Mesopotamia. The Compagnie Française des Pétroles, Royal Dutch/Shell, and Standard Oil of New Jersey would probably not spend much money looking for oil or gas in France.

The oil giants could have found petroleum in France, but it was not until after the war that they would realize it. Though the find at Saint-Marcet was modest, it did continue to produce gas until 1988. The Régie Autonome des Pétroles (RAP) was immediately formed to exploit the new resource; it set to work to extract the gas and to build a plant for its treatment near Boussens.

World War II left the Compagnie Française des Pétroles with little to do. France's share of oil from the Mesopotamian fields at Kirkouk was cut off by the British after the German invasion of France. But the Vichy government in southern France was not idle on its own account. In 1941 it created the Société Nationale des Pétroles d'Aquitaine (SNPA) to look for oil and gas in the Aquitaine region. Through the efforts of SNPA, Aquitaine was to become the oil and gas province of France.

Later in the war, when German troops occupied Vichy, the management of SNPA slackened off in its efforts to find oil. SNPA's reluctance to help in the German war effort resulted in the deportation of the company's first chairman, Pierre Angot. Like his counterpart at CFP, Jules Mény, who was also deported, Angot never returned to France.

The end of the war found the Compagnie Française des Pétroles in some disarray, with its French refining capacity in particular seriously impaired by war damage. President Charles de Gaulle was eager for the government to play an active role in restoring the country's control over its energy supplies as quickly as possible. In 1945 he created the Bureau de Recherches de Pètrole (BRP) to help the process along.

The role of BRP, which was entirely publicly funded, was—according to its founding charter—to encourage oil and gas exploration in France, its colonies, and protectorates "in the exclusive interest of the nation." Unlike RAP, BRP was not to engage in such exploration itself, but simply to identify and invest in projects that would.

De Gaulle chose Pierre Guillaumat as the first chairman of BRP. Then 36 years old, Guillaumat was to prove the single most influential figure in the history of Elf Aquitaine. (He finally retired as chairman in 1977.) Guillaumat shared a close relationship with de Gaulle. The French president had served under Guillaumat's father in the army. This personal tie was clearly a great asset for the fledgling BRP, perhaps as great an asset as the support of Prime Minister Raymond Poincaré had been for CFP's first chairman, Ernest Mercier, in the 1920s.

In the first years of its life, by far the most important investments made by BRP were in the French colony of Algeria and in equatorial Africa. Exploration in the Congo and in Gabon was largely carried out through Société des Pétroles d'Afrique Equatoriale (SPAFE), a joint venture with various French banks. Consortia were formed between SPAFE, Mobil, and Shell. In Algeria the beneficiary of BRP's funding was SN Repal, a joint venture with the colonial government and the Compagnie Française des Pétroles. Also established was Compagnie de Recherche et d'Exploitation du Pétrole du Sahara (CREPS), another oil exploration joint venture in Algeria, this time between RAP, with 65 percent, and Royal Dutch/Shell, with 35 percent.

BRP's failure to discover oil in the 1940s appeared to confirm the skepticism of those who doubted that oil would ever be discovered in the Algerian Sahara. Paradoxically, it was precisely this skepticism that had encouraged the French government to set up BRP in the first place—the privately owned oil companies, with shareholders' dividends to pay out, were not about to see large investments swallowed up by the sands of north Africa.

The job of managing BRP's still fruitless investments in Africa was, in the government's estimation, insufficiently demanding for someone of Guillaumat's ability. In 1950 he left BRP to become head of France's new Atomic Energy Commission. Eight years later, as the political situation in Algeria worsened, he became de Gaulle's minister for the army. It was not until 1960 that he returned to take charge of the much restructured BRP.

If BRP was still sifting sand in the early 1950s, SNPA was proving to be more fortunate closer to home. The Lacq gas field, discovered by SNPA in southwest France in December of 1951, was huge by French standards, with reserves estimated at 250 billion cubic meters. Extracting the gas was technically awkward on account of its highly toxic and corrosive impurities, notably hydrogen sulfide. But in the longer term SNPA turned these initial difficulties to its advantage. France became a net exporter of sulfur and the expertise SNPA acquired in treating highly sulfurous natural gas proved eminently exportable.

All the same, the initial delays must have been frustrating for SNPA's shareholders, of which the French state, owning 51 percent, was by far the largest. It took fully five years from the 1951 discovery of gas at Lacq for a salable product to be developed.

Meanwhile, the Bureau de Recherches de Pétrole was still pumping French taxpayers' money into its African investments. Its funding increased sharply after 1953, when it became a beneficiary of a new sales tax on petroleum products in France. Four years later, the government's tenacity proved justified; SN Repal discovered a huge gas field at Hassi R'Mel in November of 1956. Earlier that year, in July, the same company had struck a large quantity of oil at Hassi Messaoud.

The other forerunners of Elf Aquitaine—RAP and SNPA—also discovered oil in the Algerian desert at around the same time. In 1956 CREPS, the RAP and Shell joint venture, brought the Sahara's first marketable oil to the surface at Edjeleh. The following year, SNPA discovered oil at El Gassi.

1956 and 1957 also saw the first striking of oil in equatorial Africa, in Gabon and the Congo. But it was not until the early 1960s that important discoveries were made in the region, and then not on land but at sea, in the Gulf of Guinea.

By 1960 the French state had significant upstream oil- and gas-producing capacity. Gas from the Lacq field in Aquitaine made France almost self-sufficient in this valuable commodity, and oil and gas from North Africa was gushing and bubbling to the surface in abundance.

There were two problems, however. The first was that the various state-funded investment and exploration companies lacked the means to transport, refine, and sell their oil and gas. Upstream, they were handsomely endowed; downstream, they had nothing—no ships, no refineries, and no service stations. The second problem was that crude oil was in plentiful supply, and the heavily sulfurated Algerian oil cost more to produce and refine than oil from the Middle East. Therefore, it was hard to find buyers.

The French government concluded that these were problems for Pierre Guillaumat to solve. He re-entered the oil business as chairman of l'Union Générale des Pétroles (UGP) in 1960. UGP had three shareholders, all of them state-controlled. These were RAP, SN Repal, and the Groupement des Exploitants Pétroliers, which encompassed all the active subsidiaries of BRP, including SNPA, where BRP had become responsible for the state's investment.

Guillaumat's task was to propose ways of rationalizing these various interests and, more urgently, to supply UGP's shareholders with refining and distribution facilities. While he was working on this, the government came up with its own solution to the noncompetitive price of Algerian crude. It imposed a *devoir national* (national duty) on all French oil refiners and marketers to accept a certain amount of franc-zone crude, mostly from Algeria. One political argument in favor of the duty was that investment in oil production from such regions did not eat into French foreign currency reserves. Not surprisingly, the decision did not find favor with the chairman of CFP, Victor de Metz. The vast majority of CFP's oil output was still derived from the Middle East, outside the "franc zone."

Nevertheless, from Pierre Guillaumat's point of view, the *devoir national* ruling was obviously very helpful. It meant that the oil discoveries in North Africa and later in Equatorial Africa were not quite the boon that the French public had hoped for. But from the government's standpoint, at least the oil was sold and the wells stayed in business. Their output would no doubt be more appreciated in the future.

Pierre Guillaumat set about his primary task with alacrity. In 1960 UGP bought the French operations of Caltex, a refining and distributing operation owned jointly by Texaco and Standard Oil (California). Caltex owned a refinery at Ambes near Bordeaux, and UGP created a subsidiary, l'Union Industrielle des Pétroles (UIP), to run it. Sixty percent of UIP was owned by UGP, and forty percent by Caltex. The association with the U.S. oil companies behind Caltex would continue over many years and branch into many areas.

UGP also bought other fairly modest distribution networks— the purchase of Caltex had given it an immediate four percent market share—and built new refineries on its own account. UGP's smokestacks came to dominate the skyline at Feyzin near Lyons in 1964, at Grandpuits in 1966, and at Gargenville near Paris in 1968. Outside France, a refinery was built at Spire in the former West Germany in 1965. Algerian independence in 1962 had no immediate negative impact on the group. For the time being, the so-called Evian accords between the French and the Algerians protected France's energy interests in that country.

Large-scale rationalization took place in 1966, presided over by Pierre Guillaumat. BRP and RAP were transformed into Enterprise de Recherches d'Activités Pétrolières. The majority stake in SNPA held by BRP thus passed to ERAP. Guillaumat became chairman of both the ERAP holding company and its most dynamic subsidiary, SNPA. He was to continue to hold the two positions for 12 years. The group was still receiving funds from the sales tax on petroleum products; indeed, these support grants, as they were called, increased after 1966, when the government encouraged the group to diversify its oil supplies away from Algeria.

The French government's degree of involvement in the oil industry was by no means unique in Continental Europe at the time. The Italians had created Ente Nazionale Idrocarburi (ENI) in 1953 and given it monopoly exploration rights in the Po Valley, an area long coveted by foreign oil companies. In 1965 the Spanish had conducted an exercise similar to the restructuring in France, leading to the creation of Hispanoil.

Guillaumat and ERAP were more original in the deals they struck with oil-producing nations. ERAP's pioneering *contrats d'entreprise* were first signed with Iran in 1966 and two years later with Iraq. Others followed and were essentially service contracts under which ERAP agreed to share its exploration and production skills in return for long-term crude supplies at preferential rates. The success of this arrangement in Iraq provided a framework for the amicable resolution of Franco-Iraqi differences when the Iraqi government nationalized the assets of Compagnie Française des Pétroles, among others, in 1972.

ERAP and SNPA still lacked an instantly recognizable brand name in France. This was remedied on the night of April 27,

1967, when the Elf name and logo were unveiled at thousands of service stations throughout the country. The name "Elf" was chosen for its attractive connotations of nimbleness and sprightliness and was not an acronym.

In 1970 ERAP took control of the Antar group with its three refineries and vast distribution network. The purchase left the group with almost a quarter of the French market share for oil products.

The Antar brand name may still be seen in France today; it was considered too distinctive to throw away. Moreover, ERAP was not the only shareholder in Antar. CFP, with its long-established Total brand name, also bought a 24 percent stake.

At the beginning of the 1970s ERAP still trailed CFP; in terms of sales it was approximately three-quarters the size of the older company. That was to change in the coming decade, but first ERAP had to overcome its greatest crisis: the nationalization of its Algerian assets, which occurred in February of 1971. It was hardly unexpected, as Shell's Algerian assets had been nationalized the previous year. During the late 1960s ERAP had been diversifying its production as rapidly as possible. New business opportunities were beginning to open up in North America, Nigeria, Iran, Iraq, and in the North Sea. Nevertheless, the Algerian nationalization was a heavy blow—in a stroke the group lost two-thirds of its crude oil production, together with the huge gas reserves at Hassi R'Mel.

Guillaumat anticipated that by 1975 the group would be able to reattain its prenationalization production level of 180,000 barrels per day. Events proved him almost right, but 1971 was a difficult year.

Fortunately, the staunch political support that Guillaumat had always enjoyed from Charles de Gaulle continued under de Gaulle's successor, Georges Pompidou. On July 29, 1971, a French cabinet meeting under President Pompidou reaffirmed the government's faith in ERAP's future and gave its blessing to the further integration of SNPA and ERAP.

The government retained its confidence because SNPA withstood the loss of the Algerian oil and gas fields considerably better than other parts of the group. Oil accounted for only 22 percent of SNPA's sales in 1970. Gas was still being plentifully and profitably produced at Lacq and, since the early 1960s, SNPA had been diversifying into petrochemicals.

An encouraging sign for the future was the discovery of the Frigg gas field in the North Sea in 1971. Beginning in 1977 this would permit the group to almost double its gas output—Frigg was the same size as Lacq but could produce gas twice as fast. ERAP was entitled to half its production. In the early 1970s, however, the development of the Frigg field imposed huge demands on ERAP's budget.

The two oil price increases instigated by the Organization of Oil Exporting Countries (OPEC) cartel in 1973 and 1979 increased the value of reserves held by the group—which was renamed Société Nationale Elf Aquitaine in 1976—tenfold. But it wrought havoc with the group's refining operations. Governments everywhere launched energy conservation programs, and demand for refined oil products plummeted. The group closed down three refineries in France and a fourth at Spire in West Germany. At the same time, government-imposed price controls prevented ERAP and other oil companies operating in France from passing on the OPEC price increases in full measure to consumers.

The French government did not leave ERAP completely in the lurch. A 1974 tax on petrol sought to redistribute wealth away from the big petrol producers to the benefit of the major suppliers of fuel oil. In 1974 ERAP was by far the largest beneficiary.

SNEA made considerable diversification efforts in the 1970s. In 1973 Sanofi, a new subsidiary, was set up to invest in pharmaceuticals companies. It immediately bought an immunology research company, Laboratoire Michel Robilliard; a pharmaceuticals manufacturer, Labaz; and a minority stake in cosmetics group Yves Rocher. By the late 1980s Elf Aquitaine would become the second-largest pharmaceuticals group in France, with some 140 companies under the Sanofi umbrella.

In 1977, the year after the final merger between ERAP and SNPA to form the new Société Nationale Elf Aquitaine, Pierre Guillaumat retired. He was succeeded by Albin Chalandon, an experienced civil servant with a treasury background. Like his predecessor, Chalandon had served as a minister under Charles de Gaulle.

Chalandon raised Elf Aquitaine's profile in the United States through the 1981 acquisition of Texasgulf. The combination of Texasgulf's strength as a producer of mined sulfur and Elf's existing production at Lacq made the group the world's largest producer of this mineral. Texasgulf also had huge phosphate reserves and was one of the largest U.S. fertilizer producers. The purchase tripled Elf's overall U.S. business.

Albin Chalandon's chairmanship of Elf lasted until 1983, when Michel Pecqueur took over. Pecqueur had formerly been head of France's Atomic Energy Commission, a position held by Pierre Guillaumat in the early 1950s. The new chairman's first move was to strengthen the group's chemicals business.

"Elf Aquitaine has now truly become an oil and chemicals group," Pecqueur told shareholders at the company's annual general meeting in the spring of 1984. He admitted that it was a big gamble: the chemical companies grouped under the banner of Elf Aquitaine's new subsidiary, Atochem, had been "heavy loss makers."

Elf Aquitaine's newfound prominence in chemicals derived from a major restructuring of the largely state-controlled industry. The group acquired chlorate- and ethylene-producing capacity from the state-owned chemicals group Rhône-Poulenc, as well as further chlorate and fluorine plants from Produits Chimique Ugine Kuhlman (PCUK). As a result of Elf's expansion in these fields, consolidated turnover in 1983 increased 17 percent to FFr134.77 billion, only slightly behind Total Compagnie Française des Pétroles.

Profitability took somewhat longer to achieve. Between 1983 and 1989 Atochem passed from a FFr1.1 billion loss to a FFr2.4 billion profit after tax. Elf's 1989 report described its chemical business—France's second-largest after that of Rhône-Poulenc—as "an essential factor in the equilibrium of the group."

Under Elf Aquitaine's next chairman, Loïk Le Floch-Prigent, the group's chemicals business continued to grow apace. Le Floch-Prigent took the helm at Elf Aquitaine in June of 1989. Until 1986 he had been chairman of Rhône-Poulenc; his deputy, Serge Tchuruk, became Total's next chairman.

In August of 1989 Elf bought the U.S. specialty chemicals firm Pennwalt for US$1 billion. It then merged Pennwalt with its other U.S. chemical activities to form Atochem North America in January of 1990. At the beginning of 1990, a division of the state-owned French chemicals company Orkem was finalized. Elf picked up Orkem's petrochemicals and fertilizer businesses, while Total acquired the specialty operations, including adhesives, paints, and resins. In the first half of 1990 no less than 42 percent of Elf's FFr10.2 billion operating profits came from its chemicals business. The group, therefore, had a sizeable cushion against any deterioration of its oil business.

Since Loïk Le Floch-Prigent took the helm at Elf, the group cut back on its distribution network in France, where margins have been squeezed by the rise in discount filling stations owned by hypermarkets. The Persian Gulf crisis worsened the situation because moral pressure brought to bear by the French government on distributors prevented oil price increases from being passed on in full to the motorist.

Elf Aquitaine's base had been solidified by a number of alliances with foreign companies in 1990. Elf purchased a 25 percent stake in Cespa, Spain's leading independent oil company, giving its downstream operations an important foothold in the Spanish market.

A significant inroad into the former Soviet Union was made in 1990 when Elf pioneered the first joint exploration and production agreement between the Soviet government and a Western oil company. According to the *Oil Daily*, this agreement put Elf a step ahead of U.S. companies such as Chevron and Occidental who had "made much-publicized inroads into the U.S.S.R. without coming up with agreements on E&P." More importantly, it paved the way for further ventures in the newly formed Eastern European countries.

Elf's pharmaceutical subsidiary, Sanofi, experienced continued growth in the 1990s, including the introduction of an unprecedented eight new chemical compounds in 1990 alone. Also that year, Sanofi expanded further into the biotechnology field, purchasing the U.S. concern Genetic Systems; broke into the Japanese market for medical testing products; and acquired a 40 percent stake in Chinoin, Hungary's second-largest pharmaceutical company. More importantly, in 1991 Sanofi entered into a strategic alliance with the U.S. pharmaceutical concern Sterling Winthrop, Inc. The two companies combined their production, distribution, and marketing facilities to create Sanofi Winthrop. The alliance gave Sanofi Winthrop a research budget of FFr2.5 billion, placing it among the top ten international pharmaceutical research enterprises.

At the onset of the Persian Gulf War in 1991, oil and chemical companies found themselves in an increasingly difficult financial position. The average price of crude oil dropped 15 percent and many major economies suffered severe recessions. Elf's net income decreased five percent in 1991 to FFr8.9 billion.

Despite this setback, Le Floch-Prigent believed Elf's balanced business mix solidified its ability to withstand economically turbulent times, placing its sales figures among "the very best achieved by international oil and gas companies."

Elf continued strengthening both its upstream and downstream operations through 1991. Its production capacity was given a 27 percent boost when it purchased the Norwegian Oil Consortium (Noco). Several months later, Elf became the fourth-largest operator in the North Sea when it entered into a joint agreement with the British independent Enterprise Oil to purchase Occidental Petroleum Great Britain Inc. for US$1.35 billion in cash, plus other considerations. Elf controls two-thirds of the new company, Elf Enterprise Petroleum Ltd., while Enterprise Oil retains interest in the remaining third.

Elf gained access to an important European source of base oil in 1991 through its purchase of a 40 percent interest in a British Petroleum refinery at Dunkirk. Also that year, Elf further added to its downstream assets through an agreement with Heron PLC to add 150 new service stations to its British network, raising its market share to 5.4 percent in that country.

Temporary problems notwithstanding, half a century of public investment in the business of Elf Aquitaine was paying off in the early 1990s. The company's chairman presides over a truly diversified group that should be well equipped to withstand the heaviest of knocks from a weak economy on the road to recovery.

Principal Subsidiaries: Société Nationale Elf Aquitaine (Production); Elf Congo; Elf Italiana spa; Elf Aquitaine Norge A/S; Société Elf de Recherches et d'Exploitation des Pétroles au Cameroun; Elf Gabon; Société Africaine d'Exploration Pétrolière; Elf Nigeria Ltd.; Elf Aquitaine Inc.; Elf U.K. (Holdings) PLC; Elf Aquitaine Oman; Elf Aquitaine Colombie; Elf Aquitaine Angola; SOCAP International Ltd.; Elf Trading Inc.; Elf Trading SA (Genève); Elf France; Société des Lubrifiants Elf Aquitaine; Elf Antargaz; Elf Suisse; Elf Mineraloel GmbH; Elf Belgique; Elf Nederland; Anker Union NV; Elf Petroleum G.B.; Société Nationale des Gaz du Sud-Ouest; Société Elf France-CORIF; Elf Atlantique et Cie; Texasgulf Inc.; Atochem; Atochem North America; Sanofi Winthrop; Société Financière Auxiliaire des Pétroles-SOFAX; SOGERAP; Compagnie de Participations et d'Investissements Holding SA; Société Financière Internationale de Participation; SAFREP SA; Rivunion SA; Alphega; Norwegian Oil Consortium (Noco); Elf Enterprise Petroleum Ltd.

Further Reading: Grayson, Leslie E., *National Oil Companies,* London, John Wiley & Sons, 1981; "Direction des Relations Publiques et de la Communication, Elf Aquitaine," *L'Histoire d'Elf Aquitaine,* Paris, Elf Aquitaine, 1986; Giraud, André, and Xavier Boy de la Tour, *Géopolitique du Pétrol et du Gaz,* Paris, Editions Technip, 1987; Mangan, David, Jr., "Elf-Soviet Accord May Pave Way for Future Pacts," *Oil Daily,* May 28, 1990; Dawkins, William, "Shaping up for Competition," *Financial Times,* November 12, 1990; *Oil & Gas Journal,* November 26, 1990; *Oil & Gas Journal,* May 13, 1991; "French Companies Lead the Pack in Promoting C.I.S. Joint Ventures," *Oil & Gas Journal,* April 6, 1992.

—William Pitt
updated by Maura Troester

SOUTHAM INC.

150 Bloor Street West
Suite 900
Toronto, Ontario
Canada M5S 2Y8
(416) 927-1877
Fax: (416) 927-8563

Public Company
Incorporated: 1871 as Southam Ltd.
Employees: 12,000
Sales: C$1.17 billion (US$929.83 million)
Stock Exchanges: Toronto Montreal
SICs: 2711 Newspapers; 2721 Periodicals; 5942 Book Stores

Southam Inc. is a Canadian communications conglomerate whose primary business is newspaper publishing. Southam publishes 17 daily newspapers, including the *Montreal Gazette* and the *Windsor Star,* and 56 community newspapers. Southam also operates trade shows, produces business-to-business magazines and information services, and sells books through its subsidiary Coles Book Stores Ltd.

Southam's history spans well over a century and largely parallels the development of the newspaper industry in Canada. William Southam, a self-made man, left school in 1855 at age 12 and got his first job delivering papers for the London (Ontario) Free Press. In 1871 Southam, then 33 years old, bought a failing newspaper in Hamilton, Ontario, with partner William Carey. He paid $4,000 for his part in the venture. Southam was off to a small start but already had his eye on the *Spectator,* a much larger venture.

During this time, newspapers survived largely on government patronage. The *Spectator* and *Journal of Commerce* had prospered due to favorable government advertising contracts secured from the Conservative administration, which lasted until 1873. But by 1877 the rival Liberals ruled and advertising and printing contracts slumped. Southam and Carey were betting on a Conservative victory in the upcoming elections, which would assure the fortunes of the *Spectator.*

After becoming half-owner of the *Spectator,* Southam made sure the newspaper backed the Conservative Party in the election. The gamble paid off: on September 17, 1878, the *Specta-*

tor's presses ran late announcing the Conservative return to power.

In 1881 Southam and Carey branched out by purchasing a printing firm in Toronto, the Mail Job Printing Co. They printed railroad timetables and folders and eventually got into theater programs, posters, and even shredded paper flakes for parades. The *Spectator* also expanded by beginning a book printing business.

Then, in 1896, after the Liberal government regained power, the owners of the *Ottawa Citizen,* another Conservative government paper, feared a slump in government advertising and printing contracts. They turned to Southam as a buyer and a second newspaper was added to the company's stable. Wilson Southam, the eldest son in the family, was pegged to run the *Citizen.* He was soon joined by Harry, the fourth eldest son.

The Southam family's control over the company expanded further. In 1889, Southam's second son, Frederick Neal, was sent to Montreal to open a printing shop to serve the railway industry headquartered there. For a mere $1500, Neal was able to buy two ticket presses and a cutting machine and hire seven staff members.

In 1904 the company was reorganized and renamed Southam Ltd. Its portfolio included ownership of the *Citizen,* half of the *Spectator,* printing plants and investments in steel making and other manufacturing concerns. Five years later, the Mail Job Printing Co. in Toronto was renamed Southam Press Ltd., and operations were moved to Duncan and Adelaide Streets in Toronto.

Seeking expansion by penetrating new markets, Southam acquired other newspapers. In 1908 Southam bought a controlling interest in the *Calgary Herald,* the *Mining and Ranch Advocate,* and the *General Advertiser.* Four years later, the *Edmonton Journal* was added to its portfolio.

In the early part of the century, brothers Wilson and Harry Southam got into trouble for encouraging critical coverage from the *Citizen*'s reporters. The elder Southams hoped matters might repair themselves when the Conservative government of Robert Borden returned to power in 1911. But the Borden regime became so critical of *Citizen* coverage of its affairs that it threatened to open a rival newspaper in Ottawa.

Matters grew to a head in 1912 when founder William Southam canceled his own home subscription to the *Citizen* over its editorial trespasses. The company began a policy that grants newspaper editors independence from Southam's owners and, because of the company's size, from local pressures. The newspaper chain would have, in theory, no ''Southam editorial line.'' Instead, each management would create one for their newspaper as they saw fit.

Despite these troubles, in 1920, Southam purchased the *Winnipeg Tribune* and was well on its way to becoming among Canada's largest newspaper and communications chains. The *Tribune* had grown out of the ashes of the former *Winnipeg Sun.*

Two years later, the Southams—whose corporate vehicle was now called William Southam and Sons—pushed even further westward when they bought a controlling interest in the *Vancouver Province.* Not long after, the rival Vancouver daily, the *Sun,* ran into financial trouble under owner Robert Cromie. He knew who to turn to for help, and Frederick Neal Southam offered a lifeboat. William Southam and Sons would assume a third mortgage on the *Sun.*

Frederick Neal Southam would serve as president of William Southam and Sons from 1928 to 1945. He took over from Wilson, who had served from 1918 out of Ottawa. After the First World War, company founder William Southam began gradually ceding control to his five sons.

In the 1920s, Southam newspapers branched out into the emerging radio broadcast market. The first was the *Vancouver Province,* which broadcast on station CDED to crystal radio listeners beginning on March 13, 1922. Both the *Edmonton Journal* and the *Calgary Herald* went to the airwaves six weeks later, taking a 60 percent stake each in stations CJCA and CFAC, respectively. In 1954, Southam would acquire a 20 percent stake in station CHCT-TV in Calgary. In 1924 the *Hamilton Spectator* traded advertising space in its newspaper for the right to operate its own radio station.

Three years later, Southam went through a thorough restructuring, changing its name to the Southam Publishing Company Ltd. The main aim of this move was to gather all outstanding shares Southam held, many reflecting minority stakes in regional newspapers and broadcasting concerns, and exchange them for shares and securities of the new company.

The company also established offices in Montreal and Toronto in order to be able to sell advertising space throughout the newspaper chain. In addition, Southam sent reporters to bureaus in Ottawa, Washington, and London. Through this network, reporters could file stories for use in any of the Southam newspapers. So was born Southam News Services.

In 1945 union staff at the *Winnipeg Tribune* went on strike. Southam's head office refused to intervene, declaring the dispute a local matter. But the International Typographical Union, in solidarity with the striking Winnipeg staff, brought Southam papers in Hamilton, Ottawa, Edmonton, and Vancouver out on strike. The Vancouver strike turned bloody when printers attempted to cross the picket line and were beaten back. Trucks attempting to move newspapers from the printing plant were overturned and burned.

Earlier, in 1938, the company's name had been changed yet again to the Southam Company. Shares in the company were first issued to the public on the Toronto Stock Exchange in 1945. Three years later, Southam purchased all outstanding shares belonging to the *News of Medicine Hat,* in Alberta, for $125,000. In 1955 the company took full control of the newspaper.

By the 1960s the company was branching out into other industries. In 1960 St. Clair Balfour, then president of Southam, concluded a deal to buy Hugh C. MacLean Publications Ltd. That led shortly to the formation of Southam-MacLean Publications Ltd. The business comprised business and professional trade magazines. Under Southam's stewardship, it began conducting trade shows, seminars, and market research and opened

yet more trade publications. It also formed Videosurgery, which tapes medical operations and sells them to doctors and medical schools in North America for training and instruction.

In the next four years, Southam purchased up to 20 business publications of varying sizes, including 14 journals bought as part of Age Publishing Co. Ltd. of Toronto for $792,000. By far the largest of these acquisitions was Southam-Maclean Publications' purchase of the *Financial Times of Canada* from E.C. Ertl estate in 1961. By 1965, Southam moved its head office from Montreal to Toronto, nearer Bay Street and that city's banking and financial core.

Also in 1965, Southam formed Southstar Publishers Ltd., a joint venture with Toronto Star Ltd., to publish the *Canadian,* a weekly glossy magazine. The *Canadian* would eventually appear weekly in many Southam newspapers.

A year later, the company scooped up the North Bay Nugget after the employee-owned newspaper was put on the market. At the same time, Don Cromie, now owner of the *Vancouver Sun,* encountered financial problems of his own and turned once again to Southam for help. A handshake aboard a boat in the Vancouver harbor between Cromie and St. Clair Balfour, then managing director of Southam, solved matters. The *Province* would print a morning edition and the *Sun* would retain the afternoon slot. Both newspapers would be sold to a third company, Pacific Press Ltd., to be jointly owned by Southam and Sun Publishing. In December 1965, both Vancouver newspapers moved to a $10 million plant on Granville Street in Vancouver. Two years earlier, Don Cromie had sold his stake in Sun Publishing to F.P. Publications.

Meanwhile, across the country in Weston, Ontario, Southam bought Murray Printing & Gravure for $700,000, a move that increased Southam's printing capacity by half. The Murray plant was modernized and Southam's Toronto printing capacity was relocated to the new site.

In 1969 Southam expanded yet again by purchasing the *Windsor Star* and the *Brantford Expositor.* The buying spree continued into 1971, when the company added the *Montreal Gazette* to its stable, paying $3.7 million and 100,000 shares of the company. The Montreal newspaper had been formed almost 200 years earlier when a colleague of Benjamin Franklin, then in Montreal to win recruits to the American Revolution, stayed behind after the inventor and statesman left, and formed his own newspaper. By the end of 1971 Southam had also purchased the *Owen Sound Sun-Times* for $950,000 and the *Prince George Citizen* for $2 million.

In November 1973 the *Ottawa Citizen* moved to a modern, purpose-built plant. Here it would become the first newspaper in Canada to use video terminals for editing newspaper articles, as opposed to running a red pen over type-written copy.

In 1975 Gordon Fisher took over from Balfour as president of Southam. That same year the company purchased the *Daily Star* in Sault Ste. Marie, Ontario. In 1976 the *Hamilton Spectator* moved into a new $23 million plant, complete with a newsroom the size of a football field.

Two years later, the name of the company was changed to its current name, Southam Inc. The company also made a strategic purchase to go into book-selling, buying Coles Book Stores Ltd. at $23 a share. Coles would subsequently become the country's largest book seller, with over 250 outlets in 124 cities and towns, including 58 U.S. outlets.

Meanwhile, Southam strengthed its hold on both the major eastern and western newspaper markets. In early 1980, Southam bought a one-third interest in the *Montreal Gazette* from F.P. Publications for $13 million. This move gave it full control of Montreal's leading English-language newspaper. That same year, Southam strengthened its hold on the Vancouver newspaper market when it bought outright control of Pacific Press Ltd. for $42.25 million. A year later, the Kamploops News, in British Columbia, was added to the company's newspaper stable.

The early 1980s recession hit advertising revenues at Southam's newspaper operation, with western Canada hit the hardest. With the western newspaper sector struggling, the focus was on Southam's non-newspaper assets to perform and make up for lost advertising revenue. One competitive measure was to expand into the U.S. market; in October 1983, Southam acquired Dittler Brothers, of Atlanta, Georgia, for $67.6 million.

Southam was branching out from its core newspaper operation with gathering pace. In fact, in 1984, revenue from Southam's newspaper operations and other business segments balanced out for the first time. Such progress was welcome because labor lock-outs in Vancouver and Montreal the previous year had cost Southam $6.5 million in earnings.

In 1985 Gordon Fisher, Southam's president, died suddenly after an unexpected illness, leaving no clear successor. That opened the way for rumored takeover bids for the company and a slumping share price. The slide in stock value was eventually halted by a share exchange worth $225 million between Southam and rival Torstar Corporation. Torstar gained a 23 percent stake in Southam but signed an agreement barring it from purchasing a controlling interest in its rival for at least ten years. For Southam, the Torstar arrangement enabled the Southam family to retain control of the company while holding only 23 percent of outstanding shares.

In 1986 Southam consolidated its newspaper assets by forming the Southam Newspaper Group, led by Paddy Sherman. The company also established four other separate business segments: Southam Printing Ltd, Coles Book Stores Ltd., Southam Communications Ltd., and Southam Inc., which included a 30 percent investment in Torstar.

Sales and acquistions highlighted much of Southam's business activity in 1987. Further expansion continued as Southam expanded into the Quebec French-speaking market by publishing *Le Matin,* an up-scale tabloid daily. In total, for 1987, Southam spent $77 million on new newspaper acquisitions throughout Canada. Southam also sold its 49 percent interest in Sun Publishing Company to majority shareholder L. D. Whitehead; and Coles Book Stores sold its 48 U.S. outlets to Waldenbooks Inc. of Stamford, Connecticut.

In 1988 the company resolved a bitter, six-month-long strike at the *Montreal Gazette.* Despite this, sales for the year increased by 13.5 percent to $1.45 billion. In August of that year, Coles Book Stores launched its first Active Minds store in Calgary. The book store is aimed at younger readers. A second store soon opened in Toronto.

In 1989 a slowing Canadian economy was cited as evidence of a need for caution ahead for Southam's business plans. Hugh G. Hallward, now chairman of the company, said in the 1989 annual report: "Looking ahead to 1990, we see ... slower economic growth for Canada as a whole than in 1989, but better in the West than in the East." Hallward was essentially drawing the lines of the forthcoming recession, which hit Eastern Canada, and especially Ontario, harder than elsewhere. In late 1990 Southam sold the money-losing *Financial Times of Canada,* based in Toronto, to rival Thomson Press, for an undisclosed sum.

Troubles continued into 1991. Southam saw its advertising sales drop five percent compared with a year earlier. A number of acquisitions boosted total company sales, which jumped nine percent to $1.8 billion in fiscal 1990. But profits were down sharply to $2.7 million in 1990, compared to $90.5 million in 1989.

Further complicating Southam's troubles, the government brought an anti-trust case against the company. Southam was ordered to sell three community newspapers it had bought in 1990, all based in and around Vancouver. The government argued that Southam had monopolized the Vancouver market through its ownership of Pacific Press Limited. Divesting itself of the three newspapers, it was argued, would create room for potential competitors in the Vancouver market.

In October 1991, the 114-year tradition in which a member of the Southam family controlled the business empire ended. William Ardell, previously head of the Coles Book Stores chain and Southam Business Communications, was named to succeed John Fisher as CEO. Ardell was seen as the turnaround specialist Southam needed to restructure itself during the early 1990s recession. The downside was that Ardell had no experience running newspapers, Southam's principal business.

Uncertainty regarding the future of the company fed rumors in financial circles about impending takeover. One persistent rumor was that Torstar, with its one-third ownership of Southam, was displeased with its slumping profit line and was again entertaining takeover designs.

In 1992 Conrad Black, head of newspaper and magazine publisher Hollinger Inc., bought Torstar's 22.6 percent stake in Southam for $259 million. Black indicated at the time he was looking to hold the Southam shares for the long term, and had no takeover plans in mind.

Meanwhile, Ardell moved quickly to stem losses on the newspaper side. In November 1992 the newspaper group was split into two groups—Metro Newspapers/City and Community Newspapers, with Jim Armitage and Ray Elliot appointed presidents of the respective groups.

This followed Southam's sale of its Canadian Web Group printing operations to G.T.C. Transcontinental Group Ltd. for just under $105 million. In order to raise cash, Southam also sold its 35 percent interest in Telemedia Publishing Inc. for $18 million, and sold its entire stake in Torstar.

For the future, Southam must cut its losses if it is to maintain the loyalty of its shareholders in the face of a possible takeover bid from Hollinger Inc. Widespread cost-cutting measures continue on the newspaper side, with most of the cost savings coming from job cutbacks. For example, employees and management at Pacific Press in Vancouver are facing sale or foreclosure unless they improve their bottom line. Another contining strategy for long term growth is a commitment to debt reduction.

Principal Subsidiaries: Southam Newspaper Group; Coles Book Stores Ltd.; Southam Business Communications Ltd.

Further Reading: Charles Bruce, *News and the Southams,* Toronto, MacMillan of Canada, 1968; ''A Century of Southam,'' Gazette Canadian Printing Ltd., 1977; Peter Dunnett, *The World Newspaper Industry,* Croom Helm, London, 1988; ''No Tears for Southam-Torstar Split,'' *Globe and Mail,* July 24, 1992.

—Etan Vlessing

THE SOUTHLAND CORPORATION

Post Office Box 7119
Dallas, Texas 75221-0711
2711 Haskell Avenue
Dallas, Texas 75204
U.S.A.
(214) 828-7011
Fax: (214) 828-7848

Public Company
Incorporated: 1961
Employees: 35,646
Sales: $7.48 billion
Stock Exchanges: NASDAQ
SICs: 5411 Grocery Stores; 5541 Gasoline Service Stations

The Southland Corporation is the world's largest operator, franchisor, and licensor of convenience stores, with more than 13,700 stores in 20 countries carrying the 7-Eleven banner. The company began as a brainstorm of John Jefferson Green. In 1927 Green approached Joe C. "Jodie" Thompson, one of five founding directors of the Dallas Southland Ice Company, with a new idea. He wanted to sell milk, eggs, and bread through his retail ice dock. "You furnish the items," he suggested, "and I'll pay the power bills." Thompson agreed, and together they established the first known convenience store.

The newly formed Southland Ice Company was comprised of four separate ice companies and operated eight ice plants and 21 retail ice stations. An early attempt at advertising occurred after one Southland manager visited Alaska in 1928. Upon his return to Texas, he planted a souvenir totem pole in front of his store. The pole attracted so much attention that the employee suggested placing one at every Southland-owned retail ice dock and naming the stores "Tote'm Stores," since the consumers toted away their purchases.

Southland decided to go with the new name, sensing that it unified the company's diversified stores and provided a distinct identity, a key ingredient in the successful operation of numerous retail outlets. Jodie Thompson, secretary-treasurer of Southland Ice, unified the stores further by training staff with daily sales talks. He also chose a company uniform for ice station service men. Thompson recognized early on that consumers should receive the same quality and service at every store. During this time Southland also began to experiment with constructing and leasing gasoline stations at ten of its Dallas-area stores.

The Depression plunged Southland into bankruptcy in 1931. During a period of receivership and reorganization, Jodie Thompson was named president, a move which ensured continuity during the rocky period. The management team chosen during this time was especially strong and led Southland for a number of years. W. W. Overton Jr., a Dallas banker, helped disentangle the young company's finances by organizing the purchase of all Southland bonds for seven cents on the dollar, which eventually put ownership of the company under the control of the board of directors. Despite the financial confusion, profits from the Tote'm Stores continued to climb, and with the repeal of Prohibition in 1933, ice and beer sales surged.

Once it was on more stable footing, Southland began vertical integration with construction of Oak Farms Dairies in 1936, using public relations to market its new dairy products by offering a free movie ticket in return for six of its milk-bottle caps. A crowd of 1,600 attended the Dallas theater sponsoring the event. By 1939 Southland operated 60 Tote'm Stores in the Dallas-Fort Worth area, triple the number operating when the company had been founded 12 years earlier.

With the onset of World War II, demands for ice peaked. Southland became the chief supplier of ice for the construction and operation of Camp Hood, the U.S. Army's largest training camp. The dramatic increase in business prompted reorganization of the company. Southland bought City Ice Delivery, Ltd., which included two modern ice plants, 20 retail stations, and property on Haskell Avenue, where the new company headquarters was sited. Southland became the largest ice operator in Dallas.

By 1945 Southland owned stores scattered over north-central Texas. These stores offered convenient hours—operating from seven in the morning until 11 at night—seven days a week. When the Tracy-Locke firm was commissioned to create a new name, they chose "7-Eleven" to emphasize the company's commitment to serving customers. At this time Southland remodeled all 7-Eleven stores, doubling the amount of floor space at each retail outlet.

In the late-1940s, Americans, freed from the ration system of World War II, were eager to purchase consumer goods. Because refrigerators were not yet readily available to the public, demand for block ice peaked. Southland bought Texas Public Utilities, owners of 20 ice plants, in 1947. This acquisition made Southland the largest ice operator in Texas. In 1948 Jodie Thompson's oldest son, John P. Thompson, was named to the board of directors.

At a management meeting in Washington, D.C. in 1956, a blizzard blanketed the city. John Thompson noticed that in densely populated areas, people could walk to the stores even when the weather made driving impossible. Seven-Eleven's long operating hours and diversified stock—from canned soup to tissues to aspirin—could provide exactly what customers might need. In light of this revelation, Southland began to focus on the traffic patterns around potential store sites, choosing high-volume corners whenever possible.

Southland extended its area of operations outside of Texas during the late-1950s when John Thompson, now vice-president, introduced 7-Eleven stores in Virginia, Maryland, and eastern Pennsylvania. The company noted demographic shifts and opened more suburban stores in response to mass migration to these outlying areas. Southland also refined its marketing by studying customer traffic in its stores and eliminating products that moved slowly.

In 1961 Jodie Thompson named his sons to executive positions in Southland; John Thompson became the second president of Southland and Jere W. Thompson was elected vice-president of sales. Upon the elder Thompson's death that year, the *Dallas Morning News* credited him with transforming "the ordinary corner ice house from an ice dispensary to a multi-million-dollar drive-in grocery enterprise." His son inherited his entrepreneurial drive; John Thompson's first goal as president was to propel Southland from $100 million in annual sales to one billion dollars within ten years.

Incorporated in 1961, Southland moved quickly to national prominence. The company's unprecedented expansion began with dairy acquisitions—notably Midwest Dairy Products in 1962—yielding production plants and branches in Illinois, Arkansas, Louisiana, and Alabama.

After acquiring 100 SpeeDee Marts in California in 1963, Southland was introduced to the concept of franchising, a system already in operation at the very successful SpeeDee Mart stores. The company developed two-week training sessions for prospective franchisees, allowing greater decentralization of stores. In January of 1965, 1,519 7-Eleven stores were operating and Southland had climbed to 49th in *Fortune*'s top 50 merchandising firms.

Purchasing continued through the 1960s and 1970s, as Southland bought existing convenience market chains in Arizona, New Jersey, Colorado, Illinois, Georgia, and Tennessee. In addition, Southland experimented with its first 24-hour store, in Las Vegas, and expanded to the East Coast and Canada in 1969. By December of 1969 the number of 7-Eleven stores had exploded to 3,537. But with such growth, problems began to surface. Management noted high employee turnover and insufficient security systems in 24-hour stores. The company nonetheless remained committed to the 24-hour store, and the number of 24-hour 7-Eleven stores rose from 817 in 1972 to 3,703 by the end of 1975.

Southland reached one billion dollars in sales by 1971 and became a member of the New York Stock Exchange the following year. The first regional distribution center was opened in Florida in 1971, and by 1977 several such centers were fully functioning and serving more than 3,000 7-Eleven stores. Jere Thompson, named president of Southland in 1973, continued Southland's American retail store expansion.

Through a new computer inventory system, 7-Eleven was able to pinpoint its strengths and discover that single-purchase items were its best sellers. To make stops more convenient for customers, Southland began using microwaves for fast-food sales

and introduced self-service gasoline through its newly acquired Pak-a-Sak stores. In 1974 the five thousandth 7-Eleven store opened in Dallas at the site of John Jefferson Green's original ice dock.

Southland's success was not limited to the United States; penetration of the European market occurred with the company's purchase of a 50 percent interest in Cavenham Ltd., a manufacturing corporation controlling 840 retail outlets in Great Britain. By early 1974, Southland's international operations included 50 percent interest in 1,096 United Kingdom outlets, 75 7-Eleven stores in Canada, and four Super-7 Stores in Mexico.

Negotiations for the introduction of 7-Eleven to Japan were completed in December of 1973, when Southland granted Ito-Yokado, one of Japan's largest retailers, an area license. Like the franchise concept in the United States, area licensing worked well in Japan because of its emphasis on the individual businessperson operating a store but able to take advantage of 7-Eleven's name and established systems of management and accounting. By late 1978, 188 7-Eleven stores were open for business in Japan.

Also in 1978, Southland bought Chief Auto Parts, a California chain of 119 retail automobile-part stores. By 1986 Chief Auto Parts operated 465 stores and stood as the largest convenience retailer of automobile parts in the nation. Another Southland acquisition was Tidel Systems, a manufacturer of cash-dispensing systems and underground gasoline-tank-monitoring systems.

Southland's most significant acquisition, however, was the Citgo Petroleum Corporation, purchased in August of 1983. Southland hoped that the $780 million acquisition would provide a smooth supply of gasoline for its convenience stores. In September of 1986 Southland sold a 50-percent interest in Citgo to a subsidiary of Petroleos de Venezuela, S.A.

In mid-1987 the Thompson brothers, spurred in part by the threat of a hostile takeover bid by Canadian raider Samuel Belzburg, initiated a leveraged buyout. The buyout, which involved the formation of a temporary holding company called JT Acquisitions, was completed on December 16, 1987.

By the end of 1988 Southland had completed a series of divestitures to streamline operations, focus on convenience retailing, and pay back debt. Southland sold Chief Auto Parts, the snack foods division, the dairies group, Reddy Ice, Chemical/Food Labs, Tidel Systems, 1,000 convenience stores, and related real estate properties. Proceeds from the divestitures, as well as the monetization of royalties from the licensee in Japan, went to repay a portion of the $4 billion debt Southland had incurred through the leveraged buyout.

Southland may well have rebounded by the early 1990s were it not for competition from convenience stores operated by the major oil companies. Although these stores emphasized gasoline retailing rather than other merchandise, they did sell the primary products of convenience stores—soft drinks, cigarettes, and beer. Their sheer number and financial strength changed the nature of the convenience retailing industry. Their effort was exacerbated by the decline in the U.S. economy that began in the late-1980s. Southland, along with a number of other convenience-store chains, had limited capital to invest in its store base due to heavy debt loads.

Under President and CEO Clark J. Matthews II, the company began to work on a plan to restructure its balance sheet. In October of 1990, Southland filed a bankruptcy plan of reorganization after securing preliminary approval from its bondholders. The company emerged from bankruptcy less than five months later. As part of the reorganization, Southland exchanged its old leveraged buyout bonds for approximately half of the principal amount of new bonds—which had substantially lower interest rates. In addition Southland sold 70 percent of its common stock to IYG Holding Company of Japan for $430 million. Ito-Yokado Co., Ltd, the most profitable retailer in Japan, owns 51 percent of IYG, and Seven-Eleven Japan Co., Ltd., the long-time 7-Eleven licensee in Japan, owns 49 percent.

In 1992 Southland completed additional financing, a $400 million commercial paper facility backed by Ito-Yokado. Also in 1992, Southland decided to leave the distribution and food processing business to focus on its core business, 7-Eleven. The company sold certain distribution centers and food processing facilities to McLane Co., Inc., a subsidiary of Arkansas-based Wal-Mart stores. Southland also signed a service agreement with McLane, the country's largest convenience store distributor, to provide coast-to-coast distribution service to the company's 5,700 stores in the United States.

Matthews has capitalized on the company's nationally recognized 7-Eleven name and enhanced the quality, appearance, and service of the famous convenience store. In late 1991, Southland remodeled and remerchandised its 50 stores in Austin, Texas, to test its new physical standards, commissary food service program, and new merchandising process.

The new merchandising process, that deletes slow-moving items and introduces new products, had been refined and introduced to 7-Eleven stores across the country by the end of 1992. Due to the initial capital infusion by its majority owners in 1991, and their backing of the commercial paper facility established in 1992, Southland was able to make long-term capital investment plans for the first time in many years. The company plans to remodel 1,300 stores in selected markets in 1993 and hopes to upgrade its entire store by the end of 1996. Southland also continues to upgrade the quality and value of its fast foods because these have been identified as a good source of future profit growth.

Thus far Southland's new concepts have worked well. With the end of the recession in sight, the company is slowly returning to profitability. Market analysts have predicted an upsurge in fast food consumption and the rebound of the neighborhood convenience store, because of the growing popularity of 24-hour businesses. If convenience stores such as 7-Eleven can solve their biggest problems—a high turnover of labor and unfavorable image among women and older customers—they could well be on the road to a rapid recovery.

Principal Subsidiaries: Citgo Petroleum (50%).

Further Reading: Liles, Allen, *Oh Thank Heaven! The Story of the Southland Corporation,* Dallas, Texas, The Southland Corporation, December 1977; Annual Report: The Southland Corp., 1991; ''Bondholders Withdraw All Objections to Southland Plan (Bankruptcy Reorganization Plan),'' *Los Angeles Times,* January 24, 1991; ''Muzak Attack (7-Eleven Store in Thousand Oaks, California, Pipes in Classical Music to Discourage Loitering Youths and Criminal Activity),'' *Los Angeles Times,* November 17, 1991; ''Southland Chief Fires Top Aides to Cut Costs,'' *Wall Street Journal,* June 25, 1992; Miller, Karen Lowry, ''A New Roll of the Dice at 7-Eleven,'' *Business Week,* October 26, 1992.

—updated by Sina Dubovoj

STEELCASE INC.

P.O. Box 1967
Grand Rapids, Michigan 49501
U.S.A.
(616) 247-2710
Fax: (616) 246-9015

Private Company
Incorporated: 1912 as Metal Office Furniture Company
Employees: 20,000
Sales: $1.9 billion
SICs: 2521 Wood Office Furniture; 2522 Office Furniture
    Except Wood

Known since 1984 as "The Office Environment Company," Steelcase Inc. is the world's leading designer and manufacturer of office furniture. The company, launched in 1912 with a single product and fifteen employees, supplies thousands of products worldwide produced by 19,000 employees working in 20.6 million square feet of manufacturing, shipping, and administrative facilities in 11 countries. A network of 900 independent dealers in 68 countries sells Steelcase metal and wood office furniture, systems furniture, seating, computer support furniture, desks, tables, credenzas, filing cabinets, and office lighting. Steelcase boasts an on-time delivery rate of 98 percent. The company also offers computer-assisted programs for those who plan, provide, and manage offices; office-worker public opinion surveys; and leasing programs.

According to *A Field Guide to the Leading 400 Companies*, "This company, more than any other, is responsible for the look of the modern office. Since 1968, they've been the industry leader, earning a reputation as the General Motors of the office furniture industry." Steelcase's sales figures confirm its leadership. At $2.3 billion in worldwide sales, of which some $1.9 billion is in domestic sales, the company has more than twice the sales volume of its nearest competitor. That translates into 21 percent of total office furniture sales in North America, eight percent in Europe, and four percent in Japan.

Steelcase Inc. was incorporated as the Metal Office Furniture Company on March 16, 1912, in Grand Rapids, Michigan. Although the new company had a novel idea—fabricating furniture from sheet metal, it received little notice in "The Furniture City," which already had nearly 60 furniture manufacturers.

Peter M. Wege proposed the Metal Office Furniture Company to a group of investors. Wege had been a designer and executive at the Safe Cabinet Company and the General Fireproofing Company, both in Ohio, and had received several patents for all or portions of sheet-metal structures he had designed. He was aware of the benefits of steel furniture. At the turn of the twentieth century, mergers were leading to larger companies, larger office and administrative staffs, larger buildings, and an increased office furniture market. However, while new brick and steel construction techniques were making building exteriors less flammable and skyscrapers a reality, office interiors, cluttered with wooden furniture and other combustibles, were still being heated and lighted by open flame appliances. An added fire risk was the use of smoking materials; ashes dumped into the popular wicker wastebaskets caused many office fires. A fire in one of the higher structures was an inferno firefighters could not effectively battle.

Wege persuaded the investors, some of whom were with the Macey Furniture Company, that steel office furniture's strength, durability, and fireproof qualities made sense. The Macey Company agreed to purchase and market all of the shelving, tables, files, and fireproof safes manufactured by the new company. Metal Office Furniture Company's first officers were A. W. Hompe, president (also president of Macey Company); Peter M. Wege, vice-president and general manager; and Walter D. Idema, secretary-treasurer. Two years later, when the agreement with Macey was severed, Hompe stepped down, Wege became president and general manager, Fred W. Tobey became vice-president, and Idema remained secretary-treasurer. David D. Hunting joined Metal Office in 1914 to establish a marketing network. He became secretary in 1920, and the Wege-Idema-Hunting management team was set for the next three decades.

On August 7, 1912, the first filing cases and safes made by Metal Office were delivered to Macey sales outlets. By the end of the year, Metal Office had $13,000 in sales, and by the end of the first full year of operation, it had $76,000 in sales, an amount equal to the initial capitalization.

In 1914 Metal Office hit on an idea that solved the problem of carelessly flicked cigar and cigarette ashes: The Victor, a fireproof steel wastebasket. Touted for its strength and durability, the wastebasket could also be color coordinated with other furniture. Victor became an official trademark in 1918 and eventually became an expanded line of products. Metal Office had two other unusual products that enjoyed short-term popularity. The Liberty Bond Box was used for storing war bonds, while the Servidor was a double-doored product into which hotel guests put room service orders or clothes to be cared for. Service personnel tended to the guests' needs from the hall side without disturbing them.

The concern over fire safety led to Metal Office's first government contract and to its becoming a desk manufacturer. While businesses were slow to replace wooden furniture with the more expensive metal furniture, government architects specified it, citing the fire threat. David Hunting heard that metal furniture was to be used in the renovation of the 50-year-old Boston Customs House. Although Metal Office did not make desks, Hunting conferred with Wege and Idema and they agreed Metal

Office should submit a bid. The bid was for 192 desks at $44 each, for a total of $8,485.49.

After the lowest bidder's product was deemed unacceptable, Metal Office, as the next lowest bidder, was asked to send a sample of a desk for examination. Wege and Chris Sonne designed a desk, and a prototype was built to send to Washington the next week. Unlike the low bidder's desk, which was held together by loose bolts, theirs had welds and crimped metal and did not come apart during shipping. Metal Office got the order and filled it in 90 days.

In 1921 Metal Office hired media consultant Jim Turner to convince the public that wooden office furniture was a thing of the past. Turner coined the name Steelcase to describe the indestructible quality of the furniture. Steelcase was officially registered as a trademark in August 1921. Because office furnishers never entirely gave up their perception that offices, and especially executive offices, should have wooden furniture, the company pursued ways to make metal furniture more attractive. It implemented spray-painting in 1924 to give furniture a smoother, more even coat and in 1928 developed a wood-graining process. Metal Office manufactured fashionable roll-top desks in oak and mahogany wood-grain on metal.

During the 1930s Metal Office produced some attention-getting furniture, including a futuristic, island-based desk displayed at the World's Fair in Chicago. In 1937 the company collaborated with world-famous architect Frank Lloyd Wright to produce furniture for the "great workroom" for the offices of S. C. Johnson & Sons in Racine, Wisconsin.

Over the years, Metal Office/Steelcase won several more government contracts. During World War II, the brunt of the forced cutback in the use of steel by metal furniture manufacturers was tempered by the U.S. Navy's order for "Shipboard Furniture." The company had to recruit plant personnel to meet increased production and the loss of workers to the military. Many of the new employees were the mothers, wives, and sweethearts of soldiers.

A piece of Steelcase naval furniture was used for the historic signing of the surrender documents ending World War II. A mahogany table had been prepared on September 2, 1945, for the signing by Japanese Foreign Minister Mamoru Shigemitsu and the Supreme Commander of the Allies, General Douglas MacArthur, but the table was too small for the documents. The ceremony was completed on a Steelcase rectangular folding table from the crew's mess, spread with a green tablecloth.

Metal Office utilized what it had learned in building furniture with interchangeable parts for ships when it introduced the first standard sizing of desks based on a 15-inch multiple in 1949. The Multiple 15 concept became an industry standard; it also served as the basis for other modular furniture developed by Steelcase.

In 1954 the Metal Office Furniture Company officially changed its name to Steelcase Inc. Walter Idema thought the name change would eliminate confusion with the products of other metal furniture manufacturers. That same year, Steelcase became the first in the industry to offer office furniture in colors, announcing Sunshine Styling colors inspired by the twilight haze over the Arizona mountains: Desert Sage, Autumn Haze, and Blond Tan. The innovation was made possible by acrylic paints that made it easier for workers to change colors. In 1959 the company introduced Convertibles—auxiliary pieces with rigid steel frames and suspended cabinets and pedestals that permitted working arrangements to be individually designed to suit each worker—and Convertiwalls—steel and glass panels attached at slotted posts, which could be wired for telephone or electrical connections.

In the 1960s Steelcase product engineers developed Chromattecs, a method devised to soften the mirror-like finish of traditional chrome. The resulting new line featured "matte-textured acrylics and classic personal fabrics." In 1965 Steelcase established itself as the industry leader, achieving record sales volume for the United States and Canada. Mobiles, introduced in 1968, was the first product incorporating the concept of systems furniture. The line combined the features of Multiple 15, Sunshine Styling, and Convertibles to create more private workstations, completely furnished with desks, shelving, walls, and broadside dividers.

In 1971 Steelcase offered its first comprehensive systems furniture line, Movable Walls, and, in 1973, introduced the Series 9000 Systems Furniture line. The Designs in Wood line, introduced in 1972, addressed the negative perception of metal furniture. The furniture featured exterior hardwood paneling with drawer and pedestal interiors of steel.

In 1975 Steelcase brought out the Sensor chair, the first office chair to sense and support the body's movements according to the occupant's height, weight, and preference.

In 1992, looking to a future relying increasingly on teamwork and wireless technology, Steelcase demonstrated Harbor, a prototype product of the office of the future, and Commons, a concept that uses open space to quickly reconfigure into an ad hoc meeting area. The company also announced a partnership with Motorola, Inc. to develop wireless technology in office furniture.

Steelcase has won numerous design awards, including 26 between 1987 and 1992. The company also won the Distinguished Engineering Award from the Consulting Engineers Council of Michigan for an innovative steam-generating, waste-disposal system and a national award from the President's Council on Environmental Quality for a process that curbed pollutants in its painting process.

In the early 1990s direct descendants of Metal Office Furniture Company founders held many key executive positions in the successor firm, Steelcase Inc. They included Robert Pew (who married the daughter of investor Henry Idema), chairman; his son, Robert Pew III, president of Steelcase North American operations; Peter Wege, vice-chairman; and William Crawford, president of a design subsidiary. Only two Steelcase chief executives, Frank Merlotti and Jerry Myers, were not descended from the founders.

Frank Merlotti, who came up through the manufacturing ranks, is credited with changing how the company approached the process of product development and production. The World Class Manufacturing (WCM) plan implemented during his tenure has five principles: quality, faster throughput, elimination of waste, product group focus, and employee involvement or empowerment. The plan was put into practice at the $111 million Corporate Development Center opened in 1989. The pyramid-shaped facility has ten laboratories, giving it the most comprehensive research capability in the office furniture industry. It also provides an interdisciplinary creative environment where designers, engineers, marketers, and others work in neighborhoods focused on the development of a particular product.

Steelcase's status as a privately held company was threatened in 1992, when an estimated one million shares of the rarely traded stock passed to the brokerage firm of Robert W. Baird & Co. from the estate of an heiress of one of the founding families. Baird sold the shares to outsiders, including one buyer who accumulated 30,000 shares and distributed them to allies in an attempt to force Steelcase to go public. The descendants of the founders joined ranks and used a reverse stock split to force the outsiders to sell their Steelcase stock back to the company.

Following a 20-year boom in office furniture sales propelled by an increasing number of office jobs, Steelcase experienced flat sales in the early 1990s because of a recession and widespread corporate downsizing. Although Steelcase had to make cutbacks and short-term layoffs, it was determined to avoid the fate of the automakers. The company embarked on aggressive product development, broadened its overseas base, and continued to keep the needs of its employees and dealers a priority.

Steelcase: The First 75 Years states, "Steelcase was founded because new materials and new needs offered greater business opportunities. And these are the very ideas that have helped the company become an industry leader. In tandem with this quest to meet constantly changing needs is a strong commitment to every single member of the Steelcase family. That commitment is as fresh today as it was on that spring evening in 1912 when Metal Office Furniture Company was born."

Principal Subsidiaries: Alternative Office Furniture, Inc.; Atelier International, Ltd.; Attwood Corporation; Brayton International, Inc.; DesignTex Fabrics; Details; Hedberg Data Systems, Inc.; Interior Woodworking Corporation; Metropolitan Furniture Corporation; MFR Corporation; Steelcase Japan Ltd.; Stowe Davis; Strafor S.A. (France; owns Pohlschroeder GmbH, Germany; A.F. Sistemas, Spain; Gordon Russell, England; Euroseel, Portugal; Sanash, Morocco); Vecta Contract; Wigand Corporation.

Further Reading: Servaas, Lois, *Steelcase: The First 75 Years*, Grand Rapids: Steelcase Inc., 1987; "A Glimpse of the 'Flex' Future, At Steelcase, Offering Variable Hours, Pay and Perks Benefits the Firm and Its Workers," *Newsweek*, August 1, 1988; Moskowitz, Milton, Robert Levering and Michael Katz, editors, *Everybody's Business: A Field Guide to the 400 Leading Companies in America*, New York: Doubleday, A Currency Book, 1990; "The Best of 1989," *Business Week*, January 8, 1990; "Office Furniture Firms in Michigan Design to Ensure Business Future," *Flint Journal*, November 11, 1990; Nelson-Horchler, Joani, "Take-home Dinners (From the Company Cafeteria)," *Industry Week*, December 3, 1990; Morgan, Hal, and Kerry Tucker, *Companies That Care: The Most Family-Friendly Companies in America—What They Offer and How They Got That Way*, New York: Simon and Schuster, 1991; Sheridan, John N., "Frank Merlotti: A Master of Empowerment," *Industry Week*, January 7, 1991; "Steelcase Uses Leaves of Absence of 60 Days to Avert Big Layoffs," *Detroit Free Press*, April 5, 1991; Verespej, Michael A., "America's Best Plants: IW's Second Annual Survey. Steelcase: Grand Rapids," *Industry Week*, October 21, 1991; "The Eternal Coffee Break," *Economist*, March 7, 1992; Shellum, Bernie, "The Steelcase Way; Its Stock Battle Over, The Office Furniture Maker Forges Ahead," *Detroit Free Press*, June 8, 1992; Lyne, Jack, "Steelcase CEO Jerry Myers: Creating the Office of the Future—Now," *Site Selection and Industrial Development*, October 1992; "Steelcase Lays Off 460 More Workers," *Flint Journal*, January 21, 1993; "4 Of Top 100 in State," *Flint Journal*, January 23, 1993.

—Doris Morris Maxfield

SUN-DIAMOND GROWERS OF CALIFORNIA

5568 Gibraltar Drive
Pleasanton, California 94588-8544
U.S.A.
(510) 463-8200
Fax: (510) 463-7492

Private Company
Incorporated: 1980
Employees: 2,500
Sales: $623.2 million
SICs: 0723 Crop Preparation Services for Market; 5149
   Groceries & Related Products

Sun-Diamond Growers of California is one of the largest specialty commodity producers in the world. Once described by a *Business Week* correspondent as a "corporate fruit-salad," the company is an amalgamation of five agricultural cooperatives—Diamond Walnut Growers, Sun-Maid Growers of California, Sunsweet Growers, Valley Fig Growers, and Hazlenut Growers of Oregon—who have pooled their distribution and marketing resources. By themselves, each member of the Sun-Diamond alliance is an eminent company in its own line of business; together, they form a megacooperative with significant marketing resources at its disposal.

Sun-Diamond's history involves the coming together of individual growers to form cooperatives, which in turn formed larger cooperatives. The first of Sun-Diamond's current members to confederate were Diamond Walnut and Sunsweet, both of which were already over fifty years old when they joined forces in 1974.

Diamond Walnut was organized in 1912 by citrus and walnut grower Charles Teague, who had also been a founder of another highly successful agricultural cooperative, Sunkist Growers. The company was originally known as the California Walnut Growers Association (CWGA) and sought to stabilize walnut prices. Success came early to CWGA, aided somewhat by the outbreak of World War I, which eliminated competition from imported French walnuts. In 1918 CWGA became the first producer of walnuts to pack shelled nutmeats in airtight metal cans, and, in 1925, it began using its trademark diamond-shaped logo, stamping it on the shell of every walnut that it sold.

The outbreak of World War II posed a threat to CWGA by cutting it off from its export markets, but domestic demand helped take up the slack. The federal government purchased 1.5 million pounds of walnuts as part of its Lend-Lease program; in addition, the military used the protein-rich nutmeats as a dietary substitute to compensate for the general scarcity of meat. The supply of walnuts quickly overtook demand after the end of the war, and this oversupply required more aggressive marketing in the postwar period. In 1956 CWGA changed its name to Diamond Walnut Growers to associate itself more closely with its trademark.

Sunsweet traces its history back to 1917, when some California fruit growers formed a cooperative named California Prune and Apricot Growers in an effort to raise and stabilize what had been disastrously low prices for their commodities. Immediately, the cooperative began nationwide advertising and marketing under the brand name Sunsweet. Although the company lost members during the boom times of the 1920s, as general confidence in market conditions prompted a desire for independence, it regained many members during the Great Depression when companies sought safety in numbers. In 1934 the cooperative joined with fruit juice company Duffy-Mott to produce and market Sunsweet prune juice.

Already smarting from the worldwide depression, California Prune and Apricot took another heavy blow in 1933 when the German government banned imported fruit. Exports to Germany had accounted for as much as half of California's annual prune sales since before World War I. The company sought to improve sales with improved packaging and high profile domestic advertising campaigns, and once the United States entered World War II, the demand for dried fruit products rose again. However, as with its future associates in the walnut industry, chronic oversupply and depressed commodity prices burdened California Prune and Apricot in the postwar period. As a response, the company increased its membership in 1959 and in 1960 changed its name to Sunsweet Growers.

By the mid-1970s, both Diamond Walnut and Sunsweet had become preeminent in their respective domains. Diamond Walnut processed and marketed just over half of California's walnut crop, while Sunsweet handled about one third of the state's prune crop. Both companies felt that combined marketing would be of further benefit, and in 1974 they banded together to form Diamond/Sunsweet. The two companies did not merge assets and liabilities, but did combine their marketing operations. Diamond Walnut president and general manager A. L. Buffington became CEO of the separate cooperatives, and headquarters were established in Stockton, California.

Such combinations between agricultural cooperatives were seen as necessary in a time of increasing competition from overseas, as well as from other large cooperatives in the United States, and Diamond/Sunsweet would soon show that it felt even further growth would be necessary for it to maintain its competitive edge. Seeking an alliance that would strengthen the marketing punch of its famous Sun-Maid raisins, Sun-Maid Growers of California began courting Diamond/Sunsweet. In 1980 its sales, distribution, and administrative functions were combined with those of Diamond and Sunsweet. Sun-Maid president Frank Light became president and CEO of Sun-Diamond Growers of California. Valley Fig Growers, a cooperative of California fig growers, also joined the alliance at this time. As with the Diamond/Sunsweet alliance, the member companies pooled their marketing operations but retained autonomy over their own assets and liabilities, although the agreement substantially centralized executive power by making Light CEO of all four member cooperatives, as well as of the new concern.

Sun-Maid had a long history not unlike that of its new allies. It was formed in 1912 under the name California Associated Raisin Company (CARC) to pool advertising resources and attempt to bring price stability to a market that had suffered from highly variable commodity prices. CARC debuted with a spectacular marketing gimmick, sending a train pulling sixty raisin-laden freight cars to Chicago, with each car displaying a banner with the slogan, ''Raisins Grown by 6,000 California Growers.'' In 1915 the company introduced its longtime brand name and also its trademark, a smiling young woman wearing a red bonnet and backlit by a yellow sunburst—the Sun-Maid. In 1922, CARC changed its name to Sun-Maid Growers to link itself more explicitly with its famous logo.

Shortly thereafter, however, the Sun-Maid cooperative declared bankruptcy and was nearly dissolved. It recovered only to face financial disaster again during the depths of the Great Depression. After World War II, when both the federal and California governments acted to stabilize the raisin market, Sun-Maid once again became a steady and profitable organization. Despite its troubles, the Sun-Maid remained a popular trademark with consumers and perhaps the most famous logo in the dried fruit industry.

Sun-Maid's alliance with Diamond/Sunsweet and Valley Fig Growers produced a company with nearly $500 million in annual sales, and revenues grew sharply in the years immediately following the formation of Sun-Diamond despite a national recession and general crop oversupply. The new company owed much of its success to energetic marketing; under Frank Light's direction, Sun-Diamond significantly increased its annual advertising budget to $14 million. It also put considerable emphasis on developing new products, such as raisin bread and English muffins sold under the Sun-Maid name, and new applications for waste parts, such as distilling substandard raisins and prune pits into alcohol or selling them as cattle feed.

Sun-Diamond continued to expand, adding a relatively small cooperative, Hazlenut Growers of Oregon, to its ranks in 1984. It had also become a Fortune 500 company early in the decade. At the same time, however, sales began to slow, from $522 million in 1983 to $487 million in 1985, and low commodity prices continued to plague the company. The company also fell victim to international trade battles, as protective and retaliatory tariffs imposed by the European community cut into its export business.

Adding to these difficulties, Sun-Diamond found itself in a financial dilemma in 1985, when internal audits discovered a series of accounting errors worth $43 million. In August of that year an accounting review found that Diamond Walnut had overreported its profits for fiscal 1985 by $4.7 million, distributing more money to its member growers than it should have. Further review revealed that an inventory of unfinished walnuts sitting in Diamond Walnut's storage sheds had been overvalued by $11 million. Finally, in November, Sun-Maid discovered that it had overreported its pool proceeds by $27.3 million and had paid its members accordingly.

The loss of members' equity that followed these errors and their discovery hit Sun-Maid particularly hard. The venerable raisin cooperative suffered a mass defection, as 29 percent of its member growers chose not to renew their membership contracts after the financial disclosures. These growers accounted for about one-third of Sun-Maid's crop, forcing the company to buy processed raisins from independent growers to make up for the shortfall. Diamond Walnut suffered far less—only 50 of its 2,700 growers defected—in part because fewer of its members had their contracts up for renewal, but also because daunting conditions in the walnut market made it risky to abandon the economies of scale that a large cooperative offered.

Frank Light's tenure ended late in 1985 and the company entered a period of restructuring as the cooperatives evaluated their needs and considered revised designs for the agency agreement that defined their relationship. By 1987 the process was complete and a leaner, stronger Sun-Diamond emerged. This is the Sun-Diamond that exists today under the leadership of its president, Larry Busboom, as a service organization rather than a management organization. Greater autonomy was returned to the cooperatives, and each now has its own marketing team. Sun-Diamond provides a consolidated sales and distribution network for the cooperatives' consumer product line, and has earned a position of prominence in the agricultural commodity field. It showed healthy sales growth in the early 1990s, topping $600 million in both 1991 and 1992.

In addition, the efficacy of the concept behind Sun-Diamond has been proven. The collective safety and the economies of scale that it creates seem essential in an industry in which variable commodity prices, competition from overseas and large domestic concerns, and the vagaries of international trade can all have considerable impact on one's ability to do business. Perhaps even more important, the impact of consolidated representation for the leading brands in the business has become a powerful tool for success in today's marketplace.

Principal Subsidiaries: Diamond Walnut Growers; Hazlenut Growers of Oregon; Sun-Maid Growers of California; Sunsweet Growers; Valley Fig Growers.

Further Reading: ''What Makes Sun-Diamond Grow,'' *Business Week,* August 9, 1982; Keppel, Bruce. ''Sun-Diamond Co-op: Harvest of Discontent,'' *Los Angeles Times,* May 11, 1986.

—Douglas Sun

SUN MICROSYSTEMS, INC.

2550 Garcia Avenue
Mountain View, California 94043
U.S.A.
(415) 960-1300
Fax: (415) 969-9131

Public Company
Incorporated: 1982
Employees: 12,812
Sales: $3.58 billion
Stock Exchanges: NASDAQ/National Market System
SICs: 3571 Electronic Computers; 7372 Prepackaged
  Software

One of the fastest growing start-up companies of the 1980s, Sun Microsystems became a leader in the highly competitive arena of workstation computers within six years of its founding. Sun Microsystems, which took an unconventional approach to the computer business, pioneered the use of shared software and hardware components among competing workstation manufacturers in order to create industry standards.

Sun began as a computer project designed by Andreas Bechtolsheim while he was a graduate student at Stanford. His computer was a modification of a relatively new kind of computer, the workstation, which, like the PC (personal computer), can be utilized by single users. The workstation, however, provides users with more power. Workstations are designed for network integration and equipped with high-resolution graphics, and are fast enough to handle demanding engineering and graphics tasks. Unlike the first workstations, which had been introduced to the market only the previous year by Apollo Computer, Bechtolsheim's workstation used off-the-shelf parts, thus making it more affordable.

Bechtolsheim not only shunned custom-made hardware, but also broke with the industry tradition of adhering to proprietary operating system software. Instead, he hoped to enable different workstations brands running on a common operating system to share data. AT&T's UNIX operating system was the obvious choice; it could operate on a wide variety of computers and was already very popular among scientists and engineers because it enabled users to perform several tasks on screen at once. He began selling licenses for his computer, called the Sun

(which stood for Stanford University Network) at $10,000 each in 1981.

Within a year Bechtolsheim's project attracted the interest of Stanford MBA graduates Vinod Khosla and Scott McNealy, each of whom had some experience in the computer business. They were named president and director of manufacturing, respectively, of Sun Microsystems, Inc., upon its founding in February 1982. Bechtolsheim, who was the brains behind the hardware, became vice-president of technology. One of the first people the founders hired was Bill Joy, a Berkeley Ph.D. well known for his design of a popular version of the UNIX operating system. His task was to design the company's software.

Sun's use of standard hardware components and standard operating system software produced short-term payoffs for the fledgling company. Sun's workstations, unlike those of industry pioneer Apollo, operated on UNIX and from the outset networked easily with the hardware and software already on the market. In addition, although Sun's design could easily be copied, the strategy of using existing technologies allowed Sun to enter the market quickly with a low-priced machine. Sales grew rapidly as a result. Within six months of incorporation the company became profitable.

Sun's first workstations, the Sun-1 and Sun-2, were instant successes, achieving $8 million in sales the first year, 80 percent of which came from sales to the university market. Sun's founders, however, had their eyes on the mainstream technical market, dominated at that time by the major computer companies. Sun's first big success in this area was the contract it signed in its second year with ComputerVision, a major CAD (computer-aided design) systems supplier that had decided to drop its proprietary hardware in favor of a new platform for its software products. ComputerVision had decided to sign a contract with Apollo, but, aggressively courted by Sun executives, the company reversed its decision and accepted a counteroffer made by Sun. Thus, Sun established its reputation as a serious player in the computer business and simultaneously earned the envious wrath of its competitors.

Expanding rapidly, Sun moved out of its original location in Santa Clara to a larger building in Mountain View, which became its headquarters as the company expanded. In January 1984 Sun opened its first European sales office. In that same year Sun established a subsidiary, Sun Federal, to serve the government market. By 1991 Sun Federal was shipping more than half the workstations ordered by local, state, and federal government. Sun's informal corporate culture attracted engineers from the top universities. At the same time Sun hired additional managers who had experience working at other leading computer companies. Also in 1984 McNealy took over as president, as Khosla realized his dream of being able to retire as a millionaire before the age of 30.

During this period Sun continued to promote open systems. In 1984 it began broadly licensing Joy's design of a distributed file system software, called NFS (Network File System), that allowed data to be shared among many users in a network regardless of processor type, operating system, or communications system. NFS soon became an industry standard. Sun was so successful with this strategy that in 1984 Apollo was forced to abandon its exclusive design and instead produce a system that operated with standard software.

Between 1985 and 1989 Sun was the fastest growing company in the United States, according to *Forbes* magazine, with a compound annual growth rate of 145 percent. It had become a public company with its successful initial public offering in 1986. The following year Sun surpassed Apollo in sales, and by the close of that year it had become the leader in workstation sales. Only six years after incorporation Sun achieved $1 billion in annual sales. Part of the reason for Sun's stupendous early success was the fact that the product in which it chose to specialize, the workstation, was becoming popular just at the time Sun entered the market. Furthermore, because it was a workstation industry pioneer, it established strong relations with the most sought-after clients and the most important software developers. Sun's corporate strategy also enabled it to offer its new customers the latest technology, while its competitors had to support established clients reluctant to scrap their outdated computer systems. Industry-wide, sales of workstations rapidly displaced those of minicomputers, and the large computer companies that sold these had to compensate by offering workstations as well.

In the increasingly competitive market for workstations, where the speed of the computer is an important factor, Sun developed an even faster workstation in the late 1980s. Based on a different kind of microprocessor, this new product utilized RISC (reduced instruction set computing) architecture. RISC was simpler yet quicker than the then-prevailing CISC (complex instruction set computing) architecture. As had been the case with the workstation itself, Sun was not the first company to design a RISC-based computer (IBM had introduced a model in 1986). Sun made improvements on it, however, and designed its own RISC architecture called SPARC (scalable performance architecture); it soon dominated the market of RISC-based workstations. In April 1989 Sun introduced its SPARCstation 1, a small, low-cost desktop computer with expanded capabilities. SPARCstation 1 employed new levels of integration and miniaturized the essential electronic components. By the end of the year Sun could claim to be the world's largest supplier of RISC-based computers, with the SPARCstation the most popular workstation on the market.

As Sun was not a manufacturer of its own processors or computer chips, in 1987 it licensed Bechtolsheim's SPARC design to a few silicon chip manufacturers, which then began to produce them for Sun's needs. Then, in keeping with its tradition of the "open system," in July 1988 Sun announced that it would offer its RISC design for license to other computer makers in recognition that for RISC to succeed it needed to become a pervasive presence in the marketplace. By licensing SPARC it stimulated low-cost, high-volume production of SPARC systems and thus increased the number of third party applications available. In 1989 licensing of SPARC was turned over to a new coalition of computer companies called SPARC International, an independent testing organization founded in nearby Menlo Park, California. McNealy hoped SPARC would produce the same kind of phenomenal growth for workstations that IBM brought to PCs a decade earlier when it permitted others to copy its standard PC hardware and software designs. In April 1991,

however, Sun told its dealers it would prefer that they not sell SPARC clones. Sun claimed that small dealers would have difficulty succeeding against Sun in selling "clones" and were thus encouraging the smaller outfits to sell complementary "compatible" products, whereupon competitors charged hypocrisy in Sun's call for "open systems." Although it did not at first entirely convince other workstation companies to copy Sun's SPARC design, Sun was single-handedly making SPARC one of the international standards. By 1992 all its new workstations were based only on SPARC.

As Sun was developing its SPARCstation computer, it was also making moves to ensure the presence of improved software to take advantage of it. In 1987 Sun signed an agreement with AT&T to develop an enhanced version of the UNIX operating system to make it the software standard for workstations. AT&T even took a 19 percent equity investment in Sun in 1988 (which it sold off in 1991 upon the NCR acquisition). The product that emerged in late 1989 established a de facto high-end UNIX standard (System V Release 4.0). It was at this time that competing computer manufacturers were settling on UNIX as a universal operating system, and RISC-based hardware proved the obvious supporting standard because of its speed in handling the complexities of UNIX and its suitability for the demands of the new user interfaces and applications software. Sun Microsystems, with its RISC-based SPARCstation and involvement in upgrading UNIX, was well-positioned to take advantage of the trend. "Sun is the strongest candidate to carry the UNIX banner. It has momentum. If it can keep up the recent good work, it can continue to dominate the workstation market," wrote technology consultant Richard Shaffer in *Forbes* in 1990.

Despite the success of the SPARCstation, the year of its introduction, 1989, marked a temporary financial setback for Sun. It lost money during the difficult product transition period by launching the new SPARCstation 1 while at the same time trying to support two older product lines using different technologies. Meanwhile, it was encountering difficulties managing the chaos resulting from its explosive growth. Problems included rapid personnel hiring and training, communications problems, and reorganization pains. A new management information system did not accurately forecast parts needed to fill orders, and demand for SPARCstation 1 was misjudged. That year Sun also temporarily lost its market lead in workstation shipments when Hewlett-Packard purchased Apollo and combined their market shares.

Things improved rapidly the following year. The company reduced its product families from three to one, the SPARC systems. The SPARCstation 2, released in November 1990, had the power of a minicomputer. The financial outlook improved, with revenues up by 40 percent over the previous year, and for the first time in a long while Sun was spending less than it was taking in. By the end of 1990 Sun claimed more than a third of the total market share of workstation shipments, leaving Hewlett-Packard a distant second at 20 percent. Sun held a similar share of the world market of RISC technology with its SPARC product line. As the market continued to grow, Sun aimed at expanding at a similar rate, maintaining the same market share. Meanwhile, its stock doubled from a low of $14 in August 1989 to $37 in July 1990.

At the beginning of the 1990s Sun further widened its market objectives for its workstations beyond engineers, software developers, and chip designers, targeting commercial users such as insurance companies, brokerages, airlines, and publishers. In the spring of 1990 Sun announced a new line of low-end products designed to capture an increasing share of the vast commercial computing market, which was dominated by minicomputers and high-end PCs. Sun became the first workstation producer to introduce a low-end system for under $5,000. A month later the company announced the first color workstation for less than $10,000. It also began distributing its products through respected PC resellers. Sun was able to persuade software publishers to adapt over 2,800 programs for SPARC computer systems by 1991, including such major programs as Lotus 1-2-3, WordPerfect, and dBase IV, thus substantially broadening Sun's commercial market. By the end of 1992, when over a third of Sun's sales were to commercial as opposed to technical markets, there were more applications for Sun workstations than for any other UNIX workstation.

Business strategies in 1990 included streamlining the organization into two core management groups. Custom job-shop manufacturing was eliminated, allowing high volume from a single, elegantly designed product line to permit Sun's manufacturing system to attain economies of scale. More of the working capital and investment risk was pushed onto outside contractors that produce the printed circuit boards, boxes, and screens, leaving Sun with the relatively simple tasks of assembly and testing. It stayed out of the lucrative high-end of the workstation market to build on volume and market share in the lower end. By the close of 1990 Sun was one of the top ten computer hardware companies in the country, but unlike most of the others, it sold only workstations and servers: it did not sell PCs, minicomputers, or mainframes.

Sun had in the past attempted to build a critical mass for its technology and establish a de facto standard in hardware. In September 1991 it aimed at a similar broadening of its influence in operating system software when it announced plans to make the Sun OS operating system, a version of UNIX, run on more computers than just its own, including those running on Intel microprocessors. It was at this time that Kodak sold its UNIX software unit, Interactive Systems, to Sun. Interactive supplied UNIX System V release 4.0 for Intel-based computers, and thus the purchase of Interactive endowed Sun with needed expertise in the arena of Intel-based UNIX systems. Interactive had already previously agreed to install Sun's operating system, Solaris 2.0, onto Intel X86 architecture. With more computers using Sun's operating system, it would become easier to link Sun workstations with others in a network, and more software could be written for Sun's operating system. Sun needed a constant flow of new programs to keep its workstations sales booming, particularly now that it was facing challenges in hardware.

In 1991 Sun followed IBM and Apple by becoming a hybrid software-hardware company. This new strategy was an attempt to offset shrinking profit margins on hardware by selling software. A reorganization of the company transferred its software-selling operations to two new subsidiaries, SunSoft and Sun Technology Enterprises. SunSoft sells Sun's operating system to computer manufacturers, while Sun Technology Enterprises

supplies software for SPARC machines, such as networking, printing, imaging, and PC emulation products.

At the same time other core businesses and functions were also reorganized into subsidiaries. The largest of these was Sun Microsystems Computer Corporation, which McNealy headed in addition to his post of CEO of the parent company. Each subsidiary was set up as a separate profit and loss center having its own management to oversee product development, manufacturing, marketing, and sales.

By 1991 Sun's product line was beginning to show its age as competitors brought out machines superior in both price and performance. In the early 1990s the workstation market competition grew increasingly fierce, as it was one of the few areas of the computer industry still enjoying sales growth of more than 20 percent annually in 1991. One of the reasons for this growth was the RISC technology and the recent emphasis on serving the general-business computing market. As Sun was trying to enter the office market, however, office computing companies such as IBM, Apple, Compaq, Digital Equipment, and Hewlett-Packard were pursuing the technical market, and Sun's move into the broader commercial computing market put it into competition with the bigger computer manufacturers on their home turf. Sun has also reversed itself by moving into the high-end of the workstation market, where performance speeds are essential, using multiprocessors (two or more processors chained together) and special software. It introduced its first multiprocessor, the SPARCserver 600NO series, and new operating software for it in 1991.

By mid-1992, Sun had 21 subsidiaries around the world providing sales, service, and technical support, and overseas sales accounted for more than half of its revenues. Manufacturing was carried out at three sites: Milpitas, California; Westford, Massachusetts; and Linlithgow, Scotland. In February 1992 Sun became the first U.S. company to establish a significant presence in Moscow. Sun established an agreement with a group of 50 Russian scientists, including the Russian scientist who had developed supercomputers in the Soviet Union, who work as contractors with the company.

With such a successful first ten years for Sun, observers have expressed doubts about the company's ability to maintain its high growth rate into the late 1990s, especially in light of the proliferation of competitive workstations being offered by other manufacturers. However, although a slower rate of growth for both workstation shipments and revenue was already evident in 1992–93, Sun has laid the groundwork for establishing its SPARC processors and operating system as industry standards, and should be able take advantage of the overall growth in the workstation market for years to come.

Principal Subsidiaries: Sun Microsystems Computer Corporation; SunSoft, Inc.; Sun Technology Enterprises, Inc.; Sun Express, Inc.; Sun Microsystems Laboratories, Inc.

Further Reading: Shaffer, Richard A., ''The Case for Sun,'' *Forbes,* April 16, 1990; Fisher, Susan E., ''Vendors Court Reseller Partners as Workstations Go Mainstream,'' *PC Week,* July 30, 1990; Wrubel, Robert, ''Top Gun Once More,'' *Finance World,* October 2, 1990; Hof, Robert D., ''Where Sun

Means to be a Bigger Fireball,'' *Business Week,* April 15, 1991; Markoff, John, ''The Smart Alecks at Sun Are Regrouping,'' *New York Times,* April 28, 1991; ''Sell 'em Cheap,'' *Economist,* May 11, 1991; Hof, Robert D., ''Why Sun Can't Afford to Shine Alone,'' *Business Week,* September 9, 1991; Morrissey, Jane, ''Sun Negotiating for Interactive Unix Technology,'' *PC Week,* September 23, 1991; *Sun Microsystems: The 10-Year Success Story,* Mountain View, CA: Sun Microsystems, Inc., June 1992.

—Heather Behn Hedden

SUNDSTRAND CORPORATION

4949 Harrison Avenue
P.O. Box 7003
Rockford, Illinois 61125-7003
U.S.A.
(815) 226-6000
Fax: (815) 226-2699

Public Company
Incorporated: June 1926 as Sundstrand Machine Tool
   Company
Employees: 12,800
Sales: $1.669 billion
Stock Exchanges: New York Midwest Pacific
SICs: 3728 Aircraft Parts & Equipment Nec; 3724 Aircraft
   Engines & Engine Parts; 3812 Search & Navigation
   Equipment; 3764 Space Propulsion Units & Parts

Sundstrand is one of the world's leading manufacturers of parts and machinery for the aircraft industry. While it also produces gear drives, pumps, compressors, and electronic systems, Sundstrand derives nearly two-thirds of its sales revenue from aerospace projects. In light of shrinking defense budgets, the company has moved to reduce the volume of its military business which, in 1992, was slightly less than a quarter of total sales.

The earliest predecessor to the modern Sundstrand Corporation is the Rockford Tool Company, established in 1905 in the predominately Swedish town of Rockford, Illinois. The company was founded by an inventor and machinist named Levin Faust, who had invented a small metal chuck for carving furniture. Faust invited two young tool makers, Elmer Lutzhoff and Swan Anderson, to become partners in the venture by investing $500 each.

Although the carving chuck sold well, it failed to provide enough profit to support the company, so the three partners turned their attention to another part of furniture manufacture, designing a belt sander that proved much more successful. That year Faust also designed a buffing device that later became the company's most popular product. With sales increasing, the partners decided they needed additional capital for expansion and for funding new products, and they convinced Hugo Olson, an insurance cashier and bookkeeper, to invest $1,000 and become a full partner in the enterprise, serving as its financial advisor.

In 1909 the Rockford Tool Company gained a neighbor in its facilities, the Rockford Milling Machine Company. This company, owned by Oscar Sundstrand and his brother-in-law Edwin Cedarleaf, was also rapidly expanding and retained Hugo Olson as its financial advisor. In 1910 the Rockford Milling Machine Company relocated to a larger building where there was more room for the growing business, and the following year, on Olson's advice, the Rockford Tool Company moved to a building across the street.

In 1914 David Sundstrand, Oscar's brother and an employee at the Rockford Milling Machine Company, developed a ten-key adding machine. Its sales become so brisk that Sundstrand formed a subsidiary, Sundstrand Adding Machine Company, to accommodate the business. Eventually, the Sundstrands constructed a new four-story building for the adding machine venture a block north of its own facility.

The Rockford Milling Machine Company and the Rockford Tool Company continued on separate but related paths for nearly ten years when, in 1926, Olson suggested that the two companies merge. They were, after all, in related fields of manufacturing, and might otherwise have become competitors. All agreed, and in June of 1926, the new firm was incorporated as the Sundstrand Machine Tool Company.

In 1927, Hugo Olson was elected president of the company. A few months later, Sundstrand sold its adding machine building and brought all the company's operations under one roof. However, since it was not adequately structured to effectively market the increasingly popular adding machines, Sundstrand eventually sold the rights to the product line to Underwood-Elliot-Fisher, a manufacturer of typewriters and other office equipment. While Sundstrand continued to manufacture the adding machines for another six years, David Sundstrand left the company to work for Underwood.

During this time, in order to raise capital for new investment in plant equipment and engineering talent, the directors of the Sundstrand Machine Tool Company decided to take the company public. Once again able to concentrate on only a single core business, Sundstrand offered shares in the company for sale to investors.

During the early 1930s, Olson saw to it that Sundstrand would follow a course of expansion through diversification. The first step in this direction was an improvement in the manufacturing processes of the company's products. While many of Sundstrand's tools and other implements had been carefully made by hand, this method proved increasingly inadequate for the exact tolerances that were required for precision machine tools. In 1932, Sundstrand machinists began to experiment with hydraulic tools that enabled workers to hold pieces of metal more securely so they could be more accurately fashioned into tools. By 1934, all the company's hand-crank machinery had been replaced with hydraulic devices. Also that year, Sundstrand introduced a line of hydraulic pumps for residential oil-burning furnaces. Soon thereafter, the company introduced a complete line of hydraulic pumps, fluid motors and hydraulic transmission systems.

As a result of the Great Depression, product orders at Sundstrand dwindled, and the company was forced to drastically scale back production and lay off workers. As investment values crashed, Olson announced in Sundstrand's 1932 annual report, that "directors deemed it advisable to change the stated value per share from $17.90 to $5.00 per share." However, on the strength of its tools and hydraulics businesses, and its place as a supplier to primary industries, Sundstrand steadily recovered from the Depression. By 1933, the company was restored to profitability, and well on the way to satisfying its financial obligations. On February 8, 1936, Olson announced that the company "has no bank loans, unfunded debt, and no past due liabilities."

That year, Sundstrand acquired the American Broach and Machine Company, a tool manufacturer based in Ann Arbor, Michigan. Between 1937 and 1939, Sundstrand introduced several new machine tools, including a successful hydraulic "Rigidmill" and automatic lathe. Furthermore, in 1939, with most of American industry thoroughly on the road to recovery, demand for feed pumps, fuel units and controls was high. Sundstrand's fuel unit sales alone quadrupled between 1938 and 1939. By 1940, sales were up to $6.4 million.

Strong growth continued into the early 1940s as the United States began to take a more aggressive stand on international conflicts, particularly Japan's invasion of China. Many industries began to gear up, hopeful of supplying Britain in its war with Germany, and after Japan's surprise attack on Pearl Harbor, the United States itself was thrust into the center of the war. With its tremendous industrial capacity, demand for a full range of machinery skyrocketed.

During World War II, Sundstrand operated two shifts to meet the demand for machine tools and other products, and women were employed in the company's factories for the first time. Under the direction of a government war supply board, Sundstrand turned out aircraft engine and propeller parts, turbine blades, pistons, shell casings, and rifle barrels.

In 1943, Olson told shareholders, "During the year just closed, all our efforts were devoted to the production of equipment for war requirements and this will continue to be our policy until victory has been achieved." In an effort to increase the efficiency of that production, Sundstrand redoubled efforts to improve its machinery and manufacturing processes.

A major product of this research and development effort was the application of hydraulics to aviation engineering. In the final year of the war, and for the remainder of the 1940s, Sundstrand developed several important new products, including a variable displacement hydraulic transmission for aircraft engines. This Constant Speed Drive (CSD) was first applied on the Air Force's ten-engine B-36 bomber, to convert the aircraft's variable engine speed to a constant rate of rotation for driving electric generators. The company's newfound success in aircraft products necessitated a new Sundstrand aviation division. This was a highly profitable line, as aviation and nuclear weaponry became the nation's premier instruments of defense against the threat of Soviet attack. In 1949 Hugo Olson died and his son, Bruce F. Olson, assumed the presidency of Sundstrand.

The 1950s were a decade of expansion for Sundstrand. In 1950, with continued strength in machine tools, pumps and aviation products, Sundstrand marked sales of $16.4 million. As Sundstrand's product line gained an international clientele, Bruce Olson moved to establish the Sundstrand International Corporation, headquartered in France, in 1952. Also that year, the company returned to its founders' roots by establishing an oil pump manufacturing facility in Sweden. In 1954 the company established a separate hydraulics division, with its own manufacturing facility in Rockford. Two years later, Sundstrand opened a plant in Denver, employing 400 people in the manufacture of CSDs for both military and commercial jet aircraft markets. Furthermore, in 1957, Sundstrand built a consolidated machine tool manufacturing facility in Belvidere, Illinois, just south of Rockford. That year, with sales topping $77.5 million, the Sundstrand Machine Tool Company received a listing on the New York Stock Exchange. Two years later, shareholders voted in favor of a proposal to change the name of the company to the Sundstrand Corporation.

During the early 1960s, a team from the company's Hydraulics division experimented with applications of CSD technology on off-highway equipment. To commercialize these applications, the company merged this team with another from its Aviation division, to form a fourth operating unit, Hydro-Transmission. In 1965 Sundstrand built a separate facility in LaSalle, Illinois, especially for this division, and began supplying hydrostatic transmission components to the automotive industry. This operation was subsequently expanded to include yet another facility, located in Ames, Iowa.

In 1967, Sundstrand began an aggressive internal and external product and market diversification campaign. Internally, the company created a fifth division—Sundstrand Fluid Handling, established in 1970—to adapt certain Aviation Division products for use in other industries. The division's first product was a jet engine water injection pump, altered to pump other liquids. This new pump, called Sundyne, found many applications, particularly in the petrochemical industry. The company also established centers to produce new axial gear differentials, integrated drive generators, data recorders, cartridge pneumatic starters and milling machinery.

Externally, Sundstrand acquired United Control, a manufacturer of instruments, aviation entertainment, and avionic and flight data management systems, renaming the company Sundstrand Data Control, Inc. Sundstrand also took over Rudy Manufacturing, a producer of copper tubing, feeders, and coils for heating and cooling systems, renaming it Sundstrand Heat Transfer, Inc. Sundstrand later purchased The Falk Corporation, a leading supplier of enclosed gear drives and couplings.

The 1970s marked a turning point for Sundstrand. After the diversification and acquisition binge of the late 1960s, the company spent much of the next decade consolidating its growth. Rather than increasing sales volumes, Sundstrand concentrated instead on raising earnings, shoring up its balance sheet and maximizing market penetration. Along these lines, Sundstrand divested itself of three non-strategic divisions, selling off its machine tool operation in 1977 and its Sundstrand Compressors unit and fuel oil pump business in 1979.

Also in 1979, Bruce Olson retired, ending a 52-year run in which father and son had built Sundstrand from a small workshop into a $926 billion enterprise. Olson was succeeded as chairperson by James William Ethington, who served one year and was replaced by Evans W. Erikson.

With the massive rearmament program initiated by the Carter administration, and subsequent increases in the military budget under President Reagan, Sundstrand saw tremendous growth in its defense related businesses. This enabled the company to establish several more production sites, including facilities in Auburn, Alabama, Singapore, and Moses Lake and Redmond, Washington.

Sundstrand also took the opportunity to acquire four companies principally involved in defense aviation industry: the Task Corporation, Wulfsberg Electronics, Signatron, and the Sullair Corporation. Strategically, these companies helped to broaden Sundstrand's position as a full-line military contractor. Financially, they proved to be astute investments, as government military programs ballooned and project funding exploded. Awash in military contracts, Sundstrand also sought new opportunities to drum up more civilian business, and in 1985 it purchased the Turbomach Division of San Diego-based Solar Turbines, Inc. The acquisition of Turbomach, a manufacturer of gas turbine auxiliary power units, enabled Sundstrand to better compete in the commercial aircraft ground support market.

In 1987 Sundstrand formed a joint venture with Sauer Getriebe AG, combining the hydraulic power systems operations of both companies. While the venture operated 12 manufacturing facilities worldwide, it failed to meet Sundstrand's goals, leading the company to dissolve its interest in the business in 1989.

In 1988, Sundstrand entered a very dark period in its history. That year, a U. S. defense department auditor named Michael McConnell uncovered evidence of a massive effort by Sundstrand management to defraud the government in its procurement practices. Despite being repeatedly thwarted in his attempts to gain information on the company's government contracts, McConnell succeeded in bringing charges against the company. He charged that executives ordered managers, as a routine matter of practice, to bid low on government contracts to win those contracts, and then shift cost overruns to other existing projects through a complex accounting procedure.

Sundstrand officials initially denied all knowledge of the scheme but later pleaded guilty to the charges. The company was forced to pay back $115 million and was suspended from bidding on subsequent government contracts until remedial measures were in effect. Several Sundstrand executives left the company or were reassigned to other jobs. Chairperson Evans Erikson, who was not implicated in the affair, stepped down in 1988, and was succeeded by Don R. O'Hare.

Additional fallout from the lawsuit occurred when a group of shareholders sued officers and directors for misrepresentation of proxy materials. The suit, which caused considerable damage to the company's relationship with its shareholders, was later settled out of court.

With these unfortunate difficulties clearly behind it, Sundstrand has gone on to rebuild its reputation. Much of this task was accomplished by 1991, when Harry Stonecipher replaced O'Hare as chairperson. In January 1990, Sundstrand acquired the French company Maco-Meudon, a supplier of pneumatic contractor tools to Sullair. A year later, the company purchased the Milton Roy Company, a manufacturer of metering pumps and analytical instruments and, in 1992, acquired the Electrical Systems Division of Westinghouse.

Sundstrand is today a much sounder business than in the mid 1980s. While still suffering somewhat from the rapid decline in defense business, the company has managed to graduate toward a more stable diversity of civilian work, supplying products to Boeing, Airbus, McDonnell Douglas, and several dozen other large industrial customers.

Principal Subsidiaries: Sundstrand Aerospace Mechanical Systems; Sundstrand Electric Power Systems; Sundstrand Power Systems; Sundstrand Data Control; Milton Roy Company; The Falk Corporation; Sullair Corporation.

Further Reading: Glaberson, William, ''Sundstrand Suspended by Pentagon,'' *New York Times,* October 20, 1988; ''Sundstrand Holders' Suit Against Officials Dismissed by Judge,'' *Wall Street Journal,* March 31, 1989; Kernstock, Nicholas C., ''Sundstrand Emerges from 'Ill Wind' Inquiry with Improved Earnings and Operations,'' *Aviation Week & Space Technology,* June 11, 1990; ''Sundstrand Insurers Will Pay $15 Million to Settle Litigation,'' *Wall Street Journal,* August 10, 1990; Annual Report, 1991; *Sundstrand Corporation: A History of the Company,* Company Publication, 1992.

—John Simley

TACO BELL

17901 Von Karman
Irvine, California 92714
U.S.A.
(714) 863-4500
Fax: (714) 863-2214

Wholly Owned Subsidiary of PepsiCo Inc.
Incorporated: 1962
Employees: 70,000
Sales: $3.3 billion
SICs: 5812 Eating Places; 6794 Patent Owners & Lessors

Taco Bell is a California-based fast service restaurant chain that specializes in Mexican-style fast food. Taco Bell currently holds—with 1992 sales in the U.S. of $3.3 billion dollars—a 68 percent share of the U.S. Mexican-style restaurant market. The fast food chain is today part of the giant PepsiCo empire, a far cry from its modest beginnings as a hot dog stand.

In 1946 Glen Bell, a World War II veteran, opened a hot dog stand in San Bernardino, California. The 23-year-old Bell decided to start his own business after working for a local gas company and a railroad system. After selling a gas refrigerator bought at a discount from the gas company for $400, Bell invested the money in securing a lease for the food stand site and for buying building materials. Confident that the post-war economy would support his endeavor, "Bell's Drive In" opened its shutters for business later that year.

Bell began unassumingly, remaining a one-person operation and serving only take-out food. His first day of business brought in $20 over a 16-hour day. Working long hours—the stand's hours of operation extended from 9 am to midnight—he eventually averaged $150 a day in business during his first year.

In 1952 Bell sold his first stand and set about building an improved version. His new menu comprised hamburgers and hot dogs, then staples of the emerging fast food industry. Coincidentally, just as Bell built his second stand, the McDonald brothers were building their first fast food restaurant, also in San Bernardino. By 1955 Ray Kroc, a traveling salesman touting milk shake machines, would link up with the McDonald brothers and form the giant McDonald's hamburger chain.

The phenomenal worldwide success of the McDonald's restaurant chain would come later. But its successful beginnings in San Bernardino were enough to prompt Bell to find a niche in the fledgling Mexican-style food business. He settled on selling tacos by volume, rather than making and stuffing them individually as was the case in full-service restaurants. As Bell later noted in a 1978 speech to a Taco Bell franchise convention, "My plan for experimenting with tacos was to obtain a location in a Mexican neighborhood. That way, if tacos were successful, potential competitors would write it off to the location and assume that the idea wouldn't sell anywhere else."

After choosing a location in a Mexican neighborhood of San Bernardino, Bell began selling a chili dog from which he eventually developed his traditional taco sauce. He also developed taco shells that could be easily and quickly fried and later stuffed with ingredients. This stand was so small that Bell sold his first tacos at 19 cents each from a window on the side.

In 1953 a second stand was opened in Barstow, near San Bernardino. Tacos sold well in that locale as well, and Bell recruited Ed Hackbarth to run the stand. A year later, Bell began the construction of three Taco Tia stands in San Bernardino, Redlands, and Riverside. When the new stores were completed a year later, Bell achieved $18,000 in sales in his first month.

A small commissary was soon built to serve the three Taco Tia outlets and three other Bell's Drive Ins outlets. Here vegetables were prepared daily, as were deep taco shells and sauces. To maintain freshness, meat was cooked at the individual restaurants.

In 1956 Bell sold his three Taco Tia restaurants to fund his expansion into the Los Angeles restaurant market. A recessionary economic atmosphere, however, drove up construction costs. Bell eventually went into partnership with four members of the Los Angeles Rams professional football team to reduce his start-up risk. In 1958 they formed the El Taco restaurant chain, which included a central commissary to serve up to 100 units. Three outlets were initially opened, producing profits of $3,000 after the first year of business.

Bell wanted to remain independent, however, so in 1962 he yet again sold his share in a successful restaurant chain and, a year later, opened the first Taco Bell outlet in Downey. Eight more outlets were built in the Long Beach, Paramount, and Los Angeles regions.

During this period the concept of franchising was developing, first with car dealerships and then throughout the restaurant industry. Bell quickly seized on the idea. In 1964 Kermit Becky, a former Los Angeles policeman, purchased the first Taco Bell franchise in the South Bay area of Los Angeles. Other franchise buyers followed.

In 1965 Bell hired Robert McKay as general manager of the company to help franchise Taco Bell. McKay would later recall the challenge before him in *Forbes*: ". . . franchising was really hot. Everyone wanted franchises in the mid-sixties. Then came the shakeout a few years later and franchising no longer was the easy game it once was."

A year later, the Taco Bell chain went public on the Pacific Stock Exchange, enabling Bell to receive bank financing for the first time. Previously, all financing had been secured on a private basis. (The first Taco Bell was opened with 40 shares, each worth $100 and held mostly by Bell's family.)

In 1967 McKay was named president of Taco Bell. At that point in time the company owned 12 restaurants, with an additional 325 franchises. By 1970 Taco Bell had become a $6 million operation, producing annual profits of approximately $150,000. The fast food chain's success soon drew the attention of PepsiCo Inc., the snack food and soft drinks giant, which was seeking to diversify into the restaurant business.

In 1975 Pizza Hut, then a subsidiary of PepsiCo, launched Taco Kid, a Mexican food concept to challenge Taco Bell. The launch failed, and Pizza Hut soon had to write off its investment. PepsiCo altered its strategy and began wooing Glen Bell in order to buy Taco Bell outright. In February 1978 a deal was struck in which the Mexican fast food chain was purchased for just under $125 million in stock.

PepsiCo's strategy in acquiring Taco Bell was simple: the fast food chain dominated the Mexican food market, so PepsiCo was buying market share. For PepsiCo the challenge was to make Taco Bell less a regional ethnic food phenomenon and more a national fast food chain. Glen Bell had originally sought to set Taco Bell apart from other fast food chains, McDonald's in particular, and its preeminent position among other Mexican food chains, most all of them regional or local rivals, was already secure.

PepsiCo's decision to reposition Taco Bell was a challenge to the fast food giants on a national scale. The PepsiCo strategy emphasized that Taco Bell outlets would sport spartan simplicity in decor and menu, with a concentration on predictable quality, affordable prices, and clean and convenient surroundings. Taco Bell also moved swiftly to redesign the company logo. The old logo, a Mexican dozing under a giant sombrero, was replaced by a sparkling bell atop the company name. As Larry Higby, senior vice-president of marketing at Taco Bell, noted in *Advertising Age*: "Usually when you try to turn something around, you look to develop breakthrough advertising. But we came to exactly the opposite conclusion: we needed to look more mainstream."

The strategy worked. Taco Bell grew rapidly during the early 1980s. By 1983, when John E. Martin took over as president, the chain had 1,600 outlets in 47 U.S. states, producing a total of $918 million in sales. The average Taco Bell franchise claimed sales of $680,000 that year, a significant increase over the franchise average of $325,000 in sales only three years earlier. As a measure of market strength, Taco Bell's nearest rival in the Mexican fast food segment was Naugles, a California-based chain with only 160 outlets and 1983 sales of $84 million.

A 1985 advertising campaign typified the company's mainstream approach. The TV spots stressed that Taco Bell offered the same ingredients as its burger rivals: beef, cheese, and tomatoes. It simply served the ingredients up in a different and, according to the company, more satisfying way. The campaign's tag-line, "Just Made for You," reminded consumers that more than 60 percent of Taco Bell products were custom-made and that no dish was prepared until it was ordered to ensure freshness. By 1986 Taco Bell had grown to 2,400 outlets with just over $1.4 billion in sales. TV advertising that year called Taco Bell "the cure for the common meal," a pointed allusion to the staple foods offered by its competitors.

New Taco Bell outlets were also different from earlier models. The traditional arched windows and red-tile roofs were retained, but with the addition of exterior stucco. Interiors featured skylights, silk plants, and light-colored wood. New dishes, like seafood salad and grilled chicken, were added to menus, and drive-through windows became a standard feature.

In 1986, Taco Bell expanded overseas by opening a restaurant in London, England. Two years later, Taco Bell made widespread pricing and production changes. The resulting lower price of many of the items on the Taco Bell menu forced rival hamburger chains to follow suit. On the production side, Taco Bell began contracting out much of its food preparation—the dicing and slicing, the frying of taco shells—to get the kitchen out of the restaurant. Just-in-time inventory controls were added to all outlets, resulting in reduced overhead costs. Electronic information systems installed in all Taco Bell outlets cut down significantly on management paperwork. Staff responsibilities changed as well, as Taco Bell reversed the 70 percent kitchen and 30 percent dining room ratio in all its outlets. As Zane Leshner, the company's senior vice president for operations, commented in *Financial World* in 1991: "We no longer dedicate an awful lot of labor and space to doing things that have no customer value at all."

The strategy paid dividends for Taco Bell. The streamlining steps enabled the Mexican fast food chain to raise its profits by 25 percent annually during the late 1980s at a time when it was sharply dropping its prices.

The company's success, coming at a time when the late 1980s recession led to savage price-cutting and cutthroat competition in the fast food industry, impressed industry analysts. A 1991 article in the *Harvard Business Review* named Taco Bell as the best performer in the fast food industry at the time, surpassing traditional market leader McDonald's. The authors wrote: "If McDonald's is the epitome of the old industrialized service model, Taco Bell represents the new, redesigned model in many important respects."

To keep customers focused on Taco Bell's menu, the company in 1991 introduced a three-tiered value menu. Most products on the menu—from original tacos and bean burritos to cinnamon twists—would be sold at three main price levels: 59¢, 79¢, and 99¢. In addition, new menu items introduced in 1991 included steak burritos to lure dinner customers and a test breakfast menu. These changes helped the company to achieve 60 percent more sales in 1991 than two years earlier.

New Taco Bell outlets were also being added to the company's stable. The number had grown from 2,193 units in 1985 to 3,273 in 1990, marking an annual growth rate of 8.3 percent. In 1992 Taco Bell opened outlets in Aruba, South Korea, and Saudi Arabia, bringing the number of international locations to 11. In the United States, Taco Bell opened outlets in airports, business cafeterias, and sports stadiums. The strategy called for the company to become more than a restaurant chain: Taco Bell now hoped to be regarded as a taco distribution company.

Taco Bell has maintained its footing through the early 1990s recession, although its fast food rivals are certain to fight back. In addition, as Mexican food grows in popularity, other Mexican chains are certain to challenge Taco Bell and its 68 percent market share, attained in 1992.

However, Taco Bell has grown into a formidable force in the restaurant business, and its current economic and organizational health indicates that it is likely to remain a major player in the fast food wars for some time to come.

Principal Subsidiaries: Taco Bell Worldwide.

Further Reading: Bell, Glen, ''Getting Here,'' 1978 speech to franchise convention, Irvine, CA, Taco Bell Inc.; ''A Promising Mañana'', *Forbes,* August 1, 1977; ''Taco Bell Secures Fast-Food Presence'' *Advertising Age,* July 16, 1984; ''Taco Bell Wants to Take a Bite Out of Burgers'' *Business Week,* August 8, 1986; ''Restaurants without Kitchens'' *Financial World,* November 26, 1991; Schlesinger, Leonard, and James Heskett, ''The Service-Driven Service Company,'' *Harvard Business Review,* September-October, 1991.

—Etan Vlessing

TELECOM EIREANN

St. Stephen's Green
Dublin 2
Ireland
(01) 714444
Fax: (01) 716916

State-Owned Company
Incorporated: 1984
Employees: 13,100
Sales: IR£788 million
SICs: 4813 Telephone Communications, Except Radio

State-controlled Telecom Eireann is the dominant telecommunications network operator in Ireland. Now a thoroughly modern operation, the company suffered several years of neglect during the 1970s as an agency of the government postal service. While it has yet to undergo privatization, Telecom Eireann has passed several difficult stages in its transformation into a modern business enterprise.

The company's origins are thoroughly rooted in the development of British telecommunications, owing to British domination of Ireland throughout the 19th and early 20th centuries. Ireland has come forth from Britain's shadow and is today an emerging European industrial force. As a crucial component in Ireland's industrial infrastructure, telecommunications has grown immeasurably in value. Telecom Eireann has been at the forefront of that growth.

The establishment of telephonic communications in Ireland in the late 1800s closely followed the demise of the dominant electronic medium of the day, telegraphy. Ireland's first commercial telegraph was established by the English & Irish Magnetic Telegraph Company in 1851, linking Galway and Dublin along railway lines. The following year a submarine link was built, connecting Dublin to the English network at Holyhead, Wales.

Private ownership of telegraph systems, however, left vast areas of Ireland unserved because they were not profitable. In 1870 the British Post Office took control of the national telegraph system in an effort to spread the technology throughout Ireland, and operated at a substantial loss. Ireland, however, was the last "stepping stone" for transatlantic cables linking Europe with the United States. Important stations were established at Valentia, Ballingskelligs, and Waterville, providing direct connections between England and Germany and Nova Scotia.

Soon after Alexander Graham Bell invented the telephone in 1876, he demonstrated the device in England. The Post Office subsequently won permission to operate a telephone network under license from Bell, whose English company merged with Thomas Edison's in 1880 to form United Telephone.

Britain's Post Office understood immediately what effect the telephone would have on its telegraph monopoly and petitioned the government to allow it to take control of United Telephone. The Treasury Department, however, shocked by the projected costs of expanding the network, did not believe it was the government's place to run a telephone service. Eventually, the Post Office's involvement was limited to merely collecting licensing fees from United.

While this battle was being fought, United constructed its first exchange in Ireland, switching five lines in Dublin. So few calls were handled by this office that the switchboard operator, a young boy, frequently went off to play marbles out of boredom. The following year, the office was expanded to 20 lines and an operator was hired.

Shareholders grew impatient with United Telephone when their investments failed to show immediate returns. In 1882, acting upon shareholder discomfort, the newly formed Telephone Company of Ireland negotiated a takeover of United Telephone's Irish operations. Subsequent growth continued to be slow. By 1888 the Dublin office and three subexchanges handled only 500 customers. In addition, all lines were single-wire systems that used the earth as part of its circuit. This allowed virtually anyone with even the most rudimentary equipment to eavesdrop on conversations. Thus, the practice of "rubbernecking" became a serious impediment to sales.

In 1893 the company's backers lost faith in the company and agreed to sell the operation to National Telephone, an English concern that had previously taken over United Telephone. National attacked the privacy problem decisively by ordering a massive reconstruction program to install wires in pairs.

While the Post Office negotiated free passage rights along railway lines in Ireland, development of an intercity trunk system continued to proceed slowly because expenditures were opposed at every turn by the Treasury Department. Still, by 1900 the company managed to construct 56 exchanges in the country, principally in Dublin and southern and western Ireland. Railway companies became avid users of telephone service because it was cheaper and faster than the telegraph.

By virtue of its unusual arrangement with the government, National Telephone lived in continual fear of being taken over by the Post Office, whose intentions were clear. Only the Treasury Department kept the Post Office from acting on its ambitions. But as the profitability of telephony became ever more apparent, Treasury opposition subsided.

Finally, in 1905, the Post Office won an order to assume control of National Telephone when that company's charter expired in 1911. But when the takeover was completed in 1912, the network, which included 150 exchanges in Ireland, was saddled with widespread equipment shortages and six years of disrepair.

When World War I began in 1914, virtually all work on the telephone network ground to a halt. Only military telephony received any funding and materials. In addition, because they were strategic targets, many of the submarine cables came under attack and were disabled.

As the war drew to a close in 1918, an Anglo-Irish conflict and civil war for independence from Britain erupted. As the domestic telephone network came under attack, many exchanges were destroyed and miles of cable were knocked out. In 1922, as the conflict came to an end, a new Irish government appointed a Department of Posts & Telegraphs (P&T) to assume control of the telephone network and develop telecommunications in Ireland. Construction of the network resumed in 1924. Part of the rebuilding plan called for the establishment of an automated Strowger-type switching system in Dublin, and the assignment of five-digit telephone numbers. These switches, which eliminated the need for a switchboard operator, were installed in 1927.

The worldwide economic depression of the 1930s hit the fragile Irish economy with brutal force, causing demand for new telephones to dry up. This hardship was followed by the emerging European war some years later. As in the First World War, all civilian construction in the network was suspended in favor of military communications. After the fall of France in 1940, the P&T was called upon to wire 84 lookout posts at strategic points around Ireland where German warships could be observed or, worse, where invasion might be expected.

Despite the tremendous destruction the war caused in England, France, and Germany, Ireland emerged from the war without harm. The telephone network P&T built for the military, which included miles of new trunks, was subsequently converted to civilian use.

The huge demand for telephones after the war, coupled with P&T's conversion to underground cable systems, left P&T with virtually no available transmission facilities. As a result, when Dublin's tram system was eliminated after the war, P&T purchased the line's underground duct network for telephone cables. As part of a wider government-backed expansion plan, P&T also resolved to improve trunk service, increase subscribership from 31,000 to 100,000, and expand all operator services to 24-hours.

Despite several obstacles, continued demand for telephone service enabled the company to exceed all these goals. In 1957 P&T installed the first of its crossbar switches, which were easier to maintain than the Strowger step switches. The company began phasing out switchboards in remote areas in favor of automated switches.

P&T surveys during this time revealed low levels of usage in the network due to limited applications of the local call rate. Most calls, it was discovered, required expensive trunk connections. In 1958 the company invited G. J. Kamerbeek, an engineer with the Dutch Post Office, to propose a new rate structure for P&T. While this required extensive re-engineering of the network, it established wider local call zones. This change, as well as other pricing reforms, succeeded in raising Irish telephone subscriptions to levels comparable with other European countries.

The company began to experiment with new transmission mediums. Just as aerial cable had proven no match for Ireland's seasonal ice and wind, buried cable soon lost its appeal because of the high cost of boring trenches. In 1961 P&T installed its first microwave system, linking Althone and Galway.

The company also made other efforts to increase the number of subscribers, including reclassifying Ireland's thousand of farms as residences, thus enabling farmers to avoid high rental rates for business telephones. In addition, the ambitious Rural Automisation Programme provided for the construction of new crossbar switching facilities, for the first time, outside of rural post office facilities.

As late as 1974, a year after Ireland gained admission to the European Economic Community, all calls to and from the Continent continued to be switched through London. While this was mainly an engineering consequence of years of British domination over Ireland, the time had arrived for Ireland to declare its independence, at least in the area of international telephony. That year P&T installed its first international crossbar in Dublin, greatly facilitating call traffic with other European countries and North America.

But during this time, P&T stumbled in several areas. A series of industrial actions, including worker strikes, and a growing inability on the part of management to address these problems, led to a severe drop in service quality. Almost weekly, national and provincial newspapers berated the company for its poor service.

In 1978 the government, fearing that Ireland's telephone system was once again falling behind those of its European neighbors, commissioned a Posts and Telecommunications Review group to study the situation. The following year the group issued what became known as the Dargan Report. The study's conclusions were bleak, stating that the Irish telecommunications system was failing to keep pace with Ireland's growing economy and its customers' expectations. Urgent action was deemed necessary to avoid a crisis.

The Dargan Report recommended that P&T be separated from the civil postal system and reorganized as a state-owned company. The report specified that the new company should be operated according to modern business principles, emphasizing marketing, customer service, and high returns on equity.

In July 1979 the Irish Parliament agreed to split P&T into two entities, a postal service called An Post and a telephone company called Bord Telecom Eireann. The telephone company was given a IR£650 million development budget as part of a five-year program to construct as many as 500 new buildings, double subscriptions, drastically increase the number of trunk lines, and improve customer service. At the end of the five-year program, the Postal and Telecommunications Services Act of 1983 authorized Telecom Eireann to formally take control of Ireland's telecommunications system.

The new company benefited tremendously from a far-sighted decision made by P&T leadership some years earlier to begin the transition to digital switches, which were faster and more efficient than the mechanical switches previously used. As a result, the new company encountered none of the difficulties experienced by other European telephone companies in converting to the new system.

When Telecom Eireann took over the national system on January 1, 1984, only 309 manual exchanges remained. The last of these older switches was replaced in 1987. At last, the entire network was standardized and digital. In 1991 Telecom Eireann collected its one millionth customer.

In order to keep pace with other communications systems in the world, Telecom Eireann has devoted tremendous resources to the development of new technologies, including satellite transmission and national fiber optic networks. The company is working to bring ISDN capabilities to the network and, through its associate Broadcom Eireann Research, is involved in the Research for Advanced Communications for Europe (RACE) program. The RACE goal is to establish an integrated broadband communications network in Europe by 1995.

Telecom Eireann also has developed a national cellular phone network, called Eircell, that covers more than 90 percent of Ireland. In addition, in 1988 the company established Eirpage, a large paging operation produced in conjunction with Motorola. Other companies with whom Telecom Eireann has established partnership agreements include Nynex and France Telecom.

While Telecom Eireann is operated on many of the same principles as independent enterprises, its board is appointed by its one and only shareholder, the Irish government. As a result, much of the current board leadership is composed of inside directors, and many of the board's strategic policies and planning are products of the government, rather than the board.

Historically, the logical next step for companies that have undergone such transformation as state-owned companies, including British Telecom, NTT, and Telmex, is that they are offered for sale to public shareholders. No discussion has yet been forwarded on the matter of government sales of shares in Telecom Eireann to the public.

Two factors are working to prevent privatization of the company. First, it is likely that the Irish government has not yet seen implemented all the changes it has demanded in the telecommunications system. Secondly, the company is likely to command a much higher price in the future. The more that can be made from the sale of Telecom Eireann, the better for Irish taxpayers, whose substantial investments in the company have made it the success it is.

Principal Subsidiaries: Irish Telecommunications Investments, PC; Telecom Eireann Information Systems, Ltd.; Eircable Ltd./Cablelink, Ltd.; Telecom Ireland (US), Ltd.; Eirtrade, Ltd.; Golden Pages, Ltd.; Broadcom Eireann Research, Ltd.; Eirpage, Ltd.; Telecom Phonewatch, Ltd.; Minitel Communications, Ltd.; INET, Ltd.

Further Reading: Recalling the Telephone in Ireland—How it All Began, Dublin: Telecom Eireann, 1991; *Company History,* Dublin: Telecom Eireann, 1992; *Report and Accounts,* Dublin: Telecom Eireann, 1992.

—John Simley

TELEVISION ESPAÑOLA, S.A.

Torrespana-O'Donnell, 77
28007 Madrid
Spain
(1) 346-87-21
Fax: (1) 409-31-65

Wholly Owned Subsidiary of Radiotelevision Española
Incorporated: 1956
Employees: 5,900
Sales: PTS 1.4 trillion (US$11.96 billion)
SICs: 4833 Television Broadcasting Stations

State-owned Television Española, S.A. (TVE) is one of two subsidiaries of Radiotelevision Española, Spain's largest and most important audiovisual company. Financed by advertising, TVE has two channels, TVE 1 and La 2, and an international satellite channel broadcasting in Spanish throughout the world.

TVE began transmitting in 1956 as a monopoly from studios in Madrid. Its first channel, operating in black and white, was TVE 1. In 1962 the company created a second channel, UHF (now called La 2). The company went on to produce a variety of successful programs: in 1968 TVE's *Historias de la frivolidad* ("Tales of Frivolity") won the Golden Rose prize at the Montreaux Festival. And, first transmitting programs in color during the 1970s, the company produced *La Cabina* ("The Cabin"), which won an Emmy in 1973. Two of the most popular quiz shows the company produced were *Un millon para el mejor* ("A Million for the Best") and *La union hace la fuerza* ("Strength through Unity").

In 1982, the same year the World Soccer Cup was held in Spain, TVE constructed the Torrespana communication tower with capacity for worldwide transmission. The tower soon became a landmark on the Madrid cityscape; at 213 meters, it was among the ten tallest television towers in the world. The company built next to the tower a complex covering more than 50,000 square meters to house TVE's news services headquarters. The complex included a completely computerized central editorial office.

In the early 1980s the company continued to thrive. In 1983 *La colmena* ("The Beehive"), produced by TVE, won the Gold Bear at the Berlin Film Festival. In 1985, facing the need to expand, the company completed the Pozuelo de Alarcon center to serve production and administrative purposes. The television station proceeded to gain international recognition for its production of highly acclaimed films throughout the 1980s and into the 1990s. In 1988 TVE's *Las gallinas de Cervantes* ("The Hens of Cervantes") won the Europe prize. In 1990 TVE won the Golden Shell at the San Sebastian Film Festival with *Las Cartas de Alou* ("Alou's Letters"), a film about the experiences of an African immigrant in Spain during the 1980s.

As TVE entered the 1990s, it had three main production centers: one in Madrid, where it produced the majority of its programs; one in Barcelona (at the Catalonian Production Center); and another in the Canary Islands. The centers in Barcelona and the Canary Islands produced shows mostly for regional audiences. The company also had 15 smaller regional production centers.

In 1991 TVE had an estimated budget of $1.3 million and total broadcasting time of 260 hours per week on its two channels. 60 percent of the programs broadcast were Spanish productions; the remainder were imports. Programs transmitted on TVE 1 and La 2 reached 99 percent of homes in the Spanish part of the Iberian Peninsula and the Canary and Balearic Islands, a total of more than 11 million homes. In addition, populations in large areas of Portugal, northern Morocco, Algeria, and the south of France were able to view the two channels.

The company saw the beginning of serious competitive challenge with the end of its monopoly role in the Spanish television industry in 1990. By 1991, six regional television stations were in operation—many of them broadcasting in regional languages—as well as three private channels. The private channels included Antena 3, which began transmitting in January of 1990; Telecinco, or Tele 5; and Canal Plus, Spain's only television station requiring paid subscription.

To remain ahead in the running, the company's strategy included keeping the attention of large audiences on its first channel, TVE 1. The channel concentrated on capturing a wide audience share during Spain's secondary "prime time" slot, from 2:30 to 5:00 p.m., with general news, quiz shows, and popular Latin American soap operas. The strategy was successful: in 1990 TVE 1 had higher numbers of daily viewers and more programming hours than any other Spanish television network. It ranked first on the viewer ranking table in 1991, with an average share of television audiences of 43 percent. News and news-related programs occupied 35 percent of viewing time; drama and movies, 28 percent; quiz shows, 7 percent; programs for children, 8 percent; and cultural programs, 5 percent.

The most popular programs transmitted by TVE 1 included two quiz shows, *El precio justo* ("The Price Is Right") and *Un, dos, tres* ("One, Two, Three"), the latter almost a fixture in Spanish households, with a history of more than 20 years of transmission. Second in popularity were domestic video shows, musicals, and hit movie classics.

La 2 ranked second in numbers of daily viewers in 1990. Its audience share in 1991 was 14.2 percent. This market share, combined with that of TVE 1, allowed TVE to maintain its leadership position in the Spanish television industry with an average audience share of almost 60 percent. The channel La 2 targeted a more educated, selective audience, with programming that included documentaries, educational productions, movies for sophisticated viewers, experimental projects, and programs of regional interest. The network also provided extensive coverage of special events, including concerts, theater productions, and international affairs, and it carved a big niche in sports. The channel consecrated 20 percent of its viewing time to sports in 1990.

During prime time—8:30 p.m. to midnight in Spain and the time slot in which TVE faced its most intense challenge from competitors—La 2 offered a drama series, films, debates, or international hits such as *The Simpsons.* One program, *Tribunal Popular* (''The People's Court''), dramatized topical issues of national interest in a trial format before a panel of local celebrities.

Overall, the most popular programs the two stations offered during 1991 were: the quiz show *Un, dos, tres,* in number-one position; *Martes y Trece* (''Tuesday and Thirteen''), a comedy special featuring the camp and daring duo, Martes and Trece; *Videos de Primera,* the home video show; and the series *Las chicas de hoy en dia* (''The Girls of Today''). During 1991 the two stations averaged an overall rate of 22 million viewers per day.

In the early 1990s TVE allotted not only the largest segment of viewing time to news and news-related programming (35 percent on TVE 1 in 1991 and 30 percent of overall programming on both channels in 1990), but also the largest segment of its employees (1,200 out of 6,000). The company provided minute-by-minute coverage of the Persian Gulf War. The journalism staff in 1991 had assignments around the world, and the company had 15 international news offices. The network broadcast headline stories in three daily newscasts of 30 minutes each. TVE also provided widely popular news documentaries, including *Informe Semanal* (''Weekly Report''), *En portada* (''Front Page''), and *Metropoli.*

In 1991 TVE also participated with Latin American and European TV networks in video and film production, technical coordination, and introduction and testing of the European High Definition TV standard. TVE's Outside Broadcasting Van, helping to produce high definition programs, was frequently used by international producers. One of TVE's most noteworthy co-productions was the mini-series *Los jinetes del alba* (''Dawn Riders''), which won the silver at the 1991 International Festival of Audiovisual Programs at Cannes. The company later created two satellite stations, TVE Internacional and TVE America, in order to build better communications among the world's Spanish-speaking individuals.

The station also provided selective support for the Spanish film industry. The film *Amantes* (''Lovers''), directed by Vicente Aranda and produced by TVE, won two international prizes and the Spanish Premio Ondas de Cinematografia in 1991. In January of the same year, however, TVE began to default on both its home and overseas rights purchases. This caused traditional providers of credit to tighten their lending policies for movie producers; 30 Spanish films faced production problems and delays in 1991 because of the funding crisis.

In 1992 TVE found success in sports, providing exclusive coverage of one of the country's spotlight events, the Olympic games in Barcelona. Opening on July 25, 1992, the games were called ''the televised sports industry's biggest enterprise in the twentieth century'' by Victor Ego Ducrot in *Inter Press Service.* Overall investments in the event totalled almost $10 billion. With the exclusive rights to air the games in Spain, TVE charged about $170,000 for a 20-second commercial spot. Payments for retransmission rights were more than $635 million.

TVE's challenges for the 1990s and beyond include staying on top of rapid technological advances, keeping up with the competition in the European free market, maintaining a leadership position in the newly open Spanish market, and maintaining a share of European and Latin American productions. Watching the budget—and the competition—will be a constant necessity, but with a continued commitment to providing the public with quality productions, the station should meet not only the challenges facing it as Spain's only state-run television network, but the broader economic and cultural challenges that confront the new Spain of the 1990s.

Further Reading: ''Salute to Radiotelevision Española,'' Madrid, Radiotelevision Española, 1991; ''Electronic Media's Annual International Market Survey,'' *Crain Communications, Inc.,* May 13, 1991; ''Shortfall in ICAA Plan for Films Dropped by TVE,'' *The Financial Times Limited,* July 24, 1991; Ducrot, Victor Ego, ''Olympic Games: The TV Industry's Biggest Business Undertaking Ever,'' *Inter Press Service,* July 27, 1992.

—Dorothy Walton

TEREX CORPORATION

P.O. Box 1009
Green Bay, Wisconsin 54303
U.S.A.
(414) 435-5322
Fax: (414) 432-8094

Public Company
Incorporated: 1925 as Northwest Engineering Co.
Employees: 6,980
Sales: $784 million
Stock Exchanges: New York
SICs: 3715 Truck Trailers; 3531 Construction Machinery;
  5082 Construction & Mining Machinery

Terex Corporation designs, manufactures, and markets heavy-duty, off-highway construction, earth-moving, and material-handling equipment. In 1993, Terex and its affiliates also owned more than 50 percent of the Fruehauf Trailer Corporation, the world's largest manufacturer of truck trailers. Fruehauf operates in 19 countries and manufactures more than 325 models of truck trailers, including van, refrigerated van, platform, tank, liquid and dry-bulk tank trailers. Approximately 19 percent of the new trailer market in the United States belongs to Fruehauf. The truck maker also owns more than 20 percent of Société European de Semi-Remorques, the leading manufacturer of trailers in Europe.

Although founded in the 1920s, Terex Corporation evolved mainly from numerous acquisitions made by Chairman of the Board Randolph W. Lenz in the 1980s. Lenz, who was the company's principal shareholder with 54 percent, continued to buy such distressed or bankrupt companies into the 1990s, adding Mark Industries and the material-handling division of the Clark Equipment Company.

The story of Terex is also the story of Lenz, an ex-Marine with a degree in psychology from the University of Wisconsin. Born in 1947, Lenz began buying and selling real estate in the late 1960s. He served as president of Milwaukee-based Ranmar Enterprises, Inc. and the Network Investment Real Estate Corporation, in Brookfield, Wisconsin. It was in 1981 that Lenz moved into heavy-equipment manufacturing, buying the assets of the FWD Corporation, a bankrupt manufacturer of snow-

plows and fire trucks in Clintonville, Wisconsin. Lenz continues to hold the position of chairman of FWD.

Based on his success with FWD, Lenz began to follow a calculated strategy of buying distressed companies at fire-sale prices when he bought Northwest Engineering Co. in 1983. Northwest Engineering had been manufacturing cranes, power shovels, and draglines for more than 50 years, but the company had declared bankruptcy and was only three months from liquidation. When Lenz stepped in, however, the company's focus was changed from manufacturing and assembling new equipment to spare parts.

Northwest Engineering, in turn, bought the construction-machinery division of the Pennsylvania-based Bucyrus-Erie Company in March of 1985. At its peak, Bucyrus-Erie had employed more than 700 people, but the company had shut down its production lines in 1983, and the employees that remained were concentrating on spare parts and service. Less than a month out of bankruptcy, Northwest Engineering paid less than $9 million for a company with $20 million a year in sales. Lenz then revived the company's defunct Dynahoe product line: the new Bucyrus Construction Products (BCP) division of Northwest Engineering produced its first backhoe loader in November of 1985. By 1988, *Industry Week* reported that BCP held a 40 percent share of the market in which its products were sold.

Lenz and Terex came together in 1986 when Northwest Engineering purchased Terex USA from General Motors Corp. GM had acquired Terex, a builder of heavy-duty, earth-moving equipment, in 1953. By 1979, Terex had annual sales in excess of $500 million, and employed more than 5,000 people in the United States, Brazil, and the United Kingdom.

In 1980, in an effort to focus on its automotive business, General Motors agreed to sell Terex to IBH Holding AG, a maker of light- and medium-duty construction equipment in the former Federal Republic of Germany. However, in 1983 IBH Holding filed for bankruptcy, and with pressure from the United Auto Workers, ownership of Terex reverted to General Motors. The company was reorganized as Terex Equipment Limited, a manufacturing subsidiary in Scotland, and Terex USA, a distributor for Terex products in the Western Hemisphere. Terex USA also made some equipment and spare parts at a factory in Ohio.

When Northwest Engineering bought Terex USA in 1986, the agreement included an option to purchase Terex Equipment Limited. Northwest Engineering exercised that option in 1987. Then, in a controversial move, Lenz closed the Terex plant in Ohio, and moved all operations to Scotland. Among the items manufactured by Terex Equipment Limited were articulated dump trucks, wheeled loaders, scrapers, and other large construction vehicles.

In 1987 Northwest Engineering paid $21.9 million for Koehring Cranes & Excavators and Benton Engineering, both acquired from Koehring Co., a subsidiary of AMCA International Finance Corporation. A *Financial World* correspondent reported that Koehring had been losing almost $1 million a month for five years, and declared Lenz was able to "get well-respected

Koehring excavators and Lorain crane brand names for a song.'' Five years later the Terex concern sold what had become the Benton Harbor Engineering Division to pay off debt associated with the Koehring purchase.

The next move for Northwest Engineering came in 1988 when it bought Unit Rig and Equipment Company which was also involved in bankruptcy proceedings. Based in Tulsa, Oklahoma, Unit Rig manufactured Lectra Haul trucks and Dart loaders and haulers. That same year, Lenz changed the company's name to Terex Corporation, and Northwest Engineering became a division of Terex.

A *Forbes* reporter described Terex's rise: ''Randolph W. Lenz was an obscure Wisconsin businessman in 1983 when he was struck by a simple idea. Some of the best buy-out values in the country, Lenz reasoned, could be found among bankrupt and near-bankrupt manufacturers of earth-moving equipment companies with low prices, cleansed assets and a newly pragmatic work force of survivors. From such down-and-outers Lenz, in just six years, has built Terex Corp.''

A *Mergers & Acquisitions* correspondent—to whom Lenz described his strategy as one of ''pragmatic opportunity''—outlined what happened after a Terex takeover: ''A typical Terex acquisition means hard work after the deal is completed. Once in-house, the new business, typically in the lower technology end of the equipment field, will be streamlined to achieve production efficiencies, eliminate marginal product lines, improve marketing and reorient the work force toward the revamped operating mode.'' *Forbes* analysts were more blunt in their assessment, however, stating, ''Lenz . . . has methodically consolidated factories, slashed payrolls and shrunk product lines to those few profitable niches that his companies still retain.''

In 1989 Terex nearly tripled its size with the acquisition of yet another famous brand name. Debt-ridden Fruehauf Corp.—arguably the most recognized brand of trailer in the world—sold its trailer and maritime businesses to Terex for $231 million. Fruehauf had dominated the pre-World War II trucking industry with a market penetration estimated at nearly 90 percent. Despite trucking deregulation, an economic downturn, and increased competition in the early 1980s, Fruehauf was still reporting record annual profits. However, Fruehauf fell victim to the downside of the 1980s' practice of funding massive growth with high debt.

In 1986 corporate raider Asher Edelman purchased 9.5 percent of Fruehauf's stock—then selling for little more than $20 a share—and announced his intention to take over the company. In order to block the move, Fruehauf borrowed nearly $1.4 billion to buy back its own stock and take the company private. Stockholders who sold their stock for cash received almost $50 per share because of the attempted takeover—Edelman reportedly made a profit of almost $100 million. This left Fruehauf heavily in debt, with interest adding up to more than $100 million per year, substantially more than pre-buyout profits. By 1989, five years after posting record profits, Fruehauf was losing nearly $1 million a week, despite having raised $750 million by selling several of its smaller subsidiaries.

Terex completed its purchase of what was named the Fruehauf Trailer Corporation in July of 1989. By September, the wholly owned subsidiary was doing well enough for Terex to pre-pay $19 million in debt, and in 1990, Terex opened a new 100,000 square foot manufacturing facility in Indianola, Iowa, to build foam-insulated refrigerated vans.

In 1991 Fruehauf trailer operations accounted for nearly two-thirds of Terex's $784 million in sales. Terex also took Fruehauf public in 1991 with an initial public offering of four million shares, and began a program to convert its most effective company-owned distribution branches in the United States into independent dealerships. However, Fruehauf incurred heavy losses in 1991 and 1992, primarily attributed to a worldwide economic slowdown. In early 1993, it was reported that Terex was considering selling Fruehauf.

Two other Terex acquisitions were completed in the early 1990s. Terex added Mark Industries to its Heavy Equipment Group in 1991. The company, based in Brea, California, manufactured aerial lift equipment, including scissor lifts and boom lifts, used in construction, repair, and maintenance work in many industries. In 1992 Terex added perhaps the best-known brand of forklifts and lift trucks to its Materials Handling Group with the purchase of the material handling division of Clark Equipment Company.

Clark invented the forklift in 1928. When Terex bought the line in 1992, Clark forklifts and lift trucks were the top selling brand in North America. The Clark Materials Handling Company, with a worldwide network of independent dealers, was also a leading manufacturer and distributor of forklifts in the European market.

Soon after the purchase, Terex moved to solidify its leadership in the North American market by moving production of its internal combustion forklift trucks from Korea to Lexington, Kentucky. At the same time, Terex announced plans to invest $25 million between 1992 and 1995 to improve its forklifts and lift-trucks with advanced ergonomic features and reduced noise levels. Clark Materials Handling continued to build forklifts in Korea—in a partnership formed with Samsung in 1986—to serve the Asian market.

Despite its success in revitalizing financially troubled companies, several financial analysts in the early 1990s were concerned about Terex's ability to cope with the enormous debt it had assumed in amassing its acquisitions. At the end of 1991, Terex had long-term debt of $189.3 million. With the truck trailer industry experiencing its worst year since 1983, along with stiff price competition among manufacturers, Terex also had a net loss for that year of $33.4 million. Some analysts urged Terex to issue more stock and use the proceeds to pay off some if its long-term debt. As Michael K. Ozanian assessed in *Financial World,* ''With its track record, Wall Street would love to buy Terex equity, particularly if the proceeds were used to retire debt.'' However, Lenz reportedly did not want to dilute his own holdings and resisted that measure.

Increased highway construction and renewed interest in mass transit in the United States in 1992 and 1993 were positive signs for Terex. Much of its heavy equipment, such as graders and loaders, is used in highway and mass transit construction, while improved roadways also could increase the trucking industry's efficiency, spurring the demand for trailers.

Principal Subsidiaries: Fruehauf Trailer Corp.; Unit Rig; Terex Equipment Limited; Koehring Cranes & Excavators; Northwest Engineering; BCP Construction Products; Mark Industries; Corporate Data.

Further Reading: "Terex Rumbles On," *Engineering News Review,* August 28, 1986; Verespej, Michael A., "From 'Exile' to Profitability," *Industry Week,* August 15, 1988; Reiff, Rick, "Parlaying the Winnings," *Forbes,* July 24, 1989; Davies, Carole, "Good-Bye Fruehauf," *Ward's Auto World,* January 1990; "The Terex Prescription," *Mergers & Acquisitions,* January/February 1990; Terex Corporation Annual Report, 1991; Ozanian, Michael K., "Strip Show," *Financial World,* March 19, 1991; Wiley, Royallen, "A Casualty of the Debt-Crazed '80s," *Management Accounting,* March 1991.

—Dean Boyer

TESORO PETROLEUM CORPORATION

8700 Tesoro Drive
San Antonio, Texas 78217
U.S.A.
(512) 828-8484
Fax: (512) 828-8600

Public Company
Incorporated: 1964
Employees: 2,000
Sales: $1 billion
Stock Exchanges: New York
SICs: 2911 Petroleum Refining; 1311 Crude Petroleum &
    Natural Gas; 1381 Drilling Oil & Gas Wells

The Tesoro Petroleum Corporation is a small Texas-based oil company whose operations span an unusually broad range of activities in the petroleum industry. The company conducts exploration for and produces crude oil and natural gas in a number of countries; refines, distributes and markets petroleum products; and supplies oil field equipment. In its early years Tesoro grew rapidly through the acquisition of a wide spectrum of energy businesses. This growth weakened the company's financial status, however, and it was later forced to shed many of its subsidiaries and devote a large amount of its attention to avoiding takeover, both internal and external.

Tesoro was founded by Robert V. West, Jr., in 1964. West had earned a doctorate in chemical engineering and then spent his entire career in the petroleum industry, rising to become president of the Texstar Petroleum Company, a subsidiary of a larger company, Texstar Corporation, that was controlled by Texas wildcatter Tom Slick. After Slick's death in a plane crash, West convinced the executors of Slick's estate to sell the company West ran, with its oil-producing properties, to him. West borrowed $6.5 million to purchase the stock of Texstar Petroleum from its parent company and merged Texstar into the new company he had set up, Tesoro, which means ''treasure'' in Spanish.

In its previous incarnation, Tesoro had been a small but profitable oil and gas company. In its new form, however, the company carried such a high debt burden that it was difficult for Tesoro to save the money necessary to expand. West embarked on an effort to financially stabilize his company by joining it with another, stronger entity. After three years of searching, West found two publicly owned companies that suited his needs, and in a complicated series of transactions, the three merged. With funding from Chicago's Continental Illinois bank, the Intex Oil Company—which had been founded in California in 1939 as the Exploration and Development Company—was joined with the Sioux Oil Company and with Tesoro. The new entity took the name of Tesoro in December of 1968.

With this transformation, Tesoro became a company possessing a pool of stockholders, solid financial standing, a listing on the American Stock Exchange, and workable arrangements with investment banking houses, allowing it to raise capital for further expansion. West embarked on a ten-year spree of acquisitions in the energy business, picking up a mixed bag of companies at bargain-basement prices. The first step in this direction was taken when Tesoro sold $25 million worth of stock in late 1968. With this money, the company paid off its bank debt entirely, leaving $18 million in cash for investment.

Among Tesoro's first acquisitions were the Clymore Petroleum Corporation and the Trident Offshore Company, Ltd., in which Tesoro purchased a 55 percent interest. Tesoro's most important new venture involved the island government of Trinidad and Tobago. The company discovered that the British Petroleum Company (BP) planned to divest itself of its oil-producing operations in Trinidad and that the country's government intended to buy them. Since the Trinidadian government had no experience in the petroleum business, Tesoro was able to convince it to enter into joint ownership of the properties, forming Trinidad-Tesoro Petroleum Company Limited. Incorporated in Trinidad, the company was 50.1 percent owned by the island's government, with the remainder owned by Tesoro. Both partners contributed $50,000 to the venture, which subsequently purchased BP's holdings, including properties, equipment, and remaining oil products for $28 million. The rest of the money necessary for this purchase was raised through loans from banks and a deferred payment plan with BP. Once it had taken over BP's operations in Trinidad, Tesoro was able to restore them to profit-making status by renovating existing wells and making production less wasteful.

In addition to its operations in Trinidad, Tesoro also commenced construction of a refinery for crude oil on the west coast of Alaska at Kenai in early 1969. Building this facility took more than a year, and when it was completed, Tesoro experienced difficulty in operating it profitably. The problem of bringing crude oil to the refinery and transporting finished products to market had yet to be resolved in an economical fashion. In addition, the company faced stiff competition from the much larger Standard Oil Company (California), which owned the only other refinery in Alaska, producing a difficult competitive marketplace. ''We held our noses and went underwater for a while,'' West told *Forbes* magazine in 1973, explaining the refinery's money-losing operations. Eventually, however, prices for refined petroleum products did rise, and the Alaskan refinery became profitable.

Tesoro also continued to purchase companies with a broad range of functions in the petroleum industry, including truck and pipeline transportation, petroleum equipment manufacturing and rental, and crude oil production. In looking for acquisitions, the company sought out properties that were not only profitable, but that showed promise of continuing to return profits over the long term. Accordingly, Tesoro purchased Cardinal Transports, Inc., in early 1969. In March of the following year, the company added a Texas firm called Petroleum Distributing Company as well as the Land & Marine Rental Company and the Louisiana Barreling Company. Later that year, Tesoro invested in the Arnold Pipe Rental Company, Ltd., D&W Investments, Inc., and certain portions of Spira Chek, Inc. In early 1971 Tesoro continued its vertical integration when it took on the operation of gasoline service stations by buying the S&N Investment Company and the Digas Company, both located in southern California. These chains were subsequently expanded into many areas of the United States.

With its diverse operations, and activities in both Trinidad and Alaska running smoothly, Tesoro readied itself for further expansion with another sale of stock. In a symbolic move, the company switched its listing from the American Stock Exchange to the New York Stock Exchange, becoming the only San Antonio-based firm to be listed on the so-called Big Board. In August of 1971 Tesoro raised $32.2 million in an equity offering. With these funds, the company increased its geographical reach once again, buying Redco, a subsidiary of Asamera Oil, which owned land on Boreno in Indonesia that could be explored for oil, as well as the rights to any oil found.

West also began negotiations with an Arab ruler to refine and market crude oil produced in his country. With the expectation that these talks would bear fruit, Tesoro established in September of 1972 a wholly owned European subsidiary, Tesoro-Europe Petroleum B.V., to market petroleum products. In addition, the company bought the Dutch firm DeHumber Handelmaatschappij B.V. and four associated companies for $4 million. These companies handled wholesale and retail marketing operations. Tesoro's European interests were subsequently further expanded when the company acquired an interest in the rights to explore for petroleum in the Dutch sector of the North Sea oil field.

During this time, Tesoro continued to expand its American holdings, purchasing the Charles Wheatley Company in February of 1972. This privately owned firm manufactured valves for use in the oil industry. In May of 1973 Tesoro bought FWI, Inc., from Falcon Seaboard, Inc., in Houston. During the next year Eagle Transport Company and Turner Drill Pipe, two petroleum industry services located in Texas, were also brought on board. By the end of 1973 Tesoro was able to report that its steady pace of acquisitions in all sectors of the petroleum industry had allowed it to quintuple its earnings in just five years in business.

In 1973 the Organization of Petroleum Exporting Countries (OPEC) oil embargo caused an energy crisis in the United States, raising awareness of the importance of alternative energy sources to petroleum. Accordingly, Tesoro moved for the first time to incorporate other forms of fossil fuels in its operations. In September of 1974 the company formed Tesoro Coal Company. Four months later it increased its coal holdings when it bought the Buckhorn Hazard Coal Company.

Geographically, Tesoro moved onto yet another continent when it bought into two sizeable exploratory tracts in Bolivia. This led to the formation in 1974 of Tesoro Inter-American Production Company, which took over the company's holdings in Trinidad and also took responsibility for future operations in the Caribbean and Latin America. By the end of the 1974 fiscal year, Tesoro had gross revenues exceeding $500 million dollars and earnings of about $60 million. The company had operations in 30 states and five foreign countries.

Operating from this position of strength, Tesoro made a serious error in June of 1975, when it paid $83 million for 36.7 percent of the stock of the Commonwealth Oil Refining Company, (Corco), a Puerto Rican oil refiner and petrochemical processor that was one and a half times as large as Tesoro. Corco had been caught short by the sharp rise in petroleum prices in 1974, and its profitability had fallen, bringing the cost of its stock down as well. Tesoro sent out a team of new managers to try to turn around the fortunes of its new subsidiary.

Despite the fact that Tesoro's debt had grown in size to 1.3 times its equity, the company continued its pace of acquisitions, purchasing the GO Drilling Company of Texas, which owned three oil drilling rigs. In the following year, the company expanded its Alaskan operations when it bought the Nikiski Alaska Pipeline Company. Tesoro diversified into a third area of the energy industry, forming Tesoro Natural Gas Company in April of 1977 to purchase and transport natural gas.

By this time, however, Tesoro's financial position had become perilous, and the company's era of rapid expansion through haphazard acquisition came to a close. In 1977 Tesoro was forced to write off $59 million in Corco investments and lost $58 million overall. This bad news prompted a suit by shareholders against the company, alleging that Tesoro's Corco investment constituted mismanagement. It was clear that the company had bitten off more than it could chew.

Tesoro's lenders, concerned about the company's level of past borrowing, forced the company to liquidate many of its properties to earn cash to pay off some of its debt. Tesoro sold off its North Sea oil interests as well as an equipment manufacturer. The company was also forced to sell all but five of its American oil and gas properties, including refineries in Montana and Wyoming. This divestiture continued throughout 1978, which was capped by Corco's declaration of Chapter 11 bankruptcy. Tesoro subsequently reduced its interest in this subsidiary, surrendering its stock in 1981 and selling off its final ownership of Corco for $2.8 million in 1983. Overall, Tesoro had sacrificed a vast amount of capital in its bid to make Corco succeed.

Further difficulties arose in December of 1978 when various investigations by the Internal Revenue Service (IRS), the Securities and Exchange Commission (SEC), and the U.S. Justice Department resulted in the company having to pay tax penalties. It also had to disclose that it had paid more than $1.3 million in bribes to officials in Bolivia and other foreign countries over a six year period. This commenced a five-year federal investigation of Tesoro by a grand jury, which was not closed until February of 1984.

In an effort to rebuild, Tesoro brought in management consultants in 1979 to help it create a plan for future growth. West told

Business Week that Tesoro had undergone "a general change in philosophy" that would result in a more careful, integrated, and planned program of expansion and acquisition. As part of its new strategy, the company invested $45 million to upgrade its Alaskan refining facility, confident that the facility's remote location and ready source of raw materials in the Alaska oil fields would continue to make it a profitable enterprise.

By 1980 Tesoro had reduced its debt load to 20 percent of equity from 80 percent and was once again in the black. Belying his vow to stick to sensible investment in the petroleum industry, West made an abortive attempt to purchase Gulfstream American, a manufacturer of corporate jets, early in the year. After this was abandoned, Tesoro itself became the object of a potential corporate takeover in August when the Diamond Shamrock Corporation, a chemicals and natural resources producer, purchased 4.5 percent of the company's stock and announced that it would buy the company in an effort to move into the petroleum industry. Tesoro quickly filed two lawsuits to block this attempt. When Trinidad's government announced that it would not work with Diamond Shamrock, the attempt was dropped.

Tesoro remained in danger of corporate takeover, however. Its debt-ridden coal operation as well as new tax laws in Trinidad that penalized Trinidad-Tesoro kept earnings and the company's stock value low. Amid the disorder, speculators on Wall Street began to buy up the company's stock, anticipating its takeover or split into several parts.

In June of 1982 this speculation bore fruit when Tesoro announced a plan to sell its domestic oil, gas, and coal properties, as well as its interest in the Trinidadian company, and split its remaining holdings into two companies. The proposal, however, was subject to approval by the company's board. Ultimately, only the company's money-losing coal operations were sold, for $4.35 million, to the Shamrock Coal Company.

Despite the sale, Tesoro's persistently poor performance and low stock price continued to anger some investors, causing dissent among the ranks of the company's stockholders. When some began to agitate for replacement of Tesoro's management team through a proxy fight, Chairman Robert V. West sold a large chunk of stock in the company to a subsidiary of the Charter Company, an oil and insurance concern that was run by a friend. Subsequently, Tesoro tried to take over another small oil company, Enstar, and failed when it was sold to other suitors. The company instead purchased a 50 percent interest in offshore exploratory oil and gas properties owned by the Pel-Tex Oil Company.

In 1985 Tesoro further restructured its stock offerings to prevent any corporate takeover attempts. In addition, after years of proposals to do so, the company sold its nearly one-half share in Trinidad-Tesoro Petroleum to the island nation's government. The company announced plans to take over another oil producer but cancelled them when, later in the year, its bond ratings were lowered, reflecting a loss of confidence in Tesoro's financial health. The company reported a loss of $87 million at the end of 1985.

Matters continued to worsen in 1986, as Tesoro wrote off $44.3 million on an attempt to find oil in Trinidad and also gave up the value of its Indonesian reserves. Exploration in other areas of the world fared no better; wells in Turkey also turned up dry. In Bolivia, the country's government proved unable to pay Tesoro for its services and then announced that it would reimburse the company not in cash but in goods. Tesoro's $30 million joint venture with Pel-Tex also yielded little.

The one bright spot in the company's portfolio was its Alaskan refinery. Tesoro announced that it would upgrade the facility, which turned a profit providing fuel for the Alaska market, including substantial military operations. Nevertheless, Tesoro's 1986 balance sheet showed losses of $124.8 million, and the company continued to fend off take-over attempts. In April of 1986 Calvacade Oil made an offer to buy the company but was rejected.

In 1987 two more suitors had arrived—Oakville, a Hong Kong investment concern, and Pentane Partners, formed specifically to take over the company. Tesoro's problems had grown to include an $800 million shareholder suit, filed in July of 1987 against the company's management for corruption and securities fraud, and other legal difficulties. Tesoro won its court case but not without suffering the embarrassing revelation that it had hired prostitutes for foreign officials. In addition, an F.B.I. investigation into jury tampering was initiated, and the IRS demanded more than $50 million in back taxes.

By the end of 1987, Pentane Partners owned 9.74 percent of the company, and Oakville held 6.2 percent of Tesoro's stock. The company reported losses of $1.7 million, and joined the list of *Forbes*'s 500 poorest performing firms in sales growth. In May of 1988 Tesoro's board rejected a bid by Pentane for the remainder of the company. In the next few months, the company reached an agreement with the IRS to pay only $20.6 million in back taxes and sold its domestic oil and gas properties to American Exploration for $21 million in an effort to shore up its financial standing. By August of 1988 the company was also 5.3 percent owned by the chairman of another oil company, Stone Petroleum.

In 1988 Pentane made two additional attempts to acquire Tesoro, and the company also saw a $190 million offer by Harken Oil and Gas made and dropped. After a $56 million fine from the federal government for violating regulations on petroleum pricing and allocation, Tesoro reported a $30.52 million loss for the 1989 fiscal year.

By the following year, the company was back in the black with earnings of $22.7 million, but 1991 proved a disappointment, as the war in the Persian Gulf drove up prices for crude oil, while prices for refined products remained stable. This meant that profits on Tesoro's principal money-earning property, its Alaska refinery, were held down. The company earned only $3.9 million in 1991 and omitted its fourth quarterly dividend payment on stocks in a row. Difficulties continued in 1992, as the company laid off 60 employees and closed offices in an effort to reduce costs. As Tesoro moved into the mid-1990s, it faced a challenging business environment made more complicated the company's own legacy of bad luck and mistakes.

Principal Subsidiaries: Tesoro Alaska Petroleum Company; Tesoro Alaska Pipeline Company; Tesoro Northstore Company; Tesoro Bolivia Petroleum Company; Tesoro Exploration and Production Company; Tesoro Indonesia Petroleum Company; Tesoro Petroleum Distributing Company; Tesoro Refining, Marketing, and Supply Company; Tesoro Petroleum Companies, Inc.; Tesoro Tarakan Petroleum Company.

Further Reading: "Opportunity Talks," *Forbes,* November 15, 1973; "Tesoro Petroleum Corporation: An Address by Dr. Robert V. West, Jr., Chairman of the Board and Chief Executive Officer, at the Harvard Business School, February 19, 1975," San Antonio, TX, Tesoro Petroleum Corporation, 1975; "Tesoro Petroleum: The Irony of Becoming a Takeover Target," *Business Week,* October 6, 1980; Phalon, Richard, "'Tis a Far, Far Better Thing," *Forbes,* March 1, 1982; Burrough, Bryan, "Collapse of an Old-Boy Oil Network Places Tesoro in Vulnerable Position for Takeover," *Wall Street Journal,* June 12, 1984; Vogel, Todd, "Why Is Tesoro So Popular?," *Business Week,* December 21, 1987; Tesoro Petroleum Corporation Annual Report, 1991.

—Elizabeth Rourke

ⅦⒺ Thermo Electron

THERMO ELECTRON CORPORATION

81 Wyman Street
P.O. Box 9046
Waltham, Massachusetts 02254-9046
U.S.A.
(617) 622-1111
Fax: (617) 622-1207

Public Company
Incorporated: 1956
Employees: 7,650
Sales: $948.9 million
Stock Exchanges: New York
SICs: 3823 Process Control Instruments; 3511 Turbines &
    Turbine Generator Sets; 3845 Electromedical Equipment;
    8711 Engineering Services

Thermo Electron Corporation is a leading innovator in the practical application of heat science and energy conversion methods to the development of industrial and commercial products. The company represents the life work of Greek immigrant George Hatsopoulos, whose interest in applying technology to solving problems has led to the involvement of Thermo Electron in such fields as environmental monitoring instruments, alternative power generation, soil remediation, and artificial heart pumps. In addition to distinguishing himself as a scientist, Hatsopoulos has earned a reputation as a manager of extraordinary vision.

Hatsopoulos was born in suburban Athens in 1927 to a prosperous family of professors and politicians. He developed an interest in electronics during World War II when, upon the Nazi invasion of Greece in 1941, he constructed radios capable of tuning in Allied broadcasts—a practice punishable by imprisonment in a concentration camp. He clandestinely sold receivers to the public, and supplied transmitters to the Greek underground.

Following the war, Hatsopoulos studied electrical engineering at Greece's national technical university, Athens Polytechnic, where he developed a strong interest in thermodynamics, the science of extracting energy from heat. Perceiving that Athens Polytechnic could not meet his educational needs, Hatsopoulos

entered the Massachusetts Institute of Technology (MIT), where he became aware that there were practical applications of thermodynamics that had not yet been explored.

While still a graduate student at MIT, Hatsopoulos negotiated a $50,000 loan to found Thermo Electron. The company, which was at first based in a garage and employed only his brother John, was established to lend his thermodynamics experiments legitimacy, and in turn make grants easier to obtain. Hatsopoulos's first professional endeavors were in the new field of thermionics, the science of converting heat into electricity without the aid of moving parts. Though several completed and patented mechanisms were too expensive to market commercially, his pioneering efforts placed Thermo Electron among several major corporations as a leading patent mill in the area of thermodynamics, and helped inspire nearly 30 companies—including General Electric, North American Aviation, and General Dynamics—to enter the field.

The company survived for several years on research grants and metal fabrication work for other businesses, but was often forced to disregard profits in order to underbid competitors, acquire experience, and develop a reputation. Many Thermo Electron contracts focused on improving electrical generators and furnaces, and served to draw Thermo Electron into the business of industrial power generation and heating. Contracted by the United States government and a consortium of natural gas companies, Thermo Electron also improved industrial drying and heat-treating processes. Despite the company's status as the inventor of several new technologies, the government elected to award several subsequent contracts to larger competitors, such as GE and RCA, on the belief that the smaller organization did not have sufficient resources. In 1961 the company became the object of a takeover offer from Martin Marietta, which was interested in the application of thermionics to aerospace ventures. By this time, Thermo Electron had a staff of approximately 40 engineers and technicians, with Hatsopoulos heading the company's engineering efforts and his brother presiding over financial operations. Martin Marietta offered to purchase 51 percent of the company, retain Hatsopoulos as president, and double his salary. Hatsopoulos refused. Afterward, the government also recognized the merit of Thermo Electron, awarding it several contracts that included projects related to the space program.

In the drive to commercialize and expand, Thermo Electron began in 1963 to acquire firms whose facilities and marketing could support company breakthroughs in metallurgy and rare metals manufacturing—both of which developed from high-temperature heat conversion technology. Furthermore, in order to increase the availability of funds, Thermo Electron stock was placed on the Over-The-Counter Market in 1967 and on the New York Stock Exchange in 1980.

Much of the company's growth is directly attributable to Hatsopoulos's unique entrepreneurial philosophy: Thermo Electron engineers are encouraged to pursue their own inventions, and concepts with potential for commercial success are allotted substantial development budgets. While some of these investments fail to yield a profit, many result in inventions with great practical and commercial promise. An example of the latter is a modified Rankine-cycle steam engine that does not pollute. In 1968, four years after the engine project was initiated, the Ford Motor Company established a joint venture with Thermo Electron to apply this technology to automobiles. Enthusiasm on Wall Street drove Thermo Electron's share price to nearly ten times its value a year earlier, although stock values retreated when rising gasoline prices later led Ford to abandon the project in favor of high-efficiency engine research. Remade on a much smaller scale and powered by a miniature nuclear reactor, the steam engine was subsequently used to drive an artificial heart. When tested on animals, however, the device was found to be too hazardous for public use, and effective permanent models for humans never were developed. This work, however, led to the development of a battery-powered left ventricular-assist device, one of the most promising new product lines currently in clinical trials.

Thermo Electron's work in heat conversion and conservation technologies led to an annual grant of more than $1 million from natural gas utilities. By 1968 this support enabled the company to develop an industrial and commercial furnace division and acquire Holcroft & Company, a furnace manufacturer based in Michigan. That same year, Thermo Electron purchased Lodding Engineering, a Massachusetts manufacturer of auxiliary equipment for the paper industry. By expanding into industrial manufacturing, Thermo Electron was better able to market its innovations, test applications of its technology, and maintain quality control. By 1970 the company had diversified into other areas of primary industrial equipment manufacturing.

Hatsopoulos has demonstrated the ability to anticipate and address burgeoning public and consumer needs. Recognizing the close relationship between technology and the environment, he monitors demand for environment-oriented technologies by observing social and political events. This was best demonstrated in 1971, when Hatsopoulos predicted that ratification of the Clean Air Act would create demand for environmental monitoring devices. Consequently, Thermo Electron marketed the first instrument to detect traces of nitrogen dioxide, a common compound in automobile exhaust and smog. Later, Hatsopoulos determined that the growing dependence of the United States on foreign oil would enable oil producing nations to use their commodity as a political weapon. Hence, he stressed the development of more efficient industrial furnaces for the paper and metals industries well before the OPEC oil embargo of 1973, making the energy efficient products and patented designs of Thermo Electron the first on the furnace market. With this type of success, the company exceeded $100 million in annual sales by the mid-1970s. In 1981, revenues surpassed $230 million and profits neared $9 million.

Thermo Electron struggled for several years in a shrinking American capital goods market, however, because of an economic recession and a diminished market for capital-intensive equipment such as furnaces. In 1983 the company grossed only $182 million, leaving a scant $50,000 profit after the deduction of new business development expenditures and write-downs. At that point, Hatsopoulos decided that Thermo Electron must explore areas other than the capital goods market, and began searching for new industries. In a characteristic move, he doubled the company research and development budget. Addition-

ally, he mapped out what were determined to be the major issues of the 1980s and 1990s, and matched these issues with Thermo Electron's strengths. Consequently, Hatsopoulos decided to develop atmospheric-particle sensing devices capable of detecting small, well-concealed bombs and controlled substances such as cocaine. Company technologies also suited the development of a hazardous substance incinerator, which can be used to treat petroleum-contaminated soil. Other market-driven innovations include surgical monitors, generators that burn agricultural waste, equipment that recycles paper, and air conditioners that run on natural gas.

In a search for an improved business structure, Hatsopoulos encountered the model on which Japanese trading companies are organized. These companies, he learned, are part of huge industrial groups often including hundreds of diversified firms. Each owns a small percentage of every other company; hence, a company is owned in sum by the group. Hatsopoulos found that Japanese companies, with strong interest in mutual success, have little problem raising the funds necessary for ambitious research and development. In America, however, companies such as Thermo Electron are financially hamstrung by the limited backing of banks. Following the lead of the Japanese, he created several Thermo Electron subsidiaries beginning in 1983, selling between ten and 40 percent of each company to outside shareholders. The proceeds were used to further research and development at Thermo Electron, and nurture other subsidiaries toward public share offerings. There are now eight publicly traded subsidiaries, as well as one other one partially sold to outside investors. By separating these promising units from the larger corporation, Hatsopoulos found, he was better able to control costs, raise funds, and inspire a greater sense of mission. ''To take a company public,'' he told *CFO Magazine,* ''the company has to have an opportunity to grow at a 30 percent compounded rate for a long period. We must have the depth of management to run it as a public company, and we must have a need for the cash.'' Furthermore, none of these companies pays dividends; all shareowner profit is realized from increased share value. As a result of managerial strategies such as this, as well as product diversification, Thermo Electron has shown remarkable growth, posting revenues of $615 million in 1989, $721 million in 1990, $805 million in 1991, and $949 million in 1992. Profits in 1992 totaled $61 million.

After nearly 40 years, Thermo Electron essentially remains an idea factory. While growing tremendously in size and scope, it has almost always existed as a mini-conglomerate, a venture capital group dedicated to the solution of problems facing society. The key to the company's success, the *New York Times* noted, is that Thermo Electron ''gambles on innovative technology to attack potentially huge markets in socially important areas.''

Principal Subsidiaries: Thermo Power Corporation (52%); Thermedics Inc. (59%); ThermoTrex Corporation (62%); Thermo Energy Systems Corp. (87%); Thermo Instrument Systems Inc. (81%); Thermo Process Systems Inc. (71%); Thermo Cardiosystems Inc. (58%); Thermo Voltek Inc. (56%); Thermo FiberTek Inc. (80%).

Further Reading: Bylinsky, Gene, "Thermo Electron Corporation: From the Moon to the Steam Engine," *The Innovation Millionaires: How They Succeed,* New York, Scribner, 1976; "The Thinking Man's CEO," *Inc.,* November 1988; Hammonds, Keith H., "Inventor, Teacher, Economist—and That's Just for Starters," *Business Week,* December 18, 1989; Glazer, Sarah, "The Fabulous Hatsopoulos Boys," *CFO,* December 1989; McLaughlin, Mark, "Business Person of the Year," *New England Business,* December 1989; Feder, Barnaby J., "The Spinoff Stratagem: How Thermo Electron Copes with the High Cost of Capital," *New York Times,* November 11, 1990; "Thermo Electron Corporation: Diverse Technologies Spin Off into Growth," *Better Investing: Investment Education since 1951* 42, No. 3 (November 1992).

—John Simley

THORN APPLE VALLEY, INC.

16700 West Ten Mile Rd.
Southfield, Michigan 48075
U.S.A.
(313) 552-0700
Fax: (313) 552-0986

Public Company
Incorporated: 1959 in Michigan as Frederick Packing
   Company; 1971 in Delaware as Frederick & Herrud, Inc.;
   1977 in Michigan as Frederick & Herrud, Inc.
Employees: 3,200
Sales: $739.7 million
Stock Exchanges: NASDAQ
SICs: 2011 Meat Packing Plants; 2013 Sausages & Other
   Prepared Meats

Thorn Apple Valley, Inc., is a major producer of consumer packaged meat and poultry products in the United States. The company manufactures bacon, hot dogs, luncheon meats, hams, smoked sausages, and turkey products as well as numerous other products, marketing them under premium and other proprietary brand labels. The products are sold nationally to wholesalers, supermarkets, and food service operators. Thorn Apple also is one of the nation's largest slaughterers of hogs and sells fresh pork to other manufacturers of meat and poultry products throughout the United States.

The founder of Thorn Apple, Henry Dorfman, emigrated to the United States from Poland after World War II. He and his father escaped the Treblinka concentration camp that held many of his family members and other Polish Jews by jumping from a train. For the next three years, the two men hid in tunnels in central Poland. A master butcher by trade, Dorfman found work after the war selling meat to the United States government for officials living in Germany.

In 1949 Dorfman emigrated to the United States, settled in Detroit, and opened a butcher shop. Ten years later he and a partner bought Frederick Packing Company, a small hog slaughtering facility in Detroit. Dorfman was the the primary owner of the company and the operation's driving force. The company purchased, butchered, and sold pork to consumers and wholesalers.

In less than two years, Dorfman had repaid his purchase loan for Frederick Packing. He then began to expand the operation by acquiring other small slaughtering houses and meat processing plants located in the nation's midwestern and eastern states. Following additional acquisitions—including the purchase of Herrud and Company of Grand Rapids, Michigan, in 1969—Dorfman changed the company's name to Frederick and Herrud to better reflect the diversification of its operations into manufacturing and processing, in addition to packing. Today, the former Herrud is Thorn Apple's Grand Rapids Division and manufactures smoked sausages, hot dogs, and luncheon meats. In the early 1970s, Dorfman acquired meat businesses in North Carolina that produced deli products, smoked meat products, and bacon; these companies today make up a portion of Thorn Apple's Carolina Division in Holly Ridge, North Carolina.

In 1971 the company reincorporated in Delaware to take advantage of the tax and business benefits offered by that state's incorporation laws. Also that year, Dorfman took his company public and began trading stocks on NASDAQ. In the initial public offering, his family retained 70 percent of the shares. With some of the capital proceeds from the $16 per share purchase price, Dorfman bought two meat processing companies in Michigan and one in North Carolina. His expansion strategy involved acquiring small regional competitors that had achieved strong brand identities and consumer awareness and improving operating efficiencies by consolidating production into his existing plants. One of the company's next purchases was the Colonial hot dog brand in Massachusetts. Colonial's Boston plant was closed, and production was moved to plants in Michigan and North Carolina. In 1977 the company reincorporated again in Michigan because of changes in the state's business laws and to reflect the location of the corporate headquarters in the Detroit suburb of Southfield.

In the early 1980s many large food conglomerates were taking over independent meat packers to increase their market shares. Dorfman, by contrast, believed that future success depended on producing meats more cheaply than the conglomerates and giving consumers a better product. Despite a soft economy and a stagnant meat packing industry, he increased capital expenditures for plant modernization and improvements and devoted resources to product development and production. While this strategy resulted in several lean years for the company, Dorfman accepted the limited financial return as the cost of building a strong corporate infrastructure.

Also during this period, the company changed its image to a producer of high quality and premium brand products. To reflect this change, in 1984 Dorfman renamed the company Thorn Apple Valley, which was one of its marketing names for premium products. Later that same year, the company expanded to become vertically integrated and began operation of National Food Express, Inc., a transportation subsidiary intended to insure prompt delivery of perishable products from its Grand Rapids Division to its customers.

Despite the company's expanded market penetration, Thorn Apple's stock performed poorly, due in large part to the company's significant reliance on the unstable hog market. In 1987 the stock had declined to three dollars per share, a reduction of approximately three quarters of the original offering price three years earlier. Dorfman's son Joel wanted to take over the business and implement some new business practices to which he believed the market would react positively, but Dorfman was reluctant to step aside. However, when one of the nation's largest meat processing companies, Smithfield Foods, initiated a stock purchase for Thorn Apple at $10 a share in 1987, both Dorfmans agreed that something needed to be done. They declined Smithfield's purchase offer and set out to change the company's organizational structure and strategic posture.

Under the leadership of Joel Dorfman as president, the company operated according to a motto that was engraved on a plaque in the corporate conference room: "We are through just surviving." Because the company's decentralized structure resulted in duplicated efforts among the various Thorn Apple divisions, Joel reorganized the divisions into a centralized structure. He also made fundamental changes in plant utilization, production, marketing, and advertising.

Acquisitions continued, and in 1988 Thorn Apple began to expand into the western part of the United States with the purchase of the Tri-Miller Packing Company, a regional meat processing company in Hyrum, Utah. Tri-Miller was a successful full-line pork processor with slaughtering and production activities at its plant. Shortly thereafter Thorn Apple acquired another transportation company, Miller's Transport, Inc., to handle distribution and delivery service in the western United States.

Marketing was changed to emphasize premium products with a higher profit margin and newer items, such as turkey products, that reflected consumer preferences for leaner meats. By 1991 Thorn Apple's sales of premium products accounted for 40 percent of the company's manufactured products, up significantly from 28 percent in 1990.

The company's stock began to improve. Further changes included a tightening of the management structure, continued alterations to the marketing plan, and the establishment of a central distribution warehouse in Detroit. Plant operations were revised to eliminate plant managers, and renovations to the plants were designed to give each employee more room and time to work. Significant gains were made in the production yields of fresh pork. Yields, or the amount of meat from the hog that is able to be sold, improved three percent per hog to 59 percent between 1989 and 1991. This improved efficiency directly affected the company's bottom line; for every one percent of additional meat salvaged, revenues increased $6 million.

By December 1991 Thorn Apple completed a public offering of 300,000 shares of common stock. The net proceeds of approximately $9 million were used to reduce short-term debt, finance working capital needs, and make acquisitions. In July 1992 the company spent $3.8 million to acquire the assets of Suzannah Farms, a meat processor in Pennsauken, New Jersey, that had net sales in 1991 of $38 million. Production of the Suzannah line of products was moved to Thorn Apple's Deli and Smoked Meats Division plant in Detroit. At the same time, the company contracted with Atlanta Corporation of Elizabeth, New Jersey, the license holder for Suzannah Farms' brand name, to make hams and related meat products under the trademark Krakus. This acquisition and licensing agreement positioned Thorn Ap-

ple well to improve the company's penetration in the deli market and food service.

Financially, Thorn Apple performed well in the early 1990s. It was among the top United States food and beverage companies despite posted losses in 1990. In 1991 the company had the highest percentage of return on invested capital at 38.4 percent and the fourth best percentage sales gains, bettering such companies as Coca-Cola, Kellogg, and General Mills. Thorn Apple ranked 17th in sales among U.S. meat packers in 1991. The company achieved average annual rates of 6.7 percent growth in sales, 89.8 percent growth in earnings per share, and an improvement of 1.2 percent in net income to net sales from 1988 to 1992. Management attributed the increases to improved marketing efforts, streamlined operations, and a reduction in the volatility of fresh meat margins, which was in large part due to advances in purchasing strategies and the company's overall reduction of fresh meat in its total production mix.

In 1992 Thorn Apple enhanced profitability by maintaining its position as a low-cost producer of consumer packaged meat and poultry products and high-quality fresh pork. The company improved its manufactured product mix of consumer packaged higher-margin products such as turkey and smoked sausage and increased its capacity and sales of higher-margin value-added items such as boneless products and shelf-ready products. Sales of high-quality products were enhanced late in 1991 with the acquisition of Cavanaugh Lakeview Farms in Chelsea, Michigan, which sells gourmet meat products under the Cavanaugh name. The company's other premium brand products are marketed under the following labels: Thorn Apple Valley, Colonial, Triple M, Herrud, Bar H, Royal Crown, and Ole Virginie.

The majority of earnings in the early 1990s came from the company's manufactured products division, where strong earnings growth is dependent upon manufacturing efficiencies and increased sales volume of premium product lines. Generally, manufactured meat and poultry products have a profit margin that is three times higher than fresh pork and related by-products, which are heavily influenced by market conditions. Specifically, hog prices are cyclical and determined by supply and demand; these in turn directly affect the cost and profit margin of fresh pork and related products.

Improved operating efficiencies in manufactured products were achieved through increasing capacity and reducing ineffective production processes. Sausage and related products production at the Grand Rapids Division increased from 150,000 pounds per week to approximately 2.5 million pounds weekly in the 1990s. The Deli and Smoked Meats Division in Detroit increased from 200,000 pounds weekly to over three million pounds weekly, and bacon production was increased to over two million pounds weekly from 300,000 pounds per week at the Carolina Division. Annual hog slaughtering averaged 5,000 at the Tri-Miller subsidiary. Production of various processed meats increased to 700,000 pounds weekly since Thorn Apple's purchase of the Utah company in 1988.

Thorn Apple sells its fresh pork and manufacturing products to more than 900 customers in the United States, Canada, and several Pacific Rim countries. No single customer is responsible for more than 10 percent of the company's sales, and the 10 largest customers represent less than 30 percent of total sales. International sales for fiscal year 1992 were 1.5 percent of the company's total sales. Management expected additional opportunities for increased sales of fresh pork and processed meat in Korea, Japan, and Mexico in the mid to late 1990s to increase that total percentage.

Thorn Apple paid its first quarterly cash dividend to shareholders in 1992, which reflected a slight decline in the company's perceived need for capital. Marketing enhancements focused on customer-oriented satisfaction through the introduction of value-added products like vacuum packaged boneless pork, which is distributed to retail outlets and exported to Japan. The company also continued to develop strong wholesaler and retailer loyalty through dependable service and delivery of consistently high quality products.

Management's ultimate objective for Thorn Apple is to convince Wall Street that its cost structure and production are stable, especially in fresh pork, and that its financial performance is solid and predictable. Despite the company's gains since the late 1980s in its stock price, Thorn Apple's stock was significantly undervalued in a comparison of price-to-earnings ratios among some of the nation's top meat packers and processors. Thorn Apple's stock price relative to its net earnings per share was 8.4, which means that a share of stock is just over eight times more than a stockholder's return of net earnings. Competitors with higher price-to-earnings ratios include Con-Agra at 18.1, George Hormel at 18.6, IBP at 16.4, and Smithfield Foods at 10.6. Additional acquisitions in the Western United States, continued improvements in operating efficiencies, capacity advances, and further market penetration in selected international markets should help Thorn Apple's stock to continue to improve as the company moves toward the 21st century.

Principal Subsidiaries: Tri-Miller Packing Company; National Food Express, Inc.; Coast Refrigerated Trucking Company Inc.; Miller's Transport, Inc.

Further Reading: "Selling Out," *Inc.,* November 1990; Eberwein, Cheryl, "Thorn Apple Harvest," *Corporate Detroit,* January 1992; Gutner, Toddi, "Father Doesn't Know Best," *Forbes,* August 17, 1992.

—Allyson S. Farquhar-Boyle

TIME WARNER INC.

75 Rockefeller Plaza
New York, New York 10019
U.S.A.
(212) 484-8000
Fax: (212) 522-0907

Public Company
Incorporated: 1990
Employees: 40,215
Sales: $13.07 billion
Stock Exchanges: New York
SICs: 2721 Periodicals: Publishing, Or Publishing &
  Printing; 2731 Books: Publishing, Or Publishing &
  Printing; 4841 Cable & Other Pay Television Services;
  3652 Phonograph Records & Pre-recorded Audio Tapes &
  Discs; 7812 Motion Picture & Video Tape Production;
  3952 Lead Pencils, Crayons & Artists' materials; 3823
  Industrial Instruments for Measurements, Display &
  Control of Process Variables & Related Products; 7922
  Theatrical Producers, (Except Motion Picture) &
  Miscellaneous Theatrical Services; 7822 Motion Picture &
  Video Tape Distribution

From its inception as the thinly capitalized passion of two
young men in 1923 through its 1990 merger with Warner
Communications Inc., Time Inc. has been a steady, guiding
force in U.S. media. As the world's largest media concern, Time
Warner's mandate is to expand its global reach and transfer
more of its communications arts from print to electronic form.
In the process, Time Warner is on its way to becoming the
quintessential self-marketing media producer, due in large part
to the cultivation of synergies between Time and Warner assets.
By 1992 Time Warner claimed to be the world's leading creator
and owner of creative software copyrights, and the only media
and entertainment company to control 100 percent of its distribution.

The magazine that launched Time Inc. was conceived by Yale
University sophomores Briton Hadden and Henry Robinson
Luce during officers' training at South Carolina's Camp Jackson during World War I. "The paper," as they referred to it,
was a dream they put on hold for three years, until February of
1922, when they resigned from their positions as reporters at the
Baltimore News. Armed with $86,000 of borrowed capital,

Haddon and Luce moved to New York and prepared to launch
the weekly news magazine *Time.* The magazine's initial mandate eventually became that of the entire company: to keep the
public informed. Haddon and Luce spent a year organizing
investors, staff, and tradesmen and collecting criticism and
advice. The first, 32-page, issue of *Time* was dated March 3,
1923. Haddon was *Time*'s editor, Luce its business manager.

Just as impressive as *Time*'s expansive editorial content was the
duo's then-novel approach to marketing the publication, which
included postcard inserts soliciting subscribers and circulation
of lists of prominent charter subscribers. The magazine was
developed by a lean staff, who doubled as clerks. Luce's and
Hadden's own salaries were at subsistence level.

For its first year, *Time* prospered modestly. When *Time* was just
over a year old, it had garnered 30,000 paid subscribers. On
August 2, 1924, Luce and Hadden launched a second publication, the *Saturday Review of Literature.* Hadden, who served as
editor, determined that everything printed had to be either
directly attributable to a person or to the publication's own
authority. *Time*'s other early journalistic innovations included
the use of historical background in stories.

In 1925 Luce insisted that *Time*'s operations be moved to less-
expensive facilities in Cleveland, Ohio—a move that Hadden
and much of the publication's staff bitterly but unsuccessfully
fought. Three years later, printing of the magazine was moved
to the offices of the R. R. Donnelley company in Chicago, while
Time's editorial office was moved back to New York. Hadden
and Luce opted at the same time to switch titles and functions
temporarily. Hadden became *Time*'s business manager, overseeing the publication's daily operation, while Luce took command of *Time*'s journalistic direction.

By 1928 Time Inc. posted a net profit, after taxes, of $125,788
on revenues of $1.3 million. Making *Time* a lucrative proposi-
tion had taken its toll on Hadden, however, who began the new
year fighting off a streptococcus virus. Hadden died at the age of
31 on February 27, 1929, six years after the first issue of *Time*
was put to press.

To protect the ownership of the company, Luce and other *Time*
staffers and directors bought 2,828.5 of Hadden's 3,361 company shares at $360 a share. Hadden's family retained the
remaining 532.5 shares. Within two years, Time Inc. stock
peaked at $1,000 per share, and was split 20-to-1. In the mean-
time, Luce proposed to launch a new weekly magazine, *Fortune*, that would cater to business managers. With the Time Inc.
board's approval, Luce set out to launch *Fortune* on the eve of
the Great Depression. *Fortune*'s first issue, in February of 1930,
won satisfying acceptance among its targeted audience. In September 1931, however, Parker Lloyd-Smith, *Fortune*'s managing editor and codeveloper with Luce, committed suicide.

Also in 1931, Time was making its controversial transition to
radio. Time Inc.'s "The March of Time" radio show featured
re-enactments of historical events. The show, although popular,
was a limited run promotion that some observers felt threatened
Time's journalistic integrity. In 1935 the "March of Time"
format reappeared, as a motion picture series of short subjects.

In April of 1932 Time Inc. acquired 75 percent of *Architectural Forum*. The company completed its acquisition of that professional journal for builders the following year. Luce's personal interest in architecture had spurred Time Inc.'s acquisition of *Architectural Forum*, which he reshaped throughout the 1930s to reflect the monumental socio-political events of the day. When New Deal legislation made $3.3 billion available for construction projects, *Forum* editors rushed to press an 18-page guide explaining how builders could benefit. *Forum* editor Howard Nyers cultivated young architects and, in 1938, Frank Lloyd Wright traveled to New York and produced an issue of *Forum* devoted to the subject of his works. Although *Forum* expanded its circulation from 5,500 to almost 40,000 in the decade following Time Inc.'s acquisition of the publication, it posted only one year of profit. Luce resisted Time Inc.'s attempts to sell the publication.

In 1936 Luce began to explore the concept of a weekly photo magazine. Time subsequently brought pictures to print with the publication of *Life*, which first appeared in November 1936.

In 1937 Luce created Time Inc.'s divisional system, the corporate organization that defined Time's operations for decades. Each of the company's three fundamental publications—*Time, Fortune,* and *Life* —was assigned its own publisher, managing editor, and advertising director. Although a huge circulation success, *Life* was proving to be a major financial drain due to the unexpectedly high cost of producing the magazine. The explosive popularity of *Life* propelled Time Inc. into increasing circulation, and thus costs, pushing losses on the picture magazine into the millions. *Life* continued to lose money, a total of about $5 million, until January 1939, when the magazine turned its first profit.

While *Life* continued to lose money for Time directly, it was also the indirect cause of losses for the company as some readers of *Time* switched to *Life*. In May of 1938 the company sought to relieve *Time*'s circulation problems with the $25,000 acquisition of *Literary Digest*. About 60 percent of *Literary Digest*'s 250,000 subscribers chose to transfer their subscriptions to *Time*, bolstering that magazine's sagging circulation.

In 1938, on the news that Time Inc.'s earnings were forecasted to drop a record $2 million, *Time*'s publisher, Ralph Ingersoll, and Luce became embroiled in a fierce argument over the company's earnings. Ingersoll felt that Luce had diluted *Time*'s earning potential by siphoning off *Time*'s profits to start up and maintain publications such as *Fortune* and *Architectural Forum*. Ingersoll and Luce disagreed on editorial issues as well. In April of 1939 Ingersoll took a leave of absence from *Time* and did not return. Following Ingersoll's departure, Luce appointed himself *Time*'s publisher and editor-in-chief.

Luce, who had strong ideas about how the tumultuous events in Europe that would lead to World War II should be reported, decided later in 1939 to devote more time to the editorial direction of Time Inc.'s magazines. Thus, in September of 1939, Luce resigned as president and CEO of Time Inc., remaining editor-in-chief, and chairman Roy E. Larsen was elected to the posts that Luce had vacated. Like most other key Time Inc. executives, Larsen was younger than many of his industry peers.

Time enjoyed steady success during World War II, as its national magazines chronicled the war. Time Inc.'s publications dominated the newsstands. In 1941 *Time*'s circulation was rapidly approaching one million. *Life* had weekly sales of 3.3 million magazines, with a significant additional readership. *Fortune* had a small but influential group of 160,000 readers. The organization of 2,500 full-time employees would grow to 5,500 over the next two decades of continued expansion.

Time assumed a prominent role reporting most major news events, including World War II and the McCarthy era. There were times when the magazine clashed openly with major decision makers; President Franklin Roosevelt and *Time* criticized one another openly during the war. During the winter of 1941–1942, also in the name of covering the war, Luce and his wife, Clare Boothe Luce, reported on the state of world affairs from England and the Far East, respectively; he for *Time*, she for *Life*.

In the fall of 1942 Clare Boothe Luce was elected to Congress as a representative of the Connecticut district that her stepfather, Dr. Albert E. Austin, had served from 1938 to 1940. Her position in national politics raised the dilemma of how Time Inc.'s magazines should cover the wife of their editor-in-chief. Eventually, Luce called for a blackout on the coverage of his wife in all of Time's magazines.

In 1945 *Time* redirected the energies of its pool of wartime correspondents and photographers, organizing them into an international reporting operation under the command of C. D. Jackson. Luce simultaneously redefined the job of publisher of *Time* and appointed James A. Linen III to that position. Linen was among the first of a generation of younger managers who came up through *Time*'s editorial and sales ranks. Edward K. Thompson came up through the ranks to serve as managing editor of *Life* beginning in 1949.

Given more of a free hand than his predecessors, Thompson dismantled the periodical's divisional structure and launched the publication on its most successful decade. Soon afterward, the financially troubled *Fortune* was the subject of what Time Inc. executives referred to as a "re-think." Also in the postwar years, Luce adapted to technological advances that helped offset increases in the price of materials and wages. Despite reporting a ten-percent operating profit on a record high $120 million in revenues in 1947, Luce, ever the conservative manager, abandoned several projects, including the construction of a New York skyscraper, due to the cost.

Arguably, Time Inc.'s most important and lucrative long-term decision to diversify was the launch of *Sports Illustrated* in 1954. Sports in the United States then still tended to be seasonal, and sports marketing was relatively primitive. Despite the fact that *Sports Illustrated* did not turn its first profit for a decade, the magazine eventually became very profitable.

During the mid-1950s Time undertook to widen the appeal of longtime money-loser *Architectural Forum*. Although the company was successful in boosting circulation, the magazine continued to run at a loss. *Forum* was spun off to an existing nonprofit group in 1964. *House & Home*, a magazine Time Inc. had formed to complement *Forum* in 1952, was sold to McGraw-Hill in 1964 as well. In 1953 Time launched *Life en Español*, a companion to *Life International*. *Life en Español* was suspended in 1969, however, and *Life International* was eliminated the following year.

The post-war years also marked Time Inc.'s expansion into media other than print. In 1952 the company founded its Time-Life Broadcast subsidiary with a 50 percent interest in KOB and KOB-TV in Albuquerque, New Mexico. In a second bid for broadcast experience, Time acquired a majority interest in the Intermountain Broadcasting and Television Corporation of Salt Lake City, Utah, operators of the KDYL stations. Time acquired its first wholly owned and operated stations, KLZ-AM and KLZ-TV of Denver, Colorado, in 1954. Three years later, Time acquired the Bitner television and radio properties—WOOD in Grand Rapids, Michigan; WFBM in Indianapolis, Indiana; and WTCN in Minneapolis, Minnesota, for the then-record sum of $16 million. Eventually, Time sold its Salt Lake City and Minneapolis broadcast properties to acquire KOGO-TV in San Diego, California, and KERO-TV in Bakersfield, California.

In 1959, after recovering from his first heart attack, Luce began preparations to pass the title of editor-in-chief-to Hedley Donovan, who was then managing editor of *Fortune*. Although Luce did not finally surrender the title until 1964, in 1959 he set in motion a management reorganization that put a new generation of Time Inc. managers in control. The company prospered under its new leadership. From 1960 to 1964, net revenues jumped from $287.12 million to $412.51 million, and net income increased from $9.30 million to $26.53 million, due to sales expansion and tighter cost controls. This profitability had been enhanced by the 1961 creation of Time-Life Books, an extension of Time's already profitable book publishing operation. Time's new management initiated explosive growth. Time continued to expand overseas offices throughout the decade, and in 1962 Time acquired textbook publisher Silver Burdett Co. in a $6 million stock swap. In 1964 Hedley Donovan was appointed to succeed Luce as editor-in-chief. In January of 1968 Time bought book publisher Little, Brown and Company for $17 million worth of Time stock. In 1966 Time initiated the General Learning Corporation, a joint venture with General Electric designed to sell a variety of learning tools; it was sold in 1974 at a loss.

Luce died on February 28, 1967. Even after his death, Luce's influence was felt at the company where separation of editorial and publishing interests was considered sacrosanct. Time's new leadership continued to guide the company profitably. In October 1970 the company announced plans to sell its broadcast properties to concentrate solely on cable television—a segment of the electronic media in which it already had amassed a considerable interest. By that time, Time had created East Texas Pulp and Paper Company, a joint enterprise with the Houston Oil Company, as its own source of paper. It also had erected a new Manhattan skyscraper at Rockefeller Center and successfully fended off competition from magazines such as *Look* and the *Saturday Evening Post*. In December 1972, however, Time announced it would cease publication of *Life*, which had faced soaring production costs, shrinking advertising sales and circulation, and postal rate increases. *Life* had lost $30 million between 1969 and 1972.

Throughout the 1960s and 1970s Time Inc. acquired a number of large and small enterprises in a continuing bid to diversify. Perhaps Time Inc.'s most costly and controversial acquisition at the time was its $129 million merger in 1973 with Temple Industries, Inc., a producer of lumber, plywood, and other building materials. Time took another step toward diversification in 1978 when it acquired Inland Container Corporation for $272 million.

In November of 1972 Time's J. Richard Munro, who eventually became Time Inc.'s chairman and chief executive officer, launched the pay-TV service Home Box Office (HBO) through the Time subsidiary Sterling Information Services, Ltd. HBO was one of Time's few commercial successes. Even after Time-Life Films was phased out in the early 1980s, HBO continued to finance major films, as well as invest in a movie distribution company and join Columbia Pictures and CBS in a studio venture.

HBO, coupled with two new publications—*Money,* launched in 1972, and *People,* launched in 1974—emerged as Time's new profit centers during the 1970s and 1980s. Nicholas J. Nicholas, Jr., who had risen through Time's corporate finance ranks and would later become its president and chief operating officer in 1986, recommended that Time divest its sluggish forest-products interests to concentrate on its video and print businesses, where future growth would be focused. Consequently, Temple-Inland was formed and spun off to Time shareholders in 1983. Time Inc. was left to focus on its seven magazines and their foreign-language equivalents; American Television and Communications Corporation, one of the country's largest cable companies, which is 82 percent-owned by Time Inc.; HBO and Cinemax (begun in 1980), two of the country's most successful pay TV services; and Time-Life Books.

Time added four new magazine titles in 1988, bringing its total number of published magazines to 24. It paid $185 million for a 50-percent interest in Whittle Communications, which provided satellite public affairs and news programming directly to classrooms. It was involved in international publishing ventures with foreign-based companies such as Hachette, Arnoldo Mondadori, and Seibu. Time's growth continued through the 1980s, culminating in the 1989 agreement to acquire Warner Communications Inc. for $14 billion, creating the world's largest entertainment and media concern. Time itself had become an attractive takeover target in an era of unprecedented leveraging and hostile bids, and thus had accepted Warner's invitation to merge.

The proposed Time-Warner combination was nearly thwarted by an unsolicited takeover bid for Time from Paramount of $175 cash per share, or $10.7 billion. The raid proved unsuccessful and cost Paramount $80 million. It also required Time to rework the logistics of its merger with Warner, burdening itself with $12 billion in debt. Time and Warner engaged in a swap of each other's stock early in the merger process in an additional defensive move.

Although strategically driven, not all of Time Inc.'s board members, especially Henry Luce III and Arthur Temple, were convinced that the merger was a wise course of action. Munro and Nicholas engaged in one-on-one consultation with each director to secure unanimous approval for the January 1990 transaction. The merger created a vertically integrated company.

At the first annual shareholders meeting of Time Warner, in the spring of 1990, Munro did as expected and announced that he would step down as co-chairman and chief executive officer of Time Warner Inc., but would remain chairman of the board's executive committee. Nicholas assumed the co-chief executive title while retaining the job of president. The merger agreement called for Nicholas to succeed Time Warner chairman and co-chief executive Steven Ross as the company's sole chief executive in mid-1994.

Time Warner claimed that all of its media and entertainment franchises ranked first or second in their categories. Time Warner's cable pay-television services, HBO and Cinemax, posted record performances. Pay-TV revenues from HBO and programming continued to grow, increasing 7.6 percent in 1990. Time combined its Time-Life Books and Book-of-the-Month-Club operations. Its American Television and Communications Corporation achieved record revenues and earnings on four million basic cable and three million premium subscriptions. Time also sold off Scott, Foresman, its textbook publisher, in December 1989 for $455 million because it no longer fit into its core businesses.

In its first year as a merged entity, Time Warner created Time Warner Publishing to oversee all of the company's book and magazine publishing activities, which accounted for $3 billion of its annual combined revenues. The new unit launched such new magazines as *Martha Stewart Living* and acquired the 50-percent interest in *Health* that it did not already own. Time Warner made a small effort to begin tapping the synergies of their combined assets when, in February of 1990, Time launched *Entertainment Weekly* using Warner's tape and book subscription lists. Time Warner revealed plans to open a nationwide chain of retail stores, similar to those operated by The Walt Disney Company, to sell merchandise featuring Bugs Bunny and other Warner Brothers Looney Tunes characters, as well as other products related to the company's vast operations. Time Warner also began taking a more creative approach to cross marketing its products and publications. For instance, in November 1990 Time Warner signed an unprecedented agreement with Chrysler for advertising in seven of Time Warner's national magazines and its cable group, and to make product placements in selected Warner Brothers film releases.

To the surprise of many, within months of the merger, the highly leveraged Time Warner announced the acquisition of Lane Publishing Company, publisher of *Sunset* magazine, for $225 million—$80 million in cash and $145 million in preferred stock. In another surprising move, in April 1990 Time Warner offered to provide a $650 million bridge loan to Pathe Communications Company to help with its $1.4 billion acquisition of MGM/UA Communications Company in exchange for certain valuable MGM/UA assets, including the United Artists film library. However, Time Warner withdrew its offer, and Time Warner and Pathe eventually sued each other over the aborted agreement. In October of that year the companies opted to settle their differences out of court when Time Warner agreed to pay $125 million for the international home video rights to

1,700 titles in the United Artists and Pathe/Cannon film libraries for more than 12 years.

By late 1990, Time Warner was struggling to find ways to establish joint ventures with various international concerns. Such ventures would bring much needed new development funds into its operations while offering special expertise and foreign business connections. Management continued to promise shareholders a reduction and financial restructuring of Time Warner's $11.2 billion debt. With more than $2.5 billion in bank loans due in early 1993, one option the company had was to sell its partial stakes in businesses such as Atari, Hasbro, the Franklin Mint, Six Flags Corporation, the record clubs of Columbia House, Cineamerica theaters, and Turner Broadcasting System Inc. A weak economy in 1990 kept Time Warner from resorting to such a move as the sluggish marketplace made it impossible for them to command a premium for its business interests. Yet by the end of 1991, Time Warner's 22-percent ownership of Turner Broadcasting and its 14-percent ownership of Hasbro represented $1.6 billion of market value.

In the meantime, the company worked diligently to keep Wall Street at bay. Although initially supportive of the transaction, some Wall Street analysts soured on Time Warner six months after the merger. In May 1991 Time Warner announced an unorthodox rights offering. The company planned to issue 34.5 million shares at between $63 and $105 per share, priced according to the number of shareholders who participated. In July, following vigorous objections from the Securities and Exchange Commission and many powerful investors, Time Warner replaced the plan with a traditional $80-per-share offering. Citing the unexpected softness of media advertising, tight financing, and an uncertain economy, Time Warner officials conceded it would take them longer than expected to arrange the joint ventures and limited equity placements that would launch the merged company back into a development mode.

As a result of the $2.6 billion raised by the rights offering, which was completed in early August 1991, Time Warner's debt was significantly reduced to $8.7 billion at year's end. It helped demonstrate to potential partners that newly formed alliances would be based on long-term strategic goals.

By October 1991 Time Warner had formed a strategic alliance at the subsidiary level with its first two partners, Toshiba Corporation and C. Itoh & Co. Ltd., who agreed to invest $500 million each for a 6.25 percent stake. The agreement maintained American ownership and control. It excluded Time Warner's publishing, journalism, music, and certain other assets and called for a limited partnership, Time Warner Entertainment, which included Warner Bros. Pictures, Home Box Office, and Time Warner Cable. It was capitalized at $20 billion.

Time Inc. boasted 40 percent of the magazine industry's 1991 profits and one-third of its revenues while taking a one-time $60-million charge to cover restructuring. According to the Publisher's Information Bureau, *People, Sports Illustrated,* and *Time* weeklies led in 1991 advertising revenues. Advertising clients were offered one-stop shopping through a cross-media package that united Time Inc.'s magazine franchises with Time Warner's video, cable, programming, and book entities. Book division profits were down in 1991, despite the presence of

Warner Books' best seller *Scarlett* and Little, Brown's *Waldo* series.

More than half of the Warner Music Group's 1991 revenues came from outside the United States. In February the group bought 50 percent of Columbia House, the music and video club operator, and invested in label start-ups. Laser-disc manufacturing was added.

Warner Bros. Feature Film Division finished first in 1991 domestic box-office share. A series of partnerships were created to broaden the range of motion-picture products and international distribution. In January 1991 Warner Bros. and three European companies signed a $600-million financing, production, and distribution deal.

A new operating group, Time Warner Telecommunications, was formed in late 1991 to take advantage of the next generation of mobile voice telephone services. Quantum, a 150-channel, interactive cable service, was launched in Queens, New York, in December of 1991. Coaxial and fiber-optic cable was joined to create a two-way digital pathway into homes that allowed viewers to control what they saw and when they saw it.

Time Warner Cable had been comprised of wholly owned Warner Cable and 82-percent-owned American Television and Communications Corp. In February 1992, to help form Time Warner Entertainment, Time Warner signed a merger agreement to purchase the 18 percent of American Television and Communications that previously had been publicly owned. Viacom International Inc., a Time Warner competitor, ended its three-year, $2.4 billion antitrust lawsuit against the media giant in mid-1992. Time Warner reached a settlement with Viacom that called for greater cooperation between the two companies.

For 1991, earnings before operating results were $2.26 billion on revenues of $12.02 billion. A net loss of $99 million for the year marked an improvement from the $227 million in losses posted in 1990. In April 1992 a $1.1 billion long-term senior debt-financing lengthened the maturity of Time Warner debt.

Principal Subsidiaries: American Family Publishers; American Television and Communications Corporation; Astroworld/ Waterworld; Book of the Month Club; cable system joint ventures (50%); Cinamerica Theatres, L.P. (50%); Comedy Partners (50%); E! Entertainment Television, Inc. (44%); Hankook Ilbo Time-Life Ltd; Home Box Office Inc.; Ivy Hill Corporation; Little, Brown & Co (Canada) Ltd; Little, Brown & Co; MacDonald & Co. (Publishers) Ltd; President Inc.; Six Flags Corporation (50%); Six Flags Great Adventure; Six Flags Great America Inc.; Six Flags Magic Mountain Inc.; Six Flags Over Georgia; Six Flags Over Mid-America Inc.; Six Flags Over Texas; The Columbia House Company partnerships (50%); The Time Inc Magazine Co.; The Time Warner Cable Group; Time Canada Ltd.; Time Life International do Brazil Ltda; Time Publishing Ventures Inc.; Time Warner Enterprises; Time Warner Publishing Inc.; Time Warner Trade Publishing; Time-Life Books BV; Time-Life Inc.; Time-Life International BV; Time-Life International de Mexico SA de CV; Time-Life International GmbH; Time-Life International Ltd.; Time-Life International SA; Time-Life International SrL; Time-Life Libraries Inc.; Turner Broadcasting Systems, Inc. (22%); Warner Cable; Warner Communications Inc.; Warner Music Group Inc.; Warner Music International (Europe) Ltd.; Warner Publishing Inc.; Warner Special Products; Warner/Chappell Music Inc.; WEA Corp.; WEA Intl Inc.; WEA Manufacturing; Whittle Communications L.P. (37%).

Further Reading: Elson, Robert T., *Time Inc.: The Intimate History of a Publishing Enterprise—1923–1941,* New York, Athenaeum, 1968; Elson, Robert T., *The World of Time Inc.: The Intimate History of a Publishing Enterprise—1941–1960,* New York, Athenaeum, 1973; Prendergast, Curtis, and Geoffrey Colvin, *The World of Time Inc.: The Intimate History of a Changing Enterprise—1960–1980,* New York, Athenaeum, 1986; *Annual Report,* New York, Time Warner, 1991; Higgins, John M., "Black Ink, Slow Growth at Time Warner," *Multichannel News* 13, no. 17 (April 27, 1992); "Time Warner refinances $6.2B Debt," *Multichannel News* 13, no. 20 (May 18, 1992); Brown, Rich, "Viacom, Time Warner Bury the Hatchet," *Broadcasting* 122, no. 35 (August 24, 1992); Fabrikant, Geraldine, "Time Warner Shows Gains As It Shrinks Merger's Debt," New York Times, February 9, 1993.

—Diane C. Mermigas
updated by Anne C. Hughes

TIMEX ENTERPRISES INC.

Park Road Extension
Middlebury, Connecticut 06762
U.S.A.
(203) 573-5000
Fax: (203) 573-5143

Private Company
Incorporated: 1941 as Timex Inc.
Employees: 7,500
Sales: $400 million
SICs: 3873 Watches, Clocks, Watchcases & Parts

Timex is the largest watchmaker in the United States, controlling over a third of the country's market. For decades its image was utilitarian, but that began to change in the 1980s when it brought out lines of sports and fashion watches made popular through aggressive and innovative advertising campaigns.

Timex was founded by Norwegian shipbuilder Thomas Olsen and engineer Joakim Lehmkuhl, both of whom fled Norway to live in the United States after the German invasion of their country in 1940. The following year they purchased the nearly bankrupt Waterbury Clock Co. in Waterbury, Connecticut, seeking to aid the allied war effort by producing bomb and artillery fuses, which relied on clockwork mechanisms.

When World War II ended in 1945, Olsen, the majority shareholder, returned to Norway, while Lehmkuhl remained in the United States to run the company. During this time, Lehmkuhl decided to convert the Timex plant to mass produce inexpensive timekeeping devices. Using the simplest and most standardized production methods available, Lehmkuhl's plant incorporated a high degree of mechanization in the manufacturing process. Furthermore, the wristwatches Timex manufactured used hard alloy bearings, producing a more rugged and less expensive alternative to watches that used jewelled bearings. Timex's product and production methods eventually won Lehmkuhl a reputation as "the Henry Ford of the watch industry."

The first Timex watches rolled off the assembly line in 1949 and soon became known for their dependability. At the time, most watches were sold by jewelers, who typically marked up prices by 50 percent. To keep its prices low, Timex insisted on only a 30 percent markup, and, consequently, most jewelers refused to sell Timex watches. Robert Mohr, head of Timex's marketing operation, opted to bypass the jewelers, instead selling the watches directly to consumer outlets including drugstores, hardware stores, and even tobacco stands. During the 1950s and 1960s Mohr built a distribution network that reached nearly 250,000 outlets. By 1961, sales were up to $71 million, with after tax profits of $2.9 million.

Advertising heavily both to build its name and to sell the dependability of its watches, Timex relied chiefly on the visual impact of television. Commercials depicted Timex watches remaining functional and accurate after being attached to churning boat propellers and the hooves of galloping horses. The phrase "takes a licking and keeps on ticking" became widely known, and by the late 1960s Timex watches accounted for about half of U.S. watch sales. During this time, the company deliberately underproduced, manufacturing only 85 percent of the watches it thought it could sell. This practice created a scarcity that kept prices up and dealers tractable. In addition to the manufacture of timepieces, Timex continued to produce the clockwork mechanisms for the military that it had begun during the war. Timex facilities were also used to assemble cameras for Polaroid. In 1970 Timex had record profits of $27 million on sales of about $200 million.

However, change lay just around the corner, as the firm was facing intense competition in a changing market. Although few companies producing watches in the same price range as Timex could challenge the company for quality or popularity, digital electronic watches were rapidly overtaking the conventional watch. Timex began producing digital watches in 1972, but it had not moved as fast as its competition. In 1974 the company's net income fell by one-third to $8.7 million on sales of $348 million. By 1976 digital watch prices had fallen into the price range of the company's mechanical watches, and Timex began losing market share. Its major competitors in the electronic watch market were Texas Instruments and Fairchild Camera and Instrument Corp., both of which had more experience with electronics. A price war ensued, and by 1977 Texas Instruments had slashed the price of one of its most popular watches to ten dollars.

Also during this time, Timex management was in turmoil. Lehmkuhl had become increasingly eccentric and difficult to work with, and in 1973, Olsen's son Fred had the 78-year-old founder and chairperson removed. Furthermore, the company's three presidents were constantly at odds, and when electronics experts were brought in to help the company fight for digital watch market share, the infighting intensified and the company suffered. Timex was soon restructured to reflect Fred Olsen's belief that making electronic watches required a radically different approach than that of mechanical watches. The mechanical watch operation was thereafter isolated from the new electronic operations, a change that eventually created resentment among the employees. The restructuring also led to numerous mistakes as the isolated electronic division was unable to take advantage of the mechanical division's experience.

Consequently, Timex's electronic watches were awkwardly large and 50 percent more expensive than those offered by competing firms. Management felt sales of mechanical watches were in an irreversible decline, so they planned to keep production capacity below the level of likely sales in order to make as much money from the line as possible as the market shrunk. Advertising for mechanical watches virtually ceased, and, as spending decreased, the capital was shifted to the manufacture and sale of digital watches.

The entire watch industry had a good year in 1977, and Timex decided to slow the downsizing of mechanical watch production. However, the company failed to reinstate its advertising budget, and, as a result, its only profitable product began to decline in popularity. Timex lost $4.7 million on sales of $600 million in 1979. Sister corporation TMX Ltd., a Bermuda-based company that supplied watches and parts to Timex, also lost $5 million that year.

During this time, chief executive Robert Weltzien began diversifying the company. He bought a clock and timer operation from General Electric Co., and in early 1980 he held the company's first ever press conference, announcing that as Timex had gained experience from assembling Polaroid cameras—more than 40 million between 1952 and 1979—the company would soon begin manufacturing a new type of 35-millimeter camera. However, these moves were not enough to offset Timex's declining watch sales, and later that year Olsen flew in from Norway, fired Weltzien, and took his place as CEO. Thereafter Olsen spent two weeks a month overseeing his businesses in Norway and the other two weeks with Timex in Connecticut.

While Olsen was a brilliant long-term strategist with immense energy, he had little experience with the day to day running of an organization, and some managers became frustrated as he interfered with the details of their projects. He began closing factories, cutting wages, and selling off side businesses, as he reshaped the company into a consumer electronics concern that would sell watches, clocks, computers, and electronic products geared toward home health care.

In 1980 Commodore Computers explored the possibility of a merger or other working relationship with Timex, but Olsen declined. Instead, Timex opted to attempt duplicating Commodore's success by producing its own computer. Created by British inventor Clive Sinclair, the Timex computer was brought out at the end of 1982 and quickly achieved 500,000 sales. However, critics noted that the Timex computer was extremely limited in its capabilities and inferior to Commodore's product. After Commodore engaged Timex in a price war, Timex made little money from the venture.

In 1983 Timex brought its first home health care products to market. The products, made by Singapore subcontractors, included a $69.95 blood-pressure cuff, a $24.95 digital thermometer, and a $49.95 digital scale. Timex relied on its widely recognized name and large distribution base to give it an advantage over companies already selling similar products. The market was very competitive, however, and Timex was also hampered by the breakup of its Silicon Valley computer engineering staff due to continuing political infighting as well as the slow start of its new lab in Connecticut.

Watches still accounted for 90 percent of Timex's business in 1983. The firm's digital watches had improved considerably, and it introduced a new quartz calendar watch at $100 that was billed as the world's thinnest. While the majority of its electronic watches were more expensive than those of its competitors, Timex had succeeded in bringing out one model that sold for only $7.95.

Also in 1983, Timex endured negative press from an employee strike at its plant in Dundee, Scotland, which strikers occupied after management fired 1,900 workers. Members of the British parliament and finally Prime Minister Margaret Thatcher intervened before the six-week occupation was ended.

Throughout the 1980s, inexpensive fashion watches rapidly gained popularity and were released by a number of companies, most notably the innovative Swatch company. Timex's sales needed bolstering as some industry analysts estimated that the company only produced half as many watches as it had five years earlier. Consequently Timex began producing watches that were more fashionable, sporty, and colorful, and invested money and energy in advertising. In the spring of 1983 the company launched a $20 million television advertising campaign focusing on its new technological sophistication and style. The commercials, by Gray Advertising, playfully exaggerated the features of Timex watches. In one ad a group of joggers ran up and down the contours of a Timex sports watch; in another, a groups of people climbed out of a boat and walked across a waterproof Timex watch that served as a dock. Timex also showed its ads in movie theaters, purchasing four weeks of ad time at Screenvision Cinema Network's 4,500 theaters in 1986.

One of the firm's greatest successes during this time was its sports watches. In 1984, an Olympic games year, the company brought out the Triathlon watch, which was water resistant to 50 meters, could recall eight laps of running times, and had a 16-hour stopwatch. In its first year, 400,000 of the watches were sold at $34.95 each. Encouraged by this success, Timex brought out a ski watch that included a thermometer as well as a racing watch that could measure speeds of up to 999 miles an hour. The company launched its Atlantis 100 water resistant sports watch in 1986 with a $1 million ad shown during football's Super Bowl. This ad featured a groups of divers discovering a 65-foot replica of the watch on the bottom of the Red Sea. Five other "adventure" commercials were also produced.

In 1988 Timex brought back its "takes a licking and keeps on ticking" campaign, which had not been used in ten years. This time, however, the ads were humorous and took the premise of the old ads to extremes, one ad showing the watches being thrown to ravenous piranha. Timex also stepped up advertising for its new line of men's and women's fashion watches, influenced by those being sold by Swatch. Having formerly advertised mainly in such magazines as *Time* and *Life*, Timex began buying space in sports and fashion magazines. The ads were part of an effort to help Timex shake its staid image at a time when watchmakers like Swatch were making inroads by giving their watches a fun, quirky image. The firm spent $6 million dollars on ads during its Christmas ad campaign, representing 60 percent of its $10 million dollar annual ad budget.

Timex released new sport watches in 1988 that were aimed at niche markets while also being designed to appeal to a broader audience. One model, the Victory, included features useful in sailboat racing and a design influenced by traditional nautical instruments. While the Ironman watch was geared toward triathlon participants, the watch's memory feature and rugged styling proved so popular that Timex was soon able to claim that it was the bestselling watch in the United States.

At the end of the 1980s the color plastic watch business pioneered by Swatch was beginning to decline, but Timex continued producing colorful watches with classic styling and increased the distribution of its watches to upscale department stores. Timex remained at the top of the U.S. mass market watch sector with a share near 50 percent. Sales for 1988 topped $500 million. It was still the largest company in the $1.5 billion U.S. watch market, despite the fact that all of its watches were priced at under $75.

Although the information age initiatives the company had announced in the early 1980s had been sharply scaled back, Timex announced it would develop a wristwatch that would double as a telephone pager. It anticipated that the pager, to be developed with Motorola Inc., would be available by 1992.

In 1990, with its market share under continual pressure, Timex spent $7 million on a unique two-month print ad campaign. Again picking up on the "takes a licking" theme, the ads featured portraits of people who, along with their Timex watches, had survived serious mishaps. One woman, for example, had fallen 85 feet while rock climbing and suffered only minor injuries. The ads, by the Minneapolis based agency Fallon McElligott, appeared in 31 magazines and included several three-page spreads.

In 1992 Timex introduced a watch with a luminescent dial that glowed like a full moon at the push of a button. The watch used a dial made of zinc sulphide and copper that other companies had used on clocks, though Timex was the first to adapt it to watch size.

Although not as overwhelming a presence as it had been during the 1950s and 1960s, Timex held onto its position as the leading U.S. watchmaker as it approached the twenty-first century. The company remained adept at marketing and had succeeded in revamping its image in times of tough competition.

Further Reading: "The Great Digital Watch Shake-Out." *Business Week*, May 2, 1977; "A Reclusive Tycoon Takes Over at Timex." *Business Week*, April 14, 1980; Magnet, Myron, "Timex Takes the Torture Test." *Fortune*, June 27, 1983; White, Hooper, "Human Touch Rides New Wave." *Advertising Age*, November 7, 1983; Brown, Christie, "Sweat Chic." *Forbes*, September 5, 1988; Fahey, Alison, "Another Lickin'." *Advertising Age*, November 7, 1988; "Motorola Plans to Develop Pager Watch with Timex." *Wall Street Journal*, July 26, 1989; King, Thomas R. "Timex Hopes 'True Story' Ads Will Keep Watch Sales Ticking." *Wall Street Journal*, October 30, 1990.

—Scott Lewis

THE TORO COMPANY

8111 Lyndale Avenue South
Bloomington, Minnesota 55420-1196
U.S.A.
(612) 888-8801
Fax: (612) 887-8258

Public Company
Incorporated: 1914 as the Toro Motor Company
Employees: 3,084
Sales: $635.2 million
Stock Exchanges: New York
SICs: 3524 Lawn & Garden Equipment; 3494 Valves & Pipe
  Fittings Nec; 3052 Rubber & Plastics Hose & Belting

Long respected as a manufacturer of premium-priced lawn mowers, snow blowers, and irrigation systems, The Toro Company touts itself as "a global leader in lawn and turf care products." Toro is currently an industry leader in both turf maintenance and underground irrigation capacities for golf course establishments, and holds a strong position in the homeowner and consumer markets with such brand name lines as Toro, Lawn Boy, and Toro Wheel Horse. The company's strategies for future profitability and growth are unclear, however, after weathering a difficult downswing in fiscal 1992. Sales in the consumer products division (which accounted for roughly 55 percent of total revenue) fell nearly 19 percent, directly contributing to a $23.7 million loss in net earnings. Concurrent layoffs, plant closings, and scaled-back production have recalled Toro's battle to remain afloat during a similarly troublesome time in the early 1980s.

Under CEO Kendrick B. Melrose and President David H. Morris, the company hopes to stage a comeback akin to the one accomplished when Melrose, as newly elected president, redirected the company a decade ago. The new redirection will emphasize greater mass-merchandising efforts and lower-priced product lines.

Founded in Minneapolis in 1914, the Toro Motor Company was established by executives of the Bull Tractor Company—among them J. S. Clapper, Toro's first president—primarily to manufacture engines and other machined parts for use in the parent company's line of Bull tractors. When Bull Tractor folded in 1918—approximately the same time that Deere & Company and other competitors were fortifying their positions

in the agricultural market—Toro was forced to fend for itself. The United States's entry into World War I in 1917, however, created a demand for steam engines for merchant supply ships, a need that Toro helped to fill through the conclusion of the war. In 1920 Toro Motor became Toro Manufacturing Company. The first product to carry the company's name was the Toro (two-row) cultivator that converted to a tractor. However, a widespread economic depression among American farmers during the early 1920s left the company overstocked and in need of new products to sell. In 1921 the opportunity came for Toro to reinvent itself and become profitable for the long term. The greens committee chairman for an exclusive Minneapolis country club had approached the company with an unusual request: could a specialized tractor replace the horse-powered system then used for cutting the greens and fairways? The solution was a tractor equipped with five 30-inch lawn mowers, which enabled the groundskeeper to cut a 12-foot wide swath in a third of the time required by the earlier method. This relatively simple invention led directly to the machine-driven, gang-reel mower, the forefather of the modern power mower industry.

By 1925 the Toro name had become synonymous with turf maintenance among nearly all the major golf courses in the nation. Business was booming. The rapid growth of the company was due in large part to the establishment of a distributorship system in which regional business owners/sales representatives promoted quality Toro products while offering knowledgeable advice and service. In 1929, 13 distributorships were in place and Toro decided to go public, realizing that its research and development edge had to be maintained to thwart rising competition. The October 1929 stock market crash impeded the company's progress, but only temporarily.

In 1935 the company became Toro Manufacturing Corporation of Minnesota; two years later its engineers unveiled its most important product to date, the 76-inch Professional, an ingenious compromise between the maneuverability of walk-behind mowers and the speed and capacity of the large gang-reel units. The popular product was ultimately replaced by the Super-Pro and the 58-inch Pro.

In the years prior to World War II, the company succeeded in forming several overseas distributorships and in introducing its first power mower for the domestic consumer market. By 1942 sales had grown to $2 million and the company's commercial line—its mainstay—now served not only golf courses, but parks, schools, cemeteries, and estates. Like most American manufacturers during that period, Toro concentrated its resources on the war effort, contributing parts for tanks and other machinery. When 1945 came, Toro retooled under new owners.

Robert Gibson, Whitney Miller, and David Lilly, all veterans and all friends since their days at Dartmouth College, purchased the company in 1945 and fueled it for the next several years with youthful ambition and systematic expansion. In order to maintain the loyalty of their workers, who then numbered around 50, they named long-time employee Kenneth Goit as president. Following much-needed plant reorganization and modernization, the three owners led the company aggressively into the homeowner mower business, which market studies had shown to be a particularly promising area. From 1946 to 1950 sales climbed from $1.4 million to $7 million. Several factors contributed to this remarkable increase. The solid expansion of Toro's distribution network, which had grown to 88 members, who in turn sold to approximately 7,000 retailers, made the company a large-scale presence. In addition, the company developed and marketed Sportlawn, a popular walk-power reel mower. Finally, and most importantly, Toro acquired Milwaukee-based Whirlwind, Inc., in 1948. Whirlwind was a prominent manufacturer of a consumer rotary mower, a new design which Toro proceeded to enhance with safety features.

In 1950 Lilly succeeded Goit as president. A number of firsts highlighted the decade, including Toro's pioneering lawn and garden television advertisements, the erection of a test facility in Bloomington, Minnesota, and the creation of the Wind Tunnel housing for its Whirlwind mower, which made rear-bagging feasible for the first time. Sales increases uniformly reached double-digit percentages, despite a lukewarm entry into snow-removal equipment and a poor performance by the Tomlee Tool Company, acquired in 1954.

Toro indisputably came of age in the 1960s, aided by the power of its ad campaigns and the strength of its research and development department. Its power mower line was widely regarded by the public as the standard in engineering excellence. After achieving this goal, the half-century-old company was ready for a new dynamism. The retirement of "Mr. Toro," a charismatic salesman named "Scotty" McLaren, also augured a change in direction. The invention of the single-stage Snow Pup snowthrower in 1962 signaled the company's recommitment to establishing a winter product line, but the results were less than satisfactory (Toro would eventually succeed years later with the Snow Master). Further diversification within the golf market was another possibility. One campaign centered on the production of a deluxe golf car, the Golfmaster, that would utilize all of the company's significant design expertise. As Trace James reports in *Toro: A Diamond History,* "Toro had purchased the materials and manufactured the parts to build 1,000 Golfmasters. However, by the time the first 250 of these beauties came off the assembly line, they were so loaded with features that golf courses couldn't afford to buy them. Toro was left with work in progress for 750 cars." Through persistent sales efforts, however, the company was able to rid itself of all but four cars and turn a profit.

Finally, in 1962, Toro purchased a company that would virtually ensure Toro's lasting preeminence in the golf course industry. California-based Moist O'Matic, a manufacturer of irrigation products, brought sales above the $20 million mark that year and ultimately gave Toro the number one position in golf course irrigation equipment. This same year the company relocated to its present headquarters in Bloomington. By the end of the decade, with a greatly strengthened commercial division and the introduction of the electric start feature for its consumer mowers, Toro's sales surpassed $50 million.

The 1970s began with David McLaughlin assuming the presidency from Lilly. Growth during the decade for The Toro Company (so named in 1971) was phenomenal. The consumer snow removal business, after persistent re-engineering and re-marketing, began to thrive. Commercial turf maintenance, with the introduction of the all-hydraulic Greensmaster and Groundsmaster, experienced a renaissance. As a flurry of new products went on line, the Toro work force swelled to well over 1,000 employees. Net earnings from 1977 to 1979 almost tripled and sales reached an all-time high of $357.8 million. McLaughlin forged ahead with greatly expanded production of snowblowers. Suitable weather in which buyers could utilize the new product line proved elusive, however. Snow was a relative scarcity during the winters of 1980 and 1981 and, consequently, so were snow blower sales. Because Toro had positioned a full 40 percent of its business in this market, it suffered devastating losses, a total of $21.8 million between fiscal 1981 and fiscal 1982. To make matters worse, McLaughlin had moved Toro into the mass merchandising arena and away from its reliance on the dealer network—where lower sales but greater profits were the norm.

Melrose replaced McLaughlin in 1981 and went to work quickly, cutting salaried staff by nearly half, closing plants, and instituting a "just-in-time" inventory system to prevent future overproduction. During the mid-1980s he systematically diversified, acquiring two lighting manufacturers and establishing an outdoor electrical appliance division. The 1986 purchase of Wheel Horse (a manufacturer of lawn tractors) and Toro's entry into the lawn aeration business helped push sales above $500 million the following year. Rounding out the decade was the company's 1989 purchase of one of its chief lawn mower competitors, Outboard Marine Corporation's Lawn Boy, for $98.5 million. Melrose, along with recently elected president Morris, had succeeded in reducing the company's dependency on snowthrower sales, which fell to just nine percent of revenues, while maintaining the Toro name as the industry market leader.

The investment community, however, remained largely oblivious to the dramatic turnaround, and this was reflected in Toro's depressed stock price. Robert Magy, in his article "Toro's Second Season," recounted Melrose's befuddlement at the sluggish reaction of the investment community to Toro's recovery. This puzzlement led to the hiring in 1989 of a Chicago-based investor relations firm. "In October, the agency surveyed analysts and institutional investors in several major markets and discovered that few of them had any knowledge of Toro, and that among those who believed they did know something about the company, several thought it had collapsed early in the last decade." Thus work of a different sort, higher-profile public and investor relations, awaited Melrose. Although he quickly proved to be an effective and energetic company spokesperson, Melrose did err with over-optimistic earnings predictions.

Toro's 1990 introduction of the Toro Recycler (a high-performance mulching mower) and its high expectations for Lawn Boy as a lower-priced complement to the existing product line were among the many reasons why Melrose anticipated the company would achieve billion-dollar status by 1992. Instead, the company saw sales drop from $750 million in 1990 to $711 million in 1991 to $635 million in 1992. A series of profit projections, all of which had to be downwardly revised, seriously dampened the company's credibility during the early part of this period. Particularly harsh criticism came from *Star Tribune* writer Tony Carideo. "With each piece of negative news, Toro has trotted out explanations: A bad economy. Not enough rain. Too much rain. Not enough snow. A really bad economy. Well, maybe. But how about this? Toro makes a product that costs too much because there's a lot of R&D and advertising cost in it and because it's sold through an antiquated distributor-dealer network that raises the price even higher.'' Carideo's article appeared January 28, 1992, just after Toro had announced a major consolidation and restructuring of its Lawn Boy and Toro businesses, including a plant closing and some 450 layoffs.

More than half a year later, the company still showed signs of struggling. For its first quarter of fiscal 1993, Toro reported a net loss of $4.1 million, compared with a net loss of $6.2 million for the first quarter of fiscal 1992.

The report stated that the decline ''was expected as we consciously managed down consumer product field inventories in the quarter in preparation for several new Toro and Lawn-Boy product introductions this Spring.... [We] believe Toro will emerge from 1993 with our strong name intact, with increased market shares and with investments in new products that will ensure the future of our investment.'' Strong second quarter earnings supported that contention, as Toro reported net earnings of $1.8 million for the quarter ending January 29, 1993, versus a net loss of $11.9 million in the same quarter a year before.

Among Toro's major plans for 1993 were the introduction of the Toro Recycler II series and a wholesale assault on the mid-priced mower market through such mass merchandisers as Sears, Montgomery Ward, and Home Depot. After weathering a difficult recession, certainly a factor in Toro's stagnant performance, the company seemed prepared for a strong rebound. Yet, several analysts—Carideo excepted—were skeptical of Toro's new emphasis on mass merchandising. One likely reason was the stiff competition it would receive from Georgia-based Snapper Power Equipment Co., another high-quality manufacturer with similar plans. Whatever the outcome of its consumer line, it remained clear that Toro could ill afford to overlook possibilities for growth within its commercial line. As Dain Bosworth analyst Frank Rolfes pointed out, as many as 4,000 golf courses were to open across the United States during the 1990s (approximately four times as many as during the 1980s). Each of the courses represented potential sales of $700,000 in turf maintenance and irrigation equipment.

Principal Subsidiaries: Lawn-Boy Inc.; Toro Credit Co.; Wheel Horse Products Inc.

Further Reading: Kirsch, Sandra L., ''Toro Co.,'' *Fortune,* November 20, 1989, p. 106; James, Trace, *Toro: A Diamond History,* Bloomington, Minn.: Toro, 1989; Magy, Robert, ''Toro's Second Season,'' *Corporate Report Minnesota,* May 1990, pp. 57–63; Carideo, Anthony, ''It's Not All Sunshine for 3 Minnesota Firms,'' *Star Tribune,* May 6, 1991, p. 1D; ''Mulching Mowers Cutting an Ever-Widening Swath,'' *Star Tribune,* May 17, 1991, p. 1D; Meeks, Fleming, ''Throwing Away the Crystal Ball: Most Chief Executives Shy from Making Profit Projections. Toro Co.'s Ken Melrose Now Knows Why,'' *Forbes,* July 22, 1991, p. 60; Kurschner, Dale, ''Toro Battles Snapper for Similar Turf,'' *Minneapolis-St. Paul City Business,* September 9, 1991, pp. 1, 24; Peterson, Susan E., ''Toro Restructuring Will Shut Down Mississippi Plant, Cut 450 Workers,'' *Star Tribune,* January 22, 1992, p. 1D; Carideo, Tony, ''Toro Tackles Question of Luring Buyers Seeking a Cheaper Lawn Mower,'' *Star Tribune,* January 28, 1992, p. 2D; Howatt, Glenn, ''Toro Has First Quarterly Profit in Year; Retail Sales Still Weak,'' *Star Tribune,* May 22, 1992, p. 7D; Peterson, Susan E., ''Toro Plans to Close Distribution Center and 2 Plants,'' *Star Tribune,* July 31, 1992, p. 1D.

—Jay Pederson

TOSCO CORPORATION

72 Cummings Road
Stamford, Connecticut 06902
U.S.A.
(203) 977-1000
Fax: (203) 964-3187

Public Company
Incorporated: 1955 as Oil Shale Corporation
Employees: 1,760
Sales: $2 billion
Stock Exchanges: New York Pacific
SICs: 2911 Petroleum Refining; 2819 Industrial Inorganic
  Chemicals Nec

Tosco Corporation is one of the largest independent refiners of petroleum products in the United States. Once a major player in American efforts to develop alternative energy sources, Tosco refocused on its refining operations after enthusiasm over synthetic fuels waned in the early 1980s. The company also manufactures phosphate-based fertilizers through its Seminole Fertilizer subsidiary.

Tosco was founded in 1955 under the name Oil Shale Corporation by a group of investors headed by Hein Koolsbergen. The company was incorporated under the laws of the state of Nevada, but made its headquarters in the Los Angeles area. As its name might suggest, Oil Shale Corporation was in its beginnings a highly entrepreneurial company convinced that the practice of extracting oil out of oil-bearing shale could be a financially rewarding venture. One of its early projects was an attempt to help Brazil wean itself off of imported oil by developing its substantial oil shale deposits. The project won some early support from the U.S. government, but interest from other sources was meager and the initiative soon died out.

Oil Shale entered into a somewhat more durable alliance in 1965 when it joined West Coast oil giant Atlantic Richfield in forming the Colony Shale Oil Project. The joint venture was formed in hopes of mining a 7,000-plus acre property in a section of Colorado containing the nation's richest and most extensive known oil shale reserves. Progress on the Colony project came slowly, however, in part because of Colorado's stringent environmental laws, but also because the process of extracting oil from shale was still too expensive to make it competitive with other sources.

In the meantime, Oil Shale began to develop refining as a profitable sideline until its vision of the future of the oil industry came to fruition. It sold part of its interest in Colony Shale Oil to Atlantic Richfield for $8 million, staggered some observers in the investment community by leveraging itself to the hilt, and then went on a buying spree. In 1970 it acquired the Signal Oil & Gas refinery in Bakersfield, California, for $22.5 million. In 1976 it acquired $222 million of Phillips Petroleum's West Coast property, including the giant Avon Refinery in Concord, California. These moves gave the company a refining capacity of more than 200,000 barrels per day, making it the third-largest independent refiner in the United States and the largest supplier of gasoline to independent marketers on the West Coast. Tosco—the company changed its name to an acronym of its previous name in 1976—also drew attention for processing California crude, a thick, high-sulfur, crude oil that most refiners refused to touch. But Tosco's history of technical experimentation enabled it to find a process that could extract a broad range of gasoline products from California crude at a reasonable cost.

As Tosco underwent a major shift in operational emphasis during the 1970s, its top management changed as well. Hein Koolsbergen had served as chief executive officer virtually since the founding of the company, but critics charged that he found it difficult to adapt to the growth and maturation of his brainchild. Morton Winston, a lawyer who became a full-time executive with the company in 1964, was named president in 1971 and he and Koolsbergen quickly ran afoul of each other. In the power struggle that ensued, Winston won, becoming chief executive officer in 1976, and Koolsbergen was forced out.

Morton Winston was an anomaly in an industry in which most top managers had backgrounds in geology, engineering, or finance. As a graduate student in the early 1950s, he aspired to become a literary scholar and chairman of a college English department. Later, after a stint in the Coast Guard, he entered Harvard Law School. After graduating from Harvard in 1958, Winston spent a year clerking for Supreme Court Justice Felix Frankfurter, then joined a New York law firm that specialized in advising small, entrepreneurial companies. He made his first contacts with Oil Shale Corporation in 1961 and joined the company shortly thereafter.

As chief executive officer of Tosco, Winston made no effort to hide his unusual background in the humanities. He composed poetry in his spare time and encouraged his executives to memorize *Bartlett's Quotations.* Associates said that he conducted meetings not unlike a soft-spoken college professor conducting a class. But all the points that Winston earned on style would have gone for naught if the company had not fared well during his tenure. Despite his admission that Tosco had moved into the refining business rather later than it should have, the company nonetheless showed a tenfold increase in earnings between 1975 and 1980. The oil price shocks of the 1970s that drove the price of imported crude to dizzying heights supported Tosco's long-standing conviction that oil shale production could prove a financially viable option. As the decade drew to a close, Winston told the *Los Angeles Times* that "this company was born out of the insight that the United States would shortly be in deficit in oil. We have always been able to see what was coming. Where we have been wrong is in estimating how long it would take to get there. We have been too early.'' Tosco appeared to be in good position to collect on its shale oil bet, having patented its own process for extracting oil from shale.

The company's advancement in this area, however, was not smooth. Tosco flinched in allowing the Colony project to proceed, fearing that it would require an initial investment of $1 billion. The company also worried that future changes in Colorado's environmental regulations could drive operating costs to unacceptable levels.

In 1980 the Atlantic Richfield Company sold its 60 percent share in Colony to Exxon Corporation for $300 million. Construction began at last on a processing plant that was scheduled to be completed in 1986 or 1987. Questions about the plant, however, soon presented themselves. Rising capital costs (from 1980 to 1982, Exxon and Tosco spent $400 million between them on Colony) and a levelling off in the price of crude oil raised doubts about the economic feasibility of the project. In addition, the Reagan Administration was not sympathetic to calls for continued funding of the Synthetic Fuels Corporation, the federal agency set up by the Carter Administration to subsidize the development of synfuels. In 1982 Exxon announced that it was withdrawing from the Colony project, effectively dooming it. Without a partner of Exxon's size and prestige, Tosco could not keep the venture afloat.

The Colony project was of such size and importance that its demise seemed to signal the collapse of the entire effort to develop synthetic sources of crude oil. "It's the end of a pretty brief era," prominent oil analyst Daniel Yergin said at the time in the New York Times. After Colony's demise, only Union Oil, among major American oil companies, continued to sink money into oil shale development.

For its part, Tosco received $380 million worth of compensation from Exxon for its share of Colony. The initial agreement between the two companies had stipulated that Exxon would have to buy out its stake in the venture if it ever pulled out, and Tosco exercised that clause in the contract. Most of the money went to relieve debt and recover Tosco's own capital expenditures, while some of it went to shareholders in a special one-time dividend. Exxon's payment, however, did not obscure the fact that Tosco's gamble on oil shale—the entire reason behind the company's birth—had come to a profitless end. It now had to rely on its refinery business for direction and revenues.

During this period, Morton Winston's position at the top of the company began to look shaky. In the wake of the collapse of the Colony project, Kenneth Good, a Colorado land developer who owned nine percent of the company's outstanding shares, accused Tosco of concealing Colony's long-term risks from shareholders and pressed for Winston's removal. Tosco attempted to cope with the reality of a shale-less future by courting AZL Resources, a Phoenix-based oil and gas exploration firm. Late in 1982 it agreed to acquire Credit Immobilier, a Swiss investment concern that owned a 30 percent stake in AZL Resources. In January 1983 it acquired all remaining outstanding common shares of AZL Resources.

This attempt to recover from the Colony disaster was insufficient to forestall a major reorganization. With Tosco reeling from a first quarter loss of nearly $77 million and still saddled with more than $700 million in bank debt, Morton Winston stepped down as CEO in June 1983 and was replaced by Matthew Talbot. One of Talbot's first acts was to announce the layoffs of 15 top executives and the consolidation of Tosco's seven divisions into two.

The reorganization did little to ease Tosco's difficulties. Sagging crude oil and gasoline prices made things difficult for a company that suddenly found refining to be its sole source of support. Tosco lost over $677 million between 1983 and 1986, and, after buying out dissident shareholders inspired by Good, found itself so deeply in debt that its creditors decreed that it should hire investment banker Bear Stearns to help arrange a takeover. There were, however, no takers. The company's stock fell to $2.75 per share, down from its high of $45 in 1980. Feeling that a change of leadership was necessary, Tosco's directors forced Talbot to resign in June of 1986 and replaced him two months later with company chairman Clarence Frame. In the meantime, Tosco sold its Bakersfield refinery to Texaco for $22 million.

Although the company returned to profitability under Frame, its heavy debt load and depressed stock price forced Tosco to spend the remainder of the decade under the pall of takeover speculation. Michael Tennenbaum, a Los Angeles-based director of Bear Stearns, purchased a seven-percent stake in the company in 1987. The next year, Argus Energy, a Connecticut-based investment partnership, announced that it had acquired a 40-percent interest in Tosco. In 1989 the company acquired Seminole Fertilizer, but this did not stop the widespread takeover speculation and uncertainty over Tosco's status. Later that year, Argus Energy head man Thomas O'Malley, by now a Tosco director, succeeded Clarence Frame as chief executive officer.

One of the company's first actions under O'Malley was to announce that it was entertaining takeover bids. Tosco claimed that at least three multinational corporations made offers, but refused to announce the identity of the suitors. Informed speculation had it that one suitor was British Petroleum, which was said to be interested in establishing a presence on the West Coast through Tosco's Avon refinery. Neither party ever confirmed that this was so, however.

Tosco declared in 1991 that none of the offers it had received were satisfactory, and that it would remain independent. The company then declared that it would consolidate operations and cut administrative costs by closing down its headquarters in Santa Monica, California. Initially, Tosco declared that it would find a headquarters site in northern California, closer to the Avon refinery. But it ultimately wound up moving to Stamford, Connecticut, the home of Argus Energy.

Indeed, the move may have signalled that Tosco intended to shift geographical direction and develop a presence on the East Coast as significant as its presence on the West Coast. In December 1992 the company acquired Exxon's Bayway refinery, located in Linden, New Jersey, for $175 million. The acquisition made it the second-largest independent refiner in the United States.

Exxon's withdrawal from the Colony Shale Oil Project in 1982 and Colony's consequent collapse marked a decisive turning point for Tosco, as the company has since struggled to stabilize its fiscal health and corporate identity. What had once been a small, entrepreneurial company with a futuristic vision of how to use new technology to find alternative fuel sources has had to content itself with more traditional ways of making money in the oil business. With the acquisition of the Bayway refinery, it appears that Tosco is determined to establish itself as a major independent oil refiner.

Principal Subsidiaries: AZL Resources, Inc.; Diablo Service Corp.; Seminole Fertilizer Corp.; The Lion Group, Ltd.; The Oil Shale Corp.; Tosco Corp.; Tosco International Finance; Tosco-petro Corp.; Tosco Trading, Transportation & Supply, Inc.; Western Hemisphere Corp.

Further Reading: Grant, Linda, "Events Catching up With Tosco's Plans," *Los Angeles Times*, December 24, 1978; Chavez, Lydia, "Tosco's Winston Is an Anomaly Among Oil Industry Executives," *Los Angeles Times*, July 22, 1980; Martin, Douglas, "Exxon Abandons Shale Oil Project," *New York Times*, May 3, 1982.

—Douglas Sun

TRINITY INDUSTRIES, INCORPORATED

2525 Stemmons Freeway
Dallas, Texas 75207-2401
U.S.A.
(214) 689-0592
Fax: (214) 689-0824

Public Company
Incorporated: 1933 as Trinity Steel
Employees: 9,800
Sales: $1.19 billion
Stock Exchanges: New York
SICs: 3743 Railroad Equipment; 3441 Fabricated Structural
Metal; 3731 Ship Building & Repairing

Trinity Industries, Incorporated, is a diversified manufacturer of heavy metal products. The company's six basic business segments comprise rail car leasing and the production of rail cars, marine products, structural metal products, pressure and non-pressure tank containers, and metal components. Trinity is a leading rail car manufacturer in the United States, controlling nearly half of the national production capacity for freight cars. Tank cars and hopper cars are leading products. Marine products such as commercial boats, barges, and offshore service vessels for the United States government make up the company's second largest business segment, generating about 17 percent of revenues. Pressure and non-pressure containers for gas and chemical storage, and structural products used in construction of highways, bridges, and buildings each account for 12 percent of revenues. Metal components such as weld fittings and container heads currently make up about eight percent of the company's sales, with the remaining five percent coming from rail car leasing operations.

Trinity Industries was formed in 1958 when the Dallas Tank Company merged with Trinity Steel Company, which made metal products for the petroleum industry; the name was changed to Trinity Industries in 1966. The company has been run by W. Ray Wallace since its first year. Wallace had joined the original Trinity Steel in the late 1940s as the company's 17th employee.

After the merger, Trinity was the only publicly owned company that produced a varied line of metal products for liquefied petroleum gas (LPG). LPG, a relatively new form of fuel at that time, is used for industrial production and residential heating. Compressed natural gas and petroleum by-products can be conveniently stored and transported in specially designed tanks that permit a consumer to obtain 270 cubic feet of gas from one liquified cubic foot. As the LPG industry grew rapidly in the late 1950s and early 1960s, Trinity was the only tank manufacturer operating across a large geographical area. The company's competitors were generally smaller concerns whose markets were limited to their own regions, and Trinity, demonstrating an ability to offer consistent quality to LPG suppliers, became the industry leader.

Trinity's tank manufacturing expertise was also applied to containers for anhydrous ammonia fertilizer, which was another burgeoning industry in the 1960s. Pressure and non-pressure storage containers made up about 75 percent of Trinity's business. The company also manufactured custom metal products for the chemical and petroleum industries, and enjoyed phenomenal growth in the 1960s.

In the early 1970s Trinity broadened its operations to include construction of marine vessels and fabrication of structural steel products. In 1973 the company bought the Equitable Equipment Company, with shipyards in New Orleans and Madisonville, Louisiana, and the Mosher Steel Company of Houston, a large manufacturer of steel beams and framing. Other structural steel operations were acquired or built, including the Texas Metal Fabricating Company in 1976. Trinity subsidiaries manufactured highway guardrails and a number of products aimed at the road construction industry. By 1977 bridge girders and other structural products generated 37 percent of Trinity's sales.

In 1977 Trinity entered the rail car manufacturing business. The company had been manufacturing hopper bodies and tanks for tankers for a decade, and producing the entire rail car improved profit margins considerably. By 1980 Trinity was one of the top five rail car builders in the United States. In addition, Trinity organized a leasing subsidiary which purchased its own cars with long-term debt and leased them to various railroads on ten-year minimum contracts. The unit, which accounted for five percent of the company's profits in 1979, rapidly grew to contribute more than 50 percent in 1981.

After this initial period of growth, however, the rail car business went into a slump. Tax regulations enacted in 1981 reduced the benefits of purchasing rail cars as a tax shelter, and orders for new cars plummeted to 5,300 from 96,000 just four years earlier. Making the best of these soft market conditions, Trinity acquired several of its weakened competitors, including Pullman Standard, once the largest freight car manufacturer in the United States. In late 1986 the Greenville Steel Car Company, the Ortner Freight Car Company, and the Standard Forgings Corporation (a locomotive and rail car axle maker) were acquired. Rail cars—including tank cars, hopper cars, gondola cars, intermodal cars, and other types of freight cars—made up nearly half of Trinity Industries' sales.

During the mid- to late 1980s more rail cars were being taken out of service than were purchased, creating pent-up demand, and Trinity anticipated a massive rail car replacement program on the part of the nation's railroad operators. However, while a steady flow of orders came in each year, massive reorders were not forthcoming, and in 1985 the company reported a $6 million loss on sales of $455 million—Trinity's first loss in 27 years. By the end of the decade the situation had finally reversed itself, and the company anticipated record profits. The number of companies producing rail cars had dropped from 17 to 6 in the mid-1980s, and Trinity controlled more than half the industry's entire output capacity.

The company's other units also made significant contributions. Trinity's consistently profitable LPG container sales provided the capital for the company's rail car acquisitions; although LPG handling was a mature industry offering limited opportunities for growth, Trinity's leading position was never seriously challenged and the unit brought in steady revenues. In 1987 the Master Tank and Welding Company and certain operations of the Brighton Corporation were purchased, augmenting the container and metal components business segments. Trinity's metal components division produced weld fittings, flanges, and container heads used in piping systems and on pressure and non-pressure tank containers for the oil and gas industry. Trinity remained the American leader in this highly active market.

The marine products division continued to operate in an extremely competitive environment, and profitability was inconsistent. The company continued to bid for new types of commercial watercraft contracts, including boats for the fishing industry, tug and barge units, river hopper barges for grain transportation, and surveillance ships for the United Sates Navy. The market remained sluggish in the late years of the decade. In 1987 Trinity sold two shipyards; the company upgraded its remaining shipbuilding capacity and acquired Moss Point Marine in 1988. The marine division invested heavily in training employees and upgrading plants. In the early 1990s demand for new ships and barges increased sharply. Trinity's investment began to pay off as the marine subsidiaries showed satisfactory profits and healthy backlogs of orders.

In the structural products segment, Trinity focused on products marketed to public utility, highway, and bridge construction, and de-emphasized its products used in high-rise and other building construction. Trinity expected to profit from massive federal highway revamping. In 1992 Trinity diversified into concrete for road construction with the acquisition of the Transit Mix Concrete and Materials Company, one of the largest concrete companies in Southeastern Texas.

Although Trinity's core businesses showed disappointing growth in the 1980s, the company was able to absorb some of its stronger competitors as they went out of business without over-extending itself. The company entered the 1990s financially strong and ready to benefit from the long-anticipated modernization of the American transportation infrastructure.

Principal Subsidiaries: Beaird Industries, Incorporated; HBC Barge, Incorporated; McKees Rocks Forgings, Incorporated; Moss Point Marine, Incorporated; Standard Forged Products, Incorporated; Standard Forgings, Incorporated; Trinity-Axle Limited Partnership (90%); Trinity Industries Leasing Company; Trinity Railcar Leasing Corporation; Trinity Industries Transportation, Incorporated.

Further Reading: Rogge, Dwaine W., ''The Security I Like Best,'' *Commercial and Financial Chronicle,* March 4, 1965; Rolland, Louis J., ''Investment Background: New Records for Trinity,'' *Financial World,* July 13, 1966; Gordon, Mitchell, ''Trinity Industries Sets Sights on Seventh Straight Peak Year,'' *Barron's,* December 12, 1977; Cochran, Thomas N., ''One For Trinity,'' *Barron's,* May 9, 1988; Hannon, Kerry, ''Closely Watched Trainmaker,'' *Forbes,* April 2, 1990; ''Corporate America's Most Powerful People: Order Breaks Out,'' *Forbes,* May 28, 1990.

—Thomas Tucker

Unilever

UNILEVER PLC (UNILEVER N.V.)

P.O. Box 68
Unilever House
Blackfriars
London EC4P 4BQ
United Kingdom
(071) 822-5252
Fax: (071) 822-5898

P.O. Box 760
3000 DK Rotterdam
Netherlands
(10) 464-5911
Fax: (10) 217-4798

Public Company
Incorporated: 1929 as Unilever Ltd. and Unilever NV
Employees: 292,000
Sales: £27.56 billion/Df176.43 billion (US$40 billion)
Stock Exchanges: London Amsterdam New York Paris
   Frankfurt Brussels Zürich Luxembourg Vienna
SICs: 2841 Soap & Other Detergents; 2844 Perfumes,
   Cosmetics & Other Toilet Preparations; 2079 Shortening,
   Table Oil, Margarine & Other Edible Fats and Oils

If the adage "two heads are better than one" applies to business, then certainly Unilever is a prime example. The food and consumer products giant actually has two parent companies: Unilever PLC, based in the United Kingdom, and Unilever N.V., based in the Netherlands. The two companies, which operate virtually as a single corporation, are run by identical boards of directors, in which the chairman of each automatically becomes vice-chairman of the other. Brand-name foods, drinks, and personal products such as soap and detergent constitute the majority of Unilever's business. Unilever brands include Imperial and Promise margarines, Lipton tea, Ragú foods, detergent products such as Wisk, Sunlight, and Dove, as well as personal products like Vaseline, Pond's, and Elizabeth Taylor's Passion perfume. Unilever's other major activity is in specialty chemicals.

William Hesketh Lever, later Lord Leverhulme, was born in Bolton, England, in 1851. The founder of Lever Brothers, Lever had a personality that combined "the rationality of the business man with the restless ambitions of the explorer," according to Unilever historian Charles Wilson.

During the depression of the 1880s, Lever, then a salesman for his father's wholesale grocery business, recognized the advantages of not only selling, but also manufacturing, soap, a non-cyclical necessity item. His father, James Lever, was initially opposed to the idea, believing that they should remain grocers, not manufacturers. He softened, however, in the face of his son's determination. In 1885 William established a soap factory in Warrington as a branch of the family grocery business. Within a short time Lever was selling his soap throughout the United Kingdom, as well as in Continental Europe, North America, Australia, and South Africa.

William also began a tradition that to some degree still exists at Unilever—that of producing all its raw components. Lever Brothers, a vertically integrated company, grew to include milling operations used to crush seeds into vegetable oil for margarine as well as packaging and transporting businesses for all of its products, which then included Lux, Lifebuoy, Rinso, and Sunlight soaps.

In 1914, as the German Navy began to threaten the delivery of food imports—particularly Danish butter and Dutch margarine—to Britain, the British government asked William Lever to produce margarine. He eagerly accepted the opportunity, believing that the margarine business would be compatible with the soap business because the products both required oils and fats as raw materials. Lever Brothers' successful diversification, however, now put the company in competition with Jurgens and Van den Berghs, two leading margarine companies.

Fierce competitors in the latter half of the 19th century, Van den Berghs and Jurgens had decided in 1908 to pool their interests in an effort to make the best of the poor economic situation that existed in most of the world. Competition in the margarine industry had intensified, fueled by an increasing number of smaller firms, which were exporting their products and lowering their prices to get a piece of the market. Van den Berghs eliminated the potential for problems such as double taxation—which arose from its interests in both Holland and the United Kingdom—by creating and incorporating two parent companies for itself, one in Holland and one in England. In 1920 Jurgens and Van de Berghs decided there was strength in numbers and joined with another margarine manufacturer, Schicht, in Bohemia. In 1927 the three companies, borrowing the ideal of a dual structure from Van de Berghs, formed Margarine Union Limited, a group of Dutch firms with interests in England, and Margarine Unie N.V., located in Holland.

Through the middle and late 1920s, the oil and fat trades continued to grow. Although the activities of Margarine Unie and Margarine Union were focused on edible fats (margarine), the companies had held soap interests throughout Europe for years. Similarly, although Lever Brothers had produced margarine since World War I, its focus was soap. After two years of discussion, the companies decided that an "alliance wasted less of everybody's substance than hostility" and merged on September 2, 1929.

As it does today, the newly formed Unilever consisted of two holding companies: Unilever Limited, previously Margarine Union; and Unilever N.V., formerly Margarine Unie. The new organization included an equalization agreement to assure equal profits for shareholders of both companies, as well as identically structured boards. Unilever's parent companies were actually holding companies supervising the operations of hundreds of manufacturing and trading firms worldwide. The end result of the merger was a company that bought and processed more than a third of the world's commercial oils and fats and traded more products in more places than any other company in the world. Its manufacturing activities—which included detergents and toilet preparations, margarine and edible fats, food products, and oil milling and auxiliary businesses—were joined by a need for similar raw and refined materials, such as coconut, palm, cottonseed, and soybean oil, as well as whale oil and animal fats.

The Great Depression, which struck not long after the new company was formed, affected every aspect of Unilever's multifaceted operation: its raw material companies faced price decreases of 30 to 40 percent in the first year alone; cattle cake, sold as a product of its oil mills, suffered with the decline of the agricultural industry; margarine and other edible fats were affected by damaging competition as the price of butter plummeted; and the company's retail grocery and fish shops saw declining sales.

As prices and profits around the world threatened to collapse, Unilever had to act quickly to build up an efficient system of control. The "special committee" was established in September of 1930 to do that. Operating as a board of directors over the two boards the company already had, the special committee was designed to balance Dutch and British interests and act as an inner cabinet for the organization. It also began administering two committees established to deal with Unilever's world affairs: a continental committee to handle businesses in Europe, and an overseas committee to supervise business elsewhere.

A new generation of management led Unilever through the 1930s: Francis D'Arcy Cooper, who had been chairman of Lever Brothers since William Lever's death in 1925; Georg Schicht, the former chairman of Schicht Company; and Paul Rijkens, who succeeded Anton Jurgens as chairman of Jurgens in 1933. It was Cooper who seemed to lead the efforts to turn the various companies that comprised Unilever into one Anglo-Dutch team. It was also Cooper who convinced the board of the necessity for a reorganization in 1937, when the relationship between the profit-earning capacities of the Dutch and British companies found itself reversed.

Originally, about two-thirds of Unilever's profits were earned by the Dutch group and one-third by the British group. By 1937, however, due to increasing trade conflicts in Europe, particularly in Germany, the situation had reversed. By selling the Lever company's assets outside Great Britain, including Lever Brothers Company in the United States, to the Dutch arm of Unilever, the assets of the two groups were redistributed so that they would be nearly equal in volume and profits, which had always been the objective of the two parent companies.

Before 1945 the oils and fats industries had progressed fairly smoothly. The only major industry breakthroughs were the discovery of the hydrogenation process just before World War I, which enabled manufacturers to turn oils into hard fats, and the possibility of adding vitamins to margarine in the 1920s,

which created an opportunity for new health-related product claims. But it was not until the end of World War II that the industry in general, including Unilever, began to recognize the important relationship between marketing and research.

While Unilever's growth until the mid-1940s was a result of expanded product lines and plant capacities, its greatest achievements between 1945 and 1965 were its adaptation to new markets and technology. The decade following World War II was a period of recovery, culminating by the early 1950s in rapid economic growth in much of the Western world. Until 1955 demand continued to rise and competition was not a major issue. Afterward, however, profit margins dropped, competition in Europe and North America sharpened, and success was less assured. Unilever's strategy was to acquire companies in new areas, particularly food and chemical manufacturers.

Before the formation of Unilever, Lever Brothers had coped with overseas expansion by purchasing two factories in the United States, one in Boston and one in Philadelphia. Following World War II, Unilever found it lacked the scientific resources needed to compete with U.S. companies in research and development. Previously, key concerns for the soap industry revolved around color, scent, lather, and how well the products adapted to changing fabrics. Following the war—to the dismay of Unilever and its U.S. subsidiary, Lever Brothers Company—development efforts in the United States succeeded in creating a nonsoap, synthetic detergent powder, which had superior cleaning powers and did not form insoluble deposits in plumbing systems in hard water. The disappointment spurred Unilever to value research as highly as marketing and sales. Lever Brothers had three detergent plants in production by 1950 but remained behind in the industry for some time.

Because the primary ingredients of the new detergents were petrochemicals, Unilever now found itself involved in chemical technology. In the synthetic detergent market, each geographic area required a different kind of product depending on the way consumers washed their clothes and the type of water available to them. The new detergents gave rise to new problems, however: the foam that detergents left in sewage systems and rivers had become a major issue by the late 1950s. As a result, by 1965, Unilever had introduced biodegradable products in the United States, the United Kingdom, and West Germany.

Throughout the postwar era, Unilever continued to invest in research and research facilities. One of its major establishments—the Port Sunlight facility in Cheshire that William Lever had founded in the 1920s—researched detergents, chemicals, and timber. In Bedfordshire, the Colworth House facility continued research efforts in food preservation, animal nutrition, and health problems associated with toothpaste, shampoo, and other personal products. By 1965 the company had 11 major research establishments throughout the world, including laboratories in Continental Europe, the United Kingdom, the United States, and India.

One example of how Unilever effectively answered market demands was its continuing research in margarine. When first developed, margarine was simply a substitute for the butter that was in short supply during wartime. But when butter once again became plentiful, the product needed to offer other advantages to the consumer. Research focused on methods to improve the quality of margarine—such as making it easier to spread, more flavorful, and more nutritious. This was the primary emphasis at Unilever's Vlaardingen laboratory. By enhancing techniques used to refine soybean oil, the company succeeded in improving the raw materials available for margarine production while at the same time achieving vast savings, since soybean oil itself was inexpensive.

The advent of the European Economic Community, or Common Market, also created new opportunities for Unilever. The company held several conferences throughout the 1960s to discuss strategies for dealing with marketing, factory location, tariffs, cartels, and transport issues created by the Common Market. Of particular importance was the need to determine the best places for production under changing economic conditions. Since the late nineteenth century, when the companies that comprised Unilever had set up factories in other European countries to avoid tariff restrictions, Unilever's products had been manufactured wherever it was most economical. Under the Common Market, many of the tariff restrictions that had spawned the multinational facilities were eliminated, giving the company an opportunity to consolidate operations and concentrate production in lower-cost countries.

In the 1980s Unilever undertook a massive restructuring. The company sold most of its service and ancillary businesses, such as transport, packaging, advertising, and other services that were readily available on the market, and went on a buying spree, snapping up some 80 companies between 1984 and 1988. The restructuring was designed to concentrate the company in "those businesses that we properly understand, in which we have critical mass, and where we believe we have a strong, competitive future," Unilever PLC Chairman M. R. Angus told *Management Today* in 1988. Specifically, Unilever's core businesses are detergents, foods, toiletries, and specialty chemicals.

In addition to increasing profitability in core areas, restructuring also helped Unilever execute its biggest acquisition to date: Chesebrough-Pond's in the United States in 1986. A company with sales of nearly $3 billion, Chesebrough owned such brands as Vaseline Intensive Care, Pond's Cold Cream, and Ragú spaghetti sauce. The acquisition allowed Unilever to fill out its international personal products business, particularly in the United States, where Unilever saw a higher profit potential.

During the 1980s Unilever's detergent products posted a 50 percent growth in operating profit, while food products grew at a faster-than-normal rate. In the United States, plans to take on longtime rival Procter & Gamble were successful in 1984, when Unilever's Wisk moved P&G's Cheer out of the number two spot in the laundry detergent market. In Europe, Unilever completed its first hostile takeover attempt in 15 years, acquiring the British company Brooke Bond, the leading European tea company, for £376 million. Brooke Bond complemented Unilever's Lipton brand, the leader in the United States. Two years later, the company launched Wisk in the United Kingdom, as well as Breeze, its first soap powder introduced in the United Kingdom since the debut of Surf more than 30 years before.

In 1989 Unilever became a major player in the world's perfume and cosmetic industry through three more acquisitions. It obtained Shering-Plough's perfume business in Europe; the Calvin Klein business from Minnetonka, Inc.; and, by far the largest purchase of the three, Fabergé Inc., the American producer of Chloe, Lagerfeld, and Fendi perfumes, for $1.55 billion. The upper-end cosmetics market is a high margin business, and Unilever planned to step up marketing of its new products to raise sales.

As it entered the 1990s, Unilever had virtually completed reorganizing its European business in order to better compete after the integration of the European Economic Community in 1992. In 1991 the company further refined its operations by selling the last of its packaging businesses and by making provisions for the eventual sales of the majority of its agribusinesses.

Unilever's flexible management structure and diverse product range were integral to its survival in the rapidly changing international market. In a 1992 *Harvard Business Review* article, Chairman and Chief Executive Officer Floris A. Maljers explained Unilever's management structure: "The very nature of our products required proximity to local markets; economies of scale in certain functions justify a number of head-office departments; and the need to benefit from everybody's creativity and experience makes a sophisticated means of transferring information across our organization highly desirable. All of these factors led to our present structure: a matrix of individual managers around the world who nonetheless share a common vision and understanding of corporate strategy."

Despite poor performances by some of its subsidiaries and recessions in Europe and North America, Unilever's broad product range led to overall profit increases in both 1990 and 1991. In 1990 Unilever made substantial inroads into the newly opened markets created by the unification of Germany. The company began producing its Rama margarine at a former East German state plant in Chermnitz, established a task force to select sites for 23 Nordsee fish stores, and began distributing ice cream and frozen novelties to retailers in eastern Germany.

In 1991 Unilever entered a race with rival Proctor & Gamble to break into the newly opened markets of the former Soviet Union. Unilever purchased an 80 percent stake in the Polish detergent firm Pollena Bydgoscz for $20 million, changing the name to Lever Polaska, the first laundry detergent manufacturer to be privatized in Poland. The company earmarked approximately $24 million for product line expansions, including a fabric conditioner and household cleaning products.

Profits in Unilever's personal products division were down 11 percent in 1991, due to sluggish markets in the United States and only moderate growth in European markets. Unilever's newly purchased Elizabeth Arden and Calvin Klein, however, posted strong growth, supported by strong retailer relationships and $24 million in advertising expenditures. Such growth occurred despite an overall drop in department store cosmetic sales of nine percent from 1987 to 1992. In 1992, though, Elizabeth Arden profits began slipping, prompting the resignation of Joseph F. Ronchetti, Arden's chief executive officer since 1978. Unilever underwent further restructuring of its personal products division, creating a prestigious subdivision geared towards introducing Calvin Klein and Elizabeth Arden into overseas markets.

Unilever's fastest growing market in the early 1990s was in Asia. Although Unilever had been operating in Asia since its earliest days, the company was just beginning to tap into the region's newly acquired wealth. Asian sales of personal products, detergent, and packaged foods grew more than twice as fast as sales in the United States and Europe and were expected to double by 1997.

By 1992 Unilever was composed of some 500 companies conducting business in 75 different countries. Its flexible international management structure, marketing strategies, and product range garnered the conglomerate a reputation as one of Britain's most admired companies. "Our marketing continues to focus on the rapid transfer of successful products into new territories," Unilever's 1991 Annual Report declared, referring to its strategy as "the key to growing our business globally in the 1990s." Given its broad market base and diversified product range, Unilever seems well positioned to do just that.

Principal Subsidiaries: Unifrost GmbH; Österreichische Unilever GmbH; Nordsee GmbH; Hartog; Iglo-Ola; Lever; Union; Uni-Dan A/S; Paasivaara Oy; Suomen Unilever Oy; Astra-Calvé SA; CNF SA; Française de Soins et Parfums SA; 4P Emballages France 5A; Lever SA; Niger France SA; Compagnie des Glaces et Surgeles Alimentaires SA; Française d'Alimentation et de Boissons SA; Unilever Export France SA; Unilever France SA; Deutsche Unilever GmbH; Elida-Gibbs GmbH; 4P Folie Forchheim GmbH; 4P Nicolaus Kempten GmbH; 4P Verpackungen Ronsberg GmbH; 4P Rube Gottingen GmbH; Langnese-Iglo GmbH; Lever GmbH; Meistermarken-Werke GmbH, Spezialfabrik fur Back-und Grosskuchenbedarf; Nordsee Deutsche Hochseefischerei GmbH; Schafft Fleischwerke GmbH; Unichema Chemie GmbH; Union Deutsche Lebensmittelwerke GmbH; Lever Hellas AEBE; Elais Oleaginous Products AE; Lever Brothers (Ireland) Ltd.; W&C McDonnell Ltd.; Paul and Vincent Ltd.; HB Ice Cream Ltd.; 3C Industriale SpA; Lever Sodel SpA; Sagit SpA; Unil-It SpA; Calvé Nederland BV; Crosfield Chemie BV; Elida Gibbs BV; Zeepfabriek de Fenix BV; Inglo-Ola BV; Lever Industrial BV; Lever BV; Loders Croklaan BV; Lucas Aardenburg BV; Naarden International; National Starch & Chemical BV; Nederlandse Unilever Bedrijven BV; Quest International Nederland BV; Exportslachterij Udema BV; Unichema Chemie BV; Unilver Export BV; UniMills BV; UVG Nederland BV; Van de Bergh en Jurgens BV; Vinamul BV; Iglo Indústrias de Gelados, Lda.; Indústrias Lever Portuguesa, Lda.; Agra SA; Frigo SA; Lever España SA; Industrias Revilla SA; Pond's Española SA; Unilever España SA; Glace-Bolaget AB; Margarinbolaget AB; Lever AB; Leverindus AB; Novia Livsmedelsindustrier AB; Elida Robert Group AB; Svenska Unilever Förvaltnings AB; Astra Fett-und Oelwerke AG; Chesebrough-Pond's (Genève) SA; Elida Cosmetic AG; Lever AG; Meina Holdings AG; Sais; A. Sutter AG; Unilever (Schweiz) AG; Unilever-Is Ticaret ve Sanayi Turk Limited Sirketi; Batchelors Foods Ltd.; Birds Eye Wall's Ltd.; BOCM Silcock Ltd.; Brook Bond Foods Ltd.; Chesebrough-Pond's Ltd.; Jospeh Crosfield & Sons Ltd.; Elida Gibbs Ltd.; Erith Oil Works Ltd.; Lever Brothers Ltd.; Lever Industrial Ltd.; H. Leverton Ltd.; Lipton Export Ltd.; Lipton Tea Company Ltd.; Loders Croklaan Ltd.; Marine Harvest Ltd.; Mattessons Wall's Ltd.; Oxoid Ltd.; Plant Breeding International Cambridge Ltd.; Quest International (Fragances, Flavours, Food Ingredients) UK Ltd.; UAC Ltd.; UAC International Ltd.; UML Ltd.; Unichema Chemicals Ltd.; Unilever Export Ltd.; Unilever UK Central Resources Ltd.; United Agricultural Merchants Ltd.; Van de Berghs and Jurgens Ltd.; Vinamul Ltd.; John West Foods Ltd.; ChesebroughPond's Inc. (Canada); Lever Brothers Limited; Thomas J. Lipton Inc.; A&W Food Services of Canada Ltd.; Unilever Canada Limited; Chesebrough-Pond's Inc.; Lawry's Foods Inc.; Lever Brothers Company; Thomas J. Lipton, Inc.; National Starch and Chemical Corporation; Prince Matchabelli, Inc.; Ragú Foods, Inc.; Sequoia-Turner Corporation; Unilever Capital Corporation; Unilever United States, Inc.; Lever y Asociados sacif; Unilever Australia Ltd.; Lever Brothers Bangladesh Ltd.; Indústrias Gessy Lever Ltda.; RW King SA; Lever Chile SA; Compañia Colombiana de Grasas Cogra-Lever 5A; Plantaciones Unipalma de Los Llanos SA; Blohorn SA; CFCI SA; Uniwax SA; Hatton et Cookson SA; UAC of Ghana Ltd.; Lever Brothers Ltd. (China); Hindustan Lever Ltd.; PT Unilever Indonesia; Nippon Lever BV; Brooke Bond Kenya Ltd.; East Africa Industries Ltd.; Gailey & Roberts Ltd.; Lever Brothers (Malawi) Ltd.; Lever Brothers (Malaysia) Sdn. Bhd.; Pamol Plantations Sdn. Bhd.; Anderson Clayton & Co. SA; Pond's de Mexico SA de CV; Unilever Becumij NV; Unilever New Zealand Ltd.; Niger-Afrique SA; Pamol (Nigeria) Ltd.; Lever Brothers Pakistan Ltd.; Philippine Refining Company, Inc.; UAC of Sierra Leone Ltd.; Lever Brothers Singapore Sdn. Bhd.; Lever Solomons Ltd.; Unilever South Africa Pty. Ltd.; Lever Brothers Ltd. (Ceylon); Formosa United Industrial Corporation Ltd.; UAC of Tanzania Ltd.; Brasseries du Logone SA; Lever Brothers Ltd. (Thailand); Lever Brothers West Indies Ltd.; Gailey & Roberts Ltd. (Uganda); Sudy Lever SA; Lever-Pond's SA; Plantations Lever au Zaîre sarI; Compagnie des Margarines, Savons et Cosmétiques au Zaîre sarl; Sedec sarl; Lever Brothers Ltd.

Further Reading: Wilson, Charles, *The History of Unilever,* London, Cassell & Company, 1970; Levy, Liz, "Unilever Axes Fabergé Firm," *Marketing,* November 2, 1989; Mussey, Dagmar, "Heading Back East: Unilever Knows Way Into Reunited Germany," *Ad Age,* December 30, 1990; Unilever annual reports, 1990–91; Nayyar, Seema, "Unilever Makes Power Move on Arden," *Adweek's Marketing Week,* June 22, 1992; Zinn, Laura, "Beauty and the Beastliness," *Business Week,* June 29, 1992; Maljers, Floris A., "Inside Unilever: The Revolving Transnational Company," *Harvard Business Review,* September/October 1992; "Britain's Most Admired Companies," *The Economist,* October 17, 1992.

—updated by Maura Troester

UNIVERSAL FOODS CORPORATION

433 E. Michigan Street
Milwaukee, Wisconsin 53202
U.S.A.
(414) 271-6755
Fax: (414) 347-3785

Public Company
Incorporated: 1882 as Meadow Springs Distilling Co.
Employees: 5,924
Sales: $883 million
Stock Exchanges: New York
SICs: 2099 Food Preparations Nec; 2037 Frozen Fruits &
    Vegetables; 2034 Dehydrated Fruits, Vegetables & Soups;
    2022 Cheese—Natural & Processed

Universal Foods Corporation is a major international manufacturer and marketer of value-added food products for both commercial and consumer uses. The company's product line includes flavor and color ingredients for food processing, frozen french fried potatoes, dehydrated vegetables, and a wide range of yeast products. Universal's corporate structure is organized into six divisions: Frozen Foods, Flavor, Red Star Yeast and Products, Color, Dehydrated Products, and Red Star Specialty Products. The Frozen Foods division specializes in an assortment of fried potato forms, the vast majority of which are marketed to food service operations. The Flavor division markets exclusively to food processing companies. Its products include flavor ingredients for beverages and for bakery items. Commercial bakers make up 93 percent of the market for the Red Star Yeast and Products division. This division manufactures yeast products under the Red Star and Quick Rise brand names for baking, nutritional, and wine-making applications. The Color division operates in the marketplace primarily as Warner-Jenkinson. It supplies natural coloring ingredients for food processing as well as pharmaceutical and cosmetics uses. Universal's Dehydrated Products division, which also deals entirely with food processors, produces a line that includes dehydrated onion, garlic, chili peppers, and parsley. Red Star Specialty Products produces yeast-based products for a variety of uses, including fermentation, flavor enhancement, and diagnostics. In all of these markets, Universal ranks among the top companies in North America.

Meadow Springs Distillery, the earliest incarnation of Universal Foods, was founded in December of 1882 by three Milwaukeans: Leopold Wirth, Gustav Niemeier, and Henry Koch, Jr. At the company's first stockholders' meeting the following month, Wirth was elected to the company's presidency, Niemeier became vice-president, and Koch secretary-treasurer. Wirth was a well-known merchant in Milwaukee, dealing in horses, furs, and a variety of other items. His entry into the distillery business probably came about as a result of one of his sideline business ventures. Wirth would purchase spent grain from area distillers, use it to fatten up thin, cheaply bought cattle, then sell the cattle at a sizeable profit. Opening a distillery was a way of compacting this operation, while at the same time tapping into the growing whiskey market. The major financial backer of Meadow Springs was Adolph C. Zinn, a local financier. William Bergenthal, the owner of a distillery and a successful outlet—the Wm. Bergenthal Wholesale Liquor Company—was named to manage day-to-day operations at the distillery.

Meadow Springs sold its first barrel of whiskey on July 5, 1883. The whiskey was produced at Bergenthal's distillery. A month later, the company bought its first piece of property, a choice plot at the bottom of a hill in the Menomonee Valley. To the one building that already stood on the property, Wirth added a grain elevator, a railroad siding, and a pipeline for the spent grain. In September, Koch resigned, and Bergenthal became the company's secretary, retaining his duties as general manager. About a week later, Wirth was forced to resign as president, when a number of surprise billings and overdue claims arrived from out of town, including writs of attachment for $2,000 from the Chicago Distilling Company, and debt notices from Philip D. Armour & Co., the Chicago packing firm. A stockholder and local cattle dealer named Henry Heilbronner was elected president.

In 1886, August Bergenthal, William's brother, replaced Niemeier as vice-president of Meadow Springs. A year later, both brothers were elected to the board of directors. At the same meeting, Levi Tabor was named president. In March of that year, however, both Tabor and William Bergenthal resigned during a dispute over a company purchase. Tabor was succeeded as president by August Grau, vice-president of the Bergenthal company and a recently elected director of Meadow Springs. August Bergenthal became secretary and treasurer. Grau would remain president of the company for 35 years. In May of 1887, the name of the company was changed to National Distilling Company. Among the changes that accompanied the renaming of the firm was the addition of a filtering press for squeezing yeast. The primary line of yeast the company produced was called Red Star.

National Distilling began to expand in the 1890s. The company opened yeast distribution branches in several cities during this period, including Duluth, Chicago, Detroit, and Cleveland. National's net earnings for 1894 were over $112,000. In 1903, the company established a second manufacturing plant on the site of the recently purchased local DuPont Chemical Company facility. By 1917, National was operating over 30 yeast branches throughout the region, with major outlets in Louisville, Kansas City, and Detroit. In 1917, the government passed a measure outlawing the use of grains to make liquor, meaning that liquor could be sold, but not manufactured. Two years later, the 18th Amendment to the Constitution created prohibition. National responded by changing its name once again, this time to the name of its most important nonalcoholic product. It became Red Star Yeast and Products Company.

During prohibition, Red Star focused increasingly on yeast production and distribution. John Wiedring, the company's laboratory chief, introduced a new process for making yeast by aeration in 1918. By 1921, Red Star was operating 50 branches throughout the eastern half of the United States. The company's yeast was marketed as a health food, and sales were brisk. In July of 1922, new leadership was needed when Grau and Bergenthal died suddenly within a few weeks of each other. The presidency was assumed by Bruno Bergenthal, August's son. The company grew rapidly through the remainder of the 1920s. Its 27th Street and Cudahy manufacturing facilities were expanded and a higher quality drier was purchased during that time.

The repeal of prohibition in 1933 created a dilemma for Red Star. The company needed to decide whether to reenter the liquor distilling business or to continue to concentrate on yeast production. Beer and gin were once again brought into production in 1933. By 1937, however, Red Star had pretty much committed to yeast and vinegar as its main products. Factors leading to this shift in direction included the bottoming out of the gin market in 1935, and a legal quarrel over the use of the National Distilling name waged against the National Distillers Products Corporation of New York. With its gin department already shut down, Red Star gave up its right to the National brand name for a settlement of about $20,000.

In 1938, a policy disagreement led to Bergenthal's resignation. He was replaced as president by Charles Wirth, Jr., grandson of Leopold Wirth, one of the company's founders. Bergenthal stayed on as chairman of the board until his retirement in 1940. During World War II, the government became interested in the nutritional qualities of yeast. Since active dry yeast was less perishable than earlier forms, it was considered an excellent food item for a mobilized Army. Therefore, huge amounts of the yeast were ordered from Red Star and other companies by the government to meet the baking needs of the growing military. When the war ended, Red Star began looking for ways to diversify its product line with related baking items. The company experimented for a short time with a frozen egg department, but this venture proved to be too risky and was quickly aborted.

Charles Wirth, Jr., died of a heart attack in 1950. He was succeeded as Red Star president by his cousin, Russell Wirth. Under Russell Wirth, Red Star diversified quite a bit within the realm of yeast products. During the 1950s, the variety of products the company was marketing included packaged yeast for rolls and mixes, consumer yeast, feed yeast for livestock, nutritional yeast for cereal and baby food, and, of course, compressed and dry yeast cakes for bakers. Pillsbury, using millions of packages of yeast supplied by Red Star, was the leader among companies marketing hot roll mixes, which enjoyed a period of great popularity during the 1950s. Because of its ability to anticipate the needs of the yeast market, and to tailor its products accordingly, Red Star was one of only five to emerge among major yeast producers in the country, from a group of about 24 that existed in the 1930s.

In 1951, Red Star opened a plant in New Orleans, enabling the company to better serve the southern market, as well as reduce the cost of transporting molasses from that region. Several acquisitions in the mid-1950s elevated Red Star to the status of nationwide yeast distributors. These included the purchases of Food Industry Corporation in Dallas, San Francisco's Consumer's Yeast Corporation, and the Peerless Yeast Company, also located in California. The company went international in the 1950s as well. A yeast production plant was opened in Cuba. Red Star had interests of up to 25 percent in yeast operations in Peru, the Philippines, Iran, Korea, and elsewhere. Agreements for technical services were entered in Guatemala and Colombia. Later in the 1950s, Red Star's Cudahy plant was closed when it was discovered that Lake Michigan had eroded much of the 140-foot cliffs on which the facility rested, leaving the complex in danger of toppling into the lake. The vinegar works that operated there were sold to the Richter Vinegar Company, and, in 1957, the 10-acre plot of land on which it was built was sold to Milwaukee County.

Red Star began to diversify outside of the yeast business in the early 1960s. In 1961 and 1962, the company purchased Universal Foods Company of Chicago, a maker of institutional food products, and Chili Products Corporation of Los Angeles, a company that produced paprika and chili peppers. The company went public in 1961, making stock available for the first time to people outside the small circle of founding families and their friends. Red Star's sales that year were $12.1 million. The following year, the company's name was once again changed to reflect the wider spectrum of its activities. The new name was Universal Foods Corporation. Universal made a major acquisition with the 1963 purchase of Stella Cheese Corporation. By 1965, the company's sales had grown to $31 million.

In 1965, Robert Foote became Universal's president, and Wirth became its chairperson. Around that time, the company began marketing an active dry yeast for use in wine production. By 1967, most of the major food companies in the United States were Universal customers, including General Mills, Kraft, Hormel, Gerber, and Ralston Purina. Universal purchased the National Yeast Company, a New Jersey firm, in 1968. By that time, the company, mainly by virtue of its acquisition of Stella, controlled about 20 percent of the nation's aged Italian cheese market. It also controlled 12 percent of the market for industrial yeast, and 30 percent of the chili powder and paprika production. In September of 1968 Universal was stunned by the murder of Russell Wirth. August K. Bergenthal, Bruno's son, was convicted of the crime and sentenced to life imprisonment. It seemed that the younger Bergenthal harbored long-standing resentment regarding the events that led to his father's exit from the company's presidency.

Universal continued to grow steadily in the 1970s. Sales in the first half of the decade grew from $61 million in 1970 to $151 million in 1975. Two areas the company moved into heavily during the 1970s were soft drink bottling and gourmet foods. Universal acquired the bottling franchises for 7-Up and other beverages in a number of states, starting with Michigan. The company entered the gourmet foods market with the 1972 acquisition of Lankor International Inc., and followed this up with the acquisitions of Rema Foods Inc. and Ramsey Imports, giving Universal a substantial foothold in the fancy processed foods market. In 1976, John Murray was elected president of Universal Foods. Foote, like his predecessor Wirth, stayed on as chairperson. In 1977, production began on a line of imitation cheeses. The cheese product was made from vegetable oil at costs that were 30 to 40 percent lower than those of the real item. That year, Universal common stock was first traded on the New York Stock Exchange.

In 1979, Universal purchased Rogers Foods, a California company engaged in the dehydration of onion and garlic. The early 1980s brought the expansion of the company's bottling operations, including the addition of the St. Louis franchises for Royal Crown Cola and Canada Dry. In 1981, the company bought out one of its long-standing competitors, the Federal Yeast Company, solidifying its position as a major player in the yeast business. By 1983, three of Universal's five divisions— cheese, beverages, and fermentation—were together accounting for about three-fourths of the company's sales, each providing about a quarter of the total. Over the next couple years, Universal chose to narrow its focus somewhat. In 1983, the company dismantled its snack food division, selling off its cookie and pretzel business. The following year, Universal left the bottling business, essentially trading it for entry into the food color and flavor business. This was accomplished by dealing four 7-Up bottling plants to Philip Morris in exchange for the Warner-Jenkinson Co. plus about $10 million cash.

Universal moved into the frozen potato business in 1985 and 1986, with the purchases of Idaho Frozen Foods from Sara Lee, and of Rogers Walla Walla Inc. The two companies taken together had sold about $100 million worth of frozen potatoes to the food service industry the previous year. As the 1990s approached, Universal removed itself from a couple of the markets in which it had been operating. In 1988, the company divested its import division, which consisted of Rema Foods and Gourmet Products. In 1990 Universal got out of the cheese business, selling that division to INVUS Group, Ltd., a subsidiary of the Belgian firm R.T. Holding S.A. By that year, under chair and chief executive Guy Osborn, sales had reached over $873 million. Frozen potato products accounted for nearly 30 percent of the company's revenue for that year. In April of 1990, Universal became a major force in the flavor market with the acquisition of the British flavoring producer Felton International. Another flavor company, Fantasy Flavors, an Illinois dairy flavoring company, was acquired the following year. Also in 1991, Universal purchased the food, drug, and cosmetic color business of Morton International, Inc. Universal reported record sales in 1992, in spite of an off year for the frozen potato business. The Color division made a particularly strong showing in 1992, emerging as the market leader among North American companies in that field. Universal Foods entered 1993 poised to continue its strong record of consistent growth.

Principal Subsidiaries: Universal Frozen Foods Company; Universal Flavor Corporation; Warner-Jenkinson Company.

Further Reading: "Pizza to Go, Heavy on the Soybeans," *Forbes,* March 1, 1977; "Universal Foods Enjoys Yeasty Record of Growth," *Barron's,* February 20, 1978; "On the Rise," *Barron's,* April 20, 1981; *Universal Foods: The First 100 Years,* Milwaukee, Universal Foods Corporation, 1982; "Yeasty Prospects," *Barron's,* November 7, 1983; Brown, Paul B., "Solid, or Merely Stolid?" *Forbes,* December 5, 1983; Campanella, Frank W., "Changing the Mix," *Barron's,* August 26, 1985; Campanella, Frank W., "Big Cheese," *Barron's,* October 20, 1986; "Universal Foods to Purchase Felton's International Flavors," *Chemical Marketing Reporter,* April 9, 1990; "Universal Foods Corp.," *Barron's,* August 27, 1990; Universal Foods Corporation, *Annual Report 1992.*

—Robert R. Jacobson

USX

™

USX CORPORATION

600 Grant Street
Pittsburgh, Pennsylvania 15219
U.S.A.
(412) 433-1121
Fax: (412) 433-6847

Public Company
Incorporated: 1901 as United States Steel Corporation
Employees: 46,000
Sales: $17.84 billion
Stock Exchanges: New York Midwest Pacific Montreal
SICs: 1311 Crude Petroleum & Natural Gas; 2911 Petroleum
Refining; 3312 Blast Furnaces & Steel Mills

USX Corporation is an international diversified energy and
steel-manufacturing company. About 70 percent of sales are
derived from the oil and gas business through its Marathon Oil
Group and Delhi Group. About 30 percent of sales are from its
U.S. Steel Group, the largest integrated steel company in the
United States, which produces and sells a wide range of semi-
finished and finished steel products, coke, and taconite pellets,
as well as smaller operations in real estate, engineering, mining,
and financial services. USX's emphasis on energy dates from its
acquisitions of Marathon Oil Company in 1982 and Texas Oil &
Gas Corporation in 1986. Before these events, and its 1986
name change to USX Corporation, it was known as United
States Steel Corporation, a company founded on February 25,
1901, as the nation's largest steelmaker and the largest business
enterprise launched up to that time.

The origin of United States Steel Corporation (U.S. Steel) is
virtually an early history of the steel industry in the United
States, which in turn is closely linked to the name of Andrew
Carnegie. The quintessential 19th-century self-made man, Carnegie began as bobbin boy in a cotton mill, made a stake in the
railroad business and, in 1864, started to invest in the iron
industry. In 1873 he began to establish steel plants using the
Bessemer steelmaking process. A ruthless competitor, his Carnegie Steel Company grew to be the largest domestic steelmaker by the end of the century. In 1897 Carnegie appointed
Charles M. Schwab, a brilliant, diplomatic veteran of the steel
industry who had worked his way up through the Carnegie
organization, as president of Carnegie Steel.

At about the same time, prominent financier John Pierpont
Morgan became a major participant in the steel industry as a
result of his organization of the Federal Steel Company in 1898.
Morgan's personal representative in the steel business was
Elbert Henry Gary, a lawyer, former judge, and director of
Illinois Steel Company, one of the several steel companies co-
opted into Federal Steel, of which Gary was made president.
Carnegie, Schwab, Morgan, and Gary were the key participants
in the organization of U.S. Steel.

By 1900 the demand for steel was at peak levels, and Morgan's
ambition was to dominate this market by creating a centralized
combine, or trust. He was encouraged in this by rumors of
Carnegie's intention to retire from business. U.S. President
William McKinley was known to approve of business consolidations, and his support limited the risk of government antitrust
claims in the face of a steel-industry combination. In December
1900 Morgan attended a now-legendary dinner at New York's
University Club. During the course of the evening Schwab gave
a speech that set forth the outlines of a steel trust, the nucleus of
which would be the Carnegie and Morgan steel enterprises,
together with a number of other smaller steel, mining, and
shipping concerns. With Schwab and Gary as intermediaries
between Carnegie and Morgan, negotiations were concluded by
early February 1901 for Carnegie to sell his steel interests for
about $492 million in bonds and stock of the new company. The
organization plan was largely executed by Gary, with Morgan
arranging the financing. On February 25, 1901, United States
Steel Corporation was incorporated with an authorized capitalization of $1.4 billion, the first billion-dollar corporation in
history. The ten companies that were merged to form U.S. Steel
were American Bridge Company, American Sheet Steel
Company, American Steel Hoop Company, American Steel &
Wire Company, American Tin Plate Company, Carnegie Steel
Company, Federal Steel Company, Lake Superior Consolidated
Iron Mines, National Steel Company, and National Tube
Company.

At Morgan's urging Schwab became president of U.S. Steel,
with Gary as chairman of the board of directors and of the
executive committee. Two such strong personalities, however,
could not easily share power. In 1903 Schwab resigned and
soon took control of Bethlehem Steel Corporation, which he
eventually built into the second-largest steel producer in the
country. Gary stayed on as, in effect, chief executive officer to
lead U.S. Steel and to dominate its policies until his death in
August of 1927. His stated goal for U.S. Steel was not to create
a monopoly but to sustain trade and foster competition by
competing on a basis of efficiency and price. Steel prices did
drop significantly in the years after the company began, and,
because of competition, U.S. Steel's market share of U.S. steel
production dropped steadily over the years from about 66 percent in 1901 to about 33 percent from the 1930s to the 1950s.
U.S. Steel's sales increased from $423 million in 1902 to $1
billion during the 1920s, dropped to a low of $288 million in
1933, reached $1 billion in 1940, and climbed to about $3
billion in 1950. Except for a few deficit years, U.S. Steel's
operations have been generally profitable, though earnings have
been cyclical.

U.S. Steel's history is notable for continual acquisitions, divestitures, consolidations, reorganizations, and labor disputes. In

1901 U.S. Steel acquired the Bessemer Steamship company, a shipping concern engaged in iron-ore traffic on the Great Lakes. Shelby Steel Tube Company was purchased in 1901, Union Steel Company in 1903, and Clairton Steel Company in 1904; a number of other, smaller acquisitions were made in those early years. In 1906 U.S. Steel began construction on a large new steel plant on Lake Michigan together with a model city designed primarily for its employees. The new town was named Gary, Indiana, and was substantially completed by 1911. A major acquisition in 1907 was that of Tennessee Coal, Iron and Railroad Company, the largest steel producer in the South. A presence in the West was established by the purchase of Columbia Steel Company in 1910. In addition to steel manufacture, U.S. Steel also maintained large coal-mining operations in western Pennsylvania. These operations were based on former properties of H. C. Frick Coke Company, which included some of Carnegie's coal properties and which became a part of U.S. Steel when it was formed in 1901. The coal produced by these mines was used to fuel U.S. Steel's operations.

The 12-hour work day, standard in industry during U.S. Steel's early years, was a major labor issue. U.S. Steel's workers originally were unorganized, and Gary was a staunch enemy of unionization, the closed shop, and collective bargaining. He took a leading role among businessmen, however, by calling in 1911 for the abolition of the 12-hour work day. Little was actually done, however, and a general strike was called against the steel industry in 1919. The strike failed and was abandoned in 1920. The 12-hour work day eventually was abolished, and in 1937 U.S. Steel signed a contract with the Steel Workers Organizing Committee, which in 1942 became the United Steelworkers of America. U.S. Steel's labor relations have historically been adversarial, characterized by divisive negotiations, often bitter strikes, and settlements that were sometimes economically disastrous for the company and, in the long run, for its employees.

The U.S. government's tolerant view of big corporations ended with the administration of President Theodore Roosevelt. On Roosevelt's instructions, an antitrust investigation of U.S. Steel was begun in 1905. Gary cooperated with the investigation, but the final report to President William Howard Taft in 1911 led to a monopoly charge against U.S. Steel in the U.S. District Court of Appeals. This court's 1915 decision unanimously absolved U.S. Steel from the monopoly charge and largely vindicated Gary's claim that U.S. Steel was designed to be competitive rather than a monopolistic trust.

U.S. Steel's business boomed during World War I with sales more than doubling between 1915 and 1918 and remaining strong at about $2 billion annually through the 1920s. Gary's personal domination of U.S. Steel ended with his death in 1927. J. P. Morgan, Jr., became chairman of the board of directors from 1927 to 1932, but during this period U.S. Steel essentially was under the leadership of Myron C. Taylor, chairman of the finance committee from 1927 to 1934 and chairman of the board from 1932 until his resignation in 1938. Taylor brought about extensive changes in U.S. Steel's make-up. Numerous obsolete plants were closed, others were modernized, and a new plant was added with total capital expenditures of more than $500 million. By the end of Taylor's tenure about three-quarters of U.S. Steel's products were different or were made differently

and more efficiently than they had been in 1927, with the principal realignment being the change from heavy steel for capital goods to lighter steel for consumer goods.

After Taylor's resignation in 1938, Edward R. Stettinius, Jr., served as chairman of the board until he left in 1940 to undertake government service and eventually to become secretary of state. Benjamin F. Fairless, an important figure in U.S. Steel history, became president in 1938, and Irving S. Olds succeeded Stettinius as chairman of the board in 1940. (Olds served as chairman until 1952, when he was succeeded in that office by Fairless.)

During this period U.S. Steel's business recovered from its Depression slump, buoyed by the enormous demand for steel products generated by World War II and the postwar economic boom. Revenues more than quintupled from $611 million in 1938 to more than $3.5 billion in 1951. U.S. Steel was present in every geographical market in the United States except the East, so in 1949 it announced plans to build a large integrated steel plant in Pennsylvania on the Delaware River to be known as the Fairless Works. This plant, operational in 1952, was intended to compete with Bethlehem Steel for the eastern market and to take advantage of ocean shipment of iron ore from U.S. Steel's large ore reserves in Venezuela.

In 1951 a change intended to simplify the structure of United States Steel Corporation took place when a single company was formed from its four major operational subsidiaries. This reorganization, completed in 1953, created a tightly knit, more efficient organizational structure in place of the former aggregate of semi-independent units. In 1953 Clifford F. Hood was appointed president and chief operating officer, sharing overall responsibility for the company with board chairman Fairless and Enders W. Voorhees, who continued as chairman of the finance committee.

Fairless's tenure as chairman of the board included one of the longest strikes in U.S. Steel's history in 1952, resulting from its refusal to allow substantial wage increases and tighter closed-shop rules. Just before the strike was to begin in April 1952, President Harry S. Truman seized the company's properties in order to ensure steel production for the Korean War. This unusual action was declared unconstitutional by the U.S. Supreme Court in June 1952. An industry-wide strike ensued that was settled in August, ending a unique episode in U.S. Steel's labor history. A more productive occurrence was the ground breaking in 1953 for the building of a new research center near Pittsburgh. Fairless retired in May 1955 and was succeeded by Roger M. Blough as chairman of the board and chief executive officer.

Due to improved administrative, operating, and plant efficiencies, U.S. Steel set a postwar record for profitability in 1955, although market share continued to decline to around 30 percent. In 1958 a further corporate simplification took place when wholly owned subsidiary Universal Atlas Cement Company was merged into U.S. Steel as an operating division, as were the Union Supply Company and Homewood Stores Company subsidiaries. Profits were being squeezed between rising operating costs and relatively stable prices, and in April 1962 U.S. Steel unexpectedly announced an across-the-board price increase that triggered a storm of criticism, including an angry protest to Blough from U.S. President John F. Kennedy. Within a week U.S. Steel was forced to rescind the price increase, using the face-saving excuse that other steel companies had not agreed to support the new price level. This situation resulted from U.S. Steel's continued decline in market share to about 25 percent in 1961, together with deteriorating profitability, in part caused by excessive capital spending in relation to market volume.

In response to its difficulties U.S. Steel announced in 1963 a further reorganization and centralization of its steel divisions and sales operations in order to concentrate management resources to a greater extent on sales and consumer services. In 1964 U.S. Steel created a new chemicals division called Pittsburgh Chemical Company. Effective in 1966 United States Steel Corporation was reincorporated in Delaware to take advantage of that state's more flexible corporation laws. In 1967 Edwin H. Gott became president and chief operating officer and in 1969 he succeeded Blough as chairman of the board and CEO. Edgar B. Speer, a veteran steel man, moved up to the presidency. In 1973 Gott retired and Speer assumed his duties as chairman and CEO. Significantly, Speer immediately announced plans to expand U.S. Steel's diversification into nonsteel businesses. Prospects for long-term growth in steel were fading rapidly because of rising costs, competitive pricing, and foreign competition.

During Speer's tenure, U.S. Steel closed or sold a variety of facilities and businesses in steel, cement, fabricating, home building, plastics, and mining. Capital expenditure, much of it for environmental purposes, remained high. There was little significant diversification, however. In 1979 U.S. Steel lost $293 million. Also that year, former president David M. Roderick became chairman and CEO. He announced a major liquidation of unprofitable steel operations and increased efforts to diversify. In 1979, 13 steel facilities were closed with an $809 million write-off. Universal Atlas Cement—once the United States's largest cement company—was sold, and various real estate, timber, and mineral properties were leased or sold. The long-promised diversification move came in 1982 with United States Steel Corporation's $6.2 billion acquisition of Marathon Oil Company, a major integrated energy company with vast reserves of oil and gas. Marathon's revenues were about the same as those of U.S. Steel; thus the company's size was doubled, with steel's contribution to sales dropping to about 40 percent.

Marathon had been incorporated on August 1, 1887, as Ohio Oil Company by Ohio oil driller Henry Ernst and four of his fellow oil men, primarily in order to compete with Standard Oil Company. Ohio Oil quickly became the largest producer of crude oil in Ohio and was bought out by Standard Oil in 1889. When Standard was broken up on antitrust grounds by the U.S. government in 1911, Ohio Oil again became an independent company with veteran oil man James Donnell as president. Under Donnell and his successors Ohio Oil grew into an international integrated oil and gas company with large energy resources and extensive exploratory and retail sales operations. Its name was changed to Marathon Oil Company in 1962.

U.S. Steel continued to improve the efficiency and profitability of its steel operations with the 1983 closing of part or all of 20

obsolete plants. By 1985 Roderick had shut down more than 150 facilities and reduced steelmaking capacity by more than 30 percent. He cut 54 percent of white-collar jobs, laid off about 100,000 production workers, and sold $3 billion in assets. U.S. Steel continued its diversification program in February 1986 with the $3.6 billion acquisition of Texas Oil & Gas Corporation. Founded in 1955 as Tex-Star Oil & Gas Corporation, the company is engaged primarily in the domestic production, gathering, and transportation of natural gas. In July 1986 United States Steel Corporation changed its name to USX Corporation to reflect the company's diversification.

In October 1986 corporate raider Carl Icahn threatened to make a $7.1 billion offer for USX—after purchasing about 29 million USX shares. Roderick fought off the takeover attempt by borrowing $3.4 billion to pay off company debts with the provision that the loan would be called in the event of a takeover. Icahn gave up his attempt in January 1987 but kept his USX shares and began a long program of urging USX management to spin off or sell its under-performing steel business. In 1987 Roderick shut down about one-quarter of USX's raw steelmaking capacity, but by 1988 U.S. Steel, the steel division of USX, had become the most efficient producer of steel in the world.

In May 1989 Roderick retired and was succeeded as chairman and CEO by Charles A. Corry, a veteran of the USX restructuring. In October 1989 Corry announced a plan to sell some of Texas Oil & Gas's energy reserves in order to pay off debt and implement a large stock buyback. In June 1990 the company stated that it would consolidate Texas Oil's operations with Marathon Oil in order to cut costs. On January 31, 1991, Icahn won his long battle to have USX restructured when the company announced that it would recapitalize by issuing a separate class of stock for its U.S. Steel subsidiary although both businesses, energy and steel, would remain part of USX. In May 1991 USX shareholders approved the plan. Common shares of USX Corporation began trading as USX-Marathon Group, and new common shares of USX-U.S. Steel Group were issued. In May 1992 USX shareholders approved the creation of a third common share, USX-Delhi Group, which reflects the performance of the Delhi Gas Pipeline Corporation and related companies engaged in the gathering, processing, and transporting of natural gas.

In 1991 the two stocks rose 28 percent and the steel shares actually outperformed the oil. Several factors influenced the positive performance of the company and its stock. Marathon, unlike many of its competitors, has prepared for growth in the 1990s. The 1991 discovery of what may be a large oil field in Tunisia and two new Gulf of Mexico strikes had the early 1990s looking promising for USX-Marathon. The addition of its East Brae field in the North Sea in 1995 could also boost crude output by 25,000 barrels per day from about 200,000 barrels per day. In addition, while other oil companies reduced their exploration budgets, USX-Marathon increased its capital and exploration budget by almost one-third.

Although the outlook for steel has remained unfavorable, it has improved in the early 1990s. USX-U.S. Steel was able to reduce its fixed costs and boost productivity by cutting its raw steel capacity in half, closing four of its seven plants and reducing its total number of employees by 56 percent between 1983 and

1990. From 1991 to 1992 alone U.S. Steel reduced its operating capability by 3 million tons to 13.5 tons. The drastic cuts paid off for U.S. Steel—by 1993 the company was the lowest-cost fully integrated steel producer in the United States.

U.S. Steel has also worked to bring its quality up to par with foreign competitors, especially the Japanese, by forging joint ventures with such companies as Japan's Kobe Steel. The company also spent $1.5 billion in the early 1990s to upgrade its facilities to industry benchmark standards.

USX-U.S. Steel diversified into information technology in the fall of 1992 in order to supplant dwindling revenue. This subsidiary unit started out with 100 employees working on four major projects, including information systems consultation for another (unnamed) steelmaker. The unit planned to provide systems integration, application development, consultation, and other services to other process industries, including manufacturers of metals and forest products.

Principal Subsidiaries: Marathon Oil U.K. Ltd.; Emro Marketing Company; Carnegie Natural Gas Co.; Delhi Gas Pipeline Corp.; FWA Drilling Co., Inc.; United States Steel International, Inc.; National-Oilwell; USS-POSCO Industries; UnSS/Kobe Steel Co.; U.S. Steel Mining Co., Inc.; USX Engineers and Consultants, Inc.; USX Realty Development.

Further Reading: Cotter, Arundel, *The Authentic History of the United States Steel Corporation*, New York, Moody Magazine and Book Co., 1916; Fisher, Douglas A., *Steel Serves the Nation, 1901–1951*, Pittsburgh, United States Steel Corporation, 1951; Jackson, Stanley, *J. P Morgan*, New York, Stein and Day, 1983; Norman, James R., "U.S. Oil (& Steel)," *Forbes*, September 19, 1991; Hoffman, Thomas, "USX Diversifies into Information Services Arena," *Computerworld*, August 31, 1992; Beck, Robert J., "Industry to Trim Spending in U.S. During 1992," *Oil & Gas Journal*, February 24, 1992.

—Bernard A. Block

VALERO ENERGY CORPORATION

530 McCullough Avenue
San Antonio, Texas 78215
U.S.A.
(210) 246-2000
Fax: (210) 246-2646

Public Company
Incorporated: 1979
Employees: 1,890
Sales: $1.2 billion
Stock Exchanges: New York
SICs: 2911 Petroleum Refining; 4922 Natural Gas
   Transmission; 6719 Holding Companies, Nec

Valero Energy Corporation operates a specialized petroleum refinery in Corpus Christi, Texas. The company markets the products of this facility—primarily high-grade gasoline—and, through a half-owned subsidiary, sells, stores, and transports natural gas throughout the state of Texas.

Valero was founded as a natural gas pipeline on the last day of the year in 1979. In an effort to diversify itself into a broad-based energy firm, the company purchased a petroleum refinery shortly after its inception. Renovation and start-up of this facility in a difficult world petroleum market nearly put Valero out of business. The company subsequently sold off its gas properties to a limited partnership to retain financial stability and concentrate on its refining activities. Conditions in the petroleum industry repaid this gamble, and Valero thrived in the late 1980s and early 1990s.

The company was created by the Texas Railroad Commission, which regulates energy in Texas, to rectify the misdeeds of the Lo-Vaca Gathering Company, one subsidiary of the Coastal States Gas Corporation, Valero's corporate precursor. In the 1960s Coastal's chairman, Oscar S. Wyatt, Jr., had signed contracts to deliver gas to many customers, including several large Texas cities, at low prices, with the expectation that costs for gas would not rise. By 1972 and 1973, however, gas prices had gone up dramatically, and the company was not able to fulfill its contracts. The Texas regulatory board allowed Coastal to pass on its higher prices to customers and to make a small profit, rather than see the company go out of business. The

question of the penalty for Coastal's broken contracts became a matter of litigation that stretched through the mid-1970s.

Finally, in December of 1977, the Commission ruled that Coastal would have to refund $1.6 billion—more than the company was worth—to its customers. To satisfy this ruling, Coastal's intrastate Texas gas-gathering pipeline was spun off into a new company, Valero. Former Coastal customers were awarded 55 percent of the new company's equity, while the other half went to Coastal's shareholders, with the exception of Wyatt. In addition, Coastal was ordered to spend $230 million exploring for new gas over the next decade and a half. Any new gas found would be sold to Valero at a rate 15 percent below the current market price. Valero also got a $110 million chunk of Coastal stock.

Thus, at its birth, Valero became the largest intrastate pipeline in Texas, with 8,000 miles of transmission lines, assets worth $700 million, and start-up revenues exceeding $1 billion. In addition, Valero had the right to charge customers ten cents per million cubic feet (mcf) over its cost of gas in its first year, and 15 cents over mcf in its second, guaranteeing the company a profit of at least $23 million. Valero's stock was slated to be listed on the New York Stock Exchange shortly after its formal inaugural.

To separate itself from its corporate parent, Valero chose to locate its headquarters in San Antonio. The city was both the company's largest customer and an outpost 200 miles from Coastal's Houston home. The company's name was taken from the Mission of San Antonio de Valero, the original name of the Alamo. As its president, the company chose Bill Greehey, formerly the court-appointed head of Lo-Vaca. Greehey had been instrumental in negotiating the out-of-court settlement that resulted in Valero's formation.

Beyond Valero's basic gas business, Greehey planned to expand into gas storage and oil and gas exploration, as well as coal and oil refining. He planned to make Valero a "fully integrated energy company," as he told a *Fortune* correspondent in January of 1980.

In its first year of existence, Valero moved quickly to solidify its position and expand into the nonregulated areas of its industry. The company tapped into new supplies of gas, signing contracts in Mexico and Texas, and also added new storage facilities. Announcing that it would spend $14 million expanding its production of natural gas liquids—which at the time were selling at high prices—the company planned to build a $10.2 million processing facility and construct a 25-mile pipeline. Valero also spent $4 million on tentative moves into the gas exploration and drilling business.

Valero made its most significant investment late in 1980 when it bought a one-half interest in Saber Energy, Inc., a small marketer of gasoline, for $51 million. With its new partner, Valero planned to turn Saber's tiny gasoline-producing operation in Corpus Christi, Texas, into a state-of-the-art specialized refinery. The facility was designed to use the product at the bottom of a barrel of crude oil—a high-sulfur, tar-like substance known as atmospheric residual oil (abbreviated "resid")—as its raw material, or "feedstock." Resid was obtained as a by-product of the processing of raw crude oil and generally cost significantly less than a barrel of crude, which was the feedstock of a conventional refinery. By cracking resid in a complicated and expensive process, Saber's refinery would create high-quality gasoline. In the Saber partnership, the company made its bid to become a broad-based energy concern.

In 1981 Valero embarked on the construction of the new refining facility, which was slated to cost $100 million. In addition, the company revamped its somewhat ineffective exploration and production operation, moving aggressively to get under way and opening regional offices in Midland and Houston, Texas; Denver, Colorado; and New Orleans, Louisiana. By the end of the fiscal year, Valero's net income had risen to $97.3 million, an increase of more than 50 percent from the previous year.

By 1983 Texas was in the grip of a severe recession, and Valero's outlook was growing less rosy. The company's earnings from its core businesses—gas sales and transportation of other people's gas through Valero's pipelines—went into decline. In an effort to counteract losses, Valero joined in industry efforts to encourage the shipment of gas directly to large commercial customers, which helped somewhat to prop up its earnings.

In its new endeavors, Valero had mixed success. Although the company had spent $100 million on exploration, it had yet to benefit from these efforts. Valero's natural gas liquids business, however, proved prosperous. The company had increased its gas liquids capabilities by 50 percent, building eight plants at a cost of $150 million to stockpile ethane, butane, and propane, and these facilities contributed significantly to Valero's profits. "If not for gas liquids," Greehey told *Business Week* in 1983, "we would have been in trouble."

The biggest problem proved to be Valero's large investment in the Saber gasoline refinery. Two years into the project, estimated costs had reached $617 million, the most ever spent per barrel of oil on a refinery. Valero had taken on $550 million in debt to finance construction, and by 1983 the project was behind schedule. Experiencing difficulties meeting federal air pollution standards, the company was forced repeatedly to postpone full start-up of the facility. In addition, the economics of the refinery had shifted significantly since the project's inception. When Valero had started out, resid had been very cheap, while gasoline, the refined product, had been selling at a relatively high price. This justified large expenditures to convert one into the other. By 1983, however, the cost of Valero's raw materials had risen, and an oversupply of gasoline had driven prices for its end product down, dramatically reducing the potential profitability of the refinery.

The cost of raw materials for Valero's refinery was driven up further in 1984 when Great Britain suffered a coal strike. Unable to use coal as a fuel, British industry turned to resid instead, driving the demand and the cost of Valero's feedstock to unexpected heights, which at times exceeded the cost of straight crude oil. As a result of this stroke of bad luck, Valero's Saber refinery had still not become profitable by the middle of 1984.

Valero had certified to its lenders that the refinery was up and running two months after it had originally planned, but even after this step was taken, low gasoline prices meant that the plant was operating at a loss. In August of 1984 heavy trading of Valero's stock prompted speculation that the company would be the target of a take-over.

Saber posted losses of $53 million in the first half of 1984, and by that fall, its rapidly weakening financial condition had obligated Valero to buy out its partner. In doing so, Valero added Saber's substantial debts to its own large tally of borrowed funds, doubling its overall level of long-term indebtedness. As a result, the company was forced to omit a dividend to its shareholders in the quarter in which the consolidation was made. To placate its worried bankers, Valero agreed to limit its spending on other areas of its business while it postponed payments to the bank on its loans. With this news, the price of the company's stock sunk to its lowest point, as investors anticipated the company's possible bankruptcy.

In an effort to shore up its financial condition, in February of 1985, Valero entered into an agreement with Techniques d'Avant Garde Group SA, known as TAG, a holding company controlled by Saudi Arabian Akkram Ojjeh. TAG invested $15 million in Valero as part of an agreement that the Saudi investor would raise its interest in the company to one third if Valero could locate a cheap source of raw materials for its refinery. In a second bid to raise funds, Valero sold off a 50 percent interest in its West Texas pipeline system to InterNorth, an energy company based in Omaha, Nebraska. The sale brought the financially beleaguered company $68 million.

By late spring of 1985, more favorable conditions in the energy industry as a whole had begun to lift Valero's prospects. As costs for crude oil by-products fell and the price of gasoline rose, the Saber refinery was able to increase its earnings, posting a small operating profit for March. Despite this good news, the company temporarily suspended its production of gasoline at the Saber facility, resuming operations in June. The following month, Valero's agreement with TAG, the Saudi investor, was called off. At the end of 1985 Valero reported losses of $16.1 million.

By early 1986 Valero was also suffering from a glut in its original field, natural gas. Unable to sell the gas it had contracted at its founding in 1979 to buy from its corporate parent, Coastal, Valero refused to fulfill its contracts and in January, was sued by Coastal for $243 million in the first of a number of "take-or-pay" suits over gas purchase agreements that would not be resolved until the end of the decade.

In an effort to strengthen its financial position, Valero restructured $700 million of its debt in April of 1986 and got out of the coal business by selling off the mine it owned in Indiana. Unable to make its expensive Saber refinery profitable given conditions in the world oil market, Valero began to informally hunt for a buyer for the facility. Despite the drain on funds by the unprofitable refinery, however, improved performance in Valero's pipeline operations enabled the company to finish the year in the black, posting profits of $34.7 million.

Faced with the problem of a profitable gas business that was carrying a money-losing refinery, Valero significantly restructured itself in early 1987. The company spun off its natural gas pipeline and natural gas liquids businesses into a limited partnership, in which it would hold a 49 percent share. For this portion, Valero turned over $184 million of its own money, as well as $191 million contributed by public equity investors. The remainder of the gas partnership's funding was raised through the issuance of $550 million in notes. In addition to these moves, Valero abandoned its attempts to find oil and gas reserves, shutting down its exploration activities.

With the money from the divestiture of its gas assets, Valero was able to reduce its dangerously crippling debt load by more than $700 million, restoring its balance sheet to relative health. This meant, however, that the core of the company was its money-losing refinery. Valero lost $13.3 million in the first six months of 1987 on its refining and gasoline marketing activities.

By 1988, however, the climate for petroleum refining had improved, and Valero began to see a turn-around in its fortunes. Lower prices for its raw materials, coupled with reduced gasoline inventories and growing customer demand, enabled the company to turn a profit of $13.2 million in the first half of the year. Noting that the recent turmoil in the oil and gas industry had put many refineries out of business, Valero's leaders were confident that domestic demand for gasoline would continue to exceed refining capacity, keeping prices high. In addition, the company counted on the fact that the product it refined was high-quality, high-octane, clean-burning unleaded gas, for which it anticipated a growing demand.

On the supply side, Valero noted that prices for resid had fallen as stockpiles had grown, and the company moved to upgrade its refinery, increasing capacity. To assure future steady supplies of raw materials, the company sought to take on a foreign petroleum producer as a joint owner in the refinery. Valero ended 1988 with $30.6 million in posted profits.

The company's fortunes continued to improve in the following year. Valero's half-owned natural gas operations had profited from the deregulation of the gas industry; it increased its sales by adding customers outside Texas. The company was able to transport, through interstate gas pipeline link-ups, and sell gas to clients in other states and in Mexico. Its number of gas processing plants had grown to 11.

Valero also continued to upgrade its oil-refining facilities. The company added a device that enhanced the octane level of the gas it produced and also constructed a natural gas processing plant that split the gas into products to be used in petrochemicals or oil refining activities. In 1989 Valero announced that it would own a 20 percent stake in a planned $104 million plant for processing gases given off in the refining process in Corpus Christi, Texas. These measures, along with the reduction in Valero's debt load, allowed the company to reduce its break-even point for a barrel of refined oil from $6.00 when the plant had started up, to $3.60 in 1989. As a result of refinery upgrades and the strengthened market, Valero was able to restore its dividend payment in a sign of fiscal health in the second quarter

of that year. The company finished 1989 with profits of $41.5 million.

Valero's recovery from the severe difficulties it had experienced in the mid-1980s continued as the company moved into the 1990s. The world oil industry was thrown into turmoil in August of 1990 when Iraq invaded major oil producer Kuwait, driving up the prices of both crude oil and refined petroleum products. With this increased activity, Valero contracted for an additional $200 million investment in its refinery facilities. The company ended the year with earnings of $94.7 million, nearly double those of the year before. In a reversal of earlier conditions, petroleum refining accounted for a vast portion of the profits, while the company's interest in its natural gas partnership contributed only 20 percent of the company's returns.

The outbreak of the Allied offensive in the Persian Gulf in early 1991 immediately drove petroleum prices down. In anticipation of this effect, however, Valero had sold much of its first quarter production in advance at inflated prices and added $30 million to its balance sheet. Although Valero lost money when it was forced to shut down part of its production to make improvements to its plant, the company completed 1991 with record profits of $98.7 million.

Looking to profit from the general move toward more environmentally conscious, cleaner-burning fuels, such as natural gas and the high-octane products refined at its Corpus Christi facility, Valero continued to upgrade its plants in 1992. In addition, the company expected that by 1994 their entire gasoline output would be made up of reformulated gasoline. With an eye to further expansion, the company solidified its balance sheet by repurchasing the outstanding shares of an old stock offering and sought permission to raise money for expansion by issuing new stocks. Valero also opened an office in Mexico City, in an effort to enhance its relationship with the Mexican government and assist it in its search for clean energy.

As it moved into the mid-1990s, Valero had solidified its position in the petroleum industry. With its high-tech refinery, the company appeared well positioned to prosper in the coming years.

Principal Subsidiaries: Valero Natural Gas Partners, L.P. (49%); Valero Refining and Marketing Company.

Further Reading: ''Take That, Oscar Wyatt!,'' *Forbes,* August 21, 1978; ''Birth of a Natural Gas Giant,'' *Fortune,* January 14, 1980; ''Valero Energy: Gambling on a State-of-the-Art Refinery,'' *Business Week,* October 24, 1983; Andrew, John, ''Valero Energy Remains a Risky Investment Despite Recent Improvements, Analysts Say,'' *Wall Street Journal,* April 15, 1985; ''Valero Energy Corporation,'' *Wall Street Transcript,* October 16, 1989; Valero Energy Corporation Annual Report, 1992.

—Elizabeth Rourke

VAN CAMP SEAFOOD COMPANY, INC.

4510 Executive Dr., #300
San Diego, California 92121-3029
U.S.A.
(619) 597-4200
Fax: (619) 597-4568

Private Company
Incorporated: 1914
Employees: 2,700
Sales: $440 million (1991)
SICs: 2091 Canned & Cured Fish & Seafoods

Van Camp Seafood Company, Inc. produces Chicken of the Sea—the third most popular brand of canned tuna fish in the United States—as well as several other seafood products, such as canned salmon, crabmeat, shrimp, and oysters.

Canned tuna was first processed and marketed in 1903, the year the sardine catch suddenly dwindled. An enterprising fisherman processed the little-known tuna fish (named *thunnos* by the ancient Greeks, who considered it a rare delicacy) in San Pedro, California, the birthplace of the world's tuna industry. While the fisherman's 700 cases of tuna sold out immediately, the tuna industry faced some difficulties, particularly in keeping the fish fresh and ready for sale. As refrigeration for large volumes of fish was unavailable, the tuna had to be caught close to shore and brought back for sale quickly. However, tuna fishing is an especially slow process as tuna is one of the ocean's most migratory fish, often traveling at a rate of 45 mph. The seafood industry was revolutionized before the First World War when a method of packing fresh fish in ice was developed, enabling fishermen to fish longer hours and thereby increase their catch. This method became popular and soon tuna fishing became more lucrative.

Gilbert Van Camp, descendant of Dutch seafaring immigrants, established Van Camp Seafood Company in San Diego, California, in 1914. At this time tuna fishing was still a seasonal activity, producing albacore tuna, called the chicken of the sea because of its white meat and mild flavor. Van Camp adopted the fishermen's name for albacore tuna, "Chicken of the Sea," as the brand name of his canned tuna. He also helped to turn tuna fishing into a year-round activity by catching and canning

the more abundant yellowfin and skipjack tuna, which produced a less expensive, darker meat with a stronger flavor.

The year the Van Camp Seafood Company was established was propitious. War had broken out in Europe, and the United States soon became a major supplier of food to the blockaded allies. Food shortages at home encouraged the search for beef and pork substitutes, and tuna was declared by nutritionists a healthy alternative high in protein. By the end of the war, tuna was the most popular fish in America, and business at the Van Camp Seafood Company was booming.

As a result of the boom in the fish business, several tuna companies were established during the war, creating a more competitive environment. These companies, as well as the Van Camp Seafood Company, suffered in the recession that followed the end of the war. Nonetheless, Van Camp Seafood continued to grow. While tuna consumption declined in the heartland, it remained steady in the coastal areas. Meanwhile Van Camp Seafood did not limit itself to marketing only tuna. Several other fish varieties were canned under the Chicken of the Sea name, and Van Camp's pet food business, using tuna parts not canned for human consumption, grew.

World War II was a turning point for many companies. Shortages of meat once again made fish popular, and tuna became the preferred fish among millions of men and women in uniform, who often had their first taste of tuna in the armed forces. After the war, tuna was established as a popular and widely available food in the United States. Furthermore, through the use of the new advertising medium, television, Chicken of the Sea became a leading seafood brand.

Competition in the canned seafood business was keen. In 1965, Van Camp Seafood Company was bought by the Ralston Purina Company, a major marketer of pet food, as part of its effort to streamline its operations by processing tuna, a major ingredient in its pet food. A recession in the late 1970s coupled with severe competition led Van Camp to close down its big cannery in 1984. Four years later, an Indonesian firm, the P. T. Mantrust Company, eager for an inroad into the lucrative U.S. tuna market, bought the Van Camp Seafood Company for 260 million dollars. Americans continue to run and staff the company.

Since then, president and CEO of Van Camp Seafood, Jose Munoz, and the chief financial officer, Peter Perkinson, have overseen the rapid expansion of the company, and Chicken of the Sea tuna has become one of the top three tuna companies in the United States, with central offices in San Diego and in American Samoa. Since the 1950s, product variety has been a chief concern of Van Camp Seafood; in addition to the several varieties of canned fish it produces, it markets tuna packed in water or oil in a variety of can sizes, as well as tuna processed with a low amount of sodium.

Recently, Van Camp Seafood's industry has been affected by popular concerns for the environment. Beginning in the 1970s, environmentalists became concerned for the dolphin population, which was declining in the eastern Pacific Ocean where dolphins tend to school with the yellowfin tuna; caught along with tuna in drift nets, millions of dolphins were dying. A public letter-writing campaign begun in the 1980s, which threatened a boycott, prompted tuna companies to change their ways. In

1990, following the lead of competitor Star-Kist, Van Camp managers adopted an enlightened, though costly, policy. Declaring their tuna "dolphin safe," the company refused to purchase tuna caught by drift net fishing methods or by any other means harmful to dolphins. This forced the fishing boats of the eastern Pacific to either find new areas in which to fish or to pursue the more elusive skipjack tuna, which doesn't school with dolphins. U.S. government inspectors routinely accompany tuna fishing boats to monitor their practices and to declare whether or not tuna is dolphin safe. While the company had to raise the price of its tuna by a few cents a can, it expects the dolphin safe policy to pay off in terms of greater public trust and consumer consumption. Since this time, the company has also ensured that its cans are manufactured from recyclable materials.

At the onset of the 1990s Indonesia was second to Thailand in the exportation of tuna. Nevertheless, the Van Camp Seafood Company is an efficient, streamlined, and modern enterprise, poised to prosper as seafood becomes more important in an increasingly health conscious American diet that includes tuna salad sandwiches and even "tuna pizza."

Further Reading: "Healthy Option," *Restaurant Hospitality,* February 1991; "A Fishy Story (Killing of Dolphins Caught in Tuna Fishing Nets)," *The Economist,* May 4, 1991; Holland, Kerry L., "Exploitation on Porpoise: The Use of Purse Seine Nets by Commercial Tuna Fishermen in the Eastern Tropical Pacific Ocean," *Syracuse Journal of International Law & Commerce,* Spring 1991; Weinstein, Steve. "The 1991 Supermarket Sales Manual: Main Courses & Entrees." *Progressive Grocer,* July 1991; Magnusson, Paul; Hong, Peter, "Save the Dolphins—Or Free Trade?" *Business Week,* February 17, 1992; Conan, Kerri, "Menu Ideas: Flounder No More." *Restaurant Business,* March 1, 1992; Schwarz, Adam, "Pains of Indigestion: Indonesian Food Firm Faces Debt Problems," *Far Eastern Economic Review,* March 19, 1992; Biberman, Thor Kamban. "Van Camp Seafood Sued for Failing to Pay for Tuna," *San Diego Daily Transcript,* June 8, 1992.

—Sina Dubovoj

VECO INTERNATIONAL, INC.

813 W. Northern Lights Blvd.
Anchorage, Alaska 99503-2495
U.S.A.
(907) 277-5309
Fax: (907) 264-8130

Private Company
Incorporated: 1971
Employees: 1,000
Sales: $700 million
SICs: 1381 Drilling Oil & Gas Wells; 1389 Oil & Gas Field
   Services, Nec; 1611 Highway & Street Construction; 1623
   Water, Sewer & Utility Lines; 1629 Heavy Construction,
   Nec; 8711 Engineering Services

VECO International, Inc. is the largest oil field services company in Alaska. It modifies oil rigs, supplies support services to
drillers, and builds prefabricated modules for oil rigs and mines,
in addition to drilling in its own right. It has subsidiaries in three
states and has, since the late 1980s, been a major player in the
environmental clean-up business.

VECO traces its history to 1968 when William Allen arrived in
Alaska. A controversial man with a reputation for his business
drive, as well as pro-development activism in politics and
public affairs, Allen built VECO's fortunes as the state built its
oil revenues. Born in 1937, Allen dropped out of a New Mexico
high school at the age of 15. He took a job as a welder's
assistant in order to help support his seven brothers and sisters,
and by the time he was 23, Allen was supervising welding jobs
in Los Angeles. In 1968, he moved north with his Alaskan first
wife and began working on the Kenai Peninsula, where oil
companies would soon exploit the North Slope oil reserves.

Conditions on the North Slope then were very primitive, though
that was rapidly changing. Oil companies had paid the state
$900 million for the first lease—an amount more than three
times the entire state budget. It was at this time that executives
from ARCO approached Allen and encouraged him to go into
business with another ARCO employee, William Veltrie, to
provide the specialized support services oil drillers required to
operate in the inhospitable climate. Allen and Veltrie agreed to
the proposal, and in 1969 formed an oil field services company
called V-E Construction. The name was soon changed to VECO
and the company did well supporting the rapidly expanding
industry.

In 1973, VECO and a British company formed a joint venture
and bought a Norwegian company that did platform hookups in
the North Sea. A year later, after VECO had received its first
major contract on the North Slope, Allen bought out Veltrie and
sold his interest in the North Sea venture for $2 million. He then
used those profits to build his support operation on the North
Slope.

At this time it was still unclear whether the oil reserves in
Alaska would be developed. Conservationists were against using the reserves, while business owners had not yet made up
their minds to move full speed ahead on development. With the
worsening oil crisis in mind, Allen decided to put all his money
down on the side of the developers. ''We bet everything on the
North Slope,'' he later admitted in *Alaska Business Monthly*.

Though VECO concentrated mainly on supplying oil drillers,
Allen began to move the company into actual drilling. With the
NANA Regional Corporation—a business that pooled the
money of Alaskan natives—he formed a joint venture called
United Alaska Drilling, Inc. United Alaska Drilling was profitable, but it was perhaps most notable for the involvement of
native peoples who had often been excluded both economically
and politically in Alaska. Oil industry watchers credited Allen
for drawing native Alaskans into the oil business. Later he sold
some of VECO's interest in the drilling business to other native
corporations.

At the urging of the company's bankers—Seattle First National,
Manufacturer's Hanover Trust, and Interfirst of Dallas—VECO
also began to diversify. After reincorporating in 1981 as a
holding company called VECO International, Inc., Allen
formed several new subsidiaries, including VECO Drilling,
Inc., which bought oil drilling rigs in Colorado. Another subsidiary, Vemar, was used to purchase a Houston, Texas, business
that refit and modified oil rig platforms.

Vemar, though it had plenty of business, was having trouble.
The former owners had bid their contracts too low and the
company was losing money. Allen was able to renegotiate some
of the contracts and persuaded Penrod Drilling Corporation to
buy a share of Vemar to keep it going. In the end, Allen got the
work done, a fact which did much to solidify his reputation as a
man who made good on his word.

By the early 1980s, perhaps because of Vemar's problems,
VECO had become overextended. Faced with debts to banks
and unsecured creditors, Allen chose to pay off the unsecured
creditors and pay only interest on VECO's loans. The banks, in
turn, panicked and froze working capital. In 1982 VECO International; VECO, Inc.; and a utility subsidiary, Norcon, Inc.,
were forced into Chapter 11 bankruptcy. The proceedings, reportedly the largest such case handled by the Alaska courts up
to that time, deeply marked the company. Allen credited his and
his company's survival to the support of employees—who offered to loan the company money—and his clients.

VECO emerged from Chapter 11 stronger, if anything, than it
had been before. Allen consolidated his business, keeping top
management virtually unchanged, and switched to a group of
Alaskan banks headed by the National Bank of Alaska. By 1983
VECO had combined revenues of $92 million. In addition, by
1985, VECO had paid off all creditors 100 cents on the dollar

except, ironically, for the original banks who settled for a lower rate of payment.

In 1985 the company received a boost from changes in the market. As much of the Alaskan oil industry signed new, higher-cost agreements with labor, VECO and its subsidiaries, with their non-union workforce, were able to move away from service and support, and further into the construction business. In turn, between 1984 and 1987, VECO won the majority of large construction jobs on the North Slope. Among these were ARCO's Lisburne and West Sak projects, Standard Alaska's Endicott job, and Conoco's Milne Point endeavor. Also, VECO was awarded the contract for Alaska's Red Dog zinc mine, marking the company's move into mine construction. By 1987 VECO controlled about half of all North Slope construction. Nevertheless, its Alaskan business was less than booming, and the company was relying on its subsidiaries in different areas—including VECO Drilling in Colorado, Southwest VECO in California, and the Fairbanks utility Norcon—to bring in profits. These subsidiaries helped the company survive while the overall oil industry foundered.

As VECO grew, the company, and Allen, became a force in state politics, sometimes in controversial ways. In 1986, when the governorship and control of the Alaska state Legislature were at stake, Allen saw an opportunity to further his business aims. Leading a group of oil men who were fighting a proposal for new state taxes on the oil industry, Allen lobbied legislators and made campaign contributions to Republican candidates for the state senate. Eventually, he was caught using an employee check-off scheme to funnel $109,000 to five political candidates. The Alaska Public Offices Commission found VECO had made contributions over the legal limit and fined the company $72,000—reduced to $28,000 by the State Supreme Court. Allen had achieved his goal, however. Governor Bill Sheffield—who had accused Allen of unfair labor practices during the election—was defeated and several of Allen's candidates won. After the election, the legislature passed no new oil industry taxes.

Not all the attention VECO received was negative. In 1988, the company helped rescue three California gray whales trapped by newly-formed ice. The whales' plight provoked nationwide concern and many, including then-president Ronald Reagan, mobilized resources to help. VECO donated ice-breaking equipment, including a $3-million-dollar hovercraft which helped break and keep open an escape path for the whales. Afterwards, the story appeared in papers as far away as Florida and in such mass-circulation magazines as *People*.

Also in 1988, the company landed its first environmental clean-up contract with Cook Inlet Response Organization. This proved to be the beginning of a very lucrative area of business for VECO. It was in March of 1989 that the Exxon Valdez spilled 11 million gallons of crude oil into Alaska's Prince William Sound. Oil covered hundreds of miles of pristine coastline and the urgency of the clean-up made it highly expensive. Within weeks, Exxon named VECO lead contractor in the clean-up.

To fight the spill, VECO rented planes and fishing boats; it bought hundreds of thousands of raincoats, flashlights and garbage bags; and it hired some 10,000 workers at $16 an hour. The effort absorbed nearly the entire company's attention for

six months, and in the end, Exxon was billed more than $750 million. VECO earned $32 million for its role in the operation.

Other areas of the business benefitted from the spill as well. The Norcon utility unit experienced a turnaround, with overall sales skyrocketing from $110 million in 1988 to $960 million in 1990. Also, using what he had learned from the clean-up, in addition to the revenues earned, Allen added a new environmentally based subsidiary, VECO Environmental and Professional Services, Inc. In 1990 the new company received contracts to clean up a British Petroleum spill off of Huntington Beach, California. VECO Environmental and Professional Services subsequently advised others on an oil spill off Morocco, prepared oil-spill response plans for California companies, and sought openings for work in Eastern Europe. However, while the spill provided business openings for the company, the disaster also made life tougher for his Alaska businesses. The media questioned the effectiveness of the clean-up and the legislature passed the taxes he and other businesses had fought off in the mid-1980s.

With the oil business under attack again, and finding himself with a huge surplus of funds, Allen purchased *The Anchorage Times* in order to propound his pro-development views. His rival, *The Anchorage Daily News,* was considered anti-development, and had published probing investigations of the VECO campaign contributions scandal in 1986. Allen was proud of the *Times,* however, and explained in *Alaska Business Monthly,* "I could have sold out and went south and could have made quicker money." Instead he chose to sink all VECO's Valdez earnings into the newspaper and his pro-development campaign. Two years and about $50 million later, Allen sold his paper to the *Daily News.* Though he spent money to upgrade the facilities and pay the staff, he lost his newspaper war by failing to gain circulation or ad rates.

While the 1992 failure of *The Anchorage Times* marked a defeat for Allen and VECO, it was also the year the company won a Czechoslovakian government contract to clean up an abandoned Soviet military base. In early 1993, the *Alaska Journal of Commerce* named Bill Allen one of its "Top 25 Most Powerful Alaskans," praising him as one of the state's best, and best-known, entrepreneurs. The article described him a "restless soul" and it was wondered what he would do next. It appears clear, however, that VECO is a major player on the Alaska scene, and Allen means to make VECO a significant player in the world environmental business.

Principal Subsidiaries: VECO, Inc.; VECO Drilling, Inc.; VECO Environmental and Professional Services, Inc.; VECO Middle East, Inc.; Norcon, Inc.; Alaska United Drilling, Inc.; Eastwind, Inc.; CEC/VEPS, Inc.

Further Reading: "Don't Mess with Bill," *Alaska Business Monthly,* November 1987; "The New Forty-Niners: VECO International," *Alaska Business Monthly,* October 1990; "He's Ready To Hit the Ground Running," *Alaska Journal of Commerce,* December 11, 1989; "Anchorage Times' New Oilmen Owners May Have Purchased Trouble," *Chicago Tribune,* December 3, 1989; "Journalistic Issue In Alaska: Do Oil and Newspapers Mix?" *The New York Times,* December 18, 1989.

—Jordan Wankoff

VIACOM INTERNATIONAL INC.

1515 Broadway
New York, New York 10036
U.S.A.
(212) 258-6000
Fax: (212) 258-8718

Wholly Owned Subsidiary of National Amusements Inc.
Incorporated: 1971 as Viacom Inc.
Employees: 5,000
Sales: $1.6 billion
Stock Exchanges: American Boston
SICs: 7822 Motion Picture & Tape Distribution; 7812
    Motion Picture & Video Production; 4841 Cable & Other
    Pay Television Services; 4832 Radio Broadcasting Stations

Viacom International Inc., a subsidiary of National Amusements, Inc., is a media company owning radio and television
stations, cable systems, and pay-TV services including Showtime, The Movie Channel, and the MTV Networks. Viacom
also produces films and sells the rights to the reruns of television programs.

Viacom was formed by the Central Broadcasting System (CBS)
in the summer of 1970 to comply with regulations by the U.S.
Federal Communications Commission barring television networks from owning cable TV systems or from syndicating their
own programs in the United States. It formally became a separate company in 1971 when CBS distributed Viacom's stock to
its stockholders at the rate of one share for every seven shares of
CBS stock.

Viacom began with 70,000 stockholders and yearly sales of
$19.8 million. It had about 90,000 cable subscribers, making it
one of the largest cable operators in the United States. It also
had an enviable stable of popular, previously-run CBS television series—including *I Love Lucy*—available for syndication,
which accounted for a sizable percentage of Viacom's income.

By 1973 there were about 2,800 cable systems in the United
States, with about 7.5 million subscribers. This market fragmentation, along with the lack of an infrastructure in many communities and tough Federal regulations, slowed the development of
cable television. In 1973, Viacom had 47,000 subscribers on
Long Island, New York, but a drive to find 2,000 more added
only 250.

In 1976, to compete with Home Box Office (HBO), the leading
outlet for films in cable, Viacom established the Showtime
movie network, which sought to provide its audience with
feature films recently released in theaters. Viacom retained half
interest in the network while Warner Amex owned the other
half. Despite a federal ruling that removed many restrictions on
the choice of movies and sports available on pay-TV during this
time, allowing a wider variety of programming, Showtime lost
$825,000 in 1977. Nevertheless, Viacom earned $5.5 million
that year on sales of $58.5 million. Most of its earnings repre-
sented sales of television series, but it also reflected the growth
of its own cable systems, which at this time had about 350,000
subscribers.

Showtime continued to compete aggressively with HBO. In
1977 it began transmitting its programming to local cable stations via satellite, at a cost of $1.2 million a year. The following
year it worked out a deal with Teleprompter Corp., the largest
cable systems operator in the United States, with the result that
Teleprompter offered its customers Showtime rather than HBO.
Showtime also began offering a service channel called Front
Row. Dedicated to family programming, including classic movies and children's shows, Front Row cost consumers less than
$5 a month and was aimed at smaller cable systems where
subscribers could not afford a full-time pay-TV service.

Viacom's forays into the production of original programming in
the late 1970s and early 1980s had mixed results. The odds of
producing a successful television series or film were long, and
Viacom experienced several failures. The *Lazarus Syndrome*
and *Dear Detective* series were failures, and CBS canceled
Nurse after 14 episodes.

Cable systems were a capital-intensive business, and Viacom
constantly invested money in building its cable infrastructure—
spending $65 million in 1981 alone, for example. In the early
1980s Viacom started on a program of rapid growth across a
range of media categories. Company President Terrence A.
Elkes told *Business Week* that Viacom hoped to become a
billion dollar company in three to five years. Because management felt that cable operations were not a strong enough engine
for that growth, Viacom looked to communications and entertainment. In 1981 it bought Chicago radio station WLAK-FM
for $8 million and disclosed its minority stake in Cable Health
Network, a new advertiser-supported cable service. It also
bought Video Corp. of America for $16 million. That firm's
video production equipment stood to save Viacom a great deal
of money on production costs.

While its increased size would give Viacom clout with advertisers and advertising agencies, some industry analysts believed
that the acquisitions were partly intended to discourage takeover attempts. Buying radio and TV stations increased the
firm's debt, and added broadcast licenses to Viacom's portfolio.
The transfer of such licenses was a laborious process overseen
by the FCC, and it slowed down any attempt to quickly take
over a company.

By 1982 Showtime had 3.4 million subscribers, earning about
$10 million on sales of $140 million, and was seeking to
distinguish itself from other pay-TV sources by offering its own
series of programs. While Viacom had sales of about $210

million, syndication still accounted for a large percentage of Viacom's profits, 45 percent in 1982. The growth rate of syndication had declined, however, while that for cable had increased, and by 1982 Viacom had added 450,000 subscribers to the 90,000 it inherited from CBS, making it the ninth-largest cable operator in the United States.

However, a decline in pay-TV's popularity began in 1984, and growth in the industry was virtually halted. In early 1984, Showtime became a sister station to Warner Amex's The Movie Channel in a move calculated to increase sales for both of them. HBO and its sister channel Cinemax were being offered on 5,000 of the 5,800 cable systems in the United States, while Showtime or The Movie Channel were available on 2,700. Besides having a far larger share of the market, HBO already featured many of the films shown by Showtime and The Movie Channel, removing some of the incentive for subscribing to both groups of services. That year Viacom earned $30.9 million on revenue of $320 million.

In September 1985, Viacom purchased the MTV Networks and the other half interest in Showtime from Warner Communications, a company that needed cash because its cable interests were suffering in the unfavorable market. As part of the deal Viacom paid Warner $500 million in cash and $18 million in stock warrants. Viacom also offered $33.50 a share for the one-third of MTV stock that was publicly held. The year before Viacom bought it, MTV made $11.9 million on sales on $109.5 million. These purchases increased Viacom's debt load, making it less attractive for a takeover.

The MTV Networks included MTV, a popular music video channel, Nickelodeon, a channel geared towards children, and VH-1, a music video channel geared toward an older audience than that of MTV. The most valuable property in the MTV Network was MTV itself. Its quick pace and flashy graphics were becoming popular and highly influential in the media, and its young audience was a chief target of advertisers.

Established by Warner Amex in 1979 in response to a need for children's cable programming, Nickelodeon had not achieved any notable success until acquired by Viacom. Viacom quickly revamped Nickelodeon, giving it the slick, flashy look of MTV and unique programming that both appealed to children and distinguished the network from competitors like The Disney Channel. Viacom also introduced ''Nick at Night,'' a block of classic sitcoms aired late in the evening, popular among an adult audience. In the next few years Nickelodeon went from being the least popular channel on basic cable to the most popular.

Showtime lost about 300,000 customers between March 1985 and March 1986, and cash flow dropped dramatically. In 1986 Showtime embarked on an expensive and risky attempt to gain market share. While Showtime and arch-rival HBO had each featured exclusive presentations of some films, many films were shown on both networks. In order to eliminate this duplication Showtime gained exclusive rights to several popular films and guaranteed its customers a new film, unavailable on other movie channels, every week. However, Showtime's move increased the price of acquiring even limited rights to a film at a time when many industry observers felt that the price of buying films for pay-TV should be decreasing because the popularity of video cassette recorders had lowered their worth. Consequently, the cost of programming was raised, and Showtime was forced to increase marketing expenditures to make certain potential viewers were aware of the new policy.

Weakened by the $2 billion debt load it incurred, in part, to scare off unfriendly buyers, Viacom lost $9.9 million on sales of $919.2 million in 1986 and, ironically, became a takeover target. First Carl Icahn made an attempt to buy the company, and then a management buyout led by Terrence Elkes failed. Finally, after a six-month battle, Sumner M. Redstone, president of the National Amusements Inc. movie theater chain, bought Viacom for about $3.4 billion in March 1986. Some industry analysts felt that he had vastly overpaid, but Redstone believed Viacom had strong growth potential. Aside from its cable properties and syndication rights that now included the popular series *The Cosby Show,* Viacom owned five television and eight radio stations in major markets.

Redstone had already built National Amusements, the family business, from 50 drive-in movie theaters to a modern chain with 350 screens. Now faced with the task of turning Showtime around, he brought in Frank Biondi, former chief executive of HBO, who began organizing the company's many units into a cooperative workforce. Biondi in turn brought in HBO executive Winston Cox to run the network, and Cox immediately doubled Showtime's marketing budget. Showtime also obtained exclusive contracts with Paramount Pictures and Walt Disney films, which included the rights to air seven of the top ten films of 1986.

Redstone's banks were demanding $450 million in interest in the first two years following the takeover, but several fortuitous events aided him in paying off this debt. Shortly after the buyout Viacom began to earn millions from television stations wanting to show reruns of *The Cosby Show.* Furthermore, when Congress deregulated cable in 1987, prices for cable franchises soared. So when Redstone sold some of Viacom's assets to help pay off its debt, he was able to get large sums for them. In February 1989 Viacom's Long Island and suburban Cleveland cable systems were sold to Cablevision Systems Corp. for $545 million, or about 20 times their annual cash flow. Cablevision also bought a five percent stake in Showtime for $25 million, giving it a tangible interest in the channel's success. Further, after Redstone restructured MTV and installed a more aggressive advertising-sales staff, MTV experienced continued growth, against the expectations of many industry analysts. In 1989, for example, the MTV Networks won 15 percent of all dollars spent on cable advertising. MTV was expanding throughout the world, broadcasting to western Europe, Japan, Australia, and large portions of Latin America. It also planned to expand into eastern Europe, Poland, Brazil, Israel, and New Zealand.

These successes enabled Redstone and Biondi to significantly cut Viacom's debt by September 1989, and negotiate more favorable terms on its loans. Even so, it was rough going at first, and Viacom lost $154.4 million in 1987, though its sales increased to about $1 billion.

Under its new leadership Viacom branched out. Along with Hearst Corp. and Capital Cities/ABC Inc. it introduced Lifetime, a channel geared towards women. It also started its own production operations in 1989, Viacom Pictures, which produced about ten feature films in 1989 at a cost of about $4 million a film. These films first appeared on Showtime. Viacom's television productions also achieved success after years of mixed results. Viacom produced the hit series *Matlock* for NBC and *Jake and the Fatman* for CBS. It also added the rights for *A Different World* and *Roseanne* to its rerun stable. In addition, Viacom continued to spend heavily on new and acquired productions for Nickelodeon and MTV.

In October 1989, Viacom sold 50 percent of Showtime to TCI, a cable systems operator, for $225 million. TCI had six million subscribers, and Viacom hoped the purchase would give TCI increased incentive to market Showtime, thus giving the network a wider distribution.

By 1989 Viacom owned five television stations, 14 cable franchises and nine radio stations. In November of that year it bought five more radio stations for $121 million. Sales for the year were about $1.4 billion, with profits of $369 million. In 1990, Viacom introduced a plan that halved the cost of Showtime, but forced cable operators to dramatically increase the number of subscriptions to it. This strategy was designed to increase Showtime's market share at a time when many consumers were starting to feel that pay-TV channels were no longer worth their price.

Several months after HBO introduced its Comedy Channel in 1989, Viacom began transmitting HA!, a channel similar in format. Both channels provided comedy programs, but HA! primarily showed episodes of old sitcoms, while the Comedy Channel showed excerpts from sitcoms, movies, and stand-up comedy routines. Both channels started with subscriber bases in the low millions, and most industry analysts believed that only one of them would survive, and Viacom management expected to lose as much as $100 million over a three-year period before HA! broke even. The two companies considered merging their comedy offerings, but HBO parent Time Warner would only move forward with the idea if Viacom agreed to settle its $2.4 billion antitrust suit against HBO.

Showtime had filed the lawsuit in 1989, alleging that HBO was trying to put Showtime out of business by intimidating cable systems that carried Showtime and by trying to corner the market on Hollywood films to prevent competitors from airing them. The suit attracted wide attention and generated much negative publicity for the cable industry.

In August 1992 the suit was finally settled out of court, after having cost both sides tens of millions of dollars in legal fees. Time Warner agreed to pay Viacom $75 million and buy a Viacom cable system in Milwaukee for $95 million, about $10 million more than its estimated worth at the time. Time Warner also agreed to more widely distribute Showtime and The Movie Channel on Time Warner's cable systems, the second-largest in the United States. Furthermore, the two sides also agreed to a joint marketing campaign to try and revive the image of cable, which had suffered since deregulation.

In July 1991 Viacom announced plans to divide MTV into three cable channels by mid-1993. One channel would continue MTV's traditional mix of rock, rap, pop and heavy metal, while the other two were to focus on more specialized segments of the music audience. The cost of the move was expected to be low because it would be done with new technologies like cable compression and fiber optics that enabled more information to go through the same basic equipment. Nickelodeon, meanwhile, was going to 57.4 million homes, and was watched by more children between ages two and 11 than the children's programming on all four major networks combined. While Nickelodeon's earnings were not reported separately, the *Wall Street Journal* estimated its profits as $76 million in 1992 on sales of $190 million.

In the early 1990s the cable television industry was in a state of flux in the United States. Congress threatened reregulation, while such emerging technologies as microwave transmission threatened to bypass traditional cable systems. Nevertheless, with MTV, Nickelodeon, Showtime, and Cinemax, as well as syndicated programs in its lineup, Viacom has retained a broad consumer base and remains highly competitive.

Principal Subsidiaries: Viacom Productions Inc.

Further Reading: ''Viacom's Risky Quest for Growth,'' *Business Week,* June 21, 1982; Gubernick, Lisa, ''Sumner Redstone Scores Again,'' *Forbes,* October 31, 1988; Lieberman, David, ''Is Viacom Ready to Channel the World?'' *Business Week,* December 18, 1989.

—Scott M. Lewis

VILLAGE SUPER MARKET, INC.

733 Mountain Avenue
Springfield, New Jersey 07081
U.S.A.
(201) 467-2200
Fax: (201) 467-6582

Public Company
Incorporated: 1955
Employees: 3,950
Sales: $715 million
Stock Exchanges: NMS NASDAQ
SICs: 5411 Grocery Stores

Village Super Market, Inc., ranks among the top 100 grocery store companies in the United States. The company operates a chain of 25 supermarkets in New Jersey and Pennsylvania under the franchised name ShopRite. All the stores include traditional supermarket items, such as groceries, meats, fresh produce, dairy products, frozen foods, delicatessen, seafood, baked goods, health and beauty aids, and variety items. Some stores offer prescription pharmacies, cut flowers, in-house bakeries, small appliances, and other items. The company also operates a liquor store and a variety store.

The grocery industry of the 1930s was very different from today's large nationwide chains and distribution networks. When Nicholas and Perry Sumas, two New Jersey brothers, established Village Super Markets (VSM) in 1937, local grocers prided themselves on knowing their customers' needs and finding ways to fulfill them. In addition, grocery stores' markets were, in general, focused on food: meats, dry and canned goods, as well as fruits and vegetables in season.

In its early years, part of VSM's success in the highly competitive mid-Atlantic region can be attributed to the store's participation in the Wakefern-ShopRite food cooperative, which has long been a leader in the food industry. Village Super Market joined the newly formed cooperative in 1949. The cooperative association provided purchasing, warehousing, and marketing services to its stockholder-members, as well as the franchised ''ShopRite'' private label.

When Village Super Market incorporated in 1955, Nicholas Sumas, a co-founder, was selected as chief executive officer, president and chairman of the board. His son, James, was chosen vice-president, treasurer, and director and served on the board and several committees of the Wakefern-ShopRite cooperative.

Village's growth was strong as the company built and acquired new stores, most of which were located in the cities of Orange, Livingston, and Morris Plains in northeastern New Jersey. The Sumas brothers built their chain of supermarkets in the densely populated New Jersey counties of Morris, Essex, Union, and Somerset, which soon became part of the New York City metropolitan area.

The acquisitions and construction projects required large amounts of capital, which were eventually partially offset with the company's first stock offering.

When Village went public in 1965, it operated six supermarkets in the cities of Orange, Livingston, and Morris. The stock offering provided money for the construction of two new supermarkets in New Jersey—one in South Orange, and one in Livingston that replaced two small stores.

Throughout the 1950s and 1960s, Village Super Market was the smallest of four primary Wakefern members: Supermarkets General, Foodarama Supermarkets, and Mott's Supermarkets. The Wakefern group soon became one of the most efficient and profitable food cooperatives in the industry, with high profit margins, healthy inventory turnover, high sales per square foot, and stable return on stockholder equity.

By 1968 the Wakefern cooperative's success began to stifle its largest member, Supermarkets General. The cooperative's warehouse was too small to handle Supermarkets General's growing volume, and by 1969 the company, a 40 percent member-owner of the cooperative, left the cooperative. The power vacuum benefitted Village Super Markets, which quickly acquired four previously independent ShopRite stores, bringing its total business to eleven supermarkets, two liquor stores, three prescription pharmacy departments, and one discount store. The acquisitions capped a four-year period of growth for VSM: between 1964 and 1968 the company more than tripled its sales and earnings grew from $.75 per share to $1.50 per share during that period.

In 1973 Nicholas Sumas turned over the chief executive officership and presidency of the company to his brother and co-founder, Perry, a longtime director. Nicholas's second son, Robert, had already joined the board in 1969 as vice-president, secretary, and director in charge of finance and administration. Robert was also involved with the management of the Wakefern cooperative.

Village Super Markets encountered economic difficulties and increased competition during the 1970s. A recession, coupled with the emergence of deep-discounting among some national chains, raised the level of competition. Double- and even triple-couponing programs also drew customers from week to week.

In order to compete, VSM offered extended hours and utilized inventory control to keep costs under control; by 1978 VSM's sales were back on the rebound, growing by over 22 percent from 1977 to 1978 during a period of renewed prosperity for many publicly owned supermarkets.

In 1979 the company enjoyed record sales of over $232 million. Management saw Village Super Market's modest company size as an advantage over larger chains whose reaction time would be slowed by bureaucratic red tape. The company proved that assertion correct when, at the end of the decade, VSM was one of the first grocery companies to install computerized scanning check-out counters in its new stores.

The fifth member of the Sumas family joined the board of directors in 1980. William Sumas, son of Perry, became a vice-president and director of Village Super Market, and chaired the Bakery Committee of Wakefern. John Sumas, Perry's second son, became a vice-president and director in 1982, also serving on one of Wakefern's committees.

The new decade saw vigorous efforts to enlarge and update VSM's 19 stores along the new "superstore" format. Groceries of the 1980s and 1990s sought to offer "one-stop shopping," including everything from greeting cards to cut flowers, video-tape rentals, banking, pharmacies, and small appliances under one roof. One-stop shopping appealed to the busy lifestyles of many types of consumers, including two-income families, single individuals, and couples with no children.

Village Super Market was committed to the new format. In 1979 the leases on two stores averaging about 7,250 square feet each were allowed to lapse—VSM was building a new store in Stroudsburg, Pennsylvania, over three times as large as those two stores combined. The superstores averaged 46,000 square feet, compared to the 30,000 square-foot area of conventional groceries. The conversions cost from $1.5 million to $2.5 million each but had the potential of adding three to five percent to each store's bottom line, largely by raising per-customer sales. By 1988 VSM had converted fifteen of its nineteen stores to "superstores." The company added only one conventional store to its roster between 1982 and 1986.

In the 1980s, Village Super Markets experimented with warehouse stores, introduced generic "brand" foods, and eliminated select services in order to compete. The company also sought to reduce its labor costs by lowering wages but ran into resistance from organized labor. In 1984 the company was hit with a 24-day strike by its meat cutters, who were supported by local citizens. The strike resulted in a $294,000 pre-tax loss and Village reported that its profits plunged 98 percent in 1984, with earnings per share falling from $3.03 per share in 1983 to $.06 per share in 1984.

In 1986 Village Super Market purchased Starn's Markets, Inc., which operated a chain of three ShopRite superstores and one standard ShopRite market in southern New Jersey. The purchase brought VSM's total number of supermarkets to 25 and gave Village access to the growing Philadelphia-Atlantic City area.

The purchase helped Village Super Market celebrate its 50th anniversary with record sales and profits—and refinancing. In 1987 one million shares of Class A common stock were issued, raising $17.6 million. A private placement of 9.91 percent senior, unsecured notes that same year raised $20 million. The funds were used to pay off loans taken out during the Starn's acquisition and helped provide the company with cash for other acquisitions and new construction.

The Wakefern Food Corp. continued to be an important component of Village Super Market's success. About 85 percent of VSM's inventory was purchased from Wakefern, which grew to become the largest retailer-owned food cooperative in the United States. The cooperative's economies of scale in ware-housing, distribution, and marketing gave its 170 member stores the combined buying power of a store with $3.4 billion in sales. The ShopRite label also gained a high level of recognition over the decades through cooperative media campaigns. As an owner of Wakefern, VSM also received over 17 percent of the company's profits.

In 1990 ShopRite introduced its "Price Plus" preferred customer program, which provided electronic discounts to customers through the use of a scannable customer card. One and one-half million households joined the program within its first six months of operation, making ShopRite the national leader in this promotional area. Village Super Market opened its largest store ever, at 82,000 square feet, in Rio Grande, New Jersey, in 1991.

The Wakefern cooperative also expanded in the early 1990s, with a 210,000-square-foot perishable facility in 1990 and a 700,000-square-foot non-food warehouse completed in 1991.

Unfortunately, high unemployment, low consumer confidence, and food price deflation in the early 1990s decimated Village Super Market's profits—earnings per share in 1992 were a mere $.17. Sales in nearly all stores declined by 1.4 percent from 1991. The bright spots in VSM's annual report were its three new and/or remodeled stores in Rio Grande, Elizabeth, and Union, New Jersey. These three stores accounted for the company's entire meager sales increase.

The company continues to be principally owned and operated by six members of the Sumas family, including co-founders Nicholas and Perry. Like the grocers of the 1930s, the Sumases have several advantages over competitors with national scope. They have first-hand knowledge of local demographics and generally congenial relationships with local governments and real estate developers. Despite periods of low profits, Village has managed to pay a cash dividend to its stockholders every year since it first went public in 1965.

Further Reading: "Village Super Market, Inc.," *Commercial and Financial Chronicle,* August 16, 1965; Greene, Joan, "Shop Rite to Pathmark," *Barron's,* December 30, 1968; "Village Super Market, Inc.," *Wall Street Transcript,* March 5, 1973; Wagman, Evanne, "Fiscal '78 Net Up 17.2%, 48 Public Chains Report," *Supermarket News,* July 9, 1979; "Village Profits Plunge 98%," *Supermarket News,* November 5, 1985; "Village Super Market, Inc.," *Barron's,* January 4, 1988.

—April S. Dougal

VOLVO

AB VOLVO

S-405 08
Göteborg
Sweden
(31) 59 00 00
Fax: (31) 54 57 72

Public Company
Incorporated: 1926 as a subsidiary of AB Svenska
    Kullagerfabriken (SKF)
Employees: 60,115
Sales: SEK83 billion (US$10.95 billion)
Stock Exchanges: Stockholm London Düsseldorf Frankfurt
    Hamburg Oslo Paris NASDAQ Brussels Antwerpen Tokyo
    Zürich Basel Geneva
SICs: 3711 Motor Vehicles and Car Bodies; 3531
    Construction Machinery; 3519 Internal Combustion
    Engines, Nec; 2038 Frozen Specialties, Nec; 3724 Aircraft
    Engines and Engine Parts

Volvo is Sweden's largest industrial company and its last independent automobile manufacturer. Renowned for its practical, high quality trucks and automobiles, Volvo also is involved in several other industries, including pharmaceuticals, food, publishing, finance, and insurance. Despite recent difficulties in its core export dependent car operations, the company has proven to be a resilient and resourceful survivor.

Volvo began as a subsidiary of Svenska Kullagerfabriken (SKF), a large Swedish industrial company. In 1924, Scania Vabis ceased production of what had been Sweden's only domestically built automobile to concentrate on more profitable trucks. A year later, with the encouragement of the Swedish Association of Engineers and Architects, SKF began a confidential study of the feasibility of manufacturing its own car. Assar Gabrielsson and Gustav Larson started the project.

Gabrielsson, who had represented SKF in France and the United States, was a ball bearing salesperson who had closely studied American automobiles. Larson was an engineer with substantial experience in Britain, having worked for the English company White & Poppe.

SKF named the secret project Volvo—Latin for "I roll"—a dormant product name the company had introduced in 1915 for a line of ball bearings. Independently incorporated, hence the

title *aktiebolaget,* or "AB," the venture itself was only informally associated with SKF. The primary owners were Larson and Gabrielsson.

After agonizing over dozens of designs, the two partners settled on a simple model that would negotiate Swedish roads, with their snow, mud, steep hills, and millions of potholes, especially well. The original design, a car called the GL, or "Larson," was assembled at an abandoned SKF ball bearing factory at Hisingen, near Göteborg, from parts ordered out of various supplier catalogs from throughout Europe and the United States.

The first production model, an ÖV4, later called the "Jakob," rolled out of the factory on April 14, 1927. To the horror of all involved, it was discovered that the differential had been misconnected, resulting in a car that had three gears in reverse and only one gear for forward motion. The mistake took only ten minutes to correct. Volvo, however, could have done without the comical episode.

With 60 workers turning out five cars a week, the company proceeded with plans to manufacture a truck. The first model, introduced in 1928, was, in fact, from a design that predated the GL by four months. Volvo trucks, equipped with in-line six-cylinder engines, became extremely popular. As auto sales remained slow and their profits only marginal, the truck models consistently sold out. Profits from truck sales financed the operation for the next 20 years.

Volvo's cars and trucks were extremely sturdy and, by many measures, better assembled than American and other European models. In what was the most effective advertising of the day, Volvo models won several speed and endurance tests, racing across Sweden and speeding from Moscow to Leningrad, and later winning contests in Monte Carlo and Argentina. However, as both Larson and Gabrielsson detested automobile contests, Volvo refused to sponsor racers.

Volvo introduced a six-cylinder model, the PV651, in 1929, which proved highly successful with the lucrative taxicab market, and a larger version was soon planned. The following year, with the introduction of several new models and strong sales, Volvo purchased a controlling interest in its engine manufacturer, Pentaverken, located in Skövde. The company also purchased the Hisingen plant from SKF.

As the economy ground to a halt from the effects of the Great Depression, car sales fell into a slump. General Motors (GM), which had a Chevrolet plant in Stockholm at the time, attacked Volvo for being, in effect, "kit made." The company conducted a quick study which revealed that its cars were about 90 percent domestic content. Thus, it hit back at GM, advertising its products as "the *Swedish* cars."

Such competition kept Volvo on the alert, constantly studying other manufacturers. In 1935 it brought out a revolutionary new design: the PV36 Carioca, a streamlined art deco model, named for a popular South American dance. Later that year, the company took full control of Pentaverken and floated its first share issue on the Stockholm exchange.

While the company was introducing variations on the PV36, growing hostilities in Europe began to interrupt fuel supplies. In response, Volvo developed a means of manufacturing a combustible gas from charcoal in 1939. However, by this time the government was prohibiting the operation of private cars.

Despite the lack of crucial foreign components, Volvo continued production of cars and trucks, though mostly for military use. The company pressed on with new civilian designs in anticipation of the end of the war. Meanwhile, in 1942, Volvo took control of Svenska Flygmotor, a precision engineering company, and Köpings Mekaniska Verkstad, a gear and gearbox manufacturer.

In 1944 Volvo began taking orders for its long-awaited new model, the PV444—priced at SEK4800, the same as the 1927 ÖV4—although actual production had to wait until the end of the war the following summer. By then, however, an engineering strike crippled production, and gasoline was still under strict ration. Plans to introduce another model, the PV60, were similarly delayed in 1946 when a sheet metal supplier could not be lined up.

By 1947 these problems were alleviated, and production began, albeit slowly. Volvo now had a domestic competitor, Scania, which resumed automobile manufacturing after the war as a unit of SAAB, an aircraft manufacturer. By 1948, car sales exceeded truck and bus sales for the first time, and by 1950, Volvo employed 6,000 people and had turned out more than 100,000 vehicles, including 20,000 for export.

Gustav Larson retired from active involvement with Volvo in 1952, but continued to serve the company as an advisor. The following year, the company introduced the Duett, the first of many family estate cars designed for work and leisure. In 1954 Volvo had built a new truck factory in Göteborg, increasing annual production capacity to 15,000 vehicles, and had introduced fuel injection systems and turbochargers on its diesel engines.

In 1955 Volvo rolled out a small convertible with a plastic body and puncture proof tires called the Sport. Sales languished, however, and production was halted after only 67 had been produced. Volvo had better luck the next year with the Amazon, a welded frame sedan that borrowed heavily from other European models of the day. Later that year, Assar Gabrielsson also retired. He was succeeded by Gunnar Engellau, the head of Volvo Flygmotor.

Engellau took Volvo's helm at the height of the Suez Canal Crisis when all shipping, including oil, was refused passage. The resulting oil shortage in Sweden caused a severe drop in automobile sales. Engellau gambled that the crisis would be resolved within months, and he began laying plans for a major expansion, deciding to boldly go after export markets, especially the huge American market. Engellau was correct and, when the crisis subsided, Volvo was ready to meet the demand for new cars.

By 1959, with more than 15,000 employees, Volvo broke ground on a massive new production facility at Torslanda, near Hisingen. The following year, the company introduced a new sports car, the P1800. The car was prominently featured in the British television series *The Saint*. In fact, the car was even driven in private life by the star of the series, Roger Moore.

As other models in the product line were improved with ergonomically designed seats and new safety features—including the introduction of three-point safety belts as standard equipment in 1959—Volvo offered a revolutionary five-year engine guarantee that included coverage for damage resulting from accidents. The Swedish insurance industry, with government backing, sued Volvo for infringing on its business but, after four years of litigation, lost.

In 1963, Volvo opened a plant in Halifax, Nova Scotia, for the assembly of cars for the North American market. The initial 1956 introduction of the PV444 in the United States had been met with indifference, as most Americans still favored large, stylish vehicles such as the Buick Roadmaster. But despite its plain appearance, the PV444 was extremely well built. Subsequent models, such as the PV544, featured larger engines and windows and many new accessories. Furthermore, the company began sponsoring auto races.

The Torslanda plant, with an annual production capacity of 200,000 vehicles, opened in 1964. However, the Swedish government's decision not to join the European Economic Community stood to lock out Volvo sales on the continent due to import duties. In response, the company established an assembly plant at Ghent, Belgium, where Volvo cars would be exempt from import taxes. During this time, Volvo continued to improve its truck lines, rolling out its most powerful rig, the L495 Titan. This was followed by the tilt-cab L4571 Raske-Tiptop.

In 1966, the year before Sweden switched to right-lane driving, Volvo hit the market with a highly practical new sedan, the Volvo 144. Fitted with state-of-the-art safety features, including new safety belts and a new braking system, the 144 won Sweden's Car of the Year award. This model and its variations were especially popular in the United States, where—despite strong competition from Ford's new Mustang—the car sold for $2995. As sales jumped by 70 percent in Britain, Volvo established another assembly plant in 1968, this one in Malaysia. Meanwhile, in Sweden, Volvo's new Amazon model was leading sales.

In 1969 Volvo purchased Svenska Stålpressnings AB, which had supplied car bodies to Volvo since 1927. The following year, plans were laid for a new research and development division, the Volvo Technical Centre, which Volvo funded with between four and five percent of its sales. The VTC, as it was called, began testing hundreds of new safety features that quickly established Volvo as the world leader in automobile safety.

In 1971 Gunnar Engellau retired and was succeeded by Pehr G. Gyllenhammar. Also that year, Volvo employees gained board representation. As part of a ten year plan to maintain its feverish growth rates of the 1960s, Volvo attempted several industrial associations. The first of these occurred in 1972, when the company acquired a 33 percent interest in the Dutch auto manufacturer DAF. The company then forged links with Renault and Peugeot. While this substantially increased Volvo's production capacity within the European community, the company still regarded the United States as its largest market, bigger even than Sweden.

While auto sales were hurt severely by the oil crisis of 1973–74, its inflationary effects quickly tied up consumers' funds. This only hastened Volvo's need to find new growth markets. During this time, Volvo introduced two new models: the 265 and the DAF-built 66. In 1975 Volvo assumed greater control of DAF and changed the name of the company to Volvo Car B.V.

In 1977, Volvo proposed a merger with its Swedish rival SAAB-Scania. While the combination would produce one of Europe's largest industrial operations, effectively locking up the domestic market, SAAB didn't share Volvo's enthusiasm for the deal and allowed the matter to be dropped entirely.

Volvo next turned to Norway, where it had hoped to establish a relationship with the state oil industry and therefore tie Volvo sales to the rising fortunes of the North Sea oil business. But Volvo shareholders rejected the ill-conceived proposal even before the Norwegians had a chance to say no.

Meanwhile, Volvo restructured its operations, converting the car operation into a separate subsidiary. In 1979, with production at an all-time peak, Volvo turned out its four millionth car. It also established a closer relationship with Renault, combining research and product development and selling the French car maker a 9.9 percent interest in Volvo Car Corporation. Volvo's sales began to rise at this point, causing an increase in share values that sustained a new share issue, followed by two more in 1981 and 1982.

Volvo owed much of its strength to its reputation for quality, its 1980 introduction of the first turbocharged auto, the 240, and modifications to the popular 340. Furthermore, in 1982, a top-of-the-line sedan known as the Volvo 760 was introduced and became a symbol for Volvo quality and safety. The 240, the 340, and the 760 designs comprised the ideal range for the market.

In 1981 the Dutch government exercised its option to repurchase a majority in Volvo Car B.V., increasing its interest to 70 percent and thereby reducing Volvo's to 30 percent. During this time, Volvo continued its elaborate and expensive experiments with light components and new safety options. Many of these, tried on a series of testbed vehicles, found their way into new variations of the 300 and 700 series cars.

By 1985, Roger Holtback was promoted to head of the Volvo Car Corporation, and Håkan Frisinger was named president of AB Volvo. Under Frisinger's leadership, the company began planning a new production facility in Uddevalla, 80 kilometers northwest of Göteborg. In addition, the Dutch subsidiary introduced a new 400 series compact car.

Catalytic converters, which the company began installing in 1976, became standard on most European models in 1986. New child safety options were also incorporated into Volvo designs as were a variety of electronic sensors and controls.

Volvo's sales were extremely strong during the mid 1980s, due primarily to a devaluation in the Swedish krona. Output continued to rise until 1988, when production targets were ruined by a three-week strike. A few months later, the Uddevalla plant went on line, allowing the company to renovate the Torslanda facility, but too late to make up for lost time.

By 1990, Sweden's currency had rebounded, causing export sales to slow. The squeeze was too much for many Swedish companies to bear. In fact, in an effort to stay alive, SAAB concluded a deal with General Motors in which GM gained effective control of the company. Volvo responded by entering into a complex agreement with Renault to share the increasingly high costs of research and product development. As part of a wider reorganization, marketing responsibilities were transferred from regional sales offices back to Göteborg. Dissatisfied with these events, Holtback resigned in protest and was replaced by Björn Ahlström, head of North American operations.

Volvo concluded a deal with Mitsubishi in 1991 in which the Japanese manufacturer would take a one-third interest in the Dutch facility, allowing Mitsubishi to manufacture parts for cars it intended to assemble in Europe. The deal outraged many, including some at Renault, which resented Mitsubishi's attempts to enter the French market. The alliances also indicated that Volvo management believed it could not survive on its own.

In 1990 and 1991, Volvo introduced two new models, the 940/960 and the five-cylinder 850, which had taken more than seven years to develop. The company once again swept a series of quality and safety awards for its automobiles, and the high marks it received from automotive critics and government agencies had a considerable effect on sales. Those able to purchase one chose a Volvo because they believed it to be the safest car available.

This fact was not lost upon Volvo's marketing department. In the United States, where there were millions of young, upwardly mobile families, Volvo's reputation for safety was made the primary message of ad campaigns. As a result, the boxy Volvo gained an almost unshakable reputation for being the car of choice among America's ''yuppies.''

As economic downturns plagued Sweden, the government was faced with the precariousness of several of the country's lines of business and the possible loss of its automobile industry. To bolster the position of Swedish enterprises, the government introduced reforms to labor policies that had previously prevented Volvo and other companies from enforcing stricter absenteeism policies. This, combined with costcutting measures and the rationalization of the product line—dropping models such as the 760—helped to shore up Volvo's position. Nevertheless the company faced difficult times. Increased cooperation between Volvo and Renault—in fact, just short of a full merger—was not expected to produce tangible results before the mid 1990s.

Principal Subsidiaries: Volvo Car Corporation; Volvo Truck Corporation; Volvo Personbiler Norge AS; Volvo Laetebiler og Busser Norge AS (Norway); AB Volvo Penta; AB Volvo, Technological Development; Volvo Cars Europe Industry NV (Belgium); Volvo Cars Europe Marketing NV (Belgium); Volvo Europe Truck NV (Belgium); Volvo Penta Norden AB; Volvo Penta Industry Corporation; Volvo Personvagnar; Volvo Flygmotor AB; Volvo Canada Ltd.; Volvo GM Canada Heavy Truck Corporation; Volvo Aero Support Corporation; Volvo Lastvagner Sverige AB; Volvo Australia Holding AB; Volvo Auto OY; Volvo Personvogne Danmark A/S; Volvo Lastvogne og Busser Danmark A/S; Volvo Group Credit Sweden AB; Volvo Car Components Corporation; Volvo Deutschland GmbH (Germany); Volvo Nutzfahrzeuge Deutschland GmbH (Germany); Volvo Penta Deutschland GmbH (Germany); Volvo Badrijfawagens Nederland B.V. (Netherlands); Volvo Truck Components Corporation; Volvo Truck Parts Corporation; Volvo Cars Intercontinental AB; Volvo International Development Corporation; Alfred Berg Fondkommission AB; Ergoma AB; Volvo Group Finance Sweden AB; Volvo Bussar Sverige AB; Volvo Bus Corporation; Volvo Group Insurance Försäkrings AB; Försäkrings AB Volvia; Volvo Vehiculos Industrieles España, S.A.; Volvo Data Corporation; Volvo Transport Corporation; Volvo Cars of North America (U.S.); Volvo GM Heavy Truck Corporation (U.S.); Volvo Penta North America, Inc. (U.S.); Volvo Finance North America, Inc. (U.S.); Försäkringsaktiebolaget Volvia; Eddo Restauranger AB; Volvo Auto Oy Ab (Finland); Volvo Penta Norge AS (Norway); Volvo Continental N.V. (Belgium); Volvo European Corporate Office S.A. (France); Volvo Penta España S.A.; Volvo Automobiles France S.A.; Volvo Véhicules Industriels France S.A.; Volvo Penta France S.A.; Volvo Trucks (Great Britain) Ltd.; Volvo Bus Limited (U.K.); Volvo Parts U.K. Ltd.; Volvo Automobile (Schweiz) AG; Volvo Trucks (Schweiz) AG; Steyr Bus GesmbH (Austria); Volvo Italia SpA; Volvo Penta Italia SpA; Volvo Veicoll industriali SpA (Italy); Event Management Corporation EMC SA (Belgium); VECO Holding SA (France); Volvo North America Corporation (U.S.); Beijer Industries, Inc. (U.S.); Volvo East Asia (Pte) Ltd. (Singapore); VL Bue Asia (Pte) Ltd (Singapore); Volvo Group Finance Europe B.V. (Netherlands); Volvo (Suisse) SA (Switzerland); Volvo España S.A. (Spain); Volvo del Peru S.A.; Swedish Motor Assemblies Sdn Bhd (Malaysia); Volvo Thailand Ltd; Volvo Truck (Thailand) Co. Ltd.; Volvo Cars Japan Corporation; Volvo Penta Asia Pacific Corporation (Japan); Volvo Subamericana SACI (Argentina); Volvo Australia Pty Ltd; Volvo Distribuidora SA (Peru); Volvo do Brasil Velculoa Ltda.; Volvo Penta do Brasil Indústria e Comércio de Motores Ltda.

Further Reading: *Volvo: Sixty Years of Truckmaking,* Christer Olsson (commissioned by Volvo), Förlagshuset Norden AB, 1990; *Volvo: Cars From the '20s to the '90s,* Björn-Eric Lindh (commissioned by Volvo), Förlagshuset Norden AB, 1990; "Volvo's U.S. Chief Quits in Response to Reorganization," *Wall Street Journal,* October 1, 1990; "Volvo Searching Hard for Relief," *New York Times,* June 12, 1991; *Volvo 1927–1992,* Company Publication, 1992.

—John Simley

THE VONS COMPANIES, INCORPORATED

618 Michillinda Avenue
Arcadia, California 91007-6300
U.S.A.
(818) 821-7000
Fax: (818) 821-7933

Public Company
Incorporated: 1906 as Vons Grocery Company
Employees: 32,900
Sales: $5.6 billion
Stock Exchanges: New York
SICs: 5410 Grocery Stores

The Vons Companies, Incorporated is the ninth-largest retail supermarket chain in the United States and the largest in southern California, with a total of 346 stores throughout southern and central California and Clark County, Nevada, in 1993. Vons Supermarkets and Vons Food and Drug Stores accounted for over 80 percent of this total, a situation which was expected to change by the mid-1990s as the company expanded its Pavilions and Tianguis 'theme' chains. Vons also operates the Jerseymaid Milk Products Company, which manufactures dairy products and ice cream, and Williams Brothers, a chain of supermarkets located in the Central Coast of California.

Vons Companies' success in an increasingly competitive industry is attributable to several related factors. The company is unusually well-attuned to regional markets, and customizes product selections and displays in individual stores to reflect local customer preferences. This concept was taken one step further in 1987 with the opening of the first Tianguis superstore targeted at southern California's fast-growing Hispanic population. Throughout its history, Vons has also placed great emphasis on increasing efficiency through the use of state-of-the-art technology. Vons was one of the first retailers in the United States to introduce debit cards at checkouts, begun in the Los Angeles area in 1985, and the company continues to innovate with computerized inventory control and pricing systems. As a result of its focus on both markets and technology, the company has a turnover per square foot considerably higher than the industry average, a fact which contributed to record profits in 1991.

Vons was created by Charles Von der Ahe, an entrepreneur instrumental in the development of the modern supermarket. Von der Ahe's first experience in the grocery business was as a delivery boy in Illinois. On the way to California, where he would eventually settle, Von der Ahe worked in several markets, observing merchandising techniques and customer buying patterns first hand. In 1906, with a total capital investment of $1,200, Von der Ahe opened a small grocery store named Von's Groceteria on the corner of Seventh and Figueroa in Los Angeles. Over the next few years, he opened additional stores, implementing a number of innovative strategies which fueled dynamic growth in his business. Von der Ahe was the first grocer to introduce cash-and-carry and self-service. In leasing his open storefronts to produce vendors and butchers, Vons also pioneered the combination store concept which would later lead to his first supermarket. By 1929, the Vons Grocery Company numbered 87 stores.

Von der Ahe had the foresight to sell his stores to McMarr Stores in 1929, before the stock market crash decimated the value of commercial properties. McMarr would in turn eventually be purchased by Safeway. In the meantime, Von der Ahe enjoyed three years of retirement before being lured back into the grocery business by his sons Ted and Wil, who decided to open a new chain of Vons stores in the Los Angeles area. Von der Ahe helped his sons out with investment capital and industry expertise, and Vons stores began to multiply. The partnership culminated in the opening of a 50,300 square foot food market in downtown Los Angeles in 1948. The prototype of the supermarket, this location boasted a number of innovative features which today are taken for granted, notably self-service produce, meat, and delicatessen departments. The store confirmed the Von der Ahe family's role as innovators in the retail food industry.

In 1960, Vons merged with Shopping Bag Food Stores, bringing the total number of stores under family management to 66. Particular emphasis was placed on understanding local markets and arranging shelf space accordingly, a practice which has continued to the present day. In 1967, the merger was challenged by the Federal Trade Commission. The case went all the way to the Supreme Court, which ordered Vons to divest itself of the Shopping Bag locations immediately. In 1969, Vons was bought out by the Household Finance Corporation, now Household International, which added the chain to its Household Merchandising division.

The expansion of Vons Stores into the San Diego area during the 1970s corresponded with a period of dynamic growth when the chain widened operations to include wholesale marketing to other retailers and fast-food chains. In the mid-1970s, Vons opened a series of mid-sized units called Value Centers, which sold food and drugs in one location. This 'combo' concept would develop into Pavilions Stores in 1987. In the early 1980s, Vons expanded north into the Fresno area. In the same period, the company began to stress the importance of combining coupon promotions with in-store product demonstrations as a means of persuading more conservative customers to try new foods. Vons was among the first stores to operate its product promotion department as a profit center funded by fees from participating companies.

Vons scored a tremendous coup in 1984 when the company was designated the official supermarket of the Los Angeles Olympics. Under a deal worked out with the Olympic Committee, the chain agreed to provide food for over 12,000 athletes, coaches and trainers in the Olympic Village. Food worth $8 million was provided to the committee at cost for preparation by an independent food service organization. The balance, worth $2 million, was donated by the company. In return, Vons was guaranteed a number of exclusive merchandising and advertising opportunities. Store decor was changed to highlight the Olympic theme, and the Olympic logo was placed on a number of perishable items which were considered to have particular nutritional value.

In January 1986 top management in the Household Merchandising branch of Household International negotiated a $757 million leveraged buyout of their division. The deal, which was the largest retail buyout in the United States at the time, was masterminded by Roger E. Stangeland, who went on to become chairperson of the newly-independent Vons Companies. Stangeland had been an executive at Household International since 1961, and had been responsible for Vons Stores since 1982. While the buyout successfully separated Vons from Household International, it also burdened the company with an unacceptable level of debt. Stangeland announced that reducing the debt-to-equity ratio would be a priority over the next few years. In the meantime, he added the ten-store Pantry chain to the Vons portfolio. He also charged William S. Davila, the company's president, with developing an expanded 'combination store' concept. Started in 1986, the year of the leveraged buyout, the Pavilions sub-chain would number 28 stores by 1991.

At 75,000 square feet, the first Pavilions store was the company's largest to date. A combination store, Pavilions offered a huge food and non-food section. Different departments were identified with banners and decked with white awnings which created the effect of tented 'pavilions.' Joe Raymond, a merchandising executive with Pavilions, described the concept as "breaking away from the pack." Important features included the plain white decor, designed to focus customer attention on the items on display. The store carried a greater selection of produce than comparable stores, and shoppers were invited to sample new products at a permanently-staffed demonstration booth. In order to emphasize the freshness of the perishable goods, all food preparation was done in full view of the shopping public. At the same time, the non-foods area stressed value for money, with a large variety of health and beauty aids offered at discounts of up to 30 percent on average retail prices, and a professionally-staffed pharmacy selling prescription drugs at discounts of up to 50 percent. In some areas, Pavilions competed directly with adjacent Vons stores, a situation that traditional marketing strategists would tend to avoid. Vons executives remained unruffled, however, articulating their belief that if Pavilions did not go head-to-head with the older stores, a competitor certainly would.

In December 1986, Vons announced that a $700 million deal had been struck with Allied Supermarkets, Inc., a publicly-listed Detroit retail and wholesale food marketer. The goal of the merger was to take Vons public while controlling the company's debt load. Roger Stangeland became chair and chief

executive officer of Vons Companies Incorporated, and William S. Davila was named president and chief operating officer. Since Vons had no ambitions to expand to the midwest, Allied's Detroit assets were sold to members of the existing management. The merger achieved its goal; Vons went public on the New York Stock Exchange in early 1987.

Constantly in search of new merchandising techniques, Vons executives turned their attention to the ethnic composition of their customers in 1987. They observed that by 1990 an estimated 40 percent of southern California's population would be of Hispanic origin. In January 1987, the company opened its first Tianguis superstore in Montebello, California, designed to cater to the specific needs of Hispanic customers, especially first-generation immigrants. Tianguis, meaning marketplace in Aztec, denotes the place where the community met to shop and to socialize; commenting on the choice of name, CEO Stangeland said in August 1986 that Vons hoped to "position our stores as an important center in the community" and to "differentiate ourselves strongly from the competition." By 1991, the company was operating nine Tianguis stores throughout southern California and had plans to open two to three stores per year in the foreseeable future.

Tianguis differed from its predecessors in many ways. All advertising and store signs were bilingual, as were the stores' employees, hired from the local community. The produce section was greatly expanded to include a wide variety of Mexican herbs, fruits, and vegetables, while some product categories were eliminated completely. As in the Pavilions stores, meat preparation was done in front of customers. The grocery section included an extensive selection of Mexican imports, sharing shelf space with their U.S. counterparts. Distribution of imports was guaranteed through the early establishment of a subsidiary called Central de Abastos Internacional in 1986. To enhance the social aspect of the stores, aisles were widened to allow patrons to stop and chat. Diaper-changing rooms were installed at the back of each store since, in Vons President Davila's words, "shopping tends to be a family event for Hispanics." The introduction of the Tianguis stores was widely discussed in the industry. Vons had demonstrated once again its strength in adapting to the changing needs of the market before its competitors.

On August 29, 1988, Vons took over 172 of Safeway's southern California operations, paying $297 million in cash and giving up 11.67 million shares of Vons common stock. As a result of this transaction, the number of stores under Vons control doubled, but the company's debt load also soared. In spite of its highly-leveraged position, the company immediately embarked on an ambitious remodeling of the former Safeway stores, spending an average of $1.3 million on each location. Together with more efficient inventory control and labor scheduling, the remodeling was intended to increase per-store profitability, money which in turn would be used to pay off debt. A number of in-store innovations were also implemented, including an electronic coupon program and other cost-saving technology. The strategy worked. By November 1990, sales per square foot at the former Safeway stores had risen to $615 from an average of $447 at the time of the buyout. The industry average at the time was $550. Meanwhile, corporate finances also improved. Vons went from a $25 million loss in 1989 to a $50 million profit in 1990 and a $65 million profit in 1991. By 1991, the company's debt-to-total capitalization ratio had dropped to 60 percent. The company's financial position was also strengthened by a successful equity issue in 1991.

In January 1992, Vons acquired family-owned Williams Brothers Markets for $48 million in cash and a liability of $10 million on Williams Brothers' outstanding mortgages. The transaction was financed using Vons's existing revolving loan. Located in central California, the 18 Williams Brothers stores were well-known for their customer service and successful niche in marketing to local communities. As such, they integrated well with other stores in the Vons portfolio, while allowing Vons to expand further north.

During the course of the riots in Los Angeles in May 1992, several Vons stores were looted and burned. The cost of restoring the damaged properties, however, was largely covered by insurance. In the aftermath of the riots, attention was focused on the dearth of quality supermarkets in south central Los Angeles. Vons Companies announced that the chain would commit $100 million to developing markets in neglected areas over the next few years. Then in January 1993, an outbreak of food poisoning in Washington state that claimed the lives of three children was traced to hamburgers purchased at the Jack-in-the-Box fast-food chain, which had purchased the meat tainted with the deadly E. coli bacteria from Foodmaker, parent company of Jack-in-the-Box. Vons, as the meat processor for Foodmaker, was involved in the early stages of the investigation. After being commended by health authorities for its clean processing facility, Vons aided health authorities by tracing the source of the contaminated beef to one Foodmaker beef supplier. The incident had wide-ranging implications for United States Department of Agriculture inspection procedures, which were deemed inadequate.

In the early 1990s, Vons renewed a commitment to technological progress by announcing a dramatic increase in its Informa-tion Systems (IS) budget. IS initiatives were piloted in a number of metropolitan locations and included electronic shelf tags, which would be updated automatically when the checkout scanner price was changed. This system is expected to enhance customer service and decrease labor costs.

Vons Companies continued to run a well-managed and diversified group of supermarket chains, notable for their focus on the needs of local communities in general, and ethnic communities in particular. Having reduced its debt load and streamlined its operations through the implementation of state-of-the-art technology, Vons seemed well positioned to continue its ambitious growth strategy well into the 1990s. The company's earnings for the quarter ending January 3, 1993, nearly doubled those of the same quarter of the previous year. In October of 1991 *Fortune* magazine named Vons as one of the hundred fastest-growing companies in America. The publication identified the company's key competitive advantage as an ability to wring "ever higher sales per square foot out of its stores."

Principal Subsidiaries: Jerseymaid Milk Products Company; Central de Abastos Internacional (Mexico); 4-U Fund Incorporated; HMI Subsidiary Incorporated; R. J. Blanco; White Credit Incorporated.

Further Reading: Zwiebach, Elliott, "Vons: diversifying formats for diversified needs," *Supermarket News*, April 7, 1986; Zwiebach, Elliot, "Vons' New Accent," *Supermarket News*, February 9, 1987; Duff, Mike, "Superstores," *Supermarket Business*, January 1991; Deutschman, Alan, "America's Fastest Risers," *Fortune*, October 7, 1991; "History of the Vons Companies, Inc.," Arcadia, Vons Companies corporate document, April 1992; McDermott, Terry, "E. Coli Investigation Finds Vons Supplier," *Seattle Times,* February 23, 1993.

—Moya Verzhbinsky

VULCAN MATERIALS COMPANY

1 Metroplex Drive
Birmingham, Alabama 35209
U.S.A.
(205) 877-3000
Fax: (205) 877-3094

Public Company
Incorporated: 1956
Employees: 6,400
Sales: $1.08 billion
Stock Exchanges: New York
SICs: 1429 Crushed & Broken Stone Nec; 1442 Construction
Sand & Gravel; 2951 Asphalt Paving Mixtures & Blocks;
2812 Alkalies & Chlorine

Vulcan Materials Company, with headquarters in Birmingham, Alabama, is the largest producer of construction aggregates in the United States and a leader in the world market. Construction aggregates include crushed stone, sand and gravel, and slag, which are used in the construction of roadways, commercial buildings, and houses. The company operates quarries in 14 of the United States and, through a joint venture, runs one in Mexico. Revenue from crushed stone excavated in Vulcan quarries accounts for approximately 60 percent of the company's total sales.

Vulcan also produces chemicals for industrial use at plants in Kansas, Louisiana, and Wisconsin. These chemicals include: chlorine, caustic soda (sodium hydroxide), caustic potash (potassium hydroxide), and chlorinated solvents. The primary market for chlorine is in the treatment of water and sewage, manufacturing pulp and paper, and as a major ingredient in many other manufacturing processes. Caustic soda is used mainly in the production of alumina, soap and detergent products, and wood pulp. Caustic potash is utilized in the production of other potassium chemicals as well as in fine soaps and lotions. Finally, chlorinated solvents are employed for cleaning metals and textiles and as an intermediate chemical in the manufacture of other materials.

Vulcan Materials was created in 1956 when the Birmingham Slag Company of Birmingham, Alabama, merged with the Vulcan Detinning Company. Birmingham Slag had been founded

in 1909 by Solon Jacob and Henry Badham, two entrepreneurs who decided to turn a waste product of the steel industry, slag, into a commodity they could sell. Slag is the nonmetalic residue left behind in the process of smelting iron ore. The city of Birmingham, as it still is today, was a center for steel making, and the industry was stockpiling huge amounts of slag.

Jacob and Badham built a processing plant next to the Tennessee Coal, Iron and Railroad Company's slag pile in nearby Ensley, Alabama, and began selling the material as ballast for railroad tracks. Fortuitously, the founding of Birmingham slag occurred one year after the Ford Motor Company introduced its famous Model T automobile. When the country began demanding more paved roads, Birmingham Slag discovered that it possessed the perfect construction material.

By 1916, despite its early success, Birmingham Slag was for sale. Charles Lincoln Ireland, an Ohio banker whose family was operating stone quarries in Ohio, Kentucky, and West Virginia, purchased a controlling interest in the company. He sent his three sons—Glenn, Eugene, and Barney—to Alabama to run Birmingham Slag. Charles, in the meantime, went off to Central America to buy surplus equipment being sold after the completion of the Panama Canal. He returned with two steam shovels, a steam hoist, a star drill, and other equipment purchased at the bargain-basement price of $6,590.

The Irelands opened a new slag-processing plant in Ensley in 1918. They also opened plants in the central Alabama towns of Fairfield and Wylam and in northern Alabama near Muscle Shoals. In 1919 and 1920 the company secured contracts to process slag at three more Alabama steel mills—Republic Steel in Thomas, Central Iron and Steel Company in Holt, and Gulf States Steel Company in Alabama City. Despite plenty of post-World War I business, however, finances were tight. Records indicate that during this period the Ireland family often had to guarantee loans at the First National Bank of Birmingham personally to meet the company's payroll. Nevertheless, Birmingham Slag was ready when state legislators passed the 1922 Alabama Bond Issue for Good Roads, setting off a boom in road construction.

In 1923 Birmingham Slag formed the Montgomery Gravel Company and began providing sand and gravel for a dam being built in Cherokee Bluffs, Alabama. It expanded this business the next year by creating the Atlanta Aggregate Company to market sand and gravel in Georgia. By the 1930s Birmingham Slag also owned several ready-mixed concrete plants and was producing asphalt and concrete blocks.

In 1939 Birmingham Slag signed a contract with the newly formed Tennessee Valley Authority (TVA) to dredge part of the Tennessee River so a dam and power plant could be built at Watts Bar, thus marking yet another business expansion for the company. Birmingham Slag continued to prosper during World War II, providing aggregates and concrete for such wartime efforts as the Manhattan Project in Oak Ridge, Tennessee; the Huntsville, Alabama, Redstone Arsenal; and a major munitions depot at Fort McClellan in Anniston, Alabama.

After the war, construction of the new federal interstate highway system, proposed in the early 1950s, presented a potential bonanza for Birmingham Slag. The company, however, needed more capital than a family-owned business could muster in order to take advantage of the opportunity. In addition, Charles W. Ireland, the grandson of the Ohio banker, had become president of Birmingham Slag in 1951 and was looking for ways to lessen the inheritance taxes that family members faced. The answer presented itself in the form of a merger with the publicly traded Vulcan Detinning Company of Sewaren, New Jersey.

Vulcan Detinning had been formed in 1902 by Adolph Kern, who owned the Vulcan Metal Refining Company in Sewaren and the Vulcan Western Company of Chicago. The new company, Vulcan Detinning, used a process that had been developed in Germany to recover pure tin from tin-plated scrap. Later, Kern quietly helped establish a rival company in Pennsylvania, the Republic Chemical Company. In 1912 he left Vulcan Detinning to join Republic Chemical, taking the company's trade secrets with him and setting off a series of lawsuits. Vulcan Detinning and Republic Chemical merged in 1920, after Kern was no longer associated with either company.

William J. Buttfield—who had joined Vulcan Detinning as a director in 1912, when Kern left for Republic Chemical—guided Vulcan Detinning through the early part of the twentieth century. During the Depression of the 1930s he used his commodities brokerage background to shift the company's resources into importing coffee and rubber. Vulcan Detinning continued to pay dividends even though the Sewaren detinning plant was closed from 1932 until 1937. Employees were kept on the payroll and were occupied with the repairing and reconditioning of plant facilities. By 1940 Vulcan Detinning was again flourishing, although the Sewaren plant, reopened in 1937, was closed permanently in 1938. Buttfield is also credited with being one of the industrialists who in the months preceding the Japanese attack on Pearl Harbor, finally convinced the United States to begin stockpiling critical materials, such as tin.

The merger between Birmingham Slag and Vulcan Detinning was completed in 1956. At the time, Alfred Buttfield, the son of William J. Buttfield, was president of Vulcan Detinning. He became chairman of the board of the newly named Vulcan Materials Company.

Until the merger, Birmingham Slag, although successful, had been a modest-sized, regional company. Vulcan Materials Company was traded on the New York Stock Exchange and quickly became a company of national importance. The merger allowed Vulcan to diversify and create a business less dependent on the construction industry, as well as raise the capital for expansion. From 1956 to 1960 Vulcan's net worth increased almost seven-fold, to $72 million from $11 million. It also became the largest producer of construction aggregates material in the country.

Although Charles W. Ireland is credited with providing the vision for Vulcan's rapid growth, Bernard A. Monaghan is considered the architect. Monaghan, a Rhodes Scholar and graduate of Harvard University Law School, was the Irelands' family and corporate attorney. He negotiated the merger with Vulcan Detinning and later orchestrated the acquisition of a dozen more construction aggregate companies through the 1950s and into the early 1960s. He joined Vulcan in 1958 as executive vice-president and, soon after, became president and chief executive officer.

One of the companies with which Monaghan negotiated a merger was Lambert Brothers, Inc., an Appalachian quarrying company with a storied history. The nine Lambert brothers, from a family of 15, were low-income Smoky Mountain residents who, according to company lore, started with a mule and a wheelbarrow and built a $9 million-a-year business in one generation. During the 1930s they moved their portable rock-crushing equipment throughout the Appalachian states and as far west as Oklahoma to work on road construction. The story of their success is peppered with tales of bare-knuckled fights and high-stakes poker. By the mid 1950s Lambert Brothers was the largest rock-quarrying firm in the United States.

It was during this period of rapid expansion that Vulcan also became a chemicals manufacturer. In 1957 it bought the Union Chemical and Materials Corporation of Chicago, a construction aggregate company in the booming Midwest market that had merged with the Frontier Chemical Company. Frontier produced sodium hydroxide (caustic soda), chlorine, and hydrochloric acid for the oil industry at plants in Texas and Kansas.

The mergers with Union Chemical, Lambert Brothers, and seven other companies owned by the Lamberts were approved by Vulcan's stockholders in one fell swoop in 1957. At the time, *Fortune* magazine called it one of the most complex corporate acquisitions ever arranged. Vulcan continued its strategy of buying family-owned aggregate businesses over the next 30 years. In 1982 in a story entitled "Cinderella," a *Forbes* correspondent observed that Vulcan had created a "quasi-monopoly in the crushed stone-business" by buying more than 90 quarries in the 1950s and 1960s "when quarries were a dime a dozen."

In 1967 Vulcan purchased Aluminum and Magnesium, Inc., an Ohio-based aluminum recycler. Until 1988, when Vulcan sold its metals division, detinning and aluminum recycling had formed the nucleus of the metals processing business. Vulcan also spent ten years in oil and natural gas exploration, forming a joint venture in 1975 with Oklahoma-based Southport Exploration, Inc. Vulcan acquired Southport Exploration in 1981 but sold the business in 1985.

In July of 1987 Vulcan formally announced its Crescent Market Project, a $170 million joint venture with one of Latin America's largest construction conglomerates, Ingenieros Civiles Associados, S.C. (Grupo ICA), to quarry limestone from the wilds of the Yucatan Peninsula. Vulcan had first looked to Mexico as a potential quarry site to serve the Gulf Coast area of the United States in 1973. The idea was abandoned and then revived in 1978. In 1981 the company began a concentrated effort to locate quarry sites in the Mexican state of Quintana Roo. Afterwards, Pete Wiese, the Vulcan geologist who headed the exploration, described the effort in the company's annual magazine, *Profile*: "Quintana Roo was pretty unsettled. I had a machete and I would just get out of the car and cut through the jungle to the coast and see what I could see."

The joint venture eventually settled on a site about 45 miles south of Cancún and only a few hundred yards from ancient Mayan ruins that had been built out of the same tan limestone.

An agreement was made with the Mexican National Institute of Archeology and History to underwrite the cost of locating, mapping, and conserving the ruins. The Crescent Market Project also included construction of a deep-water port, which required dredging more than three million tons of stone from the harbor at Playa del Carmen.

Overcoming technological and logistical challenges, including Hurricane Gilbert—which battered the Yucatan coast in 1988 causing more than $400,000 damage to the stone processing plant then under construction—Vulcan and Grupo ICA began shipping stone from Mexico to the United States in 1990. Most of the Mexican limestone was destined to become construction material aggregates, but because of a high calcium content, was also being used in products as diverse as fertilizer and toothpaste.

The Mexican quarry won the National Stone Association Showplace Award in 1990, its first year of operation. In 1991 the quarry shipped 2.5 million tons of limestone, about a third of the estimated annual capacity. By late 1992 Vulcan, looking ahead to a recovering economy and refocused attention on the nation's infrastructure, was estimating that the Crescent Market Project would become profitable in 1993.

The W. H. Blount, a refitted Panamax-class vessel named for a former chief executive officer and then-chairman emeritus of Vulcan Materials, was put into operation in March of 1991 to carry limestone from the Mexican quarry. More than 700 feet long and 100 feet wide, the W. H. Blount was one of the largest self-unloading ships in service. It could carry more than 64,000 tons of limestone, or about 2,667 truckloads. A second, similar ship was put into service in late 1992.

Aside from the Crescent Market Project, which had begun in 1987, Vulcan continued with other acquisitions, taking on Texas-based White's Mines, Inc. and two affiliated companies for $89 million that year. At the time, it was the largest acquisition in the company's long history. The purchase gave Vulcan control of five more quarries, including the Uvalde limestone quarry west of San Antonio. The quarry produces rock asphalt, a stone that is naturally impregnated with asphalt, making it a natural paving material.

Three years later, in 1990, Vulcan surpassed the White's Mines acquisition by paying more than $110 million for the Reed Crushed Stone Company, Inc., and two related companies. Included in the purchase was the Reed quarry near Paducah, Kentucky, the largest single crushed-stone quarry in the country. The purchase also included a fleet of barges and a coal transshipping and blending business, putting Vulcan Materials in the coal-handling business for the first time.

Vulcan's chemical business was heavily regulated and often prompted public concerns about environmental health and safety. In 1990 Vulcan committed to reducing hazardous emissions at its chemical plants by 90 percent over the next five years, primarily by turning hydrochloric acid into calcium chloride, which can be used as a dust stabilizer and de-icer. Vulcan had been disposing of excess hydrochloric acid, a waste product of other chemical production processes, by pumping the acid into limestone deposits a mile below ground in a deep-well injection process permitted and approved by the Environmental Protection Agency (EPA). The limestone neutralized the acid; however, it was still considered a hazardous emission for reporting purposes under Title III of the Federal Superfund Amendment and Reauthorization Act. This resulted in Vulcan being listed among the worst polluters in the United States.

In order to change its status as a major polluter, Vulcan completed construction of a new calcium chloride facility at its Wichita, Kansas, chemical manufacturing complex early in 1993. Even before it opened, the plant received a Certificate for Environmental Achievement from Renew America, a national environmental organization based in Washington, D.C. The processing facility, with a capacity of 18 million pounds per year, was designed by Tetra Technologies, which also distributed the calcium chloride. Used primarily to purify drinking water, it also serves as a biocide in the fruit-processing industry and as a cleaning material in electronics.

In addition to its construction of the calcium chloride facility, Vulcan's chemicals division was phasing out production of chlorofluorocarbons (CFCs) and assisting in the development of nonozone depleting CFC replacements.

Vulcan is also a member of two major trade associations—the National Stone Association and the Chemical Manufacturers Association—that are active in addressing environmental health and safety concerns. The company participates in the Wildlife Habitat Enhancement Council, a nonprofit organization that encourages the development of wildlife sanctuaries on corporate-owned lands. In 1990 Vulcan Materials' quarry in Warrenton, Virginia, was the first site in the nation to be certified by the Wildlife Habitat Enhancement Council; Vulcan also received the Virginia Conservationist of the Year Award that year for its efforts at the quarry. As of 1992, 15 Vulcan Materials quarries had been certified by the organization.

Historically, Vulcan Material's two principal businesses have provided economic stability; construction aggregates did well when the chemical market was depressed and vice versa. However, construction spending in the United States, adjusted for inflation, decreased every year between 1986 and 1991, the longest continual decline since the Great Depression. With the economy in recession, the company recorded three straight years of lower net income, from a high of $136 million on sales of $1.05 billion in 1988 to $52.6 million on sales of $1.01 billion in 1991. In 1992 sales increased by 7 percent to $1.078 billion, while net earnings rose by 79 percent to $93.98 million. Entering 1993, the company was encouraged by indications that the economy was recovering and by a renewed national focus on rebuilding the infrastructure. The United States Congress had passed the Intermodal Surface Transportation Efficiency Act in December of 1991, and federal spending on highway construction was expected to be $18.4 billion in 1993, a 30 percent increase over 1990.

Principal Subsidiaries: Vulcan Gulf Coast Materials, Inc.

Further Reading: "The Vulcan Detinning Company," *Profile,* fall 1978; "The Merger Years 1956–1961," *Profile,* spring 1979; Carmichael, Jane, "Cinderella," *Forbes,* March 15, 1982; Blount, W. Houston, "The Past as a Challenge to the Future," speech delivered to The Newcomen Society in North

America, Birmingham, Alabama, October 13, 1982; Blevins, Dallas R. and Jessie L. Forbes, *Vulcan Materials: Alabama's Share of the Fortune* (unpublished), University of Montevallo, Alabama, 1984; Pierce, Frank, "Vulcan Materials Company: Alabama's Share of the Fortune," *Journal of the Birmingham Historical Society,* December 1985; "Interview: Pete Clemens," *Profile,* 1988; "The Crescent Market Project," *Profile,* 1988; "Interview: Bill Grayson," *Profile,* 1988; "White's Mines: Vulcan Expands in a Texas-size Way," *Profile,* 1988; "Charles Ireland: 1916–1987," *Profile,* 1988; "Barney Monaghan: 1916–1987," *Profile,* 1988; Connel, Greg, "Rolling With the Changes," *Pit & Quarry,* January 1990; Weaver, Bronwyn, "Community Involvement Rewrites Familiar Story," *Pit & Quarry,* June 1990; Archibald, Robert, and Robert Beard, "Making Waves in Gulf Coast Markets," *Pit & Quarry,* June 1991; Ransdell, Tom, "Up and Running in Mexico," *Profile,* 1992; "Obstacle Course to International Success in Mexico," *Profile,* 1992; "Protecting the Physical and Historical Environment," *Profile,* 1992; "Life in Playa del Carmen," *Profile,* 1992; "An Interview With Houston Blount," *Profile,* 1992; Bonnie, Fred, "The Low Cost of a High Public Relations Profile," *Skillings' Mining Review,* January 2, 1993; England, Ed, and Irene Preston, "The Birmingham Slag Company," *Profile;* "The Lambert Brothers," *Profile;* "Vulcan's Mideast Division," *Profile;* "The Chemicals Division/A Frontier Success Story," *Profile;* "The Campbell Limestone Company," *Profile.*

—Dean Boyer

Wattie's

WATTIE'S LTD.

277 Broadway,
New Market, Auckland
New Zealand
(9) 573 0720
Fax: 9 573 0698

Public Company
Incorporated: 1971
Employees: 5,000
Sales: NZ$773.76 million (US$400 million)
SICs: 2037 Frozen Fruits & Vegetables

Wattie's Ltd., which became a subsidiary of the multibillion dollar American firm H. J. Heinz in October 1992, is the largest and most important food processing company in New Zealand and in the Australasian territories of the southern hemisphere. With numerous markets in the Pacific Rim and in Europe, approximately half of Wattie's sales are derived from exports.

The story of Wattie's success goes back to founder James Wattie. A native New Zealander whose home was the country's North Island city of Hastings, on Hawke's Bay, Wattie was born and grew up in what happened to be New Zealand's richest fruit growing region. Fruit grew so bountifully on the Heretaunga Plains that year after year much of it lay rotting on the ground.

Entering the working world at age thirteen, during the years of the First World War when jobs were plentiful, Wattie eventually was hired by the cooperative Hawke's Bay Fruitgrowers Ltd. in Hastings. He rose through the ranks until, by the onset of the Great Depression, he had become a manager. With New Zealand in the depths of the Depression, it was the least propitious time to start up a new business, much less a new industry requiring capital and expensive machinery.

Nevertheless, Wattie came across a startling fact that led him to establish his own business. An Australian jam manufacturing firm in Auckland was importing fruit pulp from Australia, two thousand miles away, while an abundance of fruit lay rotting on the ground in nearby Hawke's Bay. Though neither Wattie nor anyone else in the Fruitgrowers cooperative had experience in processing fruit, Wattie made up his mind in 1934 to use surplus New Zealand fruit to make jam for New Zealanders.

Persuading fellow directors of the Hawke's Bay Fruitgrowers coop to raise the capital for a canning plant was a formidable task, particularly given the hard financial times in the nonindustrialized region of New Zealand. Wattie personally went from bank to bank in search of a loan and asked the cooperative to rent him a four room cottage for ten dollars a year, where the new "cannery" could be set up. The members agreed, and Wattie Canneries Ltd. was established in Hastings in September 1934.

The director of the jam manufacturing company in Auckland agreed to buy the fruit pulp processed in Hawke's Bay if it matched the quality of that imported from Australia. The company was pleased to find that it did. Importing the fruit pulp ceased, and the new Wattie Canneries Ltd. had at least one major customer.

Certainly the beginning of the new business in Hawke's Bay was rough. Wattie purchased the necessary machinery to process the fruit secondhand. However, unable to afford to manufacture its own cans, Wattie Canneries was forced to purchase them, and now and then a flawed can would turn up to the chagrin of the consumer. Fruit processing was, moreover, a highly labor intensive industry. Fruit was peeled and cored by hand, which meant that virtually every can of processed fruit was handpicked. Lastly, the fruit supply was highly dependent on the weather. One bad storm could wipe out an entire fruit crop, as happened repeatedly in the first few years of the company's existence. Overshadowing those early years was the knowledge that an earlier attempt to establish a fruit processing plant in Hawke's Bay had failed.

Nevertheless, Wattie's talents seemed to unfold once he became head of the new industry. A personable man, he knew each of his workers on a first name basis and maintained an amicable and productive relationship with them. Also, Wattie abounded in ideas and initiative. Only ten months after the company's arduous beginnings, Wattie's showed a healthy profit of nearly two thousand dollars.

Such modest success led to expansion of facilities and improved machinery. Soon new boilers were installed and processing was mechanized to the point where, by 1937, approximately 25,000 cans a day rolled off the assembly line. Wattie Canneries already was making an important contribution to the New Zealand economy.

The market for canned fruit and jam was by no means limited to underpopulated New Zealand in those early years. Though an independent country as of 1907, New Zealand had close financial and cultural ties to its mother country, Great Britain, and as a member of the British Commonwealth, New Zealand theoretically had access to markets in Great Britain and worldwide. Speculating that Great Britain would provide a good market for canned vegetables, Wattie soon was searching for land on which to raise peas, asparagus, and tomatoes.

These new product lines were extremely successful. On the eve of World War II, which New Zealand entered in September 1939, the worst of the Great Depression was over and new competitors had arrived. Though five years old, Wattie's company and the Wattie's brand had gained national recognition.

Radio proved the best medium for advertising in those early years.

Wartime demand for Wattie's food was enormous, and the challenge of meeting it would turn Wattie's from a small scale regional industry to a giant company. While in 1939 the company's production was worth $72,000, that figure had climbed to over one million dollars by 1944. Nevertheless, the challenges of producing canned fruit during wartime seemed insurmountable. Not only did the industry experience an acute labor shortage, but the raw materials indispensable to the canning, such as the all important sugar, were also difficult to come by.

Government rationing of food turned out to be one solution, while the labor shortage was gradually surmounted by the purchase of more machinery, especially for peeling and coring Wattie's fruit. The money for expansion and new equipment came when the U.S. Congress approved the Lend Lease Act in 1941, which provided Wattie Canneries with ample funds to at last establish its own can making machines capable of churning out thirty million cans annually. The company was also able to purchase land for its own farms and equip them with modern machinery, as well as to expand its original plant. Expansion was necessary once the United States entered the war, since all of Wattie's productive capacity was sold to the U.S. Joint Purchasing Board to feed the allied armed forces stationed in the Pacific.

While profits were high by the end of the war, James Wattie had long anticipated the trends of the postwar years: intense competition and the necessity of establishing new markets overseas, in addition to new product lines. With troops coming home, there also was sure to be demands for pay raises and shorter work days, which would dip into company profits. When the war ended in August 1945, Wattie immediately went in search of new markets as well as new technology, particularly during his first visit to the United States.

The 1950s and 1960s were characterized by expansion, mergers, new product lines, and Wattie's entrance into the computer age. When some employees expressed their concerns that the dramatic transformations would turn the company into a giant, impersonal monolith, Wattie maintained that for an industry to make a profit, it had to invest in new machinery, and such machinery was increasingly costly in an age of rising labor costs and shorter work days. Hence Wattie Canneries Ltd. began a program of continuous expansion.

Wattie's biggest market outside of New Zealand in the postwar years was western Europe. The demand for food products, especially canned peas and jams of all kinds, was astonishing. In 1947, Unilever of Great Britain contracted with Wattie's to purchase frozen peas under its Birdseye brand. During this time, frozen foods of all kinds were becoming enormously popular and more profitable than canned products. With the establishment of a new plant at Gisborne in 1952, in an area perfect for the growing of sweet corn, Wattie's became the first food processor in New Zealand to offer both canned and frozen corn.

Other major product lines in years to come would include tuna, baby foods, and pet food. Baby foods quickly developed into an important new industry for Wattie Canneries Ltd. as did pet food. While pet food was well established in the U.S. market, in Australasia the conventional diet of dogs and cats consisted of table scraps. New Zealand veterinarians hailed this new product line and were brought into its development. "Felix" cat food had extraordinary sales in the mid-1950s. At this time a fully staffed and equipped research and development department was established at Wattie's to put new ideas and products to the test.

By the end of the 1950s, Wattie Canneries Ltd. employed over 1,000 people and sold over 75 varieties of food products, including pet food. Sales in 1960 were valued at $10 million. Advertising was pursued aggressively, especially on the relatively new medium of television. By this time, 40 percent of Wattie's products were exported.

Australia was an extremely important market for Wattie's, particularly after the 1965 announcement of the New Zealand-Australia Free Trade Agreement, which displaced the United Kingdom as Wattie's biggest overseas customer. Other Pacific Rim countries such as Japan, Singapore, Malaysia, Taiwan, Indonesia, Borneo, and small South Pacific island nations became well established markets for Wattie's products. Japan in particular became an important Wattie's bastion after 1965, when the government of New Zealand led a goodwill mission to Japan and Taiwan. Frozen foods found the biggest market in Japan. In the 1990s, Japan displaced Australia as Wattie's most important overseas market.

Mergers were also an important feature of Wattie's evolution. In the 1960s, Wattie's took over Thompson & Hills Ltd. and S. Kirkpatrick & Co., Ltd., both subsidiaries of The Henry Jones Co-op Ltd., an important food processing industry in Melbourne with an extensive range of food processing plants in Auckland and other New Zealand cities. Several other mergers followed throughout the decade, and new product lines emerged, including the processing of meat and citrus fruits.

The largest and most complex merger, however, occurred in 1968, when the company teamed with General Foods, Ltd. of New Zealand, which had begun years earlier as a manufacturer of New Zealand's most popular brand of ice cream, "Tip Top," and Cropper-NRM, the country's largest producer of flour and flour products. This merger altered the identity of Wattie Canneries, a name that no longer adequately described the kind of enterprise Wattie's had become. Changing its name to Wattie's Industries, Ltd., the company underwent a complete reorganization in 1971.

Wattie's Industries continued to grow and prosper after James Wattie's death in 1974. By 1987, however, according to the results of a twelve month study of Wattie's Industries, the company had grown too large. That year another radical restructuring commenced, this time turning Wattie's Industries into a holding company with five major subsidiaries: Wattie Frozen Foods, Ltd.; J. Wattie Foods, Ltd.; Best Friends Pet Food Co., Ltd.; Wattie Fishing, Ltd.; and Wattie Irvine, Ltd. A year later, Wattie's Industries merged with the largest food processing giant in Australia, Goodman Fielder. The new company of Goodman Fielder, Wattie's, Ltd., entered the ranks of the top twenty food processors in the world in 1988, and was by far the largest in Australasia.

Although Wattie's half of the new industry generated $400 million worth of sales in 1992, Goodman Fielder of Australia decided to sell off its Wattie's concerns by letting the five Wattie industries (Wattie's Frozen Foods group, Wattie's Tip Top frozen desserts and ice creams, J. Wattie Foods—maker of baked beans, spaghetti, and canned vegetables—Best Friend Petfoods, and the Tegal Foods Division, processor of poultry) to float on the New Zealand stock exchange. The giant multibillion dollar food processor, H. J. Heinz of Pittsburgh, snapped up the Wattie's five food processing concerns for $300 million in October 1992. Heinz extended its foreign markets significantly with the purchase of Wattie's, and soon had a firm foothold in the increasingly lucrative southeast Asian markets. It was without doubt the biggest foreign acquisition in Heinz's long history.

Although a subsidiary of Heinz, Wattie's remained a vital industry in New Zealand, employing thousands of New Zealanders and generating multimillion dollar sales, as well as commanding a 65 percent share of the processed food market in that country. In a country with the highest environmental standards in the world, Wattie's strictly monitored and limited chemical spraying, experimented with the large scale growing and processing of organic foods, and continually sought environmentally sound and less costly alternatives to their production methods. Under the management of CEO and president David Irving, a native New Zealander, Wattie's seemed well prepared to meet consumer and community expectations.

Further Reading: Conly, Geoff, *Wattie's: The First Fifty Years*, J. Wattie Canneries, Ltd., 1984; ''Heinz Develops Asia Strategy with New Zealand Acquisition,'' *PR Newswire,* 1992; ''Heinz Buys New Zealand Food Company for Three Hundred Million,'' *The New York Times*, October 8, 1992; *The New Heinz*, Corporate Affairs Dept., 1992; *Heinz in New York*, Corporate Affairs Dept., 1992; *Annual Report: H.J. Heinz*, 1992.

—Sina Dubovoj

WEST PUBLISHING CO.

610 Opperman Drive
Eagan, Minnesota 55123
U.S.A.
(612) 687-7000
Fax: (612) 687-5388

Private Company
Incorporated: 1882 as West Publishing Co.
Employees: 5,200
Sales: $525 million (estimated)
SICs: 2731 Book Publishing

A ubiquitous and irreplaceable presence in the legal publishing industry, West Publishing Co. has held a leading position in the field of indexing and reporting court decisions, from the U. S. Supreme Court on down. Perhaps its most influential and valuable contribution has been its invention of the Key Number System, a means of methodically organizing and summarizing the thousands of judicial rulings delivered each year. This indexing grid became so widely used by lawyers that it virtually transformed the adversarial and adjudicatory processes in the United States. Now more than a century old, the Key Number System remains, through such comprehensive and regularly updated series as the *American Digest System* and the *National Reporter System,* the most prevalent and valued legal aid in the industry. Although West has struggled to maintain its position as a leading information access company in the age of computer-assisted and CD-ROM technology, the company remains known as the preeminent legal book publisher, first and foremost. Its three primary publishing divisions—Law Books, Law School, and College and School—together produce over 55 million individual volumes and pamphlets annually, an amazing legacy considering the private firm's humble beginnings.

In the post-Civil War period, the east was unrivalled for its centers of commerce, intellectual activity, and powerful publishing houses. For a firm to be established on the banks of the Mississippi in the as yet sparsely populated Midwest, create a new print medium, and successfully quell competition from the cultural and business establishment was unthinkable; yet, as historian William W. Marvin has recorded, it happened not so much in spite of as *because* of the remote, and therefore inconspicuous, location. A young St. Paul entrepreneur with experience as a traveling book salesman opened his first business in

1872, which he called John B. West, Publisher and Bookseller. West specialized in the sale of law treatises, legal forms, dictionaries, and office supplies. His most promising work, however, was in the trading of new and used court reports, a rare commodity at the time, given the notoriously sluggish official printing of state cases and verdicts. West viewed the lawyers he served as a singularly valuable market for new information; more importantly, he realized that no single publishing company offered both expedient and inclusive case reporting.

In 1876, West convinced his older brother Horatio, an accountant, to join him in a new enterprise that would help to fill at least one identifiable and easily serviced void: that of recording Minnesota Supreme Court rulings. The business now became the John B. West Co. and the chief product, an eight-page weekly pamphlet of legal excerpts entitled *The Syllabi.* By this time, West had already established himself as a valued partner of the local legal community with his "WEST" line of legal blanks, prepared with the assistance of practicing lawyers. He decided to build upon his reputation for quality, authoritativeness, and service by enlisting the expertise of a St. Paul Bar member to edit the content of *The Syllabi.* The publication became an instant hit with the law community and more than fulfilled West's initial advertisement of "prompt and reliable intelligence as to the various questions adjudicated by the Minnesota Courts at a date long prior to the publication of the State Reports." In the words of Marvin, *The Syllabi* "gave the Minnesota Bar what was then unquestionably the most complete current reporting service in the nation."

In a move that proved essential to the long-term survival of the fledgling publisher, West expanded the scope of *The Syllabi* almost immediately, replacing excerpts of Minnesota cases with complete coverage and offering selected case excerpts from neighboring Wisconsin, as a resource tool for lawyers of both states. Soon demand in Wisconsin necessitated the inclusion of all of that state's cases in excerpted form. Ironically, West's first competition came not from eastern publishers, the concerted response of which might well have proved fatal to the John B. West Company, but from a small Milwaukee printing house. Further expansion was the logical response and so, six months into publication of *The Syllabi,* the company introduced *The North Western Reporter.* This new publication was to include everything currently covered by *The Syllabi* plus all Minnesota U. S. Circuit Court decisions, selected Minnesota and Wisconsin lower court cases, and abstracts of selected cases from other states. Although the *North Western* still functioned as a legal newspaper, the concept of a permanent reference publication was soon to be realized.

Less than three years after *The Syllabi* was introduced, a new series of the *North Western* debuted offering full coverage of current decisions in Minnesota, Wisconsin, Iowa, Michigan, Nebraska, and the Dakota Territory. The flood of orders received by the company was welcome proof that a vast and enthusiastic customer base had been successfully tapped. A *Federal Reporter,* containing decisions by the U.S. Circuit and District Courts around the country, followed in 1880, as did a *U.S. Supreme Court Reporter,* in 1882. What distinguished each of these publications was West's inclusion of a uniform indexing system, complete with headnotes. The medium, particularly its comprehensiveness, was so unlike current practice by printers of state reports that it provoked widespread ridicule. Nevertheless, several publishers realized the profitability of such an approach and soon waged heated competition with West. The company maintained its advantage because of its significant market lead and also because of its low cost, fast publication, and accurate editing (state-commissioned reports were notoriously error-ridden, often having been produced without benefit of proofing departments or adequate legal knowledge).

The company's rapid growth caused the West brothers to seek outside capital to expand both its staff and manufacturing facilities. In the fall of 1882 Charles W. Ames and Peyton Boyle officially became part of the business, now incorporated as a private concern. During the next five years other *Reporter* publications were introduced, including the *Pacific, Atlantic, South Western, South Eastern,* and *Southern.* By 1887 the company was able to boast coast-to-coast coverage. In August of that year, the publisher of the *Eastern Reporter,* Wm. Gould, Jr., & Co., sold its subscription to West Publishing. In November of the following year, another major competitor, the Lawyers' Cooperative Publishing Co., ceased publication of its *New England, Central,* and *Western Reporters.* After these milestone victories, West's chief goal for the next several decades became the promotion of the *National Reporter System* as the leading case source for lawyers and judges in all U. S. jurisdictions. A major step toward this goal was the introduction in 1889 of the first permanent *Reporter* editions. Advance sheets for these editions replaced the earlier format of bindable parts but also created a lucrative albeit temporary black market for dealers who would hawk them as West's final, edited version.

While many attorneys began to accept West's publications as fundamental cases studies, many of the courts were reluctant to admit the West citations in lieu of actual State Report citations. However, by the mid-twentieth century, the *National Reporter System* was so successful that West citations had become generally accepted. In 1890, following upon the success of its *National Reporter System,* the company introduced the *American Digest* System, a singularly massive undertaking. The series, when complete, consisted of exhaustive listings and synopses of federal and state cases dating back to 1638. Typically paired to the more detailed *Reporter* volumes, the *Digest* listings were especially notable for their full-scale implementation of the Key Number System, which directed the researcher by category, topic, subtopic, and headnote to pertinent cases on record. Even before publication of its first digest volume, West entered the digest market by negotiating the rights for Little, Brown & Company's *U.S. Digest.* The success of the *National Reporter System,* and its obvious compatibility with the *American Digest System,* made effective competition difficult. The subscription list for John A. Mallory's *Complete Digest,* another potential competitor, was also purchased by West at about the same time. Mallory subsequently accepted a position with West and was crucial in perfecting the *American Digest System* classification scheme. The company closed the century on an especially high note with the unveiling of volume one of the *Century Digest,* intended as the definitive encyclopedia of all existing case law. The volume was unveiled at the American Bar Association (ABA) annual convention in 1897; the following year, the ABA offered its formal endorsement of the *American Digest System*

and West's preeminence as a legal publisher was irrevocably ensured.

In 1899 John West left the company to pursue other interests, and the presidency passed to Horatio West. In 1908 Charles W. Ames succeeded Horatio, and since that time every successor to the West presidency has been unrelated, save for a shared, longtime commitment to the private firm. Many company analysts attribute the remarkable development of the company not only to the Wests' dedication and innovations but to the early, conscientious enforcement of two policies at this time— "promotion from within" and prohibition of nepotism in management. In 1913, under Ames, West Publishing fulfilled a plan first announced in 1901: the compilation of a completely annotated, comprehensive edition of the U. S. statutes. By this time, the company was not only revamping the entire field of legal reference but also exerting an impact, through its casebooks, on the manner in which law was taught.

Ames's successor, Homer P. Clark, is generally accorded special status among West presidents. When Clark assumed the presidency in 1921 (after having served the company for nearly thirty years), he inaugurated what was to become known as the "general manager era." Until approximately 1926, when Clark's new approach to managing was adopted, the company had been ruled by a committee, no one member of which was fully cognizant of the day-to-day operations for every department. With Clark, the president gained much closer contact with department heads, thereby solving numerous communication and efficiency problems that had surfaced under the old system. Another means by which Clark ensured the long-term health of the company was through the persistent acquisition of outstanding stock held by disinterested parties and estates; the stock was then periodically reallocated to key employees, comprising a corporate-reward program that continued under Clark's successors. One of the chief editorial projects during Clark's administration was the *United States Code Annotated,* first published in 1927 after a Congressional joint committee on law revision commissioned both West and the Edward Thompson Company to pool their efforts. The original 61-volume, continually updated series now consists of some 215 permanent hardcovers, which are regularly supplemented by interim pamphlets and statutory supplements.

By the end of World War II, with Clark now serving as chairperson and Henry F. Asmussen in position as president, West began to grow rapidly. Full-time employees numbered 645 in 1945, and five years later the number had swelled to 1,172. Teletypesetting made its debut at West in 1956; further improvements in production efficiency, not to mention printing quality, came with the installation of West's first web offset press in 1962. Under then-president Lee Slater, a former business engineer, West's plant and operational layout underwent a complete modernization and overhaul. In 1968, when Slater handed control of the company to Dwight D. Opperman, West seemed well-positioned to maintain its leadership in the new technological age. When asked why he had joined the firm back in the 1950s, Opperman replied, "In law school it became apparent to me that there was one company above all others whose services were vital to the legal profession. I wanted to be a part of that company."

As the company entered the 1970s, however, technology and speed competed head-to-head with quality and longstanding service. Chief competitor Mead Data Central introduced its LEXIS service into the field of computer-assisted legal research in 1973, a full two years ahead of West. In 1975, the WEST-LAW computer-assisted legal research service was introduced. Assessing the situation for *Corporate Report Minnesota,* Brent Stahl wrote, "It is too late in the day for anyone to join West in the comprehensive court reporting field by publishing books. The cost would be prohibitive, and a workable indexing system would be difficult to devise. Computers are another story, and it is by this technology that Mead, or others, might challenge West's territory, which West gained by mastering the technology available in the 1880s." Mead did challenge West, despite the steadily rising popularity of WESTLAW, which became competitive with and perhaps even superior to LEXIS by the late 1970s. The battle between Mead and others against West became particularly heated during the middle to late 1980s due to lawsuits and countersuits revolving around the issue of Mead's attempt to use West's compilations of case reports. By 1988, however, West had negotiated a settlement agreement with Mead, after the courts had upheld the copyrightability of West's compilations, which Mead had threatened to integrate with LEXIS. Under the agreement, Mead agreed to pay an undisclosed amount to West for the use of its case report compilations.

The marketing of computerized research—in and outside the legal field—remained ripe territory for West and its Data Retrieval Corporation subsidiary during the 1990s. A 1992 arrangement with Commerce Clearing House to provide WEST-LAW users with the *Standard Federal Tax Reporter* was one way West planned to expand its subscriber base. In addition, West's pursuit of state-of-the-art software, most recently indi-cated by its unveiling of a simplified natural language search and retrieval process called WIN, promised to open new venues for West as a high-tech information access company. Yet, it is unlikely that West will ever stray too far afield from its declared domain. Given the law community's immense and ongoing investment in West's products, the company is destined to remain "Forever Associated with the Practice of Law."

Principal Subsidiaries: Data Retrieval Corporation of America; West Services, Inc. (WSI).

Further Reading: Marvin, William W., *West Publishing Co.: Origin—Growth—Leadership,* St. Paul: West Publishing Co., 1969; Stahl, Brent, "Giant with a Low Profile," *Corporate Report Minnesota,* February 1979, pp. 40–3; Willis, Judith, "WESTLAW and LEXIS Compete in Market Having Growth Potential," *St. Paul Pioneer Press & Dispatch,* March 18, 1985; Baenen, Jeff, "West Publishing's Success Brings Antitrust Lawsuit," *Star Tribune,* November 22, 1987; Pitzer, Mary J., and Zachary Schiller, "A Searing Courtroom Drama over . . . Page Numbers," *Business Week,* July 4, 1988; Ervin, John, Jr., "Publishing for the Law at West," *Publishers Weekly,* November 25, 1988; Greenhouse, Linda, "Progress Spawns Question: Who Owns the Law?" *New York Times,* February 16, 1990; *West Publishing Company: Forever Associated with the Practice of Law,* Eagan, MN: West Publishing Co., 1991; McAuliffe, Bill, "West Becomes Past in St. Paul, Present and Future in Eagan," *Star Tribune,* March 25, 1992; Woo, Junda, "Electronic Publishers of Legal Data Go to Court over Comparative Ads," *Wall Street Journal,* July 13, 1992; "West Publishing to Offer Tax Reports," *Star Tribune,* August 19, 1992; Burrow, Clive, "Legal Research, in English," *New York Times,* October 18, 1992.

—Jay Pederson

WESTMORELAND COAL COMPANY

700 The Bellevue
200 South Broad Street
Philadelphia, PA 19102
U.S.A.
(215) 545-2500
Fax: (215) 735-7175

Public Company
Incorporated: 1910 as Stonega Coke & Coal Co.
Employees: 1,226
Sales: $568.41 million
Stock Exchange: New York
SICs: 1222 Bituminous Coal—Underground

Westmoreland Coal Company is one of the coal industry's oldest independent companies. It operates mines in Virginia, West Virginia, Kentucky, and Montana, and is a major broker for smaller operations. It owns Cleancoal Terminal, an Ohio River rail-to-barge facility in Ghent, Kentucky, and has equity in Dominion Terminal, a Newport News, Virginia facility that serves both coastal and international customers. Aside from coal mining, Westmoreland has equity positions in several co-generation projects.

Westmoreland took its name from Westmoreland County in Pennsylvania, where in 1854 the company began mining coal for home heating, railroads, and, most importantly, coal gasification. Westmoreland County coal is largely bituminous, the principal grade of coal used for generating electricity and making steel. William Jasper Nicolls described Westmoreland's bituminous or ''gas-coal'' in his 1904 book, *The Story of American Coals,* as surpassing ''any in the world for its excellent gas-producing qualities.'' Westmoreland supplied this coal to fifty-eight eastern gasworks during the period just before the Civil War. In 1882 the Leisenring family accumulated major holdings in Westmoreland and maintained family control over the company for nearly a century.

In the years following 1900, when electricity began to take the place of coal in lighting homes around the nation, Westmoreland Coal Company found ample demand for its coal from railroads and steel makers. After World War I the company grew well beyond its Westmoreland County fields. On December 20, 1917, it merged with the Penn Gas Coal Company and the Manor Gas Coal Company. In 1923 and 1924 it acquired the Laurel Coal & Land Company's 11,210 acres of coal fields in Little Coal River, Boone, Crook, and Washington counties of West Virginia.

Like much of American industry, Westmoreland continued to grow during the 1920s. Profits were high, especially in relation to sales, which hovered between $1.75 and $2 million. The company's best year of the decade was 1923, when it earned $1.5 million or $7.58 per share on sales of $2.53 million.

In 1929 President E. B. Leisenring reorganized Westmoreland, creating a new company, Westmoreland Inc., to hold the land and the ten Pennsylvania coal mines, which then had a total daily capacity of 15,000 tons. The original Westmoreland Coal Company remained in existence—its stockholders also owned Westmoreland Inc.—and leased the mines and property as operations dictated.

When the Depression hit in the 1930s, declining industrial activity meant Westmoreland had fewer opportunities for sales to railroads and steel makers. In 1933, the company lost $435,000 on sales estimated at less than $3 million. Surprisingly, however, Leisenring was able to return Westmoreland to the black by 1934 when the company sold 1.74 million tons of coal and made $42,000.

In 1941, Westmoreland was operating five coal mines in Westmoreland County and had a total daily capacity of 11,000 tons. Demand increased during World War II and production jumped from 1.958 million tons in 1940 to 2.28 million tons in 1942. But after the war Westmoreland's production fell, first to 1.47 million tons in 1946, and then to 1.013 tons in 1949. The country was moving away from Westmoreland's anthracite—a variety of coal found almost exclusively in Pennsylvania and used chiefly in home heating. Railroads that had previously used anthracite switched to diesel; homeowners moved to oil or natural gas. Between 1945 and 1965 the railroads and home heating portion of the coal market fell from 20 percent to just three percent.

If Westmoreland was to grow, it would have to access bituminous coal that was used in steel making and electrical generation. The company had bituminous reserves in West Virginia and, in 1947, Leisenring leased West Virginia coal lands from Westmoreland Inc. and began constructing a mine in Logan County that would have a capacity of 2,500 tons per day.

The switch from anthracite to bituminous coal was not the only challenge the company and the coal industry faced. Through the 1950s and 1960s coal was challenged by competition from price-controlled natural gas and cheap oil from the Middle East. Nevertheless, coal remained important for the production of steel, cement, chemicals and, most importantly, electricity. In fact electric utilities tripled their demand for coal between the end of World War II and 1965.

For Westmoreland, the change from anthracite to bituminous coal and the competition from oil and natural gas led to a general decline. Dividends fell from $2.50 in 1951 to nil in

1959. Sales fell from a high of $8.5 million in 1951 to $6.5 million in 1959. The company twice reported losses during the decade and had its worst year in 1954 when it lost $370,000 on sales of $4.7 million. At the same time, however, a Westmoreland mine in West Virginia increased its volume, particularly in the higher-priced metallurgical coal used in making steel.

In 1961, Edward B. (Ted) Leisenring, Jr., succeeded his father as Westmoreland's president. Leisenring, who served as president and chief executive officer until 1978, and then as chair of the board of directors from 1978 until 1992, ran the company with a personal touch, claiming to wish to keep the company small enough that he could know his workers' names. Leisenring, a mining engineer, schooled himself on his family's company from all angles. As a young man in the 1940s he worked for more than a year as a miner in Westmoreland's Virginia mines. According to *Forbes,* Leisenring remembered sitting down during a shift at the mine to eat with an old Virginian miner. " 'Say,' the old-timer asked him, 'isn't your daddy some kind of ramrod in this outfit?' " Ted Leisenring allowed that was so. " 'Well, goddam,' the old-timer replied, 'your daddy sure must have it out for you, putting you in a crappy job like this.' "

Under Ted Leisenring's management, Westmoreland continued to move into West Virginia where by 1962 it was operating three mines in Boon and Logan Counties. Sales had risen to $8.5 million and the company had a daily capacity of 10,500 tons and reserves of 122 million tons. But the operation was barely, if at all, profitable.

Westmoreland was not the only coal company the Leisenrings controlled. They also ran Stonega Coke & Coal Co., which had been incorporated in 1910 and operated on 65,000 acres in Harlan County, Kentucky, and Wise and Lee Counties in Virginia. Bigger than Westmoreland—in 1962 it produced 2.3 million tons of coal and had sales of $11.8 million—it was in poorer shape financially. Its sales were falling and it had reported three straight years of losses.

In fact, neither company was a financial powerhouse in the 1960s. Possibly to reduce overhead, Ted Leisenring merged the two companies on April 30, 1964. Stonega was the technical successor but the new company retained the Westmoreland name. The merger was a success and, in 1964, the new, larger Westmoreland made two million dollars on sales of $25 million.

Through the mid-1960s, Westmoreland continued to grow away from its original base. It got out of Pennsylvania completely, and by the end of 1966 was producing steam and metallurgical grades from nine mines in Virginia and two in West Virginia. Fifty-one percent of Westmoreland's output went to electrical utilities, 20 percent went to industry, 16 percent became coke, eight percent was exported, and it sold five percent retail.

In the late 1960s, Westmoreland continued to expand despite declining earnings and widespread anticipation of a shaky future in the coal industry. In 1968, Leisenring paid $21 million for two small coal companies and a coal brokerage business. In 1969, he purchased another new mine with a yearly capacity of 1.5 million tons.

The early 1970s was a difficult time for much of the coal industry mainly because of the uncertainties involved in the enforcement of the Federal Coal Mine Health & Safety Act of 1969. According to *Barron's,* Westmoreland's management tagged the stretch as a "plateau of mediocrity" and claimed the act led to declines of 30 percent in the productivity of the company's underground mines. But despite these problems, the company was earning about $4 million a year and was well regarded. In 1971 the *Wall Street Transcript* called Westmoreland "outstandingly attractive."

Profits jumped significantly in 1973, 1974, and 1975 when the Arab oil embargo strengthened coal prices and Japanese buyers bid metallurgical coal into the $80 to $100 range. In the years when coal prices had been low, many large coal companies had entered into long-term, fixed-price contracts with buyers. Westmoreland, remaining optimistic about the future of coal prices, had maintained a policy of entering into only short-term "evergreen contracts"—contracts that were renegotiable on a yearly basis. When coal prices soared, Westmoreland's earlier optimism paid off. In 1974 Westmoreland earned $36 million and in 1975 it reported profits of $60 million or $8.82 a share.

In this high profit environment, Leisenring continued to expand the company. In 1974, he completed the $13 million Ferrell mine in West Virginia. The same year he began production in the West through Westmoreland Resources, a 36 percent owned (later 40 and then 60 percent) joint venture on Crow Indian lands in Montana's Powder River Basin. Always an active and a visible figure in his dealings, Leisenring personally bid on the vast low-sulfur Powder River reserves, finding that being the head of a family-controlled company helped tremendously. "I really enjoyed that experience," he told *Forbes.* "I had gone out to Montana to bid on the lease myself. We were bidding against a very big company group. To my surprise, their man had a limitation we didn't have and I found out how to bid just a little bit more and get the lease."

The down side of Westmoreland's mid-1970s success was that the price of metallurgical coal—accounting for approximately 60 percent of sales and 50 percent of tonnage—was vulnerable to the volatile nature of the steel business. Conventional wisdom would have had Westmoreland diversify in order to decrease their risks. Leisenring, however, was not conventional. "When we talk about diversifying," he told *Forbes,* "many of our shareholders get upset. They bought the stock because they want equity in the coal industry." Instead he continued to pour assets into new mining ventures such as Colorado Westmoreland Inc., a Colorado mining company created in 1977.

In the late 1970s coal prices weakened, falling far enough that by the early 1980s profits had turned to losses. In 1981 Westmoreland lost the equivalent of $2.17 a share. The losses were due in part to an explosion in the Ferrell mine in 1980, which continued to limit operations well into 1981, and to a 72-day coal miner's strike costing Westmoreland almost two million dollars a week. The situation was exacerbated by a drop in the price of metallurgical coal—Westmoreland's principal product—due to hard times in the steel industry.

Given the changing economics of the industry, Westmoreland's directors reexamined the company's priorities and set new goals: to have the safest employee accident record and to be a low cost producer/supplier. The move towards safety was already in the works when these goals were promulgated. Between 1979 and 1987 Westmoreland more than halved its accident rate. Also already in the works was a shift from metallurgical coal to steam coal, which could be distributed to the less cyclical electric utilities industry. By 1982, 82 percent of Westmoreland's sales were in steam coal.

To become a low-cost producer, Leisenring and his successor as president and chief executive officer, Pemberton Hutchinson, closed high-cost mines, laid off employees, and opened small, efficient mines. They bought coal from nonunion outside suppliers and introduced efficient longwall mining equipment which sheared coal from long underground seams and moved it to the surface via conveyors. In five years, Westmoreland's tons per manshift rate improved by more than 100 percent. And in 1987 the company produced 35 percent more coal with less than half the employees it had in 1979.

The direct mining of coal, however, was not Westmoreland's only involvement. It had a thriving coal brokerage business and in 1983 it created American Carbide Corporation to manufacture and market the carbide-tipped cutting tools used in coal mining and mine roof drilling. It was hoped that American Carbide would follow the success of Virginia Birmingham Bolt Company, which had been acquired in the merger with Stonega. Unfortunately, cutting tool prices fell and American Carbide ceased operation in 1987.

Much more successful were Dominion Terminal and Cleancoal Terminal. In 1984 Westmoreland joined with four other producers to develop the Dominion, the most modern and efficient coastal coal terminal on the East Coast. Located at Newport News, Virginia, Dominion made Westmoreland more competitive in the world market, where it was bucking a trend by increasing exports. In 1985 Westmoreland purchased Cleancoal Terminal, a rail-to-barge facility on the Ohio River between Cincinnati and Louisville. Cleancoal Terminal was profitable from its first day of operation and gave Westmoreland access to major Midwestern markets.

Coal consumption grew in the mid-1980s. The electric industry was consuming three quarters of U.S. production and a growing portion of Westmoreland's own production. Moreover, despite the high cost of pollution prevention, coal remained significantly cheaper than either oil or natural gas. To take advantage of synergies between electric generation and coal production, the company created Westmoreland Energy Inc. in 1985 to build cogeneration plants. Cogeneration plants produce power for industrial plants, hospitals, and independent communities. They sell excess electricity to power companies and provide steam for industrial processing and heating. By 1986 Westmoreland Energy president Chuck Brown had garnered commitments to three projects including one at the U.S. Army's Fort Drum in New York State.

By 1986, Leisenring and Hutchinson's cost-cutting efforts had largely paid off. "They have done what I consider to be an exemplary job of reducing their costs and handling adversity

very well," a commentator wrote in *The Wall Street Transcript*. "They are not out of the woods yet, but they have done a very good job of getting rid of the losers and reducing costs."

While cutting costs, Leisenring and Hutchinson had also worked to expand the business. In 1984 they acquired the Elk River Sewell Coal Company, a West Virginia company with a yearly capacity of one million tons. In 1987 they paid Bethlehem Steel $24 million for Kentucky Criterion Coal Company, an eastern Kentucky operation with 150 million tons of high quality, low-sulfur coal, strategically located to serve markets in the Midwest, Southeast, and Northeast.

These steps, however, were not enough to put Westmoreland solidly in the black and in 1987 the company lost $41.2 million. To reduce overhead and bring itself back into the black, in 1988 the company rededicated itself to concentrating on its core business in the southern Appalachian coal fields and disposing of non-core assets. In the spring of 1988 it sold a portion of its Kentucky reserves. In November it sold Colorado Westmoreland, Inc., its Rocky Mountains mine, to Cyprus Coal. In December it sold a 10 percent equity position in Fort Drum, and in early 1989 it sold Elk River to Upper Elk Resources.

Westmoreland reported profits through the late 1980s. After three years of progressively improving earnings and despite increased production and sales, Westmoreland lost $13.4 million in 1991—largely because of forces outside its control. At its Virginia Division's Holton Mine adverse geological conditions reduced the longwall system's productivity and led to a $12.5 million loss for the mine. At a surface mining site in West Virginia, a mining contractor went out of business and left Westmoreland with $4.8 million worth of reclamation costs.

Still working to increase efficiency, Hutchinson installed a total quality management regime in 1989, encouraging new approaches such as the Virginia Division's "replanning" program, which entails multiple, smaller, and more versatile operations. Despite efforts such as these, results for the first two quarters of 1992 were disappointing. Brokered coal sales fell, Cleancoal Terminal was in the red, and the Virginia division lost money due to adverse geological conditions. On the positive side, Criterion Coal Company, Westmoreland Resources, and the Hampton Division all reported profits. Westmoreland Energy for its part, completed three more cogeneration plants and began reporting significant earnings.

Principal Subsidiaries: ECC Leasing Corp.; Westmoreland Coal Sales Co.; Westmoreland Energy, Inc.; Criterion Coal Co.; Westmoreland Resources, Inc. (60% owned); Cleancoal Terminal Co.; Dean Processing Co.; Eastern Coal & Coke Co.; Kentucky Criterion Coal Co.; Pine Branch Mining Inc.; Roda-Dendron Coal Co.; Triport Tool Corp.; WEI-Carolina, Inc.; WEI-Carolina, Inc.; WEI-Monfort, Inc.; WEI-Roanoke Valley, Inc.

Further Reading: Nicolls, William Jasper, *The Story of American Coals*, J. B. Lippincott Company, Philadelphia, 1904; Raphael, Marvin S., *Wall Street Transcript,* April 19, 1971; Binder, Frederick Moore, *Coal Age Empire,* Pennsylvania Historical and Museum Commission, Harrisburg, 1974; Hussey, Allan F., "Westmoreland Coal Is Poised To Cash In on Heavy

Demand," *Barron's,* November 18, 1974; la Campanel, Frank W., "Steam Powered," *Barron's,* May 24, 1982; "Golden Coal," *Forbes,* April 1, 1975; Zuckerman, Stanley, "Westmoreland Coal Company," *Wall Street Transcript,* September 22, 1975; Johnson, Wayne, "Westmoreland Coal Company," *Wall Street Transcript,* May 31, 1976; "The Waiting Game," *Forbes,* October 15, 1976; Leisenring, Hutchinson, etc., "Remarks to the New York Society of Security Analysts," *Wall Street Transcript,* March 24, 1986; Hutchinson, Pemberton, "Westmoreland Coal Company," *Wall Street Transcript,* March 14, 1988.

—Jordan Wankoff

WHEELING-PITTSBURGH CORP.

34 Market Street
Wheeling, Virginia 26003
U.S.A.
(304) 234-2400
Fax: (304) 234-2442

Public Company
Incorporated: 1920 as Wheeling Steel Corp.
Sales: $957 million
Employees: 6,200
Stock Exchanges: New York
SICs: 3316 Cold-Finishing of Steel Shapes; 3312 Blast
  Furnaces & Steel Mills; 3317 Steel Pipes & Tubes

Wheeling-Pittsburgh Corp., among the top ten steel companies in America, is a major producer and supplier of flat rolled and fabricated steel products. The company was reorganized in 1991 as the result of a bankruptcy ruling, making Wheeling-Pittsburgh Corp. the holding company for Wheeling-Pittsburgh Steel. Wheeling-Pittsburgh Steel had been in Chapter 11 for more than four-and-a-half years after accumulating serious debts and undergoing well-publicized labor problems—including a controversial strike in 1985—in the first half of the 1980s. In many ways, the history of the company reflects the dramatically changing fortunes of the American steelmaking industry.

The roots of Wheeling-Pitt go back to the middle of the last century when Wheeling, West Virginia, which lies on the banks of the Ohio River, was the center of a flourishing nail manufacturing industry. In 1851 LaBelle Iron Works was established and soon became a leading nail factory. By the end of the Civil War, the nail market had begun a serious decline, and LaBelle began searching for new products to manufacture, eventually entering into the creation of steel sheets, tin plates, and galvanized roofing. This expansion was propelled by LaBelle's purchase of a three-year-old nail factory in Steubenville, Ohio and their installation of two blast furnaces at the plant. Eventually, the Steubenville plant became the site for open-hearth steelwork, plate mills, sheet mills, and tube works.

In the meantime, Alexander Glass founded the Wheeling Corrugated Company in 1901. Glass, a key figure in the early development of Wheeling-Pittsburgh, began his career at the age of 14 packing nails in a Wheeling plant. He founded Wheeling

Corrugated with a capital investment of $10,000, including $4,000 of his own money. The company began by manufacturing corrugated or "wrinkled" roofing and siding which was used to replace aging wooden structures in factories, farm buildings, and homes. The company soon diversified into the making of conductor pipes, trimmings, and ornamental steel plates, among other products. Glass turned Wheeling Corrugated into a subsidiary of the newly-formed Wheeling Steel and Iron Company in 1902. The next year saw the opening of a second Wheeling plant in nearby Martins Ferry, Ohio.

World War I was a boom period for the entire steel industry because all kinds of steel was demanded by munitions industries both at home and abroad. All over the country steel companies were rehabilitating obsolete units and buildings and installing new equipment. Wheeling Steel and Iron added six hot mills in the early days of the war and in 1918 brought six more into production. In 1917 the company would boast a record profit of $4,637,365.

On June 21, 1920, the Wheeling Steel Corporation was created, bringing together three independent companies from the area—LaBelle Iron Works, Whitaker-Glessner Company, and Wheeling Steel & Iron Company. Originally organized in 1875, Whitaker-Glessner owned a sheet-bar mill in Portsmouth as well as sheet and tin mills in Wheeling and sheet mills in Martins Ferry. Alexander Glass was appointed chairman and I.M. Scott was named president of the newly-formed Wheeling Steel Corporation, which was capitalized at $100 million.

The merger made good business sense. Whitaker-Glessner shared with Wheeling Steel and Iron the handicap of having to go outside their own processing facilities for raw material. On the other hand, LaBelle Iron Works had in abundance what the other two companies lacked: important raw material resources in the area of coal and ore properties, along with its own blast furnaces, open-hearth furnace, and modern coke byproduct facilities.

The merger came at a time when the steel industry was still riding the crest of the war years. Just prior to the merger, the three companies had declared comfortable dividends. But the boom came to an abrupt halt. The next year, 1921, saw demand dramatically fall and, at 19,224,084 tons, industry-wide steel production was less than half the previous year's output.

There was another industry-wide problem that the new company had to face: the tug-of-war between labor and management. The steel workers union was demanding that "all mills or none" in the new company be unionized immediately. Wheeling's position was that they were willing to sign scale contracts for 1921–1922 covering those of its plants that had been unionized in the past, but balked at honoring union demands at those mills that had been customarily run on an open-shop basis. Facing an intransigent management, workers at several of the mills walked off their jobs. Wheeling's immediate response was to leave the plants cold, since business was languishing anyway. Eventually non-union workers were brought in to staff the struck mills.

Weathering uncertain market conditions and the Depression, Wheeling established a foothold as number ten among the major steel manufacturers. It continued acquiring new properties, modernizing its facilities, and steadily expanded its production of flat rolled steel products. A major push was undertaken to update and streamline the physical plant since the technology was changing and competition was fierce among the top steelmakers.

One of the first major undertakings at Wheeling Steel was the installation at Steubenville of new blooming mills and a continuous sheet-bar mill which enabled the finishing mill to be independent of purchased raw material. The Portsmouth plant was also considerably upgraded; this mill had been among the first of the sheet mills to specialize in the production of high-finish sheet metal for the automotive industry. At the same time, Wheeling was acquiring new properties to add to their infrastructure. In 1927, it acquired the Riverside steel mills from the National Tube Company; this was the first time that United States Steel Corporation had disposed of a plant to a competitor.

During the war, Wheeling produced steel planking for portable airplane landing strips and fins for various bombs produced by the Allies. In 1948, as the construction industry began to shift from wood-based to steel-based structures, Wheeling began manufacturing products for the non-residential construction market.

A $200 million expansion program undertaken in 1962 and completed in 1966 modernized Wheeling's plant capabilities—but not without a painful price. In 1966 the overextended company found itself with an operating loss of $15,763,000, despite all-time record sales of $293,182,000 on recorded shipments of 1,665,000 tons. Wheeling faced a financial crisis in cash and liquidity. Commitments for further capital expenditures, without the resources to pay for them, threatened to critically undermine the entire company.

Facing this financial impasse, Wheeling looked to pull itself out of the crisis by merging with Pittsburgh Steel Company on December 5, 1968. Pittsburgh Steel, then the 16th largest steel producer, was interested in combining forces with a larger company. Founded in 1901 with facilities along the Monongahela River some 30 miles southeast of Pittsburgh, Pittsburgh Steel was at that point a small independent steelmaker with a limited product mix. During 1966 and 1967 it had produced about 2.1 million tons of raw steel a year and shipped a little less than 1.6 million tons of finished steel products. Combining forces with Wheeling would create a new company, representing the ninth largest steelmaker, with a finished capacity of more than three million tons. Meanwhile, Pittsburgh Steel had finished 1967 with a profit of $2.2 million, but had finished the previous year with a loss of close to $2.0 million.

The merger made Wheeling a stronger competitor with upgraded facilities and a more balanced product line. Wheeling's product mix was heavily based on flat-rolled products while Pittsburgh leaned towards metal-coated sheet specialty items. There were many obvious advantages to the partnership. Still, industry analysts realistically noted that both parties brought shaky economic prospects to this corporate union.

The new company began on an upbeat note. Sales volume for the two companies doubled from $505 million in 1968 to $1,037 million in 1974. However, capital expenditures continued to rise as Wheeling-Pittsburgh undertook a massive program to maintain and modernize existing facilities from raw materials through coke ovens, iron, and steel making, to production of finished products. And there was a new added expense: the increasingly formidable cost of installing new technology for environmental quality control. In 1974 and 1975, capital expenditures reached $115 million, more than double the outlay during the previous five year period.

In 1978 Dennis J. Carney, regarded as one of the most aggressive and controversial executives in U.S. steel history, became chairman of Wheeling-Pittsburgh and the company entered a dramatic new era. The company had fallen prey to erratic earnings; after the strong showing in 1974, sales volume declined to $827 million in the recession of 1975, and the following years were hardly more encouraging. Despite the marshalling of their resources, the combined efforts of both Wheeling and Pittsburgh still lay claim to an unimpressive three percent market share. And, despite prior efforts at upgrading and modernizing equipment, Wheeling-Pittsburgh continued to lag behind many of the other major steel producers in its technology.

But once again the problems faced by Wheeling-Pittsburgh were not unique to the company. The golden age of American steelmaking was over. All of the giant steel companies were feeling the pinch as supply continued to exceed demand and high labor costs and growing competition from abroad further undermined profit margins. Foreign producers were starting to land steel in the U.S. at prices lower than steel turned out in American mills; by 1984 they had captured one-quarter of all steel sold in the U.S. During that year President Reagan instituted voluntary restraint agreements, holding imports down to 20 percent of U.S. consumption. The daunting cost of modernizing steel plants was another challenge faced by most of the U.S. steel makers, who were still operating with outmoded equipment. The 1980s proved a particularly grim decade. More than 400 mills closed, an estimated 200,000 steel workers lost their jobs, and numerous steel companies bailed out into bankruptcy as the industry limped through the decade.

Carney's solution to the problems faced by Wheeling-Pittsburgh was to embark on an ambitious renovation program, financed through the company's largest capital-spending program ever. Unfortunately, the rate of long term debt far outpaced revenues as the industry entered the doldrums of the 1980s. In 1981, its net sales were $1.1 million while long-term debt stood at more than $300,000; the list of corporate creditors, an impressive roster of leading banks and insurance companies, was becoming voluminous. From 1979 to 1984 the company spent over $563 million on improvements. However, Wheeling-Pitt's losses during 1982, 1983, and 1984 alone totalled more than $172 million. At the same time, Carney was able to aggressively cut overhead and personnel costs. But his cost-cutting soon put him on a collision course with the United Steel Workers Union (USW).

During this difficult period, Carney had twice managed to persuade the USW representatives at Wheeling-Pitt to help the company by granting wage concessions in excess of $150 million. Late in 1984 Carney approached the union again but this time they balked, claiming that it was the creditors' turn to help the company. Wheeling-Pittsburgh's creditors were unwilling to shoulder the burden of bailing out the company, unless the USW agreed to cooperate.

Negotiations between the USW, Wheeling-Pittsburgh's creditors, and Carney and other top management officials eventually broke down. On April 16, 1985, Wheeling-Pittsburgh filed for Chapter 11 bankruptcy. At that point, the company was saddled with $44 million in debt against negative equity of $99 million and was unable to meet even its minimum pension funding obligations.

At the same time, the company petitioned the bankruptcy court for permission to cancel existing labor agreements and unilaterally lower wages. Several major companies, most notably Texas Air and Wilson Foods, had gone into bankruptcy proceedings in the 1980s while asking the court's permission to overturn existing contract agreements. In the case of Wheeling-Pitt, the court ruled in favor of the steelmaker.

Top management went back to the union proposing a wage and benefit rate of $17.50 per hour, down from the existing $21.40 rate. The union held their position that they would not go any lower than $18.50; furthermore, Wheeling-Pittsburgh declared that they would not be able to make a $5 million pension fund payment due at the end of July. It was at this point, with the company in bankruptcy court and a very real possibility of liquidation looming in the near future, that 8,500 steelworkers at Wheeling-Pittsburgh went on strike. The date of the walkout was July 21, 1985, and the strike received wide attention—and not only in the business community—since it was the first major strike in the steel industry in 26 years.

The strike also threw into bold relief the problems surrounding the industry. The walkout was a crucial test of the power of angry steel workers to maintain minimum wage standards in an industry that was desperate to cut costs. The bankruptcy and strike also spotlighted the controversial power of bankruptcy courts to void union contracts. Finally, the strike was anxiously monitored by steel company executives who feared that it could be the harbinger of a wave of strikes in this increasingly unstable industry.

To the distress of Wheeling-Pittsburgh's creditors and executives, the strike dragged on for almost three months. It was finally settled on October 15, 1985. Under an unusual arrangement, mill workers received a new contract with an hourly wage of $18, but they would actually continue to receive $20.33 an hour in wages and benefits. The discrepancy arose from the termination of the company's pension plans. The responsibility of meeting pension obligations was transferred from the company to the Pension Benefit Guaranty Corporation (PBGC), a federal agency that insures retirement plans. The union agreed to eliminate six hundred jobs, but won a significant voice in managing the company. The union now had the right to nominate a candidate for the board of directors and could also set up an eight-person Joint Strategic Decision Board, composed of union and management representatives, to discuss issues relating to the workers and business operation of the company.

Finally, the union helped put an abrupt end to the autocratic reign of Dennis Carney. Shortly before the settlement, Carney was asked to resign; it had become painfully obvious to company executives that the USW would not settle as long as he stayed in charge. Carney was asked to resign by Allen E. Paulson, chairman of Gulfstream Aerospace, the owner of 34 percent of Wheeling-Pitt common stock, and a principal player in the drama that was playing itself out.

While Carney left behind a controversial legacy, he did help create an important joint venture between Wheeling-Pittsburgh and Nisshin Steel Corporation. Launched in February of 1984, the Japanese firm of Nisshin Steel gained a ten percent interest in Wheeling-Pittsburgh, while Wheeling-Pittsburgh invested approximately $10 million in the Japanese steelmaker's stock. As a result of the agreement, a $40 million production line producing rust-resistant galvanized steel for the auto industry was constructed at one of Wheeling-Pittsburgh's existing plants.

The second part of the 1980s were spent under the shadow of bankruptcy as creditors and the courts worked out a reorganization plan agreeable to all parties. Under bankruptcy law protection, Wheeling-Pittsburgh was not required to pay interest on most of its debt and no longer had to worry about fulfilling pension obligations. Meanwhile, the company saw steady growth in its net sales during this period, with 1989 distinguishing itself as the second most profitable year since the two companies merged in 1968. Net sales that year were more than $1.14 million, while operating costs increased 8.7 percent, due in part to higher prices for raw materials. On January 3, 1991, five years and eight months after filing for bankruptcy, Wheeling-Pittsburgh emerged out of the court's hands.

Under the reorganization plan, the pre-Chapter 11 balance sheet of some $1.1 billion in liabilities was wiped clean. The newly-reorganized company was limited to no more than $340 million in new borrowings. The majority of its debt was reconstituted in the form of a seven year $445 million secured note. Wheeling-Pittsburgh Steel was now a subsidiary of a holding company, Wheeling-Pittsburgh Corporation. Despite the hobbling influence of the serious recession affecting the steel industry, Wheeling-Pitt emerged in its first year out of Chapter 11 as the only American integrated steel producer to record a profit ($4.7 million).

Principal Subsidiaries: Consumers Mining Co.; Mingo Oxygen Co.; Monessen Southwestern Ry Co.; Pittsburgh-Canfield Corp.; Wheeling-Empire Co.; Fort Duquesne Coal Co.; Wheeling-Pittsburgh Steel Corp.; WPC Land Co.; Pittsburgh Steel Products Co.

Further Reading: Scott, Henry Dickerson, *Iron & Steel in Wheeling,* Caslon Co., 1929; May, Earl Chapin, *Principio to Wheeling, 1715–1945, A Pageant of Iron and Steel,* Harper & Brothers, 1945; "Why Steelmakers Seek Strength in Merger," *Business Week,* February 15, 1969; "The Maverick Who Could Save Wheeling-Pitt," *Business Week,* June 4, 1984; "A Striking New Chapter in Chapter 11," *Economist,* July 27, 1985; "A Watershed Strike at Wheeling-Pitt," *Business Week,* August 3, 1985; Hoer, John P., *And the Wolf Finally Came: The Decline of the American Steel Industry,* University of Pittsburgh Press, 1988; Biesada, Alexandra, "Vultures Dance: Why Wheeling Pittsburgh Has Taken So Long to Emerge from Bankruptcy," *FW,* November 13, 1990.

—Timothy Bay

WINNEBAGO INDUSTRIES INC.

P.O. Box 152
Forest City, Iowa 50436
U.S.A.
(515) 582-3535
Fax: (515) 582-6966

Public Company
Incorporated: February 12, 1958
Employees: 2,700
Sales: $294.9 million
Stock Exchanges: New York Midwest Pacific
SICs: 3716 Motor Homes

Winnebago Industries Inc. is an Iowa-based maker of motor homes and recreation vehicles. Sold under the Winnebago, Elanté, Vectra, and Itasca brand names, these vehicles are aimed mostly at the recreational and leisure markets through an international dealer network.

Winnebago Industries was formed in Forest City, Iowa, as a community project. In the early 1950s local businesspeople were eager to establish factory jobs for those leaving farms to seek work in Minneapolis or beyond. The town—with a population of 2,500 in 1955—formed a trust, the Forest City Industrial Development, to attract industrial ventures to their area.

In these postwar years, Forest City businessman John K. Hanson had noticed the growing popularity of recreational trailers among travellers on holiday. Hanson bought two trailer models to learn more about the burgeoning industry before approaching the Industrial Development trustees with a possible venture. In October of 1957 the trustees voted to investigate making travel trailers, and Hanson became chairman of the search committee.

During a three-day drive, $20,000 came in from the Forest City community to begin the business venture. Forest City Industries was born, its board of directors including Paul Carse, president, Bob Smith, secretary, and John K. Hanson, treasurer. Smith and Hanson eventually struck a deal with Modernistic Industries Inc., a trailer factory based in California, for Modernistic Industries of Iowa to become a subsidiary. They would build Modernistic's "Aljo" brand trailers for the midwest market under supervision from California.

Work began at Modernistic Industries of Iowa on January 29, 1958. The first trailer rolled off the assembly line in mid-March. The trailer could sleep five people, had kitchen and lounging facilities, and cost $895. Because of the great demand for these trailers, a host of Forest City natives broke away to form Forest City Industries Inc., a rival to the Modernistic Industries operation. This development unsettled Modernistic management, which was led by C. T. McCreary.

The Aljo plant was shut down for Labor Day weekend and did not reopen as planned for the new 1959 model production in September. After negotiations failed to reopen the Forest City plant by February of 1959, five local businessmen purchased the trailer company, and John K. Hanson offered to manage it for the coming year. Modernistic Industries of Iowa survived the year and by 1959 it had 17 employees. On February 28, 1961, the company's name was changed to Winnebago Industries, Inc.

In 1973, Winnebago Industries, by now the continent's largest recreational vehicle maker, had amassed more than 400 acres of land holdings in Forest City, including 46.5 acres of factory floor space, or two million square feet in all. Winnebago has since increased its land holdings to 860 acres.

To encourage superior after-sales service, the company had invited more than 1,000 dealer personnel to the Forest City head office for service school classes. Also in 1973, Winnebago established two subsidiaries: Winnebago Realty Corporation and Winnebago International Corporation. The realty arm was formed to help dealers establish or enlarge outlets at selected sites, while the international arm was meant to forge overseas markets for the company's products.

In 1974 the company began to feel the full brunt of 1973's oil shortage, which discouraged sales of gas-guzzling motor homes. Compounding financial difficulties, the United States suffered a mild recession that year, further denting consumer spending. To compensate, Winnebago diversified its holdings. The Maroff Division was formed to market a new Eze-Hauler fifth-wheel trailer for use on farms. In addition, the company moved into the mass-transportation market during a time of mounting energy conservation. Winnebago buses were unveiled to encourage companies to bring employees from outlying areas to work, thus saving on gas consumption.

At the end of 1974 Winnebago's payroll stood at 1,600 people. In order to revive sales of recreational vehicles amid the OPEC oil embargo, a Grand Giveaway program was established. Under the plan, motor home buyers were offered merchandise premiums. In 1976 John Hanson removed himself from day-to-day management of the company, stepping in as vice-chairman. Gerald Boman was elected chairman of the board and John V. Hanson, son of the founder, became president and chief executive officer.

A year later, the company began constructing a 126,000-square-foot factory in Riverside, California, to build motor homes. In addition, a 66,000-square-foot plant was leased in Asheville, North Carolina, to build van conversions. Also in 1977, Winnebago celebrated the manufacture of its 100,000th motor home. Journalists from across the United States turned out for the event.

In October of that year, another boardroom shuffle saw J. Harold Bragg become chairman and chief executive officer of the company. John V. Hanson retained his position as president, but Gerald Boman became senior vice-president of the company. The change was attributed to growing demands on the company, on top of continuing shocks from the domestic energy shortage. The response required more senior managerial experience in the boardroom.

But the boardroom renewal did not succeed. In March of 1979 company founder John K. Hanson stepped in to end what he termed, according to *The Winnebago Story, 1958–1988,* "a difference in management philosophy." J. Harold Bragg and John V. Hanson were replaced by John K. Hanson, who ended his semi-retirement to become chairman and chief executive officer of the company. This boardroom crisis was a precursor of a general business downturn. In May of 1979 motor home production at Winnebago was halted for six weeks to reduce excess inventory owing to reduced consumer demand. A continuing drop in revenues led to the sale of the newly built Riverside, California, plant.

The 1980 lines of motor homes were smaller and more fuel efficient. Winnebago's new LLT trailer, for example, came in 16- and 18-foot models and had a road-to-roof height of just 86 inches. A more easily towed trailer was seen to be more fuel efficient for car owners on the highway. High interest rates and undercutting attempts at financing new vehicle purchases by consumers made 1980 a difficult trading year for Winnebago. That year, inventory, debt load, and overhead expenses were reduced. The company's work force was substantially reduced—from 4,000 employees in January of 1979 to 1,000 by August of 1980.

Remaining employees began working in quality circles in 1981 to improve productivity. That year, Winnebago had a net positive cash position of $23.7 million at its fiscal year-end. This allowed the company to invest its own funds where only a few years earlier it had to borrow amid high interest rates.

With a more assured business future, Winnebago saw yet another boardroom shuffle in 1981. John K. Hanson remained as chairman of the board, but Ronald E. Haugen assumed presidency of the company. John K. Hanson was feeling more confident about Winnebago's comeback. He was quoted as saying in *The Winnebago Story:* "We've done our homework and . . . are about to enter a period of rapid growth." An increase in sales allowed more investment in the development of fuel-efficient vehicles, and the company's work force was expanded to 1,350 people in 1982.

In the spring of 1983, the company enlisted a number of companies to manufacture a line of Winnebago brand products—from outdoor apparel to backpacks, rubberized air mattresses, picnic jugs, and coolers. Winnebago received royalties for the use of its company logo under the licensing arrangements in more than 2,000 retail outlets across the United States. Sales that year reached $239.26 million, up sharply from $146.6 million a year earlier. Earnings in 1984 were even better: profits totalled $27.8 million, or $1.10 a share (an increase of 77 percent on 1983 earnings). Rising sales were in part attributed to increased demand for the company's LeSharo and Itasca Phasar brand vehicle lines.

In order to further improve productivity, Winnebago moved part of its sewing operation from Forest City, Iowa, to Juarez, Mexico, in 1984. This was part of a long-range plan to move labor-intensive manufacturing from Forest City to cheaper labor markets.

Capital expenditure at Winnebago reached $24 million in 1985, as the company continued modernizing its manufacturing operations. Winnebago following the suit of the big three automakers in Detroit, who were developing modernized operations—including computer-aided design and manufacturing facilities. Winnebago installed a "System 85" telephone system encompassing its entire work force and dealer network. Yet another innovation was the Education Center, where Winnebago employees were instructed in the latest electronic and computer techniques being introduced on the shop floor.

Changes to the Winnebago boardroom in 1985 included John V. Hanson rejoining the company management as deputy chairman. In 1986 Gerald Gilbert became president and chief executive officer of the company, while Richard Berreth was appointed executive vice-president of operations. Also that year, Winnebago entered the *Fortune* 500 list of major United States companies, ranking number 500 in sales and 340 in net income.

In October of 1986 Winnebago diversified its portfolio by acquiring majority control of Cycle Video Inc., a satellite courier business specializing in transmitting television commercials from advertising agencies to broadcast affiliates. Also that month, Winnebago celebrated the manufacture of its 200,000th motor home. Sales for 1987 were posted at $406.4 million, leading to earnings of $19.97 million, or 78 cents per share. Changes made that year to promote increased productivity included strengthening the marketing department and expanding its training program for dealers.

More management changes occurred in 1989, following poor earnings performance a year earlier. Sales in 1988 had reached $430 million, but earnings slipped to $2.7 million, or 11 cents per share. In September, Gerald Gilbert was replaced as president and chief executive officer of the company by a seven-person management council appointed to manage day-to-day operations. John K. Hanson said of the company's performance that year, according to a 1988 annual report: "The company failed to fully participate in the growth of the motor home industry during the second half of the year."

On the international sales front, Winnebago signed a 1988 agreement with Winnebago Trading GmbH, based in Hamburg, Germany, to sell its motor vehicles in 14 European markets. The company also reached an agreement that same year with the Tokyo-based Mitsubishi Corporation to sell Winnebago products in Japan.

But the company's fortunes did not improve in 1989. Winnebago posted a loss of $4.67 million on sales of $437.5 million in 1989. The beginning of the recession that year had dented consumer confidence and demand for motor homes decreased. Still, John K. Hanson saw grounds for optimism about his company's future. The United States was seeing an increase in the population of elderly people able to afford recreational vehicles. In addition, international markets for motor homes continued to mature, especially in Europe and Japan.

That optimism was short-lived, however. Revenues for the company plunged to $332.8 million in 1990 from $437.5 million a year earlier. Earnings continued to be in the red; this time the posted loss was $17.8 million. The effects of the Persian Gulf War—which drove up the price of oil and raised fears of an oil shortage at the gas pumps—undercut sales in the motor home division. In addition, the Cycle-Sat subsidiary continued to post operating losses. To stem losses, Winnebago began an austerity program in 1990 and increased the marketing of its Warrior and Spirit micro-mini motor home models, which offered superior fuel efficiency.

Fred Dohrmann, appointed chief operating officer of Winnebago in 1990, added the position of president to his nameplate in 1991 as the company continued to struggle amid the gathering recession. Company sales, dented by the impact of the Gulf War, continued a slide of 34 percent to $222.6 million for fiscal 1991. An earnings loss in 1991 was posted at $29.3 million, or $1.18 per share.

John K. Hanson termed the year a difficult one for the company. The manufacture of commercial vehicles was discontinued to direct more investment toward the recreational motor home division, the company's core business. Sales of motor homes in 1991, at $180.8 million, represented 81.2 percent of total company sales. In 1992 sales for the company increased to $294.9 million. The company, however, continued to lose money and posted a net loss of $10.5 million. Nonetheless the recession had eased in 1992, and the Gulf War and its harmful trading effects had ended.

The prospect of recovery for the U.S. economy in 1993, and the continuing rise in the nation's elderly population, bode well for the company. At the same time, the company must concentrate on reducing its operating overheads. Heavily dependent on motor home sales, Winnebago remains vulnerable to swings in consumer confidence. And while growth in the United States market may be limited throughout the early 1990s, growth overseas will be held back by recessionary conditions in Japan and Europe. After more than three decades of successful trading, Winnebago Industries will need to work hard to maintain its ascendancy in the North American recreational motor vehicle market.

Principal Subsidiaries: Cycle-Sat Inc.; Winnebago Acceptance Corporation; Winnebago R.V., Inc.; Winnebago Realty Corporation; Winnebago Products, Inc.

Further Reading: The Winnebago Story: 1958–1988, Winnebago Industries Public Relations, 1988; Winnebago Annual Reports, 1989–92.

—Etan Vlessing

WISCONSIN DAIRIES

P.O. Box 111
Baraboo, Wisconsin 53913-0111
U.S.A.
(608) 356-8316
Fax: (608) 356-0809

Private Cooperative
Incorporated: 1963
Employees: 932
Sales: $516.00 million
SICs: 2023 Dry, Condensed & Evaporated Dairy Products;
2021 Creamery Butter; 2022 Cheese—Natural &
Processed

Wisconsin Dairies (WD) is one of the largest dairy cooperatives in the United States, a Fortune 500 company that operates 19 manufacturing plants and conducts $2 million worth of business on any given work day. It produces one third of the cheese consumed in the United States (not under its own brand name, but by selling it to major food processors and marketers) and is the nation's largest manufacturer and marketer of whey products (a by-product in cheese making) to the food processing and pharmaceutical industries in the United States and abroad. As a result, it is a world leader in the dairy industry. It is also a unique company, owned and run by 4,800 dairy farm families in Wisconsin, Minnesota, Iowa, and Illinois, who as members pay no dues and sign no contracts. In a time of difficult change for farming in the United States, WD has operated continuously in the black.

Farming cooperatives, or associations of farmers who share their resources and divide their profits equally, are as old as agriculture. Old World farmers brought the concept to the New World, and Wisconsin, heavily populated by German immigrants, saw the establishment of its first farming co-ops in the 1840s. Since that time, the success of these groups has closely followed the fortunes of the family dairy farm. As the number of Wisconsin dairy farms grew, so did the number of farming co-ops. Yet, dairy farming did not escape the general decline of the family farm that began in the 1960s, despite numerous federal price supports. In 1963 there were approximately 90,000 dairy farms in the Wisconsin; by 1985, the number was closer to 35,000. Cooperatives fared no better than the farms.

In 1963, when Wisconsin Dairies was officially established, dairy farming was still in its heyday. While its history commenced in that year, this new co-op was really the product of the merger of two parent co-ops, Wisconsin Creamery Co-op and the Wisconsin Co-op Creamery Association, each of which had been established in 1945. (These two were in turn the product of the merger of numerous other, far older, co-ops.) The decision of the two co-ops to join forces came about as the result of a coincidence. Each had independently found the need for a new dryer for dry milk processing. The boards of directors of the co-ops agreed to purchase a single dryer that would be shared. While negotiating the purchase, the two co-op directors developed a proposal for a merger. (In the end, the dryer was never purchased.) Later, they put the question of the merger to their respective cooperative members. The vote in March 1963 in favor of merger into a new cooperative entity, Wisconsin Dairies, was overwhelming. Approximately 1,700 farm families became members that day. Melvin Sprecher, who had been president of one of the merging co-ops, became chairman of WD, a position he would maintain until 1974. Vice-chairman for the next ten years would be Clarence Lehman.

At first, butter constituted a major product of WD. However, competition was keen, and reliance on butter for most of the company's sales (easy to do, since the federal government subsidized butter heavily) would not serve the co-op well in the long run. Instead, the twin themes in WD's history became diversification and expansion. Yet, until the new company could find its own niche in the marketplace, WD remained for the first several years chiefly a butter and milk producer, barely distinguishable from other dairy co-ops in the heartland. Expansion did not have to wait, though; a year after WD's official inauguration, 400 members of the Richland Co-op Creamery Company joined WD, followed through the years by 13 other mergers. The largest acquisition occurred in 1979, when 1,600 dairy farmers in Iowa and Minnesota, almost as many as the original WD in 1963, joined the company.

Cheese production gradually emerged as the mainstay of the company, since cheese consumption by the late 1960s was on the rise. By 1977, co-op members approved the construction of the company's first cheese manufacturing plant at Richland Center, Wisconsin, equipped with the latest facilities. Fifteen years after the Richland Center plant went into operation, WD was producing ten varieties of cheese, with one plant, in Clayton, Wisconsin, exclusively manufacturing mozzarella. Like all of WD's dairy products, it was not marketed under a WD brand name. (The company's only foray into retailing its products, a dairy store selling WD milk products and ice cream in Madison, Wisconsin, failed after one year.) Instead, all are sold to major food processing companies such as Kraft USA, Land O'Lakes, Kroger, and Little Caesar's Pizza.

WD was originally established in large part to eliminate duplicate services and consolidate production by means of automation, and much progress in this regard was made in WD's first decade. During this time the co-op's members also built a solid company infrastructure that would produce a cash flow healthy enough to enable the company to diversify. The organization of WD was and remains uncomplicated; ''corporate headquarters'' became a small two-story building in the heart of Baraboo, in southwest Wisconsin. The co-op members from 4,800 farm families attend annual district meetings where elections to the board of directors are held on a one person, one vote principle. The board of directors, approximately 35 to 45 representatives, select the president as well as chair of the board.

Besides district meetings, there is an annual general convention where major concerns are aired and put to a vote. Young farmers (under 35) are encouraged to become members, while current young members are involved in a special WD program to promote greater involvement in their company.

The only criterion for membership in WD is selling one's milk to the co-op. There are no contracts, annual dues, or stocks, and consequently, no single major stockholder whose voice predominates over others. However, not all who wish to join are accepted. Part of the company's efforts for greater efficiency is also its quest for higher quality. Producers of low-quality milk, either contaminated with antibiotics or bacteria, are excluded from membership. Traditionally, dairy farmers were paid for their milk based on the amount of butterfat contained. WD was one of the first co-ops in the nation to introduce cash incentives for high-quality milk in the 1970s (rather than penalizing for low quality). Researchers working with WD discovered that higher quality milk, that is, low in somatic cell counts (bacteria) and without antibiotic residues, produced superior cheese that required less milk to produce and had a longer shelf life. In 1979 only 56 percent of WD members qualified for the incentive bonus; by 1991, over 90 percent did. In 1992 members sent a record 12,000 samples of milk for lab testing before the milk was even shipped to the plant. Assistance in raising the quality of milk as well as equipment inspection are provided to members free of charge. These and other innovative strategies have been imitated widely by other dairy co-ops in the nation.

Efficiency plus a healthy cash flow and a feel for market forces have driven WD toward greater diversity, which has been the secret of the company's consistent success. Its biggest coup was the acquisition in 1984 of the Foremost whey processing plants in Wisconsin from the McKesson Corporation, based in San Francisco. This occurred just at a time when whey, a watery by-product of cheese making, was discovered to have many uses. Hundreds of uses have been developed, mainly in food processing, ice cream manufacturing, pharmaceuticals, infant formula, bakery goods, and candy. Every pound of cheese produces at least nine pounds of whey.

Historically, whey had been discarded, usually in the nearest body of water or sewage system. Concern over the environment and stricter state and federal laws in the 1970s and '80s put pressure on many businesses to find environmentally sounder means to dispose of "waste." WD's researchers began to experiment with uses for the whey. Eventually they were able to separate the valuable protein and lactose ingredients in whey and convinced the members of WD to expand into the whey business at a time when there were virtually no competitors.

With the purchase of the Foremost whey plant for only $20 million, WD gained access to many new markets. Whey and its products have replaced cheese as the mainstay of WD, and the increasing importance of whey in food processing and medicine have given WD a niche in the international market as well. In 1992 alone, WD exported whey products to over 20 countries, and the demand keeps increasing. WD has become the most important producer of whey protein concentrate in the country and is second (12 percent market share) in the production of lactose; at least half of WD's annual profit is derived from whey. WD plants turn out at least 26 whey and 11 lactose products and blends for the domestic and international markets.

While federal government price supports for agriculture have been in force since the New Deal, wholesale deregulation under the administration of President Ronald Reagan threatened to reduce and even eliminate dairy price supports. Dairy farmers have had to face the reality of continuous erosion of this "minimum wage" standard in farming. Although most of its business and profit are derived from competition on the free market, WD has always been a forceful advocate for the continuation of these critical price supports that help sustain the medium-sized, family-run farm, the bedrock of Wisconsin Dairies.

WD's efficient management and streamlined, market-oriented manufacturing operations have made the company the envy of many dairy co-ops, but it has not been without its share of problems. In the early 1990s a recession brought a significant drop in profitability, and WD faced its first ever labor dispute, which resulted in a strike in one of its cheese plants. Dozens of mergers over the years enabled WD to enter the ranks of Fortune 500 companies as one of the largest manufacturers in the United States, but bigger did not always spell better. There were signs that some of its farmer members were beginning to object to WD's growing elite of technicians, market specialists, and researchers. To offset these problems, the co-op took new steps to fine tune its business. WD's trend toward growth gave way in the early 1990s to expansion of a different sort, "strategic alliances" with non-member co-ops which had the same needs and shared the same goals (such as the agreement among WD and three other co-ops to save money by shipping their milk to the nearest plant).

WD suffered financially during the recession of the 1990s and had its share of headaches typical to a modern company. Even so, it maintained its forward-looking, highly motivated membership, and with international markets providing increasingly large and profitable outlets for its diverse array of products, it was expected to remain a strong force in the world dairy industry.

Further Reading: "Wisconsin Dairies: Its Name Spells Success," *Capital Times* (Madison, WI), April 28, 1983; Bergquist, Lee, "State Farm Cooperative Bucks Trend and Grows," *Milwaukee Sentinel,* January 8, 1985; Dryer, Jerry, "Cooperative Business Tactics Lead to High Protein Profits," *Corporate Report,* 1986; Martin, Chuck, "Milk Firms Feel Urge to Merge," *Wisconsin State Journal,* August 23, 1987; "Where There's a Will, There's a Whey," *Dairy Foods,* January, 1988; "Movers and Shakers: An Exclusive Round-Up of Leading Dairy Companies," *Dairy Foods,* April, 1988; "The Beginning of Wisconsin Dairies," *Dairy Express,* 1988; "Milk Quality and Customer Satisfaction," *Dairy Illustrated,* summer, 1991; Kimbrell, Wendy and Clem Honer, "Efficiency Experts (at Wisconsin Dairies, efficiency that results in top-quality, consistent dairy products and ingredients is the name of the game)," *Dairy Field,* March, 1992; Smith, Rod, "WD Emphasizes Need for 'Financial Fitness,' " *Feedstuffs,* August 3, 1992; Flaherty, Mike, "Whey, Once a Waste, Now Worth Millions," *Wisconsin State Journal,* August 16, 1992; *Annual Report: Wisconsin Dairies,* Baraboo, Wisconsin Dairies, 1992.

—Sina Dubovoj

Wm. **WRIGLEY** *Jr. Company*

WM. WRIGLEY JR. COMPANY

410 North Michigan Avenue
Chicago, Illinois 60611
U.S.A.
(312) 644-2121
Fax: (312) 644-7879

Public Company
Incorporated: 1919
Employees: 6,400
Sales: $1.29 billion
Stock Exchanges: New York
SICs: 2067 Chewing Gum

The Wm. Wrigley Jr. Company controls almost half the market for chewing gum in the United States. For nearly 90 years the company has maintained a narrow brand line, consisting mainly of Wrigley's Spearmint, Juicy Fruit, and Doublemint gum, promoting these brands with extremely wholesome images. In recent years the company has introduced a wider variety of flavors, but has resisted the urge to diversify into products other than chewing gum. As a result, to many, the name Wrigley means chewing gum.

William Wrigley Jr. (who never used a comma in his name) began his career in business as a mischievous teenager in Philadelphia during the 1870s. After running away from home at the age of 11 and suffering through repeated expulsions from school, the young Wrigley reportedly was told by his father after a pie throwing incident, "Your school life hasn't been a success. Let's see how work strikes you."

The elder Wrigley relegated his son to work in his soap factory, giving him the job of stirring the soap vats with a large paddle. Working ten hours a day, the boy was paid only $1.50 per week. After serving a year as a soap stirrer, Wrigley won a promotion to the sales staff. Still in his teens, the junior Wrigley drove a horse-drawn wagon loaded with soap through the crowded metropolises of the northeastern United States. Peddling soap, Wrigley soon learned the importance of gentle persuasion. He learned to make friends through kind, deferential conversation and, in the process, move tons of soap.

In 1891, at the age of 29, Wrigley moved to Chicago to establish a western agency for his father's soap business. The product, however, was shunned by local merchants who complained that, priced at only five cents per box, the soap provided them with almost no profit margin. Wrigley convinced his father to double the retail price of the soap and induce sales through premiums. Wrigley purchased 65,000 cheap red umbrellas to give away with soap purchases. While the dye in the umbrellas ran when it rained, the devices succeeded in selling a lot of soap. And, while the concept required some fine tuning, the experience confirmed to Wrigley that premiums were a good idea and an effective sales aid. "Everybody likes something extra, for nothing," he once said.

At this point Wrigley decided to strike out on his own as an independent soap wholesaler. He chose to give away baking powder as a premium and, oddly, promoted soap sales with a cookbook. Before long, demand for the baking powder outstripped demand for the soap. In 1892 Wrigley abandoned the soap business altogether to concentrate on selling baking powder. But, tiring of the business, he chose not to offer soap as the premium for baking powder. Instead, he began to search for a new premium. Wrigley probably first saw chewing gum as a young soap peddler. Long in existence, gum extracted from spruce bark had been used by Native Americans as a relaxing and habit-forming pastime.

Gum in the 1890s was still extracted from spruce gum and from paraffin, a tasteless and odorless waxy petroleum product that refused to be chewed down. These primitive gums could hold flavoring agents, such as licorice extracts, but became tasteless globs after only a few minutes of energetic chewing. At the time, only about a dozen gum companies existed. After conducting some research, Wrigley suggested to his supplier, Zeno Manufacturing, that it try making gum with chicle, a coagulated latex extract from tropical sapodilla trees. Until this time, chicle was used primarily in the manufacture of rubber.

As with the soap before it, demand for the new chicle-based "chewing candy" outstripped demand for the baking powder. In 1909 Wrigley bought out Zeno and merged the two companies into the Wm. Wrigley Jr. Company. The new company introduced two new brands to the market. The brand Vassar was targeted to women, while Lotta Gum was intended for the general market. In 1893 the company rolled out Wrigley's Spearmint, a cool minty gum that freshened the breath, and later that year introduced a sweeter fruit flavored gum called Juicy Fruit.

Juicy Fruit, first packaged in a pale grey wrapper with red lettering (the distinctive yellow package did not appear until after World War II), stood out from other brands, and the fruit extracts used in Juicy Fruit held their flavor in the chicle gum. Wrigley's Spearmint, meanwhile, was wrapped in a solid white package. Both brands, wrapped five sticks to a package, featured a design that clearly identified the gums as a Wrigley product. And both brands proved so popular that Wrigley soon found no reason to continue manufacturing Vassar or Lotta Gum.

In 1899 Wrigley was invited to join six other chewing gum manufacturers who were banding together to form a trust. He refused, and soon found himself engaged in a nearly ruinous competition with them. As he himself was once a wholesaler, Wrigley understood the importance of supporting his retailers.

Convinced that he could extend the application of premiums to dealers, Wrigley gave them free coffee grinders, cash registers, scales, lamps and other appliances. Having won their respect, if not their allegiance, Wrigley found it that much easier to foist Wrigley display cases upon retailers. But, despite his best efforts, sales remained flat. He gambled on two expensive, but ineffective, advertising campaigns—each costing in excess of $100,000—and when even these had no effect, he was left broke.

The financial panic of 1907, a drawn-out recessionary crisis that largely evaporated the demand for advertising, presented Wrigley with another opportunity to gamble. Still broke but finding advertising rates deeply discounted, Wrigley borrowed $250,000 and in three days purchased advertising space that would otherwise have cost him $1.5 million. This scale of advertising, he reasoned, would cause a reaction among consumers.

Striking quickly, with his competitors still shy from the recession, Wrigley timed his advertising campaign to run concurrent with a new dealer promotion. He sent retailers coupons for free boxes of Wrigley's Spearmint, redeemable from Wrigley distributors. When the dealers redeemed their coupons, they made themselves known to the distributors, who assembled a valuable list of retailers and methodically built relationships with them. Wrigley implored his salesmen always to be pleasant, patient, and on time, and never to argue.

In advertising, his now famous credo was, "Tell 'em quick and tell 'em often." The simple messages of his campaign, and the complex strategy behind it, were highly successful. In a matter of weeks Wrigley had grown its market from the Midwest to the entire nation. By 1910, as sales increased from $170,000 to more than $3 million, Wrigley's Spearmint became the largest-selling brand in the nation.

Looking for additional markets, Wrigley turned its attention to other English-speaking foreign markets. In Great Britain, however, the practice of chewing gum was held in low esteem. In fact, it was viewed as a guttural habit every bit as distasteful as chewing tobacco. Instead, the company turned to other British dominions and established factories in Canada in 1910 and in Australia in 1915.

Wrigley maintained a few other minor brands of chewing gum, including Sweet 16, Licorice, Pepsin, Blood Orange, Pineapple, Banana, and Lemon Cream. But lacking the marketing muscle and, consequently, the popularity of the flagship brands, these flavors gradually were phased out. In 1914, fearing stagnation in the product line, Wrigley added a new peppermint flavor, Doublemint. Wrapped in a bold green package—but with a two headed arrow logo—the new brand has been touted as "double strength," "double good," and "double distilled."

To keep the Wrigley name in the public consciousness, Wrigley bought huge public billboards, upon which he plastered his simple advertising messages: "Doublemint, Double Good" and "Chew Juicy Fruit." After 1930 Doublemint was promoted consistently with twins, double images, and even a double-talking radio comedian. Wrigley sponsored the Lone Wolf radio show, and created a fictitious Indian tribe in which more than 100,000 children were members. And in one spectacular stunt,

and possibly the birth of direct marketing, Wrigley mailed a complimentary four-stick package of gum to every household in the United States with a telephone. People with telephones, he reasoned, could afford gum. These activities helped to sustain Wrigley's gum as established national brands. They also made him very rich, particularly after taking the company public in 1919.

With his profits, Wrigley purchased a share in the Chicago Cubs baseball team in 1916 and, after buying out his partners' interests in the team, collected the talent needed to win the pennant in 1929. Before his death in 1932, and with astounding foresight, he purchased Catalina Island near Los Angeles and developed it into a major tourist attraction. These endeavors helped to keep the Wrigley family in good financial health through the difficult years of the Great Depression.

As the economy slowly recovered from the hardships of the crisis, Wrigley maintained its strong position in the market under the leadership of Wrigley's only son, Philip K. Wrigley. The company made headway into the British market, establishing a factory there in 1927 and introducing a pellet-shaped brand of gum. Called P.K, the brand was named for the company's slogan, "Packed tight, Kept right," not for Philip Wrigley's initials as many had claimed.

The company, however, entered a potentially disastrous era as the United States escalated its involvement in the war in Europe. After the Japanese bombing on Pearl Harbor, the company found shipping unavailable and quality ingredients in increasingly short supply. Production of all three brands of gum had to be severely scaled back, and then all that could be manufactured was sent to the armed forces, whose use of the gum reportedly helped to relax and revitalize them.

Left only with inferior ingredients, the company in 1944 introduced a temporary brand called Orbit. Admitting that the brand was not up to its standards, Wrigley was secure in the knowledge that Orbit would disappear when the company could again sell its premium brands. To avoid confusion or consumer dissatisfaction, Wrigley gave the new gum an entirely different package design that did not include the trademark arrow.

Soon, however, Wrigley found it impossible to produce its premium brands even for the military. For the remainder of the war, the company produced only Orbit, but continued to advertise its regular brands. In billboard and print advertisements, the company featured an empty Wrigley's Spearmint wrapper with the caption, "Remember this wrapper!" The campaign was so successful that when the war ended and the brands were reintroduced (and production of Orbit ceased), pent up demand caused consumption of Wrigley's Spearmint, Doublemint, and Juicy Fruit to exceed prewar levels.

Dedicated to maintaining the value of the company's brands to consumers, Wrigley insisted that the price of the product be held at five cents per package. This was in keeping with William Wrigley's business credo that restraint in regard to immediate profits was not only the company's most profitable policy but probably the company's only profitable policy.

By holding the line against price increases, Wrigley built strong dealer confidence in his brands and held his raw materials suppliers to more stable terms. But this was only possible because the company dominated the market for chewing gum and was able to incorporate newer, more efficient production and distribution methods. In time, Wrigley's competitors were forced to raised the price of their products. This won the company even greater loyalty from retailers and convinced many consumers to abandon their brands for Wrigley.

In 1962, dissatisfied with low sales in Britain, Wrigley launched an educational advertising campaign aimed at ending the social prejudice against gum chewing. In an effort to illustrate circumstances in which gum chewing was not socially unacceptable, the company ran a series of advertisements over the tagline, "Certainly not!" The advertisements featured barristers, businessmen, and students in scenarios where gum chewing might offend others. The advertisements were taken so seriously by the British public that many wrote to the company demanding to know when and where they could chew gum. The campaign was altered to depict acceptable circumstances for using the product, and sales began to climb.

In 1971, after charging only five cents for his product for more than 50 years, Wrigley was no longer able to extract greater efficiency from its operation. Philip Wrigley was painfully aware of price sensitivity. His father often told his managers, "We are a five-cent business, and no one in this company can afford to forget it." And so, with great consternation but no alternatives, the company raised the price of its five-stick packages from five to seven cents. Inflationary pressures brought on by the oil crisis in the early 1970s inevitably forced the company to institute additional price increases in the years that followed.

By 1974 these price increases eroded the price advantage Wrigley brands held over competitors. Upstarts such as sugar-free Trident and cinnamon-flavored Dentyne began to win market share from Wrigley brands. To meet this competition, Wrigley introduced Freedent, which had the admirable quality of not sticking to dental work. In 1976 the company rolled out Big Red, a cinnamon gum slightly hotter and in a larger stick than Dentyne. Both new brands, the first in years, came in Wrigley-style packages.

In an attempt to stave off Trident and other popular sugar-free gums, Wrigley introduced its own sugar-free brand in 1977, giving it the World War II-era name Orbit. But after xylitol, the artificial sweetener used in Orbit, was declared carcinogenic, sales of Orbit plummeted and the brand was withdrawn. Also in 1977 Philip Wrigley died. His son, named William Wrigley, assumed leadership of the company after having served as president since 1961.

Under the new Wrigley, the company began an effort to win greater market share among teen and adolescent age groups and introduced Hubba Bubba in 1979. This gum, which boasted zeppelin-sized bubbles, encountered strong competition from Bubblicious and Bubble Yum, whose manufacturers outspent Wrigley on promotion. Amidst declining sales, Hubba Bubba was transferred to Amurol, a subsidiary of the Wrigley Company. But in the 1980s Wrigley found success with new products; the company re-entered the battle for sugar-free gum chewers in 1984 when it introduced Extra, a brand sweetened with aspartame that soon gave birth to its own extensions. Over a period of years, Extra became available in a half dozen flavors.

During the 1980s Wrigley returned to heavy television promotion of its brands using the single, simple slogan, "Pure chewing satisfaction." The message remained true to William Wrigley's "Tell 'em quick, tell 'em often" advice, and gave Wrigley a wholesome, super sweet image. This conservative approach was consistent with Wrigley's reputation for quality and purity. Still sensitive to the social stigma of chewing gum in public, the company did not portray people chewing gum in its advertisements until the 1980s, and for that it used a pair of attractive young female Doublemint twins.

The company's advertising agency, BBDO Chicago (located, incidentally, in the Wrigley Building), scored a relative coup with a new campaign launched in 1990. In a series of spots, Wrigley's Spearmint was positioned as an alternative to smoking in instances where smoking is not permitted. Using words such as "House Guest," "Office Policy" and "Frequent Flyer"—with the letters O and Q substituted with a red slashed circle over a cigarette—a voice-over explains, "When I can't smoke, I enjoy pure chewing satisfaction." The Wrigley advertisement broke new ground for addressing the sticky social question of smokers' and non-smokers' rights. While steering clear of judging the virtues of smoking, the advertisements suggested new ways people could use the company's product to solve a difficult situation.

While Wrigley brands have tended to carry a more staid image, the company maintained the strongest reputation in the market for quality and specialty. After more than 100 years in business, the company—now under the stewardship of the third William Wrigley—has made no attempt to diversify into different product lines. While Wrigley's Amurol subsidiary produces novelty and specialty confectionery products such as suckers and roll candy, the company has refused to venture into the food, consumer products, or chemical industries, where its major competitors, RJR Nabisco and Warner-Lambert, are most heavily concentrated.

Principal Subsidiaries: Amurol Products Company; Four-Ten Corporation; L.A. Dreyfus Company; Northwestern Flavors, Inc.; The Wrigley Company Pty., Limited (Australia); Wrigley Austria Ges.m.b.H.; Wrigley Canada Inc.; Wrigley Chewing Gum Company Ltd. (China); The Wrigley Company Limited (U.K.); Oy Wrigley Scandinavia Ab (Finland); Wrigley S.A. (France); Wrigley G.m.b.H (Germany); Wrigley N.V. (Holland); The Wrigley Company (H.K.) Limited (Hong Kong); Wrigley Hungaria Ltd. (Hungary); Wrigley & Company, Ltd., Japan; The Wrigley Company (East Africa) Limited (Kenya); The Wrigley Company (Malaysia) Sdn. Bhd.; The Wrigley Company (N.Z.) Limited (New Zealand); Wrigley Scandinavia AS (Norway); The Wrigley Company (P.N.G.) Pty. Ltd. (Papua New Guinea); Wrigley Philippines, Inc.; Malayan Guttas Private Limited (Singapore); Wrigley Co., S.A. (Canary Islands); Wrigley Scandinavia AB (Sweden); Wrigley Taiwan Limited; Wrigley Ljubljana Ltd. (Slovenia); Wrigley Czechoslovakia, Ltd. (Prague, Czech Republic); Wrigley Poland, Limited (Poland).

Further Reading: ''The Wonder Story of Wrigley,'' *American Magazine,* March, 1920; ''William Wrigley Jr.,'' ''Chewing Gum,'' *Fortune,* April, 1932; ''Chewing Gum Is a War Material,'' *Fortune,* January, 1943; ''Impulse Item,'' *Wall Street Journal,* May 29, 1991; ''The Story of Chewing Gum and the Wm. Wrigley Jr. Company,'' Wm. Wrigley Jr. Company, 1992.

—John Simley

Worthington Industries

WORTHINGTON INDUSTRIES, INC.

1205 Dearborn Drive
Columbus, Ohio 43085
U.S.A.
(614) 438-3210
Fax: (614) 438-3136

Public Company
Incorporated: 1955 as Worthington Steel Company
Employees: 6,900
Sales: $974 million
Stock Exchanges: NASDAQ
SICs: 3316 Cold-Finishing of Steel Shapes; 3089 Plastics
  Products Nec; 3325 Steel Foundries Nec

Worthington Industries is one of the largest and strongest steel processors in the nation. Buying rolled steel coils from primary producers, Worthington custom processes steel to the precise specifications of more than 1,700 customers in the auto, appliance, office equipment, and other industries. Worthington, serving some 7,000 customers, has also become the leading manufacturer of pressure cylinders that hold gases, and has expanded into the production of components for freight and transit cars and the manufacture of custom plastic and precision metal parts.

Worthington's development largely reflects the determination, entrepreneurial skills, and exceptional management philosophy of founder and chairperson John H. McConnell, who has been at Worthington's helm from the start. Maintaining their golden rule—"we treat our customers, employees, investors, and suppliers as we would like to be treated"—McConnell built up a highly motivated, well-rewarded, and thus, highly productive work force.

Born in 1923 in New Manchester, West Virginia, the son of a steel worker, John McConnell went to work in the Weirton Steel Company mills when he graduated from high school in 1941. After three years of World War II Navy service in the Pacific, he attended Michigan State University under the GI Bill. Upon graduating in 1949, he returned to Weirton, this time in the sales department. Later he accepted a position at Shenango Steel, an independent company in Farrell, Pennsylvania, and in 1954 moved to Columbus, Ohio.

During this time, McConnell noticed that the major steel producers were busy building bigger mills and concentrating on large tonnage orders, and that interest in filling specialized orders was waning. Observing a growing need for custom steel processing services, he moved into this promising niche. In early 1955, McConnell set up business with a desk and phone in his basement in the Columbus suburb of Worthington, Ohio. Even before incorporation, he had landed an order from a thermometer company for a load of steel, which he could obtain from his old employer Weirton Steel for $1,800. McConnell had $1,200 cash on hand and figured Weirton would offer the customary 30-day payment terms. However, Weirton refused to offer credit to his new venture, and he had to rush to his bank for a $600 loan on his 1952 Oldsmobile to close the deal.

By June 1955, The Worthington Steel Company was incorporated. It ended its first year with five employees, $350,000 in sales, and a $14,000 profit. The company had already advanced from mere brokerage to rudimentary processing in rented quarters, with a slitting machine to cut the steel coils into specified widths. Four years later it moved into its first, 16,000 square-foot plant in Columbus. This was the forerunner of a complex that by the early 1990s encompassed 30 manufacturing facilities in 11 states and Canada.

From this simple start, Worthington rapidly expanded its capabilities so that it could, in McConnell's words, "do nearly everything [with steel] except actually melt [it] to prepare it for the customer's use." This included processing to the exact gauge, width, length, and shape, as well as providing the precise finish, temper (degree of hardness), and other characteristics desired by the customer. Thus, McConnell stated, "Worthington occupies a unique niche between the integrated mills, which concentrate on large, standard orders, and the metal service centers, which generally have limited processing capabilities."

The company changed its name from Worthington Steel to Worthington Industries in 1971 to mark its first diversification step: the purchase of the small, unprofitable pressure cylinder business of Lennox Industries. This operation became profitable the first year under the Worthington banner, and, before the decade was over, Worthington had become the leader in low pressure cylinders, such as propane tanks for barbecue grills. Through its cylinder business, Worthington later established a Canadian foothold in 1988 with the acquisition of Metal Flo Corp. Canada Ltd. in Guelph, Ontario, which the company renamed Worthington Cylinders of Canada.

Another diversification step was the 1978 acquisition of U-Brand Corporation which made malleable iron, plastic, and steel pipe fittings, sold through hardware and plumbing supply stores. While U-Brand generally showed moderate profits, Worthington eventually came to regard the U-Brand product lines and marketing approach as too unlike its other lines, and sold the unit to Mueller Brass. The following year Worthington purchased Advanced Coating Technology, which specialized in architectural reflective glass, a process that involved applying a steel coating to glass. As with U-Brand, Worthington later sold this operation.

More significant was the company's 1980 merger with Buckeye International, Inc., which allowed steel processor Worthington to enter into what would become its two other major business segments: plastic and metal custom products and steel castings. Molded plastic products, sold mostly to automakers, included items ranging from air conditioning louvers to dashboard assemblies, but also had applications in cellular phones, hand tools, appliances, and a wide variety of other products. Precision metal parts, similarly marketed primarily to automakers, included components of antilock brakes, power steering, and transmissions.

The primary attraction for Worthington, however, was Buckeye's position as one of the largest producers of steel castings. Worthington maintained the Buckeye name for the castings division of the business, which had applications in the production of couplers for freight cars and the increasingly profitable undercarriages for rapid transit cars.

Besides Buckeye, two 1980 acquisitions added further specialized skills to the steel castings division, Capital Die, Tool and Machine Company and I. H. Schlezinger & Sons. Capital Die designed and built specialized machinery in its tool and die plant, while marketing its services to outside customers. I. H. Schlezinger was a processor of recyclable metals.

In 1984 Worthington acquired National Rolling Mills of Malvern, Pennsylvania, which made the steel grids used in suspended ceiling systems, this business was later transferred to a joint venture with floor and ceiling products leader Armstrong World Industries, forming the acronym "WAVE" for Worthington Armstrong Venture.

Worthington started on the joint venture track in 1986 when it teamed with U.S. Steel to form Worthington Specialty Processing in Jackson, Michigan, already the site of a Worthington steel processing plant. This operation processed wide sheet steel for such uses as outer door panels in cars and appliances. Worthington entered several other joint ventures in the late 1980s. It teamed with two Japanese companies—Nissen Chemical and Sumitomo—in 1988 to form London Industries, based in London, Ohio, which made molded plastic parts for Honda and a number of other foreign companies with U.S. production facilities.

A source of major growth for the company was in cylinders and other equipment used to recover and recycle refrigeration gases. By federal law, these chemical refrigerants were required to be reclaimed during repair or replacement of air conditioning and refrigeration systems. Other promising new lines included cylinder kits for helium party balloons as well as compressed air tanks. A plant was opened in Jefferson, Ohio, in 1991 that extended the company's cylinder product line to large cylinders that could store fuel for homes situated away from gas lines. The acquisition in early 1992 of Alabama-based North American Cylinders moved Worthington into acetylene cylinders (important in welding) and high-pressure tanks. Worthington also sees growing markets for its cylinders outside North America.

Worthington's ways have generally led to steadily higher financial results. In its first year as a public company, the fiscal year ended May 1969, Worthington reported sales of $21 million and net earnings of $460,000. Sales then rose uninterrupted through the fiscal year ended May 1989, when they reached $939

million. After recessionary setbacks during the next two years, sales recovered in fiscal 1992 and were expected to top $1 billion in the May 1993 year. Earnings followed a similar path, setting new records every year except for 1982, until they encountered the slowdowns of 1990 and 1991. Earnings improved in 1992, and the May 1993 fiscal year was expected to top the fiscal 1988 record of $63 million. Worthington stock was originally offered to the public in 1968 at $7.50 a share. Through a series of stock dividends and stock splits, 100 original shares have multiplied into more than 4,800 shares, worth a total of $110,000 at the start of 1993.

As he approached his 70th birthday in May 1993, enthusiastic founder and CEO John H. McConnell gave no indication of a desire to slow down, and he continued to stress the depth and competence of Worthington management, most of which was developed in-house. Donald H. Malenick, who started as a slitting machine operator in 1959 and worked his way up through the ranks, became president and chief operating officer in 1976. The founder's son, John P. McConnell, came to the company in 1975, and, in 1992, assumed the new position of vice chairperson, with responsibility for development and oversight of emerging business opportunities. Effective June 1, 1993, John P. McConnell will assume the position of chief executive officer, while his father will continue his involvement as chairman of the board.

The elder McConnell considers the organization he has crafted to be very capable. Anchored by his "golden rule" and his strong emphasis on motivation, the company remains committed to communication—accessibility of all management from the CEO down is axiomatic—and recognition of good work, both financially and with other forms of encouragement. McConnell admitted to having little use for unions, regarding them as the result of managements that fail to meet workers' needs; by contrast, Worthington was built on a philosophy of partnership and teamwork extending to all employees.

From its inception, Worthington regularly paid all workers cash bonuses based on tonnage shipped. In 1966, to stress the importance of customer service and quell any temptation to sacrifice quality in order to rush shipments, the incentive basis was shifted to pretax profits. At the same time the production line workers were put on salary, just like office employees. The incentive plan provided workers with 40 percent or more of their annual pay. Under a separate plan, the incentive portion for managers often tops 60 percent.

Worthington has spent heavily on state-of-the-art plants and equipment. It was selected as one of five companies with "Factories that Shine" in a 1989 *Fortune* article on efforts to restore America's manufacturing leadership. Equally significant is Worthington's extensive customer service work. The company continues to be on the lookout for a wide variety of potential projects that can bring business to Worthington and improvement to the customer's operations. Plant managers spend as much as 25 percent of their time in the field. Sales personnel must first spend a few months working in the plants, so that they bring firsthand knowledge of products and operations to their talks with customers. Worthington metallurgists regularly explored with customers more efficient and cost effective means to meet their needs. They came up, for instance, with

600 WORTHINGTON INDUSTRIES, INC.

a modified automobile seat adjustment track for General Motors—Worthington's biggest customer, accounting for ten to twelve percent of volume—that resulted in savings of more than ten percent. They also suggested a change in steel composition that enabled Union Fork & Hoe Company to price its rakes more competitively, even though it meant less revenue for Worthington.

With its salary and incentive system, Worthington does not use time clocks or separate inspectors—employees carefully inspect their own work. There can be considerable peer pressure on nonperformers and new employees have to prove themselves; an employee council of nonsupervisory workers must vote to admit them to the salary plan. The team approach is credited for superior production with a rejection rate of less than one percent compared with three to five percent for the industry. Absenteeism as well as employee turnover is also exceptionally low.

Worthington also offers a high degree of job security. It has avoided layoffs during major downturns by shifting people to other parts of the company, or assigning tasks like painting, sweeping, and repairing equipment. The incentive and salary plans are not extended to the few unionized plants Worthington picked up in acquisitions; in several such plants, employees voted to decertify the unions in order to gain the team benefits.

The effectiveness of Worthington's employee policies is repeatedly cited by financial analysts in their appraisal of the company. At the same time, the company has earned acclaim from researchers more oriented toward social values. Worthington won a spot among "The 100 Best Companies to Work for in America," the 1985 compendium by Levering, Moskowitz, and Katz, and kept its place in the book's 1993 revision. Furthermore, it became one of the largest stockholdings among mutual funds requiring a positive record on environment, business ethics, employee relations, community relations, as well as financial safety and performance.

Principal Subsidiaries: The Worthington Steel Company; Worthington Specialty Processing (50%); TWB Company (50%); Worthington Cylinder Corporation; Worthington Armstrong Venture (50%); Worthington Custom Plastics, Inc.; London Industries, Inc. (60%); Worthington Precision Metals, Inc.; Buckeye Steel Castings Company.

Further Reading: McConnell, John H., . . . *And We've Only Scratched the Surface,* The Newcomen Society in North America, 1981; Robert Levering, Milton Moskowitz and Michael Katz, *The 100 Best Companies to Work for in America,* New American Library, 1985; Ramirez, Anthony, "Factories that Shine," *Fortune,* April; 24, 1989; Zipser, Andy, "Nerves of Steel," *Barron's,* February 24, 1992.

—Henry R. Hecht

INDEX TO COMPANIES AND PERSONS

Listings are arranged in alphabetical order under the company name; thus Eli Lilly & Company will be found under the letter E. Definite articles (The) and forms of incorporation that precede the name (A.B. and N.V.) are ignored for alphabetical purposes. Company names appearing in bold type have historical essays on the page numbers appearing in bold. Updates to entries that appeared in earlier volumes are signified by (upd.). The index is cumulative with volume numbers printed in bold type.

Castrén, Fredrik, **IV** 300
de Castro, Edson, **III** 133; **6** 234
Castro, Fidel, **I** 463; **II** 208, 345; **III** 196; **IV** 82
Castrol Ltd., **IV** 382–83
Castronovo, Valerio, **I** 163
Casual Corner, **V** 207–08
Catacosinos, William J., **V** 654
CATCO. *See* Crowley All Terrain Corporation.
Catell, Robert B., **6** 457
Cater, J.R., **I** 241
Cater, Richard, **6** 80
Caterpillar Belgium S.A., **III** 452
Caterpillar Inc., **I** 147, 181, 186, 422; **III** **450–53**, 458, 463, 545–46
Caterpillar of Canada Ltd., **III** 452
Caterpillar Tractor Co., **III** 450, 451–53
Caterpillar Tractor Co. Ltd., **III** 451
Cates, Louis S., **IV** 177
Cathay Insurance Co., **III** 221
Cathay Pacific Airways Limited, **I** 522; **II** 298; **6** 71, **78–80**
Cathcart, James, **III** 258
Cathcart, Silas S., **III** 519
Catherine, Queen (England), **II** 466
Catlin, Sheldon, **III** 224
Cato Oil and Grease Co., **IV** 446
Catto (Lord), **II** 428–29
Catto, Thomas (Sir), **II** 428; **IV** 685
Caudill, Bill, **6** 142
Caudill Rowlett. *See* CRSS Inc.
Caudill Rowlett Scott. *See* CRSS Inc.
Caulo, Ralph D., **IV** 624
CAV, **III** 554–55
CAV-Bosch, **III** 555
Cavallier, Camille, **III** 677
Cavedon Chemical Co., **I** 341
Cavendish International Holdings, **IV** 695
Cavendish Land, **III** 273
Cavenham Ltd., **7** 202–03
Cawoods Holdings, **III** 735
Cawthorn, Robert, **I** 668
Caxton Holdings, **IV** 641
CB&I, **7** 76–77
CB&Q. *See* Chicago, Burlington and Quincy Railroad Company.
CBC Film Sales Co., **I** 135
CBI Industries, Inc., **7 74–77**
CBM Realty Corp., **III** 643
CBS Inc., **I** 29, 488; **II** 61, 89, 102, 129–31, **132–34**, 136, 152, 166–67; **III** 55, 188; **IV** 605, 623, 652, 675, 703; **6** **157–60 (upd.)**
CBS Records, **II** 103, 134, 177; **6** 159
CBS/FOX Company, **II** 133; **6** 158
CBS/Sony, **II** 103
CBT Corp., **II** 213–14
CBWL-Hayden Stone, **II** 450
CC Soft Drinks Ltd., **I** 248
CCH Computax, **7** 93–94
CCH Legal Information Services, **7** 93
CCS Automation Systems Inc., **I** 124
CCT. *See* Crowley Caribbean Transport.
CdF-Chimie, **I** 303; **IV** 174, 198, 525
CDI Corporation, **6 139–41**
CDMS. *See* Credit and Data Marketing Services.
CE-Minerals, **IV** 109
Ceat Cavi, **III** 434
CECOS International, Inc., **V** 750
Cedar Engineering, **III** 126
Cedarleaf, Edwin, **7** 502
Cefis, Eugenio, **I** 369; **IV** 421–22

Cegedur, **IV** 174
Celanese Corp., **I 317–19**, 347
Celestial Seasonings, **II** 534
Celite Co., **III** 706; **7** 291
Celler, Emanuel, **II** 230
Cellonit-Gesellschaft Dreyfus & Cie., **I** 317
Cellular America, **6** 300
Cellulosa d'Italia, **IV** 272
Cellulose & Chemical Manufacturing Co., **I** 317
Cellulose du Pin, **III** 677, 704
Celotex Corp., **III** 766–67
Celsius Energy Company, **6** 569
CELTEX, **I** 388–89
Celtex. *See* Pricel.
Cementia, **III** 705
Cemij, **IV** 132
Cenco, Inc., **6** 188
Cenex Cooperative, **II** 536
Cengas, **6** 313
Centel Business Systems, **6** 313
Centel Cable Television, **6** 314
Centel Communications Systems, **6** 313
Centel Corporation, **6** 312–15, 593
Centel Information Systems, **6** 313
Centerior Energy Corporation, **V 567–68**
CentraBank, **II** 337
Central and South West Corporation, **V 569–70**
Central Area Power Coordination Group, **V** 677
Central Arizona Light & Power Company, **6** 545
Central Bancorp of Cincinnati, **II** 342
Central Bank for Railway Securities, **II** 281
Central Bank of Italy, **II** 403
Central Bank of London, **II** 318
Central Bank of Oman, **IV** 516
Central Coalfields Ltd., **IV** 48–49
Central Covenants, **II** 222
Central Electric & Gas Company. *See* Centel Corporation.
Central Electric and Telephone Company, Inc. *See* Centel Corporation.
Central Finance Corp. of Canada, **II** 418
Central Foam Corp., **I** 481, 563
Central Hankyu Ltd., **V** 71
Central Hardware, **III** 530
Central Hudson Gas and Electric Company, **6** 458
Central Hudson Gas And Electricity Corporation, **6 458–60**
Central Illinois Public Service Company. *See* CIPSCO Inc.
Central Independent Television plc, 7 78–80
Central India Spinning, Weaving and Manufacturing Co., **IV** 217
Central Indiana Power Company, **6** 556
Central Japan Heavy Industries, **III** 578–79; **7** 348
Central Maine Power, **6 461–64**
Central Maloney Transformer, **I** 434
Central Mining and Investment Corp., **IV** 23, 79, 95–96, 524, 565
Central National Life Insurance Co., **III** 463
Central Pacific Railroad, **II** 381
Central Planning & Design Institute, **IV** 48
Central Public Service Corporation, **6** 447
Central Soya Company, Inc., 7 81–83
Central Soya Feed Co., **7** 82

Central Telephone & Utilities Corporation, **6** 313–14. *See also* Centel Corporation.
Central Telephone Company, **6** 312–13. *See also* Centel Corporation.
Central Terminal Company, **6** 504
Central Transformer, **I** 434
Central Trust Co., **II** 313
Central Union Trust Co. of New York, **II** 313
Central West Public Service Company. *See* Centel Corporation.
Centre de Dechets Industriels Group, **IV** 296
Centre Lait, **II** 577
Century Bank, **II** 312
Century Savings Assoc. of Kansas, **II** 420
Century Tool Co., **III** 569
Century 21 Real Estate, **I** 127; **II** 679; **III** 293
CEPCO. *See* Chugoku Electric Power Company Inc.
CEPSA. *See* Compañia Española de Petroleos S.A.
CEPSA Compania Portuguesa, **IV** 397
Cera Trading Co., **III** 756
Cerberus Limited, **6** 490
Cereal Industries, **II** 466
Cerebos, **II** 565
Cerex, **IV** 290
Cermalloy, **IV** 100
Cerro Corp., **IV** 11, 136
Cerro de Pasco Corp., **IV** 33
CertainTeed Corp., **III** 677–78, 621
CertainTeed Products Corp., **III** 762
Cerveceria Polar, I 230–31
Cessna, **III** 512
Cetus, **I** 637; **III** 53; **7** 427
Cevallos, Rodrigo Borja, **IV** 510–11
Ceylan, Rasit, **IV** 563
CF AirFreight, **6** 390
CF Industries, **IV** 576
CFM. *See* Compagnie Française du Méthane.
CFP. *See* Compagnie Française des Pétroles.
CFP (Algérie), **IV** 560
CFS Continental, **II** 675
CG&E. *See* Cincinnati Gas & Electric Company.
CGCT, **I** 563
CGE, **II** 117
CGM. *See* Compagnie Générale Maritime.
CGR-MeV, **III** 635
Chace, Kenneth V., **III** 213–14
Chace, Malcolm, **V** 662
Chaco Energy Corporation, **V** 724–25
Chadbourne, H.W., **IV** 164
Chadwick's of Boston, **V** 197–98
Chaffee, Roger, **I** 79
Chalandon, Albin, **IV** 546–47; **7** 484
Challenge Corp. Ltd., **IV** 278–79
Chalmers, Floyd S., **IV** 639
Chamberlain, Joseph, **III** 493
Chamberlain, Neville, **I** 81
Chambers, Anne Cox, **IV** 596–97
Chambers, Maurice R., **III** 529–30
Chambers, Sydney, **I** 287
Champin, Marcel, **IV** 558
Champion Coated Paper Co., **IV** 263
Champion Engineering Co., **III** 582
Champion Fibre Co., **IV** 263
Champion International Corporation, **III** 215; **IV 263–65**, 334
Champion Paper and Fibre Co., **IV** 263–64

Champion Spark Plug Co., **II** 17; **III** 593
Champion Valley Farms, **II** 480
Champlin Refining and Chemicals, Inc., **IV** 393
Chance Bros., **III** 724–27
Chance Vought Aircraft Co., **I** 67–68, 84–85, 489–91
Chancellor, Christopher (Sir), **IV** 259, 669
Chanco Medical Industries, **III** 73
Chandler, Alfred D., Jr., **I** 330; **III** 626; **IV** 379
Chandler, Colby H., **III** 476–77; **7** 162
Chandler Evans, **I** 434
Chandler, Marvin, **6** 529
Chandon de Briailles, Pierre-Gabriel, **I** 271
Chang, C.S., **I** 184
Channel Master, **II** 91
Chapin, Dwight, **I** 20
Chaplin, Charlie, **I** 537; **II** 146–47
Chapman, Alvah H., Jr., **IV** 629–30
Chapman, Frank, **7** 466
Chapman, James C., **III** 599–600
Chapman, Joseph, **7** 87
Chapman, William, **V** 124
Chapman, William H., **V** 641
Chargeurs, 6 373–75
Chargeurs Réunis, **6** 373–74, 379
Charisma Communications, **6** 323
Charles A. Eaton Co., **III** 24
Charles B. Perkins Co., **II** 667
Charles Hobson, **6** 27
Charles I, Emperor (Hapsburg), **III** 207
Charles I, King (Spain), **IV** 527
Charles II, King (England), **II** 466
Charles III, King (Spain), **IV** 527
Charles Luckman Assoc., **I** 513
Charles of the Ritz Group Ltd., **I** 695–97; **III** 56
Charles Pfizer Co., **I** 96
Charles Phillips & Co. Ltd., **II** 677
Charles Schwab, **II** 228
Charles Scribner's Sons, **7** 166
Charles VI, King (Hapsburg), **III** 206
Charleston Consolidated Railway, Gas and Electric Company, **6** 574
Charleston Electric Light Company, **6** 574
Charleston Gas Light Company, **6** 574
Charlestown Foundry, **III** 690
Charley Brothers, **II** 669
Charmin Paper Co., **III** 52; **IV** 329
Charrington & Co., **I** 223
Charrington United Breweries, **I** 223
Chart House, **II** 556, 613–14
Charter Bank, **II** 348
Charter Consolidated, **IV** 23, 119–20
Charter Corp., **III** 254
Charter Oil, **II** 620
Charter Security Life Insurance Cos., **III** 293
Chartered Bank, **II** 357
Chartered Bank of India, Australia, and China, **II** 357
Chartered Co. of British New Guinea, **III** 698
Chartered Mercantile Bank of India, London and China, **II** 298
Charterhouse Petroleum, **IV** 499
Chartwell Association, **III** 16
Chartwell Land, **V 106**
Chas. A. Stevens & Co., **IV** 660
Chase & Sanborn, **II** 544
Chase Corp., **II** 402
Chase, Harris, Forbes, **II** 402
Chase Manhattan Bank N.A., **II** 248

Chase Manhattan Corporation, **I** 123, 334, 451; **II** 202, 227, **247–49**, 257, 262, 286, 317, 385; **IV** 33; **6** 52
Chase National Bank, **II** 247–48, 256, 397, 402; **III** 104, 248
Chase, Salmon P., **II** 217, 247
Chase Securities Corp., **II** 247, 397
Chase, Stephen, **II** 382
Chasen, Melvin, **6** 199
Chassagne, Yvette, **III** 393
Chastain-Roberts, **II** 669
Chateau Cheese Co. Ltd., **II** 471
Chateau Grower Winery Co., **II** 575
Chater, Catchik Paul, **IV** 699–700
Chater, Sir Paul, **6** 498–99
Chatfield & Woods Co., **IV** 311
Chatfield Paper Co., **IV** 282
Chatham and Phenix National Bank of New York, **II** 312
Chatham Bank, **II** 312
Chattanooga Gas Company, Inc., **6** 577
Chattanooga Gas Light Company, **6** 448
Chaux et Ciments de Lafarge et du Teil, **III** 703–04
Chaux et Ciments du Maroc, **III** 703
Chavez, Cesar, **I** 243; **II** 655
Cheatham, Owen, **IV** 281
Checchi, Alfred, **6** 104–05
Cheek, Joel, **II** 531
Cheeld, Chuck, **I** 98
Cheesman, Walter Scott, **6** 558
Chef Pierre, **II** 572
Chef's Orchard Airline Caterers Inc., **I** 513
Chef-Boy-Ar-Dee Quality Foods Inc., **I** 622
Cheil Sugar Co., **I** 515
Cheil Wool Textile Co., **I** 515
Chelan Power Company, **6** 596
Chemap, **III** 420
Chemcut, **I** 682
Chemical Bank, **II** 250
Chemical Bank & Trust Co., **II** 251
Chemical Bank Home Loans Ltd., **II** 234
Chemical Bank New Jersey, **II** 252
Chemical Banking Corporation, **II 250–52**, 254
Chemical Coatings Co., **I** 321
Chemical Corn Exchange Bank, **II** 251
Chemical National Assoc., Inc., **II** 251
Chemical National Bank of New York, **II** 250–51
Chemical National Co., Inc., **II** 251
Chemical New York Corp., **II** 251
Chemical Process Co.
Chemical Process Co., **IV** 409; **7** 308
Chemical Realty Co., **II** 252
Chemical Specialties Inc., **I** 512
Chemical Waste Management, **V** 753
Chemins de fer de Paris à Lyon et à la Méditerranée, **6** 424
Chemins de fer du Midi, **6** 425
Chemins de Fer Fédéraux, **V** 519
Chemisch-Pharmazeutische AG, **IV** 70
Chemische Fabrik auf Actien, **I** 681
Chemische Fabrik Friesheim Elektron AG, **IV** 229
Chemische Fabrik vormals Sandoz, **I** 671
Chemische Fabrik Wesseling AG, **IV** 70–71
Chemische Werke Hüls GmbH. *See* Hüls A.G.
Chemurgic Corporation, **6** 148
Chemway Corp., **III** 423
Chen, Steve S., **III** 130

Chen Yaosheng, **IV** 389
Chenery, Christopher T., **6** 577
Cheng, Yu Tung (Dr.), **IV** 717
Cheong, Liang Yuen, **IV** 717
Cheplin Laboratories, **III** 17
Cherokee Insurance Co., **I** 153
Cherry Co., **I** 266
Cherry Hill Cheese, **7** 429
Cherry, Wendell, **III** 81–82
Chesapeake and Ohio Railroad, **II** 329
Chesapeake and Ohio Railway, **V** 438–40
Chesebrough-Pond's, **II** 590; **7** 544
Cheshire Wholefoods, **II** 528
Chester, Colby M., **II** 531
Chester G. Luby, **I** 183
Chester Oil Co., **IV** 368
Chesterfield, Tom, **III** 670
Chetwynd (Lord), **III** 370–71
Cheung Kong (Holdings) Limited, **I** 470; **IV 693–95**
Chevalier, Alain, **I** 272
Chevalier, Maurice, **II** 155
Chevrolet Motor Division, **V** 494
Chevron Corporation, **II** 143; **IV** 367, **385–87**, 452, 464, 466, 479, 484, 490, 523, 531, 536, 539, 721
Chevron International, **IV** 563
Chevron USA Inc., **IV** 387
Cheyne, James A., **III** 358
CHF. *See* Chase, Harris, Forbes.
Chiang K'aishek, **IV** 388
Chiapparone, Paul, **III** 137
Chiba, Kazuo, **IV** 321–22
Chiba Riverment and Cement, **III** 760
Chibu Electric Power Company, Incorporated, **V 571–73**
Chicago & Calumet Terminal Railroad, **IV** 368
Chicago and Alton Railroad, **I** 456
Chicago and North Western Holdings Corporation, **6 376–78**
Chicago and North Western Railway Co., **I** 440
Chicago and North Western Transportation Company. *See* Chicago and North Western Holdings Corporation.
Chicago and Southern Airlines Inc., **I** 100; **6** 81
Chicago Bears, **IV** 703
Chicago Bridge & Iron Company, **7** 74–77
Chicago Burlington and Quincy Railroad, **III** 282; **V** 425–28
Chicago Chemical Co., **I** 373
Chicago Corp., **I** 526
Chicago Cubs, **IV** 682–83
Chicago Directory Co., **IV** 660–61
Chicago Edison, **IV** 169
Chicago Pacific Corp., **I** 530; **III** 573
Chicago Pneumatic Tool Co., **III** 427, 452; **7** 480
Chicago Radio Laboratory, **II** 123
Chicago Rock Island and Peoria Railway Co., **I** 558
Chicago Steel Works, **IV** 113
Chicago Sun-Times Distribution Systems, **6** 14
Chicago Title and Trust Co., **III** 276
Chicago Tribune. *See* Tribune Company.
Chichester, J.H.R., **III** 272
Chick, Joseph S., **6** 510
Chicopee Manufacturing Corp., **III** 35
Chief Auto Parts, **II** 661
Chiers-Chatillon-Neuves Maisons, **IV** 227
Chifley, Ben, **II** 389

Cogéma, **IV** 108
COGEMA Canada, **IV** 436
Coggeshall, James, **II** 402
Cohen, Emanuel, **II** 155
Cohen, Israel (Izzy), **II** 634–35
Cohen, John Edward (Jack), **II** 677
Cohen, Leonard, **III** 87
Cohen, Nehemiah Myer (N.M.), **II** 633–35
Cohen, Peter, **II** 450–52
Cohen, Samuel, **6** 200–01
Cohen, Stanley N., **I** 637
Cohn, Harry, **II** 135–36
Cohn, Jack, **II** 135
Coinamatic Laundry Equipment, **II** 650
Cojuangco, Antonio, **6** 106
Colaccino, Frank, **7** 113–15
Colbert, Claudette, **I** 448; **II** 155
Colbert, Jean Baptiste, **III** 675
Colbert, L.L., **I** 144
Colburn, Irwin, **III** 640
Colby, Gerard, **I** 330
Colchester Car Auctions, **II** 587
Coldwell, Banker & Company, **IV** 715; **V** 180, 182
Coldwell Banker Commercial Group, Inc., **IV** 727
Cole & Weber Inc., **I** 27
Cole, Francis W., **III** 388
Cole, Glen W., **III** 683
Cole, Walton, **IV** 669
Colebrook, James, **III** 370
Coleco Industries, **III** 506
Coleman & Co., **II** 230
Coleman Co., **III** 485
Coleman, James, **I** 244; **7** 156
Coleman, John, **III** 165; **6** 281
Coleman, Thomas, **I** 328
Coles, **V** 35
Coles, A.W., **V** 33
Coles Book Stores Ltd., **7** 486, 488–89
Coles, E.B., **V** 33
Coles, Fossey, **V** 35
Coles, George James, **V** 33
Coles Myer Ltd., **V** 33–35
Colgate & Co., **III** 23
Colgate, Bayard, **III** 23
Colgate, Bowles, **III** 23
Colgate, Samuel, **III** 23
Colgate, William, **III** 23
Colgate-Palmolive Company, **I** 260; **II** 672; **III** 23–26; **IV** 285
Colgate-Palmolive-Peet, **III** 23
Colijn, H, **IV** 132
Colin, Oswaldo R., **II** 199
College Construction Loan Insurance Assoc., **II** 455
Collegiate Arlington Sports Inc., **II** 652
Collender, H.M., **III** 442
Collett Dickenson Pearce, **I** 33
Collier, Abram, **III** 313–14
Collier, Geoffrey, **II** 428
Collier, Harry, **IV** 537
Collin, Fernand, **II** 304–05
Collins & Aikman Corp., **I** 483
Collins, Jack W., **III** 21, 22
Collins, Jackie, **IV** 672
Collins Radio, **III** 136
Collins, Ron, **6** 15
Collins, Sammy, **IV** 66–67; **7** 123–24
Collinson, Joseph, **I** 530
Collomb, Bertrand, **III** 705
Collyer, John L., **V** 232
Colman, James, **II** 566
Colman, Jeremiah, **II** 566; **III** 233

Colo-Macco. *See* CRSS Inc.
Colodny, Edwin, **I** 131–32; **6** 131–32
Cologne Reinsurance Co., **III** 273, 299
Colonia, **III** 273, 394
Colonial & General, **III** 359–60
Colonial Air Transport, **I** 89, 115
Colonial Airlines, **I** 102
Colonial Bancorp, **II** 208
Colonial Bank, **II** 236
Colonial Food Stores, **7** 373
Colonial Insurance Co., **IV** 575–76
Colonial Life Assurance Co., **III** 359
Colonial Life Insurance Co. of America, **III** 220–21
Colonial Penn Life Insurance Co., **V** 624
Colonial Stores, **II** 397
Colonial Sugar Refining Co. Ltd., **III** 686–87
Colony Communications, **7** 99
Colorado Belle Casino, **6** 204
Colorado Cooler Co., **I** 292
Colorado Electric Company. *See* Public Service Company of Colorado.
Colorado Interstate Gas Co., **IV** 394
Colorcraft, **I** 447
Colorfoto Inc., **I** 447
Colson Co., **III** 96; **IV** 135–36
Colt Industries Inc., **I** 434–36, 482, 524; **III** 435
Colt, S. Sloan, **II** 230
Columbia, **II** 135
Columbia Broadcasting System. *See* CBS Inc.
Columbia Chemical Co., **III** 731
Columbia Electric Street Railway, Light and Power Company, **6** 575
Columbia Forest Products, **IV** 358
Columbia Gas & Electric Company, **6** 466. *See also* Columbia Gas System, Inc.
Columbia Gas Light Company, **6** 574
Columbia Gas of New York, Inc., **6** 536
Columbia Gas System, Inc., **V** 580–82
Columbia Gas Transmission Corporation, **6** 467
Columbia House, **IV** 676
Columbia Insurance Co., **III** 214
Columbia News Service, **II** 132
Columbia Paper Co., **IV** 311
Columbia Phonograph, **II** 132
Columbia Phonograph Broadcasting System, **II** 132
Columbia Pictures Corp., **II** 135
Columbia Pictures Entertainment, Inc., **II** 103, 134, **135–37**, 170, 234, 619; **IV** 675
Columbia Pictures Television, **II** 137
Columbia Railroad, Gas and Electric Company, **6** 575
Columbia Recording Corp., **II** 132
Columbia River Packers, **II** 491
Columbia Savings & Loan, **II** 144
Columbia Steel Co., **IV** 28, 573; **7** 550
Columbian Chemicals Co., **IV** 179
Columbian Peanut Co., **I** 421
Columbus & Southern Ohio Electric Company (CSO), **6** 467, 481–82
Columbus Savings and Loan Society, **I** 536
Columbus-Milpar, **I** 544
Com Ed. *See* Commonwealth Edison Company.
Comalco Fabricators (Hong Kong) Ltd., **III** 758
Comalco Ltd., **IV** 59–61, 191. *See also* Commonwealth Aluminium Corp.

Comau, **I** 163
Combined American Insurance Co. of Dallas, **III** 203
Combined Casualty Co. of Philadelphia, **III** 203
Combined Communications Corp., **II** 619; **IV** 612; **7** 191
Combined Insurance Co. of America, **III** 203–04
Combined International Corp., **III** 203–04
Combined Mutual Casualty Co. of Chicago, **III** 203
Combined Registry Co., **III** 203
Combustiveis Industriais e Domésticos. *See* CIDLA.
Comcast Corporation, **7** 90–92
Comdor Flugdienst GmbH., **I** 111
Comer Motor Express, **6** 370
Comerco, **III** 21
Comet, **II** 139; **V** 106–09
Cometra Oil, **IV** 576
Comfort, Harold W., **II** 472
Cominco, **IV** 75, 141
Comitato Interministriale per la Ricostruzione, **I** 465
Comm-Quip, **6** 313
CommAir. *See* American Building Maintenance Industries, Inc.
Commander-Larabee Co., **I** 419
Commentry, **III** 676
Commerce and Industry Insurance Co., **III** 196, 203
Commerce Clearing House, Inc., **7** 93–94
Commerce Group, **III** 393
Commercial & General Life Assurance Co., **III** 371
Commercial Alliance Corp. of New York, **II** 289
Commercial Aseguradora Suizo Americana, S.A., **III** 243
Commercial Assurance, **III** 359
Commercial Bank of Australia Ltd., **II** 189, 319, 388–89
Commercial Bank of London, **II** 334
Commercial Bank of Tasmania, **II** 188
Commercial Banking Co. of Sydney, **II** 187–89
Commercial Bureau (Australia) Pty., **I** 438
Commercial Credit Corp., **III** 127–28
Commercial Exchange Bank, **II** 254
Commercial Filters Corp., **I** 512
Commercial Insurance Co. of Newark, **III** 242
Commercial Life, **III** 243
Commercial Life Assurance Co. of Canada, **III** 309
Commercial National Bank, **II** 261
Commercial National Bank & Trust Co., **II** 230
Commercial National Bank of Charlotte, **II** 336
Commercial Ship Repair Co., **I** 185
Commercial Union plc, **II** 272, 308; **III** 185, **233–35**, 350, 373; **IV** 711
Commerz- und Credit-Bank, **II** 257
Commerz- und Disconto-Bank, **II** 256–57
Commerz- und Privatbank, **II** 256
Commerzbank A.G., **II** 239, 242, **256–58**, 280, 282, 385; **IV** 222
Commerzbank Bankverein, **II** 257
Commerzfilm, **IV** 591
Commes, Thomas A., **III** 745
Commodore Business Machines Ltd., **7** 95

Epsilon Trading Corporation, **6** 81
Epstein, Max, **6** 394
Equator Bank, **II** 298
EQUICOR-Equitable HCA Corp., **III** 80, 226
Equifax Canada Inc., **6** 25
Equifax Europe, **6** 25
Equifax, Inc., 6 23–25
Equifax Insurance Systems, **6** 25
Equitable Equipment Company, **7** 540
Equitable Gas Company, **6** 493–94
Equitable General Insurance, **III** 248
Equitable Life Assurance Society of the United States, II 330; **III** 80, 229, 237, **247–49**, 274, 289, 291, 305–06, 316, 329, 359; **IV** 171, 576, 711; **6** 23
Equitable Life Leasing, **III** 249
Equitable Life Mortgage Realty Trust, **III** 248
Equitable Resources, Inc., 6 492–94
Equitable Trust Co., **II** 247, 397
Equity & Law, **III** 211
Equity Corp. Tasman, **III** 735
Equity Corporation, **6** 599
Eramet, **IV** 108
Eramet-SLN, **IV** 108
ERAP. *See* Entreprise de Recherches et d'Activités Pétrolières.
Erasco, **II** 556
Erburu, Robert, **IV** 677–78
Erdal, **II** 572
Erdölsproduktions-Gesellschaft AG, **IV** 485
Erftwerk AG, **IV** 229
Erhard, Ludwig, **IV** 193; **V** 165–66
Erhart, Charles, **I** 661
Erhart, William, **I** 96
Erho, Eino, **IV** 469
Ericson, Thorsten, **II** 2
Ericsson. *See* L.M. Ericsson.
Ericsson, Lars Magnus, **V** 334
Erie and Pennyslvania, **I** 584
Erie Railroad, **I** 584; **II** 329; **IV** 180
Erikson, Evans W., **7** 504
Eriksson, Per-Olof, **IV** 204
Eritsusha, **IV** 326
ERKA. *See* Reichs Kredit-Gesellschaft mbH.
d'Erlanger, Emile (Baron), **IV** 668
Erlick, Everett, **II** 129
Ernest Oppenheimer and Sons, **IV** 21, 79
Erni, Paul, **I** 634
Ernst & Ernst, **I** 412
Ernst, A.C., **I** 412
Ernst, Friedrich (Count of Solms-Laubach), **III** 694
Ernst, Henry, **IV** 574; **7** 551
Eroll (Lord), **IV** 259
ERPI, **7** 167
Errera-Oppenheim, Jacques, **II** 201
Erste Allgemeine, **III** 207–08
Ertan, Ismail, **IV** 563
Ertegun, Ahmet, **II** 176
Erving Distributor Products Co., **IV** 282
Erwin Wasey & Co., **I** 17, 22
Erzbergbau Salzgitter AG, **IV** 201
ES&A. *See* English, Scottish and Australian Bank Ltd.
Esanda, **II** 189
Esau, Abraham, **III** 446
ESB Inc., **IV** 112
Escambia Chemicals, **I** 298
Escamez, Alfonso, **II** 198
Escanaba Paper Co., **IV** 311
Escaut et Meuse, **IV** 227

L'Escaut, **III** 335
Escher, Alfred, **II** 267; **III** 375, 410
Escher Wyss, **III** 539, 632
Eschweiler Bergwerks-Verein AG, **IV** 25–26, 193
Escoffier Ltd., **I** 259
ESE Sports Co. Ltd., **V** 376
ESGM. *See* Elder Smith Goldsbrough Mort.
ESI Energy, Inc., **V** 623–24
Eskilstuna Separator, **III** 419
Esmark, Inc., **I** 441; **II** 448, 468–69; **6** 357
Esperance-Longdoz, **IV** 51–52
ESPN, **II** 131; **IV** 627
La Espuela Oil Company, Ltd., **IV** 81–82; **7** 186
Esquire Inc., **I** 453; **IV** 672
Esrey, William T., **V** 346
Essener Reisebüro, **II** 164
Esso
Esso, **I** 52; **II** 628; **III** 673; **IV** 276, 397, 421, 423, 432, 441, 470, 484, 486, 517–18, 531; **7** 140, 171. *See also* Standard Oil Company of New Jersey.
Esso Chemical, **IV** 439
Esso Eastern Inc., **IV** 555
Esso Exploration and Production Australia, **III** 673
Esso Exploration Turkey, **IV** 563
Esso Libya, **IV** 454
Esso Production Malaysia, **IV** 519
Esso Sirte, **IV** 454
Esso Standard, **IV** 46
Esso Standard Eastern Inc., **IV** 555
Esso Standard Sekiyu K.K., **IV** 432–33, 555
d'Estaing, Giscard, **II** 265; **IV** 618–19
Estée Lauder, **I** 696; **III** 56
Estel N.V., **IV** 105, 133
Estes, Eleanor, **IV** 622
Esteva, Pierre, **III** 393
Estlow, Edward W., **IV** 608; **7** 159
Eston Chemical, **6** 148
Etablissement Mesnel, **I** 202
Etablissement Poulenc-Frères, **I** 388
Etablissements Pierre Lemonnier S.A., **II** 532
Ethan Allen Inc., **III** 530–31
Ethicon, Inc., **III** 35
Ethyl Corp., I 334–36, 342; **IV** 289
Etimex Kunststoffwerke GmbH, **7** 141
L'Etoile, **II** 139
Etos, **II** 641
ETPM Entrêpose, **IV** 468
Euclid, **I** 147
Euler, Rudolf, **IV** 140
Euralux, **III** 209
Eurasbank, **II** 279–80
Eureka, **III** 478, 480
Eureka Insurance Co., **III** 343
Eureka Specialty Printing, **IV** 253
Eureka Tent & Awning Co., **III** 59
Euro Disney, **6** 174, 176
Euro-Pacific Finance, **II** 389
Eurobel, **II** 139; **III** 200
Eurobrokers Investment Corp., **II** 457
Eurocan Pulp & Paper Co. Ltd., **III** 648; **IV** 276, 300
Eurocard France, **II** 265
Eurocopter Holding, **7** 11
Eurocopter SA, **7** 9, 11
Eurogroup, **V** 65
Euromissile, **7** 9
Euronda, **IV** 296

Europa Metalli, **IV** 174
Europaischen Tanklager- und Transport AG, **7** 141
European and African Investments Ltd., **IV** 21
European Banking Co., **II** 186
European Banks' International Co., **II** 184–86, 295
European Coal and Steel, **II** 402
European Investment Bank, **6** 97
European Periodicals, Publicity and Advertising Corp., **IV** 641; **7** 311
European Petroleum Co., **IV** 562
European-American Banking Corp., **II** 279, 295
Europeia, **III** 403
Europemballage, **I** 600
Europensiones, **III** 348
Eurotec, **IV** 128
Eurotechnique, **III** 678
Eurovida, **III** 348
Evaluation Associates, Inc., **III** 306
Evan Picone, **III** 55
Evans, **V** 21
Evans, D. G., **6** 602
Evans, E.P., **7** 286
Evans, Harold, **IV** 652; **7** 391
Evans, Harry, **V** 59
Evans, Henry, **III** 240–41
Evans, James S., **7** 327
Evans, John J., **III** 422
Evans, Marshall, **II** 121
Evans, Maurice, **IV** 620
Evans, Mike, **I** 196
Evans, P. Wilson, **I** 373
Evans, Raymond F., **IV** 408–10; **7** 308–09
Evans, T. Mellon, **7** 286
Evans, T.R., **IV** 408; **7** 308
Evans-Aristocrat Industries, **III** 570
Eve of Roma, **III** 28
Evelyn Haddon, **IV** 91
Evelyn Wood, Inc., **7** 165, 168
Evence Coppée, **III** 704–05
Evening News Association, **IV** 612; **7** 191
L'Evèque, Edouard, **V** 441
Ever Ready Label Corp., **IV** 253
Ever Ready Ltd., **7** 209
Everaert, Pierre J., **II** 642
Everest, C.M., **IV** 463; **7** 351
Everest, Hiram Bond, **IV** 463; **7** 351
Everest, Larry, **I** 401
Everett, James, **V** 696
Everingham, Lyle, **II** 645
Eversharp, **III** 28
Evian, **6** 47, 49
Evill, William, **II** 476
Evinrude Motor Co., **III** 597–99
Evinrude, Ole, **III** 597–98
Evinrude, Ralph, **III** 598
Evinrude-ELTO, **III** 597
Evren, Kenan (Gen.), **I** 479
Ewald, Earl, **V** 672
Ewald, J.A., **III** 15
Ewaldsen, Hans, **III** 466
Ewart, Peter, **III** 359
Ewell Industries, **III** 739
Ewing, Matthew, **IV** 463; **7** 351
Ewo Breweries, **I** 469
Ex-Cell-O Corp., **IV** 297
Exacta, **III** 122
Excaliber, **6** 205
Excelsior Life Insurance Co., **III** 182
Excerpta Medica International, **IV** 610
Exchange & Discount Bank, **II** 318

Futagi Co., Ltd., **V** 96
Futagi, Hidenori, **V** 98
Futagi, Kazuichi, **V** 96
Futami, Tomio, **7** 221
The Future Now, **6** 245
Fuyo Group, **II** 274, 291–93, 391–92, 554
FWD Corporation, **7** 513
Fysh, William Hudson, **6** 109–10
Fyshe, Thomas, **II** 220

G & H Products, **III** 419
G.A.F., I 337–40, 524–25, 549; **II** 378; **III** 440
G.A. Serlachius Oy, **IV** 314–15
G&L Albu, **IV** 90
G. and T. Earle, **III** 669, 670
G&R Pasta Co., Inc., **II** 512
G.C.E. International Inc., **III** 96–97
G.C. Smith, **I** 423
G.D. Searle & Co., **I** 365–66, **686–89**; **III** 47, 53
G. H. Rinck, NV, **V** 49
G.H. Wetterau & Sons Grocery Co., **II** 681
G. Heileman Brewing Co., **I 253–55**, 270
G.I.E. Airbus Industrie, **I 41–43**, 49–52, 55–56, 70, 72, 74–76, 107, 111, 116, 121
G.L. Rexroth GmbH, **III** 566
G.P. Putnam's Sons, **II** 144
G. R. Kinney Corp., **V** 226, 352
G. Riedel Kälte- und Klimatechnik, **III** 420
G. Washington Coffee Refining Co., **I** 622
Gable, Clark, **I** 25; **II** 143, 148
Gable House Properties, **II** 141
Gabor, Eva, **III** 506
Gabor, Zsa Zsa, **III** 92
Gabriel Industries, **II** 532
Gabrielsson, Assar, **I** 209; **7** 565–66
Gabrielsson, Börje, **I** 625
GAC Corp., **II** 182; **III** 592
GAC Holdings L.P., **7** 204
Gadsen, Henry W., **I** 650
Gagarin, Yuri, **I** 79
Gage, Edwin C., **III**, **6** 365
Gage, Lyman, **II** 284
Gaherty, Geoffrey, **6** 585
Gail Borden, Jr., and Co., **II** 470
Gaillard, André, **II** 576
Gaines, Charles, **III** 167; **6** 283
Gaines Dog Food Co., **II** 531
Gainey, Daniel C., **7** 255
Gainsborough Craftsmen Ltd., **II** 569
Gair Paper Co., **I** 599
Gairns, Catherine, **II** 592
Gaisman, Henry J., **III** 27–28
Galbraith, John Kenneth, **I** 355; **IV** 252
Gale, Michael, **6** 320
Gale, Stephen F., **V** 425
Galeries Lafayette S.A., **V 57–59**
Galesburg Coulter Disc Co., **III** 439–40
Gall, Robert (Dr.), **I** 218
Gallagher, Robert, **6** 555–56
Gallaher Limited, **IV** 260; **V 398–400**
Gallaher, Tom, **V** 398
Gallatin, Albert, **II** 312
Gallatin Bank, **II** 312
Galletas, **II** 543
Gallier, Frédéric, **I** 357
Galliker, Franz, **II** 370
Gallimard, **IV** 618
Gallo. *See* E & J Gallo.
Gallo, David, **I** 244; **7** 156
Gallo, Ernest, **7** 154–56
Gallo, Joseph, **I** 242, 244; **7** 155–56

Gallo, Julio, **I** 242–44, **7** 154–56
Gallo, Robert, **I** 244; **7** 156
Gallup, George, **I** 25
Galor, **I** 676
GALP, **IV** 505
Galpin, Rodney, **II** 358
Galvanizing Co., **IV** 159
Galvin, Joe, **II** 60
Galvin Manufacturing Corp., **II** 60
Galvin, Paul, **II** 60–61
Galvin, Robert, **II** 60–62
Gamble, James, **III** 50–51, 53
Gamble, James Norris, **III** 50–51
Gamble, Theodore, **7** 429–30
Gamesa, **II** 544
Gamlestadens Fabriker, **III** 622
Gandhi, Mohandas (Mahatma), **II** 9; **IV** 218
Gandois, Jean, **I** 389–90; **IV** 174
Gandolfi, Enrico (Dr.), **IV** 422
Gang-Nail Systems, **III** 735
Gannett Co., Inc., **III** 159; **IV 612–13**, 629–30; **7 190–92 (upd.)**
Gannett, Frank, **IV** 612–13; **7** 190–91
Gannett National Service, **IV** 612
Gannett News Service, **IV** 612
Gannett Outdoor, **IV** 612
Gant, **II** 572
Gantt, H.L., **IV** 622
Gantz, William H., **I** 629
Gaon, Benny, **II** 48
Gap, Inc., **V 60–62**
Garberding, Larry, **6** 531
Garbo, Greta, **II** 143
Gardenia, **II** 587
Gardiner, Gregory John, **7** 252–53
Gardini, Raul, **IV** 422
Gärdlund, Torsten, **III** 425
Gardner Advertising. *See* Wells Rich Green BDDP.
Gardner, LeRoy U. (Dr.), **III** 707; **7** 292
Gardner Merchant, **III** 104
Gardner, Walter, **IV** 140
Gardner-Denver Co., **II** 16
Garfield, James R., **IV** 428
Garlock, **I** 435
Garner, James, **II** 173
Garnier, **III** 47
Garnier, Jules, **IV** 107
A.B. Garnisonen, **II** 352
Garrard Engineering, **II** 82
Garrett, David, **I** 100; **6** 82
Garrett, John W., **V** 438
Garrett Poultry Co., **II** 584
Garrett-Buchanan, **I** 412
Garrison, Walter R., **6** 139–40
Garrison, William Lloyd, **III** 312
Garros, Roland, **I** 54
Gartrell White, **II** 465
Garuda, **I** 107
Garuda Indonesia, **6 90–91**
Garvan, Francis P., **I** 698
Gary, Elbert Henry, **IV** 572–73; **7** 549–50
Gary Industries, **7** 4
Gary-Wheaton Corp., **II** 286
Gas Authority of India Ltd., **IV** 484
Gas Corp. of Queensland, **III** 673
Gas Energy Inc., **6** 457
Gas Group, **III** 673
Gas Light and Coke Company. *See* British Gas plc.
Gas Light Company. *See* Baltimore Gas and Electric Company.
Gas Machinery Co., **I** 412

Gas Service Company, **6** 593
Gas Supply Co., **III** 672
Gas Utilities Company, **6** 471
Gassette, Norman T., **IV** 660
Gaston, Don F., **I** 453
Gasunie. *See* N.V. Nederlandse Gasunie.
GATC. *See* General American Tank Car Company.
Gate City Company, **6** 446
Gate City Gas Works, **6** 446
Gates, Alfred, **II** 586
Gates, Charles, **II** 586
Gates, Charles Arthur, **II** 586
Gates, Leonard, **II** 586
Gates Radio Co., **II** 37
Gates, Thomas S., Jr., **II** 407
Gates, Walter, **II** 586
Gates, William, **II** 586; **6** 257–59
Gateway Corporation Ltd., **II** 612, **628–30**, 638, 642
Gateway Foodmarkets, **II** 628
Gatliff Coal Co., **6** 583
GATX, **6 394–96**
GATX Capital Corporation, **6** 394–96
GATX Leasing, **6** 395
GATX Terminals Corporation, **6** 394, 396
Gaucher, Michel, **II** 664
Gaudette, Francis J., **6** 260
Gaughler, Mr., **I** 301
de Gaulle, Charles, **I** 44–45, 189; **III** 122; **IV** 544–46, 559; **7** 481–84
Gault, Stanley C., **III** 614; **V** 248
Gaumont-British, **II** 157–58
Gauntlet Developments, **IV** 724
Gauntlett, John, **III** 737
Gauthier, C. J., **6** 529–31
Gavilan Computer Corp., **III** 124; **6** 221
Gay-Lussac, Joseph Louis, **III** 676
Gaylord, Bill, **III** 137
Gaz de France, **IV** 425; **V 626–28**
Gaziano, Joseph P., **III** 643–45
Gazit, Giora, **II** 206
Gaztelu, Candido Velazquez. *See* Velazquez Gaztelu, Candido.
GB Papers, **IV** 290
GB-Inno-BM, **II** 658; **V** 63
GBL, **IV** 499
GCFC. *See* General Cinema Finance Co.
GDF. *See* Gaz de France.
GE. *See* General Electric Company.
GE Fanuc Automation, **III** 483
GE Solid State, **II** 39
Geach, Charles, **II** 318
Gearhart Industries, **III** 499
Gearmatic, **I** 185
Geary, John, **IV** 437
Gebauer, Antonio, **II** 331
Gebrüder Kiessel GmbH, **IV** 197
Gebrüder Sulzer Aktiengesellschaft. *See* Sulzer Brothers Limited.
Gebrüder Volkart, **III** 402
Gebrueder Ahle GmbH, **III** 581
GEC. *See* General Electric Company PLC.
GEC Alsthom Electromotors, **III** 509
Geckle, Jerome W., **V** 496
GECO, **III** 618
Geco Mines Ltd., **IV** 165; **7** 398
Geddes, Auckland (Sir), **IV** 190–91
Geddes, Ford, **V** 492
Gee, Edwin, **IV** 287
Geer Drug, **III** 9–10
GEGC, **III** 434
Geginat, Hartwig, **III** 695
GEICO Corp., **III** 214, 248, 252

Langton, Bryan, **III** 95
Langworth, Richard M., **I** 145
Lanier Business Products, Inc., **II** 39
Lanier Voice Products, **II** 39
Lanier Worldwide, Inc., **II** 39
Lanigan, Robert, **I** 610
Lanne, Adolphe, **III** 210
Lanners, Fred T., **I** 331
Lannig, Charles, **I** 382
Lano Corp., **I** 446
Lansdowne (Lord), **III** 521
Lansi-Suomen Osake-Pankki, **II** 303
Lansing, Sherry, **II** 170
Lanson Pere et Fils, **II** 475
Lanterman, Joseph B., **7** 30
Lantic Industries, Inc., **II** 664
Lantic Sugar Ltd., **II** 664
Lanvin, **I** 696; **III** 48
Lanz, Kurt, **I** 348
Lanza, A.J. (Dr.), **III** 706; **7** 291
Lanzafame, Samuel, **7** 408
LAPE. *See* Líneas Aéreas Postales
    Españolas.
Lapensky, Joseph M., **I** 113; **6** 104
Lapin, Raymond H., **II** 411
Lapine Technology, **II** 51
Laporte, **I** 303
Laporte Industries Ltd., **IV** 300
LaPorte, William F., **I** 622, 624
Large, Judson, **6** 312
Larimer, William, **II** 315
Larkin, Frederick, Jr., **II** 349
Laroche Navarron, **I** 703
Larousse Group, **IV** 615
Larousse, Pierre, **IV** 614
Larousse-Nathan, **IV** 614–15
Larroque, Louis, **I** 519; **IV** 215
Larrowe Milling Co., **II** 501
Larsen & Toubro, **IV** 484
Larsen Company, **7** 128
Larsen, Ralph S., **III** 37
Larsen, Roy E., **IV** 674; **7** 527
Larson, Elwin S., **6** 455–57
Larson, Gary, **III** 13; **6** 386
Larson, Gustav, **I** 209; **7** 565–66
Larson Lumber Co., **IV** 306
Larwin Group, **III** 231
Lasala, Joseph, **II** 316
LaSalle National Bank, **II** 184
Lasell, Chester, **II** 432
Oy Läskelä Ab, **IV** 300
Lasker, Albert, **I** 12–13, 25, 36
Lasky, Jesse, **II** 154
Lasky's, **II** 141
Lasmo, **IV** 455, 499
Lasser, J.K., **IV** 671
Lassila, Jaakko, **IV** 349
Latécoère, Pierre, **V** 471
Lathière, Bernard, **I** 41
Latrobe, Ferdinand C., **III** 395
Lattès, Jean-Claude, **IV** 617, 619
Latzer, John, **7** 428–29
Latzer, Louis, **7** 428–29
Latzer, Robert, **7** 429
Laubach, Gerald, **I** 663
Lauer, John N., **V** 233
Laughlin, James, **II** 342
Lauman, J.F., **II** 681
Laura Scudder's, **7** 429
Lauren, Ralph, **III** 55
Laurentien Hotel Co., **III** 99
Laurenzo, Vince, **III** 652
Lautenberg, Frank, **III** 117–18
de Laval, Carl Gustaf Patrik, **7** 235

de Laval, Gustaf, **II** 1; **III** 417–19
Laval, Gustaf de. *See* de Laval, Gustaf.
Lavanchy, Henri-Ferdinand, **6** 9
Laventhol, David, **IV** 678
LaVoisier, Antoine, **I** 328
Law Life Assurance Society, **III** 372
Lawn Boy, **7** 535–36
Lawrence, Harding, **I** 96–97
Lawrence, John, **III** 472
Lawrence Manufacturing Co., **III** 526
Lawrence, T.E., **I** 194
Lawrence Warehouse Co., **II** 397–98
Lawrenceburg Gas Company, **6** 466
Lawrenceburg Gas Transmission
    Corporation, **6** 466
The Lawson Co., **7** 113
Lawson, Dominic, **III** 503
Lawson Milk, **II** 572
Lawyers Trust Co., **II** 230
Laxalt, Paul, **III** 188
Lay, Beirne, **I** 486
Lay, Herman, **I** 278; **III** 136
Layton, F.D., **III** 229
Lazard Bros. & Co., **IV** 658–59
Lazard Freres, **II** 268, 402, 422; **IV** 23, 79,
    659; **7** 287, 446
Lazard Freres and Company, **6** 356
Lazarus, Charles, **V** 203–06
Lazarus, Fred, **V** 26–27
Lazarus, Hyman (Judge), **IV** 581–82
Lazarus, Ralph, **V** 26
Lazarus, Wilhelm, **III** 206
Lazell, H.G. Leslie, **III** 65–66
LBS Communications, **6** 28
LDDS Communications, Inc., **7** 336
LDX NET, Inc., **IV** 576
Le Brun and Sons, **III** 291
Le Buffet System-Gastronomie, **V** 74
Lea & Perrins, **II** 475
Lea County Gas Co., **6** 580
Lea, R.W., **III** 707; **7** 292
Lead Industries Group Ltd., **III** 681; **IV**
    108
Leadership Housing Inc., **IV** 136
Leaf River Forest Products Inc., **IV** 282,
    300
Leahy, Patrick, **III** 188
Leamington Priors & Warwickshire
    Banking Co., **II** 318
Lear Inc., **II** 61
Lear, John, **I** 662
Lear Siegler Inc., I 481–83; **III** 581
Lear Siegler Seating Corp., **III** 581
Learned, Stanley, **IV** 522
Leasco Data Processing Equipment Corp.,
    III 342–44; **IV** 641–42; **7** 311
Lease International SA, **6** 358
Leaseway Transportation, **V** 494
Leatherdale, Douglas W., **III** 357
Leavey, W.M., **IV** 708
Leblanc, Nicolas, **I** 394
Leca, Dominique, **III** 393
Lecerf, Olivier, **III** 704–05
Ledder, Edward J., **I** 619–20
Ledebur, Adolf, **IV** 156
Lederle Laboratories, **I** 300–02, 657, 684
Ledoux, Fréderic, **IV** 107
Lee, Archie, **I** 233
Lee Brands, **II** 500
Lee, Byung-Chull, **I** 515–16
Lee Company, **V** 390–92
Lee, Frank A., **6** 145–46
Lee Hecht Harrison, **6** 10
Lee, Kun-Hee, **I** 516

Lee, Kyung Hoon, **III** 458
Lee, Quo Wei, **IV** 717
Lee, Sung Won, **III** 749
Lee Telephone Company, **6** 313
Lee, W. S., **V** 601
Lee, Wallace L., **6** 447–48
Lee Way Motor Freight, **I** 278
Lee, William S., **V** 601–02
Leeds & County Bank, **II** 318
Leeds & Northrup Co., **III** 644–45
Leeman, Hermann, **I** 671–72
Lees, David, **III** 495
Lefaucheux, Pierre, **I** 189
LeFauve, Richard G., **7** 462
Lefebre, Pierre, **I** 188
Lefébure, Charles, **I** 395
Lefebvre, Andre, **7** 36
Lefebvre, Gordon, **II** 15
Lefeldt, **III** 417, 418
Lefeldt, Wilhelm, **III** 417
Lefevre, Jacques, **III** 705
Legal & General Assurance Society, **III**
    272–73
Legal & General Group plc, III 272–73;
    IV 705, 712
Legal & General Life Assurance Society,
    III 272
Legal & General Netherlands, **III** 273
Legault and Masse, **II** 664
Leggett, Will, **V** 12
Lehigh Railroad, **III** 258
Lehman Bros., **I** 78, 125, 484; **II** 259, 448
Lehman Bros. Kuhn Loeb, **II** 192, 398,
    450–51
Lehman Brothers, **6** 199
Lehman, Clarence, **7** 592
Lehman, John, **I** 59, 62, 527
Lehman, Robert, **I** 89
Lehmer Company, **6** 312. *See also*
    McGraw Electric Company.
Lehmkuhl, Joakim, **7** 531
Lehn & Fink, **I** 699
Lehnkering AG, **IV** 140
Lehr, Lewis, **I** 500
Lehrman Bros., **III** 419
Lehrman, Jacob, **II** 633–34
Lehrman, Samuel, **II** 633
Lehtinen, William, **IV** 276–77
Leigh, Claude Moss, **IV** 710–11
Leigh, Vivien, **II** 148, 175
Leigh-Pemberton, Robin, **II** 334
Leinenkugel, **I** 253
Leipsner, Steven, **7** 472–73
Leisen, Mitchell, **II** 155
Leisenring, E.B., **7** 582
Leisenring, Edward B., Jr., (Ted), **7**
    583–84
Leisure Lodges, **III** 76
Leitz, **III** 583–84
Leland, Henry, **I** 171
Leman, Paul H., **IV** 11
LeMasters, Kim, **II** 134; **6** 159
Lemmen, Harvey, **7** 331
Lena Goldfields Ltd., **IV** 94
Lenard, Phillip, **I** 349
Lenc-Smith, **III** 430
Lend Lease Corporation Limited, IV
    707–09
Lend Lease Development Pty. Ltd., **IV** 708
Lendrum, Jim, **III** 704–05
Lenhartz, Rudolf, **IV** 198
Lenin, Vladimir, **IV** 299, 480
Lennings, Manfred, **III** 563
Lennon's, **II** 628

Moran Group Inc., **II** 682
MoRan Oil & Gas Co., **IV** 82–83
Morand, Paul, **IV** 618
Morehead May, James T., **I** 399
Moreland and Watson, **IV** 208
Moret, Marc, **I** 673
Moretti-Harrah Marble Co., **III** 691
Morey, Parker, **6** 548
Morgan & Cie International S.A., **II** 431
Morgan, Bill, **I** 568
Morgan, C. Powell, **7** 95
Morgan, Cary, **I** 61
Morgan Edwards, **II** 609
Morgan, Edwin B., **II** 380
Morgan family, **III** 237
Morgan, Graham, J., **III** 763
Morgan Grampian Group, **IV** 687
Morgan Grenfell (Overseas) Ltd., **II** 428
Morgan Grenfell and Co., **II** 427
Morgan Grenfell and Co. Ltd., **II** 428
Morgan Grenfell Group PLC, **II** 280,
   329, **427–29**; **IV** 21, 712
Morgan Grenfell Inc., **II** 429
Morgan Grenfell Laurie, **II** 427
Morgan Grenfell Securities, **II** 429
Morgan Guaranty International Banking
   Corp., **II** 331
Morgan Guaranty International Finance
   Corp., **II** 331
Morgan Guaranty Trust Co. of New York,
   I 26; **II** 208, 254, 262, 329–32, 339,
   428, 431, 448; **III** 80
Morgan, Harjes & Co., **II** 329
Morgan, Henry, **II** 430–31
Morgan, J.P. & Co. Inc. *See* J.P. Morgan
   & Co. Incorporated.
Morgan, James, **7** 13
Morgan, John Pierpont (J.P.), **I** 47, 61; **II**
   229, 312, 329–32, 427, 430, 447; **III**
   247; **IV** 110, 400, 572; **V** 146; **6** 605; **7**
   261, 549
Morgan, John Pierpont, Jr. (Jack), **II** 227,
   330, 427; **IV** 573; **7** 550
Morgan, Junius Spencer, **II** 329–30,
   427–28
Morgan, Lewis, Githens & Ahn, Inc., **6**
   410
Morgan Mitsubishi Development, **IV** 714
Morgan Stanley & Co., Inc., **II** 330, 408,
   430–31
Morgan Stanley Group Inc., **I** 34; **II** 211,
   403, 406–07, 428, **430–32**, 441; **IV** 295,
   447, 714
Morgan Stanley International, **II** 422
Morgan Yacht Corp., **II** 468
Morgan's Brewery, **I** 287
Morgens, Howard, **III** 52
Morgenthau, Hans, **II** 227
Mori Bank, **II** 291
Mori, Kaoru, **V** 455
Moria Informatique, **6** 229
Morison, William, **I** 497
Morita & Co., **II** 103
Morita, Akio, **II** 5, 56, 101–03; **7** 118
Morita family, **II** 103
Morita, Ko, **IV** 656
Morita, Kuzuaki, **II** 103
Moritz, Michael, **I** 145
Morley, Roger H., **IV** 398; **IV** 637
Moro, Aldo, **IV** 586
Morohashi, Shinroku, **I** 504
Morpurgo, Edgardo, **III** 207–08
Morpurgo, Giuseppe Lazzano, **III** 206
Morrill, Albert H., **II** 643–44

Morrill, Thomas C., **III** 364
Morris, Bert, **IV** 278
Morris, David H., **7** 534–35
Morris, Donald R., **IV** 311
Morris Motors, **III** 256; **7** 459
Morris, Ray, **7** 430
Morris, Robert, **V** 712; **7** 430
Morrison, Garry, **III** 214
Morrison, Harley James, **III** 51
Morrison, Harry W., **7** 355–56
Morrison Industries Ltd., **IV** 278
Morrison Knudsen Corporation, **IV** 55; **7**
   355–58
Morrison-Knudsen Engineers, **7** 356
Morrison-Knudsen International Company,
   7 356
Morrison-Knudsen Services, **7** 356
Morrow, George, **II** 497
Morrow, Richard W., **IV** 371
Morrow, Winston V., Jr., **6** 356
Morse, Arthur, **II** 297
Morse Chain Co., **III** 439
Morse, Everett, **III** 439
Morse, Frank, **III** 439
Morse, Jeremy, **II** 309
Morse, Samuel, **6** 341
Morss and White, **III** 643
Morss, Charles A., **III** 643
Morstan Development Co., Inc., **II** 432
Mortgage & Trust Co., **II** 251
Mortgage Insurance Co. of Canada, **II** 222
Mortimer, James D., **6** 505, 601
Morton, David, **IV** 12
Morton, E. James, **III** 268
Morton Foods, Inc., **II** 502
Morton Industries, **I** 370
Morton, Joy, **I** 371
Morton, Paul, **III** 247
Morton Salt, **I** 371
Morton Thiokol Inc., **I** 325, **370–72**
MOS Technology, **7** 95
Mosby-Year Book, **IV** 678
Mosconi, Enrique (Gen.), **IV** 577
Moseley, Hallgarten, Estabrook, and
   Weeden, **III** 389
Moseley, Jack, **III** 397
Mosher, Gilbert E., **III** 171; **6** 288
Mosher Steel Company, **7** 540
Mosler Safe, **III** 664–65
Mosler Safe Co., **7** 144, 146
Mosley, Leonard, **I** 330
Mosling, Bernhard A., **7** 416–17
Mosling, John, **7** 417
Mosling, Peter, **7** 418
Mosling, Stephen, **7** 418
Moss, B.S., **II** 169
Moss, Charles, **6** 51
Mossgas, **IV** 93
Mostek, **I** 85; **II** 64
Moszkowski, George, **III** 195
Mother's Oats, **II** 558–59
Motor Haulage Co., **IV** 181
Motor Transit Corp., **I** 448
Motoren-und-Turbinen-Union, **I** 151; **III**
   563
Motoren-Werke Mannheim AG, **III** 544
Motorenfabrik Deutz AG, **III** 541
Motorenfabrik Oberursel, **III** 541
Motornetic Corp., **III** 590
Motorola, Inc., **I** 534; **II** 5, 34, 44–45, 56,
   60–62, 64; **III** 455; **6** 238; **7** 119, 494,
   533
Motorola Semiconductors Japan, **II** 61
Motown Records, **II** 145

Motoyama, Kazuo, **V** 256
Moulin, Etienne, **V** 57–59
Moulton, William H., **III** 529
Mount Isa Mines, **IV** 61
Mountain, Denis, **I** 426
Mountain Fuel Resources, **6** 568–69
Mountain Fuel Supply Company, **6** 568–69
Mountain Pass Canning Co., **7** 429
Mountain State Telephone Company, **6** 300
Mountain States Telephone & Telegraph
   Co., **V** 341
Mountain States Wholesale, **II** 602
Mountbatten (Earl), **I** 469
Mounts Wire Industries, **III** 673
Mountsorrel Granite Co., **III** 734
Moussa, Pierre, **II** 259–60
Movado-Zenith-Mondia Holding, **II** 124
Moving Co. Ltd., **V** 127
MPM, **III** 735
Mr. How, **V** 191–92
Mr. M Food Stores, **7** 373
MRC Bearings, **III** 624
Mrozek, Donald J., **I** 80
Mrs. Paul's Kitchens, **II** 480
Mrs. Smith's Pie Co., **II** 525
MS-Relais, **III** 710
MS-Relais GmbH, **7** 302–03
MSAS Cargo International, **6** 415, 417
MSU. *See* Middle South Utilities.
Mt. Carmel Public Utility Company, **6** 506
Mt. Goldsworthy Mining Associates, **IV** 47
Mt. Lyell Investments, **III** 672
Mt. Lyell Mining and Railway, **III** 673
Mt. Vernon Iron Works, **II** 14
MTC Pharmaceuticals, **II** 483
Mubarrak, Hosni, **6** 86
Mueller Co., **III** 645
Mueller, Hieronymous, **7** 359
Mueller Industries, Inc., **7** **359–61**
Mueller, Louis, **I** 96
Mueller, Paul, **I** 633
Mueller, Richard, **7** 151–52
Muhammad Reza Shah Pahlevi (Shah of
   Iran), **I** 116, 195, 530, 563; **IV** 371
Muir, Malcolm, **IV** 635
Mujirushi Ryohin, **V** 188
Mukluk Freight Lines, **6** 383
Mulberger, Lorraine, **I** 269
Mule Battery Manufacturing Co., **III** 643
Mulford, Raymond, **I** 610
Mülheimer Bergwerksvereins, **I** 542
Mulholland, William, **II** 211
Mullane, Denis F., **III** 238
Mullane, Robert, **III** 431
Muller, Edouard, **II** 547; **7** 382
Müller, Heinrich, **III** 411
Mullins, Norman, **III** 671
Mullins, Tom, **IV** 170–71
Mulroney, Brian, **II** 211; **IV** 495
Multi Restaurants, **II** 664
Multimedia, **IV** 591
Multiple Access Systems Corp., **III** 109
Multiple Properties, **I** 588
Mulvaney, William Thomas, **I** 542
Mulyono, Wage, **6** 91
Mumford, Lewis, **IV** 622
Mumford, Rufus, **6** 409
Münchener Rückversicherungs-
   Gesellschaft. *See* Munich Re.
Mundt, Ray, **I** 412–13; **III** 10
Mungana Mines, **I** 438
Munich Re, **II** 239; **III** 183–84, 202,
   299–301, 400, 747

Searle, John G., **I** 686
Searle, William L., **I** 686
Searls, Fred, **7** 385
Sears, John, **V** 177
Sears plc, V 177–79
Sears, Richard W., **V** 180
Sears, Roebuck & Co., **I** 26, 146, 516,
556; **II** 18, 60, 134, 331, 411, 414; **III**
259, 265, 340, 536, 598, 653–55; **V**
180–83; **6** 12–13; **7** 166, 479
Sears, William, **V** 177
Season-all Industries, **III** 735
SEAT. *See* Sociedad Española de
Automoviles de Turismo.
Seaton, W. Bruce, **6** 354–55
Seattle Electric Company, **6** 565
Seattle Electric Light Company, **6** 565
Seaview Oil Co., **IV** 393
Seawell, William, **I** 116
SEB-Fastigheter A.B., **II** 352
Sebart, Carl, **IV** 203
SECA, **IV** 401
de Secada, C. Alexander G., **I** 550
SECDO, **III** 618
SECO Industries, **III** 614
Second Bank of the United States, **II** 213
Second National Bank, **II** 254
Secoroc, **III** 427
Le Secours, **III** 211
SecPac. *See* Security Pacific Corporation.
Secrétan, Hyacinthe, **IV** 190
Securitas Esperia, **III** 208
Securities International, Inc., **II** 440–41
Security Connecticut Life Insurance Co.,
III 276
Security Engineering, **III** 472
Security First National Bank of Los
Angeles, **II** 349
Security National Bank, **II** 251, 336
Security Pacific Bank, **II** 349
Security Pacific Corporation, **II** 349–50,
422; **III** 366
Sedgwick Group PLC, **I** 427; **III** 280, 366
See's Candies, **III** 213
Seeburg, **II** 22; **III** 430
Seefelder, Matthias, **I** 307
Seeger Refrigerator Co., **III** 653
Seeger-Orbis, **III** 624
Seekatz, Friedrich, **I** 55
Seelig, Sam, **II** 654
SEG, **I** 463
Sega Enterprises, Ltd., **7** 396
Segawa, Minoru, **II** 439–40
Seger, Eberhardt, **III** 478
Segespar, **II** 265
Sego Milk Products Company, **7** 428
de Ségur (Comtesse), **IV** 617
Seguros El Corte Inglés, **V** 52
Seiberling, Charles, **V** 244
Seiberling, Frank A., **V** 244
Seiberling Rubber Company, **V** 244
Seibert, Charles A., **III** 220
Seibu Department Stores, **II** 273
Seibu Department Stores Kansai Co., Ltd.,
V 184–85
Seibu Department Stores, Ltd., V 184–86
Seibu Distribution Companies, **V** 187
Seibu Railway Co. Ltd., V 187, 510–11,
526
Seibu Railways Group, **V** 187
Seibu Saison, **6** 207
Seidemann, William A., **7** 479
Seidl, Alois, **III** 465
Seiffert, Hans Albrecht, **II** 164

Seijo Green Plaza Co., **I** 283
Seikatsu-Soko, **V** 210
Seiko Corporation, I 488; **III 619–21**
Seiko Epson Corp., **III** 619, 621
Seiko Instruments & Electronics Co., **III**
620
Seiko Instruments Inc., **III** 619, 621
Seiko Service Centre (Australia) Pty. Ltd.,
III 620
Seiko Time (Panama) S.A., **III** 620
Seiko Time (U.K.) Ltd., **III** 620
Seiko Time AB, **III** 620
Seiko Time Corp., **III** 620
Seiko Time GmbH, **III** 620
Seiko Time Ltda., **III** 620
Seiko Time S.A., **III** 620
Seikosha Co. Ltd., **III** 619
Seine, **III** 391
Seino Transportation Company, Ltd., 6
427–29
Seipp, Walter, **II** 257
Seismograph Service Corp., **II** 86
Seiwa Fudosan Co., **I** 283
Seiyu Group, **V** 187–88
Seiyu, Ltd., V 187–89
Seiyu Stores Kansai Ltd., **V** 188
Seiyu Stores Ltd., **V** 187–88
Seiyu Stores Nagano Ltd., **V** 188
Seki, Hiromasa, **6** 30
Seki, Hironao, **6** 29
Sekimoto, Tadahiro, **II** 68
Sekisui America Corp., **III** 742
Sekisui Chemical Co., Ltd., III 741–43
Sekisui Chemical GmbH, **III** 741
Sekisui House Industry, **III** 741–42
Sekisui International Finance, **III** 742
Sekisui Malaysia Co., **III** 741
Sekisui Products, Inc., **III** 741
Sekisui Sangyo, **III** 741
Sekisui Singapore (Private) Ltd., **III** 741
SEL, **I** 193, 463
Selby, Milton, **II** 655
Selby, Prideaux, **II** 187
Selden, **I** 164, 300
Selden, George B., **I** 164
Selection Trust, **IV** 67, 380, 565
Selective Auto and Fire Insurance Co. of
America, **III** 353
Selective Insurance Co., **III** 191
Selek, Y., **I** 478
Selenia, **I** 467; **II** 86
Self Service Restaurants, **II** 613
Selfridge, **V** 94
Selfridges, **V** 177–78
Selig, Lester, **6** 394
Selikoff, I.J. (Dr.), **III** 707; **7** 292
Sella, George, **I** 301–02
Sellars, Richard, **III** 36
Selleck Nicholls, **III** 691
Seller, Robert V., **IV** 392
Sellon, John, **IV** 117–18
Sells, Boake, **V** 173
Sells, Harold, **V** 226
Seltel, **6** 33
Selznick, David O., **II** 147–48
Semenenko, Serge, **II** 208
Seminole Electric Cooperative, **6** 583
Seminole Fertilizer, **7** 537–38
Semmoto, Sachio, **7** 118, 120
Semrau and Sons, **II** 601
SEN AG, **IV** 128
Senelle-Maubeuge, **IV** 227
Senior, John Lawson, **III** 704
Senshusha, **I** 506

Sentinel Group, **6** 295
Sentinel Technologies, **III** 38
Sentinel-Star Co., **IV** 683
Sentrust, **IV** 92
Sentry, **II** 624
Senyo Kosakuki Kenkyujo, **III** 595
Seohan Development Co., **III** 516; **7** 232
Sepa, **II** 594
AB Separator, **III** 417–19
SEPIC, **I** 330
Sept, **IV** 325
Séquanaise, **III** 391
Séquanaise IARD, **III** 392
Séquanaise Vie, **III** 392
Sequoia Insurance, **III** 270
Sera-Tec, **V** 175–76
Sera-Tec Biologicals, **V** 174–75
Seraco Group, **V** 182
Serck Group, **I** 429
SEREB, **I** 45; **7** 10
Serewatt AG, **6** 491
Sergeant Drill Co., **III** 525
Sergeant, Henry Clark, **III** 525
Serlachius, Gösta, **IV** 299, 301
Serlachius, Gösta Michael, **IV** 314–15
Serlachius, Gustaf Adolf, **IV** 314
Serlachius, R. Erik, **IV** 314
Serling, Robert J., **I** 91, 98, 103, 127
Sero-Genics, Inc., **V** 174–75
Servam Corp., **7** 471–73
Servatius, Bernhard, **IV** 590–91
Servel, Inc., **III** 479
Service America Corp., 7 471–73
Service Bureau Corp., **III** 127
Service Corporation International, 6
293–95
Service Merchandise Company, Inc., V
190–92; 6 287
Service Partner, **I** 120
Service Pipe Line Co., **IV** 370
Service Q. General Service Co., **I** 109
Service Systems, **III** 103
ServiceMaster Home Systems Service, **6** 46
ServiceMaster Industries, Inc., **6** 45
Servicemaster Limited Partnership, 6
44–46
Services Maritimes des Messageries
Impériales. *See* Compagnie des
Messageries Maritimes.
Servisco, **II** 608
ServoChem A.B., **I** 387
Servomation Corporation, **7** 472–73
Sespe Oil, **IV** 569
SET, **I** 466
Sette, Pietro, **IV** 422
Settsu Marine and Fire Insurance Co., **III**
367
Setzler, Bill, **I** 405
Seubert, Edward G., **IV** 369
Seven Arts Ltd., **II** 147
Seven Arts Productions, Ltd., **II** 176
7-Eleven. *See* The Southland Corporation.
7-Eleven Japan, **V** 88–89
Seven-Up Bottling Co. of Los Angeles, **II**
121
Seven-Up Co., **I** 245, 257; **II** 468, 477
Sevin-Rosen Partners, **III** 124; **6** 221
Sewell Coal Co., **IV** 181
Sexton, Lester, **III** 321
Seyama, Seigoro, **IV** 726
Seybold, **6** 602
Seybold, L. F., **6** 602
Seybold Machine Co., **II** 37
Seydoux, Jérôme, **6** 373–75

INDEX TO INDUSTRIES

Index to Industries

747

L'air Liquide, I
Lubrizol Corporation, I
Mitsubishi Chemical Industries, Ltd., I
Monsanto Company, I
Montedison SpA, I
Morton Thiokol, Inc., I
Nalco Chemical Corporation, I
National Distillers and Chemical
  Corporation, I
Olin Corporation, I
Pennwalt Corporation, I
Perstorp A.B., I
Rhone-Poulenc S.A., I
Rohm and Haas, I
Solvay & Cie S.A., I
Sumitomo Chemical Company Ltd., I
Union Carbide Corporation, I
Vista Chemical Company, I
Witco Corporation, I

CONGLOMERATES

AEG A.G., I
Alco Standard Corporation, I
Allied-Signal Inc., I
AMFAC Inc., I
Archer-Daniels-Midland Company, I
Barlow Rand Ltd., I
Bat Industries PLC, I
BTR PLC, I
C. Itoh & Company Ltd., I
CBI Industries, Inc., 7
Colt Industries Inc., I
Delaware North Companies Incorporated, 7
Elders IXL Ltd., I
Farley Northwest Industries, Inc., I
FMC Corporation, I
Fuqua Industries, Inc., I
Gillett Holdings, Inc., 7
Greyhound Corporation, I
Gulf & Western Inc., I
Hanson PLC, III, 7 (upd.)
Hitachi Ltd., I
IC Industries, Inc., I
Instituto Nacional de Industria, I
International Telephone & Telegraph
  Corporation, I
Istituto per la Ricostruzione Industriale, I
Jardine Matheson Holdings Ltd., I
Katy Industries, Inc., I
Kidde, Inc., I
KOC Holding A.S., I
Lear Siegler, Inc., I
Litton Industries, Inc., I
Loews Corporation, I
LTV Corporation, I
Marubeni K.K., I
McKesson Corporation, I
Metromedia Company, 7
Minnesota Mining & Manufacturing
  Company, I
Mitsubishi Corporation, I
Mitsui Bussan K.K., I
NACCO Industries, Inc., 7
Nissho Iwai K.K., I
Ogden Corporation, I
Pentair, Inc., 7
Samsung Group, I
Sumitomo Corporation, I
Swire Pacific Ltd., I
Teledyne, Inc., I
Tenneco Inc., I
Textron Inc., I
Thorn Emi PLC, I
Time Warner Inc., IV; 7 (upd.)
Toshiba Corporation, I
Transamerica Corporation, I
TRW Inc., I

Unilever PLC, II; 7 (upd.)
Veba A.G., I
W.R. Grace & Company, I
Whittaker Corporation, I

CONSTRUCTION

A. Johnson & Company H.B., I
Baratt Developments PLC, I
Bechtel Group Inc., I
Bilfinger & Berger Bau A.G., I
Bouygues, I
Dillingham Corporation, I
Fairclough Construction Group PLC, I
Fluor Corporation, I
John Brown PLC, I
John Laing PLC, I
Kajima Corporation, I
Kumagai Gumi Company, Ltd., I
Linde A.G., I
Mellon-Stuart Company, I
Morrison Knudsen Corporation, 7
Ohbayashi Corporation, I
The Peninsular & Oriental Steam
  Navigation Company (Bovis Division), I
Taylor Woodrow PLC, I
Wood Hall Trust PLC, I

CONTAINERS

Ball Corporation, I
Continental Group Company, I
Crown, Cork & Seal Company, I
Metal Box PLC, I
National Can Corporation, I
Owens-Illinois, Inc., I
Primerica Corporation, I
Toyo Seikan Kaisha, Ltd., I

DRUGS

A.B. Astra, I
Abbott Laboratories, I
American Home Products, I
Baxter International, I
Becton, Dickinson & Company, I
Ciba-Geigy Ltd., I
F. Hoffmann-Laroche & Company A.G., I
Fujisawa Pharmaceutical Company Ltd., I
G.D. Searle & Company, I
Genentech, Inc., I
Glaxo Holdings PLC, I
Eli Lilly & Company, I
Marion Laboratories, Inc., I
Merck & Company, I
Miles Laboratories, I
Mylan Laboratories, I
Novo Industri A/S, I
Pfizer Inc., I
Pharmacia A.B., I
R.P. Scherer, I
Rorer Group, I
Roussel-UCLAF, I
Sandoz Ltd., I
Sankyo Company, Ltd., I
Sanofi Group, I
Schering A.G., I
Schering-Plough, I
Sigma-Aldrich, I
Smithkline Beckman Corporation, I
Squibb Corporation, I
Sterling Drug, Inc., I
Syntex Corporation, I
Takeda Chemical Industries, Ltd., I
The Upjohn Company, I
Warner-Lambert, I
The Wellcome Foundation Ltd, I

ELECTRICAL & ELECTRONICS

ABB ASEA Brown Boveri Ltd., II
Alps Electric Co., Ltd., II
AMP, Inc., II
Bicoastal Corporation, II
Compagnie Générale d'Électricite, II
Cooper Industries, Inc., II
Emerson Electric Co., II
Fuji Electric Co., Ltd., II
General Electric Company, PLC, II
General Electric Company, II
GM Hughes Electronics Corporation, II
Harris Corporation, II
Honeywell Inc., II
Intel Corporation, II
Koor Industries Ltd., II
Kyocera Corporation, II
Lucky-Goldstar, II
Matsushita Electric Industrial Co., Ltd., II
Mitsubishi Electric Corporation, II
Motorola, Inc., II
National Semiconductor Corporation, II
NEC Corporation, II
Nokia Corporation, II
Oki Electric Industry Company, Limited, II
Omron Tateisi Electronics Company, II
N.V. Philips Gloeilampenfabrieken, II
The Plessey Company, PLC, II
Racal Electronics PLC, II
Raytheon Company, II
RCA Corporation, II
Sanyo Electric Company, Ltd., II
Schneider S.A., II
Sharp Corporation, II
Siemens A.G., II
Sony Corporation, II
Sumitomo Electric Industries, Ltd., II
Tandy Corporation, II
TDK Corporation, II
Texas Instruments Incorporated, II
Thomson S.A., II
Victor Company of Japan, Ltd., II
Westinghouse Electric Corporation, II
Zenith Electronics Corporation, II

ENGINEERING & MANAGEMENT SERVICES

CDI Corporation, 6
CRSS Inc., 6
Foster Wheeler Corporation, 6
Jacobs Engineering Group Inc., 6
Ogden Corporation, 6
VECO International, Inc., 7

ENTERTAINMENT & LEISURE

British Broadcasting Corporation, 7
Cablevision Systems Corporation, 7
Capital Cities/ABC Inc., II
CBS Inc., II; 6 (upd.)
Central Independent Television plc, 7
Cineplex Odeon Corporation, 6
Columbia Pictures Entertainment, Inc., II
Comcast Corporation, 7
Continental Cablevision, Inc., 7
Granada Group PLC, II
Home Box Office Inc., 7
Japan Broadcasting Corporation, 7
Ladbroke Group PLC, II
MCA Inc., II
Media General, Inc., 7
MGM/UA Communications Company, II
National Broadcasting Company, Inc., II; 6
  (upd.)
Orion Pictures Corporation, 6
Paramount Pictures Corporation, II
Rank Organisation PLC, II

Tele-Communications, Inc., II
Television Española, S.A., 7
Touristik Union International GmbH. and
    Company K.G., II
Turner Broadcasting System, Inc., II; 6
    (upd.)
Twentieth Century Fox Film Corporation,
    II
Viacom International Inc., 7
Walt Disney Company, II; 6 (upd.)
Warner Communications Inc., II

FINANCIAL SERVICES: BANKS

Algemene Bank Nederland N.V., II
Amsterdam-Rotterdam Bank N.V., II
Australia and New Zealand Banking Group
    Ltd., II
Banca Commerciale Italiana SpA, II
Banco Bilbao Vizcaya, S.A., II
Banco Central, II
Banco do Brasil S.A., II
Bank Brussels Lambert, II
Bank Hapoalim B.M., II
Bank of Boston Corporation, II
Bank of Montreal, II
Bank of New England Corporation, II
The Bank of New York Company, Inc., II
The Bank of Nova Scotia, II
Bank of Tokyo, Ltd., II
BankAmerica Corporation, II
Bankers Trust New York Corporation, II
Banque Nationale de Paris S.A., II
Barclays PLC, II
Bayerische Hypotheken- und Wechsel-
    Bank AG, II
Bayerische Vereinsbank A.G., II
Canadian Imperial Bank of Commerce, II
The Chase Manhattan Corporation, II
Chemical Banking Corporation, II
Citicorp, II
Commerzbank A.G., II
Compagnie Financiere de Paribas, II
Continental Bank Corporation, II
Credit Agricole, II
Credit Suisse, II
Credito Italiano, II
The Dai-Ichi Kangyo Bank Ltd., II
The Daiwa Bank, Ltd., II
Deutsche Bank A.G., II
Dresdner Bank A.G., II
First Chicago Corporation, II
First Interstate Bancorp, II
The Fuji Bank, Ltd., II
Generale Bank, II
H.F. Ahmanson & Company, II
The Hongkong and Shanghai Banking
    Corporation Limited, II
The Industrial Bank of Japan, Ltd., II
J.P. Morgan & Co. Incorporated, II
Kansallis-Osake-Pankki, II
Kredietbank N.V., II
Lloyds Bank PLC, II
Long-Term Credit Bank of Japan, Ltd., II
Manufacturers Hanover Corporation, II
Mellon Bank Corporation, II
Midland Bank PLC, II
The Mitsubishi Bank, Ltd., II
The Mitsubishi Trust & Banking
    Corporation, II
The Mitsui Bank, Ltd., II
The Mitsui Trust & Banking Company,
    Ltd., II
National Westminster Bank PLC, II
NCNB Corporation, II
Nippon Credit Bank, II
Norinchukin Bank, II
PNC Financial Corporation, II

The Royal Bank of Canada, II
The Sanwa Bank, Ltd., II
Security Pacific Corporation, II
Skandinaviska Enskilda Banken, II
Société Générale, II
Standard Chartered PLC, II
The Sumitomo Bank, Ltd., II
The Sumitomo Trust & Banking Company,
    Ltd., II
Svenska Handelsbanken, II
Swiss Bank Corporation, II
The Taiyo Kobe Bank, Ltd., II
The Tokai Bank, Ltd., II
The Toronto-Dominion Bank, II
Union Bank of Switzerland, II
Wells Fargo & Company, II
Westdeutsche Landesbank Girozentrale, II
Westpac Banking Corporation, II
The Yasuda Trust and Banking Company,
    Ltd., II

FINANCIAL SERVICES: NON-BANKS

American Express Company, II
Bear Stearns Companies, Inc., II
CS First Boston Inc., II
Daiwa Securities Company, Limited, II
Drexel Burnham Lambert Incorporated, II
Federal National Mortgage Association, II
Fidelity Investments, II
Goldman, Sachs & Co., II
Household International, Inc., II
Kleinwort Benson Group PLC, II
Merrill Lynch & Co. Inc., II
Morgan Grenfell Group PLC, II
Morgan Stanley Group Inc., II
The Nikko Securities Company Limited, II
Nippon Shinpan Company, Ltd., II
Nomura Securities Company, Limited, II
Orix Corporation, II
PaineWebber Group Inc., II
Salomon Inc., II
Shearson Lehman Hutton Holdings Inc., II
Student Loan Marketing Association, II
Trilon Financial Corporation, II
Yamaichi Securities Company, Limited, II

FOOD PRODUCTS

Agway, Inc., 7
Ajinomoto Co., Inc., II
Associated British Foods PLC, II
Beatrice Company, II
Borden, Inc., II
BSN Groupe S.A., II
Cadbury Schweppes PLC, II
Campbell Soup Company, II; 7 (upd.)
Canada Packers Inc., II
Carnation Company, II
Castle & Cook, Inc., II
Central Soya Company, Inc., 7
Chiquita Brands International, Inc., 7
Conagra, Inc., II
CPC International Inc., II
Curtice-Burns Foods, Inc., 7
Dalgery, PLC, II
Dean Foods Company, 7
Del Monte Corporation, 7
Farmland Foods, Inc., 7
General Mills, Inc., II
George A. Hormel and Company, II
Gerber Products Company, 7
H.J. Heinz Company, II
Hershey Foods Corporation, II
Hillsdown Holdings, PLC, II
IBP, Inc., II
International Multifoods Corporation, 7
Itoham Foods Inc., II

Jacobs Suchard A.G., II
Kellogg Company, II
Koninklijke Wessanen N.V., II
Kraft General Foods Inc., II; 7 (upd.)
Land O'Lakes, Inc., II
Mars, Inc., 7
McCormick & Company, Incorporated, 7
McKee Foods Corporation, 7
Meiji Milk Products Company, Limited, II
Meiji Seika Kaisha, Ltd., II
Mid-America Dairymen, Inc., 7
Nabisco Foods Group, II; 7 (upd.)
Nestlé S.A., II; 7 (upd.)
Nippon Meat Packers, Inc., II
Nippon Suisan Kaisha, Limited, II
Nisshin Flour Milling Company, Ltd., II
Ocean Spray Cranberries, Inc., 7
Perdue Farms Inc., 7
Pet Incorporated, 7
Pilgrim's Pride Corporation, 7
Pillsbury Company, II
Quaker Oats Company, II
Ralston Purina Company, II
Ranks Hovis McDougall PLC, II
Reckitt & Colman PLC, II
Rich Products Corporation, 7
Roland Murten A.G., 7
Rowntree Mackintosh, II
Sara Lee Corporation, II
Savannah Foods & Industries, Inc., 7
Schwan's Sales Enterprises, Inc., 7
Smithfield Foods, Inc., 7
Snow Brand Milk Products Company,
    Limited, II
SODIMA, II
Sun-Diamond Growers of California, 7
Taiyo Fishery Company, Limited, II
Tate & Lyle PLC, II
Thorn Apple Valley, Inc., 7
Tyson Foods, Incorporated, II
Unigate PLC, II
United Biscuits (Holdings) PLC, II
United Brands Company, II
Universal Foods Corporation, 7
Van Camp Seafood Company, Inc., 7
Wattie's Ltd., 7
Wisconsin Dairies, 7
Wm. Wrigley Jr. Company, 7

FOOD SERVICES & RETAILERS

Albertson's Inc., II; 7 (upd.)
American Stores Company, II
America's Favorite Chicken Company,
    Inc., 7
ARA Services, II
Argyll Group PLC, II
Asda Group PLC, II
Bruno's Inc., 7
Burger King Corporation, II
Cargill, Inc., II
The Circle K Corporation, II
Dairy Mart Convenience Stores, Inc., 7
Domino's Pizza, Inc., 7
Edeka Zentrale A.G., II
Fleming Companies, Inc., II
Food Lion, Inc., II
The Gateway Corporation Ltd., II
George Weston Limited, II
Giant Food Inc., II
Grand Union Company, 7
The Great Atlantic & Pacific Tea
    Company, Inc., II
ICA AB, II
J Sainsbury PLC, II
KFC Corporation, 7
Koninklijke Ahold N. V., II
The Kroger Company, II

WASTE SERVICES

NOTES ON CONTRIBUTORS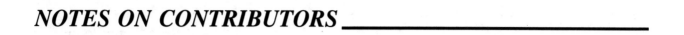

Notes on Contributors

BARBOUR, Philippe A. Commissioning editor at Gale Research International, London.

BARLOW, Margaret. Free-lance writer and editor for Book Builders Incorporated; associate editor, *Woman's Art Journal;* editor, *Open Entries.*

BAY, Timothy. Free-lance writer and editor for Book Builders Incorporated. Contributor to *New York Times,* Chicago *Tribune,* and *Newsday,* as well as various business and consumer publications.

BELSITO, Elaine. Free-lance writer and editor. Assistant managing editor, *Archives of Physical Medicine and Rehabilitation,* 1988–90.

BOWMAN, Jim. Free-lance writer and publicist specializing in business history and religion. Author of *Waste Not . . .: The Safety-Kleen Story* and other corporate histories. Chicago correspondent for Religious News Service (New York). Contributor to the *Chicago Reader, Commonweal,* the *Chicago Tribune,* and other publications. President, Society of Midland Authors; member, Chicago Press Veterans Association.

BOYER, Dean. Former newspaper reporter; free-lance writer in Seattle area.

BROWN, Susan Windisch. Free-lance writer and editor.

COHEN, Kerstan. Free-lance writer and French translator; editor for *Letter-Ex* poetry review.

DOUGAL, April S. Archivist and free-lance writer specializing in business and social history in Cleveland, Ohio.

DUBOVOJ, Sina. History contractor and free-lance writer; adjunct professor of history, Montgomery College, Rockville, Maryland.

FARQUHAR-BOYLE, Allyson S. Analyst, Mercy Health Services, Department of Strategic Planning and Analysis. Author of "Strategic Planning as a Process," *Court Management and Public Administration.*

HALL, Janet Reinhart. Free-lance writer.

HAWKINS, Dr. Richard A. Lecturer in economics, University of Wolverhampton. Author of "Socialism at Work? Corporatism, Soldier Settlers, and the Canned Pineapple Industry in South-Eastern Queensland 1917–39," *Australian Studies,* Number 4, 1990.

HECHT, Henry R. Editorial consultant and retired vice-president, editorial services, Merrill Lynch.

HEDDEN, Heather Behn. Free-lance writer. Former staff writer with the *Middle East Times* and contributor to *Business Monthly* in Cairo.

HITCHNER, Nancy. Free-lance writer and editor for Book Builders Incorporated. Former editor of *Bank Technology Report, Bank Security Report,* and other newsletters for the financial service industry. Editor of books and articles for business professionals in the fields of banking and finance, human resources, accounting, MIS, and real estate.

HUGHES, Anne C. Free-lance writer, editor, and desktop publisher in Chicago.

JACOBSON, Robert R. Free-lance writer and musician.

KALANIK, Lynn M. Advertising copywriter, Richard D. Irwin Inc., Homewood, Illinois. Creative consultant and project director, The Waterkotte Co. Inc., Pittsburgh, Pennsylvania, 1987–88.

KEELEY, Carol I. Free-lance writer and researcher; contributor to *Chicago* magazine, *Playboy,* the *Reader, Ford Times, Discovery Magazine,* the *Chicago Tribune, New American Writing, Oxford Poetry,* and *Voices International.*

KRONENBERG, Kenneth F. Free-lance writer and editor for Book Builders Incorporated. Writer and editor of English and social studies textbooks. Translator of business documents and correspondence from German into English.

LEWIS, Scott M. Free-lance writer and editor; contributing editor, *Option.* Staff editor, *Security, Distributing and Marketing,* 1989–90.

MARTIN, Jonathan. Free-lance writer; doctoral candidate in English, University of Chicago. Screenplay, *A Life of Her Own,* in production.

McDERMOTT, Marcia. Free-lance writer; CPA, MBA from University of Chicago, currently working in litigation services.

McNULTY, Mary. Editor, American Association of Law Libraries; contributor to the Chicago *Tribune.*

MAXFIELD, Doris Morris. Owner of Written Expressions, an editorial services business; contributor to numerous reference publications; editor of *Online Database*

Search Services Directory, 1983–84 and 1988, and of *Charitable Organizations in the U.S.,* 1991–92 and 1992–93.

MONAHAN, Julie. Free-lance writer specializing in business and health care for national trade and consumer magazines.

MONTGOMERY, Bruce P. Curator and director of historical collection, University of Colorado at Boulder.

NORTON, Frances E. Free-lance writer; contributor to *Evanston Arts Review* and *Helicon.*

PEDERSON, Jay P. Free-lance writer and editor.

ROURKE, Elizabeth. Free-lance writer.

SARICH, John A. Free-lance writer and editor. Graduate student in economics at the New School for Social Research.

SCHOOLMAN, Martha. Free-lance writer in Chicago.

SCHULTZ, Ron. Free-lance writer and editor for Book Builders Incorporated. Coauthor of *Cashing Out: The Entrepreneur's Guide to Going Public,* 1991, and author of *The Naked Hunch: High Pressure Decision Making,* 1993, Harper Business.

SHERMAN, Fran Shonfeld. Free-lance writer. Assistant editor, *Compton's Encyclopedia,* 1986–92; contributing editor, *Britannica Book of the Year,* annual.

SIMLEY, John. Professional researcher and corporate issues analyst. Former research editor for *International Directory of Company Histories;* contributor to *Encyclopedia of Consumer Brands.*

SMITH, Mary-Sophia. Consultant; MBA, University of Chicago.

STEIN, Wendy. Free-lance writer and editor for Book Builders Incorporated. Writer of reports, manuals, public relations materials, and catalogs for various companies. Former managing editor of periodicals department, New Readers Press. Former reporter for *Syracuse Herald-Journal* and *Herald American.*

SUN, Douglas. Assistant professor of English at California State University at Los Angeles. Author of book reviews, *Los Angeles Times,* 1988–89.

TROESTER, Maura. Chicago-based free-lance writer.

TUCKER, Thomas. Free-lance writer.

VERZHBINSKY, Moya. Free-lance writer; graduate student in business administration, University of California, Berkeley.

VLESSING, Etan. Free-lance writer and editor. Former editor of *Insight;* news editor, *Financial Weekly.*

WALTON, Dorothy. Free-lance writer with a specialty in business and legislative topics. Author of: *A Guide to Managing REO and Receivership Properties; ADA Title III: Compliance Made Practical.* Writer for *The Journal of Property Management* and for the University of Chicago Press.

WANKOFF, Jordan. Free-lance writer; coeditor of *Vice Versa* literary magazine; museum editor, *California Art Review,* 1989.